Statistical Techniques in BUSINESS & ECONOMICS

The McGraw-Hill/Irwin Series in Operations and Decision Sciences

SUPPLY CHAIN MANAGEMENT

Benton
Purchasing and Supply Chain Management
Third Edition

Bowersox, Closs, Cooper, and Bowersox
Supply Chain Logistics Management
Fourth Edition

Burt, Petcavage, and Pinkerton
Supply Management
Eighth Edition

Johnson, Leenders, and Flynn
Purchasing and Supply Management
Fourteenth Edition

Simchi-Levi, Kaminsky, and Simchi-Levi
Designing and Managing the Supply Chain: Concepts, Strategies, Case Studies
Third Edition

PROJECT MANAGEMENT

Brown and Hyer
Managing Projects: A Team-Based Approach
First Edition

Larson and Gray
Project Management: The Managerial Process
Fifth Edition

SERVICE OPERATIONS MANAGEMENT

Fitzsimmons and Fitzsimmons
Service Management: Operations, Strategy, Information Technology
Eighth Edition

MANAGEMENT SCIENCE

Hillier and Hillier
Introduction to Management Science: A Modeling and Case Studies Approach with Spreadsheets
Fifth Edition

Stevenson and Ozgur
Introduction to Management Science with Spreadsheets
First Edition

MANUFACTURING CONTROL SYSTEMS

Jacobs, Berry, Whybark, and Vollmann
Manufacturing Planning & Control for Supply Chain Management
Sixth Edition

BUSINESS RESEARCH METHODS

Cooper and Schindler
Business Research Methods
Twelfth Edition

BUSINESS FORECASTING

Wilson, Keating, and John Galt Solutions, Inc.
Business Forecasting
Sixth Edition

LINEAR STATISTICS AND REGRESSION

Kutner, Nachtsheim, and Neter
Applied Linear Regression Models
Fourth Edition

BUSINESS SYSTEMS DYNAMICS

Sterman
Business Dynamics: Systems Thinking and Modeling for a Complex World
First Edition

OPERATIONS MANAGEMENT

Cachon and Terwiesch
Matching Supply with Demand: An Introduction to Operations Management
Third Edition

Finch
Interactive Models for Operations and Supply Chain Management
First Edition

Jacobs and Chase
Operations and Supply Chain Management
Fourteenth Edition

Jacobs and Chase
Operations and Supply Chain Management: The Core
Third Edition

Jacobs and Whybark
Why ERP? A Primer on SAP Implementation
First Edition

Schroeder, Goldstein, and Rungtusanatham
Operations Management in the Supply Chain: Decisions and Cases
Sixth Edition

Stevenson
Operations Management
Eleventh Edition

Swink, Melnyk, Cooper, and Hartley
Managing Operations across the Supply Chain
Second Edition

PRODUCT DESIGN

Ulrich and Eppinger
Product Design and Development
Fifth Edition

BUSINESS MATH

Slater and Wittry
Math for Business and Finance: An Algebraic Approach
First Edition

Slater and Wittry
Practical Business Math Procedures
Eleventh Edition

Slater and Wittry
Practical Business Math Procedures, Brief Edition
Eleventh Edition

BUSINESS STATISTICS

Bowerman, O'Connell, and Murphree
Business Statistics in Practice
Seventh Edition

Bowerman, O'Connell, Murphree, and Orris
Essentials of Business Statistics
Fourth Edition

Doane and Seward
Applied Statistics in Business and Economics
Fourth Edition

Lind, Marchal, and Wathen
Basic Statistics for Business and Economics
Eighth Edition

Lind, Marchal, and Wathen
Statistical Techniques in Business and Economics
Seventeenth Edition

Jaggia and Kelly
Business Statistics: Communicating with Numbers
First Edition

Jaggia and Kelly
Essentials of Business Statistics: Communicating with Numbers
First Edition

Statistical Techniques in BUSINESS & ECONOMICS

SEVENTEENTH EDITION

DOUGLAS A. LIND
Coastal Carolina University and The University of Toledo

WILLIAM G. MARCHAL
The University of Toledo

SAMUEL A. WATHEN
Coastal Carolina University

STATISTICAL TECHNIQUES IN BUSINESS & ECONOMICS, SEVENTEENTH EDITION
Published by McGraw-Hill Education, 2 Penn Plaza, New York, NY 10121.

Some ancillaries, including electronic and print components, may not be available to customers outside the United States.

This book is printed on acid-free paper.

1 2 3 4 5 6 7 8 9 LWI 21 20 19 18 17

ISBN 978-1-259-66636-0
MHID 1-259-66636-0

Chief Product Officer, SVP Products & Markets: *G. Scott Virkler*
Vice President, General Manager, Products & Markets: *Marty Lange*
Vice President, Content Design & Delivery: *Betsy Whalen*
Managing Director: *Tim Vertovec*
Senior Brand Manager: *Charles Synovec*
Director, Product Development: Rose Koos
Product Developers: *Michele Janicek / Ryan McAndrews*
Senior Director, Digital Content Development: *Douglas Ruby*
Marketing Manager: *Trina Maurer*
Director, Content Design & Delivery: *Linda Avenarius*
Program Manager: *Mark Christianson*
Content Project Managers: *Harvey Yep (Core) / Bruce Gin (Assessment)*
Buyer: *Susan K. Culbertson*
Design: *Matt Backhaus*
Cover Image: *© Corbis / Glow Images*
Content Licensing Specialists: *Melissa Homer (Image) / Beth Thole (Text)*
Typeface: *9.5/11 Proxima Nova*
Compositor: *Aptara®, Inc.*
Printer: *LSC Communications*

All credits appearing on page or at the end of the book are considered to be an extension of the copyright page.

Library of Congress Cataloging-in-Publication Data

Names: Lind, Douglas A., author. | Marchal, William G., author. | Wathen, Samuel Adam. author.
Title: Statistical techniques in business & economics/Douglas A. Lind, Coastal Carolina University and The University of Toledo, William G. Marchal, The University of Toledo, Samuel A. Wathen, Coastal Carolina University.
Other titles: Statistical techniques in business and economics
Description: Seventeenth Edition. | Dubuque, IA : McGraw-Hill Education, [2017] | Revised edition of the authors' Statistical techniques in business & economics, [2015]
Identifiers: LCCN 2016054310| ISBN 9781259666360 (alk. paper) | ISBN 1259666360 (alk. paper)
Subjects: LCSH: Social sciences—Statistical methods. | Economics—Statistical methods. | Commercial statistics.
Classification: LCC HA29 .M268 2017 | DDC 519.5—dc23 LC record available at https://lccn.loc.gov/2016054310

The Internet addresses listed in the text were accurate at the time of publication. The inclusion of a website does not indicate an endorsement by the authors or McGraw-Hill Education, and McGraw-Hill Education does not guarantee the accuracy of the information presented at these sites.

mheducation.com/highered

DEDICATION

To Jane, my wife and best friend, and our sons, their wives, and our grandchildren: Mike and Sue (Steve and Courtney), Steve and Kathryn (Kennedy, Jake, and Brady), and Mark and Sarah (Jared, Drew, and Nate).

Douglas A. Lind

To Oscar Sambath Marchal, Julian Irving Horowitz, Cecilia Marchal Nicholson and Andrea.

William G. Marchal

To my wonderful family: Barb, Hannah, and Isaac.

Samuel A. Wathen

A NOTE FROM THE AUTHORS

Over the years, we received many compliments on this text and understand that it's a favorite among students. We accept that as the highest compliment and continue to work very hard to maintain that status.

The objective of *Statistical Techniques in Business and Economics* is to provide students majoring in management, marketing, finance, accounting, economics, and other fields of business administration with an introductory survey of descriptive and inferential statistics. To illustrate the application of statistics, we use many examples and exercises that focus on business applications, but also relate to the current world of the college student. A previous course in statistics is not necessary, and the mathematical requirement is first-year algebra.

In this text, we show beginning students every step needed to be successful in a basic statistics course. This step-by-step approach enhances performance, accelerates preparedness, and significantly improves motivation. Understanding the concepts, seeing and doing plenty of examples and exercises, and comprehending the application of statistical methods in business and economics are the focus of this book.

The first edition of this text was published in 1967. At that time, locating relevant business data was difficult. That has changed! Today, locating data is not a problem. The number of items you purchase at the grocery store is automatically recorded at the checkout counter. Phone companies track the time of our calls, the length of calls, and the identity of the person called. Credit card companies maintain information on the number, time and date, and amount of our purchases. Medical devices automatically monitor our heart rate, blood pressure, and temperature from remote locations. A large amount of business information is recorded and reported almost instantly. CNN, USA Today, and MSNBC, for example, all have websites that track stock prices in real time.

Today, the practice of data analytics is widely applied to "big data." The practice of data analytics requires skills and knowledge in several areas. Computer skills are needed to process large volumes of information. Analytical skills are needed to evaluate, summarize, organize, and analyze the information. Critical thinking skills are needed to interpret and communicate the results of processing the information.

Our text supports the development of basic data analytical skills. In this edition, we added a new section at the end of each chapter called Data Analytics. As you work through the text, this section provides the instructor and student with opportunities to apply statistical knowledge and statistical software to explore several business environments. Interpretation of the analytical results is an integral part of these exercises.

A variety of statistical software is available to complement our text. Microsoft Excel includes an add-in with many statistical analyses. Megastat is an add-in available for Microsoft Excel. Minitab and JMP are stand-alone statistical software available to download for either PC or MAC computers. In our text, Microsoft Excel, Minitab, and Megastat are used to illustrate statistical software analyses. When a software application is presented, the software commands for the application are available in Appendix C. We use screen captures within the chapters, so the student becomes familiar with the nature of the software output.

Because of the availability of computers and software, it is no longer necessary to dwell on calculations. We have replaced many of the calculation examples with interpretative ones, to assist the student in understanding and interpreting the statistical results. In addition, we place more emphasis on the conceptual nature of the statistical topics. While making these changes, we still continue to present, as best we can, the key concepts, along with supporting interesting and relevant examples.

WHAT'S NEW IN THE SEVENTEENTH EDITION?

We have made many changes to examples and exercises throughout the text. The section on "Enhancements" to our text details them. The major change to the text is in response to user interest in the area of data analytics. Our approach is to provide instructors and students with the opportunity to combine statistical knowledge, computer and statistical software skills, and interpretative and critical thinking skills. A set of new and revised exercises is included at the end of chapters 1 through 18 in a section titled "Data Analytics."

In these sections, exercises refer to three data sets. The North Valley Real Estate sales data set lists 105 homes currently on the market. The Lincolnville School District bus data lists information on 80 buses in the school district's bus fleet. The authors designed these data so that students will be able to use statistical software to explore the data and find realistic relationships in the variables. The Baseball Statistics for the 2016 season is updated from the previous edition.

The intent of the exercises is to provide the basis of a continuing case analysis. We suggest that instructors select one of the data sets and assign the corresponding exercises as each chapter is completed. Instructor feedback regarding student performance is important. Students should retain a copy of each chapter's results and interpretations to develop a portfolio of discoveries and findings. These will be helpful as students progress through the course and use new statistical techniques to further explore the data. The ideal ending for these continuing data analytics exercises is a comprehensive report based on the analytical findings.

We know that working with a statistics class to develop a very basic competence in data analytics is challenging. Instructors will be teaching statistics. In addition, instructors will be faced with choosing statistical software and supporting students in developing or enhancing their computer skills. Finally, instructors will need to assess student performance based on assignments that include both statistical and written components. Using a mentoring approach may be helpful.

We hope that you and your students find this new feature interesting and engaging.

HOW ARE CHAPTERS ORGANIZED TO ENGAGE STUDENTS AND PROMOTE LEARNING?

Chapter Learning Objectives

Each chapter begins with a set of learning objectives designed to provide focus for the chapter and motivate student learning. These objectives, located in the margins next to the topic, indicate what the student should be able to do after completing each section in the chapter.

▲ **MERRILL LYNCH** recently completed a study of online investment portfolios for a sample of clients. For the 70 participants in the study, organize these data into a frequency distribution. (See Exercise 43 and LO2-3.)

LEARNING OBJECTIVES

When you have completed this chapter, you will be able to:

LO2-1 Summarize qualitative variables with frequency and relative frequency tables.

LO2-2 Display a frequency table using a bar or pie chart.

LO2-3 Summarize quantitative variables with frequency and relative frequency distributions.

LO2-4 Display a frequency distribution using a histogram or frequency polygon.

Chapter Opening Exercise

A representative exercise opens the chapter and shows how the chapter content can be applied to a real-world situation.

Introduction to the Topic

Each chapter starts with a review of the important concepts of the previous chapter and provides a link to the material in the current chapter. This step-by-step approach increases comprehension by providing continuity across the concepts.

INTRODUCTION

The United States automobile retailing industry is highly competitive. It is dominated by megadealerships that own and operate 50 or more franchises, employ over 10,000 people, and generate several billion dollars in annual sales. Many of the top dealerships are publicly owned with shares traded on the New York Stock Exchange or NASDAQ. In 2014, the largest megadealership was AutoNation (ticker symbol AN), followed by Penske Auto Group (PAG), Group 1 Automotive, Inc. (ticker symbol GPI), and the privately owned Van Tuyl Group.

These large corporations use statistics and analytics to summarize and analyze data and information to support their decisions. As an example, we will look at the Applewood Auto group. It owns four dealerships and sells a wide range of vehicles. These include the popular Korean brands Kia and Hyundai, BMW and Volvo sedans and luxury SUVs, and a full line of Ford and Chevrolet cars and trucks.

Example/Solution

After important concepts are introduced, a solved example is given. This example provides a how-to illustration and shows a relevant business application that helps students answer the question, "How can I apply this concept?"

EXAMPLE

The service departments at Tionesta Ford Lincoln and Sheffield Motors Inc., two of the four Applewood Auto Group dealerships, were both open 24 days last month. Listed below is the number of vehicles serviced last month at the two dealerships. Construct dot plots and report summary statistics to compare the two dealerships.

Tionesta Ford Lincoln					
Monday	**Tuesday**	**Wednesday**	**Thursday**	**Friday**	**Saturday**
23	33	27	28	39	26
30	32	28	33	35	32
29	25	36	31	32	27
35	32	35	37	36	30

Self-Reviews

Self-Reviews are interspersed throughout each chapter and follow Example/Solution sections. They help students monitor their progress and provide immediate reinforcement for that particular technique. Answers are in Appendix E.

SELF-REVIEW 4–2

The Quality Control department of Plainsville Peanut Company is responsible for checking the weight of the 8-ounce jar of peanut butter. The weights of a sample of nine jars produced last hour are:

7.69	7.72	7.8	7.86	7.90	7.94	7.97	8.06	8.09

(a) What is the median weight?
(b) Determine the weights corresponding to the first and third quartiles.

Statistics in Action

Statistics in Action articles are scattered throughout the text, usually about two per chapter. They provide unique, interesting applications and historical insights in the field of statistics.

STATISTICS IN ACTION

If you wish to get some attention at the next gathering you attend, announce that you believe that at least two people present were born on the same date—that is, the same day of the year but not necessarily the same year. If there are 30 people in the room, the probability of a duplicate is .706. If there are 60 people in the room,

Definitions

Definitions of new terms or terms unique to the study of statistics are set apart from the text and highlighted for easy reference and review. They also appear in the Glossary at the end of the book.

JOINT PROBABILITY A probability that measures the likelihood two or more events will happen concurrently.

Formulas

Formulas that are used for the first time are boxed and numbered for reference. In addition, a formula card is bound into the back of the text that lists all the key formulas.

SPECIAL RULE OF MULTIPLICATION $P(A \text{ and } B) = P(A)P(B)$ **[5–5]**

Exercises

Exercises are included after sections within the chapter and at the end of the chapter. Section exercises cover the material studied in the section. Many exercises have data files available to import into statistical software. They are indicated with the FILE icon. Answers to the odd-numbered exercises are in Appendix D.

EXERCISES

For Exercises 47–52, do the following:

a. Compute the sample variance.
b. Determine the sample standard deviation.

47. Consider these values a sample: 7, 2, 6, 2, and 3.
48. The following five values are a sample: 11, 6, 10, 6, and 7.
49. FILE Dave's Automatic Door, referred to in Exercise 37, installs automatic garage door openers. Based on a sample, following are the times, in minutes, required to install 10 door openers: 28, 32, 24, 46, 44, 40, 54, 38, 32, and 42.
50. FILE The sample of eight companies in the aerospace industry, referred to in Exercise 38, was surveyed as to their return on investment last year. The results are 10.6, 12.6, 14.8, 18.2, 12.0, 14.8, 12.2, and 15.6.

Computer Output

The text includes many software examples, using Excel, MegaStat®, and Minitab. The software results are illustrated in the chapters. Instructions for a particular software example are in Appendix C.

APPLEWOOD AUTO GROUP

	A	B	C	D	E	F	G	H
1	Age	Profit	Location	Vehicle-Type	Previous		Profit	
2	21	$1,387	Tionesta	Sedan	0			
3	23	$1,754	Sheffield	SUV	1		Mean	1843.17
4	24	$1,817	Sheffield	Hybrid	1		Standard Error	47.97
5	25	$1,040	Sheffield	Compact	0		Median	1882.50
6	26	$1,273	Kane	Sedan	1		Mode	1915.00
7	27	$1,529	Sheffield	Sedan	1		Standard Deviation	643.63
8	27	$3,082	Kane	Truck	0		Sample Variance	414256.61
9	28	$1,951	Kane	SUV	1		Kurtosis	-0.22
10	28	$2,692	Tionesta	Compact	0		Skewness	-0.24
11	29	$1,342	Kane	Sedan	2		Range	2998
12	29	$1,206	Sheffield	Sedan	0		Minimum	294
13	30	$443	Kane	Sedan	3		Maximum	3292
14	30	$1,621	Sheffield	Truck	1		Sum	331770
15	30	$754	Olean	Sedan	2		Count	180

HOW DOES THIS TEXT REINFORCE STUDENT LEARNING?

BY CHAPTER

Chapter Summary

Each chapter contains a brief summary of the chapter material, including vocabulary, definitions, and critical formulas.

CHAPTER SUMMARY

I. A random variable is a numerical value determined by the outcome of an experiment.
II. A probability distribution is a listing of all possible outcomes of an experiment and the probability associated with each outcome.
  A. A discrete probability distribution can assume only certain values. The main features are:
    1. The sum of the probabilities is 1.00.
    2. The probability of a particular outcome is between 0.00 and 1.00.
    3. The outcomes are mutually exclusive.
  B. A continuous distribution can assume an infinite number of values within a specific range.
III. The mean and variance of a probability distribution are computed as follows.
  A. The mean is equal to:

$$\mu = \Sigma[xP(x)] \qquad \textbf{(6–1)}$$

  B. The variance is equal to:

$$\sigma^2 = \Sigma[(x - \mu)^2P(x)] \qquad \textbf{(6–2)}$$

Pronunciation Key

This section lists the mathematical symbol, its meaning, and how to pronounce it. We believe this will help the student retain the meaning of the symbol and generally enhance course communications.

PRONUNCIATION KEY

SYMBOL	MEANING	PRONUNCIATION
$P(A)$	Probability of *A*	*P* of *A*
$P(\sim A)$	Probability of not *A*	*P* of not *A*
$P(A$ and $B)$	Probability of *A* and *B*	*P* of *A* and *B*
$P(A$ or $B)$	Probability of *A* or *B*	*P* of *A* or *B*
$P(A\|B)$	Probability of *A* given *B* has happened	*P* of *A* given *B*
${}_nP_r$	Permutation of *n* items selected *r* at a time	*Pnr*
${}_nC_r$	Combination of *n* items selected *r* at a time	*Cnr*

Chapter Exercises

Generally, the end-of-chapter exercises are the most challenging and integrate the chapter concepts. The answers and worked-out solutions for all odd-numbered exercises are in Appendix D at the end of the text. Many exercises are noted with a data file icon in the margin. For these exercises, there are data files in Excel format located on the text's website, www.mhhe.com/Lind17e. These files help students use statistical software to solve the exercises.

CHAPTER EXERCISES

25. According to the local union president, the mean gross income of plumbers in the Salt Lake City area follows the normal probability distribution with a mean of $45,000 and a standard deviation of $3,000. A recent investigative reporter for KYAK TV found, for a sample of 120 plumbers, the mean gross income was $45,500. At the .10 significance level, is it reasonable to conclude that the mean income is not equal to $45,000? Determine the *p*-value.

26. FILE Rutter Nursery Company packages its pine bark mulch in 50-pound bags. From a long history, the production department reports that the distribution of the bag weights follows the normal distribution and the standard deviation of the packaging process is 3 pounds per bag. At the end of each day, Jeff Rutter, the production manager, weighs 10 bags and computes the mean weight of the sample. Below are the weights of 10 bags from today's production.

45.6	47.7	47.6	46.3	46.2	47.4	49.2	55.8	47.5	48.5

  a. Can Mr. Rutter conclude that the mean weight of the bags is less than 50 pounds? Use the .01 significance level.
  b. In a brief report, tell why Mr. Rutter can use the *z* distribution as the test statistic.
  c. Compute the *p*-value.

27. A new weight-watching company, Weight Reducers International, advertises that those who join will lose an average of 10 pounds after the first two weeks. The standard deviation is 2.8 pounds. A random sample of 50 people who joined the weight reduction program revealed a mean loss of 9 pounds. At the .05 level of significance, can we

Data Analytics

The goal of the Data Analytics sections is to develop analytical skills. The exercises present a real world context with supporting data. The data sets are printed in Appendix A and available to download from the text's website www.mhhe.com/Lind17e. Statistical software is required to analyze the data and respond to the exercises. Each data set is used to explore questions and discover findings that relate to a real world context. For each business context, a story is uncovered as students progress from chapters one to seventeen.

DATA ANALYTICS

(The data for these exercises are available at the text website: www.mhhe.com/lind17e.)

74. Refer to the North Valley Real Estate data, which report information on homes sold during the last year.
  a. The mean selling price (in $ thousands) of the homes was computed earlier to be $357.0, with a standard deviation of $160.7. Use the normal distribution to estimate the percentage of homes selling for more than $500.000. Compare this to the actual results. Is price normally distributed? Try another test. If price is normally distributed, how many homes should have a price greater than the mean? Compare this to the actual number of homes. Construct a frequency distribution of price. What do you observe?
  b. The mean days on the market is 30 with a standard deviation of 10 days. Use

Software Commands

Software examples using Excel, MegaStat®, and Minitab are included throughout the text. The explanations of the computer input commands are placed at the end of the text in Appendix C.

12–2. The Excel commands for the one-way ANOVA on page 400 are:
  a. Key in data into four columns labeled *Northern, WTA, Pocono,* and *Branson.*
  b. Select the **Data** tab on the top menu. Then, on the far right, select **Data Analysis.** Select **ANOVA: Single Factor,** then click **OK.**
  c. In the subsequent dialog box, make the input range *A1:D8,* click on **Grouped by Columns,** click on **Labels in first row,** the **Alpha** text box is *0.05,* and finally select **Output Range** as *F1* and click **OK.**

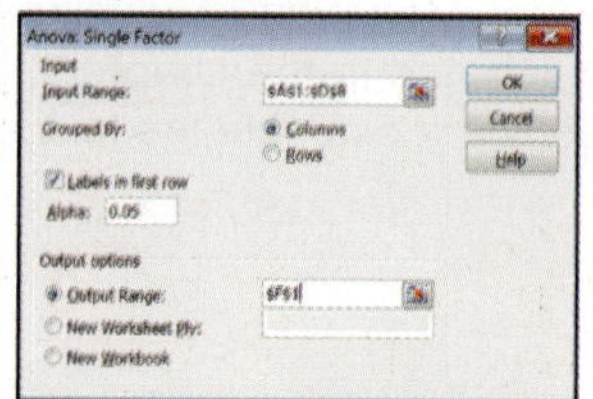

Answers to Self-Review

The worked-out solutions to the Self-Reviews are provided at the end of the text in Appendix E.

16–7 a.

		Rank			
x	y	x	y	d	d^2
805	23	5.5	1	4.5	20.25
777	62	3.0	9	−6.0	36.00
820	60	8.5	8	0.5	0.25
682	40	1.0	4	−3.0	9.00
777	70	3.0	10	−7.0	49.00
810	28	7.0	2	5.0	25.00
805	30	5.5	3	2.5	6.25
840	42	10.0	5	5.0	25.00
777	55	3.0	7	−4.0	16.00
820	51	8.5	6	2.5	6.25
				0	193.00

BY SECTION

Section Reviews

After selected groups of chapters (1–4, 5–7, 8 and 9, 10–12, 13 and 14, 15 and 16, and 17 and 18), a Section Review is included. Much like a review before an exam, these include a brief **overview** of the chapters and **problems for review.**

A REVIEW OF CHAPTERS 1–4

This section is a review of the major concepts and terms introduced in Chapters 1–4. Chapter 1 began by describing the meaning and purpose of statistics. Next we described the different types of variables and the four levels of measurement. Chapter 2 was concerned with describing a set of observations by organizing it into a frequency distribution and then portraying the frequency distribution as a histogram or a frequency polygon. Chapter 3 began by describing measures of location, such as the mean, weighted mean, median, geometric mean, and mode. This chapter also included measures of dispersion, or spread. Discussed in this section were the range, variance, and standard deviation. Chapter 4 included several graphing techniques such as dot plots, box plots, and scatter diagrams. We also discussed the coefficient of skewness, which reports the lack of symmetry in a set of data.

Throughout this section we stressed the importance of statistical software, such as Excel and Minitab. Many computer outputs in these chapters demonstrated how quickly and effectively a large data set can be organized into a frequency

Cases

The review also includes continuing cases and several small cases that let students make decisions using tools and techniques from a variety of chapters.

CASES

A. Century National Bank

The following case will appear in subsequent review sections. Assume that you work in the Planning Department of the Century National Bank and report to Ms. Lamberg. You will need to do some data analysis and prepare a short written report. Remember, Mr. Selig is the president of the bank, so you will want to ensure that your report is complete and accurate. A copy of the data appears in Appendix A.6.

Century National Bank has offices in several cities in the Midwest and the southeastern part of the United States. Mr. Dan Selig, president and CEO, would like to know the characteristics of his checking account customers. What is the balance of a typical customer?

How many other bank services do the checking account customers use? Do the customers use the ATM service and, if so, how often? What about debit cards? Who

2. Determine the mean and median of the checking account balances. Compare the mean and the median balances for the four branches. Is there a difference among the branches? Be sure to explain the difference between the mean and the median in your report.
3. Determine the range and the standard deviation of the checking account balances. What do the first and third quartiles show? Determine the coefficient of skewness and indicate what it shows. Because Mr. Selig does not deal with statistics daily, include a brief description and interpretation of the standard deviation and other measures.

B. Wildcat Plumbing Supply Inc.: Do We Have Gender Differences?

Wildcat Plumbing Supply has served the plumbing needs of Southwest Arizona for more than 40 years

Practice Test

The Practice Test is intended to give students an idea of content that might appear on a test and how the test might be structured. The Practice Test includes both objective questions and problems covering the material studied in the section.

PRACTICE TEST

There is a practice test at the end of each review section. The tests are in two parts. The first part contains several objective questions, usually in a fill-in-the-blank format. The second part is problems. In most cases, it should take 30 to 45 minutes to complete the test. The problems require a calculator. Check the answers in the Answer Section in the back of the book.

Part 1—Objective

1. The science of collecting, organizing, presenting, analyzing, and interpreting data to assist in making effective decisions is called ______. 1. ______
2. Methods of organizing, summarizing, and presenting data in an informative way are called ______. 2. ______
3. The entire set of individuals or objects of interest or the measurements obtained from all individuals or objects of interest are called the ______ 3. ______

Required=Results

©Getty Images/iStockphoto

McGraw-Hill Connect®
Learn Without Limits

Connect is a teaching and learning platform that is proven to deliver better results for students and instructors.

Connect empowers students by continually adapting to deliver precisely what they need, when they need it, and how they need it, so your class time is more engaging and effective.

73% of instructors who use **Connect** require it; instructor satisfaction **increases** by 28% when **Connect** is required.

Connect's Impact on Retention Rates, Pass Rates, and Average Exam Scores

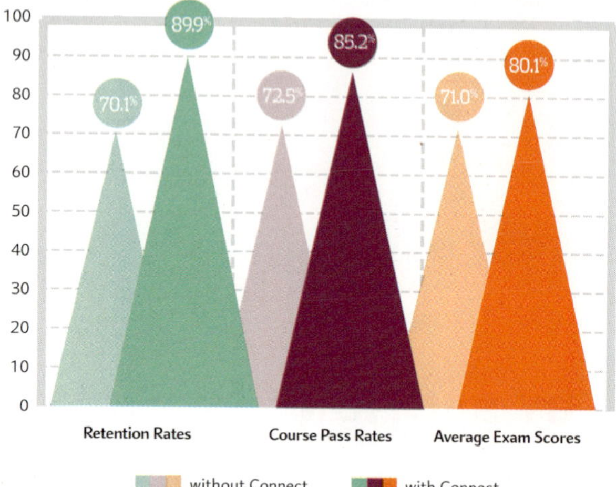

Using **Connect** improves retention rates by **19.8%**, passing rates by **12.7%**, and exam scores by **9.1%**.

Analytics

Connect Insight®

Connect Insight is Connect's new one-of-a-kind visual analytics dashboard—now available for both instructors and students—that provides at-a-glance information regarding student performance, which is immediately actionable. By presenting assignment, assessment, and topical performance results together with a time metric that is easily visible for aggregate or individual results, Connect Insight gives the user the ability to take a just-in-time approach to teaching and learning, which was never before available. Connect Insight presents data that empowers students and helps instructors improve class performance in a way that is efficient and effective.

Impact on Final Course Grade Distribution

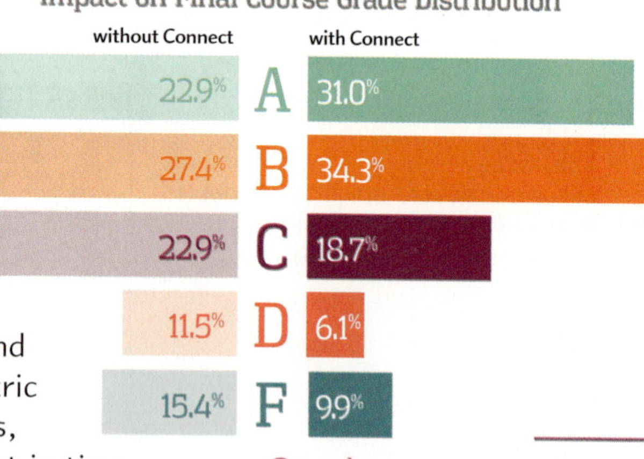

Students can view their results for any **Connect** course.

Mobile

Connect's new, intuitive mobile interface gives students and instructors flexible and convenient, anytime–anywhere access to all components of the Connect platform.

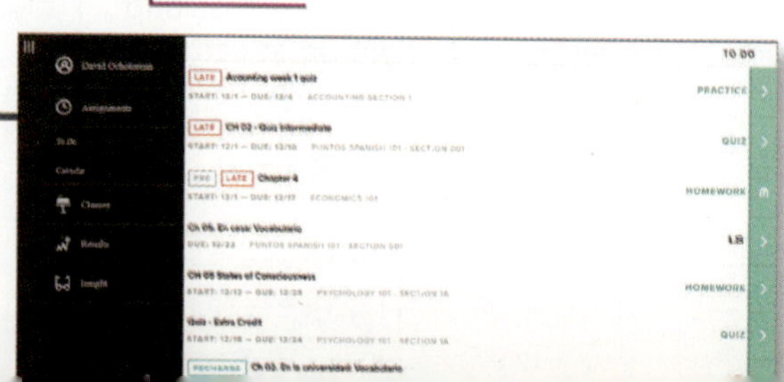

Adaptive

THE **ADAPTIVE READING EXPERIENCE** DESIGNED TO TRANSFORM THE WAY STUDENTS READ

More students earn **A's** and **B's** when they use McGraw-Hill Education **Adaptive** products.

SmartBook®

Proven to help students improve grades and study more efficiently, SmartBook contains the same content within the print book, but actively tailors that content to the needs of the individual. SmartBook's adaptive technology provides precise, personalized instruction on what the student should do next, guiding the student to master and remember key concepts, targeting gaps in knowledge and offering customized feedback, and driving the student toward comprehension and retention of the subject matter. Available on tablets, SmartBook puts learning at the student's fingertips—anywhere, anytime.

Over **8 billion questions** have been answered, making McGraw-Hill Education products more intelligent, reliable, and precise.

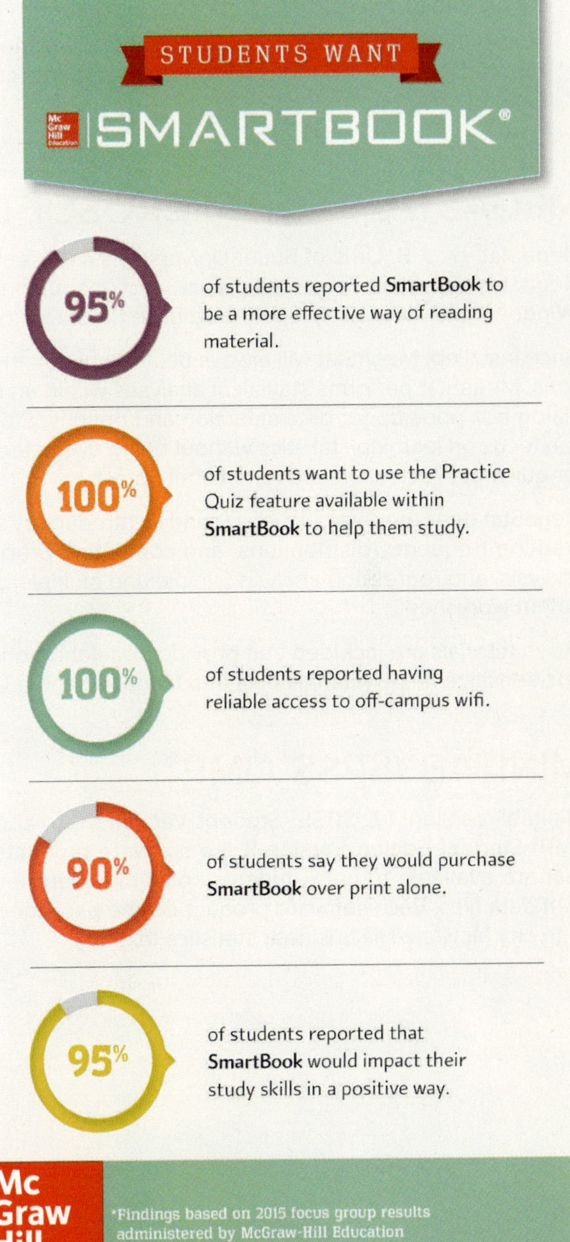

www.mheducation.com

INSTRUCTOR LIBRARY

The *Connect*® *Business Statistics* Instructor Library is your repository for additional resources to improve student engagement in and out of class. You can select and use any asset that enhances your lecture, including:

- **Solutions Manual** The Solutions Manual, carefully revised by the authors, contains solutions to all basic, intermediate, and challenge problems found at the end of each chapter.
- **Test Bank** The Test Bank, revised by Wendy Bailey of Troy University, contains hundreds of true/false, multiple choice and short-answer/discussions, updated based on the revisions of the authors. The level of difficulty varies, as indicated by the easy, medium, and difficult labels.
- **Powerpoint Presentations** Prepared by Stephanie Campbell of Mineral Area College, the presentations contain exhibits, tables, key points, and summaries in a visually stimulating collection of slides.
- **Excel Templates** There are templates for various end of chapter problems that have been set as Excel spreadsheets—all denoted by an icon. Students can easily download, save the files and use the data to solve end of chapter problems.

MEGASTAT® FOR MICROSOFT EXCEL®

MegaStat® by J. B. Orris of Butler University is a full-featured Excel statistical analysis add-in that is available on the MegaStat website at www.mhhe.com/megastat (for purchase). MegaStat works with recent versions of Microsoft Excel® (Windows and Mac OS X). See the website for details on supported versions.

Once installed, MegaStat will always be available on the Excel add-ins ribbon with no expiration date or data limitations. MegaStat performs statistical analyses within an Excel workbook. When a MegaStat menu item is selected, a dialog box pops up for data selection and options. Since MegaStat is an easy-to-use extension of Excel, students can focus on learning statistics without being distracted by the software. Ease-of-use features include Auto Expand for quick data selection and Auto Label detect.

MegaStat does most calculations found in introductory statistics textbooks, such as computing descriptive statistics, creating frequency distributions, and computing probabilities as well as hypothesis testing, ANOVA, chi-square analysis, and regression analysis (simple and multiple). MegaStat output is carefully formatted and appended to an output worksheet.

Video tutorials are included that provide a walkthrough using MegaStat for typical business statistics topics. A context-sensitive help system is built into MegaStat and a User's Guide is included in PDF format.

MINITAB®/SPSS®/JMP®

Minitab® Version 17, SPSS® Student Version 18.0, and JMP® Student Edition Version 8 are software products that are available to help students solve the exercises with data files. Each software product can be packaged with any McGraw-Hill business statistics text.

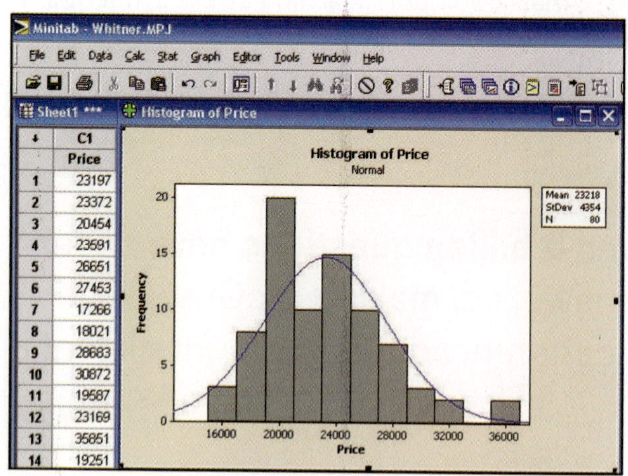

ACKNOWLEDGMENTS

This edition of *Statistical Techniques in Business and Economics* is the product of many people: students, colleagues, reviewers, and the staff at McGraw-Hill Education. We thank them all. We wish to express our sincere gratitude to the reviewers:

Stefan Ruediger
Arizona State University
Anthony Clark
St. Louis Community College
Umair Khalil
West Virginia University
Leonie Stone
SUNY Geneseo
Golnaz Taghvatalab
Central Michigan University
John Yarber
Northeast Mississippi Community College
John Beyers
University of Maryland
Mohammad Kazemi
University of North Carolina Charlotte
Anna Terzyan
Loyola Marymount University
Lee O. Cannell
El Paso Community College

Their suggestions and thorough reviews of the previous edition and the manuscript of this edition make this a better text.

Special thanks go to a number of people. Shelly Moore, College of Western Idaho, and John Arcaro, Lakeland Community College, accuracy checked the *Connect* exercises. Ed Pappanastos, Troy University, built new data sets and revised Smartbook. Rene Ordonez, Southern Oregon University, built the *Connect* guided examples. Wendy Bailey, Tory University, prepared the test bank. Stephanie Campbell, Mineral Area College, prepared the Powerpoint decks. Vickie Fry, Westmoreland County Community College, provided countless hours of digital accuracy checking and support.

We also wish to thank the staff at McGraw-Hill. This includes Dolly Womack, Senior Brand Manager; Michele Janicek, Product Developer Coordinator; Camille Corum and Ryan McAndrews, Product Developers; Harvey Yep and Bruce Gin, Content Project Managers; and others we do not know personally, but who have made valuable contributions.

ENHANCEMENTS TO STATISTICAL TECHNIQUES IN BUSINESS & ECONOMICS, 17E

MAJOR CHANGES MADE TO INDIVIDUAL CHAPTERS:

CHAPTER 1 What Is Statistics?

- Revised Self-Review 1-2.
- New Section describing Business Analytics and its integration with the text.
- Updated exercises 2, 3, 17, and 19.
- New Data Analytics section with new data and questions.

CHAPTER 2 Describing Data: Frequency Tables, Frequency Distributions, and Graphic Presentation

- Revised chapter introduction.
- Added more explanation about cumulative relative frequency distributions.
- Updated exercises 47 and 48 using real data.
- New Data Analytics section with new data and questions.

CHAPTER 3 Describing Data: Numerical Measures

- Updated Self-Review 3-2.
- Updated Exercises 16, 18, 73, 77, and 82.
- New Data Analytics section with new data and questions.

CHAPTER 4 Describing Data: Displaying and Exploring Data

- Updated exercise 22 with 2016 New York Yankee player salaries.
- New Data Analytics section with new data and questions.

CHAPTER 5 A Survey of Probability Concepts

- Revised the Example/Solution in the section on Bayes Theorem.
- Updated exercises 45 and 58 using real data.
- New Data Analytics section with new data and questions.

CHAPTER 6 Discrete Probability Distributions

- Expanded discussion of random variables.
- Revised the Example/Solution in the section on Poisson distribution.
- Updated exercises 18, 58, and 68.
- New Data Analytics section with new data and questions.

CHAPTER 7 Continuous Probability Distributions

- Revised Self-Review 7-1.
- Revised the Example/Solutions using Uber as the context.
- Updated exercises 19, 22, 28, 36, 47, and 64.
- New Data Analytics section with new data and questions.

CHAPTER 8 Sampling Methods and the Central Limit Theorem

- New Data Analytics section with new data and questions.

CHAPTER 9 Estimation and Confidence Intervals

- New Self-Review 9-3 problem description.
- Updated exercises 5, 6, 12, 14, 23, 24, 33, 41, 43, and 61.
- New Data Analytics section with new data and questions.

CHAPTER 10 One-Sample Tests of Hypothesis

- Revised the Example/Solutions using an airport, cell phone parking lot as the context.
- Revised the section on Type II error to include an additional example.
- New Type II error exercises, 23 and 24.
- Updated exercises 19, 31, 32, and 43.
- New Data Analytics section with new data and questions.

CHAPTER 11 Two-Sample Tests of Hypothesis

- Updated exercises 5, 9, 12, 26, 27, 30, 32, 34, 40, 42, and 46.
- New Data Analytics section with new data and questions.

CHAPTER 12 Analysis of Variance

- Revised Self-Reviews 12-1 and 12-3.
- Updated exercises 10, 21, 24, 33, 38, 42, and 44.
- New Data Analytics section with new data and questions.

CHAPTER 13 Correlation and Linear Regression

- Added new conceptual formula, to relate the standard error to the regression ANOVA table.
- Updated exercises 36, 41, 42, 43, and 57.
- New Data Analytics section with new data and questions.

CHAPTER 14 Multiple Regression Analysis

- Updated exercises 19, 21, 23, 24, and 25.
- New Data Analytics section with new data and questions.

CHAPTER 15 Nonparametric Methods: Nominal Level Hypothesis Tests

- Updated the context of Manelli Perfume Company Example/Solution.
- Revised the "Hypothesis Test of Unequal Expected Frequencies" Example/Solution.
- Updated exercises 3, 31, 42, 46, and 61.
- New Data Analytics section with new data and questions.

CHAPTER 16 Nonparametric Methods: Analysis of Ordinal Data

- Revised the "Sign Test" Example/Solution.
- Revised the "Testing a Hypothesis About a Median" Example/Solution.
- Revised the "Wilcoxon Rank-Sum Test for Independent Populations" Example/Solution.
- Revised Self-Reviews 16-3 and 16-6.
- Updated exercise 25.
- New Data Analytics section with new data and questions.

CHAPTER 17 Index Numbers

- Revised Self-Reviews 17-1, 17-2, 17-3, 17-4, 17-5, 17-6, 17-7.
- Updated dates, illustrations, and examples.
- New Data Analytics section with new data and questions.

CHAPTER 18 Time Series and Forecasting

- Updated dates, illustrations, and examples.
- New Data Analytics section with new data and questions.

CHAPTER 19 Statistical Process Control and Quality Management

- Updated 2016 Malcolm Baldridge National Quality Award winners.
- Updated exercises 13, 22, and 25.

BRIEF CONTENTS

CONTENTS

What is Statistics?

1

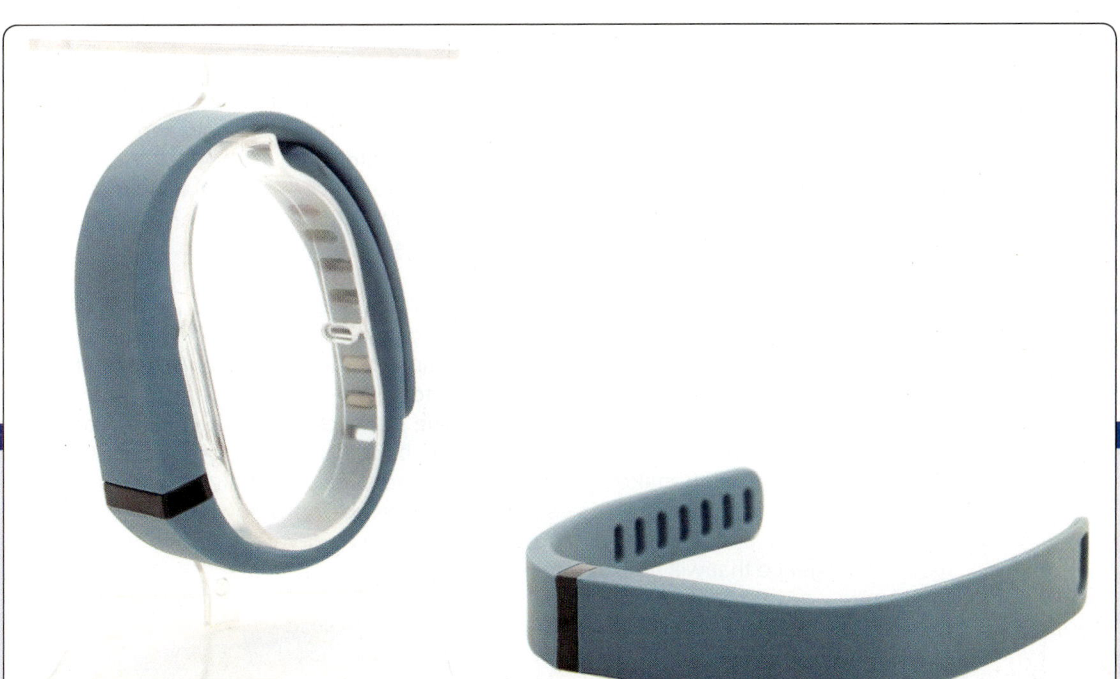

© Kelvin Wong/Shutterstock.com

▲ **BEST BUY** sells Fitbit wearable technology products that track a person's physical activity and sleep quality. The Fitbit technology collects daily information on a person's number of steps so that a person can track calories consumed. The information can be synced with a cell phone and displayed with a Fitbit app. Assume you know the daily number of Fitbit Flex 2 units sold last month at the Best Buy store in Collegeville, Pennsylvania. Describe a situation where the number of units sold is considered a sample. Illustrate a second situation where the number of units sold is considered a population. (See Exercise 11 and LO1-3.)

LEARNING OBJECTIVES

When you have completed this chapter, you will be able to:

LO1-1 Explain why knowledge of statistics is important.

LO1-2 Define statistics and provide an example of how statistics is applied.

LO1-3 Differentiate between descriptive and inferential statistics.

LO1-4 Classify variables as qualitative or quantitative, and discrete or continuous.

LO1-5 Distinguish between nominal, ordinal, interval, and ratio levels of measurement.

LO1-6 List the values associated with the practice of statistics.

© Gregor Schuster/Getty Images RF

INTRODUCTION

Suppose you work for a large company and your supervisor asks you to decide if a new version of a smartphone should be produced and sold. You start by thinking about the product's innovations and new features. Then, you stop and realize the consequences of the decision. The product will need to make a profit so the pricing and the costs of production and distribution are all very important. The decision to introduce the product is based on many alternatives. So how will you know? Where do you start?

Without a long experience in the industry, beginning to develop an intelligence that will make you an expert is essential. You select three other people to work with and meet with them. The conversation focuses on what you need to know and what information and data you need. In your meeting, many questions are asked. How many competitors are already in the market? How are smartphones priced? What design features do competitors' products have? What features does the market require? What do customers want in a smartphone? What do customers like about the existing products? The answers will be based on business intelligence consisting of data and information collected through customer surveys, engineering analysis, and market research. In the end, your presentation to support your decision regarding the introduction of a new smartphone is based on the statistics that you use to summarize and organize your data, the statistics that you use to compare the new product to existing products, and the statistics to estimate future sales, costs, and revenues. The statistics will be the focus of the conversation that you will have with your supervisor about this very important decision.

As a decision maker, you will need to acquire and analyze data to support your decisions. The purpose of this text is to develop your knowledge of basic statistical techniques and methods and how to apply them to develop the business and personal intelligence that will help you make decisions.

LO1-1

Explain why knowledge of statistics is important.

WHY STUDY STATISTICS?

If you look through your university catalogue, you will find that statistics is required for many college programs. As you investigate a future career in accounting, economics, human resources, finance, business analytics, or other business area, you also will discover that statistics is required as part of these college programs. So why is statistics a requirement in so many disciplines?

A major driver of the requirement for statistics knowledge is the technologies available for capturing data. Examples include the technology that Google uses to track how Internet users access websites. As people use Google to search the Internet, Google records every search and then uses these data to sort and prioritize the results for future Internet searches. One recent estimate indicates that Google processes 20,000 terabytes of information per day. Big-box retailers like Target, Walmart, Kroger, and others scan every purchase and use the data to manage the distribution of products, to make decisions about marketing and sales, and to track daily and even hourly sales. Police departments collect and use data to provide city residents with maps that communicate information about crimes committed and their location. Every organization is collecting and using data to develop knowledge and intelligence that will help people make informed decisions, and to track the implementation of their decisions. The graphic to the left shows the amount of data generated every minute (www.domo.com). A good working knowledge of statistics is useful for summarizing and organizing data to provide information that is useful and supportive of decision making. Statistics is used to make valid comparisons and to predict the outcomes of decisions.

In summary, there are at least three reasons for studying statistics: (1) data are collected everywhere and require statistical knowledge to make the information useful, (2) statistical techniques are used to make professional and personal decisions, and (3) no matter what your career, you will need a knowledge of statistics to understand the world and to be conversant in your career. An understanding of statistics and statistical method will help you make more effective personal and professional decisions.

LO1-2
Define statistics and provide an example of how statistics is applied.

WHAT IS MEANT BY STATISTICS?

This question can be rephrased in two, subtly different ways: what are statistics and what is statistics? To answer the first question, a statistic is a number used to communicate a piece of information. Examples of **statistics** are:

- The inflation rate is 2%.
- Your grade point average is 3.5.
- The price of a new Tesla Model S sedan is $79,570.

STATISTICS IN ACTION

A feature of our textbook is called *Statistics in Action*. Read each one carefully to get an appreciation of the wide application of statistics in management, economics, nursing, law enforcement, sports, and other disciplines.

- In 2015, *Forbes* published a list of the richest Americans. William Gates, founder of Microsoft Corporation, is the richest. His net worth is estimated at $76.0 billion. (www.forbes.com)
- In 2015, the four largest privately owned American companies, ranked by revenue, were Cargill, Koch Industries, Dell, and Albertsons. (www.forbes.com)
- In the United States, a typical high school graduate earns $668 per week, a typical college graduate with a bachelor's degree earns $1,101 per week, and a typical college graduate with a master's degree earns $1,326 per week. (www.bls.gov/emp/ep_chart_001.htm)

Each of these statistics is a numerical fact and communicates a very limited piece of information that is not very useful by itself. However, if we recognize that each of these statistics is part of a larger discussion, then the question "what **is** statistics" is applicable. Statistics is the set of knowledge and skills used to organize, summarize, and analyze data. The results of statistical analysis will start interesting conversations in the search for knowledge and intelligence that will help us make decisions. For example:

- The inflation rate for the calendar year was 0.7%. By applying statistics we could compare this year's inflation rate to the past observations of inflation. Is it higher, lower, or about the same? Is there a trend of increasing or decreasing inflation? Is there a relationship between interest rates and government bonds?
- Your grade point average (GPA) is 3.5. By collecting data and applying statistics, you can determine the required GPA to be admitted to the Master of Business Administration program at the University of Chicago, Harvard, or the University of Michigan. You can determine the likelihood that you would be admitted to a particular program. You may be interested in interviewing for a management position with Procter & Gamble. What GPA does Procter & Gamble require for college graduates with a bachelor's degree? Is there a range of acceptable GPAs?
- You are budgeting for a new car. You would like to own an electric car with a small carbon footprint. The price for the Tesla Model S Sedan is $79,570. By collecting additional data and applying statistics, you can analyze the alternatives. For example, another choice is a hybrid car that runs on both gas and electricity such as a 2015 Toyota Prius. It can be purchased for about $28,659. Another hybrid, the Chevrolet Volt, costs $33,995. What are the differences in the cars' specifications? What additional information can be collected and summarized so that you can make a good purchase decision?

Another example of using statistics to provide information to evaluate decisions is the distribution and market share of Frito-Lay products. Data are collected on each of the Frito-Lay product lines. These data include the market share and the pounds of product sold. Statistics is used to present this information in a bar chart in Chart 1–1. It clearly shows Frito-Lay's dominance in the potato, corn, and tortilla chip markets. It also shows the absolute measure of pounds of each product line consumed in the United States.

These examples show that statistics is more than the presentation of numerical information. Statistics is about collecting and processing information to create a conversation, to stimulate additional questions, and to provide a basis for making decisions. Specifically, we define **statistics** as:

STATISTICS The science of collecting, organizing, presenting, analyzing, and interpreting data to assist in making more effective decisions.

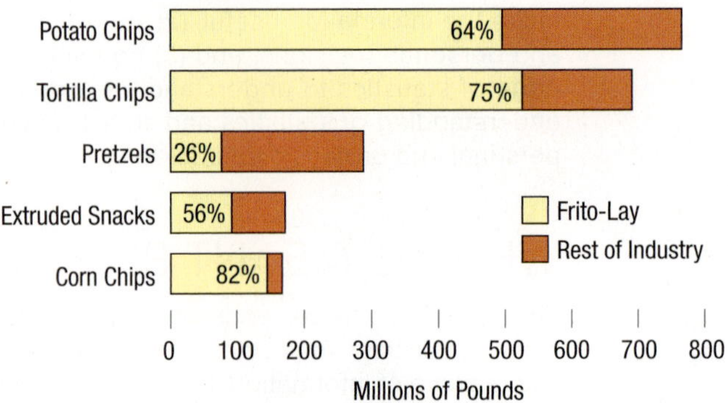

CHART 1–1 Frito-Lay Volume and Share of Major Snack Chip Categories in U.S. Supermarkets

In this book, you will learn the basic techniques and applications of statistics that you can use to support your decisions, both personal and professional. To start, we will differentiate between descriptive and inferential statistics.

LO1-3
Differentiate between descriptive and inferential statistics.

TYPES OF STATISTICS

When we use statistics to generate information for decision making from data, we use either descriptive statistics or inferential statistics. Their application depends on the questions asked and the type of data available.

Descriptive Statistics

Masses of unorganized data—such as the census of population, the weekly earnings of thousands of computer programmers, and the individual responses of 2,000 registered voters regarding their choice for president of the United States—are of little value as is. However, descriptive statistics can be used to organize data into a meaningful form. We define **descriptive statistics** as:

> **DESCRIPTIVE STATISTICS** Methods of organizing, summarizing, and presenting data in an informative way.

The following are examples that apply descriptive statistics to summarize a large amount of data and provide information that is easy to understand.

- There are a total of 46,837 miles of interstate highways in the United States. The interstate system represents only 1% of the nation's total roads but carries more than 20% of the traffic. The longest is I-90, which stretches from Boston to Seattle, a distance of 3,099 miles. The shortest is I-878 in New York City, which is 0.70 mile in length. Alaska does not have any interstate highways, Texas has the most interstate miles at 3,232, and New York has the most interstate routes with 28.
- The average person spent $133.91 on traditional Valentine's Day merchandise in 2014. This is an increase of $2.94 from 2013. As in previous years, men spent more than twice the amount women spent on the holiday. The average man spent $108.38 to impress the people in his life while women only spent $48.41.

Statistical methods and techniques to generate descriptive statistics are presented in Chapters 2 and 4. These include organizing and summarizing data with frequency distributions and presenting frequency distributions with charts and graphs. In addition, statistical measures to summarize the characteristics of a distribution are discussed in Chapter 3.

Inferential Statistics

Sometimes we must make decisions based on a limited set of data. For example, we would like to know the operating characteristics, such as fuel efficiency measured by miles per gallon, of sport utility vehicles (SUVs) currently in use. If we spent a lot of time, money, and effort, all the owners of SUVs could be surveyed. In this case, our goal would be to survey the **population** of SUV owners.

POPULATION The entire set of individuals or objects of interest or the measurements obtained from all individuals or objects of interest.

However, based on inferential statistics, we can survey a limited number of SUV owners and collect a **sample** from the population.

SAMPLE A portion, or part, of the population of interest.

Samples often are used to obtain reliable estimates of population parameters. (Sampling is discussed in Chapter 8.) In the process, we make trade-offs between the time, money, and effort to collect the data and the error of estimating a population parameter. The process of sampling SUVs is illustrated in the following graphic. In this example, we would like to know the mean or average SUV fuel efficiency. To estimate the mean of the population, six SUVs are sampled and the mean of their MPG is calculated.

STATISTICS IN ACTION

Where did statistics get its start? In 1662 John Graunt published an article called "Natural and Political Observations Made upon Bills of Mortality." The author's "observations" were the result of a study and analysis of a weekly church publication called "Bill of Mortality," which listed births, christenings, and deaths and their causes. Graunt realized that the Bills of Mortality represented only a fraction of all births and deaths in London. However, he used the data to reach broad conclusions or inferences about the impact of disease, such as the plague, on the general population. His logic is an example of statistical inference. His analysis and interpretation of the data are thought to mark the start of statistics.

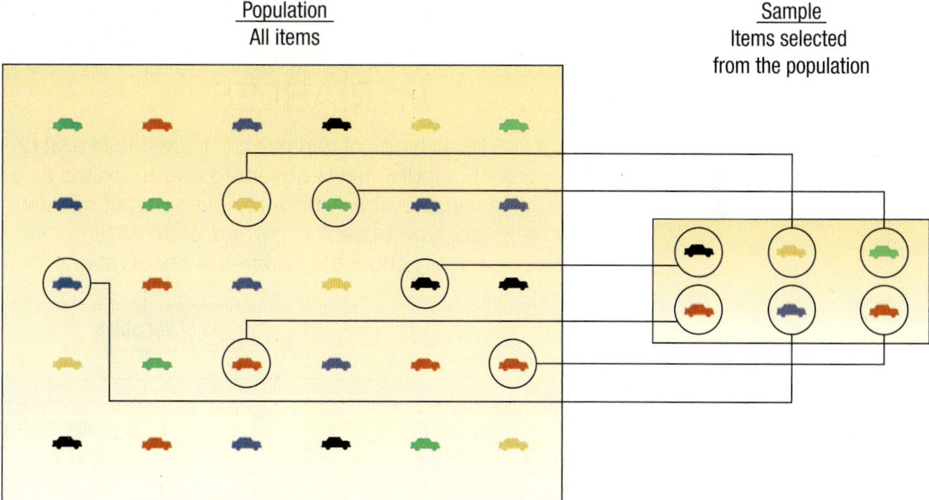

So, the sample of six SUVs represents evidence from the population that we use to reach an inference or conclusion about the average MPG for all SUVs. The process of sampling from a population with the objective of estimating properties of a population is called **inferential statistics.**

INFERENTIAL STATISTICS The methods used to estimate a property of a population on the basis of a sample.

Inferential statistics is widely applied to learn something about a population in business, agriculture, politics, and government, as shown in the following examples:

- Television networks constantly monitor the popularity of their programs by hiring Nielsen and other organizations to sample the preferences of TV viewers. For example, 9.0% of a sample of households with TVs watched The Big Bang Theory during the week of November 2, 2015 (www.nielsen.com). These program ratings are used to make decisions about advertising rates and whether to continue or cancel a program.
- In 2015, a sample of U.S. Internal Revenue Service tax preparation volunteers were tested with three standard tax returns. The sample indicated that tax returns were completed with a 49% accuracy rate. In other words there were errors on about half of the returns. In this example, the statistics are used to make decisions about how to improve the accuracy rate by correcting the most common errors and improving the training of volunteers.

A feature of our text is self-review problems. There are a number of them interspersed throughout each chapter. The first self-review follows. Each self-review tests your comprehension of preceding material. The answer and method of solution are given in Appendix E. You can find the answer to the following self-review in 1–1 in Appendix E. We recommend that you solve each one and then check your answer.

SELF-REVIEW 1–1

The answers are in Appendix E.

The Atlanta-based advertising firm Brandon and Associates asked a sample of 1,960 consumers to try a newly developed chicken dinner by Boston Market. Of the 1,960 sampled, 1,176 said they would purchase the dinner if it is marketed.

(a) Is this an example of descriptive statistics or inferential statistics? Explain.
(b) What could Brandon and Associates report to Boston Market regarding acceptance of the chicken dinner in the population?

LO1-4
Classify variables as qualitative or quantitative, and discrete or continuous.

TYPES OF VARIABLES

There are two basic types of variables: (1) qualitative and (2) quantitative (see Chart 1–2). When an object or individual is observed and recorded as a nonnumeric characteristic, it is a qualitative variable or an attribute. Examples of qualitative variables are gender, beverage preference, type of vehicle owned, state of birth, and eye color. When a variable is qualitative, we usually count the number of observations for each category and determine

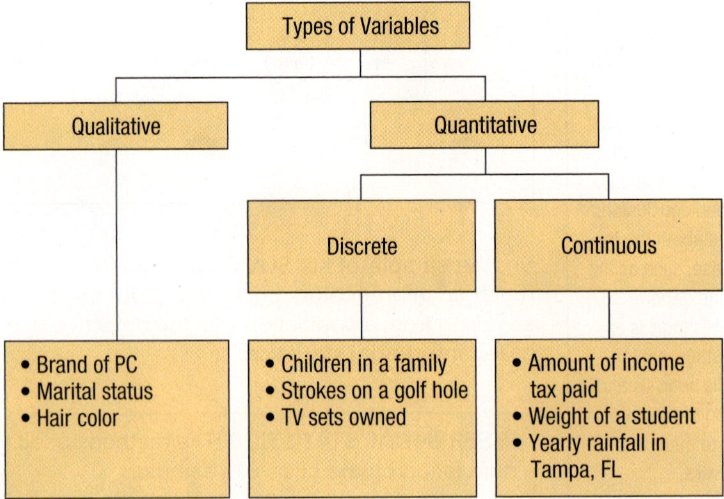

CHART 1–2 Summary of the Types of Variables

what percent are in each category. For example, if we observe the variable eye color, what percent of the population has blue eyes and what percent has brown eyes? If the variable is type of vehicle, what percent of the total number of cars sold last month were SUVs? Qualitative variables are often summarized in charts and bar graphs (Chapter 2).

When a variable can be reported numerically, it is called a quantitative variable. Examples of quantitative variables are the balance in your checking account, the number of gigabytes of data used on your cell phone plan last month, the life of a car battery (such as 42 months), and the number of people employed by a company.

Quantitative variables are either discrete or continuous. Discrete variables can assume only certain values, and there are "gaps" between the values. Examples of discrete variables are the number of bedrooms in a house (1, 2, 3, 4, etc.), the number of cars arriving at Exit 25 on I-4 in Florida near Walt Disney World in an hour (326, 421, etc.), and the number of students in each section of a statistics course (25 in section A, 42 in section B, and 18 in section C). We count, for example, the number of cars arriving at Exit 25 on I-4, and we count the number of statistics students in each section. Notice that a home can have 3 or 4 bedrooms, but it cannot have 3.56 bedrooms. Thus, there is a "gap" between possible values. Typically, discrete variables are counted.

Observations of a continuous variable can assume any value within a specific range. Examples of continuous variables are the air pressure in a tire and the weight of a shipment of tomatoes. Other examples are the ounces of raisins in a box of raisin bran cereal and the duration of flights from Orlando to San Diego. Grade point average (GPA) is a continuous variable. We could report the GPA of a particular student as 3.2576952. The usual practice is to round to 3 places—3.258. Typically, continuous variables result from measuring.

LO1-5
Distinguish between nominal, ordinal, interval, and ratio levels of measurement.

LEVELS OF MEASUREMENT

Data can be classified according to levels of measurement. The level of measurement determines how data should be summarized and presented. It also will indicate the type of statistical analysis that can be performed. Here are two examples of the relationship between measurement and how we apply statistics. There are six colors of candies in a bag of M&Ms. Suppose we assign brown a value of 1, yellow 2, blue 3, orange 4, green 5, and red 6. What kind of variable is the color of an M&M? It is a qualitative variable. Suppose someone summarizes M&M color by adding the assigned color values, divides the sum by the number of M&Ms, and reports that the mean color is 3.56. How do we interpret this statistic? You are correct in concluding that it has no meaning as a measure of M&M color. As a qualitative variable, we can only report the count and percentage of each color in a bag of M&Ms. As a second example, in a high school track meet there are eight competitors in the 400-meter run. We report the order of finish and that the mean finish is 4.5. What does the mean finish tell us? Nothing! In both of these instances, we have not used the appropriate statistics for the level of measurement.

© Ron Buskirk/Alamy Stock Photo

There are four levels of measurement: nominal, ordinal, interval, and ratio. The lowest, or the most primitive, measurement is the nominal level. The highest is the ratio level of measurement.

Nominal-Level Data

For the **nominal level of measurement,** observations of a qualitative variable are measured and recorded as labels or names. The labels or names can only be classified and counted. There is no particular order to the labels.

NOMINAL LEVEL OF MEASUREMENT Data recorded at the nominal level of measurement is represented as labels or names. They have no order. They can only be classified and counted.

The classification of the six colors of M&M milk chocolate candies is an example of the nominal level of measurement. We simply classify the candies by color. There is no natural order. That is, we could report the brown candies first, the orange first, or any of the other colors first. Recording the variable gender is another example of the nominal level of measurement. Suppose we count the number of students entering a football game with a student ID and report how many are men and how many are women. We could report either the men or the women first. For the data measured at the nominal level, we are limited to counting the number in each category of the variable. Often, we convert these counts to percentages. For example, a random sample of M&M candies reports the following percentages for each color:

Color	Percent in a bag
Blue	24%
Green	20%
Orange	16%
Yellow	14%
Red	13%
Brown	13%

To process the data for a variable measured at the nominal level, we often numerically code the labels or names. For example, if we are interested in measuring the home state for students at East Carolina University, we would assign a student's home state of Alabama a code of 1, Alaska a code of 2, Arizona a 3, and so on. Using this procedure with an alphabetical listing of states, Wisconsin is coded 49 and Wyoming 50. Realize that the number assigned to each state is still a label or name. The reason we assign numerical codes is to facilitate counting the number of students from each state with statistical software. Note that assigning numbers to the states does not give us license to manipulate the codes as numerical information. Specifically, in this example, $1 + 2 = 3$ corresponds to Alabama + Alaska = Arizona. Clearly, the nominal level of measurement does not permit any mathematical operation that has any valid interpretation.

Ordinal-Level Data

The next higher level of measurement is the **ordinal level.** For this level of measurement a qualitative variable or attribute is either ranked or rated on a relative scale.

ORDINAL LEVEL OF MEASUREMENT Data recorded at the ordinal level of measurement is based on a relative ranking or rating of items based on a defined attribute or qualitative variable. Variables based on this level of measurement are only ranked or counted.

Best Business Climate

1. Florida
2. Utah
3. Texas
4. Georgia
5. Indiana
6. Tennessee
7. Nebraska
8. North Carolina
9. Virginia
10. Washington

For example, many businesses make decisions about where to locate their facilities; in other words, where is the best place for their business? Business Facilities (www.businessfacilities.com) publishes a list of the top 10 states for the "best business climate." The 2016 rankings are shown to the left. They are based on the evaluation of many different factors, including the cost of labor, business tax climate, quality of life, transportation infrastructure, educated workforce, and economic growth potential.

This is an example of an ordinal scale because the states are ranked in order of best to worst business climate. That is, we know the relative order of the states based on the attribute. For example, in 2016 Florida had the best business climate and Utah was second. Indiana was fifth, and that was better than Tennessee but not as good as Georgia. Notice we cannot say that Florida's business climate is five times better than Indiana's business climate because the magnitude of the differences between the states is not known. To put it another way, we do not know if the magnitude of the difference between Louisiana and Utah is the same as between Texas and Georgia.

Another example of the ordinal level measure is based on a scale that measures an attribute. This type of scale is used when students rate instructors on a variety of attributes. One attribute may be: "Overall, how do you rate the quality of instruction in this class?" A student's response is recorded on a relative scale of inferior, poor, good, excellent, and superior. An important characteristic of using a relative measurement scale is that we cannot distinguish the magnitude of the differences between groups. We do not know if the difference between "Superior" and "Good" is the same as the difference between "Poor" and "Inferior."

Table 1–1 lists the frequencies of 60 student ratings of instructional quality for Professor James Brunner in an Introduction to Finance course. The data are summarized based on the order of the scale used to rate the instructor. That is, they are summarized by the number of students who indicated a rating of superior (6), good (26), and so on. We also can convert the frequencies to percentages. About 43.3% (26/60) of the students rated the instructor as good.

TABLE 1–1 Rating of a Finance Professor

Rating	Frequency	Percentage
Superior	6	10.0%
Good	26	43.3%
Average	16	26.7%
Poor	9	15.0%
Inferior	3	5.0%

Interval-Level Data

The **interval level of measurement** is the next highest level. It includes all the characteristics of the ordinal level, but, in addition, the difference or interval between values is meaningful.

INTERVAL LEVEL OF MEASUREMENT For data recorded at the interval level of measurement, the interval or the distance between values is meaningful. The interval level of measurement is based on a scale with a known unit of measurement.

The Fahrenheit temperature scale is an example of the interval level of measurement. Suppose the high temperatures on three consecutive winter days in Boston are 28, 31, and 20 degrees Fahrenheit. These temperatures can be easily ranked, but we can also determine the interval or distance between temperatures. This is possible because 1 degree Fahrenheit represents a constant unit of measurement. That is, the distance between 10 and 15 degrees Fahrenheit is 5 degrees, and is the same as the 5-degree distance between 50 and 55 degrees Fahrenheit. It is also important to note that 0 is just a point on the scale. It does not represent the absence of the condition. The measurement of zero degrees Fahrenheit does not represent the absence of heat or cold. But by our own measurement scale, it is cold! A major limitation of a variable measured at the interval level is that we cannot make statements similar to 20 degrees Fahrenheit is twice as warm as 10 degrees Fahrenheit.

Another example of the interval scale of measurement is women's dress sizes. Listed below is information on several dimensions of a standard U.S. woman's dress.

Size	Bust (in)	Waist (in)	Hips (in)
8	32	24	35
10	34	26	37
12	36	28	39
14	38	30	41
16	40	32	43
18	42	34	45
20	44	36	47
22	46	38	49
24	48	40	51
26	50	42	53
28	52	44	55

Why is the "size" scale an interval measurement? Observe that as the size changes by two units (say from size 10 to size 12 or from size 24 to size 26), each of the measurements increases by 2 inches. To put it another way, the intervals are the same.

There is no natural zero point for dress size. A "size 0" dress does not have "zero" material. Instead, it would have a 24-inch bust, 16-inch waist, and 27-inch hips. Moreover, the ratios are not reasonable. If you divide a size 28 by a size 14, you do not get the same answer as dividing a size 20 by a size 10. Neither ratio is equal to two, as the "size" number would suggest. In short, if the distances between the numbers make sense, but the ratios do not, then you have an interval scale of measurement.

Ratio-Level Data

Almost all quantitative variables are recorded on the **ratio level of measurement.** The ratio level is the "highest" level of measurement. It has all the characteristics of the interval level, but, in addition, the 0 point and the ratio between two numbers are both meaningful.

RATIO LEVEL OF MEASUREMENT Data recorded at the ratio level of measurement are based on a scale with a known unit of measurement and a meaningful interpretation of zero on the scale.

Examples of the ratio scale of measurement include wages, units of production, weight, changes in stock prices, distance between branch offices, and height. Money is also a good illustration. If you have zero dollars, then you have no money, and a wage of $50 per hour is two times the wage of $25 per hour. Weight also is measured at the ratio level of measurement. If a scale is correctly calibrated, then it will read 0 when nothing is on the scale. Further, something that weighs 1 pound is half as heavy as something that weighs 2 pounds.

Table 1–2 illustrates the ratio scale of measurement for the variable, annual income for four father-and-son combinations. Observe that the senior Lahey earns twice as much as his son. In the Rho family, the son makes twice as much as the father.

TABLE 1–2 Father–Son Income Combinations

Name	Father	Son
Lahey	$80,000	$ 40,000
Nale	90,000	30,000
Rho	60,000	120,000
Steele	75,000	130,000

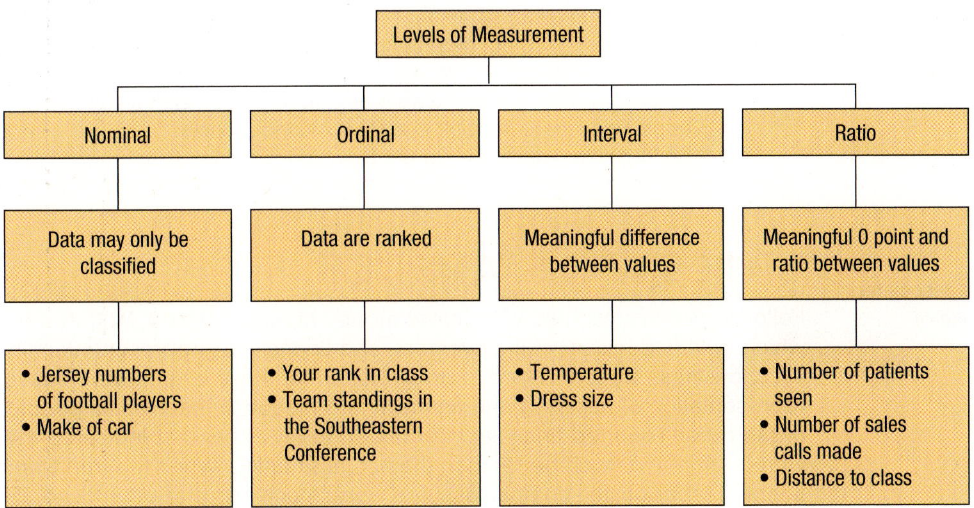

CHART 1–3 Summary and Examples of the Characteristics for Levels of Measurement

Chart 1–3 summarizes the major characteristics of the various levels of measurement. The level of measurement will determine the type of statistical methods that can be used to analyze a variable. Statistical methods to analyze variables measured on a nominal level are discussed in Chapter 15; methods for ordinal-level variables are discussed in Chapter 16. Statistical methods to analyze variables measured on an interval or ratio level are presented in Chapters 9 through 14.

SELF-REVIEW 1–2

(a) The mean age of people who listen to talk radio is 42.1 years. What level of measurement is used to assess the variable age?

(b) In a survey of luxury-car owners, 8% of the U.S. population owned luxury cars. In California and Georgia, 14% of people owned luxury cars. Two variables are included in this information. What are they and how are they measured?

EXERCISES

The answers to the odd-numbered exercises are in Appendix D.

1. What is the level of measurement for each of the following variables?
- **a.** Student IQ ratings.
- **b.** Distance students travel to class.
- **c.** The jersey numbers of a sorority soccer team.
- **d.** A student's state of birth.
- **e.** A student's academic class—that is, freshman, sophomore, junior, or senior.
- **f.** Number of hours students study per week.

2. *Slate* is a daily magazine on the Web. Its business activities can be described by a number of variables. What is the level of measurement for each of the following variables?
- **a.** The number of hits on their website on Saturday between 8:00 am and 9:00 am.
- **b.** The departments, such as food and drink, politics, foreign policy, sports, etc.
- **c.** The number of weekly hits on the Sam's Club ad.
- **d.** The number of years each employee has been employed with Slate.

3. On the Web, go to your favorite news source and find examples of each type of variable. Write a brief memo that lists the variables and describes them in terms of qualitative or quantitative, discrete or continuous, and the measurement level.

4. For each of the following, determine whether the group is a sample or a population.
   a. The participants in a study of a new cholesterol drug.
   b. The drivers who received a speeding ticket in Kansas City last month.
   c. People on welfare in Cook County (Chicago), Illinois.
   d. The 30 stocks that make up the Dow Jones Industrial Average.

LO1-6
List the values associated with the practice of statistics.

ETHICS AND STATISTICS

Following events such as Wall Street money manager Bernie Madoff's Ponzi scheme, which swindled billions from investors, and financial misrepresentations by Enron and Tyco, business students need to understand that these events were based on the misrepresentation of business and financial information. In each case, people within each organization reported financial information to investors that indicated the companies were performing much better than the actual situation. When the true financial information was reported, the companies were worth much less than advertised. The result was many investors lost all or nearly all of the money they had invested.

The article "Statistics and Ethics: Some Advice for Young Statisticians," in *The American Statistician* 57, no. 1 (2003), offers guidance. The authors advise us to practice statistics with integrity and honesty, and urge us to "do the right thing" when collecting, organizing, summarizing, analyzing, and interpreting numerical information. The real contribution of statistics to society is a moral one. Financial analysts need to provide information that truly reflects a company's performance so as not to mislead individual investors. Information regarding product defects that may be harmful to people must be analyzed and reported with integrity and honesty. The authors of *The American Statistician* article further indicate that when we practice statistics, we need to maintain "an independent and principled point-of-view" when analyzing and reporting findings and results.

As you progress through this text, we will highlight ethical issues in the collection, analysis, presentation, and interpretation of statistical information. We also hope that, as you learn about using statistics, you will become a more informed consumer of information. For example, you will question a report based on data that do not fairly represent the population, a report that does not include all relevant statistics, one that includes an incorrect choice of statistical measures, or a presentation that introduces bias in a deliberate attempt to mislead or misrepresent.

BASIC BUSINESS ANALYTICS

A knowledge of statistics is necessary to support the increasing need for companies and organizations to apply business analytics. Business analytics is used to process and analyze data and information to support a story or narrative of a company's business, such as "what makes us profitable," "how will our customers respond to a change in marketing"? In addition to statistics, an ability to use computer software to summarize, organize, analyze, and present the findings of statistical analysis is essential. In this text, we will be using very elementary applications of business analytics using common and available computer software. Throughout our text, we will use Microsoft Excel and, occasionally, Minitab. Universities and colleges usually offer access to Microsoft Excel. Your computer already may be packaged with Microsoft Excel. If not, the Microsoft Office package with Excel often is sold at a reduced academic price through your university or college. In this text, we use Excel for the majority of the applications. We also use an Excel "Add-in" called MegaStat. If your instructor requires this package, it is available at www.mhhe.com/megastat. This add-in gives Excel the capability to produce additional statistical reports. Occasionally, we use Minitab to illustrate an application. See www.minitab.com for further information. Minitab also offers discounted academic pricing. The 2016 version of Microsoft Excel supports the analyses in our text. However, earlier versions of Excel for Apple Mac computers do not have the necessary add-in. If you do not have Excel 2016 and are using an Apple Mac computer with Excel, you can download the free, trial version of Stat Plus at www.analystsoft.com. It is a statistical software package that will integrate with Excel for Mac computers.

The following example shows the application of Excel to perform a statistical summary. It refers to sales information from the Applewood Auto Group, a multi-location car sales and service company. The Applewood information has sales information for 180 vehicle sales. Each sale is described by several variables: the age of the buyer, whether the buyer is a repeat customer, the location of the dealership for the sale, the type of vehicle sold, and the profit for the sale. The following shows Excel's summary of statistics for the variable profit. The summary of profit shows the mean profit per vehicle was $1,843.17, the median profit was slightly more at $1,882.50, and profit ranged from $294 to $3,292.

APPLEWOOD AUTO GROUP.xlsx

	A	B	C	D	E	F	G	H
1	Age	Profit	Location	Vehicle-Type	Previous		Profit	
2	33	$1,889	Olean	SUV	1			
3	47	$1,461	Kane	Sedan	0		Mean	1843.17
4	44	$1,532	Tionesta	SUV	3		Standard Error	47.97
5	53	$1,220	Olean	Sedan	0		Median	1882.50
6	51	$1,674	Sheffield	Sedan	1		Mode	1915.00
7	41	$2,389	Kane	Truck	1		Standard Deviation	643.63
8	58	$2,058	Kane	SUV	1		Sample Variance	414256.61
9	35	$1,919	Tionesta	SUV	1		Kurtosis	-0.22
10	45	$1,266	Olean	Sedan	0		Skewness	-0.24
11	54	$2,991	Tionesta	Sedan	0		Range	2998
12	56	$2,695	Kane	Sedan	2		Minimum	294
13	41	$2,165	Tionesta	SUV	0		Maximum	3292
14	38	$1,766	Sheffield	SUV	0		Sum	331770
15	48	$1,952	Tionesta	Compact	1		Count	180

Throughout the text, we will motivate the use of computer software to summarize, describe, and present information and data. The applications of Excel are supported by instructions so that you can learn how to apply Excel to do statistical analysis. The instructions are presented in Appendix C of this text. These data and other data sets and files are available on the text's student website, www.mhhe.com/lind17e.

CHAPTER SUMMARY

I. Statistics is the science of collecting, organizing, presenting, analyzing, and interpreting data to assist in making more effective decisions.

II. There are two types of statistics.
- **A.** Descriptive statistics are procedures used to organize and summarize data.
- **B.** Inferential statistics involve taking a sample from a population and making estimates about a population based on the sample results.
  - **1.** A population is an entire set of individuals or objects of interest or the measurements obtained from all individuals or objects of interest.
  - **2.** A sample is a part of the population.

III. There are two types of variables.
- **A.** A qualitative variable is nonnumeric.
  - **1.** Usually we are interested in the number or percent of the observations in each category.
  - **2.** Qualitative data are usually summarized in graphs and bar charts.

B. There are two types of quantitative variables and they are usually reported numerically.

1. Discrete variables can assume only certain values, and there are usually gaps between values.

2. A continuous variable can assume any value within a specified range.

IV. There are four levels of measurement.

A. With the nominal level, the data are sorted into categories with no particular order to the categories.

B. The ordinal level of measurement presumes that one classification is ranked higher than another.

C. The interval level of measurement has the ranking characteristic of the ordinal level of measurement plus the characteristic that the distance between values is a constant size.

D. The ratio level of measurement has all the characteristics of the interval level, plus there is a 0 point and the ratio of two values is meaningful.

CHAPTER EXERCISES

5. Explain the difference between qualitative and quantitative variables. Give an example of qualitative and quantitative variables.

6. Explain the difference between a sample and a population.

7. Explain the difference between a discrete and a continuous variable. Give an example of each not included in the text.

8. For the following situations, would you collect information using a sample or a population? Why?

a. Statistics 201 is a course taught at a university. Professor Rauch has taught nearly 1,500 students in the course over the past 5 years. You would like to know the average grade for the course.

b. As part of a research project, you need to report the average profit as a percentage of revenue for the #1-ranked corporation in the Fortune 500 for each of the last 10 years.

c. You are looking forward to graduation and your first job as a salesperson for one of five large pharmaceutical corporations. Planning for your interviews, you will need to know about each company's mission, profitability, products, and markets.

d. You are shopping for a new MP3 music player such as the Apple iPod. The manufacturers advertise the number of music tracks that can be stored in the memory. Usually, the advertisers assume relatively short, popular songs to estimate the number of tracks that can be stored. You, however, like Broadway musical tunes and they are much longer. You would like to estimate how many Broadway tunes will fit on your MP3 player.

9. Exits along interstate highways were formerly numbered successively from the western or southern border of a state. However, the Department of Transportation has recently changed most of them to agree with the numbers on the mile markers along the highway.

a. What level of measurement were data on the consecutive exit numbers?

b. What level of measurement are data on the milepost numbers?

c. Discuss the advantages of the newer system.

10. A poll solicits a large number of college undergraduates for information on the following variables: the name of their cell phone provider (AT&T, Verizon, and so on), the numbers of minutes used last month (200, 400, for example), and their satisfaction with the service (Terrible, Adequate, Excellent, and so forth). What is the level of measurement for each of these three variables?

11. Best Buy sells Fitbit wearable technology products that track a person's activity. For example, the Fitbit technology collects daily information on a person's number of steps so that a person can track calories consumed. The information can be synced with a cell phone and displayed with a Fitbit app. Assume you know the daily number of Fitbit Flex

2 units sold last month at the Best Buy store in Collegeville, Pennsylvania. Describe a situation where the number of units sold is considered a sample. Illustrate a second situation where the number of units sold is considered a population.

12. Using the concepts of sample and population, describe how a presidential election is unlike an "exit" poll of the electorate.

13. Place these variables in the following classification tables. For each table, summarize your observations and evaluate if the results are generally true. For example, salary is reported as a continuous quantitative variable. It is also a continuous ratio-scaled variable.

a. Salary
b. Gender
c. Sales volume of MP3 players
d. Soft drink preference
e. Temperature
f. SAT scores
g. Student rank in class
h. Rating of a finance professor
i. Number of home video screens

	Discrete Variable	Continuous Variable
Qualitative		
Quantitative		a. Salary

	Discrete	Continuous
Nominal		
Ordinal		
Interval		
Ratio		a. Salary

14. Using data from such publications as the *Statistical Abstract of the United States, Forbes,* or any news source, give examples of variables measured with nominal, ordinal, interval, and ratio scales.

15. The Struthers Wells Corporation employs more than 10,000 white-collar workers in its sales offices and manufacturing facilities in the United States, Europe, and Asia. A sample of 300 U.S. workers revealed 120 would accept a transfer to a location outside the United States. On the basis of these findings, write a brief memo to Ms. Wanda Carter, Vice President of Human Services, regarding all white-collar workers in the firm and their willingness to relocate.

16. AVX Home Entertainment, Inc., recently began a "no-hassles" return policy. A sample of 500 customers who recently returned items showed 400 thought the policy was fair, 32 thought it took too long to complete the transaction, and the rest had no opinion. On the basis of this information, make an inference about customer reaction to the new policy.

17. FILE *The Wall Street Journal*'s website, www.wsj.com, reported the number of cars and light-duty trucks sold through October of 2014 and October of 2015. The top sixteen manufacturers are listed here. Sales data often is reported in this way to compare current sales to last year's sales.

Manufacturer	Year-to-Date Sales Through October 2015	Through October 2014
General Motors Corp.	2,562,840	2,434,707
Ford Motor Company	2,178,587	2,065,612
Toyota Motor Sales USA Inc.	2,071,446	1,975,368
Chrysler	1,814,268	1,687,313
American Honda Motor Co Inc.	1,320,217	1,281,777
Nissan North America Inc.	1,238,535	1,166,389
Hyundai Motor America	638,195	607,539
Kia Motors America Inc.	526,024	489,711
Subaru of America Inc.	480,331	418,497
Volkswagen of America Inc.	294,602	301,187
Mercedes-Benz	301,915	281,728
BMW of North America Inc.	279,395	267,193
Mazda Motor of America Inc.	267,158	259,751
Audi of America Inc.	165,103	146,133
Mitsubishi Motors N A, Inc.	80,683	64,564
Volvo	53,803	47,823

a. Using computer software, compare the October 2015 sales to the October 2014 sales for each manufacturer by computing the difference. Make a list of the manufacturers that increased sales compared to 2014; make a list of manufacturers that decreased sales.

b. Using computer software, compare 2014 sales to 2015 sales for each manufacturer by computing the percentage change in sales. Make a list of the manufacturers in order of increasing percentage changes. Which manufacturers are in the top five in percentage change? Which manufacturers are in the bottom five in percentage change?

c. Using computer software, first sort the data using the 2015 year-to-date sales. Then, design a bar graph to illustrate the 2014 and 2015 year-to-date sales for the top 12 manufacturers. Also, design a bar graph to illustrate the percentage change for the top 12 manufacturers. Compare these two graphs and prepare brief written comments.

18. The following chart depicts the average amounts spent by consumers on holiday gifts.

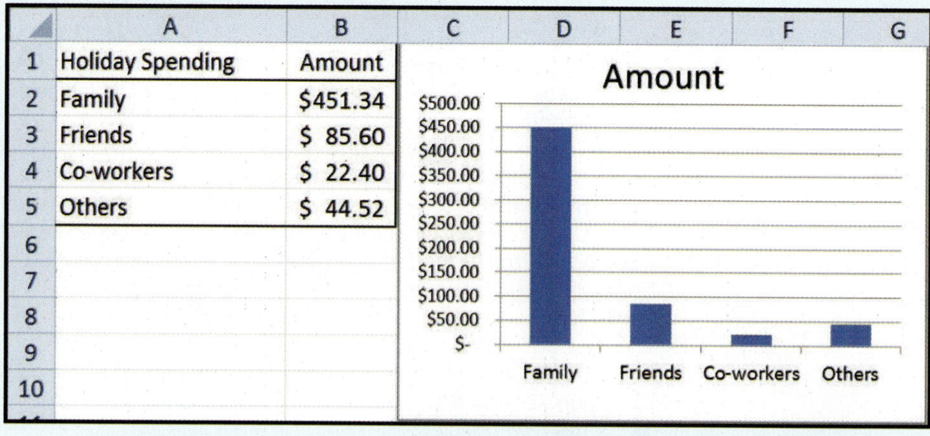

Holiday Spending	Amount
Family	$451.34
Friends	$ 85.60
Co-workers	$ 22.40
Others	$ 44.52

Write a brief report summarizing the amounts spent during the holidays. Be sure to include the total amount spent and the percent spent by each group.

19. The following chart depicts the earnings in billions of dollars for ExxonMobil for the period 2003 until 2014. Write a brief report discussing the earnings at ExxonMobil during the period. Was one year higher than the others? Did the earnings increase, decrease, or stay the same over the period?

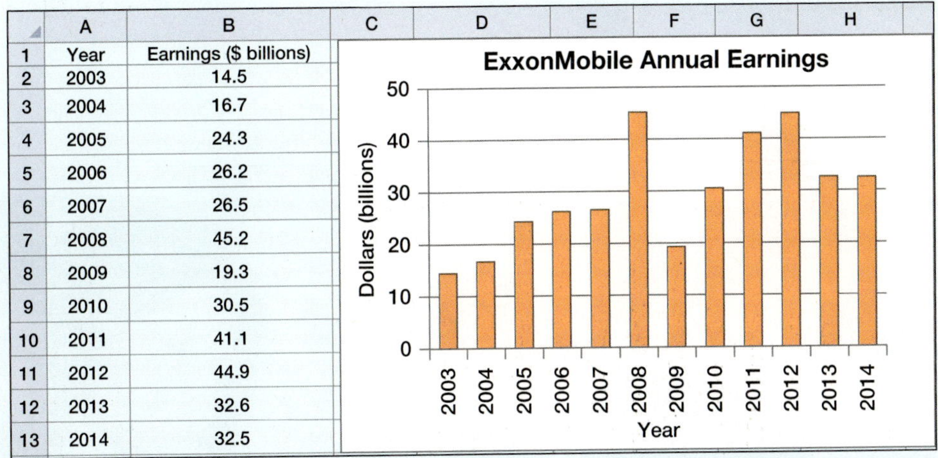

	A	B
1	Year	Earnings ($ billions)
2	2003	14.5
3	2004	16.7
4	2005	24.3
5	2006	26.2
6	2007	26.5
7	2008	45.2
8	2009	19.3
9	2010	30.5
10	2011	41.1
11	2012	44.9
12	2013	32.6
13	2014	32.5

DATA ANALYTICS

20. FILE Refer to the North Valley Real Estate data, which report information on homes sold in the area last year. Consider the following variables: selling price, number of bedrooms, township, and mortgage type.
    a. Which of the variables are qualitative and which are quantitative?
    b. How is each variable measured? Determine the level of measurement for each of the variables.
21. FILE Refer to the Baseball 2016 data, which report information on the 30 Major League Baseball teams for the 2016 season. Consider the following variables: number of wins, payroll, season attendance, whether the team is in the American or National League, and the number of home runs hit.
    a. Which of these variables are quantitative and which are qualitative?
    b. Determine the level of measurement for each of the variables.
22. FILE Refer to the Lincolnville School District bus data, which report information on the school district's bus fleet.
    a. Which of the variables are qualitative and which are quantitative?
    b. Determine the level of measurement for each variable.

2 Describing Data:

FREQUENCY TABLES, FREQUENCY DISTRIBUTIONS, AND GRAPHIC PRESENTATION

© rido/123RF

▲ **MERRILL LYNCH** recently completed a study of online investment portfolios for a sample of clients. For the 70 participants in the study, organize these data into a frequency distribution. (See Exercise 43 and **LO2-3**.)

LEARNING OBJECTIVES

When you have completed this chapter, you will be able to:

LO2-1 Summarize qualitative variables with frequency and relative frequency tables.

LO2-2 Display a frequency table using a bar or pie chart.

LO2-3 Summarize quantitative variables with frequency and relative frequency distributions.

LO2-4 Display a frequency distribution using a histogram or frequency polygon.

INTRODUCTION

The United States automobile retailing industry is highly competitive. It is dominated by megadealerships that own and operate 50 or more franchises, employ over 10,000 people, and generate several billion dollars in annual sales. Many of the top dealerships are publicly owned with shares traded on the New York Stock Exchange or NASDAQ. In 2014, the largest megadealership was AutoNation (ticker symbol AN), followed by Penske Auto Group (PAG), Group 1 Automotive, Inc. (ticker symbol GPI), and the privately owned Van Tuyl Group.

© Justin Sullivan/Getty Images

These large corporations use statistics and analytics to summarize and analyze data and information to support their decisions. As an example, we will look at the Applewood Auto group. It owns four dealerships and sells a wide range of vehicles. These include the popular Korean brands Kia and Hyundai, BMW and Volvo sedans and luxury SUVs, and a full line of Ford and Chevrolet cars and trucks.

Ms. Kathryn Ball is a member of the senior management team at Applewood Auto Group, which has its corporate offices adjacent to Kane Motors. She is responsible for tracking and analyzing vehicle sales and the profitability of those vehicles. Kathryn would like to summarize the profit earned on the vehicles sold with tables, charts, and graphs that she would review monthly. She wants to know the profit per vehicle sold, as well as the lowest and highest amount of profit. She is also interested in describing the demographics of the buyers. What are their ages? How many vehicles have they previously purchased from one of the Applewood dealerships? What type of vehicle did they purchase?

The Applewood Auto Group operates four dealerships:

- ***Tionesta Ford Lincoln*** sells Ford and Lincoln cars and trucks.
- ***Olean Automotive Inc.*** has the Nissan franchise as well as the General Motors brands of Chevrolet, Cadillac, and GMC Trucks.
- ***Sheffield Motors Inc.*** sells Buick, GMC trucks, Hyundai, and Kia.
- ***Kane Motors*** offers the Chrysler, Dodge, and Jeep line as well as BMW and Volvo.

APPLEWOOD AUTO GROUP

	A	B	C	D	E
1	Age	Profit	Location	Vehicle-Type	Previous
2	21	$1,387	Tionesta	Sedan	0
3	23	$1,754	Sheffield	SUV	1
4	24	$1,817	Sheffield	Hybrid	1
5	25	$1,040	Sheffield	Compact	0
6	26	$1,273	Kane	Sedan	1
7	27	$1,529	Sheffield	Sedan	1
8	27	$3,082	Kane	Truck	0
9	28	$1,951	Kane	SUV	1
10	28	$2,692	Tionesta	Compact	0
11	29	$1,206	Sheffield	Sedan	0
12	29	$1,342	Kane	Sedan	2
13	30	$443	Kane	Sedan	3
14	30	$754	Olean	Sedan	2
15	30	$1,621	Sheffield	Truck	1

Every month, Ms. Ball collects data from each of the four dealerships and enters them into an Excel spreadsheet. Last month the Applewood Auto Group sold 180 vehicles at the four dealerships. A copy of the first few observations appears to the left. The variables collected include:

- ***Age***—the age of the buyer at the time of the purchase.
- ***Profit***—the amount earned by the dealership on the sale of each vehicle.
- ***Location***—the dealership where the vehicle was purchased.
- ***Vehicle type***—SUV, sedan, compact, hybrid, or truck.
- ***Previous***—the number of vehicles previously purchased at any of the four Applewood dealerships by the consumer.

The entire data set is available at the McGraw-Hill website (www.mhhe.com/lind17e) and in Appendix A.4 at the end of the text.

LO2-1

Summarize qualitative variables with frequency and relative frequency tables.

CONSTRUCTING FREQUENCY TABLES

Recall from Chapter 1 that techniques used to describe a set of data are called descriptive statistics. Descriptive statistics organize data to show the general pattern of the data, to identify where values tend to concentrate, and to expose extreme or unusual data values. The first technique we discuss is a **frequency table.**

FREQUENCY TABLE A grouping of qualitative data into mutually exclusive and collectively exhaustive classes showing the number of observations in each class.

In Chapter 1, we distinguished between qualitative and quantitative variables. To review, a qualitative variable is nonnumeric, that is, it can only be classified into distinct categories. Examples of qualitative data include political affiliation (Republican, Democrat, Independent, or other), state of birth (Alabama, . . . , Wyoming), and method of payment for a purchase at Barnes & Noble (cash, digital wallet, debit, or credit). On the other hand, quantitative variables are numerical in nature. Examples of quantitative data relating to college students include the price of their textbooks, their age, and the number of credit hours they are registered for this semester.

In the Applewood Auto Group data set, there are five variables for each vehicle sale: age of the buyer, amount of profit, dealer that made the sale, type of vehicle sold, and number of previous purchases by the buyer. The dealer and the type of vehicle are *qualitative* variables. The amount of profit, the age of the buyer, and the number of previous purchases are *quantitative* variables.

© Steve Cole/Getty Images RF

Suppose Ms. Ball wants to summarize last month's sales by location. The first step is to sort the vehicles sold last month according to their location and then tally, or count, the number sold at each location of the four locations: Tionesta, Olean, Sheffield, or Kane. The four locations are used to develop a frequency table with four mutually exclusive (distinctive) classes. Mutually exclusive classes means that a particular vehicle can be assigned to only one class. In addition, the frequency table must be collectively exhaustive. That is every vehicle sold last month is accounted for in the table. If every vehicle is included in the frequency table, the table will be collectively exhaustive and the total number of vehicles will be 180. How do we obtain these counts? Excel provides a tool called a Pivot Table that will quickly and accurately establish the four classes and do the counting. The Excel results follow in Table 2–1. The table shows a total of 180 vehicles and, of the 180 vehicles, 52 were sold at Kane Motors.

TABLE 2–1 Frequency Table for Vehicles Sold Last Month at Applewood Auto Group by Location

Location	Number of Cars
Kane	52
Olean	40
Sheffield	45
Tionesta	43
Total	180

Relative Class Frequencies

You can convert class frequencies to relative class frequencies to show the fraction of the total number of observations in each class. A relative frequency captures the relationship between a class frequency and the total number of observations. In the vehicle sales example, we may want to know the percentage of total cars sold at each of the four locations. To convert a frequency table to a relative frequency table, each of the class frequencies is divided by the total number of observations. Again, this is easily accomplished using Excel. The fraction of vehicles sold last month at the Kane location is 0.289, found by 52 divided by 180. The relative frequency for each location is shown in Table 2–2.

TABLE 2–2 Relative Frequency Table of Vehicles Sold by Location Last Month at Applewood Auto Group

Location	Number of Cars	Relative Frequency	Found by
Kane	52	.289	52/180
Olean	40	.222	40/180
Sheffield	45	.250	45/180
Tionesta	43	.239	43/180
Total	180	1.000	

LO2-2
Display a frequency table using a bar or pie chart.

GRAPHIC PRESENTATION OF QUALITATIVE DATA

The most common graphic form to present a qualitative variable is a **bar chart.** In most cases, the horizontal axis shows the variable of interest. The vertical axis shows the frequency or fraction of each of the possible outcomes. A distinguishing feature of a bar chart is there is distance or a gap between the bars. That is, because the variable of interest is qualitative, the bars are not adjacent to each other. Thus, a bar chart graphically describes a frequency table using a series of uniformly wide rectangles, where the height of each rectangle is the class frequency.

BAR CHART A graph that shows qualitative classes on the horizontal axis and the class frequencies on the vertical axis. The class frequencies are proportional to the heights of the bars.

We use the Applewood Auto Group data as an example (Chart 2–1). The variables of interest are the location where the vehicle was sold and the number of vehicles sold at each location. We label the horizontal axis with the four locations and scale the vertical axis with the number sold. The variable location is of nominal scale, so the order of the locations on the horizontal axis does not matter. In Chart 2–1, the locations are listed alphabetically. The locations could also be in order of decreasing or increasing frequencies.

The height of the bars, or rectangles, corresponds to the number of vehicles at each location. There were 52 vehicles sold last month at the Kane location, so the height of the Kane bar is 52; the height of the bar for the Olean location is 40.

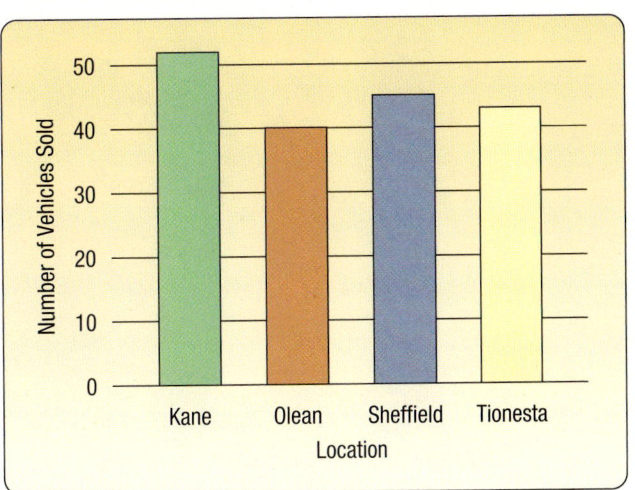

CHART 2–1 Number of Vehicles Sold by Location

Another useful type of chart for depicting qualitative information is a **pie chart.**

PIE CHART A chart that shows the proportion or percentage that each class represents of the total number of frequencies.

We explain the details of constructing a pie chart using the information in Table 2–3, which shows the frequency and percent of cars sold by the Applewood Auto Group for each vehicle type.

TABLE 2–3 Vehicle Sales by Type at Applewood Auto Group

Vehicle Type	Number Sold	Percent Sold
Sedan	72	40
SUV	54	30
Compact	27	15
Truck	18	10
Hybrid	9	5
Total	180	100

The first step to develop a pie chart is to mark the percentages 0, 5, 10, 15, and so on evenly around the circumference of a circle (see Chart 2–2). To plot the 40% of total sales represented by sedans, draw a line from the center of the circle to 0 and another line from the center of the circle to 40%. The area in this "slice" represents the number of sedans sold as a percentage of the total sales. Next, add the SUV's percentage of total sales, 30%, to the sedan's percentage of total sales, 40%. The result is 70%. Draw a line from the center of the circle to 70%, so the area between 40 and 70 shows the sales of SUVs as a percentage of total sales. Continuing, add the 15% of total sales for compact vehicles, which gives us a total of 85%. Draw a line from the center of the circle to 85, so the "slice" between 70% and 85% represents the number of compact vehicles sold as a percentage of the total sales. The remaining 10% for truck sales and 5% for hybrid sales are added to the chart using the same method.

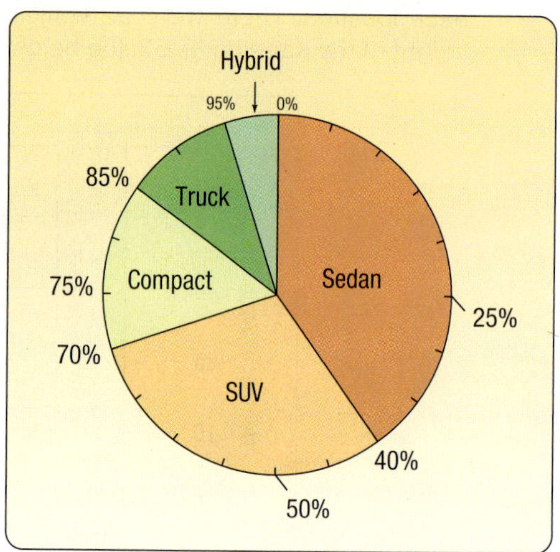

CHART 2–2 Pie Chart of Vehicles by Type

Because each slice of the pie represents the relative frequency of each vehicle type as a percentage of the total sales, we can easily compare them:

- The largest percentage of sales is for sedans.
- Sedans and SUVs together account for 70% of vehicle sales.
- Hybrids account for 5% of vehicle sales, in spite of being on the market for only a few years.

We can use Excel software to quickly count the number of cars for each vehicle type and create the frequency table, bar chart, and pie chart shown in the following summary. The Excel tool is called a Pivot Table. The instructions to produce these descriptive statistics and charts are given in Appendix C.

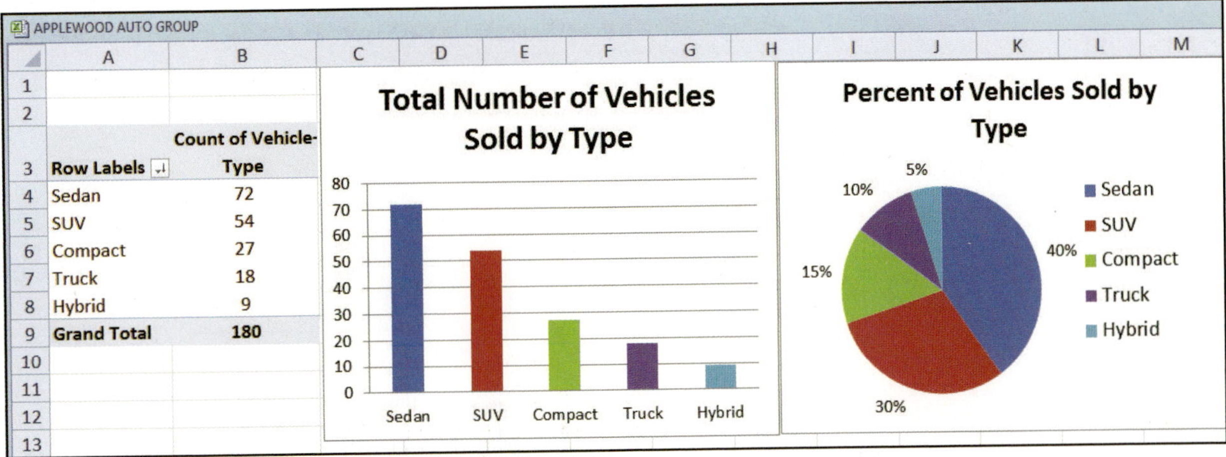

Row Labels	Count of Vehicle-Type
Sedan	72
SUV	54
Compact	27
Truck	18
Hybrid	9
Grand Total	**180**

Pie and bar charts both serve to illustrate frequency and relative frequency tables. When is a pie chart preferred to a bar chart? In most cases, pie charts are used to show and compare the relative differences in the percentage of observations for each value or class of a qualitative variable. Bar charts are preferred when the goal is to compare the number or frequency of observations for each value or class of a qualitative variable. The following Example/Solution shows another application of bar and pie charts.

EXAMPLE

SkiLodges.com is test marketing its new website and is interested in how easy its website design is to navigate. It randomly selected 200 regular Internet users and asked them to perform a search task on the website. Each person was asked to rate the relative ease of navigation as poor, good, excellent, or awesome. The results are shown in the following table:

Awesome	102
Excellent	58
Good	30
Poor	10

1. What type of measurement scale is used for ease of navigation?
2. Draw a bar chart for the survey results.
3. Draw a pie chart for the survey results.

SOLUTION

The data are measured on an ordinal scale. That is, the scale is ranked in relative ease of navigation when moving from "awesome" to "poor." The interval between each rating is unknown so it is impossible, for example, to conclude that a rating of good is twice the value of a poor rating.

We can use a bar chart to graph the data. The vertical scale shows the relative frequency and the horizontal scale shows the values of the ease-of-navigation variable.

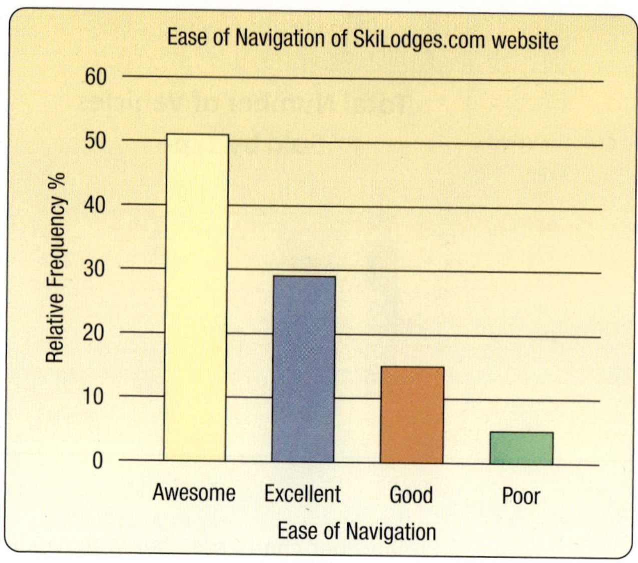

A pie chart can also be used to graph these data. The pie chart emphasizes that more than half of the respondents rate the relative ease of using the website awesome.

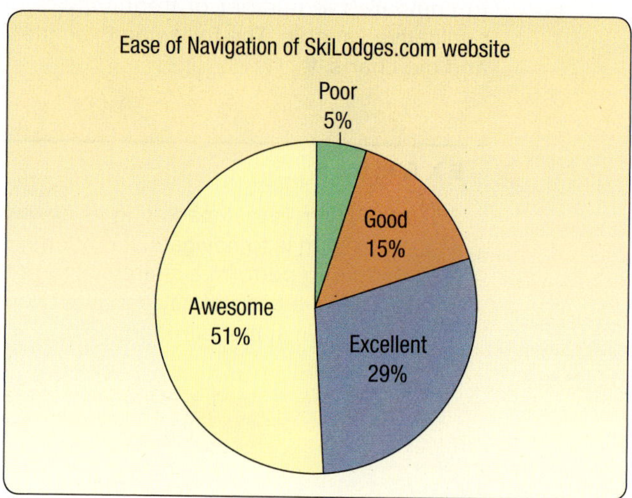

SELF-REVIEW 2–1

The answers are in Appendix E.

DeCenzo Specialty Food and Beverage Company has been serving a cola drink with an additional flavoring, Cola-Plus, that is very popular among its customers. The company is interested in customer preferences for Cola-Plus versus Coca-Cola, Pepsi, and a lemon-lime beverage. They ask 100 randomly sampled customers to take a taste test and select the beverage they prefer most. The results are shown in the following table:

Beverage	Number
Cola-Plus	40
Coca-Cola	25
Pepsi	20
Lemon-Lime	15
Total	100

(a) Is the data qualitative or quantitative? Why?
(b) What is the table called? What does it show?
(c) Develop a bar chart to depict the information.
(d) Develop a pie chart using the relative frequencies.

EXERCISES

The answers to the odd-numbered exercises are at the end of the book in Appendix D.

1. A pie chart shows the relative market share of cola products. The "slice" for Pepsi-Cola has a central angle of 90 degrees. What is its market share?

2. In a marketing study, 100 consumers were asked to select the best digital music player from the iPod, the iRiver, and the Magic Star MP3. To summarize the consumer responses with a frequency table, how many classes would the frequency table have?

3. A total of 1,000 residents in Minnesota were asked which season they preferred. One hundred liked winter best, 300 liked spring, 400 liked summer, and 200 liked fall. Develop a frequency table and a relative frequency table to summarize this information.

4. Two thousand frequent business travelers are asked which midwestern city they prefer: Indianapolis, Saint Louis, Chicago, or Milwaukee. One hundred liked Indianapolis best, 450 liked Saint Louis, 1,300 liked Chicago, and the remainder preferred Milwaukee. Develop a frequency table and a relative frequency table to summarize this information.

5. Wellstone Inc. produces and markets replacement covers for cell phones in five different colors: bright white, metallic black, magnetic lime, tangerine orange, and fusion red. To estimate the demand for each color, the company set up a kiosk in the Mall of America for several hours and asked randomly selected people which cover color was their favorite. The results follow:

Bright white	130
Metallic black	104
Magnetic lime	325
Tangerine orange	455
Fusion red	286

a. What is the table called?
b. Draw a bar chart for the table.
c. Draw a pie chart.
d. If Wellstone Inc. plans to produce 1 million cell phone covers, how many of each color should it produce?

6. A small business consultant is investigating the performance of several companies. The fourth-quarter sales for last year (in thousands of dollars) for the selected companies were:

Company	Fourth-Quarter Sales ($ thousands)
Hoden Building Products	$ 1,645.2
J & R Printing Inc.	4,757.0
Long Bay Concrete Construction	8,913.0
Mancell Electric and Plumbing	627.1
Maxwell Heating and Air Conditioning	24,612.0
Mizelle Roofing & Sheet Metals	191.9

The consultant wants to include a chart in his report comparing the sales of the six companies. Use a bar chart to compare the fourth-quarter sales of these corporations and write a brief report summarizing the bar chart.

LO2-3
Summarize quantitative variables with frequency and relative frequency distributions.

CONSTRUCTING FREQUENCY DISTRIBUTIONS

In Chapter 1 and earlier in this chapter, we distinguished between qualitative and quantitative data. In the previous section, using the Applewood Automotive Group data, we summarized two qualitative variables: the location of the sale and the type of vehicle sold. We created frequency and relative frequency tables and depicted the results in bar and pie charts.

The Applewood Auto Group data also includes several quantitative variables: the age of the buyer, the profit earned on the sale of the vehicle, and the number of previous purchases. Suppose Ms. Ball wants to summarize last month's sales by profit earned for each vehicle. We can describe profit using a **frequency distribution.**

FREQUENCY DISTRIBUTION A grouping of quantitative data into mutually exclusive and collectively exhaustive classes showing the number of observations in each class.

How do we develop a frequency distribution? The following example shows the steps to construct a frequency distribution. Remember, our goal is to construct tables, charts, and graphs that will quickly summarize the data by showing the location, extreme values, and shape of the data's distribution.

EXAMPLE

Ms. Kathryn Ball of the Applewood Auto Group wants to summarize the quantitative variable profit with a frequency distribution and display the distribution with charts and graphs. With this information, Ms. Ball can easily answer the following questions: What is the typical profit on each sale? What is the largest or maximum profit on any sale? What is the smallest or minimum profit on any sale? Around what value do the profits tend to cluster?

SOLUTION

To begin, we need the profits for each of the 180 vehicle sales listed in Table 2–4. This information is called raw or ungrouped data because it is simply a listing

TABLE 2–4 Profit on Vehicles Sold Last Month by the Applewood Auto Group

Maximum

$1,387	$2,148	$2,201	$ 963	$ 820	$2,230	$3,043	$2,584	$2,370
1,754	2,207	996	1,298	1,266	2,341	1,059	2,666	2,637
1,817	2,252	2,813	1,410	1,741	3,292	1,674	2,991	1,426
1,040	1,428	323	1,553	1,772	1,108	1,807	934	2,944
1,273	1,889	352	1,648	1,932	1,295	2,056	2,063	2,147
1,529	1,166	482	2,071	2,350	1,344	2,236	2,083	1,973
3,082	1,320	1,144	2,116	2,422	1,906	2,928	2,856	2,502
1,951	2,265	1,485	1,500	2,446	1,952	1,269	2,989	783
2,692	1,323	1,509	1,549	369	2,070	1,717	910	1,538
1,206	1,760	1,638	2,348	978	2,454	1,797	1,536	2,339
1,342	1,919	1,961	2,498	1,238	1,606	1,955	1,957	2,700
443	2,357	2,127	294	1,818	1,680	2,199	2,240	2,222
754	2,866	2,430	1,115	1,824	1,827	2,482	2,695	2,597
1,621	732	1,704	1,124	1,907	1,915	2,701	1,325	2,742
870	1,464	1,876	1,532	1,938	2,084	3,210	2,250	1,837
1,174	1,626	2,010	1,688	1,940	2,639	377	2,279	2,842
1,412	1,762	2,165	1,822	2,197	842	1,220	2,626	2,434
1,809	1,915	2,231	1,897	2,646	1,963	1,401	1,501	1,640
2,415	2,119	2,389	2,445	1,461	2,059	2,175	1,752	1,821
1,546	1,766	335	2,886	1,731	2,338	1,118	2,058	2,487

Minimum

of the individual, observed profits. It is possible to search the list and find the smallest or minimum profit ($294) and the largest or maximum profit ($3,292), but that is about all. It is difficult to determine a typical profit or to visualize where the profits tend to cluster. The raw data are more easily interpreted if we summarize the data with a frequency distribution. The steps to create this frequency distribution follow.

Step 1: **Decide on the number of classes.** A useful recipe to determine the number of classes (k) is the "2 to the k rule." This guide suggests you select the smallest number (k) for the number of classes such that 2^k (in words, 2 raised to the power of k) is greater than the number of observations (n). In the Applewood Auto Group example, there were 180 vehicles sold. So $n = 180$. If we try $k = 7$, which means we would use 7 classes, $2^7 = 128$, which is less than 180. Hence, 7 is too few classes. If we let $k = 8$, then $2^8 = 256$, which is greater than 180. So the recommended number of classes is 8.

Step 2: **Determine the class interval.** Generally, the **class interval** is the same for all classes. The classes all taken together must cover at least the distance from the minimum value in the data up to the maximum value. Expressing these words in a formula:

$$i \geq \frac{\text{Maximum Value} - \text{Minimum Value}}{k}$$

where i is the class interval, and k is the number of classes.

For the Applewood Auto Group, the minimum value is $294 and the maximum value is $3,292. If we need 8 classes, the interval should be:

$$i \geq \frac{\text{Maximum Value} - \text{Minimum Value}}{k} = \frac{\$3{,}292 - \$294}{8} = \$374.75$$

In practice, this interval size is usually rounded up to some convenient number, such as a multiple of 10 or 100. The value of $400 is a reasonable choice.

Step 3: **Set the individual class limits.** State clear class limits so you can put each observation into only one category. This means you must avoid overlapping or unclear class limits. For example, classes such as "$1,300–$1,400" and "$1,400–$1,500" should not be used because it is not clear whether the value $1,400 is in the first or second class. In this text, we will generally use the format $1,300 **up to** $1,400 and $1,400 **up to** $1,500 and so on. With this format, it is clear that $1,399 goes into the first class and $1,400 in the second.

Because we always round the class interval up to get a convenient class size, we cover a larger than necessary range. For example, using 8 classes with an interval of $400 in the Applewood Auto Group example results in a range of 8($400) = $3,200. The actual range is $2,998, found by ($3,292 - $294). Comparing that value to $3,200, we have an excess of $202. Because we need to cover only the range (*Maximum* - *Minimum*), it is natural to put approximately equal amounts of the excess in each of the two tails. Of course, we also should select convenient class limits. A guideline is to make the lower limit of the first class a multiple of the class interval. Sometimes this is not possible, but the lower limit should at least be rounded. So here are the classes we could use for these data.

Classes
\$ 200 up to \$ 600
600 up to 1,000
1,000 up to 1,400
1,400 up to 1,800
1,800 up to 2,200
2,200 up to 2,600
2,600 up to 3,000
3,000 up to 3,400

Step 4: **Tally the vehicle profit into the classes and determine the number of observations in each class.** To begin, the profit from the sale of the first vehicle in Table 2–4 is \$1,387. It is tallied in the \$1,000 up to \$1,400 class. The second profit in the first row of Table 2–4 is \$2,148. It is tallied in the \$1,800 up to \$2,200 class. The other profits are tallied in a similar manner. When all the profits are tallied, the table would appear as:

Profit	Frequency
\$ 200 up to \$ 600	𝍸 |||
600 up to 1,000	𝍸 𝍸 |
1,000 up to 1,400	𝍸 𝍸 𝍸 𝍸 |||
1,400 up to 1,800	𝍸 𝍸 𝍸 𝍸 𝍸 𝍸 𝍸 |||
1,800 up to 2,200	𝍸 𝍸 𝍸 𝍸 𝍸 𝍸 𝍸 𝍸 𝍸
2,200 up to 2,600	𝍸 𝍸 𝍸 𝍸 𝍸 ||
2,600 up to 3,000	𝍸 𝍸 𝍸 ||||
3,000 up to 3,400	||||

The number of observations in each class is called the **class frequency.** In the \$200 up to \$600 class there are 8 observations, and in the \$600 up to \$1,000 class there are 11 observations. Therefore, the class frequency in the first class is 8 and the class frequency in the second class is 11. There are a total of 180 observations in the entire set of data. So the sum of all the frequencies should be equal to 180. The results of the frequency distribution are in Table 2–5.

TABLE 2–5 Frequency Distribution of Profit for Vehicles Sold Last Month at Applewood Auto Group

Profit	Frequency
\$ 200 up to \$ 600	8
600 up to 1,000	11
1,000 up to 1,400	23
1,400 up to 1,800	38
1,800 up to 2,200	45
2,200 up to 2,600	32
2,600 up to 3,000	19
3,000 up to 3,400	4
Total	180

Now that we have organized the data into a frequency distribution (see Table 2–5), we can summarize the profits of the vehicles for the Applewood Auto Group. Observe the following:

1. The profits from vehicle sales range between \$200 and \$3,400.
2. The vehicle profits are classified using a class interval of \$400. The class interval is determined by subtracting consecutive lower or upper class limits. For

example, the lower limit of the first class is $200, and the lower limit of the second class is $600. The difference is the class interval of $400.

3. The profits are concentrated between $1,000 and $3,000. The profit on 157 vehicles, or 87%, was within this range.
4. For each class, we can determine the typical profit or **class midpoint.** It is halfway between the lower or upper limits of two consecutive classes. It is computed by adding the lower or upper limits of consecutive classes and dividing by 2. Referring to Table 2–5, the lower class limit of the first class is $200, and the next class limit is $600. The class midpoint is $400, found by ($600 + $200)/2. The midpoint best represents, or is typical of, the profits of the vehicles in that class. Applewood sold 8 vehicles with a typical profit of $400.
5. The largest concentration, or highest frequency, of vehicles sold is in the $1,800 up to $2,200 class. There are 45 vehicles in this class. The class midpoint is $2,000. So we say that the typical profit in the class with the highest frequency is $2,000.

By presenting this information to Ms. Ball, we give her a clear picture of the distribution of the vehicle profits for last month.

We admit that arranging the information on profits into a frequency distribution does result in the loss of some detailed information. That is, by organizing the data into a frequency distribution, we cannot pinpoint the exact profit on any vehicle, such as $1,387, $2,148, or $2,201. Further, we cannot tell that the actual minimum profit for any vehicle sold is $294 or that the maximum profit was $3,292. However, the lower limit of the first class and the upper limit of the last class convey essentially the same meaning. Likely, Ms. Ball will make the same judgment if she knows the smallest profit is about $200 that she will if she knows the exact profit is $292. The advantages of summarizing the 180 profits into a more understandable and organized form more than offset this disadvantage.

When we summarize raw data with frequency distributions, equal class intervals are preferred. However, in certain situations unequal class intervals may be necessary to avoid a large number of classes with very small frequencies. Such is the case in Table 2–6. The U.S. Internal Revenue Service uses unequal-sized class intervals for adjusted gross income on individual tax returns to summarize the number of individual tax returns. If we use our method to find equal class intervals, the 2^k rule results in 25 classes, and

STATISTICS IN ACTION

In 1788, James Madison, John Jay, and Alexander Hamilton anonymously published a series of essays entitled *The Federalist.* These Federalist papers were an attempt to convince the people of New York that they should ratify the Constitution. In the course of history, the authorship of most of these papers became known, but 12 remained contested. Through the use of statistical analysis, and particularly studying the frequency distributions of various words, we can now conclude that James Madison is the likely author of the 12 papers. In fact, the statistical evidence that Madison is the author is overwhelming.

TABLE 2–6 Adjusted Gross Income for Individuals Filing Income Tax Returns

Adjusted Gross Income	Number of Returns (in thousands)
No adjusted gross income	178.2
$ 1 up to 5,000	1,204.6
5,000 up to 10,000	2,595.5
10,000 up to 15,000	3,142.0
15,000 up to 20,000	3,191.7
20,000 up to 25,000	2,501.4
25,000 up to 30,000	1,901.6
30,000 up to 40,000	2,502.3
40,000 up to 50,000	1,426.8
50,000 up to 75,000	1,476.3
75,000 up to 100,000	338.8
100,000 up to 200,000	223.3
200,000 up to 500,000	55.2
500,000 up to 1,000,000	12.0
1,000,000 up to 2,000,000	5.1
2,000,000 up to 10,000,000	3.4
10,000,000 or more	0.6

a class interval of $400,000, assuming $0 and $10,000,000 as the minimum and maximum values for adjusted gross income. Using equal class intervals, the first 13 classes in Table 2–6 would be combined into one class of about 99.9% of all tax returns and 24 classes for the 0.1% of the returns with an adjusted gross income above $400,000. Using equal class intervals does not provide a good understanding of the raw data. In this case, good judgment in the use of unequal class intervals, as demonstrated in Table 2–6, is required to show the distribution of the number of tax returns filed, especially for incomes under $500,000.

SELF-REVIEW 2–2

In the first quarter of last year, the 11 members of the sales staff at Master Chemical Company earned the following commissions:

$1,650 $1,475 $1,510 $1,670 $1,595 $1,760 $1,540 $1,495 $1,590 $1,625 $1,510

(a) What are the values such as $1,650 and $1,475 called?
(b) Using $1,400 up to $1,500 as the first class, $1,500 up to $1,600 as the second class, and so forth, organize the quarterly commissions into a frequency distribution.
(c) What are the numbers in the right column of your frequency distribution called?
(d) Describe the distribution of quarterly commissions, based on the frequency distribution. What is the largest concentration of commissions earned? What is the smallest, and the largest? What is the typical amount earned?

Relative Frequency Distribution

It may be desirable, as we did earlier with qualitative data, to convert class frequencies to relative class frequencies to show the proportion of the total number of observations in each class. In our vehicle profits, we may want to know what percentage of the vehicle profits are in the $1,000 up to $1,400 class. To convert a frequency distribution to a *relative* frequency distribution, each of the class frequencies is divided by the total number of observations. From the distribution of vehicle profits, Table 2–5, the relative frequency for the $1,000 up to $1,400 class is 0.128, found by dividing 23 by 180. That is, profit on 12.8% of the vehicles sold is between $1,000 and $1,400. The relative frequencies for the remaining classes are shown in Table 2–7.

TABLE 2–7 Relative Frequency Distribution of Profit for Vehicles Sold Last Month at Applewood Auto Group

Profit	Frequency	Relative Frequency	Found by
$ 200 up to $ 600	8	.044	8/180
600 up to 1,000	11	.061	11/180
1,000 up to 1,400	23	.128	23/180
1,400 up to 1,800	38	.211	38/180
1,800 up to 2,200	45	.250	45/180
2,200 up to 2,600	32	.178	32/180
2,600 up to 3,000	19	.106	19/180
3,000 up to 3,400	4	.022	4/180
Total	180	1.000	

APPLEWOOD AUTO GROUP

	A	B	C
1	Profit Class	Frequency	Relative Frequency
2	200-600	8	4.44%
3	600-1000	11	6.11%
4	1000-1400	23	12.78%
5	1400-1800	38	21.11%
6	1800-2200	45	25.00%
7	2200-2600	32	17.78%
8	2600-3000	19	10.56%
9	3000-3400	4	2.22%
10	Grand Total	180	100.00%

There are many software packages that perform statistical calculations. Throughout this text, we will show the output from Microsoft Excel, MegaStat (a Microsoft Excel add-in), and Minitab (a statistical software package). Because Excel is most readily available, it is used most frequently.

Within the earlier Graphic Presentation of Qualitative Data section, we used the Pivot Table tool in Excel to create a frequency table. To create the table to the left, we use the same Excel tool to compute frequency and relative frequency distributions for the profit variable in the Applewood Auto Group data. The necessary steps are given in the Software Commands section in Appendix C.

SELF-REVIEW 2–3

Barry Bonds of the San Francisco Giants established a new single-season Major League Baseball home run record by hitting 73 home runs during the 2001 season. Listed below is the sorted distance of each of the 73 home runs.

320	320	347	350	360	360	360	361	365	370
370	375	375	375	375	380	380	380	380	380
380	390	390	391	394	396	400	400	400	400
405	410	410	410	410	410	410	410	410	410
410	410	411	415	415	416	417	417	420	420
420	420	420	420	420	420	429	430	430	430
430	430	435	435	436	440	440	440	440	440
450	480	488							

(a) For this data, show that seven classes would be used to create a frequency distribution using the 2^k rule.
(b) Show that a class interval of 30 would summarize the data in seven classes.
(c) Construct frequency and relative frequency distributions for the data with seven classes and a class interval of 30. Start the first class with a lower limit of 300.
(d) How many home runs traveled a distance of 360 up to 390 feet?
(e) What percentage of the home runs traveled a distance of 360 up to 390 feet?
(f) What percentage of the home runs traveled a distance of 390 feet or more?

EXERCISES

This **FILE** icon indicates that the data are available at the text website: www.mhhe.com/Lind17e. You will be able to download the data directly into Excel or Minitab from this site.

7. A set of data consists of 38 observations. How many classes would you recommend for the frequency distribution?

8. A set of data consists of 45 observations between \$0 and \$29. What size would you recommend for the class interval?

9. A set of data consists of 230 observations between \$235 and \$567. What class interval would you recommend?

10. A set of data contains 53 observations. The minimum value is 42 and the maximum value is 129. The data are to be organized into a frequency distribution.
   a. How many classes would you suggest?
   b. What would you suggest as the lower limit of the first class?

11. **FILE** Wachesaw Manufacturing Inc. produced the following number of units in the last 16 days.

27	27	27	28	27	25	25	28
26	28	26	28	31	30	26	26

The information is to be organized into a frequency distribution.
   a. How many classes would you recommend?
   b. What class interval would you suggest?
   c. What lower limit would you recommend for the first class?
   d. Organize the information into a frequency distribution and determine the relative frequency distribution.
   e. Comment on the shape of the distribution.

12. **FILE** The Quick Change Oil Company has a number of outlets in the metropolitan Seattle area. The daily number of oil changes at the Oak Street outlet in the past 20 days are:

65	98	55	62	79	59	51	90	72	56
70	62	66	80	94	79	63	73	71	85

The data are to be organized into a frequency distribution.

a. How many classes would you recommend?
b. What class interval would you suggest?
c. What lower limit would you recommend for the first class?
d. Organize the number of oil changes into a frequency distribution.
e. Comment on the shape of the frequency distribution. Also determine the relative frequency distribution.

13. **FILE** The manager of the BiLo Supermarket in Mt. Pleasant, Rhode Island, gathered the following information on the number of times a customer visits the store during a month. The responses of 51 customers were:

5	3	3	1	4	4	5	6	4	2	6	6	6	7	1
1	14	1	2	4	4	4	5	6	3	5	3	4	5	6
8	4	7	6	5	9	11	3	12	4	7	6	5	15	1
1	10	8	9	2	12									

a. Starting with 0 as the lower limit of the first class and using a class interval of 3, organize the data into a frequency distribution.
b. Describe the distribution. Where do the data tend to cluster?
c. Convert the distribution to a relative frequency distribution.

14. **FILE** The food services division of Cedar River Amusement Park Inc. is studying the amount of money spent per day on food and drink by families who visit the amusement park. A sample of 40 families who visited the park yesterday revealed they spent the following amounts:

$77	$18	$63	$84	$38	$54	$50	$59	$54	$56	$36	$26	$50	$34	$44
41	58	58	53	51	62	43	52	53	63	62	62	65	61	52
60	60	45	66	83	71	63	58	61	71					

a. Organize the data into a frequency distribution, using seven classes and 15 as the lower limit of the first class. What class interval did you select?
b. Where do the data tend to cluster?
c. Describe the distribution.
d. Determine the relative frequency distribution.

LO2-4
Display a distribution using a histogram or frequency polygon.

GRAPHIC PRESENTATION OF A DISTRIBUTION

Sales managers, stock analysts, hospital administrators, and other busy executives often need a quick picture of the distributions of sales, stock prices, or hospital costs. These distributions can often be depicted by the use of charts and graphs. Three charts that will help portray a frequency distribution graphically are the histogram, the frequency polygon, and the cumulative frequency polygon.

Histogram

A **histogram** for a frequency distribution based on quantitative data is similar to the bar chart showing the distribution of qualitative data. The classes are marked on the horizontal axis and the class frequencies on the vertical axis. The class frequencies are represented by the heights of the bars. However, there is one important difference based on the nature of the data. Quantitative data are usually measured using scales that are continuous, not discrete. Therefore, the horizontal axis represents all possible values, and the bars are drawn adjacent to each other to show the continuous nature of the data.

HISTOGRAM A graph in which the classes are marked on the horizontal axis and the class frequencies on the vertical axis. The class frequencies are represented by the heights of the bars, and the bars are drawn adjacent to each other.

EXAMPLE

Below is the frequency distribution of the profits on vehicle sales last month at the Applewood Auto Group.

Profit	Frequency
$ 200 up to $ 600	8
600 up to 1,000	11
1,000 up to 1,400	23
1,400 up to 1,800	38
1,800 up to 2,200	45
2,200 up to 2,600	32
2,600 up to 3,000	19
3,000 up to 3,400	4
Total	180

Construct a histogram. What observations can you reach based on the information presented in the histogram?

SOLUTION

The class frequencies are scaled along the vertical axis (*Y*-axis) and either the class limits or the class midpoints along the horizontal axis. To illustrate the construction of the histogram, the first three classes are shown in Chart 2–3.

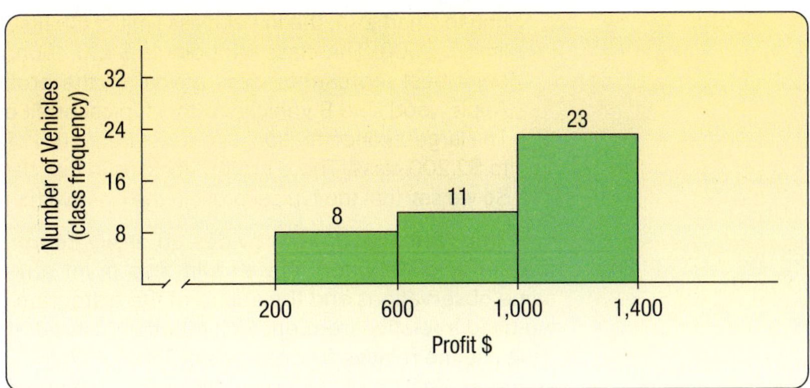

CHART 2–3 Construction of a Histogram

From Chart 2–3 we note the profit on eight vehicles was $200 up to $600. Therefore, the height of the column for that class is 8. There are 11 vehicle sales where the profit was $600 up to $1,000. So, logically, the height of that column is 11. The height of the bar represents the number of observations in the class.

This procedure is continued for all classes. The complete histogram is shown in Chart 2–4. Note that there is no space between the bars. This is a feature of the histogram. Why is this so? Because the variable profit, plotted on the horizontal axis, is a continuous variable. In a bar chart, the scale of measurement is usually nominal and the vertical bars are separated. This is an important distinction between the histogram and the bar chart.

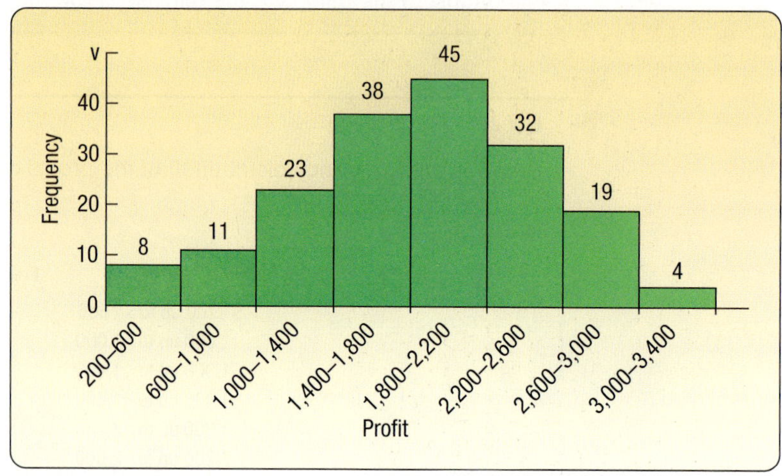

CHART 2–4 Histogram of the Profit on 180 Vehicles Sold at the Applewood Auto Group

We can make the following statements using Chart 2–4. They are the same as the observations based on Table 2–5.

1. The profits from vehicle sales range between $200 and $3,400.
2. The vehicle profits are classified using a class interval of $400. The class interval is determined by subtracting consecutive lower or upper class limits. For example, the lower limit of the first class is $200, and the lower limit of the second class is $600. The difference is the class interval or $400.
3. The profits are concentrated between $1,000 and $3,000. The profit on 157 vehicles, or 87%, was within this range.
4. For each class, we can determine the typical profit or class midpoint. It is halfway between the lower or upper limits of two consecutive classes. It is computed by adding the lower or upper limits of consecutive classes and dividing by 2. Referring to Chart 2–4, the lower class limit of the first class is $200, and the next class limit is $600. The class midpoint is $400, found by ($600 + $200)/2. The midpoint best represents, or is typical of, the profits of the vehicles in that class. Applewood sold 8 vehicles with a typical profit of $400.
5. The largest concentration, or highest frequency of vehicles sold, is in the $1,800 up to $2,200 class. There are 45 vehicles in this class. The class midpoint is $2,000. So we say that the typical profit in the class with the highest frequency is $2,000.

Thus, the histogram provides an easily interpreted visual representation of a frequency distribution. We should also point out that we would have made the same observations and the shape of the histogram would have been the same had we used a relative frequency distribution instead of the actual frequencies. That is, if we use the relative frequencies of Table 2–7, the result is a histogram of the same shape as Chart 2–4. The only difference is that the vertical axis would have been reported in percentage of vehicles instead of the number of vehicles. The Excel commands to create Chart 2–4 are given in Appendix C.

STATISTICS IN ACTION

Florence Nightingale is known as the founder of the nursing profession. However, she also saved many lives by using statistical analysis. When she encountered an unsanitary condition or an undersupplied hospital, she improved the conditions and then used statistical data to document the improvement. Thus, she was able to convince others of the need for medical reform, particularly in the area of sanitation. She developed original graphs to demonstrate that, during the Crimean War, more soldiers died from unsanitary conditions than were killed in combat.

Frequency Polygon

A **frequency polygon** also shows the shape of a distribution and is similar to a histogram. It consists of line segments connecting the points formed by the intersections of the class midpoints and the class frequencies. The construction of a frequency polygon is illustrated in Chart 2–5. We use the profits from the cars sold last month at the Applewood Auto Group. The midpoint of each class is scaled on the *X*-axis and the class frequencies on the *Y*-axis. Recall that the class midpoint is the value at the center of a class and represents the typical values in that class. The class frequency is the number of observations in a particular class. The profit earned on the vehicles sold last month by the Applewood Auto Group is repeated below.

Profit	Midpoint	Frequency
$ 200 up to $ 600	$ 400	8
600 up to 1,000	800	11
1,000 up to 1,400	1,200	23
1,400 up to 1,800	1,600	38
1,800 up to 2,200	2,000	45
2,200 up to 2,600	2,400	32
2,600 up to 3,000	2,800	19
3,000 up to 3,400	3,200	4
Total		180

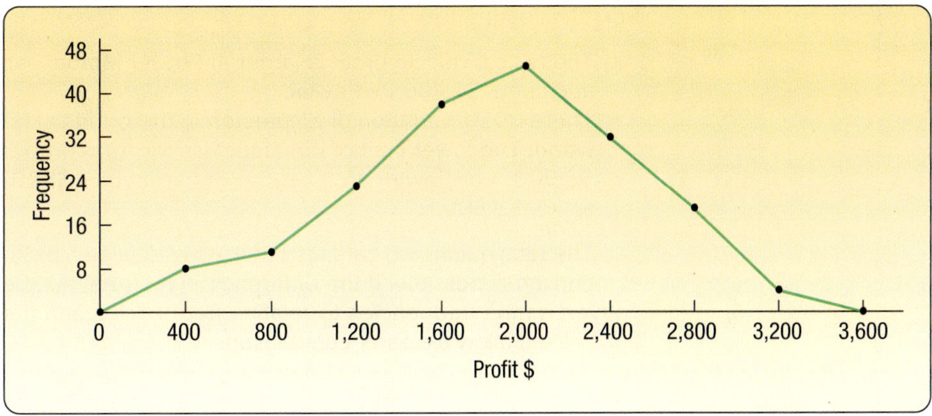

CHART 2–5 Frequency Polygon of Profit on 180 Vehicles Sold at Applewood Auto Group

As noted previously, the $200 up to $600 class is represented by the midpoint $400. To construct a frequency polygon, move horizontally on the graph to the midpoint, $400, and then vertically to 8, the class frequency, and place a dot. The *x* and the *y* values of this point are called the *coordinates*. The coordinates of the next point are $x = 800$ and $y = 11$. The process is continued for all classes. Then the points are connected in order. That is, the point representing the lowest class is joined to the one representing the second class and so on. Note in Chart 2–5 that, to complete the frequency polygon, midpoints of $0 and $3,600 are added to the *X*-axis to "anchor" the polygon at zero frequencies. These two values, $0 and $3,600, were derived by subtracting the class interval of $400 from the lowest midpoint ($400) and by adding $400 to the highest midpoint ($3,200) in the frequency distribution.

Both the histogram and the frequency polygon allow us to get a quick picture of the main characteristics of the data (highs, lows, points of concentration, etc.). Although the two representations are similar in purpose, the histogram has the advantage of depicting each class as a rectangle, with the height of the rectangular bar representing

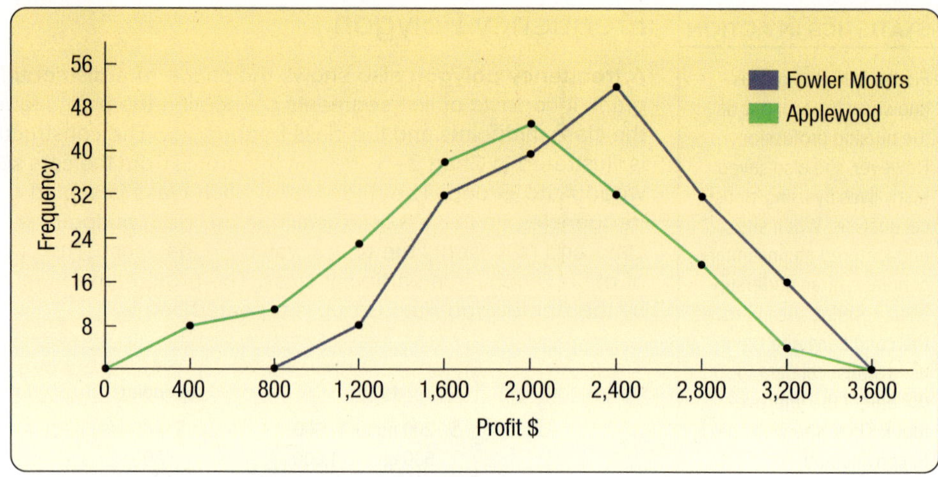

CHART 2–6 Distribution of Profit at Applewood Auto Group and Fowler Motors

the number in each class. The frequency polygon, in turn, has an advantage over the histogram. It allows us to compare directly two or more frequency distributions. Suppose Ms. Ball wants to compare the profit per vehicle sold at Applewood Auto Group with a similar auto group, Fowler Auto in Grayling, Michigan. To do this, two frequency polygons are constructed, one on top of the other, as in Chart 2–6. Two things are clear from the chart:

- The typical vehicle profit is larger at Fowler Motors—about $2,000 for Applewood and about $2,400 for Fowler.
- There is less variation or dispersion in the profits at Fowler Motors than at Applewood. The lower limit of the first class for Applewood is $0 and the upper limit is $3,600. For Fowler Motors, the lower limit is $800 and the upper limit is the same: $3,600.

The total number of cars sold at the two dealerships is about the same, so a direct comparison is possible. If the difference in the total number of cars sold is large, then converting the frequencies to relative frequencies and then plotting the two distributions would allow a clearer comparison.

SELF-REVIEW 2–4

The annual imports of a selected group of electronic suppliers are shown in the following frequency distribution.

Imports ($ millions)	Number of Suppliers
2 up to 5	6
5 up to 8	13
8 up to 11	20
11 up to 14	10
14 up to 17	1

(a) Portray the imports as a histogram.
(b) Portray the imports as a relative frequency polygon.
(c) Summarize the important facets of the distribution (such as classes with the highest and lowest frequencies).

EXERCISES

15. Molly's Candle Shop has several retail stores in the coastal areas of North and South Carolina. Many of Molly's customers ask her to ship their purchases. The following chart shows the number of packages shipped per day for the last 100 days. For example, the first class shows that there were 5 days when the number of packages shipped was 0 up to 5.

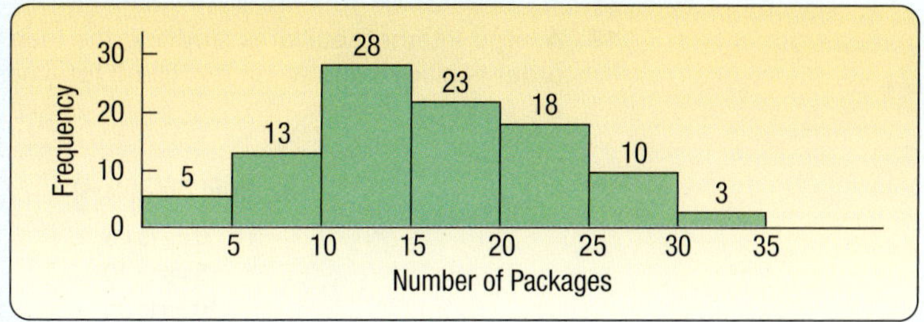

a. What is this chart called?
b. What is the total number of packages shipped?
c. What is the class interval?
d. What is the number of packages shipped in the 10 up to 15 class?
e. What is the relative frequency of packages shipped in the 10 up to 15 class?
f. What is the midpoint of the 10 up to 15 class?
g. On how many days were there 25 or more packages shipped?

16. The following chart shows the number of patients admitted daily to Memorial Hospital through the emergency room.

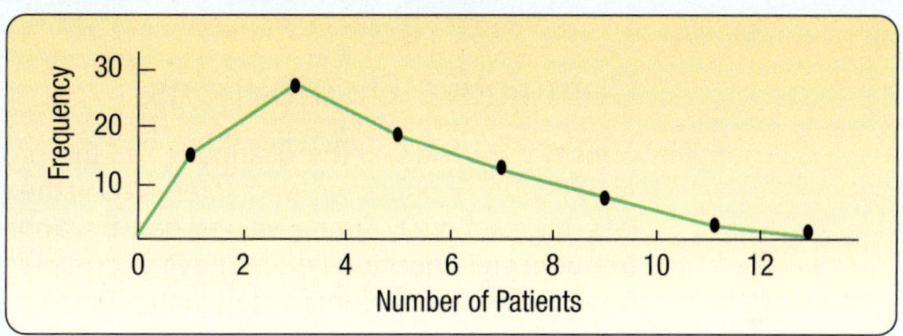

a. What is the midpoint of the 2 up to 4 class?
b. How many days were 2 up to 4 patients admitted?
c. What is the class interval?
d. What is this chart called?

17. The following frequency distribution reports the number of frequent flier miles, reported in thousands, for employees of Brumley Statistical Consulting Inc. during the most recent quarter.

Frequent Flier Miles (000)	Number of Employees
0 up to 3	5
3 up to 6	12
6 up to 9	23
9 up to 12	8
12 up to 15	2
Total	50

a. How many employees were studied?
b. What is the midpoint of the first class?
c. Construct a histogram.
d. A frequency polygon is to be drawn. What are the coordinates of the plot for the first class?
e. Construct a frequency polygon.
f. Interpret the frequent flier miles accumulated using the two charts.

18. A large Internet retailer is studying the lead time (elapsed time between when an order is placed and when it is filled) for a sample of recent orders. The lead times are reported in days.

Lead Time (days)	Frequency
0 up to 5	6
5 up to 10	7
10 up to 15	12
15 up to 20	8
20 up to 25	7
Total	40

a. How many orders were studied?
b. What is the midpoint of the first class?
c. What are the coordinates of the first class for a frequency polygon?
d. Draw a histogram.
e. Draw a frequency polygon.
f. Interpret the lead times using the two charts.

Cumulative Distributions

Consider once again the distribution of the profits on vehicles sold by the Applewood Auto Group. Suppose we were interested in the number of vehicles that sold for a profit of less than $1,400. These values can be approximated by developing a **cumulative frequency distribution** and portraying it graphically in a **cumulative frequency polygon.** Or, suppose we were interested in the profit earned on the lowest-selling 40% of the vehicles. These values can be approximated by developing a **cumulative relative frequency distribution** and portraying it graphically in a **cumulative relative frequency polygon.**

EXAMPLE

The frequency distribution of the profits earned at Applewood Auto Group is repeated from Table 2–5.

Profit	Frequency
$ 200 up to $ 600	8
600 up to 1,000	11
1,000 up to 1,400	23
1,400 up to 1,800	38
1,800 up to 2,200	45
2,200 up to 2,600	32
2,600 up to 3,000	19
3,000 up to 3,400	4
Total	180

Construct a cumulative frequency polygon to answer the following question: sixty of the vehicles earned a profit of less than what amount? Construct a cumulative relative frequency polygon to answer this question: seventy-five percent of the vehicles sold earned a profit of less than what amount?

SOLUTION

As the names imply, a cumulative frequency distribution and a cumulative frequency polygon require *cumulative frequencies.* To construct a cumulative frequency distribution, refer to the preceding table and note that there were eight vehicles in which the profit earned was less than $600. Those 8 vehicles, plus the 11 in the next higher class, for a total of 19, earned a profit of less than $1,000. The cumulative frequency for the next higher class is 42, found by 8 + 11 + 23. This process is continued for all the classes. All the vehicles earned a profit of less than $3,400. (See Table 2–8.)

TABLE 2–8 Cumulative Frequency Distribution for Profit on Vehicles Sold Last Month at Applewood Auto Group

Profit	Cumulative Frequency	Found by
Less than $ 600	8	8
Less than 1,000	19	8 + 11
Less than 1,400	42	8 + 11 + 23
Less than 1,800	80	8 + 11 + 23 + 38
Less than 2,200	125	8 + 11 + 23 + 38 + 45
Less than 2,600	157	8 + 11 + 23 + 38 + 45 + 32
Less than 3,000	176	8 + 11 + 23 + 38 + 45 + 32 + 19
Less than 3,400	180	8 + 11 + 23 + 38 + 45 + 32 + 19 + 4

To construct a cumulative relative frequency distribution, we divide the cumulative frequencies by the total number of observations, 180. As shown in Table 2-9, the cumulative relative frequency of the fourth class is 80/180 = 44%. This means that 44% of the vehicles sold for less than $1,800.

TABLE 2–9 Cumulative Relative Frequency Distribution for Profit on Vehicles Sold Last Month at Applewood Auto Group

Profit	Cumulative Frequency	Cumulative Relative Frequency
Less than $ 600	8	8/180 = 0.044 = 4.4%
Less than $1,000	19	19/180 = 0.106 = 10.6%
Less than $1,400	42	42/180 = 0.233 = 23.3%
Less than $1,800	80	80/180 = 0.444 = 44.4%
Less than $2,200	125	125/180 = 0.694 = 69.4%
Less than $2,600	157	157/180 = 0.872 = 87.2%
Less than $3,000	176	176/180 = 0.978 = 97.8%
Less than $3,400	180	180/180 = 1.000 = 100%

To plot a cumulative frequency distribution, scale the upper limit of each class along the *X*-axis and the corresponding cumulative frequencies along the *Y*-axis. To provide additional information, you can label the vertical axis on the right in terms of cumulative relative frequencies. In the Applewood Auto Group, the vertical axis on the left is labeled from 0 to 180 and on the right from 0 to 100%. Note, as an example, that 50% on the right axis should be opposite 90 vehicles on the left axis.

To begin, the first plot is at $x = 200$ and $y = 0$. None of the vehicles sold for a profit of less than $200. The profit on 8 vehicles was less than $600, so the next plot is at $x = 600$ and $y = 8$. Continuing, the next plot is $x = 1{,}000$ and $y = 19$. There were 19 vehicles that sold for a profit of less than $1,000. The rest of the points are plotted and then the dots connected to form Chart 2–7.

We should point out that the shape of the distribution is the same if we use cumulative relative frequencies instead of the cumulative frequencies. The only difference is that the vertical axis is scaled in percentages. In the following charts, a percentage scale is added to the right side of the graphs to help answer questions about cumulative relative frequencies.

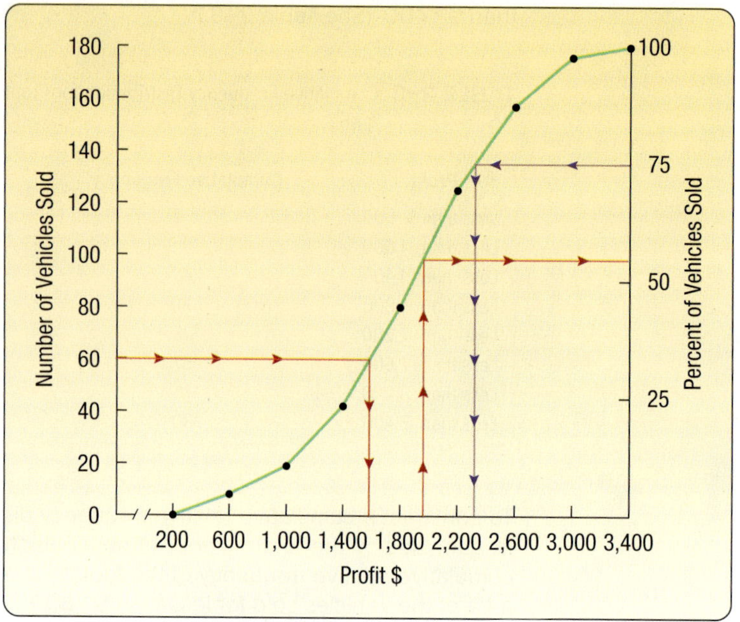

CHART 2–7 Cumulative Frequency Polygon for Profit on Vehicles Sold Last Month at Applewood Auto Group

Using Chart 2–7 to find the amount of profit on 75% of the cars sold, draw a horizontal line from the 75% mark on the right-hand vertical axis over to the polygon, then drop down to the *X*-axis and read the amount of profit. The value on the *X*-axis is about $2,300, so we estimate that 75% of the vehicles sold earned a profit of $2,300 or less for the Applewood group.

To find the highest profit earned on 60 of the 180 vehicles, we use Chart 2–7 to locate the value of 60 on the left-hand vertical axis. Next, we draw a horizontal line from the value of 60 to the polygon and then drop down to the *X*-axis and read the profit. It is about $1,600, so we estimate that 60 of the vehicles sold for a profit of less than $1,600. We can also make estimates of the percentage of vehicles that sold for less than a particular amount. To explain, suppose we want to estimate the percentage of vehicles that sold for a profit of less than $2,000. We begin by locating the value of $2,000 on the *X*-axis, move vertically to the polygon, and then horizontally to the vertical axis on the right. The value is about 56%, so we conclude 56% of the vehicles sold for a profit of less than $2,000.

SELF-REVIEW 2–5

A sample of the hourly wages of 15 employees at Home Depot in Brunswick, Georgia, was organized into the following table.

Hourly Wages	Number of Employees
\$ 8 up to \$10	3
10 up to 12	7
12 up to 14	4
14 up to 16	1

(a) What is the table called?
(b) Develop a cumulative frequency distribution and portray the distribution in a cumulative frequency polygon.
(c) On the basis of the cumulative frequency polygon, how many employees earn less than \$11 per hour?

EXERCISES

19. The following cumulative frequency and the cumulative relative frequency polygon for the distribution of hourly wages of a sample of certified welders in the Atlanta, Georgia, area is shown in the graph.

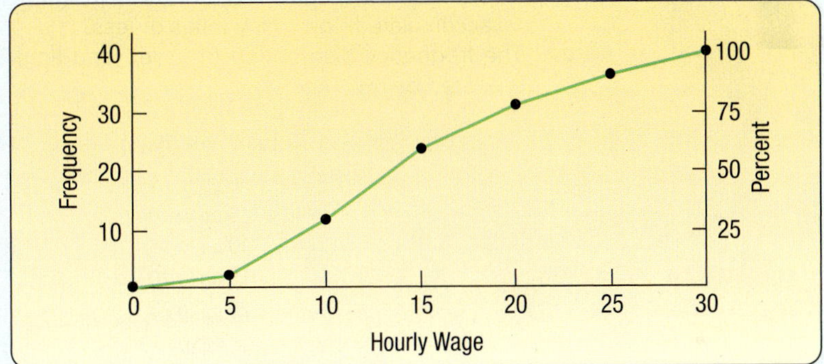

a. How many welders were studied?
b. What is the class interval?
c. About how many welders earn less than \$10.00 per hour?
d. About 75% of the welders make less than what amount?
e. Ten of the welders studied made less than what amount?
f. What percent of the welders make less than \$20.00 per hour?

20. The cumulative frequency and the cumulative relative frequency polygon for a distribution of selling prices (\$000) of houses sold in the Billings, Montana, area is shown in the graph.

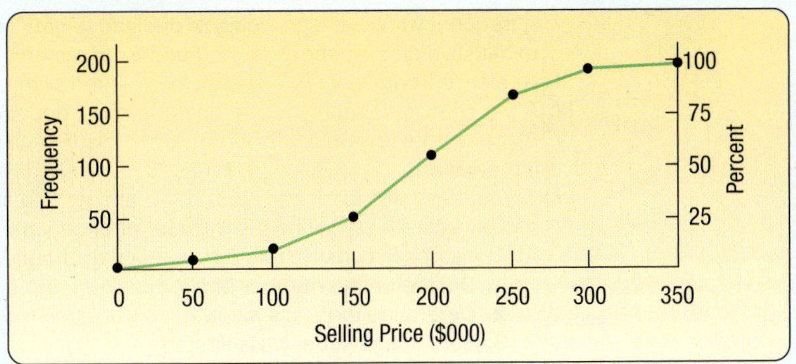

a. How many homes were studied?
b. What is the class interval?
c. One hundred homes sold for less than what amount?
d. About 75% of the homes sold for less than what amount?
e. Estimate the number of homes in the $150,000 up to $200,000 class.
f. About how many homes sold for less than $225,000?

21. The frequency distribution representing the number of frequent flier miles accumulated by employees at Brumley Statistical Consulting Inc. is repeated from Exercise 17.

Frequent Flier Miles (000)	Frequency
0 up to 3	5
3 up to 6	12
6 up to 9	23
9 up to 12	8
12 up to 15	2
Total	50

a. How many employees accumulated less than 3,000 miles?
b. Convert the frequency distribution to a cumulative frequency distribution.
c. Portray the cumulative distribution in the form of a cumulative frequency polygon.
d. Based on the cumulative relative frequencies, about 75% of the employees accumulated how many miles or less?

22. The frequency distribution of order lead time of the retailer from Exercise 18 is repeated below.

Lead Time (days)	Frequency
0 up to 5	6
5 up to 10	7
10 up to 15	12
15 up to 20	8
20 up to 25	7
Total	40

a. How many orders were filled in less than 10 days? In less than 15 days?
b. Convert the frequency distribution to cumulative frequency and cumulative relative frequency distributions.
c. Develop a cumulative frequency polygon.
d. About 60% of the orders were filled in less than how many days?

CHAPTER SUMMARY

I. A frequency table is a grouping of qualitative data into mutually exclusive and collectively exhaustive classes showing the number of observations in each class.
II. A relative frequency table shows the fraction of the number of frequencies in each class.
III. A bar chart is a graphic representation of a frequency table.
IV. A pie chart shows the proportion each distinct class represents of the total number of observations.
V. A frequency distribution is a grouping of data into mutually exclusive and collectively exhaustive classes showing the number of observations in each class.
  A. The steps in constructing a frequency distribution are
    1. Decide on the number of classes.
    2. Determine the class interval.
    3. Set the individual class limits.
    4. Tally the raw data into classes and determine the frequency in each class.

B. The class frequency is the number of observations in each class.
C. The class interval is the difference between the limits of two consecutive classes.
D. The class midpoint is halfway between the limits of consecutive classes.

VI. A relative frequency distribution shows the percent of observations in each class.

VII. There are several methods for graphically portraying a frequency distribution.
A. A histogram portrays the frequencies in the form of a rectangle or bar for each class. The height of the rectangles is proportional to the class frequencies.
B. A frequency polygon consists of line segments connecting the points formed by the intersection of the class midpoint and the class frequency.
C. A graph of a cumulative frequency distribution shows the number of observations less than a given value.
D. A graph of a cumulative relative frequency distribution shows the percent of observations less than a given value.

CHAPTER EXERCISES

23. Describe the similarities and differences of qualitative and quantitative variables. Be sure to include the following:
a. What level of measurement is required for each variable type?
b. Can both types be used to describe both samples and populations?

24. Describe the similarities and differences between a frequency table and a frequency distribution. Be sure to include which requires qualitative data and which requires quantitative data.

25. Alexandra Damonte will be building a new resort in Myrtle Beach, South Carolina. She must decide how to design the resort based on the type of activities that the resort will offer to its customers. A recent poll of 300 potential customers showed the following results about customers' preferences for planned resort activities:

Like planned activities	63
Do not like planned activities	135
Not sure	78
No answer	24

a. What is the table called?
b. Draw a bar chart to portray the survey results.
c. Draw a pie chart for the survey results.
d. If you are preparing to present the results to Ms. Damonte as part of a report, which graph would you prefer to show? Why?

26. FILE Speedy Swift is a package delivery service that serves the greater Atlanta, Georgia, metropolitan area. To maintain customer loyalty, one of Speedy Swift's performance objectives is on-time delivery. To monitor its performance, each delivery is measured on the following scale: early (package delivered before the promised time), on-time (package delivered within 5 minutes of the promised time), late (package delivered more than 5 minutes past the promised time), or lost (package never delivered). Speedy Swift's objective is to deliver 99% of all packages either early or on-time. Speedy collected the following data for last month's performance:

On-time	On-time	Early	Late	On-time	On-time	On-time	On-time	Late	On-time
Early	On-time	On-time	Early	On-time	On-time	On-time	On-time	On-time	On-time
Early	On-time	Early	On-time	On-time	On-time	Early	On-time	On-time	On-time
Early	On-time	On-time	Late	Early	Early	On-time	On-time	On-time	Early
On-time	Late	Late	On-time	On-time	On-time	On-time	On-time	On-time	On-time
On-time	Late	Early	On-time	Early	On-time	Lost	On-time	On-time	On-time
Early	Early	On-time	On-time	Late	Early	Lost	On-time	On-time	On-time
On-time	On-time	Early	On-time	Early	On-time	Early	On-time	Late	On-time
On-time	Early	On-time	On-time	On-time	Late	On-time	Early	On-time	On-time
On-time	On-time	On-time	On-time	On-time	Early	Early	On-time	On-time	On-time

a. What kind of variable is delivery performance? What scale is used to measure delivery performance?
b. Construct a frequency table for delivery performance for last month.
c. Construct a relative frequency table for delivery performance last month.
d. Construct a bar chart of the frequency table for delivery performance for last month.
e. Construct a pie chart of on-time delivery performance for last month.
f. Write a memo reporting the results of the analyses. Include your tables and graphs with written descriptions of what they show. Conclude with a general statement of last month's delivery performance as it relates to Speedy Swift's performance objectives.

27. A data set consists of 83 observations. How many classes would you recommend for a frequency distribution?

28. A data set consists of 145 observations that range from 56 to 490. What size class interval would you recommend?

29. FILE The following is the number of minutes to commute from home to work for a group of 25 automobile executives.

28	25	48	37	41	19	32	26	16	23	23	29	36
31	26	21	32	25	31	43	35	42	38	33	28	

a. How many classes would you recommend?
b. What class interval would you suggest?
c. What would you recommend as the lower limit of the first class?
d. Organize the data into a frequency distribution.
e. Comment on the shape of the frequency distribution.

30. FILE The following data give the weekly amounts spent on groceries for a sample of 45 households.

$271	$363	$159	$ 76	$227	$337	$295	$319	$250
279	205	279	266	199	177	162	232	303
192	181	321	309	246	278	50	41	335
116	100	151	240	474	297	170	188	320
429	294	570	342	279	235	434	123	325

a. How many classes would you recommend?
b. What class interval would you suggest?
c. What would you recommend as the lower limit of the first class?
d. Organize the data into a frequency distribution.

31. FILE A social scientist is studying the use of iPods by college students. A sample of 45 students revealed they played the following number of songs yesterday.

4	6	8	7	9	6	3	7	7	6	7	1	4	7	7
4	6	4	10	2	4	6	3	4	6	8	4	3	3	6
8	8	4	6	4	6	5	5	9	6	8	8	6	5	10

Organize the information into a frequency distribution.
a. How many classes would you suggest?
b. What is the most suitable class interval?
c. What is the lower limit of the initial class?
d. Create the frequency distribution.
e. Describe the shape of the distribution.

32. FILE David Wise handles his own investment portfolio, and has done so for many years. Listed below is the holding time (recorded to the nearest whole year) between purchase and sale for his collection of 36 stocks.

8	8	6	11	11	9	8	5	11	4	8	5	14	7	12	8	6	11	9	7
9	15	8	8	12	5	9	8	5	9	10	11	3	9	8	6				

a. How many classes would you propose?
b. What class interval would you suggest?
c. What quantity would you use for the lower limit of the initial class?

d. Using your responses to parts (a), (b), and (c), create a frequency distribution.
e. Describe the shape of the frequency distribution.

33. FILE You are exploring the music in your iTunes library. The total play counts over the past year for the 27 songs on your "smart playlist" are shown below. Make a frequency distribution of the counts and describe its shape. It is often claimed that a small fraction of a person's songs will account for most of their total plays. Does this seem to be the case here?

128	56	54	91	190	23	160	298	445	50
578	494	37	677	18	74	70	868	108	71
466	23	84	38	26	814	17			

34. FILE The monthly issues of the *Journal of Finance* are available on the Internet. The table below shows the number of times an issue was downloaded over the last 33 months. Suppose that you wish to summarize the number of downloads with a frequency distribution.

312	2,753	2,595	6,057	7,624	6,624	6,362	6,575	7,760	7,085	7,272
5,967	5,256	6,160	6,238	6,709	7,193	5,631	6,490	6,682	7,829	7,091
6,871	6,230	7,253	5,507	5,676	6,974	6,915	4,999	5,689	6,143	7,086

a. How many classes would you propose?
b. What class interval would you suggest?
c. What quantity would you use for the lower limit of the initial class?
d. Using your responses to parts (a), (b), and (c), create a frequency distribution.
e. Describe the shape of the frequency distribution.

35. The following histogram shows the scores on the first exam for a statistics class.

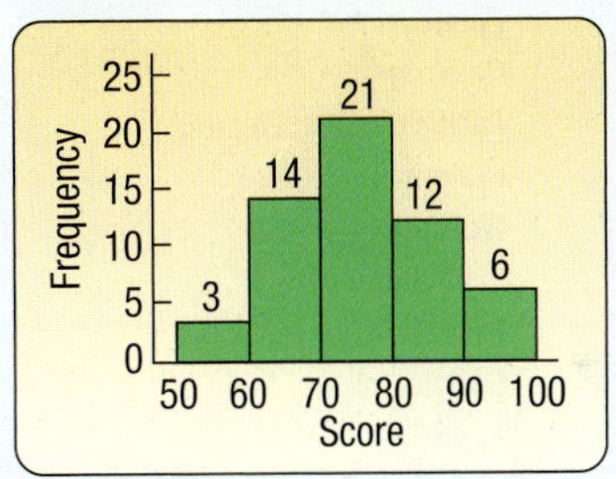

a. How many students took the exam?
b. What is the class interval?
c. What is the class midpoint for the first class?
d. How many students earned a score of less than 70?

36. The following chart summarizes the selling price of homes sold last month in the Sarasota, Florida, area.

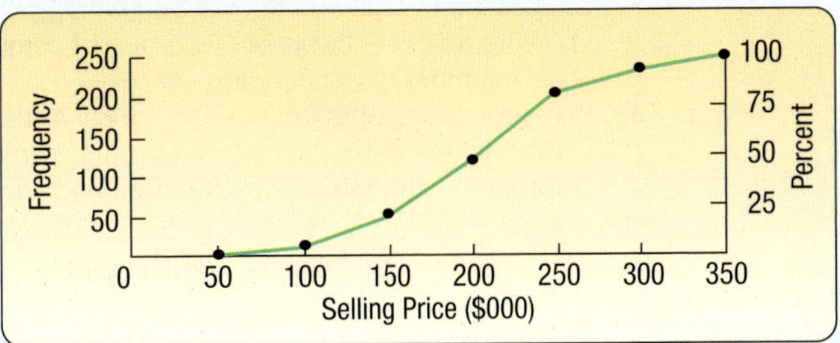

a. What is the chart called?
b. How many homes were sold during the last month?
c. What is the class interval?
d. About 75% of the houses sold for less than what amount?
e. One hundred seventy-five of the homes sold for less than what amount?

37. **FILE** A chain of sport shops catering to beginning skiers, headquartered in Aspen, Colorado, plans to conduct a study of how much a beginning skier spends on his or her initial purchase of equipment and supplies. Based on these figures, it wants to explore the possibility of offering combinations, such as a pair of boots and a pair of skis, to induce customers to buy more. A sample of 44 cash register receipts revealed these initial purchases:

$140	$ 82	$265	$168	$ 90	$114	$172	$230	$142
86	125	235	212	171	149	156	162	118
139	149	132	105	162	126	216	195	127
161	135	172	220	229	129	87	128	126
175	127	149	126	121	118	172	126	

a. Arrive at a suggested class interval.
b. Organize the data into a frequency distribution using a lower limit of $70.
c. Interpret your findings.

38. **FILE** The numbers of outstanding shares for 24 publicly traded companies are listed in the following table.

Company	Number of Outstanding Shares (millions)	Company	Number of Outstanding Shares (millions)
Southwest Airlines	738	Costco	436
FirstEnergy	418	Home Depot	1,495
Harley Davidson	226	DTE Energy	172
Entergy	178	Dow Chemical	1,199
Chevron	1,957	Eastman Kodak	272
Pacific Gas and Electric	430	American Electric Power	485
DuPont	932	ITT Corporation	93
Westinghouse	22	Ameren	243
Eversource	314	Virginia Electric and Power	575
Facebook	1,067	Public Service Electric & Gas	506
Google, Inc.	64	Consumers Energy	265
Apple	941	Starbucks	744

a. Using the number of outstanding shares, summarize the companies with a frequency distribution.
b. Display the frequency distribution with a frequency polygon.
c. Create a cumulative frequency distribution of the outstanding shares.
d. Display the cumulative frequency distribution with a cumulative frequency polygon.
e. Based on the cumulative relative frequency distribution, 75% of the companies have less than "what number" of outstanding shares?
f. Write a brief analysis of this group of companies based on your statistical summaries of "number of outstanding shares."

39. A recent survey showed that the typical American car owner spends $2,950 per year on operating expenses. Below is a breakdown of the various expenditure items. Draw an appropriate chart to portray the data and summarize your findings in a brief report.

Expenditure Item	Amount
Fuel	$ 603
Interest on car loan	279
Repairs	930
Insurance and license	646
Depreciation	492
Total	$2,950

40. **FILE** Midland National Bank selected a sample of 40 student checking accounts. Below are their end-of-the-month balances.

$404	$ 74	$234	$149	$279	$215	$123	$ 55	$ 43	$321
87	234	68	489	57	185	141	758	72	863
703	125	350	440	37	252	27	521	302	127
968	712	503	489	327	608	358	425	303	203

a. Tally the data into a frequency distribution using $100 as a class interval and $0 as the starting point.
b. Draw a cumulative frequency polygon.
c. The bank considers any student with an ending balance of $400 or more a "preferred customer." Estimate the percentage of preferred customers.
d. The bank is also considering a service charge to the lowest 10% of the ending balances. What would you recommend as the cutoff point between those who have to pay a service charge and those who do not?

41. Residents of the state of South Carolina earned a total of $69.5 billion in adjusted gross income. Seventy-three percent of the total was in wages and salaries; 11% in dividends, interest, and capital gains; 8% in IRAs and taxable pensions; 3% in business income pensions; 2% in Social Security; and the remaining 3% from other sources. Develop a pie chart depicting the breakdown of adjusted gross income. Write a paragraph summarizing the information.

42. **FILE** A recent study of home technologies reported the number of hours of personal computer usage per week for a sample of 60 persons. Excluded from the study were people who worked out of their home and used the computer as a part of their work.

9.3	5.3	6.3	8.8	6.5	0.6	5.2	6.6	9.3	4.3
6.3	2.1	2.7	0.4	3.7	3.3	1.1	2.7	6.7	6.5
4.3	9.7	7.7	5.2	1.7	8.5	4.2	5.5	5.1	5.6
5.4	4.8	2.1	10.1	1.3	5.6	2.4	2.4	4.7	1.7
2.0	6.7	1.1	6.7	2.2	2.6	9.8	6.4	4.9	5.2
4.5	9.3	7.9	4.6	4.3	4.5	9.2	8.5	6.0	8.1

a. Organize the data into a frequency distribution. How many classes would you suggest? What value would you suggest for a class interval?
b. Draw a histogram. Describe your result.

43. **FILE** Merrill Lynch recently completed a study regarding the size of online investment portfolios (stocks, bonds, mutual funds, and certificates of deposit) for a sample of clients in the 40 up to 50 years old age group. Listed following is the value of all the investments in thousands of dollars for the 70 participants in the study.

$669.9	$ 7.5	$ 77.2	$ 7.5	$125.7	$516.9	$ 219.9	$645.2
301.9	235.4	716.4	145.3	26.6	187.2	315.5	89.2
136.4	616.9	440.6	408.2	34.4	296.1	185.4	526.3
380.7	3.3	363.2	51.9	52.2	107.5	82.9	63.0
228.6	308.7	126.7	430.3	82.0	227.0	321.1	403.4
39.5	124.3	118.1	23.9	352.8	156.7	276.3	23.5
31.3	301.2	35.7	154.9	174.3	100.6	236.7	171.9
221.1	43.4	212.3	243.3	315.4	5.9	1,002.2	171.7
295.7	437.0	87.8	302.1	268.1	899.5		

a. Organize the data into a frequency distribution. How many classes would you suggest? What value would you suggest for a class interval?
b. Draw a histogram. Financial experts suggest that this age group of people have at least five times their salary saved. As a benchmark, assume an investment portfolio of $500,000 would support retirement in 10–15 years. In writing, summarize your results.

44. A total of 5.9% of the prime-time viewing audience watched shows on ABC, 7.6% watched shows on CBS, 5.5% on Fox, 6.0% on NBC, 2.0% on Warner Brothers, and 2.2% on UPN. A total of 70.8% of the audience watched shows on other cable networks, such as CNN and ESPN. You can find the latest information on TV viewing from the following website: **http://www.nielsen.com/us/en/top10s.html/**. Develop a pie chart or a bar chart to depict this information. Write a paragraph summarizing your findings.

45. Refer to the following chart:

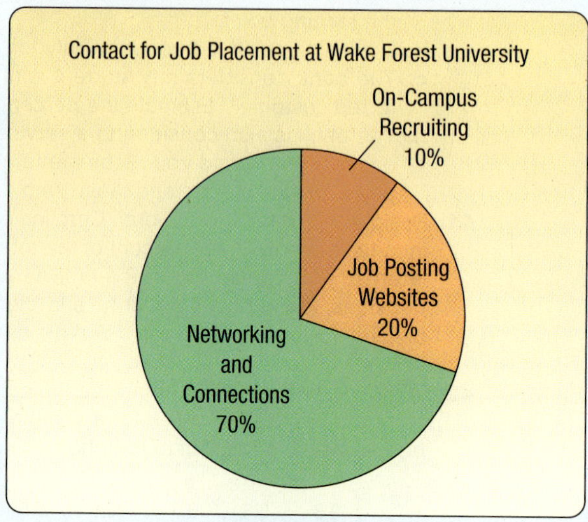

a. What is the name given to this type of chart?

b. Suppose that 1,000 graduates will start a new job shortly after graduation. Estimate the number of graduates whose first contact for employment occurred through networking and other connections.

c. Would it be reasonable to conclude that about 90% of job placements were made through networking, connections, and job posting websites? Cite evidence.

46. The following chart depicts the annual revenues, by type of tax, for the state of Georgia.

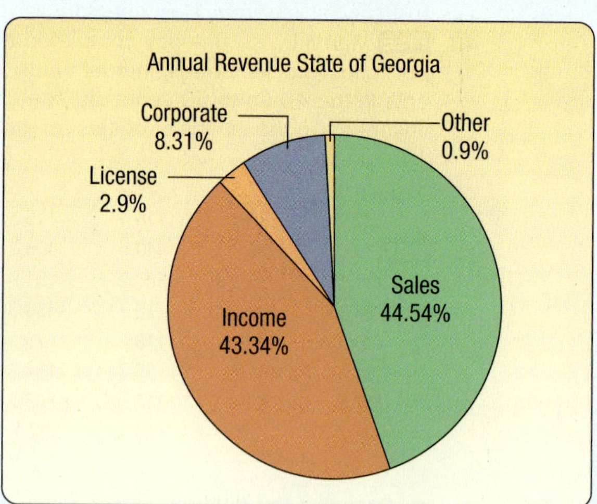

a. What percentage of the state revenue is accounted for by sales tax and individual income tax?

b. Which category will generate more revenue: corporate taxes or license fees?

c. The total annual revenue for the state of Georgia is $6.3 billion. Estimate the amount of revenue in billions of dollars for sales taxes and for individual taxes.

47. In 2014, the United States exported a total of $376 billion worth of products to Canada. The five largest categories were:

Product	Amount
Vehicles	$63.3
Machinery	59.7
Electrical machinery	36.6
Mineral fuel and oil	24.8
Plastic	17.0

a. Use a software package to develop a bar chart.
b. What percentage of the United States' total exports to Canada is represented by the two categories "Machinery" and "Electrical Machinery"?
c. What percentage of the top five exported products do "Machinery" and "Electrical Machinery" represent?

48. FILE In the United States, the industrial revolution of the early 20th century changed farming by making it more efficient. For example, in 1910 U.S. farms used 24.2 million horses and mules and only about 1,000 tractors. By 1960, 4.6 million tractors were used and only 3.2 million horses and mules. An outcome of making farming more efficient is the reduction of the number of farms from over 6 million in 1920 to about 2.2 million farms today. Listed below is the number of farms, in thousands, for each of the 50 states. Summarize the data and write a paragraph that describes your findings.

50	12	5	28	59	19	35	22	80	5
8	48	3	75	25	77	46	68	10	69
77	25	13	20	35	6	52	61	36	38
88	1	75	246	59	50	44	98	74	2
32	42	7	31	28	9	8	44	25	37

49. One of the most popular candies in the United States is M&M's produced by the Mars Company. In the beginning M&M's were all brown. Now they are produced in red, green, blue, orange, brown, and yellow. Recently, the purchase of a 14-ounce bag of M&M's Plain had 444 candies with the following breakdown by color: 130 brown, 98 yellow, 96 red, 35 orange, 52 blue, and 33 green. Develop a chart depicting this information and write a paragraph summarizing the results.

50. FILE The number of families who used the Minneapolis YWCA day care service was recorded during a 30-day period. The results are as follows:

31	49	19	62	24	45	23	51	55	60
40	35	54	26	57	37	43	65	18	41
50	56	4	54	39	52	35	51	63	42

a. Construct a cumulative frequency distribution.
b. Sketch a graph of the cumulative frequency polygon.
c. How many days saw fewer than 30 families utilize the day care center?
d. Based on cumulative relative frequencies, how busy were the highest 80% of the days?

DATA ANALYTICS

51. FILE Refer to the North Valley Real Estate data that reports information on homes sold during the last year. For the variable *price*, select an appropriate class interval and organize the selling prices into a frequency distribution. Write a brief report summarizing your findings. Be sure to answer the following questions in your report.
a. Around what values of price do the data tend to cluster?
b. Based on the frequency distribution, what is the typical selling price in the first class? What is the typical selling price in the last class?

c. Draw a cumulative relative frequency distribution. Using this distribution, fifty percent of the homes sold for what price or less? Estimate the lower price of the top ten percent of homes sold. About what percent of the homes sold for less than $300,000?

d. Refer to the variable *bedrooms*. Draw a bar chart showing the number of homes sold with 2, 3, 4 or more bedrooms. Write a description of the distribution.

52. **FILE** Refer to the Baseball 2016 data that report information on the 30 Major League Baseball teams for the 2016 season. Create a frequency distribution for the *Team Salary* variable and answer the following questions.

a. What is the typical salary for a team? What is the range of the salaries?

b. Comment on the shape of the distribution. Does it appear that any of the teams have a salary that is out of line with the others?

c. Draw a cumulative relative frequency distribution of team salary. Using this distribution, forty percent of the teams have a salary of less than what amount? About how many teams have a total salary of more than $220 million?

53. **FILE** Refer to the Lincolnville School District bus data. Select the variable referring to the number of *miles traveled since the last maintenance*, and then organize these data into a frequency distribution.

a. What is a typical amount of miles traveled? What is the range?

b. Comment on the shape of the distribution. Are there any outliers in terms of miles driven?

c. Draw a cumulative relative frequency distribution. Forty percent of the buses were driven fewer than how many miles? How many buses were driven less than 10,500 miles?

d. Refer to the variables regarding the bus *manufacturer* and the bus *capacity.* Draw a pie chart of each variable and write a description of your results.

Describing Data:

NUMERICAL MEASURES

© Andy Lyons/Getty Images

▲ **THE KENTUCKY DERBY** is held the first Saturday in May at Churchill Downs in Louisville, Kentucky. The race track is one and one-quarter miles. The table in Exercise 82 shows the winners since 1990, their margin of victory, the winning time, and the payoff on a $2 bet. Determine the mean and median for the variables winning time and payoff on a $2 bet. (See Exercise 82 and **LO3-1**.)

LEARNING OBJECTIVES

When you have completed this chapter, you will be able to:

LO3-1 Compute and interpret the mean, the median, and the mode.

LO3-2 Compute a weighted mean.

LO3-3 Compute and interpret the geometric mean.

LO3-4 Compute and interpret the range, variance, and standard deviation.

LO3-5 Explain and apply Chebyshev's theorem and the Empirical Rule.

LO3-6 Compute the mean and standard deviation of grouped data.

INTRODUCTION

> **STATISTICS IN ACTION**
>
> Did you ever meet the "average" American man? Well, his name is Robert (that is the nominal level of measurement) and he is 31 years old (that is the ratio level), is 69.5 inches tall (again the ratio level of measurement), weighs 172 pounds, wears a size 9½ shoe, has a 34-inch waist, and wears a size 40 suit. In addition, the average man eats 4 pounds of potato chips, watches 1,456 hours of TV, and eats 26 pounds of bananas each year, and also sleeps 7.7 hours per night.
>
> The average American woman is 5′ 4″ tall and weighs 140 pounds, while the average American model is 5′ 11″ tall and weighs 117 pounds. On any given day, almost half of the women in the United States are on a diet. Idolized in the 1950s, Marilyn Monroe would be considered overweight by today's standards. She fluctuated between a size 14 and a size 18 dress, and was a healthy and attractive woman.

Chapter 2 began our study of descriptive statistics. To summarize raw data into a meaningful form, we organized qualitative data into a frequency table and portrayed the results in a bar chart. In a similar fashion, we organized quantitative data into a frequency distribution and portrayed the results in a histogram. We also looked at other graphical techniques such as pie charts to portray qualitative data and frequency polygons to portray quantitative data.

This chapter is concerned with two numerical ways of describing quantitative variables, namely, **measures of location** and **measures of dispersion.** Measures of location are often referred to as averages. The purpose of a measure of location is to pinpoint the center of a distribution of data. An average is a measure of location that shows the central value of the data. Averages appear daily on TV, on various websites, in the newspaper, and in other journals. Here are some examples:

- The average U.S. home changes ownership every 11.8 years.
- An American receives an average of 568 pieces of mail per year.
- The average American home has more TV sets than people. There are 2.73 TV sets and 2.55 people in the typical home.
- The average American couple spends $20,398 for their wedding, while their budget is 50% less. This does not include the cost of a honeymoon or engagement ring.
- The average price of a theater ticket in the United States is $8.31, according to the National Association of Theater Owners.

© Andersen Ross/Getty Images RF

If we consider only measures of location in a set of data, or if we compare several sets of data using central values, we may draw an erroneous conclusion. In addition to measures of location, we should consider the **dispersion**—often called the *variation* or the *spread*—in the data. As an illustration, suppose the average annual income of executives for Internet-related companies is $80,000, and the average income for executives in pharmaceutical firms is also $80,000. If we looked only at the average incomes, we might wrongly conclude that the distributions of the two salaries are the same. However, we need to examine the dispersion or spread of the distributions of salary. A look at the salary ranges indicates that this conclusion of equal distributions is not correct. The salaries for the executives in the Internet firms range from $70,000 to $90,000, but salaries for the marketing executives in pharmaceuticals range from $40,000 to $120,000. Thus, we conclude that although the average salaries are the same for the two industries, there is much more spread or dispersion in salaries for the pharmaceutical executives. To describe the dispersion, we will consider the range, the variance, and the standard deviation.

LO3-1
Compute and interpret the mean, the median, and the mode.

MEASURES OF LOCATION

We begin by discussing measures of location. There is not just one measure of location; in fact, there are many. We will consider five: the arithmetic mean, the median, the mode, the weighted mean, and the geometric mean. The arithmetic mean is the most widely used and widely reported measure of location. We study the mean as both a population parameter and a sample statistic.

The Population Mean

Many studies involve all the values in a population. For example, there are 12 sales associates employed at the Reynolds Road Carpet Outlet. The mean amount of commission they earned last month was $1,345. This is a population value because we considered the commission of *all* the sales associates. Other examples of a population mean would be:

- The mean closing price for Johnson & Johnson stock for the last 5 days is $95.47.
- The mean number of hours of overtime worked last week by the six welders in the welding department of Butts Welding Inc. is 6.45 hours.
- Caryn Tirsch began a website last month devoted to organic gardening. The mean number of hits on her site for the 31 days in July was 84.36.

For raw data—that is, data that have not been grouped in a frequency distribution—the population mean is the sum of all the values in the population divided by the number of values in the population. To find the population mean, we use the following formula.

$$\text{Population mean} = \frac{\text{Sum of all the values in the population}}{\text{Number of values in the population}}$$

Instead of writing out in words the full directions for computing the population mean (or any other measure), it is more convenient to use the shorthand symbols of mathematics. The mean of the population using mathematical symbols is:

POPULATION MEAN $$\mu = \frac{\Sigma x}{N} \qquad \textbf{(3–1)}$$

where:

μ represents the population mean. It is the Greek lowercase letter "mu."
N is the number of values in the population.
x represents any particular value.
Σ is the Greek capital letter "sigma" and indicates the operation of adding.
Σx is the sum of the x values in the population.

Any measurable characteristic of a population is called a **parameter.** The mean of a population is an example of a parameter.

PARAMETER A characteristic of a population.

EXAMPLE

There are 42 exits on I-75 through the state of Kentucky. Listed below are the distances between exits (in miles).

11	4	10	4	9	3	8	10	3	14	1	10	3	5
2	2	5	6	1	2	2	3	7	1	3	7	8	10
1	4	7	5	2	2	5	1	1	3	3	1	2	1

Why is this information a population? What is the mean number of miles between exits?

SOLUTION

This is a population because we are considering all the exits on I-75 in Kentucky. We add the distances between each of the 42 exits. The total distance is 192 miles. To find the arithmetic mean, we divide this total by 42. So the arithmetic mean is 4.57 miles, found by 192/42. From formula (3–1):

$$\mu = \frac{\Sigma x}{N} = \frac{11 + 4 + 10 + \cdots + 1}{42} = \frac{192}{42} = 4.57$$

How do we interpret the value of 4.57? It is the typical number of miles between exits. Because we considered all the exits on I-75 in Kentucky, this value is a population parameter.

© Bloomberg/Getty Images

The Sample Mean

As explained in Chapter 1, we often select a sample from the population to estimate a specific characteristic of the population. Smucker's quality assurance department needs to be assured that the amount of orange marmalade in the jar labeled as containing 12 ounces actually contains that amount. It would be very expensive and time-consuming to check the weight of each jar. Therefore, a sample of 20 jars is selected, the mean of the sample is determined, and that value is used to estimate the amount in each jar.

For raw data—that is, ungrouped data—*the mean is the sum of all the sampled values divided by the total number of sampled values.* To find the mean for a sample:

$$\text{Sample mean} = \frac{\text{Sum of all the values in the sample}}{\text{Number of values in the sample}}$$

The mean of a sample and the mean of a population are computed in the same way, but the shorthand notation used is different. The formula for the mean of a *sample* is:

SAMPLE MEAN $$\bar{x} = \frac{\Sigma x}{n}$$ **(3–2)**

where:

$\bar{x}$ represents the sample mean. It is read "x bar."
n is the number of values in the sample.
x represents any particular value.
Σ is the Greek capital letter "sigma" and indicates the operation of adding.
Σx is the sum of the x values in the sample.

The mean of a sample, or any other measure based on sample data, is called a **statistic.** If the mean weight of a sample of 10 jars of Smucker's orange marmalade is 11.5 ounces, this is an example of a statistic.

STATISTIC A characteristic of a sample.

EXAMPLE

Verizon is studying the number of monthly minutes used by clients in a particular cell phone rate plan. A random sample of 12 clients showed the following number of minutes used last month.

90	77	94	89	119	112
91	110	92	100	113	83

What is the arithmetic mean number of minutes used last month?

SOLUTION

Using formula (3–2), the sample mean is:

$$\text{Sample mean} = \frac{\text{Sum of all values in the sample}}{\text{Number of values in the sample}}$$

$$\bar{x} = \frac{\Sigma x}{n} = \frac{90 + 77 + \cdots + 83}{12} = \frac{1{,}170}{12} = 97.5$$

The arithmetic mean number of minutes used last month by the sample of cell phone users is 97.5 minutes.

Properties of the Arithmetic Mean

The arithmetic mean is a widely used measure of location. It has several important properties:

1. **To compute a mean, the data must be measured at the interval or ratio level.** Recall from Chapter 1 that ratio-level data include such data as ages, incomes, and weights, with the distance between numbers being constant.
2. **All the values are included in computing the mean.**
3. **The mean is unique.** That is, there is only one mean in a set of data. Later in the chapter, we will discover a measure of location that might appear twice, or more than twice, in a set of data.
4. **The sum of the deviations of each value from the mean is zero.** Expressed symbolically:

$$\Sigma(x - \bar{x}) = 0$$

As an example, the mean of 3, 8, and 4 is 5. Then:

$$\begin{aligned}\Sigma(x - \bar{x}) &= (3 - 5) + (8 - 5) + (4 - 5)\\ &= -2 + 3 - 1\\ &= 0\end{aligned}$$

Thus, we can consider the mean as a balance point for a set of data. To illustrate, we have a long board with the numbers 1, 2, 3, . . . , 9 evenly spaced on it. Suppose three bars of equal weight were placed on the board at numbers 3, 4, and 8, and the balance point was set at 5, the mean of the three numbers. We would find that the board is balanced perfectly! The deviations below the mean (−3) are equal to the deviations above the mean (+3). Shown schematically:

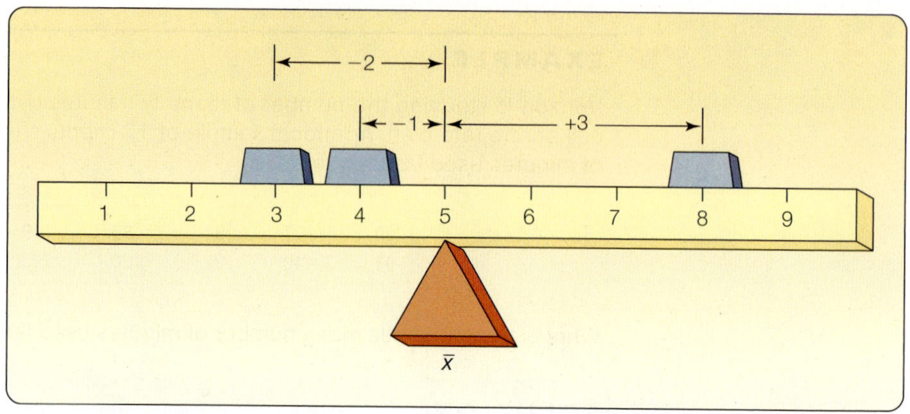

The mean does have a weakness. Recall that the mean uses the value of every item in a sample, or population, in its computation. If one or two of these values are either extremely large or extremely small compared to the majority of data, the mean might not be an appropriate average to represent the data. For example, suppose the annual incomes of a sample of financial planners at Merrill Lynch are $62,900, $61,600, $62,500, $60,800, and $1,200,000. The mean income is $289,560. Obviously, it is not representative of this group because all but one financial planner has an income in the $60,000 to $63,000 range. One income ($1.2 million) is unduly affecting the mean.

SELF-REVIEW 3–1

1. The annual incomes of a sample of middle-management employees at Westinghouse are $62,900, $69,100, $58,300, and $76,800.
   (a) Give the formula for the sample mean.
   (b) Find the sample mean.
   (c) Is the mean you computed in (b) a statistic or a parameter? Why?
   (d) What is your best estimate of the population mean?
2. The six students in Computer Science 411 are a population. Their final course grades are 92, 96, 61, 86, 79, and 84.
   (a) Give the formula for the population mean.
   (b) Compute the mean course grade.
   (c) Is the mean you computed in (b) a statistic or a parameter? Why?

EXERCISES

The answers to the odd-numbered exercises are in Appendix D.

1. Compute the mean of the following population values: 6, 3, 5, 7, 6.

2. Compute the mean of the following population values: 7, 5, 7, 3, 7, 4.

3. **a.** Compute the mean of the following sample values: 5, 9, 4, 10.
b. Show that $\Sigma(x - \bar{x}) = 0$.

4. **a.** Compute the mean of the following sample values: 1.3, 7.0, 3.6, 4.1, 5.0.
b. Show that $\Sigma(x - \bar{x}) = 0$.

5. Compute the mean of the following sample values: 16.25, 12.91, 14.58.

6. Suppose you go to the grocery store and spend $61.85 for the purchase of 14 items. What is the mean price per item?

For Exercises 7–10, (a) compute the arithmetic mean and (b) indicate whether it is a statistic or a parameter.

7. There are 10 salespeople employed by Midtown Ford. The number of new cars sold last month by the respective salespeople were: 15, 23, 4, 19, 18, 10, 10, 8, 28, 19.
8. A mail-order company counted the number of incoming calls per day to the company's toll-free number during the first 7 days in May: 14, 24, 19, 31, 36, 26, 17.
9. **FILE** The Cambridge Power and Light Company selected a random sample of 20 residential customers. Following are the amounts, to the nearest dollar, the customers were charged for electrical service last month:

54	48	58	50	25	47	75	46	60	70
67	68	39	35	56	66	33	62	65	67

10. **FILE** A Human Resources manager at Metal Technologies studied the overtime hours of welders. A sample of 15 welders showed the following number of overtime hours worked last month.

13	13	12	15	7	15	5	12
6	7	12	10	9	13	12	

11. AAA Heating and Air Conditioning completed 30 jobs last month with a mean revenue of $5,430 per job. The president wants to know the total revenue for the month. Based on the limited information, can you compute the total revenue? What is it?
12. A large pharmaceutical company hires business administration graduates to sell its products. The company is growing rapidly and dedicates only 1 day of sales training for new salespeople. The company's goal for new salespeople is $10,000 per month. The goal is based on the current mean sales for the entire company, which is $10,000 per month. After reviewing the retention rates of new employees, the company finds that only 1 in 10 new employees stays longer than 3 months. Comment on using the current mean sales per month as a sales goal for new employees. Why do new employees leave the company?

The Median

We have stressed that, for data containing one or two very large or very small values, the arithmetic mean may not be representative. The center for such data is better described by a measure of location called the **median.**

To illustrate the need for a measure of location other than the arithmetic mean, suppose you are seeking to buy a condominium in Palm Aire. Your real estate agent says that the typical price of the units currently available is $110,000. Would you still want to look? If you had budgeted your maximum purchase price at $75,000, you might think they are out of your price range. However, checking the prices of the individual units might change your mind. They are $60,000, $65,000, $70,000, and $80,000, and a superdeluxe penthouse costs $275,000. The arithmetic mean price is $110,000, as the real estate agent reported, but one price ($275,000) is pulling the arithmetic mean upward, causing it to be an unrepresentative average. It does seem that a price around $70,000 is a more typical or representative average, and it is. In cases such as this, the median provides a more valid measure of location.

MEDIAN The midpoint of the values after they have been ordered from the minimum to the maximum values.

The median price of the units available is $70,000. To determine this, we order the prices from the minimum value ($60,000) to the maximum value ($275,000) and select the middle value ($70,000). For the median, the data must be at least an ordinal level of measurement.

Prices Ordered from Minimum to Maximum		Prices Ordered from Maximum to Minimum
$ 60,000		$275,000
65,000		80,000
70,000	← Median →	70,000
80,000		65,000
275,000		60,000

Note that there is the same number of prices below the median of $70,000 as above it. The median is, therefore, unaffected by extremely low or high prices. Had the highest price been $90,000, or $300,000, or even $1 million, the median price would still be $70,000. Likewise, had the lowest price been $20,000 or $50,000, the median price would still be $70,000.

In the previous illustration, there are an *odd* number of observations (five). How is the median determined for an *even* number of observations? As before, the observations are ordered. Then by convention to obtain a unique value we calculate the mean of the two middle observations. So for an even number of observations, the median may not be one of the given values.

EXAMPLE

Facebook is a popular social networking website. Users can add friends and send them messages, and update their personal profiles to notify friends about themselves and their activities. A sample of 10 adults revealed they spent the following number of hours last month using Facebook.

3	5	7	5	9	1	3	9	17	10

Find the median number of hours.

SOLUTION

Note that the number of adults sampled is even (10). The first step, as before, is to order the hours using Facebook from the minimum value to the maximum value. Then identify the two middle times. The arithmetic mean of the two middle observations gives us the median hours. Arranging the values from minimum to maximum:

1	3	3	5	5	7	9	9	10	17

The median is found by averaging the two middle values. The middle values are 5 hours and 7 hours, and the mean of these two values is 6. We conclude that the typical adult Facebook user spends 6 hours per month at the website. Notice that the median is not one of the values. Also, half of the times are below the median and half are above it.

The major properties of the median are:

1. **It is not affected by extremely large or small values.** Therefore, the median is a valuable measure of location when such values do occur.
2. **It can be computed for ordinal-level data or higher.** Recall from Chapter 1 that ordinal-level data can be ranked from low to high.

The Mode

The **mode** is another measure of location.

MODE The value of the observation that appears most frequently.

The mode is especially useful in summarizing nominal-level data. As an example of its use for nominal-level data, a company has developed five bath oils. The bar chart in Chart 3–1 shows the results of a marketing survey designed to find which bath oil consumers prefer. The largest number of respondents favored Lamoure, as evidenced by the highest bar. Thus, Lamoure is the mode.

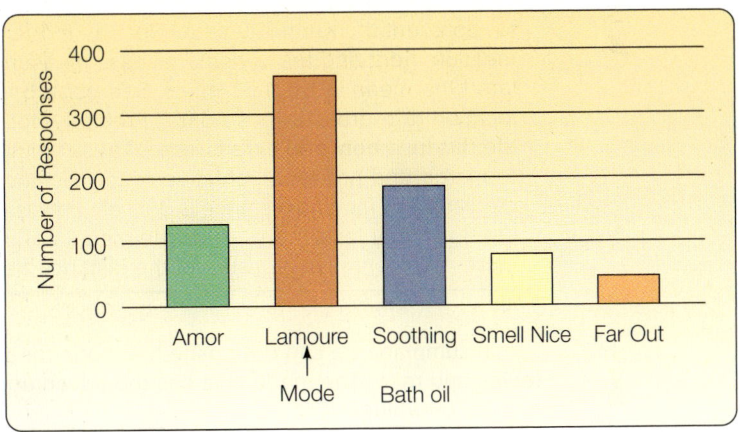

CHART 3–1 Number of Respondents Favoring Various Bath Oils

EXAMPLE

Recall the data regarding the distance in miles between exits on I-75 in Kentucky. The information is repeated below.

11	4	10	4	9	3	8	10	3	14	1	10	3	5
2	2	5	6	1	2	2	3	7	1	3	7	8	10
1	4	7	5	2	2	5	1	1	3	3	1	2	1

What is the modal distance?

SOLUTION

The first step is to organize the distances into a frequency table. This will help us determine the distance that occurs most frequently.

Distance in Miles between Exits	Frequency
1	8
2	7
3	7
4	3
5	4
6	1
7	3
8	2
9	1
10	4
11	1
14	1
Total	42

The distance that occurs most often is 1 mile. This happens eight times—that is, there are eight exits that are 1 mile apart. So the modal distance between exits is 1 mile.

Which of the three measures of location (mean, median, or mode) best represents the central location of these data? Is the mode the best measure of location to represent the Kentucky data? No. The mode assumes only the nominal scale of measurement and the variable miles is measured using the ratio scale. We calculated the mean to be 4.57 miles. See page 54. Is the mean the best measure of location to represent these data? Probably not. There are several cases in which the distance between exits is large. These values are affecting the mean, making it too large and not representative of the distances between exits. What about the median? The median distance is 3 miles. That is, half of the distances between exits are 3 miles or less. In this case, the median of 3 miles between exits is probably a more representative measure of the distance between exits.

In summary, we can determine the mode for all levels of data—nominal, ordinal, interval, and ratio. The mode also has the advantage of not being affected by extremely high or low values.

The mode does have disadvantages, however, that cause it to be used less frequently than the mean or median. For many sets of data, there is no mode because no value appears more than once. For example, there is no mode for this set of price data because every value occurs once: \$19, \$21, \$23, \$20, and \$18. Conversely, for some data sets there is more than one mode. Suppose the ages of the individuals in a stock investment club are 22, 26, 27, 27, 31, 35, and 35. Both the ages 27 and 35 are modes. Thus, this grouping of ages is referred to as *bimodal* (having two modes). One would question the use of two modes to represent the location of this set of age data.

SELF-REVIEW 3–2

1. A sample of single persons in Towson, Texas, receiving Social Security payments revealed these monthly benefits: \$852, \$598, \$580, \$1,374, \$960, \$878, and \$1,130.
   (a) What is the median monthly benefit?
   (b) How many observations are below the median? Above it?
2. The number of work stoppages in the United States over the last 10 years are 22, 20, 21, 15, 5, 11, 19, 19, 15, and 11.
   (a) What is the median number of stoppages?
   (b) How many observations are below the median? Above it?
   (c) What is the modal number of work stoppages?

EXERCISES

13. What would you report as the modal value for a set of observations if there were a total of:
    a. 10 observations and no two values were the same?
    b. 6 observations and they were all the same?
    c. 6 observations and the values were 1, 2, 3, 3, 4, and 4?

For Exercises 14–16, determine the (a) mean, (b) median, and (c) mode.

14. The following is the number of oil changes for the last 7 days at the Jiffy Lube located at the corner of Elm Street and Pennsylvania Avenue.

41	15	39	54	31	15	33

15. The following is the percent change in net income from last year to this year for a sample of 12 construction companies in Denver.

5	1	−10	−6	5	12	7	8	6	5	−1	11

16. The following are the ages of the 10 people in the Java Coffee Shop at the Southwyck Shopping Mall at 10 a.m.

21	41	20	23	24	33	37	42	23	29

17. **FILE** Several indicators of long-term economic growth in the United States and their annual percent change are listed below.

Economic Indicator	Percent Change	Economic Indicator	Percent Change
Inflation	4.5%	Real GNP	2.9%
Exports	4.7	Investment (residential)	3.6
Imports	2.3	Investment (nonresidential)	2.1
Real disposable income	2.9	Productivity (total)	1.4
Consumption	2.7	Productivity (manufacturing)	5.2

    a. What is the median percent change?
    b. What is the modal percent change?

18. **FILE** Sally Reynolds sells real estate along the coastal area of Northern California. Below are her total annual commissions between 2005 and 2015. Find the mean, median, and mode of the commissions she earned for the 11 years.

Year	Amount (thousands)
2005	292.16
2006	233.80
2007	206.97
2008	202.67
2009	164.69
2010	206.53
2011	237.51
2012	225.57
2013	255.33
2014	248.14
2015	269.11

19. **FILE** The accounting firm of Rowatti and Koppel specializes in income tax returns for self-employed professionals, such as physicians, dentists, architects, and lawyers. The firm employs 11 accountants who prepare the returns. For last year, the number of returns prepared by each accountant was:

58	75	31	58	46	65	60	71	45	58	80

Find the mean, median, and mode for the number of returns prepared by each accountant. If you could report only one, which measure of location would you recommend reporting?

20. **FILE** The demand for the video games provided by Mid-Tech Video Games Inc. has exploded in the last several years. Hence, the owner needs to hire several new technical people to keep up with the demand. Mid-Tech gives each applicant a special test that Dr. McGraw, the designer of the test, believes is closely related to the ability to create video games. For the general population, the mean on this test is 100. Below are the scores on this test for the applicants.

95	105	120	81	90	115	99	100	130	10

The president is interested in the overall quality of the job applicants based on this test. Compute the mean and the median scores for the 10 applicants. What would you report to the president? Does it seem that the applicants are better than the general population?

The Relative Positions of the Mean, Median, and Mode

Refer to the histogram in Chart 3–2. It is a symmetric distribution, which is also mound-shaped. This distribution *has the same shape on either side of the center*. If the histogram were folded in half, the two halves would be identical. For any symmetric distribution, the mode, median, and mean are located at the center and are always equal. They are all equal to 30 years in Chart 3–2. We should point out that there are symmetric distributions that are not mound-shaped.

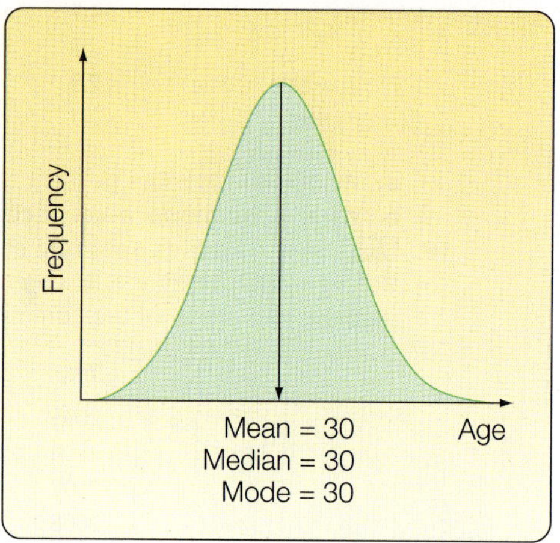

CHART 3–2 A Symmetric Distribution

The number of years corresponding to the highest point of the curve is the *mode* (30 years). Because the distribution is symmetrical, the *median* corresponds to the point where the distribution is cut in half (30 years). Also, because the arithmetic mean is the balance point of a distribution (as shown in the Properties of the Arithmetic Mean section on page 56), and the distribution is symmetric, the arithmetic mean is 30. Logically, any of the three measures would be appropriate to represent the distribution's center.

If a distribution is nonsymmetrical, or **skewed,** the relationship among the three measures changes. In a **positively skewed distribution,** such as the distribution of weekly income in Chart 3–3, the arithmetic mean is the largest of the three measures. Why? Because the mean is influenced more than the median or mode by a few extremely high values. The median is generally the next largest measure in a positively skewed frequency distribution. The mode is the smallest of the three measures.

If the distribution is highly skewed, the mean would not be a good measure to use. The median and mode would be more representative.

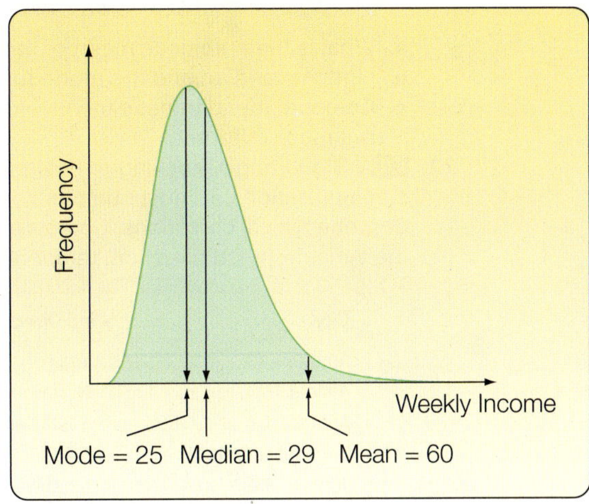

CHART 3–3 A Positively Skewed Distribution

Conversely, if a distribution is **negatively skewed,** such as the distribution of tensile strength in Chart 3–4, the mean is the lowest of the three measures. The mean is, of course, influenced by a few extremely low observations. The median is greater than the arithmetic mean, and the modal value is the largest of the three measures. Again, if the distribution is highly skewed, the mean should not be used to represent the data.

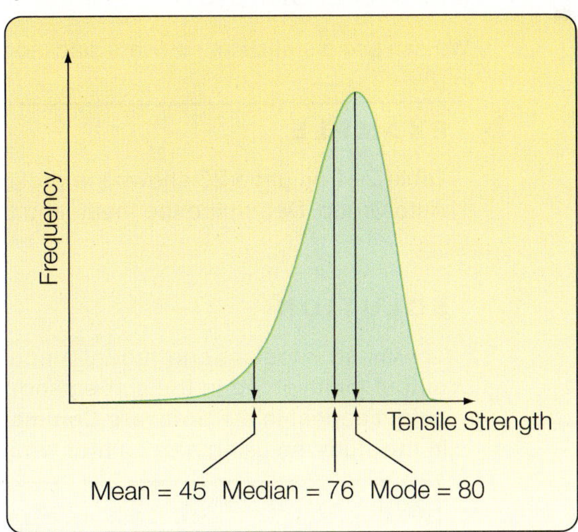

CHART 3–4 A Negatively Skewed Distribution

SELF-REVIEW 3–3

The weekly sales from a sample of Hi-Tec electronic supply stores were organized into a frequency distribution. The mean of weekly sales was computed to be $105,900, the median $105,000, and the mode $104,500.

(a) Sketch the sales in the form of a smoothed frequency polygon. Note the location of the mean, median, and mode on the *X*-axis.

(b) Is the distribution symmetrical, positively skewed, or negatively skewed? Explain.

EXERCISES

21. FILE The unemployment rate in the state of Alaska by month is given in the table below:

Jan	Feb	Mar	Apr	May	Jun	Jul	Aug	Sep	Oct	Nov	Dec
8.7	8.8	8.7	7.8	7.3	7.8	6.6	6.5	6.5	6.8	7.3	7.6

a. What is the arithmetic mean of the Alaska unemployment rates?
b. Find the median and the mode for the unemployment rates.
c. Compute the arithmetic mean and median for just the winter (Dec–Mar) months. Is it much different?

22. **FILE** Big Orange Trucking is designing an information system for use in "in-cab" communications. It must summarize data from eight sites throughout a region to describe typical conditions. Compute an appropriate measure of central location for the variables wind direction, temperature, and pavement.

City	Wind Direction	Temperature	Pavement
Anniston, AL	West	89	Dry
Atlanta, GA	Northwest	86	Wet
Augusta, GA	Southwest	92	Wet
Birmingham, AL	South	91	Dry
Jackson, MS	Southwest	92	Dry
Meridian, MS	South	92	Trace
Monroe, LA	Southwest	93	Wet
Tuscaloosa, AL	Southwest	93	Trace

Software Solution

We can use a statistical software package to find many measures of location.

EXAMPLE

Table 2–4 on page 26 shows the profit on the sales of 180 vehicles at Applewood Auto Group. Determine the mean and the median selling price.

SOLUTION

The mean, median, and modal amounts of profit are reported in the following output (highlighted in the screen shot). (Reminder: The instructions to create the output appear in the **Software Commands** in Appendix C.) There are 180 vehicles in the study, so using a calculator would be tedious and prone to error.

APPLEWOOD AUTO GROUP

	A	B	C	D	E	F	G	H
1	Age	Profit	Location	Vehicle-Type	Previous		*Profit*	
2	21	$1,387	Tionesta	Sedan	0			
3	23	$1,754	Sheffield	SUV	1		Mean	1843.17
4	24	$1,817	Sheffield	Hybrid	1		Standard Error	47.97
5	25	$1,040	Sheffield	Compact	0		Median	1882.50
6	26	$1,273	Kane	Sedan	1		Mode	1915.00
7	27	$1,529	Sheffield	Sedan	1		Standard Deviation	643.63
8	27	$3,082	Kane	Truck	0		Sample Variance	414256.61
9	28	$1,951	Kane	SUV	1		Kurtosis	-0.22
10	28	$2,692	Tionesta	Compact	0		Skewness	-0.24
11	29	$1,342	Kane	Sedan	2		Range	2998
12	29	$1,206	Sheffield	Sedan	0		Minimum	294
13	30	$443	Kane	Sedan	3		Maximum	3292
14	30	$1,621	Sheffield	Truck	1		Sum	331770
15	30	$754	Olean	Sedan	2		Count	180

The mean profit is \$1,843.17 and the median is \$1,882.50. These two values are less than \$40 apart, so either value is reasonable. We can also see from the Excel output that there were 180 vehicles sold and their total profit was \$331,770.00. We will describe the meaning of standard error, standard deviation, and other measures reported on the output later in this chapter and in later chapters.

What can we conclude? The typical profit on a vehicle is about \$1,850. Management at Applewood might use this value for revenue projections. For example, if the dealership could increase the number of vehicles sold in a month from 180 to 200, this would result in an additional estimated \$37,000 of revenue, found by 20(\$1,850).

LO3-2
Compute a weighted mean.

THE WEIGHTED MEAN

The weighted mean is a convenient way to compute the arithmetic mean when there are several observations of the same value. To explain, suppose the nearby Wendy's Restaurant sold medium, large, and Biggie-sized soft drinks for \$1.84, \$2.07, and \$2.40, respectively. Of the last 10 drinks sold, 3 were medium, 4 were large, and 3 were Biggie-sized. To find the mean price of the last 10 drinks sold, we could use formula (3–2).

$$\bar{x} = \frac{\$1.84 + \$1.84 + \$1.84 + \$2.07 + \$2.07 + \$2.07 + \$2.07 + \$2.40 + \$2.40 + \$2.40}{10}$$

$$\bar{x} = \frac{\$21.00}{10} = \$2.10$$

The mean selling price of the last 10 drinks is \$2.10.

An easier way to find the mean selling price is to determine the weighted mean. That is, we multiply each observation by the number of times it occurs. We will refer to the weighted mean as $\bar{x}_w$. This is read "x bar sub w."

$$\bar{x}_w = \frac{3(\$1.84) + 4(\$2.07) + 3(\$2.40)}{10} = \frac{\$21.00}{10} = \$2.10$$

In this case, the weights are frequency counts. However, any measure of importance could be used as a weight. In general, the weighted mean of a set of numbers designated $x_1, x_2, x_3, \ldots, x_n$ with the corresponding weights $w_1, w_2, w_3, \ldots, w_n$ is computed by:

WEIGHTED MEAN

$$\bar{x}_w = \frac{w_1x_1 + w_2x_2 + w_3x_3 + \cdots + w_nx_n}{w_1 + w_2 + w_3 + \cdots + w_n} \qquad \textbf{(3–3)}$$

This may be shortened to:

$$\bar{x}_w = \frac{\Sigma(wx)}{\Sigma w}$$

Note that the denominator of a weighted mean is always the sum of the weights.

EXAMPLE

The Carter Construction Company pays its hourly employees \$16.50, \$19.00, or \$25.00 per hour. There are 26 hourly employees, 14 of whom are paid at the \$16.50 rate, 10 at the \$19.00 rate, and 2 at the \$25.00 rate. What is the mean hourly rate paid the 26 employees?

SOLUTION

To find the mean hourly rate, we multiply each of the hourly rates by the number of employees earning that rate. From formula (3–3), the mean hourly rate is

$$\bar{x}_w = \frac{14(\$16.50) + 10(\$19.00) + 2(\$25.00)}{14 + 10 + 2} = \frac{\$471.00}{26} = \$18.1154$$

The weighted mean hourly wage is rounded to \$18.12.

SELF-REVIEW 3–4

Springers sold 95 Antonelli men's suits for the regular price of \$400. For the spring sale, the suits were reduced to \$200 and 126 were sold. At the final clearance, the price was reduced to \$100 and the remaining 79 suits were sold.

(a) What was the weighted mean price of an Antonelli suit?

(b) Springers paid \$200 a suit for the 300 suits. Comment on the store's profit per suit if a salesperson receives a \$25 commission for each one sold.

EXERCISES

23. In June, an investor purchased 300 shares of Oracle (an information technology company) stock at \$20 per share. In August, she purchased an additional 400 shares at \$25 per share. In November, she purchased an additional 400 shares, but the stock declined to \$23 per share. What is the weighted mean price per share?

24. The Bookstall Inc. is a specialty bookstore concentrating on used books sold via the Internet. Paperbacks are \$1.00 each, and hardcover books are \$3.50. Of the 50 books sold last Tuesday morning, 40 were paperback and the rest were hardcover. What was the weighted mean price of a book?

25. The Loris Healthcare System employs 200 persons on the nursing staff. Fifty are nurse's aides, 50 are practical nurses, and 100 are registered nurses. Nurse's aides receive \$8 an hour, practical nurses \$15 an hour, and registered nurses \$24 an hour. What is the weighted mean hourly wage?

26. Andrews and Associates specialize in corporate law. They charge \$100 an hour for researching a case, \$75 an hour for consultations, and \$200 an hour for writing a brief. Last week one of the associates spent 10 hours consulting with her client, 10 hours researching the case, and 20 hours writing the brief. What was the weighted mean hourly charge for her legal services?

LO3-3
Compute and interpret the geometric mean.

THE GEOMETRIC MEAN

The geometric mean is useful in finding the average change of percentages, ratios, indexes, or growth rates over time. It has a wide application in business and economics because we are often interested in finding the percentage changes in sales, salaries, or economic figures, such as the gross domestic product, which compound or build on each other. The geometric mean of a set of *n* positive numbers is defined as the *n*th root of the product of *n* values. The formula for the geometric mean is written:

GEOMETRIC MEAN $$GM = \sqrt[n]{(x_1)(x_2) \cdots (x_n)}$$ **(3–4)**

The geometric mean will always be less than or equal to (never more than) the arithmetic mean. Also, all the data values must be positive.

As an example of the geometric mean, suppose you receive a 5% increase in salary this year and a 15% increase next year. The average annual percent increase is 9.886%, not 10.0%. Why is this so? We begin by calculating the geometric mean. Recall, for example, that a 5% increase in salary is 105%. We will write it as 1.05.

$$GM = \sqrt{(1.05)(1.15)} = 1.09886$$

This can be verified by assuming that your monthly earning was \$3,000 to start and you received two increases of 5% and 15%.

$$\begin{aligned} \text{Raise 1} &= \$3{,}000(.05) = \$150.00 \\ \text{Raise 2} &= \$3{,}150(.15) = \underline{\ \ 472.50} \\ \text{Total} & \qquad\qquad\quad\ \ \$622.50 \end{aligned}$$

Your total salary increase is \$622.50. This is equivalent to:

$$\begin{aligned} \$3{,}000.00(.09886) &= \$296.59 \\ \$3{,}296.58(.09886) &= \underline{\ \ 325.91} \\ & \quad\ \$622.50 \end{aligned}$$

The following example shows the geometric mean of several percentages.

EXAMPLE

The return on investment earned by Atkins Construction Company for four successive years was 30%, 20%, −40%, and 200%. What is the geometric mean rate of return on investment?

SOLUTION

The number 1.3 represents the 30% return on investment, which is the "original" investment of 1.0 plus the "return" of 0.3. The number 0.6 represents the loss of 40%, which is the original investment of 1.0 less the loss of 0.4. This calculation assumes the total return each period is reinvested or becomes the base for the next period. In other words, the base for the second period is 1.3 and the base for the third period is (1.3)(1.2) and so forth.

Then the geometric mean rate of return is 29.4%, found by

$$GM = \sqrt[n]{(x_1)(x_2)\cdots(x_n)} = \sqrt[4]{(1.3)(1.2)(0.6)(3.0)} = \sqrt[4]{2.808} = 1.294$$

The geometric mean is the fourth root of 2.808. So, the average rate of return (compound annual growth rate) is 29.4%.

Notice also that if you compute the arithmetic mean [(30 + 20 − 40 + 200)/4 = 52.5], you would have a much larger number, which would overstate the true rate of return!

A second application of the geometric mean is to find an average percentage change over a period of time. For example, if you earned \$45,000 in 2004 and \$100,000 in 2016, what is your annual rate of increase over the period? It is 6.88%. The rate of increase is determined from the following formula.

RATE OF INCREASE OVER TIME

$$GM = \sqrt[n]{\frac{\text{Value at end of period}}{\text{Value at start of period}}} - 1 \qquad \textbf{(3–5)}$$

In formula 3-5 above, n is the number of periods. An example will show the details of finding the average annual percent increase.

EXAMPLE

During the decade of the 1990s, and into the 2000s, Las Vegas, Nevada, was one of the fastest-growing cities in the United States. The population increased from 258,295 in 1990 to 613,599 in 2014. This is an increase of 355,304 people, or a 137.56% increase over the period. The population has more than doubled. What is the average *annual* percent increase?

SOLUTION

There are 24 years between 1990 and 2014, so $n = 24$. Then the geometric mean formula (3–5) as applied to this problem is:

$$GM = \sqrt[n]{\frac{\text{Value at end of period}}{\text{Value at start of period}}} - 1.0 = \sqrt[24]{\frac{613{,}599}{258{,}295}} - 1.0 = 1.0367 - 1.0 = .0367$$

To summarize, the steps to compute the geometric mean are:

1. Divide the value at the end of the period by the value at the beginning of the period.
2. Find the *n*th root of the ratio, where *n* is the number of periods.
3. Subtract one.

The value of .0367 indicates that the average annual growth over the period was 3.67%. To put it another way, the population of Las Vegas increased at a rate of 3.67% per year from 1990 to 2014.

SELF-REVIEW 3–5

1. The percent increase in sales for the last 4 years at Combs Cosmetics were 4.91, 5.75, 8.12, and 21.60.
   (a) Find the geometric mean percent increase.
   (b) Find the arithmetic mean percent increase.
   (c) Is the arithmetic mean equal to or greater than the geometric mean?
2. Production of Cablos trucks increased from 23,000 units in 1996 to 120,520 in 2016. Find the geometric mean annual percent increase.

EXERCISES

27. Compute the geometric mean of the following monthly percent increases: 8, 12, 14, 26, and 5.

28. Compute the geometric mean of the following weekly percent increases: 2, 8, 6, 4, 10, 6, 8, and 4.

29. Listed below is the percent increase in sales for the MG Corporation over the last 5 years. Determine the geometric mean percent increase in sales over the period.

9.4	13.8	11.7	11.9	14.7

30. In 2001, a total of 40,244,000 taxpayers in the United States filed their individual tax returns electronically. By the year 2015, the number increased to 128,653,000. What is the geometric mean annual increase for the period?

31. The Consumer Price Index is reported monthly by the U.S. Bureau of Labor Statistics. It reports the change in prices for a market basket of goods from one period to another. The index for 2000 was 172.2. By 2015, it increased to 236.525. What was the geometric mean annual increase for the period?

32. JetBlue Airways is an American low-cost airline headquartered in New York City. Its main base is John F. Kennedy International Airport. JetBlue's revenue in 2002 was $635.2 million. By 2014, revenue had increased to $5,817.0 million. What was the geometric mean annual increase for the period?

33. In 2000, there were 720,000 cell phone subscribers worldwide. By 2015, the number of cell phone subscribers increased to 752,000,000. What is the geometric mean annual increase for the period?

34. The information below shows the cost for a year of college in public and private colleges in 2002–03 and 2015–16. What is the geometric mean annual increase for the period for the two types of colleges? Compare the rates of increase.

Type of College	2002–03	2015–16
Public	$ 4,960	$23,893
Private	18,056	32,405

LO3-4
Compute and interpret the range, variance, and standard deviation.

WHY STUDY DISPERSION?

A measure of location, such as the mean, median, or mode, only describes the center of the data. It is valuable from that standpoint, but it does not tell us anything about the spread of the data. For example, if your nature guide told you that the river ahead averaged 3 feet in depth, would you want to wade across on foot without additional information? Probably not. You would want to know something about the variation in the depth. Is the maximum depth of the river 3.25 feet and the minimum 2.75 feet? If that is the case, you would probably agree to cross. What if you learned the river depth ranged from 0.50 foot to 5.5 feet? Your decision would probably be not to cross. Before making a decision about crossing the river, you want information on both the typical depth and the dispersion in the depth of the river.

STATISTICS IN ACTION

The U.S. Postal Service has tried to become more "user friendly" in the last several years. A recent survey showed that customers were interested in more *consistency* in the time it takes to make a delivery. Under the old conditions, a local letter might take only one day to deliver, or it might take several. "Just tell me how many days ahead I need to mail the birthday card to Mom so it gets there on her birthday, not early, not late," was a common complaint. The level of consistency is measured by the standard deviation of the delivery times.

A small value for a measure of dispersion indicates that the data are clustered closely, say, around the arithmetic mean. The mean is therefore considered representative of the data. Conversely, a large measure of dispersion indicates that the mean is not reliable. Refer to Chart 3–5. The 100 employees of Hammond Iron Works Inc., a steel fabricating company, are organized into a histogram based on the number of years of employment with the company. The mean is 4.9 years, but the spread of the data is from 6 months to 16.8 years. The mean of 4.9 years is not very representative of all the employees.

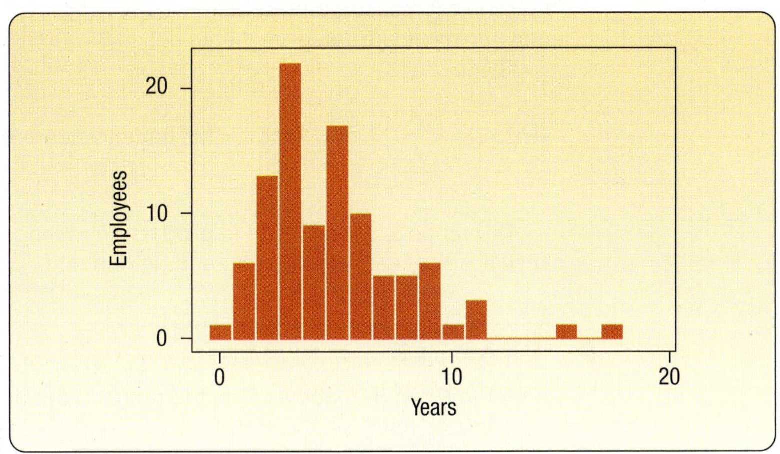

CHART 3–5 Histogram of Years of Employment at Hammond Iron Works Inc.

A second reason for studying the dispersion in a set of data is to compare the spread in two or more distributions. Suppose, for example, that the new Vision Quest LCD computer monitor is assembled in Baton Rouge and also in Tucson. The arithmetic mean hourly output in both the Baton Rouge plant and the Tucson plant is 50. Based on

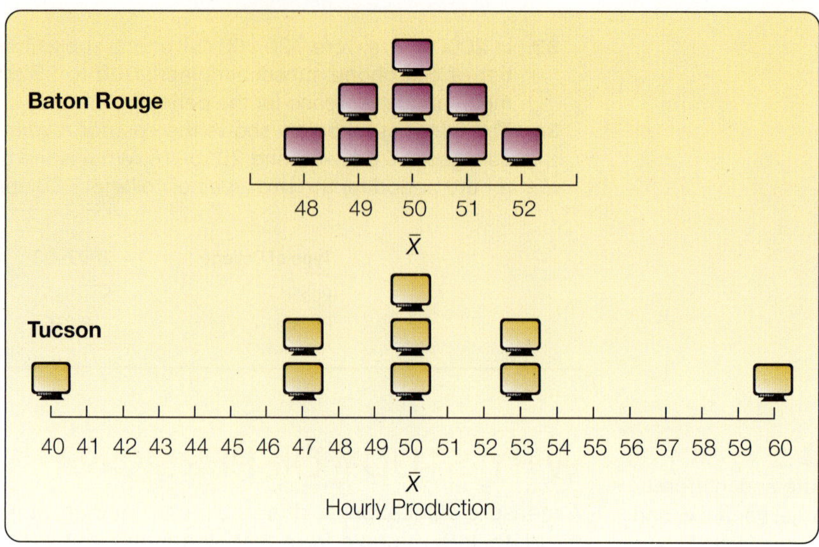

CHART 3–6 Hourly Production of Computer Monitors at the Baton Rouge and Tucson Plants

the two means, you might conclude that the distributions of the hourly outputs are identical. Production records for 9 hours at the two plants, however, reveal that this conclusion is not correct (see Chart 3–6). Baton Rouge production varies from 48 to 52 assemblies per hour. Production at the Tucson plant is more erratic, ranging from 40 to 60 per hour. Therefore, the hourly output for Baton Rouge is clustered near the mean of 50; the hourly output for Tucson is more dispersed.

We will consider several measures of dispersion. The range is based on the maximum and minimum values in the data set; that is, only two values are considered. The variance and the standard deviation use all the values in a data set and are based on deviations from the arithmetic mean.

Range

The simplest measure of dispersion is the **range.** It is the difference between the maximum and minimum values in a data set. In the form of an equation:

RANGE Range = Maximum value − Minimum value **(3–6)**

The range is widely used in production management and control applications because it is very easy to calculate and understand.

EXAMPLE

Refer to Chart 3–6 above. Find the range in the number of computer monitors produced per hour for the Baton Rouge and the Tucson plants. Interpret the two ranges.

SOLUTION

The range of the hourly production of computer monitors at the Baton Rouge plant is 4, found by the difference between the maximum hourly production of 52 and the minimum of 48. The range in the hourly production for the Tucson plant is 20 computer monitors, found by 60 − 40. We therefore conclude that (1) there is less dispersion in the hourly production in the Baton Rouge plant than in the Tucson plant because the range of 4 computer monitors is less than a range of 20 computer monitors and (2) the production is clustered more closely around the mean of 50 at the Baton Rouge plant than at the Tucson plant (because a range of 4 is less than a range of 20). Thus, the mean production in the Baton Rouge plant (50 computer monitors) is a more representative measure of location than the mean of 50 computer monitors for the Tucson plant.

Variance

A limitation of the range is that it is based on only two values, the maximum and the minimum; it does not take into consideration all of the values. The **variance** does. It measures the mean amount by which the values in a population, or sample, vary from their mean. In terms of a definition:

VARIANCE The arithmetic mean of the squared deviations from the mean.

The following example illustrates how the variance is used to measure dispersion.

EXAMPLE

© Sorbis/Shutterstock.com

The chart below shows the number of cappuccinos sold at the Starbucks in the Orange County airport and the Ontario, California, airport between 4 and 5 p.m. for a sample of 5 days last month.

California Airports	
Orange County	Ontario
20	20
40	45
50	50
60	55
80	80

Determine the mean, median, range, and variance for each location. Comment on the similarities and differences in these measures.

SOLUTION

The mean, median, and range for each of the airport locations are reported as part of an Excel spreadsheet.

	A	B	C
1		California Airports	
2		Orange County	Ontario
3		20	20
4		40	45
5		50	50
6		60	55
7		80	80
8			
9	Mean	50	50
10	Median	50	50
11	Range	60	60

Notice that all three of the measures are exactly the same. Does this indicate that there is no difference in the two sets of data? We get a clearer picture if we calculate the variance. First, for Orange County:

F	G	H
Calculation of Variance for Orange County		
Number Sold	Each Value - Mean	Squared Deviation
20	20 - 50 = -30	900
40	40 - 50 = -10	100
50	50 - 50 = 0	0
60	60 - 50 = 10	100
80	80 - 50 = 30	900
	Total	2000

$$\text{Variance} = \frac{\Sigma(x-\mu)^2}{N} = \frac{(-30^2)+(-10^2)+0^2+10^2+30^2}{5} = \frac{2{,}000}{5} = 400$$

The variance is 400. That is, the average squared deviation from the mean is 400.

The following shows the detail of determining the variance for the number of cappuccinos sold at the Ontario Airport.

Calculation of Variance for Ontario		
Number Sold	Each Value - Mean	Squared Deviation
20	20 - 50 = -30	900
45	45 - 50 = -5	25
50	50 - 50 = 0	0
55	55 - 50 = 5	25
80	80 - 50 = 30	900
	Total	1850

$$\text{Variance} = \frac{\Sigma(x-\mu)^2}{N} = \frac{(-30^2)+(-5^2)+0^2+5^2+30^2}{5} = \frac{1{,}850}{5} = 370$$

So the mean, median, and range of the cappuccinos sold are the same at the two airports, but the variances are different. The variance at Orange County is 400, but it is 370 at Ontario.

Let's interpret and compare the results of our measures for the two Starbucks airport locations. The mean and median of the two locations are exactly the same, 50 cappuccinos sold. These measures of location suggest the two distributions are the same. The range for both locations is also the same, 60. However, recall that the range provides limited information about the dispersion because it is based on only two values, the minimum and maximum.

The variances are not the same for the two airports. The variance is based on the differences between each observation and the arithmetic mean. It shows the closeness or clustering of the data relative to the mean or center of the distribution. Compare the variance for Orange County of 400 to the variance for Ontario of 370. Based on the variance, we conclude that the dispersion for the sales distribution of the Ontario Starbucks is more concentrated—that is, nearer the mean of 50—than for the Orange County location.

The variance has an important advantage over the range. It uses all the values in the computation. Recall that the range uses only the highest and the lowest values.

SELF-REVIEW 3–6

The weights of containers being shipped to Ireland are (in thousands of pounds):

95	103	105	110	104	105	112	90

(a) What is the range of the weights?
(b) Compute the arithmetic mean weight.
(c) Compute the variance of the weights.

EXERCISES

For Exercises 35–38, calculate the (a) range, (b) arithmetic mean, (c) variance, and (d) interpret the statistics.

35. **FILE** During last weekend's sale, there were five customer service representatives on duty at the Electronic Super Store. The numbers of HDTVs these representatives sold were 5, 8, 4, 10, and 3.

36. **FILE** The Department of Statistics at Western State University offers eight sections of basic statistics. Following are the numbers of students enrolled in these sections: 34, 46, 52, 29, 41, 38, 36, and 28.

37. **FILE** Dave's Automatic Door installs automatic garage door openers. The following list indicates the number of minutes needed to install 10 door openers: 28, 32, 24, 46, 44, 40, 54, 38, 32, and 42.

38. **FILE** All eight companies in the aerospace industry were surveyed as to their return on investment last year. The results are: 10.6%, 12.6%, 14.8%, 18.2%, 12.0%, 14.8%, 12.2%, and 15.6%.

39. **FILE** Ten young adults living in California rated the taste of a newly developed sushi pizza topped with tuna, rice, and kelp on a scale of 1 to 50, with 1 indicating they did not like the taste and 50 that they did. The ratings were:

34	39	40	46	33	31	34	14	15	45

In a parallel study, 10 young adults in Iowa rated the taste of the same pizza. The ratings were:

28	25	35	16	25	29	24	26	17	20

As a market researcher, compare the potential for sushi pizza in the two markets.

40. **FILE** The personnel files of all eight employees at the Pawnee location of Acme Carpet Cleaners Inc. revealed that during the last 6-month period they lost the following number of days due to illness:

2	0	6	3	10	4	1	2

All eight employees during the same period at the Chickpee location of Acme Carpets revealed they lost the following number of days due to illness:

2	0	1	0	5	0	1	0

As the director of human resources, compare the two locations. What would you recommend?

Population Variance

In the previous example, we developed the concept of variance as a measure of dispersion. Similar to the mean, we can calculate the variance of a population or the variance of a sample. The formula to compute the population variance is:

POPULATION VARIANCE $$\sigma^2 = \frac{\Sigma(x - \mu)^2}{N}$$ **(3–7)**

where:

σ^2 is the population variance (σ is the lowercase Greek letter sigma). It is read as "sigma squared."
x is the value of a particular observation in the population.
μ is the arithmetic mean of the population.
N is the number of observations in the population.

The process for computing the variance is implied by the formula.

1. Begin by finding the mean.
2. Find the difference between each observation and the mean, and square that difference.
3. Sum all the squared differences.
4. Divide the sum of the squared differences by the number of items in the population.

So the population variance is the mean of the squared difference between each value and the mean. For populations whose values are near the mean, the variance will be small. For populations whose values are dispersed from the mean, the population variance will be large.

The variance overcomes the weakness of the range by using all the values in the population, whereas the range uses only the maximum and minimum values. We overcome the issue where $\Sigma(x - \mu) = 0$ by squaring the differences. Squaring the differences will always result in nonnegative values. The following is another example that illustrates the calculation and interpretation of the variance.

EXAMPLE

The number of traffic citations issued last year by month in Beaufort County, South Carolina, is reported below.

Citations by Month

January	February	March	April	May	June	July	August	September	October	November	December
19	17	22	18	28	34	45	39	38	44	34	10

Determine the population variance.

SOLUTION

Because we are studying all the citations for a year, the data comprise a population. To determine the population variance, we use formula (3–7). The table below details the calculations.

Month	Citations (x)	$x - \mu$	$(x - \mu)^2$
January	19	−10	100
February	17	−12	144
March	22	−7	49
April	18	−11	121
May	28	−1	1
June	34	5	25
July	45	16	256
August	39	10	100
September	38	9	81
October	44	15	225
November	34	5	25
December	10	−19	361
Total	348	0	1,488

1. We begin by determining the arithmetic mean of the population. The total number of citations issued for the year is 348, so the mean number issued per month is 29.

$$\mu = \frac{\Sigma x}{N} = \frac{19 + 17 + \cdots + 10}{12} = \frac{348}{12} = 29$$

2. Next we find the difference between each observation and the mean. This is shown in the third column of the table. Recall on page 55 in this chapter, the Verizon example showed that the sum of the differences between each value and the mean is 0. This principle is repeated here. The sum of the differences between the mean and the number of citations each month is 0.
3. The next step is to square the difference for each month. That is shown in the fourth column of the table. All the squared differences will be positive. Note that squaring a negative value, or multiplying a negative value by itself, always results in a positive value.
4. The squared differences are totaled. The total of the fourth column is 1,488. That is the term $\Sigma(x - \mu)^2$.
5. Finally, we divide the squared differences by N, the number of observations in the population.

$$\sigma^2 = \frac{\Sigma(x - \sigma)^2}{N} = \frac{1{,}488}{12} = 124$$

So, the population variance for the number of citations is 124.

Like the range, the variance can be used to compare the dispersion in two or more sets of observations. For example, the variance for the number of citations issued in Beaufort County was just computed to be 124. If the variance in the number of citations issued in Marlboro County, South Carolina, is 342.9, we conclude that (1) there is less dispersion in the distribution of the number of citations issued in Beaufort County than in Marlboro County (because 124 is less than 342.9) and (2) the number of citations in Beaufort County is more closely clustered around the mean of 29 than for the number of citations issued in Marlboro County. Thus the mean number of citations issued in Beaufort County is a more representative measure of location than the mean number of citations in Marlboro County.

Population Standard Deviation

When we compute the variance, it is important to understand the unit of measure and what happens when the differences in the numerator are squared. That is, in the previous example, the number of monthly citations is the variable. When we calculate the variance, the unit of measure for the variance is citations squared. Using "squared citations" as a unit of measure is cumbersome.

There is a way out of this difficulty. By taking the square root of the population variance, we can transform it to the same unit of measurement used for the original data. The square root of 124 citations squared is 11.14 citations. The units are now simply citations. The square root of the population variance is the **population standard deviation.**

POPULATION STANDARD DEVIATION

$$\sigma = \sqrt{\frac{\Sigma(x - \mu)^2}{N}} \quad \textbf{(3–8)}$$

SELF-REVIEW 3–7

The Philadelphia office of PricewaterhouseCoopers hired five accounting trainees this year. Their monthly starting salaries were $3,536; $3,173; $3,448; $3,121; and $3,622.

(a) Compute the population mean.
(b) Compute the population variance.
(c) Compute the population standard deviation.
(d) The Pittsburgh office hired six trainees. Their mean monthly salary was $3,550, and the standard deviation was $250. Compare the two groups.

EXERCISES

41. Consider these five values a population: 8, 3, 7, 3, and 4.
  a. Determine the mean of the population.
  b. Determine the variance.

42. Consider these six values a population: 13, 3, 8, 10, 8, and 6.
  a. Determine the mean of the population.
  b. Determine the variance.

43. The annual report of Dennis Industries cited these primary earnings per common share for the past 5 years: $2.68, $1.03, $2.26, $4.30, and $3.58. If we assume these are population values, what is:
  a. The arithmetic mean primary earnings per share of common stock?
  b. The variance?

44. Referring to Exercise 43, the annual report of Dennis Industries also gave these returns on stockholder equity for the same 5-year period (in percent): 13.2, 5.0, 10.2, 17.5, and 12.9.
  a. What is the arithmetic mean return?
  b. What is the variance?

45. Plywood Inc. reported these returns on stockholder equity for the past 5 years: 4.3, 4.9, 7.2, 6.7, and 11.6. Consider these as population values.
  a. Compute the range, the arithmetic mean, the variance, and the standard deviation.
  b. Compare the return on stockholder equity for Plywood Inc. with that for Dennis Industries cited in Exercise 44.

46. The annual incomes of the five vice presidents of TMV Industries are $125,000; $128,000; $122,000; $133,000; and $140,000. Consider this a population.
  a. What is the range?
  b. What is the arithmetic mean income?
  c. What is the population variance? The standard deviation?
  d. The annual incomes of officers of another firm similar to TMV Industries were also studied. The mean was $129,000 and the standard deviation $8,612. Compare the means and dispersions in the two firms.

Sample Variance and Standard Deviation

The formula for the population mean is $\mu = \Sigma x/N$. We just changed the symbols for the sample mean; that is, $\bar{x} = \Sigma x/n$. Unfortunately, the conversion from the population variance to the sample variance is not as direct. It requires a change in the denominator. Instead of substituting n (number in the sample) for N (number in the population), the denominator is $n - 1$. Thus the formula for the **sample variance** is:

SAMPLE VARIANCE $$s^2 = \frac{\Sigma(x - \bar{x})^2}{n - 1} \qquad \textbf{(3–9)}$$

where:

- s^2 is the sample variance.
- x is the value of each observation in the sample.
- $\bar{x}$ is the mean of the sample.
- n is the number of observations in the sample.

Why is this change made in the denominator? Although the use of n is logical since $\bar{x}$ is used to estimate μ, it tends to underestimate the population variance, σ^2. The use of $(n - 1)$ in the denominator provides the appropriate correction for this tendency. Because the primary use of sample statistics like s^2 is to estimate population parameters like σ^2, $(n - 1)$ is preferred to n in defining the sample variance. We will also use this convention when computing the sample standard deviation.

EXAMPLE

The hourly wages for a sample of part-time employees at Home Depot are \$12, \$20, \$16, \$18, and \$19. What is the sample variance?

SOLUTION

The sample variance is computed by using formula (3–9).

$$\bar{x} = \frac{\Sigma x}{n} = \frac{\$85}{5} = \$17$$

Hourly Wage (x)	$x - \bar{x}$	$(x - \bar{x})^2$
\$12	−\$5	25
20	3	9
16	−1	1
18	1	1
19	2	4
\$85	0	40

$$s^2 = \frac{\Sigma(x - \bar{x})^2}{n - 1} = \frac{40}{5 - 1}$$

$$= 10 \text{ in dollars squared}$$

The sample standard deviation is used as an estimator of the population standard deviation. As noted previously, the population standard deviation is the square root of the population variance. Likewise, the *sample standard deviation is the square root of the sample variance*. The sample standard deviation is determined by:

SAMPLE STANDARD DEVIATION $$s = \sqrt{\frac{\Sigma(x - \bar{x})^2}{n - 1}} \quad \textbf{(3–10)}$$

EXAMPLE

The sample variance in the previous example involving hourly wages was computed to be 10. What is the sample standard deviation?

SOLUTION

The sample standard deviation is $3.16, found by $\sqrt{10}$. Note again that the sample variance is in terms of dollars squared, but taking the square root of 10 gives us $3.16, which is in the same units (dollars) as the original data.

Software Solution

On page 64, we used Excel to determine the mean, median, and mode of profit for the Applewood Auto Group data. You also will note that it lists the sample variance and sample standard deviation. Excel, like most other statistical software, assumes the data are from a sample.

APPLEWOOD AUTO GROUP

	A	B	C	D	E	F	G	H
1	Age	Profit	Location	Vehicle-Type	Previous		Profit	
2	21	$1,387	Tionesta	Sedan	0			
3	23	$1,754	Sheffield	SUV	1		Mean	1843.17
4	24	$1,817	Sheffield	Hybrid	1		Standard Error	47.97
5	25	$1,040	Sheffield	Compact	0		Median	1882.50
6	26	$1,273	Kane	Sedan	1		Mode	1915.00
7	27	$1,529	Sheffield	Sedan	1		Standard Deviation	643.63
8	27	$3,082	Kane	Truck	0		Sample Variance	414256.61
9	28	$1,951	Kane	SUV	1		Kurtosis	-0.22
10	28	$2,692	Tionesta	Compact	0		Skewness	-0.24
11	29	$1,342	Kane	Sedan	2		Range	2998
12	29	$1,206	Sheffield	Sedan	0		Minimum	294
13	30	$443	Kane	Sedan	3		Maximum	3292
14	30	$1,621	Sheffield	Truck	1		Sum	331770
15	30	$754	Olean	Sedan	2		Count	180

SELF-REVIEW 3–8

The years of service for a sample of seven employees at a State Farm Insurance claims office in Cleveland, Ohio, are 4, 2, 5, 4, 5, 2, and 6. What is the sample variance? Compute the sample standard deviation.

EXERCISES

For Exercises 47–52, do the following:

a. Compute the sample variance.
b. Determine the sample standard deviation.

47. Consider these values a sample: 7, 2, 6, 2, and 3.
48. The following five values are a sample: 11, 6, 10, 6, and 7.
49. FILE Dave's Automatic Door, referred to in Exercise 37, installs automatic garage door openers. Based on a sample, following are the times, in minutes, required to install 10 door openers: 28, 32, 24, 46, 44, 40, 54, 38, 32, and 42.
50. FILE The sample of eight companies in the aerospace industry, referred to in Exercise 38, was surveyed as to their return on investment last year. The results are 10.6, 12.6, 14.8, 18.2, 12.0, 14.8, 12.2, and 15.6.
51. FILE The Houston, Texas, Motel Owner Association conducted a survey regarding weekday motel rates in the area. Listed below is the room rate for business-class guests for a sample of 10 motels.

$101	$97	$103	$110	$78	$87	$101	$80	$106	$88

52. FILE A consumer watchdog organization is concerned about credit card debt. A survey of 10 young adults with credit card debt of more than $2,000 showed they paid an average of just over $100 per month against their balances. Listed below are the amounts each young adult paid last month.

$110	$126	$103	$93	$99	$113	$87	$101	$109	$100

LO3-5
Explain and apply Chebyshev's theorem and the Empirical Rule.

INTERPRETATION AND USES OF THE STANDARD DEVIATION

The standard deviation is commonly used as a measure to compare the spread in two or more sets of observations. For example, the standard deviation of the biweekly amounts invested in the Dupree Paint Company profit-sharing plan is computed to be $7.51. Suppose these employees are located in Georgia. If the standard deviation for a group of employees in Texas is $10.47, and the means are about the same, it indicates that the amounts invested by the Georgia employees are not dispersed as much as those in Texas (because $7.51 < $10.47). Since the amounts invested by the Georgia employees are clustered more closely about the mean, the mean for the Georgia employees is a more reliable measure than the mean for the Texas group.

STATISTICS IN ACTION

Most colleges report the "average class size." This information can be misleading because average class size can be found in several ways. If we find the number of students *in each class* at a particular university, the result is the mean number of students per class. If we compile a list of the class sizes for each student and find the mean class size, we might find the mean to be quite different. One school found the mean number of students in each of its 747 classes to be 40. But when

(*continued*)

Chebyshev's Theorem

We have stressed that a small standard deviation for a set of values indicates that these values are located close to the mean. Conversely, a large standard deviation reveals that the observations are widely scattered about the mean. The Russian mathematician P. L. Chebyshev (1821–1894) developed a theorem that allows us to determine the minimum proportion of the values that lie within a specified number of standard deviations of the mean. For example, according to **Chebyshev's theorem,** at least three out of every four, or 75%, of the values must lie between the mean plus two standard deviations and the mean minus two standard deviations. This relationship applies regardless of the shape of the distribution. Further, at least eight of nine values, or 88.9%, will lie between plus three standard deviations and minus three standard deviations of the mean. At least 24 of 25 values, or 96%, will lie between plus and minus five standard deviations of the mean.

Chebyshev's theorem states:

CHEBYSHEV'S THEOREM For any set of observations (sample or population), the proportion of the values that lie within k standard deviations of the mean is at least $1 - 1/k^2$, where k is any value greater than 1.

EXAMPLE

Dupree Paint Company employees contribute a mean of \$51.54 to the company's profit-sharing plan every two weeks. The standard deviation of biweekly contributions is \$7.51. At least what percent of the contributions lie within plus 3.5 standard deviations and minus 3.5 standard deviations of the mean, that is between \$25.26 and \$77.83?

SOLUTION

About 92%, found by

$$1 - \frac{1}{k^2} = 1 - \frac{1}{(3.5)^2} = 1 - \frac{1}{12.25} = 0.92$$

(*continued from p. 79*)

it found the mean from a list of the class sizes of each student, it was 147. Why the disparity? Because there are few students in the small classes and a larger number of students in the larger classes, which has the effect of increasing the mean class size when it is calculated this way. A school could reduce this mean class size for each student by reducing the number of students in each class. That is, cut out the large freshman lecture classes.

The Empirical Rule

Chebyshev's theorem applies to any set of values; that is, the distribution of values can have any shape. However, for a symmetrical, bell-shaped distribution such as the one in Chart 3–7, we can be more precise in explaining the dispersion about the mean. These relationships involving the standard deviation and the mean are described by the **Empirical Rule,** sometimes called the **Normal Rule.**

EMPIRICAL RULE For a symmetrical, bell-shaped frequency distribution, approximately 68% of the observations will lie within plus and minus one standard deviation of the mean; about 95% of the observations will lie within plus and minus two standard deviations of the mean; and practically all (99.7%) will lie within plus and minus three standard deviations of the mean.

These relationships are portrayed graphically in Chart 3–7 for a bell-shaped distribution with a mean of 100 and a standard deviation of 10.

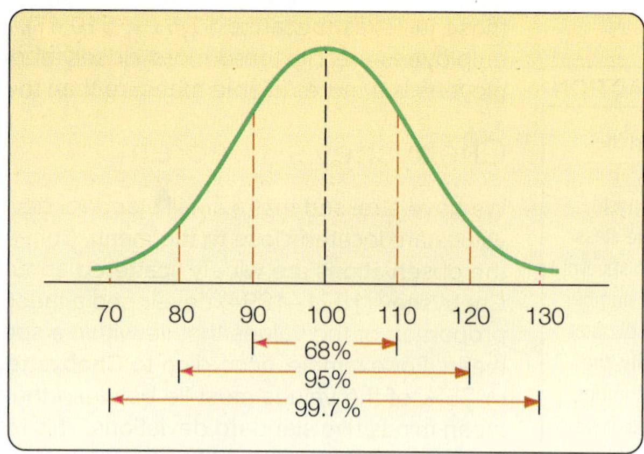

CHART 3–7 A Symmetrical, Bell-Shaped Curve Showing the Relationships between the Standard Deviation and the Percentage of Observations

Applying the Empirical Rule, if a distribution is symmetrical and bell-shaped, practically all of the observations lie between the mean plus and minus three standard deviations. Thus, if $\overline{x} = 100$ and $s = 10$, practically all the observations lie between 100 + 3(10) and 100 – 3(10), or 70 and 130. The estimated range is therefore 60, found by 130 – 70.

Conversely, if we know that the range is 60 and the distribution is bell-shaped, we can approximate the standard deviation by dividing the range by 6. For this illustration: range ÷ 6 = 60 ÷ 6 = 10, the standard deviation.

EXAMPLE

A sample of the rental rates at University Park Apartments approximates a symmetrical, bell-shaped distribution. The sample mean is $500; the standard deviation is $20. Using the Empirical Rule, answer these questions:

1. About 68% of the monthly rentals are between what two amounts?
2. About 95% of the monthly rentals are between what two amounts?
3. Almost all of the monthly rentals are between what two amounts?

SOLUTION

1. About 68% are between $480 and $520, found by $\bar{x} \pm 1s = \$500 \pm 1(\$20)$.
2. About 95% are between $460 and $540, found by $\bar{x} \pm 2s = \$500 \pm 2(\$20)$.
3. Almost all (99.7%) are between $440 and $560, found by $\bar{x} \pm 3s = \$500 \pm 3(\$20)$.

SELF-REVIEW 3–9

The Pitney Pipe Company is one of several domestic manufacturers of PVC pipe. The quality control department sampled 600 10-foot lengths. At a point 1 foot from the end of the pipe, they measured the outside diameter. The mean was 14.0 inches and the standard deviation 0.1 inch.

(a) If we do not know the shape of the distribution of outside pipe diameters, at least what percent of the observations will be between 13.85 inches and 14.15 inches?

(b) If we assume that the distribution of diameters is symmetrical and bell-shaped, about 95% of the observations will be between what two values?

EXERCISES

53. According to Chebyshev's theorem, at least what percent of any set of observations will be within 1.8 standard deviations of the mean?

54. The mean income of a group of sample observations is $500; the standard deviation is $40. According to Chebyshev's theorem, at least what percent of the incomes will lie between $400 and $600?

55. The distribution of the weights of a sample of 1,400 cargo containers is symmetric and bell-shaped. According to the Empirical Rule, what percent of the weights will lie:

a. Between $\bar{x} - 2s$ and $\bar{x} + 2s$?

b. Between $\bar{x}$ and $\bar{x} + 2s$? Above $\bar{x} + 2s$?

56. The following graph portrays the distribution of the number of spicy chicken sandwiches sold at a nearby Wendy's for the last 141 days. The mean number of sandwiches sold per day is 91.9 and the standard deviation is 4.67.

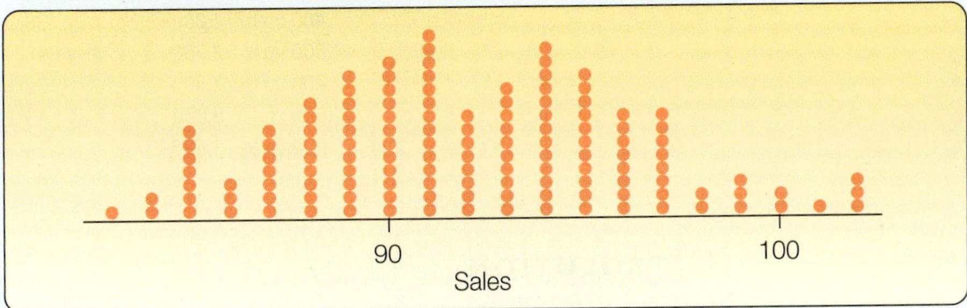

If we use the Empirical Rule, sales will be between what two values on 68% of the days? Sales will be between what two values on 95% of the days?

LO3-6

Compute the mean and standard deviation of grouped data.

THE MEAN AND STANDARD DEVIATION OF GROUPED DATA

STATISTICS IN ACTION

During the 2016 Major League Baseball season, DJ LeMahieu of the Colorado Rockies had the highest batting average at .348. Tony Gwynn hit .394 in the strike-shortened season of 1994, and Ted Williams hit .406 in 1941. No one has hit over .400 since 1941. The mean batting average has remained constant at about .260 for more than 100 years, but the standard deviation declined from .049 to .031. This indicates less dispersion in the batting averages today and helps explain the lack of any .400 hitters in recent times.

In most instances, measures of location, such as the mean, and measures of dispersion, such as the standard deviation, are determined by using the individual values. Statistical software packages make it easy to calculate these values, even for large data sets. However, sometimes we are given only the frequency distribution and wish to estimate the mean or standard deviation. In the following discussion, we show how we can estimate the mean and standard deviation from data organized into a frequency distribution. We should stress that a mean or a standard deviation from grouped data is an *estimate* of the corresponding actual values.

Arithmetic Mean of Grouped Data

To approximate the arithmetic mean of data organized into a frequency distribution, we begin by assuming the observations in each class are represented by the *midpoint* of the class. The mean of a sample of data organized in a frequency distribution is computed by:

ARITHMETIC MEAN OF GROUPED DATA

$$\bar{x} = \frac{\Sigma fM}{n} \qquad \textbf{(3–11)}$$

where:

- $\bar{x}$ is the sample mean.
- M is the midpoint of each class.
- f is the frequency in each class.
- fM is the frequency in each class times the midpoint of the class.
- Σfm is the sum of these products.
- n is the total number of frequencies.

EXAMPLE

The computations for the arithmetic mean of data grouped into a frequency distribution will be shown based on the Applewood Auto Group profit data. Recall in Chapter 2, in Table 2–7 on page 30, we constructed a frequency distribution for the vehicle profit. The information is repeated below. Determine the arithmetic mean profit per vehicle.

Profit	Frequency
$ 200 up to $ 600	8
600 up to 1,000	11
1,000 up to 1,400	23
1,400 up to 1,800	38
1,800 up to 2,200	45
2,200 up to 2,600	32
2,600 up to 3,000	19
3,000 up to 3,400	4
Total	180

SOLUTION

The mean vehicle selling price can be estimated from data grouped into a frequency distribution. To find the estimated mean, assume the midpoint of each class is representative of the data values in that class. Recall that the midpoint of a class is halfway between the lower class limits of two consecutive classes. To find the midpoint of a particular class, we add the lower limits of two consecutive classes and divide by 2. Hence, the midpoint of the first class is \$400, found by (\$200 + \$600)/2. We assume the value of \$400 is representative of the eight values in that class. To put it another way, we assume the sum of the eight values in this class is \$3,200, found by 8(\$400). We continue the process of multiplying the class midpoint by the class frequency for each class and then sum these products. The results are summarized in Table 3–1.

TABLE 3–1 Profit on 180 Vehicles Sold Last Month at Applewood Auto Group

Profit	Frequency (*f*)	Midpoint (*M*)	*fM*
\$ 200 up to \$ 600	8	\$ 400	\$ 3,200
600 up to 1,000	11	800	8,800
1,000 up to 1,400	23	1,200	27,600
1,400 up to 1,800	38	1,600	60,800
1,800 up to 2,200	45	2,000	90,000
2,200 up to 2,600	32	2,400	76,800
2,600 up to 3,000	19	2,800	53,200
3,000 up to 3,400	4	3,200	12,800
Total	180		\$333,200

Solving for the arithmetic mean using formula (3–11), we get:

$$\bar{x} = \frac{\Sigma fM}{n} = \frac{\$333{,}200}{180} = \$1{,}851.11$$

We conclude that the mean profit per vehicle is about \$1,851.

Standard Deviation of Grouped Data

To calculate the standard deviation of data grouped into a frequency distribution, we need to adjust formula (3–10) slightly. We weight each of the squared differences by the number of frequencies in each class. The formula is:

STANDARD DEVIATION, GROUPED DATA

$$s = \sqrt{\frac{\Sigma f(M - \bar{x})^2}{n - 1}} \qquad \textbf{(3–12)}$$

where:

- s is the sample standard deviation.
- M is the midpoint of the class.
- f is the class frequency.
- n is the number of observations in the sample.
- $\bar{x}$ is the sample mean.

EXAMPLE

Refer to the frequency distribution for the Applewood Auto Group profit data reported in Table 3–1. Compute the standard deviation of the vehicle selling prices.

SOLUTION

Following the same practice used earlier for computing the mean of data grouped into a frequency distribution, f is the class frequency, M the class midpoint, and n the number of observations.

Profit	Frequency (f)	Midpoint (M)	fM	$(M-\bar{x})$	$(M-\bar{x})^2$	$f(M-\bar{x})^2$
\$ 200 up to \$ 600	8	400	3,200	−1,451	2,105,401	16,843,208
600 up to 1,000	11	800	8,800	−1,051	1,104,601	12,150,611
1,000 up to 1,400	23	1,200	27,600	−651	423,801	9,747,423
1,400 up to 1,800	38	1,600	60,800	−251	63,001	2,394,038
1,800 up to 2,200	45	2,000	90,000	149	22,201	999,045
2,200 up to 2,600	32	2,400	76,800	549	301,401	9,644,832
2,600 up to 3,000	19	2,800	53,200	949	900,601	17,111,419
3,000 up to 3,400	4	3,200	12,800	1,349	1,819,801	7,279,204
Total	180		333,200			76,169,780

To find the standard deviation:

Step 1: Subtract the mean from the class midpoint. That is, find $(M-\bar{x})$ = (\$400 − \$1,851 = −\$1,451) for the first class, for the second class (\$800 − \$1,851 = −\$1,051), and so on.

Step 2: Square the difference between the class midpoint and the mean. For the first class, it would be $(\$400 - \$1{,}851)^2 = 2{,}105{,}401$, for the second class $(\$800 - \$1{,}851)^2 = 1{,}104{,}601$, and so on.

Step 3: Multiply the squared difference between the class midpoint and the mean by the class frequency. For the first class, the value is $8(\$400 - \$1{,}851)^2 = 16{,}843{,}208$; for the second, $11(\$800 - \$1{,}851)^2 = 12{,}150{,}611$, and so on.

Step 4: Sum the $f(M-\bar{x})^2$. The total is 76,169,920. To find the standard deviation, we insert these values in formula (3–12).

$$s = \sqrt{\frac{\Sigma f(M-\bar{x})^2}{n-1}} = \sqrt{\frac{76{,}169{,}780}{180-1}} = 652.33$$

The mean and the standard deviation calculated from the data grouped into a frequency distribution are usually close to the values calculated from raw data. The grouped data result in some loss of information. For the vehicle profit example, the mean profit reported in the Excel output on page 64 is \$1,843.17 and the standard deviation is \$643.63. The respective values estimated from data grouped into a frequency distribution are \$1,851.11 and \$652.33. The difference in the means is \$7.94, or about 0.4%. The standard deviations differ by \$8.70, or 1.4%. Based on the percentage difference, the estimates are very close to the actual values.

SELF-REVIEW 3–10

The net incomes of a sample of twenty container shipping companies were organized into the following table:

Net Income (\$ millions)	Number of Companies
2 up to 6	1
6 up to 10	4
10 up to 14	10
14 up to 18	3
18 up to 22	2

(a) What is the table called?
(b) Based on the distribution, what is the estimate of the arithmetic mean net income?
(c) Based on the distribution, what is the estimate of the standard deviation?

EXERCISES

57. When we compute the mean of a frequency distribution, why do we refer to this as an *estimated* mean?

58. Estimate the mean and the standard deviation of the following frequency distribution showing the number of times students eat at campus dining places in a month.

Class	Frequency
0 up to 5	2
5 up to 10	7
10 up to 15	12
15 up to 20	6
20 up to 25	3

59. Estimate the mean and the standard deviation of the following frequency distribution showing the ages of the first 60 people in line on Black Friday at a retail store.

Class	Frequency
20 up to 30	7
30 up to 40	12
40 up to 50	21
50 up to 60	18
60 up to 70	12

60. SCCoast, an Internet provider in the Southeast, developed the following frequency distribution on the age of Internet users. Estimate the mean and the standard deviation.

Age (years)	Frequency
10 up to 20	3
20 up to 30	7
30 up to 40	18
40 up to 50	20
50 up to 60	12

61. The IRS was interested in the number of individual tax forms prepared by small accounting firms. The IRS randomly sampled 50 public accounting firms with 10 or fewer employees in the Dallas–Fort Worth area. The following frequency table reports the results of the study. Estimate the mean and the standard deviation.

Number of Clients	Frequency
20 up to 30	1
30 up to 40	15
40 up to 50	22
50 up to 60	8
60 up to 70	4

62. Advertising expenses are a significant component of the cost of goods sold. Listed below is a frequency distribution showing the advertising expenditures for 60 manufacturing companies located in the Southwest. Estimate the mean and the standard deviation of advertising expenses.

Advertising Expenditure ($ millions)	Number of Companies
25 up to 35	5
35 up to 45	10
45 up to 55	21
55 up to 65	16
65 up to 75	8
Total	60

ETHICS AND REPORTING RESULTS

In Chapter 1, we discussed the ethical and unbiased reporting of statistical results. While you are learning about how to organize, summarize, and interpret data using statistics, it is also important to understand statistics so that you can be an intelligent consumer of information.

In this chapter, we learned how to compute numerical descriptive statistics. Specifically, we showed how to compute and interpret measures of location for a data set: the mean, median, and mode. We also discussed the advantages and disadvantages for each statistic. For example, if a real estate developer tells a client that the average home in a particular subdivision sold for $150,000, we assume that $150,000 is a representative selling price for all the homes. But suppose that the client also asks what the median sales price is, and the median is $60,000. Why was the developer only reporting the mean price? This information is extremely important to a person's decision making when buying a home. Knowing the advantages and disadvantages of the mean, median, and mode is important as we report statistics and as we use statistical information to make decisions.

We also learned how to compute measures of dispersion: range, variance, and standard deviation. Each of these statistics also has advantages and disadvantages. Remember that the range provides information about the overall spread of a distribution. However, it does not provide any information about how the data are clustered or concentrated around the center of the distribution. As we learn more about statistics, we need to remember that when we use statistics we must maintain an independent and principled point of view. Any statistical report requires objective and honest communication of the results.

CHAPTER SUMMARY

I. A measure of location is a value used to describe the central tendency of a set of data.

A. The arithmetic mean is the most widely reported measure of location.

1. It is calculated by adding the values of the observations and dividing by the total number of observations.

a. The formula for the population mean of ungrouped or raw data is

$$\mu = \frac{\Sigma x}{N} \quad \textbf{(3–1)}$$

b. The formula for the sample mean is

$$\bar{x} = \frac{\Sigma x}{n} \quad \textbf{(3–2)}$$

c. The formula for the sample mean of data in a frequency distribution is

$$\bar{x} = \frac{\Sigma fM}{n} \tag{3–11}$$

2. The major characteristics of the arithmetic mean are:
   a. At least the interval scale of measurement is required.
   b. All the data values are used in the calculation.
   c. A set of data has only one mean. That is, it is unique.
   d. The sum of the deviations from the mean equals 0.

B. The median is the value in the middle of a set of ordered data.
   1. To find the median, sort the observations from minimum to maximum and identify the middle value.
   2. The major characteristics of the median are:
      a. At least the ordinal scale of measurement is required.
      b. It is not influenced by extreme values.
      c. Fifty percent of the observations are larger than the median.
      d. It is unique to a set of data.

C. The mode is the value that occurs most often in a set of data.
   1. The mode can be found for nominal-level data.
   2. A set of data can have more than one mode.

D. The weighted mean is found by multiplying each observation by its corresponding weight.
   1. The formula for determining the weighted mean is

$$\bar{x}_w = \frac{w_1x_1 + w_2x_2 + w_3x_3 + \cdots + w_nx_n}{w_1 + w_2 + w_3 + \cdots + w_n} \tag{3–3}$$

E. The geometric mean is the *n*th root of the product of *n* positive values.
   1. The formula for the geometric mean is

$$GM = \sqrt[n]{(x_1)(x_2)(x_3)\cdots(x_n)} \tag{3–4}$$

   2. The geometric mean is also used to find the rate of change from one period to another.

$$GM = \sqrt[n]{\frac{\text{Value at end of period}}{\text{Value at beginning of period}}} - 1 \tag{3–5}$$

   3. The geometric mean is always equal to or less than the arithmetic mean.

II. The dispersion is the variation or spread in a set of data.

A. The range is the difference between the maximum and minimum values in a set of data.
   1. The formula for the range is

$$\text{Range} = \text{Maximum value} - \text{Minimum value} \tag{3–6}$$

   2. The major characteristics of the range are:
      a. Only two values are used in its calculation.
      b. It is influenced by extreme values.
      c. It is easy to compute and to understand.

B. The variance is the mean of the squared deviations from the arithmetic mean.
   1. The formula for the population variance is

$$\sigma^2 = \frac{\Sigma(x - \mu)^2}{N} \tag{3–7}$$

   2. The formula for the sample variance is

$$s^2 = \frac{\Sigma(x - \bar{x})^2}{n - 1} \tag{3–9}$$

   3. The major characteristics of the variance are:
      a. All observations are used in the calculation.
      b. The units are somewhat difficult to work with; they are the original units squared.

C. The standard deviation is the square root of the variance.
   1. The major characteristics of the standard deviation are:
      a. It is in the same units as the original data.
      b. It is the square root of the average squared distance from the mean.
      c. It cannot be negative.
      d. It is the most widely reported measure of dispersion.

2. The formula for the sample standard deviation is

$$s = \sqrt{\frac{\Sigma(x - \bar{x})^2}{n - 1}} \quad \textbf{(3–10)}$$

3. The formula for the standard deviation of grouped data is

$$s = \sqrt{\frac{\Sigma f(M - \bar{x})^2}{n - 1}} \quad \textbf{(3–12)}$$

III. We use the standard deviation to describe a frequency distribution by applying Chebyshev's theorem or the Empirical Rule.

A. Chebyshev's theorem states that regardless of the shape of the distribution, at least $1 - 1/k^2$ of the observations will be within k standard deviations of the mean, where k is greater than 1.

B. The Empirical Rule states that for a bell-shaped distribution about 68% of the values will be within one standard deviation of the mean, 95% within two, and virtually all within three.

PRONUNCIATION KEY

SYMBOL	MEANING	PRONUNCIATION
μ	Population mean	*mu*
Σ	Operation of adding	*sigma*
Σx	Adding a group of values	*sigma x*
$\bar{x}$	Sample mean	*x bar*
$\bar{x}_w$	Weighted mean	*x bar sub w*
GM	Geometric mean	*G M*
ΣfM	Adding the product of the frequencies and the class midpoints	*sigma f M*
σ^2	Population variance	*sigma squared*
σ	Population standard deviation	*sigma*

CHAPTER EXERCISES

63. The accounting firm of Crawford and Associates has five senior partners. Yesterday the senior partners saw six, four, three, seven, and five clients, respectively.

a. Compute the mean and median number of clients seen by the partners.
b. Is the mean a sample mean or a population mean?
c. Verify that $\Sigma(x - \mu) = 0$.

64. Owens Orchards sells apples in a large bag by weight. A sample of seven bags contained the following numbers of apples: 23, 19, 26, 17, 21, 24, 22.

a. Compute the mean and median number of apples in a bag.
b. Verify that $\Sigma(x - \bar{x}) = 0$.

65. **FILE** A sample of households that subscribe to United Bell Phone Company for landline phone service revealed the following number of calls received per household last week. Determine the mean and the median number of calls received.

52	43	30	38	30	42	12	46	39	37
34	46	32	18	41	5				

66. **FILE** The Citizens Banking Company is studying the number of times the ATM located in a Loblaws Supermarket at the foot of Market Street is used per day. Following are the number of times the machine was used daily over each of the last 30 days. Determine the mean number of times the machine was used per day.

83	64	84	76	84	54	75	59	70	61
63	80	84	73	68	52	65	90	52	77
95	36	78	61	59	84	95	47	87	60

67. FILE A recent study of the laundry habits of Americans included the time in minutes of the wash cycle. A sample of 40 observations follows. Determine the mean and the median of a typical wash cycle.

35	37	28	37	33	38	37	32	28	29
39	33	32	37	33	35	36	44	36	34
40	38	46	39	37	39	34	39	31	33
37	35	39	38	37	32	43	31	31	35

68. FILE Trudy Green works for the True-Green Lawn Company. Her job is to solicit lawn-care business via the telephone. Listed below is the number of appointments she made in each of the last 25 hours of calling. What is the arithmetic mean number of appointments she made per hour? What is the median number of appointments per hour? Write a brief report summarizing the findings.

9	5	2	6	5	6	4	4	7	2	3	6	3
4	4	7	8	4	4	5	5	4	8	3	3	

69. The Split-A-Rail Fence Company sells three types of fence to homeowners in suburban Seattle, Washington. Grade A costs $5.00 per running foot to install, Grade B costs $6.50 per running foot, and Grade C, the premium quality, costs $8.00 per running foot. Yesterday, Split-A-Rail installed 270 feet of Grade A, 300 feet of Grade B, and 100 feet of Grade C. What was the mean cost per foot of fence installed?

70. Rolland Poust is a sophomore in the College of Business at Scandia Tech. Last semester he took courses in statistics and accounting, 3 hours each, and earned an A in both. He earned a B in a 5-hour history course and a B in a 2-hour history of jazz course. In addition, he took a 1-hour course dealing with the rules of basketball so he could get his license to officiate high school basketball games. He got an A in this course. What was his GPA for the semester? Assume that he receives 4 points for an A, 3 for a B, and so on. What measure of central tendency did you calculate? What method did you use?

71. The table below shows the percent of the labor force that is unemployed and the size of the labor force for three counties in northwest Ohio. Jon Elsas is the Regional Director of Economic Development. He must present a report to several companies that are considering locating in northwest Ohio. What would be an appropriate unemployment rate to show for the entire region?

County	Percent Unemployed	Size of Workforce
Wood	4.5	15,300
Ottawa	3.0	10,400
Lucas	10.2	150,600

72. FILE The American Diabetes Association recommends a blood glucose reading of less than 130 for those with Type 2 diabetes. Blood glucose measures the amount of sugar in the blood. Below are the readings for February for a person recently diagnosed with Type 2 diabetes.

112	122	116	103	112	96	115	98	106	111
106	124	116	127	116	108	112	112	121	115
124	116	107	118	123	109	109	106		

a. What is the arithmetic mean glucose reading?
b. What is the median glucose reading?
c. What is the modal glucose reading?

73. The first Super Bowl was played in 1967. The cost for a 30-second commercial was $42,000. The cost of a 30-second commercial for Super Bowl 50 was $4.6 million. What was the geometric mean rate of increase for the 50 year period?

74. A recent article suggested that, if you earn $25,000 a year today and the inflation rate continues at 3% per year, you'll need to make $33,598 in 10 years to have the same buying power. You would need to make $44,771 if the inflation rate jumped to 6%. Confirm that these statements are accurate by finding the geometric mean rate of increase.

75. The ages of a sample of Canadian tourists flying from Toronto to Hong Kong were 32, 21, 60, 47, 54, 17, 72, 55, 33, and 41.

a. Compute the range.
b. Compute the standard deviation.

76. The weights (in pounds) of a sample of five boxes being sent by UPS are 12, 6, 7, 3, and 10.

a. Compute the range.
b. Compute the standard deviation.

77. **FILE** The enrollments of the 13 public universities in the state of Ohio are listed below.

College	Enrollment
University of Akron	26,106
Bowling Green State University	18,864
Central State University	1,718
University of Cincinnati	44,354
Cleveland State University	17,194
Kent State University	41,444
Miami University	23,902
Ohio State University	62,278
Ohio University	36,493
Shawnee State University	4,230
University of Toledo	20,595
Wright State University	17,460
Youngstown State University	12,512

a. Is this a sample or a population?
b. What is the mean enrollment?
c. What is the median enrollment?
d. What is the range of the enrollments?
e. Compute the standard deviation.

78. Health issues are a concern of managers, especially as they evaluate the cost of medical insurance. A recent survey of 150 executives at Elvers Industries, a large insurance and financial firm located in the Southwest, reported the number of pounds by which the executives were overweight. Compute the mean and the standard deviation.

Pounds Overweight	Frequency
0 up to 6	14
6 up to 12	42
12 up to 18	58
18 up to 24	28
24 up to 30	8

79. **FILE** The Apollo space program lasted from 1967 until 1972 and included 13 missions. The missions lasted from as little as 7 hours to as long as 301 hours. The duration of each flight is listed below.

9	195	241	301	216	260	7	244	192	147
10	295	142							

a. Explain why the flight times are a population.
b. Find the mean and median of the flight times.
c. Find the range and the standard deviation of the flight times.

80. **FILE** Creek Ratz is a very popular restaurant located along the coast of northern Florida. They serve a variety of steak and seafood dinners. During the summer beach season, they do not take reservations or accept "call ahead" seating. Management of the restaurant is concerned with the time a patron must wait before being seated for dinner. Listed below is the wait time, in minutes, for the 25 tables seated last Saturday night.

28	39	23	67	37	28	56	40	28	50
51	45	44	65	61	27	24	61	34	44
64	25	24	27	29					

a. Explain why the times are a population.
b. Find the mean and median of the times.
c. Find the range and the standard deviation of the times.

81. **FILE** A sample of 25 undergraduates reported the following dollar amounts of entertainment expenses last year:

684	710	688	711	722	698	723	743	738	722	696	721	685
763	681	731	736	771	693	701	737	717	752	710	697	

a. Find the mean, median, and mode of this information.
b. What are the range and standard deviation?
c. Use the Empirical Rule to establish an interval that includes about 95% of the observations.

82. **FILE** The Kentucky Derby is held the first Saturday in May at Churchill Downs in Louisville, Kentucky. The race track is one and one-quarter miles. The following table shows the winners since 1990, their margin of victory, the winning time, and the payoff on a $2 bet.

Year	Winner	Winning Margin (lengths)	Winning Time (minutes)	Payoff on a $2 Win Bet
1990	Unbridled	3.5	2.03333	10.80
1991	Strike the Gold	1.75	2.05000	4.80
1992	Lil E. Tee	1	2.05000	16.80
1993	Sea Hero	2.5	2.04000	12.90
1994	Go For Gin	2	2.06000	9.10
1995	Thunder Gulch	2.25	2.02000	24.50
1996	Grindstone	nose	2.01667	5.90
1997	Silver Charm	head	2.04000	4.00
1998	Real Quiet	0.5	2.03667	8.40
1999	Charismatic	neck	2.05333	31.30
2000	Fusaichi Pegasus	1.5	2.02000	2.30
2001	Monarchos	4.75	1.99950	10.50
2002	War Emblem	4	2.01883	20.50
2003	Funny Cide	1.75	2.01983	12.80
2004	Smarty Jones	2.75	2.06767	4.10
2005	Giacomo	0.5	2.04583	50.30
2006	Barbaro	6.5	2.02267	6.10
2007	Street Sense	2.25	2.03617	4.90
2008	Big Brown	4.75	2.03033	6.80
2009	Mine That Bird	6.75	2.04433	103.20
2010	Super Saver	2.50	2.07417	18.00
2011	Animal Kingdom	2.75	2.034	43.80
2012	I'll Have Another	1.5	2.03050	32.60
2013	Orb	2.5	2.04817	12.80
2014	California Chrome	1.75	2.0610	7.00
2015	American Pharaoh	1.00	2.05033	7.80

a. Determine the mean and median for the variables winning time and payoff on a $2 bet.
b. Determine the range and standard deviation of the variables winning time and payoff on a $2 bet.
c. Refer to the variable winning margin. What is the level of measurement? What measure of location would be most appropriate?

83. **FILE** The manager of the local Walmart Supercenter is studying the number of items purchased by customers in the evening hours. Listed below is the number of items for a sample of 30 customers.

15	8	6	9	9	4	18	10	10	12
12	4	7	8	12	10	10	11	9	13
5	6	11	14	5	6	6	5	13	5

a. Find the mean and the median of the number of items.
b. Find the range and the standard deviation of the number of items.
c. Organize the number of items into a frequency distribution. You may want to review the guidelines in Chapter 2 for establishing the class interval and the number of classes.
d. Find the mean and the standard deviation of the data organized into a frequency distribution. Compare these values with those computed in part (a). Why are they different?

84. The following frequency distribution reports the electricity cost for a sample of 50 two-bedroom apartments in Albuquerque, New Mexico, during the month of May last year.

Electricity Cost	Frequency
$ 80 up to $100	3
100 up to 120	8
120 up to 140	12
140 up to 160	16
160 up to 180	7
180 up to 200	4
Total	50

a. Estimate the mean cost.
b. Estimate the standard deviation.
c. Use the Empirical Rule to estimate the proportion of costs within two standard deviations of the mean. What are these limits?

85. Bidwell Electronics Inc. recently surveyed a sample of employees to determine how far they lived from corporate headquarters. The results are shown below. Compute the mean and the standard deviation.

Distance (miles)	Frequency	M
0 up to 5	4	2.5
5 up to 10	15	7.5
10 up to 15	27	12.5
15 up to 20	18	17.5
20 up to 25	6	22.5

DATA ANALYTICS

86. **FILE** Refer to the North Valley Real Estate data and prepare a report on the sales prices of the homes. Be sure to answer the following questions in your report.
a. Around what values of price do the data tend to cluster? What is the mean sales price? What is the median sales price? Is one measure more representative of the typical sales prices than the others?
b. What is the range of sales prices? What is the standard deviation? About 95% of the sales prices are between what two values? Is the standard deviation a useful statistic for describing the dispersion of sales price?
c. Repeat (a) and (b) using FICO score.

87. FILE Refer to the Baseball 2016 data, which report information on the 30 Major League Baseball teams for the 2016 season. Refer to the variable team salary.

a. Prepare a report on the team salaries. Be sure to answer the following questions in your report.

1. Around what values do the data tend to cluster? Specifically what is the mean team salary? What is the median team salary? Is one measure more representative of the typical team salary than the others?

2. What is the range of the team salaries? What is the standard deviation? About 95% of the salaries are between what two values?

b. Refer to the information on the average salary for each year. In 2000 the average player salary was $1.99 million. By 2016 the average player salary had increased to $4.40 million. What was the rate of increase over the period?

88. FILE Refer to the Lincolnville School District bus data. Prepare a report on the maintenance cost for last month. Be sure to answer the following questions in your report.

a. Around what values do the data tend to cluster? Specifically what was the mean maintenance cost last month? What is the median cost? Is one measure more representative of the typical cost than the others?

b. What is the range of maintenance costs? What is the standard deviation? About 95% of the maintenance costs are between what two values?

Describing Data:

DISPLAYING AND EXPLORING DATA

© Denis Vrublevski/Shutterstock.com

MCGIVERN JEWELERS recently posted an advertisement on a social media site reporting the shape, size, price, and cut grade for 33 of its diamonds in stock. Develop a box plot of the variable price and comment on the result. (See Exercise 37 and LO4-4.)

LEARNING OBJECTIVES

When you have completed this chapter, you will be able to:

LO4-1 Construct and interpret a dot plot.

LO4-2 Construct and describe a stem-and-leaf display.

LO4-3 Identify and compute measures of position.

LO4-4 Construct and analyze a box plot.

LO4-5 Compute and interpret the coefficient of skewness.

LO4-6 Create and interpret a scatter diagram.

LO4-7 Develop and explain a contingency table.

INTRODUCTION

Chapter 2 began our study of descriptive statistics. In order to transform raw or ungrouped data into a meaningful form, we organize the data into a frequency distribution. We present the frequency distribution in graphic form as a histogram or a frequency polygon. This allows us to visualize where the data tend to cluster, the largest and the smallest values, and the general shape of the data.

In Chapter 3, we first computed several measures of location, such as the mean, median, and mode. These measures of location allow us to report a typical value in the set of observations. We also computed several measures of dispersion, such as the range, variance, and standard deviation. These measures of dispersion allow us to describe the variation or the spread in a set of observations.

We continue our study of descriptive statistics in this chapter. We study (1) dot plots, (2) stem-and-leaf displays, (3) percentiles, and (4) box plots. These charts and statistics give us additional insight into where the values are concentrated as well as the general shape of the data. Then we consider bivariate data. In bivariate data, we observe two variables for each individual or observation. Examples include the number of hours a student studied and the points earned on an examination; if a sampled product meets quality specifications and the shift on which it is manufactured; or the amount of electricity used in a month by a homeowner and the mean daily high temperature in the region for the month. These charts and graphs provide useful insights as we use business analytics to enhance our understanding of data.

LO4-1
Construct and interpret a dot plot.

DOT PLOTS

Recall for the Applewood Auto Group data, we summarized the profit earned on the 180 vehicles sold with a frequency distribution using eight classes. When we organized the data into the eight classes, we lost the exact value of the observations. A **dot plot,** on the other hand, groups the data as little as possible, and we do not lose the identity of an individual observation. To develop a dot plot, we display a dot for each observation along a horizontal number line indicating the possible values of the data. If there are identical observations or the observations are too close to be shown individually, the dots are "piled" on top of each other. This allows us to see the shape of the distribution, the value about which the data tend to cluster, and the largest and smallest observations. Dot plots are most useful for smaller data sets, whereas histograms tend to be most useful for large data sets. An example will show how to construct and interpret dot plots.

EXAMPLE

The service departments at Tionesta Ford Lincoln and Sheffield Motors Inc., two of the four Applewood Auto Group dealerships, were both open 24 days last month. Listed below is the number of vehicles serviced last month at the two dealerships. Construct dot plots and report summary statistics to compare the two dealerships.

Tionesta Ford Lincoln					
Monday	Tuesday	Wednesday	Thursday	Friday	Saturday
23	33	27	28	39	26
30	32	28	33	35	32
29	25	36	31	32	27
35	32	35	37	36	30

Sheffield Motors Inc.					
Monday	**Tuesday**	**Wednesday**	**Thursday**	**Friday**	**Saturday**
31	35	44	36	34	37
30	37	43	31	40	31
32	44	36	34	43	36
26	38	37	30	42	33

SOLUTION

The Minitab system provides a dot plot and outputs the mean, median, maximum, and minimum values, and the standard deviation for the number of cars serviced at each dealership over the last 24 working days.

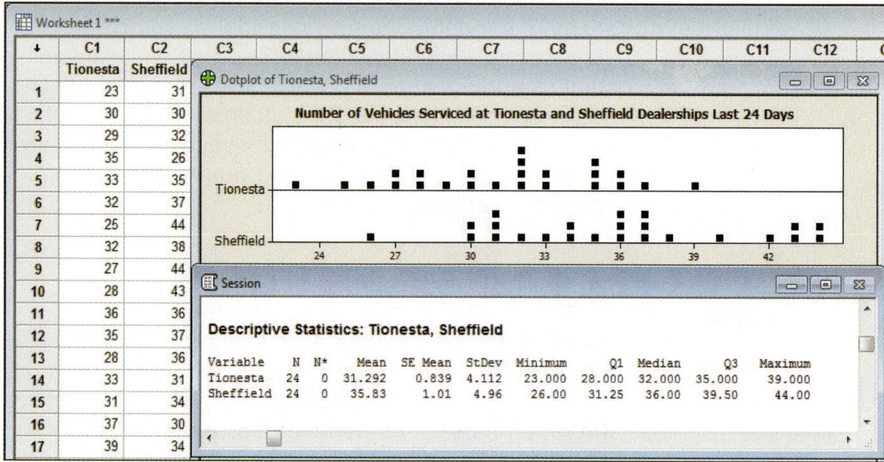

The dot plots, shown in the center of the output, graphically illustrate the distributions for each dealership. The plots show the difference in the location and dispersion of the observations. By looking at the dot plots, we can see that the number of vehicles serviced at the Sheffield dealership is more widely dispersed and has a larger mean than at the Tionesta dealership. Several other features of the number of vehicles serviced are:

- Tionesta serviced the fewest cars in any day, 23.
- Sheffield serviced 26 cars during their slowest day, which is 4 cars less than the next lowest day.
- Tionesta serviced exactly 32 cars on four different days.
- The numbers of cars serviced cluster around 36 for Sheffield and 32 for Tionesta.

From the descriptive statistics, we see Sheffield serviced a mean of 35.83 vehicles per day. Tionesta serviced a mean of 31.292 vehicles per day during the same period. So Sheffield typically services 4.54 more vehicles per day. There is also more dispersion, or variation, in the daily number of vehicles serviced at Sheffield than at Tionesta. How do we know this? The standard deviation is larger at Sheffield (4.96 vehicles per day) than at Tionesta (4.112 cars per day).

LO4-2
Construct and describe a stem-and-leaf display.

STEM-AND-LEAF DISPLAYS

In Chapter 2, we showed how to organize data into a frequency distribution so we could summarize the raw data into a meaningful form. The major advantage to organizing the data into a frequency distribution is we get a quick visual picture of the shape of the distribution without doing any further calculation. To put it another way, we can see where the data are concentrated and also determine whether there are any extremely large or small values. There are two disadvantages, however, to organizing the data into a frequency distribution: (1) we lose the exact identity of each value and (2) we are not sure how the values within each class are distributed. To explain, the Theater of the Republic in Erie, Pennsylvania, books live theater and musical performances. The theater's capacity is 160 seats. Last year, among the forty-five performances, there were eight different plays and twelve different bands. The following frequency distribution shows that between eighty up to ninety people attended two of the forty-five performances; there were seven performances where ninety up to one hundred people attended. However, is the attendance within this class clustered about 90, spread evenly throughout the class, or clustered near 99? We cannot tell.

Attendance	Frequency
80 up to 90	2
90 up to 100	7
100 up to 110	6
110 up to 120	9
120 up to 130	8
130 up to 140	7
140 up to 150	3
150 up to 160	3
Total	45

One technique used to display quantitative information in a condensed form and provide more information than the frequency distribution is the **stem-and-leaf display.** An advantage of the stem-and-leaf display over a frequency distribution is we do not lose the identity of each observation. In the above example, we would not know the identity of the values in the 90 up to 100 class. To illustrate the construction of a stem-and-leaf display using the number people attending each performance, suppose the seven observations in the 90 up to 100 class are 96, 94, 93, 94, 95, 96, and 97. The **stem** value is the leading digit or digits, in this case 9. The **leaves** are the trailing digits. The stem is placed to the left of a vertical line and the leaf values to the right.

The values in the 90 up to 100 class would appear as follows:

9 | 6 4 3 4 5 6 7

It is also customary to sort the values within each stem from smallest to largest. Thus, the second row of the stem-and-leaf display would appear as follows:

9 | 3 4 4 5 6 6 7

With the stem-and-leaf display, we can quickly observe that 94 people attended two performances and the number attending ranged from 93 to 97. A stem-and-leaf display is similar to a frequency distribution with more information, that is, the identity of the observations is preserved.

STEM-AND-LEAF DISPLAY A statistical technique to present a set of data. Each numerical value is divided into two parts. The leading digit(s) becomes the stem and the trailing digit the leaf. The stems are located along the vertical axis, and the leaf values are stacked against each other along the horizontal axis.

The following example explains the details of developing a stem-and-leaf display.

EXAMPLE

Listed in Table 4–1 is the number of people attending each of the 45 performances at the Theater of the Republic last year. Organize the data into a stem-and-leaf display. Around what values does attendance tend to cluster? What is the smallest attendance? The largest attendance?

TABLE 4–1 Number of People Attending Each of the 45 Performances at the Theater of the Republic

96	93	88	117	127	95	113	96	108	94	148	156
139	142	94	107	125	155	155	103	112	127	117	120
112	135	132	111	125	104	106	139	134	119	97	89
118	136	125	143	120	103	113	124	138			

SOLUTION

From the data in Table 4–1, we note that the smallest attendance is 88. So we will make the first stem value 8. The largest attendance is 156, so we will have the stem values begin at 8 and continue to 15. The first number in Table 4–1 is 96, which has a stem value of 9 and a leaf value of 6. Moving across the top row, the second value is 93 and the third is 88. After the first 3 data values are considered, the chart is as follows.

Stem	Leaf
8	8
9	6 3
10	
11	
12	
13	
14	
15	

Organizing all the data, the stem-and-leaf chart looks as follows.

Stem	Leaf
8	8 9
9	6 3 5 6 4 4 7
10	8 7 3 4 6 3
11	7 3 2 7 2 1 9 8 3
12	7 5 7 0 5 5 0 4
13	9 5 2 9 4 6 8
14	8 2 3
15	6 5 5

The usual procedure is to sort the leaf values from the smallest to largest. The last line, the row referring to the values in the 150s, would appear as:

15	5	5	6

The final table would appear as follows, where we have sorted all of the leaf values.

Stem	Leaf
8	8 9
9	3 4 4 5 6 6 7
10	3 3 4 6 7 8
11	1 2 2 3 3 7 7 8 9
12	0 0 4 5 5 5 7 7
13	2 4 5 6 8 9 9
14	2 3 8
15	5 5 6

You can draw several conclusions from the stem-and-leaf display. First, the minimum number of people attending is 88 and the maximum is 156. There were two performances with less than 90 people attending, and three performances with 150 or more. You can observe, for example, that for the three performances with more than 150 people attending, the actual attendances were 155, 155, and 156. The concentration of attendance is between 110 and 130. There were fifteen performances with attendance between 110 and 119 and eight performances between 120 and 129. We can also tell that within the 120 to 129 group the actual attendances were spread evenly throughout the class. That is, 120 people attended two performances, 124 people attended one performance, 125 people attended three performances, and 127 people attended two performances.

We also can generate this information on the Minitab software system. We have named the variable *Attendance*. The Minitab output is below. You can find the Minitab commands that will produce this output in Appendix C.

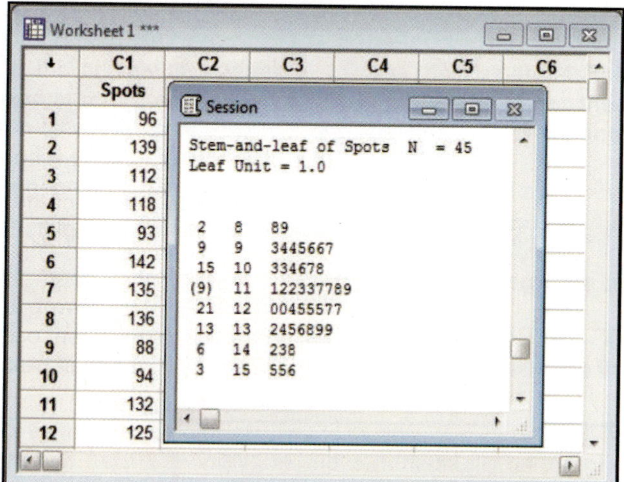

The Minitab solution provides some additional information regarding cumulative totals. In the column to the left of the stem values are numbers such as 2, 9, 15, and so on. The number 9 indicates there are 9 observations that have occurred before the value of 100. The number 15 indicates that 15 observations have occurred prior to 110. About halfway down the column the number 9 appears in parentheses. The parentheses indicate that the middle value or median appears in that row and there are nine values in this group. In this case, we describe the middle value as the value below which half of the observations occur. There are a total of 45 observations, so the middle value, if the data were arranged from smallest to largest, would be the 23rd observation; its value is 118. After the median, the values begin to decline. These values represent the "more than" cumulative totals. There are 21 observations of 120 or more, 13 of 130 or more, and so on.

Which is the better choice, a dot plot or a stem-and-leaf chart? This is really a matter of personal choice and convenience. For presenting data, especially with a large number of observations, you will find dot plots are more frequently used. You will see dot plots in analytical literature, marketing reports, and occasionally in annual reports. If you are doing a quick analysis for yourself, stem-and-leaf tallies are handy and easy, particularly on a smaller set of data.

SELF-REVIEW 4–1

© Somos/Veer/Getty Images RF

1. The number of employees at each of the 142 Home Depot stores in the Southeast region is shown in the following dot plot.

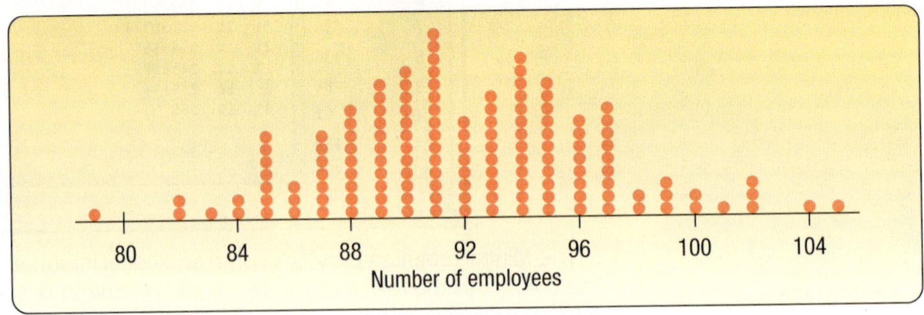

   (a) What are the maximum and minimum numbers of employees per store?
   (b) How many stores employ 91 people?
   (c) Around what values does the number of employees per store tend to cluster?
2. The rate of return for 21 stocks is:

8.3	9.6	9.5	9.1	8.8	11.2	7.7	10.1	9.9	10.8	
10.2	8.0	8.4	8.1	11.6	9.6	8.8	8.0	10.4	9.8	9.2

Organize this information into a stem-and-leaf display.
(a) How many rates are less than 9.0?
(b) List the rates in the 10.0 up to 11.0 category.
(c) What is the median?
(d) What are the maximum and the minimum rates of return?

EXERCISES

1. Describe the differences between a histogram and a dot plot. When might a dot plot be better than a histogram?
2. Describe the differences between a histogram and a stem-and-leaf display.
3. Consider the following chart.

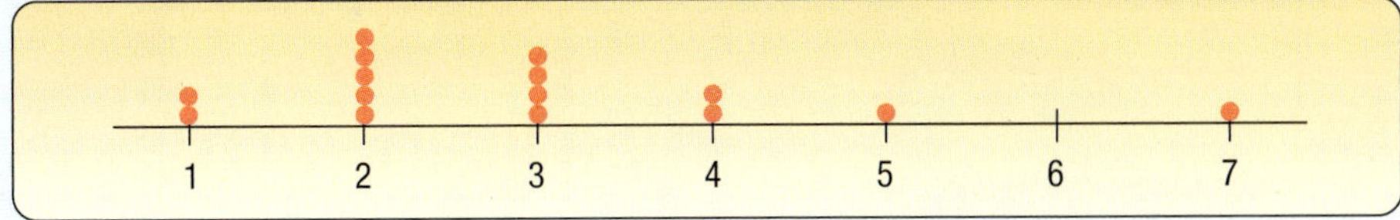

   a. What is this chart called?
   b. How many observations are in the study?
   c. What are the maximum and the minimum values?
   d. Around what values do the observations tend to cluster?
4. The following chart reports the number of cell phones sold at a big-box retail store for the last 26 days.

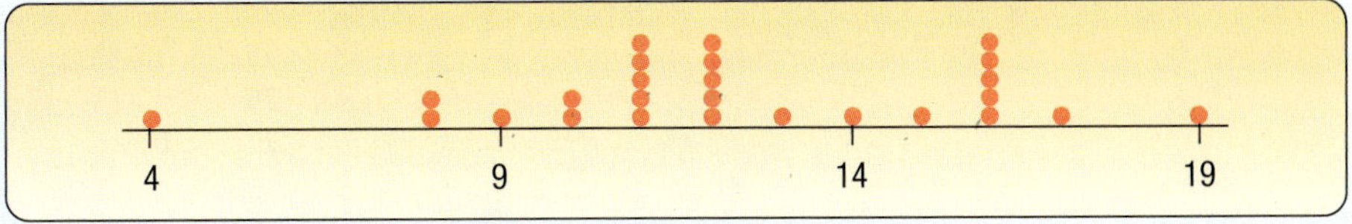

   a. What are the maximum and the minimum numbers of cell phones sold in a day?
   b. What is a typical number of cell phones sold?
5. The first row of a stem-and-leaf chart appears as follows: 62 | 1 3 3 7 9. Assume whole number values.
   a. What is the "possible range" of the values in this row?
   b. How many data values are in this row?
   c. List the actual values in this row of data.
6. The third row of a stem-and-leaf chart appears as follows: 21 | 0 1 3 5 7 9. Assume whole number values.
   a. What is the "possible range" of the values in this row?
   b. How many data values are in this row?
   c. List the actual values in this row of data.
7. The following stem-and-leaf chart shows the number of units produced per day in a factory.

Stem	Leaf
3	8
4	
5	6
6	0133559
7	0236778
8	59
9	00156
10	36

   a. How many days were studied?
   b. How many observations are in the first class?

c. What are the minimum value and the maximum value?
d. List the actual values in the fourth row.
e. List the actual values in the second row.
f. How many values are less than 70?
g. How many values are 80 or more?
h. What is the median?
i. How many values are between 60 and 89, inclusive?

8. The following stem-and-leaf chart reports the number of prescriptions filled per day at the pharmacy on the corner of Fourth and Main Streets.

Stem	Leaf
12	689
13	123
14	6889
15	589
16	35
17	24568
18	268
19	13456
20	034679
21	2239
22	789
23	00179
24	8
25	13
26	
27	0

a. How many days were studied?
b. How many observations are in the last class?
c. What are the maximum and the minimum values in the entire set of data?
d. List the actual values in the fourth row.
e. List the actual values in the next to the last row.
f. On how many days were less than 160 prescriptions filled?
g. On how many days were 220 or more prescriptions filled?
h. What is the middle value?
i. How many days did the number of filled prescriptions range between 170 and 210?

9. **FILE** A survey of the number of phone calls made by a sample of 16 Verizon subscribers last week revealed the following information. Develop a stem-and-leaf chart. How many calls did a typical subscriber make? What were the maximum and the minimum number of calls made?

52	43	30	38	30	42	12	46	39
37	34	46	32	18	41	5		

10. **FILE** Aloha Banking Co. is studying ATM use in suburban Honolulu. Yesterday, for a sample of 30 ATM's, the bank counted the number of times each machine was used. The data is presented in the table. Develop a stem-and-leaf chart to summarize the data. What were the typical, minimum, and maximum number of times each ATM was used?

83	64	84	76	84	54	75	59	70	61
63	80	84	73	68	52	65	90	52	77
95	36	78	61	59	84	95	47	87	60

LO4-3

Identify and compute measures of position.

MEASURES OF POSITION

The standard deviation is the most widely used measure of dispersion. However, there are other ways of describing the variation or spread in a set of data. One method is to determine the *location* of values that divide a set of observations into equal parts. These measures include **quartiles, deciles,** and **percentiles.**

Quartiles divide a set of observations into four equal parts. To explain further, think of any set of values arranged from the minimum to the maximum. In Chapter 3, we called the middle value of a set of data arranged from the minimum to the maximum the median. That is, 50% of the observations are larger than the median and 50% are smaller. The median is a measure of location because it pinpoints the center of the data. In a similar fashion, **quartiles** divide a set of observations into four equal parts. The first quartile, usually labeled Q_1, is the value below which 25% of the observations occur, and the third quartile, usually labeled Q_3, is the value below which 75% of the observations occur.

Similarly, **deciles** divide a set of observations into 10 equal parts and **percentiles** into 100 equal parts. So if you found that your GPA was in the 8th decile at your university, you could conclude that 80% of the students had a GPA lower than yours and 20% had a higher GPA. If your GPA was in the 92nd percentile, then 92% of students had a GPA less than your GPA and only 8% of students had a GPA greater than your GPA. Percentile scores are frequently used to report results on such national standardized tests as the SAT, ACT, GMAT (used to judge entry into many master of business administration programs), and LSAT (used to judge entry into law school).

Quartiles, Deciles, and Percentiles

To formalize the computational procedure, let L_p refer to the location of a desired percentile. So if we want to find the 92nd percentile we would use L_{92}, and if we wanted the median, the 50th percentile, then L_{50}. For a number of observations, n, the location of the *Pth* percentile, can be found using the formula:

LOCATION OF A PERCENTILE $$L_p = (n + 1)\frac{P}{100} \qquad \textbf{[4–1]}$$

An example will help to explain further.

EXAMPLE

Morgan Stanley is an investment company with offices located throughout the United States. Listed below are the commissions earned last month by a sample of 15 brokers at the Morgan Stanley office in Oakland, California.

$2,038	$1,758	$1,721	$1,637	$2,097	$2,047	$2,205	$1,787	$2,287
1,940	2,311	2,054	2,406	1,471	1,460			

Locate the median, the first quartile, and the third quartile for the commissions earned.

SOLUTION

The first step is to sort the data from the smallest commission to the largest.

$1,460	$1,471	$1,637	$1,721	$1,758	$1,787	$1,940	$2,038
2,047	2,054	2,097	2,205	2,287	2,311	2,406	

© Ramin Talaie/Getty Images

The median value is the observation in the center and is the same as the 50th percentile, so P equals 50. So the median or L_{50} is located at $(n + 1)(50/100)$, where n is the number of observations. In this case, that is position number 8, found by $(15 + 1)(50/100)$. The eighth-largest commission is $2,038. So we conclude this is the median and that half the brokers earned commissions more than $2,038 and half earned less than $2,038. The result using formula (4–1) to find the median is the same as the method presented in Chapter 3.

Recall the definition of a quartile. Quartiles divide a set of observations into four equal parts. Hence 25% of the observations will be less than the first quartile. Seventy-five percent of the observations will be less than the third quartile. To locate the first quartile, we use formula (4–1), where $n = 15$ and $P = 25$:

$$L_{25} = (n + 1)\frac{P}{100} = (15 + 1)\frac{25}{100} = 4$$

and to locate the third quartile, $n = 15$ and $P = 75$:

$$L_{75} = (n + 1)\frac{P}{100} = (15 + 1)\frac{75}{100} = 12$$

Therefore, the first and third quartile values are located at positions 4 and 12, respectively. The fourth value in the ordered array is $1,721 and the twelfth is $2,205. These are the first and third quartiles.

In the above example, the location formula yielded a whole number. That is, we wanted to find the first quartile and there were 15 observations, so the location formula indicated we should find the fourth ordered value. What if there were 20 observations in the sample, that is $n = 20$, and we wanted to locate the first quartile? From the location formula (4–1):

$$L_{25} = (n + 1)\frac{P}{100} = (20 + 1)\frac{25}{100} = 5.25$$

We would locate the fifth value in the ordered array and then move .25 of the distance between the fifth and sixth values and report that as the first quartile. Like the median, the quartile does not need to be one of the actual values in the data set.

To explain further, suppose a data set contained the six values 91, 75, 61, 101, 43, and 104. We want to locate the first quartile. We order the values from the minimum to the maximum: 43, 61, 75, 91, 101, and 104. The first quartile is located at

$$L_{25} = (n + 1)\frac{P}{100} = (6 + 1)\frac{25}{100} = 1.75$$

The position formula tells us that the first quartile is located between the first and the second values and it is .75 of the distance between the first and the second values. The first value is 43 and the second is 61. So the distance between these two values is 18. To locate the first quartile, we need to move .75 of the distance between the first and second values, so .75(18) = 13.5. To complete the procedure, we add 13.5 to the first value, 43, and report that the first quartile is 56.5.

We can extend the idea to include both deciles and percentiles. To locate the 23rd percentile in a sample of 80 observations, we would look for the 18.63 position.

$$L_{23} = (n + 1)\frac{P}{100} = (80 + 1)\frac{23}{100} = 18.63$$

STATISTICS IN ACTION

John W. Tukey (1915–2000) received a PhD in mathematics from Princeton in 1939. However, when he joined the Fire Control Research Office during World War II, his interest in abstract mathematics shifted to applied statistics. He developed effective numerical and graphical methods for studying patterns in data. Among the graphics he developed are the stem-and-leaf diagram and the box-and-whisker plot or box plot. From 1960 to 1980, Tukey headed the statistical division of NBC's election night vote projection team. He became renowned in 1960 for preventing an early call of victory for Richard Nixon in the presidential election won by John F. Kennedy.

To find the value corresponding to the 23rd percentile, we would locate the 18th value and the 19th value and determine the distance between the two values. Next, we would multiply this difference by 0.63 and add the result to the smaller value. The result would be the 23rd percentile.

Statistical software is very helpful when describing and summarizing data. Excel, Minitab, and MegaStat, a statistical analysis Excel add-in, all provide summary statistics that include quartiles. For example, the Minitab summary of the Morgan Stanley commission data, shown below, includes the first and third quartiles, and other statistics. Based on the reported quartiles, 25% of the commissions earned were less than $1,721 and 75% were less than $2,205. These are the same values we calculated using formula (4–1).

Sheet1 ***

↓	C1
	Commissions
1	1460
2	1471
3	1637
4	1721

Session

Descriptive Statistics: Commissions

Variable	N	N*	Mean	SE Mean	StDev	Minimum	Q1	Median	Q3	Maximum
Commissions	15	0	1947.9	77.1	298.8	1460.0	1721.0	2038.0	2205.0	2406.0

Morgan Stanley Commissions		
1460	Equation 4-1	
2047	Quartile 1	1721
1471	Quartile 3	2205
2054		
1637		
2097	Alternate Method	
1721	Quartile 1	1739.5
2205	Quartile 3	2151
1758		
2287		
1787		
2311		
1940		
2406		
2038		

There are ways other than formula (4–1) to locate quartile values. For example, another method uses $0.25n + 0.75$ to locate the position of the first quartile and $0.75n + 0.25$ to locate the position of the third quartile. We will call this the *Excel Method.* In the Morgan Stanley data, this method would place the first quartile at position 4.5 ($.25 \times 15 + .75$) and the third quartile at position 11.5 ($.75 \times 15 + .25$). The first quartile would be interpolated as 0.5, or one-half the difference between the fourth- and the fifth-ranked values. Based on this method, the first quartile is $1739.5, found by ($1,721 + 0.5[$1,758 − $1,721]). The third quartile, at position 11.5, would be $2,151, or one-half the distance between the eleventh- and the twelfth-ranked values, found by ($2,097 + 0.5[$2,205 − $2,097]). Excel, as shown in the Morgan Stanley and Applewood examples, can compute quartiles using either of the two methods. **Please note the text uses formula (4–1) to calculate quartiles.**

Is the difference between the two methods important? No. Usually it is just a nuisance. In general, both methods calculate values that will support the statement that approximately 25% of the values are less than the value of the first quartile, and approximately 75% of the data values are less than the value of the third quartile. When the sample is large, the difference in the results from the two methods is small. For example, in the Applewood Auto Group data there are 180 vehicles. The quartiles computed using both methods are shown to the left. Based on the variable profit, 45 of the 180 values (25%) are less than both values of the first quartile, and 135 of the 180 values (75%) are less than both values of the third quartile.

Applewood			
Age	Profit		
21	$1,387		
23	$1,754		
24	$1,817	Equation 4-1	
25	$1,040	Quartile 1	1415.5
26	$1,273	Quartile 3	2275.5
27	$1,529		
27	$3,082	Alternate Method	
28	$1,951	Quartile 1	1422.5
28	$2,692	Quartile 3	2268.5
29	$1,342		

When using Excel, be careful to understand the method used to calculate quartiles. Excel 2013 and Excel 2016 offer both methods. The Excel function, ***Quartile.exc,*** will result in the same answer as Equation 4–1. The Excel function, *Quartile.inc*, will result in the Excel Method answers.

SELF-REVIEW 4–2

The Quality Control department of Plainsville Peanut Company is responsible for checking the weight of the 8-ounce jar of peanut butter. The weights of a sample of nine jars produced last hour are:

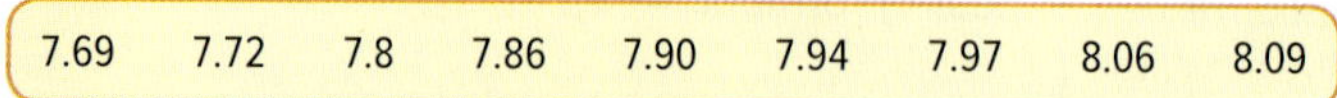

7.69	7.72	7.8	7.86	7.90	7.94	7.97	8.06	8.09

(a) What is the median weight?
(b) Determine the weights corresponding to the first and third quartiles.

EXERCISES

11. FILE Determine the median and the first and third quartiles in the following data.

46	47	49	49	51	53	54	54	55	55	59

12. FILE Determine the median and the first and third quartiles in the following data.

5.24	6.02	6.67	7.30	7.59	7.99	8.03	8.35	8.81	9.45
9.61	10.37	10.39	11.86	12.22	12.71	13.07	13.59	13.89	15.42

13. FILE The Thomas Supply Company Inc. is a distributor of gas-powered generators. As with any business, the length of time customers take to pay their invoices is important. Listed below, arranged from smallest to largest, is the time, in days, for a sample of The Thomas Supply Company Inc. invoices.

13	13	13	20	26	27	31	34	34	34	35	35	36	37	38
41	41	41	45	47	47	47	50	51	53	54	56	62	67	82

a. Determine the first and third quartiles.
b. Determine the second decile and the eighth decile.
c. Determine the 67th percentile.

14. FILE Kevin Horn is the national sales manager for National Textbooks Inc. He has a sales staff of 40 who visit college professors all over the United States. Each Saturday morning he requires his sales staff to send him a report. This report includes, among other things, the number of professors visited during the previous week. Listed below, ordered from smallest to largest, are the number of visits last week.

38	40	41	45	48	48	50	50	51	51	52	52	53	54	55	55	55	56	56	57
59	59	59	62	62	62	63	64	65	66	66	67	67	69	69	71	77	78	79	79

a. Determine the median number of calls.
b. Determine the first and third quartiles.
c. Determine the first decile and the ninth decile.
d. Determine the 33rd percentile.

LO4-4
Construct and analyze a box plot.

BOX PLOTS

A **box plot** is a graphical display, based on quartiles, that helps us picture a set of data. To construct a box plot, we need only five statistics: the minimum value, Q_1 (the first quartile), the median, Q_3 (the third quartile), and the maximum value. An example will help to explain.

EXAMPLE

Alexander's Pizza offers free delivery of its pizza within 15 miles. Alex, the owner, wants some information on the time it takes for delivery. How long does a typical delivery take? Within what range of times will most deliveries be completed? For a sample of 20 deliveries, he determined the following information:

$$\text{Minimum value} = 13 \text{ minutes}$$
$$Q_1 = 15 \text{ minutes}$$
$$\text{Median} = 18 \text{ minutes}$$
$$Q_3 = 22 \text{ minutes}$$
$$\text{Maximum value} = 30 \text{ minutes}$$

Develop a box plot for the delivery times. What conclusions can you make about the delivery times?

SOLUTION

The first step in drawing a box plot is to create an appropriate scale along the horizontal axis. Next, we draw a box that starts at Q_1 (15 minutes) and ends at Q_3 (22 minutes). Inside the box we place a vertical line to represent the median (18 minutes). Finally, we extend horizontal lines from the box out to the minimum value (13 minutes) and the maximum value (30 minutes). These horizontal lines outside of the box are sometimes called "whiskers" because they look a bit like a cat's whiskers.

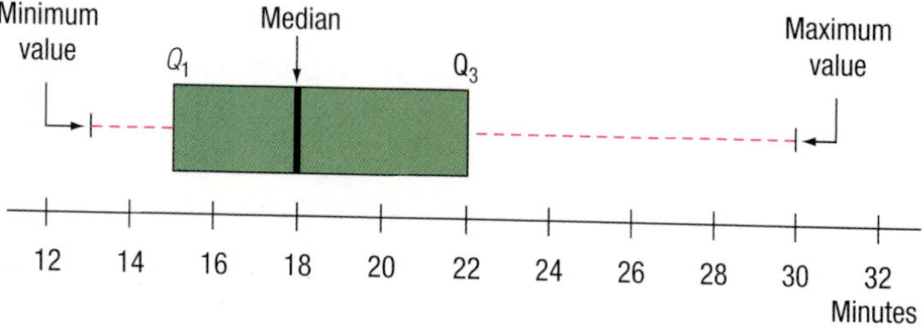

The box plot also shows the interquartile range of delivery times between Q1 and Q3. The **interquartile range** is 7 minutes and indicates that 50% of the deliveries are between 15 and 22 minutes.

The box plot also reveals that the distribution of delivery times is positively skewed. In Chapter 3, we defined skewness as the lack of symmetry in a set of data. How do we know this distribution is positively skewed? In this case, there are actually two pieces of information that suggest this. First, the dashed line to the right of the box from 22 minutes (Q_3) to the maximum time of 30 minutes is longer than the dashed line from the left of 15 minutes (Q_1) to the minimum value of 13 minutes. To put it another way, the 25% of the data larger than the third quartile is more spread out than the 25% less than the first quartile. A second indication of positive skewness is that the median is not in the center of the box. The distance from the first quartile to the median is smaller than the distance from the median to the third quartile. We know that the number of delivery times between 15 minutes and 18 minutes is the same as the number of delivery times between 18 minutes and 22 minutes.

EXAMPLE

Refer to the Applewood Auto Group data. Develop a box plot for the variable age of the buyer. What can we conclude about the distribution of the age of the buyer?

SOLUTION

Minitab was used to develop the following chart and summary statistics.

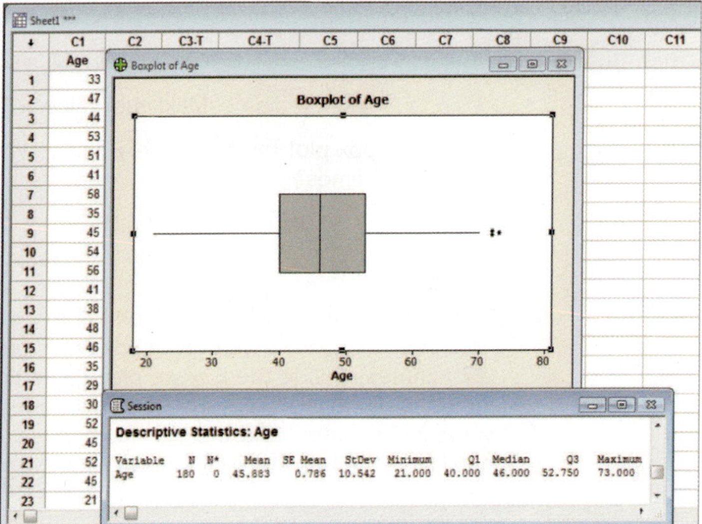

The median age of the purchaser is 46 years, 25% of the purchasers are less than 40 years of age, and 25% are more than 52.75 years of age. Based on the summary information and the box plot, we conclude:

- Fifty percent of the purchasers are between the ages of 40 and 52.75 years.
- The distribution of ages is fairly symmetric. There are two reasons for this conclusion. The length of the whisker above 52.75 years (Q_3) is about the same length as the whisker below 40 years (Q_1). Also, the area in the box between 40 years and the median of 46 years is about the same as the area between the median and 52.75.

There are three asterisks (*) above 70 years. What do they indicate? In a box plot, an asterisk identifies an **outlier.** An outlier is a value that is inconsistent with the rest of the data. It is defined as a value that is more than 1.5 times the interquartile range smaller than Q_1 or larger than Q_3. In this example, an outlier would be a value larger than 71.875 years, found by:

$$\textit{Outlier} > Q_3 + 1.5(Q_3 - Q_1) = 52.75 + 1.5(52.75 - 40) = 71.875$$

An outlier would also be a value less than 20.875 years.

$$\textit{Outlier} < Q_1 - 1.5(Q_3 - Q_1) = 40 - 1.5(52.75 - 40) = 20.875$$

From the box plot, we conclude there are three purchasers 72 years of age or older and none less than 21 years of age. Technical note: In some cases, a single asterisk may represent more than one observation because of the limitations of the software and space available. It is a good idea to check the actual data. In this instance, there are three purchasers 72 years old or older; two are 72 and one is 73.

SELF-REVIEW 4–3

The following box plot shows the assets in millions of dollars for credit unions in Seattle, Washington.

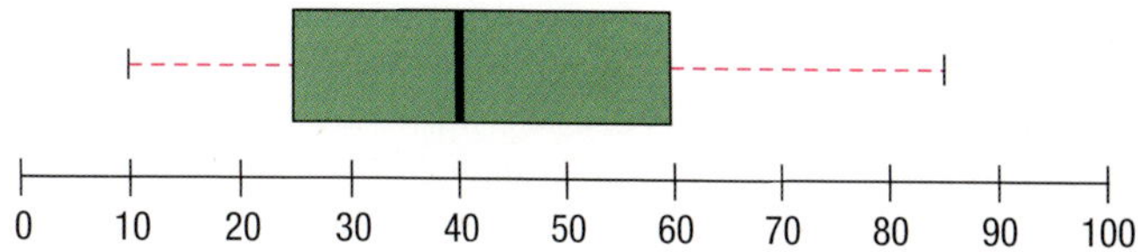

What are the smallest and largest values, the first and third quartiles, and the median? Would you agree that the distribution is symmetrical? Are there any outliers?

EXERCISES

15. The box plot below shows the amount spent for books and supplies per year by students at four-year public colleges.

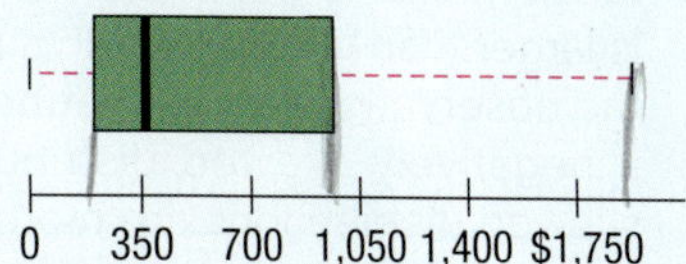

a. Estimate the median amount spent.
b. Estimate the first and third quartiles for the amount spent.
c. Estimate the interquartile range for the amount spent.
d. Beyond what point is a value considered an outlier?
e. Identify any outliers and estimate their value.
f. Is the distribution symmetrical or positively or negatively skewed?

16. The box plot shows the undergraduate in-state tuition per credit hour at four-year public colleges.

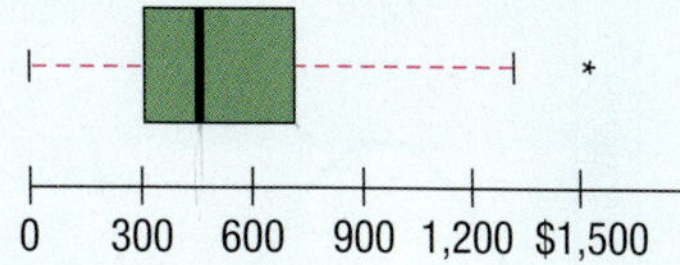

a. Estimate the median.
b. Estimate the first and third quartiles.
c. Determine the interquartile range.
d. Beyond what point is a value considered an outlier?
e. Identify any outliers and estimate their value.
f. Is the distribution symmetrical or positively or negatively skewed?

17. In a study of the gasoline mileage of model year 2016 automobiles, the mean miles per gallon was 27.5 and the median was 26.8. The smallest value in the study was 12.70 miles per gallon, and the largest was 50.20. The first and third quartiles were 17.95 and 35.45 miles per gallon, respectively. Develop a box plot and comment on the distribution. Is it a symmetric distribution?

18. FILE A sample of 28 time shares in the Orlando, Florida, area revealed the following daily charges for a one-bedroom suite. For convenience, the data are ordered from smallest to largest. Construct a box plot to represent the data. Comment on the distribution. Be sure to identify the first and third quartiles and the median.

$116	$121	$157	$192	$207	$209	$209
229	232	236	236	239	243	246
260	264	276	281	283	289	296
307	309	312	317	324	341	353

LO4-5 Compute and interpret the coefficient of skewness.

SKEWNESS

In Chapter 3, we described measures of central location for a distribution of data by reporting the mean, median, and mode. We also described measures that show the amount of spread or variation in a distribution, such as the range and the standard deviation.

Another characteristic of a distribution is the shape. There are four shapes commonly observed: symmetric, positively skewed, negatively skewed, and bimodal. In a **symmetric** distribution the mean and median are equal and the data values are evenly spread around these values. The shape of the distribution below the mean and median is a mirror image of distribution above the mean and median. A distribution of values is **skewed to the right** or **positively skewed** if there is a single peak, but the values extend much farther to the right of the peak than to the left of the peak. In this case, the mean is larger than the median. In a **negatively skewed** distribution there is a single peak, but the observations extend farther to the left, in the negative direction, than to the right. In a negatively skewed distribution, the mean is smaller than the median. Positively skewed distributions are more common. Salaries often follow this pattern. Think of the salaries of those employed in a small company of about 100 people. The president and a few top executives would have very large salaries relative to the other workers and hence the distribution of salaries would exhibit positive skewness. A **bimodal distribution** will have two or more peaks. This is often the case when the values are from two or more populations. This information is summarized in Chart 4–1.

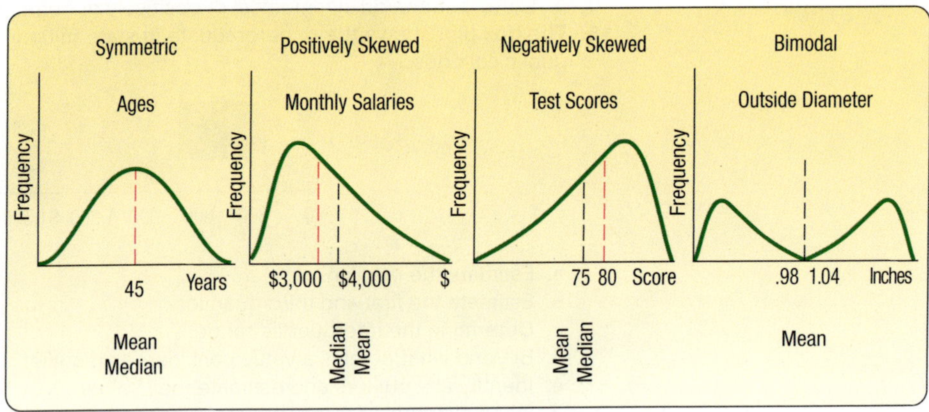

CHART 4–1 Shapes of Frequency Polygons

There are several formulas in the statistical literature used to calculate skewness. The simplest, developed by Professor Karl Pearson (1857–1936), is based on the difference between the mean and the median.

STATISTICS IN ACTION

The late Stephen Jay Gould (1941–2002) was a professor of zoology and professor of geology at Harvard University. In 1982, he was diagnosed with cancer and had an expected survival time of 8 months. However, never to be discouraged, his research showed that the distribution of survival time is dramatically skewed to the right and showed that not only do 50% of similar cancer patients survive more than 8 months, but that the survival time could be years rather than months! In fact, Dr. Gould lived another 20 years. Based on his experience, he wrote a widely published essay titled "The Median Is Not the Message."

PEARSON'S COEFFICIENT OF SKEWNESS

$$sk = \frac{3(\bar{x} - \text{Median})}{s} \qquad [4\text{–}2]$$

Using this relationship, the coefficient of skewness can range from −3 up to 3. A value near −3, such as −2.57, indicates considerable negative skewness. A value such as 1.63 indicates moderate positive skewness. A value of 0, which will occur when the mean and median are equal, indicates the distribution is symmetrical and there is no skewness present.

In this text, we present output from Minitab and Excel. Both of these software packages compute a value for the coefficient of skewness based on the cubed deviations from the mean. The formula is:

SOFTWARE COEFFICIENT OF SKEWNESS

$$sk = \frac{n}{(n-1)(n-2)}\left[\sum\left(\frac{x-\bar{x}}{s}\right)^3\right] \qquad [4\text{–}3]$$

Formula (4–3) offers an insight into skewness. The right-hand side of the formula is the difference between each value and the mean, divided by the standard deviation. That is the portion $(x - \bar{x})/s$ of the formula. This idea is called **standardizing.** We will discuss the idea of standardizing a value in more detail in Chapter 7 when we describe the normal probability distribution. At this point, observe that the result is to report the difference between each value and the mean in units of the standard deviation. If this difference is positive, the particular value is larger than the mean; if the value is negative, the standardized quantity is smaller than the mean. When we cube these values, we retain the information on the direction of the difference. Recall that in the formula for the standard deviation [see formula (3–10)] we squared the difference between each value and the mean, so that the result was all nonnegative values.

If the set of data values under consideration is symmetric, when we cube the standardized values and sum over all the values, the result would be near zero. If there are several large values, clearly separate from the others, the sum of the cubed differences would be a large positive value. If there are several small values clearly separate from the others, the sum of the cubed differences will be negative.

An example will illustrate the idea of skewness.

EXAMPLE

Following are the earnings per share for a sample of 15 software companies for the year 2016. The earnings per share are arranged from smallest to largest.

\$0.09	\$0.13	\$0.41	\$0.51	\$ 1.12	\$ 1.20	\$ 1.49	\$3.18
3.50	6.36	7.83	8.92	10.13	12.99	16.40	

Compute the mean, median, and standard deviation. Find the coefficient of skewness using Pearson's estimate and the software methods. What is your conclusion regarding the shape of the distribution?

SOLUTION

These are sample data, so we use formula (3–2) to determine the mean

$$\bar{x} = \frac{\Sigma x}{n} = \frac{\$74.26}{15} = \$4.95$$

The median is the middle value in a set of data, arranged from smallest to largest. In this case, there is an odd-number of observations, so the middle value is the median. It is \$3.18.

We use formula (3–10) on page 78 to determine the sample standard deviation.

$$s = \sqrt{\frac{\Sigma(x - \bar{x})^2}{n - 1}} = \sqrt{\frac{(\$0.09 - \$4.95)^2 + \cdots + (\$16.40 - \$4.95)^2}{15 - 1}} = \$5.22$$

Pearson's coefficient of skewness is 1.017, found by

$$sk = \frac{3(\bar{x} - \text{Median})}{s} = \frac{3(\$4.95 - \$3.18)}{\$5.22} = 1.017$$

This indicates there is moderate positive skewness in the earnings per share data.

We obtain a similar, but not exactly the same, value from the software method. The details of the calculations are shown in Table 4–2. To begin, we find the difference between each earnings per share value and the mean and divide this result by the standard deviation. We have referred to this as standardizing. Next, we cube, that is, raise to the third power, the result of the first step. Finally, we sum the cubed values. The details for the first company, that is, the company with an earnings per share of \$0.09, are:

$$\left(\frac{x - \bar{x}}{s}\right)^3 = \left(\frac{0.09 - 4.95}{5.22}\right)^3 = (-0.9310)^3 = -0.8070$$

TABLE 4–2 Calculation of the Coefficient of Skewness

Earnings per Share	$\frac{(x - \bar{x})}{s}$	$\left(\frac{x - \bar{x}}{s}\right)^3$
0.09	−0.9310	−0.8070
0.13	−0.9234	−0.7873
0.41	−0.8697	−0.6579
0.51	−0.8506	−0.6154
1.12	−0.7337	−0.3950
1.20	−0.7184	−0.3708
1.49	−0.6628	−0.2912
3.18	−0.3391	−0.0390
3.50	−0.2778	−0.0214
6.36	0.2701	0.0197
7.83	0.5517	0.1679
8.92	0.7605	0.4399
10.13	0.9923	0.9772
12.99	1.5402	3.6539
16.40	2.1935	10.5537
		11.8274

When we sum the 15 cubed values, the result is 11.8274. That is, the term $\Sigma[(x - \bar{x})/s]^3 = 11.8274$. To find the coefficient of skewness, we use formula (4–3), with $n = 15$.

$$sk = \frac{n}{(n - 1)(n - 2)} \Sigma \left(\frac{x - \bar{x}}{s}\right)^3 = \frac{15}{(15 - 1)(15 - 2)}(11.8274) = 0.975$$

We conclude that the earnings per share values are somewhat positively skewed. The following Minitab summary reports the descriptive measures, such as the mean, median, and standard deviation of the earnings per share data. Also included are the coefficient of skewness and a histogram with a bell-shaped curve superimposed.

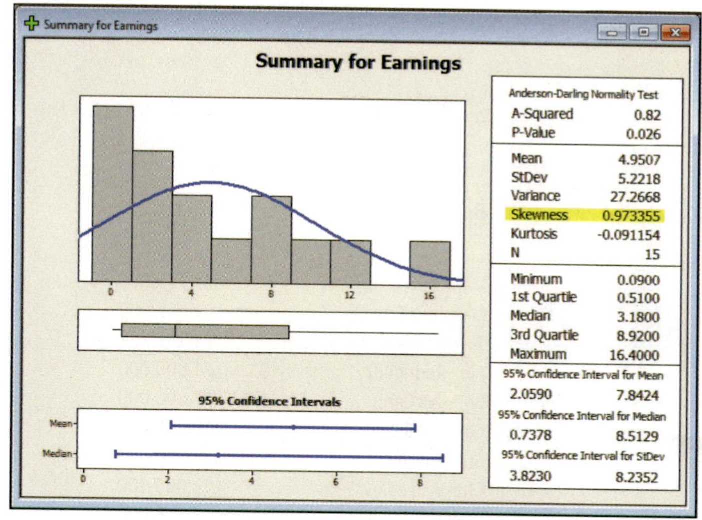

SELF-REVIEW 4–4

A sample of five data entry clerks employed in the Horry County Tax Office revised the following number of tax records last hour: 73, 98, 60, 92, and 84.

(a) Find the mean, median, and the standard deviation.
(b) Compute the coefficient of skewness using Pearson's method.
(c) Calculate the coefficient of skewness using the software method.
(d) What is your conclusion regarding the skewness of the data?

EXERCISES

For Exercises 19–22:

a. Determine the mean, median, and the standard deviation.
b. Determine the coefficient of skewness using Pearson's method.
c. Determine the coefficient of skewness using the software method.

19. FILE The following values are the starting salaries, in $000, for a sample of five accounting graduates who accepted positions in public accounting last year.

36.0	26.0	33.0	28.0	31.0

20. FILE Listed below are the salaries, in $000, for a sample of 15 chief financial officers in the electronics industry.

$516.0	$548.0	$566.0	$534.0	$586.0	$529.0
546.0	523.0	538.0	523.0	551.0	552.0
486.0	558.0	574.0			

21. **FILE** Listed below are the commissions earned ($000) last year by the 15 sales representatives at Furniture Patch Inc.

$ 3.9	$ 5.7	$ 7.3	$10.6	$13.0	$13.6	$15.1	$15.8	$17.1
17.4	17.6	22.3	38.6	43.2	87.7			

22. **FILE** Listed below are the salaries for the 2016 New York Yankees Major League Baseball team.

Player	Salary	Player	Salary
CC Sabathia	$25,000,000	Dustin Ackley	$3,200,000
Mark Teixeira	23,125,000	Martin Prado	3,000,000
Masahiro Tanaka	22,000,000	Didi Gregorius	2,425,000
Jacoby Ellsbury	21,142,857	Aaron Hicks	574,000
Alex Rodriguez	21,000,000	Austin Romine	556,000
Brian McCann	17,000,000	Chasen Shreve	533,400
Carlos Beltran	15,000,000	Greg Bird	525,300
Brett Gardner	13,500,000	Luis Severino	521,300
Chase Headley	13,000,000	Bryan Mitchell	516,650
Aroldis Chapman	11,325,000	Kirby Yates	511,900
Andrew Miller	9,000,000	Mason Williams	509,700
Starlin Castro	7,857,143	Ronald Torreyes	508,600
Nathan Eovaldi	5,600,000	John Barbato	507,500
Michael Pineda	4,300,000	Dellin Betances	507,500
Ivan Nova	4,100,000	Luis Cessa	507,500

LO4-6
Create and interpret a scatter diagram.

DESCRIBING THE RELATIONSHIP BETWEEN TWO VARIABLES

In Chapter 2 and the first section of this chapter, we presented graphical techniques to summarize the distribution of a single variable. We used a histogram in Chapter 2 to summarize the profit on vehicles sold by the Applewood Auto Group. Earlier in this chapter, we used dot plots and stem-and-leaf displays to visually summarize a set of data. Because we are studying a single variable, we refer to this as **univariate** data.

© Steve Mason/Getty Images RF

There are situations where we wish to study and visually portray the relationship between two variables. When we study the relationship between two variables, we refer to the data as **bivariate.** Data analysts frequently wish to understand the relationship between two variables. Here are some examples:

- Tybo and Associates is a law firm that advertises extensively on local TV. The partners are considering increasing their advertising budget. Before doing so, they would like to know the relationship between the amount spent per month on advertising and the total amount of billings for that month. To put it another way, will increasing the amount spent on advertising result in an increase in billings?

- Coastal Realty is studying the selling prices of homes. What variables seem to be related to the selling price of homes? For example, do larger homes sell for more than smaller ones? Probably. So Coastal might study the relationship between the area in square feet and the selling price.
- Dr. Stephen Givens is an expert in human development. He is studying the relationship between the height of fathers and the height of their sons. That is, do tall fathers tend to have tall children? Would you expect LeBron James, the 6′8″, 250 pound professional basketball player, to have relatively tall sons?

One graphical technique we use to show the relationship between variables is called a **scatter diagram.**

To draw a scatter diagram, we need two variables. We scale one variable along the horizontal axis (*X*-axis) of a graph and the other variable along the vertical axis (*Y*-axis). Usually one variable depends to some degree on the other. In the third example above, the height of the son *depends* on the height of the father. So we scale the height of the father on the horizontal axis and that of the son on the vertical axis.

We can use statistical software, such as Excel, to perform the plotting function for us. *Caution:* You should always be careful of the scale. By changing the scale of either the vertical or the horizontal axis, you can affect the apparent visual strength of the relationship.

Following are three scatter diagrams (Chart 4–2). The one on the left shows a rather strong positive relationship between the age in years and the maintenance cost last year for a sample of 10 buses owned by the city of Cleveland, Ohio. Note that as the age of the bus increases, the yearly maintenance cost also increases. The example in the center, for a sample of 20 vehicles, shows a rather strong indirect relationship between the odometer reading and the auction price. That is, as the number of miles driven increases, the auction price decreases. The example on the right depicts the relationship between the height and yearly salary for a sample of 15 shift supervisors. This graph indicates there is little relationship between their height and yearly salary.

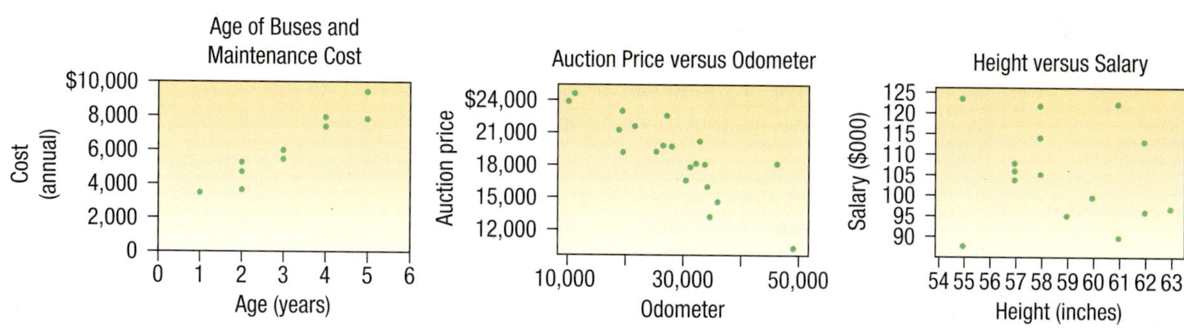

CHART 4–2 Three Examples of Scatter Diagrams.

EXAMPLE

In the introduction to Chapter 2, we presented data from the Applewood Auto Group. We gathered information concerning several variables, including the profit earned from the sale of 180 vehicles sold last month. In addition to the amount of profit on each sale, one of the other variables is the age of the purchaser. Is there a relationship between the profit earned on a vehicle sale and the age of the purchaser? Would it be reasonable to conclude that more profit is made on vehicles purchased by older buyers?

SOLUTION

We can investigate the relationship between vehicle profit and the age of the buyer with a scatter diagram. We scale age on the horizontal, or X-axis, and the profit on the vertical, or Y-axis. We assume profit depends on the age of the purchaser. As people age, they earn more income and purchase more expensive cars which, in turn, produce higher profits. We use Excel to develop the scatter diagram. The Excel commands are in Appendix C.

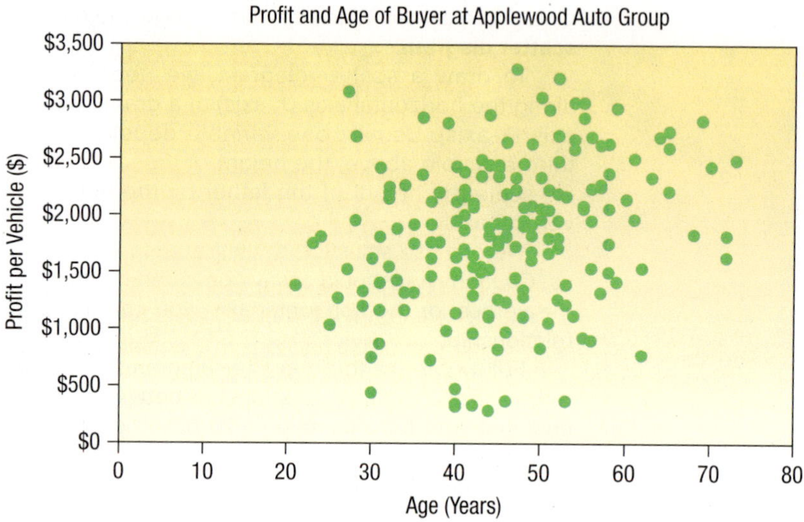

The scatter diagram shows a rather weak positive relationship between the two variables. It does not appear there is much relationship between the vehicle profit and the age of the buyer. In Chapter 13, we will study the relationship between variables more extensively, even calculating several numerical measures to express the relationship between variables.

In the preceding example, there is a weak positive, or direct, relationship between the variables. There are, however, many instances where there is a relationship between the variables, but that relationship is inverse or negative. For example:

- The value of a vehicle and the number of miles driven. As the number of miles increases, the value of the vehicle decreases.
- The premium for auto insurance and the age of the driver. Auto rates tend to be the highest for younger drivers and less for older drivers.
- For many law enforcement personnel, as the number of years on the job increases, the number of traffic citations decreases. This may be because personnel become more liberal in their interpretations or they may be in supervisor positions and not in a position to issue as many citations. But in any event, as age increases, the number of citations decreases.

LO4-7
Develop and explain a contingency table.

CONTINGENCY TABLES

A scatter diagram requires that both of the variables be at least interval scale. In the Applewood Auto Group example, both age and vehicle profit are ratio scale variables. Height is also ratio scale as used in the discussion of the relationship between the height of fathers and the height of their sons. What if we wish to study the relationship between two variables when one or both are nominal or ordinal scale? In this case, we tally the results in a **contingency table.**

CONTINGENCY TABLE A table used to classify observations according to two identifiable characteristics.

A contingency table is a cross-tabulation that simultaneously summarizes two variables of interest. For example:

- Students at a university are classified by gender and class (freshman, sophomore, junior, or senior).
- A product is classified as acceptable or unacceptable and by the shift (day, afternoon, or night) on which it is manufactured.
- A voter in a school bond referendum is classified as to party affiliation (Democrat, Republican, other) and the number of children that voter has attending school in the district (0, 1, 2, etc.).

EXAMPLE

There are four dealerships in the Applewood Auto Group. Suppose we want to compare the profit earned on each vehicle sold by the particular dealership. To put it another way, is there a relationship between the amount of profit earned and the dealership?

SOLUTION

In a contingency table, both variables only need to be nominal or ordinal. In this example, the variable dealership is a nominal variable and the variable profit is a ratio variable. To convert profit to an ordinal variable, we classify the variable profit into two categories, those cases where the profit earned is more than the median and those cases where it is less. On page 64, we calculated the median profit for all sales last month at Applewood Auto Group to be $1,882.50.

Contingency Table Showing the Relationship between Profit and Dealership

Above/Below Median Profit	Kane	Olean	Sheffield	Tionesta	Total
Above	25	20	19	26	90
Below	27	20	26	17	90
Total	52	40	45	43	180

By organizing the information into a contingency table, we can compare the profit at the four dealerships. We observe the following:

- From the Total column on the right, 90 of the 180 cars sold had a profit above the median and half below. From the definition of the median, this is expected.
- For the Kane dealership, 25 out of the 52, or 48%, of the cars sold were sold for a profit more than the median.
- The percentage of profits above the median for the other dealerships are 50% for Olean, 42% for Sheffield, and 60% for Tionesta.

We will return to the study of contingency tables in Chapter 5 during the study of probability and in Chapter 15 during the study of nonparametric methods of analysis.

SELF-REVIEW 4–5

The rock group Blue String Beans is touring the United States. The following chart shows the relationship between concert seating capacity and revenue in $000 for a sample of concerts.

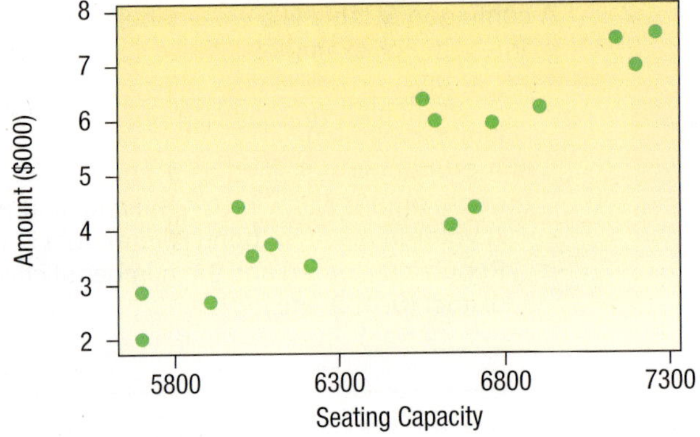

(a) What is the diagram called?
(b) How many concerts were studied?
(c) Estimate the revenue for the concert with the largest seating capacity.
(d) How would you characterize the relationship between revenue and seating capacity? Is it strong or weak, direct or inverse?

EXERCISES

23. FILE Develop a scatter diagram for the following sample data. How would you describe the relationship between the values?

x-Value	*y*-Value	*x*-Value	*y*-Value
10	6	11	6
8	2	10	5
9	6	7	2
11	5	7	3
13	7	11	7

24. Silver Springs Moving and Storage Inc. is studying the relationship between the number of rooms in a move and the number of labor hours required for the move. As part of the analysis, the CFO of Silver Springs developed the following scatter diagram.

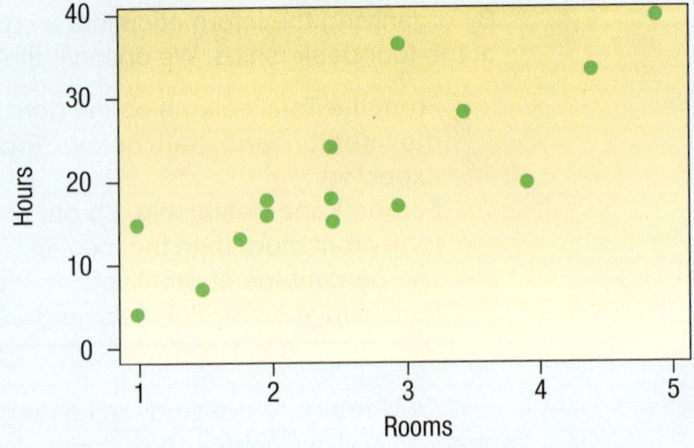

a. How many moves are in the sample?
b. Does it appear that more labor hours are required as the number of rooms increases, or do labor hours decrease as the number of rooms increases?

25. The Director of Planning for Devine Dining Inc. wishes to study the relationship between the gender of a guest and whether the guest orders dessert. To investigate the relationship, the manager collected the following information on 200 recent customers.

	Gender		
Dessert Ordered	**Male**	**Female**	**Total**
Yes	32	15	47
No	68	85	153
Total	100	100	200

a. What is the level of measurement of the two variables?
b. What is the above table called?
c. Does the evidence in the table suggest men are more likely to order dessert than women? Explain why.

26. Ski Resorts of Vermont Inc. is considering a merger with Gulf Shores Beach Resorts Inc. of Alabama. The board of directors surveyed 50 stockholders concerning their position on the merger. The results are reported below.

	Opinion			
Number of Shares Held	**Favor**	**Oppose**	**Undecided**	**Total**
Under 200	8	6	2	16
200 up to 1,000	6	8	1	15
Over 1,000	6	12	1	19
Total	20	26	4	50

a. What level of measurement is used in this table?
b. What is this table called?
c. What group seems most strongly opposed to the merger?

CHAPTER SUMMARY

I. A dot plot shows the range of values on the horizontal axis and the number of observations for each value on the vertical axis.
  A. Dot plots report the details of each observation.
  B. They are useful for comparing two or more data sets.

II. A stem-and-leaf display is an alternative to a histogram.
  A. The leading digit is the stem and the trailing digit the leaf.
  B. The advantages of a stem-and-leaf display over a histogram include:
    1. The identity of each observation is not lost.
    2. The digits themselves give a picture of the distribution.
    3. The cumulative frequencies are also shown.

III. Measures of location also describe the shape of a set of observations.
  A. Quartiles divide a set of observations into four equal parts.
    1. Twenty-five percent of the observations are less than the first quartile, 50% are less than the second quartile, and 75% are less than the third quartile.
    2. The interquartile range is the difference between the third quartile and the first quartile.
  B. Deciles divide a set of observations into 10 equal parts and percentiles into 100 equal parts.

IV. A box plot is a graphic display of a set of data.

A. A box is drawn enclosing the regions between the first quartile and the third quartile.

1. A line is drawn inside the box at the median value.

2. Dotted line segments are drawn from the third quartile to the largest value to show the highest 25% of the values and from the first quartile to the smallest value to show the lowest 25% of the values.

B. A box plot is based on five statistics: the maximum and minimum values, the first and third quartiles, and the median.

V. The coefficient of skewness is a measure of the symmetry of a distribution.

A. There are two formulas for the coefficient of skewness.

1. The formula developed by Pearson is:

$$sk = \frac{3(\bar{x} - \text{Median})}{s} \qquad \textbf{[4–2]}$$

2. The coefficient of skewness computed by statistical software is:

$$sk = \frac{n}{(n-1)(n-2)}\left[\Sigma\left(\frac{x-\bar{x}}{s}\right)^3\right] \qquad \textbf{[4–3]}$$

VI. A scatter diagram is a graphic tool to portray the relationship between two variables.

A. Both variables are measured with interval or ratio scales.

B. If the scatter of points moves from the lower left to the upper right, the variables under consideration are directly or positively related.

C. If the scatter of points moves from the upper left to the lower right, the variables are inversely or negatively related.

VII. A contingency table is used to classify nominal-scale observations according to two characteristics.

PRONUNCIATION KEY

SYMBOL	MEANING	PRONUNCIATION
L_p	Location of percentile	*L* sub *p*
Q_1	First quartile	*Q* sub 1
Q_3	Third quartile	*Q* sub 3

CHAPTER EXERCISES

27. A sample of students attending Southeast Florida University is asked the number of social activities in which they participated last week. The chart below was prepared from the sample data.

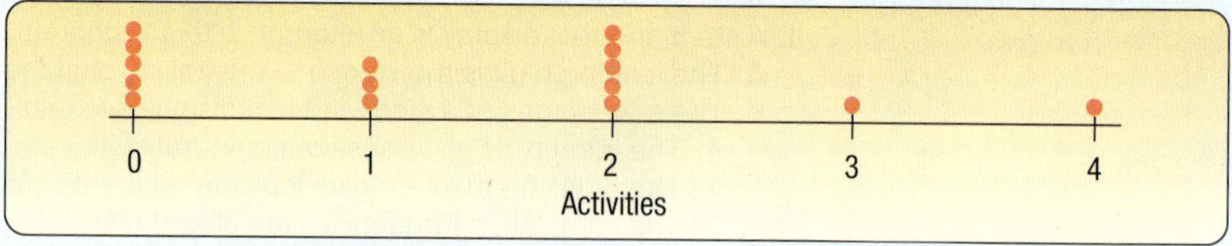

a. What is the name given to this chart?

b. How many students were in the study?

c. How many students reported attending no social activities?

28. Doctor's Care is a walk-in clinic, with locations in Georgetown, Moncks Corner, and Aynor, at which patients may receive treatment for minor injuries, colds, and flu, as well as physical examinations. The following charts report the number of patients treated in each of the three locations last month.

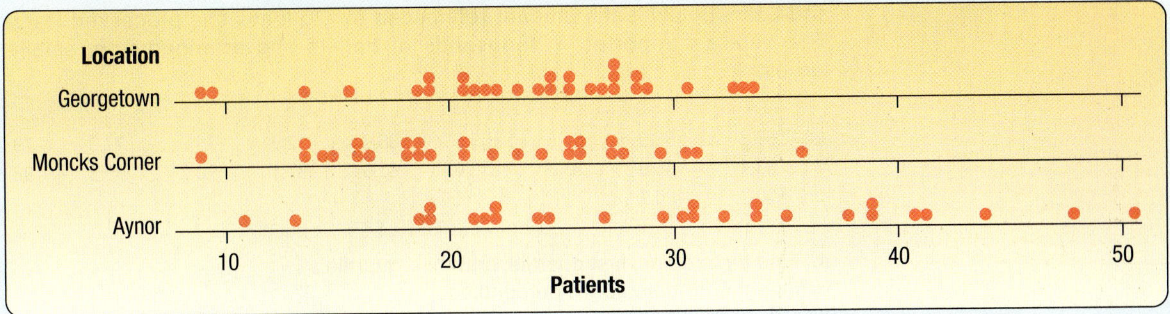

Describe the number of patients served at the three locations each day. What are the maximum and minimum numbers of patients served at each of the locations?

29. FILE Below is the number of customers who visited Smith's True-Value hardware store in Bellville, Ohio, over the last twenty-three days. Make a stem-and-leaf display of this variable.

46	52	46	40	42	46	40	37	46	40	52	32	37	32	52
40	32	52	40	52	46	46	52							

30. FILE The top 25 companies (by market capitalization) operating in the Washington, DC, area along with the year they were founded and the number of employees are given below. Make a stem-and-leaf display of each of these variables and write a short description of your findings.

Company Name	Year Founded	Employees
AES Corp.	1981	30,000
American Capital Ltd.	1986	484
AvalonBay Communities Inc.	1978	1,767
Capital One Financial Corp.	1995	31,800
Constellation Energy Group Inc.	1816	9,736
Coventry Health Care Inc.	1986	10,250
Danaher Corp.	1984	45,000
Dominion Resources Inc.	1909	17,500
Fannie Mae	1938	6,450
Freddie Mac	1970	5,533
Gannett Co.	1906	49,675
General Dynamics Corp.	1952	81,000
Genworth Financial Inc.	2004	7,200
Harman International Industries Inc.	1980	11,246
Host Hotels & Resorts Inc.	1927	229
Legg Mason	1899	3,800
Lockheed Martin Corp.	1995	140,000
Marriott International Inc.	1927	151,000
MedImmune LLC	1988	2,516
NII Holdings Inc.	1996	7,748
Norfolk Southern Corp.	1982	30,594
Pepco Holdings Inc.	1896	5,057
Sallie Mae	1972	11,456
T. Rowe Price Group Inc.	1937	4,605
The Washington Post Co.	1877	17,100

31. FILE In recent years, due to low interest rates, many homeowners refinanced their home mortgages. Linda Lahey is a mortgage officer at Down River Federal Savings and Loan. Below is the amount refinanced for 20 loans she processed last week. The data are reported in thousands of dollars and arranged from smallest to largest.

59.2	59.5	61.6	65.5	66.6	72.9	74.8	77.3	79.2
83.7	85.6	85.8	86.6	87.0	87.1	90.2	93.3	98.6
100.2	100.7							

a. Find the median, first quartile, and third quartile.
b. Find the 26th and 83rd percentiles.
c. Draw a box plot of the data.

32. **FILE** A study is made by the recording industry in the United States of the number of music CDs owned by 25 senior citizens and 30 young adults. The information is reported below.

Seniors									
28	35	41	48	52	81	97	98	98	99
118	132	133	140	145	147	153	158	162	174
177	180	180	187	188					

Young Adults									
81	107	113	147	147	175	183	192	202	209
233	251	254	266	283	284	284	316	372	401
417	423	490	500	507	518	550	557	590	594

a. Find the median and the first and third quartiles for the number of CDs owned by senior citizens. Develop a box plot for the information.
b. Find the median and the first and third quartiles for the number of CDs owned by young adults. Develop a box plot for the information.
c. Compare the number of CDs owned by the two groups.

33. **FILE** The corporate headquarters of *Bank.com,* an on-line banking company, is located in downtown Philadelphia. The director of human resources is making a study of the time it takes employees to get to work. The city is planning to offer incentives to each downtown employer if they will encourage their employees to use public transportation. Below is a listing of the time to get to work this morning according to whether the employee used public transportation or drove a car.

Public Transportation									
23	25	25	30	31	31	32	33	35	36
37	42								

Private									
32	32	33	34	37	37	38	38	38	39
40	44								

a. Find the median and the first and third quartiles for the time it took employees using public transportation. Develop a box plot for the information.
b. Find the median and the first and third quartiles for the time it took employees who drove their own vehicle. Develop a box plot for the information.
c. Compare the times of the two groups.

34. The following box plot shows the number of daily newspapers published in each state and the District of Columbia. Write a brief report summarizing the number published. Be sure to include information on the values of the first and third quartiles,

the median, and whether there is any skewness. If there are any outliers, estimate their value.

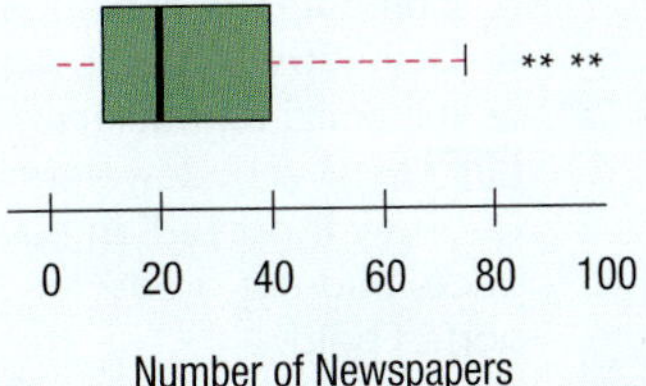

35. Walter Gogel Company is an industrial supplier of fasteners, tools, and springs. The amounts of its invoices vary widely, from less than $20.00 to more than $400.00. During the month of January the company sent out 80 invoices. Here is a box plot of these invoices. Write a brief report summarizing the invoice amounts. Be sure to include information on the values of the first and third quartiles, the median, and whether there is any skewness. If there are any outliers, approximate the value of these invoices.

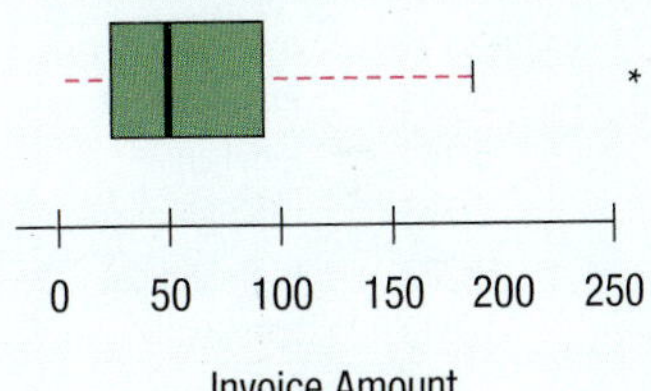

36. FILE The American Society of PeriAnesthesia Nurses (ASPAN; www.aspan.org) is a national organization serving nurses practicing in ambulatory surgery, preanesthesia, and postanesthesia care. The organization consists of the 40 components listed below.

State/Region	Membership	State/Region	Membership
Alabama	95	New Jersey, Bermuda	517
Arizona	399	Alaska, Idaho, Montana, Oregon, Washington	708
Maryland, Delaware, DC	531	New York	891
Connecticut	239	Ohio	708
Florida	631	Oklahoma	171
Georgia	384	Arkansas	68
Hawaii	73	California	1,165
Illinois	562	New Mexico	79
Indiana	270	Pennsylvania	575
Iowa	117	Rhode Island	53
Kentucky	197	Colorado	409
Louisiana	258	South Carolina	237
Michigan	411	Texas	1,026
Massachusetts	480	Tennessee	167
Maine	97	Utah	67
Minnesota, Dakotas	289	Virginia	414
Missouri, Kansas	282	Vermont, New Hampshire	144
Mississippi	90	Wisconsin	311
Nebraska	115	West Virginia	62
North Carolina	542		
Nevada	106		

Use statistical software to answer the following questions.

a. Find the mean, median, and standard deviation of the number of members per component.

b. Find the coefficient of skewness, using the software. What do you conclude about the shape of the distribution of component size?

c. Compute the first and third quartiles using formula (4–1).

d. Develop a box plot. Are there any outliers? Which components are outliers? What are the limits for outliers?

37. FILE McGivern Jewelers is located in the Levis Square Mall just south of Toledo, Ohio. Recently it posted an advertisement on a social media site reporting the shape, size, price, and cut grade for 33 of its diamonds currently in stock. The information is reported below.

Shape	Size (carats)	Price	Cut Grade	Shape	Size (carats)	Price	Cut Grade
Princess	5.03	$44,312	Ideal cut	Round	0.77	$2,828	Ultra ideal cut
Round	2.35	20,413	Premium cut	Oval	0.76	3,808	Premium cut
Round	2.03	13,080	Ideal cut	Princess	0.71	2,327	Premium cut
Round	1.56	13,925	Ideal cut	Marquise	0.71	2,732	Good cut
Round	1.21	7,382	Ultra ideal cut	Round	0.70	1,915	Premium cut
Round	1.21	5,154	Average cut	Round	0.66	1,885	Premium cut
Round	1.19	5,339	Premium cut	Round	0.62	1,397	Good cut
Emerald	1.16	5,161	Ideal cut	Round	0.52	2,555	Premium cut
Round	1.08	8,775	Ultra ideal cut	Princess	0.51	1,337	Ideal cut
Round	1.02	4,282	Premium cut	Round	0.51	1,558	Premium cut
Round	1.02	6,943	Ideal cut	Round	0.45	1,191	Premium cut
Marquise	1.01	7,038	Good cut	Princess	0.44	1,319	Average cut
Princess	1.00	4,868	Premium cut	Marquise	0.44	1,319	Premium cut
Round	0.91	5,106	Premium cut	Round	0.40	1,133	Premium cut
Round	0.90	3,921	Good cut	Round	0.35	1,354	Good cut
Round	0.90	3,733	Premium cut	Round	0.32	896	Premium cut
Round	0.84	2,621	Premium cut				

a. Develop a box plot of the variable price and comment on the result. Are there any outliers? What is the median price? What are the values of the first and the third quartiles?

b. Develop a box plot of the variable size and comment on the result. Are there any outliers? What is the median price? What are the values of the first and the third quartiles?

c. Develop a scatter diagram between the variables price and size. Be sure to put price on the vertical axis and size on the horizontal axis. Does there seem to be an association between the two variables? Is the association direct or indirect? Does any point seem to be different from the others?

d. Develop a contingency table for the variables shape and cut grade. What is the most common cut grade? What is the most common shape? What is the most common combination of cut grade and shape?

38. FILE Listed below is the amount of commissions earned last month for the eight members of the sales staff at Best Electronics. Calculate the coefficient of skewness using both methods. Hint: Use of a spreadsheet will expedite the calculations.

980.9	1,036.5	1,099.5	1,153.9	1,409.0	1,456.4	1,718.4	1,721.2

39. FILE Listed below is the number of car thefts in a large city over the last week. Calculate the coefficient of skewness using both methods. Hint: Use of a spreadsheet will expedite the calculations.

3	12	13	7	8	3	8

40. The manager of Information Services at Wilkin Investigations, a private investigation firm, is studying the relationship between the age (in months) of a combination printer, copier, and fax machine and its monthly maintenance cost. For a sample of 15 machines, the manager developed the following chart. What can the manager conclude about the relationship between the variables?

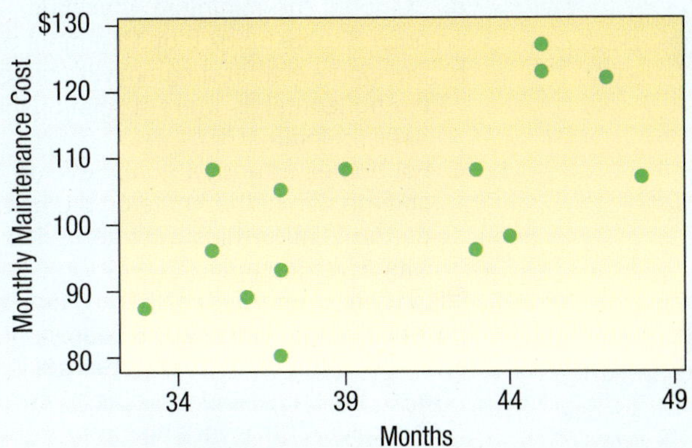

41. FILE An auto insurance company reported the following information regarding the age of a driver and the number of accidents reported last year. Develop a scatter diagram for the data and write a brief summary.

Age	Accidents	Age	Accidents
16	4	23	0
24	2	27	1
18	5	32	1
17	4	22	3

42. Wendy's offers eight different condiments (mustard, catsup, onion, mayonnaise, pickle, lettuce, tomato, and relish) on hamburgers. A store manager collected the following information on the number of condiments ordered and the age group of the customer. What can you conclude regarding the information? Who tends to order the most or least number of condiments?

	Age			
Number of Condiments	Under 18	18 up to 40	40 up to 60	60 or older
0	12	18	24	52
1	21	76	50	30
2	39	52	40	12
3 or more	71	87	47	28

43. Here is a table showing the number of employed and unemployed workers 20 years or older by gender in the United States.

	Number of Workers (000)	
Gender	Employed	Unemployed
Men	70,415	4,209
Women	61,402	3,314

a. How many workers were studied?
b. What percent of the workers were unemployed?
c. Compare the percent unemployed for the men and the women.

DATA ANALYTICS

44. FILE Refer to the North Valley real estate data recorded on homes sold during the last year. Prepare a report on the selling prices of the homes based on the answers to the following questions.

a. Compute the minimum, maximum, median, and the first and the third quartiles of price. Create a box plot. Comment on the distribution of home prices.

b. Develop a scatter diagram with price on the vertical axis and the size of the home on the horizontal. Is there a relationship between these variables? Is the relationship direct or indirect?

c. For homes without a pool, develop a scatter diagram with price on the vertical axis and the size of the home on the horizontal. Do the same for homes with a pool. How do the relationships between price and size for homes without a pool and homes with a pool compare?

45. FILE Refer to the Baseball 2016 data that report information on the 30 Major League Baseball teams for the 2016 season.

a. In the data set, the year opened, is the first year of operation for that stadium. For each team, use this variable to create a new variable, stadium age, by subtracting the value of the variable, year opened, from the current year. Develop a box plot with the new variable, age. Are there any outliers? If so, which of the stadiums are outliers?

b. Using the variable, salary, create a box plot. Are there any outliers? Compute the quartiles using formula (4–1). Write a brief summary of your analysis.

c. Draw a scatter diagram with the variable, wins, on the vertical axis and salary on the horizontal axis. What are your conclusions?

d. Using the variable, wins, draw a dot plot. What can you conclude from this plot?

46. FILE Refer to the Lincolnville School District bus data.

a. Referring to the maintenance cost variable, develop a box plot. What are the minimum, first quartile, median, third quartile, and maximum values? Are there any outliers?

b. Using the median maintenance cost, develop a contingency table with bus manufacturer as one variable and whether the maintenance cost was above or below the median as the other variable. What are your conclusions?

A REVIEW OF CHAPTERS 1–4

This section is a review of the major concepts and terms introduced in Chapters 1–4. Chapter 1 began by describing the meaning and purpose of statistics. Next we described the different types of variables and the four levels of measurement. Chapter 2 was concerned with describing a set of observations by organizing it into a frequency distribution and then portraying the frequency distribution as a histogram or a frequency polygon. Chapter 3 began by describing measures of location, such as the mean, weighted mean, median, geometric mean, and mode. This chapter also included measures of dispersion, or spread. Discussed in this section were the range, variance, and standard deviation. Chapter 4 included several graphing techniques such as dot plots, box plots, and scatter diagrams. We also discussed the coefficient of skewness, which reports the lack of symmetry in a set of data.

Throughout this section we stressed the importance of statistical software, such as Excel and Minitab. Many computer outputs in these chapters demonstrated how quickly and effectively a large data set can be organized into a frequency distribution, several of the measures of location or measures of variation calculated, and the information presented in graphical form.

PROBLEMS

1. **FILE** The duration in minutes of a sample of 50 power outages last year in the state of South Carolina is listed below.

124	14	150	289	52	156	203	82	27	248
39	52	103	58	136	249	110	298	251	157
186	107	142	185	75	202	119	219	156	78
116	152	206	117	52	299	58	153	219	148
145	187	165	147	158	146	185	186	149	140

Use a statistical software package such as Excel or Minitab to help answer the following questions.

a. Determine the mean, median, and standard deviation.
b. Determine the first and third quartiles.
c. Develop a box plot. Are there any outliers? Do the amounts follow a symmetric distribution or are they skewed? Justify your answer.
d. Organize the distribution of funds into a frequency distribution.
e. Write a brief summary of the results in parts a to d.

2. **FILE** Listed below are the 45 U.S. presidents and their age as they began their terms in office.

Number	Name	Age	Number	Name	Age
1	Washington	57	24	Cleveland	55
2	J. Adams	61	25	McKinley	54
3	Jefferson	57	26	T. Roosevelt	42
4	Madison	57	27	Taft	51
5	Monroe	58	28	Wilson	56
6	J. Q. Adams	57	29	Harding	55
7	Jackson	61	30	Coolidge	51
8	Van Buren	54	31	Hoover	54
9	W. H. Harrison	68	32	F. D. Roosevelt	51
10	Tyler	51	33	Truman	60
11	Polk	49	34	Eisenhower	62
12	Taylor	64	35	Kennedy	43
13	Fillmore	50	36	L. B. Johnson	55
14	Pierce	48	37	Nixon	56
15	Buchanan	65	38	Ford	61
16	Lincoln	52	39	Carter	52
17	A. Johnson	56	40	Reagan	69
18	Grant	46	41	G. H. W. Bush	64
19	Hayes	54	42	Clinton	46
20	Garfield	49	43	G. W. Bush	54
21	Arthur	50	44	Obama	47
22	Cleveland	47	45	Trump	70
23	B. Harrison	55			

Use a statistical software package such as Excel or Minitab to help answer the following questions.

a. Determine the mean, median, and standard deviation.
b. Determine the first and third quartiles.
c. Develop a box plot. Are there any outliers? Do the amounts follow a symmetric distribution or are they skewed? Justify your answer.
d. Organize the distribution of ages into a frequency distribution.
e. Write a brief summary of the results in parts a to d.

3. FILE Listed below is the 2014 median household income for the 50 states and the District of Columbia. https://www.census.gov/hhes/www/income/data/historical/household/

State	Amount	State	Amount
Alabama	42,278	Montana	51,102
Alaska	67,629	Nebraska	56,870
Arizona	49,254	Nevada	49,875
Arkansas	44,922	New Hampshire	73,397
California	60,487	New Jersey	65,243
Colorado	60,940	New Mexico	46,686
Connecticut	70,161	New York	54,310
Delaware	57,522	North Carolina	46,784
D.C.	68,277	North Dakota	60,730
Florida	46,140	Ohio	49,644
Georgia	49,555	Oklahoma	47,199
Hawaii	71,223	Oregon	58,875
Idaho	53,438	Pennsylvania	55,173
Illinois	54,916	Rhode Island	58,633
Indiana	48,060	South Carolina	44,929
Iowa	57,810	South Dakota	53,053
Kansas	53,444	Tennessee	43,716
Kentucky	42,786	Texas	53,875
Louisiana	42,406	Utah	63,383
Maine	51,710	Vermont	60,708
Maryland	76,165	Virginia	66,155
Massachusetts	63,151	Washington	59,068
Michigan	52,005	West Virginia	39,552
Minnesota	67,244	Wisconsin	58,080
Mississippi	35,521	Wyoming	55,690
Missouri	56,630		

Use a statistical software package such as Excel or Minitab to help answer the following questions.

a. Determine the mean, median, and standard deviation.

b. Determine the first and third quartiles.

c. Develop a box plot. Are there any outliers? Do the amounts follow a symmetric distribution or are they skewed? Justify your answer.

d. Organize the distribution of funds into a frequency distribution.

e. Write a brief summary of the results in parts a to d.

4. A sample of 12 homes sold last week in St. Paul, Minnesota, revealed the following information. Draw a scatter diagram. Can we conclude that, as the size of the home (reported below in thousands of square feet) increases, the selling price (reported in $ thousands) also increases?

Home Size (thousands of square feet)	Selling Price ($ thousands)	Home Size (thousands of square feet)	Selling Price ($ thousands)
1.4	100	1.3	110
1.3	110	0.8	85
1.2	105	1.2	105
1.1	120	0.9	75
1.4	80	1.1	70
1.0	105	1.1	95

5. Refer to the following diagram.

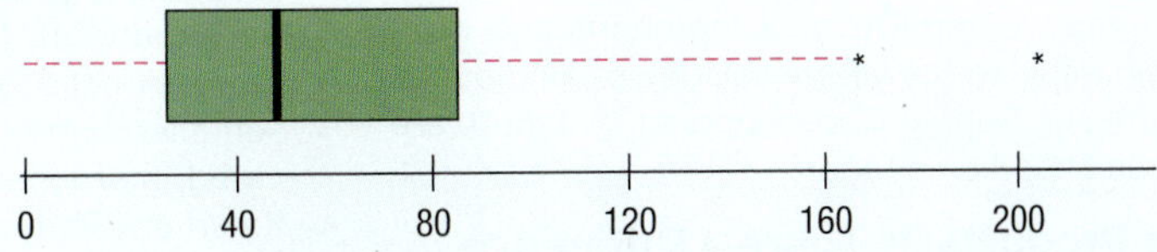

a. What is the graph called?
b. What are the median, and first and third quartile values?
c. Is the distribution positively skewed? Tell how you know.
d. Are there any outliers? If yes, estimate these values.
e. Can you determine the number of observations in the study?

CASES

A. Century National Bank

The following case will appear in subsequent review sections. Assume that you work in the Planning Department of the Century National Bank and report to Ms. Lamberg. You will need to do some data analysis and prepare a short written report. Remember, Mr. Selig is the president of the bank, so you will want to ensure that your report is complete and accurate. A copy of the data appears in Appendix A.6.

Century National Bank has offices in several cities in the Midwest and the southeastern part of the United States. Mr. Dan Selig, president and CEO, would like to know the characteristics of his checking account customers. What is the balance of a typical customer?

How many other bank services do the checking account customers use? Do the customers use the ATM service and, if so, how often? What about debit cards? Who uses them, and how often are they used?

To better understand the customers, Mr. Selig asked Ms. Wendy Lamberg, director of planning, to select a sample of customers and prepare a report. To begin, she has appointed a team from her staff. You are the head of the team and responsible for preparing the report. You select a random sample of 60 customers. In addition to the balance in each account at the end of last month, you determine (1) the number of ATM (automatic teller machine) transactions in the last month; (2) the number of other bank services (a savings account, a certificate of deposit, etc.) the customer uses; (3) whether the customer has a debit card (this is a bank service in which charges are made directly to the customer's account); and (4) whether or not interest is paid on the checking account. The sample includes customers from the branches in Cincinnati, Ohio; Atlanta, Georgia; Louisville, Kentucky; and Erie, Pennsylvania.

1. Develop a graph or table that portrays the checking balances. What is the balance of a typical customer? Do many customers have more than $2,000 in their accounts? Does it appear that there is a difference in the distribution of the accounts among the four branches? Around what value do the account balances tend to cluster?
2. Determine the mean and median of the checking account balances. Compare the mean and the median balances for the four branches. Is there a difference among the branches? Be sure to explain the difference between the mean and the median in your report.
3. Determine the range and the standard deviation of the checking account balances. What do the first and third quartiles show? Determine the coefficient of skewness and indicate what it shows. Because Mr. Selig does not deal with statistics daily, include a brief description and interpretation of the standard deviation and other measures.

B. Wildcat Plumbing Supply Inc.: Do We Have Gender Differences?

Wildcat Plumbing Supply has served the plumbing needs of Southwest Arizona for more than 40 years. The company was founded by Mr. Terrence St. Julian and is run today by his son Cory. The company has grown from a handful of employees to more than 500 today. Cory is concerned about several positions within the company where he has men and women doing essentially the same job but at different pay. To investigate, he collected the information below. Suppose you are a student intern in the Accounting Department and have been given the task to write a report summarizing the situation.

Yearly Salary ($000)	Women	Men
Less than 30	2	0
30 up to 40	3	1
40 up to 50	17	4
50 up to 60	17	24
60 up to 70	8	21
70 up to 80	3	7
80 or more	0	3

To kick off the project, Mr. Cory St. Julian held a meeting with his staff and you were invited. At this meeting, it was suggested that you calculate several measures of location, create charts or draw graphs such as a cumulative frequency distribution, and determine the quartiles for both men and women. Develop the charts and write the report summarizing the yearly salaries of employees at Wildcat Plumbing Supply. Does it appear that there are pay differences based on gender?

C. Kimble Products: Is There a Difference In the Commissions?

At the January national sales meeting, the CEO of Kimble Products was questioned extensively regarding the company policy for paying commissions to its sales representatives. The company sells sporting goods to two major markets. There are 40 sales representatives who call directly on large-volume customers, such as the athletic departments at major colleges and universities and professional sports franchises. There are 30 sales representatives who represent the company to retail stores located in shopping malls and large discounters such as Kmart and Target.

Upon his return to corporate headquarters, the CEO asked the sales manager for a report comparing the commissions earned last year by the two parts of the sales team. The information is reported below. Write a brief report. Would you conclude that there is a difference? Be sure to include information in the report on both the central tendency and dispersion of the two groups.

Commissions Earned by Sales Representatives Calling on Athletic Departments ($)

354	87	1,676	1,187	69	3,202	680	39	1,683	1,106
883	3,140	299	2,197	175	159	1,105	434	615	149
1,168	278	579	7	357	252	1,602	2,321	4	392
416	427	1,738	526	13	1,604	249	557	635	527

Commissions Earned by Sales Representatives Calling on Large Retailers ($)

1,116	681	1,294	12	754	1,206	1,448	870	944	1,255
1,213	1,291	719	934	1,313	1,083	899	850	886	1,556
886	1,315	1,858	1,262	1,338	1,066	807	1,244	758	918

PRACTICE TEST

There is a practice test at the end of each review section. The tests are in two parts. The first part contains several objective questions, usually in a fill-in-the-blank format. The second part is problems. In most cases, it should take 30 to 45 minutes to complete the test. The problems require a calculator. Check the answers in the Answer Section in the back of the book.

Part 1—Objective

1. The science of collecting, organizing, presenting, analyzing, and interpreting data to assist in making effective decisions is called ________. 1. ________
2. Methods of organizing, summarizing, and presenting data in an informative way are called ________. 2. ________
3. The entire set of individuals or objects of interest or the measurements obtained from all individuals or objects of interest are called the ________. 3. ________
4. List the two types of variables. 4. ________
5. The number of bedrooms in a house is an example of a ________. (discrete variable, continuous variable, qualitative variable—pick one) 5. ________
6. The jersey numbers of Major League Baseball players are an example of what level of measurement? 6. ________
7. The classification of students by eye color is an example of what level of measurement? 7. ________
8. The sum of the differences between each value and the mean is always equal to what value? 8. ________
9. A set of data contained 70 observations. How many classes would the 2^k method suggest to construct a frequency distribution? 9. ________
10. What percent of the values in a data set are always larger than the median? 10. ________
11. The square of the standard deviation is the ________. 11. ________
12. The standard deviation assumes a negative value when ________. (all the values are negative, at least half the values are negative, or never—pick one.) 12. ________
13. Which of the following is least affected by an outlier? (mean, median, or range—pick one) 13. ________

Part 2—Problems

1. The Russell 2000 index of stock prices increased by the following amounts over the last 3 years.

18%	4%	2%

What is the geometric mean increase for the 3 years? ________

2. The information below refers to the selling prices ($000) of homes sold in Warren, Pennsylvania, during 2016.

Selling Price ($000)	Frequency
120.0 up to 150.0	4
150.0 up to 180.0	18
180.0 up to 210.0	30
210.0 up to 240.0	20
240.0 up to 270.0	17
270.0 up to 300.0	10
300.0 up to 330.0	6

a. What is the class interval? ______
b. How many homes were sold in 2016? ______
c. How many homes sold for less than $210,000? ______
d. What is the relative frequency of the 210 up to 240 class? ______
e. What is the midpoint of the 150 up to 180 class? ______
f. The selling prices range between what two amounts? ______

3. A sample of eight college students revealed they owned the following number of CDs.

52	76	64	79	80	74	66	69

a. What is the mean number of CDs owned? ______
b. What is the median number of CDs owned? ______
c. What is the 40th percentile? ______
d. What is the range of the number of CDs owned? ______
e. What is the standard deviation of the number of CDs owned? ______

4. An investor purchased 200 shares of the Blair Company for $36 each in July of 2013, 300 shares at $40 each in September 2015, and 500 shares at $50 each in January 2016. What is the investor's weighted mean price per share? ______

5. During the 50th Super Bowl, 30 million pounds of snack food were eaten. The chart below depicts this information.

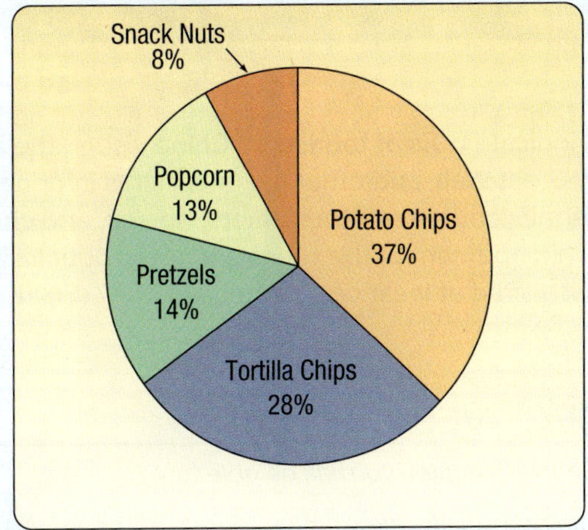

a. What is the name given to this graph? ______
b. Estimate, in millions of pounds, the amount of potato chips eaten during the game. ______
c. Estimate the relationship of potato chips to popcorn. (twice as much, half as much, three times, none of these—pick one) ______
d. What percent of the total do potato chips and tortilla chips comprise? ______

A Survey of Probability Concepts

RECENT SURVEYS indicate 60% of tourists to China visited the Forbidden City, the Temple of Heaven, the Great Wall, and other historical sites in or near Beijing. Forty percent visited Xi'an and its magnificent terra-cotta soldiers, horses, and chariots, which lay buried for over 2,000 years. Thirty percent of the tourists went to both Beijing and Xi'an. What is the probability that a tourist visited at least one of these places? (See Exercise 76 and LO5-3.)

LEARNING OBJECTIVES

When you have completed this chapter, you will be able to:

LO5-1 Define the terms *probability, experiment, event,* and *outcome.*

LO5-2 Assign probabilities using a classical, empirical, or subjective approach.

LO5-3 Calculate probabilities using the rules of addition.

LO5-4 Calculate probabilities using the rules of multiplication.

LO5-5 Compute probabilities using a contingency table.

LO5-6 Calculate probabilities using Bayes' theorem.

LO5-7 Determine the number of outcomes using principles of counting.

INTRODUCTION

The emphasis in Chapters 2, 3, and 4 is on descriptive statistics. In Chapter 2, we organize the profits on 180 vehicles sold by the Applewood Auto Group into a frequency distribution. This frequency distribution shows the smallest and the largest profits and where the largest concentration of data occurs. In Chapter 3, we use numerical measures of location and dispersion to locate a typical profit on vehicle sales and to examine the variation in the profit of a sale. We describe the variation in the profits with such measures of dispersion as the range and the standard deviation. In Chapter 4, we develop charts and graphs, such as a scatter diagram or a dot plot, to further describe the data graphically.

Descriptive statistics is concerned with summarizing data collected from past events. We now turn to the second facet of statistics, namely, *computing the chance that something will occur in the future*. This facet of statistics is called **statistical inference** or **inferential statistics.**

Seldom does a decision maker have complete information to make a decision. For example:

© Ballda/Shutterstock.com

- Toys and Things, a toy and puzzle manufacturer, recently developed a new game based on sports trivia. It wants to know whether sports buffs will purchase the game. "Slam Dunk" and "Home Run" are two of the names under consideration. To investigate, the president of Toys and Things decided to hire a market research firm. The firm selected a sample of 800 consumers from the population and asked each respondent for a reaction to the new game and its proposed titles. Using the sample results, the company can estimate the proportion of the population that will purchase the game.
- The quality assurance department of a U.S. Steel mill must assure management that the quarter-inch wire being produced has an acceptable tensile strength. Clearly, not all the wire produced can be tested for tensile strength because testing requires the wire to be stretched until it breaks—thus destroying it. So a random sample of 10 pieces is selected and tested. Based on the test results, all the wire produced is deemed to be either acceptable or unacceptable.
- Other questions involving uncertainty are: Should the daytime drama *Days of Our Lives* be discontinued immediately? Will a newly developed mint-flavored cereal be profitable if marketed? Will Charles Linden be elected to county auditor in Batavia County?

STATISTICS IN ACTION

Government statistics show there are about 1.7 automobile-caused fatalities for every 100,000,000 vehicle-miles. If you drive 1 mile to the store to buy your lottery ticket and then return home, you have driven 2 miles. Thus the probability that you will join this statistical group on your next 2-mile round trip is $2 \times 1.7/100{,}000{,}000 = 0.000000034$. This can also be stated as "One in 29,411,765." Thus, if you drive to the store to buy your Powerball ticket, your chance of being killed (or killing someone else) is more than 4 times greater than the chance that you will win the Powerball Jackpot, one chance in 120,526,770.
http://www.durangobill.com/PowerballOdds.html

Statistical inference deals with conclusions about a population based on a sample taken from that population. (The populations for the preceding illustrations are all consumers who like sports trivia games, all the quarter-inch steel wire produced, all television viewers who watch soaps, all who purchase breakfast cereal, and so on.)

Because there is uncertainty in decision making, it is important that all the known risks involved be scientifically evaluated. Helpful in this evaluation is *probability theory,* often referred to as the science of uncertainty. Probability theory allows the decision maker to analyze the risks and minimize the gamble inherent, for example, in marketing a new product or accepting an incoming shipment possibly containing defective parts.

Because probability concepts are so important in the field of statistical inference (to be discussed starting with Chapter 8), this chapter introduces the basic language of probability, including such terms as *experiment, event, subjective probability,* and *addition* and *multiplication rules*.

LO5-1
Define the terms *probability, experiment, event,* and *outcome.*

WHAT IS A PROBABILITY?

No doubt you are familiar with terms such as *probability, chance,* and *likelihood.* They are often used interchangeably. The weather forecaster announces that there is a 70% chance of rain for Super Bowl Sunday. Based on a survey of consumers who tested a newly developed toothpaste with a banana flavor, the probability is .03 that, if marketed, it will be a financial success. (This means that the chance of the banana-flavor toothpaste being accepted by the public is rather remote.) What is a **probability?** In general, it is a numerical value that describes the chance that something will happen.

PROBABILITY A value between zero and one, inclusive, describing the relative possibility (chance or likelihood) an event will occur.

A probability is frequently expressed as a decimal, such as .70, .27, or .50, or a percent such as 70%, 27% or 50%. It also may be reported as a fraction such as 7/10, 27/100, or 1/2. It can assume any number from 0 to 1, inclusive. Expressed as a percentage, the range is between 0% and 100%, inclusive. If a company has only five sales regions, and each region's name or number is written on a slip of paper and the slips put in a hat, the probability of selecting one of the five regions is 1. The probability of selecting from the hat a slip of paper that reads "Pittsburgh Steelers" is 0. Thus, the probability of 1 represents something that is certain to happen, and the probability of 0 represents something that cannot happen.

The closer a probability is to 0, the more improbable it is the event will happen. The closer the probability is to 1, the more likely it will happen. The relationship is shown in the following diagram along with a few of our personal beliefs. You might, however, select a different probability for Slo Poke's chances to win the Kentucky Derby or for an increase in federal taxes.

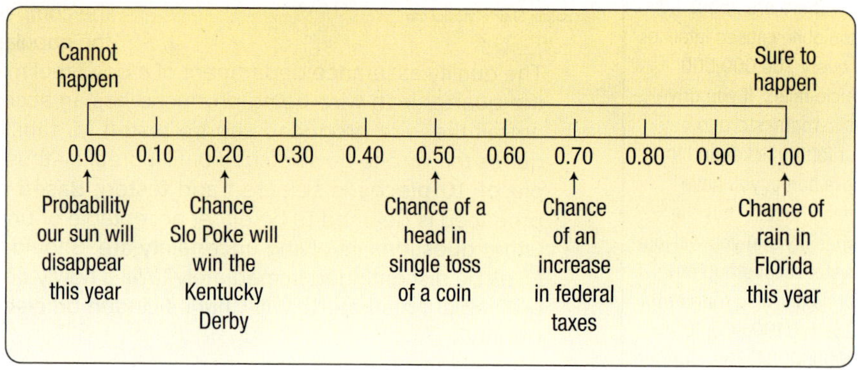

Sometimes, the likelihood of an event is expressed using the term *odds*. To explain, someone says the odds are "five to two" that an event will occur. This means that in a total of seven trials (5 + 2), the event will occur five times and not occur two times. Using odds, we can compute the probability that the event occurs as 5/(5 + 2) or 5/7. So, if the odds in favor of an event are x to y, the probability of the event is $x/(x + y)$.

Three key words are used in the study of probability: **experiment, outcome,** and **event.** These terms are used in our everyday language, but in statistics they have specific meanings.

EXPERIMENT A process that leads to the occurrence of one and only one of several possible results.

This definition is more general than the one used in the physical sciences, where we picture someone manipulating test tubes or microscopes. In reference to probability, an experiment has two or more possible results, and it is uncertain which will occur.

OUTCOME A particular result of an experiment.

For example, the tossing of a coin is an experiment. You are unsure of the outcome. When a coin is tossed, one particular outcome is a "head." The alternative outcome is a "tail." Similarly, asking 500 college students if they would travel more than 100 miles to attend a Mumford and Sons concert is an experiment. In this experiment, one possible outcome is that 273 students indicate they would travel more than 100 miles to attend the concert. Another outcome is that 317 students would attend the concert. Still another outcome is that 423 students indicate they would attend the concert. When one or more of the experiment's outcomes are observed, we call this an event.

EVENT A collection of one or more outcomes of an experiment.

Examples to clarify the definitions of the terms *experiment, outcome,* and *event* are presented in the following figure.

In the die-rolling experiment, there are six possible outcomes, but there are many possible events. When counting the number of members of the board of directors for Fortune 500 companies over 60 years of age, the number of possible outcomes can be anywhere from zero to the total number of members. There are an even larger number of possible events in this experiment.

Experiment	Roll a die	Count the number of members of the board of directors for Fortune 500 companies who are over 60 years of age
All possible outcomes	Observe a 1 Observe a 2 Observe a 3 Observe a 4 Observe a 5 Observe a 6	None is over 60 One is over 60 Two are over 60 ... 29 are over 60 ... ... 48 are over 60 ...
Some possible events	Observe an even number Observe a number greater than 4 Observe a number 3 or less	More than 13 are over 60 Fewer than 20 are over 60

SELF-REVIEW 5–1

Video Games Inc. recently developed a new video game. Its playability is to be tested by 80 veteran game players.

(a) What is the experiment?
(b) What is one possible outcome?
(c) Suppose 65 of the 80 players testing the new game said they liked it. Is 65 a probability?
(d) The probability that the new game will be a success is computed to be −1.0. Comment.
(e) Specify one possible event.

LO5-2
Assign probabilities using a classical, empirical, or subjective approach.

APPROACHES TO ASSIGNING PROBABILITIES

In this section, we describe three ways to assign a probability to an event: classical, empirical, and subjective. The classical and empirical methods are objective and are based on information and data. The subjective method is based on a person's belief or estimate of an event's likelihood.

Classical Probability

Classical probability is based on the assumption that the outcomes of an experiment are *equally likely*. Using the classical viewpoint, the probability of an event happening is computed by dividing the number of favorable outcomes by the number of possible outcomes:

CLASSICAL PROBABILITY

$$\text{Probability of an event} = \frac{\text{Number of favorable outcomes}}{\text{Total number of possible outcomes}} \quad \textbf{[5–1]}$$

EXAMPLE

Consider an experiment of rolling a six-sided die. What is the probability of the event "an even number of spots appear face up"?

SOLUTION

The possible outcomes are:

There are three "favorable" outcomes (a two, a four, and a six) in the collection of six equally likely possible outcomes. Therefore:

$$\text{Probability of an even number} = \frac{3}{6} \begin{array}{l} \leftarrow \text{Number of favorable outcomes} \\ \leftarrow \text{Total number of possible outcomes} \end{array}$$
$$= .5$$

The **mutually exclusive** concept appeared earlier in our study of frequency distributions in Chapter 2. Recall that we create classes so that a particular value is included in only one of the classes and there is no overlap between classes. Thus, only one of several events can occur at a particular time.

MUTUALLY EXCLUSIVE The occurrence of one event means that none of the other events can occur at the same time.

The variable "gender" presents mutually exclusive outcomes, male and female. An employee selected at random is either male or female but cannot be both. A manufactured part is acceptable or unacceptable. The part cannot be both acceptable and unacceptable at the same time. In a sample of manufactured parts, the event of selecting an unacceptable part and the event of selecting an acceptable part are mutually exclusive.

If an experiment has a set of events that includes every possible outcome, such as the events "an even number" and "an odd number" in the die-tossing experiment, then the set of events is **collectively exhaustive.** For the die-tossing experiment, every outcome will be either even or odd. So the set is collectively exhaustive.

COLLECTIVELY EXHAUSTIVE At least one of the events must occur when an experiment is conducted.

If the set of events is collectively exhaustive and the events are mutually exclusive, the sum of the probabilities is 1. Historically, the classical approach to probability was developed and applied in the 17th and 18th centuries to games of chance, such as cards and dice. It is unnecessary to do an experiment to determine the probability of an event occurring using the classical approach because the total number of outcomes is known before the experiment. The flip of a coin has two possible outcomes; the roll of a die has six possible outcomes. We can logically arrive at the probability of getting a tail on the toss of one coin or three heads on the toss of three coins.

The classical approach to probability can also be applied to lotteries. In South Carolina, one of the games of the Education Lottery is "Pick 3." A person buys a lottery ticket and selects three numbers between 0 and 9. Once per week, the three numbers are randomly selected from a machine that tumbles three containers each with balls numbered 0 through 9. One way to win is to match the numbers and the order of the numbers. Given that 1,000 possible outcomes exist (000 through 999), the probability of winning with any three-digit number is 0.001, or 1 in 1,000.

Empirical Probability

Empirical or relative frequency is the second type of objective probability. It is based on the number of times an event occurs as a proportion of a known number of trials.

EMPIRICAL PROBABILITY The probability of an event happening is the fraction of the time similar events happened in the past.

The formula to determine an empirical probability is:

$$\text{Empirical probability} = \frac{\text{Number of times the event occurs}}{\text{Total number of observations}}$$

The empirical approach to probability is based on what is called the **law of large numbers.** The key to establishing probabilities empirically is that more observations will provide a more accurate estimate of the probability.

LAW OF LARGE NUMBERS Over a large number of trials, the empirical probability of an event will approach its true probability.

To explain the law of large numbers, suppose we toss a fair coin. The result of each toss is either a head or a tail. With just one toss of the coin the empirical probability for heads is either zero or one. If we toss the coin a great number of times, the probability of the outcome of heads will approach .5. The following table reports the results of seven different experiments of flipping a fair coin 1, 10, 50, 100, 500, 1,000, and 10,000 times and then computing the relative frequency of heads. Note as we increase the number of trials, the empirical probability of a head appearing approaches .5, which is its value based on the classical approach to probability.

Number of Trials	Number of Heads	Relative Frequency of Heads
1	0	.00
10	3	.30
50	26	.52
100	52	.52
500	236	.472
1,000	494	.494
10,000	5,027	.5027

What have we demonstrated? Based on the classical definition of probability, the likelihood of obtaining a head in a single toss of a fair coin is .5. Based on the empirical or relative frequency approach to probability, the probability of the event happening approaches the same value based on the classical definition of probability.

This reasoning allows us to use the empirical or relative frequency approach to finding a probability. Here are some examples.

- Last semester, 80 students registered for Business Statistics 101 at Scandia University. Twelve students earned an A. Based on this information and the empirical approach to assigning a probability, we estimate the likelihood a student at Scandia will earn an A is .15.
- Stephen Curry of the Golden State Warriors made 363 out of 400 free throw attempts during the 2015–16 NBA season. Based on the empirical approach to probability, the likelihood of him making his next free throw attempt is .908.

Life insurance companies rely on past data to determine the acceptability of an applicant as well as the premium to be charged. Mortality tables list the likelihood a person of a particular age will die within the upcoming year. For example, the likelihood a 20-year-old female will die within the next year is .00105.

The empirical concept is illustrated with the following example.

EXAMPLE

On February 1, 2003, the Space Shuttle *Columbia* exploded. This was the second disaster in 113 space missions for NASA. On the basis of this information, what is the probability that a future mission is successfully completed?

SOLUTION

We use letters or numbers to simplify the equations. *P* stands for probability and *A* represents the event of a successful mission. In this case, *P*(*A*) stands for the probability a future mission is successfully completed.

$$\text{Probability of a successful flight} = \frac{\text{Number of successful flights}}{\text{Total number of flights}}$$

$$P(A) = \frac{111}{113} = .98$$

We can use this as an estimate of probability. In other words, based on past experience, the probability is .98 that a future space shuttle mission will be safely completed.

Subjective Probability

If there is little or no experience or information on which to base a probability, it is estimated subjectively. Essentially, this means an individual evaluates the available opinions and information and then estimates or assigns the probability. This probability is called a **subjective probability.**

SUBJECTIVE CONCEPT OF PROBABILITY The likelihood (probability) of a particular event happening that is assigned by an individual based on whatever information is available.

Illustrations of subjective probability are:

1. Estimating the likelihood the New England Patriots will play in the Super Bowl next year.
2. Estimating the likelihood you are involved in an automobile accident during the next 12 months.
3. Estimating the likelihood the U.S. budget deficit will be reduced by half in the next 10 years.

The types of probability are summarized in Chart 5–1. A probability statement always assigns a likelihood to an event that has not yet occurred. There is, of course, considerable latitude in the degree of uncertainty that surrounds this probability, based primarily on the knowledge possessed by the individual concerning the underlying process. The individual possesses a great deal of knowledge about the toss of a die and can state that the probability that a one-spot will appear face up on the toss of a true die is one-sixth. But we know very little concerning the acceptance in the marketplace of a new and untested product. For example, even though a market research director tests a newly developed product in 40 retail stores and states that there is a 70% chance that the product will have sales of more than 1 million units, she has limited knowledge of how consumers will react when it is marketed nationally. In both cases (the case of the person rolling a die and the testing of a new product), the individual is assigning a probability value to an event of interest, and a difference exists only in the predictor's confidence in the precision of the estimate. However, regardless of the viewpoint, the same laws of probability (presented in the following sections) will be applied.

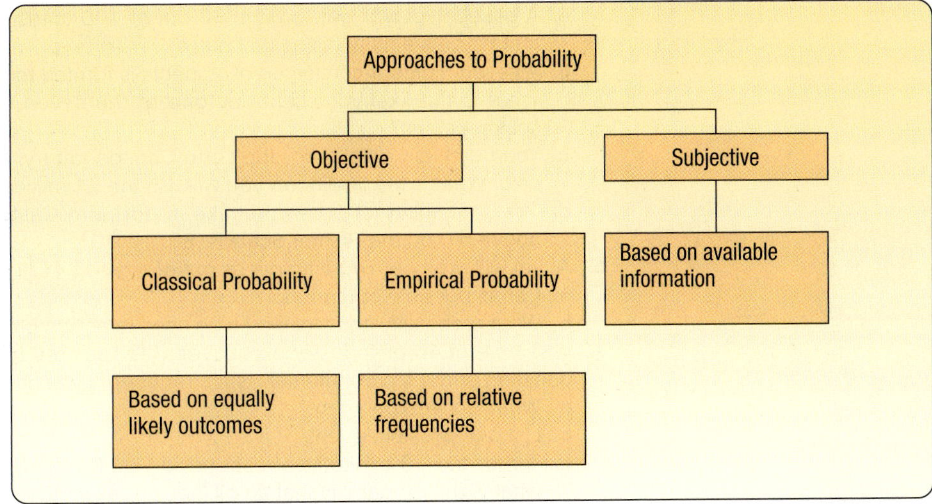

CHART 5–1 Summary of Approaches to Probability

SELF-REVIEW 5–2

1. One card will be randomly selected from a standard 52-card deck. What is the probability the card will be a queen? Which approach to probability did you use to answer this question?
2. The Center for Child Care reports on 539 children and the marital status of their parents. There are 333 married, 182 divorced, and 24 widowed parents. What is the probability a particular child chosen at random will have a parent who is divorced? Which approach did you use?
3. What is the probability you will save one million dollars by the time you retire? Which approach to probability did you use to answer this question?

EXERCISES

1. Some people are in favor of reducing federal taxes to increase consumer spending and others are against it. Two persons are selected and their opinions are recorded. Assuming no one is undecided, list the possible outcomes.

2. A quality control inspector selects a part to be tested. The part is then declared acceptable, repairable, or scrapped. Then another part is tested. List the possible outcomes of this experiment regarding two parts.

3. FILE A survey of 34 students at the Wall College of Business showed the following majors:

Accounting	10
Finance	5
Economics	3
Management	6
Marketing	10

From the 34 students, suppose you randomly select a student.

a. What is the probability he or she is a management major?
b. Which concept of probability did you use to make this estimate?

4. A large company must hire a new president. The Board of Directors prepares a list of five candidates, all of whom are equally qualified. Two of these candidates are members of a minority group. To avoid bias in the selection of the candidate, the company decides to select the president by lottery.

a. What is the probability one of the minority candidates is hired?
b. Which concept of probability did you use to make this estimate?

5. In each of the following cases, indicate whether classical, empirical, or subjective probability is used.

a. A baseball player gets a hit in 30 out of 100 times at bat. The probability is .3 that he gets a hit in his next at bat.
b. A seven-member committee of students is formed to study environmental issues. What is the likelihood that any one of the seven is randomly chosen as the spokesperson?
c. You purchase a ticket for the Lotto Canada lottery. Over 5 million tickets were sold. What is the likelihood you will win the $1 million jackpot?
d. The probability of an earthquake in northern California in the next 10 years above 5.0 on the Richter Scale is .80.

6. A firm will promote two employees out of a group of six men and three women.

a. List all possible outcomes.
b. What probability concept would be used to assign probabilities to the outcomes?

7. A sample of 40 oil industry executives was selected to test a questionnaire. One question about environmental issues required a yes or no answer.

a. What is the experiment?
b. List one possible event.
c. Ten of the 40 executives responded yes. Based on these sample responses, what is the probability that an oil industry executive will respond yes?
d. What concept of probability does this illustrate?
e. Are each of the possible outcomes equally likely and mutually exclusive?

8. **FILE** A sample of 2,000 licensed drivers revealed the following number of speeding violations.

Number of Violations	Number of Drivers
0	1,910
1	46
2	18
3	12
4	9
5 or more	5
Total	2,000

   a. What is the experiment?
   b. List one possible event.
   c. What is the probability that a particular driver had exactly two speeding violations?
   d. What concept of probability does this illustrate?

9. Bank of America customers select their own three-digit personal identification number (PIN) for use at ATMs.
   a. Think of this as an experiment and list four possible outcomes.
   b. What is the probability that a customer will pick 259 as their PIN?
   c. Which concept of probability did you use to answer (b)?

10. An investor buys 100 shares of AT&T stock and records its price change daily.
   a. List several possible events for this experiment.
   b. Which concept of probability did you use in (a)?

LO5-3
Calculate probabilities using the rules of addition.

RULES OF ADDITION FOR COMPUTING PROBABILITIES

There are two rules of addition, the special rule of addition and the general rule of addition. We begin with the special rule of addition.

Special Rule of Addition

When we use the **special rule of addition,** the events must be *mutually exclusive*. Recall that mutually exclusive means that when one event occurs, none of the other events can occur at the same time. An illustration of mutually exclusive events in the die-tossing experiment is the events "a number 4 or larger" and "a number 2 or smaller." If the outcome is in the first group {4, 5, and 6}, then it cannot also be in the second group {1 and 2}. Another illustration is a product coming off the assembly line cannot be defective and satisfactory at the same time.

If two events A and B are mutually exclusive, the special rule of addition states that the probability of one *or* the other event's occurring equals the sum of their probabilities. This rule is expressed in the following formula:

SPECIAL RULE OF ADDITION $$P(A \text{ or } B) = P(A) + P(B) \quad [5\text{–}2]$$

For three mutually exclusive events designated A, B, and C, the rule is written:

$$P(A \text{ or } B \text{ or } C) = P(A) + P(B) + P(C)$$

An example will show the details.

EXAMPLE

© Ian Dagnall/Alamy Stock Photo

A machine fills plastic bags with a mixture of beans, broccoli, and other vegetables. Most of the bags contain the correct weight, but because of the variation in the size of the beans and other vegetables, a package might be underweight or overweight. A check of 4,000 packages filled in the past month revealed:

Weight	Event	Number of Packages	Probability of Occurrence	
Underweight	*A*	100	.025	← $\frac{100}{4,000}$
Satisfactory	*B*	3,600	.900	
Overweight	*C*	300	.075	
		4,000	1.000	

What is the probability that a particular package will be either underweight or overweight?

SOLUTION

The outcome "underweight" is the event *A*. The outcome "overweight" is the event *C*. Applying the special rule of addition:

$$P(A \text{ or } C) = P(A) + P(C) = .025 + .075 = .10$$

Note that the events are mutually exclusive, meaning that a package of mixed vegetables cannot be underweight, satisfactory, and overweight at the same time. They are also collectively exhaustive; that is, a selected package must be either underweight, satisfactory, or overweight.

English logician J. Venn (1834–1923) developed a diagram to portray graphically the outcome of an experiment. The *mutually exclusive* concept and various other rules for combining probabilities can be illustrated using this device. To construct a Venn diagram, a space is first enclosed representing the total of all possible outcomes. This space is usually in the form of a rectangle. An event is then represented by a circular area that is drawn inside the rectangle proportional to the probability of the event. The following Venn diagram represents the *mutually exclusive* concept. There is no overlapping of events, meaning that the events are mutually exclusive. In the following Venn diagram, assume the events *A*, *B*, and *C* are about equally likely.

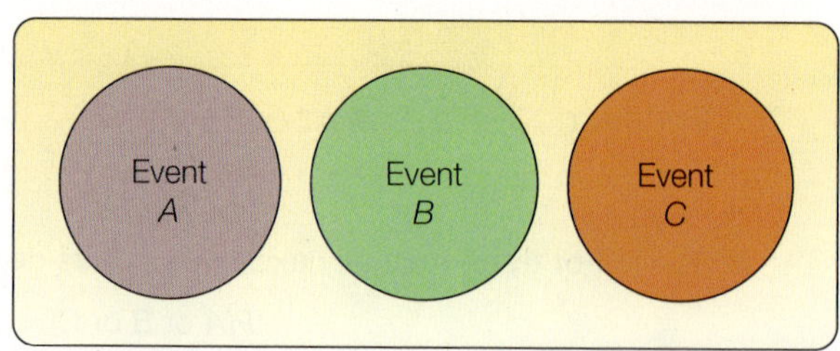

Complement Rule

The probability that a bag of mixed vegetables selected is underweight, $P(A)$, plus the probability that it is not an underweight bag, written $P(\sim A)$ and read "not A," must logically equal 1. This is written:

$$P(A) + P(\sim A) = 1$$

This can be revised to read:

COMPLEMENT RULE $$P(A) = 1 - P(\sim A) \qquad \textbf{[5–3]}$$

This is the **complement rule.** It is used to determine the probability of an event occurring by subtracting the probability of the event not occurring from 1. This rule is useful because sometimes it is easier to calculate the probability of an event happening by determining the probability of it not happening and subtracting the result from 1. Notice that the events A and $\sim A$ are mutually exclusive and collectively exhaustive. Therefore, the probabilities of A and $\sim A$ sum to 1. A Venn diagram illustrating the complement rule is shown as:

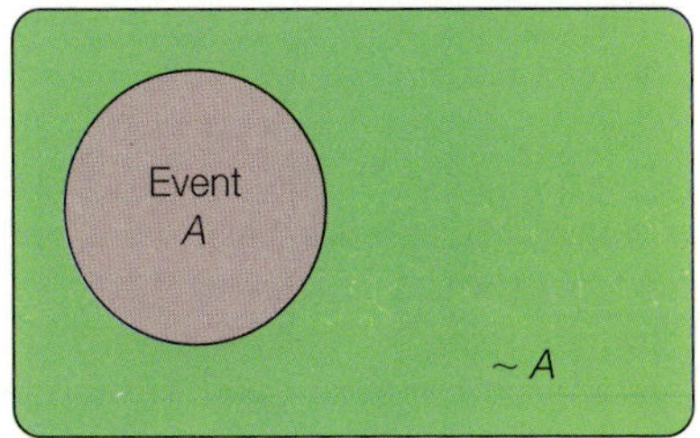

EXAMPLE

Referring to the previous example/solution, the probability a bag of mixed vegetables is underweight is .025 and the probability of an overweight bag is .075. Use the complement rule to show the probability of a satisfactory bag is .900. Show the solution using a Venn diagram.

SOLUTION

The probability the bag is unsatisfactory equals the probability the bag is overweight plus the probability it is underweight. That is, $P(A \text{ or } C) = P(A) + P(C) = .025 + .075 = .100$. The bag is satisfactory if it is not underweight or overweight, so $P(B) = 1 - [P(A) + P(C)] = 1 - [.025 + .075] = 0.900$. The Venn diagram portraying this situation is:

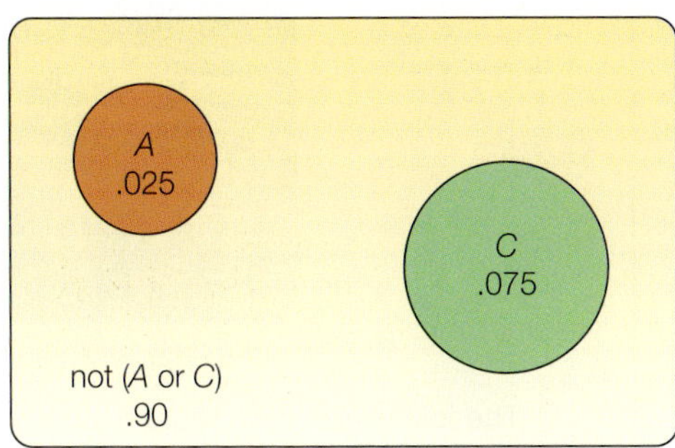

SELF-REVIEW 5–3

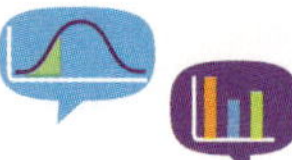

A sample of employees of Worldwide Enterprises is to be surveyed about a new health care plan. The employees are classified as follows:

Classification	Event	Number of Employees
Supervisors	A	120
Maintenance	B	50
Production	C	1,460
Management	D	302
Secretarial	E	68

(a) What is the probability that the first person selected is:
   (i) either in maintenance or a secretary?
   (ii) not in management?
(b) Draw a Venn diagram illustrating your answers to part (a).
(c) Are the events in part (a)(i) complementary or mutually exclusive or both?

The General Rule of Addition

The outcomes of an experiment may not be mutually exclusive. For example, the Florida Tourist Commission selected a sample of 200 tourists who visited the state during the year. The survey revealed that 120 tourists went to Disney World and 100 went to Busch Gardens near Tampa. What is the probability that a person selected visited either Disney World or Busch Gardens? If the special rule of addition is used, the probability of selecting a tourist who went to Disney World is .60, found by 120/200. Similarly, the probability of a tourist going to Busch Gardens is .50. The sum of these probabilities is 1.10. We know, however, that this probability cannot be greater than 1. The explanation is that many tourists visited both attractions and are being counted twice! A check of the survey responses revealed that 60 out of 200 sampled did, in fact, visit both attractions.

To answer our question, "What is the probability a selected person visited either Disney World or Busch Gardens?" (1) add the probability that a tourist visited Disney World and the probability he or she visited Busch Gardens, and (2) subtract the probability of visiting both. Thus:

$$P(\text{Disney or Busch}) = P(\text{Disney}) + P(\text{Busch}) - P(\text{both Disney and Busch})$$
$$= .60 + .50 - .30 = .80$$

When two events both occur, the probability is called a **joint probability.** The probability (.30) that a tourist visits both attractions is an example of a joint probability.

STATISTICS IN ACTION

If you wish to get some attention at the next gathering you attend, announce that you believe that at least two people present were born on the same date—that is, the same day of the year but not necessarily the same year. If there are 30 people in the room, the probability of a duplicate is .706. If there are 60 people in the room, the probability is .994 that at least two people share the same birthday. With as few as 23 people the chances are even, that is .50, that at least two people share the same birthday. Hint: To compute this, find the probability everyone was born on a different day and use the complement rule. Try this in your class.

© Rostislav Glinsky/Shutterstock.com

The following Venn diagram shows two events that are not mutually exclusive. The two events overlap to illustrate the joint event that some people have visited both attractions.

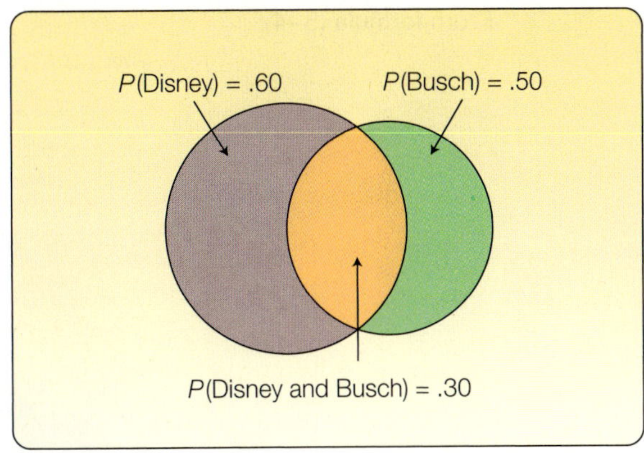

JOINT PROBABILITY A probability that measures the likelihood two or more events will happen concurrently.

So the general rule of addition, which is used to compute the probability of two events that are not mutually exclusive, is:

GENERAL RULE OF ADDITION $P(A \text{ or } B) = P(A) + P(B) - P(A \text{ and } B)$ **[5–4]**

For the expression $P(A$ or $B)$, the word *or* suggests that *A* may occur or *B* may occur. This also includes the possibility that *A* and *B* may occur. This use of *or* is sometimes called an **inclusive.** You could also write $P(A$ or B or both) to emphasize that the union of the events includes the intersection of *A* and *B*.

If we compare the general and special rules of addition, the important difference is determining if the events are mutually exclusive. If the events *are* mutually exclusive, then the joint probability $P(A$ and $B)$ is 0 and we could use the special rule of addition. Otherwise, we must account for the joint probability and use the general rule of addition.

EXAMPLE

What is the probability that a card chosen at random from a standard deck of cards will be either a king or a heart?

SOLUTION

We may be inclined to add the probability of a king and the probability of a heart. But this creates a problem. If we do that, the king of hearts is counted with the kings and also with the hearts. So, if we simply add the probability of a king (there are 4 in a deck of 52 cards) to the probability of a heart (there are 13 in a deck of 52 cards) and report that 17 out of 52 cards meet the requirement, we have counted the king of hearts twice. We need to subtract 1 card from the 17 so the king of hearts is counted only once. Thus, there are 16 cards that are either hearts or kings. So the probability is 16/52 = .3077.

Card	Probability	Explanation
King	$P(A)$ = 4/52	4 kings in a deck of 52 cards
Heart	$P(B)$ = 13/52	13 hearts in a deck of 52 cards
King of Hearts	$P(A$ and $B)$ = 1/52	1 king of hearts in a deck of 52 cards

From formula (5–4):

$$\begin{aligned} P(A \text{ or } B) &= P(A) + P(B) - P(A \text{ and } B) \\ &= 4/52 + 13/52 - 1/52 \\ &= 16/52, \text{ or } .3077 \end{aligned}$$

A Venn diagram portrays these outcomes, which are not mutually exclusive.

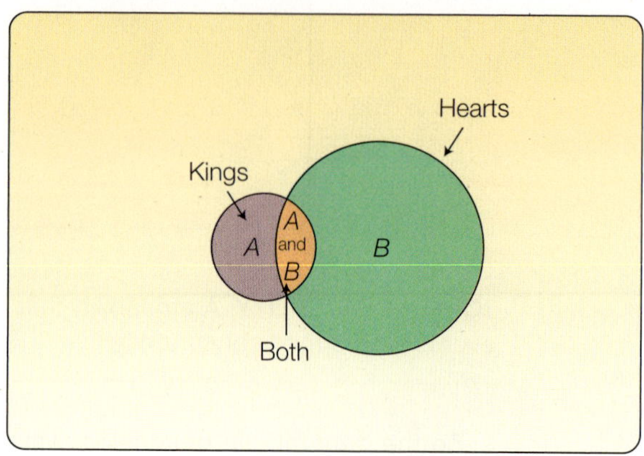

SELF-REVIEW 5–4

Routine physical examinations are conducted annually as part of a health service program for General Concrete Inc. employees. It was discovered that 8% of the employees need corrective shoes, 15% need major dental work, and 3% need both corrective shoes and major dental work.

(a) What is the probability that an employee selected at random will need either corrective shoes or major dental work?

(b) Show this situation in the form of a Venn diagram.

EXERCISES

11. The events A and B are mutually exclusive. Suppose $P(A) = .30$ and $P(B) = .20$. What is the probability of either A or B occurring? What is the probability that neither A nor B will happen?

12. The events X and Y are mutually exclusive. Suppose $P(X) = .05$ and $P(Y) = .02$. What is the probability of either X or Y occurring? What is the probability that neither X nor Y will happen?

13. **FILE** A study of 200 advertising firms revealed their income after taxes:

Income after Taxes	Number of Firms
Under $1 million	102
$1 million to $20 million	61
$20 million or more	37

a. What is the probability an advertising firm selected at random has under $1 million in income after taxes?

b. What is the probability an advertising firm selected at random has either an income between $1 million and $20 million, or an income of $20 million or more? What rule of probability was applied?

14. The chair of the board of directors says, "There is a 50% chance this company will earn a profit, a 30% chance it will break even, and a 20% chance it will lose money next quarter."

a. Use an addition rule to find the probability the company will not lose money next quarter.

b. Use the complement rule to find the probability it will not lose money next quarter.

15. Suppose the probability you will get an A in this class is .25 and the probability you will get a B is .50. What is the probability your grade will be above a C?

16. Two coins are tossed. If A is the event "two heads" and B is the event "two tails," are A and B mutually exclusive? Are they complements?
17. The probabilities of the events A and B are .20 and .30, respectively. The probability that both A and B occur is .15. What is the probability of either A or B occurring?
18. Let $P(X) = .55$ and $P(Y) = .35$. Assume the probability that they both occur is .20. What is the probability of either X or Y occurring?
19. Suppose the two events A and B are mutually exclusive. What is the probability of their joint occurrence?
20. A student is taking two courses, history and math. The probability the student will pass the history course is .60, and the probability of passing the math course is .70. The probability of passing both is .50. What is the probability of passing at least one?
21. The aquarium at Sea Critters Depot contains 140 fish. Eighty of these fish are green swordtails (44 female and 36 male) and 60 are orange swordtails (36 female and 24 males). A fish is randomly captured from the aquarium:
    a. What is the probability the selected fish is a green swordtail?
    b. What is the probability the selected fish is male?
    c. What is the probability the selected fish is a male green swordtail?
    d. What is the probability the selected fish is either a male or a green swordtail?
22. A National Park Service survey of visitors to the Rocky Mountain region revealed that 50% visit Yellowstone Park, 40% visit the Tetons, and 35% visit both.
    a. What is the probability a vacationer will visit at least one of these attractions?
    b. What is the probability .35 called?
    c. Are the events mutually exclusive? Explain.

LO5-4
Calculate probabilities using the rules of multiplication.

RULES OF MULTIPLICATION TO CALCULATE PROBABILITY

In this section, we discuss the rules for computing the likelihood that two events both happen, or their joint probability. For example, 16% of the 2016 tax returns were prepared by H&R Block and 75% of those returns showed a refund. What is the likelihood a person's tax form was prepared by H&R Block and the person received a refund? Venn diagrams illustrate this as the intersection of two events. To find the likelihood of two events happening, we use the rules of multiplication. There are two rules of multiplication: the special rule and the general rule.

Special Rule of Multiplication

The special rule of multiplication requires that two events A and B are **independent.** Two events are independent if the occurrence of one event does not alter the probability of the occurrence of the other event.

INDEPENDENCE The occurrence of one event has no effect on the probability of the occurrence of another event.

One way to think about independence is to assume that events A and B occur at different times. For example, when event B occurs after event A occurs, does A have any effect on the likelihood that event B occurs? If the answer is no, then A and B are independent events. To illustrate independence, suppose two coins are tossed. The outcome of a coin toss (head or tail) is unaffected by the outcome of any other prior coin toss (head or tail).

For two independent events A and B, the probability that A and B will both occur is found by multiplying the two probabilities. This is the **special rule of multiplication** and is written symbolically as:

SPECIAL RULE OF MULTIPLICATION $$P(A \text{ and } B) = P(A)P(B) \qquad [5\text{–}5]$$

For three independent events, A, B, and C, the special rule of multiplication used to determine the probability that all three events will occur is:

$$P(A \text{ and } B \text{ and } C) = P(A)P(B)P(C)$$

EXAMPLE

A survey by the American Automobile Association (AAA) revealed 60% of its members made airline reservations last year. Two members are selected at random. What is the probability both made airline reservations last year?

SOLUTION

The probability the first member made an airline reservation last year is .60, written $P(R_1) = .60$, where R_1 refers to the fact that the first member made a reservation. The probability that the second member selected made a reservation is also .60, so $P(R_2) = .60$. Because the number of AAA members is very large, you may assume that R_1 and R_2 are independent. Consequently, using formula (5–5), the probability they both make a reservation is .36, found by:

$$P(R_1 \text{ and } R_2) = P(R_1)P(R_2) = (.60)(.60) = .36$$

All possible outcomes can be shown as follows. R means a reservation is made, and $\sim R$ means no reservation is made.

With the probabilities and the complement rule, we can compute the joint probability of each outcome. For example, the probability that neither member makes a reservation is .16. Further, the probability of the first or the second member (special addition rule) making a reservation is .48 (.24 + .24). You can also observe that the outcomes are mutually exclusive and collectively exhaustive. Therefore, the probabilities sum to 1.00.

Outcomes	Joint Probability	
R_1 R_2	(.60)(.60) =	.36
R_1 $\sim R_2$	(.60)(.40) =	.24
$\sim R_1$ R_2	(.40)(.60) =	.24
$\sim R_1$ $\sim R_2$	(.40)(.40) =	.16
Total		1.00

STATISTICS IN ACTION

In 2000 George W. Bush won the U.S. presidency by the slimmest of margins. Many election stories resulted, some involving voting irregularities, others raising interesting election questions. In a local Michigan election, there was a tie between two candidates for an elected position. To break the tie, the candidates drew a slip of paper from a box that contained two slips of paper, one marked "Winner" and the other unmarked. To determine which candidate drew first, election officials flipped a coin. The winner of the coin flip also drew the winning slip of paper. But was the coin flip really necessary? No, because the two events are independent. Winning the coin flip did not alter the probability of either candidate drawing the winning slip of paper.

SELF-REVIEW 5–5

From experience, Teton Tire knows the probability is .95 that a particular XB-70 tire will last 60,000 miles before it becomes bald or fails. An adjustment is made on any tire that does not last 60,000 miles. You purchase four XB-70s. What is the probability all four tires will last at least 60,000 miles?

General Rule of Multiplication

If two events are not independent, they are referred to as **dependent.** To illustrate dependency, suppose there are 10 cans of soda in a cooler; 7 are regular and 3 are diet. A can is selected from the cooler. The probability of selecting a can of diet soda is 3/10, and the probability of selecting a can of regular soda is 7/10. Then a second can is selected from the cooler, without returning the first. The probability the second is diet depends on whether the first one selected was diet or not. The probability that the second is diet is:

2/9, if the first can is diet. (Only two cans of diet soda remain in the cooler.)
3/9, if the first can selected is regular. (All three diet sodas are still in the cooler.)

The fraction 2/9 (or 3/9) is called a **conditional probability** because its value is conditional on (dependent on) whether a diet or regular soda was the first selection from the cooler.

CONDITIONAL PROBABILITY The probability of a particular event occurring, given that another event has occurred.

In the general rule of multiplication, the conditional probability is required to compute the joint probability of two events that are not independent. For two events, A and B, that are not independent, the conditional probability is represented as $P(B|A)$, and expressed as the probability of B given A. Or the probability of B is conditional on the occurrence and effect of event A. Symbolically, the general rule of multiplication for two events that are not independent is:

GENERAL RULE OF MULTIPLICATION $P(A \text{ and } B) = P(A)P(B|A)$ **[5–6]**

EXAMPLE

A golfer has 12 golf shirts in his closet. Suppose 9 of these shirts are white and the others blue. He gets dressed in the dark, so he just grabs a shirt and puts it on. He plays golf two days in a row and does not launder and return the used shirts to the closet. What is the likelihood both shirts selected are white?

SOLUTION

The event that the first shirt selected is white is W_1. The probability is $P(W_1) = 9/12$ because 9 of the 12 shirts are white. The event that the second shirt selected is also white is identified as W_2. The conditional probability that the second shirt selected is white, given that the first shirt selected is also white, is $P(W_2|W_1) = 8/11$. Why is this so? Because after the first shirt is selected, there are only 11 shirts remaining in the closet and 8 of these are white. To determine the probability of 2 white shirts being selected, we use formula (5–6).

$$P(W_1 \text{ and } W_2) = P(W_1)P(W_2|W_1) = \left(\frac{9}{12}\right)\left(\frac{8}{11}\right) = .55$$

So the likelihood of selecting two shirts and finding them both to be white is .55.

We can extend the general rule of multiplication to more than two events. For three events A, B, and C, the formula is:

$$P(A \text{ and } B \text{ and } C) = P(A)P(B|A)P(C|A \text{ and } B)$$

In the case of the golf shirt example, the probability of selecting three white shirts without replacement is:

$$P(W_1 \text{ and } W_2 \text{ and } W_3) = P(W_1)P(W_2|W_1)P(W_3|W_1 \text{ and } W_2) = \left(\frac{9}{12}\right)\left(\frac{8}{11}\right)\left(\frac{7}{10}\right) = .38$$

So the likelihood of selecting three shirts without replacement and all being white is .38.

SELF-REVIEW 5–6

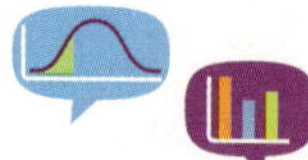

The board of directors of Tarbell Industries consists of eight men and four women. A four-member search committee is to be chosen at random to conduct a nationwide search for a new company president.

(a) What is the probability all four members of the search committee will be women?
(b) What is the probability all four members will be men?
(c) Does the sum of the probabilities for the events described in parts (a) and (b) equal 1? Explain.

LO5-5
Compute probabilities using a contingency table.

CONTINGENCY TABLES

Often we tally the results of a survey in a two-way table and use the results of this tally to determine various probabilities. We described this idea on page 116 in Chapter 4. To review, we refer to a two-way table as a **contingency table.**

CONTINGENCY TABLE A table used to classify sample observations according to two or more identifiable categories or classes.

A contingency table is a cross-tabulation that simultaneously summarizes two variables of interest and their relationship. The level of measurement can be nominal. Below are several examples.

- One hundred fifty adults were asked their gender and the number of Facebook accounts they used. The following table summarizes the results.

	Gender		
Facebook Accounts	**Men**	**Women**	**Total**
0	20	40	60
1	40	30	70
2 or more	10	10	20
Total	70	80	150

- The American Coffee Producers Association reports the following information on age and the amount of coffee consumed in a month.

	Coffee Consumption			
Age (Years)	**Low**	**Moderate**	**High**	**Total**
Under 30	36	32	24	92
30 up to 40	18	30	27	75
40 up to 50	10	24	20	54
50 and over	26	24	29	79
Total	90	110	100	300

According to this table, each of the 300 respondents is classified according to two criteria: (1) age and (2) the amount of coffee consumed.

The following example shows how the rules of addition and multiplication are used when we employ contingency tables.

EXAMPLE

Last month, the National Association of Theater Managers conducted a survey of 500 randomly selected adults. The survey asked respondents their age and the number of times they saw a movie in a theater. The results are summarized in Table 5–1.

TABLE 5–1 Number of Movies Attended per Month by Age

		Age		
Movies per Month	**Less than 30 B_1**	**30 up to 60 B_2**	**60 or Older B_3**	**Total**
0 A_1	15	50	10	75
1 or 2 A_2	25	100	75	200
3, 4, or 5 A_3	55	60	60	175
6 or more A_4	5	15	30	50
Total	100	225	175	500

The association is interested in understanding the probabilities that an adult will see a movie in a theater, especially for adults 60 and older. This information is useful for making decisions regarding discounts on tickets and concessions for seniors.

Determine the probability of:

1. Selecting an adult who attended 6 or more movies per month.
2. Selecting an adult who attended 2 or fewer movies per month.
3. Selecting an adult who attended 6 or more movies per month **or** is 60 years of age or older.
4. Selecting an adult who attended 6 or more movies per month **given** the person is 60 years of age or older.
5. Selecting an adult who attended 6 or more movies per month **and** is 60 years of age or older.

Determine the independence of:

6. Number of movies per month attended and the age of the adult.

SOLUTION

Table 5–1 is called a contingency table. In a contingency table, an individual or an object is classified according to two criteria. In this example, a sampled adult is classified by age and by the number of movies attended per month. The rules of addition [formulas (5–2) and (5–4)] and the rules of multiplication [formulas (5–5) and (5–6)] allow us to answer the various probability questions based on the contingency table.

1. To find the probability that a randomly selected adult attended 6 or more movies per month, focus on the row labeled "6 or more" (also labeled A_4) in Table 5–1. The table shows that 50 of the total of 500 adults are in this class. Using the empirical approach, the probability is computed:

$$P(\text{6 or more}) = P(A_4) = \frac{50}{500} = .10$$

This probability indicates 10% of the 500 adults attend 6 or more movies per month.

2. To determine the probability of randomly selecting an adult who went to 2 or fewer movies per month, two outcomes must be combined: attending 0 movies per month and attending 1 or 2 movies per month. These two outcomes are mutually exclusive. That is, a person can only be classified as attending 0

movies per month, or 1 or 2 movies per month, not both. Because the two outcomes are mutually exclusive, we use the special rule of addition [formula (5–2)] by adding the probabilities of attending no movies and attending 1 or 2 movies:

$$P[(\text{attending 0}) \text{ or } (\text{attending 1 or 2})] = P(A_1) + P(A_2) = \left(\frac{75}{500} + \frac{200}{500}\right) = .55$$

So 55% of the adults in the sample attended 2 or fewer movies a month.

3. To determine the probability of randomly selecting an adult who went to "6 or more" movies per month or whose age is "60 or older," we again use the rules of addition. However, in this case the outcomes are **not** mutually exclusive. Why is this? Because a person can attend more than 6 movies per month, be 60 or older, or be both. So the two groups are not mutually exclusive because it is possible that a person would be counted in both groups. To determine this probability, the general rule of addition [formula (5–4)] is used.

$$P[(\text{6 or more}) \text{ or } (\text{60 or older})] = P(A_4) + P(B_3) - P(A_4 \text{ and } B_3)$$
$$= \left(\frac{50}{500} + \frac{175}{500} - \frac{30}{500}\right) = .39$$

So 39% of the adults are either 60 or older, attend 6 or more movies per month, or both.

4. To determine the probability of selecting a person who attends 6 or more movies per month given that the person is 60 or older, focus only on the column labeled B_3 in Table 5–1. That is, we are only interested in the 175 adults who are 60 or older. Of these 175 adults, 30 attended 6 or more movies. Using the general rule of multiplication [formula (5–6)]:

$$P[(\text{6 or more}) \text{ given } (\text{60 or older})] = P(A_4|B_3) = \frac{30}{175} = .17$$

Of the 500 adults, 17% of adults who are 60 or older attend 6 or more movies per month. This is called a conditional probability because the probability is based on the "condition" of being the age of 60 or older. Recall that in part (1), 10% of all adults attend 6 or more movies per month; here we see that 17% of adults who are 60 or older attend movies. This is valuable information for theater managers regarding the characteristics of their customers.

5. The probability a person attended 6 or more movies and is 60 or older is based on two conditions and they must both happen. That is, the two outcomes "6 or more movies" (A_4) and "60 or older" (B_3) must occur jointly. To find this joint probability we use the special rule of multiplication [formula (5–6)].

$$P[(\text{6 or more}) \text{ and } (\text{60 or older})] = P(A_4 \text{ and } B_3) = P(A_4)P(B_3|A_4)$$

To compute the joint probability, first compute the simple probability of the first outcome, A_4, randomly selecting a person who attends 6 or more movies. To find the probability, refer to row A_4 in Table 5–1. There are 50 of 500 adults that attended 6 or more movies. So $P(A_4) = 50/500$.

Next, compute the conditional probability $P(B_3|A_4)$. This is the probability of selecting an adult who is 60 or older given that the person attended 6 or more movies. The conditional probability is:

$$P[(\text{60 or older}) \text{ given } (\text{60 or more})] = P(B_3|A_4) = 30/50$$

Using these two probabilities, the joint probability that an adult attends 6 or more movies and is 60 or older is:

$$P[(\text{6 or more}) \text{ and } (\text{60 or older})] = P(A_4 \text{ and } B_3) = P(A_4)P(B_3|A_4)$$
$$= (50/500)(30/50) = .06$$

Based on the sample information from Table 5–1, the probability that an adult is both over 60 and attended 6 or more movies is 6%. It is important to know that the 6% is relative to all 500 adults.

Is there another way to determine this joint probability without using the special rule of multiplication formula? Yes. Look directly at the cell where row A_4, attends 6 or more movies, and column B_3, 60 or older, intersect. There are 30 adults in this cell that meet both criteria, so $P(A_4 \text{ and } B_3) = 30/500 = .06$. This is the same as computed with the formula.

6. Are the events independent? We can answer this question with the help of the results in part 4. In part 4 we found the probability of selecting an adult who was 60 or older given that the adult attended 6 or more movies was .17. If age is not a factor in movie attendance then we would expect the probability of a person who is 30 or less that attended 6 or more movies to also be 17%. That is, the two conditional probabilities would be the same. The probability that an adult attends 6 or more movies per month given the adult is less than 30 years old is:

$$P[(\text{6 or more}) \text{ given } (\text{less than 30})] = \frac{5}{100} = .05$$

Because these two probabilities are not the same, the number of movies attended and age are not independent. To put it another way, for the 500 adults, age is related to the number of movies attended. In Chapter 15, we investigate this concept of independence in greater detail.

SELF-REVIEW 5–7

Refer to Table 5–1 on page 151 to find the following probabilities.

(a) What is the probability of selecting an adult that is 30 up to 60 years old?
(b) What is the probability of selecting an adult who is under 60 years of age?
(c) What is the probability of selecting an adult who is less than 30 years old or attended no movies?
(d) What is the probability of selecting an adult who is less than 30 years old and went to no movies?

Tree Diagrams

A **tree diagram** is a visual that is helpful in organizing and calculating probabilities for problems similar to the previous example/solution. This type of problem involves several stages and each stage is illustrated with a branch of the tree. The branches of a tree diagram are labeled with probabilities. We will use the information in Table 5–1 to show the construction of a tree diagram.

1. We begin the construction by drawing a box with the variable, age, on the left to represent the root of the tree (see Chart 5–2).
2. There are three main branches going out from the root. The upper branch represents the outcome that an adult is less than 30 years old. The branch is labeled with the probability, $P(B_1) = 100/500$. The next branch represents the outcome that adults are 30 up to 60 years old. This branch is labeled with the probability $P(B_2) = 225/500$. The remaining branch is labeled $P(B_3) = 175/500$.
3. Four branches "grow" out of each of the four main branches. These branches represent the four categories of movies attended per month—0; 1 or 2; 3, 4, or 5; and 6 or more. The upper branches of the tree represent the conditional probabilities that an adult did not attend any movies given they are less than 30 years old. These are written $P(A_1|B_1)$, $P(A_2|B_1)$, $P(A_3|B_1)$, and $P(A_4|B_1)$ where A_1 refers to attending no movies; A_2 attending 1 or 2 movies per month; A_3 attending 3, 4, or 5 movies

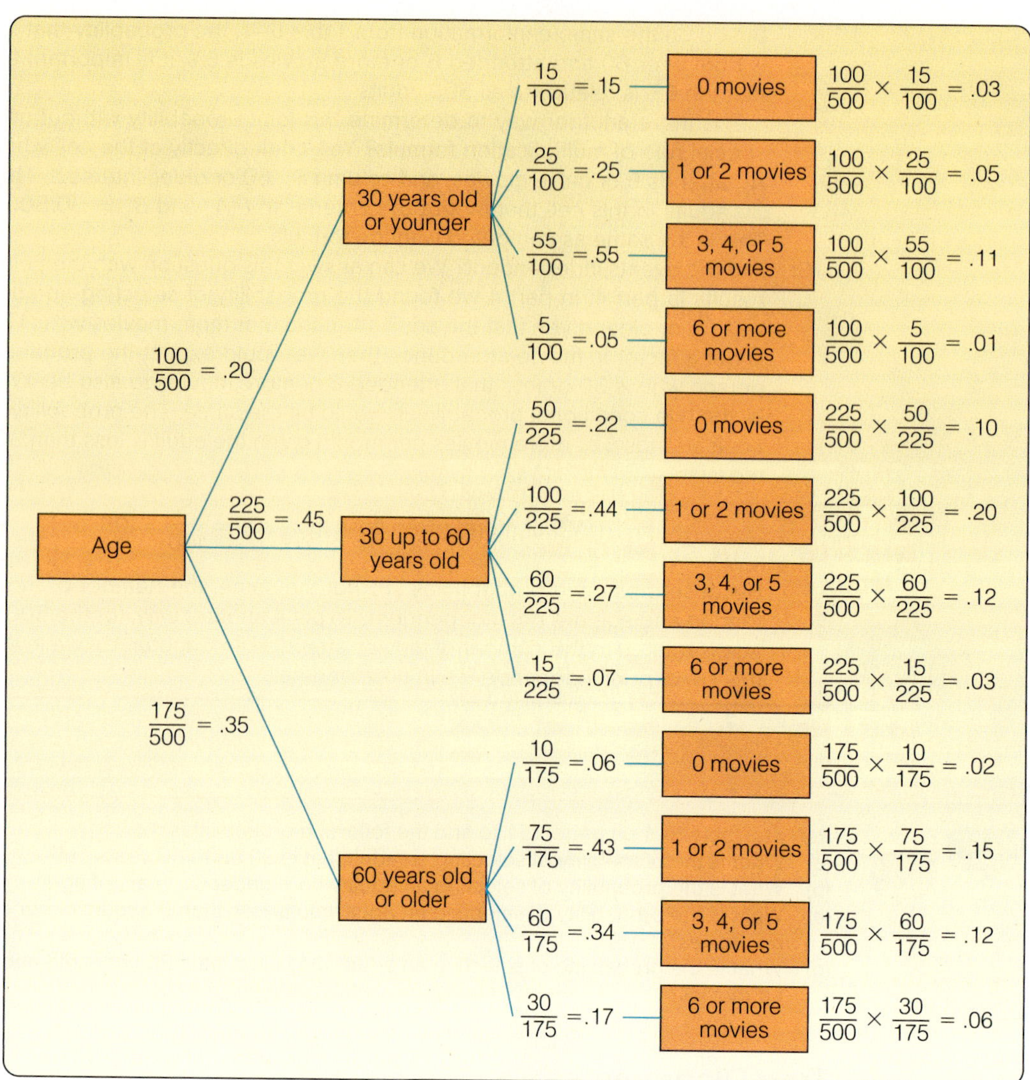

CHART 5–2 Tree Diagram Showing Age and Number of Movies Attended

per month; and A_4 attending 6 or more movies per month. For the upper branch of the tree, these probabilities are 15/100, 25/100, 55/100, and 5/100. We write the conditional probabilities in a similar fashion on the other branches.

4. Finally we determine the various joint probabilities. For the top branches, the events are an adult attends no movies per month and is 30 years old or younger; an adult attends 1 or 2 movies and is 30 years old or younger; an adult attends 3, 4, or 5 movies per month and is 30 years old or younger; and an adult attends 6 or more movies per month and is 30 years old or younger. These joint probabilities are shown on the right side of Chart 5–2. To explain, the joint probability that a randomly selected adult is less than 30 years old and attends 0 movies per month is:

$$P(B_1 \text{ and } A_1) = P(B_1)P(A_1|B_1) = \left(\frac{100}{500}\right)\left(\frac{15}{100}\right) = .03$$

The tree diagram summarizes all the probabilities based on the contingency table in Table 5–1. For example, the conditional probabilities show that the 60-and-older group has the highest percentage, 17%, attending 6 or movies per month. The

30-to-60-year-old group has the highest percentage, 22%, of seeing no movies per month. Based on the joint probabilities, 20% of the adults sampled attend 1 or 2 movies per month and are 30 up to 60 years of age. As you can see, there are many observations that we can make based on the information presented in the tree diagram.

SELF-REVIEW 5–8

Consumers were surveyed on the relative number of visits to a Sears store (often, occasional, and never) and if the store was located in an enclosed mall (yes and no). When variables are measured nominally, such as these data, the results are usually summarized in a contingency table.

	Enclosed Mall		
Visits	**Yes**	**No**	**Total**
Often	60	20	80
Occasional	25	35	60
Never	5	50	55
	90	105	195

What is the probability of selecting a shopper who:

(a) Visited a Sears store often?
(b) Visited a Sears store in an enclosed mall?
(c) Visited a Sears store in an enclosed mall or visited a Sears store often?
(d) Visited a Sears store often, given that the shopper went to a Sears store in an enclosed mall?

In addition:

(e) Are the number of visits and the enclosed mall variables independent?
(f) What is the probability of selecting a shopper who visited a Sears store often and it was in an enclosed mall?
(g) Draw a tree diagram and determine the various joint probabilities.

EXERCISES

23. Suppose $P(A) = .40$ and $P(B|A) = .30$. What is the joint probability of A and B?

24. Suppose $P(X_1) = .75$ and $P(Y_2|X_1) = .40$. What is the joint probability of X_1 and Y_2?

25. A local bank reports that 80% of its customers maintain a checking account, 60% have a savings account, and 50% have both. If a customer is chosen at random, what is the probability the customer has either a checking or a savings account? What is the probability the customer does not have either a checking or a savings account?

26. All Seasons Plumbing has two service trucks that frequently need repair. If the probability the first truck is available is .75, the probability the second truck is available is .50, and the probability that both trucks are available is .30, what is the probability neither truck is available?

27. FILE Refer to the following table.

	First Event			
Second Event	A_1	A_2	A_3	**Total**
B_1	2	1	3	6
B_2	1	2	1	4
Total	3	3	4	10

a. Determine $P(A_1)$.
b. Determine $P(B_1|A_2)$.
c. Determine $P(B_2 \text{ and } A_3)$.

28. Three defective electric toothbrushes were accidentally shipped to a drugstore by Cleanbrush Products along with 17 nondefective ones.
    a. What is the probability the first two electric toothbrushes sold will be returned to the drugstore because they are defective?
    b. What is the probability the first two electric toothbrushes sold will not be defective?
29. **FILE** Each salesperson at Puchett, Sheets, and Hogan Insurance Agency is rated either below average, average, or above average with respect to sales ability. Each salesperson also is rated with respect to his or her potential for advancement—either fair, good, or excellent. These traits for the 500 salespeople were cross-classified into the following table.

	Potential for Advancement		
Sales Ability	**Fair**	**Good**	**Excellent**
Below average	16	12	22
Average	45	60	45
Above average	93	72	135

    a. What is this table called?
    b. What is the probability a salesperson selected at random will have above average sales ability and excellent potential for advancement?
    c. Construct a tree diagram showing all the probabilities, conditional probabilities, and joint probabilities.
30. An investor owns three common stocks. Each stock, independent of the others, has equally likely chances of (1) increasing in value, (2) decreasing in value, or (3) remaining the same value. List the possible outcomes of this experiment. Estimate the probability at least two of the stocks increase in value.
31. **FILE** A survey of 545 college students asked: What is your favorite winter sport? And, what type of college do you attend? The results are summarized below:

	Favorite Winter Sport			
College Type	**Snowboarding**	**Skiing**	**Ice Skating**	**Total**
Junior College	68	41	46	155
Four-Year College	84	56	70	210
Graduate School	59	74	47	180
Total	211	171	163	545

    Using these 545 students as the sample, a student from this study is randomly selected.
    a. What is the probability of selecting a student whose favorite sport is skiing?
    b. What is the probability of selecting a junior-college student?
    c. If the student selected is a four-year-college student, what is the probability that the student prefers ice skating?
    d. If the student selected prefers snowboarding, what is the probability that the student is in junior college?
    e. If a graduate student is selected, what is the probability that the student prefers skiing or ice skating?
32. If you ask three strangers about their birthdays, what is the probability (a) All were born on Wednesday? (b) All were born on different days of the week? (c) None was born on Saturday?

LO5-6
Calculate probabilities using Bayes' theorem.

BAYES' THEOREM

In the 18th century, Reverend Thomas Bayes, an English Presbyterian minister, pondered this question: Does God really exist? Being interested in mathematics, he attempted to develop a formula to arrive at the probability God does exist based on evidence available to him on earth. Later Pierre-Simon Laplace refined Bayes' work and gave it the name "Bayes' theorem." The formula for **Bayes' theorem** is:

BAYES' THEOREM
$$P(A_i \mid B) = \frac{P(A_i)P(B \mid A_i)}{P(A_1)P(B \mid A_1) + P(A_2)P(B \mid A_2)} \qquad \textbf{[5–7]}$$

Assume in formula (5–7) that the events A_1 and A_2 are mutually exclusive and collectively exhaustive, and A_i refers to either event A_1 or A_2. Hence A_1 and A_2 are in this case complements. The meaning of the symbols used is illustrated by the following example.

Suppose 5% of the population of Umen, a fictional Third World country, have a disease that is peculiar to that country. We will let A_1 refer to the event "has the disease" and A_2 refer to the event "does not have the disease." Thus, we know that if we select a person from Umen at random, the probability the individual chosen has the disease is .05, or $P(A_1) = .05$. This probability, $P(A_1) = P(\text{has the disease}) = .05$, is called the **prior probability.** It is given this name because the probability is assigned before any empirical data are obtained.

PRIOR PROBABILITY The initial probability based on the present level of information.

The prior probability a person is not afflicted with the disease is therefore .95, or $P(A_2) = .95$, found by 1 − .05.

There is a diagnostic technique to detect the disease, but it is not very accurate. Let B denote the event "test shows the disease is present." Assume that historical evidence shows that if a person actually has the disease, the probability that the test will indicate the presence of the disease is .90. Using the conditional probability definitions developed earlier in this chapter, this statement is written as:

$$P(B|A_1) = .90$$

Assume the probability is .15 that for a person who actually does not have the disease the test will indicate the disease is present.

$$P(B|A_2) = .15$$

Let's randomly select a person from Umen and perform the test. The test results indicate the disease is present. What is the probability the person actually has the disease? In symbolic form, we want to know $P(A_1|B)$, which is interpreted as: $P(\text{has the disease} \mid \text{the test results are positive})$. The probability $P(A_1|B)$ is called a **posterior probability.**

POSTERIOR PROBABILITY A revised probability based on additional information.

With the help of Bayes' theorem, formula (5–7), we can determine the posterior probability.

$$P(A_1 \mid B) = \frac{P(A_1)P(B \mid A_1)}{P(A_1)P(B \mid A_1) + P(A_2)P(B \mid A_2)}$$
$$= \frac{(.05)(.90)}{(.05)(.90) + (.95)(.15)} = \frac{.0450}{.1875} = .24$$

STATISTICS IN ACTION

A recent study by the National Collegiate Athletic Association (NCAA) reported that of 150,000 senior boys playing on their high school basketball team, 64 would make a professional team. To put it another way, the odds of a high school senior basketball player making a professional team are 1 in 2,344. From the same study:

1. The odds of a high school senior basketball player playing some college basketball are about 1 in 40.
2. The odds of a high school senior playing college basketball as a senior in college are about 1 in 60.
3. If you play basketball as a senior in college, the odds of making a professional team are about 1 in 37.5.

So the probability that a person has the disease, given that he or she tested positive, is .24. How is the result interpreted? If a person is selected at random from the population, the probability that he or she has the disease is .05. If the person is tested and the test result is positive, the probability that the person actually has the disease is increased about fivefold, from .05 to .24.

In the preceding problem, we had only two mutually exclusive and collectively exhaustive events, A_1 and A_2. If there are n such events, $A_1, A_2, \ldots, A_n$, Bayes' theorem, formula (5–7), becomes

$$P(A_i \mid B) = \frac{P(A_i)P(B \mid A_i)}{P(A_1)P(B \mid A_1) + P(A_2)P(B \mid A_2) + \cdots + P(A_n)P(B \mid A_n)}$$

With the preceding notation, the calculations for the Umen problem are summarized in the following table.

Event, A_i	Prior Probability, $P(A_i)$	Conditional Probability, $P(B \mid A_i)$	Joint Probability, $P(A_i$ and $B)$	Posterior Probability, $P(A_i \mid B)$
Disease, A_1	.05	.90	.0450	.0450/.1875 = .24
No disease, A_2	.95	.15	.1425	.1425/.1875 = .76
			$P(B)$ = .1875	1.00

Another illustration of Bayes' theorem follows.

EXAMPLE

© McGraw-Hill Education/ Marker Dierker, photographer

A manufacturer of cell phones purchases a microchip, called the LS-24, from three suppliers: Hall Electronics, Schuller Sales, and Crawford Components. Forty-five percent of the LS-24 chips are purchased from Hall Electronics, 30% from Schuller Sales, and the remaining 25% from Crawford Components. The manufacturer has extensive histories on the three suppliers and knows that 3% of the LS-24 chips from Hall Electronics are defective, 6% of chips from Schuller Sales are defective, and 4% of the chips purchased from Crawford Components are defective.

When the LS-24 chips arrive from the three suppliers, they are placed directly in a bin and not inspected or otherwise identified by supplier. A worker selects a chip for installation and finds it defective. What is the probability that it was manufactured by Schuller Sales?

SOLUTION

As a first step, let's summarize some of the information given in the problem statement.

- There are three mutually exclusive and collectively exhaustive events, that is, three suppliers.

  A_1 The LS-24 was purchased from Hall Electronics.
  A_2 The LS-24 was purchased from Schuller Sales.
  A_3 The LS-24 was purchased from Crawford Components.

- The prior probabilities are:

  $P(A_1) = .45$ The probability the LS-24 was manufactured by Hall Electronics.
  $P(A_2) = .30$ The probability the LS-24 was manufactured by Schuller Sales.
  $P(A_3) = .25$ The probability the LS-24 was manufactured by Crawford Components.

- The additional information can be either:

  B_1 The LS-24 is defective, or
  B_2 The LS-24 is not defective.

- The following conditional probabilities are given.

  $P(B_1|A_1) = .03$ The probability that an LS-24 chip produced by Hall Electronics is defective.
  $P(B_1|A_2) = .06$ The probability that an LS-24 chip produced by Schuller Sales is defective.
  $P(B_1|A_3) = .04$ The probability that an LS-24 chip produced by Crawford Components is defective.

- A chip is selected from the bin. Because the chips are not identified by supplier, we are not certain which supplier manufactured the chip. We want to determine the probability that the defective chip was purchased from Schuller Sales. The probability is written $P(A_2|B_1)$.

Look at Schuller's quality record. It is the worst of the three suppliers. They produce 30 percent of the product, but 6% are defective. Now that we have found a defective LS-24 chip, we suspect that $P(A_2|B_1)$ is greater than the 30% of $P(A_2)$. That is, we expect the revised probability to be greater than .30. But how much greater? Bayes' theorem can give us the answer. As a first step, consider the tree diagram in Chart 5–3.

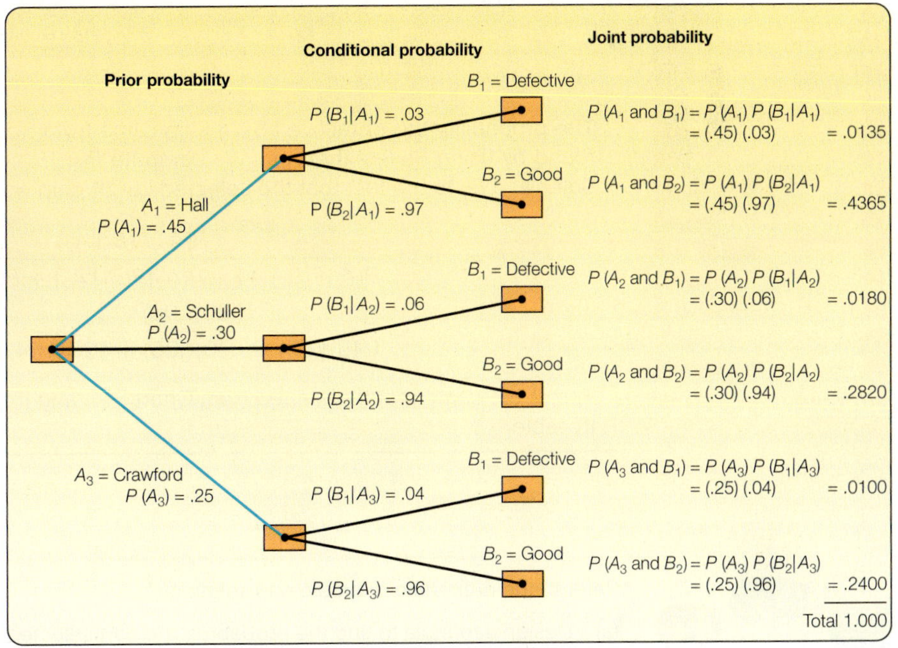

CHART 5–3 Tree Diagram of the Cell Phone Manufacturing Problem

REVISION OF CHART 5-3

The events are dependent, so the prior probability in the first branch is multiplied by the conditional probability in the second branch to obtain the joint probability. The joint probability is reported in the last column of Chart 5–3. To construct the tree diagram of Chart 5–3, we used a time sequence that moved from the supplier to the determination of whether the chip was defective.

What we need to do is reverse the time process. That is, instead of moving from left to right in Chart 5–3, we need to move from right to left. We have a defective chip, and we want to determine the likelihood that it was purchased from Schuller Sales. How is that accomplished? We first look at the joint probabilities as relative frequencies out of 10,000 cases. For example, the likelihood of a defective LS-24 chip that was produced by Hall Electronics is .0135. So of 10,000 cases, we would expect to find 135 defective chips produced by Hall Electronics. We observe that in 415 of 10,000 cases the LS-24 chip selected for assembly is defective, found by 135 + 180 + 100. Of these 415 defective chips, 180 were produced by Schuller Sales. Thus, the probability that the defective LS-24 chip was purchased from Schuller Sales is 180/415 = .4337. We have now determined the revised probability of $P(A_2|B_1)$. Before we found the defective chip, the likelihood that it was purchased from Schuller Sales was .30. This likelihood has been increased to .4337. What have we accomplished by using Bayes' Theorem? Once we found the defective part, we conclude that it is much more likely it is a product of Schuller Sales. The increase in the probability is rather dramatic moving from .30 to .4337.

This information is summarized in the following table.

Event, A_i	Prior Probability, $P(A_i)$	Conditional Probability, $P(B_1 \mid A_i)$	Joint Probability, $P(A_i \text{ and } B_1)$	Posterior Probability, $P(A_i \mid B_1)$
Hall	.45	.03	.0135	.0135/.0415 = .3235
Schuller	.30	.06	.0180	.0180/.0415 = .4337
Crawford	.25	.04	.0100	.0100/.0415 = .2410
			$P(B_1)$ = .0415	1.0000

The probability the defective LS-24 chip came from Schuller Sales can be formally found by using Bayes' theorem. We compute $P(A_2|B_1)$, where A_2 refers to Schuller Sales and B_1 to the fact that the selected LS-24 chip was defective.

$$P(A_2 \mid B_1) = \frac{P(A_2)P(B_1 \mid A_2)}{P(A_1)P(B_1 \mid A_1) + P(A_2)P(B_1 \mid A_2) + P(A_3)(B_1 \mid A_3)}$$

$$= \frac{(.30)(.06)}{(.45)(.03) + (.30)(.06) + (.25)(.04)} = \frac{.0180}{.04850} = .4337$$

This is the same result obtained from Chart 5–3 and from the conditional probability table.

SELF-REVIEW 5–9

Refer to the preceding example and solution.

(a) Design a formula to find the probability the part selected came from Crawford Components, given that it was a good chip.

(b) Compute the probability using Bayes' theorem.

EXERCISES

33. $P(A_1) = .60$, $P(A_2) = .40$, $P(B_1|A_1) = .05$, and $P(B_1|A_2) = .10$. Use Bayes' theorem to determine $P(A_1|B_1)$.

34. $P(A_1) = .20$, $P(A_2) = .40$, $P(A_3) = .40$, $P(B_1|A_1) = .25$, $P(B_1|A_2) = .05$, and $P(B_1|A_3) = .10$. Use Bayes' theorem to determine $P(A_3|B_1)$.

35. The Ludlow Wildcats baseball team, a minor league team in the Cleveland Indians organization, plays 70% of their games at night and 30% during the day. The team wins 50% of their night games and 90% of their day games. According to today's newspaper, they won yesterday. What is the probability the game was played at night?

36. Dr. Stallter has been teaching basic statistics for many years. She knows that 80% of the students will complete the assigned problems. She has also determined that among those who do their assignments, 90% will pass the course. Among those students who do not do their homework, 60% will pass. Mike Fishbaugh took statistics last semester from Dr. Stallter and received a passing grade. What is the probability that he completed the assignments?

37. The credit department of Lion's Department Store in Anaheim, California, reported that 30% of their sales are cash, 30% are paid with a credit card, and 40% with a debit card. Twenty percent of the cash purchases, 90% of the credit card purchases, and 60% of the debit card purchases are for more than \$50. Ms. Tina Stevens just purchased a new dress that cost \$120. What is the probability that she paid cash?

38. One-fourth of the residents of the Burning Ridge Estates leave their garage doors open when they are away from home. The local chief of police estimates that 5% of the garages with open doors will have something stolen, but only 1% of those closed will have something stolen. If a garage is robbed, what is the probability the doors were left open?

LO5-7
Determine the number of outcomes using principles of counting.

PRINCIPLES OF COUNTING

If the number of possible outcomes in an experiment is small, it is relatively easy to count them. There are six possible outcomes, for example, resulting from the roll of a die, namely:

If, however, there are a large number of possible outcomes, such as the number of heads and tails for an experiment with 10 tosses, it would be tedious to count all the possibilities. They could have all heads, one head and nine tails, two heads and eight tails, and so on. To facilitate counting, we describe three formulas: the multiplication formula (not to be confused with the multiplication *rule* described earlier in the chapter), the permutation formula, and the combination formula.

The Multiplication Formula

We begin with the **multiplication formula.**

MULTIPLICATION FORMULA If there are *m* ways of doing one thing and *n* ways of doing another thing, there are *m* x *n* ways of doing both.

In terms of a formula:

MULTIPLICATION FORMULA Total number of arrangements = $(m)(n)$ **[5–8]**

This can be extended to more than two events. For three events *m*, *n*, and *o*:

$$\text{Total number of arrangements} = (m)(n)(o)$$

EXAMPLE

An automobile dealer wants to advertise that for $29,999 you can buy a convertible, a two-door sedan, or a four-door model with your choice of either wire wheel covers or solid wheel covers. Based on the number of models and wheel covers, how many different vehicles can the dealer offer?

SOLUTION

Of course, the dealer could determine the total number of different cars by picturing and counting them. There are six.

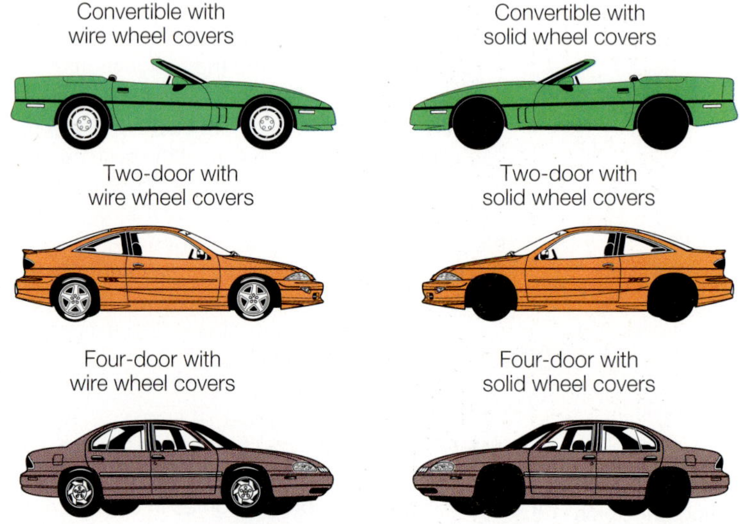

We can employ the multiplication formula as a check (where m is the number of models and n the wheel cover type). From formula (5–8):

$$\text{Total possible arrangements} = (m)(n) = (3)(2) = 6$$

It was not difficult to count all the possible model and wheel cover combinations in this example. Suppose, however, that the dealer decided to offer eight models and six types of wheel covers. It would be tedious to picture and count all the possible alternatives. Instead, the multiplication formula can be used. In this case, there are $(m)(n) = (8)(6) = 48$ possible arrangements.

Note in the preceding applications of the multiplication formula that there were *two or more groupings from which you made selections*. The automobile dealer, for example, offered a choice of models and a choice of wheel covers. If a home builder offered you four different exterior styles of a home to choose from and three interior floor plans, the multiplication formula would be used to find how many different arrangements were possible. There are 12 possibilities.

SELF-REVIEW 5–10

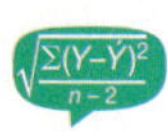

1. The Women's Shopping Network on cable TV offers sweaters and slacks for women. The sweaters and slacks are offered in coordinating colors. If sweaters are available in five colors and the slacks are available in four colors, how many different outfits can be advertised?

2. Pioneer manufactures three models of Wifi Internet radios, two MP3 docking stations, four different sets of speakers, and three CD carousel changers. When the four types of components are sold together, they form a "system." How many different systems can the electronics firm offer?

The Permutation Formula

The multiplication formula is applied to find the number of possible arrangements for two or more groups. In contrast, we use the **permutation formula** to find the number of possible arrangements when there is a single group of objects. Illustrations of this type of problem are:

- Three electronic parts, a transistor, an LED, and a synthesizer, are assembled into a plug-in component for a HDTV. The parts can be assembled in any order. How many different ways can the three parts be assembled?
- A machine operator must make four safety checks before starting his machine. It does not matter in which order the checks are made. In how many different ways can the operator make the checks?

One order for the first illustration might be the transistor first, the LED second, and the synthesizer third. This arrangement is called a **permutation.**

PERMUTATION Any arrangement of r objects selected from a single group of n possible objects.

Note that the arrangements *a b c* and *b a c* are different permutations. The formula to count the total number of different permutations is:

PERMUTATION FORMULA $${}_nP_r = \frac{n!}{(n-r)!} \qquad \textbf{[5–9]}$$

where:

n is the total number of objects.
r is the number of objects selected.

Before we solve the two problems illustrated, the permutations and combinations (to be discussed shortly) use a notation called *n factorial*. It is written $n!$ and means the product of $n(n-1)(n-2)(n-3)\cdots(1)$. For instance, $5! = 5 \cdot 4 \cdot 3 \cdot 2 \cdot 1 = 120$.

Many of your calculators have a button with $x!$ that will perform this calculation for you. It will save you a great deal of time. For example the Texas Instrument Pro Scientific calculator has the following key:

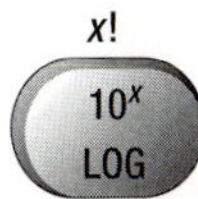

It is the "third function," so check your users' manual or the Internet for instructions.

The factorial notation can also be canceled when the same number appears in both the numerator and the denominator, as shown below.

$$\frac{6!3!}{4!} = \frac{6 \cdot 5 \cdot \cancel{4} \cdot \cancel{3} \cdot \cancel{2} \cdot \cancel{1}(3 \cdot 2 \cdot 1)}{\cancel{4} \cdot \cancel{3} \cdot \cancel{2} \cdot \cancel{1}} = 180$$

By definition, zero factorial, written 0!, is 1. That is, $0! = 1$.

EXAMPLE

Referring to the group of three electronic parts that are to be assembled in any order, in how many different ways can they be assembled?

SOLUTION

There are three electronic parts to be assembled, so $n = 3$. Because all three are to be inserted into the plug-in component, $r = 3$. Solving using formula (5–9) gives:

$${}_nP_r = \frac{n!}{(n-r)!} = \frac{3!}{(3-3)!} = \frac{3!}{0!} = \frac{3!}{1} = 6$$

We can check the number of permutations arrived at by using the permutation formula. We determine how many "spaces" have to be filled and the possibilities for each "space." In the problem involving three electronic parts, there are three locations in the plug-in unit for the three parts. There are three possibilities for the first place, two for the second (one has been used up), and one for the third, as follows:

$$(3)(2)(1) = 6 \text{ permutations}$$

The six ways in which the three electronic parts, lettered A, B, C, can be arranged are:

ABC	*BAC*	*CAB*	*ACB*	*BCA*	*CBA*

In the previous example, we selected and arranged all the objects, that is $n = r$. In many cases, only some objects are selected and arranged from the n possible objects. We explain the details of this application in the following example.

EXAMPLE

The Fast Media Company is producing a one-minute video advertisement. In the production process, eight different video segments were made. To make the one-minute ad, they can only select three of the eight segments. How many different ways can the eight video segments be arranged in the three spaces available in the ad?

SOLUTION

There are eight possibilities for the first available space in the ad, seven for the second space (one has been used up), and six for the third space. Thus:

$$(8)(7)(6) = 336,$$

that is, there are a total of 336 different possible arrangements. This could also be found by using formula (5–9). If $n = 8$ video segments and $r = 3$ spaces available, the formula leads to

$${}_nP_r = \frac{n!}{(n-r)!} = \frac{8!}{(8-3)!} = \frac{8!}{5!} = \frac{(8)(7)(6)\cancel{5!}}{\cancel{5!}} = 336$$

The Combination Formula

If the order of the selected objects is *not* important, any selection is called a **combination.** Logically, the number of combinations is always less than the number of permutations. The formula to count the number of r object combinations from a set of n objects is:

COMBINATION FORMULA $${}_nC_r = \frac{n!}{r!(n-r)!} \qquad \textbf{[5–10]}$$

For example, if executives Able, Baker, and Chauncy are to be chosen as a committee to negotiate a merger, there is only one possible combination of these three; the committee of Able, Baker, and Chauncy is the same as the committee of Baker, Chauncy, and Able. Using the combination formula:

$$_nC_r = \frac{n!}{r!(n-r)!} = \frac{3 \cdot 2 \cdot 1}{3 \cdot 2 \cdot 1(1)} = 1$$

EXAMPLE

The Grand 16 movie theater uses teams of three employees to work the concession stand each evening. There are seven employees available to work each evening. How many different teams can be scheduled to staff the concession stand?

SOLUTION

According to formula (5–10), there are 35 combinations, found by

$$_7C_3 = \frac{n!}{r!(n-r)!} = \frac{7!}{3!(7-3)!} = \frac{7!}{3!4!} = 35$$

The seven employees taken three at a time would create the possibility of 35 different teams.

When the number of permutations or combinations is large, the calculations are tedious. Computer software and handheld calculators have "functions" to compute these numbers. The Excel output for the selection of three video segments for the eight available at the Fast Media Company is shown below. There are a total of 336 arrangements.

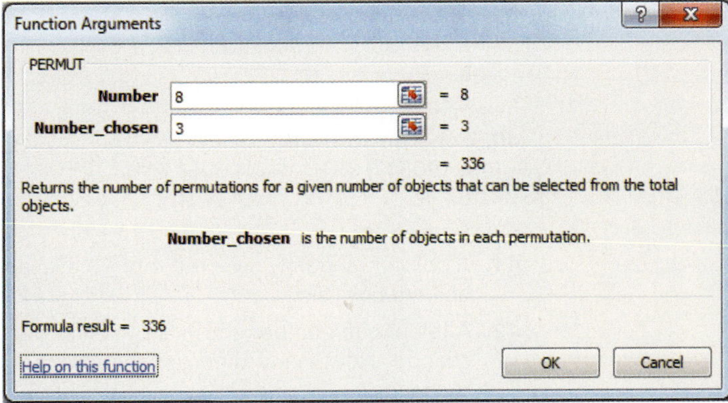

Below is the output for the number of teams at the Grand 16 movie theater. Three employees are chosen from seven possible employees.

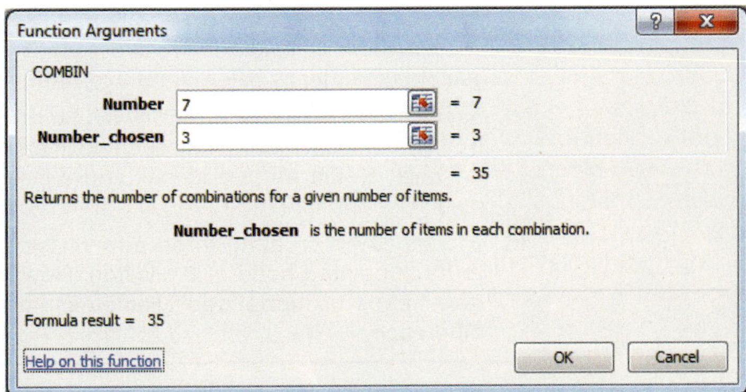

SELF-REVIEW 5–11

1. A musician wants to write a score based on only five chords: B-flat, C, D, E, and G. However, only three chords out of the five will be used in succession, such as C, B-flat, and E. Repetitions, such as B-flat, B-flat, and E, will not be permitted.
   (a) How many permutations of the five chords, taken three at a time, are possible?
   (b) Using formula (5–9), how many permutations are possible?
2. The 10 numbers 0 through 9 are to be used in code groups of four to identify an item of clothing. Code 1083 might identify a blue blouse, size medium; the code group 2031 might identify a pair of pants, size 18; and so on. Repetitions of numbers are not permitted. That is, the same number cannot be used twice (or more) in a total sequence. For example, 2256, 2562, or 5559 would not be permitted. How many different code groups can be designed?
3. In the preceding example/solution involving the Grand 16 movie theater, there were 35 possible teams of three taken from seven employees.
   (a) Use formula (5–10) to show this is true.
   (b) The manager of the theater wants to plan for staffing the concession stand with teams of five employees on the weekends to serve the larger crowds. From the seven employees, how many teams of five employees are possible?
4. In a lottery game, three numbers are randomly selected from a tumbler of balls numbered 1 through 50.
   (a) How many permutations are possible?
   (b) How many combinations are possible?

EXERCISES

39. Solve the following:
- **a.** 40!/35!
- **b.** ${}_7P_4$
- **c.** ${}_5C_2$

40. Solve the following:
- **a.** 20!/17!
- **b.** ${}_9P_3$
- **c.** ${}_7C_2$

41. A pollster randomly selected 4 of 10 available people. How many different groups of 4 are possible?

42. A telephone number consists of seven digits, the first three representing the exchange. How many different telephone numbers are possible within the 537 exchange?

43. An overnight express company must include five cities on its route. How many different routes are possible, assuming that it does not matter in which order the cities are included in the routing?

44. A representative of the Environmental Protection Agency (EPA) wants to select samples from 10 landfills. The director has 15 landfills from which she can collect samples. How many different samples are possible?

45. Sam Snead's restaurant in Conway, South Carolina, offers an early bird special from 4–6 pm each week day evening. If each patron selects a Starter Selection (4 options), an Entrée (8 options), and a Dessert (3 options), how many different meals are possible?

46. A company is creating three new divisions and seven managers are eligible to be appointed head of a division. How many different ways could the three new heads be appointed? Hint: Assume the division assignment makes a difference.

CHAPTER SUMMARY

I. A probability is a value between 0 and 1 inclusive that represents the likelihood a particular event will happen.

- **A.** An experiment is the observation of some activity or the act of taking some measurement.
- **B.** An outcome is a particular result of an experiment.
- **C.** An event is the collection of one or more outcomes of an experiment.

II. There are three definitions of probability.

- **A.** The classical definition applies when there are *n* equally likely outcomes to an experiment.
- **B.** The empirical definition occurs when the number of times an event happens is divided by the number of observations.
- **C.** A subjective probability is based on whatever information is available.

III. Two events are mutually exclusive if by virtue of one event happening the other cannot happen.

IV. Events are independent if the occurrence of one event does not affect the occurrence of another event.

V. The rules of addition refer to the probability that any of two or more events can occur.

- **A.** The special rule of addition is used when events are mutually exclusive.

$$P(A \text{ or } B) = P(A) + P(B) \qquad \textbf{[5–2]}$$

- **B.** The general rule of addition is used when the events are not mutually exclusive.

$$P(A \text{ or } B) = P(A) + P(B) - P(A \text{ and } B) \qquad \textbf{[5–4]}$$

- **C.** The complement rule is used to determine the probability of an event happening by subtracting the probability of the event not happening from 1.

$$P(A) = 1 - P(\sim A) \qquad \textbf{[5–3]}$$

VI. The rules of multiplication are applied when two or more events occur simultaneously.

- **A.** The special rule of multiplication refers to events that are independent.

$$P(A \text{ and } B) = P(A)P(B) \qquad \textbf{[5–5]}$$

- **B.** The general rule of multiplication refers to events that are not independent.

$$P(A \text{ and } B) = P(A)P(B|A) \qquad \textbf{[5–6]}$$

- **C.** A joint probability is the likelihood that two or more events will happen at the same time.
- **D.** A conditional probability is the likelihood that an event will happen, given that another event has already happened.
- **E.** Bayes' theorem is a method of revising a probability, given that additional information is obtained. For two mutually exclusive and collectively exhaustive events:

$$P(A_1 \mid B) = \frac{P(A_1)P(B \mid A_1)}{P(A_1)P(B \mid A_1) + P(A_2)P(B \mid A_2)} \qquad \textbf{[5–7]}$$

VII. There are three counting rules that are useful in determining the number of outcomes in an experiment.

- **A.** The multiplication rule states that if there are *m* ways one event can happen and *n* ways another event can happen, then there are *mn* ways the two events can happen.

$$\text{Number of arrangements} = (m)(n) \qquad \textbf{[5–8]}$$

- **B.** A permutation is an arrangement in which the order of the objects selected from a specific pool of objects is important.

$$_nP_r = \frac{n!}{(n-r)!} \qquad \textbf{[5–9]}$$

- **C.** A combination is an arrangement where the order of the objects selected from a specific pool of objects is not important.

$$_nC_r = \frac{n!}{r!(n-r)!} \qquad \textbf{[5–10]}$$

PRONUNCIATION KEY

SYMBOL	MEANING	PRONUNCIATION
$P(A)$	Probability of *A*	*P* of *A*
$P(\sim A)$	Probability of not *A*	*P* of not *A*
$P(A \text{ and } B)$	Probability of *A* and *B*	*P* of *A* and *B*
$P(A \text{ or } B)$	Probability of *A* or *B*	*P* of *A* or *B*
$P(A \mid B)$	Probability of *A* given *B* has happened	*P* of *A* given *B*
${}_nP_r$	Permutation of *n* items selected *r* at a time	*Pnr*
${}_nC_r$	Combination of *n* items selected *r* at a time	*Cnr*

CHAPTER EXERCISES

47. The marketing research department at Pepsico plans to survey teenagers about a newly developed soft drink. Each will be asked to compare it with his or her favorite soft drink.

a. What is the experiment?

b. What is one possible event?

48. The number of times a particular event occurred in the past is divided by the number of occurrences. What is this approach to probability called?

49. The probability that the cause and the cure for all cancers will be discovered before the year 2020 is .20. What viewpoint of probability does this statement illustrate?

50. FILE Berdine's Chicken Factory has several stores in the Hilton Head, South Carolina, area. When interviewing applicants for server positions, the owner would like to include information on the amount of tip a server can expect to earn per check (or bill). A study of 500 recent checks indicated the server earned the following amounts in tips per 8-hour shift.

Amount of Tip	Number
$0 up to $ 20	200
20 up to 50	100
50 up to 100	75
100 up to 200	75
200 or more	50
Total	500

a. What is the probability of a tip of $200 or more?

b. Are the categories "$0 up to $20," "$20 up to $50," and so on considered mutually exclusive?

c. If the probabilities associated with each outcome were totaled, what would that total be?

d. What is the probability of a tip of up to $50?

e. What is the probability of a tip of less than $200?

51. Winning all three "Triple Crown" races is considered the greatest feat of a pedigree racehorse. After a successful Kentucky Derby, Corn on the Cob is a heavy favorite at 2 to 1 odds to win the Preakness Stakes.

a. If he is a 2 to 1 favorite to win the Belmont Stakes as well, what is his probability of winning the Triple Crown?

b. What do his chances for the Preakness Stakes have to be in order for him to be "even money" to earn the Triple Crown?

52. The first card selected from a standard 52-card deck is a king.

a. If it is returned to the deck, what is the probability that a king will be drawn on the second selection?

b. If the king is not replaced, what is the probability that a king will be drawn on the second selection?

c. What is the probability that a king will be selected on the first draw from the deck and another king on the second draw (assuming that the first king was not replaced)?

53. Armco, a manufacturer of traffic light systems, found that under accelerated-life tests, 95% of the newly developed systems lasted 3 years before failing to change signals properly.

a. If a city purchased four of these systems, what is the probability all four systems would operate properly for at least 3 years?

b. Which rule of probability does this illustrate?

c. Using letters to represent the four systems, write an equation to show how you arrived at the answer to part (a).

54. Refer to the following picture.

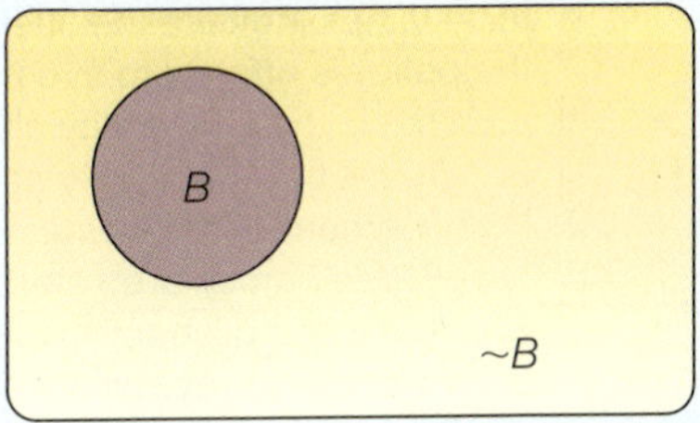

a. What is the picture called?

b. What rule of probability is illustrated?

c. *B* represents the event of choosing a family that receives welfare payments. What does $P(B) + P(\sim B)$ equal?

55. In a management trainee program at Claremont Enterprises, 80% of the trainees are female and 20% male. Ninety percent of the females attended college, and 78% of the males attended college.

a. A management trainee is selected at random. What is the probability that the person selected is a female who did not attend college?

b. Are gender and attending college independent? Why?

c. Construct a tree diagram showing all the probabilities, conditional probabilities, and joint probabilities.

d. Do the joint probabilities total 1.00? Why?

56. Assume the likelihood that any flight on Delta Airlines arrives within 15 minutes of the scheduled time is .90. We randomly selected a Delta flight on four different days.

a. What is the likelihood all four of the selected flights arrived within 15 minutes of the scheduled time?

b. What is the likelihood that none of the selected flights arrived within 15 minutes of the scheduled time?

c. What is the likelihood at least one of the selected flights did not arrive within 15 minutes of the scheduled time?

57. There are 100 employees at Kiddie Carts International. Fifty-seven of the employees are hourly workers, 40 are supervisors, 2 are secretaries, and the remaining employee is the president. Suppose an employee is selected:

a. What is the probability the selected employee is an hourly worker?

b. What is the probability the selected employee is either an hourly worker or a supervisor?

c. Refer to part (b). Are these events mutually exclusive?

d. What is the probability the selected employee is neither an hourly worker nor a supervisor?

58. DJ LeMahieu of the Colorado Rockies had the highest batting average in the 2016 Major League Baseball season. His average was .348. So assume the probability of getting a hit is .348 for each time he batted. In a particular game, assume he batted three times.

a. This is an example of what type of probability?

b. What is the probability of getting three hits in a particular game?

c. What is the probability of not getting any hits in a game?

d. What is the probability of getting at least one hit?

59. Four women's college basketball teams are participating in a single-elimination holiday basketball tournament. If one team is favored in its semifinal match by odds of 2 to 1 and another squad is favored in its contest by odds of 3 to 1, what is the probability that:
   a. Both favored teams win their games?
   b. Neither favored team wins its game?
   c. At least one of the favored teams wins its game?

60. There are three clues labeled "daily double" on the game show *Jeopardy.* If three equally matched contenders play, what is the probability that:
   a. A single contestant finds all three "daily doubles"?
   b. The returning champion gets all three of the "daily doubles"?
   c. Each of the players selects precisely one of the "daily doubles"?

61. Brooks Insurance Inc. wishes to offer life insurance to men age 60 via the Internet. Mortality tables indicate the likelihood of a 60-year-old man surviving another year is .98. If the policy is offered to five men age 60:
   a. What is the probability all five men survive the year?
   b. What is the probability at least one does not survive?

62. Forty percent of the homes constructed in the Quail Creek area include a security system. Three homes are selected at random:
   a. What is the probability all three of the selected homes have a security system?
   b. What is the probability none of the three selected homes has a security system?
   c. What is the probability at least one of the selected homes has a security system?
   d. Did you assume the events to be dependent or independent?

63. Refer to Exercise 62, but assume there are 10 homes in the Quail Creek area and 4 of them have a security system. Three homes are selected at random:
   a. What is the probability all three of the selected homes have a security system?
   b. What is the probability none of the three selected homes has a security system?
   c. What is the probability at least one of the selected homes has a security system?
   d. Did you assume the events to be dependent or independent?

64. There are 20 families living in the Willbrook Farms Development. Of these families, 10 prepared their own federal income taxes for last year, 7 had their taxes prepared by a local professional, and the remaining 3 by H&R Block.
   a. What is the probability of selecting a family that prepared their own taxes?
   b. What is the probability of selecting two families, both of which prepared their own taxes?
   c. What is the probability of selecting three families, all of which prepared their own taxes?
   d. What is the probability of selecting two families, neither of which had their taxes prepared by H&R Block?

65. The board of directors of Saner Automatic Door Company consists of 12 members, 3 of whom are women. A new policy and procedures manual is to be written for the company. A committee of three is randomly selected from the board to do the writing.
   a. What is the probability that all members of the committee are men?
   b. What is the probability that at least one member of the committee is a woman?

66. **FILE** A recent survey reported in *BloombergBusinessweek* dealt with the salaries of CEOs at large corporations and whether company shareholders made money or lost money.

	CEO Paid More Than $1 Million	CEO Paid Less Than $1 Million	Total
Shareholders made money	2	11	13
Shareholders lost money	4	3	7
Total	6	14	20

If a company is randomly selected from the list of 20 studied, what is the probability:
   a. The CEO made more than $1 million?
   b. The CEO made more than $1 million or the shareholders lost money?
   c. The CEO made more than $1 million given the shareholders lost money?
   d. Of selecting two CEOs and finding they both made more than $1 million?

67. Althoff and Roll, an investment firm in Augusta, Georgia, advertises extensively in the *Augusta Morning Gazette,* the newspaper serving the region. The *Gazette* marketing staff estimates that 60% of Althoff and Roll's potential market read the newspaper. It is further estimated that 85% of those who read the *Gazette* remember the Althoff and Roll advertisement.

a. What percent of the investment firm's potential market sees and remembers the advertisement?

b. What percent of the investment firm's potential market sees, but does not remember, the advertisement?

68. An Internet company located in Southern California has season tickets to the Los Angeles Lakers basketball games. The company president always invites one of the four vice presidents to attend games with him, and claims he selects the person to attend at random. One of the four vice presidents has not been invited to attend any of the last five Lakers home games. What is the likelihood this could be due to chance?

69. A computer-supply retailer purchased a batch of 1,000 CD-R disks and attempted to format them for a particular application. There were 857 perfect CDs, 112 CDs were usable but had bad sectors, and the remainder could not be used at all.

a. What is the probability a randomly chosen CD is not perfect?

b. If the disk is not perfect, what is the probability it cannot be used at all?

70. An investor purchased 100 shares of Fifth Third Bank stock and 100 shares of Santee Electric Cooperative stock. The probability the bank stock will appreciate over a year is .70. The probability the electric utility will increase over the same period is .60. Assume the two events are independent.

a. What is the probability both stocks appreciate during the period?

b. What is the probability the bank stock appreciates but the utility does not?

c. What is the probability at least one of the stocks appreciates?

71. Flashner Marketing Research Inc. specializes in providing assessments of the prospects for women's apparel shops in shopping malls. Al Flashner, president, reports that he assesses the prospects as good, fair, or poor. Records from previous assessments show that 60% of the time the prospects were rated as good, 30% of the time fair, and 10% of the time poor. Of those rated good, 80% made a profit the first year; of those rated fair, 60% made a profit the first year; and of those rated poor, 20% made a profit the first year. Connie's Apparel was one of Flashner's clients. Connie's Apparel made a profit last year. What is the probability that it was given an original rating of poor?

72. Two boxes of men's Old Navy shirts were received from the factory. Box 1 contained 25 mesh polo shirts and 15 Super-T shirts. Box 2 contained 30 mesh polo shirts and 10 Super-T shirts. One of the boxes was selected at random, and a shirt was chosen at random from that box to be inspected. The shirt was a mesh polo shirt. Given this information, what is the probability that the mesh polo shirt came from Box 1?

73. With each purchase of a large pizza at Tony's Pizza, the customer receives a coupon that can be scratched to see if a prize will be awarded. The probability of winning a free soft drink is 0.10, and the probability of winning a free large pizza is 0.02. You plan to eat lunch tomorrow at Tony's. What is the probability:

a. That you will win either a large pizza or a soft drink?

b. That you will not win a prize?

c. That you will not win a prize on three consecutive visits to Tony's?

d. That you will win at least one prize on one of your next three visits to Tony's?

74. For the daily lottery game in Illinois, participants select three numbers between 0 and 9. A number cannot be selected more than once, so a winning ticket could be, say, 307 but not 337. Purchasing one ticket allows you to select one set of numbers. The winning numbers are announced on TV each night.

a. How many different outcomes (three-digit numbers) are possible?

b. If you purchase a ticket for the game tonight, what is the likelihood you will win?

c. Suppose you purchase three tickets for tonight's drawing and select a different number for each ticket. What is the probability that you will not win with any of the tickets?

75. Several years ago, Wendy's Hamburgers advertised that there are 256 different ways to order your hamburger. You may choose to have, or omit, any combination of the following on your hamburger: mustard, ketchup, onion, pickle, tomato, relish, mayonnaise, and lettuce. Is the advertisement correct? Show how you arrive at your answer.

76. Recent surveys indicate 60% of tourists to China visited the Forbidden City, the Temple of Heaven, the Great Wall, and other historical sites in or near Beijing. Forty percent visited Xi'an with its magnificent terra-cotta soldiers, horses, and chariots, which lay buried for over 2,000 years. Thirty percent of the tourists went to both Beijing and Xi'an. What is the probability that a tourist visited at least one of these places?

77. A new chewing gum has been developed that is helpful to those who want to stop smoking. If 60% of those people chewing the gum are successful in stopping smoking, what is the probability that in a group of four smokers using the gum at least one quits smoking?

78. Reynolds Construction Company has agreed not to erect all "look-alike" homes in a new subdivision. Five exterior designs are offered to potential home buyers. The builder has standardized three interior plans that can be incorporated in any of the five exteriors. How many different ways can the exterior and interior plans be offered to potential home buyers?

79. A new sports car model has defective brakes 15% of the time and a defective steering mechanism 5% of the time. Let's assume (and hope) that these problems occur independently. If one or the other of these problems is present, the car is called a "lemon." If both of these problems are present, the car is a "hazard." Your instructor purchased one of these cars yesterday. What is the probability it is:

a. A lemon?
b. A hazard?

80. The state of Maryland has license plates with three numbers followed by three letters. How many different license plates are possible?

81. There are four people being considered for the position of chief executive officer of Dalton Enterprises. Three of the applicants are over 60 years of age. Two are female, of which only one is over 60.

a. What is the probability that a candidate is over 60 and female?
b. Given that the candidate is male, what is the probability he is less than 60?
c. Given that the person is over 60, what is the probability the person is female?

82. Tim Bleckie is the owner of Bleckie Investment and Real Estate Company. The company recently purchased four tracts of land in Holly Farms Estates and six tracts in Newburg Woods. The tracts are all equally desirable and sell for about the same amount.

a. What is the probability that the next two tracts sold will be in Newburg Woods?
b. What is the probability that of the next four sold at least one will be in Holly Farms?
c. Are these events independent or dependent?

83. A computer password consists of four characters. The characters can be one of the 26 letters of the alphabet. Each character may be used more than once. How many different passwords are possible?

84. A case of 24 cans contains 1 can that is contaminated. Three cans are to be chosen randomly for testing.

a. How many different combinations of three cans could be selected?
b. What is the probability that the contaminated can is selected for testing?

85. A puzzle in the newspaper presents a matching problem. The names of 10 U.S. presidents are listed in one column, and their vice presidents are listed in random order in the second column. The puzzle asks the reader to match each president with his vice president. If you make the matches randomly, how many matches are possible? What is the probability all 10 of your matches are correct?

86. Two components, A and B, operate in series. Being in series means that for the system to operate, both components A and B must work. Assume the two components are independent. What is the probability the system works under these conditions? The probability A works is .90 and the probability B functions is also .90.

87. Horwege Electronics Inc. purchases TV picture tubes from four different suppliers. Tyson Wholesale supplies 20% of the tubes, Fuji Importers 30%, Kirkpatricks 25%, and Parts Inc. 25%. Tyson Wholesale tends to have the best quality, as only 3% of its tubes arrive defective. Fuji Importers' tubes are 4% defective, Kirkpatricks' 7%, and Parts Inc.'s are 6.5% defective.

a. What is the overall percent defective?

b. A defective picture tube was discovered in the latest shipment. What is the probability that it came from Tyson Wholesale?

88. ABC Auto Insurance classifies drivers as good, medium, or poor risks. Drivers who apply to them for insurance fall into these three groups in the proportions 30%, 50%, and 20%, respectively. The probability a "good" driver will have an accident is .01, the probability a "medium" risk driver will have an accident is .03, and the probability a "poor" driver will have an accident is .10. The company sells Mr. Brophy an insurance policy and he has an accident. What is the probability Mr. Brophy is:

a. A "good" driver?
b. A "medium" risk driver?
c. A "poor" driver?

89. You take a trip by air that involves three independent flights. If there is an 80% chance each specific leg of the trip is on time, what is the probability all three flights arrive on time?

90. The probability a D-Link network server is down is .05. If you have three independent servers, what is the probability that at least one of them is operational?

91. Twenty-two percent of all light emitting diode (LED) displays are manufactured by Samsung. What is the probability that in a collection of three independent LED HDTV purchases, at least one is a Samsung?

DATA ANALYTICS

92. **FILE** Refer to the North Valley Real Estate data, which report information on homes sold during the last year.

a. Sort the data into a table that shows the number of homes that have a pool versus the number that don't have a pool in each of the five townships. If a home is selected at random, compute the following probabilities.

1. The home has a pool.
2. The home is in Township 1 or has a pool.
3. Given that it is in Township 3, that it has a pool.
4. The home has a pool and is in Township 3.

b. Sort the data into a table that shows the number of homes that have a garage attached versus those that don't in each of the five townships. If a home is selected at random, compute the following probabilities:

1. The home has a garage attached.
2. The home does not have a garage attached, given that it is in Township 5.
3. The home has a garage attached and is in Township 3.
4. The home does not have a garage attached or is in Township 2.

93. **FILE** Refer to the Baseball 2016 data, which reports information on the 30 Major League Baseball teams for the 2016 season. Set up three variables:

- Divide the teams into two groups, those that had a winning season and those that did not. That is, create a variable to count the teams that won 81 games or more, and those that won 80 or less.
- Create a new variable for attendance, using three categories: attendance less than 2.0 million, attendance of 2.0 million up to 3.0 million, and attendance of 3.0 million or more.
- Create a variable that shows the teams that play in a stadium less than 20 years old versus one that is 20 years old or more.

Answer the following questions.

a. Create a table that shows the number of teams with a winning season versus those with a losing season by the three categories of attendance. If a team is selected at random, compute the following probabilities:

1. The team had a winning season.
2. The team had a winning season or attendance of more than 3.0 million.
3. The team had a winning season given attendance was more than 3.0 million.
4. The team has a winning season and attracted fewer than 2.0 million fans.

b. Create a table that shows the number of teams with a winning season versus those that play in new or old stadiums. If a team is selected at random, compute the following probabilities:

1. Selecting a team with a stadium that is at least 20 years old.
2. The likelihood of selecting a team with a winning record and playing in a new stadium.
3. The team had a winning record or played in a new stadium.

94. FILE Refer to the Lincolnville school bus data. Set up a variable that divides the age of the buses into three groups: new (less than 5 years old), medium (5 but less than 10 years), and old (10 or more years). The median maintenance cost is $4,179. Based on this value, create a variable for those less than or equal to the median (low maintenance) and those more than the median (high maintenance cost). Finally, develop a table to show the relationship between maintenance cost and age of the bus.

a. What percentage of the buses are less than five years old?
b. What percentage of the buses less than five years old have low maintenance costs?
c. What percentage of the buses ten or more years old have high maintenance costs?
d. Does maintenance cost seem to be related to the age of the bus? Hint: Compare the maintenance cost of the old buses with the cost of the new buses? Would you conclude maintenance cost is independent of the age?

Discrete Probability Distributions

6

© JGI/Jamie Grill/Getty Images

▲ **RECENT STATISTICS SUGGEST** that 15% of those who visit a retail site on the Web make a purchase. A retailer wished to verify this claim. To do so, she selected a sample of 16 "hits" to her site and found that 4 had actually made a purchase. What is the likelihood of exactly four purchases? How many purchases should she expect? What is the likelihood that four or more "hits" result in a purchase? (See Exercise 49 and LO6-4.)

LEARNING OBJECTIVES

When you have completed this chapter, you will be able to:

LO6-1 Identify the characteristics of a probability distribution.

LO6-2 Distinguish between discrete and continuous random variables.

LO6-3 Compute the mean, variance, and standard deviation of a discrete probability distribution.

LO6-4 Explain the assumptions of the binomial distribution and apply it to calculate probabilities.

LO6-5 Explain the assumptions of the hypergeometric distribution and apply it to calculate probabilities.

LO6-6 Explain the assumptions of the Poisson distribution and apply it to calculate probabilities.

INTRODUCTION

Chapters 2 through 4 are devoted to descriptive statistics. We describe raw data by organizing the data into a frequency distribution and portraying the distribution in tables, graphs, and charts. Also, we compute a measure of location—such as the arithmetic mean, median, or mode—to locate a typical value near the center of the distribution. The range and the standard deviation are used to describe the spread in the data. These chapters focus on describing *something that has already happened.*

Starting with Chapter 5, the emphasis changes—we begin examining *something that could happen.* We note that this facet of statistics is called *statistical inference.* The objective is to make inferences (statements) about a population based on a number of observations, called a sample, selected from the population. In Chapter 5, we state that a probability is a value between 0 and 1 inclusive, and we examine how probabilities can be combined using rules of addition and multiplication.

This chapter begins the study of **probability distributions.** A probability distribution is like a relative frequency distribution. However, instead of describing the past, it is used to provide estimates of the likelihood of future events. Probability distributions can be described by measures of location and dispersion so we show how to compute a distribution's mean, variance, and standard deviation. We also discuss three frequently occurring discrete probability distributions: the binomial, hypergeometric, and Poisson.

LO6-1

Identify the characteristics of a probability distribution.

WHAT IS A PROBABILITY DISTRIBUTION?

A probability distribution defines or describes the likelihoods for a range of possible future outcomes. For example, Spalding Golf Products, Inc. assembles golf clubs with three components: a club head, a shaft, and a grip. From experience five percent of the shafts received from their Asian supplier are defective. As part of Spalding's statistical process control they inspect twenty shafts from each arriving shipment. From experience, we know that the probability of a defective shaft is five percent. Therefore, in a sample of twenty shafts, we would expect one shaft to be defective and the other nineteen shafts to be acceptable. But, by using a probability distribution we can completely describe the range of possible outcomes. For example, we would know the probability that none of the twenty shafts are defective, or that two, or three, or four, or continuing up to twenty shafts in the sample are defective. Given the small probability of a defective shaft, the probability distribution would show that there is a very small probability of four or more defective shafts.

PROBABILITY DISTRIBUTION A listing of all the outcomes of an experiment and the probability associated with each outcome.

The important characteristics of a probability distribution are:

CHARACTERISTICS OF A PROBABILITY DISTRIBUTION

1. The probability of a particular outcome is between 0 and 1 inclusive.
2. The outcomes are mutually exclusive.
3. The list of outcomes is exhaustive. So the sum of the probabilities of the outcomes is equal to 1.

How can we generate a probability distribution? The following example will explain.

EXAMPLE

Suppose we are interested in the number of heads showing face up on three tosses of a coin. This is the experiment. The possible results are zero heads, one head, two heads, and three heads. What is the probability distribution for the number of heads?

SOLUTION

There are eight possible outcomes. A tail might appear face up on the first toss, another tail on the second toss, and another tail on the third toss of the coin. Or we might get a tail, tail, and head, in that order. We use the multiplication formula for counting outcomes (5–8). There are (2)(2)(2) or 8 possible results. These results are shown in the following table.

Possible Result	Coin Toss First	Coin Toss Second	Coin Toss Third	Number of Heads
1	T	T	T	0
2	T	T	H	1
3	T	H	T	1
4	T	H	H	2
5	H	T	T	1
6	H	T	H	2
7	H	H	T	2
8	H	H	H	3

Note that the outcome "zero heads" occurred only once, "one head" occurred three times, "two heads" occurred three times, and the outcome "three heads" occurred only once. That is, "zero heads" happened one out of eight times. Thus, the probability of zero heads is one-eighth, the probability of one head is three-eighths, and so on. The probability distribution is shown in Table 6–1. Because one of these outcomes must happen, the total of the probabilities of all possible events is 1.000. This is always true. The same information is shown in Chart 6–1.

TABLE 6–1 Probability Distribution for the Events of Zero, One, Two, and Three Heads Showing Face Up on Three Tosses of a Coin

Number of Heads, x	Probability of Outcome, $P(x)$
0	$\frac{1}{8}$ = .125
1	$\frac{3}{8}$ = .375
2	$\frac{3}{8}$ = .375
3	$\frac{1}{8}$ = .125
Total	$\frac{8}{8}$ = 1.000

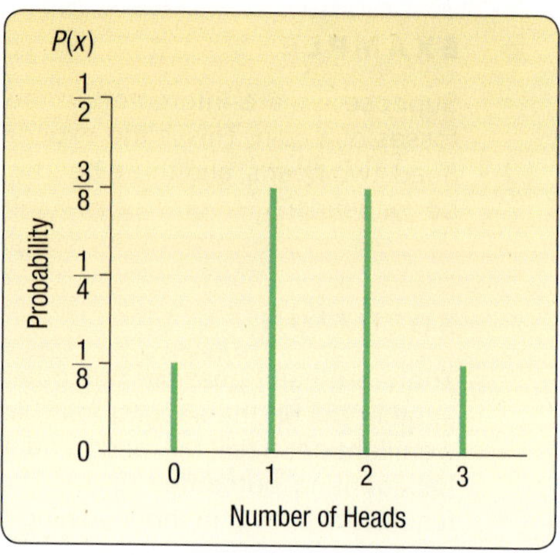

CHART 6–1 Graphical Presentation of the Number of Heads Resulting from Three Tosses of a Coin and the Corresponding Probability

Refer to the coin-tossing example in Table 6–1. We write the probability of x as $P(x)$. So the probability of zero heads is $P(0 \text{ heads}) = .125$, and the probability of one head is $P(1 \text{ head}) = .375$, and so forth. The sum of these mutually exclusive probabilities is 1; that is, from Table 6–1, $.125 + .375 + .375 + .125 = 1.00$.

SELF-REVIEW 6–1

The possible outcomes of an experiment involving the roll of a six-sided die are a one-spot, a two-spot, a three-spot, a four-spot, a five-spot, and a six-spot.

(a) Develop a probability distribution for the number of possible spots.
(b) Portray the probability distribution graphically.
(c) What is the sum of the probabilities?

LO6-2
Distinguish between discrete and continuous random variables.

RANDOM VARIABLES

In any experiment of chance, the outcomes occur randomly. So it is often called a *random variable*. For example, rolling a single die is an experiment: Any one of six possible outcomes can occur. Some experiments result in outcomes that are measured with quantitative variables (such as dollars, weight, or number of children), and other experimental outcomes are measured with qualitative variables (such as color or religious preference). A few examples will further illustrate what is meant by a **random variable.**

- The number of employees absent from the day shift on Monday, the number might be 0, 1, 2, 3, . . . The number absent is the random variable.
- The hourly wage of a sample of 50 plumbers in Jacksonville, FL. The hourly wage is the random variable.
- The number of defective lightbulbs produced in an hour at the Cleveland Electric Company, Inc.
- The grade level (Freshman, Sophomore, Junior, or Senior) of the members of the St. James High School Varsity girls' basketball team. The grade level is the random variable and notice that it is a qualitative variable.
- The number of participants in the 2016 New York City Marathon.
- The daily number of drivers charged with driving under the influence of alcohol in Brazoria County, Texas, last month.

A random variable is defined as follows:

RANDOM VARIABLE A variable measured or observed as the result of an experiment. By chance, the variable can have different values.

In Chapter 5 we defined the terms *experiment, outcome,* and *event.* Consider the example we just described regarding the experiment of tossing a fair coin three times. In this case the *random variable* is the number of heads that appear in the three tosses. There are eight possible outcomes to this experiment. These outcomes are shown in the following diagram.

Possible *outcomes* for three coin tosses

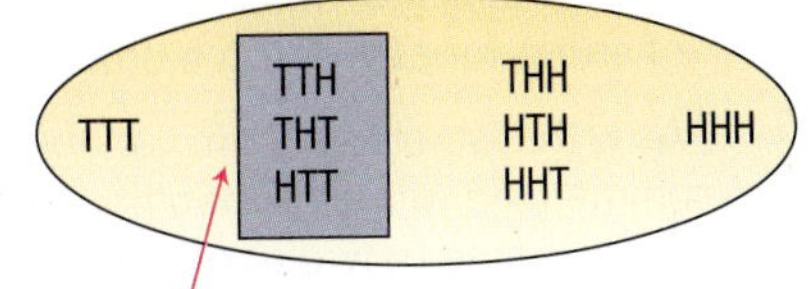

The *event* {one head} occurs and the *random variable* $x = 1$.

So, one possible outcome is that a tail appears on each toss: TTT. This single outcome would describe the event of zero heads appearing in three tosses. Another possible outcome is a head followed by two tails: HTT. If we wish to determine the event of exactly one head appearing in the three tosses, we must consider the three possible outcomes: TTH, THT, and HTT. These three outcomes describe the event of exactly one head appearing in three tosses.

In this experiment, the random variable is the number of heads in three tosses. The random variable can have four different values, 0, 1, 2, or 3. The outcomes of the experiment are unknown. But, using probability, we can compute the probability of a single head in three tosses as 3/8 or 0.375. As shown in Chapter 5, the probability of each value of the random variable can be computed to create a probability distribution for the random variable, number of heads in three tosses of a coin.

There are two types of random variables: *discrete* or *continuous.*

Discrete Random Variable

A discrete random variable can assume only a certain number of separated values. For example, the Bank of the Carolinas counts the number of credit cards carried for a group of customers. The data are summarized with the following relative frequency table.

Number of Credit Cards	Relative Frequency
0	.03
1	.10
2	.18
3	.21
4 or more	.48
Total	1.00

In this frequency table, the number of cards carried is the **discrete random variable.**

DISCRETE RANDOM VARIABLE A random variable that can assume only certain clearly separated values.

A discrete random variable can, in some cases, assume fractional or decimal values. To be a discrete random variable, these values must be separated—that is, have distance between them. As an example, a department store offers coupons with discounts of 10%, 15%, and 25%. In terms of probability, we could compute the probability that a customer would use a 10% coupon versus a 15% or 25% coupon.

Continuous Random Variable

On the other hand, a **continuous random variable** can assume an infinite number of values within a given range. It is measured on a continuous interval or ratio scale. Examples include:

- The times of commercial flights between Atlanta and Los Angeles are 4.67 hours, 5.13 hours, and so on. The random variable is the time in hours and is measured on a continuous scale of time.
- The annual snowfall in Minneapolis, Minnesota. The random variable is the amount of snow, measured on a continuous scale.

As with discrete random variables, the likelihood of a continuous random variable can be summarized with a **probability distribution.** For example, with a probability distribution for the flight time between Atlanta and Los Angeles, we could say that there is a probability of 0.90 that the flight will be less than 4.5 hours. This also implies that there is a probability of 0.10 that the flight will be more than 4.5 hours. With a probability of snowfall in Minneapolis, we could say that there is probability of 0.25 that the annual snowfall will exceed 48 inches. This also implies that there is a probability of 0.75 that annual snowfall will be less than 48 inches. Notice that these examples refer to a continuous range of values.

LO6-3
Compute the mean, variance, and standard deviation of a probability distribution.

THE MEAN, VARIANCE, AND STANDARD DEVIATION OF A DISCRETE PROBABILITY DISTRIBUTION

In Chapter 3, we discussed measures of location and variation for a frequency distribution. The mean reports the central location of the data, and the variance describes the spread in the data. In a similar fashion, a probability distribution is summarized by its mean and variance. We identify the mean of a probability distribution by the lowercase Greek letter mu (μ) and the standard deviation by the lowercase Greek letter sigma (σ).

Mean

The mean is a typical value used to represent the central location of a probability distribution. It also is the long-run average value of the random variable. The mean of a probability distribution is also referred to as its **expected value.** It is a weighted average where the possible values of a random variable are weighted by their corresponding probabilities of occurrence.

The mean of a discrete probability distribution is computed by the formula:

MEAN OF A PROBABILITY DISTRIBUTION $$\mu = \Sigma[xP(x)] \qquad \textbf{(6–1)}$$

where $P(x)$ is the probability of a particular value x. In other words, multiply each x value by its probability of occurrence, and then add these products.

Variance and Standard Deviation

The mean is a typical value used to summarize a discrete probability distribution. However, it does not describe the amount of spread (variation) in a distribution. The variance does this. The formula for the variance of a probability distribution is:

VARIANCE OF A PROBABILITY DISTRIBUTION $$\sigma^2 = \Sigma[(x - \mu)^2 P(x)] \qquad \textbf{(6–2)}$$

The computational steps are:

1. Subtract the mean from each value of the random variable, and square this difference.
2. Multiply each squared difference by its probability.
3. Sum the resulting products to arrive at the variance.

The standard deviation, σ, is found by taking the positive square root of σ^2; that is, $\sigma = \sqrt{\sigma^2}$

An example will help explain the details of the calculation and interpretation of the mean and standard deviation of a probability distribution.

EXAMPLE

© Thinkstock/JupiterImages RF

John Ragsdale sells new cars for Pelican Ford. John usually sells the largest number of cars on Saturday. He has developed the following probability distribution for the number of cars he expects to sell on a particular Saturday.

Number of Cars Sold, x	Probability, $P(x)$
0	.1
1	.2
2	.3
3	.3
4	.1
	1.0

1. What type of distribution is this?
2. On a typical Saturday, how many cars does John expect to sell?
3. What is the variance of the distribution?

SOLUTION

1. This is a discrete probability distribution for the random variable called "number of cars sold." Note that John expects to sell only within a certain range of cars; he does not expect to sell 5 cars or 50 cars. Further, he cannot sell half a car. He can sell only 0, 1, 2, 3, or 4 cars. Also, the outcomes are mutually exclusive—he cannot sell a total of both 3 and 4 cars on the same Saturday. The sum of the possible outcomes total 1. Hence, these circumstance qualify as a probability distribution.
2. The mean number of cars sold is computed by weighting the number of cars sold by the probability of selling that number and adding or summing the products, using formula (6–1):

$$\begin{aligned}\mu &= \Sigma[xP(x)]\\ &= 0(.1) + 1(.2) + 2(.3) + 3(.3) + 4(.1)\\ &= 2.1\end{aligned}$$

These calculations are summarized in the following table.

Number of Cars Sold, x	Probability, $P(x)$	$x \cdot P(x)$
0	.1	0.0
1	.2	0.2
2	.3	0.6
3	.3	0.9
4	.1	0.4
	1.0	$\mu = 2.1$

How do we interpret a mean of 2.1? This value indicates that, over a large number of Saturdays, John Ragsdale expects to sell a mean of 2.1 cars a day. Of course, it is not possible for him to sell *exactly* 2.1 cars on any particular Saturday. However, the expected value can be used to predict the arithmetic mean number of cars sold on Saturdays in the long run. For example, if John works 50 Saturdays during a year, he can expect to sell (50) (2.1) or 105 cars just on Saturdays. Thus, the mean is sometimes called the expected value.

3. The following table illustrates the steps to calculate the variance using formula (6–2). The first two columns repeat the probability distribution. In column three, the mean is subtracted from each value of the random variable. In column four, the differences from column three are squared. In the fifth column, each squared difference in column four is multiplied by the corresponding probability. The variance is the sum of the values in column five.

Number of Cars Sold, x	Probability, $P(x)$	$(x - \mu)$	$(x - \mu)^2$	$(x - \mu)^2P(x)$
0	.1	0 − 2.1	4.41	0.441
1	.2	1 − 2.1	1.21	0.242
2	.3	2 − 2.1	0.01	0.003
3	.3	3 − 2.1	0.81	0.243
4	.1	4 − 2.1	3.61	0.361
				$\sigma^2 = 1.290$

Recall that the standard deviation, σ, is the positive square root of the variance. In this example, $\sqrt{\sigma^2} = \sqrt{1.290} = 1.136$ cars. How do we apply a standard deviation of 1.136 cars? If salesperson Rita Kirsch also sold a mean of 2.1 cars on Saturdays, and the standard deviation in her sales was 1.91 cars, we would conclude that there is more variability in the Saturday sales of Ms. Kirsch than in those of Mr. Ragsdale (because 1.91 > 1.136).

SELF-REVIEW 6–2

The Pizza Palace offers three sizes of cola. The smallest size sells for $1.99, the medium for $2.49, and the large for $2.89. Thirty percent of the drinks sold are small, 50% are medium, and 20% are large. Create a probability distribution for the random variable price and answer the following questions.

(a) Is this a discrete probability distribution? Indicate why or why not.
(b) Compute the mean amount charged for a cola.
(c) What is the variance in the amount charged for a cola? The standard deviation?

EXERCISES

1. **FILE** Compute the mean and variance of the following discrete probability distribution.

x	$P(x)$
0	.2
1	.4
2	.3
3	.1

2. **FILE** Compute the mean and variance of the following discrete probability distribution.

x	$P(x)$
2	.5
8	.3
10	.2

3. **FILE** Compute the mean and variance of the following probability distribution.

x	*P*(*x*)
5	.1
10	.3
15	.2
20	.4

4. Which of these variables are discrete and which are continuous random variables?
   a. The number of new accounts established by a salesperson in a year.
   b. The time between customer arrivals to a bank ATM.
   c. The number of customers in Big Nick's barber shop.
   d. The amount of fuel in your car's gas tank.
   e. The number of minorities on a jury.
   f. The outside temperature today.
5. **FILE** The information below is the number of daily emergency service calls made by the volunteer ambulance service of Walterboro, South Carolina, for the last 50 days. To explain, there were 22 days on which there were two emergency calls, and 9 days on which there were three emergency calls.

Number of Calls	Frequency
0	8
1	10
2	22
3	9
4	1
Total	50

   a. Convert this information on the number of calls to a probability distribution.
   b. Is this an example of a discrete or continuous probability distribution?
   c. What is the mean number of emergency calls per day?
   d. What is the standard deviation of the number of calls made daily?
6. **FILE** The director of admissions at Kinzua University in Nova Scotia estimated the distribution of student admissions for the fall semester on the basis of past experience. What is the expected number of admissions for the fall semester? Compute the variance and the standard deviation of the number of admissions.

Admissions	Probability
1,000	.6
1,200	.3
1,500	.1

7. **FILE** Belk Department Store is having a special sale this weekend. Customers charging purchases of more than $50 to their Belk credit card will be given a special Belk Lottery card. The customer will scratch off the card, which will indicate the amount to be taken off the total amount of the purchase. Listed below are the amount of the prize and the percent of the time that amount will be deducted from the total amount of the purchase.

Prize Amount	Probability
$ 10	.50
25	.40
50	.08
100	.02

a. What is the mean amount deducted from the total purchase amount?
b. What is the standard deviation of the amount deducted from the total purchase?

8. **FILE** The Downtown Parking Authority of Tampa, Florida, reported the following information for a sample of 250 customers on the number of hours cars are parked and the amount they are charged.

Number of Hours	Frequency	Amount Charged
1	20	$ 3
2	38	6
3	53	9
4	45	12
5	40	14
6	13	16
7	5	18
8	36	20
	250	

a. Convert the information on the number of hours parked to a probability distribution. Is this a discrete or a continuous probability distribution?
b. Find the mean and the standard deviation of the number of hours parked. How would you answer the question: How long is a typical customer parked?
c. Find the mean and the standard deviation of the amount charged.

LO6-4
Explain the assumptions of the binomial distribution and apply it to calculate probabilities.

BINOMIAL PROBABILITY DISTRIBUTION

The **binomial probability distribution** is a widely occurring discrete probability distribution. To describe experimental outcomes with a binomial distribution, there are four requirements. The first requirement is there are only two possible outcomes on a particular experimental trial. For example, on a test, a true/false question is either answered correctly or incorrectly. In a resort, a housekeeping supervisor reviews an employee's work and evaluates it as acceptable or unacceptable. A key characteristic of the two outcomes is that they must be mutually exclusive. This means that the answer to a true/false question must be either correct or incorrect but cannot be both correct and incorrect at the same time. Another example is the outcome of a sales call. Either a customer purchases or does not purchase the product, but the sale cannot result in both outcomes. Frequently, we refer to the two possible outcomes of a binomial experiment as a "success" and a "failure." However, this distinction does not imply that one outcome is good and the other is bad, only that there are two mutually exclusive outcomes.

The second binomial requirement is that the random variable is the number of successes for a fixed and known number of trials. For example, we flip a coin five times and count the number of times a head appears in the five flips, we randomly select 10 employees and count the number who are older than 50 years of age, or we randomly select 20 boxes of Kellogg's Raisin Bran and count the number that weigh more than the amount indicated on the package. In each example, we count the number of successes from the fixed number of trials.

A third requirement is that we know the probability of a success and it is the same for each trial. Three examples are:

- For a test with 10 true/false questions, we know there are 10 trials and the probability of correctly guessing the answer for any of the 10 trials is 0.5. Or, for a test with 20 multiple-choice questions with four options and only one correct answer, we know that there are 20 trials and the probability of randomly guessing the correct answer for each of the 20 trials is 0.25.

- Bones Albaugh is a Division I college basketball player who makes 70% of his foul shots. If he has five opportunities in tonight's game, the likelihood he will be successful on each of the five attempts is 0.70.
- In a recent poll, 18% of adults indicated a Snickers bar was their favorite candy bar. We select a sample of 15 adults and ask each for his or her favorite candy bar. The likelihood a Snickers bar is the answer for each adult is 0.18.

© David Madison/Digital Vision/Getty Images

The final requirement of a binomial probability distribution is that each trial is *independent* of any other trial. Independent means there is no pattern to the trials. The outcome of a particular trial does not affect the outcome of any other trial. Two examples are:

- A young family has two children, both boys. The probability of a third birth being a boy is still .50. That is, the gender of the third child is independent of the gender of the other two.
- Suppose 20% of the patients served in the emergency room at Waccamaw Hospital do not have insurance. If the second patient served on the afternoon shift today did not have insurance, that does not affect the probability the third, the tenth, or any of the other patients will or will not have insurance.

BINOMIAL PROBABILITY EXPERIMENT

1. An outcome on each trial of an experiment is classified into one of two mutually exclusive categories—a success or a failure.
2. The random variable is the number of successes in a fixed number of trials.
3. The probability of success is the same for each trial.
4. The trials are independent, meaning that the outcome of one trial does not affect the outcome of any other trial.

How Is a Binomial Probability Computed?

To construct a particular binomial probability, we use (1) the number of trials and (2) the probability of success on each trial. For example, if the Hannah Landscaping Company plants 10 Norfolk pine trees today knowing that 90% of these trees survive, we can compute the binomial probability that exactly 8 trees survive. In this case the number of trials is the 10 trees, the probability of success is .90, and the number of successes is eight. In fact, we can compute a binomial probability for any number of successes from 0 to 10 surviving trees.

A binomial probability is computed by the formula:

BINOMIAL PROBABILITY FORMULA $$P(x) = {}_nC_x \pi^x (1 - \pi)^{n-x} \quad \textbf{(6–3)}$$

where:

C denotes a combination.
n is the number of trials.
x is the random variable defined as the number of successes.
π is the probability of a success on each trial.

We use the Greek letter π (pi) to denote a binomial population parameter. Do not confuse it with the mathematical constant 3.1416.

EXAMPLE

There are five flights daily from Pittsburgh via American Airlines into the Bradford Regional Airport in Bradford, Pennsylvania. Suppose the probability that any flight arrives late is .20. What is the probability that none of the flights are late today? What is the probability that exactly one of the flights is late today?

SOLUTION

We can use formula (6–3). The probability that a particular flight is late is .20, so let $\pi = .20$. There are five flights, so $n = 5$, and X, the random variable, refers to the number of successes. In this case, a "success" is a flight that arrives late. The random variable, x, can be equal to 0 late flights in the five trials, 1 late flight in the five trials, or 2, 3, 4, or 5. The probability for no late arrivals, $x = 0$, is,

$$P(0) = {}_nC_x(\pi)^x(1 - \pi)^{n-x}$$
$$= {}_5C_0(.20)^0(1 - .20)^{5-0} = (1)(1)(.3277) = .3277$$

The probability that exactly one of the five flights will arrive late today is .4096, found by

$$P(1) = {}_nC_x(\pi)^x(1 - \pi)^{n-x}$$
$$= {}_5C_1(.20)^1(1 - .20)^{5-1} = (5)(.20)(.4096) = .4096$$

The entire binomial probability distribution with $\pi = .20$ and $n = 5$ is shown in the following bar chart. We observe that the probability of exactly three late flights is .0512 and from the bar chart that the distribution of the number of late arrivals is positively skewed.

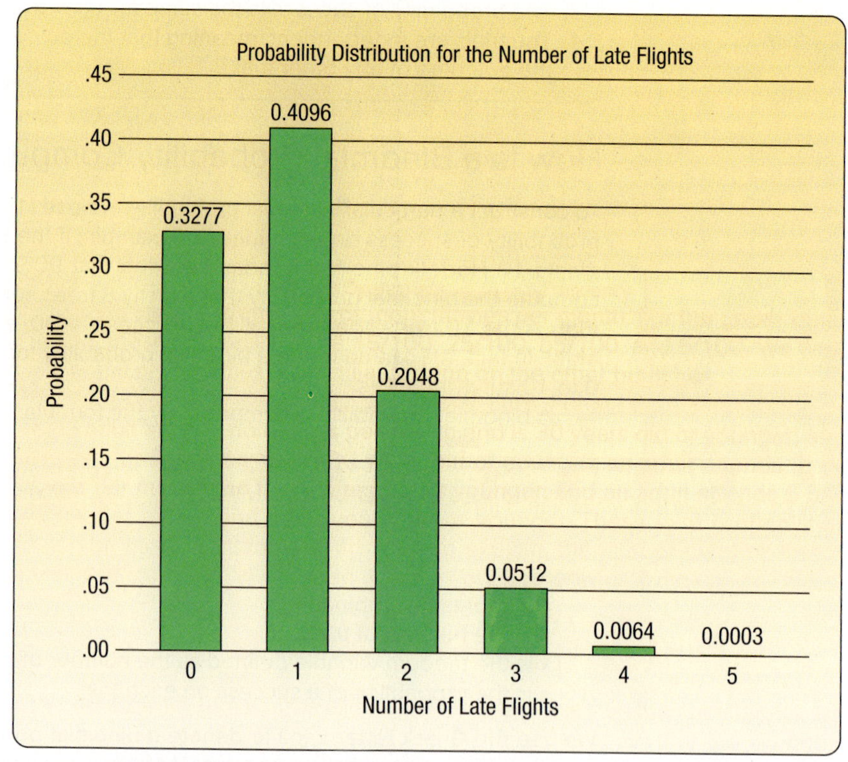

The mean (μ) and the variance (σ^2) of a binomial distribution are computed in a "shortcut" fashion by:

MEAN OF A BINOMIAL DISTRIBUTION $$\mu = n\pi \quad \text{(6–4)}$$

VARIANCE OF A BINOMIAL DISTRIBUTION $$\sigma^2 = n\pi(1 - \pi) \quad \text{(6–5)}$$

For the example regarding the number of late flights, recall that $\pi = .20$ and $n = 5$. Hence:

$$\mu = n\pi = (5)(.20) = 1.0$$

$$\sigma^2 = n\pi(1 - \pi) = 5(.20)(1 - .20) = .7997$$

The mean of 1.0 and the variance of .7997 can be verified from formulas (6–1) and (6–2). The probability distribution from the bar chart shown earlier and the details of the calculations are shown below.

Number of Late Flights, x	$P(x)$	$xP(x)$	$x - \mu$	$(x - \mu)^2$	$(x - \mu)^2P(x)$
0	0.3277	0.0000	−1	1	0.3277
1	0.4096	0.4096	0	0	0
2	0.2048	0.4096	1	1	0.2048
3	0.0512	0.1536	2	4	0.2048
4	0.0064	0.0256	3	9	0.0576
5	0.0003	0.0015	4	16	0.0048
		$\mu = 1.0000$			$\sigma^2 = 0.7997$

Binomial Probability Tables

Formula (6–3) can be used to build a binomial probability distribution for any value of n and π. However, for a larger n, the calculations take more time. For convenience, the tables in Appendix B.1 show the result of using the formula for various values of n and π. Table 6–2 shows part of Appendix B.1 for $n = 6$ and various values of π.

TABLE 6–2 Binomial Probabilities for $n = 6$ and Selected Values of π

	$n = 6$ Probability										
$x\backslash\pi$	**.05**	.1	.2	.3	.4	.5	.6	.7	.8	.9	.95
0	**.735**	.531	.262	.118	.047	.016	.004	.001	.000	.000	.000
1	**.232**	.354	.393	.303	.187	.094	.037	.010	.002	.000	.000
2	**.031**	.098	.246	.324	.311	.234	.138	.060	.015	.001	.000
3	**.002**	.015	.082	.185	.276	.313	.276	.185	.082	.015	.002
4	**.000**	.001	.015	.060	.138	.234	.311	.324	.246	.098	.031
5	**.000**	.000	.002	.010	.037	.094	.187	.303	.393	.354	.232
6	**.000**	.000	.000	.001	.004	.016	.047	.118	.262	.531	.735

EXAMPLE

In the Southwest, 5% of all cell phone calls are dropped. What is the probability that out of six randomly selected calls, none was dropped? Exactly one? Exactly two? Exactly three? Exactly four? Exactly five? Exactly six out of six?

SOLUTION

The binomial conditions are met: (a) there are only two possible outcomes (a particular call is either dropped or not dropped), (b) there are a fixed number of trials (6), (c) there is a constant probability of success (.05), and (d) the trials are independent.

Refer to Table 6–2 on the previous page for the probability of exactly zero dropped calls. Go down the left margin to an x of 0. Now move horizontally to the column headed by a π of .05 to find the probability. It is .735. The values in Table 6–2 are rounded to three decimal places.

The probability of exactly one dropped call in a sample of six calls is .232. The complete binomial probability distribution for $n = 6$ and $\pi = .05$ is:

Number of Dropped Calls, x	Probability of Occurrence, $P(x)$	Number of Dropped Calls, x	Probability of Occurrence, $P(x)$
0	.735	4	.000
1	.232	5	.000
2	.031	6	.000
3	.002		

Of course, there is a slight chance of getting exactly five dropped calls out of six random selections. It is .00000178, found by inserting the appropriate values in the binomial formula:

$$P(5) = {}_6C_5(.50)^5(.95)^1 = (6)(.05)^5(.95) = .00000178$$

For six out of the six, the exact probability is .000000016. Thus, the probability is very small that five or six calls will be dropped in six trials.

We can compute the mean or expected value of the distribution of the number defective:

$$\mu = n\pi = (6)(.05) = 0.30$$

$$\sigma^2 = n\pi(1 - \pi) = 6(.05)(.95) = 0.285$$

SELF-REVIEW 6–3

Ninety-five percent of the employees at the J. M. Smucker Company plant on Laskey Road have their bimonthly wages sent directly to their bank by electronic funds transfer. This is also called direct deposit. Suppose we select a random sample of seven employees.

(a) Does this situation fit the assumptions of the binomial distribution?
(b) What is the probability that all seven employees use direct deposit?
(c) Use formula (6–3) to determine the exact probability that four of the seven sampled employees use direct deposit.
(d) Use Excel to verify your answers to parts (b) and (c).

Appendix B.1 is limited. It gives probabilities for n values from 1 to 15 and π values of .05, .10, . . . , .90, and .95. A software program can generate the probabilities for a specified number of successes, given n and π. The Excel output on the next page shows the probability when $n = 40$ and $\pi = .09$. Note that the number of successes stops at 15 because the probabilities for 16 to 40 are very close to 0. The instructions are detailed in the Software Commands in Appendix C.

	A	B
1	Success	Probability
2	0	0.0230
3	1	0.0910
4	2	0.1754
5	3	0.2198
6	4	0.2011
7	5	0.1432
8	6	0.0826
9	7	0.0397
10	8	0.0162
11	9	0.0057
12	10	0.0017
13	11	0.0005
14	12	0.0001
15	13	0.0000
16	14	0.0000
17	15	0.0000

Several additional points should be made regarding the binomial probability distribution.

1. If n remains the same but π increases from .05 to .95, the shape of the distribution changes. Look at Table 6–3 and Chart 6–2. The distribution for a π of .05 is positively skewed. As π approaches .50, the distribution becomes symmetrical. As π goes beyond .50 and moves toward .95, the probability distribution becomes negatively skewed. Table 6–3 highlights probabilities for $n = 10$ and a π of .05, .10, .20, .50, and .70. The graphs of these probability distributions are shown in Chart 6–2.

TABLE 6–3 Probability of 0, 1, 2, . . . Successes for a π of .05, .10, .20, .50, and .70, and an n of 10

$x\backslash\pi$	.05	.1	.2	.3	.4	.5	.6	.7	.8	.9	.95
0	.599	.349	.107	.028	.006	.001	.000	.000	.000	.000	.000
1	.315	.387	.268	.121	.040	.010	.002	.000	.000	.000	.000
2	.075	.194	.302	.233	.121	.044	.011	.001	.000	.000	.000
3	.010	.057	.201	.267	.215	.117	.042	.009	.001	.000	.000
4	.001	.011	.088	.200	.251	.205	.111	.037	.006	.000	.000
5	.000	.001	.026	.103	.201	.246	.201	.103	.026	.001	.000
6	.000	.000	.006	.037	.111	.205	.251	.200	.088	.011	.001
7	.000	.000	.001	.009	.042	.117	.215	.267	.201	.057	.010
8	.000	.000	.000	.001	.011	.044	.121	.233	.302	.194	.075
9	.000	.000	.000	.000	.002	.010	.040	.121	.268	.387	.315
10	.000	.000	.000	.000	.000	.001	.006	.028	.107	.349	.599

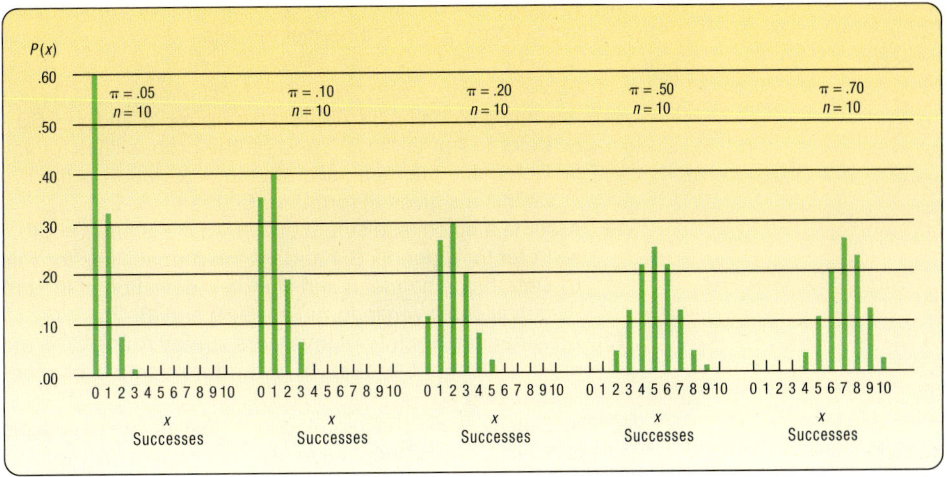

CHART 6–2 Graphing the Binomial Probability Distribution for a π of .05, .10, .20, .50, and .70, and an n of 10

2. If π, the probability of success, remains the same but n becomes larger, the shape of the binomial distribution becomes more symmetrical. Chart 6–3 shows a situation where π remains constant at .10 but n increases from 7 to 40.

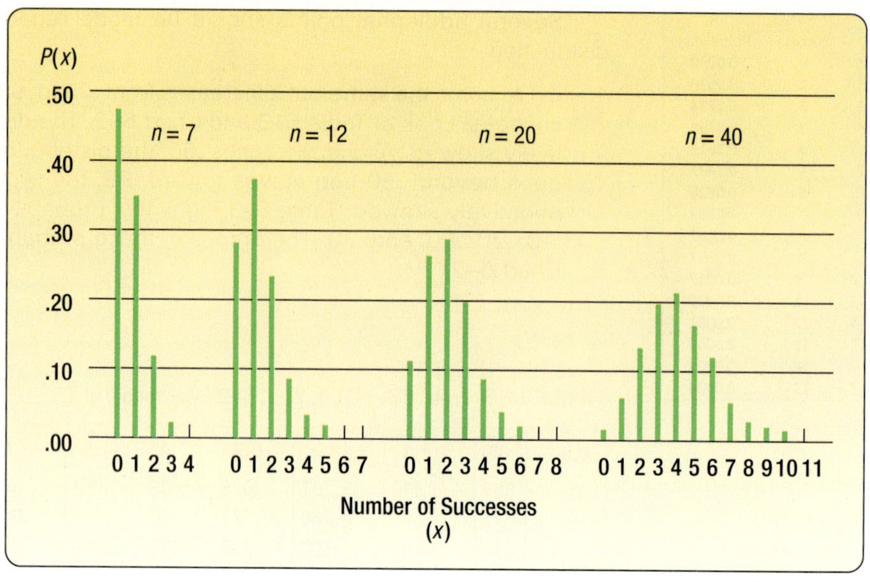

CHART 6–3 Chart Representing the Binomial Probability Distribution for a π of .10 and an n of 7, 12, 20, and 40

EXERCISES

9. In a binomial situation, $n = 4$ and $\pi = .25$. Determine the probabilities of the following events using the binomial formula.
   a. $x = 2$
   b. $x = 3$

10. In a binomial situation, $n = 5$ and $\pi = .40$. Determine the probabilities of the following events using the binomial formula.
   a. $x = 1$
   b. $x = 2$

11. Assume a binomial distribution where $n = 3$ and $\pi = .60$.
   a. Refer to Appendix B.1, and list the probabilities for values of x from 0 to 3.
   b. Determine the mean and standard deviation of the distribution from the general definitions given in formulas (6–1) and (6–2).

12. Assume a binomial distribution where $n = 5$ and $\pi = .30$.
   a. Refer to Appendix B.1 and list the probabilities for values of x from 0 to 5.
   b. Determine the mean and standard deviation of the distribution from the general definitions given in formulas (6–1) and (6–2).

13. An American Society of Investors survey found 30% of individual investors have used a discount broker. In a random sample of nine individuals, what is the probability:
   a. Exactly two of the sampled individuals have used a discount broker?
   b. Exactly four of them have used a discount broker?
   c. None of them has used a discount broker?

14. **FILE** The U.S. Postal Service reports 95% of first-class mail within the same city is delivered within 2 days of the time of mailing. Six letters are randomly sent to different locations.
   a. What is the probability that all six arrive within 2 days?
   b. What is the probability that exactly five arrive within 2 days?
   c. Find the mean number of letters that will arrive within 2 days.
   d. Compute the variance and standard deviation of the number that will arrive within 2 days.

15. **FILE** Industry standards suggest that 10% of new vehicles require warranty service within the first year. Jones Nissan in Sumter, South Carolina, sold 12 Nissans yesterday.
    a. What is the probability that none of these vehicles requires warranty service?
    b. What is the probability exactly one of these vehicles requires warranty service?
    c. Determine the probability that exactly two of these vehicles require warranty service.
    d. Compute the mean and standard deviation of this probability distribution.
16. **FILE** A telemarketer makes six phone calls per hour and is able to make a sale on 30% of these contacts. During the next 2 hours, find:
    a. The probability of making exactly four sales.
    b. The probability of making no sales.
    c. The probability of making exactly two sales.
    d. The mean number of sales in the 2-hour period.
17. **FILE** A recent survey by the American Accounting Association revealed 23% of students graduating with a major in accounting select public accounting. Suppose we select a sample of 15 recent graduates.
    a. What is the probability two select public accounting?
    b. What is the probability five select public accounting?
    c. How many graduates would you expect to select public accounting?
18. **FILE** It is reported that 41% of American households use a cell phone exclusively for their telephone service. In a sample of eight households,
    a. Find the probability that no household uses a cell phone as their exclusive telephone service.
    b. Find the probability that exactly 5 households exclusively use a cell phone for telephone service.
    c. Find the mean number of households exclusively using cell phones.

Cumulative Binomial Probability Distributions

We may wish to know the probability of correctly guessing the answers to 6 *or more* true/false questions out of 10. Or we may be interested in the probability of *selecting less than two* defectives at random from production during the previous hour. In these cases, we need cumulative frequency distributions similar to the ones developed in the Chapter 2, Cumulative Distribution section on page 38. The following example will illustrate.

EXAMPLE

A study by the Illinois Department of Transportation concluded that 76.2% of front seat occupants used seat belts. That is, both occupants of the front seat were using their seat belts. Suppose we decide to compare that information with current usage. We select a sample of 12 vehicles.

1. What is the probability the front seat occupants in exactly 7 of the 12 vehicles selected are wearing seat belts?
2. What is the probability the front seat occupants in at least 7 of the 12 vehicles are wearing seat belts?

SOLUTION

This situation meets the binomial requirements.

- In a particular vehicle, both the front seat occupants are either wearing seat belts or they are not. There are only two possible outcomes.
- There are a fixed number of trials, 12 in this case, because 12 vehicles are checked.
- The probability of a "success" (occupants wearing seat belts) is the same from one vehicle to the next: 76.2%.
- The trials are independent. If the fourth vehicle selected in the sample has all the occupants wearing their seat belts, this does not have any effect on the results for the fifth or tenth vehicle.

To find the likelihood the occupants of *exactly* 7 of the sampled vehicles are wearing seat belts, we use formula (6–3). In this case, $n = 12$ and $\pi = .762$.

$$P(x = 7) = {}_{12}C_7(.762)^7(1 - .762)^{12-7} = 792(.149171)(.000764) = .0902$$

So we conclude the likelihood that the occupants of exactly 7 of the 12 sampled vehicles will be wearing their seat belts is about 9%.

To find the probability that the occupants in seven or more of the vehicles will be wearing seat belts, we use formula (6–3) from this chapter as well as the special rule of addition from the previous chapter. See formula (5-2) on page 141.

Because the events are mutually exclusive (meaning that a particular sample of 12 vehicles cannot have both a *total* of 7 and a *total* of 8 vehicles where the occupants are wearing seat belts), we find the probability of 7 vehicles where the occupants are wearing seat belts, the probability of 8, and so on up to the probability that occupants of all 12 sample vehicles are wearing seat belts. The probability of each of these outcomes is then totaled.

$$\begin{aligned} P(x \geq 7) &= P(x = 7) + P(x = 8) + P(x = 9) + P(x = 10) + P(x = 11) + P(x = 12) \\ &= .0902 + .1805 + .2569 + .2467 + .1436 + .0383 \\ &= .9562 \end{aligned}$$

So the probability of selecting 12 cars and finding that the occupants of 7 or more vehicles were wearing seat belts is .9562. This information is shown on the following Excel spreadsheet. There is a slight difference in the software answer due to rounding. The Excel commands are similar to those detailed in the Software Commands in Appendix C.

Cumulative Binomial.xlsx

	A	B	C	D
1	Success	Probability		
2	0	0.0000		
3	1	0.0000		
4	2	0.0000		
5	3	0.0002		
6	4	0.0017		
7	5	0.0088		
8	6	0.0329		
9	7	0.0902		
10	8	0.1805		
11	9	0.2569		
12	10	0.2467		
13	11	0.1436		
14	12	0.0383		
15		0.9563		

Sum of Probabilities for 7 or more successes

SELF-REVIEW 6–4

A recent study revealed that 40% of women in the San Diego metropolitan area who work full time also volunteer in the community. Suppose we randomly select eight women in the San Diego area.

(a) What are the values for n and π?
(b) What is the probability exactly three of the women volunteer in the community?
(c) What is the probability at least one of the women volunteers in the community?

EXERCISES

19. In a binomial distribution, $n = 8$ and $\pi = .30$. Find the probabilities of the following events.
  a. $x = 2$.
  b. $x \le 2$ (the probability that x is equal to or less than 2).
  c. $x \ge 3$ (the probability that x is equal to or greater than 3).

20. In a binomial distribution, $n = 12$ and $\pi = .60$. Find the following probabilities.
  a. $x = 5$.
  b. $x \le 5$.
  c. $x \ge 6$.

21. **FILE** In a recent study, 90% of the homes in the United States were found to have large-screen TVs. In a sample of nine homes, what is the probability that:
  a. All nine have large-screen TVs?
  b. Less than five have large-screen TVs?
  c. More than five have large-screen TVs?
  d. At least seven homes have large-screen TVs?

22. **FILE** A manufacturer of window frames knows from long experience that 5% of the production will have some type of minor defect that will require an adjustment. What is the probability that in a sample of 20 window frames:
  a. None will need adjustment?
  b. At least one will need adjustment?
  c. More than two will need adjustment?

23. **FILE** The speed with which utility companies can resolve problems is very important. GTC, the Georgetown Telephone Company, reports it can resolve customer problems the same day they are reported in 70% of the cases. Suppose the 15 cases reported today are representative of all complaints.
  a. How many of the problems would you expect to be resolved today? What is the standard deviation?
  b. What is the probability 10 of the problems can be resolved today?
  c. What is the probability 10 or 11 of the problems can be resolved today?
  d. What is the probability more than 10 of the problems can be resolved today?

24. **FILE** It is asserted that 80% of the cars approaching an individual toll booth in New Jersey are equipped with an E-ZPass transponder. Find the probability that in a sample of six cars:
  a. All six will have the transponder.
  b. At least three will have the transponder.
  c. None will have a transponder.

LO6-5
Explain the assumptions of the hypergeometric distribution and apply it to calculate probabilities.

HYPERGEOMETRIC PROBABILITY DISTRIBUTION

For the binomial distribution to be applied, the probability of a success must stay the same for each trial. For example, the probability of guessing the correct answer to a true/false question is .50. This probability remains the same for each question on an examination. Likewise, suppose that 40% of the registered voters in a precinct are

Republicans. If 27 registered voters are selected at random, the probability of choosing a Republican on the first selection is .40. The chance of choosing a Republican on the next selection is also .40, assuming that the sampling is done *with replacement,* meaning that the person selected is put back in the population before the next person is selected.

Most sampling, however, is done *without replacement.* Thus, if the population is small, the probability of a success will change for each observation. For example, if the population consists of 20 items, the probability of selecting a particular item from that population is 1/20. If the sampling is done without replacement, after the first selection there are only 19 items remaining; the probability of selecting a particular item on the second selection is only 1/19. For the third selection, the probability is 1/18, and so on. This assumes that the population is **finite**—that is, the number in the population is known and relatively small in number. Examples of a finite population are 2,842 Republicans in the precinct, 9,241 applications for medical school, and the eighteen Dakota 4x4 Crew Cabs at Helfman Dodge Chrysler Jeep in Houston, Texas.

Recall that one of the criteria for the binomial distribution is that the probability of success remains the same from trial to trial. Because the probability of success does not remain the same from trial to trial when sampling is from a relatively small population without replacement, the binomial distribution should not be used. Instead, the **hypergeometric distribution** is applied. Therefore, (1) if a sample is selected from a finite population without replacement and (2) if the size of the sample n is more than 5% of the size of the population N, then the hypergeometric distribution is used to determine the probability of a specified number of successes or failures. It is especially appropriate when the size of the population is small.

The formula for the hypergeometric distribution is:

HYPERGEOMETRIC DISTRIBUTION

$$P(x) = \frac{({}_SC_x)({}_{N-S}C_{n-x})}{{}_NC_n} \qquad [6\text{–}6]$$

where:

N is the size of the population.
S is the number of successes in the population.
x is the number of successes in the sample. It may be 0, 1, 2, 3, ...
n is the size of the sample or the number of trials.
C is the symbol for a combination.

In summary, a hypergeometric probability distribution has these characteristics:

HYPERGEOMETRIC PROBABILITY EXPERIMENT

1. An outcome on each trial of an experiment is classified into one of two mutually exclusive categories—a success or a failure.
2. The random variable is the number of successes in a fixed number of trials.
3. The trials are not independent.
4. We assume that we sample from a finite population without replacement and $n/N > 0.05$. So, the probability of a success *changes* for each trial.

The following example illustrates the details of determining a probability using the hypergeometric distribution.

EXAMPLE

PlayTime Toys Inc. employs 50 people in the Assembly Department. Forty of the employees belong to a union and 10 do not. Five employees are selected at random to form a committee to meet with management regarding shift starting times. What is the probability that four of the five selected for the committee belong to a union?

© Howard Berman/Getty Images

SOLUTION

The population in this case is the 50 Assembly Department employees. An employee can be selected for the committee only once. Hence, the sampling is done without replacement. Thus, the probability of selecting a union employee, for example, changes from one trial to the next. The hypergeometric distribution is appropriate for determining the probability. In this problem,

N is 50, the number of employees.
S is 40, the number of union employees.
x is 4, the number of union employees selected.
n is 5, the number of employees selected.

We wish to find the probability 4 of the 5 committee members belong to a union. Inserting these values into formula (6–6):

$$P(4) = \frac{({}_{40}C_4)({}_{50-40}C_{5-4})}{{}_{50}C_5} = \frac{(91{,}390)(10)}{2{,}118{,}760} = .431$$

Thus, the probability of selecting 5 assembly workers at random from the 50 workers and finding 4 of the 5 are union members is .431.

Table 6–4 shows the hypergeometric probabilities of finding 0, 1, 2, 3, 4, and 5 union members on the committee.

TABLE 6–4 Hypergeometric Probabilities ($n = 5$, $N = 50$, and $S = 40$) for the Number of Union Members on the Committee

Union Members	Probability
0	.000
1	.004
2	.044
3	.210
4	.431
5	.311
	1.000

Table 6–5 shows a comparison of the results using the binomial distribution and the hypergeometric distribution. Because 40 of the 50 Assembly Department employees belong to the union, we let $\pi = .80$ for the binomial distribution. The binomial probabilities for Table 6–5 come from the binomial distribution with $n = 5$ and $\pi = .80$.

TABLE 6–5 Hypergeometric and Binomial Probabilities for PlayTime Toys Inc. Assembly Department

Number of Union Members on Committee	Hypergeometric Probability, $P(x)$	Binomial Probability ($n = 5$ and $\pi = .80$)
0	.000	.000
1	.004	.006
2	.044	.051
3	.210	.205
4	.431	.410
5	.311	.328
	1.000	1.000

As Table 6–5 shows, when the binomial requirement of a constant probability of success cannot be met, the hypergeometric distribution should be used. There are clear differences between the probabilities.

However, under certain conditions the results of the binomial distribution can be used to approximate the hypergeometric. This leads to a rule of thumb: if selected items are not returned to the population, the binomial distribution can be used to closely approximate the hypergeometric distribution when $n < .05N$. In other words, the binomial will closely approximate the hypergeometric distribution if the sample is less than 5% of the population. For example, if the population, N, is 150, the number of successes in the population, S, is 120, and the sample size, n, is five, then the rule of thumb is true. That is, $5 < 0.05(150)$, or $5 < 7.5$. The sample size is less than 5% of the population. In the following table, hypergeometric and binomial probability distributions are compared for this situation. The probabilities are very close.

TABLE 6–6 A Comparison of Hypergeometric and Binomial Probabilities When the Sample Size is Less than 0.05(n)

x	Hypergeometric Probability, $P(x)$	Binomial Probability ($n = 5$ and $\pi = .80 = (120/150)$
0	.000	.000
1	.006	.006
2	.049	.051
3	.206	.205
4	.417	.410
5	.322	.328
	1.000	1.000

	A	B
1	Union Members	Probability
2	0	0.000
3	1	0.004
4	2	0.044
5	3	0.210
6	4	0.431
7	5	0.311

A hypergeometric distribution can be created using Excel. See the output for Table 6–5 on the left. The necessary steps are given in Appendix C in the back of the text.

SELF-REVIEW 6–5

Horwege Discount Brokers plans to hire five new financial analysts this year. There is a pool of 12 approved applicants, and George Horwege, the owner, decides to randomly select those who will be hired. There are eight men and four women among the approved applicants. What is the probability that three of the five hired are men?

EXERCISES

25. A CD contains 10 songs; 6 are classical and 4 are rock and roll. In a sample of three songs, what is the probability that exactly two are classical? Assume the samples are drawn without replacement.
26. A population consists of 15 items, 10 of which are acceptable. In a sample of four items, what is the probability that exactly three are acceptable? Assume the samples are drawn without replacement.
27. The Riverton Branch of the National Bank of Wyoming has 10 real estate loans over $1,000,000. Of these 10 loans, 3 are "underwater." A loan is underwater if the amount of the loan is greater than the value of the property. The chief loan officer decided to randomly select two of these loans to determine if they met all banking standards. What is the probability that neither of the selected loans is underwater?
28. The Computer Systems Department has eight faculty, six of whom are tenured. Dr. Vonder, the chairman, wants to establish a committee of three department faculty members to review the curriculum. If she selects the committee at random:
    a. What is the probability all members of the committee are tenured?
    b. What is the probability that at least one member is not tenured? (Hint: For this question, use the complement rule.)
29. Keith's Florists has 15 delivery trucks, used mainly to deliver flowers and flower arrangements in the Greenville, South Carolina, area. Of these 15 trucks, 6 have brake problems. A sample of five trucks is randomly selected. What is the probability that two of those tested have defective brakes?
30. The game called Lotto sponsored by the Louisiana Lottery Commission pays its largest prize when a contestant matches all 6 of the 40 possible numbers. Assume there are 40 ping-pong balls each with a single number between 1 and 40. Any number appears only once, and the winning balls are selected without replacement.
    a. The commission reports that the probability of matching all the numbers are 1 in 3,838,380. What is this in terms of probability?
    b. Use the hypergeometric formula to find this probability.

    The lottery commission also pays if a contestant matches four or five of the six winning numbers. Hint: Divide the 40 numbers into two groups, winning numbers and nonwinning numbers.
    c. Find the probability, again using the hypergeometric formula, for matching 4 of the 6 winning numbers.
    d. Find the probability of matching 5 of the 6 winning numbers.

LO6-6
Explain the assumptions of the Poisson distribution and apply it to calculate probabilities.

POISSON PROBABILITY DISTRIBUTION

The **Poisson probability distribution** describes the number of times some event occurs during a specified interval. Examples of an interval may be time, distance, area, or volume.

The distribution is based on two assumptions. The first assumption is that the probability is proportional to the length of the interval. The second assumption is that the intervals are independent. To put it another way, the longer the interval, the larger the probability, and the number of occurrences in one interval does not affect the other intervals. This distribution is a limiting form of the binomial distribution when the probability of a success is very small and n is large. It is often referred to as the "law of improbable events," meaning that the probability, π, of a particular event's happening is quite small. The Poisson distribution is a discrete probability distribution because it is formed by counting.

STATISTICS IN ACTION

Near the end of World War II, the Germans developed rocket bombs, which were fired at the city of London. The Allied military command didn't know whether these bombs were fired at random or whether they had an aiming device. To investigate, the city of London was divided into 586 square regions. The distribution of hits in each square was recorded as follows:

Hits	0	1	2	3	4	5
Regions	229	221	93	35	7	1

To interpret, the above chart indicates that 229 regions were not hit with one of the bombs. Seven regions were hit four times. Using the Poisson distribution, with a mean of 0.93 hits per region, the expected number of hits is as follows:

Hits	0	1	2	3	4	5 or more
Regions	231.2	215.0	100.0	31.0	7.2	1.6

Because the actual number of hits was close to the expected number of hits, the military command concluded that the bombs were falling at random. The Germans had not developed a bomb with an aiming device.

The Poisson probability distribution has these characteristics:

POISSON PROBABILITY EXPERIMENT

1. The random variable is the number of times some event occurs during a defined interval.
2. The probability of the event is proportional to the size of the interval.
3. The intervals do not overlap and are independent.

This probability distribution has many applications. It is used as a model to describe the distribution of errors in data entry, the number of scratches and other imperfections in newly painted car panels, the number of defective parts in outgoing shipments, the number of customers waiting to be served at a restaurant or waiting to get into an attraction at Disney World, and the number of accidents on I–75 during a three-month period.

The Poisson distribution is described mathematically by the formula:

POISSON DISTRIBUTION $$P(x) = \frac{\mu^x e^{-\mu}}{x!} \quad \textbf{(6–7)}$$

where:

μ (mu) is the mean number of occurrences (successes) in a particular interval.
e is the constant 2.71828 (base of the Napierian logarithmic system).
x is the number of occurrences (successes).
$P(x)$ is the probability for a specified value of x.

The mean number of successes, μ, is found by $n\pi$, where n is the total number of trials and π the probability of success.

MEAN OF A POISSON DISTRIBUTION $$\mu = n\pi \quad \textbf{(6–8)}$$

The variance of the Poisson is equal to its mean. If, for example, the probability that a check cashed by a bank will bounce is .0003, and 10,000 checks are cashed, the mean and the variance for the number of bad checks is 3.0, found by $\mu = n\pi = 10{,}000(.0003) = 3.0$.

Recall that for a binomial distribution there are a fixed number of trials. For example, for a four-question multiple-choice test there can only be zero, one, two, three, or four successes (correct answers). The random variable, x, for a Poisson distribution, however, can assume an *infinite number of values*—that is, 0, 1, 2, 3, 4, 5, . . . However, *the probabilities become very small after the first few occurrences* (successes).

EXAMPLE

Budget Airlines is a seasonal airline that operates flights from Myrtle Beach, South Carolina, to various cities in the northeast. The destinations include Boston, Pittsburgh, Buffalo, and both LaGuardia and JFK airports in New York City. Recently Budget has been concerned about the number of lost bags. Ann Poston from the Analytics Department was asked to study the issue. She randomly selected a sample of 500 flights and found that a total of twenty bags were lost on the sampled flights.

Show that this situation follows the Poisson distribution. What is the mean number of bags lost per flight? What is the likelihood that no bags are lost on a flight? What is the probability at least one bag is lost?

SOLUTION

To begin, let's confirm that the Budget Airlines situation follows a Poisson Distribution. Refer to the highlighted box labeled Poisson Probability Experiment in this section. We count the number of bags lost on a particular flight. On most flights there were no bags lost, on a few flights one was lost, and perhaps in very rare circumstances more than one bag was lost. The continuum or interval is a particular flight. Each flight is assumed to be independent of any other flight.

Based on the sample information we can estimate the mean number of bags lost per flight. There were 20 bags lost in 500 flights so the mean number of bags lost per flight is .04, found by 20/500. Hence $\mu = .04$.

We use formula (6–7) to find the probability of any number of lost bags. In this case x, the number of lost bags is 0.

$$P(0) = \frac{\mu^x e^{-\mu}}{x!} = \frac{.04^0 e^{-0.04}}{0!} = .9608$$

The probability of exactly one lost bag is:

$$P(1) = \frac{\mu^x e^{-\mu}}{x!} = \frac{.04^0 e^{-0.04}}{1!} = .0384$$

The probability of one or more lost bags is:

$$1 - P(0) = 1 - \frac{\mu^x e^{-\mu}}{x!} = 1 - \frac{.04^0 e^{-0.04}}{0!} = 1 - .9608 = .0392$$

These probabilities can also be found using Excel. The commands to compute Poisson probabilities are in Appendix C.

	A	B
1	Success	Probability
2	0	0.9608
3	1	0.0384
4	2	0.0008
5	3	0.0000
6	4	0.0000
7	5	0.0000
8	6	0.0000
9	7	0.0000

Part of Appendix B.2 is repeated as Table 6–7. For certain values of μ, the mean of the Poisson distribution, we can read the probability directly from the table. Turning to another example, NewYork-LA Trucking Company finds the mean number of breakdowns on the New York to Los Angeles route is 0.30. From Table 6–7 we can locate the probability of no breakdowns on a particular run. First find the column headed "0.30" then read down that column to the row labeled "0". The value at the intersection is .7408, so this value is the probability of no breakdowns on a particular run. The probability of one breakdown is .2222.

TABLE 6–7 Poisson Table for Various Values of μ (from Appendix B.2)

	μ								
x	**0.1**	**0.2**	**0.3**	**0.4**	**0.5**	**0.6**	**0.7**	**0.8**	**0.9**
0	0.9048	0.8187	0.7408	0.6703	0.6065	0.5488	0.4966	0.4493	0.4066
1	0.0905	0.1637	0.2222	0.2681	0.3033	0.3293	0.3476	0.3595	0.3659
2	0.0045	0.0164	0.0333	0.0536	0.0758	0.0988	0.1217	0.1438	0.1647
3	0.0002	0.0011	0.0033	0.0072	0.0126	0.0198	0.0284	0.0383	0.0494
4	0.0000	0.0001	0.0003	0.0007	0.0016	0.0030	0.0050	0.0077	0.0111
5	0.0000	0.0000	0.0000	0.0001	0.0002	0.0004	0.0007	0.0012	0.0020
6	0.0000	0.0000	0.0000	0.0000	0.0000	0.0000	0.0001	0.0002	0.0003
7	0.0000	0.0000	0.0000	0.0000	0.0000	0.0000	0.0000	0.0000	0.0000

Earlier in this section, we mentioned that the Poisson probability distribution is a limiting form of the binomial. That is, we could estimate a binomial probability using the Poisson. In the following example, we use the Poisson distribution to estimate a binomial probability when *n*, the number of trials, is large and π, the probability of a success, small.

EXAMPLE

Coastal Insurance Company underwrites insurance for beachfront properties along the Virginia, North and South Carolina, and Georgia coasts. It uses the estimate that the probability of a named Category III hurricane (sustained winds of more than 110 miles per hour) or higher striking a particular region of the coast (for example, St. Simons Island, Georgia) in any one year is .05. If a homeowner takes a 30-year mortgage on a recently purchased property in St. Simons, what is the likelihood that the owner will experience at least one hurricane during the mortgage period?

SOLUTION

To use the Poisson probability distribution, we begin by determining the mean or expected number of storms meeting the criterion hitting St. Simons during the 30-year period. That is:

$$\mu = n\pi = 30(.05) = 1.5$$

where:

n is the number of years, 30 in this case.
π is the probability a hurricane meeting the strength criteria comes ashore.
μ is the mean or expected number of storms in a 30-year period.

To find the probability of at least one storm hitting St. Simons Island, Georgia, we first find the probability of no storms hitting the coast and subtract that value from 1.

$$P(x \geq 1) = 1 - P(x = 0) = 1 - \frac{\mu^0 e^{-1.5}}{0!} = 1 - .2231 = .7769$$

We conclude that the likelihood a hurricane meeting the strength criteria will strike the beachfront property at St. Simons during the 30-year period when the mortgage is in effect is .7769. To put it another way, the probability St. Simons will be hit by a Category III or higher hurricane during the 30-year period is a little more than 75%.

We should emphasize that the continuum, as previously described, still exists. That is, there are expected to be 1.5 storms hitting the coast per 30-year period. The continuum is the 30-year period.

In the preceding case, we are actually using the Poisson distribution as an estimate of the binomial. Note that we've met the binomial conditions outlined on page 183.

- There are only two possible outcomes: a hurricane hits the St. Simons area or it does not.
- There are a fixed number of trials, in this case 30 years.
- There is a constant probability of success; that is, the probability of a hurricane hitting the area is .05 each year.
- The years are independent. That means if a named storm strikes in the fifth year, that has no effect on any other year.

To find the probability of at least one storm striking the area in a 30-year period using the binomial distribution:

$$P(x \geq 1) = 1 - P(x = 0) = 1 - [{}_{30}C_0(.05)^0(.95)^{30}] = 1 - [(1)(1)(.2146)] = .7854$$

The probability of at least one hurricane hitting the St. Simons area during the 30-year period using the binomial distribution is .7854.

Which answer is correct? Why should we look at the problem both ways? The binomial is the more "technically correct" solution. The Poisson can be thought of as an approximation for the binomial, when n, the number of trials is large, and π, the probability of a success, is small. We look at the problem using both distributions to emphasize the convergence of the two discrete distributions. In some instances, using the Poisson may be the quicker solution, and as you see there is little practical difference in the answers. In fact, as n gets larger and π smaller, the difference between the two distributions gets smaller.

The Poisson probability distribution is always positively skewed and the random variable has no specific upper limit. In the lost bags example/solution, the Poisson distribution, with $\mu = 0.04$, is highly skewed. As μ becomes larger, the Poisson distribution becomes more symmetrical. For example, Chart 6–4 shows the distributions of

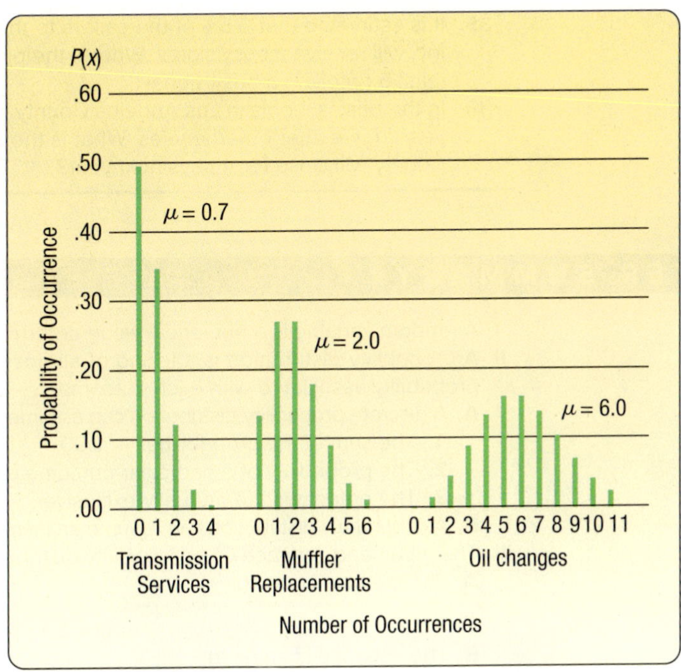

CHART 6–4 Poisson Probability Distributions for Means of 0.7, 2.0, and 6.0

the number of transmission services, muffler replacements, and oil changes per day at Avellino's Auto Shop. They follow Poisson distributions with means of 0.7, 2.0, and 6.0, respectively.

In summary, the Poisson distribution is a family of discrete distributions. All that is needed to construct a Poisson probability distribution is the mean number of defects, errors, or other random variable, designated as μ.

SELF-REVIEW 6–6

From actuary tables, Washington Insurance Company determined the likelihood that a man age 25 will die within the next year is .0002. If Washington Insurance sells 4,000 policies to 25-year-old men this year, what is the probability they will pay on exactly one policy?

EXERCISES

31. In a Poisson distribution $\mu = 0.4$.
- **a.** What is the probability that $x = 0$?
- **b.** What is the probability that $x > 0$?

32. In a Poisson distribution $\mu = 4$.
- **a.** What is the probability that $x = 2$?
- **b.** What is the probability that $x \leq 2$?
- **c.** What is the probability that $x > 2$?

33. Ms. Bergen is a loan officer at Coast Bank and Trust. From her years of experience, she estimates that the probability is .025 that an applicant will not be able to repay his or her installment loan. Last month she made 40 loans.
- **a.** What is the probability that three loans will be defaulted?
- **b.** What is the probability that at least three loans will be defaulted?

34. Automobiles arrive at the Elkhart exit of the Indiana Toll Road at the rate of two per minute. The distribution of arrivals approximates a Poisson distribution.
- **a.** What is the probability that no automobiles arrive in a particular minute?
- **b.** What is the probability that at least one automobile arrives during a particular minute?

35. It is estimated that 0.5% of the callers to the Customer Service department of Dell Inc. will receive a busy signal. What is the probability that of today's 1,200 callers at least 5 received a busy signal?

36. In the past, schools in Los Angeles County have closed an average of 3 days each year for weather emergencies. What is the probability that schools in Los Angeles County will close for 4 days next year?

CHAPTER SUMMARY

I. A random variable is a numerical value determined by the outcome of an experiment.

II. A probability distribution is a listing of all possible outcomes of an experiment and the probability associated with each outcome.
- **A.** A discrete probability distribution can assume only certain values. The main features are:
  1. The sum of the probabilities is 1.00.
  2. The probability of a particular outcome is between 0.00 and 1.00.
  3. The outcomes are mutually exclusive.
- **B.** A continuous distribution can assume an infinite number of values within a specific range.

III. The mean and variance of a probability distribution are computed as follows.
- **A.** The mean is equal to:

$$\mu = \Sigma[xP(x)] \quad \textbf{(6–1)}$$

- **B.** The variance is equal to:

$$\sigma^2 = \Sigma[(x - \mu)^2P(x)] \quad \textbf{(6–2)}$$

IV. The binomial distribution has the following characteristics.

A. Each outcome is classified into one of two mutually exclusive categories.

B. The distribution results from a count of the number of successes in a fixed number of trials.

C. The probability of a success remains the same from trial to trial.

D. Each trial is independent.

E. A binomial probability is determined as follows:

$$P(x) = {}_nC_x \pi^x (1 - \pi)^{n-x} \quad \textbf{(6–3)}$$

F. The mean is computed as:

$$\mu = n\pi \quad \textbf{(6–4)}$$

G. The variance is

$$\sigma^2 = n\pi(1 - \pi) \quad \textbf{(6–5)}$$

V. The hypergeometric distribution has the following characteristics.

A. There are only two possible outcomes.

B. The probability of a success is not the same on each trial.

C. The distribution results from a count of the number of successes in a fixed number of trials.

D. It is used when sampling without replacement from a finite population.

E. A hypergeometric probability is computed from the following equation:

$$P(x) = \frac{({}_SC_x)({}_{N-S}C_{n-x})}{({}_NC_n)} \quad \textbf{(6–6)}$$

VI. The Poisson distribution has the following characteristics.

A. It describes the number of times some event occurs during a specified interval.

B. The probability of a "success" is proportional to the length of the interval.

C. Nonoverlapping intervals are independent.

D. It is a limiting form of the binomial distribution when n is large and π is small.

E. A Poisson probability is determined from the following equation:

$$P(x) = \frac{\mu^x e^{-\mu}}{x!} \quad \textbf{(6–7)}$$

F. The mean and the variance are:

$$\mu = n\pi$$
$$\sigma^2 = n\pi \quad \textbf{(6–8)}$$

CHAPTER EXERCISES

37. What is the difference between a random variable and a probability distribution?

38. For each of the following indicate whether the random variable is discrete or continuous.

a. The length of time to get a haircut.

b. The number of cars a jogger passes each morning while running.

c. The number of hits for a team in a high school girls' softball game.

d. The number of patients treated at the South Strand Medical Center between 6 and 10 p.m. each night.

e. The distance your car traveled on the last fill-up.

f. The number of customers at the Oak Street Wendy's who used the drive-through facility.

g. The distance between Gainesville, Florida, and all Florida cities with a population of at least 50,000.

39. FILE An investment will be worth \$1,000, \$2,000, or \$5,000 at the end of the year. The probabilities of these values are .25, .60, and .15, respectively. Determine the mean and variance of the investment's dollar value.

40. The following notice appeared in the golf shop at a Myrtle Beach, South Carolina, golf course.

Blackmoor Golf Club Members

The golf shop is holding a raffle to win a
TaylorMade M1 10.5° Regular Flex Driver ($300 value).
Tickets are $5.00 each.
Only 80 tickets will be sold.
Please see the golf shop to get your tickets!

John Underpar buys a ticket.

a. What are Mr. Underpar's possible monetary outcomes?
b. What are the probabilities of the possible outcomes?
c. Summarize Mr. Underpar's "experiment" as a probability distribution.
d. What is the mean or expected value of the probability distribution? Explain your result.
e. If all 80 tickets are sold, what is the expected return to the Club?

41. **FILE** Croissant Bakery Inc. offers special decorated cakes for birthdays, weddings, and other occasions. It also has regular cakes available in its bakery. The following table gives the total number of cakes sold per day and the corresponding probability. Compute the mean, variance, and standard deviation of the number of cakes sold per day.

Number of Cakes Sold in a Day	Probability
12	.25
13	.40
14	.25
15	.10

42. **FILE** The payouts for the Powerball lottery and their corresponding odds and probabilities of occurrence are shown below. The price of a ticket is $1.00. Find the mean and standard deviation of the payout. Hint: Don't forget to include the cost of the ticket and its corresponding probability.

Divisions	Payout	Odds	Probability
Five plus Powerball	$50,000,000	146,107,962	0.000000006844
Match 5	200,000	3,563,609	0.000000280614
Four plus Powerball	10,000	584,432	0.000001711060
Match 4	100	14,255	0.000070145903
Three plus Powerball	100	11,927	0.000083836351
Match 3	7	291	0.003424657534
Two plus Powerball	7	745	0.001340482574
One plus Powerball	4	127	0.007812500000
Zero plus Powerball	3	69	0.014285714286

43. In a recent study, 35% of people surveyed indicated chocolate was their favorite flavor of ice cream. Suppose we select a sample of 10 people and ask them to name their favorite flavor of ice cream.

a. How many of those in the sample would you expect to name chocolate?
b. What is the probability exactly four of those in the sample name chocolate?
c. What is the probability four or more name chocolate?

44. **FILE** Thirty percent of the population in a southwestern community are Spanish-speaking Americans. A Spanish-speaking person is accused of killing a non-Spanish-speaking American and goes to trial. Of the first 12 potential jurors, only 2 are Spanish-speaking Americans, and 10 are not. The defendant's lawyer challenges the jury selection, claiming bias against her client. The government lawyer disagrees, saying that the probability of this particular jury composition is common. Compute the probability and discuss the assumptions.

45. An auditor for Health Maintenance Services of Georgia reports 40% of policyholders 55 years or older submit a claim during the year. Fifteen policyholders are randomly selected for company records.

a. How many of the policyholders would you expect to have filed a claim within the last year?

b. What is the probability that 10 of the selected policyholders submitted a claim last year?

c. What is the probability that 10 or more of the selected policyholders submitted a claim last year?

d. What is the probability that more than 10 of the selected policyholders submitted a claim last year?

46. Tire and Auto Supply is considering a 2-for-1 stock split. Before the transaction is finalized, at least two-thirds of the 1,200 company stockholders must approve the proposal. To evaluate the likelihood the proposal will be approved, the CFO selected a sample of 18 stockholders. He contacted each and found 14 approved of the proposed split. What is the likelihood of this event, assuming two-thirds of the stockholders approve?

47. A federal study reported that 7.5% of the U.S. workforce has a drug problem. A drug enforcement official for the state of Indiana wished to investigate this statement. In her sample of 20 employed workers:

a. How many would you expect to have a drug problem? What is the standard deviation?

b. What is the likelihood that *none* of the workers sampled has a drug problem?

c. What is the likelihood *at least one* has a drug problem?

48. The Bank of Hawaii reports that 7% of its credit card holders will default at some time in their life. The Hilo branch just mailed out 12 new cards today.

a. How many of these new cardholders would you expect to default? What is the standard deviation?

b. What is the likelihood that *none* of the cardholders will default?

c. What is the likelihood *at least one* will default?

49. Recent statistics suggest that 15% of those who visit a retail site on the internet to make a purchase. A retailer wished to verify this claim. To do so, she selected a sample of 16 "hits" to her site and found that 4 had actually made a purchase.

a. What is the likelihood of exactly four purchases?

b. How many purchases should she expect?

c. What is the likelihood that four or more "hits" result in a purchase?

50. In Chapter 19, we discuss *acceptance sampling.* Acceptance sampling is a statistical method used to monitor the quality of purchased parts and components. To ensure the quality of incoming parts, a purchaser or manufacturer normally samples 20 parts and allows one defect.

a. What is the likelihood of accepting a lot that is 1% defective?

b. If the quality of the incoming lot was actually 2%, what is the likelihood of accepting it?

c. If the quality of the incoming lot was actually 5%, what is the likelihood of accepting it?

51. Unilever Inc. recently developed a new body wash with a scent of ginger. Their research indicates that 30% of men like the new scent. To further investigate, Unilever's marketing research group randomly selected 15 men and asked them if they liked the scent. What is the probability that six or more men like the ginger scent in the body wash?

52. Dr. Richmond, a psychologist, is studying the daytime television viewing habits of college students. She believes 45% of college students watch soap operas during the afternoon. To further investigate, she selects a sample of 10.

a. Develop a probability distribution for the number of students in the sample who watch soap operas.

b. Find the mean and the standard deviation of this distribution.

c. What is the probability of finding exactly four students who watch soap operas?

d. What is the probability less than half of the students selected watch soap operas?

53. FILE A recent study conducted by Penn, Shone, and Borland, on behalf of LastMinute.com, revealed that 52% of business travelers plan their trips less than two weeks before departure. The study is to be replicated in the tri-state area with a sample of 12 frequent business travelers.

a. Develop a probability distribution for the number of travelers who plan their trips within two weeks of departure.

b. Find the mean and the standard deviation of this distribution.

c. What is the probability exactly 5 of the 12 selected business travelers plan their trips within two weeks of departure?

d. What is the probability 5 or fewer of the 12 selected business travelers plan their trips within two weeks of departure?

54. The Internal Revenue Service is studying the category of charitable contributions. A sample of 25 returns is selected from young couples between the ages of 20 and 35 who had an adjusted gross income of more than $100,000. Of these 25 returns, five had charitable contributions of more than $1,000. Four of these returns are selected for a comprehensive audit.

a. Explain why the hypergeometric distribution is appropriate.

b. What is the probability exactly one of the four audited had a charitable deduction of more than $1,000?

c. What is the probability at least one of the audited returns had a charitable contribution of more than $1,000?

55. The law firm of Hagel and Hagel is located in downtown Cincinnati. There are 10 partners in the firm; 7 live in Ohio and 3 in northern Kentucky. Ms. Wendy Hagel, the managing partner, wants to appoint a committee of 3 partners to look into moving the firm to northern Kentucky. If the committee is selected at random from the 10 partners, what is the probability that:

a. One member of the committee lives in northern Kentucky and the others live in Ohio?

b. At least one member of the committee lives in northern Kentucky?

56. Topten is a leading source on energy-efficient products. Their list of the top seven vehicles in terms of fuel efficiency for 2017 includes three Hondas.

a. Determine the probability distribution for the number of Hondas in a sample of two cars chosen from the top seven.

b. What is the likelihood that in the sample of two at least one Honda is included?

57. The position of chief of police in the city of Corry, Pennsylvania, is vacant. A search committee of Corry residents is charged with the responsibility of recommending a new chief to the city council. There are 12 applicants, 4 of whom are either female or members of a minority. The search committee decides to interview all 12 of the applicants. To begin, they randomly select four applicants to be interviewed on the first day, and none of the four is female or a member of a minority. The local newspaper, the *Corry Press*, suggests discrimination in an editorial. What is the likelihood of this occurrence?

58. **FILE** Listed below is the population by state for the 15 states with the largest population. Also included is whether that state's border touches the Gulf of Mexico, the Atlantic Ocean, or the Pacific Ocean (coastline).

Rank	State	Population	Coastline
1	California	38,802,500	Yes
2	Texas	26,956,958	Yes
3	Florida	19,893,297	Yes
4	New York	19,746,227	Yes
5	Illinois	12,880,580	No
6	Pennsylvania	12,787,209	No
7	Ohio	11,594,163	No
8	Georgia	10,097,343	Yes
9	North Carolina	9,943,964	Yes
10	Michigan	9,909,877	No
11	New Jersey	8,938,175	Yes
12	Virginia	8,326,289	Yes
13	Washington	7,061,530	Yes
14	Massachusetts	6,745,408	Yes
15	Arizona	6,731,484	No

Note that 5 of the 15 states do not have any coastline. Suppose three states are selected at random. What is the probability that:

a. None of the states selected has any coastline?

b. Exactly one of the selected states has a coastline?

c. At least one of the selected states has a coastline?

59. The sales of Lexus automobiles in the Detroit area follow a Poisson distribution with a mean of 3 per day.
   a. What is the probability that no Lexus is sold on a particular day?
   b. What is the probability that for 5 consecutive days at least one Lexus is sold?

60. Suppose 1.5% of the antennas on new Nokia cell phones are defective. For a random sample of 200 antennas, find the probability that:
   a. None of the antennas is defective.
   b. Three or more of the antennas are defective.

61. A study of the checkout lines at the Safeway Supermarket in the South Strand area revealed that between 4 and 7 p.m. on weekdays there is an average of four customers waiting in line. What is the probability that you visit Safeway today during this period and find:
   a. No customers are waiting?
   b. Four customers are waiting?
   c. Four or fewer are waiting?
   d. Four or more are waiting?

62. An internal study by the Technology Services department at Lahey Electronics revealed company employees receive an average of two non-work-related e-mails per hour. Assume the arrival of these e-mails is approximated by the Poisson distribution.
   a. What is the probability Linda Lahey, company president, received exactly one non-work-related e-mail between 4 p.m. and 5 p.m. yesterday?
   b. What is the probability she received five or more non-work-related e-mails during the same period?
   c. What is the probability she did not receive any non-work-related e-mails during the period?

63. Recent crime reports indicate that 3.1 motor vehicle thefts occur each minute in the United States. Assume that the distribution of thefts per minute can be approximated by the Poisson probability distribution.
   a. Calculate the probability exactly *four* thefts occur in a minute.
   b. What is the probability there are *no* thefts in a minute?
   c. What is the probability there is *at least one* theft in a minute?

64. Recent difficult economic times have caused an increase in the foreclosure rate of home mortgages. Statistics from the Penn Bank and Trust Company show their monthly foreclosure rate is now 1 loan out of every 136 loans. Last month the bank approved 300 loans.
   a. How many foreclosures would you expect the bank to have last month?
   b. What is the probability of exactly two foreclosures?
   c. What is the probability of at least one foreclosure?

65. The National Aeronautics and Space Administration (NASA) has experienced two disasters. The *Challenger* exploded over the Atlantic Ocean in 1986, and the *Columbia* disintegrated on reentry over East Texas in 2003. Based on the first 113 missions, and assuming failures occur at the same rate, consider the next 23 missions. What is the probability of exactly two failures? What is the probability of no failures?

66. According to the "January theory," if the stock market is up for the month of January, it will be up for the year. If it is down in January, it will be down for the year. According to an article in *The Wall Street Journal,* this theory held for 29 out of the last 34 years. Suppose there is no truth to this theory; that is, the probability it is either up or down is .50. What is the probability this could occur by chance? You will probably need a software package such as Excel or Minitab.

67. During the second round of the 1989 U.S. Open golf tournament, four golfers scored a hole in one on the sixth hole. The odds of a professional golfer making a hole in one are estimated to be 3,708 to 1, so the probability is 1/3,709. There were 155 golfers participating in the second round that day. Estimate the probability that four golfers would score a hole in one on the sixth hole.

68. According to sales information in the first quarter of 2016, 2.7% of new vehicles sold in the United States were hybrids. This is down from 3.3% for the same period a year earlier. An analyst's review of the data indicates that the reasons for the sales decline include the low price of gasoline and the higher price of a hybrid compared to similar vehicles. Let's assume these statistics remain the same for 2017. That is, 2.7 percent of new car sales are hybrids in the first quarter of 2017. For a sample of 40 vehicles sold in the Richmond, Virginia area:

a. How many vehicles would you expect to be hybrid?

b. Use the Poisson distribution to find the probability that five of the sales were hybrid vehicles.

c. Use the binomial distribution to find the probability that five of the sales were hybrid vehicles.

69. A recent CBS News survey reported that 67% of adults felt the U.S. Treasury should continue making pennies. Suppose we select a sample of 15 adults.

a. How many of the 15 would we expect to indicate that the Treasury should continue making pennies? What is the standard deviation?

b. What is the likelihood that exactly eight adults would indicate the Treasury should continue making pennies?

c. What is the likelihood at least eight adults would indicate the Treasury should continue making pennies?

DATA ANALYTICS

70. FILE Refer to the North Valley Real Estate data, which report information on homes sold in the area last year.

a. Create a probability distribution for the number of bedrooms. Compute the mean and the standard deviation of this distribution.

b. Create a probability distribution for the number of bathrooms. Compute the mean and the standard deviation of this distribution.

71. FILE Refer to the Baseball 2016 data. Compute the mean number of home runs per game. To do this, first find the mean number of home runs per team for 2016. Next, divide this value by 162 (a season comprises 162 games). Then multiply by 2 because there are two teams in each game. Use the Poisson distribution to estimate the number of home runs that will be hit in a game. Find the probability that:

a. There are no home runs in a game.

b. There are two home runs in a game.

c. There are at least four home runs in a game.

Continuous Probability Distributions

7

© Ilene MacDonald/Alamy Stock Photo

▲ **CRUISE SHIPS** of the Royal Viking line report that 80% of their rooms are occupied during September. For a cruise ship having 800 rooms, what is the probability that 665 or more are occupied in September? (See Exercise 60 and LO7-4.)

LEARNING OBJECTIVES

When you have completed this chapter, you will be able to:

LO7-1 Describe the uniform probability distribution and use it to calculate probabilities.

LO7-2 Describe the characteristics of a normal probability distribution.

LO7-3 Describe the standard normal probability distribution and use it to calculate probabilities.

LO7-4 Approximate the binomial probability distribution using the standard normal probability distribution to calculate probabilities.

LO7-5 Describe the exponential probability distribution and use it to calculate probabilities.

INTRODUCTION

Chapter 6 began our study of probability distributions. We consider three *discrete* probability distributions: binomial, hypergeometric, and Poisson. These distributions are based on discrete random variables, which can assume only clearly separated values. For example, we select for study 10 small businesses that began operations during the year 2014. The number still operating in 2017 can be 0, 1, 2, . . . , 10. There cannot be 3.7, 12, or −7 still operating in 2017. In this example, only certain outcomes are possible and these outcomes are represented by clearly separated values. In addition, the result is usually found by counting the number of successes. We count the number of the businesses in the study that are still in operation in 2017.

We continue our study of probability distributions by examining *continuous* probability distributions. A continuous probability distribution usually results from measuring something, such as the distance from the dormitory to the classroom, the weight of an individual, or the amount of bonus earned by CEOs. As an example, at Dave's Inlet Fish Shack flounder is the featured, fresh-fish menu item. The distribution of the amount of flounder sold per day has a mean of 10.0 pounds per day and a standard deviation of 3.0 pounds per day. This distribution is continuous because Dave, the owner, "measures" the amount of flounder sold each day. It is important to realize that a continuous random variable has an infinite number of values within a particular range. So, for a continuous random variable, probability is for a range of values. The probability for a specific value of a continuous random variable is 0.

This chapter shows how to use three continuous probability distributions: the uniform probability distribution, the normal probability distribution, and the exponential probability distribution.

LO7-1
Describe the uniform probability distribution and use it to calculate probabilities.

THE FAMILY OF UNIFORM PROBABILITY DISTRIBUTIONS

The uniform probability distribution is the simplest distribution for a continuous random variable. This distribution is rectangular in shape and is completely defined by its minimum and maximum values. Here are some examples that follow a uniform distribution.

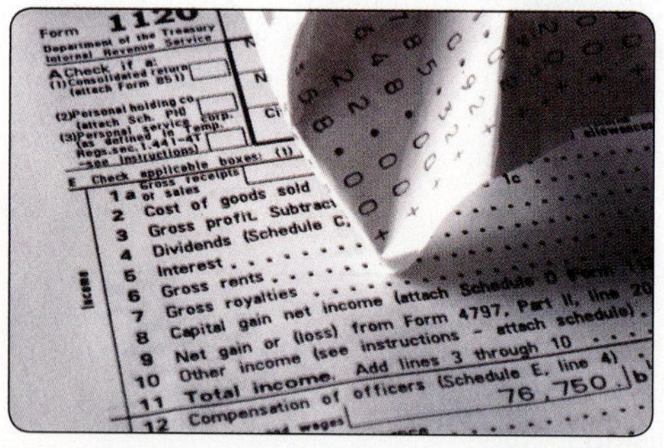

© C. Sherburne/PhotoLink/Getty Imagess

- The sales of gasoline at the Kwik Fill in Medina, New York, follow a uniform distribution that varies between 2,000 and 5,000 gallons per day. The random variable is the number of gallons sold per day and is continuous within the interval between 2,000 gallons and 5,000 gallons.
- Volunteers at the Grand Strand Public Library prepare federal income tax forms. The time to prepare form 1040-EZ follows a uniform distribution over the interval between 10 minutes and 30 minutes. The random variable is the number of minutes to complete the form, and it can assume any value between 10 and 30.

A uniform distribution is shown in Chart 7–1. The distribution's shape is rectangular and has a minimum value of a and a maximum of b. Also notice in Chart 7–1 the height of the distribution is constant or uniform for all values between a and b.

The mean of a uniform distribution is located in the middle of the interval between the minimum and maximum values. It is computed as:

MEAN OF THE UNIFORM DISTRIBUTION $$\mu = \frac{a + b}{2} \qquad \textbf{(7–1)}$$

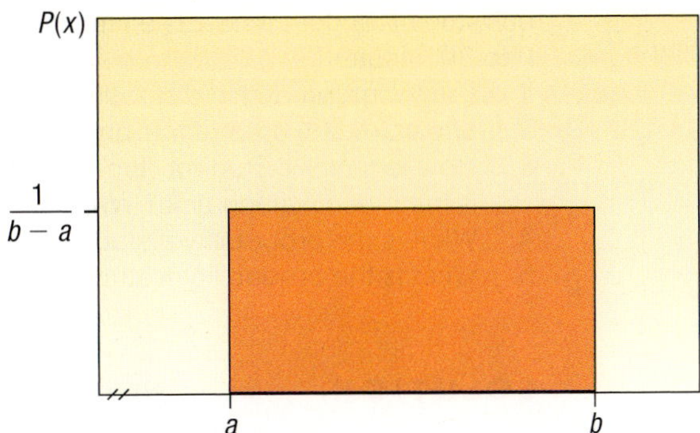

CHART 7–1 A Continuous Uniform Distribution

The standard deviation describes the dispersion of a distribution. In the uniform distribution, the standard deviation is also related to the interval between the maximum and minimum values.

STANDARD DEVIATION OF THE UNIFORM DISTRIBUTION

$$\sigma = \sqrt{\frac{(b - a)^2}{12}} \quad \textbf{(7–2)}$$

The equation for the uniform probability distribution is:

UNIFORM DISTRIBUTION

$$P(x) = \frac{1}{b - a} \text{ if } a \leq x \leq b \text{ and 0 elsewhere} \quad \textbf{(7–3)}$$

As we described in Chapter 6, probability distributions are useful for making probability statements concerning the values of a random variable. For distributions describing a continuous random variable, areas within the distribution represent probabilities. In the uniform distribution, its rectangular shape allows us to apply the area formula for a rectangle. Recall that we find the area of a rectangle by multiplying its length by its height. For the uniform distribution, the height of the rectangle is $P(x)$, which is $1/(b - a)$. The length or base of the distribution is $b - a$. So if we multiply the height of the distribution by its entire range to find the area, the result is always 1.00. To put it another way, the total area within a continuous probability distribution is equal to 1.00. In general

$$\text{Area} = (\text{height})(\text{base}) = \frac{1}{(b - a)}(b - a) = 1.00$$

So if a uniform distribution ranges from 10 to 15, the height is 0.20, found by 1/(15 − 10). The base is 5, found by 15 − 10. The total area is:

$$\text{Area} = (\text{height})(\text{base}) = \frac{1}{(15 - 10)}(15 - 10) = 1.00$$

The following example illustrates the features of a uniform distribution and how we use it to calculate probabilities.

EXAMPLE

Southwest Arizona State University provides bus service to students while they are on campus. A bus arrives at the North Main Street and College Drive stop every 30 minutes between 6 a.m. and 11 p.m. during weekdays. Students arrive at the bus stop at random times. The time that a student waits is uniformly distributed from 0 to 30 minutes.

1. Draw a graph of this distribution.
2. Show that the area of this uniform distribution is 1.00.
3. How long will a student "typically" have to wait for a bus? In other words, what is the mean waiting time? What is the standard deviation of the waiting times?
4. What is the probability a student will wait more than 25 minutes?
5. What is the probability a student will wait between 10 and 20 minutes?

SOLUTION

In this case, the random variable is the length of time a student must wait. Time is measured on a continuous scale, and the wait times may range from 0 minutes up to 30 minutes.

1. The graph of the uniform distribution is shown in Chart 7–2. The horizontal line is drawn at a height of .0333, found by 1/(30 – 0). The range of this distribution is 30 minutes.

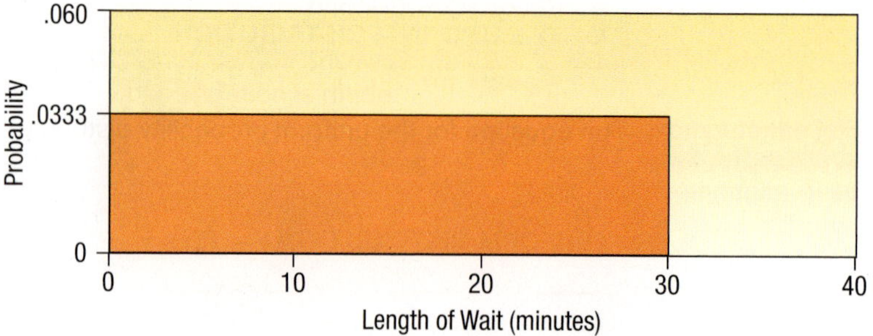

CHART 7–2 Uniform Probability Distribution of Student Waiting Times

2. The times students must wait for the bus are uniform over the interval from 0 minutes to 30 minutes, so in this case a is 0 and b is 30.

$$\text{Area} = (\text{height})(\text{base}) = \frac{1}{(30 - 0)}(30 - 0) = 1.00$$

3. To find the mean, we use formula (7–1).

$$\mu = \frac{a + b}{2} = \frac{0 + 30}{2} = 15$$

The mean of the distribution is 15 minutes, so the typical wait time for bus service is 15 minutes.

To find the standard deviation of the wait times, we use formula (7–2).

$$\sigma = \sqrt{\frac{(b - a)^2}{12}} = \sqrt{\frac{(30 - 0)^2}{12}} = 8.66$$

The standard deviation of the distribution is 8.66 minutes. This measures the variation in the student wait times.

4. The area within the distribution for the interval 25 to 30 represents this particular probability. From the area formula:

$$P(25 < \text{wait time} < 30) = (\text{height})(\text{base}) = \frac{1}{(30 - 0)}(5) = .1667$$

So the probability a student waits between 25 and 30 minutes is .1667. This conclusion is illustrated by the following graph.

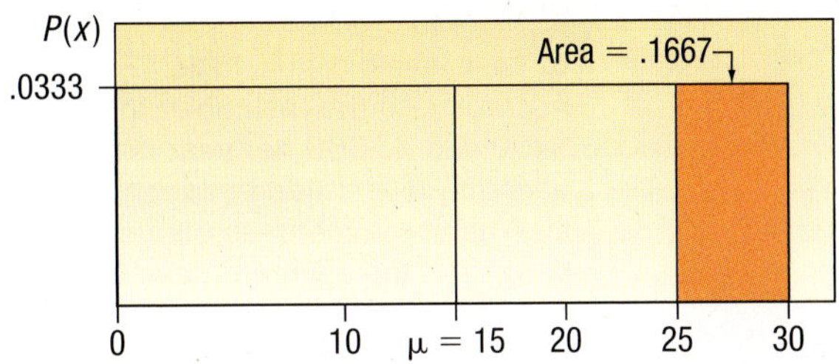

5. The area within the distribution for the interval 10 to 20 represents the probability.

$$P(10 < \text{wait time} < 20) = (\text{height})(\text{base}) = \frac{1}{(30 - 0)}(10) = .3333$$

We can illustrate this probability as follows.

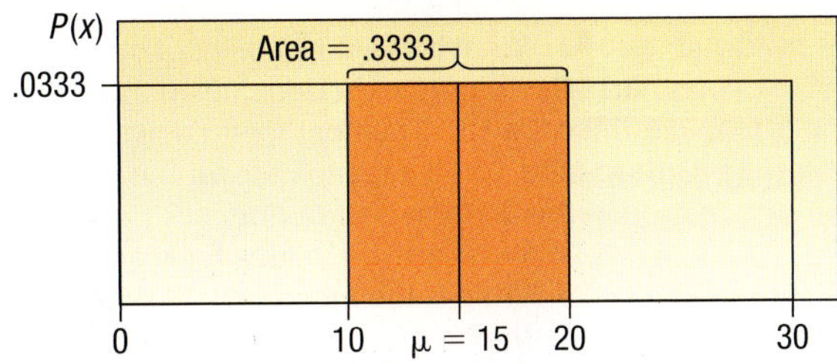

SELF-REVIEW 7–1

Microwave ovens only last so long. The life-time of a microwave oven follows a uniform distribution between 8 and 14 years.

(a) Draw this uniform distribution. What are the height and base values?
(b) Show the total area under the curve is 1.00.
(c) Calculate the mean and the standard deviation of this distribution.
(d) What is the probability a particular microwave oven lasts between 10 and 14 years?
(e) What is the probability a microwave oven will last less than 9 years?

EXERCISES

1. A uniform distribution is defined over the interval from 6 to 10.
   a. What are the values for *a* and *b*?
   b. What is the mean of this uniform distribution?
   c. What is the standard deviation?
   d. Show that the total area is 1.00.
   e. Find the probability of a value more than 7.
   f. Find the probability of a value between 7 and 9.

2. A uniform distribution is defined over the interval from 2 to 5.
   a. What are the values for *a* and *b*?
   b. What is the mean of this uniform distribution?
   c. What is the standard deviation?
   d. Show that the total area is 1.00.
   e. Find the probability of a value more than 2.6.
   f. Find the probability of a value between 2.9 and 3.7.

3. The closing price of Schnur Sporting Goods Inc. common stock is uniformly distributed between $20 and $30 per share. What is the probability that the stock price will be:
   a. More than $27?
   b. Less than or equal to $24?
4. According to the Insurance Institute of America, a family of four spends between $400 and $3,800 per year on all types of insurance. Suppose the money spent is uniformly distributed between these amounts.
   a. What is the mean amount spent on insurance?
   b. What is the standard deviation of the amount spent?
   c. If we select a family at random, what is the probability they spend less than $2,000 per year on insurance per year?
   d. What is the probability a family spends more than $3,000 per year?
5. The April rainfall in Flagstaff, Arizona, follows a uniform distribution between 0.5 and 3.00 inches.
   a. What are the values for *a* and *b*?
   b. What is the mean amount of rainfall for the month? What is the standard deviation?
   c. What is the probability of less than an inch of rain for the month?
   d. What is the probability of *exactly* 1.00 inch of rain?
   e. What is the probability of more than 1.50 inches of rain for the month?
6. Customers experiencing technical difficulty with their Internet cable service may call an 800 number for technical support. It takes the technician between 30 seconds and 10 minutes to resolve the problem. The distribution of this support time follows the uniform distribution.
   a. What are the values for *a* and *b* in minutes?
   b. What is the mean time to resolve the problem? What is the standard deviation of the time?
   c. What percent of the problems take more than 5 minutes to resolve?
   d. Suppose we wish to find the middle 50% of the problem-solving times. What are the end points of these two times?

LO7-2

Describe the characteristics of a normal probability distribution.

THE FAMILY OF NORMAL PROBABILITY DISTRIBUTIONS

Next we consider the normal probability distribution. Unlike the uniform distribution [see formula (7–3)] the normal probability distribution has a very complex formula.

NORMAL PROBABILITY DISTRIBUTION

$$P(x) = \frac{1}{\sigma\sqrt{2\pi}} e^{-\left[\frac{(x-\mu)^2}{2\sigma^2}\right]} \quad \textbf{(7–4)}$$

However, do not be bothered by how complex this formula looks. You are already familiar with many of the values. The symbols μ and σ refer to the mean and the standard deviation, as usual. The Greek symbol π is a constant and its value is approximately 22/7 or 3.1416. The letter *e* is also a constant. It is the base of the natural log system and is approximately equal to 2.718. *x* is the value of a continuous random variable. So a normal distribution is based on—that is, it is defined by—its mean and standard deviation.

You will not need to make calculations using formula (7–4). Instead you will use a table, given in Appendix B.3, to find various probabilities. These probabilities can also be calculated using Excel functions as well as other statistical software.

STATISTICS IN ACTION

Many variables are approximately, normally distributed, such as IQ scores, life expectancies, and adult height. This implies that nearly all observations occur within 3 standard deviations of the mean. On the other hand, observations that occur beyond 3 standard deviations from the mean are extremely rare. For example, the mean adult male height is 68.2 inches (about 5 feet 8 inches) with a standard deviation of 2.74. This means that almost all males are between 60.0 inches (5 feet) and 76.4 inches (6 feet 4 inches). LeBron James, a professional basketball player with the Cleveland Cavaliers, is 80 inches, or 6 feet 8 inches, which is clearly beyond 3 standard deviations from the mean. The height of a standard doorway is 6 feet 8 inches, and should be high enough for almost all adult males, except for a rare person like LeBron James.

As another example, the driver's seat in most vehicles is set to comfortably fit a person who is at least 159 cm (62.5 inches) tall. The distribution of heights of adult women is approximately a normal distribution with a mean of 161.5 cm and a standard deviation of 6.3 cm. Thus about 35% of adult women will not fit comfortably in the driver's seat.

The normal probability distribution has the following characteristics:

- It is **bell-shaped** and has a single peak at the center of the distribution. The arithmetic mean, median, and mode are equal and located in the center of the distribution. The total area under the curve is 1.00. Half the area under the normal curve is to the right of this center point and the other half, to the left of it.
- It is **symmetrical** about the mean. If we cut the normal curve vertically at the center value, the shapes of the curves will be mirror images. Also, the area of each half is 0.5.
- It falls off smoothly in either direction from the central value. That is, the distribution is **asymptotic:** The curve gets closer and closer to the *X*-axis but never actually touches it. To put it another way, the tails of the curve extend indefinitely in both directions.
- The location of a normal distribution is determined by the mean, μ. The dispersion or spread of the distribution is determined by the standard deviation, σ.

These characteristics are shown graphically in Chart 7–3.

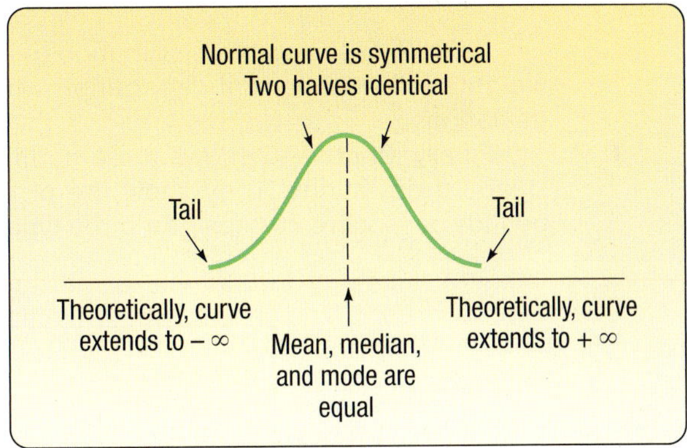

CHART 7–3 Characteristics of a Normal Distribution

There is not just one normal probability distribution, but rather a "family" of them. For example, in Chart 7–4 the probability distributions of length of employee service in three different plants are compared. In the Camden plant, the mean is 20 years and the standard deviation is 3.1 years. There is another normal probability distribution for the length of service in the Dunkirk plant, where $\mu = 20$ years and $\sigma = 3.9$ years. In the Elmira plant, $\mu = 20$ years and $\sigma = 5.0$ years. Note that the means are the same but the standard deviations are different. As the standard deviation gets smaller, the distribution becomes more narrow and "peaked."

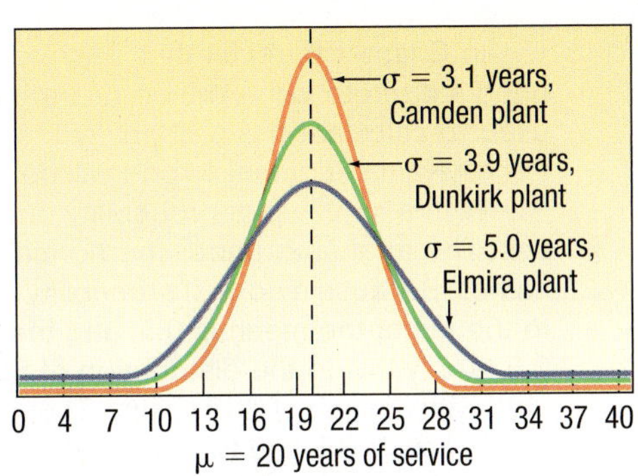

CHART 7–4 Normal Probability Distributions with Equal Means but Different Standard Deviations

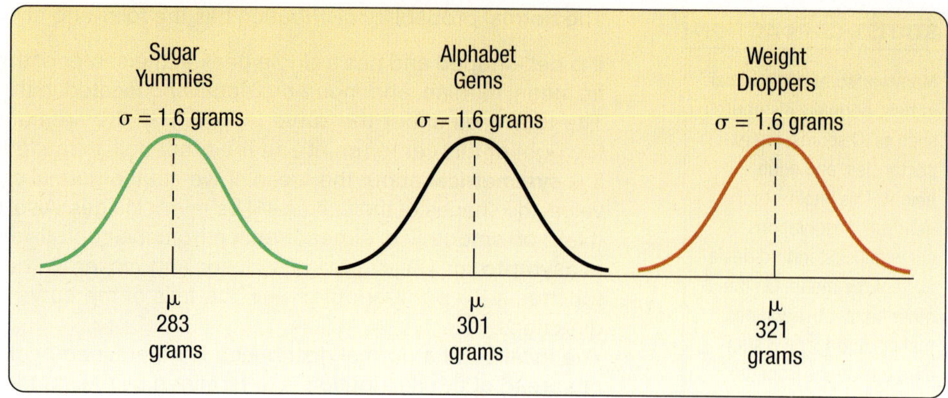

CHART 7–5 Normal Probability Distributions Having Different Means but Equal Standard Deviations

Chart 7–5 shows the distribution of box weights of three different cereals. The weights follow a normal distribution with different means but identical standard deviations.

Finally, Chart 7–6 shows three normal distributions having different means and standard deviations. They show the distribution of tensile strengths, measured in pounds per square inch (psi), for three types of cables.

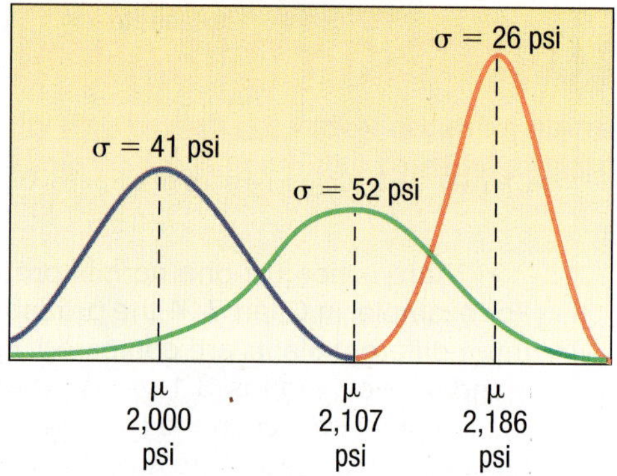

CHART 7–6 Normal Probability Distributions with Different Means and Standard Deviations

In Chapter 6, recall that discrete probability distributions show the specific likelihood a discrete value will occur. For example, on page 186 the binomial distribution is used to calculate the probability that none of the five flights arriving at the Bradford Pennsylvania Regional Airport will be late.

With a continuous probability distribution, areas below the curve define probabilities. The total area under the normal curve is 1.0. This accounts for all possible outcomes. Because a normal probability distribution is symmetric, the area under the curve to the left of the mean is 0.5, and the area under the curve to the right of the mean is 0.5. Apply this to the distribution of Sugar Yummies in Chart 7–5. It is normally distributed with a mean of 283 grams. Therefore, the probability of filling a box with more than 283 grams is 0.5 and the probability of filling a box with less than 283 grams is 0.5. We also can determine the probability that a box weighs between 280 and 286 grams. However, to determine this probability we need to know about the standard normal probability distribution.

LO7-3
Describe the standard normal probability distribution and use it to calculate probabilities.

THE STANDARD NORMAL PROBABILITY DISTRIBUTION

The number of normal distributions is unlimited, each having a different mean (μ), standard deviation (σ), or both. While it is possible to provide a limited number of probability tables for discrete distributions such as the binomial and the Poisson, providing tables for the infinite number of normal distributions is impractial. Fortunately, one member of the family can be used to determine the probabilities for all normal probability distributions. It is called the **standard normal probability distribution,** and it is unique because it has a mean of 0 and a standard deviation of 1.

Any *normal probability distribution* can be converted into a *standard normal probability distribution* by subtracting the mean from each observation and dividing this difference by the standard deviation. The results are called ***z* values** or ***z* scores.**

***z* VALUE** The signed distance between a selected value, designated *x,* and the mean, μ, divided by the standard deviation, σ.

So, a *z* value is the distance from the mean, measured in units of the standard deviation. The formula for this conversion is:

STANDARD NORMAL VALUE $$z = \frac{x - \mu}{\sigma} \tag{7–5}$$

where:

x is the value of any particular observation or measurement.
μ is the mean of the distribution.
σ is the standard deviation of the distribution.

STATISTICS IN ACTION

An individual's skills depend on a combination of many hereditary and environmental factors, each having about the same amount of weight or influence on the skills. Thus, much like a binomial distribution with a large number of trials, many skills and attributes follow the normal distribution. For example, the SAT Reasoning Test is the most widely used standardized test for college admissions in the United States. Scores are based on a normal distribution with a mean of 1,500 and a standard deviation of 300.

As we noted in the preceding definition, a *z* value expresses the distance or difference between a particular value of *x* and the arithmetic mean in units of the standard deviation. Once the normally distributed observations are standardized, the *z* values are normally distributed with a mean of 0 and a standard deviation of 1. Therefore, the *z* distribution has all the characteristics of any normal probability distribution. These characteristics are listed on page 215 in the Family of Normal Probability Distributions section. The table in Appendix B.3 lists the probabilities for the standard normal probability distribution. A small portion of this table follows.

TABLE 7–1 Areas under the Normal Curve

z	0.00	0.01	0.02	0.03	0.04	0.05	. . .
1.3	0.4032	0.4049	0.4066	0.4082	0.4099	0.4115	
1.4	0.4192	0.4207	0.4222	0.4236	0.4251	0.4265	
1.5	0.4332	0.4345	0.4357	0.4370	0.4382	0.4394	
1.6	0.4452	0.4463	0.4474	0.4484	0.4495	0.4505	
1.7	0.4554	0.4564	0.4573	0.4582	0.4591	0.4599	
1.8	0.4641	0.4649	0.4656	0.4664	0.4671	0.4678	
1.9	0.4713	0.4719	0.4726	0.4732	0.4738	0.4744	
⋮							

Applications of the Standard Normal Distribution

The standard normal distribution is very useful for determining probabilities for any normally distributed random variable. The basic procedure is to find the z value for a particular value of the random variable based on the mean and standard deviation of its distribution. Then, using the z value, we can use the standard normal distribution to find various probabilities. The following example/solution describes the details of the application.

EXAMPLE

In recent years a new type of taxi service has evolved in more than 300 cities worldwide, where the customer is connected directly with a driver via a smartphone. The idea was first developed by Uber Technologies, which is headquartered in San Francisco, California. It uses the Uber mobile app, which allows customers with a smartphone to submit a trip request which is then routed to a Uber driver who picks up the customer and takes the customer to the desired location. No cash is involved, the payment for the transaction is handled via a digital payment.

Suppose the weekly income of Uber drivers follows the normal probability distribution with a mean of \$1,000 and a standard deviation of \$100. What is the z value of income for a driver who earns \$1,100 per week? For a driver who earns \$900 per week?

SOLUTION

Using formula (7–5), the z values corresponding to the two x values (\$1,100 and \$900) are:

For $x = \$1,100$:

$$z = \frac{x - \mu}{\sigma} = \frac{\$1,100 - \$1,000}{\$100} = 1.00$$

For $x = \$900$:

$$z = \frac{x - \mu}{\sigma} = \frac{\$900 - \$1,000}{\$100} = -1.00$$

The z of 1.00 indicates that a weekly income of \$1,100 is one standard deviation above the mean, and a z of -1.00 shows that a \$900 income is one standard deviation below the mean. Note that both incomes (\$1,100 and \$900) are the same distance (\$100) from the mean.

SELF-REVIEW 7–2

A recent national survey concluded that the typical person consumes 48 ounces of water per day. Assume daily water consumption follows a normal probability distribution with a standard deviation of 12.8 ounces.

(a) What is the z value for a person who consumes 64 ounces of water per day? Based on this z value, how does this person compare to the national average?

(b) What is the z value for a person who consumes 32 ounces of water per day? Based on this z value, how does this person compare to the national average?

The Empirical Rule

The Empirical Rule is introduced on page 80 of Chapter 3. It states that if a random variable is normally distributed, then:

1. Approximately 68% of the observations will lie within plus and minus one standard deviation of the mean.

2. About 95% of the observations will lie within plus and minus two standard deviations of the mean.
3. Practically all, or 99.7% of the observations, will lie within plus and minus three standard deviations of the mean.

Now, knowing how to apply the standard normal probability distribution, we can verify the Empirical Rule. For example, one standard deviation from the mean is the same as a z value of 1.00. When we refer to the standard normal probability table, a z value of 1.00 corresponds to a probability of 0.3413. So what percent of the observations will lie within plus and minus one standard deviation of the mean? We multiply (2)(0.3413), which equals 0.6826, or approximately 68% of the observations are within plus and minus one standard deviation of the mean.

The Empirical Rule is summarized in the following graph.

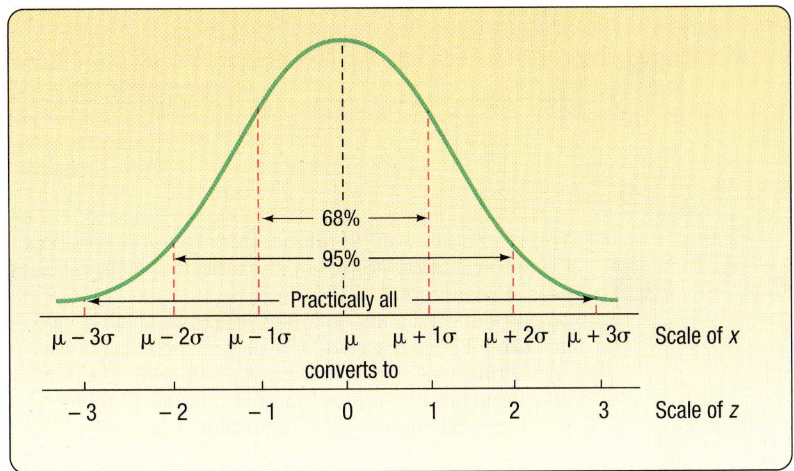

Transforming measurements to standard normal deviates changes the scale. The conversions are also shown in the graph. For example, $\mu + 1\sigma$ is converted to a z value of 1.00. Likewise, $\mu - 2\sigma$ is transformed to a z value of −2.00. Note that the center of the z distribution is zero, indicating no deviation from the mean, μ.

EXAMPLE

As part of its quality assurance program, the Autolite Battery Company conducts tests on battery life. For a particular D-cell alkaline battery, the mean life is 19 hours. The useful life of the battery follows a normal distribution with a standard deviation of 1.2 hours. Answer the following questions.

1. About 68% of the batteries failed between what two values?
2. About 95% of the batteries failed between what two values?
3. Virtually all of the batteries failed between what two values?

SOLUTION

We can use the Empirical Rule to answer these questions.

1. About 68% of the batteries will fail between 17.8 and 20.2 hours, found by $19.0 \pm 1(1.2)$ hours.
2. About 95% of the batteries will fail between 16.6 and 21.4 hours, found by $19.0 \pm 2(1.2)$ hours.
3. Practically all failed between 15.4 and 22.6 hours, found by $19.0 \pm 3(1.2)$ hours.

This information is summarized on the following chart.

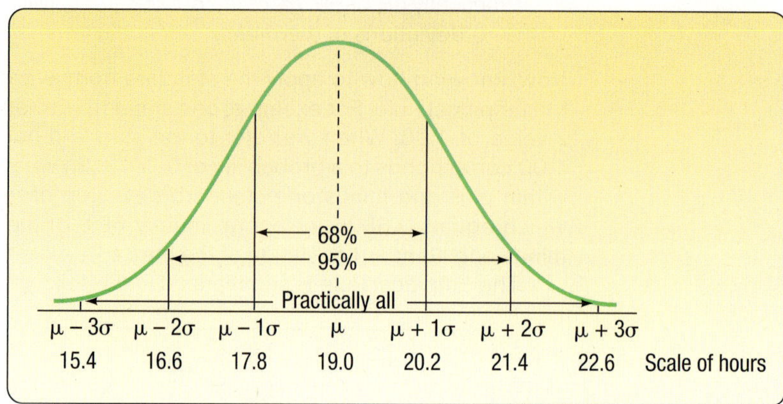

SELF-REVIEW 7–3

The distribution of the annual incomes of a group of middle-management employees at Compton Plastics approximates a normal distribution with a mean of $47,200 and a standard deviation of $800.

(a) About 68% of the incomes lie between what two amounts?
(b) About 95% of the incomes lie between what two amounts?
(c) Virtually all of the incomes lie between what two amounts?
(d) What are the median and the modal incomes?
(e) Is the distribution of incomes symmetrical?

EXERCISES

7. Explain what is meant by this statement: "There is not just one normal probability distribution but a 'family' of them."

8. List the major characteristics of a normal probability distribution.

9. The mean of a normal probability distribution is 500; the standard deviation is 10.
  a. About 68% of the observations lie between what two values?
  b. About 95% of the observations lie between what two values?
  c. Practically all of the observations lie between what two values?

10. The mean of a normal probability distribution is 60; the standard deviation is 5.
  a. About what percent of the observations lie between 55 and 65?
  b. About what percent of the observations lie between 50 and 70?
  c. About what percent of the observations lie between 45 and 75?

11. The Kamp family has twins, Rob and Rachel. Both Rob and Rachel graduated from college 2 years ago, and each is now earning $50,000 per year. Rachel works in the retail industry, where the mean salary for executives with less than 5 years' experience is $35,000 with a standard deviation of $8,000. Rob is an engineer. The mean salary for engineers with less than 5 years' experience is $60,000 with a standard deviation of $5,000. Compute the z values for both Rob and Rachel and comment on your findings.

12. A recent article in the *Cincinnati Enquirer* reported that the mean labor cost to repair a heat pump is $90 with a standard deviation of $22. Monte's Plumbing and Heating Service completed repairs on two heat pumps this morning. The labor cost for the first was $75 and it was $100 for the second. Assume the distribution of labor costs follows the normal probability distribution. Compute z values for each and comment on your findings.

Finding Areas under the Normal Curve

The next application of the standard normal distribution involves finding the area in a normal distribution between the mean and a selected value, which we identify as x. The following example/solution will illustrate the details.

EXAMPLE

In the first example/solution described on page 218 in this section, we reported that the weekly income of Uber drivers followed the normal distribution with a mean of $1,000 and a standard deviation of $100. That is, $\mu = \$1{,}000$ and $\sigma = \$100$. What is the likelihood of selecting a driver whose weekly income is between $1,000 and $1,100?

SOLUTION

We have already converted $1,100 to a z value of 1.00 using formula (7–5). To repeat:

$$z = \frac{x - \mu}{\sigma} = \frac{\$1{,}100 - \$1{,}000}{\$100} = 1.00$$

The probability associated with a z of 1.00 is available in Appendix B.3. A portion of Appendix B.3 follows. To locate the probability, go down the left column to 1.0, and then move horizontally to the column headed .00. The value is .3413.

z	0.00	0.01	0.02
⋮	⋮	⋮	⋮
0.7	.2580	.2611	.2642
0.8	.2881	.2910	.2939
0.9	.3159	.3186	.3212
1.0	.3413	.3438	.3461
1.1	.3643	.3665	.3686
⋮	⋮	⋮	⋮

The area under the normal curve between $1,000 and $1,100 is .3413. We could also say 34.13% of Uber drivers earn between $1,000 and $1,100 weekly, or the likelihood of selecting a driver and finding his or her income is between $1,000 and $1,100 is .3413.

This information is summarized in the following diagram.

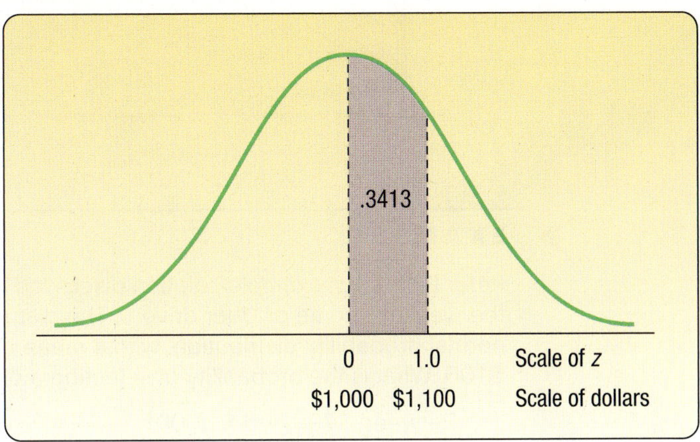

STATISTICS IN ACTION

Many processes, such as filling soda bottles and canning fruit, are normally distributed. Manufacturers must guard against both over- and underfilling. If they put too much in the can or bottle, they are giving away their product. If they put too little in, the customer may feel cheated and the government may question the label description. "Control charts," with limits drawn three standard deviations above and below the mean, are routinely used to monitor this type of production process.

In the example/solution just completed, we are interested in the probability between the mean and a given value. Let's change the question. Instead of wanting to know the probability of selecting a random driver who earned between $1,000 and $1,100, suppose we wanted the probability of selecting a driver who earned less than $1,100. In probability notation, we write this statement as *P*(weekly income < $1,100). The method of solution is the same. We find the probability of selecting a driver who earns between $1,000, the mean, and $1,100. This probability is .3413. Next, recall that half the area, or probability, is above the mean and half is below. So the probability of selecting a driver earning less than $1,000 is .5000. Finally, we add the two probabilities, so .3413 + .5000 = .8413. About 84% of Uber drivers earn less than $1,100 per week. See the following diagram.

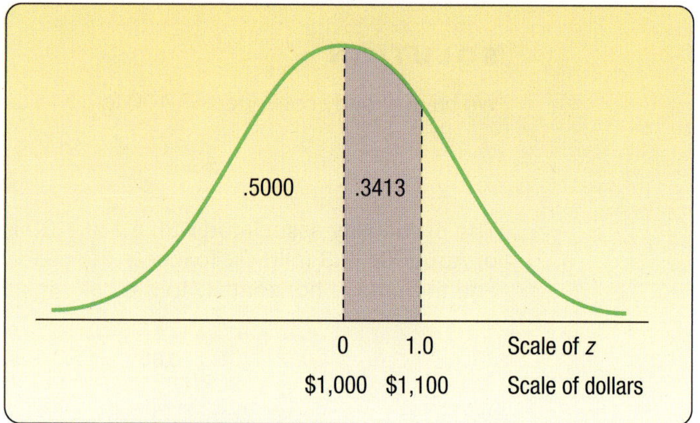

Excel will calculate this probability. The necessary commands are in the **Software Commands** in Appendix C. The answer is .8413, the same as we calculated.

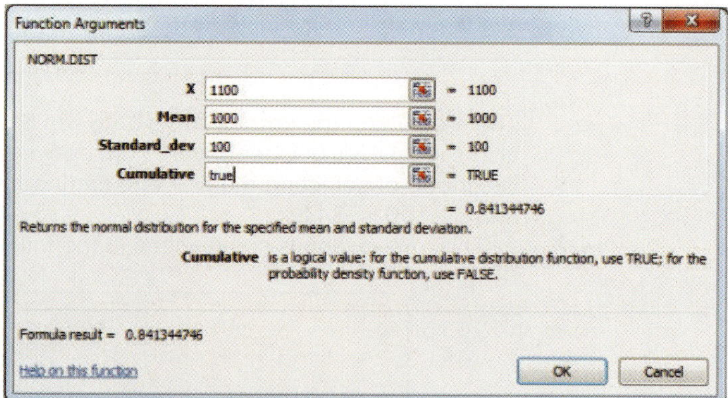

EXAMPLE

Refer to the first example/solution discussed on page 218 in this section regarding the weekly income of Uber drivers. The distribution of weekly incomes follows the normal probability distribution, with a mean of $1,000 and a standard deviation of $100. What is the probability of selecting a driver whose income is:

1. Between $790 and $1,000?
2. Less than $790?

SOLUTION

We begin by finding the z value corresponding to a weekly income of \$790. From formula (7–5):

$$z = \frac{x - \mu}{s} = \frac{\$790 - \$1{,}000}{\$100} = -2.10$$

See Appendix B.3. Move down the left margin to the row 2.1 and across that row to the column headed 0.00. The value is .4821. So the area under the standard normal curve corresponding to a z value of 2.10 is .4821. However, because the normal distribution is symmetric, the area between 0 and a negative z value is the same as that between 0 and the corresponding positive z value. The likelihood of finding a driver earning between \$790 and \$1,000 is .4821. In probability notation, we write $P(\$790 < \text{weekly income} < \$1{,}000) = .4821$.

z	0.00	0.01	0.02
⋮	⋮	⋮	⋮
2.0	.4772	.4778	.4783
2.1	.4821	.4826	.4830
2.2	.4861	.4864	.4868
2.3	.4893	.4896	.4898
⋮	⋮	⋮	⋮

The mean divides the normal curve into two identical halves. The area under the half to the left of the mean is .5000, and the area to the right is also .5000. Because the area under the curve between \$790 and \$1,000 is .4821, the area below \$790 is .0179, found by .5000 – .4821. In probability notation, we write $P(\text{weekly income} < \$790) = .0179$.

So we conclude that 48.21% of the Uber drivers have weekly incomes between \$790 and \$1,000. Further, we can anticipate that 1.79% earn less than \$790 per week. This information is summarized in the following diagram.

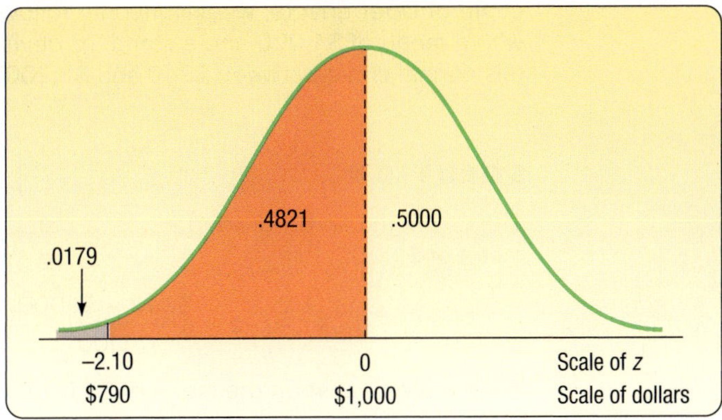

SELF-REVIEW 7–4

The temperature of coffee sold at the Coffee Bean Cafe follows the normal probability distribution, with a mean of 150 degrees. The standard deviation of this distribution is 5 degrees.

(a) What is the probability that the coffee temperature is between 150 degrees and 154 degrees?

(b) What is the probability that the coffee temperature is more than 164 degrees?

EXERCISES

13. A normal population has a mean of 20.0 and a standard deviation of 4.0.
  a. Compute the z value associated with 25.0.
  b. What proportion of the population is between 20.0 and 25.0?
  c. What proportion of the population is less than 18.0?

14. A normal population has a mean of 12.2 and a standard deviation of 2.5.
  a. Compute the z value associated with 14.3.
  b. What proportion of the population is between 12.2 and 14.3?
  c. What proportion of the population is less than 10.0?

15. A recent study of the hourly wages of maintenance crew members for major airlines showed that the mean hourly salary was $20.50, with a standard deviation of $3.50. Assume the distribution of hourly wages follows the normal probability distribution. If we select a crew member at random, what is the probability the crew member earns:
  a. Between $20.50 and $24.00 per hour?
  b. More than $24.00 per hour?
  c. Less than $19.00 per hour?

16. The mean of a normal probability distribution is 400 pounds. The standard deviation is 10 pounds.
  a. What is the area between 415 pounds and the mean of 400 pounds?
  b. What is the area between the mean and 395 pounds?
  c. What is the probability of selecting a value at random and discovering that it has a value of less than 395 pounds?

Another application of the normal distribution involves combining two areas, or probabilities. One of the areas is to the right of the mean and the other to the left.

EXAMPLE

Continuing the example/solution first discussed on page 218 using the weekly income of Uber drivers, weekly income follows the normal probability distribution, with a mean of $1,000 and a standard deviation of $100. What is the area under this normal curve between $840 and $1,200?

SOLUTION

The problem can be divided into two parts. For the area between $840 and the mean of $1,000:

$$z = \frac{\$840 - \$1{,}000}{\$100} = \frac{-\$160}{\$100} = -1.60$$

For the area between the mean of $1,000 and $1,200:

$$z = \frac{\$1{,}200 - \$1{,}000}{\$100} = \frac{\$200}{\$100} = 2.00$$

The area under the curve for a z of −1.60 is .4452 (from Appendix B.3). The area under the curve for a z of 2.00 is .4772. Adding the two areas: .4452 + .4772 = .9224. Thus, the probability of selecting an income between $840 and $1,200 is .9224. In probability notation, we write $P(\$840 < \text{weekly income} < \$1{,}200) = .4452 + .4772 = .9224$. To summarize, 92.24% of the drivers have weekly incomes between $840 and $1,200. This is shown in a diagram:

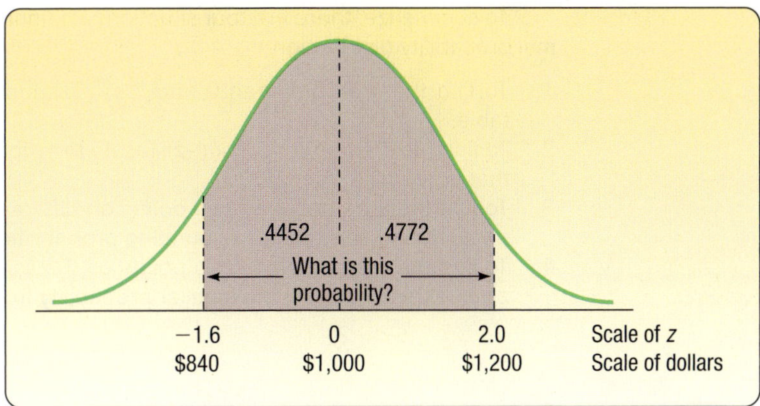

Another application of the normal distribution involves determining the area between values on the *same* side of the mean.

EXAMPLE

Returning to the weekly income distribution of Uber drivers ($\mu = \$1{,}000$, $\sigma = \$100$), what is the area under the normal curve between \$1,150 and \$1,250?

SOLUTION

The situation is again separated into two parts, and formula (7–5) is used. First, we find the z value associated with a weekly income of \$1,250:

$$z = \frac{\$1{,}250 - \$1{,}000}{\$100} = 2.50$$

Next we find the z value for a weekly income of \$1,150:

$$z = \frac{\$1{,}150 - \$1{,}000}{\$100} = 1.50$$

From Appendix B.3, the area associated with a z value of 2.50 is .4938. So the probability of a weekly income between \$1,000 and \$1,250 is .4938. Similarly, the area associated with a z value of 1.50 is .4332, so the probability of a weekly income between \$1,000 and \$1,150 is .4332. The probability of a weekly income between \$1,150 and \$1,250 is found by subtracting the area associated with a z value of 1.50 (.4332) from that associated with a z of 2.50 (.4938). Thus, the probability of a weekly income between \$1,150 and \$1,250 is .0606. In probability notation, we write $P(\$1{,}150 < \text{weekly income} < \$1{,}250) = .4938 - .4332 = .0606$.

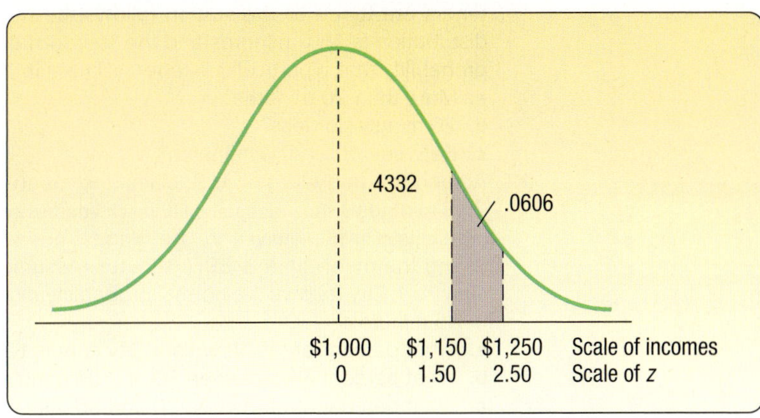

To summarize, there are four situations for finding the area under the standard normal probability distribution.

1. To find the area between 0 and z or $(-z)$, look up the probability directly in the table.
2. To find the area beyond z or $(-z)$, locate the probability of z in the table and subtract that probability from .5000.
3. To find the area between two points on different sides of the mean, determine the z values and add the corresponding probabilities.
4. To find the area between two points on the same side of the mean, determine the z values and subtract the smaller probability from the larger.

SELF-REVIEW 7–5

Refer to Self-Review 7–4. The temperature of coffee sold at the Coffee Bean Cafe follows the normal probability distribution with a mean of 150 degrees. The standard deviation of this distribution is 5 degrees.

(a) What is the probability the coffee temperature is between 146 degrees and 156 degrees?
(b) What is the probability the coffee temperature is more than 156 but less than 162 degrees?

EXERCISES

17. A normal distribution has a mean of 50 and a standard deviation of 4.
a. Compute the probability of a value between 44.0 and 55.0.
b. Compute the probability of a value greater than 55.0.
c. Compute the probability of a value between 52.0 and 55.0.

18. A normal population has a mean of 80.0 and a standard deviation of 14.0.
a. Compute the probability of a value between 75.0 and 90.0.
b. Compute the probability of a value of 75.0 or less.
c. Compute the probability of a value between 55.0 and 70.0.

19. Suppose the Internal Revenue Service reported that the mean tax refund for the year 2016 was $2,800. Assume the standard deviation is $450 and that the amounts refunded follow a normal probability distribution.
a. What percent of the refunds are more than $3,100?
b. What percent of the refunds are more than $3,100 but less than $3,500?
c. What percent of the refunds are more than $2,250 but less than $3,500?

20. The distribution of the number of viewers for the *American Idol* television show follows a normal distribution with a mean of 29 million and a standard deviation of 5 million. What is the probability next week's show will:
a. Have between 30 and 34 million viewers?
b. Have at least 23 million viewers?
c. Exceed 40 million viewers?

21. WNAE, an all-news AM station, finds that the distribution of the lengths of time listeners are tuned to the station follows the normal distribution. The mean of the distribution is 15.0 minutes and the standard deviation is 3.5 minutes. What is the probability that a particular listener will tune in for:
a. More than 20 minutes?
b. 20 minutes or less?
c. Between 10 and 12 minutes?

22. Among the thirty largest U.S. cities, the mean one-way commute time to work is 25.8 minutes. **https://deepblue.lib.umich.edu/bitstream/handle/2027.42/112057/103196.pdf?sequence=1&isAllowed=y**. The longest one-way travel time is in New York City, where the mean time is 39.7 minutes. Assume the distribution of travel times in New York City follows the normal probability distribution and the standard deviation is 7.5 minutes.
a. What percent of the New York City commutes are for less than 30 minutes?
b. What percent are between 30 and 35 minutes?
c. What percent are between 30 and 50 minutes?

The previous example/solutions require finding the percent of the observations located between two observations or the percent of the observations above, or below, a particular observation x. A further application of the normal distribution involves finding the value of the observation x when the percent above or below the observation is given.

EXAMPLE

Layton Tire and Rubber Company wishes to set a minimum mileage guarantee on its new MX100 tire. Tests reveal the mean mileage is 67,900 with a standard deviation of 2,050 miles and that the distribution of miles follows the normal probability distribution. Layton wants to set the minimum guaranteed mileage so that no more than 4% of the tires will have to be replaced. What minimum guaranteed mileage should Layton announce?

© JupiterImages/Getty Images

SOLUTION

The facets of this case are shown in the following diagram, where x represents the minimum guaranteed mileage.

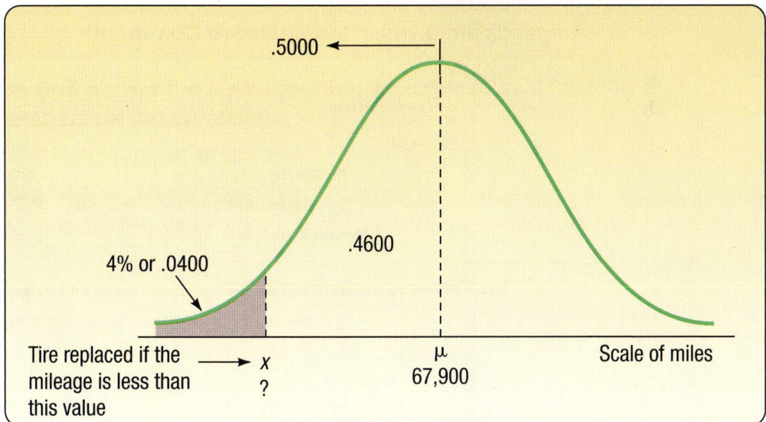

Inserting these values in formula (7–5) for z gives:

$$z = \frac{x - \mu}{\sigma} = \frac{x - 67{,}900}{2{,}050}$$

There are two unknowns in this equation, z and x. To find x, we first find z, and then solve for x. Recall from the characteristics of a normal curve that the area to the left of μ is .5000. The area between μ and x is .4600, found by .5000 − .0400. Now refer to Appendix B.3. Search the body of the table for the area closest to .4600. The closest area is .4599. Move to the margins from this value and read the z value of 1.75. Because the value is to the left of the mean, it is actually −1.75. These steps are illustrated in Table 7–2.

TABLE 7–2 Selected Areas under the Normal Curve

z ...	.03	.04	.05	.06
⋮	⋮	⋮	⋮	⋮
1.5	.4370	.4382	.4394	.4406
1.6	.4484	.4495	.4505	.4515
1.7	.4582	.4591	.4599	.4608
1.8	.4664	.4671	.4678	.4686

Knowing that the distance between μ and x is -1.75σ or $z = -1.75$, we can now solve for x (the minimum guaranteed mileage):

$$z = \frac{x - 67{,}900}{2{,}050}$$

$$-1.75 = \frac{x - 67{,}900}{2{,}050}$$

$$-1.75(2{,}050) = x - 67{,}900$$

$$x = 67{,}900 - 1.75(2{,}050) = 64{,}312$$

So Layton can advertise that it will replace for free any tire that wears out before it reaches 64,312 miles, and the company will know that only 4% of the tires will be replaced under this plan.

Excel will also find the mileage value. See the following output. The necessary commands are given in the **Software Commands** in Appendix C.

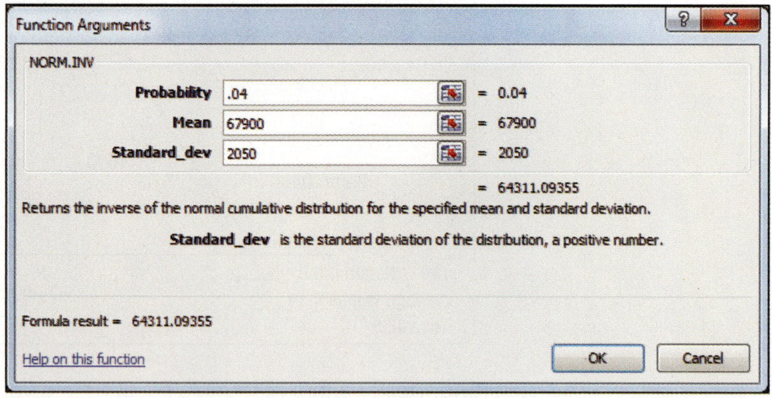

SELF-REVIEW 7–6

An analysis of the final test scores for Introduction to Business reveals the scores follow the normal probability distribution. The mean of the distribution is 75 and the standard deviation is 8. The professor wants to award an A to students whose score is in the highest 10%. What is the dividing point for those students who earn an A and those earning a B?

EXERCISES

23. A normal distribution has a mean of 50 and a standard deviation of 4. Determine the value below which 95% of the observations will occur.

24. A normal distribution has a mean of 80 and a standard deviation of 14. Determine the value above which 80% of the values will occur.

25. Assume that the hourly cost to operate a commercial airplane follows the normal distribution with a mean of \$2,100 per hour and a standard deviation of \$250. What is the operating cost for the lowest 3% of the airplanes?

26. The SAT Reasoning Test is perhaps the most widely used standardized test for college admissions in the United States. Scores are based on a normal distribution with a mean of 1500 and a standard deviation of 300. Clinton College would like to offer an honors scholarship to students who score in the top 10% of this test. What is the minimum score that qualifies for the scholarship?

27. According to media research, the typical American listened to 195 hours of music in the last year. This is down from 290 hours 4 years earlier. Dick Trythall is a big country and western music fan. He listens to music while working around the house, reading, and riding in his truck. Assume the number of hours spent listening to music follows a normal probability distribution with a standard deviation of 8.5 hours.

   a. If Dick is in the top 1% in terms of listening time, how many hours did he listen last year?

   b. Assume that the distribution of times 4 years earlier also follows the normal probability distribution with a standard deviation of 8.5 hours. How many hours did the 1% who listen to the *least* music actually listen?

28. For the most recent year available, the mean annual cost to attend a private university in the United States was \$42,224. Assume the distribution of annual costs follows the normal probability distribution and the standard deviation is \$4,500. Ninety-five percent of all students at private universities pay less than what amount?

29. In economic theory, a "hurdle rate" is the minimum return that a person requires before he or she will make an investment. A research report says that annual returns from a specific class of common equities are distributed according to a normal distribution with a mean of 12% and a standard deviation of 18%. A stock screener would like to identify a hurdle rate such that only 1 in 20 equities is above that value. Where should the hurdle rate be set?

30. The manufacturer of a laser printer reports the mean number of pages a cartridge will print before it needs replacing is 12,200. The distribution of pages printed per cartridge closely follows the normal probability distribution and the standard deviation is 820 pages. The manufacturer wants to provide guidelines to potential customers as to how long they can expect a cartridge to last. How many pages should the manufacturer advertise for each cartridge if it wants to be correct 99% of the time?

LO7-4
Approximate the binomial probability distribution using the standard normal probability distribution to calculate probabilities.

THE NORMAL APPROXIMATION TO THE BINOMIAL

Chapter 6 describes the binomial probability distribution, which is a discrete distribution. The table of binomial probabilities in Appendix B.1 goes successively from an n of 1 to an n of 15. If a problem involved taking a sample of 60, generating a binomial distribution for that large a number would be very time-consuming. A more efficient approach is to apply the *normal approximation to the binomial*.

We can use the normal distribution (a continuous distribution) as a substitute for a binomial distribution (a discrete distribution) for large values of n because, as n increases, a binomial distribution gets closer and closer to a normal distribution. Chart 7–7 depicts the change in the shape of a binomial distribution with $\pi = .50$ from

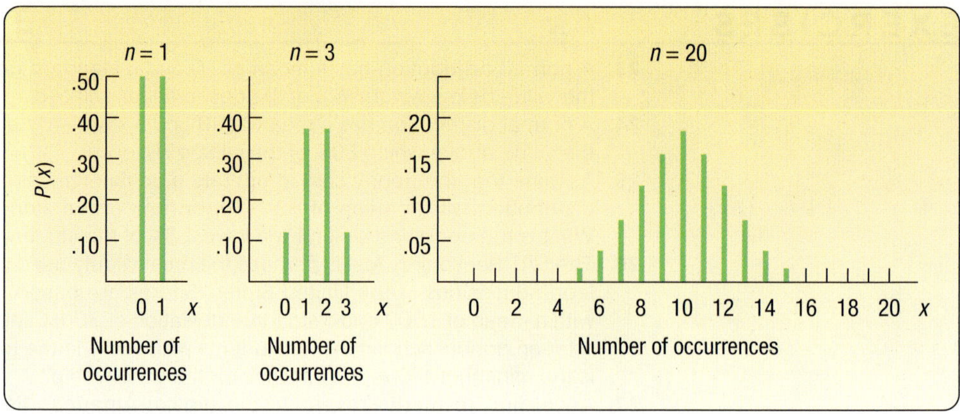

CHART 7–7 Binomial Distributions for an n of 1, 3, and 20, Where $\pi = .50$

an n of 1, to an n of 3, to an n of 20. Notice how the case where $n = 20$ approximates the shape of the normal distribution.

When can we use the normal approximation to the binomial? The normal probability distribution is a good approximation to the binomial probability distribution when $n\pi$ and $n(1 - \pi)$ are both at least 5. However, before we apply the normal approximation, we must make sure that our distribution of interest is in fact a binomial distribution. Recall from Chapter 6 that four criteria must be met:

1. There are only two mutually exclusive outcomes to an experiment: a "success" and a "failure."
2. The distribution results from counting the number of successes in a fixed number of trials.
3. The probability of a success, π, remains the same from trial to trial.
4. Each trial is independent.

Continuity Correction Factor

To show the application of the normal approximation to the binomial and the need for a correction factor, suppose the management of the Santoni Pizza Restaurant found that 70% of its new customers return for another meal. For a week in which 80 new (first-time) customers dined at Santoni's, what is the probability that 60 or more will return for another meal?

Notice the binomial conditions are met: (1) There are only two possible outcomes—a customer either returns for another meal or does not return. (2) We can count the number of successes, meaning, for example, that 57 of the 80 customers return. (3) The trials are independent, meaning that if the 34th person returns for a second meal, that does not affect whether the 58th person returns. (4) The probability of a customer returning remains at .70 for all 80 customers.

Therefore, we could use the binomial formula (6–3) described on page 185.

$$P(x) = {}_nC_x\,(\pi)^x\,(1 - \pi)^{n-x}$$

To find the probability 60 or more customers return for another pizza, we need to first find the probability exactly 60 customers return. That is:

$$P(x = 60) = {}_{80}C_{60}\,(.70)^{60}\,(1 - .70)^{20} = .063$$

Next we find the probability that exactly 61 customers return. It is:

$$P(x = 61) = {}_{80}C_{61}\,(.70)^{61}\,(1 - .70)^{19} = .048$$

We continue this process until we have the probability that all 80 customers return. Finally, we add the probabilities from 60 to 80. Solving the preceding problem in this manner is tedious. We can also use statistical software packages to find the various probabilities. Listed below are the binomial probabilities for $n = 80$, $\pi = .70$, and x, the number of customers returning, ranging from 43 to 68. The probability of any number of customers less than 43 or more than 68 returning is less than .001. We can assume these probabilities are 0.000.

Number Returning	Probability	Number Returning	Probability
43	.001	56	.097
44	.002	57	.095
45	.003	58	.088
46	.006	59	.077
47	.009	60	.063
48	.015	61	.048
49	.023	62	.034
50	.033	63	.023
51	.045	64	.014
52	.059	65	.008
53	.072	66	.004
54	.084	67	.002
55	.093	68	.001

We can find the probability of 60 or more returning by summing .063 + .048 + . . . + .001, which is .197. However, a look at the plot below shows the similarity of this distribution to a normal distribution. All we need do is "smooth out" the discrete probabilities into a continuous distribution. Furthermore, working with a normal distribution will involve far fewer calculations than working with the binomial.

The trick is to let the discrete probability for 56 customers be represented by an area under the continuous curve between 55.5 and 56.5. Then let the probability for 57 customers be represented by an area between 56.5 and 57.5, and so on. This is just the opposite of rounding off the numbers to a whole number.

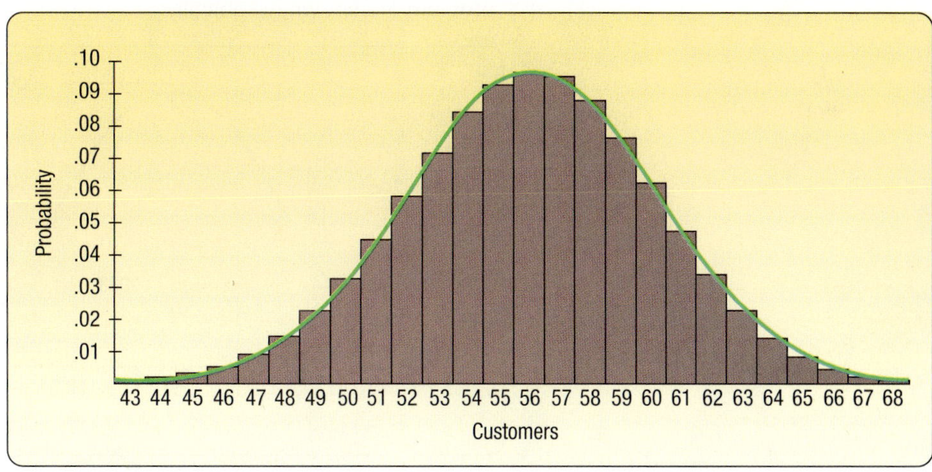

Because we use the normal distribution to determine the binomial probability of 60 or more successes, we must subtract, in this case, .5 from 60. The value .5 is called the **continuity correction factor.** This small adjustment is made because a continuous distribution (the normal distribution) is being used to approximate a discrete distribution (the binomial distribution).

CONTINUITY CORRECTION FACTOR The value .5 subtracted or added, depending on the question, to a selected value when a discrete probability distribution is approximated by a continuous probability distribution.

How to Apply the Correction Factor

Only four cases may arise. These cases are:

1. For the probability *at least* x occur, use the area *above* $(x - .5)$.
2. For the probability that *more than* x occur, use the area *above* $(x + .5)$.
3. For the probability that x *or fewer* occur, use the area *below* $(x + .5)$.
4. For the probability that *fewer than* x occur, use the area *below* $(x - .5)$.

To use the normal distribution to approximate the probability that 60 or more first-time Santoni customers out of 80 will return, follow the procedure shown below.

Step 1: Find the z value corresponding to an x of 59.5 using formula (7–5), and formulas (6–4) and (6–5) for the mean and the variance of a binomial distribution:

$$\mu = n\pi = 80(.70) = 56$$
$$\sigma^2 = n\pi(1 - \pi) = 80(.70)(1 - .70) = 16.8$$
$$\sigma = \sqrt{16.8} = 4.10$$
$$z = \frac{x - \mu}{\sigma} = \frac{59.5 - 56}{4.10} = 0.85$$

Step 2: Determine the area under the normal curve between a μ of 56 and an x of 59.5. From step 1, we know that the z value corresponding to 59.5 is 0.85. So we go to Appendix B.3 and read down the left margin to 0.8, and then we go horizontally to the area under the column headed by .05. That area is .3023.

Step 3: Calculate the area beyond 59.5 by subtracting .3023 from .5000 (.5000 − .3023 = .1977). Thus, .1977 is the probability that 60 or more first-time Santoni customers out of 80 will return for another meal. In probability notation, $P(\text{customers} > 59.5) = .5000 - .3023 = .1977$. The facets of this problem are shown graphically:

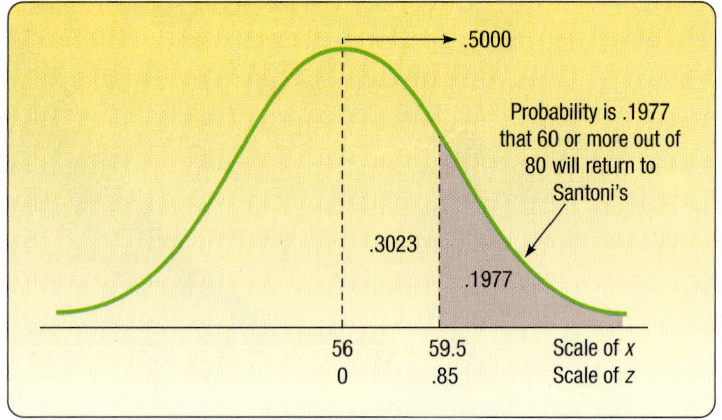

No doubt you will agree that using the normal approximation to the binomial is a more efficient method of estimating the probability of 60 or more first-time customers returning. The result compares favorably with that computed on page 230 using the binomial distribution. The probability using the binomial distribution is .197, whereas the probability using the normal approximation is .1977.

SELF-REVIEW 7–7

A study by Great Southern Home Insurance revealed that none of the stolen goods were recovered by the homeowners in 80% of reported thefts.

(a) During a period in which 200 thefts occurred, what is the probability that no stolen goods were recovered in 170 or more of the robberies?

(b) During a period in which 200 thefts occurred, what is the probability that no stolen goods were recovered in 150 or more robberies?

EXERCISES

31. Assume a binomial probability distribution with $n = 50$ and $\pi = .25$. Compute the following:

a. The mean and standard deviation of the random variable.

b. The probability that x is 15 or more.

c. The probability that x is 10 or less.

32. Assume a binomial probability distribution with $n = 40$ and $\pi = .55$. Compute the following:

a. The mean and standard deviation of the random variable.

b. The probability that x is 25 or greater.

c. The probability that x is 15 or less.

d. The probability that x is between 15 and 25, inclusive.

33. Dottie's Tax Service specializes in federal tax returns for professional clients, such as physicians, dentists, accountants, and lawyers. A recent audit by the IRS of the returns she prepared indicated that an error was made on 7% of the returns she prepared last year. Assuming this rate continues into this year and she prepares 80 returns, what is the probability that she makes errors on:

a. More than six returns?

b. At least six returns?

c. Exactly six returns?

34. Shorty's Muffler advertises it can install a new muffler in 30 minutes or less. However, the work standards department at corporate headquarters recently conducted a study and found that 20% of the mufflers were not installed in 30 minutes or less. The Maumee branch installed 50 mufflers last month. If the corporate report is correct:

a. How many of the installations at the Maumee branch would you expect to take more than 30 minutes?

b. What is the likelihood that fewer than eight installations took more than 30 minutes?

c. What is the likelihood that eight or fewer installations took more than 30 minutes?

d. What is the likelihood that exactly 8 of the 50 installations took more than 30 minutes?

35. A study conducted by the nationally known Taurus Health Club revealed that 30% of its new members are 15 pounds overweight. A membership drive in a metropolitan area resulted in 500 new members.

a. It has been suggested that the normal approximation to the binomial be used to determine the probability that 175 or more of the new members are 15 pounds overweight. Does this problem qualify as a binomial problem? Explain.

b. What is the probability that 175 or more of the new members are 15 pounds overweight?

c. What is the probability that 140 or more new members are 15 pounds overweight?

36. The website, herecomestheguide.com, suggested that couples planning their wedding should expect eighty percent of those who are sent an invitation to respond that they will attend. Rich and Stacy are planning to be married later this year. They plan to send 200 invitations.

a. How many guests would you expect to accept the invitation?

b. What is the standard deviation?

c. What is the probability 150 or more will accept the invitation?

d. What is the probability exactly 150 will accept the invitation?

LO7-5
Describe the exponential probability distribution and use it to calculate probabilities.

THE FAMILY OF EXPONENTIAL DISTRIBUTIONS

So far in this chapter, we have considered two continuous probability distributions, the uniform and the normal. The next continuous distribution we consider is the exponential distribution. This continuous probability distribution usually describes times between events in a sequence. The actions occur independently at a constant rate per unit of time or length. Because time is never negative, an exponential random variable is always positive. The exponential distribution usually describes situations such as:

- The service time for customers at the information desk of the Dallas Public Library.
- The time between "hits" on a website.
- The lifetime of a kitchen appliance.
- The time until the next phone call arrives in a customer service center.

The exponential probability distribution is positively skewed. That differs from the uniform and normal distributions, which were both symmetric. Moreover, the distribution is described by only one parameter, which we will identify as λ (pronounced "lambda"). λ is often referred to as the "rate" parameter. The following chart shows the change in the shape of the exponential distribution as we vary the value of λ from 1/3 to 1 to 2. Observe that as we decrease λ, the shape of the distribution is "less skewed."

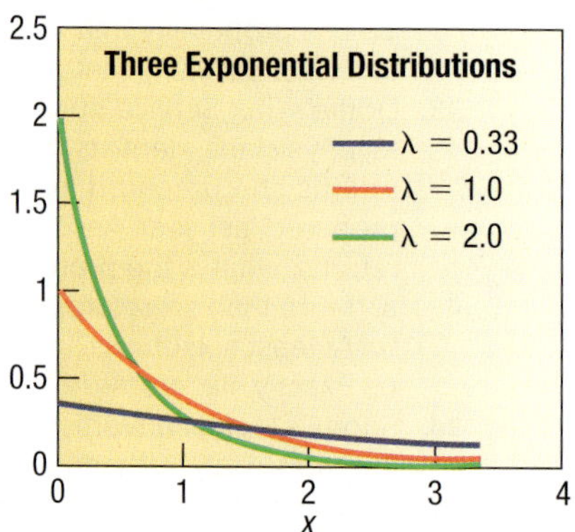

© Robert Cicchetti/Shutterstock.com

Another feature of the exponential distribution is its close relationship to the Poisson distribution. The Poisson is a discrete probability distribution and also has a single parameter, μ. We described the Poisson distribution starting in Chapter 6 on page 197. It too is a positively skewed distribution. To explain the relationship between the Poisson and the exponential distributions, suppose customers arrive at a family restaurant during the dinner hour at a rate of six per hour. The Poisson distribution would have a mean of six. For a time interval of one hour, we can use the Poisson distribution to find the probability that one, or two, or ten customers arrive. But suppose instead of studying the number of customers *arriving in an hour,* we wish to study the time *between their arrivals*. The time between arrivals is a continuous distribution because time is measured as a continuous random variable. If customers arrive at a rate of six per hour, then logically the typical or mean time between arrivals is 1/6 of an hour, or 10 minutes. We need to be careful here to be consistent with our units, so let's stay with 1/6 of an hour. So in general, if we know customers arrive at a certain rate per hour, which we call μ, then we can expect the mean time between arrivals to be $1/\mu$. The rate parameter λ is equal to $1/\mu$. So in our restaurant arrival example, the mean time between customer arrivals is $\lambda = 1/6$ of an hour.

The graph of the exponential distribution starts at the value of λ when the random variable's (x) value is 0. The distribution declines steadily as we move to the right with increasing values of x. Formula (7–6) describes the exponential probability distribution with λ as rate parameter. As we described with the Poisson distribution on page 197, e is a mathematical constant equal to 2.71828. It is the base for the natural logarithm system. It is a pleasant surprise that both the mean and the standard deviation of the exponential probability distribution are equal to $1/\lambda$.

EXPONENTIAL DISTRIBUTION $P(x) = \lambda e^{-\lambda x}$ **(7–6)**

With continuous distributions, we do not address the probability that a distinct value will occur. Instead, areas or regions below the graph of the probability distribution between two specified values give the probability the random variable is in that interval. A table, such as Appendix B.3 for the normal distribution, is not necessary for the exponential distribution. The area under the exponential density function is found by a formula and the necessary calculations can be accomplished with a handheld calculator with an e^x key. Most statistical software packages will also calculate exponential probabilities by inputting the rate parameter, λ, only. The probability of obtaining an arrival value less than a particular value of x is:

FINDING A PROBABILITY USING THE EXPONENTIAL DISTRIBUTION $P(\text{Arrival time} < x) = 1 - e^{-\lambda x}$ **(7–7)**

EXAMPLE

Orders for prescriptions arrive at a pharmacy website according to an exponential probability distribution at a mean of one every 20 seconds. Find the probability the next order arrives in less than 5 seconds. Find the probability the next order arrives in more than 40 seconds.

SOLUTION

To begin, we determine the rate parameter λ, which in this case is 1/20. To find the probability, we insert 1/20 for λ and 5 for x in formula (7–7).

$$P(\text{Arrival time} < 5) = 1 - e^{-\frac{1}{20}(5)} = 1 - e^{-0.25} = 1 - .7788 = .2212$$

So we conclude there is a 22% chance the next order will arrive in less than 5 seconds. The region is identified as the colored area under the curve.

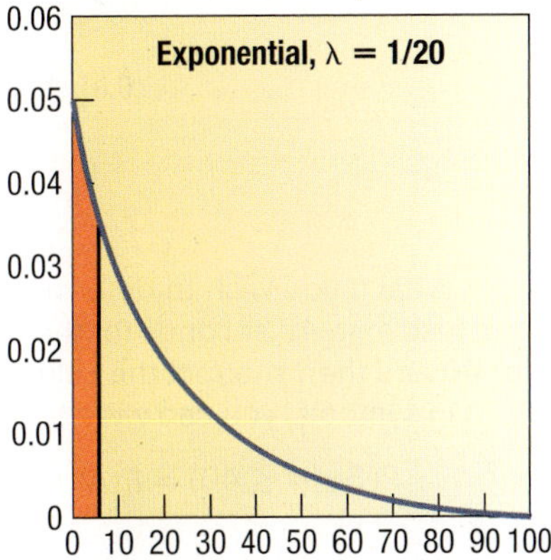

The preceding computations addressed the area in the left-tail area of the exponential distribution with $\lambda = 1/20$ and the area between 0 and 5—that is, the area that is below 5 seconds. What if you are interested in the right-tail area? It is found using the complement rule. See formula (5–3) in Chapter 5. To put it another way, to find the probability the next order will arrive in more than 40 seconds, we find the probability the order arrives in less than 40 seconds and subtract the result from 1.00. We show this in two steps.

1. Find the probability an order is received *in less than* 40 seconds.

$$P(\text{Arrival} < 40) = 1 - e^{-\frac{1}{20}(40)} = 1 - .1353 = .8647$$

2. Find the probability an order is received *in more than* 40 seconds.

$$P(\text{Arrival} > 40) = 1 - P(\text{Arrival} < 40) = 1 - .8647 = .1353$$

We conclude that the likelihood that it will be 40 seconds or more before the next order is received at the pharmacy is 13.5%.

In the preceding example/solution, when we apply the exponential probability distribution to compute the probability that the arrival time is greater than 40 seconds, you probably observed that there is some redundancy. In general, if we wish to find the likelihood of a time greater than some value x, such as 40, the complement rule is applied as follows:

$$P(\text{Arrival} > x) = 1 - P(\text{Arrival} < x) = 1 - (1 - e^{-\lambda x}) = e^{-\lambda x}$$

In other words, when we subtract formula (7–7) from 1 to find the area in the right tail, the result is $e^{-\lambda x}$. Thus, the probability that more than 40 seconds go by before the next order arrives is computed without the aid of the complement rule as follows:

$$P(\text{Arrival} > 40) = e^{-\frac{1}{20}(40)} = .1353$$

The result is shown in the following graph.

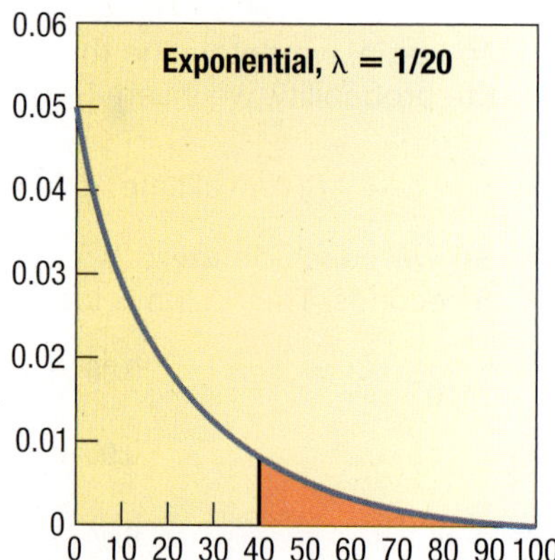

What if you wish to determine the probability that it will take more than 5 seconds but less than 40 seconds for the next order to arrive? Use formula (7–7) with an x value of 40 and then subtract the value of formula (7–7) when x is 5.

In symbols, you can write this as:

$$P(5 \le x \le 40) = P(\text{Arrival} \le 40) - P(\text{Arrival} \le 5)$$

$$= \left(1 - e^{-\frac{1}{20}(40)}\right) - \left(1 - e^{-\frac{1}{20}(5)}\right) = .8647 - .2212 = .6435$$

We conclude that about 64% of the time, the time between orders will be between 5 seconds and 40 seconds.

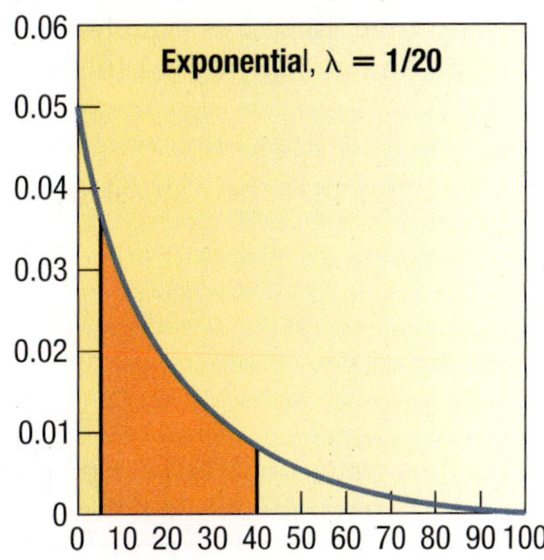

Previous examples require finding the percentage of the observations located between two values or the percentage of the observations above or below a particular value, x. We can also use formula (7–7) in "reverse" to find the value of the observation x when the percentage above or below the observation is given. The following example/solution illustrates this situation.

EXAMPLE

Compton Computers wishes to set a minimum lifetime guarantee on its new power supply unit. Quality testing shows the time to failure follows an exponential distribution with a mean of 4,000 hours. Compton wants a warranty period such that only 5% of the power supply units fail during that period. What value should they set for the warranty period?

SOLUTION

Note that 4,000 hours is a mean and not a rate. Therefore, we must compute λ as 1/4,000, or 0.00025 failure per hour. A diagram of the situation is shown below, where x represents the minimum guaranteed lifetime.

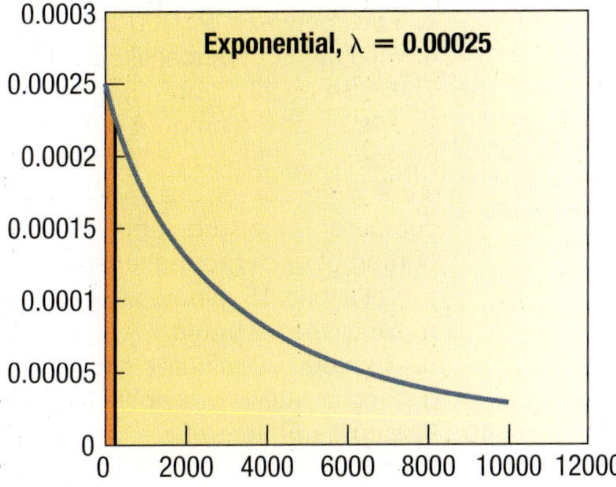

We use formula (7–7) and essentially work backward for the solution. In this case, the rate parameter is 4,000 hours and we want the area, as shown in the diagram, to be .05.

$$P(\text{Arrival time} < x) = 1 - e^{(-\lambda x)}$$

$$= 1 - e^{-\frac{1}{4{,}000}(x)} = .05$$

Next, we solve this equation for x. So, we subtract 1 from both sides of the equation and multiply by -1 to simplify the signs. The result is:

$$.95 = e^{-\frac{1}{4{,}000}(x)}$$

Next, we take the natural log of both sides and solve for x:

$$\ln(.95) = -\frac{1}{4{,}000}x$$
$$-(.051293294) = -\frac{1}{4{,}000}x$$
$$x = 205.17$$

In this case, $x = 205.17$. Hence, Compton can set the warranty period at 205 hours and expect about 5% of the power supply units to be returned.

SELF-REVIEW 7–8

The time between ambulance arrivals at the Methodist Hospital emergency room follows an exponential distribution with a mean of 10 minutes.

(a) What is the likelihood the next ambulance will arrive in 15 minutes or less?
(b) What is the likelihood the next ambulance will arrive in more than 25 minutes?
(c) What is the likelihood the next ambulance will arrive in more than 15 minutes but less than 25?
(d) Find the 80th percentile for the time between ambulance arrivals. (This means only 20% of the runs are longer than this time.)

EXERCISES

37. Waiting times to receive food after placing an order at the local Subway sandwich shop follow an exponential distribution with a mean of 60 seconds. Calculate the probability a customer waits:

- **a.** Less than 30 seconds.
- **b.** More than 120 seconds.
- **c.** Between 45 and 75 seconds.
- **d.** Fifty percent of the patrons wait less than how many seconds? What is the median?

38. The lifetime of LCD TV sets follows an exponential distribution with a mean of 100,000 hours. Compute the probability a television set:

- **a.** Fails in less than 10,000 hours.
- **b.** Lasts more than 120,000 hours.
- **c.** Fails between 60,000 and 100,000 hours of use.
- **d.** Find the 90th percentile. So 10% of the TV sets last more than what length of time?

39. The Bureau of Labor Statistics' *American Time Use Survey*, www.bls.gov/data, showed that the amount of time spent using a computer for leisure varied greatly by age. Individuals age 75 and over averaged 0.3 hour (18 minutes) per day using a computer for leisure. Individuals ages 15 to 19 spend 1.0 hour per day using a computer for leisure. If these times follow an exponential distribution, find the proportion of each group that spends:

- **a.** Less than 15 minutes per day using a computer for leisure.
- **b.** More than 2 hours.
- **c.** Between 30 minutes and 90 minutes using a computer for leisure.
- **d.** Find the 20th percentile. Eighty percent spend more than what amount of time?

40. The cost per item at a supermarket follows an exponential distribution. There are many inexpensive items and a few relatively expensive ones. The mean cost per item is \$3.50. What is the percentage of items that cost:

- **a.** Less than \$1?
- **b.** More than \$4?
- **c.** Between \$2 and \$3?
- **d.** Find the 40th percentile. Sixty percent of the supermarket items cost more than what amount?

CHAPTER SUMMARY

I. The uniform distribution is a continuous probability distribution with the following characteristics.

A. It is rectangular in shape.

B. The mean and the median are equal.

C. It is completely described by its minimum value *a* and its maximum value *b*.

D. It is described by the following equation for the region from *a* to *b*:

$$P(x) = \frac{1}{b - a} \tag{7–3}$$

E. The mean and standard deviation of a uniform distribution are computed as follows:

$$\mu = \frac{(a + b)}{2} \tag{7–1}$$

$$\sigma = \sqrt{\frac{(b - a)^2}{12}} \tag{7–2}$$

II. The normal probability distribution is a continuous distribution with the following characteristics.

A. It is bell-shaped and has a single peak at the center of the distribution.

B. The distribution is symmetric.

C. It is asymptotic, meaning the curve approaches but never touches the *X*-axis.

D. It is completely described by its mean and standard deviation.

E. There is a family of normal probability distributions.

1. Another normal probability distribution is created when either the mean or the standard deviation changes.

2. The normal probability distribution is described by the following formula:

$$P(x) = \frac{1}{\sigma\sqrt{2\pi}} e^{-\left[\frac{(x - \mu)^2}{2\sigma^2}\right]} \tag{7–4}$$

III. The standard normal probability distribution is a particular normal distribution.

A. It has a mean of 0 and a standard deviation of 1.

B. Any normal probability distribution can be converted to the standard normal probability distribution by the following formula.

$$z = \frac{x - \mu}{\sigma} \tag{7–5}$$

C. By standardizing a normal probability distribution, we can report the distance of a value from the mean in units of the standard deviation.

IV. The normal probability distribution can approximate a binomial distribution under certain conditions.

A. $n\pi$ and $n(1 - \pi)$ must both be at least 5.

1. *n* is the number of observations.

2. π is the probability of a success.

B. The four conditions for a binomial probability distribution are:

1. There are only two possible outcomes.

2. π (pi) remains the same from trial to trial.

3. The trials are independent.

4. The distribution results from a count of the number of successes in a fixed number of trials.

C. The mean and variance of a binomial distribution are computed as follows:

$$\mu = n\pi$$

$$\sigma^2 = n\pi(1 - \pi)$$

D. The continuity correction factor of .5 is used to extend the continuous value of *x* one-half unit in either direction. This correction compensates for approximating a discrete distribution by a continuous distribution.

V. The exponential probability distribution describes times between events in a sequence.
 A. The actions occur independently at a constant rate per unit of time or length.
 B. The probabilities are computed using the formula:

$$P(x) = \lambda e^{-\lambda x} \quad \textbf{(7–6)}$$

 C. It is nonnegative, is positively skewed, declines steadily to the right, and is asymptotic.
 D. The area under the curve is given by the formula

$$P(\text{Arrival time} < x) = 1 - e^{-\lambda x} \quad \textbf{(7–7)}$$

 E. Both the mean and standard deviation are:

$$\mu = 1/\lambda$$
$$\sigma^2 = 1/\lambda$$

CHAPTER EXERCISES

41. The amount of cola in a 12-ounce can is uniformly distributed between 11.96 ounces and 12.05 ounces.
 a. What is the mean amount per can?
 b. What is the standard deviation amount per can?
 c. What is the probability of selecting a can of cola and finding it has less than 12 ounces?
 d. What is the probability of selecting a can of cola and finding it has more than 11.98 ounces?
 e. What is the probability of selecting a can of cola and finding it has more than 11.00 ounces?

42. A tube of Listerine Tartar Control toothpaste contains 4.2 ounces. As people use the toothpaste, the amount remaining in any tube is random. Assume the amount of toothpaste remaining in the tube follows a uniform distribution. From this information, we can determine the following information about the amount remaining in a toothpaste tube without invading anyone's privacy.
 a. How much toothpaste would you expect to be remaining in the tube?
 b. What is the standard deviation of the amount remaining in the tube?
 c. What is the likelihood there is less than 3.0 ounces remaining in the tube?
 d. What is the probability there is more than 1.5 ounces remaining in the tube?

43. Many retail stores offer their own credit cards. At the time of the credit application, the customer is given a 10% discount on the purchase. The time required for the credit application process follows a uniform distribution with the times ranging from 4 minutes to 10 minutes.
 a. What is the mean time for the application process?
 b. What is the standard deviation of the process time?
 c. What is the likelihood a particular application will take less than 6 minutes?
 d. What is the likelihood an application will take more than 5 minutes?

44. The time patrons at the Grande Dunes Hotel in the Bahamas spend waiting for an elevator follows a uniform distribution between 0 and 3.5 minutes.
 a. Show that the area under the curve is 1.00.
 b. How long does the typical patron wait for elevator service?
 c. What is the standard deviation of the waiting time?
 d. What percent of the patrons wait for less than a minute?
 e. What percent of the patrons wait more than 2 minutes?

45. The net sales and the number of employees for aluminum fabricators with similar characteristics are organized into frequency distributions. Both are normally distributed. For the net sales, the mean is $180 million and the standard deviation is $25 million. For the number of employees, the mean is 1,500 and the standard deviation is 120. Clarion Fabricators had sales of $170 million and 1,850 employees.
 a. Convert Clarion's sales and number of employees to z values.
 b. Locate the two z values.
 c. Compare Clarion's sales and number of employees with those of the other fabricators.

46. The accounting department at Weston Materials Inc., a national manufacturer of unattached garages, reports that it takes two construction workers a mean of 32 hours and a standard deviation of 2 hours to erect the Red Barn model. Assume the assembly times follow the normal distribution.

a. Determine the z values for 29 and 34 hours. What percent of the garages take between 32 hours and 34 hours to erect?

b. What percent of the garages take between 29 hours and 34 hours to erect?

c. What percent of the garages take 28.7 hours or less to erect?

d. Of the garages, 5% take how many hours or more to erect?

47. In 2015 The United States Department of Agriculture issued a report (http://www.cnpp.usda.gov/sites/default/files/CostofFoodMar2015.pdf) indicating a family of four spent an average of about $890 per month on food. Assume the distribution of food expenditures for a family of four follows the normal distribution, with a standard deviation of $90 per month.

a. What percent of the families spend more than $430 but less than $890 per month on food?

b. What percent of the families spend less than $830 per month on food?

c. What percent spend between $830 and $1,000 per month on food?

d. What percent spend between $900 and $1,000 per month on food?

48. A study of long-distance phone calls made from General Electric Corporate Headquarters in Fairfield, Connecticut, revealed the length of the calls, in minutes, follows the normal probability distribution. The mean length of time per call was 4.2 minutes and the standard deviation was 0.60 minute.

a. What is the probability that calls last between 4.2 and 5 minutes?

b. What is the probability that calls last more than 5 minutes?

c. What is the probability that calls last between 5 and 6 minutes?

d. What is the probability that calls last between 4 and 6 minutes?

e. As part of her report to the president, the director of communications would like to report the length of the longest (in duration) 4% of the calls. What is this time?

49. Shaver Manufacturing Inc. offers dental insurance to its employees. A recent study by the human resource director shows the annual cost per employee per year followed the normal probability distribution, with a mean of $1,280 and a standard deviation of $420 per year.

a. What is the probability that annual dental expenses are more than $1,500?

b. What is the probability that annual dental expenses are between $1,500 and $2,000?

c. Estimate the probability that an employee had no annual dental expenses.

d. What was the cost for the 10% of employees who incurred the highest dental expense?

50. The annual commissions earned by sales representatives of Machine Products Inc., a manufacturer of light machinery, follow the normal probability distribution. The mean yearly amount earned is $40,000 and the standard deviation is $5,000.

a. What percent of the sales representatives earn more than $42,000 per year?

b. What percent of the sales representatives earn between $32,000 and $42,000?

c. What percent of the sales representatives earn between $32,000 and $35,000?

d. The sales manager wants to award the sales representatives who earn the largest commissions a bonus of $1,000. He can award a bonus to 20% of the representatives. What is the cutoff point between those who earn a bonus and those who do not?

51. According to the South Dakota Department of Health, the number of hours of TV viewing per week is higher among adult women than adult men. A recent study showed women spent an average of 34 hours per week watching TV, and men, 29 hours per week. Assume that the distribution of hours watched follows the normal distribution for both groups, and that the standard deviation among the women is 4.5 hours and is 5.1 hours for the men.

a. What percent of the women watch TV less than 40 hours per week?

b. What percent of the men watch TV more than 25 hours per week?

c. How many hours of TV do the 1% of women who watch the most TV per week watch? Find the comparable value for the men.

52. According to a government study among adults in the 25- to 34-year age group, the mean amount spent per year on reading and entertainment is $1,994. Assume that the distribution of the amounts spent follows the normal distribution with a standard deviation of $450.
    a. What percent of the adults spend more than $2,500 per year on reading and entertainment?
    b. What percent spend between $2,500 and $3,000 per year on reading and entertainment?
    c. What percent spend less than $1,000 per year on reading and entertainment?
53. Management at Gordon Electronics is considering adopting a bonus system to increase production. One suggestion is to pay a bonus on the highest 5% of production based on past experience. Past records indicate weekly production follows the normal distribution. The mean of this distribution is 4,000 units per week and the standard deviation is 60 units per week. If the bonus is paid on the upper 5% of production, the bonus will be paid on how many units or more?
54. Fast Service Truck Lines uses the Ford Super Duty F-750 exclusively. Management made a study of the maintenance costs and determined the number of miles traveled during the year followed the normal distribution. The mean of the distribution was 60,000 miles and the standard deviation 2,000 miles.
    a. What percent of the Ford Super Duty F-750s logged 65,200 miles or more?
    b. What percent of the trucks logged more than 57,060 but less than 58,280 miles?
    c. What percent of the Fords traveled 62,000 miles or less during the year?
    d. Is it reasonable to conclude that any of the trucks were driven more than 70,000 miles? Explain.
55. Best Electronics Inc. offers a "no hassle" returns policy. The daily number of customers returning items follows the normal distribution. The mean number of customers returning items is 10.3 per day and the standard deviation is 2.25 per day.
    a. For any day, what is the probability that eight or fewer customers returned items?
    b. For any day, what is the probability that the number of customers returning items is between 12 and 14?
    c. Is there any chance of a day with no customer returns?
56. A recent news report indicated that 20% of all employees steal from their company each year. If a company employs 50 people, what is the probability that:
    a. Fewer than five employees steal?
    b. More than five employees steal?
    c. Exactly five employees steal?
    d. More than 5 but fewer than 15 employees steal?
57. The *Orange County Register,* as part of its Sunday health supplement, reported that 64% of American men over the age of 18 consider nutrition a top priority in their lives. Suppose we select a sample of 60 men. What is the likelihood that:
    a. 32 or more consider nutrition important?
    b. 44 or more consider nutrition important?
    c. More than 32 but fewer than 43 consider nutrition important?
    d. Exactly 44 consider diet important?
58. It is estimated that 10% of those taking the quantitative methods portion of the CPA examination fail that section. Sixty students are taking the exam this Saturday.
    a. How many would you expect to fail? What is the standard deviation?
    b. What is the probability that exactly two students will fail?
    c. What is the probability at least two students will fail?
59. The Georgetown, South Carolina, Traffic Division reported 40% of high-speed chases involving automobiles result in a minor or major accident. If 50 high-speed chases occur in a year, what is the probability that 25 or more will result in a minor or major accident?
60. Cruise ships of the Royal Viking line report that 80% of their rooms are occupied during September. For a cruise ship having 800 rooms, what is the probability that 665 or more are occupied in September?
61. The goal at U.S. airports handling international flights is to clear these flights within 45 minutes. Let's interpret this to mean that 95% of the flights are cleared in 45 minutes, so 5% of the flights take longer to clear. Let's also assume that the distribution is approximately normal.
    a. If the standard deviation of the time to clear an international flight is 5 minutes, what is the mean time to clear a flight?

b. Suppose the standard deviation is 10 minutes, not the 5 minutes suggested in part (a). What is the new mean?

c. A customer has 30 minutes from the time her flight lands to catch her limousine. Assuming a standard deviation of 10 minutes, what is the likelihood that she will be cleared in time?

62. The funds dispensed at the ATM machine located near the checkout line at the Kroger's in Union, Kentucky, follows a normal probability distribution with a mean of $4,200 per day and a standard deviation of $720 per day. The machine is programmed to notify the nearby bank if the amount dispensed is very low (less than $2,500) or very high (more than $6,000).

a. What percent of the days will the bank be notified because the amount dispensed is very low?

b. What percent of the time will the bank be notified because the amount dispensed is high?

c. What percent of the time will the bank not be notified regarding the amount of funds dispersed?

63. The weights of canned hams processed at Henline Ham Company follow the normal distribution, with a mean of 9.20 pounds and a standard deviation of 0.25 pound. The label weight is given as 9.00 pounds.

a. What proportion of the hams actually weigh less than the amount claimed on the label?

b. The owner, Glen Henline, is considering two proposals to reduce the proportion of hams below label weight. He can increase the mean weight to 9.25 and leave the standard deviation the same, or he can leave the mean weight at 9.20 and reduce the standard deviation from 0.25 pound to 0.15. Which change would you recommend?

64. A recent Gallup study (http://www.gallup.com/poll/175286/hour-workweek-actually-longer-seven-hours.aspx) found the typical American works an average of 46.7 hour per week. The study did not report the shape of the distribution of hours worked or the standard deviation. It did however indicate that 40% of the workers worked less than 40 hours a week and that 18 percent worked more than 60 hours.

a. If we assume that the distribution of hours worked is normally distributed, and knowing 40% of the workers worked less than 40 hours, find the standard deviation of the distribution.

b. If we assume that the distribution of hours worked is normally distributed and 18% of the workers worked more than 60 hours, find the standard deviation of the distribution.

c. Compare the standard deviations computed in parts *a* and *b*. Is the assumption that the distribution of hours worked is approximately normal reasonable? Why?

65. Most four-year automobile leases allow up to 60,000 miles. If the lessee goes beyond this amount, a penalty of 20 cents per mile is added to the lease cost. Suppose the distribution of miles driven on four-year leases follows the normal distribution. The mean is 52,000 miles and the standard deviation is 5,000 miles.

a. What percent of the leases will yield a penalty because of excess mileage?

b. If the automobile company wanted to change the terms of the lease so that 25% of the leases went over the limit, where should the new upper limit be set?

c. One definition of a low-mileage car is one that is 4 years old and has been driven less than 45,000 miles. What percent of the cars returned are considered low-mileage?

66. The price of shares of Bank of Florida at the end of trading each day for the last year followed the normal distribution. Assume there were 240 trading days in the year. The mean price was $42.00 per share and the standard deviation was $2.25 per share.

a. What is the probability that the end-of-day trading price is over $45.00? Estimate the number of days in a year when the trading price finished above $45.00.

b. What percent of the days was the price between $38.00 and $40.00?

c. What is the minimum share price for the top 15% of end-of-day trading prices?

67. The annual sales of romance novels follow the normal distribution. However, the mean and the standard deviation are unknown. Forty percent of the time sales are more than 470,000, and 10% of the time sales are more than 500,000. What are the mean and the standard deviation?

68. In establishing warranties on HDTVs, the manufacturer wants to set the limits so that few will need repair at the manufacturer's expense. On the other hand, the warranty period must be long enough to make the purchase attractive to the buyer. For a new HDTV, the mean number of months until repairs are needed is 36.84 with a standard deviation of 3.34 months. Where should the warranty limits be set so that only 10% of the HDTVs need repairs at the manufacturer's expense?

69. DeKorte Tele-Marketing Inc. is considering purchasing a machine that randomly selects and automatically dials telephone numbers. DeKorte Tele-Marketing makes most of its calls during the evening, so calls to business phones are wasted. The manufacturer of the machine claims that its programming reduces the calling to business phones to 15% of all calls. To test this claim, the director of purchasing at DeKorte programmed the machine to select a sample of 150 phone numbers. What is the likelihood that more than 30 of the phone numbers selected are those of businesses, assuming the manufacturer's claim is correct?

70. A carbon monoxide detector in the Wheelock household activates once every 200 days on average. Assume this activation follows the exponential distribution. What is the probability that:

a. There will be an alarm within the next 60 days?
b. At least 400 days will pass before the next alarm?
c. It will be between 150 and 250 days until the next warning?
d. Find the median time until the next activation.

71. "Boot time" (the time between the appearance of the Bios screen to the first file that is loaded in Windows) on Eric Mouser's personal computer follows an exponential distribution with a mean of 27 seconds. What is the probability his "boot" will require:

a. Less than 15 seconds?
b. More than 60 seconds?
c. Between 30 and 45 seconds?
d. What is the point below which only 10% of the boots occur?

72. The time between visits to a U.S. emergency room for a member of the general population follows an exponential distribution with a mean of 2.5 years. What proportion of the population:

a. Will visit an emergency room within the next 6 months?
b. Will not visit the ER over the next 6 years?
c. Will visit an ER next year, but not this year?
d. Find the first and third quartiles of this distribution.

73. The times between failures on a personal computer follow an exponential distribution with a mean of 300,000 hours. What is the probability of:

a. A failure in less than 100,000 hours?
b. No failure in the next 500,000 hours?
c. The next failure occurring between 200,000 and 350,000 hours?
d. What are the mean and standard deviation of the time between failures?

DATA ANALYTICS

(The data for these exercises are available at the text website: www.mhhe.com/lind17e.)

74. Refer to the North Valley Real Estate data, which report information on homes sold during the last year.

a. The mean selling price (in $ thousands) of the homes was computed earlier to be $357.0, with a standard deviation of $160.7. Use the normal distribution to estimate the percentage of homes selling for more than $500.000. Compare this to the actual results. Is price normally distributed? Try another test. If price is normally distributed, how many homes should have a price greater than the mean? Compare this to the actual number of homes. Construct a frequency distribution of price. What do you observe?

b. The mean days on the market is 30 with a standard deviation of 10 days. Use the normal distribution to estimate the number of homes on the market more than 24 days. Compare this to the actual results. Try another test. If days on the market is normally distributed, how many homes should be on the market more than the mean number of days? Compare this to the actual number of homes. Does the normal distribution yield a good approximation of the actual results? Create a frequency distribution of days on the market. What do you observe?

75. Refer to the Baseball 2016 data, which report information on the 30 Major League Baseball teams for the 2016 season.

a. The mean attendance per team for the season was 2.439 million, with a standard deviation of 0.618 million. Use the normal distribution to estimate the number of teams with attendance of more than 3.5 million. Compare that estimate with the actual number. Comment on the accuracy of your estimate.

b. The mean team salary was $121 million, with a standard deviation of $40.0 million. Use the normal distribution to estimate the number of teams with a team salary of more than $100 million. Compare that estimate with the actual number. Comment on the accuracy of the estimate.

76. Refer to the Lincolnville School District bus data.

a. Refer to the maintenance cost variable. The mean maintenance cost for last year is $4,552 with a standard deviation of $2332. Estimate the number of buses with a maintenance cost of more than $6,000. Compare that with the actual number. Create a frequency distribution of maintenance cost. Is the distribution normally distributed?

b. Refer to the variable on the number of miles driven since the last maintenance. The mean is 11,121 and the standard deviation is 617 miles. Estimate the number of buses traveling more than 11,500 miles since the last maintenance. Compare that number with the actual value. Create a frequency distribution of miles since maintenance cost. Is the distribution normally distributed?

A REVIEW OF CHAPTERS 5–7

The chapters in this section consider methods of dealing with uncertainty. In Chapter 5, we describe the concept of probability. A *probability* is a value between 0 and 1 that expresses the likelihood a particular event will occur. We also looked at methods to calculate probabilities using rules of addition and multiplication; presented principles of counting, including permutations and combinations; and described situations for using Bayes' theorem.

Chapter 6 describes *discrete* probability distributions. Discrete probability distributions list all possible outcomes of an experiment and the probability associated with each outcome. We describe three discrete probability distributions: the *binomial distribution,* the *hypergeometric distribution,* and the *Poisson distribution.* The requirements for the binomial distribution are there are only two possible outcomes for each trial, there is a constant probability of success, there are a fixed number of trials, and the trials are independent. The binomial distribution lists the probabilities for the number of successes in a fixed number of trials. The hypergeometric distribution is similar to the binomial, but the probability of success is not constant, so the trials are not independent. The Poisson distribution is characterized by a small probability of success in a large number of trials. It has the following characteristics: the random variable is the number of times some event occurs in a fixed interval, the probability of a success is proportional to the size of the interval, and the intervals are independent and do not overlap.

Chapter 7 describes three continuous probability distributions: the *uniform distribution,* the *normal distribution,* and the *exponential distribution.* The uniform probability distribution is rectangular in shape and is defined by minimum and maximum values. The mean and the median of a uniform probability distribution are equal, and it does not have a mode.

A normal probability distribution is the most widely used and widely reported distribution. Its major characteristics are that it is bell-shaped and symmetrical, completely described by its mean and standard deviation, and asymptotic, that is, it falls smoothly in each direction from its peak but never touches the horizontal axis. There is a family of normal probability distributions—each with its own mean and standard deviation. There are an unlimited number of normal probability distributions.

To find the probabilities for any normal probability distribution, we convert a normal distribution to a *standard normal probability distribution* by computing z values. A z value is the distance between x and the mean in units of the standard deviation. The standard normal probability distribution has a mean of 0 and a standard deviation of 1. It is useful because the probability for any event from a normal probability distribution can be computed using standard normal probability tables (see Appendix B.3).

The exponential probability distribution describes the time between events in a sequence. These events occur independently at a constant rate per unit of time or length. The exponential probability distribution is positively skewed, with λ as the "rate" parameter. The mean and standard deviation are equal and are the reciprocal of λ.

PROBLEMS

1. Proactine, a new medicine for acne, is claimed by the manufacturer to be 80% effective. It is applied to the affected area of a sample of 15 people. What is the probability that:
   a. All 15 will show significant improvement?
   b. Fewer than 9 of 15 will show significant improvement?
   c. 12 or more people will show significant improvement?
2. Customers at the Bank of Commerce of Idaho Falls, Idaho, default at a rate of .005 on small home-improvement loans. The bank has approved 400 small home-improvement loans. Assuming the Poisson probability distribution applies to this problem:
   a. What is the probability that no homeowners out of the 400 will default?
   b. How many of the 400 are expected not to default?
   c. What is the probability that three or more homeowners will default on their small home-improvement loans?
3. A study of the attendance at the University of Alabama's basketball games revealed that the distribution of attendance is normally distributed with a mean of 10,000 and a standard deviation of 2,000.
   a. What is the probability a particular game has an attendance of 13,500 or more?
   b. What percent of the games have an attendance between 8,000 and 11,500?
   c. Ten percent of the games have an attendance of how many or less?
4. **FILE** Daniel-James Insurance Company will insure an offshore ExxonMobil oil production platform against weather losses for one year. The president of Daniel-James estimates the following losses for that platform (in millions of dollars) with the accompanying probabilities:

Amount of Loss ($ millions)	Probability of Loss
0	.98
40	.016
300	.004

   a. What is the expected amount Daniel-James will have to pay to ExxonMobil in claims?
   b. What is the likelihood that Daniel-James will actually lose less than the expected amount?
   c. Given that Daniel-James suffers a loss, what is the likelihood that it is for $300 million?
   d. Daniel-James has set the annual premium at $2.0 million. Does that seem like a fair premium? Will it cover its risk?
5. **FILE** The distribution of the number of school-age children per family in the Whitehall Estates area of Grand Junction, Colorado, is:

Number of children	0	1	2	3	4
Percent of families	40	30	15	10	5

   a. Determine the mean and standard deviation of the number of school-age children per family in Whitehall Estates.
   b. A new school is planned in Whitehall Estates. An estimate of the number of school-age children is needed. There are 500 family units. How many children would you estimate?
   c. Some additional information is needed about only the families having children. Convert the preceding distribution to one for families with children. What is the mean number of children among families that have children?
6. The following table shows a breakdown of the 114th U.S. Congress by party affiliation. (There are two independent senators included in the count of Democratic senators. There is one vacant House seat.)

	Party		
	Democrats	Republicans	Total
House	188	246	434
Senate	46	54	100
Total	234	300	534

a. A member of Congress is selected at random. What is the probability of selecting a Republican?

b. Given that the person selected is a member of the House of Representatives, what is the probability he or she is a Republican?

c. What is the probability of selecting a member of the House of Representatives or a Democrat?

CASES

A. Century National Bank

Refer to the Century National Bank data. Is it reasonable that the distribution of checking account balances approximates a normal probability distribution? Determine the mean and the standard deviation for the sample of 60 customers. Compare the actual distribution with the theoretical distribution. Cite some specific examples and comment on your findings.

Divide the account balances into three groups, of about 20 each, with the smallest third of the balances in the first group, the middle third in the second group, and those with the largest balances in the third group. Next, develop a table that shows the number in each of the categories of the account balances by branch. Does it appear that account balances are related to the branch? Cite some examples and comment on your findings.

B. Elections Auditor

An item such as an increase in taxes, recall of elected officials, or an expansion of public services can be placed on the ballot if a required number of valid signatures are collected on the petition. Unfortunately, many people will sign the petition even though they are not registered to vote in that particular district, or they will sign the petition more than once.

Sara Ferguson, the elections auditor in Venango County, must certify the validity of these signatures after the petition is officially presented. Not surprisingly, her staff is overloaded, so she is considering using statistical methods to validate the pages of 200 signatures, instead of validating each individual signature. At a recent professional meeting, she found that, in some communities in the state, election officials were checking only five signatures on each page and rejecting the entire page if two or more signatures were invalid. Some people are concerned that five may not be enough to make a good decision. They suggest that you should check 10 signatures and reject the page if 3 or more are invalid.

In order to investigate these methods, Sara asks her staff to pull the results from the last election and sample 30 pages. It happens that the staff selected 14 pages from the Avondale district, 9 pages from the Midway district, and 7 pages from the Kingston district. Each page had 200 signatures, and the data below show the number of invalid signatures on each.

Use the data to evaluate Sara's two proposals. Calculate the probability of rejecting a page under each of the approaches. Would you get about the same results by examining every single signature? Offer a plan of your own, and discuss how it might be better or worse than the two plans proposed by Sara.

Avondale	Midway	Kingston
9	19	38
14	22	39
11	23	41
8	14	39
14	22	41
6	17	39
10	15	39
13	20	
8	18	
8		
9		
12		
7		
13		

C. Geoff Applies Data Analytics

Geoff Brown is the manager for a small telemarketing firm and is evaluating the sales rate of experienced workers in order to set minimum standards for new hires. During the past few weeks, he has recorded the number of successful calls per hour for the staff. These data appear next along with some summary statistics he worked out with a statistical software package. Geoff has been a student at the local community college and has heard of many different kinds of probability distributions (binomial, normal, hypergeometric, Poisson, etc.). Could you give Geoff some advice on which distribution to use to fit these data as well as possible and how to decide when a probationary employee should be accepted as having reached full production status? This is important because it means a pay raise for the employee, and there have been some probationary employees in the past who have quit because of discouragement that they would never meet the standard.

Successful sales calls per hour during the week of August 14:

4	2	3	1	4	5	5	2	3	2	2	4	5	2	5	3	3	0
1	3	2	8	4	5	2	2	4	1	5	5	4	5	1	2	4	

Descriptive statistics:

N	MEAN	MEDIAN	STANDARD DEVIATION
35	3.229	3.000	1.682
MIN	MAX	1ST QUARTILE	3RD QUARTILE
0.0	8.0	2.0	5.0

Analyze the distribution of sales calls. Which distribution do you think Geoff should use for his analysis? Support your recommendation with your analysis. What standard should be used to determine if an employee has reached "full production" status? Explain your recommendation.

D. CNP Bank Card

Before banks issue a credit card, they usually rate or score the customer in terms of his or her projected probability of being a profitable customer. A typical scoring table appears below.

Age	**Under 25** (12 pts.)	**25–29** (5 pts.)	**30–34** (0 pts.)	**35+** (18 pts.)
Time at same address	**<1 yr.** (9 pts.)	**1–2 yrs.** (0 pts.)	**3–4 yrs.** (13 pts.)	**5+ yrs.** (20 pts.)
Auto age	**None** (18 pts.)	**0–1yr.** (12 pts.)	**2–4 yrs.** (13 pts.)	**5+ yrs.** (3 pts.)
Monthly car payment	**None** (15 pts.)	**$1–$99** (6 pts.)	**$100–$299** (4 pts.)	**$300+** (0 pts.)
Housing cost	**$1–$199** (0 pts.)	**$200–$399** (10 pts.)	**Owns** (12 pts.)	**Lives with relatives** (24 pts.)
Checking/ savings accounts	**Both** (15 pts.)	**Checking only** (3 pts.)	**Savings only** (2 pts.)	**Neither** (0 pts.)

The score is the sum of the points on the six items. For example, Tracy Brown is under 25 years old (12 pts.), has lived at the same address for 2 years (0 pts.), owns a 4-year-old car (13 pts.), with car payments of $75 (6 pts.), housing cost of $450 (10 pts.), and a checking account (3 pts.). She would score 44.

A second chart is then used to convert scores into the probability of being a profitable customer. A sample chart of this type appears below.

Score	30	40	50	60	70	80	90
Probability	.70	.78	.85	.90	.94	.95	.96

Tracy's score of 44 would translate into a probability of being profitable of approximately .81. In other words, 81% of customers like Tracy will make money for the bank card operations.

Here are the interview results for three potential customers.

Name	David Born	Edward Brendan	Ann McLaughlin
Age	42	23	33
Time at same address	9	2	5
Auto age	2	3	7
Monthly car payment	$140	$99	$175
Housing cost	$450	$650	Owns clear
Checking/savings accounts	Both	Checking only	Neither

1. Score each of these customers and estimate their probability of being profitable.
2. What is the probability that all three are profitable?
3. What is the probability that none of them are profitable?
4. Find the entire probability distribution for the number of profitable customers among this group of three.
5. Write a brief summary of your findings.

PRACTICE TEST

Part 1—Objective

1. Under what conditions will a probability be greater than 1 or 100%? 1. ________
2. An ________ is the observation of some activity or the act of taking some type of measurement. 2. ________
3. An ________ is the collection of one or more outcomes to an experiment. 3. ________
4. A ________ probability is the likelihood that two or more events will happen at the same time. 4. ________
5. In a (5a) ________, the order in which the events are counted is important, but in a (5b) ________, it is not important. 5. a. ________ 5. b. ________
6. In a discrete probability distribution, the sum of the possible outcomes is equal to ________. 6. ________
7. Which of the following is *NOT* a requirement of the binomial distribution? (constant probability of success, three or more outcomes, the result of counts) 7. ________
8. How many normal distributions are there? (1, 10, 30, 1,000, or infinite—pick one) 8. ________
9. How many standard normal distributions are there? (1, 10, 30, 1,000, or infinite—pick one) 9. ________
10. What is the probability of finding a *z* value between 0 and −0.76? 10. ________
11. What is the probability of finding a *z* value greater than 1.67? 11. ________
12. Two events are ____________ if the occurrence of one event does not affect the occurrence of another event. 12. ________

13. Two events are ______________ if by virtue of one event happening the other cannot happen. **13.** ______________

14. Which of the following is not true regarding the normal probability distribution? (asymptotic, family of distributions, only two outcomes, 50% of the observations greater than the mean) **14.** ______________

15. Which of the following statements best describes the shape of a normal probability distribution? (bell-shaped, uniform, V-shaped, no constant shape) **15.** ______________

Part 2—Problems

1. Fred Friendly, CPA, has 20 tax returns to prepare before the April 15th deadline. It is late at night so he decides to do two more before going home. In his stack of accounts, 12 are personal, 5 are businesses, and 3 are for charitable organizations. If he selects the two returns at random, what is the probability:
   a. Both are businesses?
   b. At least one is a business?
2. The IRS reports that 15% of returns where the adjusted gross income is more than $1,000,000 will be subject to a computer audit. For the year 2017, Fred Friendly, CPA, completed 16 returns where the adjusted gross income was more than $1,000,000.
   a. What is the probability exactly one of these returns will be audited?
   b. What is the probability at least one will be audited?
3. Fred works in a tax office with five other CPAs. There are five parking spots beside the office. In how many different ways can the cars belonging to the CPAs be arranged in the five spots? Assume they all drive to work.
4. Fred decided to study the number of exemptions claimed on personal tax returns he prepared in 2017. The data are summarized in the following table.

Exemptions	Percent
1	20
2	50
3	20
4	10

   a. What is the mean number of exemptions per return?
   b. What is the variance of the number of exemptions per return?
5. In a memo to all those involved in tax preparation, the IRS indicated that the mean amount of refund was $1,600 with a standard deviation of $850. Assume the distribution of the amounts returned follows the normal distribution.
   a. What percent of the refunds were between $1,600 and $2,000?
   b. What percent of the refunds were between $900 and $2,000?
   c. According to the above information, what percent of the refunds were less than $0; that is, the taxpayer owed the IRS.
6. For the year 2017, Fred Friendly completed a total of 80 returns. He developed the following table summarizing the relationship between number of dependents and whether or not the client received a refund.

	Dependents			
Refund	**1**	**2**	**3 or more**	**Total**
Yes	20	20	10	50
No	10	20	0	30
Total	30	40	10	80

   a. What is the name given to this table?
   b. What is the probability of selecting a client who received a refund?
   c. What is the probability of selecting a client who received a refund or had one dependent?
   d. Given that the client received a refund, what is the probability he or she had one dependent?
   e. What is the probability of selecting a client who did *not* receive a refund and had one dependent?
7. The IRS offers taxpayers the choice of allowing the IRS to compute the amount of their tax refund. During the busy filing season, the number of returns received at the Springfield Service Center that request this service follows a Poisson distribution with a mean of three per day. What is the probability that on a particular day:
   a. There are no requests?
   b. Exactly three requests appear?
   c. Five or more requests take place?
   d. There are no requests on two consecutive days?

Sampling Methods and the Central Limit Theorem

© ecopix/ullstein bild/The Image Works

▲ **THE NIKE** annual report says that the average American buys 6.5 pairs of sports shoes per year. Suppose a sample of 81 customers is surveyed and the population standard deviation of sports shoes purchased per year is 2.1 What is the standard error of the mean in this experiment? (See Exercise 45 and **LO8-4**.)

LEARNING OBJECTIVES

When you have completed this chapter, you will be able to:

LO8-1 Explain why populations are sampled and describe four methods to sample a population.

LO8-2 Define sampling error.

LO8-3 Demonstrate the construction of a sampling distribution of the sample mean.

LO8-4 Recite the central limit theorem and define the mean and standard error of the sampling distribution of the sample mean.

LO8-5 Apply the central limit theorem to calculate probabilities.

INTRODUCTION

Chapters 2 through 4 emphasize techniques to describe data. To illustrate these techniques, we organize the profits for the sale of 180 vehicles by the four dealers included in the Applewood Auto Group into a frequency distribution and compute measures of location and dispersion. Such measures as the mean and the standard deviation describe the typical profit and the spread in the profits. In these chapters, the emphasis is on describing the distribution of the data. That is, we describe something that has already happened.

In Chapter 5, we begin to lay the foundation for statistical inference with the study of probability. Recall that in statistical inference our goal is to determine something about a *population* based only on the *sample*. The population is the entire group of individuals or objects under consideration, and the sample is a part or subset of that population. Chapter 6 extends the probability concepts by describing three discrete probability distributions: the binomial, the hypergeometric, and the Poisson. Chapter 7 describes three continuous probability distributions: the uniform, normal, and exponential. Probability distributions encompass all possible outcomes of an experiment and the probability associated with each outcome. We use probability distributions to evaluate the likelihood something occurs in the future.

This chapter begins our study of sampling. Sampling is a process of selecting items from a population so we can use this information to make judgments or inferences about the population. We begin this chapter by discussing methods of selecting a sample from a population. Next, we construct a distribution of the sample mean to understand how the sample means tend to cluster around the population mean. Finally, we show that for any population the shape of this sampling distribution tends to follow the normal probability distribution.

LO8-1
Explain why populations are sampled and describe four methods to sample a population.

SAMPLING METHODS

In Chapter 1, we said the purpose of inferential statistics is to find something about a population based on a sample. A sample is a portion or part of the population of interest. In many cases, sampling is more feasible than studying the entire population. In this section, we discuss the reasons for sampling, and then several methods for selecting a sample.

Reasons to Sample

When studying characteristics of a population, there are many practical reasons why we prefer to select portions or samples of a population to observe and measure. Here are some of the reasons for sampling:

1. **To contact the whole population would be time-consuming.** A candidate for a national office may wish to determine her chances for election. A sample poll using the regular staff and field interviews of a professional polling firm would take only 1 or 2 days. Using the same staff and interviewers and working 7 days a week, it would take nearly 200 years to contact all the voting population! Even if a large staff of interviewers could be assembled, the benefit of contacting all of the voters would probably not be worth the time.
2. **The cost of studying all the items in a population may be prohibitive.** Public opinion polls and consumer testing organizations, such as Harris Interactive Inc., CBS News Polls, and Zogby Analytics, usually contact fewer than 2,000 of the nearly 60 million families in the United States. One consumer panel–type organization charges $40,000 to mail samples and tabulate responses to test a product (such as breakfast cereal, cat food, or perfume). The same product test using all 60 million families would be too expensive to be worthwhile.
3. **The physical impossibility of checking all items in the population.** Some populations are infinite. It would be impossible to check all the water in Lake Erie for bacterial levels, so we select samples at various locations. The populations of fish, birds, snakes, deer, and the like are large and are constantly moving, being

© David Epperson/Getty Images

born, and dying. Instead of even attempting to count all the ducks in Canada or all the fish in Lake Pontchartrain, we make estimates using various techniques—such as counting all the ducks on a pond selected at random, tracking fish catches, or netting fish at predetermined places in the lake.

4. **The destructive nature of some tests.** If the wine tasters at the Sutter Home Winery in California drank all the wine to evaluate the vintage, they would consume the entire crop, and none would be available for sale. In the area of industrial production, steel plates, wires, and similar products must have a certain minimum tensile strength. To ensure that the product meets the minimum standard, the Quality Assurance Department selects a sample from the current production. Each piece is stretched until it breaks and the breaking point (usually measured in pounds per square inch) recorded. Obviously, if all the wire or all the plates were tested for tensile strength, none would be available for sale or use. For the same reason, only a few seeds are tested for germination by Burpee Seeds Inc. prior to the planting season.
5. **The sample results are adequate.** Even if funds were available, it is doubtful the additional accuracy of a 100% sample—that is, studying the entire population—is essential in most problems. For example, the federal government uses a sample of grocery stores scattered throughout the United States to determine the monthly index of food prices. The prices of bread, beans, milk, and other major food items are included in the index. It is unlikely that the inclusion of all grocery stores in the United States would significantly affect the index because the prices of milk, bread, and other major foods usually do not vary by more than a few cents from one chain store to another.

Simple Random Sampling

The most widely used sampling method is a **simple random sampling.**

SIMPLE RANDOM SAMPLE A sample selected so that each item or person in the population has the same chance of being included.

To illustrate the selection process for a simple random sample, suppose the population of interest is the 750 Major League Baseball players on the active rosters of the 30 teams at the end of the 2017 season. The president of the players' union wishes to form a committee of 10 players to study the issue of concussions. One way of ensuring that every player in the population has the same chance of being chosen to serve on the Concussion Committee is to write each name of the 750 players on a slip of paper and place all the slips of paper in a box. After the slips of paper have been thoroughly mixed, the first selection is made by drawing a slip of paper from the box identifying the first player. The slip of paper is not returned to the box. This process is repeated nine more times to form the committee. (Note that the probability of each selection does increase slightly because the slip is not replaced. However, the differences are very small because the population is 750. The probability of each selection is about 0.0013, rounded to four decimal places.)

Of course, the process of writing all the players' names on a slip of paper is very time-consuming. A more convenient method of selecting a random sample is to use a **table of random numbers** such as the one in Appendix B.4. In this case the union president would prepare a list of all 750 players and number each of the players from 1 to 750 with a computer application. Using a table of random numbers, we would randomly pick a starting place in the table, and then select 10 three-digit numbers between 001 and 750. A computer can also generate random numbers. These numbers would correspond with the 10 players in the list that will be asked to participate on the committee. As the name simple random sampling implies, the probability of selecting any number between 001 and 750 is the same. Thus, the probability of selecting the player assigned the number 131 is

STATISTICS IN ACTION

To insure that an unbiased, representative sample is selected from a population, lists of random numbers are needed. In 1927, L. Tippett published the first book of random numbers. In 1938, R. A. Fisher and F. Yates published 15,000 random digits generated using two decks of cards. In 1955, RAND Corporation published a million random digits, generated by the random frequency pulses of an electronic roulette wheel. Since then, computer programs have been developed for generating digits that are "almost" random and hence are called *pseudo-random*. The question of whether a computer program can be used to generate numbers that are truly random remains a debatable issue.

the same as the probability of selecting player 722 or player 382. Using random numbers to select players for the committee removes any bias from the selection process.

The following example shows how to select random numbers using a portion of a random number table illustrated below. First, we choose a starting point in the table. One way of selecting the starting point is to close your eyes and point at a number in the table. Any starting point will do. Another way is to randomly pick a column and row. Suppose the time is 3:04. Using the hour, three o'clock, pick the third column and then, using the minutes, four, move down to the fourth row of numbers. The number is 03759. Because there are only 750 players, we will use the first three digits of a five-digit random number. Thus, 037 is the number of the first player to be a member of the sample. To continue selecting players, we could move in any direction. Suppose we move right. The first three digits of the number to the right of 03759 are 447. Player number 447 is the second player selected to be on the committee. The next three-digit number to the right is 961. You skip 961 as well as the next number 784 because there are only 750 players. The third player selected is number 189. We continue this process until we have 10 players.

50525	57454	28455	68226	34656	38884	39018
72507	53380	53827	42486	54465	71819	91199
34986	74297	00144	38676	89967	98869	39744
68851	27305	03759	44723	96108	78489	18910
06738	62879	03910	17350	49169	03850	18910
11448	10734	05837	24397	10420	16712	94496
		Starting point	Second player			Third player

Statistical packages such as Minitab and spreadsheet packages such as Excel have software that will select a simple random sample. The following example/solution uses Excel to select a random sample from a list of the data.

EXAMPLE

Jane and Joe Miley operate the Foxtrot Inn, a bed and breakfast in Tryon, North Carolina. There are eight rooms available for rent at this B&B. For each day of June 2017, the number of rooms rented is listed. Use Excel to select a sample of five nights during the month of June.

June	Rentals	June	Rentals	June	Rentals
1	0	11	3	21	3
2	2	12	4	22	2
3	3	13	4	23	3
4	2	14	4	24	6
5	3	15	7	25	0
6	4	16	0	26	4
7	2	17	5	27	1
8	3	18	3	28	1
9	4	19	6	29	3
10	7	20	2	30	3

SOLUTION

Excel will select the random sample and report the results. On the first sampled date, four of the eight rooms were rented. On the second sampled date in June, seven rooms were rented. The information is reported in column D of the Excel spreadsheet. The Excel steps are listed in the **Software Commands** in Appendix C. The Excel system performs the sampling *with* replacement. This means it is possible for the same day to appear more than once in a sample.

	A	B	C	D
1	Day of June	Rentals		Sample
2	1	0		4
3	2	2		7
4	3	3		4
5	4	2		3
6	5	3		1
7	6	4		
8	7	2		
9	8	3		
10	9	4		
11	10	7		
12	11	3		
13	12	4		
14	13	4		
15	14	4		

SELF-REVIEW 8–1

The following roster lists the students enrolled in an introductory course in business statistics. Three students will be randomly selected and asked questions about course content and method of instruction.

(a) The numbers 00 through 45 are handwritten on slips of paper and placed in a bowl. The three numbers selected are 31, 7, and 25. Which students are in the sample?
(b) Now use the table of random digits, Appendix B.4, to select your own sample.
(c) What would you do if you encountered the number 59 in the table of random digits?

STAT 264 BUSINESS STATISTICS
9:00 AM - 9:50 AM MW; 118 CARLSON HALL; PROFESSOR LIND

RANDOM NUMBER	NAME	CLASS RANK	RANDOM NUMBER	NAME	CLASS RANK
00	ANDERSON, RAYMOND	SO	23	MEDLEY, CHERYL ANN	SO
01	ANGER, CHERYL RENEE	SO	24	MITCHELL, GREG R	FR
02	BALL, CLAIRE JEANETTE	FR	25	MOLTER, KRISTI MARIE	SO
03	BERRY, CHRISTOPHER G	FR	26	MULCAHY, STEPHEN ROBERT	SO
04	BOBAK, JAMES PATRICK	SO	27	NICHOLAS, ROBERT CHARLES	JR
05	BRIGHT, M. STARR	JR	28	NICKENS, VIRGINIA	SO
06	CHONTOS, PAUL JOSEPH	SO	29	PENNYWITT, SEAN PATRICK	SO
07	DETLEY, BRIAN HANS	JR	30	POTEAU, KRIS E	JR
08	DUDAS, VIOLA	SO	31	PRICE, MARY LYNETTE	SO
09	DULBS, RICHARD ZALFA	JR	32	RISTAS, JAMES	SR
10	EDINGER, SUSAN KEE	SR	33	SAGER, ANNE MARIE	SO
11	FINK, FRANK JAMES	SR	34	SMILLIE, HEATHER MICHELLE	SO
12	FRANCIS, JAMES P	JR	35	SNYDER, LEISHA KAY	SR
13	GAGHEN, PAMELA LYNN	JR	36	STAHL, MARIA TASHERY	SO
14	GOULD, ROBYN KAY	SO	37	ST. JOHN, AMY J	SO
15	GROSENBACHER, SCOTT ALAN	SO	38	STURDEVANT, RICHARD K	SO
16	HEETFIELD, DIANE MARIE	SO	39	SWETYE, LYNN MICHELE	SO
17	KABAT, JAMES DAVID	JR	40	WALASINSKI, MICHAEL	SO
18	KEMP, LISA ADRIANE	FR	41	WALKER, DIANE ELAINE	SO
19	KILLION, MICHELLE A	SO	42	WARNOCK, JENNIFER MARY	SO
20	KOPERSKI, MARY ELLEN	SO	43	WILLIAMS, WENDY A	SO
21	KOPP, BRIDGETTE ANN	SO	44	YAP, HOCK BAN	SO
22	LEHMANN, KRISTINA MARIE	JR	45	YODER, ARLAN JAY	JR

STATISTICS IN ACTION

Random and unbiased sampling methods are extremely important to make valid statistical inferences. In 1936, the *Literary Digest* conducted a straw vote to predict the outcome of the presidential race between Franklin Roosevelt and Alfred Landon. Ten million ballots in the form of returnable postcards were sent to addresses taken from *Literary Digest* subscribers, telephone directories and automobile registrations. In 1936 not many people could afford a telephone or an automobile. Thus, the population that was sampled did not represent the population of voters. A second problem was with the non-responses. More than 10 million people were sent surveys, and more than 2.3 million responded. However, no attempt was made to see whether those responding represented a cross-section of all the voters. On Election Day, Roosevelt won with 61% of the vote. Landon had 39%. In the mid-1930s people who had telephones and drove automobiles clearly did not represent American voters!

Systematic Random Sampling

The simple random sampling procedure is awkward in some research situations. For example, Stood's Grocery Market needs to sample their customers to study the length of time customers spend in the store. Simple random sampling is not an effective method. Practically, we do not have a list of customers, so assigning random numbers to customers is impossible. Instead, we can use **systematic random sampling** to select a representative sample. Using this method for Stood's Grocery Market, we decide to select 100 customers over 4 days, Monday through Thursday. We will select 25 customers a day and begin the sampling at different times each day: 8 a.m., 11 a.m., 4 p.m., and 7 p.m. We write the 4 times and 4 days on slips of paper and put them in two hats—one hat for the days and the other hat for the times. We select one slip from each hat. This ensures that the time of day is randomly assigned for each day. Suppose we selected 4 p.m. for the starting time on Monday. Next we select a random number between 1 and 10; it is 6. Our selection process begins on Monday at 4 p.m. by selecting the sixth customer to enter the store. Then, we select every 10th (16th, 26th, 36th) customer until we reach the goal of 25 customers. For each of these sampled customers, we measure the length of time the customer spends in the store.

SYSTEMATIC RANDOM SAMPLE A random starting point is selected, and then every *k*th member of the population is selected.

Simple random sampling is used in the selection of the days, the times, and the starting point. But the systematic procedure is used to select the actual customer.

Before using systematic random sampling, we should carefully observe the physical order of the population. When the physical order is related to the population characteristic, then systematic random sampling should not be used because the sample could be biased. For example, if we wanted to audit the invoices in a file drawer that were ordered in increasing dollar amounts, systematic random sampling would not guarantee an unbiased random sample. Other sampling methods should be used.

Stratified Random Sampling

When a population can be clearly divided into groups based on some characteristic, we may use **stratified random sampling.** It guarantees each group is represented in the sample. The groups are called **strata.** For example, college students can be grouped as full time or part time; as male or female; or as freshman, sophomore, junior, or senior. Usually the strata are formed based on members' shared attributes or characteristics. A random sample from each stratum is taken in a number proportional to the stratum's size when compared to the population. Once the strata are defined, we apply simple random sampling within each group or stratum to collect the sample.

STRATIFIED RANDOM SAMPLE A population is divided into subgroups, called strata, and a sample is randomly selected from each stratum.

For instance, we might study the advertising expenditures for the 352 largest companies in the United States. The objective of the study is to determine whether firms with high returns on equity (a measure of profitability) spend more on advertising than firms with low returns on equity. To make sure the sample is a fair representation of the 352 companies, the companies are grouped on percent return on equity. Table 8–1 shows the strata and the relative frequencies. If simple random sampling is used, observe that firms in the 3rd and 4th strata have a high chance of selection (probability of 0.87) while firms in the other strata have a small chance of selection (probability of 0.13). We might not select any firms in stratum 1 or 5 *simply by chance*. However, stratified random sampling will guarantee that at least one firm in each of strata 1 and

TABLE 8–1 Number Selected for a Proportional Stratified Random Sample

Stratum	Profitability (return on equity)	Number of Firms	Relative Frequency	Number Sampled
1	30% and over	8	0.02	1*
2	20 up to 30%	35	0.10	5*
3	10 up to 20%	189	0.54	27
4	0 up to 10%	115	0.33	16
5	Deficit	5	0.01	1
Total		352	1.00	50

*0.02 of 50 = 1, 0.10 of 50 = 5, etc.

5 is represented in the sample. Let's say that 50 firms are selected for intensive study. Then based on probability, 1 firm, or (0.02)(50), should be randomly selected from stratum 1. We would randomly select 5, or (0.10)(50), firms from stratum 2. In this case, the number of firms sampled from each stratum is proportional to the stratum's relative frequency in the population. Stratified sampling has the advantage, in some cases, of more accurately reflecting the characteristics of the population than does simple random or systematic random sampling.

Cluster Sampling

Another common type of sampling is **cluster sampling.** It is often employed to reduce the cost of sampling a population scattered over a large geographic area.

CLUSTER SAMPLING A population is divided into clusters using naturally occurring geographic or other boundaries. Then, clusters are randomly selected and a sample is collected by randomly selecting from each cluster.

Suppose you want to determine the views of residents in the greater Chicago, Illinois, metropolitan area about state and federal environmental protection policies. Selecting a random sample of residents in this region and personally contacting each one would be time-consuming and very expensive. Instead, you could employ cluster sampling by subdividing the region into small units, perhaps by counties. These are often called *primary units.*

There are 12 counties in the greater Chicago metropolitan area. Suppose you randomly select 3 counties. The 3 chosen are La Porte, Cook, and Kenosha (see Chart 8–1 below). Next, you select a random sample of the residents in each of these counties and interview them. This is also referred to as sampling through an *intermediate unit.* In this case, the intermediate unit is the county. (Note that this is a combination of cluster sampling and simple random sampling.)

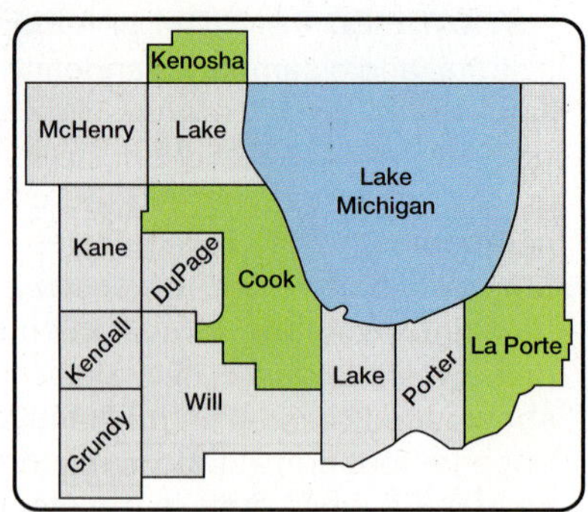

CHART 8–1 The Counties of the Greater Chicago, Illinois, Metropolitan Area

The discussion of sampling methods in the preceding sections did not include all the sampling methods available to a researcher. Should you become involved in a major research project in marketing, finance, accounting, or other areas, you would need to consult books devoted solely to sample theory and sample design.

SELF-REVIEW 8–2

Refer to Self-Review 8–1 and the class roster on page 254. Suppose a systematic random sample will select every ninth student enrolled in the class. Initially, the fourth student on the list was selected at random. That student is numbered 03. Remembering that the random numbers start with 00, which students will be chosen to be members of the sample?

EXERCISES

1. The following is a list of 24 Marco's Pizza stores in Lucas County. The stores are identified by numbering them 00 through 23. Also noted is whether the store is corporate-owned (C) or manager-owned (M). A sample of four locations is to be selected and inspected for customer convenience, safety, cleanliness, and other features.

ID No.	Address	Type	ID No.	Address	Type
00	2607 Starr Av	C	12	2040 Ottawa River Rd	C
01	309 W Alexis Rd	C	13	2116 N Reynolds Rd	C
02	2652 W Central Av	C	14	3678 Rugby Dr	C
03	630 Dixie Hwy	M	15	1419 South Av	C
04	3510 Dorr St	C	16	1234 W Sylvania Av	C
05	5055 Glendale Av	C	17	4624 Woodville Rd	M
06	3382 Lagrange St	M	18	5155 S Main	M
07	2525 W Laskey Rd	C	19	106 E Airport Hwy	C
08	303 Louisiana Av	C	20	6725 W Central	M
09	149 Main St	C	21	4252 Monroe	C
10	835 S McCord Rd	M	22	2036 Woodville Rd	C
11	3501 Monroe St	M	23	1316 Michigan Av	M

   a. The random numbers selected are 08, 18, 11, 54, 02, 41, and 54. Which stores are selected?
   b. Use the table of random numbers to select your own sample of locations.
   c. Using systematic random sampling, every seventh location is selected starting with the third store in the list. Which locations will be included in the sample?
   d. Using stratified random sampling, select three locations. Two should be corporate-owned and one should be manager-owned.

2. The following is a list of 29 hospitals in the Cincinnati, Ohio, and Northern Kentucky region. Each hospital is assigned a number, 00 through 28. The hospitals are classified by type, either a general medical/surgical hospital (M/S) or a specialty hospital (S). We are interested in estimating the average number of full- and part-time nurses employed in the area hospitals.

ID Number	Name	Address	Type	ID Number	Name	Address	Type
00	Bethesda North	10500 Montgomery Cincinnati, Ohio 45242	M/S	04	Mercy Hospital– Hamilton	100 Riverfront Plaza Hamilton, Ohio 45011	M/S
01	Ft. Hamilton–Hughes	630 Eaton Avenue Hamilton, Ohio 45013	M/S	05	Middletown Regional	105 McKnight Drive Middletown, Ohio 45044	M/S
02	Jewish Hospital– Kenwood	4700 East Galbraith Rd. Cincinnati, Ohio 45236	M/S	06	Clermont Mercy Hospital	3000 Hospital Drive Batavia, Ohio 45103	M/S
03	Mercy Hospital– Fairfield	3000 Mack Road Fairfield, Ohio 45014	M/S	07	Mercy Hospital– Anderson	7500 State Road Cincinnati, Ohio 45255	M/S

ID Number	Name	Address	Type	ID Number	Name	Address	Type
08	Bethesda Oak Hospital	619 Oak Street Cincinnati, Ohio 45206	M/S	19	St. Luke's Hospital West	7380 Turfway Drive Florence, Kentucky 41075	M/S
09	Children's Hospital Medical Center	3333 Burnet Avenue Cincinnati, Ohio 45229	M/S	20	St. Luke's Hospital East	85 North Grand Avenue Ft. Thomas, Kentucky 41042	M/S
10	Christ Hospital	2139 Auburn Avenue Cincinnati, Ohio 45219	M/S	21	Care Unit Hospital	3156 Glenmore Avenue Cincinnati, Ohio 45211	S
11	Deaconess Hospital	311 Straight Street Cincinnati, Ohio 45219	M/S	22	Emerson Behavioral Science	2446 Kipling Avenue Cincinnati, Ohio 45239	S
12	Good Samaritan Hospital	375 Dixmyth Avenue Cincinnati, Ohio 45220	M/S	23	Pauline Warfield Lewis Center for Psychiatric Treat.	1101 Summit Road Cincinnati, Ohio 45237	S
13	Jewish Hospital	3200 Burnet Avenue Cincinnati, Ohio 45229	M/S	24	Children's Psychiatric No. Kentucky	502 Farrell Drive Covington, Kentucky 41011	S
14	University Hospital	234 Goodman Street Cincinnati, Ohio 45267	M/S	25	Drake Center Rehab—Long Term	151 W. Galbraith Road Cincinnati, Ohio 45216	S
15	Providence Hospital	2446 Kipling Avenue Cincinnati, Ohio 45239	M/S	26	No. Kentucky Rehab Hospital—Short Term	201 Medical Village Edgewood, Kentucky	S
16	St. Francis–St. George Hospital	3131 Queen City Avenue Cincinnati, Ohio 45238	M/S	27	Shriners Burns Institute	3229 Burnet Avenue Cincinnati, Ohio 45229	S
17	St. Elizabeth Medical Center, North Unit	401 E. 20th Street Covington, Kentucky 41014	M/S	28	VA Medical Center	3200 Vine Cincinnati, Ohio 45220	S
18	St. Elizabeth Medical Center, South Unit	One Medical Village Edgewood, Kentucky 41017	M/S				

a. A sample of five hospitals is to be randomly selected. The random numbers are 09, 16, 00, 49, 54, 12, and 04. Which hospitals are included in the sample?

b. Use a table of random numbers to develop your own sample of five hospitals.

c. Using systematic random sampling, every fifth location is selected starting with the second hospital in the list. Which hospitals will be included in the sample?

d. Using stratified random sampling, select five hospitals. Four should be medical and surgical hospitals and one should be a specialty hospital. Select an appropriate sample.

3. Listed below are the 35 members of the Metro Toledo Automobile Dealers Association. We would like to estimate the mean revenue from dealer service departments. The members are identified by numbering them 00 through 34.

ID Number	Dealer	ID Number	Dealer	ID Number	Dealer
00	Dave White Acura	11	Thayer Chevrolet/Toyota	23	Kistler Ford, Inc.
01	Autofair Nissan	12	Spurgeon Chevrolet Motor Sales, Inc.	24	Lexus of Toledo
02	Autofair Toyota-Suzuki	13	Dunn Chevrolet	25	Mathews Ford Oregon, Inc.
03	George Ball's Buick GMC Truck	14	Don Scott Chevrolet	26	Northtown Chevrolet
04	York Automotive Group	15	Dave White Chevrolet Co.	27	Quality Ford Sales, Inc.
05	Bob Schmidt Chevrolet	16	Dick Wilson Infinity	28	Rouen Chrysler Jeep Eagle
06	Bowling Green Lincoln Mercury Jeep Eagle	17	Doyle Buick	29	Saturn of Toledo
07	Brondes Ford	18	Franklin Park Lincoln Mercury	30	Ed Schmidt Jeep Eagle
08	Brown Honda	19	Genoa Motors	31	Southside Lincoln Mercury
09	Brown Mazda	20	Great Lakes Ford Nissan	32	Valiton Chrysler
10	Charlie's Dodge	21	Grogan Towne Chrysler	33	Vin Divers
		22	Hatfield Motor Sales	34	Whitman Ford

a. We want to select a random sample of five dealers. The random numbers are 05, 20, 59, 21, 31, 28, 49, 38, 66, 08, 29, and 02. Which dealers would be included in the sample?

b. Use the table of random numbers to select your own sample of five dealers.
c. Using systematic random sampling, every seventh dealer is selected starting with the fourth dealer in the list. Which dealers are included in the sample?

4. Listed next are the 27 Nationwide Insurance agents in the El Paso, Texas metropolitan area. The agents are numbered 00 through 26. We would like to estimate the mean number of years employed with Nationwide.

ID Number	Agent	ID Number	Agent	ID Number	Agent
00	**Bly Scott** 3332 W Laskey Rd	10	**Heini Bernie** 7110 W Centra	20	**Schwab Dave** 572 W Dussel Dr
01	**Coyle Mike** 5432 W Central Av	11	**Hinckley Dave** 14 N Holland Sylvania Rd	21	**Seibert John H** 201 S Main
02	**Denker Brett** 7445 Airport Hwy	12	**Joehlin Bob** 3358 Navarre Av	22	**Smithers Bob** 229 Superior St
03	**Denker Rollie** 7445 Airport Hwy	13	**Keisser David** 3030 W Sylvania Av	23	**Smithers Jerry** 229 Superior St
04	**Farley Ron** 1837 W Alexis Rd	14	**Keisser Keith** 5902 Sylvania Av	24	**Wright Steve** 105 S Third St
05	**George Mark** 7247 W Central Av	15	**Lawrence Grant** 342 W Dussel Dr	25	**Wood Tom** 112 Louisiana Av
06	**Gibellato Carlo** 6616 Monroe St	16	**Miller Ken** 2427 Woodville Rd	26	**Yoder Scott** 6 Willoughby Av
07	**Glemser Cathy** 5602 Woodville Rd	17	**O'Donnell Jim** 7247 W Central Av		
08	**Green Mike** 4149 Holland Sylvania Rd	18	**Priest Harvey** 5113 N Summit St		
09	**Harris Ev** 2026 Albon Rd	19	**Riker Craig** 2621 N Reynolds Rd		

a. We want to select a random sample of four agents. The random numbers are 02, 59, 51, 25, 14, 29, 77, 69, and 18. Which dealers would be included in the sample?
b. Use the table of random numbers to select your own sample of four agents.
c. Using systematic random sampling, every fifth dealer is selected starting with the third dealer in the list. Which dealers are included in the sample?

LO8-2
Define sampling error.

SAMPLING "ERROR"

In the previous section, we discussed sampling methods that are used to select a sample that is an unbiased representation of the population. In each method, the selection of every possible sample of a specified size from a population has a known chance or probability. This is another way to describe an unbiased sampling method.

Samples are used to estimate population characteristics. For example, the mean of a sample is used to estimate the population mean. However, since the sample is a part or portion of the population, it is unlikely that the sample mean would be *exactly equal* to the population mean. Similarly, it is unlikely that the sample standard deviation would be *exactly equal* to the population standard deviation. We can therefore expect a difference between a *sample statistic* and its corresponding *population parameter*. This difference is called **sampling error.**

SAMPLING ERROR The difference between a sample statistic and its corresponding population parameter.

The following example/solution clarifies the idea of sampling error.

EXAMPLE

Refer to the example/solution on page 253, where we studied the number of rooms rented at the Foxtrot Inn bed and breakfast in Tryon, North Carolina. The population is the number of rooms rented each of the 30 days in June 2017. Find the mean of the population. Select three random samples of 5 days. Calculate the mean rooms rented for each sample and compare it to the population mean. What is the sampling error in each case?

SOLUTION

During the month, there were a total of 94 rentals. So the mean number of units rented per night is 3.13. This is the population mean. Hence we designate this value with the Greek letter μ.

$$\mu = \frac{\Sigma x}{N} = \frac{0 + 2 + 3 + \cdots + 3}{30} = \frac{94}{30} = 3.13$$

The first random sample of five nights resulted in the following number of rooms rented: 4, 7, 4, 3, and 1. The mean of this sample is 3.80 rooms, which we designate as $\bar{x}_1$. The bar over the *x* reminds us that it is a sample mean and the subscript 1 indicates it is the mean of the first sample.

$$\bar{x}_1 = \frac{\Sigma x}{n} = \frac{4 + 7 + 4 + 3 + 1}{5} = \frac{19}{5} = 3.80$$

The sampling error for the first sample is the difference between the population mean (3.13) and the first sample mean (3.80). Hence, the sampling error is $(\bar{x}_1 - \mu) = 3.80 - 3.13 = 0.67$. The second random sample of 5 days from the population of all 30 days in June revealed the following number of rooms rented: 3, 3, 2, 3, and 6. The mean of these five values is 3.40, found by

$$\bar{x}_2 = \frac{\Sigma x}{n} = \frac{3 + 3 + 2 + 3 + 6}{5} = 3.40$$

The sampling error is $(\bar{x}_2 - \mu) = 3.4 - 3.13 = 0.27$. In the third random sample, the mean was 1.80 and the sampling error was -1.33.

Each of these differences, 0.67, 0.27, and -1.33, is the sampling error made in estimating the population mean. Sometimes these errors are positive values, indicating that the sample mean overestimated the population mean; other times they are negative values, indicating the sample mean was less than the population mean.

June	Rentals	June	Rentals	June	Rentals		Sample 1	Sample 2	Sample 3
1	0	11	3	21	3		4	3	0
2	2	12	4	22	2		7	3	0
3	3	13	4	23	3		4	2	3
4	2	14	4	24	6		3	3	3
5	3	15	7	25	0		1	6	3
6	4	16	0	26	4	Total	19	17	9
7	2	17	5	27	1	Mean	3.80	3.40	1.80
8	3	18	3	28	1	Sampling Error	0.67	0.27	-1.33
9	4	19	6	29	3				
10	7	20	2	30	3				

In this case, where we have a population of 30 values and samples of 5 values, there is a very large number of possible samples—142,506 to be exact! To find this value, use the combination formula (5–10) on page 164. Each of the 142,506 different samples has the same chance of being selected. Each sample may have a different sample mean and therefore a different sampling error. The value of the sampling error is based on the particular one of the 142,506 different possible samples selected. Therefore, the sampling errors are random and occur by chance. If you summed the sampling errors for all 142,506 samples, the result would equal zero. This is true because the sample mean is an *unbiased estimator* of the population mean.

LO8-3
Demonstrate the construction of a sampling distribution of the sample mean.

SAMPLING DISTRIBUTION OF THE SAMPLE MEAN

In the previous section, we defined sampling error and presented the results when we compared a sample statistic, such as the sample mean, to the population mean. To put it another way, when we use the sample mean to estimate the population mean, how can we determine how accurate the estimate is? How does:

- A quality-assurance supervisor decide if a machine is filling 20-ounce bottles with 20 ounces of cola based only on a sample of 10 filled bottles?
- FiveThirtyEight.com or Gallup make accurate statements about the demographics of voters in a presidential race based on relatively small samples from a voting population of nearly 90 million?

To answer these questions, we first develop a *sampling distribution of the sample mean*.

The sample means in the previous example/solution varied from one sample to the next. The mean of the first sample of 5 days was 3.80 rooms, and the second sample mean was 3.40 rooms. The population mean was 3.13 rooms. If we organized the means of all possible samples of 5 days into a probability distribution, the result is called the **sampling distribution of the sample mean.**

SAMPLING DISTRIBUTION OF THE SAMPLE MEAN A probability distribution of all possible sample means of a given sample size.

The following example/solution illustrates the construction of a sampling distribution of the sample mean. We have intentionally used a small population to highlight the relationship between the population mean and the various sample means.

EXAMPLE

Tartus Industries has seven production employees (considered the population). The hourly earnings of each employee are given in Table 8–2.

TABLE 8–2 Hourly Earnings of the Production Employees of Tartus Industries

Employee	Hourly Earnings	Employee	Hourly Earnings
Joe	$14	Jan	14
Sam	14	Art	16
Sue	16	Ted	18
Bob	16		

1. What is the population mean?
2. What is the sampling distribution of the sample mean for samples of size 2?
3. What is the mean of the sampling distribution?
4. What observations can be made about the population and the sampling distribution?

SOLUTION

Here are the solutions to the questions.

1. The population is small so it is easy to calculate the population mean. It is $15.43, found by:

$$\mu = \frac{\Sigma x}{N} = \frac{\$14 + \$14 + \$16 + \$16 + \$14 + \$16 + \$18}{7} = \$15.43$$

We identify the population mean with the Greek letter μ. Recall from earlier chapters, Greek letters are used to represent population parameters.

2. To arrive at the sampling distribution of the sample mean, we need to select all possible samples of 2 without replacement from the population, then compute the mean of each sample. There are 21 possible samples, found by using formula (5–10) on page 164.

$$_{N}C_{n} = \frac{N!}{n!(N-n)!} = \frac{7!}{2!(7-2)!} = 21$$

where $N = 7$ is the number of items in the population and $n = 2$ is the number of items in the sample.

TABLE 8–3 Sample Means for All Possible Samples of 2 Employees

Sample	Employees	Hourly Earnings	Sum	Mean	Sample	Employees	Hourly Earnings	Sum	Mean
1	Joe, Sam	$14, $14	$28	$14	12	Sue, Bob	16,16	32	16
2	Joe, Sue	14, 16	30	15	13	Sue, Jan	16,14	30	15
3	Joe, Bob	14, 16	30	15	14	Sue, Art	16,16	32	16
4	Joe, Jan	14, 14	28	14	15	Sue, Ted	16,18	34	17
5	Joe, Art	14, 16	30	15	16	Bob, Jan	16,14	30	15
6	Joe, Ted	14, 18	32	16	17	Bob, Art	16,16	32	16
7	Sam, Sue	14, 16	30	15	18	Bob, Ted	16,18	34	17
8	Sam, Bob	14, 16	30	15	19	Jan, Art	14,16	30	15
9	Sam, Jan	14,14	28	14	20	Jan, Ted	14,18	32	16
10	Sam, Art	14,16	30	15	21	Art, Ted	16,18	34	17
11	Sam, Ted	14,18	32	16					

The 21 sample means from all possible samples of 2 that can be drawn from the population of 7 employees are shown in Table 8–3. These 21 sample means are used to construct a probability distribution. This is called the sampling distribution of the sample mean, and it is summarized in Table 8–4.

TABLE 8–4 Sampling Distribution of the Sample Mean for $n = 2$

Sample Mean	Number of Means	Probability
$14	3	.1429
15	9	.4285
16	6	.2857
17	3	.1429
	21	1.0000

3. Using the data in Table 8–3, the mean of the sampling distribution of the sample mean is obtained by summing the various sample means and dividing the sum by the number of samples. The mean of all the sample means is usually written $\mu_{\bar{x}}$. The μ reminds us that it is a population value because we have considered all possible samples of two employees from the population of seven employees. The subscript $\bar{x}$ indicates that it is the sampling distribution of the sample mean.

$$\mu_{\bar{x}} = \frac{\text{Sum of all sample means}}{\text{Total number of samples}} = \frac{\$14 + \$15 + \$15 + \cdots + \$16 + \$17}{21}$$

$$= \frac{\$324}{21} = \$15.43$$

4. Refer to Chart 8–2. It shows the population distribution based on the data in Table 8–2 and the distribution of the sample mean based on the data in Table 8–4. These observations can be made:
   a. The mean of the distribution of the sample mean ($15.43) is equal to the mean of the population: $\mu = \mu_{\bar{X}}$.
   b. The spread in the distribution of the sample mean is less than the spread in the population values. The sample means range from $14 to $17 while the population values vary from $14 up to $18. If we continue to increase the sample size, the spread of the distribution of the sample mean becomes smaller.
   c. The shape of the sampling distribution of the sample mean and the shape of the frequency distribution of the population values are different. The distribution of the sample mean tends to be more bell-shaped and to approximate the normal probability distribution.

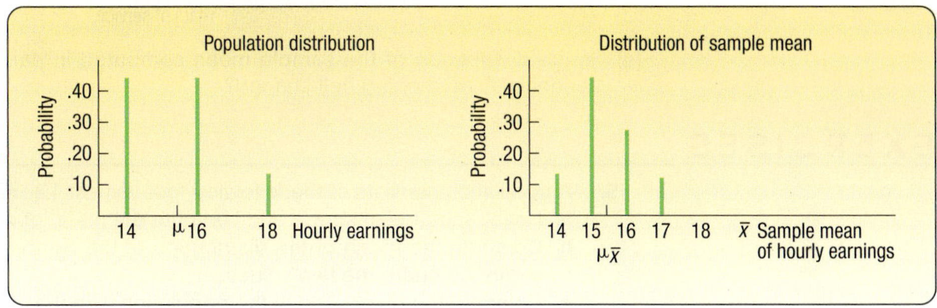

CHART 8–2 Distributions of Population Values and Sample Means

In summary, we took all possible random samples from a population and for each sample calculated a sample statistic (the mean amount earned). This example illustrates important relationships between the population distribution and the sampling distribution of the sample mean:

1. The mean of the sample means is exactly equal to the population mean.
2. The dispersion of the sampling distribution of the sample mean is narrower than the population distribution.
3. The sampling distribution of the sample mean tends to become bell-shaped and to approximate the normal probability distribution.

Given a bell-shaped or normal probability distribution, we will be able to apply concepts from Chapter 7 to determine the probability of selecting a sample with a specified sample mean. In the next section, we will show the importance of sample size as it relates to the sampling distribution of the sample mean.

SELF-REVIEW 8–3

The years of service of the five executives employed by Standard Chemicals are:

Name	Years
Mr. Snow	20
Ms. Tolson	22
Mr. Kraft	26
Ms. Irwin	24
Mr. Jones	28

(a) Using the combination formula, how many samples of size 2 are possible?
(b) List all possible samples of two executives from the population and compute their means.
(c) Organize the means into a sampling distribution.
(d) Compare the population mean and the mean of the sample means.
(e) Compare the dispersion in the population with that in the distribution of the sample mean.
(f) A chart portraying the population values follows. Is the distribution of population values normally distributed (bell-shaped)?

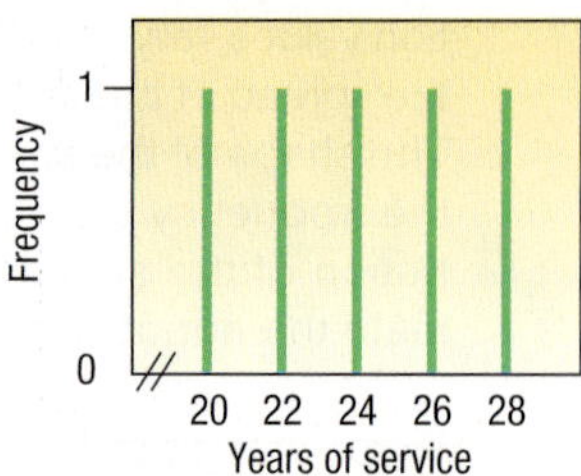

(g) Is the distribution of the sample mean computed in part (c) starting to show some tendency toward being bell-shaped?

EXERCISES

5. A population consists of the following four values: 12, 12, 14, and 16.
   a. List all samples of size 2, and compute the mean of each sample.
   b. Compute the mean of the distribution of the sample mean and the population mean. Compare the two values.
   c. Compare the dispersion in the population with that of the sample mean.

6. A population consists of the following five values: 2, 2, 4, 4, and 8.
   a. List all samples of size 2, and compute the mean of each sample.
   b. Compute the mean of the distribution of sample means and the population mean. Compare the two values.
   c. Compare the dispersion in the population with that of the sample means.

7. A population consists of the following five values: 12, 12, 14, 15, and 20.
   a. List all samples of size 3, and compute the mean of each sample.
   b. Compute the mean of the distribution of sample means and the population mean. Compare the two values.
   c. Compare the dispersion in the population with that of the sample means.

8. A population consists of the following five values: 0, 0, 1, 3, 6.
   a. List all samples of size 3, and compute the mean of each sample.
   b. Compute the mean of the distribution of sample means and the population mean. Compare the two values.
   c. Compare the dispersion in the population with that of the sample means.

9. In the law firm Tybo and Associates, there are six partners. Listed is the number of cases each partner actually tried in court last month.

Partner	Number of Cases
Ruud	3
Wu	6
Sass	3
Flores	3
Wilhelms	0
Schueller	1

   a. How many different samples of size 3 are possible?
   b. List all possible samples of size 3, and compute the mean number of cases in each sample.
   c. Compare the mean of the distribution of sample means to the population mean.
   d. On a chart similar to Chart 8–2, compare the dispersion in the population with that of the sample means.

10. There are five sales associates at Mid-Motors Ford. The five associates and the number of cars they sold last week are:

Sales Associate	Cars Sold
Peter Hankish	8
Connie Stallter	6
Juan Lopez	4
Ted Barnes	10
Peggy Chu	6

a. How many different samples of size 2 are possible?
b. List all possible samples of size 2, and compute the mean of each sample.
c. Compare the mean of the sampling distribution of the sample mean with that of the population.
d. On a chart similar to Chart 8–2, compare the dispersion in sample means with that of the population.

LO8-4
Recite the central limit theorem and define the mean and standard error of the sampling distribution of the sample mean.

THE CENTRAL LIMIT THEOREM

In this section, we examine the **central limit theorem.** Its application to the sampling distribution of the sample mean, introduced in the previous section, allows us to use the normal probability distribution to create confidence intervals for the population mean (described in Chapter 9) and perform tests of hypothesis (described in Chapter 10). The central limit theorem states that, for large random samples, the shape of the sampling distribution of the sample mean is close to the normal probability distribution. The approximation is more accurate for large samples than for small samples. This is one of the most useful conclusions in statistics. We can reason about the distribution of the sample mean with absolutely no information about the shape of the population distribution from which the sample is taken. In other words, the central limit theorem is true for all population distributions.

CENTRAL LIMIT THEOREM If all samples of a particular size are selected from any population, the sampling distribution of the sample mean is approximately a normal distribution. This approximation improves with larger samples.

To further illustrate the central limit theorem, if the population follows a normal probability distribution, then for any sample size the sampling distribution of the sample mean will also be normal. If the population distribution is symmetrical (but not normal), you will see the normal shape of the distribution of the sample mean emerge with samples as small as 10. On the other hand, if you start with a distribution that is skewed or has thick tails, it may require samples of 30 or more to observe the normality feature. This concept is summarized in Chart 8–3 for various population shapes. Observe the convergence to a normal distribution regardless of the shape of the population distribution.

The idea that a distribution of sample means will converge to normality when the population is not normal is illustrated in Charts 8–4, 8–5, and 8–6. We will discuss this example in more detail shortly, but Chart 8–4 is a graph of a discrete probability distribution that is positively skewed. There are many possible samples of 5 that might be selected from this population. Suppose we randomly select 25 samples of size 5 from the population portrayed in Chart 8–4 and compute the mean of each sample. These results are shown in Chart 8–5. Notice that the shape of the distribution of sample means has changed from the shape of the original population even though we selected only 25 of the many possible samples. To put it another way, we selected 25 random samples of $n = 5$ from a population that is positively skewed and found the distribution

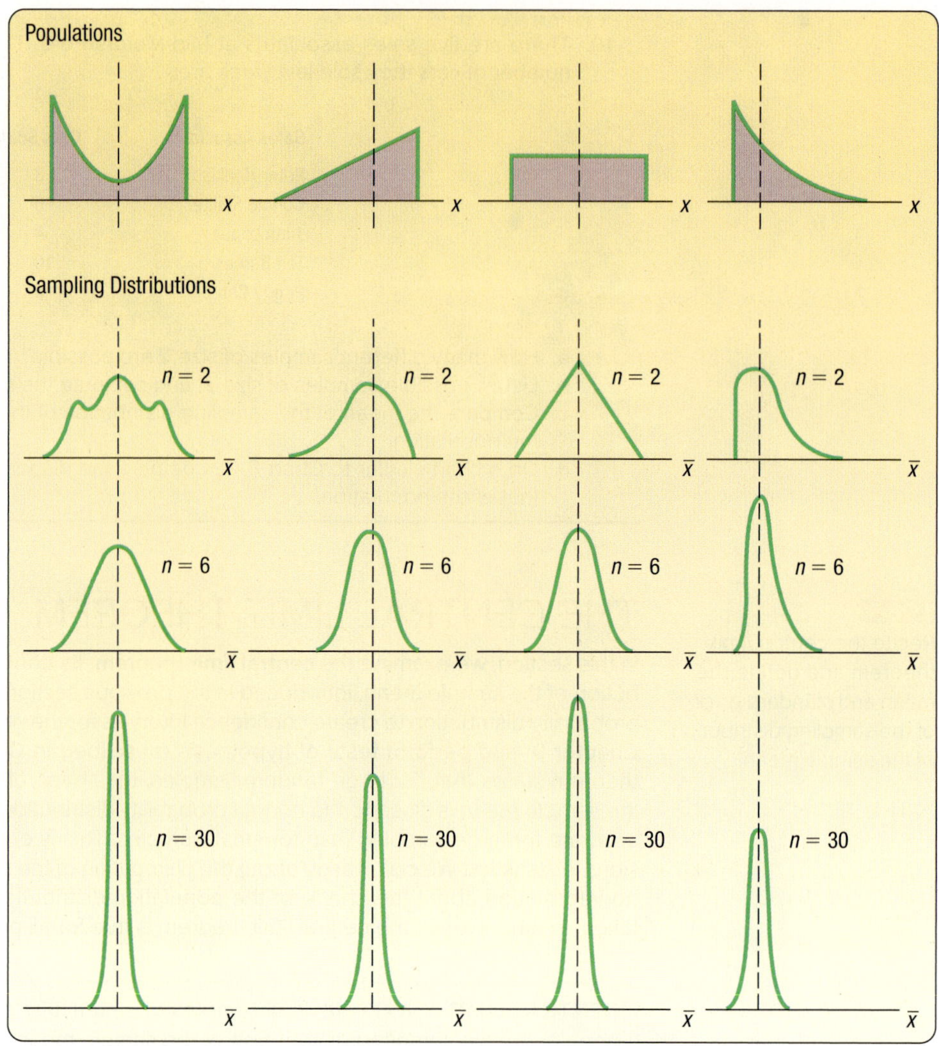

CHART 8–3 Results of the Central Limit Theorem for Several Populations

of sample means is different from the shape of the population. As we take larger samples, that is, $n = 20$ instead of $n = 5$, we will find the distribution of the sample mean will approach the normal distribution. Chart 8–6 shows the results of 25 random samples of 20 observations each from the same population. Observe the clear trend toward the normal probability distribution. This is the point of the central limit theorem. The following example/solution will underscore this condition.

EXAMPLE

Ed Spence began his sprocket business 20 years ago. The business has grown over the years and now employs 40 people. Spence Sprockets Inc. faces some major decisions regarding health care for these employees. Before making a final decision on what health care plan to purchase, Ed decides to form a committee of five representative employees. The committee will be asked to study the health care issue carefully and make a recommendation as to what plan best fits the employees' needs. Ed feels the views of newer employees toward health care may differ from those of more experienced employees. If Ed randomly selects this committee, what can he expect in terms of the mean years with Spence Sprockets for those on the committee? How does the shape of the distribution of years of service of all employees (the population) compare with the shape of the sampling distribution of the mean? The years of service (rounded to the nearest year) of the 40 employees currently on the Spence Sprockets Inc. payroll are as follows.

11	4	18	2	1	2	0	2	2	4
3	4	1	2	2	3	3	19	8	3
7	1	0	2	7	0	4	5	1	14
16	8	9	1	1	2	5	10	2	3

SOLUTION

Chart 8–4 shows a histogram for the frequency distribution of the years of service for the population of 40 current employees. This distribution is positively skewed. Why? Because the business has grown in recent years, the distribution shows that 29 of the 40 employees have been with the company less than 6 years. Also, there are 11 employees who have worked at Spence Sprockets for more than 6 years. In particular, four employees have been with the company 12 years or more (count the frequencies above 12). So there is a long tail in the distribution of service years to the right, that is, the distribution is positively skewed.

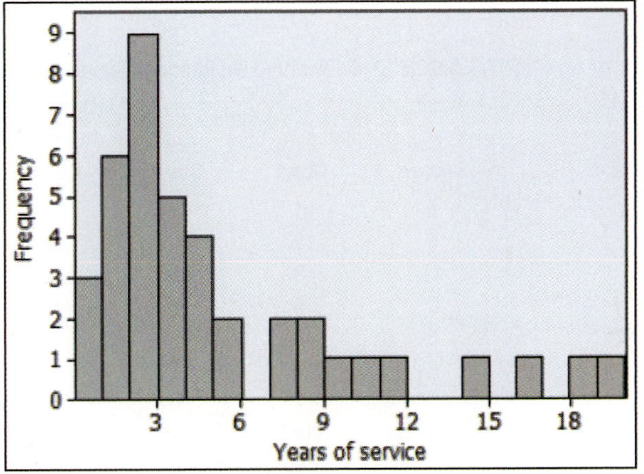

CHART 8–4 Years of Service for Spence Sprockets Inc. Employees

Let's consider the first of Ed Spence's problems. He would like to form a committee of five employees to look into the health care question and suggest what type of health care coverage would be most appropriate for the majority of workers. How should he select the committee? If he selects the committee randomly, what might he expect in terms of mean years of service for those on the committee?

To begin, Ed writes the years of service for each of the 40 employees on pieces of paper and puts them into an old baseball hat. Next, he shuffles the pieces of paper and randomly selects five slips of paper. The years of service for these five employees are 1, 9, 0, 19, and 14 years. Thus, the mean years of service for these five sampled employees is 8.60 years. How does that compare with the population mean? At this point, Ed does not know the population mean, but the number of employees in the population is only 40, so he decides to calculate the mean years of service for *all* his employees. It is 4.8 years, found by adding the years of service for *all* the employees and dividing the total by 40.

$$\mu = \frac{11 + 4 + 18 + \cdots + 2 + 3}{40} = 4.80$$

The difference between a sample mean ($\bar{x}$) and the population mean (μ) is called **sampling error**. In other words, the difference of 3.80 years between the sample mean of 8.60 and the population mean of 4.80 is the sampling error. It is due to chance. Thus, if Ed selected these five employees to constitute the committee, their mean years of service would be larger than the population mean.

What would happen if Ed put the five pieces of paper back into the baseball hat and selected another sample? Would you expect the mean of this second sample to be exactly the same as the previous one? Suppose he selects another sample of five employees and finds the years of service in this sample to be 7, 4, 4, 1, and 3. This sample mean is 3.80 years. The result of selecting 25 samples of five employees and computing the mean for each sample is shown in Table 8–5 and Chart 8–5. There are actually 658,008 possible samples of 5 from the population of 40 employees, found by the combination formula (5–10) for 40 things taken 5 at a time. Notice the difference in the shape of the population and the distribution of these sample means. The population of the years of service for employees (Chart 8–4) is positively skewed, but the distribution of these 25 sample means does not reflect the same positive skew. There is also a difference in the range of the sample means versus the range of the population. The population ranged from 0 to 19 years, whereas the sample means range from 1.6 to 8.6 years.

TABLE 8–5 Twenty-Five Random Samples of Five Employees

	Sample Data						
Sample	**Obs 1**	**Obs 2**	**Obs 3**	**Obs 4**	**Obs 5**	**Sum**	**Mean**
A	1	9	0	19	14	43	8.6
B	7	4	4	1	3	19	3.8
C	8	19	8	2	1	38	7.6
D	4	18	2	0	11	35	7.0
E	4	2	4	7	18	35	7.0
F	1	2	0	3	2	8	1.6
G	2	3	2	0	2	9	1.8
H	11	2	9	2	4	28	5.6
I	9	0	4	2	7	22	4.4
J	1	1	1	11	1	15	3.0
K	2	0	0	10	2	14	2.8
L	0	2	3	2	16	23	4.6
M	2	3	1	1	1	8	1.6
N	3	7	3	4	3	20	4.0
O	1	2	3	1	4	11	2.2
P	19	0	1	3	8	31	6.2
Q	5	1	7	14	9	36	7.2
R	5	4	2	3	4	18	3.6
S	14	5	2	2	5	28	5.6
T	2	1	1	4	7	15	3.0
U	3	7	1	2	1	14	2.8
V	0	1	5	1	2	9	1.8
W	0	3	19	4	2	28	5.6
X	4	2	3	4	0	13	2.6
Y	1	1	2	3	2	9	1.8

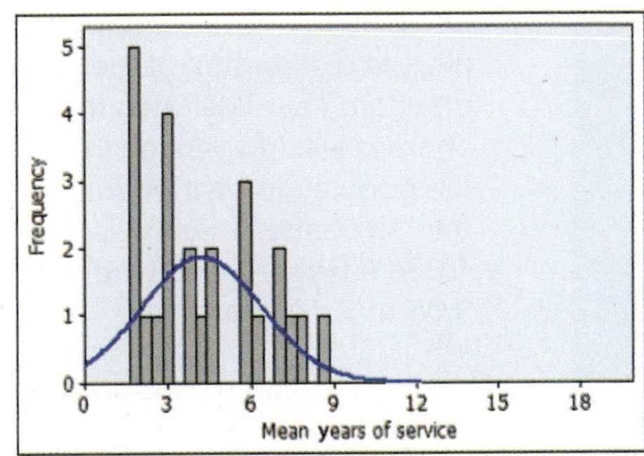

CHART 8–5 Histogram of Mean Years of Service for 25 Samples of Five Employees

Now let's change the example by increasing the size of each sample from 5 employees to 20. Table 8–6 reports the result of selecting 25 samples of 20 employees each and computing their sample means. These sample means are shown graphically in Chart 8–6. Compare the shape of this distribution to the population (Chart 8–4) and to the distribution of sample means where the sample is $n = 5$ (Chart 8–5). You should observe two important features:

1. The shape of the distribution of the sample mean is different from that of the population. In Chart 8–4, the distribution of all employees is positively skewed. However, as we select random samples from this population, the shape of the

TABLE 8–6 Twenty-Five Random Samples of 20 Employees

	Sample Data							
Sample	**Obs 1**	**Obs 2**	**Obs 3**	**–**	**Obs 19**	**Obs 20**	**Sum**	**Mean**
A	3	8	3	–	4	16	79	3.95
B	2	3	8	–	3	1	65	3.25
C	14	5	0	–	19	8	119	5.95
D	9	2	1	–	1	3	87	4.35
E	18	1	2	–	3	14	107	5.35
F	10	4	4	–	2	1	80	4.00
G	5	7	11	–	2	4	131	6.55
H	3	0	2	–	16	5	85	4.25
I	0	0	18	–	2	3	80	4.00
J	2	7	2	–	3	2	81	4.05
K	7	4	5	–	1	2	84	4.20
L	0	3	10	–	0	4	81	4.05
M	4	1	2	–	1	2	88	4.40
N	3	16	1	–	11	1	95	4.75
O	2	19	2	–	2	2	102	5.10
P	2	18	16	–	4	3	100	5.00
Q	3	2	3	–	3	1	102	5.10
R	2	3	1	–	0	2	73	3.65
S	2	14	19	–	0	7	142	7.10
T	0	1	3	–	2	0	61	3.05
U	1	0	1	–	9	3	65	3.25
V	1	9	4	–	2	11	137	6.85
W	8	1	9	–	8	7	107	5.35
X	4	2	0	–	2	5	86	4.30
Y	1	2	1	–	1	18	101	5.05

distribution of the sample mean changes. As we increase the size of the sample, the distribution of the sample mean approaches the normal probability distribution. This illustrates the central limit theorem.

2. There is less dispersion in the sampling distribution of the sample mean than in the population distribution. In the population, the years of service ranged from 0 to 19 years. When we selected samples of 5, the sample means ranged from 1.6 to 8.6 years, and when we selected samples of 20, the means ranged from 3.05 to 7.10 years.

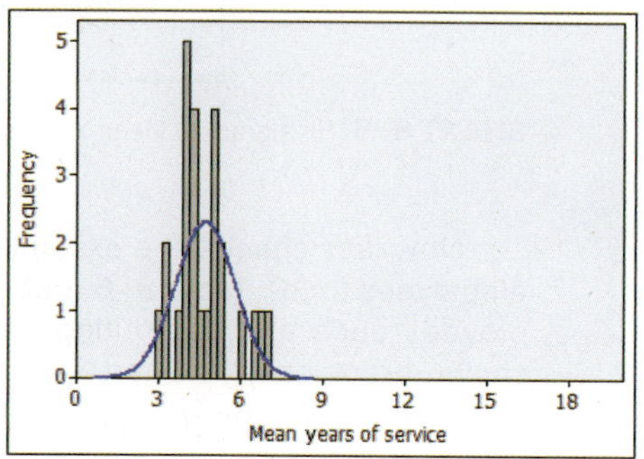

CHART 8–6 Histogram of Mean Years of Service for 25 Samples of 20 Employees

We can also compare the mean of the sample means to the population mean. The mean of the 25 samples of 20 employees reported in Table 8–6 is 4.676 years.

$$\mu_{\bar{x}} = \frac{3.95 + 3.25 + \cdots + 4.30 + 5.05}{25} = 4.676$$

We use the symbol $\mu_{\bar{x}}$ to identify the mean of the distribution of the sample mean. The subscript reminds us that the distribution is of the sample mean. It is read "mu sub x bar." We observe that the mean of the sample means, 4.676 years, is very close to the population mean of 4.80.

What should we conclude from this example? The central limit theorem indicates that, regardless of the shape of the population distribution, the sampling distribution of the sample mean will move toward the normal probability distribution. The larger the number of observations sampled or selected, the stronger the convergence. The Spence Sprockets Inc. example shows how the central limit theorem works. We began with a positively skewed population (Chart 8–4). Next, we selected 25 random samples of 5 observations, computed the mean of each sample, and finally organized these 25 sample means into a histogram (Chart 8–5). We observe that the shape of the sampling distribution of the sample mean is very different from that of the population. The population distribution is positively skewed compared to the nearly normal shape of the sampling distribution of the sample mean.

To further illustrate the effects of the central limit theorem, we increased the number of observations in each sample from 5 to 20. We selected 25 samples of 20 observations each and calculated the mean of each sample. Finally, we organized these sample means into a histogram (Chart 8–6). The shape of the histogram in Chart 8–6 is clearly moving toward the normal probability distribution.

If you go back to Chapter 6 where several binomial distributions with a "success" proportion of .10 are shown in Chart 6–3 on page 190, you can see yet another demonstration of the central limit theorem. Observe as n increases from 7 through 12 and 20 up to 40 that the profile of the probability distributions moves closer and closer to a normal probability distribution. Chart 8–6 also shows the convergence to normality as n increases. This again reinforces the fact that, as more observations are sampled from any population distribution, the shape of the sampling distribution of the sample mean will get closer and closer to a normal distribution.

The **central limit theorem,** defined on page 265, does not say anything about the dispersion of the sampling distribution of the sample mean or about the comparison of the mean of the sampling distribution of the sample mean to the mean of the population. However, in our Spence Sprockets example, we did observe that there was less dispersion in the distribution of the sample mean than in the population distribution by noting the difference in the range in the population and the range of the sample means. We observe that the mean of the sample means is close to the mean of the population. It can be demonstrated that the mean of the sampling distribution is exactly equal to the population mean (i.e., $\mu_{\bar{x}} = \mu$), and if the standard deviation in the population is σ, the standard deviation of the sample means is $\sigma/\sqrt{n}$ where n is the number of observations in each sample. We refer to $\sigma/\sqrt{n}$ as the **standard error of the mean.** Its longer name is actually the *standard deviation of the sampling distribution of the sample mean.*

STANDARD ERROR OF THE MEAN

$$\sigma_{\bar{x}} = \frac{\sigma}{\sqrt{n}} \qquad \textbf{(8–1)}$$

In this section, we also came to other important conclusions.

1. The mean of the distribution of sample means will be *exactly* equal to the population mean if we are able to select all possible samples of the same size from a given population. That is:

$$\mu = \mu_{\bar{x}}$$

   Even if we do not select all samples, we can expect the mean of the distribution of sample means to be close to the population mean.
2. There will be less dispersion in the sampling distribution of the sample mean than in the population. If the standard deviation of the population is σ, the standard deviation of the distribution of sample means is $\sigma/\sqrt{n}$. Note that when we increase the size of the sample, the standard error of the mean decreases.

SELF-REVIEW 8–4

Refer to the Spence Sprockets Inc. data on page 267. Select 10 random samples of five employees each. Use the methods described earlier in the chapter and the Table of Random Numbers (Appendix B.4) to find the employees to include in the sample. Compute the mean of each sample and plot the sample means on a chart similar to Chart 8–4. What is the mean of your 10 sample means?

EXERCISES

11. FILE Appendix B.4 is a table of random numbers that are uniformly distributed. Hence, each digit from 0 to 9 has the same likelihood of occurrence.

   a. Draw a graph showing the population distribution of random numbers. What is the population mean?
   b. Following are the first 10 rows of five digits from the table of random numbers in Appendix B.4. Assume that these are 10 random samples of five values each. Determine the mean of each sample and plot the means on a chart similar to

Chart 8–4. Compare the mean of the sampling distribution of the sample mean with the population mean.

0	2	7	1	1
9	4	8	7	3
5	4	9	2	1
7	7	6	4	0
6	1	5	4	5
1	7	1	4	7
1	3	7	4	8
8	7	4	5	5
0	8	9	9	9
7	8	8	0	4

12. FILE Scrapper Elevator Company has 20 sales representatives who sell its product throughout the United States and Canada. The number of units sold last month by each representative is listed below. Assume these sales figures to be the population values.

2	3	2	3	3	4	2	4	3	2	2	7	3	4	5	3	3	3	3	5

a. Draw a graph showing the population distribution.
b. Compute the mean of the population.
c. Select five random samples of 5 each. Compute the mean of each sample. Use the methods described in this chapter and Appendix B.4 to determine the items to be included in the sample.
d. Compare the mean of the sampling distribution of the sample mean to the population mean. Would you expect the two values to be about the same?
e. Draw a histogram of the sample means. Do you notice a difference in the shape of the distribution of sample means compared to the shape of the population distribution?

13. Consider all of the coins (pennies, nickels, quarters, etc.) in your pocket or purse as a population. Make a frequency table beginning with the current year and counting backward to record the ages (in years) of the coins. For example, if the current year is 2017, then a coin with 2015 stamped on it is 2 years old.
a. Draw a histogram or other graph showing the population distribution.
b. Randomly select five coins and record the mean age of the sampled coins. Repeat this sampling process 20 times. Now draw a histogram or other graph showing the distribution of the sample means.
c. Compare the shapes of the two histograms.

14. Consider the digits in the phone numbers on a randomly selected page of your local phone book a population. Make a frequency table of the final digit of 30 randomly selected phone numbers. For example, if a phone number is 555-9704, record a 4.
a. Draw a histogram or other graph of this population distribution. Using the uniform distribution, compute the population mean and the population standard deviation.
b. Also record the sample mean of the final four digits (9704 would lead to a mean of 5). Now draw a histogram or other graph showing the distribution of the sample means.
c. Compare the shapes of the two histograms.

LO8-5
Apply the central limit theorem to calculate probabilities.

USING THE SAMPLING DISTRIBUTION OF THE SAMPLE MEAN

The previous discussion is important because most business decisions are made on the basis of sample information. Here are some examples.

1. Arm & Hammer Company wants to ensure that its laundry detergent actually contains 100 fluid ounces, as indicated on the label. Historical summaries from the filling process indicate the mean amount per container is 100 fluid ounces and the standard deviation is 2 fluid ounces. At 10 a.m., a quality technician measures 40 containers and finds the mean amount per container is 99.8 fluid ounces. Should the technician shut down the filling operation?
2. A. C. Nielsen Company provides information to organizations advertising on television. Prior research indicates that adult Americans watch an average of 6.0 hours per day of television. The standard deviation is 1.5 hours. What is the probability that we could randomly select a sample of 50 adults and find that they watch an average of 6.5 hours or more of television per day?
3. Haughton Elevator Company wishes to develop specifications for the number of people who can ride in a new oversized elevator. Suppose the mean weight of an adult is 160 pounds and the standard deviation is 15 pounds. However, the distribution of weights does not follow the normal probability distribution. It is positively skewed. For a sample of 30 adults, what is the likelihood that their mean weight is 170 pounds or more?

We can answer the questions in each of these situations using the ideas discussed in the previous section. In each case, we have a population with information about its mean and standard deviation. Using this information and sample size, we can determine the distribution of sample means and compute the probability that a sample mean will fall within a certain range. The sampling distribution will be normally distributed under two conditions:

1. When the samples are taken from populations known to follow the normal distribution. In this case, the size of the sample is not a factor.
2. When the shape of the population distribution is not known, sample size is important. In general, the sampling distribution will be normally distributed as the sample size approaches infinity. In practice, a sampling distribution will be close to a normal distribution with samples of at least 30 observations.

We use formula (7–5) from the previous chapter to convert any normal distribution to the standard normal distribution. Using formula (7–5) to compute z values, we can use the standard normal table, Appendix B.3, to find the probability that an observation is within a specific range. The formula for finding a z value is:

$$z = \frac{x - \mu}{\sigma}$$

In this formula, x is the value of the random variable, μ is the population mean, and σ is the population standard deviation.

However, when we sample from populations, we are interested in the distribution of $\overline{X}$, the sample mean, instead of X, the value of one observation. That is the first change we make in formula (7–5). The second is that we use the standard error of the mean of n observations instead of the population standard deviation. That is, we use $\sigma/\sqrt{n}$ in the denominator rather than σ. Therefore, to find the likelihood of a sample mean within a specified range, we first use the following formula to find the corresponding z value. Then we use Appendix B.3 or statistical software to determine the probability.

FINDING THE z VALUE OF $\bar{x}$ WHEN THE POPULATION STANDARD DEVIATION IS KNOWN

$$z = \frac{\bar{x} - \mu}{\sigma/\sqrt{n}} \quad \textbf{(8–2)}$$

The following example/solution will show the application.

EXAMPLE

The Quality Assurance Department for Cola, Inc. maintains records regarding the amount of cola in its jumbo bottle. The actual amount of cola in each bottle is critical but varies a small amount from one bottle to the next. Cola, Inc. does not wish to underfill the bottles because it will have a problem with truth in labeling. On the other hand, it cannot overfill each bottle because it would be giving cola away, hence reducing its profits. Records maintained by the Quality Assurance Department indicate that the amount of cola follows the normal probability distribution. The mean amount per bottle is 31.2 ounces and the population standard deviation is 0.4 ounce. At 8 a.m. today the quality technician randomly selected 16 bottles from the filling line. The mean amount of cola contained in the bottles is 31.38 ounces. Is this an unlikely result? Is it likely the process is putting too much soda in the bottles? To put it another way, is the sampling error of 0.18 ounce unusual?

SOLUTION

We use the results of the previous section to find the likelihood that we could select a sample of 16 (n) bottles from a normal population with a mean of 31.2 (μ) ounces and a population standard deviation of 0.4 (σ) ounce and find the sample mean to be 31.38 ($\bar{x}$) or more. We use formula (8–2) to find the value of z.

$$z = \frac{\bar{x} - \mu}{\sigma/\sqrt{n}} = \frac{31.38 - 31.20}{0.4/\sqrt{16}} = 1.80$$

The numerator of this equation, $\bar{x} - \mu = 31.38 - 31.20 = .18$, is the sampling error. The denominator, $\sigma/\sqrt{n} = 0.4/\sqrt{16} = 0.1$, is the standard error of the sampling distribution of the sample mean. So the z values express the sampling error in standard units—in other words, the standard error.

Next, we compute the likelihood of a z value greater than 1.80. In Appendix B.3, locate the probability corresponding to a z value of 1.80. It is .4641. The likelihood of a z value greater than 1.80 is .0359, found by .5000 − .4641.

What do we conclude? It is unlikely, less than a 4% chance, we could select a sample of 16 observations from a normal population with a mean of 31.2 ounces and a population standard deviation of 0.4 ounce and find the sample mean equal to or greater than 31.38 ounces. We conclude the process is putting too much cola in the bottles. The quality technician should see the production supervisor about reducing the amount of soda in each bottle. This information is summarized in Chart 8–7.

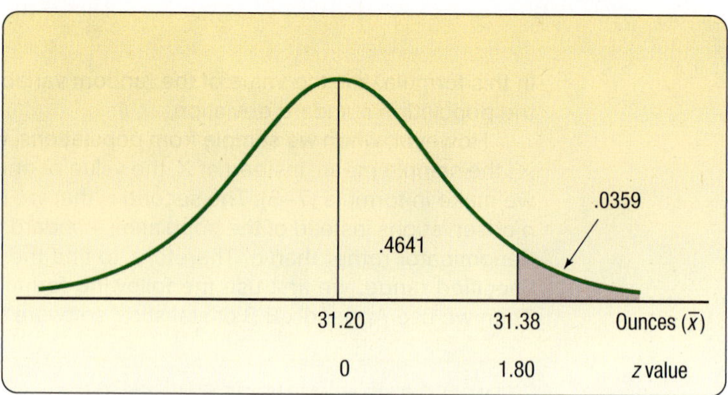

CHART 8–7 Sampling Distribution of the Mean Amount of Cola in a Jumbo Bottle

SELF-REVIEW 8–5

Refer to the Cola, Inc. information. Suppose the quality technician selected a sample of 16 jumbo bottles that averaged 31.08 ounces. What can you conclude about the filling process?

EXERCISES

15. A normal population has a mean of 60 and a standard deviation of 12. You select a random sample of 9. Compute the probability the sample mean is:

a. Greater than 63.
b. Less than 56.
c. Between 56 and 63.

16. A normal population has a mean of 75 and a standard deviation of 5. You select a sample of 40. Compute the probability the sample mean is:

a. Less than 74.
b. Between 74 and 76.
c. Between 76 and 77.
d. Greater than 77.

17. In a certain section of Southern California, the distribution of monthly rent for a one-bedroom apartment has a mean of $2,200 and a standard deviation of $250. The distribution of the monthly rent does not follow the normal distribution. In fact, it is positively skewed. What is the probability of selecting a sample of 50 one-bedroom apartments and finding the mean to be at least $1,950 per month?

18. According to an IRS study, it takes a mean of 330 minutes for taxpayers to prepare, copy, and electronically file a 1040 tax form. This distribution of times follows the normal distribution and the standard deviation is 80 minutes. A consumer watchdog agency selects a random sample of 40 taxpayers.

a. What is the standard error of the mean in this example?
b. What is the likelihood the sample mean is greater than 320 minutes?
c. What is the likelihood the sample mean is between 320 and 350 minutes?
d. What is the likelihood the sample mean is greater than 350 minutes?

CHAPTER SUMMARY

I. The characteristics of the *F* distribution are:

- **A.** There are many reasons for sampling a population.
- **B.** The results of a sample may adequately estimate the value of the population parameter, thus saving time and money.
- **C.** It may be too time-consuming to contact all members of the population.
- **D.** It may be impossible to check or locate all the members of the population.
- **E.** The cost of studying all the items in the population may be prohibitive.
- **F.** Often testing destroys the sampled item and it cannot be returned to the population.

II. In an unbiased or probability sample, all members of the population have a chance of being selected for the sample. There are several probability sampling methods.

- **A.** In a simple random sample, all members of the population have the same chance of being selected for the sample.
- **B.** In a systematic sample, a random starting point is selected, and then every *k*th item thereafter is selected for the sample.
- **C.** In a stratified sample, the population is divided into several groups, called strata, and then a random sample is selected from each stratum.
- **D.** In cluster sampling, the population is divided into primary units, then samples are drawn from the primary units.

III. The sampling error is the difference between a population parameter and a sample statistic.

IV. The sampling distribution of the sample mean is a probability distribution of all possible sample means of the same sample size.

A. For a given sample size, the mean of all possible sample means selected from a population is equal to the population mean.

B. There is less variation in the distribution of the sample mean than in the population distribution.

C. The standard error of the mean measures the variation in the sampling distribution of the sample mean. The standard error is found by:

$$\sigma_{\bar{x}} = \frac{\sigma}{\sqrt{n}} \quad \textbf{(8–1)}$$

D. If the population follows a normal distribution, the sampling distribution of the sample mean will also follow the normal distribution for samples of any size. If the population is not normally distributed, the sampling distribution of the sample mean will approach a normal distribution when the sample size is at least 30. Assume the population standard deviation is known. To determine the probability that a sample mean falls in a particular region, use the following formula.

$$z = \frac{\bar{x} - \mu}{\sigma/\sqrt{n}} \quad \textbf{(8–2)}$$

PRONUNCIATION KEY

SYMBOL	MEANING	PRONUNCIATION
$\mu_{\bar{x}}$	Mean of the sampling distribution of the sample mean	*mu sub x bar*
$\sigma_{\bar{x}}$	Population standard error of the sample mean	*sigma sub x bar*

CHAPTER EXERCISES

19. The 25 retail stores located in the North Towne Square Mall numbered 00 through 24 are:

00	Elder-Beerman	09	Lion Store	18	County Seat
01	Sears	10	Bootleggers	19	Kid Mart
02	Deb Shop	11	Formal Man	20	Lerner
03	Frederick's of Hollywood	12	Leather Ltd.	21	Coach House Gifts
04	Petries	13	Barnes and Noble	22	Spencer Gifts
05	Easy Dreams	14	Pat's Hallmark	23	CPI Photo Finish
06	Summit Stationers	15	Things Remembered	24	Regis Hairstylists
07	E. B. Brown Opticians	16	Pearle Vision Express		
08	Kay-Bee Toy & Hobby	17	Dollar Tree		

a. If the following random numbers are selected, which retail stores should be contacted for a survey? 11, 65, 86, 62, 06, 10, 12, 77, and 04

b. Select a random sample of four retail stores. Use Appendix B.4.

c. A systematic sampling procedure will be used. The first store will be selected and then every third store. Which stores will be in the sample?

20. The Medical Assurance Company is investigating the cost of a routine office visit to family-practice physicians in the Rochester, New York, area. The following is a list of 39 family-practice physicians in the region. Physicians are to be randomly selected and contacted regarding their charges. The 39 physicians have been coded from 00 to 38. Also noted is whether they are in practice by themselves (S), have a partner (P), or are in a group practice (G).

Number	Physician	Type of Practice	Number	Physician	Type of Practice
00	R. E. Scherbarth, M.D.	S	20	Gregory Yost, M.D.	P
01	Crystal R. Goveia, M.D.	P	21	J. Christian Zona, M.D.	P
02	Mark D. Hillard, M.D.	P	22	Larry Johnson, M.D.	P
03	Jeanine S. Huttner, M.D.	P	23	Sanford Kimmel, M.D.	P
04	Francis Aona, M.D.	P	24	Harry Mayhew, M.D.	S
05	Janet Arrowsmith, M.D.	P	25	Leroy Rodgers, M.D.	S
06	David DeFrance, M.D.	S	26	Thomas Tafelski, M.D.	S
07	Judith Furlong, M.D.	S	27	Mark Zilkoski, M.D.	G
08	Leslie Jackson, M.D.	G	28	Ken Bertka, M.D.	G
09	Paul Langenkamp, M.D.	S	29	Mark DeMichiei, M.D.	G
10	Philip Lepkowski, M.D.	S	30	John Eggert, M.D.	P
11	Wendy Martin, M.D.	S	31	Jeanne Fiorito, M.D.	P
12	Denny Mauricio, M.D.	P	32	Michael Fitzpatrick, M.D.	P
13	Hasmukh Parmar, M.D.	P	33	Charles Holt, D.O.	P
14	Ricardo Pena, M.D.	P	34	Richard Koby, M.D.	P
15	David Reames, M.D.	P	35	John Meier, M.D.	P
16	Ronald Reynolds, M.D.	G	36	Douglas Smucker, M.D.	S
17	Mark Steinmetz, M.D.	G	37	David Weldy, M.D.	P
18	Geza Torok, M.D.	S	38	Cheryl Zaborowski, M.D.	P
19	Mark Young, M.D.	P			

a. The random numbers obtained from Appendix B.4 are 31, 94, 43, 36, 03, 24, 17, and 09. Which physicians should be contacted?

b. Select a random sample of four physicians using the random numbers of Appendix B.4.

c. Using systematic random sampling, every fifth physician is selected starting with the fourth physician in the list. Which physicians will be contacted?

d. Select a sample that includes two physicians in solo practice (S), two in partnership (P), and one in group practice (G). Explain your procedure.

21. A population consists of the following three values: 1, 2, and 3.

a. Sampling with replacement, list all possible samples of size 2 and compute the mean of every sample.

b. Find the means of the distribution of the sample mean and the population mean. Compare the two values.

c. Compare the dispersion of the population with that of the sample mean.

d. Describe the shapes of the two distributions.

22. Based on all student records at Camford University, students spend an average of 5.5 hours per week playing organized sports. The population's standard deviation is 2.2 hours per week. Based on a sample of 121 students, Healthy Lifestyles Incorporated (HLI) would like to apply the central limit theorem to make various estimates.

a. Compute the standard error of the sample mean.

b. What is the chance HLI will find a sample mean between 5 and 6 hours?

c. Calculate the probability that the sample mean will be between 5.3 and 5.7 hours.

d. How strange would it be to obtain a sample mean greater than 6.5 hours?

23. The manufacturer of eComputers, an economy-priced computer, recently completed the design for a new laptop model. eComputer's top management would like some assistance in pricing the new laptop. Two market research firms were contacted and asked to prepare a pricing strategy. Marketing-Gets-Results tested the new eComputers laptop with 50 randomly selected consumers who indicated they plan to purchase a laptop within the next year. The second marketing research firm, called Marketing-Reaps-Profits, test-marketed the new eComputers laptop with 200 current laptop owners. Which of the marketing research companies' test results will be more useful? Discuss why.

24. Answer the following questions in one or two well-constructed sentences.
- **a.** What happens to the standard error of the mean if the sample size is increased?
- **b.** What happens to the distribution of the sample means if the sample size is increased?
- **c.** When using sample means to estimate the population mean, what is the benefit of using larger sample sizes?

25. There are 25 motels in Goshen, Indiana. The number of rooms in each motel follows:

90	72	75	60	75	72	84	72	88	74	105	115	68	74	80	64	104	82	48	58	60	80	48	58	100

- **a.** Using a table of random numbers (Appendix B.4), select a random sample of five motels from this population.
- **b.** Obtain a systematic sample by selecting a random starting point among the first five motels and then select every fifth motel.
- **c.** Suppose the last five motels are "cut-rate" motels. Describe how you would select a random sample of three regular motels and two cut-rate motels.

26. As a part of their customer-service program, United Airlines randomly selected 10 passengers from today's 9 a.m. Chicago–Tampa flight. Each sampled passenger will be interviewed about airport facilities, service, and so on. To select the sample, each passenger was given a number on boarding the aircraft. The numbers started with 001 and ended with 250.
- **a.** Select 10 usable numbers at random using Appendix B.4.
- **b.** The sample of 10 could have been chosen using a systematic sample. Choose the first number using Appendix B.4, and then list the numbers to be interviewed.
- **c.** Evaluate the two methods by giving the advantages and possible disadvantages.
- **d.** What other way could a random sample be selected from the 250 passengers?

27. Suppose your statistics instructor gave six examinations during the semester. You received the following exam scores (percent correct): 79, 64, 84, 82, 92, and 77. To compute your final course grade, the instructor decided to randomly select two exam scores, compute their mean, and use this score to determine your final course grade.
- **a.** Compute the population mean.
- **b.** How many different samples of two test grades are possible?
- **c.** List all possible samples of size 2 and compute the mean of each.
- **d.** Compute the mean of the sample means and compare it to the population mean.
- **e.** If you were a student, would you like this arrangement? Would the result be different from dropping the lowest score? Write a brief report.

28. At the downtown office of First National Bank, there are five tellers. Last week, the tellers made the following number of errors each: 2, 3, 5, 3, and 5.
- **a.** How many different samples of two tellers are possible?
- **b.** List all possible samples of size 2 and compute the mean of each.
- **c.** Compute the mean of the sample means and compare it to the population mean.

29. The Quality Control Department employs five technicians during the day shift. Listed below is the number of times each technician instructed the production foreman to shut down the manufacturing process last week.

Technician	Shutdowns	Technician	Shutdowns
Taylor	4	Rousche	3
Hurley	3	Huang	2
Gupta	5		

- **a.** How many different samples of two technicians are possible from this population?
- **b.** List all possible samples of two observations each and compute the mean of each sample.
- **c.** Compare the mean of the sample means with the population mean.
- **d.** Compare the shape of the population distribution with the shape of the distribution of the sample means.

30. The Appliance Center has six sales representatives at its North Jacksonville outlet. The following table lists the number of refrigerators sold by each representative last month.

Sales Representative	Number Sold	Sales Representative	Number Sold
Zina Craft	54	Jan Niles	48
Woon Junge	50	Molly Camp	50
Ernie DeBrul	52	Rachel Myak	52

a. How many samples of size 2 are possible?
b. Select all possible samples of size 2 and compute the mean number sold.
c. Organize the sample means into a frequency distribution.
d. What is the mean of the population? What is the mean of the sample means?
e. What is the shape of the population distribution?
f. What is the shape of the distribution of the sample mean?

31. Power +, Inc. produces AA batteries used in remote-controlled toy cars. The mean life of these batteries follows the normal probability distribution with a mean of 35.0 hours and a standard deviation of 5.5 hours. As a part of its quality assurance program, Power +, Inc. tests samples of 25 batteries.
a. What can you say about the shape of the distribution of the sample mean?
b. What is the standard error of the distribution of the sample mean?
c. What proportion of the samples will have a mean useful life of more than 36 hours?
d. What proportion of the samples will have a mean useful life greater than 34.5 hours?
e. What proportion of the samples will have a mean useful life between 34.5 and 36.0 hours?

32. Majesty Video Production Inc. wants the mean length of its advertisements to be 30 seconds. Assume the distribution of ad length follows the normal distribution with a population standard deviation of 2 seconds. Suppose we select a sample of 16 ads produced by Majesty.
a. What can we say about the shape of the distribution of the sample mean time?
b. What is the standard error of the mean time?
c. What percent of the sample means will be greater than 31.25 seconds?
d. What percent of the sample means will be greater than 28.25 seconds?
e. What percent of the sample means will be greater than 28.25 but less than 31.25 seconds?

33. Recent studies indicate that the typical 50-year-old woman spends $350 per year for personal-care products. The distribution of the amounts spent follows a normal distribution with a standard deviation of $45 per year. We select a random sample of 40 women. The mean amount spent for those sampled is $335. What is the likelihood of finding a sample mean this large or larger from the specified population?

34. Information from the American Institute of Insurance indicates the mean amount of life insurance per household in the United States is $165,000. This distribution follows the normal distribution with a standard deviation of $40,000.
a. If we select a random sample of 50 households, what is the standard error of the mean?
b. What is the expected shape of the distribution of the sample mean?
c. What is the likelihood of selecting a sample with a mean of at least $167,000?
d. What is the likelihood of selecting a sample with a mean of more than $155,000?
e. Find the likelihood of selecting a sample with a mean of more than $155,000 but less than $167,000.

35. In the United States, the mean age of men when they marry for the first time follows the normal distribution with a mean of 29 years. The standard deviation of the distribution is 2.5 years. For a random sample of 60 men, what is the likelihood that the age when they were first married is less than 29.3. years?

36. A recent study by the Greater Los Angeles Taxi Drivers Association showed that the mean fare charged for service from Hermosa Beach to Los Angeles International Airport is $21 and the standard deviation is $3.50. We select a sample of 15 fares.
a. What is the likelihood that the sample mean is between $20 and $23?
b. What must you assume to make the above calculation?

37. Crossett Trucking Company claims that the mean weight of its delivery trucks when they are fully loaded is 6,000 pounds and the standard deviation is 150 pounds. Assume that the population follows the normal distribution. Forty trucks are randomly selected and weighed. Within what limits will 95% of the sample means occur?

38. The mean amount purchased by a typical customer at Churchill's Grocery Store is $23.50, with a standard deviation of $5.00. Assume the distribution of amounts purchased follows the normal distribution. For a sample of 50 customers, answer the following questions.

a. What is the likelihood the sample mean is at least $25.00?

b. What is the likelihood the sample mean is greater than $22.50 but less than $25.00?

c. Within what limits will 90% of the sample means occur?

39. The mean performance score on a physical fitness test for Division I student-athletes is 947 with a standard deviation of 205. If you select a random sample of 60 of these students, what is the probability the mean is below 900?

40. Suppose we roll a fair die two times.

a. How many different samples are there?

b. List each of the possible samples and compute the mean.

c. On a chart similar to Chart 8–2, compare the distribution of sample means with the distribution of the population.

d. Compute the mean and the standard deviation of each distribution and compare them.

41. FILE Following is a list of the 50 states with the numbers 0 through 49 assigned to them.

Number	State	Number	State
0	Alabama	25	Montana
1	Alaska	26	Nebraska
2	Arizona	27	Nevada
3	Arkansas	28	New Hampshire
4	California	29	New Jersey
5	Colorado	30	New Mexico
6	Connecticut	31	New York
7	Delaware	32	North Carolina
8	Florida	33	North Dakota
9	Georgia	34	Ohio
10	Hawaii	35	Oklahoma
11	Idaho	36	Oregon
12	Illinois	37	Pennsylvania
13	Indiana	38	Rhode Island
14	Iowa	39	South Carolina
15	Kansas	40	South Dakota
16	Kentucky	41	Tennessee
17	Louisiana	42	Texas
18	Maine	43	Utah
19	Maryland	44	Vermont
20	Massachusetts	45	Virginia
21	Michigan	46	Washington
22	Minnesota	47	West Virginia
23	Mississippi	48	Wisconsin
24	Missouri	49	Wyoming

a. You wish to select a sample of eight from this list. The selected random numbers are 45, 15, 81, 09, 39, 43, 90, 26, 06, 45, 01, and 42. Which states are included in the sample?

b. Select a systematic sample of every sixth item using the digit 02 as the starting point. Which states are included?

42. Human Resource Consulting (HRC) surveyed a random sample of 60 Twin Cities construction companies to find information on the costs of their health care plans. One of the items being tracked is the annual deductible that employees must pay. The Minnesota Department of Labor reports that historically the mean deductible amount per employee is $502 with a standard deviation of $100.

a. Compute the standard error of the sample mean for HRC.
b. What is the chance HRC finds a sample mean between $477 and $527?
c. Calculate the likelihood that the sample mean is between $492 and $512.
d. What is the probability the sample mean is greater than $550?

43. Over the past decade, the mean number of hacking attacks experienced by members of the Information Systems Security Association is 510 per year with a standard deviation of 14.28 attacks. The number of attacks per year is normally distributed. Suppose nothing in this environment changes.
a. What is the likelihood this group will suffer an average of more than 600 attacks in the next 10 years?
b. Compute the probability the mean number of attacks over the next 10 years is between 500 and 600.
c. What is the possibility they will experience an average of less than 500 attacks over the next 10 years?

44. An economist uses the price of a gallon of milk as a measure of inflation. She finds that the average price is $3.82 per gallon and the population standard deviation is $0.33. You decide to sample 40 convenience stores, collect their prices for a gallon of milk, and compute the mean price for the sample.
a. What is the standard error of the mean in this experiment?
b. What is the probability that the sample mean is between $3.78 and $3.86?
c. What is the probability that the difference between the sample mean and the population mean is less than $0.01?
d. What is the likelihood the sample mean is greater than $3.92?

45. Nike's annual report says that the average American buys 6.5 pairs of sports shoes per year. Suppose a sample of 81 customers is surveyed and the population standard deviation of sports shoes purchased per year is 2.1.
a. What is the standard error of the mean in this experiment?
b. What is the probability that the sample mean is between 6 and 7 pairs of sports shoes?
c. What is the probability that the difference between the sample mean and the population mean is less than 0.25 pair?
d. What is the likelihood the sample mean is greater than 7 pairs?

DATA ANALYTICS

46. FILE Refer to the North Valley Real Estate data, which report information on the homes sold last year. Assume the 105 homes is a population. Compute the population mean and the standard deviation of price. Select a sample of 10 homes. Compute the mean. Determine the likelihood of a sample mean price this high or higher.

47. FILE Refer to the Baseball 2016 data, which report information on the 30 Major League Baseball teams for the 2016 season. Over the last decade, the mean attendance per team followed a normal distribution with a mean of 2.45 million per team and a standard deviation of .71 million. Compute the mean attendance per team for the 2016 season. Determine the likelihood of a sample mean attendance this large or larger from the population.

48. FILE Refer to the Lincolnville School District bus data. Information provided by manufacturers of school buses suggests the mean maintenance cost per year is $4,400 per bus with a standard deviation of $1,000. Compute the mean maintenance cost for the Lincolnville buses. Does the Lincolnville data seem to be in line with that reported by the manufacturer? Specifically, what is the probability of Lincolnville's mean annual maintenance cost, or greater, given the manufacturer's data?

Estimation and Confidence Intervals

THE AMERICAN RESTAURANT ASSOCIATION collected information on the number of meals eaten outside the home per week by young married couples. A survey of 60 couples showed the sample mean number of meals eaten outside the home was 2.76 meals per week, with a standard deviation of 0.75 meal per week. Construct a 99% confidence interval for the population mean. (See Exercise 36 and LO9-2.)

LEARNING OBJECTIVES

When you have completed this chapter, you will be able to:

LO9-1 Compute and interpret a point estimate of a population mean.

LO9-2 Compute and interpret a confidence interval for a population mean.

LO9-3 Compute and interpret a confidence interval for a population proportion.

LO9-4 Calculate the required sample size to estimate a population proportion or population mean.

LO9-5 Adjust a confidence interval for finite populations.

STATISTICS IN ACTION

On all new cars, a fuel economy estimate is prominently displayed on the window sticker as required by the Environmental Protection Agency (EPA). Often, fuel economy is a factor in a consumer's choice of a new car because of fuel costs or environmental concerns. The fuel estimates for a 2016 BMW 328i Sedan (4-cylinder, automatic) are 23 miles per gallon (mpg) in the city and 35 on the highway. The EPA recognizes that actual fuel economy may differ from the estimates by noting, "No test can simulate all possible combinations of conditions and climate, driver behavior, and car care habits. Actual mileage depends on how, when, and where the vehicle is driven. The EPA has found that the mpg obtained by most drivers will be within a few mpg of the estimates."

INTRODUCTION

The previous chapter began our discussion of sampling. We introduced both the reasons for, and the methods of, sampling. The reasons for sampling were:

- Contacting the entire population is too time-consuming.
- Studying all the items in the population is often too expensive.
- The sample results are usually adequate.
- Certain tests are destructive.
- Checking all the items is physically impossible.

There are several methods of sampling. Simple random sampling is the most widely used method. With this type of sampling, each member of the population has the same chance of being selected to be a part of the sample. Other methods of sampling include systematic sampling, stratified sampling, and cluster sampling.

Chapter 8 assumes information about the population, such as the mean, the standard deviation, or the shape of the population, is known. In most business situations, such information is not available. In fact, one purpose of sampling is to estimate some of these values. For example, you select a sample from a population and use the mean of the sample to estimate the mean of the population.

This chapter considers several important aspects of sampling. We begin by studying **point estimates.** A point estimate is a single value (point) computed from sample information and used to estimate a population value. For example, we may be interested in the number of hours worked by consultants employed by Boston Consulting Group. Using simple random sampling, we select 50 consultants and ask each of them how many hours they worked last week. The sample's mean is a point estimate of the unknown population mean. A more informative approach is to present a range of values where we expect the population parameter to occur. Such a range of values is called a **confidence interval.**

Frequently in business we need to determine the size of a sample. How many voters should a polling organization contact to forecast the election outcome? How many products do we need to examine to ensure our quality level? This chapter also develops a strategy for determining the appropriate number of observations in the sample.

LO9-1

Compute and interpret a point estimate of a population mean.

POINT ESTIMATE FOR A POPULATION MEAN

A point estimate is a single statistic used to estimate a population parameter. Suppose Best Buy Inc. wants to estimate the mean age of people who purchase LCD HDTV televisions. They select a random sample of 75 recent purchases, determine the age of each buyer, and compute the mean age of the buyers in the sample. The mean of this sample is a **point estimate** of the population mean.

> **POINT ESTIMATE** The statistic, computed from sample information, that estimates a population parameter.

The following examples illustrate point estimates of population means.

1. Tourism is a major source of income for many Caribbean countries, such as Barbados. Suppose the Bureau of Tourism for Barbados wants an estimate of the mean amount spent by tourists visiting the country. It would not be feasible to contact each tourist. Therefore, 500 tourists are randomly selected as they depart the country and asked in detail about their spending while visiting Barbados. The mean amount spent by the sample of 500 tourists is an estimate of the unknown population parameter. That is, we let the sample mean serve as a point estimate of the population mean.

2. Litchfield Home Builders Inc. builds homes in the southeastern region of the United States. One of the major concerns of new buyers is the date when the home will be completed. Recently, Litchfield has been telling customers, "Your home will be completed 45 working days from the date we begin installing drywall." The customer relations department at Litchfield wishes to compare this pledge with recent experience. A sample of 50 homes completed this year revealed that the point estimate of the population mean is 46.7 working days from the start of drywall to the completion of the home. Is it reasonable to conclude that the population mean is still 45 days and that the difference between the sample mean (46.7 days) and the proposed population mean (45 days) is sampling error? In other words, is the sample mean significantly different from the population mean?

© Andersen Ross/Getty Images RF

3. Recent medical studies indicate that exercise is an important part of a person's overall health. The director of human resources at OCF, a large glass manufacturer, wants an estimate of the number of hours per week employees spend exercising. A sample of 70 employees reveals the mean number of hours of exercise last week is 3.3. This value is a point estimate of the unknown population mean.

The sample mean, $\bar{x}$, is not the only point estimate of a population parameter. For example, p, a sample proportion, is a point estimate of π, the population proportion; and s, the sample standard deviation, is a point estimate of σ, the population standard deviation.

LO9-2
Compute and interpret a confidence interval for a population mean.

CONFIDENCE INTERVALS FOR A POPULATION MEAN

A point estimate, however, tells only part of the story. While we expect the point estimate to be close to the population parameter, we would like to measure how close it really is. A confidence interval serves this purpose. For example, we estimate the mean yearly income for construction workers in the New York–New Jersey area is $85,000. The range of this estimate might be from $81,000 to $89,000. We can describe how confident we are that the population parameter is in the interval. We might say, for instance, that we are 90% confident that the mean yearly income of construction workers in the New York–New Jersey area is between $81,000 and $89,000.

> **CONFIDENCE INTERVAL** A range of values constructed from sample data so that the population parameter is likely to occur within that range at a specified probability. The specified probability is called the *level of confidence*.

To compute a confidence interval for a population mean, we will consider two situations:

- We use sample data to estimate μ with $\bar{x}$ and the population standard deviation (σ) is known.
- We use sample data to estimate μ with $\bar{x}$ and the population standard deviation is unknown. In this case, we substitute the sample standard deviation (s) for the population standard deviation (σ).

There are important distinctions in the assumptions between these two situations. We first consider the case where σ is known.

Population Standard Deviation, Known σ

A confidence interval is computed using two statistics: the sample mean, $\bar{x}$, and the standard deviation. From previous chapters, you know that the standard deviation is an important statistic because it measures the dispersion, or variation, of a population or sampling distribution. In computing a confidence interval, the standard deviation is used to compute the limits of the confidence interval.

To demonstrate the idea of a confidence interval, we start with one simplifying assumption. That assumption is that we know the value of the population standard deviation, σ. Typically, we know the population standard deviation in situations where we have a long history of collected data. Examples are data from monitoring processes that fill soda bottles or cereal boxes, and the results of the SAT Reasoning Test (for college admission). Knowing σ allows us to simplify the development of a confidence interval because we can use the standard normal distribution from Chapter 8.

Recall that the sampling distribution of the sample mean is the distribution of all sample means, $\bar{x}$, of sample size n from a population. The population standard deviation, σ, is known. From this information, and the central limit theorem, we know that the sampling distribution follows the normal probability distribution with a mean of μ and a standard deviation $\sigma/\sqrt{n}$. Also recall that this value is called the standard error.

The results of the central limit theorem allow us to make the following general confidence interval statements using z-statistics:

1. Ninety-five percent of all confidence intervals computed from random samples selected from a population will contain the population mean. These intervals are computed using a z-statistic equal to 1.96.
2. Ninety percent of all confidence intervals computed from random samples selected from a population will contain the population mean. These confidence intervals are computed using a z-statistic equal to 1.65.

These confidence interval statements provide examples of *levels of confidence* and are called a **95% confidence interval** and a **90% confidence interval.** The *95%* and *90%* are the levels of confidence and refer to the percentage of similarly constructed intervals that would include the parameter being estimated—in this case, μ, the population mean.

How are the values of 1.96 and 1.65 obtained? First, let's look for the z value for a 95% confidence interval. The following diagram and Table 9–1 will help explain. Table 9–1 is a reproduction of the standard normal table in Appendix B. However, many rows and columns have been eliminated to allow us to better focus on particular rows and columns.

1. First, we divide the confidence level in half, so .9500/2 = .4750.
2. Next, we find the value .4750 in the body of Table 9–1. Note that .4750 is located in the table at the intersection of a row and a column.
3. Locate the corresponding row value in the left margin, which is 1.9, and the column value in the top margin, which is .06. Adding the row and column values gives us a z value of 1.96.
4. Thus, the probability of finding a z value between 0 and 1.96 is .4750.
5. Likewise, because the normal distribution is symmetric, the probability of finding a z value between −1.96 and 0 is also .4750.
6. When we add these two probabilities, the probability that a z value is between −1.96 and 1.96 is .9500.

For the 90% level of confidence, we follow the same steps. First, one-half of the desired confidence interval is .4500. A search of Table 9–1 does not reveal this exact value. However, it is between two values, .4495 and .4505. As in step three, we locate each value in the table. The first, .4495, corresponds to a z value of 1.64 and the second, .4505, corresponds to a z value of 1.65. To be conservative, we will select the larger of the two z values, 1.65, and the exact level of confidence is 90.1%, or 2(0.4505). Next, the probability of finding a z value between −1.65 and 0 is .4505, and the probability that a z value is between −1.65 and 1.65 is .9010.

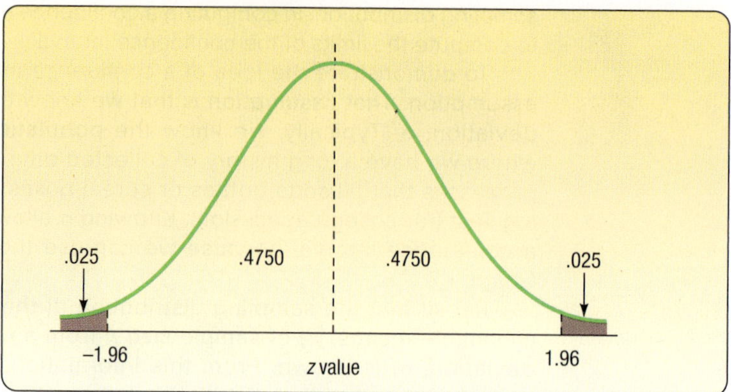

TABLE 9–1 The Standard Normal Table for Selected Values

z	0.00	0.01	0.02	0.03	0.04	0.05	0.06	0.07
⋮	⋮	⋮	⋮	⋮	⋮	⋮	⋮	⋮
1.5	0.4332	0.4345	0.4357	0.4370	0.4382	0.4394	0.4406	0.4418
1.6	0.4452	0.4463	0.4474	0.4484	0.4495	0.4505	0.4515	0.4525
1.7	0.4554	0.4564	0.4573	0.4582	0.4591	0.4599	0.4608	0.4616
1.8	0.4641	0.4649	0.4656	0.4664	0.4671	0.4678	0.4686	0.4693
1.9	0.4713	0.4719	0.4726	0.4732	0.4738	0.4744	0.4750	0.4756
2.0	0.4772	0.4778	0.4783	0.4788	0.4793	0.4798	0.4803	0.4808
2.1	0.4821	0.4826	0.4830	0.4834	0.4838	0.4842	0.4846	0.4850
2.2	0.4861	0.4864	0.4868	0.4871	0.4875	0.4878	0.4881	0.4884

How do we determine a 95% confidence interval? The width of the interval is determined by two factors: (1) the level of confidence, as described in the previous section, and (2) the size of the standard error of the mean. To find the standard error of the mean, recall from the previous chapter [see formula (8–1) on page 271] that the standard error of the mean reports the variation in the distribution of sample means. It is really the standard deviation of the distribution of sample means. The formula is repeated below:

$$\sigma_{\bar{x}} = \frac{\sigma}{\sqrt{n}}$$

where:

- $\sigma_{\bar{x}}$ is the symbol for the standard error of the mean. We use a Greek letter because it is a population value, and the subscript $\bar{x}$ reminds us that it refers to a sampling distribution of the sample means.
- σ is the population standard deviation.
- n is the number of observations in the sample.

The size of the standard error is affected by two values. The first is the standard deviation of the population. The larger the population standard deviation, σ, the larger $\sigma/\sqrt{n}$. If the population is homogeneous, resulting in a small population standard deviation, the standard error will also be small. However, the standard error is also affected by the number of observations in the sample. A large number of observations in the sample will result in a small standard error of estimate, indicating that there is less variability in the sample means.

We can summarize the calculation for a 95% confidence interval using the following formula:

$$\bar{x} \pm 1.96\frac{\sigma}{\sqrt{n}}$$

Similarly, a 90.1% confidence interval is computed as follows:

$$\bar{x} \pm 1.65 \frac{\sigma}{\sqrt{n}}$$

The values 1.96 and 1.65 are z values corresponding to the 95% and the 90.1% confidence intervals, respectively. However, we are not restricted to these values. We can select any confidence level between 0 and 100% and find the corresponding value for z. In general, a confidence interval for the population mean when the population follows the normal distribution and the population standard deviation is known is computed by:

CONFIDENCE INTERVAL FOR A POPULATION MEAN WITH σ KNOWN

$$\bar{x} \pm z \frac{\sigma}{\sqrt{n}} \quad \textbf{(9–1)}$$

Courtesy Del Monte Corporation

To explain these ideas, consider the following example. Del Monte Foods distributes diced peaches in 4.5-ounce plastic cups. To ensure that each cup contains at least the required amount, Del Monte sets the filling operation to dispense 4.51 ounces of peaches and gel in each cup. Of course, not every cup will contain exactly 4.51 ounces of peaches and gel. Some cups will have more and others less. From historical data, Del Monte knows that 0.04 ounce is the standard deviation of the filling process and that the amount, in ounces, follows the normal probability distribution. The quality control technician selects a sample of 64 cups at the start of each shift, measures the amount in each cup, computes the mean fill amount, and then develops a 95% confidence interval for the population mean. Using the confidence interval, is the process filling the cups to the desired amount? This morning's sample of 64 cups had a sample mean of 4.507 ounces. Based on this information, the 95% confidence interval is:

$$\bar{x} \pm 1.96 \frac{\sigma}{\sqrt{n}} = 4.507 \pm 1.96 \frac{0.04}{\sqrt{64}} = 4.507 \pm 0.0098$$

The 95% confidence interval estimates that the population mean is between 4.4972 ounces and 4.5168 ounces of peaches and gel. Recall that the process is set to fill each cup with 4.51 ounces. Because the desired fill amount of 4.51 ounces is in this interval, we conclude that the filling process is achieving the desired results. In other words, it is reasonable to conclude that the sample mean of 4.507 could have come from a population distribution with a mean of 4.51 ounces.

In this example, we observe that the population mean of 4.51 ounces is in the confidence interval. But this is not always the case. If we selected 100 samples of 64 cups from the population, calculated the sample mean, and developed a confidence interval based on each sample, we would expect to find the population mean in about 95 of the 100 intervals. Or, in contrast, about five of the intervals would not contain the population mean. From Chapter 8, this is called sampling error. The following example details repeated sampling from a population.

EXAMPLE

The American Management Association (AMA) is studying the income of store managers in the retail industry. A random sample of 49 managers reveals a sample mean of $45,420. The standard deviation of this population is $2,050. The association would like answers to the following questions:

1. What is the population mean?
2. What is a reasonable range of values for the population mean?
3. How do we interpret these results?

SOLUTION

Generally, distributions of salary and income are positively skewed because a few individuals earn considerably more than others, thus skewing the distribution in the positive direction. Fortunately, the central limit theorem states that the sampling distribution of the mean becomes a normal distribution as sample size increases. In this instance, a sample of 49 store managers is large enough that we can assume that the sampling distribution will follow the normal distribution. Now to answer the questions posed in the example.

1. **What is the population mean?** In this case, we do not know. We do know the sample mean is \$45,420. Hence, our best estimate of the unknown population value is the corresponding sample statistic. Thus, the sample mean of \$45,420 is a *point estimate* of the unknown population mean.
2. **What is a reasonable range of values for the population mean?** The AMA decides to use the 95% level of confidence. To determine the corresponding confidence interval, we use formula (9–1):

$$\bar{x} \pm z\frac{\sigma}{\sqrt{n}} = \$45{,}420 \pm 1.96\frac{\$2{,}050}{\sqrt{49}} = \$45{,}420 \pm \$574$$

   The confidence interval limits are \$44,846 and \$45,994 determined by subtracting \$574 and adding \$574 to the sample mean. The degree or level of confidence is 95% and the confidence interval is from \$44,846 to \$45,994. The value, \$574, is called the margin of error.
3. **How do we interpret these results?** Suppose we select many samples of 49 store managers, perhaps several hundred. For each sample, we compute the mean and then construct a 95% confidence interval, such as we did in the previous section. We could expect about 95% of these confidence intervals to contain the *population* mean. About 5% of the intervals would not contain the population mean annual income, which is μ. However, a particular confidence interval either contains the population parameter or it does not. The following diagram shows the results of selecting samples from the population of store managers in the retail industry, computing the mean of each, and then, using formula (9–1), determining a 95% confidence interval for the population mean. Note that not all intervals include the population mean. Both the endpoints of the fifth sample are less than the population mean. We attribute this to sampling error, and it is the risk we assume when we select the level of confidence.

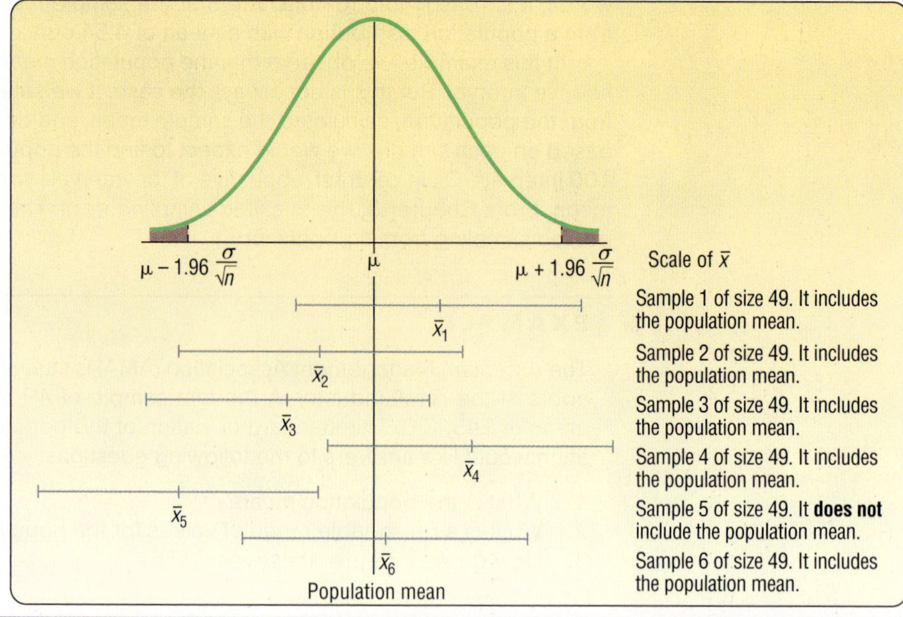

A Computer Simulation

With statistical software, we can create random samples of a desired sample size, *n*, from a population. For each sample of *n* observations with corresponding numerical values, we can calculate the sample mean. With the sample mean, population standard deviation, and confidence level, we can determine the confidence interval for each sample. Then, using all samples and the confidence intervals, we can find the frequency that the population mean is included in the confidence intervals. The following example does just that.

EXAMPLE

From many years in the automobile leasing business, Town Bank knows that the mean distance driven on an automobile with a four-year lease is 50,000 miles and the standard deviation is 5,000 miles. These are population values. Suppose Town Bank would like to experiment with the idea of sampling to estimate the population mean of 50,000 miles. Town Bank decides to choose a sample size of 30 observations and a 95% confidence interval to estimate the population mean. Based on the experiment, we want to count the number of confidence intervals that include the population mean of 50,000. We expect about 95%, or 57 of the 60 intervals, will include the population mean. To make the calculations easier to understand, we'll conduct the study in thousands of miles, instead of miles.

SOLUTION

Using statistical software, 60 random samples of 30 observations, $n = 30$, are generated and the sample means for each sample computed. Then, using the *n* of 30 and a standard error of 0.913 ($\sigma/\sqrt{n} = 5/\sqrt{30}$), a 95% confidence interval is computed for each sample. The results of the experiment are shown next.

	Sample Observations													Sample	95% Confidence Limits	
Sample	**1**	**2**	**3**	**4**	**5**	**–**	**–**	**–**	**26**	**27**	**28**	**29**	**30**	**Mean**	**Lower Limit**	**Upper Limit**
1	56	47	47	48	58	–	–	–	55	62	48	61	57	51.6	49.811	53.389
2	55	51	52	40	53	–	–	–	47	54	55	55	45	50.77	48.981	52.559
3	42	46	48	46	41	–	–	–	50	52	50	47	45	48.63	46.841	50.419
4	52	49	55	47	49	–	–	–	46	56	49	43	50	49.9	48.111	51.689
5	48	50	53	48	45	–	–	–	46	51	61	49	47	49.03	47.241	50.819
6	49	44	47	46	48	–	–	–	51	44	51	52	43	47.73	45.941	49.519
7	50	53	39	50	46	–	–	–	55	47	43	50	57	50.2	48.411	51.989
8	47	51	49	58	44	–	–	–	49	57	54	48	48	51.17	49.381	52.959
9	51	44	47	56	45	–	–	–	45	51	49	49	52	50.33	48.541	52.119
10	45	44	52	52	56	–	–	–	52	51	52	50	48	50	48.211	51.789
11	43	52	54	46	54	–	–	–	43	46	49	52	52	51.2	49.411	52.989
12	57	53	48	42	55	–	–	–	49	44	46	46	48	49.8	48.011	51.589
13	53	39	47	51	53	–	–	–	42	44	44	55	58	49.6	47.811	51.389
14	56	55	45	43	57	–	–	–	48	51	52	55	47	49.03	47.241	50.819
15	49	50	39	45	44	–	–	–	49	43	44	51	51	49.37	47.581	51.159
16	46	44	55	53	55	–	–	–	44	53	53	43	44	50.13	48.341	51.919
17	64	52	55	55	43	–	–	–	58	46	52	58	55	52.47	50.681	54.259
18	57	51	60	40	53	–	–	–	50	51	53	46	52	50.1	48.311	51.889
19	50	49	51	57	45	–	–	–	53	52	40	45	52	49.6	47.811	51.389
20	45	46	53	57	49	–	–	–	49	43	43	53	48	49.47	47.681	51.259
21	52	45	51	52	45	–	–	–	43	49	49	58	53	50.43	48.641	52.219
22	48	48	52	49	40	–	–	–	50	47	54	51	45	47.53	45.741	49.319

(continued)

23	48	50	50	53	44	–	–	–	48	57	52	44	39	49.1	47.311	50.889
24	51	51	40	54	52	–	–	–	54	45	50	57	48	50.13	48.341	51.919
25	48	63	41	52	41	–	–	–	48	50	48	44	53	49.33	47.541	51.119
26	47	45	48	59	49	–	–	–	44	47	49	55	42	49.63	47.841	51.419
27	52	45	60	51	52	–	–	–	52	50	54	46	52	49.4	47.611	51.189
28	46	48	46	57	51	–	–	–	51	50	51	41	52	49.33	47.541	51.119
29	46	48	45	42	48	–	–	–	49	43	59	46	50	48.27	46.481	50.059
30	55	48	47	48	48	–	–	–	47	59	54	51	42	50.53	48.741	52.319
31	58	49	56	46	46	–	–	–	44	51	47	51	46	50.77	48.981	52.559
32	53	54	52	58	55	–	–	–	53	52	45	44	51	50	48.211	51.789
33	50	57	56	51	51	–	–	–	58	47	50	56	46	49.7	47.911	51.489
34	61	48	49	53	54	–	–	–	46	46	56	45	54	50.03	48.241	51.819
35	43	42	43	46	49	–	–	–	49	49	56	51	45	49.43	47.641	51.219
36	39	48	48	51	44	–	–	–	54	52	47	50	52	50.07	48.281	51.859
37	48	43	57	42	54	–	–	–	52	50	59	50	52	50.17	48.381	51.959
38	55	43	49	57	45	–	–	–	41	51	51	52	52	49.5	47.711	51.289
39	47	49	58	54	54	–	–	–	50	56	51	56	58	50.37	48.581	52.159
40	47	56	41	50	54	–	–	–	46	56	61	61	45	51.6	49.811	53.389
41	48	47	42	47	62	–	–	–	44	47	49	55	43	49.43	47.641	51.219
42	46	49	43	36	52	–	–	–	45	51	46	51	43	47.67	45.881	49.459
43	44	48	49	48	51	–	–	–	47	52	51	48	49	49.63	47.841	51.419
44	45	52	54	54	49	–	–	–	49	45	53	50	52	49.07	47.281	50.859
45	54	46	54	45	48	–	–	–	55	38	56	50	62	49.53	47.741	51.319
46	48	50	49	52	51	–	–	–	53	57	58	46	50	49.9	48.111	51.689
47	54	55	46	55	50	–	–	–	56	54	50	55	51	50.5	48.711	52.289
48	45	47	47	63	44	–	–	–	45	53	42	53	50	50.1	48.311	51.889
49	47	47	48	54	56	–	–	–	50	48	54	49	51	49.93	48.141	51.719
50	45	61	51	45	54	–	–	–	55	52	47	45	53	51.03	49.241	52.819
51	49	62	43	49	48	–	–	–	49	58	42	58	52	51.07	49.281	52.859
52	54	52	62	43	54	–	–	–	51	57	49	58	55	50.17	48.381	51.959
53	46	50	59	56	46	–	–	–	50	51	52	54	53	50.47	48.681	52.259
54	52	50	48	48	58	–	–	–	58	52	43	61	54	51.77	49.981	53.559
55	45	44	46	56	46	–	–	–	43	45	63	48	56	49.37	47.581	51.159
56	60	50	56	51	43	–	–	–	45	43	49	59	54	50.37	48.581	52.159
57	59	56	43	47	52	–	–	–	49	54	50	50	57	49.53	47.741	51.319
58	52	55	48	51	40	–	–	–	53	51	51	52	47	49.77	47.981	51.559
59	53	50	44	53	52	–	–	–	47	50	55	46	51	50.07	48.281	51.859
60	55	54	50	52	43	–	–	–	57	50	48	47	53	52.07	50.281	53.859

To explain, in the first row, the statistical software computed 30 random observations from a population distribution with a mean of 50 and a standard deviation of 5. To conserve space, only observations 1 through 5 and 26 through 30 are listed. The first sample's mean is computed and listed as 51.6. In the next columns, the upper and lower limits of the 95% confidence interval for the first sample are shown. The confidence interval calculation for the first sample follows:

$$\bar{x} \pm 1.96 \frac{\sigma}{\sqrt{n}} = 51.6 \pm 1.96 \frac{5}{\sqrt{30}} = 51.6 \pm 1.789$$

This calculation is repeated for all samples. The results of the experiment show that 93.33%, or 56 of the sixty confidence intervals include the population mean of 50. 93.33% is close to the estimate that 95%, or 57, of the intervals will include the population mean. Using the complement, we expected 5%, or three, of the intervals would not include the population mean. The experiment resulted in 6.67%, or four, of the 60 intervals that did not include the population mean. The particular intervals, 6, 17, 22, and 42, are highlighted in yellow. This is another example of sampling error, or the possibility that a particular random sample may not be a good representation of the population. In each of these four samples, the mean of the sample is either much less or much more than the population mean. Because of random sampling, the mean of the sample is not a good estimate of the population mean, and the confidence interval based on the sample's mean does not include the population mean.

SELF-REVIEW 9–1

The Bun-and-Run is a franchise fast-food restaurant located in the Northeast specializing in half-pound hamburgers, fish sandwiches, and chicken sandwiches. Soft drinks and French fries also are available. The Marketing Department of Bun-and-Run Inc. reports that the distribution of daily sales for their restaurants follows the normal distribution and that the population standard deviation is $3,000. A sample of 40 franchises showed the mean daily sales to be $20,000.

(a) What is the population mean of daily sales for Bun-and-Run franchises?
(b) What is the best estimate of the population mean? What is this value called?
(c) Develop a 95% confidence interval for the population mean of daily sales.
(d) Interpret the confidence interval.

EXERCISES

1. A sample of 49 observations is taken from a normal population with a standard deviation of 10. The sample mean is 55. Determine the 99% confidence interval for the population mean.

2. A sample of 81 observations is taken from a normal population with a standard deviation of 5. The sample mean is 40. Determine the 95% confidence interval for the population mean.

3. A sample of 250 observations is selected from a normal population with a population standard deviation of 25. The sample mean is 20.
- **a.** Determine the standard error of the mean.
- **b.** Explain why we can use formula (9–1) to determine the 95% confidence interval.
- **c.** Determine the 95% confidence interval for the population mean.

4. Suppose you know σ and you want an 85% confidence level. What value would you use as z in formula (9–1)?

5. A research firm conducted a survey to determine the mean amount Americans spend on coffee during a week. They found the distribution of weekly spending followed the normal distribution with a population standard deviation of $5. A sample of 49 Americans revealed that $\bar{x} = \$20$.
- **a.** What is the point estimate of the population mean? Explain what it indicates.
- **b.** Using the 95% level of confidence, determine the confidence interval for μ. Explain what it indicates.

6. Refer to the previous exercise. Instead of 49, suppose that 64 Americans were surveyed about their weekly expenditures on coffee. Assume the sample mean remained the same.
- **a.** What is the 95% confidence interval estimate of μ?
- **b.** Explain why this confidence interval is narrower than the one determined in the previous exercise.

7. Bob Nale is the owner of Nale's Quick Fill. Bob would like to estimate the mean number of gallons of gasoline sold to his customers. Assume the number of gallons sold follows the normal distribution with a population standard deviation of 2.30 gallons. From his records, he selects a random sample of 60 sales and finds the mean number of gallons sold is 8.60.
- **a.** What is the point estimate of the population mean?
- **b.** Develop a 99% confidence interval for the population mean.
- **c.** Interpret the meaning of part (b).

8. Dr. Patton is a professor of English. Recently she counted the number of misspelled words in a group of student essays. She noted the distribution of misspelled words per essay followed the normal distribution with a population standard deviation of 2.44 words per essay. For her 10 a.m. section of 40 students, the mean number of misspelled words was 6.05. Construct a 95% confidence interval for the mean number of misspelled words in the population of student essays.

Population Standard Deviation, σ Unknown

In the previous section, we assumed the population standard deviation was known. In the case involving Del Monte 4.5-ounce cups of peaches, there would likely be a long history of measurements in the filling process. Therefore, it is reasonable to assume the standard deviation of the population is available. However, in most sampling situations the population standard deviation (σ) is not known. Here are some examples where we wish to estimate the population means and it is unlikely we would know the population standard deviations. Suppose each of these studies involves students at West Virginia University.

- The Dean of the Business College wants to estimate the mean number of hours full-time students work at paying jobs each week. He selects a sample of 30 students, contacts each student, and asks them how many hours they worked last week. From the sample information, he can calculate the sample mean, but it is not likely he would know or be able to find the *population* standard deviation (σ) required in formula (9–1).
- The Dean of Students wants to estimate the distance the typical commuter student travels to class. She selects a sample of 40 commuter students, contacts each, and determines the one-way distance from each student's home to the center of campus. From the sample data, she calculates the mean travel distance, that is, $\bar{x}$. It is unlikely the standard deviation of the population would be known or available, again making formula (9–1) unusable.
- The Director of Student Loans wants to estimate the mean amount owed on student loans at the time of his/her graduation. The director selects a sample of 20 graduating students and contacts each to find the information. From the sample information, the director can estimate the mean amount. However, to develop a confidence interval using formula (9–1), the population standard deviation is necessary. It is not likely this information is available.

STATISTICS IN ACTION

The *t* distribution was created by William Gosset who was born in England in 1876 and died there in 1937. He worked for many years at Arthur Guinness, Sons and Company. In fact, in his later years he was in charge of the Guinness Brewery in London. Guinness preferred its employees to use pen names when publishing papers, so in 1908, when Gosset wrote "The Probable Error of a Mean," he used the name "Student." In this paper, he first described the properties of the *t* distribution and used it to monitor the brewing process so that the beer met Guinness' quality standards.

Fortunately we can use the sample standard deviation to estimate the population standard deviation. That is, we use s, the sample standard deviation, to estimate σ, the population standard deviation. But in doing so, we cannot use formula (9–1). Because we do not know σ, we cannot use the z distribution. However, there is a remedy. We use the sample standard deviation and replace the z distribution with the t distribution.

The t distribution is a continuous probability distribution, with many similar characteristics to the z distribution. William Gosset, an English brewmaster, was the first to study the t distribution. He was particularly concerned with the exact behavior of the distribution of the following statistic:

$$t = \frac{\bar{x} - \mu}{s/\sqrt{n}}$$

where s is an estimate of σ. He noticed differences between estimating σ based on s, especially when s was calculated from a very small sample. The t distribution and the standard normal distribution are shown graphically in Chart 9–1. Note particularly that the t distribution is flatter, more spread out, than the standard normal distribution. This is because the standard deviation of the t distribution is larger than that of the standard normal distribution.

The following characteristics of the t distribution are based on the assumption that the population of interest is normal, or nearly normal.

- It is, like the *z* distribution, a continuous distribution.
- It is, like the *z* distribution, bell-shaped and symmetrical.
- There is not one *t* distribution, but rather a family of *t* distributions. All *t* distributions have a mean of 0, but their standard deviations differ according to the sample size, *n*. There is a *t* distribution for a sample size of 20, another for a sample size of 22, and so on. The standard deviation for a *t* distribution with 5 observations is larger than for a *t* distribution with 20 observations.
- The *t* distribution is more spread out and flatter at the center than the standard normal distribution (see Chart 9–1). As the sample size increases, however, the *t* distribution approaches the standard normal distribution because the errors in using *s* to estimate σ decrease with larger samples.

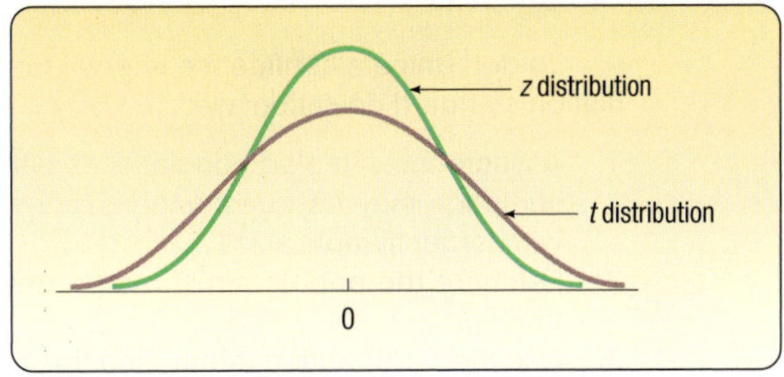

CHART 9–1 The Standard Normal Distribution and Student's *t* Distribution

Because Student's *t* distribution has a greater spread than the *z* distribution, the value of *t* for a given level of confidence is larger in magnitude than the corresponding *z* value. Chart 9–2 shows the values of *z* for a 95% level of confidence and of *t* for the

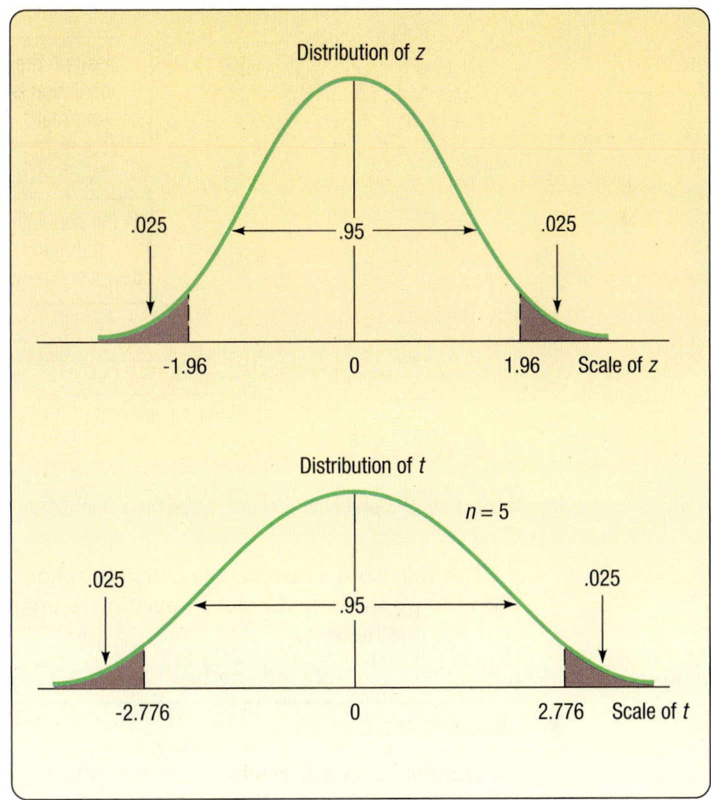

CHART 9–2 Values of *z* and *t* for the 95% Level of Confidence

same level of confidence when the sample size is $n = 5$. How we obtained the actual value of t will be explained shortly. For now, observe that for the same level of confidence the t distribution is flatter or more spread out than the standard normal distribution. Note that the 95% confidence interval using a t statistic will be wider compared to an interval using a z statistic.

To develop a confidence interval for the population mean using the t distribution, we adjust formula (9–1) as follows.

CONFIDENCE INTERVAL FOR THE POPULATION MEAN, σ UNKNOWN

$$\bar{x} \pm t\frac{s}{\sqrt{n}} \tag{9–2}$$

To determine a confidence interval for the population mean with an unknown population standard deviation, we:

1. Assume the sampled population is either normal or approximately normal. This assumption may be questionable for small sample sizes, and becomes more valid with larger sample sizes.
2. Estimate the population standard deviation (σ) with the sample standard deviation (s).
3. Use the t distribution rather than the z distribution.

We should be clear at this point. We base the decision on whether to use the t or the z on whether or not we know σ, the population standard deviation. If we know the population standard deviation, then we use z. If we do not know the population standard deviation, then we must use t. Chart 9–3 summarizes the decision-making process.

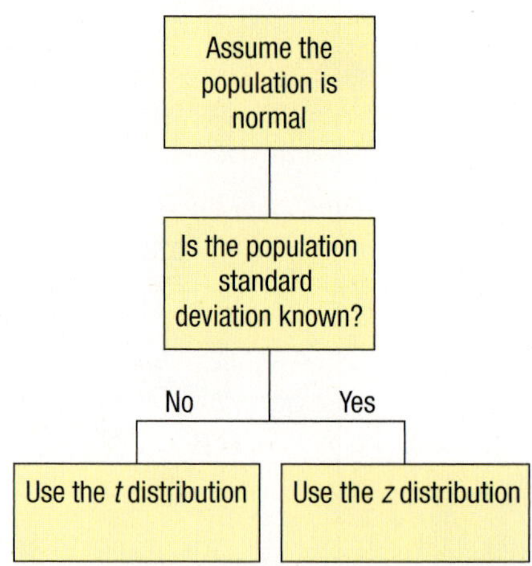

CHART 9–3 Determining When to Use the z Distribution or the t Distribution

The following example will illustrate a confidence interval for a population mean when the population standard deviation is unknown and how to find the appropriate value of t in a table.

EXAMPLE

A tire manufacturer wishes to investigate the tread life of its tires. A sample of 10 tires driven 50,000 miles revealed a sample mean of 0.32 inch of tread remaining with a standard deviation of 0.09 inch. Construct a 95% confidence interval for the population mean. Would it be reasonable for the manufacturer to conclude that after 50,000 miles the population mean amount of tread remaining is 0.30 inch?

SOLUTION

To begin, we assume the population distribution is normal. In this case, we don't have a lot of evidence, but the assumption is probably reasonable. We know the sample standard deviation is .09 inch. We use formula (9–2):

$$\bar{x} \pm t\frac{s}{\sqrt{n}}$$

From the information given, $\bar{x} = 0.32$, $s = 0.09$, and $n = 10$. To find the value of t, we use Appendix B.5, a portion of which is reproduced in Table 9–2. Appendix B.5 is also reproduced on the inside back cover of the text. The first step for locating t is to move across the columns identified for "Confidence Intervals" to the level of confidence requested. In this case, we want the 95% level of confidence, so we move to the column headed "95%." The column on the left margin is identified as "*df.*" This refers to the number of degrees of freedom. The number of degrees of freedom is the number of observations in the sample minus the number of samples, written $n - 1$. In this case, it is $10 - 1 = 9$. Why did we decide there were 9 degrees of freedom? When sample statistics are being used, it is necessary to determine the number of values that are *free to vary.*

TABLE 9–2 A Portion of the *t* Distribution

	Confidence Intervals				
	80%	90%	95%	98%	99%
	Level of Significance for One-Tailed Test				
df	0.10	0.05	0.025	0.010	0.005
	Level of Significance for Two-Tailed Test				
	0.20	0.10	0.05	0.02	0.01
1	3.078	6.314	12.706	31.821	63.657
2	1.886	2.920	4.303	6.965	9.925
3	1.638	2.353	3.182	4.541	5.841
4	1.533	2.132	2.776	3.747	4.604
5	1.476	2.015	2.571	3.365	4.032
6	1.440	1.943	2.447	3.143	3.707
7	1.415	1.895	2.365	2.998	3.499
8	1.397	1.860	2.306	2.896	3.355
9	1.383	1.833	2.262	2.821	3.250
10	1.372	1.812	2.228	2.764	3.169

To illustrate the meaning of degrees of freedom: Assume that the mean of four numbers is known to be 5. The four numbers are 7, 4, 1, and 8. The deviations of these numbers from the mean must total 0. The deviations of +2, −1, −4, and +3 do total 0. If the deviations of +2, −1, and −4 are known, then the value of +3 is fixed (restricted) in order to satisfy the condition that the sum of the deviations must equal 0. Thus, 1 degree of freedom is lost in a sampling problem involving the standard deviation of the sample because one number (the arithmetic mean) is known. For a 95% level of confidence and 9 degrees of freedom, we select the row with 9 degrees of freedom. The value of t is 2.262.

To determine the confidence interval, we substitute the values in formula (9–2).

$$\bar{x} \pm t\frac{s}{\sqrt{n}} = 0.32 \pm 2.262\frac{0.09}{\sqrt{10}} = 0.32 \pm 0.64$$

The endpoints of the confidence interval are 0.256 and 0.384. How do we interpret this result? If we repeated this study 200 times, calculating the 95% confidence interval with each sample's mean and the standard deviation, we expect 190 of the intervals would include the population mean. Ten of the intervals would not include the population mean. This is the effect of sampling error. A further interpretation is to conclude that the population mean is in this interval. The manufacturer can be reasonably sure (95% confident) that the mean remaining tread depth is between 0.256 and 0.384 inch. Because the value of 0.30 is in this interval, it is possible that the mean of the population is 0.30.

Here is another example to clarify the use of confidence intervals. Suppose an article in your local newspaper reported that the mean time to sell a residential property in the area is 60 days. You select a random sample of 20 homes sold in the last year and find the mean selling time is 65 days. Based on the sample data, you develop a 95% confidence interval for the population mean. You find that the endpoints of the confidence interval are 62 days and 68 days. How do you interpret this result? You can be reasonably confident the population mean is within this range. The value proposed for the population mean, that is, 60 days, is not included in the interval. It is not likely that the population mean is 60 days. The evidence indicates the statement by the local newspaper may not be correct. To put it another way, it seems unreasonable to obtain the sample you did from a population that had a mean selling time of 60 days.

The following example will show additional details for determining and interpreting a confidence interval. We used Minitab to perform the calculations.

EXAMPLE

The manager of the Inlet Square Mall, near Ft. Myers, Florida, wants to estimate the mean amount spent per shopping visit by customers. A sample of 20 customers reveals the following amounts spent.

$48.16	$42.22	$46.82	$51.45	$23.78	$41.86	$54.86
37.92	52.64	48.59	50.82	46.94	61.83	61.69
49.17	61.46	51.35	52.68	58.84	43.88	

What is the best estimate of the population mean? Determine a 95% confidence interval. Interpret the result. Would it be reasonable to conclude that the population mean is $50? What about $60?

SOLUTION

The mall manager assumes that the population of the amounts spent follows the normal distribution. This is a reasonable assumption in this case. Additionally, the

SOLUTION

First, note the population is finite. That is, there is a limit to the number of people residing in Scandia, in this case 250.

1. We do not know the population mean. This is the value we wish to estimate. The best estimate we have of the population mean is the sample mean, which is \$450.
2. The formula to find the confidence interval for a population mean follows.

$$\bar{x} \pm t\frac{s}{\sqrt{n}}\left(\sqrt{\frac{N-n}{N-1}}\right)$$

   In this case, we know $\bar{x} = 450$, $s = 75$, $N = 250$, and $n = 40$. We do not know the population standard deviation, so we use the t distribution. To find the appropriate value of t, we use Appendix B.5, and move across the top row to the column headed 90%. The degrees of freedom are $df = n - 1 = 40 - 1 = 39$, so we move to the cell where the df row of 39 intersects with the column headed 90%. The value is 1.685. Inserting these values in the formula:

$$\bar{x} \pm t\frac{s}{\sqrt{n}}\left(\sqrt{\frac{N-n}{N-1}}\right)$$

$$= \$450 \pm 1.685\frac{\$75}{\sqrt{40}}\left(\sqrt{\frac{250-40}{250-1}}\right) = \$450 \pm \$19.98\sqrt{.8434} = \$450 \pm \$18.35$$

   The endpoints of the confidence interval are \$431.65 and \$468.35.
3. It is likely that the population mean is more than \$431.65 but less than \$468.35. To put it another way, could the population mean be \$445? Yes, but it is not likely that it is \$425. Why is this so? Because the value \$445 is within the confidence interval and \$425 is not within the confidence interval.

SELF-REVIEW 9–5

The same study of church contributions in Scandia revealed that 15 of the 40 families sampled attend church regularly. Construct the 95% confidence interval for the proportion of families attending church regularly.

EXERCISES

27. Thirty-six items are randomly selected from a population of 300 items. The sample mean is 35 and the sample standard deviation 5. Develop a 95% confidence interval for the population mean.

28. Forty-nine items are randomly selected from a population of 500 items. The sample mean is 40 and the sample standard deviation 9. Develop a 99% confidence interval for the population mean.

29. The attendance at the Savannah Colts minor league baseball game last night was 400. A random sample of 50 of those in attendance revealed that the mean number of soft drinks consumed per person was 1.86, with a standard deviation of 0.50. Develop a 99% confidence interval for the mean number of soft drinks consumed per person.

30. There are 300 welders employed at Maine Shipyards Corporation. A sample of 30 welders revealed that 18 graduated from a registered welding course. Construct the 95% confidence interval for the proportion of all welders who graduated from a registered welding course.

CHAPTER SUMMARY

I. A point estimate is a single value (statistic) used to estimate a population value (parameter).

II. A confidence interval is a range of values within which the population parameter is expected to occur.

- **A.** The factors that determine the width of a confidence interval for a mean are:
  - **1.** The number of observations in the sample, *n*.
  - **2.** The variability in the population, usually estimated by the sample standard deviation, *s*.
  - **3.** The level of confidence.
    - **a.** To determine the confidence limits when the population standard deviation is known, we use the *z* distribution. The formula is

$$\bar{x} \pm z\frac{\sigma}{\sqrt{n}} \quad \textbf{(9–1)}$$

    - **b.** To determine the confidence limits when the population standard deviation is unknown, we use the *t* distribution. The formula is

$$\bar{x} \pm t\frac{s}{\sqrt{n}} \quad \textbf{(9–2)}$$

III. The major characteristics of the *t* distribution are:

- **A.** It is a continuous distribution.
- **B.** It is mound-shaped and symmetrical.
- **C.** It is flatter, or more spread out, than the standard normal distribution.
- **D.** There is a family of *t* distributions, depending on the number of degrees of freedom.

IV. A proportion is a ratio, fraction, or percent that indicates the part of the sample or population that has a particular characteristic.

- **A.** A sample proportion, *p*, is found by *x*, the number of successes, divided by *n*, the number of observations.
- **B.** We construct a confidence interval for a sample proportion from the following formula.

$$p \pm z\sqrt{\frac{p(1-p)}{n}} \quad \textbf{(9–4)}$$

V. We can determine an appropriate sample size for estimating both means and proportions.

- **A.** There are three factors that determine the sample size when we wish to estimate the mean.
  - **1.** The margin of error, *E*.
  - **2.** The desired level of confidence.
  - **3.** The variation in the population.
  - **4.** The formula to determine the sample size for the mean is

$$n = \left(\frac{z\sigma}{E}\right)^2 \quad \textbf{(9–5)}$$

- **B.** There are three factors that determine the sample size when we wish to estimate a proportion.
  - **1.** The margin of error, *E*.
  - **2.** The desired level of confidence.
  - **3.** A value for π to calculate the variation in the population.
  - **4.** The formula to determine the sample size for a proportion is

$$n = \pi(1-\pi)\left(\frac{z}{E}\right)^2 \quad \textbf{(9–6)}$$

VI. For a finite population, the standard error is adjusted by the factor: $\sqrt{\frac{N-n}{N-1}}$

CHAPTER EXERCISES

31. A random sample of 85 group leaders, supervisors, and similar personnel at General Motors revealed that, on average, they spent 6.5 years in a particular job before being promoted. The standard deviation of the sample was 1.7 years. Construct a 95% confidence interval.

32. A state meat inspector in Iowa has been given the assignment of estimating the mean net weight of packages of ground chuck labeled "3 pounds." Of course, he realizes that the weights cannot always be precisely 3 pounds. A sample of 36 packages reveals the mean weight to be 3.01 pounds, with a standard deviation of 0.03 pound.

a. What is the estimated population mean?

b. Determine a 95% confidence interval for the population mean.

33. As part of their business promotional package, the Milwaukee Chamber of Commerce would like an estimate of the mean cost per month to lease a one-bedroom apartment. The mean cost per month for a random sample of 40 apartments currently available for lease was $884. The standard deviation of the sample was $50.

a. Develop a 98% confidence interval for the population mean.

b. Would it be reasonable to conclude that the population mean is $950 per month?

34. A recent survey of 50 executives who were laid off during a recent recession revealed it took a mean of 26 weeks for them to find another position. The standard deviation of the sample was 6.2 weeks. Construct a 95% confidence interval for the population mean. Is it reasonable that the population mean is 28 weeks? Justify your answer.

35. Marty Rowatti recently assumed the position of director of the YMCA of South Jersey. He would like some current data on how long current members of the YMCA have been members. To investigate, suppose he selects a random sample of 40 current members. The mean length of membership for the sample is 8.32 years and the standard deviation is 3.07 years.

a. What is the mean of the population?

b. Develop a 90% confidence interval for the population mean.

c. The previous director, in the summary report she prepared as she retired, indicated the mean length of membership was now "almost 10 years." Does the sample information substantiate this claim? Cite evidence.

36. The American Restaurant Association collected information on the number of meals eaten outside the home per week by young married couples. A survey of 60 couples showed the sample mean number of meals eaten outside the home was 2.76 meals per week, with a standard deviation of 0.75 meal per week. Construct a 99% confidence interval for the population mean.

37. The National Collegiate Athletic Association (NCAA) reported that college football assistant coaches spend a mean of 70 hours per week on coaching and recruiting during the season. A random sample of 50 assistant coaches showed the sample mean to be 68.6 hours, with a standard deviation of 8.2 hours.

a. Using the sample data, construct a 99% confidence interval for the population mean.

b. Does the 99% confidence interval include the value suggested by the NCAA? Interpret this result.

c. Suppose you decided to switch from a 99% to a 95% confidence interval. Without performing any calculations, will the interval increase, decrease, or stay the same? Which of the values in the formula will change?

38. The Human Relations Department of Electronics Inc. would like to include a dental plan as part of the benefits package. The question is: How much does a typical employee and his or her family spend per year on dental expenses? A sample of 45 employees reveals the mean amount spent last year was $1,820, with a standard deviation of $660.

a. Construct a 95% confidence interval for the population mean.

b. The information from part (a) was given to the president of Electronics Inc. He indicated he could afford $1,700 of dental expenses per employee. Is it possible that the population mean could be $1,700? Justify your answer.

39. A student conducted a study and reported that the 95% confidence interval for the mean ranged from 46 to 54. He was sure that the mean of the sample was 50, that the standard deviation of the sample was 16, and that the sample size was at least 30, but could not remember the exact number. Can you help him out?

40. A recent study by the American Automobile Dealers Association surveyed a random sample of 20 dealers. The data revealed a mean amount of profit per car sold was $290, with a standard deviation of $125. Develop a 95% confidence interval for the population mean of profit per car.

41. A study of 25 graduates of four-year public colleges revealed the mean amount owed by a student in student loans was $55,051. The standard deviation of the sample was $7,568. Construct a 90% confidence interval for the population mean. Is it reasonable to conclude that the mean of the population is actually $55,000? Explain why or why not.

42. An important factor in selling a residential property is the number of times real estate agents show a home. A sample of 15 homes recently sold in the Buffalo, New York, area revealed the mean number of times a home was shown was 24 and the standard deviation of the sample was 5 people. Develop a 98% confidence interval for the population mean.

43. **FILE** In 2003, the Accreditation Council for Graduate Medical Education (ACGME) implemented new rules limiting work hours for all residents. A key component of these rules is that residents should work no more than 80 hours per week. The following is the number of weekly hours worked in 2017 by a sample of residents at the Tidelands Medical Center.

84	86	84	86	79	82	87	81	84	78	74	86

   a. What is the point estimate of the population mean for the number of weekly hours worked at the Tidelands Medical Center?
   b. Develop a 90% confidence interval for the population mean.
   c. Is the Tidelands Medical Center within the ACGME guideline? Why?

44. **FILE** PrintTech, Inc. is introducing a new line of ink-jet printers and would like to promote the number of pages a user can expect from a print cartridge. A sample of 10 cartridges revealed the following number of pages printed.

2,698	2,028	2,474	2,395	2,372	2,475	1,927	3,006	2,334	2,379

   a. What is the point estimate of the population mean?
   b. Develop a 95% confidence interval for the population mean.

45. **FILE** Dr. Susan Benner is an industrial psychologist. She is currently studying stress among executives of Internet companies. She has developed a questionnaire that she believes measures stress. A score above 80 indicates stress at a dangerous level. A random sample of 15 executives revealed the following stress level scores.

94	78	83	90	78	99	97	90	97	90	93	94	100	75	84

   a. Find the mean stress level for this sample. What is the point estimate of the population mean?
   b. Construct a 95% confidence level for the population mean.
   c. According to Dr. Benner's test, is it reasonable to conclude that the mean stress level of Internet executives is 80? Explain.

46. Pharmaceutical companies promote their prescription drugs using television advertising. In a survey of 80 randomly sampled television viewers, 10 indicated that they asked their physician about using a prescription drug they saw advertised on TV. Develop a 95% confidence interval for the proportion of viewers who discussed a drug seen on TV with their physician. Is it reasonable to conclude that 25% of the viewers discuss an advertised drug with their physician?

47. HighTech, Inc. randomly tests its employees about company policies. Last year in the 400 random tests conducted, 14 employees failed the test. Develop a 99% confidence interval for the proportion of applicants that fail the test. Would it be reasonable to conclude that 5% of the employees cannot pass the company policy test? Explain.

48. During a national debate on changes to health care, a cable news service performs an opinion poll of 500 small-business owners. It shows that 65% of small-business owners do not approve of the changes. Develop a 95% confidence interval for the proportion opposing health care changes. Comment on the result.

49. There are 20,000 eligible voters in York County, South Carolina. A random sample of 500 York County voters revealed 350 plan to vote to return Louella Miller to the state senate. Construct a 99% confidence interval for the proportion of voters in the county who plan to vote for Ms. Miller. From this sample information, is it reasonable to conclude that Ms. Miller will receive a majority of the votes?

50. In a poll to estimate presidential popularity, each person in a random sample of 1,000 voters was asked to agree with one of the following statements:

1. The president is doing a good job.
2. The president is doing a poor job.
3. I have no opinion.

A total of 560 respondents selected the first statement, indicating they thought the president was doing a good job.

a. Construct a 95% confidence interval for the proportion of respondents who feel the president is doing a good job.

b. Based on your interval in part (a), is it reasonable to conclude that a majority of the population believes the president is doing a good job?

51. Police Chief Edward Wilkin of River City reports 500 traffic citations were issued last month. A sample of 35 of these citations showed the mean amount of the fine was $54, with a standard deviation of $4.50. Construct a 95% confidence interval for the mean amount of a citation in River City.

52. The First National Bank of Wilson has 650 checking account customers. A recent sample of 50 of these customers showed 26 have a Visa card with the bank. Construct the 99% confidence interval for the proportion of checking account customers who have a Visa card with the bank.

53. It is estimated that 60% of U.S. households subscribe to cable TV. You would like to verify this statement for your class in mass communications. If you want your estimate to be within 5 percentage points, with a 95% level of confidence, how many households should you sample?

54. You need to estimate the mean number of travel days per year for salespeople. The mean of a small pilot study was 150 days, with a standard deviation of 14 days. If you must estimate the population mean within 2 days, how many salespeople should you sample? Use the 90% confidence level.

55. You want to estimate the mean family income in a rural area of central Indiana. The question is, how many families should be sampled? In a pilot sample of 10 families, the standard deviation of the sample was $500. The sponsor of the survey wants you to use the 95% confidence level. The estimate is to be within $100. How many families should be interviewed?

56. *Families USA,* a monthly magazine that discusses issues related to health and health costs, surveyed 20 of its subscribers. It found that the annual health insurance premiums for a family with coverage through an employer averaged $10,979. The standard deviation of the sample was $1,000.

a. Based on this sample information, develop a 90% confidence interval for the population mean yearly premium.

b. How large a sample is needed to find the population mean within $250 at 99% confidence?

57. Passenger comfort is influenced by the amount of pressurization in an airline cabin. Higher pressurization permits a closer-to-normal environment and a more relaxed flight. A study by an airline user group recorded the equivalent air pressure on 30 randomly chosen flights. The study revealed a mean equivalent air pressure of 8,000 feet with a standard deviation of 300 feet.

a. Develop a 99% confidence interval for the population mean equivalent air pressure.

b. How large a sample is needed to find the population mean within 25 feet at 95% confidence?

58. A survey of 25 randomly sampled judges employed by the state of Florida found that they earned an average wage (including benefits) of $65.00 per hour. The sample standard deviation was $6.25 per hour.
    a. What is the population mean? What is the best estimate of the population mean?
    b. Develop a 99% confidence interval for the population mean wage (including benefits) for these employees.
    c. How large a sample is needed to assess the population mean with an allowable error of $1.00 at 95% confidence?
59. Based on a sample of 50 U.S. citizens, the American Film Institute found that a typical American spent 78 hours watching movies last year. The standard deviation of this sample was 9 hours.
    a. Develop a 95% confidence interval for the population mean number of hours spent watching movies last year.
    b. How large a sample should be used to be 90% confident the sample mean is within 1.0 hour of the population mean?
60. Dylan Jones kept careful records of the fuel efficiency of his new car. After the first nine times he filled up the tank, he found the mean was 23.4 miles per gallon (mpg) with a sample standard deviation of 0.9 mpg.
    a. Compute the 95% confidence interval for his mpg.
    b. How many times should he fill his gas tank to obtain a margin of error below 0.1 mpg?
61. A survey of 36 randomly selected iPhone owners showed that the purchase price has a mean of $650 with a sample standard deviation of $24.
    a. Compute the standard error of the sample mean.
    b. Compute the 95% confidence interval for the mean.
    c. How large a sample is needed to estimate the population mean within $10?
62. You plan to conduct a survey to find what proportion of the workforce has two or more jobs. You decide on the 95% confidence level and a margin of error of 2%. A pilot survey reveals that 5 of the 50 sampled hold two or more jobs. How many in the workforce should be interviewed to meet your requirements?
63. A study conducted several years ago reported that 21 percent of public accountants changed companies within 3 years. The American Institute of CPA's would like to update the study. They would like to estimate the population proportion of public accountants who changed companies within 3 years with a margin of error of 3% and a 95% level of confidence.
    a. To update this study, the files of how many public accountants should be studied?
    b. How many public accountants should be contacted if no previous estimates of the population proportion are available?
64. As part of an annual review of its accounts, a discount brokerage selected a random sample of 36 customers and reviewed the value of their accounts. The mean was $32,000 with a sample standard deviation of $8,200. What is a 90% confidence interval for the mean account value of the population of customers?
65. The National Weight Control Registry tries to mine secrets of success from people who lost at least 30 pounds and kept it off for at least a year. It reports that out of 2,700 registrants, 459 were on a low-carbohydrate diet (less than 90 grams a day).
    a. Develop a 95% confidence interval for the proportion of people on a low-carbohydrate diet.
    b. Is it possible that the population percentage is 18%?
    c. How large a sample is needed to estimate the proportion within 0.5%?
66. Near the time of an election, a cable news service performs an opinion poll of 1,000 probable voters. It shows that the Republican contender has an advantage of 52% to 48%.
    a. Develop a 95% confidence interval for the proportion favoring the Republican candidate.
    b. Estimate the probability that the Democratic candidate is actually leading.
    c. Repeat the above analysis based on a sample of 3,000 probable voters.
67. A sample of 352 subscribers to *Wired* magazine shows the mean time spent using the Internet is 13.4 hours per week, with a sample standard deviation of 6.8 hours. Find the 95% confidence interval for the mean time *Wired* subscribers spend on the Internet.
68. The Tennessee Tourism Institute (TTI) plans to sample information center visitors entering the state to learn the fraction of visitors who plan to camp in the state. Current estimates are that 35% of visitors are campers. How many visitors would you sample to estimate the population proportion of campers with a 95% confidence level and an allowable error of 2%?

DATA ANALYTICS

69. **FILE** Refer to the North Valley Real Estate data, which reports information on homes sold in the area during the last year. Select a random sample of twenty homes.
    - **a.** Based on your random sample of twenty homes, develop a 95% confidence interval for the mean selling price of the homes.
    - **b.** Based on your random sample of twenty homes, develop a 95% confidence interval for the mean days on the market.
    - **c.** Based on your random sample of twenty homes, develop a 95% confidence interval for the proportion of homes with a pool.
    - **d.** Suppose that North Valley Real Estate employs several agents. Each agent will be randomly assigned twenty homes to sell. The agents are highly motivated to sell homes based on the commissions they earn. They are also concerned about the twenty homes they are assigned to sell. Using the confidence intervals you created, write a general memo informing the agents about the characteristics of the homes they may be assigned to sell.
    - **e.** What would you do if your confidence intervals did not include the mean of all 105 homes? How could this happen?
70. **FILE** Refer to the Baseball 2016 data, which report information on the 30 Major League Baseball teams for the 2016 season. Assume the 2016 data represents a sample.
    - **a.** Develop a 95% confidence interval for the mean number of home runs per team.
    - **b.** Develop a 95% confidence interval for the mean batting average by each team.
    - **c.** Develop a 95% confidence interval for the mean earned run average (ERA) for each team.
71. **FILE** Refer to the Lincolnville School District bus data.
    - **a.** Develop a 95% confidence interval for the mean bus maintenance cost.
    - **b.** Develop a 95% confidence interval for the mean bus odometer miles.
    - **c.** Write a business memo to the state transportation official to report your results.

A REVIEW OF CHAPTERS 8–9

We began Chapter 8 by describing the reasons sampling is necessary. We sample because it is often impossible to study every item, or individual, in some populations. For example, to contact all U.S. bank officers and record their annual incomes would be too expensive and time-consuming, . Also, sampling often destroys the product. A drug manufacturer cannot test the properties of each vitamin tablet manufactured because there would be none left to sell. Therefore, to estimate a population parameter, we select a sample from the population. A sample is a part of the population. Care must be taken to ensure that every member of our population has a chance of being selected; otherwise, the conclusions might be biased. A number of probability-type sampling methods can be used, including *simple random, systematic, stratified,* and *cluster sampling.*

Regardless of the sampling method selected, a sample statistic is seldom equal to the corresponding population parameter. For example, the mean of a sample is seldom exactly the same as the mean of the population. The difference between this sample statistic and the population parameter is the *sampling error.*

In Chapter 8, we demonstrated that, if we select all possible samples of a specified size from a population and calculate the mean of these samples, the result will be exactly equal to the population mean. We also showed that the dispersion in the distribution of the sample means is equal to the population standard deviation divided by the square root of the sample size. This result is called the standard error of the mean. There is less dispersion in the distribution of the sample means than in the population. In addition, as we increase the number of observations in each sample, we decrease the variation in the sampling distribution.

The central limit theorem is the foundation of statistical inference. It states that, if the population from which we select the samples follows the normal probability distribution, the distribution of the sample means will also follow the normal distribution. If the population is not normal, it will approach the normal probability distribution as we increase the size of the sample.

Our focus in Chapter 9 was point estimates and interval estimates. A point estimate is a single value used to estimate a population parameter. An interval estimate is a range of values within which we expect the population parameter to occur. For example, based on a sample, we estimate that the mean annual income of all professional house painters in Atlanta, Georgia (the population), is $45,300. That estimate is called a *point estimate.* If we state that the population mean is probably in the interval between $45,200 and $45,400, that estimate is called an *interval estimate.* The two endpoints ($45,200 and $45,400) are the *confidence limits* for the population mean. We also described procedures for establishing a confidence interval for a population mean when the population standard deviation is not known and for a population proportion. In this chapter, we also provided a method to determine the necessary sample size based on the dispersion in the population, the level of confidence desired, and the desired precision of the estimate or margin of error.

PROBLEMS

1. A recent study indicated that women took an average of 8.6 weeks of unpaid leave from their jobs after the birth of a child. Assume that this distribution follows the normal probability distribution with a standard deviation of 2.0 weeks. We select a sample of 35 women who recently returned to work after the birth of a child. What is the likelihood that the mean of this sample is at least 8.8 weeks?
2. The manager of Tee Shirt Emporium reports that the mean number of shirts sold per week is 1,210, with a standard deviation of 325. The distribution of sales follows the normal distribution. What is the likelihood of selecting a sample of 25 weeks and finding the sample mean to be 1,100 or less?
3. The owner of the Gulf Stream Café wished to estimate the mean number of lunch customers per day. A sample of 40 days revealed a mean of 160 per day, with a standard deviation of 20 per day. Develop a 98% confidence interval for the mean number of customers per day.
4. The manager of the local Hamburger Express wishes to estimate the mean time customers spend at the drive-through window. A sample of 20 customers experienced a mean waiting time of 2.65 minutes, with a standard deviation of 0.45 minute. Develop a 90% confidence interval for the mean waiting time.
5. Defiance Tool and Die has 293 sales offices throughout the world. The VP of Sales is studying the usage of its copy machines. A random sample of six of the sales offices revealed the following number of copies made in each selected office last week.

826	931	1,126	918	1,011	1,101

   Develop a 95% confidence interval for the mean number of copies per week.
6. John Kleman is the host of KXYZ Radio 55 AM drive-time news in Denver. During his morning program, John asks listeners to call in and discuss current local and national news. This morning, John was concerned with the number of hours children under 12 years of age watch TV per day. The last five callers reported that their children watched the following number of hours of TV last night.

3.0	3.5	4.0	4.5	3.0

   Would it be reasonable to develop a confidence interval from these data to show the mean number of hours of TV watched? If yes, construct an appropriate confidence interval and interpret the result. If no, why would a confidence interval not be appropriate?
7. Historically, Widgets Manufacturing Inc. produces 250 widgets per day. Recently the new owner bought a new machine to produce more widgets per day. A sample of 16 days' production revealed a mean of 240 units with a standard deviation of 35. Construct a confidence interval for the mean number of widgets produced per day. Does it seem reasonable to conclude that the mean daily widget production has changed? Justify your conclusion.
8. A manufacturer of cell phone batteries wants to estimate the useful life of its battery (in thousands of hours). The estimate is to be within 0.10 (100 hours). Assume a 95% level of confidence and that the standard deviation of the useful life of the battery is 0.90 (900 hours). Determine the required sample size.
9. The manager of a home improvement store wishes to estimate the mean amount of money spent in the store. The estimate is to be within $4.00 with a 95% level of confidence. The manager does not know the standard deviation of the amounts spent. However, he does estimate that the range is from $5.00 up to $155.00. How large of a sample is needed?
10. In a sample of 200 residents of Georgetown County, 120 reported they believed the county real estate taxes were too high. Develop a 95% confidence interval for the proportion of residents who believe the tax rate is too high. Does it seem reasonable to conclude that 50% of the voters believe that taxes are too high?
11. In recent times, the percent of buyers purchasing a new vehicle via the Internet has been large enough that local automobile dealers are concerned about its impact on their business. The information needed is an estimate of the proportion of purchases via the Internet. How large of a sample of purchasers is necessary for the estimate to be

within 2 percentage points with a 98% level of confidence? Current thinking is that about 8% of the vehicles are purchased via the Internet.

12. Historically, the proportion of adults over the age of 24 who smoke has been .30. In recent years, much information has been published and aired on radio and TV that smoking is not good for one's health. A sample of 500 adults revealed only 25% of those sampled smoked. Develop a 98% confidence interval for the proportion of adults who currently smoke. Does it seem reasonable to conclude that the proportion of adults who smoke has changed?

13. The auditor of the state of Ohio needs an estimate of the proportion of residents who regularly play the state lottery. Historically, about 40% regularly play, but the auditor would like some current information. How large a sample is necessary for the estimate to be within 3 percentage points, with a 98% level of confidence?

CASES

Century National Bank

Refer to the description of Century National Bank at the end of the Review of Chapters 1–4 on page 129. When Mr. Selig took over as president of Century several years ago, the use of debit cards was just beginning. He would like an update on the use of these cards. Develop a 95% confidence interval for the proportion of customers using these cards. On the basis of the confidence interval, is it reasonable to conclude that more than half of the customers use a debit card? Write a brief report interpreting the results.

PRACTICE TEST

Part 1—Objective

1. If each item in the population has the same chance of being selected, this is called a ________. **1.** ________
2. The difference between the population mean and the sample mean is called the ________. **2.** ________
3. The ________ is the standard deviation of the distribution of sample means. **3.** ________
4. If the sample size is increased, the variance of the sample means will ________. (become smaller, become larger, not change) **4.** ________
5. A single value used to estimate a population parameter is called a ________. **5.** ________
6. A range of values within which the population parameter is expected to occur is called a ________. **6.** ________
7. Which of the following does *not* affect the width of a confidence interval? (sample size, variation in the population, level of confidence, size of population) **7.** ________
8. The fraction of a population that has a particular characteristic is called a ________. **8.** ________
9. Which of the following is not a characteristic of the *t* distribution? (positively skewed, continuous, mean of zero, based on degrees of freedom) **9.** ________
10. To determine the required sample size of a proportion when no estimate of the population proportion is available, what value is used? **10.** ________

Part 2—Problems

1. Americans spend an average (mean) of 12.2 minutes (per day) in the shower. The distribution of times follows the normal distribution with a population standard deviation of 2.3 minutes. What is the likelihood that the mean time per day for a sample of 12 Americans was 11 minutes or less?
2. A recent study of 26 Conway, South Carolina, residents revealed they had lived at their current address an average of 9.3 years. The standard deviation of the sample was 2 years.
   - **a.** What is the population mean?
   - **b.** What is the best estimate of the population mean?
   - **c.** What is the standard error of estimate?
   - **d.** Develop a 90% confidence interval for the population mean.
3. A recent federal report indicated that 27% of children ages 2 to 5 ate a vegetable at least five times a week. How large a sample is needed to estimate the true population proportion within 2% with a 98% level of confidence? Be sure to use the information contained in the federal report.
4. The Philadelphia Area Transit Authority wishes to estimate the proportion of central city workers that use public transportation to get to work. A sample of 100 workers revealed that 64 used public transportation. Develop a 95% confidence interval for the population proportion.

10 One-Sample Tests of Hypothesis

DOLE PINEAPPLE INC. is concerned that the 16-ounce can of sliced pineapple is being overfilled. Assume the standard deviation of the process is .03 ounce. The quality control department took a random sample of 50 cans and found that the arithmetic mean weight was 16.05 ounces. At the 5% level of significance, can we conclude that the mean weight is greater than 16 ounces? Determine the *p*-value. (See Exercise 26 and LO10-4.)

LEARNING OBJECTIVES

When you have completed this chapter, you will be able to:

LO10-1 Explain the process of testing a hypothesis.

LO10-2 Apply the six-step procedure for testing a hypothesis.

LO10-3 Distinguish between a one-tailed and a two-tailed test of hypothesis.

LO10-4 Conduct a test of a hypothesis about a population mean.

LO10-5 Compute and interpret a *p*-value.

LO10-6 Use a *t* statistic to test a hypothesis.

LO10-7 Compute the probability of a Type II error.

INTRODUCTION

Chapter 8 began our study sampling and statistical inference. We described how we could select a random sample to estimate the value of a population parameter. For example, we selected a sample of five employees at Spence Sprockets, found the number of years of service for each sampled employee, computed the mean years of service, and used the sample mean to estimate the mean years of service for all employees. In other words, we estimated a population parameter from a sample statistic.

Chapter 9 continued the study of statistical inference by developing a confidence interval. A confidence interval is a range of values within which we expect the population parameter to occur. In this chapter, rather than develop a range of values within which we expect the population parameter to occur, we develop a procedure to test the validity of a statement about a population parameter. Some examples of statements we might want to test are:

- The mean speed of automobiles passing milepost 150 on the West Virginia Turnpike is 68 miles per hour.
- The mean number of miles driven by those leasing a Chevy TrailBlazer for 3 years is 32,000 miles.
- The mean time an American family lives in a particular single-family dwelling is 11.8 years.
- In 2016, the mean starting salary for a graduate from a four-year business program is $51,541.
- According to the Kelley Blue Book (www.kbb.com), a 2017 Ford Edge averages 21 miles per gallon in the city.
- The mean cost to remodel a kitchen is $20,000.

© Russell Ilig/Getty Images

This chapter and several of the following chapters cover statistical hypothesis testing. We begin by defining what we mean by a statistical hypothesis and statistical hypothesis testing. Next, we outline the steps in statistical hypothesis testing. Then we conduct tests of hypothesis for means. In the last section of the chapter, we describe possible errors due to sampling in hypothesis testing.

LO10-1
Explain the process of testing a hypothesis.

WHAT IS HYPOTHESIS TESTING?

The terms *hypothesis testing* and *testing a hypothesis* are used interchangeably. Hypothesis testing starts with a statement, or assumption, about a population parameter—such as the population mean. This statement is referred to as a hypothesis.

HYPOTHESIS A statement about a population parameter subject to verification.

A hypothesis might be that the mean monthly commission of sales associates in retail electronics stores, such as hhgregg, is $2,000. We cannot contact all hhgregg sales associates to determine that the mean is $2,000. The cost of locating and interviewing every hhgregg electronics sales associate in the United States would be exorbitant. To test the validity of the hypothesis ($\mu = \$2{,}000$), we must select a sample from the population of all hhgregg electronics sales associates, calculate sample statistics, and based on certain decision rules reject or fail to reject the hypothesis. A sample mean of $1,000 per month is much less than $2,000 per month and we would most likely reject the hypothesis. However, suppose the sample mean is $1,995. Can we attribute the $5 difference between $1,995 and $2,000 to sampling error? Or is this difference of $5 statistically significant?

HYPOTHESIS TESTING A procedure based on sample evidence and probability theory to determine whether the hypothesis is a reasonable statement.

LO10-2
Apply the six-step procedure for testing a hypothesis.

SIX-STEP PROCEDURE FOR TESTING A HYPOTHESIS

There is a six-step procedure that systematizes hypothesis testing; when we get to step 6 we are ready to interpret the results of the test based on the decision to reject or not reject the hypothesis. However, hypothesis testing as used by statisticians does not provide proof that something is true, in the manner in which a mathematician "proves" a statement. It does provide a kind of "proof beyond a reasonable doubt," in the manner of the court system. Hence, there are specific rules of evidence, or procedures, that are followed. The steps are shown in the following diagram. We will discuss in detail each of the steps.

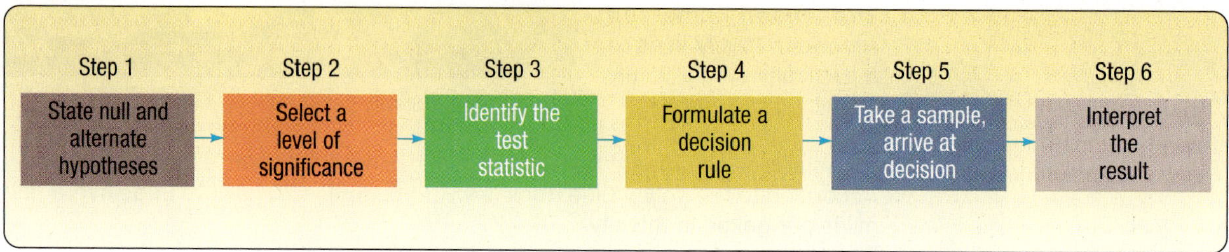

Step 1: State the Null Hypothesis (H_0) and the Alternate Hypothesis (H_1)

The first step is to state the hypothesis being tested. It is called the **null hypothesis,** designated H_0, and read "*H sub zero.*" The capital letter *H* stands for hypothesis, and the subscript zero implies "no difference." There is usually a "not" or a "no" term in the null hypothesis, meaning that there is "no change." For example, the null hypothesis is that the mean number of miles driven on the steel-belted tire is not different from 60,000. The null hypothesis would be written H_0: $\mu = 60{,}000$. Generally speaking, the null hypothesis is developed for the purpose of testing. We either reject or fail to reject the null hypothesis. The null hypothesis is a statement that is not rejected unless our sample data provide convincing evidence that it is false.

We should emphasize that, if the null hypothesis is not rejected on the basis of the sample data, we cannot say that the null hypothesis is true. To put it another way, failing to reject the null hypothesis does not prove that H_0 is true; it means we have *failed to disprove* H_0. To prove without any doubt the null hypothesis is true, the population parameter would have to be known. To actually determine it, we would have to test, survey, or count every item in the population. This is usually not feasible. The alternative is to take a sample from the population.

Often, the **null hypothesis** begins by stating, "There is no *significant* difference between . . ." or "The mean impact strength of the glass is not *significantly* different from. . . ." When we select a sample from a population, the sample statistic is usually numerically different from the hypothesized population parameter. As an illustration, suppose the hypothesized impact strength of a glass plate is 70 psi, and the mean impact strength of a sample of 12 glass plates is 69.5 psi. We must make a decision about the difference of 0.5 psi. Is it a true difference, that is, a significant difference, or is the difference between the sample statistic (69.5) and the hypothesized population parameter (70.0) due to chance (sampling)? To answer this question, we conduct a test of significance, commonly referred to as a test of hypothesis. To define what is meant by a null hypothesis:

NULL HYPOTHESIS A statement about the value of a population parameter developed for the purpose of testing numerical evidence.

The **alternate hypothesis** describes what you will conclude if you reject the null hypothesis. It is written H_1 and is read "*H sub one.*" It is also referred to as the research hypothesis. The alternate hypothesis is accepted if the sample data provide us with enough statistical evidence that the null hypothesis is false.

ALTERNATE HYPOTHESIS A statement that is accepted if the sample data provide sufficient evidence that the null hypothesis is false.

The following example will help clarify what is meant by the null hypothesis and the alternate hypothesis. A recent article indicated the mean age of U.S. commercial aircraft is 15 years. To conduct a statistical test regarding this statement, the first step is to determine the null and the alternate hypotheses. The null hypothesis represents the current or reported condition. It is written H_0: $\mu = 15$. The alternate hypothesis is that the statement is not true, that is, H_1: $\mu \neq 15$. It is important to remember that no matter how the problem is stated, *the null hypothesis will always contain the equal sign.* The equal sign (=) will never appear in the alternate hypothesis. Why? Because the null hypothesis is the statement being tested, and we need a specific value to include in our calculations. We turn to the alternate hypothesis only if the data suggest the null hypothesis is untrue.

Step 2: Select a Level of Significance

After setting up the null hypothesis and alternate hypothesis, the next step is to state the level of significance.

LEVEL OF SIGNIFICANCE The probability of rejecting the null hypothesis when it is true.

The level of significance is designated α, the Greek letter alpha. It is also sometimes called the level of risk. This may be a more appropriate term because it is the risk you take of rejecting the null hypothesis when it is really true.

There is no one level of significance that is applied to all tests. A decision is made to use the .05 level (often stated as the 5% level), the .01 level, the .10 level, or any other level between 0 and 1. Traditionally, the .05 level is selected for consumer research projects, .01 for quality assurance, and .10 for political polling. You, the researcher, must decide on the level of significance *before* formulating a decision rule and collecting sample data.

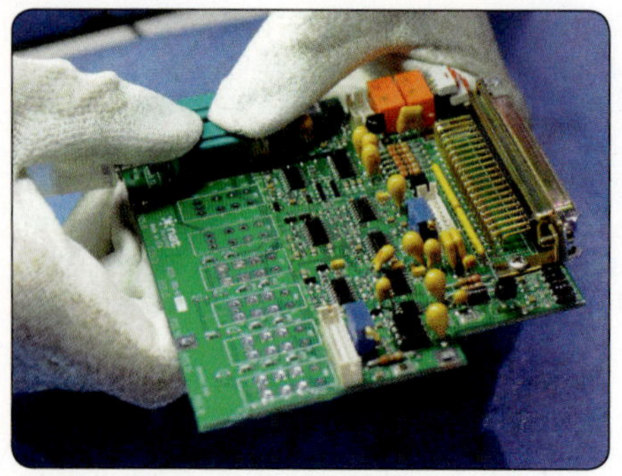
© Jim Stern/Bloomberg via Getty Images

To illustrate how it is possible to reject a true hypothesis, suppose a firm manufacturing personal computers uses a large number of printed circuit boards. Suppliers bid on the boards, and the one with the lowest bid is awarded a sizable contract. Suppose the contract specifies that the computer manufacturer's quality-assurance department will randomly sample all incoming shipments of circuit boards. If more than 6% of the boards sampled are substandard, the shipment will be rejected. The null hypothesis is that the incoming shipment of boards meets the quality standards of the contract and contains 6% or less defective boards. The alternate hypothesis is that more than 6% of the boards are defective.

A shipment of 4,000 circuit boards was received from Allied Electronics, and the quality assurance department selected a random sample of 50 circuit boards for testing. Of the 50 circuit boards sampled, 4 boards, or 8%, were substandard. The shipment was rejected because it exceeded the maximum of 6% substandard printed circuit boards. If the shipment was actually substandard, then the decision to return the boards to the supplier was correct.

However, because of sampling error, there is a small probability of an incorrect decision. Suppose there were only 40, or 4%, defective boards in the shipment (well under the 6% threshold) and 4 of these 40 were randomly selected in the sample of 50. The sample evidence indicates that the percentage of defective boards is 8% (4 out of 50 is 8%) so we reject the shipment. But, in fact, of the 4,000 boards, there are only 40 defective units. The true defect rate is 1.00%. In this instance our sample evidence estimates 8% defective but there is only 1% defective in the population. Based on the sample evidence, an incorrect decision was made. In terms of hypothesis testing, we rejected the null hypothesis when we should have failed to reject the null hypothesis. By rejecting a true null hypothesis, we committed a Type I error. The probability of committing a Type I error is represented by the Greek letter alpha (α).

TYPE I ERROR Rejecting the null hypothesis, H_0, when it is true.

The other possible error in hypothesis testing is called Type II error. The probability of committing a Type II error is designated by the Greek letter beta (β).

TYPE II ERROR Not rejecting the null hypothesis when it is false.

The firm manufacturing personal computers would commit a Type II error if, unknown to the manufacturer, an incoming shipment of printed circuit boards from Allied Electronics contained 15% substandard boards, yet the shipment was accepted. How could this happen? A random sample of 50 boards could have 2 (4%) substandard boards, and 48 good boards. According to the stated procedure, because the sample contained less than 6% substandard boards, the decision is to accept the shipment. This is a Type II error. While this event is extremely unlikely, it is possible based on the process of randomly sampling from a population. In a later section, we show how to calculate the probability of a Type II error.

In retrospect, the researcher cannot study every item or individual in the population. Thus, there is a possibility of two types of error—a Type I error, wherein the null hypothesis is rejected when it should not be rejected, and a Type II error, wherein the null hypothesis is not rejected when it should have been rejected.

We often refer to the probability of these two possible errors as *alpha,* α, and *beta,* β. Alpha (α) is the probability of making a Type I error, and beta (β) is the probability of making a Type II error. The following table summarizes the decisions the researcher could make and the possible consequences.

Null Hypothesis	Researcher: Does Not Reject H_0	Researcher: Rejects H_0
H_0 is true	Correct decision	Type I error
H_0 is false	Type II error	Correct decision

Step 3: Select the Test Statistic

There are many **test statistics**. In this chapter, we use both z and t as the test statistics. In later chapters, we will use such test statistics as F and χ^2, called chi-square.

TEST STATISTIC A value, determined from sample information, used to determine whether to reject the null hypothesis.

In hypothesis testing for the mean (μ) when σ is known, the test statistic z is computed by:

TESTING A MEAN, σ KNOWN

$$z = \frac{\bar{x} - \mu}{\sigma/\sqrt{n}} \quad \textbf{(10–1)}$$

The z value is based on the sampling distribution of $\bar{x}$, which follows the normal distribution with a mean ($\mu_{\bar{x}}$) equal to μ and a standard deviation $\sigma_{\bar{x}}$, which is equal to $\sigma/\sqrt{n}$. We can thus determine whether the difference between $\bar{x}$ and μ is statistically significant by finding the number of standard deviations $\bar{x}$ is from μ, using formula (10–1).

Step 4: Formulate the Decision Rule

A decision rule is a statement of the specific conditions under which the null hypothesis is rejected and the conditions under which it is not rejected. The region or area of rejection defines the location of all those values that are so large or so small that the probability of their occurrence under a true null hypothesis is rather remote.

Chart 10–1 portrays the rejection region for a test of significance that will be conducted later in the chapter.

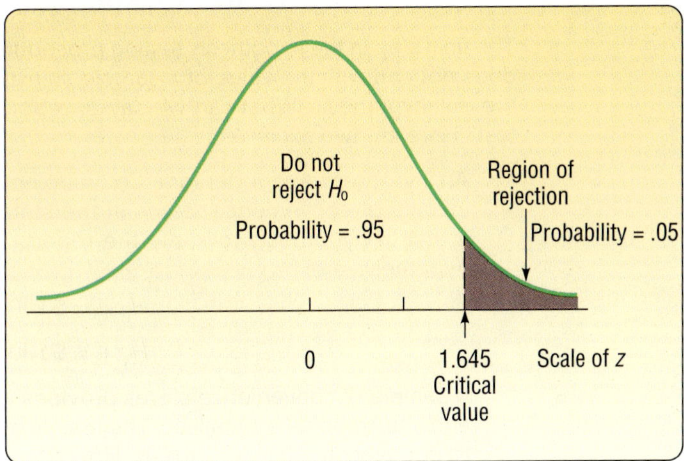

CHART 10–1 Sampling Distribution of the Statistic z, a Right-Tailed Test, .05 Level of Significance

STATISTICS IN ACTION

During World War II, allied military planners needed estimates of the number of German tanks. The information provided by traditional spying methods was not reliable, but statistical methods proved to be valuable. For example, espionage and reconnaissance led analysts to estimate that 1,550 tanks were produced during June 1941. However, using the serial numbers of captured tanks and statistical analysis, military planners estimated that only 244 tanks were produced. The actual number produced, as determined from German production records, was 271. The estimate using statistical analysis turned out to be much more accurate. A similar type of analysis was used to estimate the number of Iraqi tanks destroyed during Desert Storm.

Note in the chart that:

- The area where the null hypothesis is not rejected is to the left of 1.645. We will explain how to get the 1.645 value shortly.
- The area of rejection is to the right of 1.645.
- A one-tailed test is being applied. (This will also be explained later.)
- The .05 level of significance was chosen.
- The sampling distribution of the statistic z follows the normal probability distribution.
- The value 1.645 separates the regions where the null hypothesis is rejected and where it is not rejected.
- The value 1.645 is the **critical value.**

CRITICAL VALUE The dividing point between the region where the null hypothesis is rejected and the region where it is not rejected.

Step 5: Make a Decision

The fifth step in hypothesis testing is to compute the value of the test statistic, compare its value to the critical value, and make a decision to reject or not to reject the null hypothesis. Referring to Chart 10–1, if, based on sample information, z is computed to be 2.34, the null hypothesis is rejected at the .05 level of significance. The decision to reject H_0 was made because 2.34 lies in the region of rejection, that is, beyond 1.645. We reject the null hypothesis, reasoning that it is highly improbable that a computed z value this large is due to sampling error (chance).

Had the computed value been 1.645 or less, say 0.71, the null hypothesis is not rejected. It is reasoned that such a small computed value could be attributed to chance, that is, sampling error. As we have emphasized, only one of two decisions is possible in hypothesis testing—either reject or do not reject the null hypothesis.

However, because the decision is based on a sample, it is always possible to make either of two decision errors. It is possible to make a Type I error when the null hypothesis is rejected when it should not be rejected. Or it is also possible to make a Type II error when the null hypothesis is not rejected and it should have been rejected. Fortunately, we select the probability of making a Type I error, α (alpha), and we can compute the probabilities associated with a Type II error, β (beta).

Step 6: Interpret the Result

The final step in the hypothesis testing procedure is to interpret the results. The process does not end with the value of a sample statistic or the decision to reject or not reject the null hypothesis. What can we say or report based on the results of the statistical test? Here are two examples:

- An investigative reporter for a Colorado newspaper reports that the mean monthly income of convenience stores in the state is \$130,000. You decide to conduct a test of hypothesis to verify the report. The null hypothesis and the alternate hypothesis are:

  $$H_0: \mu = \$130{,}000$$
  $$H_1: \mu \neq \$130{,}000$$

  A sample of convenience stores provides a sample mean and standard deviation, and you compute a z statistic. The results of the hypothesis test result in a decision to not reject the null hypothesis. How do you interpret the result? Be cautious with

STATISTICS IN ACTION

LASIK is a 15-minute surgical procedure that uses a laser to reshape an eye's cornea with the goal of improving eyesight. Research shows that about 5% of all surgeries involve complications such as glare, corneal haze, overcorrection or undercorrection of vision, and loss of vision. In a statistical sense, the research tests a null hypothesis that the surgery will not improve eyesight with the alternative hypothesis that the surgery will improve eyesight. The sample data of LASIK surgery shows that 5% of all cases result in complications. The 5% represents a Type I error rate. When a person decides to have the surgery, he or she expects to reject the null hypothesis. In 5% of future cases, this expectation will not be met. (Source: *American Academy of Ophthalmology Journal*, Vol. 16, no. 43.)

your interpretation because by not rejecting the null hypothesis, you did not prove the null hypothesis to be true. Based on the sample data, the difference between the sample mean and hypothesized population mean was not large enough to reject the null hypothesis.

- In a recent speech to students, the dean of the College of Business reported that the mean credit card debt for college students is \$3,000. You decide to conduct a test of the dean's statement or hypothesis to investigate the statement's truth. The null hypothesis and the alternate hypothesis are:

$$H_0: \mu = \$3,000$$
$$H_1: \mu \neq \$3,000$$

A random sample of college students provides a sample mean and standard deviation, and you compute a *z* statistic. The hypothesis test results in a decision to reject the null hypothesis. How do you interpret the result? The sample evidence does not support the dean's statement. Based on the sample data, the mean amount of student credit card debt is different from \$3,000. You have disproved the null hypothesis with a stated probability of a Type I error, α. That is, there is a small probability that the decision to reject the null hypothesis was an error due to random sampling.

SUMMARY OF THE STEPS IN HYPOTHESIS TESTING

1. Establish the null hypothesis (H_0) and the alternate hypothesis (H_1).
2. Select the level of significance, that is, α.
3. Select an appropriate test statistic.
4. Formulate a decision rule based on steps 1, 2, and 3 above.
5. Make a decision regarding the null hypothesis based on the sample information.
6. Interpret the results of the test.

Before actually conducting a test of hypothesis, we describe the difference between a one-tailed and a two-tailed hypothesis test.

LO10-3 Distinguish between a one-tailed and a two-tailed test of hypothesis.

ONE-TAILED AND TWO-TAILED HYPOTHESIS TESTS

Refer to Chart 10–1. It shows a one-tailed test. It is called a one-tailed test because the rejection region is only in one tail of the curve. In this case, it is in the right, or upper, tail of the curve. To illustrate, suppose that the packaging department at General Foods Corporation is concerned that some boxes of Grape Nuts are significantly overweight. The cereal is packaged in 453-gram boxes, so the null hypothesis is $H_0: \mu \leq 453$. This is read, "the population mean (μ) is equal to or less than 453." The alternate hypothesis is, therefore, $H_1: \mu > 453$. This is read, "μ is greater than 453." Note that the inequality sign in the alternate hypothesis (>) points to the region of rejection in the upper tail. (See Chart 10–1.) Also observe that the null hypothesis includes the equal sign. That is, $H_0: \mu \leq 453$. The equality condition always appears in H_0, never in H_1.

Chart 10–2 portrays a situation where the rejection region is in the left (lower) tail of the standard normal distribution. As an illustration, consider the problem of automobile manufacturers, large automobile leasing companies, and other organizations that purchase large quantities of tires. They want the tires to average, say, 60,000 miles of wear under normal usage. They will, therefore, reject a shipment of tires if tests reveal that the mean life of the tires is significantly below 60,000 miles. They gladly accept a shipment if the mean life is greater than 60,000 miles! They are not concerned with this possibility, however. They are concerned only if they have sample evidence to conclude

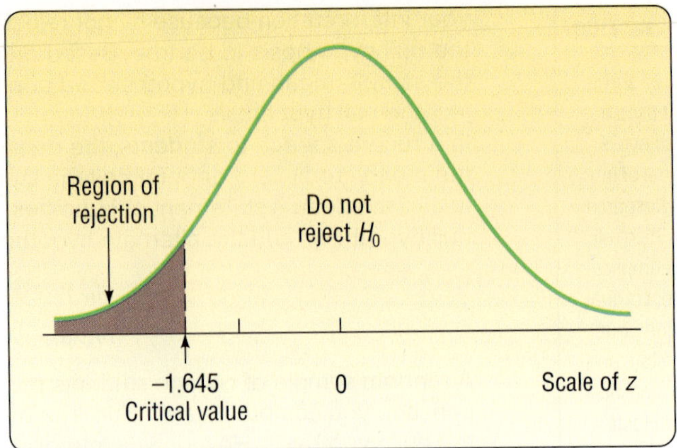

CHART 10–2 Sampling Distribution for the Statistic z, Left-Tailed Test, .05 Level of Significance

that the tires will average less than 60,000 miles of useful life. Thus, the test is set up to satisfy the concern of the automobile manufacturers that *the mean life of the tires is not less than 60,000 miles.* This statement appears in the null hypothesis. The null and alternate hypotheses in this case are written H_0: $\mu \geq 60{,}000$ and H_1: $\mu < 60{,}000$.

One way to determine the location of the rejection region is to look at the direction in which the inequality sign in the alternate hypothesis is pointing (either < or >). In the tire wear problem, it is pointing to the left, and the rejection region is therefore in the left tail.

In summary, a test is *one-tailed* when the alternate hypothesis, H_1, states a direction, such as:

H_0: The mean income of female stockbrokers is *less than or equal to* \$65,000 per year.
H_1: The mean income of female stockbrokers is *greater than* \$65,000 per year.

If no direction is specified in the alternate hypothesis, we use a *two-tailed* test. Changing the previous problem to illustrate, we can say:

H_0: The mean income of female stockbrokers is \$65,000 per year.
H_1: The mean income of female stockbrokers is *not equal to* \$65,000 per year.

If the null hypothesis is rejected and H_1 accepted in the two-tailed case, the mean income could be significantly greater than \$65,000 per year or it could be significantly less than \$65,000 per year. To accommodate these two possibilities, the 5% area of rejection is divided equally into the two tails of the sampling distribution (2.5% each). Chart 10–3 shows the two areas and the critical values. Note that the total area in the normal distribution is 1.0000, found by .9500 + .0250 + .0250.

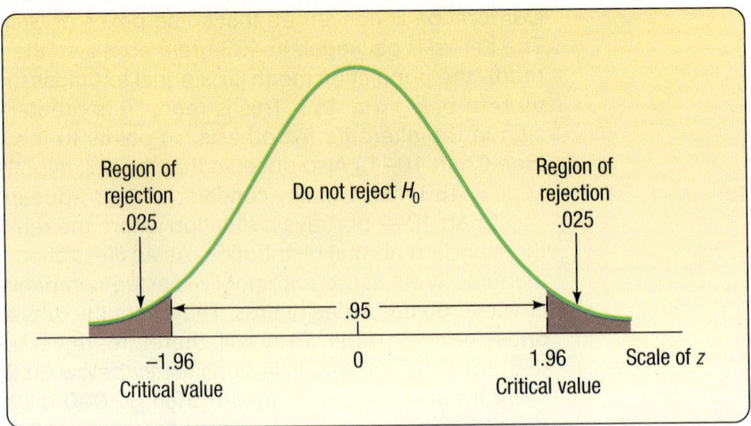

CHART 10–3 Regions of Nonrejection and Rejection for a Two-Tailed Test, .05 Level of Significance

LO10-4
Conduct a test of a hypothesis about a population mean.

HYPOTHESIS TESTING FOR A POPULATION MEAN: KNOWN POPULATION STANDARD DEVIATION

A Two-Tailed Test

An example will show the details of the six-step hypothesis testing procedure. We also wish to use a two-tailed test. That is, we are *not* concerned whether the sample results are larger or smaller than the proposed population mean. Rather, we are interested in whether it is *different from* the proposed value for the population mean. We begin, as we did in the previous chapter, with a situation in which we have historical information about the population and in fact know its standard deviation.

EXAMPLE

Jamestown Steel Company manufactures and assembles desks and other office equipment at several plants in western New York State. The weekly production of the Model A325 desk at the Fredonia Plant follows a normal probability distribution with a mean of 200 and a standard deviation of 16. Recently, because of market expansion, new production methods have been introduced and new employees hired. The vice president of manufacturing would like to investigate whether there has been a *change* in the weekly production of the Model A325 desk. Is the mean number of desks produced at the Fredonia Plant *different from* 200 at the .01 significance level?

© Robert Nicholas/Getty Images

SOLUTION

In this example, we know two important pieces of information: (1) the population of weekly production follows the normal distribution and (2) the standard deviation of this normal distribution is 16 desks per week. So it is appropriate to use the z statistic. We use the statistical hypothesis testing procedure to investigate whether the production rate has changed from 200 per week.

Step 1: State the null hypothesis and the alternate hypothesis. The null hypothesis is "The population mean is 200." The alternate hypothesis is "The mean is different from 200" or "The mean is not 200." These two hypotheses are written:

$$H_0: \mu = 200$$

$$H_1: \mu \neq 200$$

This is a *two-tailed test* because the alternate hypothesis does not state a direction. In other words, it does not state whether the mean production is greater than 200 or less than 200. The vice president wants only to find out whether the production rate is different from 200.

Before moving to Step 2, we wish to emphasize two points.

- The null hypothesis has the equal sign. Why? Because the value we are testing is always in the null hypothesis. Logically, the alternate hypothesis never contains the equal sign.
- Both the null hypothesis and the alternate hypothesis contain Greek letters—in this case μ, which is the symbol for the population mean. Tests of hypothesis **always** refer to population parameters, never to sample statistics. To put it another way, you will never see the symbol $\bar{x}$ as part of the null hypothesis or the alternate hypothesis.

Step 2: Select the level of significance. In the example description, the significance level selected is .01. This is α, the probability of committing a Type I error, and it is the probability of rejecting a true null hypothesis.

Step 3: Select the test statistic. The test statistic is z when the population standard deviation is known. Transforming the production data to standard units (z values) permits their use not only in this problem but also in other hypothesis-testing problems. Formula (10–1) for z is repeated next with the various letters identified.

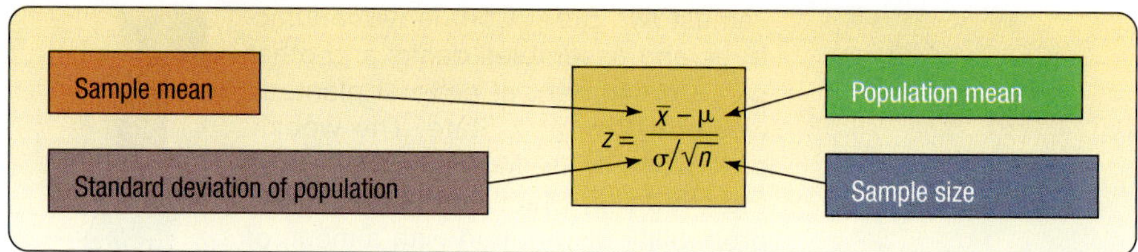

Step 4: Formulate the decision rule. We formulate the decision rule by first determining the critical values of z. Because this is a two-tailed test, half of .01, or .005, is placed in each tail. The area where H_0 is not rejected, located between the two tails, is therefore .99. Using the Student's t Distribution table in Appendix B.5, move to the top margin called "Level of Significance for Two-Tailed Tests, α," select the column with $\alpha = .01$, and move to the last row, which is labeled ∞, or infinite degrees of freedom. The z value in this cell is 2.576. For your convenience, Appendix B.5, Student's t Distribution, is repeated in the inside back cover. All the facets of this problem are shown in the diagram in Chart 10–4.

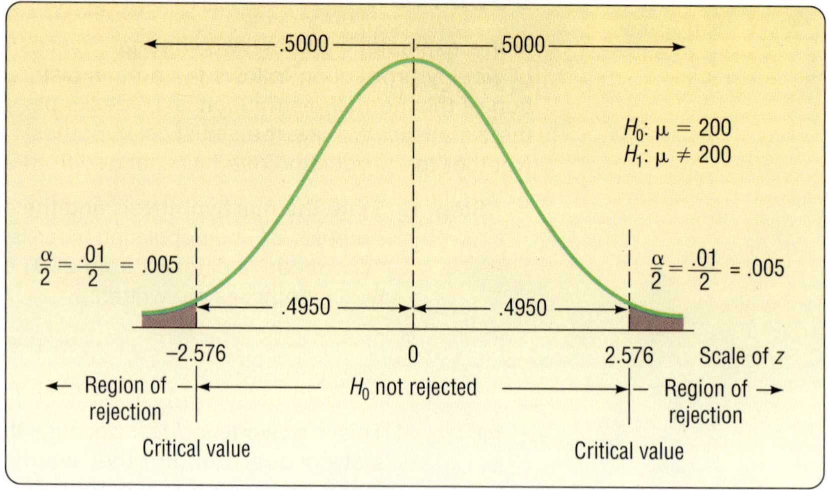

CHART 10–4 Decision Rule for the .01 Significance Level

The decision rule is: if the computed value of z is not between −2.576 and 2.576, reject the null hypothesis. If z falls between −2.576 and 2.576, do not reject the null hypothesis.

Step 5: Make a decision. Take a sample from the population (weekly production), compute a test statistic, apply the decision rule, and arrive at a decision to reject H_0 or not to reject H_0. The mean number of desks produced last year (50 weeks because the plant was shut down 2 weeks for vacation) is 203.5. The standard deviation of the population is 16 desks per week. Computing the z value from formula (10–1):

$$z = \frac{\bar{x} - \mu}{\sigma/\sqrt{n}} = \frac{203.5 - 200}{16/\sqrt{50}} = 1.547$$

Because 1.547 is between −2.576 and 2.576, we decide not to reject H_0.

Step 6: Interpret the result. We did not reject the null hypothesis, so we have failed to show that the population mean has changed from 200 per week. To put it another way, the difference between the population mean of 200 per week and the sample mean of 203.5 could simply be due to chance. What should we tell the vice president? The sample information fails to indicate that the new production methods resulted in a change in the 200-desks-per-week production rate.

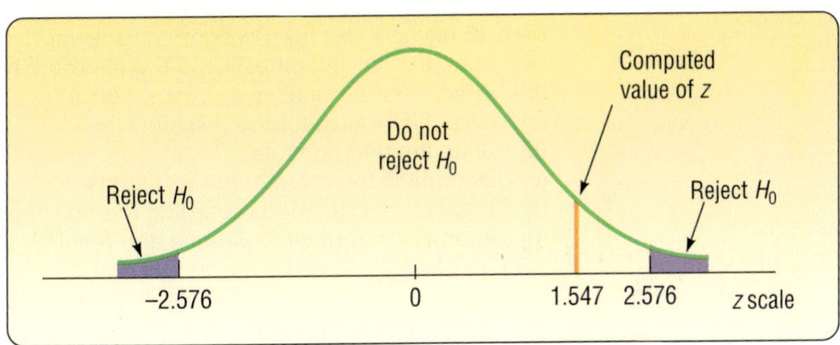

Did we prove that the assembly rate is still 200 per week? Not really. *We failed to disprove the null hypothesis.* Failing to disprove the hypothesis that the population mean is 200 is not the same thing as proving it to be true. For example, in the U.S. judicial system, a person is presumed innocent until proven guilty. The trial starts with a null hypothesis that the individual is innocent. If the individual is acquitted, the trial did not provide enough evidence to reject the presumption of innocence and conclude that the individual was not innocent or guilty as charged. That is what we do in statistical hypothesis testing when we do not reject the null hypothesis. The correct interpretation is that, based on the evidence or sample information, we have failed to disprove the null hypothesis.

We selected the significance level, .01 in this case, before setting up the decision rule and sampling the population. This is the appropriate strategy. The significance level should be set by the investigator, but it should be determined *before* gathering the sample evidence and not changed based on the sample evidence.

How does the hypothesis testing procedure just described compare with that of confidence intervals discussed in the previous chapter? When we conducted the test of hypothesis regarding the production of desks, we changed the units from desks per week to a z value. Then we compared the computed value of the test statistic (1.547) to that of the critical values (−2.576 and 2.576). Because the computed value of the test statistic was in the region where the null hypothesis was not rejected, we concluded that the population mean could be 200. To use the confidence interval approach, on the other hand, we would develop a confidence interval, based on formula (9–1). See page 287. The interval would be from 197.671 to 209.329, found by $203.5 \pm 2.576(16/\sqrt{50})$. Note that the proposed population value, 200, is within this interval. Hence, we would conclude that the population mean could reasonably be 200.

In general, H_0 is rejected if the confidence interval does not include the hypothesized value. If the confidence interval includes the hypothesized value, then H_0 is not rejected. So the "do not reject region" for a test of hypothesis is equivalent to the proposed population value occurring in the confidence interval.

SELF-REVIEW 10–1

Heinz, a manufacturer of ketchup, uses a particular machine to dispense 16 ounces of its ketchup into containers. From many years of experience with the particular dispensing machine, Heinz knows the amount of product in each container follows a normal distribution with a mean of 16 ounces and a standard deviation of 0.15 ounce. A sample of 50 containers filled last hour revealed the mean amount per container was 16.017 ounces. Does this evidence suggest that the mean amount dispensed is different from 16 ounces? Use the .05 significance level.

© Kevin Lorenzi/Bloomberg/Getty Images

(a) State the null hypothesis and the alternate hypothesis.
(b) What is the probability of a Type I error?
(c) Give the formula for the test statistic.
(d) State the decision rule.
(e) Determine the value of the test statistic.
(f) What is your decision regarding the null hypothesis?
(g) Interpret, in a single sentence, the result of the statistical test.

A One-Tailed Test

In the previous example/solution, we emphasized that we were concerned only with reporting to the vice president whether there had been a change in the mean number of desks assembled at the Fredonia Plant. We were not concerned with whether the change was an increase or a decrease in the production.

To illustrate a one-tailed test, let's change the problem. Suppose the vice president wants to know whether there has been an *increase* in the number of units assembled. Can we conclude, because of the improved production methods, that the mean number of desks assembled in the last 50 weeks was more than 200? Look at the difference in the way the problem is formulated. In the first case, we wanted to know whether there was a *difference* in the mean number assembled, but now we want to know whether there has been an *increase*. Because we are investigating different questions, we will set our hypotheses differently. The biggest difference occurs in the alternate hypothesis. Before, we stated the alternate hypothesis as "different from"; now we want to state it as "greater than." In symbols:

A two-tailed test:	A one-tailed test:
H_0: $\mu = 200$	H_0: $\mu \leq 200$
H_1: $\mu \neq 200$	H_1: $\mu > 200$

The critical values for a one-tailed test are different from a two-tailed test at the same significance level. In the previous example/solution, we split the significance level in half and put half in the lower tail and half in the upper tail. In a one-tailed test, we put all the rejection region in one tail. See Chart 10–5.

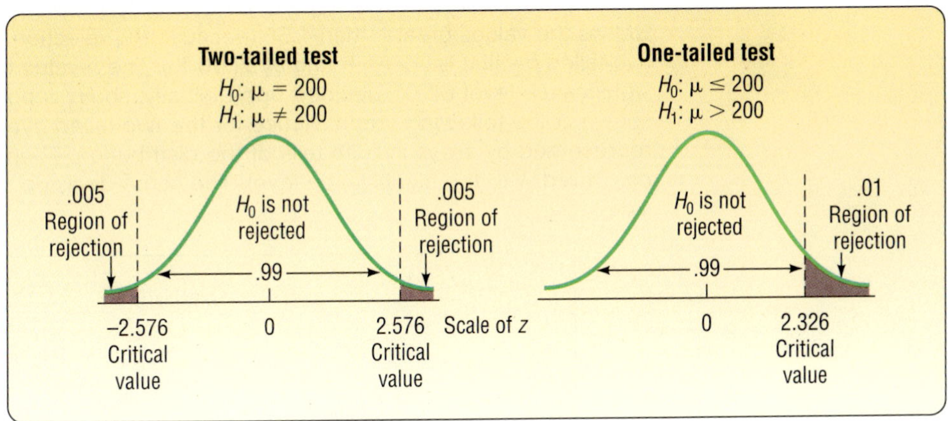

CHART 10–5 Rejection Regions for Two-Tailed and One-Tailed Tests, $\alpha = .01$

For the one-tailed test, the critical value of z is 2.326. Using the Student's t Distribution table in Appendix B.5, move to the top heading called "Level of Significance for One-Tailed Tests, α," select the column with $\alpha = .01$, and move to the last row, which is labeled ∞, or infinite degrees of freedom. The z value in this cell is 2.326.

LO10-5
Compute and interpret a *p*-value.

p-VALUE IN HYPOTHESIS TESTING

In testing a hypothesis, we compare the test statistic to a critical value. A decision is made to either reject or not reject the null hypothesis. So, for example, if the critical value is 1.96 and the computed value of the test statistic is 2.19, the decision is to reject the null hypothesis.

In recent years, spurred by the availability of computer software, additional information is often reported on the strength of the rejection. That is, how confident are we in rejecting the null hypothesis? This approach reports the probability (assuming that the null hypothesis is true) of getting a value of the test statistic at least as extreme as the value actually obtained. This process compares the probability, called the ***p*-value,** with the significance level. If the *p*-value is smaller than the significance level, H_0 is rejected. If it is larger than the significance level, H_0 is not rejected.

STATISTICS IN ACTION

There is a difference between *statistically significant* and *practically significant.* To explain, suppose we develop a new diet pill and test it on 100,000 people. We conclude that the typical person taking the pill for 2 years lost 1 pound. Do you think many people would be interested in taking the pill to lose 1 pound? The results of using the new pill were statistically significant but not practically significant.

***p*-VALUE** The probability of observing a sample value as extreme as, or more extreme than, the value observed, given that the null hypothesis is true.

Determining the *p*-value not only results in a decision regarding H_0, but it gives us additional insight into the strength of the decision. A very small *p*-value, such as .0001, indicates that there is little likelihood the H_0 is true. On the other hand, a *p*-value of .2033 means that H_0 is not rejected, and there is little likelihood that it is false.

How do we find the *p*-value? To calculate *p*-values, we will need to use the z table (Appendix B.3) and, to use this table, we will round z test statistics to two decimals. To illustrate how to compute a *p*-value, we will use the example where we tested the null hypothesis that the mean number of desks produced per week at Fredonia was 200.

We did not reject the null hypothesis because the computed z test statistic of 1.547 fell in the region between −2.576 and 2.576. We agreed not to reject the null hypothesis if the z test statistic fell in this region. Rounding 1.547 to 1.55 and using the z table, the probability of finding a z value of 1.55 or more is .0606, found by .5000 − .4394. To put it another way, the probability of obtaining an $\bar{x}$ greater than 203.5 if $\mu = 200$ is .0606. To compute the p-value, we need to be concerned with the region less than −1.55 as well as the values greater than 1.55 (because the rejection region is in both tails). The two-tailed p-value is .1212, found by 2(.0606). The p-value of .1212 is greater than the significance level of .01 decided upon initially, so H_0 is not rejected. The details are shown in the following graph. Notice for the two-tailed hypothesis test, the p-value is represented by areas in both tails of the distribution. Then the p-value can easily be compared with the significance level. The same decision rule is used as in the one-sided test.

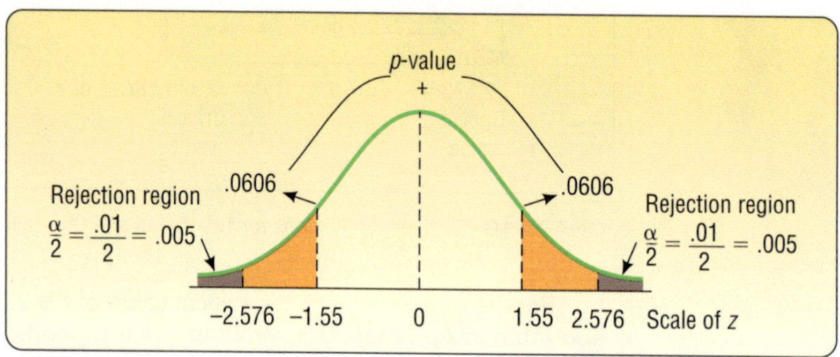

A p-value is a way to express the likelihood that H_0 is false. But how do we interpret a p-value? We have already said that if the p-value is less than the significance level, then we reject H_0; if it is greater than the significance level, then we do not reject H_0. Also, if the p-value is very large, then it is likely that H_0 is true. If the p-value is small, then it is likely that H_0 is not true. The following box will help to interpret p-values.

INTERPRETING THE WEIGHT OF EVIDENCE AGAINST H_0

If the p-value is less than

(a) .10, we have *some* evidence that H_0 is not true.
(b) .05, we have *strong* evidence that H_0 is not true.
(c) .01, we have *very strong* evidence that H_0 is not true.
(d) .001, we have *extremely strong* evidence that H_0 is not true.

SELF-REVIEW 10–2

Refer to Self-Review 10–1.

(a) Suppose the next to the last sentence is changed to read: Does this evidence suggest that the mean amount dispensed is *more than* 16 ounces? State the null hypothesis and the alternate hypothesis under these conditions.
(b) What is the decision rule under the new conditions stated in part (a)?
(c) A second sample of 50 filled containers revealed the mean to be 16.040 ounces. What is the value of the test statistic for this sample?
(d) What is your decision regarding the null hypothesis?
(e) Interpret, in a single sentence, the result of the statistical test.
(f) What is the p-value? What is your decision regarding the null hypothesis based on the p-value? Is this the same conclusion reached in part (d)?

EXERCISES

For Exercises 1–4, answer the questions: (a) Is this a one- or two-tailed test? (b) What is the decision rule? (c) What is the value of the test statistic? (d) What is your decision regarding H_0? (e) What is the *p*-value? Interpret it.

1. A sample of 36 observations is selected from a normal population. The sample mean is 49, and the population standard deviation is 5. Conduct the following test of hypothesis using the .05 significance level.

$$H_0: \mu = 50$$
$$H_1: \mu \neq 50$$

2. A sample of 36 observations is selected from a normal population. The sample mean is 12, and the population standard deviation is 3. Conduct the following test of hypothesis using the .01 significance level.

$$H_0: \mu \leq 10$$
$$H_1: \mu > 10$$

3. A sample of 36 observations is selected from a normal population. The sample mean is 21, and the population standard deviation is 5. Conduct the following test of hypothesis using the .05 significance level.

$$H_0: \mu \leq 20$$
$$H_1: \mu > 20$$

4. A sample of 64 observations is selected from a normal population. The sample mean is 215, and the population standard deviation is 15. Conduct the following test of hypothesis using the .025 significance level.

$$H_0: \mu \geq 220$$
$$H_1: \mu < 220$$

For Exercises 5–8: (a) State the null hypothesis and the alternate hypothesis. (b) State the decision rule. (c) Compute the value of the test statistic. (d) What is your decision regarding H_0? (e) What is the *p*-value? Interpret it.

5. The manufacturer of the X-15 steel-belted radial truck tire claims that the mean mileage the tire can be driven before the tread wears out is 60,000 miles. Assume the mileage wear follows the normal distribution and the standard deviation of the distribution is 5,000 miles. Crosset Truck Company bought 48 tires and found that the mean mileage for its trucks is 59,500 miles. Is Crosset's experience different from that claimed by the manufacturer at the .05 significance level?
6. The waiting time for customers at MacBurger Restaurants follows a normal distribution with a population standard deviation of 1 minute. At the Warren Road MacBurger, the quality-assurance department sampled 50 customers and found that the mean waiting time was 2.75 minutes. At the .05 significance level, can we conclude that the mean waiting time is less than 3 minutes?
7. A recent national survey found that high school students watched an average (mean) of 6.8 movies per month with a population standard deviation of 1.8. The distribution of number of movies watched per month follows the normal distribution. A random sample of 36 college students revealed that the mean number of movies watched last month was 6.2. At the .05 significance level, can we conclude that college students watch fewer movies a month than high school students?
8. At the time she was hired as a server at the Grumney Family Restaurant, Beth Brigden was told, "You can average $80 a day in tips." Assume the population of daily tips is normally distributed with a standard deviation of $9.95. Over the first 35 days she was employed at the restaurant, the mean daily amount of her tips was $84.85. At the .01 significance level, can Ms. Brigden conclude that her daily tips average more than $80?

LO10-6
Use a t statistic to test a hypothesis.

HYPOTHESIS TESTING FOR A POPULATION MEAN: POPULATION STANDARD DEVIATION UNKNOWN

In the preceding example, we knew σ, the population standard deviation, and that the population followed the normal distribution. In most cases, however, the population standard deviation is unknown. Thus, σ must be based on prior studies or estimated by the sample standard deviation, s. The population standard deviation in the following example is not known, so the sample standard deviation is used to estimate σ.

To find the value of the test statistic, we use the t distribution and revise formula (10–1) as follows:

TESTING A MEAN, σ UNKNOWN

$$t = \frac{\bar{x} - \mu}{s/\sqrt{n}} \qquad \textbf{(10–2)}$$

with $n - 1$ degrees of freedom, where:

$\bar{x}$ is the sample mean.
μ is the hypothesized population mean.
s is the sample standard deviation.
n is the number of observations in the sample.

We encountered this same situation when constructing confidence intervals in the previous chapter. See pages 292–294 in Chapter 9. We summarized this problem in Chart 9–3 on page 294. Under these conditions, the correct statistical procedure is to replace the standard normal distribution with the t distribution. To review, the major characteristics of the t distribution are:

- It is a continuous distribution.
- It is bell-shaped and symmetrical.
- There is a family of t distributions. Each time the degrees of freedom change, a new distribution is created.
- As the number of degrees of freedom increases, the shape of the t distribution approaches that of the standard normal distribution.
- The t distribution is flatter, or more spread out, than the standard normal distribution.

The following example/solution shows the details.

EXAMPLE

The McFarland Insurance Company Claims Department reports the mean cost to process a claim is \$60. An industry comparison showed this amount to be larger than most other insurance companies, so the company instituted cost-cutting measures. To evaluate the effect of the cost-cutting measures, the supervisor of the Claims Department selected a random sample of 26 claims processed last month and recorded the cost to process each claim. The sample information is reported below.

\$45	\$49	\$62	\$40	\$43	\$61
48	53	67	63	78	64
48	54	51	56	63	69
58	51	58	59	56	57
38	76				

At the .01 significance level, is it reasonable to conclude that the mean cost to process a claim is now less than \$60?

SOLUTION

We will use the six-step hypothesis testing procedure.

Step 1: State the null hypothesis and the alternate hypothesis. The null hypothesis is that the population mean is at least \$60. The alternate hypothesis is that the population mean is less than \$60. We can express the null and alternate hypotheses as follows:

$$H_0: \mu \geq \$60$$

$$H_1: \mu < \$60$$

The test is *one*-tailed because we want to determine whether there has been a *reduction* in the cost. The inequality in the alternate hypothesis points to the region of rejection in the left tail of the distribution.

Step 2: Select the level of significance. We decided on the .01 significance level.

Step 3: Select the test statistic. The test statistic in this situation is the *t* distribution. Why? First, it is reasonable to conclude that the distribution of the cost per claim follows the normal distribution. We can confirm this from the histogram in the center of the following Minitab output. Observe the normal distribution superimposed on the frequency distribution.

We do not know the standard deviation of the population. So we substitute the sample standard deviation. The value of the test statistic is computed by formula (10–2):

$$t = \frac{\bar{x} - \mu}{s/\sqrt{n}}$$

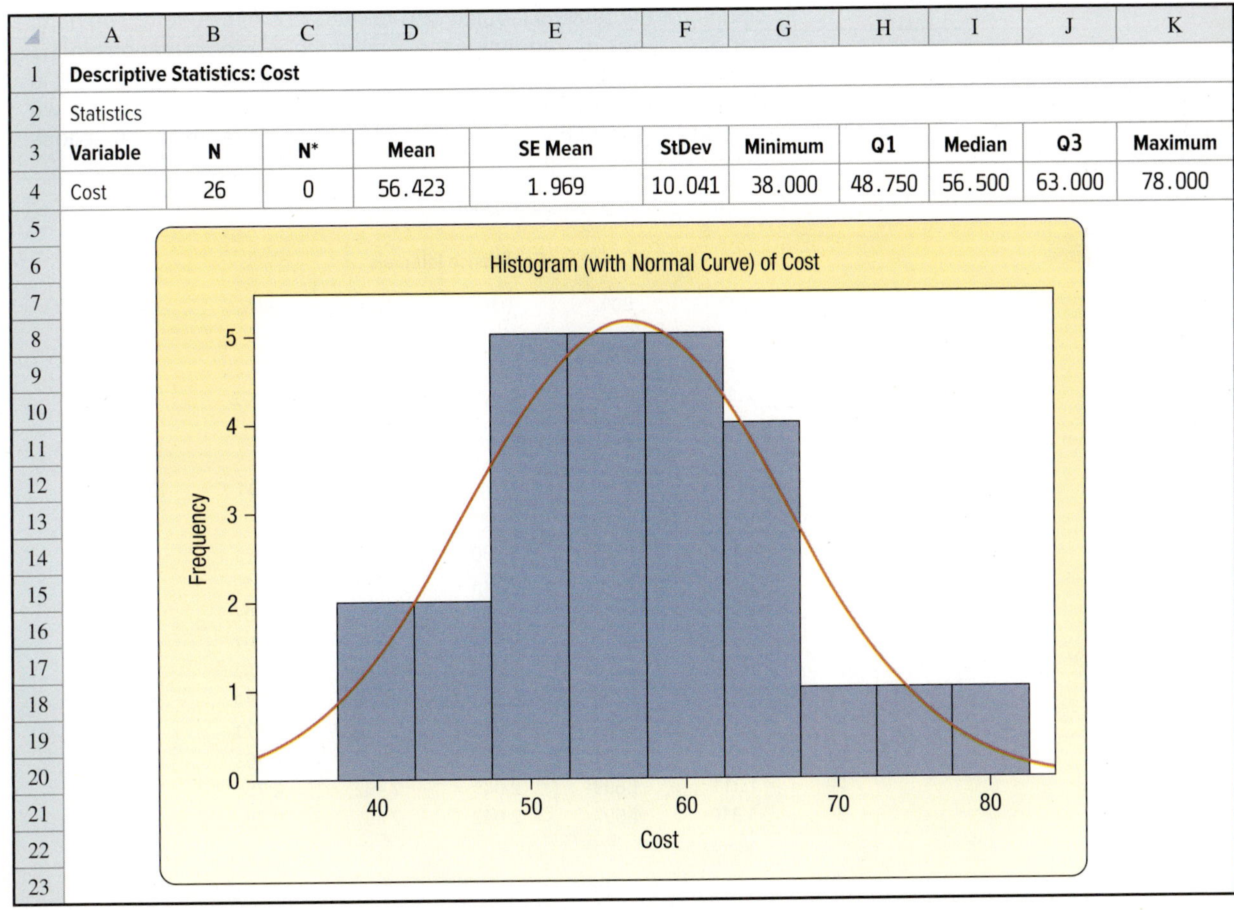

Descriptive Statistics: Cost

Statistics

Variable	N	N*	Mean	SE Mean	StDev	Minimum	Q1	Median	Q3	Maximum
Cost	26	0	56.423	1.969	10.041	38.000	48.750	56.500	63.000	78.000

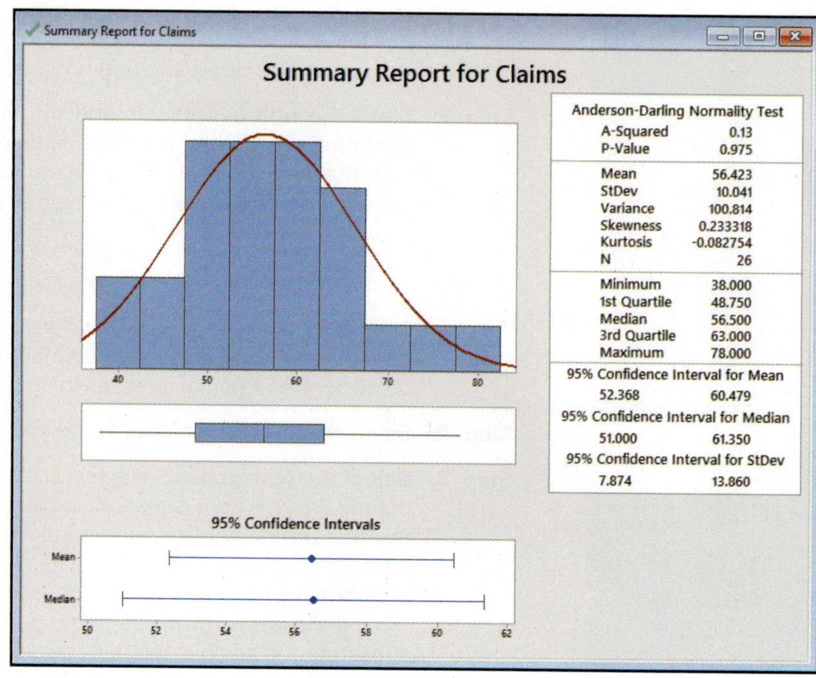

Step 4: Formulate the decision rule. The critical values of t are given in Appendix B.5, a portion of which is shown in Table 10–1. Appendix B.5 is also repeated in the back inside cover of the text. The far left column of the table is labeled "*df*" for degrees of freedom. The number of degrees of freedom is the total number of observations in the sample minus the number of populations sampled, written $n - 1$. In this case, the number of observations in the sample is 26, and we sampled 1 population, so there are $26 - 1 = 25$ degrees of freedom.

TABLE 10–1 A Portion of the *t* Distribution Table

	Confidence Intervals					
	80%	90%	95%	98%	99%	99.9%
	Level of Significance for One-Tailed Test, α					
df	0.10	0.05	0.025	0.01	0.005	0.0005
	Level of Significance for Two-Tailed Test, α					
	0.20	0.10	0.05	0.02	0.01	0.001
⋮	⋮	⋮	⋮	⋮	⋮	⋮
21	1.323	1.721	2.080	2.518	2.831	3.819
22	1.321	1.717	2.074	2.508	2.819	3.792
23	1.319	1.714	2.069	2.500	2.807	3.768
24	1.318	1.711	2.064	2.492	2.797	3.745
25	1.316	1.708	2.060	2.485	2.787	3.725
26	1.315	1.706	2.056	2.479	2.779	3.707
27	1.314	1.703	2.052	2.473	2.771	3.690
28	1.313	1.701	2.048	2.467	2.763	3.674
29	1.311	1.699	2.045	2.462	2.756	3.659
30	1.310	1.697	2.042	2.457	2.750	3.646

To find the critical value, first locate the row with the appropriate degrees of freedom. This row is shaded in Table 10–1. Next, determine whether the test is one-tailed or two-tailed. In this case, we have a one-tailed test, so find the portion of the table that is labeled "one-tailed." Locate the column with the selected significance level. In this example, the significance level is .01. Move down the column labeled "0.01" until it intersects the row with 25 degrees of freedom. The value is 2.485. Because this is a one-sided test and the rejection region is in the left tail, the critical value is negative. The decision rule is to reject H_0 if the value of t is less than −2.485.

Step 5: Make a decision. From the Minitab output, the mean cost per claim for the sample of 26 observations is \$56.423. The standard deviation of this sample is \$10.041. We insert these values in formula (10–2) and compute the value of t:

$$t = \frac{\overline{x} - \mu}{s/\sqrt{n}} = \frac{\$56.423 - \$60}{\$10.041/\sqrt{26}} = -1.816$$

Because −1.816 lies in the region to the right of the critical value of −2.485 (see Chart 10–6), the null hypothesis is not rejected at the .01 significance level.

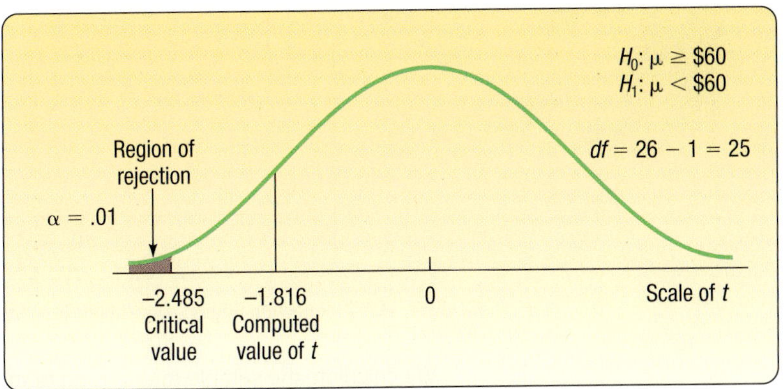

CHART 10–6 Rejection Region, *t* Distribution, .01 Significance Level

Step 6: Interpret the result. We have not disproved the null hypothesis. The sample of claims could have been selected from a population with a mean cost of \$60 per claim. To put it another way, the difference of \$3.577 (\$56.423 – \$60.00) between the sample mean and the population mean could be due to sampling error. The test results do not allow the claims department manager to conclude that the cost-cutting measures have been effective.

In the previous example, the mean and the standard deviation were computed using Minitab. The following example/solution shows the details when the sample mean and sample standard deviation are calculated from sample data.

EXAMPLE

The Myrtle Beach International Airport provides a cell phone parking lot where people can wait for a message to pick up arriving passengers. To decide if the cell phone lot has enough parking places, the manager of airport parking needs to know if the mean time in the lot is more than 15 minutes. A sample of 12 recent customers showed they were in the lot the following lengths of time, in minutes.

30	24	28	22	14	2	39	23	23	28	12	31

At the .05 significance level, is it reasonable to conclude that the mean time in the lot is more than 15 minutes?

SOLUTION

We begin by stating the null hypothesis and the alternate hypothesis. In this case, the question is whether the population mean could be more than 15 minutes. So this is a one-tailed test. We state the two hypotheses as follows:

$$H_0: \mu \leq 15$$

$$H_1: \mu > 15$$

There are 11 degrees of freedom, found by $n - 1 = 12 - 1 = 11$. The critical t value is 1.796, found by referring to Appendix B.5 for a one-tailed test, using $\alpha = .05$ with 11 degrees of freedom. The decision rule is: Reject the null hypothesis if the computed t is greater than 1.796. This information is summarized in Chart 10–7.

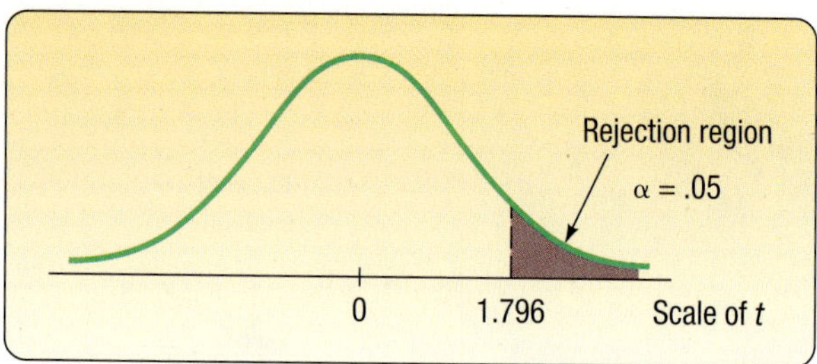

CHART 10–7 Rejection Region, One-Tailed Test, Student's t Distribution, $\alpha = .05$

We calculate the sample mean using formula (3–2) and the sample standard deviation using formula (3–8). The sample mean is 23 minutes, and the sample standard deviation is 9.835 minutes. The details of the calculations are shown in Table 10–2.

TABLE 10–2 Calculations of Sample Mean and Standard Deviation Parking Times

Customer	x, Minutes	$(x - \bar{x})^2$
Chmura	30	49
Will	24	1
Crompton	28	25
Craver	22	1
Cao	14	81
Nowlin	2	441
Esposito	39	256
Colvard	23	0
Hoefle	23	0
Lawler	28	25
Trask	12	121
Grullon	31	64
Total	276	1064

$$\bar{x} = \frac{\Sigma x}{n} = \frac{276}{12} = 23$$

$$s = \sqrt{\frac{\Sigma(x - \bar{x})^2}{n - 1}} = \sqrt{\frac{1064}{12 - 1}} = 9.835$$

Now we are ready to compute the value of t, using formula (10–2).

$$t = \frac{\bar{x} - \mu}{s/\sqrt{n}} = \frac{23 - 15}{9.835/\sqrt{12}} = 2.818$$

The null hypothesis that the population mean is less than or equal to 15 minutes is rejected because the computed t value of 2.818 lies in the area to the right of 1.796. We conclude that the time customers spend in the lot is more than 15 minutes. This result indicates that the airport may need to add more parking places.

SELF-REVIEW 10–3

The mean life of a battery used in a digital clock is 305 days. The lives of the batteries follow the normal distribution. The battery was recently modified to last longer. A sample of 20 of the modified batteries had a mean life of 311 days with a standard deviation of 12 days. Did the modification increase the mean life of the battery?

(a) State the null hypothesis and the alternate hypothesis.

(b) Show the decision rule graphically. Use the .05 significance level.

(c) Compute the value of t. What is your decision regarding the null hypothesis? Briefly summarize your results.

EXERCISES

9. Given the following hypotheses:

$$H_0: \mu \leq 10$$
$$H_1: \mu > 10$$

A random sample of 10 observations is selected from a normal population. The sample mean was 12 and the sample standard deviation 3. Using the .05 significance level:

a. State the decision rule.

b. Compute the value of the test statistic.

c. What is your decision regarding the null hypothesis?

10. Given the following hypotheses:

$$H_0: \mu = 400$$
$$H_1: \mu \neq 400$$

A random sample of 12 observations is selected from a normal population. The sample mean was 407 and the sample standard deviation 6. Using the .01 significance level:

a. State the decision rule.

b. Compute the value of the test statistic.

c. What is your decision regarding the null hypothesis?

11. The Rocky Mountain district sales manager of Rath Publishing Inc., a college textbook publishing company, claims that the sales representatives make an average of 40 sales calls per week on professors. Several reps say that this estimate is too low. To investigate, a random sample of 28 sales representatives reveals that the mean number of calls made last week was 42. The standard deviation of the sample is 2.1 calls. Using the .05 significance level, can we conclude that the mean number of calls per salesperson per week is more than 40?

12. The management of White Industries is considering a new method of assembling its golf cart. The present method requires a mean time of 42.3 minutes to assemble a cart. The mean assembly time for a random sample of 24 carts, using the new method, was 40.6 minutes, and the standard deviation of the sample was 2.7 minutes. Using the .10 level of significance, can we conclude that the assembly time using the new method is faster?

13. The mean income per person in the United States is $50,000, and the distribution of incomes follows a normal distribution. A random sample of 10 residents of Wilmington, Delaware, had a mean of $60,000 with a standard deviation of $10,000. At the .05 level of significance, is that enough evidence to conclude that residents of Wilmington, Delaware, have more income than the national average?

14. **FILE** Most air travelers now use e-tickets. Electronic ticketing allows passengers to not worry about a paper ticket, and it costs the airline companies less to handle than paper ticketing. However, in recent times the airlines have received complaints from passengers regarding their e-tickets, particularly when connecting flights and a change of airlines were involved. To investigate the problem, an independent watchdog agency contacted a random sample of 20 airports and collected information on the number of complaints the airport had with e-tickets for the month of March. The information is reported below.

14	14	16	12	12	14	13	16	15	14
12	15	15	14	13	13	12	13	10	13

At the .05 significance level, can the watchdog agency conclude the mean number of complaints per airport is less than 15 per month?

a. What assumption is necessary before conducting a test of hypothesis?
b. Plot the number of complaints per airport in a frequency distribution or a dot plot. Is it reasonable to conclude that the population follows a normal distribution?
c. Conduct a test of hypothesis and interpret the results.

A Statistical Software Solution

The Minitab statistical software system, used in earlier chapters and the previous section, provides an efficient method for conducting a one-sample test of hypothesis for a population mean. The steps to generate the following output are shown in Appendix C.

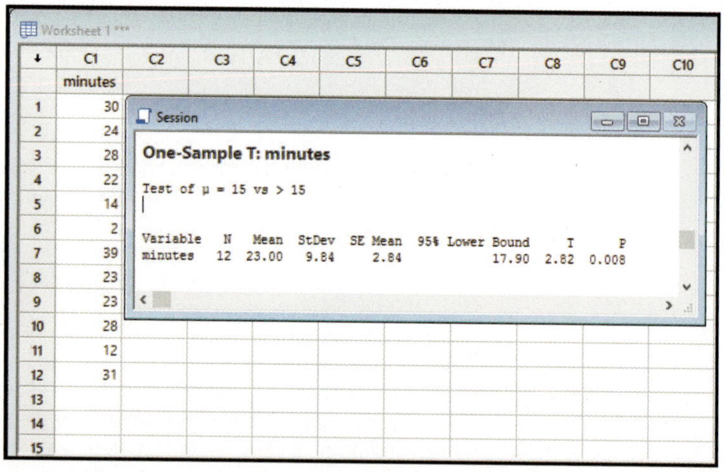

Worksheet 1 ***

↓	C1 minutes
1	30
2	24
3	28
4	22
5	14
6	2
7	39
8	23
9	23
10	28
11	12
12	31
13	
14	
15	

Session

One-Sample T: minutes

```
Test of μ = 15 vs > 15

Variable   N   Mean  StDev  SE Mean  95% Lower Bound     T      P
minutes   12  23.00   9.84     2.84            17.90  2.82  0.008
```

An additional feature of most statistical software packages is to report the *p*-value, which gives additional information on the null hypothesis. The *p*-value is the probability of a *t* value as extreme or more extreme than the computed *t* value, given that the null hypothesis is true. Using the Minitab analysis from the previous cell phone parking lot example, the *p*-value of .008 is the likelihood of a *t* value of 2.82 or larger, given a population mean of 15. Thus, comparing the *p*-value to the significance level tells us whether the null hypothesis was close to being rejected, barely rejected, and so on.

To explain further, refer to the diagram below. The *p*-value of .008 is the brown shaded area and the significance level is the total amber and brown shaded area. Because the *p*-value of .008 is less than the significance level of .05, the null hypothesis is rejected. Had the *p*-value been larger—say, .06, .19, or .57—than the significance level, the null hypothesis would not be rejected.

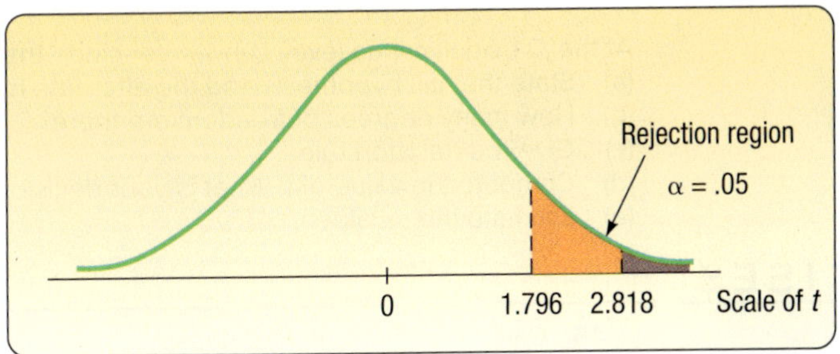

In the preceding example, the alternate hypothesis was one-sided, and the upper (right) tail of the *t* distribution contained the rejection region. The *p*-value is the area to the right of 2.818 for a *t* distribution with 11 degrees of freedom.

What if we were conducting a two-sided test, so that the rejection region is in both the upper and the lower tails? That is, in the cell phone parking lot example, if H_1 were stated as $\mu \neq 15$, we would have reported the *p*-value as the area to the right of 2.818 plus the value to the left of −2.818. Both of these values are .008, so the *p*-value is .008 + .008 = .016.

How can we estimate a *p*-value without a computer? To illustrate, recall that, in the example/solution regarding the length of time at the cell phone parking lot, we rejected the null hypothesis that $\mu \leq 15$ and accepted the alternate hypothesis that $\mu > 15$. The significance level was .05, so logically the *p*-value is less than .05. To estimate the *p*-value more accurately, go to Appendix B.5 and find the row with 11 degrees of freedom. The computed *t* value of 2.818 is between 2.718 and 3.106. (A portion of Appendix B.5 is reproduced as Table 10–3.) The one-tailed significance level corresponding to 2.718 is .01, and for 3.106 it is .005. Therefore, the *p*-value is between .005 and .01. The usual practice is to report that the *p*-value is less than the larger of the two significance levels. So we would report "the *p*-value is less than .01."

TABLE 10–3 A Portion of Student's *t* Distribution

	Confidence Intervals					
	80%	**90%**	**95%**	**98%**	**99%**	**99.9%**
	Level of Significance for One-Tailed Test, α					
	0.10	**0.05**	**.0025**	**0.01**	**0.005**	**0.0005**
df	Level of Significance for Two-Tailed Test, α					
	0.20	**0.10**	**0.05**	**0.02**	**0.01**	**0.001**
⋮	⋮	⋮	⋮	⋮	⋮	⋮
9	1.383	1.833	2.262	2.821	3.250	4.781
10	1.372	1.812	2.228	2.764	3.169	4.587
11	1.363	1.796	2.201	2.718	3.106	4.437
12	1.356	1.782	2.179	2.681	3.055	4.318
13	1.350	1.771	2.160	2.650	3.012	4.221
14	1.345	1.761	2.145	2.624	2.977	4.140
15	1.341	1.753	2.131	2.602	2.947	4.073

SELF-REVIEW 10–4

A machine is set to fill a small bottle with 9.0 grams of medicine. A sample of eight bottles revealed the following amounts (grams) in each bottle.

9.2	8.7	8.9	8.6	8.8	8.5	8.7	9.0

At the .01 significance level, can we conclude that the mean weight is less than 9.0 grams?

(a) State the null hypothesis and the alternate hypothesis.
(b) How many degrees of freedom are there?
(c) Give the decision rule.
(d) Compute the value of t. What is your decision regarding the null hypothesis?
(e) Estimate the p-value.

EXERCISES

15. Given the following hypotheses:

$$H_0: \mu \geq 20$$
$$H_1: \mu > 20$$

A random sample of five resulted in the following values: 18, 15, 12, 19, and 21. Assume a normal population. Using the .01 significance level, can we conclude the population mean is less than 20?

a. State the decision rule.
b. Compute the value of the test statistic.
c. What is your decision regarding the null hypothesis?
d. Estimate the p-value.

16. Given the following hypotheses:

$$H_0: \mu = 100$$
$$H_1: \mu \neq 100$$

A random sample of six resulted in the following values: 118, 105, 112, 119, 105, and 111. Assume a normal population. Using the .05 significance level, can we conclude the mean is different from 100?

a. State the decision rule.
b. Compute the value of the test statistic.
c. What is your decision regarding the null hypothesis?
d. Estimate the p-value.

17. FILE The amount of water consumed each day by a healthy adult follows a normal distribution with a mean of 1.4 liters. A health campaign promotes the consumption of at least 2.0 liters per day. A sample of 10 adults after the campaign shows the following consumption in liters:

1.5	1.6	1.5	1.4	1.9	1.4	1.3	1.9	1.8	1.7

At the .01 significance level, can we conclude that water consumption has increased? Calculate and interpret the p-value.

18. FILE The liquid chlorine added to swimming pools to combat algae has a relatively short shelf life before it loses its effectiveness. Records indicate that the mean shelf life of a 5-gallon jug of chlorine is 2,160 hours (90 days). As an experiment, Holdlonger was added to the chlorine to find whether it would increase the shelf life. A sample of nine jugs of chlorine had these shelf lives (in hours):

2,159	2,170	2,180	2,179	2,160	2,167	2,171	2,181	2,185

At the .025 level, has Holdlonger increased the shelf life of the chlorine? Estimate the p-value.

19. FILE A Washington, D.C., "think tank" announces the typical teenager sent 67 text messages per day in 2017. To update that estimate, you phone a sample of 12 teenagers and ask them how many text messages they sent the previous day. Their responses were:

51	175	47	49	44	54	145	203	21	59	42	100

At the .05 level, can you conclude that the mean number is greater than 67? Estimate the *p*-value and describe what it tells you.

20. FILE Hugger Polls contends that an agent conducts a mean of 53 in-depth home surveys every week. A streamlined survey form has been introduced, and Hugger wants to evaluate its effectiveness. The number of in-depth surveys conducted during a week by a random sample of 15 agents are:

53	57	50	55	58	54	60	52	59	62	60	60	51	59	56

At the .05 level of significance, can we conclude that the mean number of interviews conducted by the agents is more than 53 per week? Estimate the *p*-value.

LO10-7

Compute the probability of a Type II error.

TYPE II ERROR

Recall that the level of significance, identified by the symbol α, is the probability that the null hypothesis is rejected when it is true. This is called a Type I error. The most common levels of significance are .05 and .01 and are set by the researcher at the outset of the test.

In a hypothesis-testing situation there is also the possibility that a null hypothesis is not rejected when it is actually false. This is called a Type II error. The probability of a Type II error is identified by the Greek letter beta (β). In contrast to selecting a value for α in the hypothesis testing procedure, the value of β is calculated after the hypothesis testing procedure is finished. The following example illustrates the details of determining the value of β.

EXAMPLE

Western Wire Products purchases steel bars to make cotter pins. Past experience indicates that the mean tensile strength of all incoming shipments is 10,000 psi and that the standard deviation, σ, is 400 psi. To monitor the quality of the cotter pins, samples of 100 pins are randomly selected and tested for their strength. In our hypothesis testing procedure the hypotheses are:

$$H_0: \mu = 10{,}000$$

$$H_1: \mu \neq 10{,}000$$

To determine if a shipment of steel bars meets the quality standard, Western Wire Products set up a rule for the quality-control inspector to follow: "Take a sample of 100 steel bars. Test each of the bars for tensile strength. Using a .05 significance level, accept the shipment if the sample mean ($\bar{x}$) strength falls between 9,922 psi and 10,078 psi." These values are the critical values for the hypothesis test. If the sample mean is more than 10,078 or less than 9,922, the hypothesis is rejected and we conclude that the shipment does not meet the quality standard.

Refer to Chart 10–8, Graph A. Given that the population mean is 10,000 psi, designated μ_0, with a standard deviation of 400, the distribution shows the regions where the hypothesis is rejected and where it is not rejected, that is, whether the shipment meets the quality standard for tensile strength.

Suppose that the result of testing 100 bars results in a sample mean of 9,900 psi. Clearly, based on Graph A, the shipment does not meet the quality standard and is rejected with a .05 probability of a Type I error, a small chance of rejecting the shipment in error. To calculate the Type II error, we assume that the sample mean of 9,900 psi is the true population mean. Compare Graph A and Graph B. Graph A represents the company's distribution of tensile strength centered on 10,000 psi. Graph B, based on the sample data, suggests that the distribution is centered on 9,900 psi.

Now, let's use Graph B to determine the probability of a Type II error, β. From the quality standards we know that 9,922 psi is used to reject the null hypothesis. Any sample mean greater than 9,922 and less than 10,078 is accepted. If the distribution is really centered on 9,900 psi, it is possible to find sample means more than 9,922, and we would fail to reject the null hypothesis, $\mu = 10{,}000$. This is the area in Graph B labeled "Probability of β" where the null hypothesis would not be rejected. The graph indicates that the probability of a Type II error is .2912. We can also calculate the power of the test as $(1 - \beta)$. The power is the probability of not making a Type II error, rejecting the null hypothesis correctly. Here, the power of the test is .7088.

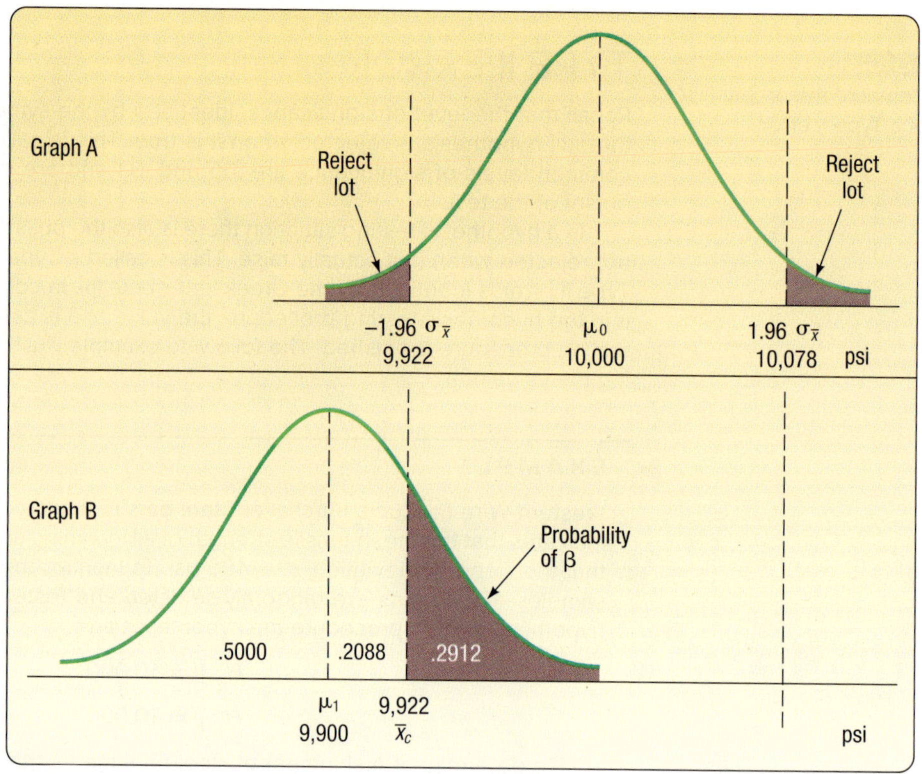

CHART 10–8 Charts Showing Type I and Type II Errors

SOLUTION

The probability of committing a Type II error, is represented by the shaded area in Chart 10–8, Graph B. It is computed by determining the area under the normal curve that lies above 9,922 pounds. The calculation of the areas under the normal curve was discussed in Chapter 7. Reviewing briefly, first determine the probability of the sample mean falling between 9,900 and 9,922. Then this probability is subtracted from .5000 (which represents all the area to the right of the mean of 9,900) to arrive at the probability of making a Type II error.

The number of standard errors (z value) between the mean of the incoming lot (9,900), designated by μ_1, and $\bar{x}_C$, representing the critical value for 9,922, is computed by:

TYPE II ERROR

$$z = \frac{\bar{x}_c - \mu_1}{\sigma/\sqrt{n}} \quad \textbf{(10–3)}$$

With $n = 100$ and $\sigma = 400$, the value of z is 0.55:

$$z = \frac{\bar{x}_c - \mu_1}{\sigma/\sqrt{n}} = \frac{9{,}922 - 9{,}900}{400/\sqrt{100}} = \frac{22}{40} = 0.55$$

The area under the curve between 9,900 and 9,922 (a z value of 0.55) is .2088. The area under the curve beyond 9,922 pounds is .5000 − .2088, or .2912; this is the probability of making a Type II error—that is, accepting an incoming lot of steel bars, based on the company's standard of 10,000 psi, when the sample suggests that the population mean is 9,900 psi and the shipment should be rejected.

Let's use another example, illustrated in Chart 10–9. Suppose the testing of a sample of 100 bars results in a mean of 10,120 psi. Based on the company's standards, represented in Graph A, the shipment should be rejected. The sample mean of 10,120 is more than the critical value of 10,078. Based on the sample mean, Graph C shows the distribution of sample means based on the distribution centered on the sample mean, 10,120.

If the distribution is centered on the sample mean of 10,120, there is a probability that a sample mean could be less than the upper critical value of 10,078. In Graph C, this is labeled, β. To find the probability, we calculate the z value of 10,078 in Graph C:

$$z = \frac{\bar{x}_c - \mu_1}{\sigma/\sqrt{n}} = \frac{10{,}078 - 10{,}120}{400/\sqrt{100}} = -1.05$$

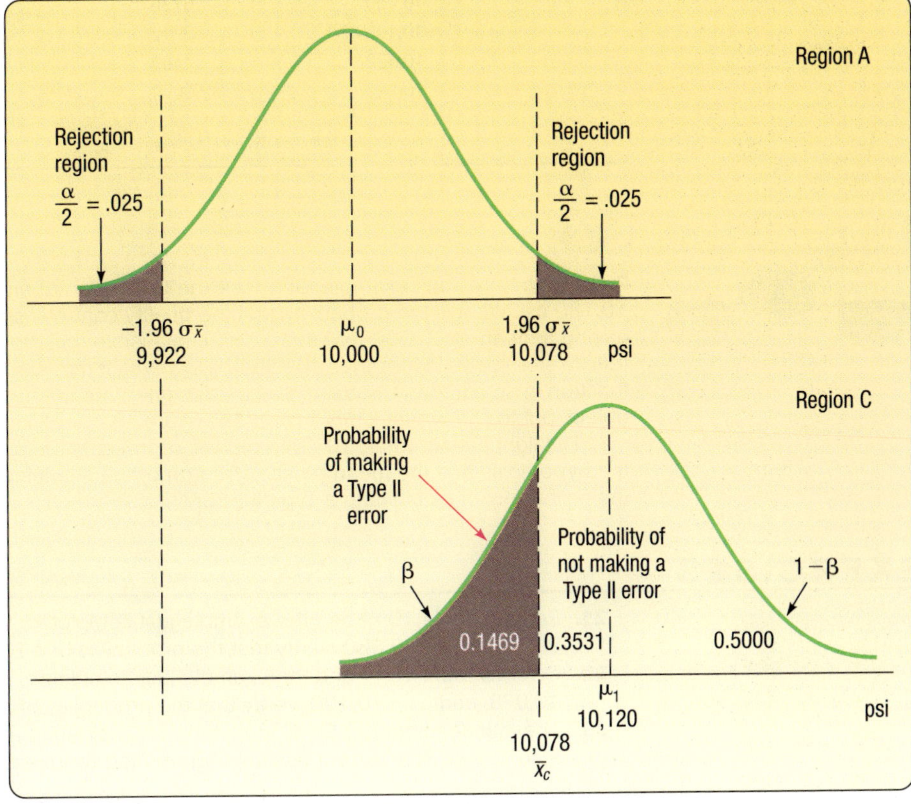

CHART 10–9 Type I and Type II Errors (Another Example)

The probability that z is less than -1.05 is .1469, found by .5000 − .3531. Therefore, β, or the probability of a Type II error, is .1469. The power of the test is 1.000 − .1469 or .8531. Caution: If the difference between μ_0 and μ_1 is relatively small, the probability of a Type II error may occur in both tails. This eventuality is not considered here.

Using the methods illustrated by Charts 10–8 Region B and 10–9 Region C, the probability of a Type II error can be determined for any sample mean used as an estimate of μ_1.

To review, in hypothesis testing, we select the probability of making a Type I error, α. Naturally, we pick small probabilities, typically less than 0.10. The probability of a Type II error depends on the sample result. The larger the difference between the hypothesized mean and the sample mean, the smaller the probability of a Type II error, failing to reject the null hypothesis when it should have been rejected.

For this example/solution, Table 10–4 shows the probabilities of a Type II error and the power of the test for selected values of μ_1. The right column gives the probability of not making a Type II error, which is also known as the power of a test.

TABLE 10–4 Probabilities of a Type II Error for $\mu_0 = 10{,}000$ Pounds and Selected Alternative Means, .05 Level of Significance

Selected Mean (μ_1)	Probability of Type II Error (β)	Power of a Test ($1 - \beta$)
9,820	.0054	.9946
9,880	.1469	.8531
9,900	.2912	.7088
9,940	.6736	.3264
10,000	—*	—
10,060	.6736	.3264
10,100	.2912	.7088
10,120	.1469	.8531
10,180	.0054	.9946

*It is not possible to make a Type II error when $\mu_1 = \mu_0$.

SELF-REVIEW 10–5

Refer to the previous example. Suppose the true mean of an incoming lot of steel bars is 10,180 psi. What is the probability that the quality control inspector will accept the bars as having a mean of 10,000 psi? (It sounds implausible that steel bars will be rejected if the tensile strength is higher than specified. However, it may be that the cotter pin has a dual function in an outboard motor. It may be designed not to shear off if the motor hits a small object, but to shear off if it hits a rock. Therefore, the steel should not be *too* strong.)

The light area in Chart 10–9, Region C, represents the probability of falsely accepting the hypothesis that the mean tensile strength of the incoming steel is 10,000 psi. What is the probability of committing a Type II error?

EXERCISES

21. Refer to Table 10–4 and the example just completed. With $n = 100$, $\sigma = 400$, $\bar{x}_c = 9{,}922$ and $\mu_1 = 9{,}880$, verify that the probability of a Type II error is .1469.

22. Refer to Table 10–4 and the example just completed. With $n = 100$, $\sigma = 400$, $\bar{x}_c = 10{,}078$, and $\mu_1 = 10{,}100$, verify that the probability of a Type II error is .2912.

23. The management of KSmall Industries is considering a new method of assembling a computer. The current assembling method requires a mean time of 60 minutes with a standard deviation of 2.7 minutes. Using the new method, the mean assembly time for a random sample of 24 computers was 58 minutes. Using the .10 level of significance, can we conclude that the assembly time using the new method is faster? What is the probability of a Type II error?

24. A recent national survey found that parents read an average (mean) of 10 books per month to their children under five years old. The population standard deviation is 5. The distribution of books read per month follows the normal distribution. A random sample of 25 households revealed that the mean number of books read last month was 12. At the .01 significance level, can we conclude that parents read more than the average number of books to their children? What is the probability of a Type II error?

CHAPTER SUMMARY

I. The objective of hypothesis testing is to verify the validity of a statement about a population parameter.

II. The steps to conduct a test of hypothesis are:

A. State the null hypothesis (H_0) and the alternate hypothesis (H_1).

B. Select the level of significance.

1. The level of significance is the likelihood or probability of rejecting a true null hypothesis.

2. The most frequently used probabilities used as significance levels are .01, .05, and .10. As a probability, any value between 0 and 1.00 is possible, but we prefer small probabilities of making a Type I error.

C. Select the test statistic.

1. A test statistic is a value calculated from sample information used to determine whether to reject the null hypothesis.

2. Two test statistics were considered in this chapter.

a. The standard normal distribution (the z distribution) is used when the population follows the normal distribution and the population standard deviation is known.

b. The t distribution is used when the population follows the normal distribution and the population standard deviation is unknown.

D. State the decision rule.

1. The decision rule indicates the condition or conditions when the null hypothesis is rejected.

2. In a two-tailed test, the rejection region is evenly split between the upper and lower tails.

3. In a one-tailed test, all of the rejection region is in either the upper or the lower tail.

E. Select a sample, compute the value of the test statistic, and make a decision regarding the null hypothesis.

F. Interpret the results of your decision.

III. A p-value is the probability that the value of the test statistic is as extreme as the value computed, when the null hypothesis is true.

IV. When testing a hypothesis about a population mean:

A. If the population standard deviation, σ, is known, the test statistic is the standard normal distribution and is determined from:

$$z = \frac{\bar{x} - \mu}{\sigma/\sqrt{n}} \quad \textbf{(10–1)}$$

B. If the population standard deviation is not known, s is substituted for σ. The test statistic is the t distribution, and its value is determined from:

$$t = \frac{\bar{x} - \mu}{s/\sqrt{n}} \quad \textbf{(10–2)}$$

The major characteristics of the t distribution are:

1. It is a continuous distribution.
2. It is mound-shaped and symmetrical.
3. It is flatter, or more spread out, than the standard normal distribution.
4. There is a family of t distributions, depending on the number of degrees of freedom.

V. There are two types of errors that can occur in a test of hypothesis.

A. A Type I error occurs when a true null hypothesis is rejected.

1. The probability of making a Type I error is equal to the level of significance.
2. This probability is designated by the Greek letter α.

B. A Type II error occurs when a false null hypothesis is not rejected.

1. The probability of making a Type II error is designated by the Greek letter β.
2. The likelihood of a Type II error must be calculated comparing the hypothesized distribution to an alternate distribution based on sample results.

PRONUNCIATION KEY

SYMBOL	MEANING	PRONUNCIATION
H_0	Null hypothesis	*H sub zero*
H_1	Alternate hypothesis	*H sub one*
$\alpha/2$	Two-tailed significance level	*Alpha divided by 2*
$\bar{x}_c$	Limit of the sample mean	*x bar sub c*
μ_0	Assumed population mean	*mu sub zero*

CHAPTER EXERCISES

25. According to the local union president, the mean gross income of plumbers in the Salt Lake City area follows the normal probability distribution with a mean of \$45,000 and a standard deviation of \$3,000. A recent investigative reporter for KYAK TV found, for a sample of 120 plumbers, the mean gross income was \$45,500. At the .10 significance level, is it reasonable to conclude that the mean income is not equal to \$45,000? Determine the p-value.

26. **FILE** Rutter Nursery Company packages its pine bark mulch in 50-pound bags. From a long history, the production department reports that the distribution of the bag weights follows the normal distribution and the standard deviation of the packaging process is 3 pounds per bag. At the end of each day, Jeff Rutter, the production manager, weighs 10 bags and computes the mean weight of the sample. Below are the weights of 10 bags from today's production.

45.6	47.7	47.6	46.3	46.2	47.4	49.2	55.8	47.5	48.5

a. Can Mr. Rutter conclude that the mean weight of the bags is less than 50 pounds? Use the .01 significance level.
b. In a brief report, tell why Mr. Rutter can use the z distribution as the test statistic.
c. Compute the p-value.

27. A new weight-watching company, Weight Reducers International, advertises that those who join will lose an average of 10 pounds after the first two weeks. The standard deviation is 2.8 pounds. A random sample of 50 people who joined the weight reduction program revealed a mean loss of 9 pounds. At the .05 level of significance, can we conclude that those joining Weight Reducers will lose less than 10 pounds? Determine the p-value.

28. Dole Pineapple Inc. is concerned that the 16-ounce can of sliced pineapple is being overfilled. Assume the standard deviation of the process is .03 ounce. The quality-control department took a random sample of 50 cans and found that the arithmetic mean weight was 16.05 ounces. At the 5% level of significance, can we conclude that the mean weight is greater than 16 ounces? Determine the p-value.

29. According to a recent survey, Americans get a mean of 7 hours of sleep per night. A random sample of 50 students at West Virginia University revealed the mean length of time slept last night was 6 hours and 48 minutes (6.8 hours). The standard deviation of the sample was 0.9 hour. At the 5% level of significance, is it reasonable to conclude that students at West Virginia sleep less than the typical American? Compute the *p*-value.

30. A statewide real estate sales agency, Farm Associates, specializes in selling farm property in the state of Nebraska. Its records indicate that the mean selling time of farm property is 90 days. Because of recent drought conditions, the agency believes that the mean selling time is now greater than 90 days. A statewide survey of 100 recently sold farms revealed a mean selling time of 94 days, with a standard deviation of 22 days. At the .10 significance level, has there been an increase in selling time?

31. According to the Census Bureau, 3.13 people reside in the typical American household. A sample of 25 households in Arizona retirement communities showed the mean number of residents per household was 2.86 residents. The standard deviation of this sample was 1.20 residents. At the .05 significance level, is it reasonable to conclude the mean number of residents in the retirement community household is less than 3.13 persons?

32. A recent article in *Vitality* magazine reported that the mean amount of leisure time per week for American men is 40.0 hours. You believe this figure is too large and decide to conduct your own test. In a random sample of 60 men, you find that the mean is 37.8 hours of leisure per week and that the standard deviation of the sample is 12.2 hours. Can you conclude that the information in the article is untrue? Use the .05 significance level. Determine the *p*-value and explain its meaning.

33. **FILE** A recent survey by nerdwallet.com indicated Americans paid a mean of $6,658 interest on credit card debt in 2017. A sample of 12 households with children revealed the follow amounts. At the .05 significance level is it reasonable to conclude that these households paid more interest?

7077	5744	6753	7381	7625	6636	7164	7348	8060	5848	9275	7052

34. **FILE** A recent article in *The Wall Street Journal* reported that the home equity loan rate is now less than 4%. A sample of eight small banks in the Midwest revealed the following home equity loan rates (in percent):

3.6	4.1	5.3	3.6	4.9	4.6	5.0	4.4

At the .01 significance level, can we conclude that the home equity loan rate for small banks is less than 4%? Estimate the *p*-value.

35. **FILE** A recent study revealed the typical American coffee drinker consumes an average of 3.1 cups per day. A sample of 12 senior citizens revealed they consumed the following amounts of coffee, reported in cups, yesterday.

3.1	3.3	3.5	2.6	2.6	4.3	4.4	3.8	3.1	4.1	3.1	3.2

At the .05 significance level, do these sample data suggest there is a difference between the national average and the sample mean from senior citizens?

36. **FILE** The postanesthesia care area (recovery room) at St. Luke's Hospital in Maumee, Ohio, was recently enlarged. The hope was that the change would increase the mean number of patients served per day to more than 25. A random sample of 15 days revealed the following numbers of patients.

25	27	25	26	25	28	28	27	24	26	25	29	25	27	24

At the .01 significance level, can we conclude that the mean number of patients per day is more than 25? Estimate the *p*-value and interpret it.

37. **FILE** www.golfsmith.com receives an average of 6.5 returns per day from online shoppers. For a sample of 12 days, it received the following numbers of returns.

0	4	3	4	9	4	5	9	1	6	7	10

At the .01 significance level, can we conclude the mean number of returns is less than 6.5?

38. **FILE** During recent seasons, Major League Baseball has been criticized for the length of the games. A report indicated that the average game lasts 3 hours and 30 minutes. A sample of 17 games revealed the following times to completion. (Note that the minutes have been changed to fractions of hours, so that a game that lasted 2 hours and 24 minutes is reported at 2.40 hours.)

2.98	2.40	2.70	2.25	3.23	3.17	2.93	3.18	2.80
2.38	3.75	3.20	3.27	2.52	2.58	4.45	2.45	

Can we conclude that the mean time for a game is less than 3.50 hours? Use the .05 significance level.

39. **FILE** Watch Corporation of Switzerland claims that its watches on average will neither gain nor lose time during a week. A sample of 18 watches provided the following gains (+) or losses (–) in seconds per week.

−0.38	−0.20	−0.38	−0.32	+0.32	−0.23	+0.30	+0.25	−0.10
−0.37	−0.61	−0.48	−0.47	−0.64	−0.04	−0.20	−0.68	+0.05

Is it reasonable to conclude that the mean gain or loss in time for the watches is 0? Use the .05 significance level. Estimate the *p*-value.

40. **FILE** Listed below is the annual rate of return (reported in percent) for a sample of 12 taxable mutual funds.

4.63	4.15	4.76	4.70	4.65	4.52	4.70	5.06	4.42	4.51	4.24	4.52

Using the .05 significance level, is it reasonable to conclude that the mean rate of return is more than 4.50%?

41. **FILE** Many grocery stores and large retailers such as Kroger and Walmart have installed self-checkout systems so shoppers can scan their own items and cash out themselves. How do customers like this service and how often do they use it? Listed below is the number of customers using the service for a sample of 15 days at a Walmart location.

120	108	120	114	118	91	118	92	104	104
112	97	118	108	117					

Is it reasonable to conclude that the mean number of customers using the self-checkout system is more than 100 per day? Use the .05 significance level.

42. **FILE** For a recent year, the mean fare to fly from Charlotte, North Carolina, to Chicago, Illinois, on a discount ticket was $267. A random sample of 13 round-trip discount fares on this route last month shows:

$321	$286	$290	$330	$310	$250	$270	$280	$299	$265	$291	$275	$281

At the .01 significance level, can we conclude that the mean fare has increased? What is the *p*-value?

43. The publisher of *Celebrity Living* claims that the mean sales for personality magazines that feature people such as Megan Fox or Jennifer Lawrence are 1.5 million copies per week. A sample of 10 comparable titles shows a mean weekly sales last week of 1.3 million copies with a standard deviation of 0.9 million copies. Do these data contradict the publisher's claim? Use the 0.01 significance level.

44. A United Nations report shows the mean family income for Mexican migrants to the United States is $27,000 per year. A FLOC (Farm Labor Organizing Committee) evaluation of 25 Mexican family units reveals a mean to be $30,000 with a sample standard deviation of $10,000. Does this information disagree with the United Nations report? Apply the 0.01 significance level.

45. FILE The number of "destination weddings" has skyrocketed in recent years. For example, many couples are opting to have their weddings in the Caribbean. A Caribbean vacation resort recently advertised in *Bride Magazine* that the cost of a Caribbean wedding was less than $30,000. Listed below is a total cost in $000 for a sample of 8 Caribbean weddings.

29.7	29.4	31.7	29.0	29.1	30.5	29.1	29.8

At the .05 significance level, is it reasonable to conclude the mean wedding cost is less than $30,000 as advertised?

46. The American Water Works Association reports that the per capita water use in a single-family home is 69 gallons per day. Legacy Ranch is a relatively new housing development. The builders installed more efficient water fixtures, such as low-flush toilets, and subsequently conducted a survey of the residences. Thirty-six owners responded, and the sample mean water use per day was 64 gallons with a standard deviation of 8.8 gallons per day. At the .10 level of significance, is that enough evidence to conclude that residents of Legacy Ranch use less water on average?

47. A cola-dispensing machine is set to dispense 9.00 ounces of cola per cup, with a standard deviation of 1.00 ounce. The manufacturer of the machine would like to set the control limit in such a way that, for samples of 36, 5% of the sample means will be greater than the upper control limit, and 5% of the sample means will be less than the lower control limit.

a. At what value should the control limit be set?
b. If the population mean shifts to 8.6, what is the probability of detecting the change?
c. If the population mean shifts to 9.6, what is the probability of detecting the change?

48. The owners of the Westfield Mall wished to study customer shopping habits. From earlier studies, the owners were under the impression that a typical shopper spends 0.75 hour at the mall, with a standard deviation of 0.10 hour. Recently the mall owners added some specialty restaurants designed to keep shoppers in the mall longer. The consulting firm, Brunner and Swanson Marketing Enterprises, was hired to evaluate the effects of the restaurants. A sample of 45 shoppers by Brunner and Swanson revealed that the mean time spent in the mall had increased to 0.80 hour.

a. Develop a hypothesis test to determine if the mean time spent in the mall changed. Use the .10 significance level.
b. Suppose the mean shopping time actually increased from 0.75 hour to 0.79 hours. What is the probability of making a Type II error?
c. When Brunner and Swanson reported the information in part (b) to the mall owners, the owners believed that the probability of making a Type II error was too high. How could this probability be reduced?

49. The following null and alternate hypotheses are given.

$$H_0: \mu \leq 50$$
$$H_1: \mu > 50$$

Suppose the population standard deviation is 10. The probability of a Type I error is set at .01 and the probability of a Type II error at .30. Assume that the population mean shifts from 50 to 55. How large a sample is necessary to meet these requirements?

50. An insurance company, based on past experience, estimates the mean damage for a natural disaster in its area is $5,000. After introducing several plans to prevent loss, it randomly samples 200 policyholders and finds the mean amount per claim was $4,800 with a standard deviation of $1,300. Does it appear the prevention plans were effective in reducing the mean amount of a claim? Use the .05 significance level.

51. A national grocer's magazine reports the typical shopper spends 8 minutes in line waiting to check out. A sample of 24 shoppers at the local Farmer Jack's showed a mean of 7.5 minutes with a standard deviation of 3.2 minutes. Is the waiting time at the local Farmer Jack's less than that reported in the national magazine? Use the .05 significance level.

DATA ANALYTICS

52. FILE The North Valley Real Estate data reports information on the homes sold last year.

a. Adam Marty recently joined North Valley Real Estate and was assigned twenty homes to market and show. When he was hired, North Valley assured him that the twenty homes would be fairly assigned to him. When he reviewed the selling prices of his assigned homes, he thought that the prices were much below the average of $357,000. Adam was able to find the data of how the other agents in the firm were assigned to the homes. Use statistical inference to analyze the "fairness" that homes were assigned to the agents.

53. FILE Refer to the Baseball 2016 data, which report information on the 30 Major League Baseball teams for the 2016 season.

a. Conduct a test of hypothesis to determine whether the mean salary of the teams was different from $100.0 million. Use the .05 significance level.

b. Using a 5% significance level, conduct a test of hypothesis to determine whether the mean attendance was more than 2,000,000 per team.

54. FILE Refer to the Lincolnville School District bus data.

a. Select the variable for the number of miles traveled last month. Conduct a hypothesis test to determine whether the mean miles traveled last month equals 10,000. Use the .01 significance level. Find the *p*-value and explain what it means.

b. A study of school bus fleets reports that the average per bus maintenance cost is $4,000 per year. Using the maintenance cost variable, conduct a hypothesis test to determine whether the mean maintenance cost for Lincolnville's bus fleet is more than $4,000 at the .05 significance level. Determine the *p*-value and report the results.

Two-Sample Tests of Hypothesis

11

© JGI/Blend Images LLC RF

▲ **GIBBS BABY FOOD COMPANY** wishes to compare the weight gain of infants using its brand versus its competitor's. A sample of 40 babies using the Gibbs products revealed a mean weight gain of 7.6 pounds in the first three months after birth. For the Gibbs brand, the population standard deviation of the sample is 2.3 pounds. A sample of 55 babies using the competitor's brand revealed a mean increase in weight of 8.1 pounds. The population standard deviation is 2.9 pounds. At the .05 significance level, can we conclude that babies using the Gibbs brand gained less weight? (See Exercise 3 and LO11-1.)

LEARNING OBJECTIVES

When you have completed this chapter, you will be able to:

LO11-1 Test a hypothesis that two independent population means are equal, assuming that the population standard deviations are known and equal.

LO11-2 Test a hypothesis that two independent population means are equal, with unknown population standard deviations.

LO11-3 Test a hypothesis about the mean population difference between paired or dependent observations.

LO11-4 Explain the difference between dependent and independent samples.

INTRODUCTION

Chapter 10 began our study of hypothesis testing. We described the nature of hypothesis testing and conducted tests of a hypothesis in which we compared the results of a single sample to a population value. That is, we selected a single random sample from a population and conducted a test of whether the proposed population value was reasonable. Recall in Chapter 10 that we selected a sample of the number of desks assembled per week at Jamestown Steel Company to determine whether there was a change in the production rate. Similarly, we sampled the cost to process insurance claims to determine if cost-cutting measures resulted in a mean less than the current $60 per claim. In both cases, we compared the results of a *single* sample statistic to a population parameter.

© John Lund/Drew Kelly/Blend Images LLC RF

In this chapter, we expand the idea of hypothesis testing to two populations. That is, we select random samples from two different populations to determine whether the population means are equal. Some questions we might want to test are:

1. Is there a difference in the mean value of residential real estate sold by male agents and female agents in south Florida?
2. At Grabit Software, Inc., do customer service employees receive more calls for assistance during the morning or afternoon?
3. In the fast-food industry, is there a difference in the mean number of days absent between young workers (under 21 years of age) and older workers (more than 60 years of age)?
4. Is there an increase in the production rate if music is piped into the production area?

We begin this chapter with the case in which we select random samples from two independent populations and wish to investigate whether these populations have the same mean.

LO11-1 Test a hypothesis that two independent population means are equal, assuming that the population standard deviations are known and equal.

TWO-SAMPLE TESTS OF HYPOTHESIS: INDEPENDENT SAMPLES

A city planner in Tampa, Florida wishes to know whether there is a difference in the mean hourly wage rate of plumbers and electricians in central Florida. A financial accountant wishes to know whether the mean rate of return for domestic, U.S., mutual funds is different from the mean rate of return on global mutual funds. In each of these cases, there are two independent populations. In the first case, the plumbers represent one population and the electricians, the other. In the second case, domestic, U.S., mutual funds are one population and global mutual funds, the other.

To investigate the question in each of these cases, we would select a random sample from each population and compute the mean of the two samples. If the two population means are the same, that is, the mean hourly rate is the same for the plumbers and the electricians, we would expect the *difference* between the two sample means to be zero. But what if our sample results yield a difference other than zero? Is that difference due to chance or is it because there is a real difference in the hourly earnings? A two-sample test of means will help to answer this question.

Return to the results of Chapter 8. Recall that we showed that a distribution of sample means would tend to approximate the normal distribution. We need to again assume that a distribution of sample means will follow the normal distribution. It can be shown mathematically that the distribution of the differences between sample means for two normal distributions is also normal.

We can illustrate this theory in terms of the city planner in Tampa, Florida. To begin, let's assume some information that is not usually available. Suppose that the population of plumbers has a mean of $30.00 per hour and a standard deviation of $5.00 per hour. The population of electricians has a mean of $29.00 and a standard deviation of $4.50. Now, from this information it is clear that the two population means are not the same. The plumbers actually earn $1.00 per hour more than the electricians. But we cannot expect to uncover this difference each time we sample the two populations.

Suppose we select a random sample of 40 plumbers and a random sample of 35 electricians and compute the mean of each sample. Then, we determine the difference between the sample means. It is this difference between the sample means that holds our interest. If the populations have the same mean, then we would expect the difference between the two sample means to be zero. If there is a difference between the population means, then we expect to find a difference between the sample means.

To understand the theory, we need to take several pairs of samples, compute the mean of each, determine the difference between the sample means, and study the distribution of the differences in the sample means. Because of the Central Limit Theorem in Chapter 8, we know that the distribution of the sample means follows the normal distribution. If the two distributions of sample means follow the normal distribution, then we can reason that the distribution of their differences will also follow the normal distribution. This is the first hurdle.

The second hurdle refers to the mean of this distribution of differences. If we find the mean of this distribution is zero, that implies that there is no difference in the two populations. On the other hand, if the mean of the distribution of differences is equal to some value other than zero, either positive or negative, then we conclude that the two populations do not have the same mean.

To report some concrete results, let's return to the city planner in Tampa, Florida. Table 11–1 shows the result of selecting 20 different samples of 40 plumbers and 35 electricians, computing the mean of each sample, and finding the difference

TABLE 11–1 The Mean Hourly Earnings of 20 Random Samples of Plumbers and Electricians and the Differences between the Means

Sample	Plumbers	Electricians	Difference
1	$29.80	$28.76	$1.04
2	30.32	29.40	0.92
3	30.57	29.94	0.63
4	30.04	28.93	1.11
5	30.09	29.78	0.31
6	30.02	28.66	1.36
7	29.60	29.13	0.47
8	29.63	29.42	0.21
9	30.17	29.29	0.88
10	30.81	29.75	1.06
11	30.09	28.05	2.04
12	29.35	29.07	0.28
13	29.42	28.79	0.63
14	29.78	29.54	0.24
15	29.60	29.60	0.00
16	30.60	30.19	0.41
17	30.79	28.65	2.14
18	29.14	29.95	−0.81
19	29.91	28.75	1.16
20	28.74	29.21	−0.47

between the two sample means. In the first case, the sample of 40 plumbers has a mean of \$29.80, and for the 35 electricians the mean is \$28.76. The difference between the sample means is \$1.04. This process was repeated 19 more times. Observe that in 17 of the 20 cases, the differences are positive because the mean of the plumbers is larger than the mean of the electricians. In two cases, the differences are negative because the mean of the electricians is larger than the mean of the plumbers. In one case, the means are equal.

Our final hurdle is that we need to know something about the *variability* of the distribution of differences. To put it another way, what is the standard deviation of this distribution of differences? Statistical theory shows that when we have independent populations, as in this case, the distribution of the differences has a variance (standard deviation squared) equal to the sum of the two individual variances. This means that we can add the variances of the two sampling distributions. To put it another way, the variance of the difference in sample means ($\bar{x}_1 - \bar{x}_2$) is equal to the sum of the variance for the plumbers and the variance for the electricians.

VARIANCE OF THE DISTRIBUTION OF DIFFERENCES IN MEANS

$$\sigma^2_{\bar{x}_1-\bar{x}_2} = \frac{\sigma_1^2}{n_1} + \frac{\sigma_2^2}{n_2} \qquad \textbf{(11–1)}$$

The term $\sigma^2_{\bar{x}_1-\bar{x}_2}$ looks complex but need not be difficult to interpret. The σ^2 portion reminds us that it is a variance, and the subscript $\bar{x}_1 - \bar{x}_2$ that it is a distribution of differences in the sample means.

We can put this equation in a more usable form by taking the square root, so that we have the standard deviation or "standard error" of the distribution of differences. Finally, we standardize the distribution of the differences. The result is the following equation.

TWO-SAMPLE TEST OF MEANS—KNOWN σ

$$z = \frac{\bar{x}_1 - \bar{x}_2}{\sqrt{\dfrac{\sigma_1^2}{n_1} + \dfrac{\sigma_2^2}{n_2}}} \qquad \textbf{(11–2)}$$

Before we present an example, let's review the assumptions necessary for using formula (11–2).

- The two populations follow normal distributions.
- The two samples are unrelated, that is, independent.
- The standard deviations for both populations are known.

The following example shows the details of the test of hypothesis for two population means and shows how to interpret the results.

EXAMPLE

Customers at the FoodTown Supermarket have a choice when paying for their groceries. They may check out and pay using the standard cashier-assisted checkout, or they may use the new Fast Lane procedure. In the standard procedure, a FoodTown employee scans each item and puts it on a short conveyor, where another employee puts it in a bag and then into the grocery cart. In the Fast Lane procedure,

© Teschner/Agencja Fotograficzna Caro/Alamy Stock Photo

the customer scans each item, bags it, and places the bags in the cart him- or herself. The Fast Lane procedure is designed to reduce the time a customer spends in the checkout line.

The Fast Lane facility was recently installed at the Byrne Road FoodTown location. The store manager would like to know if the mean checkout time using the standard checkout method is longer than using the Fast Lane. She gathered the following sample information. The time is measured from when the customer enters the line until all his or her bags are in the cart. Hence the time includes both waiting in line and checking out. What is the *p*-value?

Customer Type	Sample Size	Sample Mean	Population Standard Deviation
Standard	50	5.50 minutes	0.40 minute
Fast Lane	100	5.30 minutes	0.30 minute

SOLUTION

We use the six-step hypothesis-testing procedure to investigate the question.

Step 1: State the null hypothesis and the alternate hypothesis. The null hypothesis is that the mean standard checkout time is less than or equal to the mean Fast Lane checkout time. In other words, the difference of 0.20 minute between the mean checkout time for the standard method and the mean checkout time for Fast Lane is due to chance. The alternate hypothesis is that the mean checkout time is larger for those using the standard method. We will let μ_S refer to the mean checkout time for the population of standard customers and μ_F the mean checkout time for the Fast Lane customers. The null and alternative hypotheses are:

$$H_0: \mu_S \leq \mu_F$$
$$H_1: \mu_S > \mu_F$$

Step 2: Select the level of significance. The significance level is the probability that we reject the null hypothesis when it is actually true. This likelihood is determined prior to selecting the sample or performing any calculations. The .05 and .01 significance levels are the most common, but other values, such as .02 and .10, are also used. In theory, we may select any value between 0 and 1 for the significance level. In this case, we selected the .01 significance level.

Step 3: Determine the test statistic. In Chapter 10, we used the standard normal distribution (that is, *z*) and *t* as test statistics. In this case, we use the *z* distribution as the test statistic because we assume the two population distributions are both normal and the standard deviations of both populations are known.

Step 4: Formulate a decision rule. The decision rule is based on the null and the alternate hypotheses (i.e., one-tailed or two-tailed test), the level of significance, and the test statistic used. We selected the .01 significance level and the *z* distribution as the test statistic, and we wish to determine whether the mean checkout time is longer using the standard method. We set the alternate hypothesis to indicate that the mean checkout time is longer for those using the standard method than the Fast Lane method. Hence, the rejection region is in the upper tail of the standard normal distribution (a one-tailed test). To find the critical value, go to Student's *t* distribution

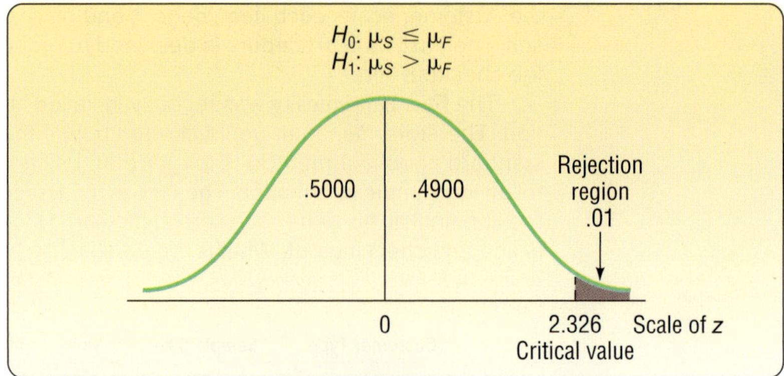

CHART 11–1 Decision Rule for One-Tailed Test at .01 Significance Level

(Appendix B.5). In the table headings, find the row labeled **"Level of Significance for One-Tailed Test"** and select the column for an alpha of .01. Go to the bottom row with infinite degrees of freedom. The z critical value is 2.326. So the decision rule is to reject the null hypothesis if the value of the test statistic exceeds 2.326. Chart 11–1 depicts the decision rule.

Step 5: Make the decision regarding H_0. FoodTown randomly selected 50 customers using the standard checkout and computed a sample mean checkout time of 5.5 minutes, and 100 customers using the Fast Lane checkout and computed a sample mean checkout time of 5.3 minutes. We assume that the population standard deviations for the two methods is known. We use formula (11-2) to compute the value of the test statistic.

$$z = \frac{\bar{x}_S - \bar{x}_F}{\sqrt{\frac{\sigma_S^2}{n_S} + \frac{\sigma_F^2}{n_F}}} = \frac{5.5 - 5.3}{\sqrt{\frac{0.40^2}{50} + \frac{0.30^2}{100}}} = \frac{0.2}{0.064031} = 3.123$$

The computed value of 3.123 is larger than the critical value of 2.326. Our decision is to reject the null hypothesis and accept the alternate hypothesis.

Step 6: Interpret the result. The difference of .20 minute between the mean checkout times is too large to have occurred by chance. We conclude the Fast Lane method is faster.

What is the p-value for the test statistic? Recall that the p-value is the probability of finding a value of the test statistic this extreme when the null hypothesis is true. To calculate the p-value, we need the probability of a z value larger than 3.123. From Appendix B.3, we cannot find the probability associated with 3.123. The largest value available is 3.09. The area corresponding to 3.09 is .4990. In this case, we can report that the p-value is less than .0010, found by .5000 – .4990. We conclude that there is very little likelihood that the null hypothesis is true! The checkout time is less using the fast lane.

STATISTICS IN ACTION

Do you live to work or work to live? A recent poll of 802 working Americans revealed that, among those who considered their work as a career, the mean number of hours worked per day was 8.7. Among those who considered their work as a job, the mean number of hours worked per day was 7.6.

In summary, the criteria for using formula (11–2) are:

1. **The samples are from independent populations.** This means the checkout time for the Fast Lane customers is unrelated to the checkout time for the other customers. For example, Mr. Smith's checkout time does not affect any other customer's checkout time.

2. **Both populations follow the normal distribution.** In the FoodTown example, the population of times in both the standard checkout line and the Fast Lane follow normal distributions.
3. **Both population standard deviations are known.** In the FoodTown example, the population standard deviation of the Fast Lane times was 0.30 minute. The population standard deviation of the standard checkout times was 0.40 minute.

SELF-REVIEW 11–1

Tom Sevits is the owner of the Appliance Patch. Recently Tom observed a difference in the dollar value of sales between the men and women he employs as sales associates. A sample of 40 days revealed the men sold a mean of $1,400 worth of appliances per day. For a sample of 50 days, the women sold a mean of $1,500 worth of appliances per day. Assume the population standard deviation for men is $200 and for women $250. At the .05 significance level, can Mr. Sevits conclude that the mean amount sold per day is larger for the women?

(a) State the null hypothesis and the alternate hypothesis.
(b) What is the decision rule?
(c) What is the value of the test statistic?
(d) What is your decision regarding the null hypothesis?
(e) What is the *p*-value?
(f) Interpret the result.

EXERCISES

1. A sample of 40 observations is selected from one population with a population standard deviation of 5. The sample mean is 102. A sample of 50 observations is selected from a second population with a population standard deviation of 6. The sample mean is 99. Conduct the following test of hypothesis using the .04 significance level.

$$H_0: \mu_1 = \mu_2$$
$$H_1: \mu_1 \neq \mu_2$$

a. Is this a one-tailed or a two-tailed test?
b. State the decision rule.
c. Compute the value of the test statistic.
d. What is your decision regarding H_0?
e. What is the *p*-value?

2. A sample of 65 observations is selected from one population with a population standard deviation of 0.75. The sample mean is 2.67. A sample of 50 observations is selected from a second population with a population standard deviation of 0.66. The sample mean is 2.59. Conduct the following test of hypothesis using the .08 significance level.

$$H_0: \mu_1 \leq \mu_2$$
$$H_1: \mu_1 > \mu_2$$

a. Is this a one-tailed or a two-tailed test?
b. State the decision rule.
c. Compute the value of the test statistic.
d. What is your decision regarding H_0?
e. What is the *p*-value?

Note: Use the six-step hypothesis-testing procedure to solve the following exercises.

3. Gibbs Baby Food Company wishes to compare the weight gain of infants using its brand versus its competitor's. A sample of 40 babies using the Gibbs products revealed a mean weight gain of 7.6 pounds in the first three months after birth. For the Gibbs brand, the population standard deviation of the sample is 2.3 pounds. A sample of 55 babies using the competitor's brand revealed a mean increase in weight of 8.1 pounds. The population standard deviation is 2.9 pounds. At the .05 significance level, can we conclude that babies using the Gibbs brand gained less weight? Compute the *p*-value and interpret it.

4. As part of a study of corporate employees, the director of human resources for PNC Inc. wants to compare the distance traveled to work by employees at its office in downtown Cincinnati with the distance for those in downtown Pittsburgh. A sample of 35 Cincinnati employees showed they travel a mean of 370 miles per month. A sample of 40 Pittsburgh employees showed they travel a mean of 380 miles per month. The population standard deviations for the Cincinnati and Pittsburgh employees are 30 and 26 miles, respectively. At the .05 significance level, is there a difference in the mean number of miles traveled per month between Cincinnati and Pittsburgh employees?

5. Do married and unmarried women spend the same amount of time per week using Facebook? A random sample of 45 married women who use Facebook spent an average of 3.0 hours per week on this social media website. A random sample of 39 unmarried women who regularly use Facebook spent an average of 3.4 hours per week. Assume that the weekly Facebook time for married women has a population standard deviation of 1.2 hours, and the population standard deviation for unmarried, regular Facebook users is 1.1 hours per week. Using the .05 significance level, do married and unmarried women differ in the amount of time per week spent on Facebook? Find the *p*-value and interpret the result.

6. Mary Jo Fitzpatrick is the vice president for Nursing Services at St. Luke's Memorial Hospital. Recently she noticed in the job postings for nurses that those that are unionized seem to offer higher wages. She decided to investigate and gathered the following information.

Group	Sample Size	Sample Mean Wage	Population Standard Deviation
Union	40	\$20.75	\$2.25
Nonunion	45	\$19.80	\$1.90

Would it be reasonable for her to conclude that union nurses earn more? Use the .02 significance level. What is the *p*-value?

LO11-2
Test a hypothesis that two independent population means are equal, with unknown population standard deviations.

COMPARING POPULATION MEANS WITH UNKNOWN POPULATION STANDARD DEVIATIONS

In the previous section, we used the standard normal distribution and *z* as the test statistic to test a hypothesis that two population means from independent populations were equal. The hypothesis tests presumed that the populations were normally distributed and that we knew the population standard deviations. However, in most cases, we do not know the population standard deviations. We can overcome this problem, as we did in the one-sample case in the previous chapter, by substituting the sample standard deviation (s) for the population standard deviation (σ). See formula (10–2) on page 334.

Two-Sample Pooled Test

In this section, we describe another method for comparing the sample means of two independent populations to determine if the sampled populations could reasonably have the same mean. The method described does *not* require that we know the standard deviations of the populations. This gives us a great deal more flexibility when investigating the difference in sample means. There are two major differences in this test and the previous test described in this chapter.

1. We assume the sampled populations have equal but unknown standard deviations. Because of this assumption, we combine or "pool" the sample standard deviations.
2. We use the t distribution as the test statistic.

The formula for computing the value of the test statistic t is similar to formula (11–2), but an additional calculation is necessary. The two sample standard deviations are pooled to form a single estimate of the unknown population standard deviation. In essence, we compute a weighted mean of the two sample standard deviations and use this value as an estimate of the unknown population standard deviation. The weights are the degrees of freedom that each sample provides. Why do we need to pool the sample standard deviations? Because we assume that the two populations have equal standard deviations, the best estimate we can make of that value is to combine or pool all the sample information we have about the value of the population standard deviation.

The following formula is used to pool the sample standard deviations. Notice that two factors are involved: the number of observations in each sample and the sample standard deviations themselves.

POOLED VARIANCE

$$s_p^2 = \frac{(n_1 - 1)s_1^2 + (n_2 - 1)s_2^2}{n_1 + n_2 - 2} \quad \textbf{(11–3)}$$

where:

s_1^2 is the variance (standard deviation squared) of the first sample.
s_2^2 is the variance of the second sample.

The value of t is computed from the following equation.

TWO-SAMPLE TEST OF MEANS—UNKNOWN σ'S

$$t = \frac{\bar{x}_1 - \bar{x}_2}{\sqrt{s_p^2\left(\frac{1}{n_1} + \frac{1}{n_2}\right)}} \quad \textbf{(11–4)}$$

where:

$\bar{x}_1$ is the mean of the first sample.
$\bar{x}_2$ is the mean of the second sample.
n_1 is the number of observations in the first sample.
n_2 is the number of observations in the second sample.
s_p^2 is the pooled estimate of the population variance.

The number of degrees of freedom in the test is the total number of items sampled minus the total number of samples. Because there are two samples, there are $n_1 + n_2 - 2$ degrees of freedom.

To summarize, there are three requirements or assumptions for the test.

1. The sampled populations are approximately normally distributed.
2. The sampled populations are independent.
3. The standard deviations of the two populations are equal.

The following example/solution explains the details of the test.

EXAMPLE

Owens Lawn Care Inc. manufactures and assembles lawnmowers that are shipped to dealers throughout the United States and Canada. Two different procedures have been proposed for mounting the engine on the frame of the lawnmower. The question is: Is there a difference in the mean time to mount the engines on the frames of the lawnmowers? The first procedure was developed by longtime Owens employee Herb Welles (designated as procedure W), and the other procedure was developed by Owens Vice President of Engineering William Atkins (designated as procedure A). To evaluate the two methods, we conduct a time and motion study. A sample of five employees is timed using the Welles method and six using the Atkins method. The results, in minutes, are shown below. Is there a difference in the mean mounting times? Use the .10 significance level.

Welles (minutes)	Atkins (minutes)
2	3
4	7
9	5
3	8
2	4
	3

SOLUTION

Following the six steps to test a hypothesis, the null hypothesis states that there is no difference in mean mounting times between the two procedures. The alternate hypothesis indicates that there is a difference.

$$H_0: \mu_W = \mu_A$$
$$H_1: \mu_W \neq \mu_A$$

The required assumptions are:

- The observations in the Welles sample are *independent* of the observations in the Atkins sample.
- The two populations follow the normal distribution.
- The two populations have equal standard deviations.

Is there a difference between the mean assembly times using the Welles and the Atkins methods? The degrees of freedom are equal to the total number of items sampled minus the number of samples. In this case, that is $n_W + n_A - 2$. Five assemblers used the Welles method and six the Atkins method. Thus, there are 9 degrees of freedom, found by 5 + 6 − 2. The critical values of t, from Appendix B.5 for $df = 9$, a two-tailed test, and the .10 significance level, are −1.833 and 1.833. The decision rule is portrayed graphically in Chart 11–2. We do not reject the null hypothesis if the computed value of t falls between −1.833 and 1.833.

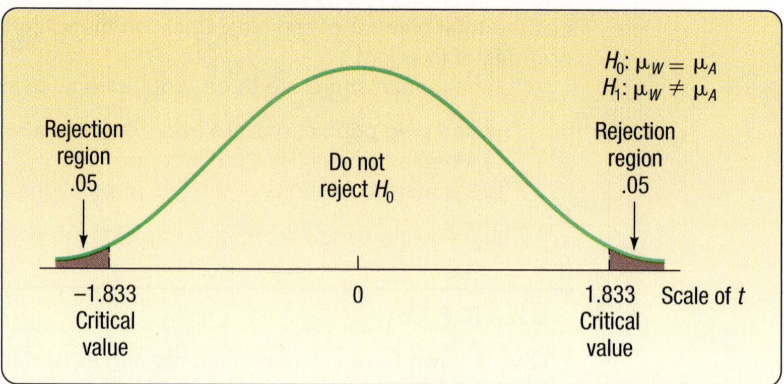

CHART 11–2 Regions of Rejection, Two-Tailed Test, $df = 9$, and .10 Significance Level

We use three steps to compute the value of t.

Step 1: Calculate the sample standard deviations. To compute the sample standard deviations, we use formula (3–9). See the details below.

Welles Method		Atkins Method	
x_W	$(x_W - \bar{x}_W)^2$	x_A	$(x_A - \bar{x}_A)^2$
2	$(2-4)^2 = 4$	3	$(3-5)^2 = 4$
4	$(4-4)^2 = 0$	7	$(7-5)^2 = 4$
9	$(9-4)^2 = 25$	5	$(5-5)^2 = 0$
3	$(3-4)^2 = 1$	8	$(8-5)^2 = 9$
2	$(2-4)^2 = 4$	4	$(4-5)^2 = 1$
20	34	3	$(3-5)^2 = 4$
		30	22

$$\bar{x}_W = \frac{\Sigma x_W}{n_W} = \frac{20}{5} = 4 \qquad \bar{x}_A = \frac{\Sigma x_A}{n_A} = \frac{30}{6} = 5$$

$$s_W = \sqrt{\frac{\Sigma(x_W - \bar{x}_W)^2}{n_W - 1}} = \sqrt{\frac{34}{5-1}} = 2.9155 \qquad s_A = \sqrt{\frac{\Sigma(x_A - \bar{x}_A)^2}{n_A - 1}} = \sqrt{\frac{22}{6-1}} = 2.0976$$

Step 2: Pool the sample variances. We use formula (11–3) to pool the sample variances (standard deviations squared).

$$s_p^2 = \frac{(n_W - 1)s_W^2 + (n_A - 1)s_A^2}{n_W + n_A - 2} = \frac{(5-1)(2.9155)^2 + (6-1)(2.0976)^2}{5+6-2} = 6.2222$$

Step 3: Determine the value of *t*. The mean mounting time for the Welles method is 4.00 minutes, found by $\bar{x}_W = 20/5$. The mean mounting time for the Atkins method is 5.00 minutes, found by $\bar{x}_A = 30/6$. We use formula (11–4) to calculate the value of t.

$$t = \frac{\bar{x}_W - \bar{x}_A}{\sqrt{s_p^2\left(\frac{1}{n_W} + \frac{1}{n_A}\right)}} = \frac{4.00 - 5.00}{\sqrt{6.2222\left(\frac{1}{5} + \frac{1}{6}\right)}} = -0.662$$

The decision is not to reject the null hypothesis because −0.662 falls in the region between −1.833 and 1.833. Our conclusion is that the sample data failed to show a difference between the mean assembly times of the two methods.

We also can estimate the p-value using Appendix B.5. Locate the row with 9 degrees of freedom, and use the two-tailed test column. Find the t value, without regard to the sign, that is closest to our computed value of 0.662. It is 1.383, corresponding to a significance level of .20. Thus, even had we used the 20% significance level, we would not have rejected the null hypothesis of equal means. We can report that the p-value is greater than .20.

Excel has a procedure called "t-Test: Two Sample Assuming Equal Variances" that will perform the calculations of formulas (11–3) and (11–4) as well as find the sample means and sample variances. The details of the procedure are provided in Appendix C. The data are input in the first two columns of the Excel spreadsheet. They are labeled "Welles" and "Atkins." The output follows. The value of t, called the "t Stat," is −0.662, and the two-tailed p-value is .525. As we would expect, the p-value is larger than the significance level of .10. The conclusion is not to reject the null hypothesis.

welles and atkins.xlsx

	A	B	C	D	E	F
1	Welles	Atkins		t-Test: Two-Sample Assuming Equal Variances		
2	2	3				
3	4	7			*Welles*	*Atkins*
4	9	5		Mean	4.000	5.000
5	3	8		Variance	8.500	4.400
6	2	4		Observations	5.000	6.000
7		3		Pooled Variance	6.222	
8				Hypothesized Mean Difference	0.000	
9				df	9.000	
10				t Stat	-0.662	
11				P(T<=t) one-tail	0.262	
12				t Critical one-tail	1.833	
13				P(T<=t) two-tail	0.525	
14				t Critical two-tail	2.262	

SELF-REVIEW 11–2

The production manager at Bellevue Steel, a manufacturer of wheelchairs, wants to compare the number of defective wheelchairs produced on the day shift with the number on the afternoon shift. A sample of the production from 6 day shifts and 8 afternoon shifts revealed the following number of defects.

Day	5	8	7	6	9	7		
Afternoon	8	10	7	11	9	12	14	9

At the .05 significance level, is there a difference in the mean number of defects per shift?

(a) State the null hypothesis and the alternate hypothesis.
(b) What is the decision rule?
(c) What is the value of the test statistic?
(d) What is your decision regarding the null hypothesis?
(e) What is the *p*-value?
(f) Interpret the result.
(g) What are the assumptions necessary for this test?

EXERCISES

For Exercises 7 and 8: (a) state the decision rule, (b) compute the pooled estimate of the population variance, (c) compute the test statistic, (d) state your decision about the null hypothesis, and (e) estimate the *p*-value.

7. The null and alternate hypotheses are:

$$H_0: \mu_1 = \mu_2$$
$$H_1: \mu_1 \neq \mu_2$$

A random sample of 10 observations from one population revealed a sample mean of 23 and a sample standard deviation of 4. A random sample of 8 observations from another population revealed a sample mean of 26 and a sample standard deviation of 5. At the .05 significance level, is there a difference between the population means?

8. The null and alternate hypotheses are:

$$H_0: \mu_1 = \mu_2$$
$$H_1: \mu_1 \neq \mu_2$$

A random sample of 15 observations from the first population revealed a sample mean of 350 and a sample standard deviation of 12. A random sample of 17 observations from the second population revealed a sample mean of 342 and a sample standard deviation of 15. At the .10 significance level, is there a difference in the population means?

Note: Use the six-step hypothesis testing procedure for the following exercises.

9. **FILE** Listed below are the 25 players on the opening-day roster of the 2016 New York Yankees Major League Baseball team, their salaries, and fielding positions.

Player	Position	Salary (US$)
C.C. Sabathia	Starting Pitcher	$25,000,000
Mark Teixeira	First Base	$23,125,000
Masahiro Tanaka	Starting Pitcher	$22,000,000
Jacoby Ellsbury	Center Field	$21,142,857
Alex Rodriguez	Designated Hitter	$21,000,000
Brian McCann	Catcher	$17,000,000
Carlos Beltran	Right Field	$15,000,000
Brett Gardner	Left Field	$13,500,000
Chase Headley	Third Base	$13,000,000
Andrew Miller	Relief Pitcher	$ 9,000,000
Starlin Castro	Second Base	$ 7,857,142
Nathan Eovaldi	Starting Pitcher	$ 5,600,000
Michael Pineda	Starting Pitcher	$ 4,300,000
Ivan Nova	Relief Pitcher	$ 4,100,000
Dustin Ackley	Left Field	$ 3,200,000
Didi Gregorius	Shortstop	$ 2,425,000
Aaron Hicks	Center Field	$ 574,000
Austin Romine	Catcher	$ 556,000
Chasen Shreve	Relief Pitcher	$ 533,400
Luis Severino	Starting Pitcher	$ 521,300
Kirby Yates	Relief Pitcher	$ 511,900
Ronald Torreyes	Second Base	$ 508,600
Johnny Barbato	Relief Pitcher	$ 507,500
Dellin Betances	Relief Pitcher	$ 507,500
Luis Cessa	Relief Pitcher	$ 507,500

Sort the players into two groups, all pitchers (relief and starting) and position players (all others). Assume equal population standard deviations for the pitchers and the position players. Test the hypothesis that mean salaries of pitchers and position players are equal using the .01 significance level.

10. A recent study compared the time spent together by single- and dual-earner couples. According to the records kept by the wives during the study, the mean amount of time spent together watching television among the single-earner couples was 61 minutes per day, with a standard deviation of 15.5 minutes. For the dual-earner couples, the mean number of minutes spent watching television was 48.4 minutes, with a standard deviation of 18.1 minutes. At the .01 significance level, can we conclude that the single-earner couples on average spend more time watching television together? There were 15 single-earner and 12 dual-earner couples studied.

11. FILE Ms. Lisa Monnin is the budget director for Nexus Media Inc. She would like to compare the daily travel expenses for the sales staff and the audit staff. She collected the following sample information.

Sales ($)	131	135	146	165	136	142	
Audit ($)	130	102	129	143	149	120	139

At the .10 significance level, can she conclude that the mean daily expenses are greater for the sales staff than the audit staff? What is the *p*-value?

12. FILE The Tampa Bay (Florida) Area Chamber of Commerce wanted to know whether the mean weekly salary of nurses was larger than that of school teachers. To investigate, they collected the following information on the amounts earned last week by a sample of school teachers and a sample of nurses.

School Teachers ($)	1,095	1,076	1,077	1,125	1,034	1,059	1,052	1,070	1,079	1,080	1.092	1,082
Nurses ($)	1,091	1,140	1,071	1,021	1,100	1,109	1,075	1,079				

Is it reasonable to conclude that the mean weekly salary of nurses is higher? Use the .01 significance level. What is the *p*-value?

Unequal Population Standard Deviations

In the previous sections, it was necessary to assume that the populations had equal standard deviations. To put it another way, we did not know the population standard deviations, but we assumed they were equal. In many cases, this is a reasonable assumption, but what if it is not? In the next chapter, we present a formal method to test the assumption of equal variances. If the variances are not equal, we describe a test of hypothesis that does not require either the equal variance or the normality assumption in Chapter 16.

If it is not reasonable to assume the population standard deviations are equal, then we use a statistic very much like formula (11–2). The sample standard deviations, s_1 and s_2, are used in place of the respective population standard deviations. In addition, the degrees of freedom are adjusted downward by a rather complex approximation formula. The effect is to reduce the number of degrees of freedom in the test, which will require a larger value of the test statistic to reject the null hypothesis.

The formula for the *t* statistic is:

TEST STATISTIC FOR NO DIFFERENCE IN MEANS, UNEQUAL VARIANCES

$$t = \frac{\bar{x}_1 - \bar{x}_2}{\sqrt{\frac{s_1^2}{n_1} + \frac{s_2^2}{n_2}}} \qquad \textbf{(11–5)}$$

The degrees of freedom statistic is found by:

DEGREES OF FREEDOM FOR UNEQUAL VARIANCE TEST

$$df = \frac{[(s_1^2/n_1) + (s_2^2/n_2)]^2}{\frac{(s_1^2/n_1)^2}{n_1 - 1} + \frac{(s_2^2/n_2)^2}{n_2 - 1}} \qquad \textbf{(11–6)}$$

where n_1 and n_2 are the respective sample sizes and s_1 and s_2 are the respective sample standard deviations. If necessary, this fraction is rounded down to an integer value. An example will explain the details.

EXAMPLE

Personnel in a consumer testing laboratory are evaluating the absorbency of paper towels. They wish to compare a set of store brand towels to a similar group of name brand ones. For each brand they dip a ply of the paper into a tub of fluid, allow the paper to drain back into the vat for 2 minutes, and then evaluate the amount of liquid the paper has taken up from the vat. A random sample of nine store brand paper towels absorbed the following amounts of liquid in milliliters.

8	8	3	1	9	7	5	5	12

An independent random sample of 12 name brand towels absorbed the following amounts of liquid in milliliters:

12	11	10	6	8	9	9	10	11	9	8	10

Use the .10 significance level and test if there is a difference in the mean amount of liquid absorbed by the two types of paper towels.

SOLUTION

To begin, let's assume that the amounts of liquid absorbed follow the normal probability distribution for both the store brand and the name brand towels. We do not know either of the population standard deviations, so we are going to use the t distribution as the test statistic. The assumption of equal population standard deviations does not appear reasonable. The amount of absorption in the store brand ranges from 1 ml to 12 ml. For the name brand, the amount of absorption ranges from 6 ml to 12 ml. That is, there is considerably more variation in the amount of absorption in the store brand than in the name brand. We observe the difference in the variation in the following dot plot provided by Minitab. The software commands to create a Minitab dot plot are given in Appendix C, Chapter 4, 4-1.

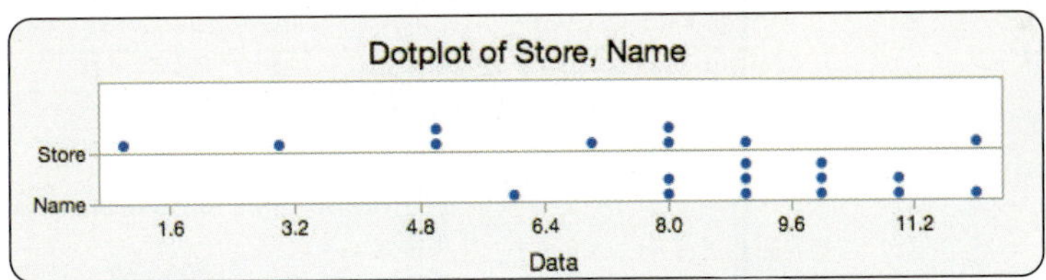

So we decide to use the t distribution and assume that the population standard deviations are not the same.

In the six-step hypothesis testing procedure, the first step is to state the null hypothesis and the alternate hypothesis. The null hypothesis is that there is no difference in the mean amount of liquid absorbed between the two types of paper towels. The alternate hypothesis is that there is a difference.

$$H_0: \mu_1 = \mu_2$$
$$H_0: \mu_1 \neq \mu_2$$

The significance level is .10 and the test statistic follows the t distribution. Because we do not wish to assume equal population standard deviations, we adjust the degrees of freedom using formula (11–6). To do so, we need to find the sample standard deviations. We can use statistical software to quickly find these results.

The respective sample sizes are $n_1 = 9$ and $n_2 = 12$ and the respective standard deviations are 3.321 ml and 1.621 ml.

Variable	n	Mean	Standard Deviation
Store	9	6.444	3.321
Name	12	9.417	1.621

Inserting this information into formula (11–6):

$$df = \frac{[(s_1^2/n_1) + (s_2^2/n_2)]^2}{\dfrac{(s_1^2/n_1)^2}{n_1 - 1} + \dfrac{(s_2^2/n_2)^2}{n_2 - 1}} = \frac{[(3.321^2/9) + (1.621^2/12)]^2}{\dfrac{(3.321^2/9)^2}{9 - 1} + \dfrac{(1.621^2/12)^2}{12 - 1}} = \frac{1.4444^2}{.1877 + .0044} = 10.86$$

The usual practice is to round down to the integer, so we use 10 degrees of freedom. From Appendix B.5 with 10 degrees of freedom, a two-tailed test, and the .10 significance level, the critical t values are −1.812 and 1.812. Our decision rule is to reject the null hypothesis if the computed value of t is less than −1.812 or greater than 1.812.

To find the value of the test statistic, we use formula (11–5). Recall that the mean amount of absorption for the store paper towels is 6.444 ml and 9.417 ml for the brand.

$$t = \frac{\bar{x}_1 - \bar{x}_2}{\sqrt{\dfrac{s_1^2}{n_1} + \dfrac{s_2^2}{n_2}}} = \frac{6.444 - 9.417}{\sqrt{\dfrac{3.321^2}{9} + \dfrac{1.621^2}{12}}} = -2.474$$

The computed value of t is less than the lower critical value, so our decision is to reject the null hypothesis. We conclude that the mean absorption rate for the two towels is not the same.

For this analysis there are many calculations. Statistical software often provides an option to compare two population means with different standard deviations. The Minitab output for this example follows.

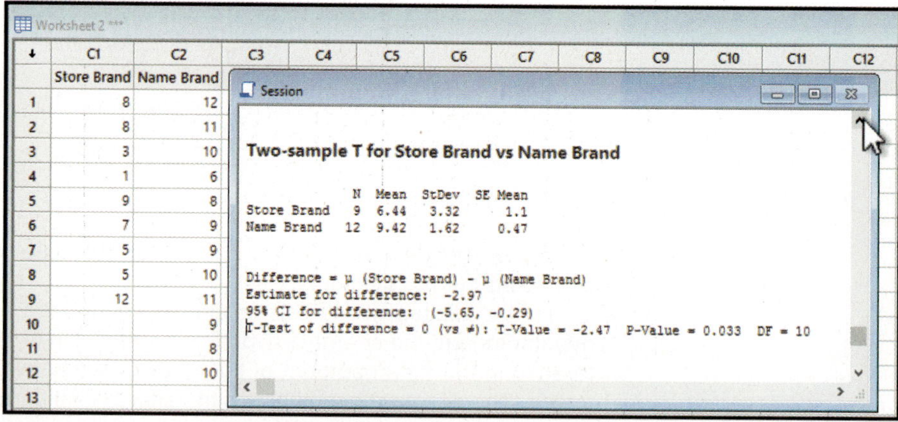

SELF-REVIEW 11–3

It is often useful for companies to know who their customers are and how they became customers. A credit card company is interested in whether the owner of the card applied for the card on his or her own or was contacted by a telemarketer. The company obtained the following sample information regarding end-of-the-month balances for the two groups.

Source	Sample Size	Mean	Standard Deviation
Applied	10	$1,568	$356
Contacted	8	1,967	857

Is it reasonable to conclude the mean balance is larger for the credit card holders that were contacted by telemarketers than for those who applied on their own for the card? Assume the population standard deviations are not the same. Use the .05 significance level.

(a) State the null hypothesis and the alternate hypothesis.
(b) How many degrees of freedom are there?
(c) What is the decision rule?
(d) What is the value of the test statistic?
(e) What is your decision regarding the null hypothesis?
(f) Interpret the result.

EXERCISES

For exercises 13 and 14, assume the sample populations do not have equal standard deviations and use the .05 significance level: (a) determine the number of degrees of freedom, (b) state the decision rule, (c) compute the value of the test statistic, and (d) state your decision about the null hypothesis.

13. The null and alternate hypotheses are:

$$H_0: \mu_1 = \mu_2$$
$$H_1: \mu_1 \neq \mu_2$$

A random sample of 15 items from the first population showed a mean of 50 and a standard deviation of 5. A sample of 12 items for the second population showed a mean of 46 and a standard deviation of 15.

14. The null and alternate hypotheses are:

$$H_0: \mu_1 \leq \mu_2$$
$$H_1: \mu_1 > \mu_2$$

A random sample of 20 items from the first population showed a mean of 100 and a standard deviation of 15. A sample of 16 items for the second population showed a mean of 94 and a standard deviation of 8. Use the .05 significant level.

15. A recent survey compared the costs of adoption through public and private agencies. For a sample of 16 adoptions through a public agency, the mean cost was $21,045, with a standard deviation of $835. For a sample of 18 adoptions through a private agency, the mean cost was $22,840, with a standard deviation of $1,545. Can we conclude the mean cost is larger for adopting children through a private agency? Use the .05 significance level.

16. **FILE** Suppose you are an expert on the fashion industry and wish to gather information to compare the amount earned per month by models featuring Liz Claiborne attire with those of Calvin Klein. The following is the amount ($000) earned per month by a sample of 15 Claiborne models:

$5.0	$4.5	$3.4	$3.4	$6.0	$3.3	$4.5	$4.6	$3.5	$5.2
4.8	4.4	4.6	3.6	5.0					

The following is the amount ($000) earned by a sample of 12 Klein models.

$3.1	$3.7	$3.6	$4.0	$3.8	$3.8	$5.9	$4.9	$3.6	$3.6
2.3	4.0								

Is it reasonable to conclude that Claiborne models earn more? Use the .05 significance level and assume the population standard deviations are not the same.

LO11-3
Test a hypothesis about the mean population difference between paired or dependent observations.

TWO-SAMPLE TESTS OF HYPOTHESIS: DEPENDENT SAMPLES

In the Owens Lawn Care example/solution on page 361, we tested the difference between the means from two independent populations. We compared the mean time required to mount an engine using the Welles method to the time to mount the engine using the Atkins method. The samples were *independent,* meaning that the sample of assembly times using the Welles method was in no way related to the sample of assembly times using the Atkins method.

There are situations, however, in which the samples are not independent. To put it another way, the samples are *dependent* or *related*. As an example, Nickel Savings and Loan employs two firms, Schadek Appraisals and Bowyer Real Estate, to appraise the value of the real estate properties on which it makes loans. It is important that these two firms be similar in their appraisal values. To review the consistency of the two appraisal firms, Nickel Savings randomly selects 10 homes and has both Schadek Appraisals and Bowyer Real Estate appraise the values of the selected homes. For each home, there will be a pair of appraisal values. That is, for each home there will be an appraised value from both Schadek Appraisals and Bowyer Real Estate. The appraised values depend on, or are related to, the home selected. This is also referred to as a **paired sample.**

© Photodisc/Getty Images

For hypothesis testing, we are interested in the distribution of the *differences* in the appraised value of each home. Hence, there is only one sample. To put it more formally, we are investigating whether the mean of the distribution of differences in the appraised values is 0. The sample is made up of the *differences* between the appraised values determined by Schadek Appraisals and the values from Bowyer Real Estate. If the two appraisal firms are reporting similar estimates, then sometimes Schadek Appraisals will be the higher value and sometimes Bowyer Real Estate will have the higher value. However, the mean of the distribution of differences will be 0. On the other hand, if one of the firms consistently reports larger appraisal values, then the mean of the distribution of the differences will not be 0.

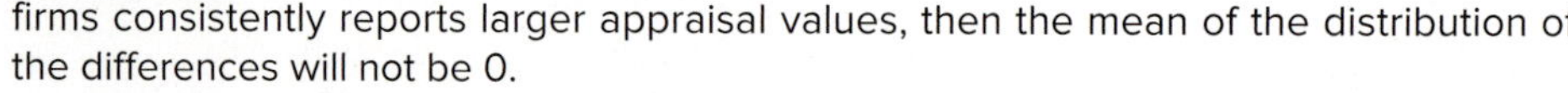

We will use the symbol μ_d to indicate the population mean of the distribution of differences. We assume the distribution of the population of differences is approximately normally distributed. The test statistic follows the *t* distribution and we calculate its value from the following formula:

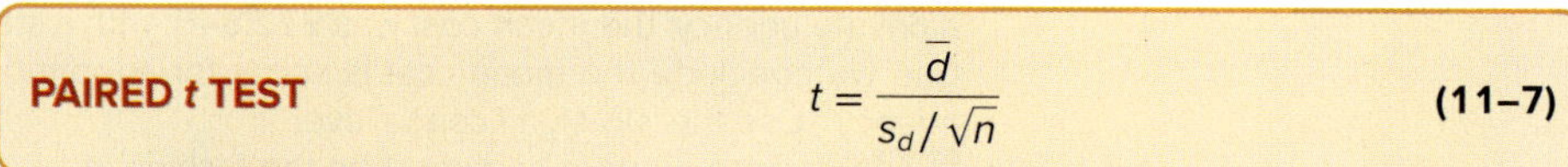

PAIRED *t* TEST $$t = \frac{\bar{d}}{s_d / \sqrt{n}}$$ **(11–7)**

There are $n - 1$ degrees of freedom and

- $\bar{d}$ is the mean of the difference between the paired or related observations.
- s_d is the standard deviation of the differences between the paired or related observations.
- n is the number of paired observations.

The standard deviation of the differences is computed by the familiar formula for the standard deviation [see formula (3–9)], except d is substituted for x. The formula is:

$$s_d = \sqrt{\frac{\Sigma(d - \bar{d})^2}{n - 1}}$$

The following example illustrates this test.

EXAMPLE

Recall that Nickel Savings and Loan wishes to compare the two companies it uses to appraise the value of residential homes. Nickel Savings selected a sample of 10 residential properties and scheduled both firms for an appraisal. The results, reported in \$000, are:

Home	Schadek	Bowyer
A	235	228
B	210	205
C	231	219
D	242	240
E	205	198
F	230	223
G	231	227
H	210	215
I	225	222
J	249	245

At the .05 significance level, can we conclude there is a difference between the firms' mean appraised home values?

SOLUTION

The first step is to state the null and the alternate hypotheses. In this case, a two-tailed alternative is appropriate because we are interested in determining whether there is a *difference* in the firms' appraised values. We are not interested in showing whether one particular firm appraises property at a higher value than the other. The question is whether the sample differences in the appraised values could have come from a population with a mean of 0. If the population mean of the differences is 0, then we conclude that there is no difference between the two firms' appraised values. The null and alternate hypotheses are:

$$H_0: \mu_d = 0$$
$$H_1: \mu_d \neq 0$$

There are 10 homes appraised by both firms, so $n = 10$, and $df = n - 1 = 10 - 1 = 9$. We have a two-tailed test, and the significance level is .05. To determine the critical value, go to Appendix B.5 and move across the row with 9 degrees of freedom to the column for a two-tailed test and the .05 significance level. The value at the intersection is 2.262. This value appears in the box in Table 11–2. The decision rule is to reject the null hypothesis if the computed value of t is less than −2.262 or greater than 2.262. Here are the computational details.

Home	Schadek	Bowyer	Difference, d	$(d - \bar{d})$	$(d - \bar{d})^2$
A	235	228	7	2.4	5.76
B	210	205	5	0.4	0.16
C	231	219	12	7.4	54.76
D	242	240	2	−2.6	6.76
E	205	198	7	2.4	5.76
F	230	223	7	2.4	5.76
G	231	227	4	−0.6	0.36
H	210	215	−5	−9.6	92.16
I	225	222	3	−1.6	2.56
J	249	245	4	−0.6	0.36
			46	0	174.40

$$\bar{d} = \frac{\Sigma d}{n} = \frac{46}{10} = 4.60$$

$$s_d = \sqrt{\frac{\Sigma(d - \bar{d})^2}{n - 1}} = \sqrt{\frac{174.4}{10 - 1}} = 4.402$$

Using formula (11–7), the value of the test statistic is 3.305, found by

$$t = \frac{\bar{d}}{s_d/\sqrt{n}} = \frac{4.6}{4.402/\sqrt{10}} = \frac{4.6}{1.3920} = 3.305$$

Because the computed t falls in the rejection region, the null hypothesis is rejected. The population distribution of differences does not have a mean of 0. We conclude that there is a difference between the firms' mean appraised home values. The largest difference of $12,000 is for Home 3. Perhaps that would be an appropriate place to begin a more detailed review.

To find the p-value, we use Appendix B.5 and the section for a two-tailed test. Move along the row with 9 degrees of freedom and find the values of t that are closest to our calculated value. For a .01 significance level, the value of t is 3.250. The computed value is larger than this value, but smaller than the value of 4.781 corresponding to the .001 significance level. Hence, the p-value is less than .01. This information is highlighted in Table 11–2.

TABLE 11–2 A Portion of the t Distribution from Appendix B.5

	Confidence Intervals					
	80%	90%	95%	98%	99%	
	Level of Significance for One-Tailed Test					
df	0.10	0.05	0.025	0.01	0.005	
	Level of Significance for Two-Tailed Test					
	0.20	0.10	0.05	0.02	0.01	0.001
1	3.078	6.314	12.706	31.821	63.657	636.619
2	1.886	2.920	4.303	6.965	9.925	31.599
3	1.638	2.353	3.182	4.541	5.841	12.924
[illegible]	[illegible]	2.132	2.776	3.747	4.604	8.610
[illegible]	[illegible]	2.015	2.571	3.365	4.032	6.869
6	1.440	1.943	2.447	3.143	3.707	5.959
7	1.415	895	2.365	2.998	3.499	5.408
8	1.397	1.860	2.306	2.896	3.355	5.041
9	1.383	1.833	2.262	2.821	3.250	4.781
10	1.372	1.812	2.228	2.764	3.169	4.587

Critical t-statistic for 0.05

p-value between 0.01 and 0.001

Excel's statistical analysis software has a procedure called "t-Test: Paired Two-Sample for Means" that will perform the calculations of formula (11–7). The output from this procedure is given below.

The computed value of t is 3.305, and the two-tailed p-value is .009. Because the p-value is less than .05, we reject the hypothesis that the mean of the distribution of the differences between the appraised values is zero. In fact, this p-value is between .01 and .001. There is a small likelihood that the null hypothesis is true.

	A	B	C	D	E	F	G
1	Home	Schadek	Bowyer		t-Test: Paired Two-Sample for Means		
2	A	235	228				
3	B	210	205			*Schadek*	*Bowyer*
4	C	231	219		Mean	226.800	222.200
5	D	242	240		Variance	208.844	204.178
6	E	205	198		Observations	10.000	10.000
7	F	230	223		Pearson Correlation	0.953	
8	G	231	227		Hypothesized Mean Difference	0.000	
9	H	210	215		df	9.000	
10	I	225	222		t Stat	3.305	
11	J	249	245		P(T<=t) one-tail	0.005	
12					t Critical one-tail	1.833	
13					P(T<=t) two-tail	0.009	
14					t Critical two-tail	2.262	
15							

LO11-4

Explain the difference between dependent and independent samples.

COMPARING DEPENDENT AND INDEPENDENT SAMPLES

Beginning students are often confused by the difference between tests for independent samples [formula (11–4)] and tests for dependent samples [formula (11–7)]. How do we tell the difference between dependent and independent samples? There are two types of dependent samples: (1) those characterized by a measurement, an intervention of some type, and then another measurement; and (2) a matching or pairing of the observations. To explain further:

1. The first type of dependent sample is characterized by a measurement followed by an intervention of some kind and then another measurement. This could be called a "before" and "after" study. Two examples will help to clarify. Suppose we want to show that, by placing speakers in the production area and playing soothing music, we are able to increase production. We begin by selecting a sample of workers and measuring their output under the current conditions. The speakers are then installed in the production area, and we again measure the output of the same workers. There are two measurements, before placing the speakers in the production area and after. The intervention is placing speakers in the production area.

   A second example involves an educational firm that offers courses designed to increase test scores and reading ability. Suppose the firm wants to offer a course that will help high school juniors increase their SAT scores. To begin, each student takes the SAT in the junior year in high school. During the summer between the junior and senior year, they participate in the course that gives them tips on taking tests. Finally, during the fall of their senior year in high school, they retake the SAT. Again, the procedure is characterized by a measurement (taking the SAT as a junior), an intervention (the summer workshops), and another measurement (taking the SAT during their senior year).
2. The second type of dependent sample is characterized by matching or pairing observations. The previous example/solution regarding Nickel Savings illustrates dependent samples. A property is selected and both firms appraise the same property. As a second example, suppose an industrial psychologist wishes to study the intellectual similarities of newly married couples. She selects a sample of newlyweds. Next, she administers a standard intelligence test to both the man and woman to determine the difference in the scores. Notice the matching that occurred: comparing the scores that are paired or matched by marriage.

Why do we prefer dependent samples to independent samples? By using dependent samples, we are able to reduce the variation in the sampling distribution. To illustrate, we will use the Nickel Savings and Loan example/solution just completed. Suppose we assume that we have two independent samples of real estate property for appraisal and conduct the following test of hypothesis, using formula (11–4). The null and alternate hypotheses are:

$$H_0: \mu_1 = \mu_2$$
$$H_1: \mu_1 \neq \mu_2$$

There are now two independent samples of 10 each. So the number of degrees of freedom is 10 + 10 − 2 = 18. From Appendix B.5, for the .05 significance level, H_0 is rejected if t is less than −2.101 or greater than 2.101.

We use Excel to find the means and standard deviations of the two independent samples as shown in the Chapter 3 section of Appendix C. The Excel instructions to find the pooled variance and the value of the "t Stat" are in the Chapter 11 section in Appendix C. These values are highlighted in yellow.

	A	B	C	D	E	F	G	H
1	Home	Schadek	Bowyer		t-Test: Two-Sample Assuming Equal Variances			
2	A	235	228					
3	B	210	205			*Schadek*	*Bowyer*	
4	C	231	219		Mean	226.800	222.200	
5	D	242	240		Variance	208.844	204.178	
6	E	205	198		Observations	10.000	10.000	
7	F	230	223		Pooled Variance	206.511		
8	G	231	227		Hypothesized Mean Difference	0.000		
9	H	210	215		df	18.000		
10	I	225	222		t Stat	0.716		
11	J	249	245		P(T<=t) one-tail	0.242		
12					t Critical one-tail	1.734		
13	Mean =	226.80	222.20		P(T<=t) two-tail	0.483		
14	S =	14.45	14.29		t Critical two-tail	2.101		
15								

The mean of the appraised value of the 10 properties by Schadek is \$226,800, and the standard deviation is \$14,500. For Bowyer Real Estate, the mean appraised value is \$222,200, and the standard deviation is \$14,290. To make the calculations easier, we use \$000 instead of \$. The value of the pooled estimate of the variance from formula (11–3) is

$$s_p^2 = \frac{(n_1 - 1)s_1^2 + (n_2 - 1)s_2^2}{n_1 + n_2 - 2} = \frac{(10 - 1)(14.45^2) + (10 - 1)(14.29)^2}{10 + 10 - 2} = 206.50$$

From formula (11–4), t is 0.716.

$$t = \frac{\bar{x}_1 - \bar{x}_2}{\sqrt{s_p^2\left(\frac{1}{n_1} + \frac{1}{n_2}\right)}} = \frac{226.8 - 222.2}{\sqrt{206.50\left(\frac{1}{10} + \frac{1}{10}\right)}} = \frac{4.6}{6.4265} = 0.716$$

The computed t (0.716) is less than 2.101, so the null hypothesis is not rejected. We cannot show that there is a difference in the mean appraisal value. That is not the same conclusion that we got before! Why does this happen? The numerator is the same in the paired observations test (4.6). However, the denominator is smaller. In the paired test, the denominator is 1.3920 (see the calculations on page 372 in the previous section). In the case of the independent samples, the denominator is 6.4265. There is more variation or uncertainty. This accounts for the difference in the t values and the difference in the statistical decisions. The denominator measures the standard error of the statistic. When the samples are *not* paired, two kinds of variation are present: differences between the two appraisal firms and the difference in the value of the real estate. Properties numbered 4 and 10 have relatively high values, whereas number 5 is relatively low. These data show how different the values of the property are, but we are really interested in the difference between the two appraisal firms.

In sum, when we can pair or match observations that measure differences for a common variable, a hypothesis test based on dependent samples is more sensitive to detecting a significant difference than a hypothesis test based on independent samples. In the case of comparing the property valuations by Schadek Appraisals and Bowyer Real Estate, the hypothesis test based on dependent samples eliminates the variation between the values of the properties and focuses only on the comparisons in the two appraisals for each property. There is a bit of bad news here. In the dependent samples test, the degrees of freedom are half of what they are if the samples are not paired. For the real estate example, the degrees of freedom drop from 18 to 9 when the observations are paired. However, in most cases, this is a small price to pay for a better test.

SELF-REVIEW 11–4

Advertisements by Core Fitness Center claim that completing its course will result in losing weight. A random sample of eight recent participants showed the following weights before and after completing the course. At the .01 significance level, can we conclude the students lost weight?

Name	Before	After
Hunter	155	154
Cashman	228	207
Mervine	141	147
Massa	162	157
Creola	211	196
Peterson	164	150
Redding	184	170
Poust	172	165

(a) State the null hypothesis and the alternate hypothesis.
(b) What is the critical value of *t*?
(c) What is the computed value of *t*?
(d) Interpret the result. What is the *p*-value?
(e) What assumption needs to be made about the distribution of the differences?

EXERCISES

17. The null and alternate hypotheses are:

$$H_0: \mu_d \leq 0$$
$$H_1: \mu_d > 0$$

The following sample information shows the number of defective units produced on the day shift and the afternoon shift for a sample of four days last month.

	Day			
	1	2	3	4
Day shift	10	12	15	19
Afternoon shift	8	9	12	15

At the .05 significance level, can we conclude there are more defects produced on the day shift?

18. The null and alternate hypotheses are:

$$H_0: \mu_d = 0$$
$$H_1: \mu_d \neq 0$$

The following paired observations show the number of traffic citations given for speeding by Officer Dhondt and Officer Meredith of the South Carolina Highway Patrol for the last five months.

	Number of Citations Issued				
	May	**June**	**July**	**August**	**September**
Officer Dhondt	30	22	25	19	26
Officer Meredith	26	19	20	15	19

At the .05 significance level, is there a difference in the mean number of citations given by the two officers?

Note: Use the six-step hypothesis testing procedure to solve the following exercises.

19. **FILE** The management of Discount Furniture, a chain of discount furniture stores in the Northeast, designed an incentive plan for salespeople. To evaluate this innovative plan, 12 salespeople were selected at random, and their weekly incomes before and after the plan were recorded.

Salesperson	Before	After
Sid Mahone	$320	$340
Carol Quick	290	285
Tom Jackson	421	475
Andy Jones	510	510
Jean Sloan	210	210
Jack Walker	402	500
Peg Mancuso	625	631
Anita Loma	560	560
John Cuso	360	365
Carl Utz	431	431
A. S. Kushner	506	525
Fern Lawton	505	619

Was there a significant increase in the typical salesperson's weekly income due to the innovative incentive plan? Use the .05 significance level. Estimate the *p*-value, and interpret it.

20. **FILE** The federal government recently granted funds for a special program designed to reduce crime in high-crime areas. A study of the results of the program in eight high-crime areas of Miami, Florida, yielded the following results.

	Number of Crimes by Area							
	A	**B**	**C**	**D**	**E**	**F**	**G**	**H**
Before	14	7	4	5	17	12	8	9
After	2	7	3	6	8	13	3	5

Has there been a decrease in the number of crimes since the inauguration of the program? Use the .01 significance level. Estimate the *p*-value.

CHAPTER SUMMARY

I. In comparing two population means, we wish to know whether they could be equal.

A. We are investigating whether the distribution of the difference between the means could have a mean of 0.

B. The test statistic follows the standard normal distribution if the population standard deviations are known.

1. The two populations follow normal distributions.

2. The samples are from independent populations.

3. The formula to compute the value of z is

$$z = \frac{\bar{x}_1 - \bar{x}_2}{\sqrt{\frac{\sigma_1^2}{n_1} + \frac{\sigma_2^2}{n_2}}} \qquad \textbf{(11–2)}$$

II. The test statistic to compare two means is the t distribution if the population standard deviations are not known.

A. Both populations are approximately normally distributed.

B. The populations must have equal standard deviations.

C. The samples are independent.

D. Finding the value of t requires two steps.

1. The first step is to pool the standard deviations according to the following formula:

$$s_p^2 = \frac{(n_1 - 1)s_1^2 + (n_2 - 1)s_2^2}{n_1 + n_2 - 2} \qquad \textbf{(11–3)}$$

2. The value of t is computed from the following formula:

$$t = \frac{\bar{x}_1 - \bar{x}_2}{\sqrt{s_p^2\left(\frac{1}{n_1} + \frac{1}{n_2}\right)}} \qquad \textbf{(11–4)}$$

3. The degrees of freedom for the test are $n_1 + n_2 - 2$.

III. If we cannot assume the population standard deviations are equal, we adjust the degrees of freedom and the formula for finding t.

A. We determine the degrees of freedom based on the following formula.

$$df = \frac{[(s_1^2/n_1) + (s_2^2/n_2)]^2}{\frac{(s_1^2/n_1)^2}{n_1 - 1} + \frac{(s_2^2/n_2)^2}{n_2 - 1}} \qquad \textbf{(11–6)}$$

B. The value of the test statistic is computed from the following formula.

$$t = \frac{\bar{x}_1 - \bar{x}_2}{\sqrt{\frac{s_1^2}{n_1} + \frac{s_2^2}{n_2}}} \qquad \textbf{(11–5)}$$

IV. For dependent samples, we assume the population distribution of the paired differences has a mean of 0.

A. We first compute the mean and the standard deviation of the sample differences.

B. The value of the test statistic is computed from the following formula:

$$t = \frac{\bar{d}}{s_d/\sqrt{n}} \qquad \textbf{(11–7)}$$

PRONUNCIATION KEY

SYMBOL	MEANING	PRONUNCIATION
s_p^2	Pooled sample variance	*s squared sub p*
$\bar{X}_1$	Mean of the first sample	*x bar sub 1*
$\bar{X}_2$	Mean of the second sample	*x bar sub 2*
$\bar{d}$	Mean of the difference between dependent observations	*d bar*
s_d	Standard deviation of the difference between dependent observations	*s sub d*

CHAPTER EXERCISES

21. A recent study focused on the number of times men and women who live alone buy take-out dinner in a month. Assume that the distributions follow the normal probability distribution and the population standard deviations are equal. The information is summarized below.

Statistic	Men	Women
Sample mean	24.51	22.69
Sample standard deviation	4.48	3.86
Sample size	35	40

At the .01 significance level, is there a difference in the mean number of times men and women order take-out dinners in a month? What is the *p*-value?

22. Clark Heter is an industrial engineer at Lyons Products. He would like to determine whether there are more units produced on the night shift than on the day shift. The mean number of units produced by a sample of 54 day-shift workers was 345. The mean number of units produced by a sample of 60 night-shift workers was 351. Assume the population standard deviation of the number of units produced on the day shift is 21 and 28 on the night shift. Using the .05 significance level, is the number of units produced on the night shift larger?

23. Fry Brothers Heating and Air Conditioning Inc. employs Larry Clark and George Murnen to make service calls to repair furnaces and air-conditioning units in homes. Tom Fry, the owner, would like to know whether there is a difference in the mean number of service calls they make per day. A random sample of 40 days last year showed that Larry Clark made an average of 4.77 calls per day. For a sample of 50 days George Murnen made an average of 5.02 calls per day. Assume the population standard deviation for Larry Clark is 1.05 calls per day and 1.23 calls per day for George Murnen. At the .05 significance level, is there a difference in the mean number of calls per day between the two employees? What is the *p*-value?

24. A coffee manufacturer is interested in whether the mean daily consumption of regular-coffee drinkers is less than that of decaffeinated-coffee drinkers. Assume the population standard deviation for those drinking regular coffee is 1.20 cups per day and 1.36 cups per day for those drinking decaffeinated coffee. A random sample of 50 regular-coffee drinkers showed a mean of 4.35 cups per day. A sample of 40 decaffeinated-coffee drinkers showed a mean of 5.84 cups per day. Use the .01 significance level. Compute the *p*-value.

25. A cell phone company offers two plans to its subscribers. At the time new subscribers sign up, they are asked to provide some demographic information. The mean yearly income for a sample of 40 subscribers to Plan A is $57,000 with a standard deviation of $9,200. For a sample of 30 subscribers to Plan B, the mean income is $61,000 with a standard deviation of $7,100. At the .05 significance level, is it reasonable to conclude the mean income of those selecting Plan B is larger? What is the *p*-value?

26. A computer manufacturer offers technical support that is available 24 hours a day, 7 days a week. Timely resolution of these calls is important to the company's image. For 35 calls that were related to software, technicians resolved the issues in a mean time of 18 minutes with a standard deviation of 4.2 minutes. For 45 calls related to hardware, technicians resolved the problems in a mean time of 15.5 minutes with a standard deviation of 3.9 minutes. At the .05 significance level, does it take longer to resolve software issues? What is the *p*-value?

27. Music streaming services are the most popular way to listen to music. Data gathered over the last 12 months show Apple Music was used by an average of 1.65 million households with a sample standard deviation of 0.56 million family units. Over the same 12 months Spotify was used by an average of 2.2 million families with a sample standard deviation of 0.30 million. Assume the population standard deviations are not the same. Using a significance level of .05, test the hypothesis of no difference in the mean number of households picking either service.

28. Businesses such as General Mills, Kellogg's, and Betty Crocker regularly use coupons to build brand allegiance and stimulate sales. Marketers believe that the users of paper coupons are different from the users of e-coupons accessed through the Internet. One survey recorded the age of each person who redeemed a coupon along with the type of coupon (either paper or electronic). The sample of 25 traditional paper-coupon clippers had a mean age of 39.5 with a standard deviation of 4.8. The sample of 35 e-coupon users had a mean age of 33.6 years with a standard deviation of 10.9. Assume the population standard deviations are not the same. Using a significance level of .01, test the hypothesis of no difference in the mean ages of the two groups of coupon clients.

29. The owner of Bun 'N' Run Hamburgers wishes to compare the sales per day at two locations. The mean number sold for 10 randomly selected days at the Northside site was 83.55, and the standard deviation was 10.50. For a random sample of 12 days at the Southside location, the mean number sold was 78.80 and the standard deviation was 14.25. At the .05 significance level, is there a difference in the mean number of hamburgers sold at the two locations? What is the *p*-value?

30. **FILE** Educational Technology, Inc. sells software to provide guided homework problems for a statistics course. They would like to know if students who use the software score better on exams. A sample of students who used the software had the following exam scores: 86, 78, 66, 83, 84, 81, 84, 109, 65, and 102. Students who did not use the software had the following exam scores: 91, 71, 75, 76, 87, 79, 73, 76, 79, 78, 87, 90, 76, and 72. Assume the population standard deviations are not the same. At the .10 significance level, can we conclude that there is a difference in the mean exam scores for the two groups of students?

31. **FILE** The Willow Run Outlet Mall has two Haggar Outlet Stores, one located on Peach Street and the other on Plum Street. The two stores are laid out differently, but both store managers claim their layout maximizes the amounts customers will purchase on impulse. A sample of 10 customers at the Peach Street store revealed they spent the following amounts on impulse purchases: $17.58, $19.73, $12.61, $17.79, $16.22, $15.82, $15.40, $15.86, $11.82, and $15.85. A sample of 14 customers at the Plum Street store revealed they spent the following amounts on impulse purchases: $18.19, $20.22, $17.38, $17.96, $23.92, $15.87, $16.47, $15.96, $16.79, $16.74, $21.40, $20.57, $19.79, and $14.83. At the .01 significance level, is there a difference in the mean amounts purchased on impulse at the two stores?

32. **FILE** Grand Strand Family Medical Center treats minor medical emergencies for visitors to the Myrtle Beach area. There are two facilities, one in the Little River Area and the other in Murrells Inlet. The Quality Assurance Department wishes to compare the mean waiting time for patients at the two locations. Samples of the waiting times for each location, reported in minutes, follow:

Location	Waiting Time											
Little River	31	28	29	22	29	18	32	25	29	26		
Murrells Inlet	22	23	26	27	26	25	30	29	23	23	27	22

Assume the population standard deviations are not the same. At the .05 significance level, is there a difference in the mean waiting time?

33. **FILE** Commercial Bank and Trust Company is studying the use of its automatic teller machines (ATMs). Of particular interest is whether young adults (under 25 years) use the machines more than senior citizens. To investigate further, samples of customers under 25 years of age and customers over 60 years of age were selected. The number of ATM transactions last month was determined for each selected individual, and the results are shown below. At the .01 significance level, can bank management conclude that younger customers use the ATMs more?

Under 25	10	10	11	15	7	11	10	9			
Over 60	4	8	7	7	4	5	1	7	4	10	5

34. **FILE** Two of the teams competing in the *America's Cup* race are Team Oracle U.S.A. and Land Rover BAR. They race their boats over a part of the course several times. Below are a sample of times in minutes for each boat. Assume the population standard deviations are not the same. At the .05 significance level, can we conclude that there is a difference in their mean times?

Boat	Time (minutes)											
Land Rover BAR	12.9	12.5	11.0	13.3	11.2	11.4	11.6	12.3	14.2	11.3		
Team Oracle	14.1	14.1	14.2	17.4	15.8	16.7	16.1	13.3	13.4	13.6	10.8	19.0

35. **FILE** The manufacturer of an MP3 player wanted to know whether a 10% reduction in price is enough to increase the sales of its product. To investigate, the owner randomly selected eight outlets and sold the MP3 player at the reduced price. At seven randomly selected outlets, the MP3 player was sold at the regular price. Reported below is the number of units sold last month at the regular and reduced prices at the randomly selected outlets. At the .01 significance level, can the manufacturer conclude that the price reduction resulted in an increase in sales?

Regular price	138	121	88	115	141	125	96	
Reduced price	128	134	152	135	114	106	112	120

36. **FILE** A number of minor automobile accidents occur at various high-risk intersections in Teton County despite traffic lights. The Traffic Department claims that a modification in the type of light will reduce these accidents. The county commissioners have agreed to a proposed experiment. Eight intersections were chosen at random, and the lights at those intersections were modified. The numbers of minor accidents during a six-month period before and after the modifications were:

	Number of Accidents							
	A	**B**	**C**	**D**	**E**	**F**	**G**	**H**
Before modification	5	7	6	4	8	9	8	10
After modification	3	7	7	0	4	6	8	2

At the .01 significance level, is it reasonable to conclude that the modification reduced the number of traffic accidents?

37. FILE Lester Hollar is vice president for human resources for a large manufacturing company. In recent years, he has noticed an increase in absenteeism that he thinks is related to the general health of the employees. Four years ago, in an attempt to improve the situation, he began a fitness program in which employees exercise during their lunch hour. To evaluate the program, he selected a random sample of eight participants and found the number of days each was absent in the six months before the exercise program began and in the six months following the exercise program. Below are the results. At the .05 significance level, can he conclude that the number of absences has declined? Estimate the *p*-value.

Employee	Before	After
Bauman	6	5
Briggs	6	2
Dottellis	7	1
Lee	7	3
Perralt	4	3
Rielly	3	6
Steinmetz	5	3
Stoltz	6	7

38. FILE The president of the American Insurance Institute wants to compare the yearly costs of auto insurance offered by two leading companies. He selects a sample of 15 families, some with only a single insured driver, others with several teenage drivers, and pays each family a stipend to contact the two companies and ask for a price quote. To make the data comparable, certain features, such as the deductible amount and limits of liability, are standardized. The data for the sample of families and their two insurance quotes are reported below. At the .10 significance level, can we conclude that there is a difference in the amounts quoted?

Family	Midstates Car Insurance	Gecko Mutual Insurance
Becker	$2,090	$1,610
Berry	1,683	1,247
Cobb	1,402	2,327
Debuck	1,830	1,367
DuBrul	930	1,461
Eckroate	697	1,789
German	1,741	1,621
Glasson	1,129	1,914
King	1,018	1,956
Kucic	1,881	1,772
Meredith	1,571	1,375
Obeid	874	1,527
Price	1,579	1,767
Phillips	1,577	1,636
Tresize	860	1,188

39. Fairfield Homes is developing two parcels near Pigeon Fork, Tennessee. In order to test different advertising approaches, it uses different media to reach potential buyers. The mean annual family income for 15 people making inquiries at the first development is $150,000, with a standard deviation of $40,000. A corresponding sample of 25 people at the second development had a mean of $180,000, with a standard deviation of $30,000. Assume the population standard deviations are the same. At the .05 significance level, can Fairfield conclude that the population means are different?

40. A candy company taste-tested two chocolate bars, one with almonds and one without almonds. A panel of testers rated the bars on a scale of 0 to 5, with 5 indicating the highest taste rating. Assume the population standard deviations are equal. At the .05 significance level, do the ratings show a difference between chocolate bars with or without almonds?

With Almonds	Without Almonds
3	0
1	4
2	4
3	3
1	4
1	
2	

41. FILE An investigation of the effectiveness of an antibacterial soap in reducing operating room contamination resulted in the accompanying table. The new soap was tested in a sample of eight operating rooms in the greater Seattle area during the last year. The following table reports the contamination levels before and after the use of the soap for each operating room.

	Operating Room							
	A	B	C	D	E	F	G	H
Before	6.6	6.5	9.0	10.3	11.2	8.1	6.3	11.6
After	6.8	2.4	7.4	8.5	8.1	6.1	3.4	2.0

At the .05 significance level, can we conclude the contamination measurements are lower after use of the new soap?

42. FILE The following data on annual rates of return were collected from eleven randomly selected stocks listed on the New York Stock Exchange ("the big board") and twelve randomly selected stocks listed on NASDAQ. Assume the population standard deviations are the same. At the .10 significance level, can we conclude that the annual rates of return are higher on the big board?

NYSE	NASDAQ
15.0	8.8
10.7	6.0
20.2	14.4
18.6	19.1
19.1	17.6
8.7	17.8
17.8	15.9
13.8	17.9
22.7	21.6
14.0	6.0
26.1	11.9
	23.4

43. FILE The city of Laguna Beach operates two public parking lots. The Ocean Drive parking lot can accommodate up to 125 cars and the Rio Rancho parking lot can accommodate up to 130 cars. City planners are considering increasing the size of the lots and changing the fee structure. To begin, the Planning Office would like some information on the number of cars in the lots at various times of the day. A junior planner officer is assigned the task of visiting the two lots at random times of the day and evening and counting the number of cars in the lots. The study lasted over a period of one month. Below is the number of cars in the lots for 25 visits of the Ocean Drive lot and 28 visits of the Rio Rancho lot. Assume the population standard deviations are equal.

Ocean Drive												
89	115	93	79	113	77	51	75	118	105	106	91	54
63	121	53	81	115	67	53	69	95	121	88	64	
Rio Rancho												
128	110	81	126	82	114	93	40	94	45	84	71	74
92	66	69	100	114	113	107	62	77	80	107	90	129
105	124											

Is it reasonable to conclude that there is a difference in the mean number of cars in the two lots? Use the .05 significance level.

44. FILE The amount of income spent on housing is an important component of the cost of living. The total costs of housing for homeowners might include mortgage payments, property taxes, and utility costs (water, heat, electricity). An economist selected a sample of 20 homeowners in New England and then calculated these total housing costs as a percent of monthly income, 5 years ago and now. The information is reported below. Is it reasonable to conclude the percent is less now than 5 years ago?

Homeowner	Five Years Ago	Now	Homeowner	Five Years Ago	Now
Holt	17%	10%	Lozier	35%	32%
Pierse	20	39	Cieslinski	16	32
Merenick	29	37	Rowatti	23	21
Lanoue	43	27	Koppel	33	12
Fagan	36	12	Rumsey	44	40
Bobko	43	41	McGinnis	44	42
Kippert	45	24	Pierce	28	22
San Roman	19	26	Roll	29	19
Kurimsky	49	28	Lang	39	35
Davison	49	26	Miller	22	12

45. FILE The CVS Pharmacy located on US 17 in Murrells Inlet has been one of the busiest pharmaceutical retail stores in South Carolina for many years. To try and capture more business in the area, CVS top management opened another store about 6 miles west on SC 707. After a few months, CVS management decided to compare the business volume at the two stores. One way to measure business volume is to count the number of cars in the store parking lots on random days and times. The results of the survey from the last 3 months of the year are reported below. To explain, the first observation was on October 2 at 20:52 military time (8:52 p.m.). At that time there were four cars in the US 17 lot and nine cars in the SC 707 lot. At the .05 significance level, is it reasonable to conclude that, based on vehicle counts, the US 17 store has more business volume than the SC 707 store?

Date	Time	Vehicle Count US 17	Vehicle Count SC 707
Oct 2	20:52	4	9
Oct 11	19:30	5	7
Oct 15	22:08	9	12
Oct 19	11:42	4	5
Oct 25	15:32	10	8
Oct 26	11:02	9	15
Nov 3	11:22	13	7
Nov 5	19:09	20	3
Nov 8	15:10	15	14
Nov 9	13:18	15	11
Nov 15	22:38	13	11
Nov 17	18:46	16	12
Nov 21	15:44	17	8
Nov 22	15:34	15	3
Nov 27	21:42	20	6
Nov 29	9:57	17	13
Nov 30	17:58	5	9
Dec 3	19:54	7	13
Dec 15	18:20	11	6
Dec 16	18:25	14	15
Dec 17	11:08	8	8
Dec 22	21:20	10	3
Dec 24	15:21	4	6
Dec 25	20:21	7	9
Dec 30	14:25	19	4

46. FILE A goal of financial literacy for children is to learn how to manage money wisely. One question is: How much money do children have to manage? A recent study by Schnur Educational Research Associates randomly sampled 15 children between 8 and 10 years old and 18 children between 11 and 14 years old and recorded their monthly allowance. Is it reasonable to conclude that the mean allowance received by children between 11 and 14 years is more than the allowance received by children between 8 and 10 years? Use the .01 significance level. What is the *p*-value?

8–10 Years	11–14 Years	8–10 Years	11–14 Years
26	49	26	41
33	44	25	38
30	42	27	44
26	38	29	39
34	39	34	50
26	41	32	49
27	39		41
27	38		42
30	38		30

DATA ANALYTICS

47. FILE The North Valley Real Estate data reports information on the homes sold last year.

- **a.** At the .05 significance level, can we conclude that there is a difference in the mean selling price of homes with a pool and homes without a pool?
- **b.** At the .05 significance level, can we conclude that there is a difference in the mean selling price of homes with an attached garage and homes without an attached garage?
- **c.** At the .05 significance level, can we conclude that there is a difference in the mean selling price of homes that are in default on the mortgage?

48. FILE Refer to the Baseball 2016 data, which report information on the 30 Major League Baseball teams for the 2016 season.

- **a.** At the .05 significance level, can we conclude that there is a difference in the mean salary of teams in the American League versus teams in the National League?
- **b.** At the .05 significance level, can we conclude that there is a difference in the mean home attendance of teams in the American League versus teams in the National League?
- **c.** Compute the mean and the standard deviation of the number of wins for the 10 teams with the highest salaries. Do the same for the 10 teams with the lowest salaries. At the .05 significance level, is there a difference in the mean number of wins for the two groups? At the .05 significance level, is there a difference in the mean attendance for the two groups?

49. FILE Refer to the Lincolnville School District bus data. Is there a difference in the mean maintenance cost for the diesel versus the gasoline buses? Use the .05 significance level.

12 Analysis of Variance

© Alexander Hassenstein/Getty Images

▲ **ONE VARIABLE THAT GOOGLE** uses to rank pages on the Internet is page speed, the time it takes for a web page to load into your browser. A source for women's clothing is redesigning their page to improve the images that show its products and to reduce its load time. The new page is clearly faster, but initial tests indicate there is more variation in the time to load. A sample of 16 different load times showed that the standard deviation of the load time was 22 hundredths of a second for the new page and 12 hundredths of a second for the current page. At the .05 significance level, can we conclude that there is more variation in the load time of the new page? (See Exercise 24 and **LO12-1**.)

LEARNING OBJECTIVES

When you have completed this chapter, you will be able to:

LO12-1 Apply the *F* distribution to test a hypothesis that two population variances are equal.

LO12-2 Use ANOVA to test a hypothesis that three or more population means are equal.

LO12-3 Use confidence intervals to test and interpret differences between pairs of population means.

LO12-4 Use a blocking variable in a two-way ANOVA to test a hypothesis that three or more population means are equal.

LO12-5 Perform a two-way ANOVA with interaction and describe the results.

INTRODUCTION

In this chapter, we continue our discussion of hypothesis testing. Recall that in Chapters 10 and 11 we examined the general theory of hypothesis testing. We described the case where a sample was selected from the population. We used the *z* distribution (the standard normal distribution) or the *t* distribution to determine whether it was reasonable to conclude that the population mean was equal to a specified value. We tested whether two population means are the same. In this chapter, we expand our idea of hypothesis tests. We describe a test for variances and then a test that simultaneously compares several population means to determine if they are equal.

LO12-1

Apply the *F* distribution to test a hypothesis that two population variances are equal.

COMPARING TWO POPULATION VARIANCES

In Chapter 11, we tested hypotheses about equal population means. The tests differed based on our assumptions regarding whether the population standard deviations or variances were equal or unequal. In this chapter, the assumption about equal population variances is also important. In this section, we present a way to statistically test this assumption. The test is based on the *F* distribution.

The *F* Distribution

The probability distribution used in this chapter is the *F* distribution. It was named to honor Sir Ronald Fisher, one of the founders of modern-day statistics. The test statistic for several situations follows this probability distribution. It is used to test whether two samples are from populations having equal variances, and it is also applied when we want to compare several population means simultaneously. The simultaneous comparison of several population means is called **analysis of variance (ANOVA).** In both of these situations, the populations must follow a normal distribution, and the data must be at least interval-scale.

What are the characteristics of the *F* distribution?

1. **There is a family of *F* distributions.** A particular member of the family is determined by two parameters: the degrees of freedom in the numerator and the degrees of freedom in the denominator. The shape of the distribution is illustrated by the following graph. There is one *F* distribution for the combination of 29 degrees of freedom in the numerator (*df*) and 28 degrees of freedom in the denominator. There is another *F* distribution for 19 degrees of freedom in the numerator and 6 degrees of freedom in the denominator. The final distribution shown has 6 degrees of freedom in the numerator and 6 degrees of freedom in the denominator. We will describe the concept of degrees of freedom later in the chapter. Note that the shapes of the distributions change as the degrees of freedom change.

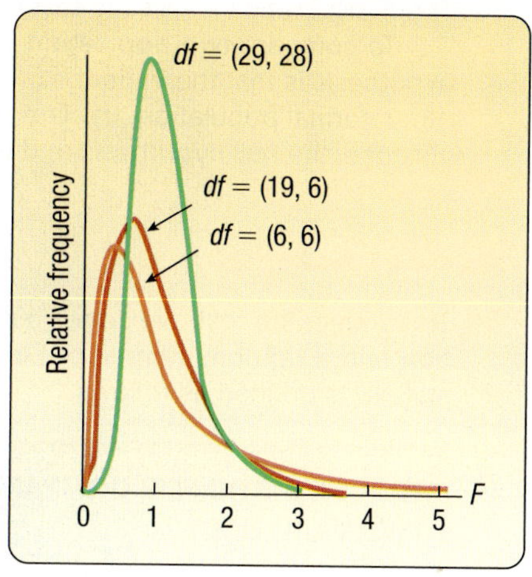

2. **The F distribution is continuous.** This means that the value of F can assume an infinite number of values between zero and positive infinity.
3. **The F statistic cannot be negative.** The smallest value F can assume is 0.
4. **The F distribution is positively skewed.** The long tail of the distribution is to the right-hand side. As the number of degrees of freedom increases in both the numerator and denominator, the distribution approaches a normal distribution.
5. **The F distribution is asymptotic.** As the values of F increase, the distribution approaches the horizontal axis but never touches it. This is similar to the behavior of the normal probability distribution, described in Chapter 7.

Testing a Hypothesis of Equal Population Variances

The first application of the F distribution that we describe occurs when we test the hypothesis that the variance of one normal population equals the variance of another normal population. The following examples will show the use of the test:

- A health services corporation manages two hospitals in Knoxville, Tennessee: St. Mary's North and St. Mary's South. In each hospital, the mean waiting time in the Emergency Department is 42 minutes. The hospital administrator believes that the St. Mary's North Emergency Department has more variation in waiting time than St. Mary's South.
- The mean rate of return on two types of common stock may be the same, but there may be more variation in the rate of return in one than the other. A sample of 10 technology and 10 utility stocks shows the same mean rate of return, but there is likely more variation in the technology stocks.
- An on-line newspaper found that men and women spend about the same amount of time per day accessing news apps. However, the same report indicated the times of men had nearly twice as much variation compared to the times of women.

© McGraw-Hill Education/ John Flournoy, photographer John Flournoy

The F distribution is also used to test the assumption that the variances of two normal populations are equal. Recall that in the previous chapter the t test to investigate whether the means of two independent populations differed assumes that the variances of the two normal populations are the same. See this list of assumptions on page 361. The F distribution is used to test the assumption that the variances are equal.

To compare two population variances, we first state the null hypothesis. The null hypothesis is that the variance of one normal population, σ_1^2, equals the variance of another normal population, σ_2^2. The alternate hypothesis is that the variances differ. In this instance, the null hypothesis and the alternate hypothesis are:

$$H_0: \sigma_1^2 = \sigma_2^2$$
$$H_1: \sigma_1^2 \neq \sigma_2^2$$

To conduct the test, we select a random sample of observations, n_1, from one population and a random sample of observations, n_2, from the second population. The test statistic is defined as follows.

TEST STATISTIC FOR COMPARING TWO VARIANCES

$$F = \frac{s_1^2}{s_2^2} \qquad \textbf{(12–1)}$$

The terms s_1^2 and s_2^2 are the respective sample variances. If the null hypothesis is true, the test statistic follows the F distribution with $n_1 - 1$ and $n_2 - 1$ degrees of freedom. To reduce the size of the table of critical values, the *larger* sample variance is placed in the numerator; hence, the tabled F ratio is always larger than 1.00. Thus, the right-tail critical value is the only one required. The critical value of F for a two-tailed test is found by dividing the significance level in half ($\alpha/2$) and then referring to the appropriate degrees of freedom in Appendix B.6. An example will illustrate.

EXAMPLE

Lammers Limos offers limousine service from Government Center in downtown Toledo, Ohio, to Metro Airport in Detroit. Sean Lammers, president of the company, is considering two routes. One is via U.S. 25 and the other via I-75. He wants to study the time it takes to drive to the airport using each route and then compare the results. He collected the following sample data, which is reported in minutes. Using the .10 significance level, is there a difference in the variation in the driving times for the two routes?

© Daniel Acker/Bloomberg/Getty Images RF

U.S. Route 25	Interstate 75
52	59
67	60
56	61
45	51
70	56
54	63
64	57
	65

SOLUTION

The mean driving times along the two routes are nearly the same. The mean time is 58.29 minutes for the U.S. 25 route and 59.0 minutes along the I-75 route. However, in evaluating travel times, Mr. Lammers is also concerned about the variation in the travel times. The first step is to compute the two sample variances. We'll use formula (3–9) to compute the sample standard deviations. To obtain the sample variances, we square the standard deviations.

U.S. ROUTE 25

$$\bar{x} = \frac{\Sigma x}{n} = \frac{408}{7} = 58.29 \qquad s = \sqrt{\frac{\Sigma(x - \bar{x})^2}{n - 1}} = \sqrt{\frac{485.43}{7 - 1}} = 8.9947$$

INTERSTATE 75

$$\bar{x} = \frac{\Sigma x}{n} = \frac{472}{8} = 59.00 \qquad s = \sqrt{\frac{\Sigma(x - \bar{x})^2}{n - 1}} = \sqrt{\frac{134}{8 - 1}} = 4.3753$$

There is more variation, as measured by the standard deviation, in the U.S. 25 route than in the I-75 route. This is consistent with his knowledge of the two routes; the U.S. 25 route contains more stoplights, whereas I-75 is a limited-access interstate highway. However, the I-75 route is several miles longer. It is important that the service offered be both timely and consistent, so he decides to conduct a statistical test to determine whether there really is a difference in the variation of the two routes.

We use the six-step hypothesis test procedure.

Step 1: We begin by stating the null hypothesis and the alternate hypothesis. The test is two-tailed because we are looking for a difference in the variation of the two routes. We are *not* trying to show that one route has more variation than the other. For this example/solution, the subscript 1 indicates information for U.S. 25; the subscript 2 indicates information for I-75.

$$H_0: \sigma_1^2 = \sigma_2^2$$
$$H_1: \sigma_1^2 \neq \sigma_2^2$$

Step 2: We selected the .10 significance level.

Step 3: The appropriate test statistic follows the F distribution.

Step 4: The critical value is obtained from Appendix B.6, a portion of which is reproduced as Table 12–1. Because we are conducting a two-tailed test, the tabled significance level is .05, found by $\alpha/2 = .10/2 = .05$. There are $n_1 - 1 = 7 - 1 = 6$ degrees of freedom in the numerator and $n_2 - 1 = 8 - 1 = 7$ degrees of freedom in the denominator. To find the critical value, move horizontally across the top portion of the F table (Table 12–1 or Appendix B.6) for the .05 significance level to 6 degrees of freedom in the numerator. Then move down that column to the critical value opposite 7 degrees of freedom in the denominator. The critical value is 3.87. Thus, the decision rule is: Reject the null hypothesis if the ratio of the sample variances exceeds 3.87.

TABLE 12–1 Critical Values of the F Distribution, $\alpha = .05$

Degrees of Freedom for Denominator	Degrees of Freedom for Numerator			
	5	**6**	**7**	**8**
1	230	234	237	239
2	19.3	19.3	19.4	19.4
3	9.01	8.94	8.89	8.85
4	6.26	6.16	6.09	6.04
5	5.05	4.95	4.88	4.82
6	4.39	4.28	4.21	4.15
7	3.97	3.87	3.79	3.73
8	3.69	3.58	3.50	3.44
9	3.48	3.37	3.29	3.23
10	3.33	3.22	3.14	3.07

Step 5: Next we compute the ratio of the two sample variances, determine the value of the test statistic, and make a decision regarding the null hypothesis. Note that formula (12–1) refers to the sample *variances*, but we calculated the sample *standard deviations*. We need to square the standard deviations to determine the variances.

$$F = \frac{s_1^2}{s_2^2} = \frac{(8.9947)^2}{(4.3753)^2} = 4.23$$

The decision is to reject the null hypothesis because the computed F value (4.23) is larger than the critical value (3.87).

Step 6: We conclude there is a difference in the variation in the time to travel the two routes. Mr. Lammers will want to consider this in his scheduling.

The usual practice is to determine the F ratio by putting the larger of the two sample variances in the numerator. This will force the F ratio to be at least 1.00. This allows us to always use the right tail of the F distribution, thus avoiding the need for more extensive F tables.

A logical question arises: Is it possible to conduct one-tailed tests? For example, suppose in the previous example we suspected that the variance of the times using the U.S. 25 route, σ_1^2, is larger than the variance of the times along the I-75 route, σ_2^2. We would state the null and the alternate hypothesis as

$$H_0: \sigma_1^2 \leq \sigma_2^2$$
$$H_1: \sigma_1^2 > \sigma_2^2$$

The test statistic is computed as s_1^2/s_2^2. Notice that we labeled the population with the suspected large variance as population 1. So s_1^2 appears in the numerator. The F ratio will be larger than 1.00, so we can use the upper tail of the F distribution. Under these conditions, it is not necessary to divide the significance level in half. Because Appendix B.6 gives us only the .05 and .01 significance levels, we are restricted to these levels for one-tailed tests and .10 and .02 for two-tailed tests unless we consult a more complete table or use statistical software to compute the F statistic.

The Excel software has a procedure to perform a test of variances. Below is the output. The computed value of F is the same as that determined by using formula (12–1). The result of the one-tail hypothesis test is to reject the null hypothesis. The F of 4.23 is greater than the critical value of 3.87. Also, the p-value is less than 0.05. We conclude the variance of travel times on U.S. 25 is greater than the variance of travel times on I-75.

Variance Test

	A	B	C	D	E	F	G
1	U.S. 25	Interstate 75		F-Test Two-Sample for Variances			
2	52	59			*U.S. 25*	*Interstate 75*	
3	67	60		Mean	58.29	59.00	
4	56	61		Variance	80.90	19.14	
5	45	51		Observations	7.00	8.00	
6	70	56		df	6.00	7.00	
7	54	63		F	4.23		
8	64	57		P(F<=f) one-tail	0.04		
9		65		F Critical one-tail	3.87		
10							

SELF-REVIEW 12–1

Steele Electric Products Inc. assembles cell phones. For the last 10 days, Mark Nagy completed a mean of 39 phones per day, with a standard deviation of 2 per day. Debbie Richmond completed a mean of 38.5 phones per day, with a standard deviation of 1.5 per day. At the .05 significance level, can we conclude that there is more variation in Mark's daily production?

EXERCISES

1. What is the critical F value when the sample size for the numerator is six and the sample size for the denominator is four? Use a two-tailed test and the .10 significance level.
2. What is the critical F value when the sample size for the numerator is four and the sample size for the denominator is seven? Use a one-tailed test and the .01 significance level.
3. The following hypotheses are given.

$$H_0: \sigma_1^2 = \sigma_2^2$$
$$H_1: \sigma_1^2 \neq \sigma_2^2$$

A random sample of eight observations from the first population resulted in a standard deviation of 10. A random sample of six observations from the second population resulted in a standard deviation of 7. At the .02 significance level, is there a difference in the variation of the two populations?

4. The following hypotheses are given.

$$H_0: \sigma_1^2 \leq \sigma_2^2$$
$$H_1: \sigma_1^2 > \sigma_2^2$$

A random sample of five observations from the first population resulted in a standard deviation of 12. A random sample of seven observations from the second population showed a standard deviation of 7. At the .01 significance level, is there more variation in the first population?

5. Arbitron Media Research Inc. conducted a study of the iPod listening habits of men and women. One facet of the study involved the mean listening time. It was discovered that the mean listening time for a sample of 10 men was 35 minutes per day. The standard deviation was 10 minutes per day. The mean listening time for a sample of 12 women was also 35 minutes, but the standard deviation of the sample was 12 minutes. At the .10 significance level, can we conclude that there is a difference in the variation in the listening times for men and women?

6. A stockbroker at Critical Securities reported that the mean rate of return on a sample of 10 oil stocks was 12.6% with a standard deviation of 3.9%. The mean rate of return on a sample of 8 utility stocks was 10.9% with a standard deviation of 3.5%. At the .05 significance level, can we conclude that there is more variation in the oil stocks?

LO12-2
Use ANOVA to test a hypothesis that three or more population means are equal.

ANOVA: ANALYSIS OF VARIANCE

The *F* distribution is used to perform a wide variety of hypothesis tests. For example, when testing the equality of three or more population means, the Analysis of Variance (ANOVA) technique is used and the *F* statistic is used as the test statistic.

ANOVA Assumptions

The ANOVA to test the equality of three or more population means requires that three assumptions are true:

1. The populations follow the normal distribution.
2. The populations have equal standard deviations (σ).
3. The populations are independent.

When these conditions are met, *F* is used as the distribution of the test statistic.

Why do we need to study ANOVA? Why can't we just use the test of differences in population means discussed in the previous chapter? We could compare the population means two at a time. The major reason is the unsatisfactory buildup of Type I error. To explain further, suppose we have four different methods (A, B, C, and D) of training new recruits to be firefighters. We randomly assign each of the 40 recruits in this year's class to one of the four methods. At the end of the training program, we administer a test to measure understanding of firefighting techniques to the four groups. The question is: Is there a difference in the mean test scores among the four groups? An answer to this question will allow us to compare the four training methods.

Using the *t* distribution to compare the four population means, we would have to conduct six different *t* tests. That is, we would need to compare the mean scores for the four methods as follows: A versus B, A versus C, A versus D, B versus C, B versus D, and C versus D. For each *t* test, suppose we choose an $\alpha = .05$. Therefore, the probability of a Type I error, rejecting the null when it is true, is .05. The complement is the probability of .95 that we do not reject the null when it is true. Because we conduct six separate (independent) tests, the probability that all six tests result in correct decisions is:

$$P(\text{All correct}) = (.95)(.95)(.95)(.95)(.95)(.95) = .735$$

To find the probability of at least one error due to sampling, we subtract this result from 1. Thus, the probability of at least one incorrect decision due to sampling is 1 − .735 = .265. To summarize, if we conduct six independent tests using the *t* distribution, the likelihood of rejecting a true null hypothesis because of sampling error is an unsatisfactory .265. The ANOVA technique allows us to compare population means simultaneously at a selected significance level. It avoids the buildup of Type I error associated with testing many hypotheses.

ANOVA was first developed for applications in agriculture, and many of the terms related to that context remain. In particular, the term *treatment* is used to identify the different populations being examined. For example, treatment refers to how a plot of ground was treated with a particular type of fertilizer. The following illustration will clarify the term *treatment* and demonstrate an application of ANOVA.

EXAMPLE

Joyce Kuhlman manages a regional financial center. She wishes to compare the productivity, as measured by the number of customers served, among three employees. Four days are randomly selected and the number of customers served by each employee is recorded. The results are:

Wolfe	White	Korosa
55	66	47
54	76	51
59	67	46
56	71	48

SOLUTION

Is there a difference in the mean number of customers served? Chart 12–1 illustrates how the populations would appear if there were a difference in the treatment means. Note that the populations follow the normal distribution and the variation in each population is the same. However, the means are *not* the same.

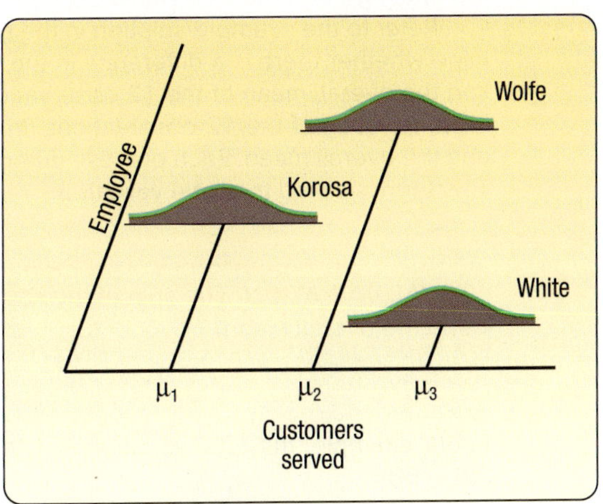

CHART 12–1 Case Where Treatment Means Are Different

Suppose there is no difference in the treatment means. This would indicate that the population means are the same. This is shown in Chart 12–2. Note again that the populations follow the normal distribution and the variation in each of the populations is the same.

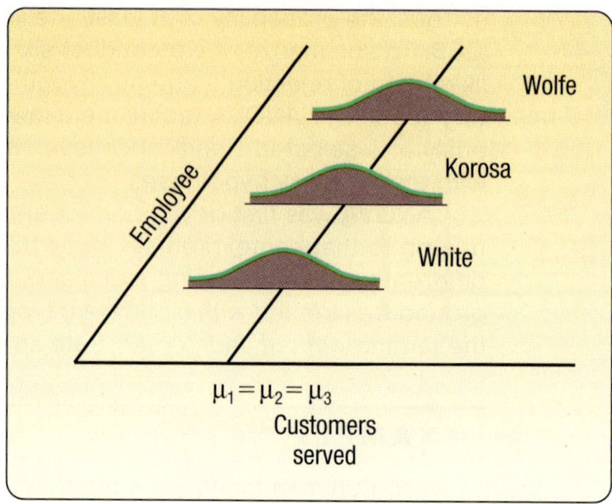

CHART 12–2 Case Where Treatment Means Are the Same

The ANOVA Test

How does the ANOVA test work? Recall that we want to determine whether the various sample means came from a single population or populations with different means. We actually compare these sample means through their variances. To explain, on page 392 we listed the assumptions required for ANOVA. One of those assumptions was that the standard deviations of the various normal populations had to be the same. We take advantage of this requirement in the ANOVA test. The underlying strategy is to estimate the population variance (standard deviation squared) two ways and then find the ratio of these two estimates. If this ratio is about 1, then logically the two estimates are the same, and we conclude that the population means are the same. If the ratio is quite different from 1, then we conclude that the population means are not the same. The *F* distribution serves as a referee by indicating when the ratio of the sample variances is too much greater than 1 to have occurred by chance.

Refer to the example/solution in the previous section. The manager wants to determine whether there is a difference in the mean number of customers served. To begin, find the overall mean of the 12 observations. It is 58, found by $(55 + 54 + \cdots + 48)/12$. Next, for each of the 12 observations find the difference between the particular value and the overall mean. Each of these differences is squared and these squares summed. This term is called the **total variation.**

> **TOTAL VARIATION** The sum of the squared differences between each observation and the overall mean.

In our example, the total variation is 1,082, found by $(55 - 58)^2 + (54 - 58)^2 + \cdots + (48 - 58)^2$.

Next, break this total variation into two components: variation due to the **treatment variation** and **random variation.**

TREATMENT VARIATION The sum of the squared differences between each treatment mean and the grand or overall mean.

The variation due to treatments is also called variation between treatment means. In this example, we first square the difference between each treatment mean and the overall mean. The mean for Wolfe is 56 customers, found by (55 + 54 + 59 + 56)/4. The other means are 70 and 48, respectively. Then, each of the squared differences is multiplied by the number of observations in each treatment. In this case, the value is 4. Last, these values are summed together. This term is 992. The sum of the squares due to the treatments is:

$$4(56 - 58)^2 + 4(70 - 58)^2 + 4(48 - 58)^2 = 992$$

If there is considerable variation among the treatment means compared to the overall mean, it is logical that this term will be a large value. If the treatment means are similar, this value will be small. The smallest possible value would be zero. This would occur when all the treatment means are the same. In this case, all the treatment means would also equal the overall mean.

The other source of variation is referred to as **random variation,** or the error component.

RANDOM VARIATION The sum of the squared differences between each observation and its treatment mean.

In the example, this term is the sum of the squared differences between each value and the mean for each treatment or employee. This is also called the variation within the treatments. The error variation is 90.

$$(55 - 56)^2 + (54 - 56)^2 + \cdots + (48 - 48)^2 = 90$$

We determine the test statistic, which is the ratio of the two estimates of the population variance, from the following equation.

$$F = \frac{\begin{array}{c}\text{Estimate of the population variance}\\ \text{based on the differences between the treatment means}\end{array}}{\begin{array}{c}\text{Estimate of the population variance}\\ \text{based on the variation within the treatments}\end{array}}$$

Our first estimate of the population variance is based on the treatments, that is, the difference *between* the means. It is 992/2. Why did we divide by 2? Recall from Chapter 3, to find a sample variance [see formula (3–9)], we divide by the number of observations minus one. In this case, there are three treatments, so we divide by 2. Our first estimate of the population variance is 992/2.

The variance estimate *within* the treatments is the random variation divided by the total number of observations less the number of treatments—that is, 90/(12 − 3). Hence, our second estimate of the population variance is 90/9. This is actually a generalization of formula (11–4), we pooled the sample variances from two populations.

The last step is to take the ratio of these two estimates.

$$F = \frac{992/2}{90/9} = 49.6$$

Because this ratio is quite different from 1, we can conclude that the treatment means are not the same. There is a difference in the mean number of customers served by the three employees.

Here's another example, which deals with samples of different sizes.

EXAMPLE

Recently airlines cut services, such as meals and snacks during flights, and started charging for checked luggage. A group of four carriers hired Brunner Marketing Research Inc. to survey passengers regarding their level of satisfaction with a recent flight. The survey included questions on ticketing, boarding, in-flight service, baggage handling, pilot communication, and so forth. Twenty-five questions offered a range of possible answers: excellent, good, fair, or poor. A response of excellent was given a score of 4, good a 3, fair a 2, and poor a 1. These responses were then totaled, so the total score was an indication of the satisfaction with the flight. The greater the score, the higher the level of satisfaction with the service. The highest possible score was 100.

Brunner randomly selected and surveyed passengers from the four airlines. Below is the sample information. Is there a difference in the mean satisfaction level among the four airlines? Use the .01 significance level.

Northern	WTA	Pocono	Branson
94	75	70	68
90	68	73	70
85	77	76	72
80	83	78	65
	88	80	74
		68	65
		65	

SOLUTION

We will use the six-step hypothesis-testing procedure.

Step 1: State the null hypothesis and the alternate hypothesis. The null hypothesis is that the mean scores are the same for the four airlines.

$$H_0: \mu_N = \mu_W = \mu_P = \mu_B$$

The alternate hypothesis is that the mean scores are not all the same for the four airlines.

H_1: The mean scores are not all equal.

We can also think of the alternate hypothesis as "at least two mean scores are not equal."

If the null hypothesis is not rejected, we conclude that there is no difference in the mean scores for the four airlines. If H_0 is rejected, we conclude that there is a difference in at least one pair of mean scores, but at this point we do not know which pair or how many pairs differ.

Step 2: Select the level of significance. We selected the .01 significance level.

Step 3: Determine the test statistic. The test statistic follows the F distribution.

Step 4: Formulate the decision rule. To determine the decision rule, we need the critical value. The critical value for the F statistic is found in Appendix B.6. The critical values for the .05 significance level are found on the first page and the .01 significance level on the second page. To use this table, we need to know the degrees of freedom in the numerator and the denominator. The degrees of freedom in the numerator equal the number of treatments, designated as k, minus 1.

The degrees of freedom in the denominator are the total number of observations, n, minus the number of treatments. For this problem, there are four treatments and a total of 22 observations.

Degrees of freedom in the numerator $= k - 1 = 4 - 1 = 3$

Degrees of freedom in the denominator $= n - k = 22 - 4 = 18$

Refer to Appendix B.6 and the .01 significance level. Move horizontally across the top of the page to 3 degrees of freedom in the numerator. Then move down that column to the row with 18 degrees of freedom. The value at this intersection is 5.09. So the decision rule is to reject H_0 if the computed value of F exceeds 5.09.

Step 5: Select the sample, perform the calculations, and make a decision. It is convenient to summarize the calculations of the F statistic in an **ANOVA table.** The format for an ANOVA table is as follows. Statistical software packages also use this format.

ANOVA Table

Source of Variation	Sum of Squares	Degrees of Freedom	Mean Square	F
Treatments	SST	$k - 1$	SST/$(k - 1)$ = MST	MST/MSE
Error	SSE	$n - k$	SSE/$(n - k)$ = MSE	
Total	SS total	$n - 1$		

There are three values, or sum of squares, used to compute the test statistic F. You can determine these values by obtaining SS total and SSE, then finding SST by subtraction. The SS total term is the total variation, SST is the variation due to the treatments, and SSE is the variation within the treatments or the random error.

We usually start the process by finding SS total. This is the sum of the squared differences between each observation and the overall mean. The formula for finding SS total is:

$$\text{SS total} = \Sigma(x - \bar{x}_G)^2 \quad \textbf{(12–2)}$$

where:

x is each sample observation.

$\bar{x}_G$ is the overall or grand mean.

Next determine SSE or the sum of the squared errors. This is the sum of the squared differences between each observation and its respective treatment mean. The formula for finding SSE is:

$$\text{SSE} = \Sigma(x - \bar{x}_c)^2 \quad \textbf{(12–3)}$$

where:

$\bar{x}_c$ is the sample mean for treatment c.

The SSE is calculated:

$$\text{SSE} = \Sigma(x - \bar{x}_N)^2 + \Sigma(x - \bar{x}_W)^2 + \Sigma(x - \bar{x}_P)^2 + \Sigma(x - \bar{x}_B)^2$$

The detailed calculations of SS total and SSE for this example follow. To determine the values of SS total and SSE we start by calculating the overall or grand mean. There are 22 observations and the total is 1,664, so the grand mean is 75.64.

$$\bar{x}_G = \frac{1{,}664}{22} = 75.64$$

	Northern	WTA	Pocono	Branson	Total
	94	75	70	68	
	90	68	73	70	
	85	77	76	72	
	80	83	78	65	
		88	80	74	
			68	65	
			65		
Column total	349	391	510	414	1,664
n	4	5	7	6	22
Mean	87.25	78.20	72.86	69.00	75.64

Grand Mean

Next we find the deviation of each observation from the grand mean, square those deviations, and sum this result for all 22 observations. For example, the first sampled passenger had a score of 94 and the overall or grand mean is 75.64. So $(x - \bar{x}_G) = 94 - 75.64 = 18.36$. For the last passenger, $(x - \bar{x}_G) = 65 - 75.64 = -10.64$. The calculations for all other passengers follow.

Northern	WTA	Pocono	Branson
18.36	−0.64	−5.64	−7.64
14.36	−7.64	−2.64	−5.64
9.36	1.36	0.36	−3.64
4.36	7.36	2.36	−10.64
	12.36	4.36	−1.64
		−7.64	−10.64
		−10.64	

Then square each of these differences and sum all the values. Thus, for the first passenger:

$$(x - \bar{x}_G)^2 = (94 - 75.64)^2 = (18.36)^2 = 337.09$$

Finally, sum all the squared differences as formula (12–2) directs. Our SS total value is 1,485.10.

	Northern	WTA	Pocono	Branson	Total
	337.09	0.41	31.81	58.37	
	206.21	58.37	6.97	31.81	
	87.61	1.85	0.13	13.25	
	19.01	54.17	5.57	113.21	
		152.77	19.01	2.69	
			58.37	113.21	
			113.21		
Total	649.92	267.57	235.07	332.54	1,485.10

SS Total

To compute the term SSE, find the deviation between each observation and its treatment mean. In the example, the mean of the first treatment (that is, the passengers on Northern Airlines) is 87.25, found by $\bar{x}_N = 349/4$. The subscript N refers to Northern Airlines.

The first passenger rated Northern a 94, so $(x - \bar{x}_N) = (94 - 87.25) = 6.75$. The first passenger in the WTA group responded with a total score of 75, so $(x - \bar{x}_W) = (75 - 78.20) = -3.2$. The detail for all the passengers follows.

Northern	WTA	Pocono	Branson
6.75	−3.2	−2.86	−1
2.75	−10.2	0.14	1
−2.25	−1.2	3.14	3
−7.25	4.8	5.14	−4
	9.8	7.14	5
		−4.86	−4
		−7.86	

Each of these values is squared and then summed for all 22 observations. The four column totals can also be summed to find SSE. The values are shown in the following table.

	Northern	WTA	Pocono	Branson	Total
	45.5625	10.24	8.18	1	
	7.5625	104.04	0.02	1	
	5.0625	1.44	9.86	9	
	52.5625	23.04	26.42	16	
		96.04	50.98	25	
			23.62	16	SSE
			61.78		
Total	110.7500	234.80	180.86	68	594.41

So the SSE value is 594.41. That is, $\Sigma(x - \bar{x}_c)^2 = 594.41$.

Finally, we determine SST, the sum of the squares due to the treatments, by subtraction.

$$\text{SST} = \text{SS total} - \text{SSE} \qquad \textbf{(12–4)}$$

For this example:

$$\text{SST} = \text{SS total} - \text{SSE} = 1{,}485.10 - 594.41 = 890.69.$$

To find the computed value of F, work your way across the ANOVA table. The degrees of freedom for the numerator and the denominator are the same as in step 4 on page 396 when we were finding the critical value of F. The term **mean square** is another expression for an estimate of the variance. The mean square for treatments is SST divided by its degrees of freedom. The result is the **mean square for treatments** and is written MST. Compute the **mean square error** in a similar fashion. To be precise, divide SSE by its degrees of freedom. To complete the process and find F, divide MST by MSE.

Insert the particular values of F into an ANOVA table and compute the value of F as follows.

Source of Variation	Sum of Squares	Degrees of Freedom	Mean Square	F
Treatments	890.69	3	296.90	8.99
Error	594.41	18	33.02	
Total	1,485.10	21		

STATISTICS IN ACTION

Have you ever waited in line for a telephone and it seemed like the person using the phone talked on and on? There is evidence that people actually talk longer on public telephones when someone is waiting. In a recent survey, researchers measured the length of time that 56 shoppers in a mall spent on the phone (1) when they were alone, (2) when a person was using the adjacent phone, and (3) when a person was using an adjacent phone and someone was waiting to use the phone. The study, using the one-way ANOVA technique, showed that the mean time using the telephone was significantly less when the person was alone.

The computed value of F is 8.99, which is greater than the critical value of 5.09, so the null hypothesis is rejected.

Step 6: Interpret the result. We conclude the population means are not all equal. At this point, the results of the ANOVA only show that at least one pair of mean satisfaction scores are not the same among the four airlines. We cannot statistically show which airlines differ in satisfaction or which airlines have the highest or lowest satisfaction scores. The techniques for determining how the airlines differ are presented in the next section.

The calculations in the previous example/solution are tedious if the number of observations in each treatment is large. Many statistical software packages will perform the calculations and output the results. In the following illustration, Excel is used to calculate the descriptive statistics and ANOVA for the previous example/solution involving airlines and passenger ratings. There are some slight differences between the output and the previous calculations. These differences are due to rounding.

Airline Anova

	A	B	C	D	E	F	G	H	I	J	K	L	M
1	Northern	WTA	Pocono	Branson		Anova: Single Factor							
2	94	75	70	68									
3	90	68	73	70		SUMMARY							
4	85	77	76	72		*Groups*	*Count*	*Sum*	*Average*	*Variance*			
5	80	83	78	65		Northern	4	349	87.250	36.917			
6		88	80	74		WTA	5	391	78.200	58.700			
7			68	65		Pocono	7	510	72.857	30.143			
8			65			Branson	6	414	69.000	13.600			
9													
10						ANOVA							
11						*Source of Variation*	*SS*	*df*	*MS*	*F*	*P-value*	*F crit*	
12						Between Groups	890.684	3	296.895	8.99	0.0007	3.160	
13						Within Groups	594.407	18	33.023				
14													
15						Total	1485.091	21					
16													

Notice Excel uses the term "Between Groups" for treatments and "Within Groups" for error. However, they have the same meanings. The p-value is .0007. This is the probability of finding a value of the test statistic this large or larger when the null hypothesis is true. To put it another way, it is the likelihood of calculating an F value larger than 8.99 with 3 degrees of freedom in the numerator and 18 degrees of freedom in the denominator. So when we reject the null hypothesis in this instance, there is a very small likelihood of committing a Type I error!

SELF-REVIEW 12–2

Citrus Clean is a new all-purpose cleaner being test-marketed by placing displays in three different locations within various supermarkets. The number of 12-ounce bottles sold from each location within the supermarket is reported below.

Near Bread	Near Beer	With Cleaners
18	12	26
14	18	28
19	10	30
17	16	32

At the .05 significance level, is there a difference in the mean number of bottles sold at the three locations?

(a) State the null hypothesis and the alternate hypothesis.
(b) What is the decision rule?
(c) Compute the values of SS total, SST, and SSE.
(d) Develop an ANOVA table.
(e) What is your decision regarding the null hypothesis?

EXERCISES

7. The following are four observations collected from each of three treatments. Test the hypothesis that the treatment means are equal. Use the .05 significance level.

Treatment 1	Treatment 2	Treatment 3
8	3	3
6	2	4
10	4	5
9	3	4

   a. State the null and the alternate hypotheses.
   b. What is the decision rule?
   c. Compute SST, SSE, and SS total.
   d. Complete an ANOVA table.
   e. State your decision regarding the null hypothesis.

8. The following are six observations collected from treatment 1, four observations collected from treatment 2, and five observations collected from treatment 3. Test the hypothesis at the .05 significance level that the treatment means are equal.

Treatment 1	Treatment 2	Treatment 3
9	13	10
7	20	9
11	14	15
9	13	14
12		15
10		

   a. State the null and the alternate hypotheses.
   b. What is the decision rule?
   c. Compute SST, SSE, and SS total.
   d. Complete an ANOVA table.
   e. State your decision regarding the null hypothesis.

9. FILE A real estate developer is considering investing in a shopping mall on the outskirts of Atlanta, Georgia. Three parcels of land are being evaluated. Of particular importance is the income in the area surrounding the proposed mall. A random sample of four families is selected near each proposed mall. Following are the sample results. At the .05 significance level, can the developer conclude there is a difference in the mean income? Use the usual six-step hypothesis testing procedure.

Southwyck Area ($000)	Franklin Park ($000)	Old Orchard ($000)
64	74	75
68	71	80
70	69	76
60	70	78

10. FILE The manager of a computer software company wishes to study the number of hours per week senior executives by type of industry spend at their desktop computers. The manager selected a sample of five executives from each of three

industries. At the .05 significance level, can she conclude there is a difference in the mean number of hours spent per week by industry?

Banking	Retail	Insurance
32	28	30
30	28	28
30	26	26
32	28	28
30	30	30

LO12-3
Use confidence intervals to test and interpret differences between pairs of population means.

INFERENCES ABOUT PAIRS OF TREATMENT MEANS

Suppose we carry out the ANOVA procedure, make the decision to reject the null hypothesis, and conclude that all the treatment means are not the same. Sometimes we may be satisfied with this conclusion, but in other instances we may want to know which treatment means differ. This section provides the details for this analysis.

Recall in the previous example/solution regarding airline passenger ratings, we concluded that there was a difference in the treatment means. That is, the null hypothesis was rejected and the alternate hypothesis accepted. The conclusion is that at least one of the airline's mean level of satisfaction is different for the others. Now, the question is which of the four airlines differ?

Several procedures are available to answer this question. The simplest is through the use of confidence intervals, that is, formula (9–2). From the computer output of the example on page 400, the sample mean score for those passengers rating Northern's service is 87.25, and for those rating Branson's service, the sample mean score is 69.00. Is there enough disparity to justify the conclusion that there is a significant difference in the mean satisfaction scores of the two airlines?

The t distribution, described in Chapters 10 and 11, is used as the basis for this test. Recall that one of the assumptions of ANOVA is that the population variances are the same for all treatments. This common population value is the **mean square error,** or MSE, and is determined by SSE/($n - k$). A confidence interval for the difference between two populations is found by:

CONFIDENCE INTERVAL FOR THE DIFFERENCE IN TREATMENT MEANS

$$(\bar{x}_1 - \bar{x}_2) \pm t\sqrt{\text{MSE}\left(\frac{1}{n_1} + \frac{1}{n_2}\right)} \quad \textbf{(12–5)}$$

where:

$\bar{x}_1$ is the mean of the first sample.
$\bar{x}_2$ is the mean of the second sample.
t is obtained from Appendix B.5. The degrees of freedom are equal to $n - k$.
MSE is the mean square error term obtained from the ANOVA table [SSE/($n - k$)].
n_1 is the number of observations in the first sample.
n_2 is the number of observations in the second sample.

How do we decide whether there is a difference in the treatment means? If the confidence interval includes zero, there is *not* a difference between the treatment means. For example, if the left endpoint of the confidence interval has a negative sign and the right endpoint has a positive sign, the interval includes zero and the two means do not differ. So if we develop a confidence interval from formula (12–5) and find the difference in the sample means was 5.00—that is, if $\bar{x}_1 - \bar{x}_2 = 5$ and

$t\sqrt{\text{MSE}\left(\frac{1}{n_1}+\frac{1}{n_2}\right)} = 12$—the confidence interval would range from −7.00 up to 17.00. To put it in symbols:

$$(\bar{x}_1 - \bar{x}_2) \pm t\sqrt{\text{MSE}\left(\frac{1}{n_1}+\frac{1}{n_2}\right)} = 5.00 \pm 12.00 = -7.00 \text{ up to } 17.00$$

Note that zero is in this interval. Therefore, we conclude that there is no significant difference in the selected treatment means.

On the other hand, if the endpoints of the confidence interval have the same sign, this indicates that the treatment means differ. For example, if $\bar{x}_1 - \bar{x}_2 = -0.35$ and $t\sqrt{\text{MSE}\left(\frac{1}{n_1}+\frac{1}{n_2}\right)} = 0.25$, the confidence interval would range from −0.60 up to −0.10. Because −0.60 and −0.10 have the same sign, both negative, zero is not in the interval and we conclude that these treatment means differ.

Using the previous airline example, let us compute the confidence interval for the difference between the mean scores of passengers on Northern and Branson. With a 95% level of confidence, the endpoints of the confidence interval are 10.457 and 26.043.

$$(\bar{x}_N - \bar{x}_B) \pm t\sqrt{\text{MSE}\left(\frac{1}{n_N}+\frac{1}{n_B}\right)} = (87.25 - 69.00) \pm 2.101\sqrt{33.023\left(\frac{1}{4}+\frac{1}{6}\right)}$$
$$= 18.25 \pm 7.793$$

where:

$\bar{x}_N$ is 87.25.
$\bar{x}_B$ is 69.00.
t is 2.101: from Appendix B.5 with $(n - k) = 22 - 4 = 18$ degrees of freedom.
MSE is 33.023: from the ANOVA table with $\text{SSE}/(n - k) = 594.4/18$.
n_N is 4.
n_B is 6.

The 95% confidence interval ranges from 10.457 up to 26.043. Both endpoints are positive; hence, we can conclude these treatment means differ significantly. That is, passengers on Northern Airlines rated service significantly different from those on Branson Airlines.

The confidence intervals for the differences between each pair of means can be obtained directly using statistical software. The following confidence intervals were computed using the one-way ANOVA in Minitab. Statistical software, such as Minitab, offers a variety of methods to control Type I error when making multiple comparisons. The following analysis used Fisher's method to compare means.

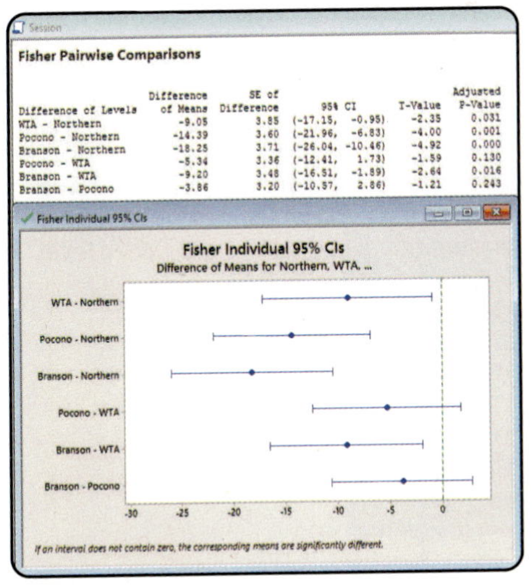
Session

Fisher Pairwise Comparisons

Difference of Levels	Difference of Means	SE of Difference	95% CI	T-Value	Adjusted P-Value
WTA - Northern	-9.05	3.85	(-17.15, -0.95)	-2.35	0.031
Pocono - Northern	-14.39	3.60	(-21.96, -6.83)	-4.00	0.001
Branson - Northern	-18.25	3.71	(-26.04, -10.46)	-4.92	0.000
Pocono - WTA	-5.34	3.36	(-12.41, 1.73)	-1.59	0.130
Branson - WTA	-9.20	3.48	(-16.51, -1.89)	-2.64	0.016
Branson - Pocono	-3.86	3.20	(-10.57, 2.86)	-1.21	0.243

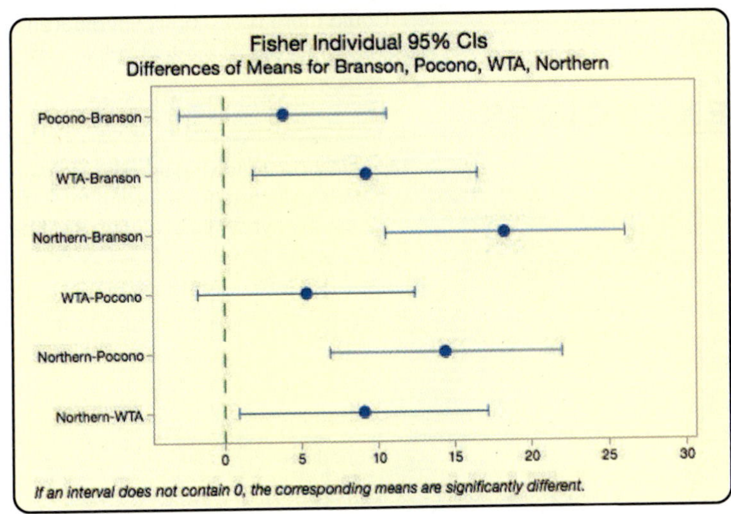

The output shows the confidence intervals for the difference between each pair of treatment means. The first row shows the confidence interval that compares WTA and Northern. It shows a confidence interval that does not include zero. It also shows the *p*-value for a hypothesis test that the means of WTA and Northern are equal. The hypothesis is rejected because a *p*-value of 0.031 is less than an assumed α of 0.05. Both results indicate that the WTA and Northern means are significantly different. Reviewing the entire table, only two pairs of means are not significantly different: Pocono and WTA, and Branson and Pocono. All other confidence intervals do not include zero and have *p*-values less than 0.05. Therefore, all other pairs of means are significantly different.

The graphic illustrates the results of the confidence interval analysis. Each confidence interval is represented by its endpoints and treatment mean. Note that a difference of zero is illustrated with the vertical dotted line. Two of the intervals include zero, Pocono and WTA, and Branson and Pocono. The others do not include zero so the means are significantly different. The following pairs of means are different: WTA and Northern, Pocono and Northern, Branson and Northern, and Branson and WTA.

We should emphasize that this investigation is a step-by-step process. The initial step is to conduct the ANOVA test. Only if the null hypothesis that the treatment means are equal is rejected should any analysis of the individual treatment means be attempted.

SELF-REVIEW 12–3

The following data are the semester tuition charges ($000) for a sample of five private colleges in the Northeast region of the United States, four in the Southeast region, and five in the West region. At the .05 significance level, can we conclude there is a difference in the mean tuition rates for the various regions?

Northeast ($000)	Southeast ($000)	West ($000)
40	38	37
41	39	38
42	40	36
40	38	37
42		36

(a) State the null and the alternate hypotheses.
(b) What is the decision rule?
(c) Develop an ANOVA table. What is the value of the test statistic?
(d) What is your decision regarding the null hypothesis?
(e) Could there be a significant difference between the mean tuition in the Northeast and that of the West? If so, develop a 95% confidence interval for that difference.

EXERCISES

11. FILE The following are three observations collected from treatment 1, five observations collected from treatment 2, and four observations collected from treatment 3. Test the hypothesis that the treatment means are equal at the .05 significance level.

Treatment 1	Treatment 2	Treatment 3
8	3	3
11	2	4
10	1	5
	3	4
	2	

a. State the null hypothesis and the alternate hypothesis.
b. What is the decision rule?
c. Compute SST, SSE, and SS total.
d. Complete an ANOVA table.
e. State your decision regarding the null hypothesis.
f. If H_0 is rejected, can we conclude that treatment 1 and treatment 2 differ? Use the 95% level of confidence.

12. **FILE** The following are six observations collected from treatment 1, ten observations collected from treatment 2, and eight observations collected from treatment 3. Test the hypothesis that the treatment means are equal at the .05 significance level.

Treatment 1	Treatment 2	Treatment 3
3	9	6
2	6	3
5	5	5
1	6	5
3	8	5
1	5	4
	4	1
	7	5
	6	
	4	

a. State the null hypothesis and the alternate hypothesis.
b. What is the decision rule?
c. Compute SST, SSE, and SS total.
d. Complete an ANOVA table.
e. State your decision regarding the null hypothesis.
f. If H_0 is rejected, can we conclude that treatment 2 and treatment 3 differ? Use the 95% level of confidence.

13. A senior accounting major at Midsouth State University has job offers from four CPA firms. To explore the offers further, she asked a sample of recent trainees how many months each worked for the firm before receiving a raise in salary. The sample information is submitted to Minitab with the following results:

```
Analysis of Variance
Source    DF      SS       MS       F        P
Factor     3   32.33    10.78    2.36    0.133
Error     10   45.67     4.57
Total     13   78.00
```

At the .05 level of significance, is there a difference in the mean number of months before a raise was granted among the four CPA firms?

14. **FILE** A stock analyst wants to determine whether there is a difference in the mean return on equity for three types of stock: utility, retail, and banking stocks. The following output is obtained:

Analysis of Variance

Source	DF	Adj SS	Adj MS	F-Value	P-Value
Factor	2	303.697	151.848	5.50	0.0202
Error	12	331.381	27.615		
Total	14	635.077			

Means

Factor	N	Mean	StDev	95% CI
bank	5	5.318	3.904	(0.198, 10.438)
utility	5	9.3160	1.5376	(4.1956, 14.4364)
retail	5	16.212	8.077	(11.092, 21.332)

Pooled StDev = 5.25500

Fisher Individual Tests for Differences of Means

Difference of Levels	Difference of Means	SE of Difference	95% CI	T-Value	Adjusted P-Value
utility-bank	3.998	3.324	(-3.243, 11.239)	1.20	0.2522
retail-bank	10.894	3.324	(3.653, 18.135)	3.28	0.0066
retail-utility	6.896	3.324	(-0.345, 14.137)	2.07	0.0602

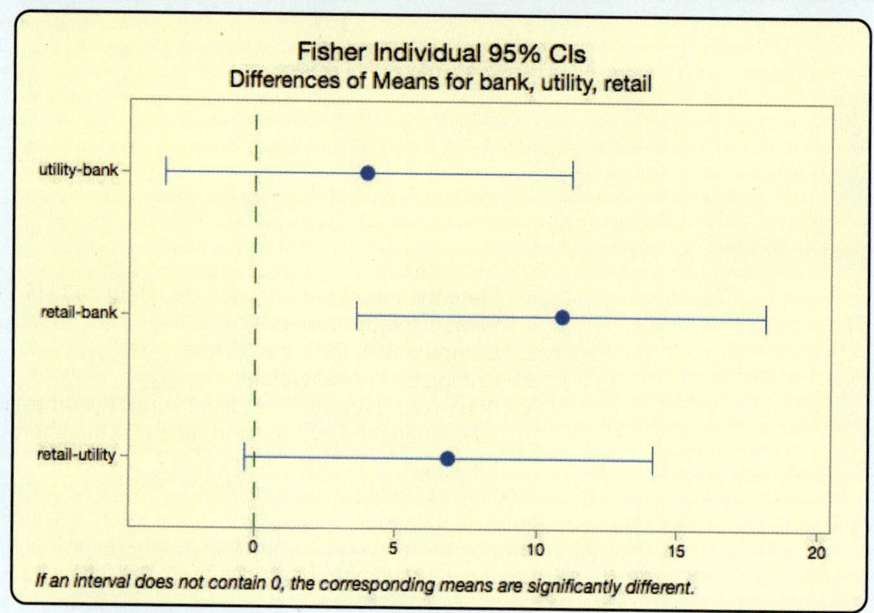

a. Using the .05 level of significance, is there a difference in the mean return on equity among the three types of stock?

b. Can the analyst conclude there is a difference between the mean return on equity for utility and retail stocks? For utility and banking stocks? For banking and retail stocks? Explain.

LO12-4 Use a blocking variable in a two-way ANOVA to test a hypothesis that three or more population means are equal.

TWO-WAY ANALYSIS OF VARIANCE

In the example/solution in the previous section, we divided the total variation in passenger ratings of the airlines into two categories: the variation between the treatments and the variation within the treatments. We also called the variation within the treatments the error or the random variation. To put it another way, we considered only two sources of variation: that due to the treatments and the random differences. In the airline passenger ratings example, there may be other causes of variation. These factors might include, for example, the season of the year, the particular airport, or the number of passengers on the flight.

The benefit of considering other factors is that we can reduce the error variance. That is, if we can reduce the denominator of the *F* statistic (reducing the error variance or, more directly, the SSE term), the value of *F* will be larger, causing us to reject the hypothesis of equal treatment means. In other words, if we can explain more of the variation, then there is less "error." An example will clarify the reduction in the error variance.

EXAMPLE

WARTA, the Warren Area Regional Transit Authority, is expanding bus service from the suburb of Starbrick into the central business district of Warren. There are four routes being considered from Starbrick to downtown Warren: (1) via U.S. 6, (2) via the West End, (3) via the Hickory Street Bridge, and (4) via Route 59. WARTA conducted several tests to determine whether there was a difference in the mean travel times along the four routes. Because there will be many different drivers, the test was set up so each driver drove along each of the four routes. Below is the travel time, in minutes, for each driver–route combination.

© John A. Rizzo/Getty Images RF

	Travel Time from Starbrick to Warren (minutes)			
Driver	**U.S. 6**	**West End**	**Hickory St.**	**Rte. 59**
Deans	18	17	21	22
Snaverly	16	23	23	22
Ormson	21	21	26	22
Zollaco	23	22	29	25
Filbeck	25	24	28	28

At the .05 significance level, is there a difference in the mean travel time along the four routes? If we remove the effect of the drivers, is there a difference in the mean travel time?

SOLUTION

To begin, we conduct a test of hypothesis using a one-way ANOVA. That is, we consider only the four routes. Under this condition, differences in travel times are due to either treatment or random variation. In this example/solution, the subscripts correspond to the treatments or routes: 1 for U.S. 6, 2 for West End, 3 for Hickory Street, and 4 for Route 59. The null hypothesis and the alternate hypothesis for comparing the mean travel time along the four routes are:

H_0: $\mu_1 = \mu_2 = \mu_3 = \mu_4$
H_1: Not all treatment means are the same.

There are four routes, so the numerator degrees of freedom is $(k - 1) = (4 - 1) = 3$. There are 20 observations, so the degrees of freedom in the denominator is

$(n - k) = (20 - 4) = 16$. From Appendix B.6, at the .05 significance level, the critical value of F is 3.24. The decision rule is to reject the null hypothesis if the computed F test statistic's value is greater than 3.24.

We use Excel to perform the calculations and output the results. The computed value of F is 2.483, so we decide to not reject the null hypothesis. We conclude there is no difference in the mean travel time along the four routes. There is no reason to conclude that any one of the routes is faster than any other.

Drivers and Routes.xlsx

	Routes			
Driver	U.S 6	West End	Hickory St.	Route 59
Deans	18	17	21	22
Snaverly	16	23	23	22
Ormson	21	21	26	22
Zollaco	23	22	29	25
Filbeck	25	24	28	28

Anova: Single Factor

SUMMARY

Groups	Count	Sum	Average	Variance
U.S 6	5	103	20.6	13.3
West End	5	107	21.4	7.3
Hickory St.	5	127	25.4	11.3
Route 59	5	119	23.8	7.2

ANOVA

Source of Variation	SS	df	MS	F	P-value	F crit
Between Groups	72.8	3	24.267	2.483	0.098	3.239
Within Groups	156.4	16	9.775			
Total	229.2	19				

Treatment (Block)

Error

From the above Excel output, the mean travel times along the routes were 20.6 minutes along U.S. 6, 21.4 minutes along the West End route, 25.4 minutes using Hickory Street, and 23.8 minutes using Route 59. We conclude these differences could reasonably be attributed to chance. From the ANOVA table, we note SST is 72.8, SSE is 156.4, and SS total is 229.2.

In this example, we only considered the variation due to the treatments (routes) and took all the remaining variation to be random. If we include the effect or variance of the drivers, this would allow us to reduce the SSE term, and the computed values of the F statistics would be larger.

In this case, we let the drivers be the **blocking variable.** To include the variance due to the drivers, we need to determine the sum of squares due to the blocks. In a two-way ANOVA, the sum of squares due to blocks is found by the following formula.

BLOCKING VARIABLE A second treatment variable that when included in the ANOVA analysis will have the effect of reducing the SSE term.

$$\text{SSB} = k\Sigma(\bar{x}_b - \bar{x}_G)^2 \qquad \textbf{(12–6)}$$

where:

k is the number of treatments.
b is the number of blocks.
$\bar{x}_b$ is the sample mean of block b.
$\bar{x}_G$ is the overall or grand mean.

From the calculations on the next page, the means for the respective drivers are 19.5 minutes, 21 minutes, 22.5 minutes, 24.75 minutes, and 26.25 minutes. The overall mean is 22.8 minutes, found by adding the travel time for all 20 drives (456 minutes) and dividing by 20.

Travel Time from Starbrick to Warren (minutes)						
Driver	U.S. 6	West End	Hickory St.	Rte. 59	Driver Sums	Driver Means
Deans	18	17	21	22	78	19.50
Snaverly	16	23	23	22	84	21.00
Ormson	21	21	26	22	90	22.50
Zollaco	23	22	29	25	99	24.75
Filbeck	25	24	28	28	105	26.25

Substituting this information into formula (12–6) we determine SSB, the sum of squares due to the drivers (the blocking variable), is 119.7.

$$\begin{aligned} SSB &= k\Sigma(\bar{x}_b - \bar{x}_G)^2 \\ &= 4(19.5 - 22.8)^2 + 4(21.0 - 22.8)^2 + 4(22.5 - 22.8)^2 \\ &\quad + 4(24.75 - 22.8)^2 + 4(26.25 - 22.8)^2 \\ &= 119.7 \end{aligned}$$

The SSE term is found by subtraction.

SUM OF SQUARES ERROR, TWO-WAY $SSE = SS\ total - SST - SSB$ **(12–7)**

The same format is used in the two-way ANOVA table as in the one-way case, except there is an additional row for the blocking variable. SS total and SST are calculated as before, and SSB is found from formula (12–6). The values for the various components of the ANOVA table are computed as follows.

Source of Variation	Sum of Squares	Degrees of Freedom	Mean Square	*F*
Treatments	SST	$k - 1$	$SST/(k - 1) = MST$	MST/MSE
Blocks	SSB	$b - 1$	$SSB/(b - 1) = MSB$	MSB/MSE
Error	SSE	$(k - 1)(b - 1)$	$SSE/[(k - 1)(b - 1)] = MSE$	
Total	SS total	$n - 1$		

SSE is found by formula (12–7).

$$SSE = SS\ total - SST - SSB = 229.2 - 72.8 - 119.7 = 36.7$$

Source of Variation	(1) Sum of Squares	(2) Degrees of Freedom	(3) Mean Square (1)/(2)
Treatments	72.8	3	24.27
Blocks	119.7	4	29.93
Error	36.7	12	3.06
Total	229.2	19	

There is disagreement at this point. If the purpose of the blocking variable (the drivers in this example) was only to reduce the error variation, we should not conduct a test of hypothesis for the difference in block means. That is, if our goal was to reduce the MSE term, then we should not test a hypothesis regarding the blocking variable. On the other hand, we may wish to give the blocks the same status as the treatments and conduct a hypothesis test. In the latter case, when the blocks are important enough to be considered as a second factor, we refer to this as a **two-factor experiment.** In many cases the decision is not clear. In our example we are concerned about the difference in the travel time for the different drivers, so we will conduct the hypothesis test of equal block means. The subscripts are the first letter of each driver's name. The two sets of hypotheses are:

1. H_0: The treatment means are equal ($\mu_1 = \mu_2 = \mu_3 = \mu_4$).
   H_1: At least one treatment mean is different.
2. H_0: The block means are equal ($\mu_D = \mu_S = \mu_O = \mu_Z = \mu_F$).
   H_1: At least one block mean is different.

First, we will test the hypothesis concerning the treatment means. There are $(k - 1) = (4 - 1) = 3$ degrees of freedom in the numerator and $(b - 1)(k - 1) = (5 - 1)(4 - 1) = 12$ degrees of freedom in the denominator. Using the .05 significance level, the critical value of F is 3.49. The null hypothesis that the mean times for the four routes are the same is rejected if the F ratio exceeds 3.49.

$$F = \frac{\text{MST}}{\text{MSE}} = \frac{24.27}{3.06} = 7.93$$

The null hypothesis is rejected and we conclude that at least one of the route's mean travel times is different from the other routes. WARTA will want to conduct some tests to determine which treatment means differ.

Next, we test to find whether the travel times for the various drivers are equal. The degrees of freedom in the numerator for blocks are $(b - 1) = (5 - 1) = 4$. The degrees of freedom for the denominator are the same as before: $(b - 1)(k - 1) = (5 - 1)(4 - 1) = 12$. The null hypothesis that the block means are the same is rejected if the F ratio exceeds 3.26.

$$F = \frac{\text{MSB}}{\text{MSE}} = \frac{29.93}{3.06} = 9.78$$

The null hypothesis about the block means is rejected, and we conclude that at least one driver's mean travel time is different from the other drivers. Thus, WARTA management can conclude, based on the sample results, that there is a difference in the mean travel times of drivers.

The Excel spreadsheet has a two-factor ANOVA procedure. The output for the WARTA example just completed follows. This output also includes the p-values. The p-value for the null hypothesis regarding the drivers is .001 and .004 for the routes. These p-values confirm that the null hypotheses for treatments and blocks should both be rejected because the p-value is less than the significance level.

Drivers and Routes.xlsx

	Routes			
Driver	U.S 6	West End	Hickory St.	Route 59
Deans	18	17	21	22
Snaverly	16	23	23	22
Ormson	21	21	26	22
Zollaco	23	22	29	25
Filbeck	25	24	28	28

Anova: Two-Factor Without Replication

SUMMARY	Count	Sum	Average	Variance
Deans	4	78	19.50	5.67
Snaverly	4	84	21.00	11.33
Ormson	4	90	22.50	5.67
Zollaco	4	99	24.75	9.58
Filbeck	4	105	26.25	4.25
U.S 6	5	103	20.60	13.30
West End	5	107	21.40	7.30
Hickory St.	5	127	25.40	11.30
Route 59	5	119	23.80	7.20

ANOVA

Source of Variation	SS	df	MS	F	P-value	F crit
Rows	119.7	4	29.925	9.785	0.001	3.259
Columns	72.8	3	24.267	7.935	0.004	3.490
Error	36.7	12	3.058			
Total	229.2	19				

Block (Driver)

Treatment (Route)

SELF-REVIEW 12–4

Vive Shampoo sells three shampoos, one each for dry, normal, and oily hair. Sales, in millions of dollars, for the past 5 months are given in the following table. Using the .05 significance level, test whether the mean sales differ for the three types of shampoo or by month.

	Sales ($ million)		
Month	**Dry**	**Normal**	**Oily**
June	7	9	12
July	11	12	14
August	13	11	8
September	8	9	7
October	9	10	13

EXERCISES

For exercises 15 and 16, conduct a test of hypothesis to determine whether the block or the treatment means differ. Using the .05 significance level: (a) state the null and alternate hypotheses for treatments; (b) state the decision rule for treatments; and (c) state the null and alternate hypotheses for blocks. Also, state the decision rule for blocks, then: (d) compute SST, SSB, SS total, and SSE; (e) complete an ANOVA table; and (f) give your decision regarding the two sets of hypotheses and interpret the results.

15. The following data was collected for a two-factor ANOVA with two treatments and three blocks.

	Treatment	
Block	**1**	**2**
A	46	31
B	37	26
C	44	35

16. The following data was collected for a two-factor ANOVA with three treatments and three blocks.

	Treatment		
Block	**1**	**2**	**3**
A	12	14	8
B	9	11	9
C	7	8	8

17. **FILE** Chapin Manufacturing Company operates 24 hours a day, 5 days a week. The workers rotate shifts each week. Management is interested in whether there is a difference in the number of units produced when the employees work on various shifts. A sample of five workers is selected and their output recorded on each shift. At the .05 significance level, can we conclude there is a difference in the mean production rate by shift or by employee?

	Units Produced		
Employee	**Day**	**Afternoon**	**Night**
Skaff	31	25	35
Lum	33	26	33
Clark	28	24	30
Treece	30	29	28
Morgan	28	26	27

18. FILE There are three hospitals in the Tulsa, Oklahoma, area. The following data show the number of outpatient surgeries performed on Monday, Tuesday, Wednesday, Thursday, and Friday at each hospital last week. At the .05 significance level, can we conclude there is a difference in the mean number of surgeries performed by hospital or by day of the week?

	Number of Surgeries Performed		
Day	St. Luke's	St. Vincent	Mercy
Monday	14	18	24
Tuesday	20	24	14
Wednesday	16	22	14
Thursday	18	20	22
Friday	20	28	24

LO12-5
Perform a two-way ANOVA with interaction and describe the results.

TWO-WAY ANOVA WITH INTERACTION

In the previous section, we studied the separate or independent effects of two variables, or factors, on a response variable, travel time. In the example/solution, the two factors were the bus routes and the drivers and the response was travel time. The analysis shows two significant results. First, the mean travel times between routes, averaged over all drivers, are different. Second, the mean travel times between the five drivers, averaged over all the routes, are different. What could explain these differences? The differences between routes may simply be related to differences in the distance of the routes. We really didn't study the distance of the various routes. Perhaps the differences are explained by how fast, on average, the drivers drive regardless of the route.

There is another effect that may influence travel time that we have not considered. This is called the **interaction effect** between route and driver on travel time. That is, differences in travel time may depend on both the driver and the route. For example, it is possible that one of the drivers is especially good driving one of the routes. Perhaps one driver knows how to effectively time the traffic lights or how to avoid heavily congested intersections for one or more of the routes. In this case, differences in mean travel time may depend on the combined effect of driver and route. The results of the interaction of driver and route can provide interesting information.

INTERACTION The effect of one factor on a response variable differs depending on the value of another factor.

Interaction Plots

An everyday illustration of interaction is the effect of diet and exercise on body weight. It is generally agreed that body weight (the response variable) can be affected by two factors, diet and exercise. However, research shows there is also a combined or *interaction* effect of diet and exercise on weight loss. That is, the amount of weight loss will be different and depend on diet AND whether people exercise.

The following graph, or interaction plot, illustrates the interaction of diet and exercise. First, for people who do not exercise, the mean weight losses for Diet 1 and Diet 2 are plotted. These are connected with the blue line. Clearly, there is a difference in weight loss for the two diets. Second, for people who did exercise, the mean weight losses for Diet 1 and Diet 2 are plotted. These are connected with the green line. Again, there is a clear difference in weight loss between Diet 1 and Diet 2 for people who exercise. The plot also shows an interaction effect between diet and exercise on weight loss. Notice the two lines are not parallel to each other. For Diet 1, the mean weight loss is more when people also exercise. For Diet 2, the mean weight loss is also more when people also exercise, but the weight loss is much greater than for Diet 1. So, what is the effect of diet and exercise on weight loss? It depends on the combined, or interaction, effects of diet and exercise.

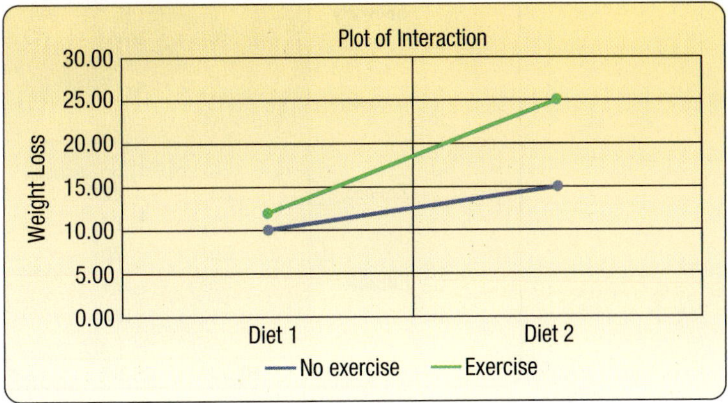

How would the interaction plot look if there were no interaction? The following graph shows an analysis of diet and exercise with no interaction.

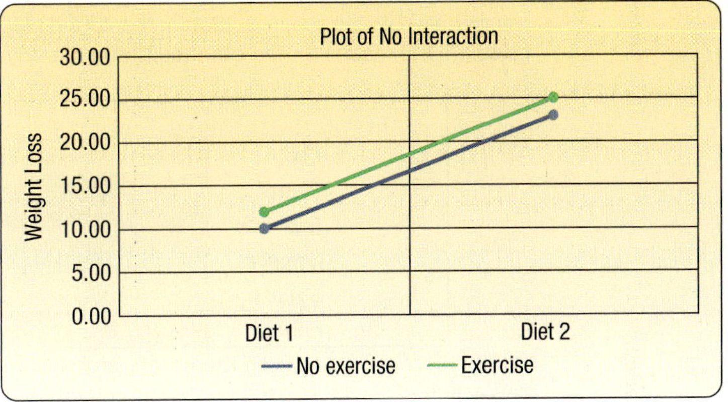

In this case the lines are parallel. Comparing the means, the effect of exercise on weight loss for Diet 1 and Diet 2 is the same. The estimated weight loss is about two pounds. In addition, the effect of diet is the same whether people exercise or not. It is about 13 pounds.

Testing for Interaction

To test for an interaction effect, we use a two-way ANOVA with interaction. To illustrate, we return to the previous WARTA example/solution. Restating the issue facing WARTA management: They want to expand bus service from downtown Warren to Starbrick. So far they have concluded, based on statistical analysis, that there is a difference in the mean travel time along the four proposed routes and a difference in the mean travel times of the five drivers. But it is possible that the combination, or the interaction between routes and drivers, has a significant effect on mean travel time.

In this analysis, we call the two variables, route and driver, **factors.** We refer to the variable, travel time, as the **response** variable. To test for interaction, the sample data must be replicated for each route. In this case, each driver drives each route three times so there are three observed times for each route/driver combination. This information is summarized in the following Excel spreadsheet.

	Routes				
	US 6	West End	Hickory St	Route 59	Means for Drivers
Deans	18	17	21	22	
	15	14	20	19	
	21	20	22	25	19.50
Snaverly	16	23	23	22	
	19	19	24	20	
	13	25	22	24	20.83
Ormson	21	21	26	22	
	19	23	24	24	
	14	25	28	20	22.25
Zollaco	23	22	29	25	
	21	24	30	20	
	25	20	28	26	24.42
Filbeck	25	24	28	28	
	24	25	29	30	Grand Mean
	26	23	27	26	26.25
Means for Routes	20.00	21.67	25.40	23.53	22.65

To evaluate interaction effects, a useful first step is to plot the means for each driver/route combination. For the driver/route combination Driver Deans using Route 6, the mean is 18 minutes, found by (18 + 15 + 21)/3. For the driver/route combination Driver Filbeck using Route 59, the mean is 28 minutes, found by (28 + 30 + 26)/3. In a similar manner we calculate the means for the other cells and summarize the results in the following table.

	Routes			
Drivers	US 6	West End	Hickory St	Route 59
Deans	18	17	21	22
Snaverly	16	22.33	23	22
Ormson	18	23	26	22
Zollaco	23	22	29	23.67
Filbeck	25	24	28	28

The graph below shows the interaction plot using the information in the above table. The vertical axis is the travel time in minutes. The four routes are labeled on the horizontal axis and each line plots the mean travel times for each driver for all four routes. For example, the green line reports average travel times for Deans for each of the four routes.

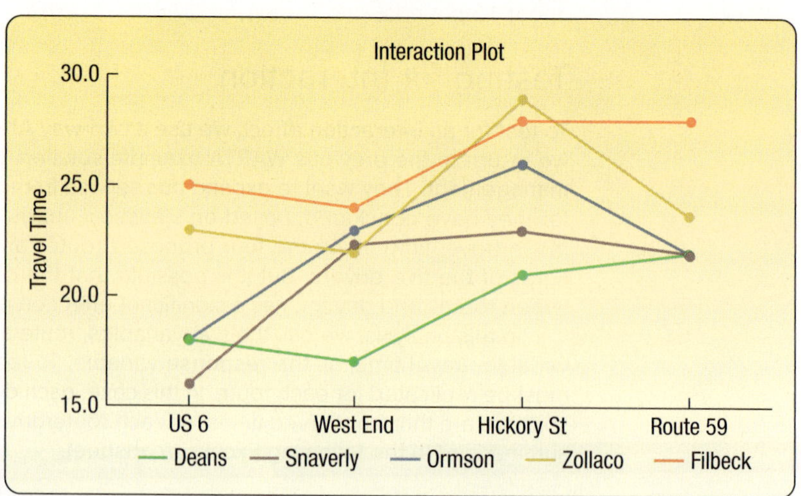

From the graph, what observations can be made about the interaction of driver and route on travel time? Most importantly, the lines are not parallel. Because the five lines are clearly not parallel, there is an interaction effect of driver and route on travel time; that is, travel time depends on the combined effect of driver and route.

Note the differences in travel times. For the U.S. 6 route, Snaverly has the lowest or fastest mean travel time. Deans has the lowest mean travel time for the West End and Hickory Street routes. Zollaco has the slowest average time for the Hickory Street route. There are many other observations that lead to the general observation that travel time is related to the combined effects of driver AND route. The critical question is whether the observed interactions are significant or the differences are due to chance.

Hypothesis Tests for Interaction

The next step is to conduct statistical tests to further investigate the possible interaction effects. In summary, our study of travel times has several questions:

- Is there an interaction effect of routes and drivers on mean travel times?
- Are the mean travel times for drivers the same?
- Are the mean travel times for the routes the same?

Of the three questions, we are most interested in the test for interactions.

We formalize these ideas into three sets of hypotheses:

1. H_0: There is no interaction between drivers and routes.
   H_1: There is interaction between drivers and routes.
2. H_0: The driver means are equal.
   H_1: At least one driver travel time mean is different.
3. H_0: The route means are equal.
   H_1: At least one route travel time mean is different.

We test each of these hypotheses as we did in the previous section using the F distribution. The tests are summarized with the following ANOVA table. It is similar to the two-way ANOVA in the previous section with the addition of the Interaction source of variation. In addition, we refer to the driver effect as **Factor A** and the route effect as **Factor B.** Each of these hypotheses is tested using the familiar F statistic.

Source of Variation	Sum of Squares	*df*	Mean Square	*F*
Factor A (driver)	SSA	$k - 1$	MSA = SSA/(k − 1)	MSA/MSE
Factor B (route)	SSB	$b - 1$	MSB = SSA/(b − 1)	MSB/MSE
Interaction	SSI	$(k - 1)(b - 1)$	MSI = SSI/[(k − 1)(b − 1)]	MSI/MSE
Error	SSE	$n - kb$	MSE = SSE/(n − kb)	
Total		$n - 1$		

To test the hypotheses for a two-way ANOVA with interaction, we use the ANOVA: Two-Factor with Replication in the Data Analysis add-in for Excel. The details of using Excel are summarized in Appendix C. The following ANOVA table shows the results of the analysis. We use the p-values to test each hypothesis. Using the .05 significance level, the null hypotheses are rejected if the computed p-value is less than .05.

ANOVA						
Source of Variation	*SS*	*df*	*MS*	*F*	*P-value*	*F crit*
Drivers	353.5667	4	88.39167	17.21916	0.0000	2.605975
Routes	244.9833	3	81.66111	15.90801	0.0000	2.838745
Interaction	125.7667	12	10.48056	2.041667	0.0456	2.003459
Error	205.3333	40	5.133333			
Total	929.65	59				

Reviewing the results of the ANOVA, the *p*-value for the interaction effect of .0456 is less than our significance level of .05, so our decision is to reject the null hypothesis of no interaction and conclude that the combination of route and driver has a significant effect on the response variable, travel time.

A significant interaction effect provides important information about the combined effects of the variables. If interaction is present, then a test of differences in the factor means using a one-way ANOVA for each level of the other factor is the next step. This analysis requires some time and work to complete, but the results are usually enlightening.

We will continue the analysis by conducting a one-way ANOVA for each route by testing the hypothesis H_0: Driver travel times are equal. The results follow.

US 6; H_0: Driver times are equal

Source of Variation	*SS*	*df*	*MS*	*F*	*P-value*	*F crit*
Between Groups	174	4	43.5	6.04167	0.010	3.478
Within Groups	72	10	7.2			
Total	246	14				

West End; H_0: Driver times are equal

Source of Variation	*SS*	*df*	*MS*	*F*	*P-value*	*F crit*
Between Groups	88.6667	4	22.1667	4.05488	0.033	3.478
Within Groups	54.6667	10	5.46667			
Total	143.333	14				

Hickory; H_0: Driver times are equal

Source of Variation	*SS*	*df*	*MS*	*F*	*P-value*	*F crit*
Between Groups	135.6	4	33.9	21.1875	0.000	3.478
Within Groups	16	10	1.6			
Total	151.6	14				

Route 59; H_0: Driver times are equal

Source of Variation	*SS*	*df*	*MS*	*F*	*P-value*	*F crit*
Between Groups	81.0667	4	20.2667	3.23404	0.060	3.478
Within Groups	62.6667	10	6.26667			
Total	143.733	14				

The results of the one-way ANOVA show there are significant differences in the mean travel times among the drivers for every route, except Route 59 with a *p*-value of 0.06. A review of the interaction plot may reveal some of the differences. For example, for the West End route, the graph suggests that Deans has the best mean travel time. Further statistical analysis would test pairs of mean travel times to determine the significant differences between driver travel times for each route that has a significant *p*-value.

SELF-REVIEW 12–5

See the following ANOVA table.

ANOVA					
Source of Variation	**SS**	***df***	**MS**	***F***	***p*-value**
Factor A	6.41	3	2.137	3.46	0.0322
Factor B	5.01	2	2.507	4.06	0.0304
Interaction	33.15	6	5.525	8.94	0.0000
Error	14.83	24	0.618		
Total	59.41	35			

Use the .05 significance level to answer the following questions.

(a) How many levels does Factor A have? Is there a significant difference among the Factor A means? How do you know?

(b) How many levels does Factor B have? Is there a significant difference among the Factor B means? How do you know?

(c) How many observations are there in each cell? Is there a significant interaction between Factor A and Factor B on the response variable? How do you know?

EXERCISES

19. FILE Consider the following sample data for a two-factor ANOVA analysis. There are two levels (heavy and light) of factor A (weight), and three levels (small, medium, and large) of factor B (size). For each combination of size and weight, there are three observations.

		Size		
		Small	**Medium**	**Large**
Weight	Heavy	23	20	11
		21	32	20
		25	26	20
	Light	13	20	11
		32	17	23
		17	15	8

Compute an ANOVA with statistical software, and use the .05 significance level to answer the following questions.

a. Is there a difference in the Size means?

b. Is there a difference in the Weight means?

c. Is there a significant interaction between Weight and Size?

20. Consider the following partially completed two-way ANOVA table. Suppose there are four levels of Factor A and three levels of Factor B. The number of replications per cell is 5. Complete the table and test to determine if there is a significant difference in Factor A means, Factor B means, or the interaction means. Use the .05 significance level. (Hint: estimate the values from the *F* table.)

ANOVA				
Source	**SS**	***df***	**MS**	***F***
Factor A	75			
Factor B	25			
Interaction	300			
Error	600			
Total	1000			

21. **FILE** A vending machine company sells its packaged foods in a variety of different machines. The company is considering three types of new vending machines. Management wants to know if the different machines affect sales. These vending machines are designated as J-1000, D-320, and UV-57. Management also wants to know if the position of the machines indoors or outdoors affects sales. Each of six similar locations was randomly assigned a machine and position combination. The data below are the number of purchases over four days.

Position/Machine	J-1000	D-320	UV-57
Inside	33, 40, 30, 31	29, 28, 33, 33	47, 39, 39, 45
Outside	43, 36, 41, 40	48, 45, 40, 44	37, 32, 36, 35

   a. Draw the interaction graph. Based on your observations, is there an interaction effect? Based on the graph, describe the interaction effect of machine and position.
   b. Compute an ANOVA with statistical software, and use the 0.05 level to test for position, machine, and interaction effects on sales. Report the statistical results.
   c. Compare the inside and outside mean sales for each machine using statistical techniques. What do you conclude?

22. **FILE** A large company is organized into three functional areas: manufacturing, marketing, and research and development. The employees claim that the company pays women less than men for similar jobs. The company randomly selected four males and four females in each area and recorded their weekly salaries in dollars.

Area/Gender	Female	Male
Manufacturing	1016, 1007, 875, 968	978, 1056, 982, 748
Marketing	1045, 895, 848, 904	1154, 1091, 878, 876
Research and Development	770, 733, 844, 771	926, 1055, 1066, 1088

   a. Draw the interaction graph. Based on your observations, is there an interaction effect? Based on the graph, describe the interaction effect of gender and area on salary.
   b. Compute an ANOVA with statistical software, and use the 0.05 level to test for gender, area, and interaction effects on salary. Report the statistical results.
   c. Compare the male and female mean salary for each area using statistical techniques. What do you recommend to the distributor?

CHAPTER SUMMARY

I. The characteristics of the F distribution are:
   A. It is continuous.
   B. Its values cannot be negative.
   C. It is positively skewed.
   D. There is a family of F distributions. Each time the degrees of freedom in either the numerator or the denominator change, a new distribution is created.

II. The F distribution is used to test whether two population variances are the same.
   A. The sampled populations must follow the normal distribution.
   B. The larger of the two sample variances is placed in the numerator, forcing the ratio to be at least 1.00.
   C. The value of F is computed using the following equation:

$$F = \frac{s_1^2}{s_2^2} \quad \textbf{(12–1)}$$

III. A one-way ANOVA is used to compare several treatment means.
  A. A treatment is a source of variation.
  B. The assumptions underlying ANOVA are:
    1. The samples are from populations that follow the normal distribution.
    2. The populations have equal standard deviations.
    3. The populations are independent.
  C. The information for finding the value of *F* is summarized in an ANOVA table.
    1. The formula for SS total, the sum of squares total, is:

$$\text{SS total} = \Sigma(x - \bar{x}_G)^2 \quad \textbf{(12–2)}$$

    2. The formula for SSE, the sum of squares error, is:

$$\text{SSE} = \Sigma(x - \bar{x}_c)^2 \quad \textbf{(12–3)}$$

    3. The formula for the SST, the sum of squares treatment, is found by subtraction.

$$\text{SST} = \text{SS total} - \text{SSE} \quad \textbf{(12–4)}$$

    4. This information is summarized in the following ANOVA table and the value of *F* is determined.

Source of Variation	Sum of Squares	Degrees of Freedom	Mean Square	F
Treatments	SST	$k - 1$	SST/(k − 1) = MST	MST/MSE
Error	SSE	$n - k$	SSE/(n − k) = MSE	
Total	SS total	$n - 1$		

IV. If a null hypothesis of equal treatment means is rejected, we can identify the pairs of means that differ from the following confidence interval.

$$(\bar{x}_1 - \bar{x}_2) \pm t\sqrt{\text{MSE}\left(\frac{1}{n_1} + \frac{1}{n_2}\right)} \quad \textbf{(12–5)}$$

V. In a two-way ANOVA, we consider a second treatment variable.
  A. The second treatment variable is called the blocking variable.
  B. It is determined using the following equation:

$$\text{SSB} = k\Sigma(\bar{x}_b - \bar{x}_G)^2 \quad \textbf{(12–6)}$$

  C. The SSE term, or sum of squares error, is found from the following equation.

$$\text{SSE} = \text{SS total} - \text{SST} - \text{SSB} \quad \textbf{(12–7)}$$

  D. The *F* statistics for the treatment variable and the blocking variable are determined in the following table.

Source of Variation	Sum of Squares	Degrees of Freedom	Mean Square	F
Treatments	SST	$k - 1$	SST/(k − 1) = MST	MST/MSE
Blocks	SSB	$b - 1$	SSB/(b − 1) = MSB	MSB/MSE
Error	SSE	$(k - 1)(b - 1)$	SSE/[(k − 1)(b − 1)] = MSE	
Total	SS total	$n - 1$		

VI. In a two-way ANOVA with repeated observations, we consider two treatment variables and the possible interaction between the variables. The complete ANOVA table including interactions is:

Source	Sum of Squares	df	Mean Square	F
Factor A	SSA	$k - 1$	SSA/(k − 1) = MSA	MSA/MSE
Factor B	SSB	$b - 1$	SSB/(b − 1) = MSB	MSB/MSE
Interaction	SSI	$(k - 1)(b - 1)$	SSI/[(k − 1)(b − 1)] = MSI	MSI/MSE
Error	SSE	$n - kb$	SSE/(n − kb) = MSE	
Total	SS total	$n - 1$		

PRONUNCIATION KEY

SYMBOL	MEANING	PRONUNCIATION
SS total	Sum of squares total	*S S total*
SST	Sum of squares treatment	*S S T*
SSE	Sum of squares error	*S S E*
MSE	Mean square error	*M S E*
SSB	Block sum of squares	*S S B*
SSI	Sum of squares interaction	*S S I*

CHAPTER EXERCISES

23. A real estate agent in the coastal area of Georgia wants to compare the variation in the selling price of homes on the oceanfront with those one to three blocks from the ocean. A sample of 21 oceanfront homes sold within the last year revealed the standard deviation of the selling prices was $45,600. A sample of 18 homes, also sold within the last year, that were one to three blocks from the ocean revealed that the standard deviation was $21,330. At the .01 significance level, can we conclude that there is more variation in the selling prices of the oceanfront homes?

24. One variable that Google uses to rank pages on the Internet is page speed, the time it takes for a web page to load into your browser. A source for women's clothing is redesigning their page to improve the images that show its products and to reduce its load time. The new page is clearly faster, but initial tests indicate there is more variation in the time to load. A sample of 16 different load times showed that the standard deviation of the load time was 22 hundredths of a second for the new page and 12 hundredths of a second for the current page. At the .05 significance level, can we conclude that there is more variation in the load time of the new page?

25. **FILE** There are two Chevrolet dealers in Jamestown, New York. The mean monthly sales at Sharkey Chevy and Dave White Chevrolet are about the same. However, Tom Sharkey, the owner of Sharkey Chevy, believes his sales are more consistent. Below are the numbers of new cars sold at Sharkey in the last 7 months and for the last 8 months at Dave White. Do you agree with Mr. Sharkey? Use the .01 significance level.

Sharkey	98	78	54	57	68	64	70	
Dave White	75	81	81	30	82	46	58	101

26. Random samples of five were selected from each of three populations. The sum of squares total was 100. The sum of squares due to the treatments was 40.

a. Set up the null hypothesis and the alternate hypothesis.
b. What is the decision rule? Use the .05 significance level.
c. Create the ANOVA table. What is the value of *F*?
d. What is your decision regarding the null hypothesis?

27. In an ANOVA table, the MSE is equal to 10. Random samples of six were selected from each of four populations, where the sum of squares total was 250.

a. Set up the null hypothesis and the alternate hypothesis.
b. What is the decision rule? Use the .05 significance level.
c. Create the ANOVA table. What is the value of *F*?
d. What is your decision regarding the null hypothesis?

28. The following is a partial ANOVA table.

Source	Sum of Squares	*df*	Mean Square	*F*
Treatment		2		
Error			20	
Total	500	11		

Complete the table and answer the following questions. Use the .05 significance level.

a. How many treatments are there?

b. What is the total sample size?

c. What is the critical value of *F*?

d. Write out the null and alternate hypotheses.

e. What is your conclusion regarding the null hypothesis?

29. **FILE** A consumer organization wants to know whether there is a difference in the price of a particular toy at three different types of stores. The price of the toy was checked in a sample of five discount stores, five variety stores, and five department stores. The results are shown below. Use the .05 significance level.

Discount	Variety	Department
$12	$15	$19
13	17	17
14	14	16
12	18	20
15	17	19

30. **FILE** Jacob Lee is a frequent traveler between Los Angeles and San Diego. For the past month, he wrote down the flight times in minutes on three different airlines. The results are:

Goust	Jet Red	Cloudtran
51	50	52
51	53	55
52	52	60
42	62	64
51	53	61
57	49	49
47	50	49
47	49	
50	58	
60	54	
54	51	
49	49	
48	49	
48	50	

a. Use the .05 significance level and the six-step hypothesis-testing process to check if there is a difference in the mean flight times among the three airlines.

b. Develop a 95% confidence interval for the difference in the means between Goust and Cloudtran.

31. **FILE** The City of Maumee comprises four districts. Chief of Police Andy North wants to determine whether there is a difference in the mean number of crimes committed among the four districts. He examined the records from six randomly selected days and recorded the number of crimes. At the .05 significance level, can Chief North conclude that there is a difference in the mean number of crimes among the four districts?

Number of Crimes			
Rec Center	**Key Street**	**Monclova**	**Whitehouse**
13	21	12	16
15	13	14	17
14	18	15	18
15	19	13	15
14	18	12	20
15	19	15	18

32. **FILE** A study of the effect of television commercials on 12-year-old children measured their attention span, in seconds. The commercials were for clothes, food, and toys. At the .05 significance level, is there a difference in the mean attention span of the children for the various commercials? Are there significant differences between pairs of means? Would you recommend dropping one of the three commercial types?

Clothes	Food	Toys
26	45	60
21	48	51
43	43	43
35	53	54
28	47	63
31	42	53
17	34	48
31	43	58
20	57	47
	47	51
	44	51
	54	

33. **FILE** When only two treatments are involved, ANOVA and the Student's *t* test (Chapter 11) result in the same conclusions. Also, for computed test statistics, $t^2 = F$. To demonstrate this relationship, use the following example. Fourteen randomly selected students enrolled in a history course were divided into two groups, one consisting of 6 students who took the course in the normal lecture format. The other group of 8 students took the course in a distance format. At the end of the course, each group was examined with a 50-item test. The following is a list of the number correct for each of the two groups.

Traditional Lecture	Distance
37	50
35	46
41	49
40	44
35	41
34	42
	45
	43

a. Using analysis of variance techniques, test H_0 that the two mean test scores are equal; $\alpha = .05$.
b. Using the *t* test from Chapter 11, compute *t*.
c. Interpret the results.

34. There are four auto body shops in Bangor, Maine, and all claim to promptly repair cars. To check if there is any difference in repair times, customers are randomly selected from each repair shop and their repair times in days are recorded. The output from a statistical software package is:

Summary				
Groups	**Sample Size**	**Sum**	**Average**	**Variance**
Body Shop A	3	15.4	5.133333	0.323333
Body Shop B	4	32	8	1.433333
Body Shop C	5	25.2	5.04	0.748
Body Shop D	4	25.9	6.475	0.595833

ANOVA					
Source of Variation	**SS**	***df***	**MS**	***F***	***p*-value**
Between Groups	23.37321	3	7.791069	9.612506	0.001632
Within Groups	9.726167	12	0.810514		
Total	33.09938	15			

Is there evidence to suggest a difference in the mean repair times at the four body shops? Use the .05 significance level.

35. The fuel efficiencies for a sample of 27 compact, midsize, and large cars are entered into a statistical software package. Analysis of variance is used to investigate if there is a difference in the mean miles per gallon of the three car sizes. What do you conclude? Use the .01 significance level.

Summary				
Groups	**Sample Size**	**Sum**	**Average**	**Variance**
Compact	12	268.3	22.35833	9.388106
Midsize	9	172.4	19.15556	7.315278
Large	6	100.5	16.75	7.303

Additional results are shown below.

ANOVA					
Source of Variation	**SS**	***df***	**MS**	***F***	***p*-value**
Between Groups	136.4803	2	68.24014	8.258752	0.001866
Within Groups	198.3064	24	8.262766		
Total	334.7867	26			

36. Three assembly lines are used to produce a certain component for an airliner. To examine the production rate, a random sample of six hourly periods is chosen for each assembly line and the number of components produced during these periods for each line is recorded. The output from a statistical software package is:

Summary				
Groups	**Sample Size**	**Sum**	**Average**	**Variance**
Line A	6	250	41.66667	0.266667
Line B	6	260	43.33333	0.666667
Line C	6	249	41.5	0.7

ANOVA					
Source of Variation	**SS**	***df***	**MS**	***F***	***p*-value**
Between Groups	12.33333	2	6.166667	11.32653	0.001005
Within Groups	8.166667	15	0.544444		
Total	20.5	17			

a. Use a .01 level of significance to test if there is a difference in the mean production of the three assembly lines.

b. Develop a 99% confidence interval for the difference in the means between Line B and Line C.

37. FILE The postal service sorts mail as Priority Mail Express, Priority Mail, First-Class Mail, or Standard Mail. Over a period of 3 weeks, 18 of each type were mailed from the Network Distribution Center in Atlanta, Georgia, to Des Moines, Iowa. The total delivery time in days was recorded. Minitab was used to perform the ANOVA. The results follow:

Analysis of Variance

Source	DF	Adj SS	Adj MS	F-Value	P-Value
Factor	3	35.7678	11.9226	13.62	<0.0001
Error	68	59.5167	0.8752		
Total	71	95.2844			

Model Summary

S	R-sq	R-sq(adj)	R-sq(pred)
0.935545	37.54%	34.78%	29.97%

Means

Factor	N	Mean	StDev	95% CI
Priority Mail Express	18	1.2556	0.6271	(0.8155, 1.6956)
Priority Mail	18	1.9944	0.9434	(1.5544, 2.4345)
First-Class Mail	18	2.8611	1.0600	(2.4211, 3.3011)
Standard Mail	18	3.0000	1.0460	(2.5600, 3.4400)

Pooled StDev = 0.935545

Fisher Individual Tests for Differences of Means

Difference of Levels	Difference of Means	SE of Difference	95% CI	T-Value	Adjusted P-Value
Priority Mail-Priority Mail Express	0.7389	0.3118	(0.1166, 1.3612)	2.37	0.0207
First-Class Mail-Priority Mail Express	1.6056	0.3118	(0.9833, 2.2278)	5.15	<0.0001
Standard Mail-Priority Mail Express	1.7444	0.3118	(1.1222, 2.3667)	5.59	<0.0001
First-Class Mail-Priority Mail	0.8667	0.3118	(0.2444, 1.4890)	2.78	0.0070
Standard Mail-Priority Mail	1.0056	0.3118	(0.3833, 1.6278)	3.22	0.0019
Standard Mail-First-Class Mail	0.1389	0.3118	(-0.4834, 0.7612)	0.45	0.6575

Simultaneous confidence level = 80.02%

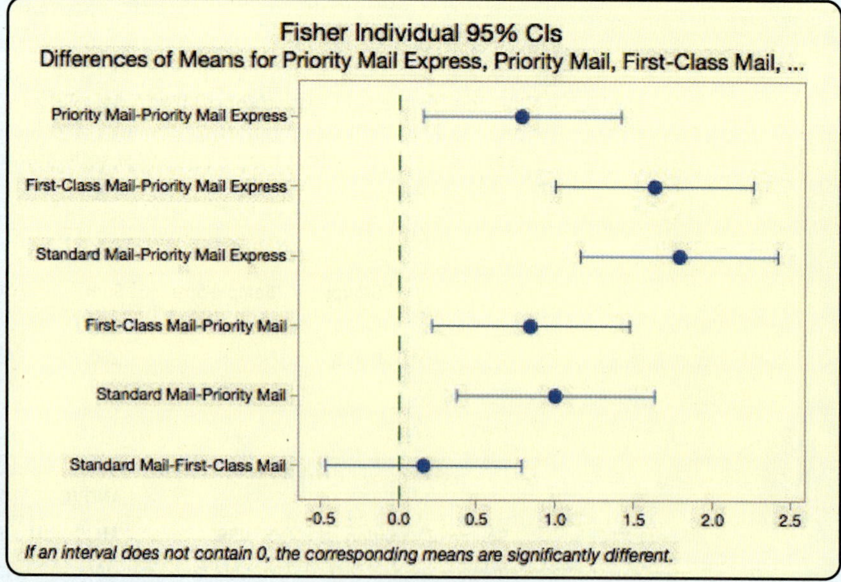

Using the ANOVA results, compare the average delivery times of the four different types of mail.

38. **FILE** To prevent spam from entering your email inbox, you use a filter. You are interested in knowing if the number of spam emails differs by day of the week. The number of spam emails by day of week is counted and recorded. Minitab is used to perform the data analysis. Here are the results:

Analysis of Variance

Source	DF	Adj SS	Adj MS	F-Value	P-Value
Factor	6	2266.92	377.820	9.29	<0.0001
Error	48	1952.43	40.676		
Total	54	4219.35			

Means

Factor	N	Mean	StDev	95% CI
Monday	10	76.400	4.452	(72.345, 80.455)
Tuesday	9	60.444	4.333	(56.170, 64.719)
Wednesday	7	74.286	4.231	(69.439, 79.132)
Thursday	8	60.750	6.251	(56.216, 65.284)
Friday	8	74.000	7.838	(69.466, 78.534)
Saturday	5	64.000	7.036	(58.265, 69.735)
Sunday	8	69.125	9.372	(64.591, 73.659)

Pooled StDev = 6.37774

Grouping Information Using the Fisher LSD Method and 95% Confidence

Factor	N	Mean	Grouping			
Monday	10	76.400	A			
Wednesday	7	74.286	A	B		
Friday	8	74.000	A	B		
Sunday	8	69.125		B	C	
Saturday	5	64.000			C	D
Thursday	8	60.750				D
Tuesday	9	60.444				D

Means that do not share a letter are significantly different.

Fisher Individual Tests for Differences of Means

Difference of Levels	Difference of Means	SE of Difference	95% CI	T-Value	Adjusted P-Value
Tuesday-Monday	-15.956	2.930	(-21.847, -10.064)	-5.44	<0.0001
Wednesday-Monday	-2.114	3.143	(-8.434, 4.205)	-0.67	0.5044
Thursday-Monday	-15.650	3.025	(-21.733, -9.567)	-5.17	<0.0001
Friday-Monday	-2.400	3.025	(-8.483, 3.683)	-0.79	0.4315
Saturday-Monday	-12.400	3.493	(-19.424, -5.376)	-3.55	0.0009
Sunday-Monday	-7.275	3.025	(-13.358, -1.192)	-2.40	0.0201
Wednesday-Tuesday	13.841	3.214	(7.379, 20.304)	4.31	<0.0001
Thursday-Tuesday	0.306	3.099	(-5.925, 6.537)	0.10	0.9219
Friday-Tuesday	13.556	3.099	(7.325, 19.787)	4.37	<0.0001
Saturday-Tuesday	3.556	3.557	(-3.597, 10.708)	1.00	0.3226
Sunday-Tuesday	8.681	3.099	(2.450, 14.912)	2.80	0.0073
Thursday-Wednesday	-13.536	3.301	(-20.172, -6.899)	-4.10	0.0002
Friday-Wednesday	-0.286	3.301	(-6.922, 6.351)	-0.09	0.9314
Saturday-Wednesday	-10.286	3.734	(-17.794, -2.777)	-2.75	0.0083
Sunday-Wednesday	-5.161	3.301	(-11.797, 1.476)	-1.56	0.1245
Friday-Thursday	13.250	3.189	(6.838, 19.662)	4.16	0.0001
Saturday-Thursday	3.250	3.636	(-4.060, 10.560)	0.89	0.3759
Sunday-Thursday	8.375	3.189	(1.963, 14.787)	2.63	0.0115
Saturday-Friday	-10.000	3.636	(-17.310, -2.690)	-2.75	0.0084
Sunday-Friday	-4.875	3.189	(-11.287, 1.537)	-1.53	0.1329
Sunday-Saturday	5.125	3.636	(-2.185, 12.435)	1.41	0.1651

Simultaneous confidence level = 57.84%

Using the ANOVA results, compare the average number of spam emails for each day of the week.

39. **FILE** Shank's Inc., a nationwide advertising firm, wants to know whether the size of an advertisement and the color of the advertisement make a difference in the response of magazine readers. A random sample of readers is shown ads of four different colors and three different sizes. Each reader is asked to give the particular combination of size and color a rating between 1 and 10. Assume that the ratings follow the normal distribution. The rating for each combination is shown in the following table (for example, the rating for a small red ad is 2).

	Color of Ad			
Size of Ad	**Red**	**Blue**	**Orange**	**Green**
Small	2	3	3	8
Medium	3	5	6	7
Large	6	7	8	8

Is there a difference in the effectiveness of an advertisement by color and by size? Use the .05 level of significance.

40. **FILE** There are four McBurger restaurants in the Columbus, Georgia, area. The numbers of burgers sold at the respective restaurants for each of the last 6 weeks are shown below. At the .05 significance level, is there a difference in the mean number sold among the four restaurants when the factor of week is considered?

	Restaurant			
Week	**Metro**	**Interstate**	**University**	**River**
1	124	160	320	190
2	234	220	340	230
3	430	290	290	240
4	105	245	310	170
5	240	205	280	180
6	310	260	270	205

a. Is there a difference in the treatment means?
b. Is there a difference in the block means?

41. **FILE** The city of Tucson, Arizona, employs people to assess the value of homes for the purpose of calculating real estate tax. The city manager sends each assessor to the same five homes and then compares the results. The information is given below, in thousands of dollars. Can we conclude that there is a difference in the assessors? Use the .05 significance level.

	Assessor			
Home	**Zawodny**	**Norman**	**Cingle**	**Holiday**
A	$53.0	$55.0	$49.0	$45.0
B	50.0	51.0	52.0	53.0
C	48.0	52.0	47.0	53.0
D	70.0	68.0	65.0	64.0
E	84.0	89.0	92.0	86.0

a. Is there a difference in the treatment means?
b. Is there a difference in the block means?

42. **FILE** A task requires the completion of four activities. A teacher would like to know if differences in the sequence of the four activities results in different task completion times. The teacher selects three students and demonstrates the activities in random order to the students. Then each student completes the task with each of the activity sequences. The completion times are recorded. The following table shows the minutes for each student to complete each task.

	Time (minutes)		
Sequence	Allen	Carla	Henry
A	22.4	20.8	21.5
B	17.0	19.4	20.7
C	19.2	20.2	21.2
D	20.3	18.6	20.4

Using the .05 level of significance:

a. Is there a difference in the task completion times among the different sequences?

b. Is there a difference in task completion times between the students?

43. FILE A research firm wants to compare the miles per gallon of unleaded regular, mid-grade, and super premium gasolines. Because of differences in the performance of different automobiles, seven different automobiles were selected and treated as blocks. Therefore, each brand of gasoline was tested with each type of automobile. The results of the trials, in miles per gallon, are shown in the following table. At the .05 significance level, is there a difference in the gasolines or automobiles?

Automobile	Regular	Mid-grade	Super Premium
1	21	23	26
2	23	22	25
3	24	25	27
4	24	24	26
5	26	26	30
6	26	24	27
7	28	27	32

44. FILE Each of three supermarket chains in the Denver area claims to have the lowest overall prices. As part of an investigative study on supermarket advertising, a local television station conducted a study by randomly selecting nine grocery items. Then, on the same day, an intern was sent to each of the three stores to purchase the nine items. From the receipts, the following data was recorded. At the .05 significance level, is there a difference in the mean price for the nine items between the three supermarkets?

Item	Super$	Ralph's	Lowblaws
1	$1.12	$1.02	$1.07
2	1.14	1.10	1.21
3	1.72	1.97	2.08
4	2.22	2.09	2.32
5	2.40	2.10	2.30
6	4.04	4.32	4.15
7	5.05	4.95	5.05
8	4.68	4.13	4.67
9	5.52	5.46	5.86

45. **FILE** Listed below are the weights (in grams) of a sample of M&M's Plain candies, classified according to color. Use a statistical software system to determine whether there is a difference in the mean weights of candies of different colors. Use the .05 significance level.

Red	Orange	Yellow	Brown	Tan	Green
0.946	0.902	0.929	0.896	0.845	0.935
1.107	0.943	0.960	0.888	0.909	0.903
0.913	0.916	0.938	0.906	0.873	0.865
0.904	0.910	0.933	0.941	0.902	0.822
0.926	0.903	0.932	0.838	0.956	0.871
0.926	0.901	0.899	0.892	0.959	0.905
1.006	0.919	0.907	0.905	0.916	0.905
0.914	0.901	0.906	0.824	0.822	0.852
0.922	0.930	0.930	0.908		0.965
1.052	0.883	0.952	0.833		0.898
0.903		0.939			
0.895		0.940			
		0.882			
		0.906			

46. There are four radio stations in Midland. The stations have different formats (hard rock, classical, country/western, and easy listening), but each is concerned with the number of minutes of music played per hour. From a sample of 10 randomly selected hours from each station, the sum of squared differences between each observation and the mean for its respective radio station, $\Sigma(x - \bar{x}_c)^2$, are:

Hard rock station:	126.29	Country/western station:	166.79
Classical station:	233.34	Easy listening station:	77.57

The total sum of squares for the data is: SS total = 1,099.61.

a. Determine SSE.
b. Determine SST.
c. Complete an ANOVA table.
d. At the .05 significance level, is there a difference in the treatment means?
e. If the mean for the hard rock station is 51.32 and the mean for the country/western station is 50.85, determine if there is a difference using the .05 significance level.

47. **FILE** The American Accounting Association recently conducted a study to compare the weekly wages of men and women employed in either the public or private sector of accounting. Random samples of five men and five women were selected in each group.

	Sector	
Gender	**Public**	**Private**
Men	$ 978	$1,335
	1,035	1,167
	964	1,236
	996	1,317
	1,117	1,192
Women	$ 863	$1,079
	975	1,160
	999	1,063
	1,019	1,110
	1,037	1,093

a. Draw an interaction plot of men and women means by sector.
b. Compute an ANOVA with statistical software and, using the .05 significance level, test the interaction effect of gender and sector on wages.
c. Based on your results in part (b), conduct the appropriate tests of hypotheses for differences in factor means.
d. Interpret the results in a brief report.

48. FILE Robert Altoff is vice president of engineering for a manufacturer of household washing machines. As part of a new product development project, he wishes to determine the optimal length of time for the washing cycle. Included in the project is a study of the relationship between the detergent used (four brands) and the length of the washing cycle (18, 20, 22, or 24 minutes). In order to run the experiment, 32 standard household laundry loads (having equal amounts of dirt and the same total weights) are randomly assigned to the 16 detergent–washing cycle combinations. The results (in pounds of dirt removed) are shown below.

	Cycle Time (min)			
Detergent Brand	**18**	**20**	**22**	**24**
A	0.13	0.12	0.19	0.15
	0.11	0.11	0.17	0.18
B	0.14	0.15	0.18	0.20
	0.10	0.14	0.17	0.18
C	0.16	0.15	0.18	0.19
	0.17	0.14	0.19	0.21
D	0.09	0.12	0.16	0.15
	0.13	0.13	0.16	0.17

a. Draw an interaction plot of the detergent means by cycle time.
b. Compute the ANOVA with statistical software and, using the .05 significance level, test the interaction effect of brand and cycle time on "dirt removed."
c. Based on your results in part (b), conduct the appropriate tests of hypotheses for differences in factor means.
d. Interpret the results in a brief report.

DATA ANALYTICS

49. FILE The North Valley Real Estate data reports information on the homes sold last year.
a. At the .02 significance level, is there a difference in the variability of the selling prices of the homes that have a pool versus those that do not have a pool?
b. At the .02 significance level, is there a difference in the variability of the selling prices of the homes with an attached garage versus those that do not have an attached garage?
c. At the .05 significance level, is there a difference in the mean selling price of the homes among the five townships?
d. Adam Marty recently joined North Valley Real Estate and was assigned twenty homes to market and show. When he was hired, North Valley assured him that the twenty homes would be fairly assigned to him. When he reviewed the selling prices of his assigned homes, he thought that the prices were much below the average of $357,000. Adam was able to find the data of the homes assigned to agents in the firm. Use statistical inference to compare the mean price of homes assigned to him to the mean price of homes assigned to the other agents. What do the results indicate? How is your analysis defining fairness?
e. Home buyers finance the purchase of their home with a mortgage. In this data, the mortgages are either a fixed rate mortgage paid over 30 years, or an adjustable rate mortgage. The adjustable rate mortgage provides a lower introductory interest rate for the first five years of occupancy. Then, in the fifth year, the rate is adjusted to the current rate plus an additional percent. Usually, the adjusted rate is higher than

the "introductory" rate. With this information, we may predict that the average years of occupancy would be different for home owners based on the type of mortgage and whether they defaulted on the mortgage. Use the data to evaluate this prediction.

50. FILE Refer to the Baseball 2016 data, which report information on the 30 Major League Baseball teams for the 2016 season.
   - **a.** At the .10 significance level, is there a difference in the variation in team salary among the American and National League teams?
   - **b.** Create a variable that classifies a team's total attendance into three groups: less than 2.0 (million), 2.0 up to 3.0, and 3.0 or more. At the .05 significance level, is there a difference in the mean number of games won among the three groups?
   - **c.** Using the same attendance variable developed in part (b), is there a difference in the mean number of home runs hit per team? Use the .05 significance level.
   - **d.** Using the same attendance variable developed in part (b), is there a difference in the mean salary of the three groups? Use the .05 significance level.

51. FILE Refer to the Lincolnville School District bus data.
   - **a.** Conduct a test of hypothesis to reveal whether the mean maintenance cost is equal for each of the bus manufacturers. Use the .01 significance level.
   - **b.** Conduct a test of hypothesis to determine whether the mean miles traveled since the last maintenance is equal for each bus manufacturer. Use the .05 significance level.

A REVIEW OF CHAPTERS 10–12

This section is a review of the major concepts and terms introduced in Chapters 10, 11, and 12. Chapter 10 began our study of hypothesis testing. A hypothesis is an assumption about a characteristic of a population. In statistical hypothesis testing, we begin by making a statement about the value of the population parameter in the null hypothesis. We establish the null hypothesis for the purpose of testing. When we complete the testing, our decision is either to reject or to fail to reject the null hypothesis. If we reject the null hypothesis, we conclude that the alternate hypothesis is true. The alternate hypothesis is "accepted" only if we show that the null hypothesis is false. We also refer to the alternate hypothesis as the research hypothesis. Most of the time we want to prove the alternate hypothesis.

In Chapter 10, we selected random samples from a single population and tested whether it was reasonable that the population parameter under study equaled a particular value. For example, we wish to investigate whether the mean tenure of those holding the position of CEO in large firms is 12 years. We select a sample of CEOs, compute the sample mean, and compare the mean of the sample to the population. The single population under consideration is the length of tenure of CEOs of large firms. We described methods for conducting the test when the population standard deviation was available and when it was not available.

In Chapter 11, we extended the idea of hypothesis testing to whether two independent random samples came from populations having the same or equal population means. For example, St. Mathews Hospital operates an urgent care facility on both the north and south sides of Knoxville, Tennessee. The research question is: Is the mean waiting time for patients visiting the two facilities the same? To investigate, we select a random sample from each of the facilities and compute the sample means. We test the null hypothesis that the mean waiting time is the same at the two facilities. The alternate hypothesis is that the mean waiting time is not the same for the two facilities. If the population standard deviations are known, we use the z distribution as the test statistic. If the population standard deviations are not known, the test statistic follows the t distribution.

Our discussion in Chapter 11 also concerned dependent samples. The test statistic is the t distribution and we assume that the distribution of differences follows the normal distribution. One typical paired sample problem calls for recording an individual's blood pressure before administering medication and then again afterward in order to evaluate the effectiveness of the medication. We also considered the case of testing two population proportions. For example, the production manager wished to compare the proportion of defects on the day shift with that of the second shift.

Chapter 11 dealt with the difference between two population means. Chapter 12 presented tests for variances and a procedure called the *analysis of variance,* or *ANOVA*. ANOVA is used to simultaneously determine whether several independent normal populations have the same mean. This is accomplished by comparing the variances of the random samples selected from these populations. We apply the usual hypothesis-testing procedure, but we use the F distribution as the test statistic. Often the calculations are tedious, so a statistical software package is recommended.

As an example of analysis of variance, a test could be conducted to resolve whether there is any difference in effectiveness among five fertilizers on the weight of popcorn ears. This type of analysis is referred to as *one-factor ANOVA* because we are able to draw conclusions about only one factor, called a *treatment*. If we want to draw conclusions about the simultaneous effects of more than one factor or variable, we use the *two-factor ANOVA* technique. Both the one-factor and two-factor tests use the *F distribution* as the distribution of the test statistic. The *F* distribution is also the distribution of the test statistic used to find whether one normal population has more variation than another.

An additional feature of the two-factor ANOVA is the possibility that interactions may exist between the factors. There is an *interaction* if the response to one of the factors depends on the level of the other factor. Fortunately, the ANOVA is easily extended to include a test for interactions.

PROBLEMS

For problems 1–6, state: (a) the null and the alternate hypotheses, (b) the decision rule, and (c) the decision regarding the null hypothesis, (d) then interpret the result.

1. A machine is set to produce tennis balls so the mean bounce is 36 inches when the ball is dropped from a platform of a certain height. The production supervisor suspects that the mean bounce has changed and is less than 36 inches. As an experiment, a sample of 12 balls was dropped from the platform and the mean height of the bounce was 35.5 inches, with a standard deviation of 0.9 inch. At the .05 significance level, can the supervisor conclude that the mean bounce height is less than 36 inches?
2. **FILE** It was hypothesized that road construction workers, on the average, spend 20 minutes of each hour not engaged in productive work. Some claimed the nonproductive time is greater than 20 minutes. An actual study was conducted at a construction site, using a stopwatch and other ways of checking the work habits. A random check of workers revealed the following unproductive times, in minutes, during a one-hour period (exclusive of regularly scheduled breaks):

10	25	17	20	28	30	18	23	18

   Using the .05 significance level, is it reasonable to conclude the mean unproductive time is greater than 20 minutes?
3. Stiktite, Inc. plans a test of the mean holding power of two glues designed for plastic. First, a small plastic hook was coated at one end with Epox glue and fastened to a sheet of plastic. After it dried, weight was added to the hook until it separated from the sheet of plastic. The weight was then recorded. This was repeated until 12 hooks were tested. The same procedure was followed for Holdtite glue, but only 10 hooks were used. The sample results, in pounds, were:

	Epox	Holdtite
Sample size	12	10
Sample mean	250	252
Sample standard deviation	5	8

   At the .01 significance level, is there a difference between the mean holding power of Epox and that of Holdtite?
4. **FILE** Pittsburgh Paints wishes to test an additive formulated to increase the life of paints used in the hot and arid conditions of the Southwest. The top half of a piece of wood was painted using the regular paint. The bottom half was painted with the paint including the additive. The same procedure was followed for a total of 10 pieces. Then each

piece was subjected to brilliant light. The data, the number of hours each piece lasted before it faded beyond a certain point, follow:

	Number of Hours by Sample									
	A	B	C	D	E	F	G	H	I	J
Without additive	325	313	320	340	318	312	319	330	333	319
With additive	323	313	326	343	310	320	313	340	330	315

Using the .05 significance level, determine whether the additive is effective in prolonging the life of the paint.

5. **FILE** A Buffalo, New York, cola distributor is featuring a special sale on 12-packs. She wonders where in the grocery store to place the cola for maximum attention. Should it be near the front door of the grocery stores, in the cola section, at the checkout registers, or near the milk and other dairy products? Four stores with similar total sales cooperated in an experiment. In one store, the 12-packs were stacked near the front door, in another they were placed near the checkout registers, and so on. Sales were checked at specified times in each store for exactly four minutes. The results were:

Cola at the Door	In Soft Drink Section	Near Registers	Dairy Section
$6	$ 5	$ 7	$10
8	10	10	9
3	12	9	6
7	4	4	11
	9	5	
		7	

The Buffalo distributor wants to find out whether there is a difference in the mean sales for cola stacked at the four locations in the store. Use the .05 significance level.

6. **FILE** Williams Corporation is investigating the effects of educational background on employee performance. A potential relevant variable in this case is the self-rated social status of the employee. The company has recorded the annual sales volumes (in $000) achieved by sales employees in each of the categories below. Perform a complete two-way analysis of variance (including the possibility of interactions) on the data and describe what your results suggest.

	School Type		
Self-Rated Social Status	Ivy League	State-supported	Small Private
Low	62, 61	68, 64	70, 70
Medium	68, 64	74, 68	62, 65
High	70, 71	57, 60	57, 56

7. A school supervisor is reviewing initial wages of former students (in $000). Samples were taken over 3 years for four different majors (accounting, administration, finance, and marketing). For each combination of major and year, three former students were sampled.

Major/Year	2014	2015	2016
Accounting	75.4, 69.8, 62.3	73.9, 78.8, 62.0	64.2, 80.8, 68.2
Administration	61.5, 59.9, 62.1	63.9, 57.6, 66.5	74.2, 67.5, 58.1
Finance	63.6, 70.2, 72.2	69.2, 72.5, 67.2	74.7, 66.4, 77.9
Marketing	71.3, 69.2, 66.4	74.0, 67.6, 61.7	60.0, 61.3, 62.5

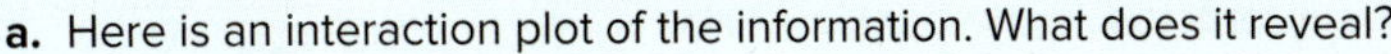

a. Here is an interaction plot of the information. What does it reveal?

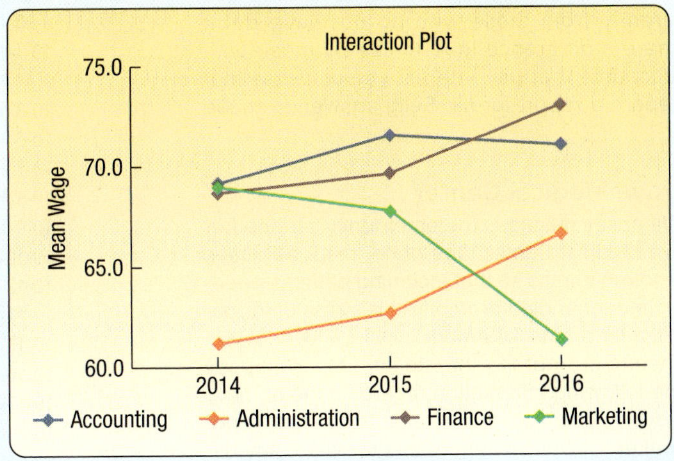

b. Write out all of the pairs of null and alternative hypotheses you would apply for a two-way ANOVA.

c. Here is the statistical software output. Use the 0.05 level to check for interactions.

Source	DF	SS	MS	F	P
Major	3	329.20	109.732	3.39	0.034
Year	2	7.32	3.659	0.11	0.894
Interaction	6	183.57	30.595	0.94	0.482
Error	24	777.29	32.387		
Total	35	1297.37			

d. If proper, test the other hypotheses at the .05 significance level. If it is not appropriate, describe why you should not do the tests.

CASES

A. Century National Bank

Refer to the description of Century National Bank on page 129 at the end of the Review of Chapters 1–4.

With many other options available, customers no longer let their money sit in a checking account. For many years the mean checking balance has been $1,600. Do the sample data indicate that the mean account balance has declined from this value?

Recent years have also seen an increase in the use of ATM machines. When Mr. Selig took over the bank, the mean number of transactions per month per customer was 8; now he believes it has increased to more than 10. In fact, the advertising agency that prepares TV commercials for Century would like to use this on the new commercial being designed. Is there sufficient evidence to conclude that the mean number of transactions per customer is more than 10 per month? Could the advertising agency say the mean is more than 9 per month?

The bank has branch offices in four different cities: Cincinnati, Ohio; Atlanta, Georgia; Louisville, Kentucky; and Erie, Pennsylvania. Mr. Selig would like to know whether there is a difference in the mean checking account balances among the four branches. If there are differences, between which branches do these differences occur?

Mr. Selig is also interested in the bank's ATMs. Is there a difference in ATM use among the branches? Also, do customers who have debit cards tend to use ATMs differently from those who do not have debit cards? Is there a difference in ATM use by those with checking accounts that pay interest versus those that do not? Prepare a report for Mr. Selig answering these questions.

B. Bell Grove Medical Center

Ms. Gene Dempsey manages the emergency care center at Bell Grove Medical Center. One of her responsibilities is to have enough nurses so that incoming patients needing service can be handled promptly. It is stressful for patients to wait a long time for emergency care even when their care needs are not life threatening. Ms. Dempsey gathered the following information regarding the number of patients over the last several weeks. The center is not open on weekends. Does it appear that there are any differences in the number of patients served by the day of the week? If there are differences, which days seem to be the busiest? Write a brief report summarizing your findings.

Date	Day	Patients
9-29-16	Monday	38
9-30-16	Tuesday	28
10-1-16	Wednesday	28
10-2-16	Thursday	30
10-3-16	Friday	35
10-6-16	Monday	35
10-7-16	Tuesday	25
10-8-16	Wednesday	22
10-9-16	Thursday	21
10-10-16	Friday	32
10-13-16	Monday	37
10-14-16	Tuesday	29
10-15-16	Wednesday	27
10-16-16	Thursday	28
10-17-16	Friday	35
10-20-16	Monday	37
10-21-16	Tuesday	26
10-22-16	Wednesday	28
10-23-16	Thursday	23
10-24-16	Friday	33

PRACTICE TEST

Part 1—Objective

1. A statement about the value of a population parameter that always includes the equal sign is called the ________. 1. ________
2. The likelihood of rejecting a true null hypothesis is called the ________. 2. ________
3. Assuming the null hypothesis is true, the likelihood of finding a value of the test statistic at least as extreme as the one found in the sample is called the ________. 3. ________
4. When conducting a test of hypothesis about a single population mean, the z distribution is used as the test statistic only when the ________ is known. 4. ________
5. In a two-sample test of hypothesis for means, if the population standard deviations are not known, *what must we assume about the shape of the populations?* 5. ________
6. A value calculated from sample information used to determine whether to reject the null hypothesis is called the ________. 6. ________
7. In a two-tailed test, the rejection region is ________. (all in the upper tail, all in the lower tail, split evenly between the two tails, none of these—pick one) 7. ________
8. Which of the following is not a characteristic of the F distribution? (continuous, positively skewed, range from $-\infty$ to ∞, family of distributions) 8. ________
9. To perform a one-way ANOVA, the treatments must be ________. (independent, mutually exclusive, continuous) 9. ________
10. In a one-way ANOVA, there are four treatments and six observations in each treatment. What are the degrees of freedom for the F distribution? 10. ________

Part 2—Problems

For problems 1 and 2, state the null and alternate hypotheses and the decision rule, make a decision regarding the null hypothesis, and interpret the result.

1. The Park Manager at Fort Fisher State Park in North Carolina believes the typical summer visitor spends more than 90 minutes in the park. A sample of 18 visitors during the months of June, July, and August revealed the mean time in the park for visitors was 96 minutes, with a standard deviation of 12 minutes. At the .01 significance level, is it reasonable to conclude the mean time in the park is greater than 90 minutes?
2. Is there a difference in the mean miles traveled per week by each of two taxicab companies operating in the Grand Strand area? The *Sun News*, the local paper, is investigating and obtained the following sample information. At the

.05 significance level, is it reasonable to conclude there is a difference in the mean miles traveled? Assume equal population variances.

Variable	Yellow Cab	Horse and Buggy Cab Company
Sample size	14	12
Mean miles	837	797
Standard deviation	30	40

3. The results of a one-way ANOVA are reported below. Use the .05 significance level.

ANOVA				
Source of Variation	**SS**	***df***	**MS**	***F***
Between groups	6.892202	2	3.446101	4.960047
Within groups	12.50589	18	0.694772	
Total	19.3981	20		

Answer the following questions.

a. How many treatments are in the study?
b. What is the total sample size?
c. What is the critical value of *F*?
d. Write out the null hypothesis and the alternate hypothesis.
e. What is your decision regarding the null hypothesis?
f. Why can we conclude the treatment means differ?

Correlation and Linear Regression

▲ **TRAVELAIR.COM** samples domestic airline flights to explore the relationship between airfare and distance. The service would like to know if there is a correlation between airfare and flight distance. If there is a correlation, what percentage of the variation in airfare is accounted for by distance? How much does each additional mile add to the fare? (See Exercise 61 and LO13-2, LO13-3, and LO13-5.)

LEARNING OBJECTIVES

When you have completed this chapter, you will be able to:

LO13-1 Explain the purpose of correlation analysis.

LO13-2 Calculate a correlation coefficient to test and interpret the relationship between two variables.

LO13-3 Apply regression analysis to estimate the linear relationship between two variables.

LO13-4 Evaluate the significance of the slope of the regression equation.

LO13-5 Evaluate a regression equation's ability to predict using the standard estimate of the error and the coefficient of determination.

LO13-6 Calculate and interpret confidence and prediction intervals.

LO13-7 Use a log function to transform a nonlinear relationship.

INTRODUCTION

Chapters 2 through 4 presented *descriptive statistics.* We organized raw data into a frequency distribution and computed several measures of location and measures of dispersion to describe the major characteristics of the distribution. In Chapters 5 through 7, we described probability, and from probability statements, we created probability distributions. In Chapters 8 through 12, we studied *statistical inference,* where we collected a sample to estimate a population parameter such as the population mean or population proportion. In addition, we used the sample data to test a hypothesis about a population mean or a population proportion, the difference between two population means, or the equality of several population means. Each of these tests involved just *one* interval- or ratio-level variable, such as the profit made on a car sale, the income of bank presidents, or the number of patients admitted each month to a particular hospital.

In this chapter, we shift the emphasis to the study of relationships between two interval- or ratio-level variables. In all business fields, identifying and studying relationships between variables can provide information on ways to increase profits, methods to decrease costs, or variables to predict demand. In marketing products, many firms use price reductions through coupons and discount pricing to increase sales. In this example, we are interested in the relationship between two variables: price reductions and sales. To collect the data, a company can test-market a variety of price reduction methods and observe sales. We hope to confirm a relationship that decreasing price leads to increased sales. In economics, you will find many relationships between two variables that are the basis of economics, such as price and demand.

STATISTICS IN ACTION

The space shuttle *Challenger* exploded on January 28, 1986. An investigation of the cause examined four contractors: Rockwell International for the shuttle and engines, Lockheed Martin for ground support, Martin Marietta for the external fuel tanks, and Morton Thiokol for the solid fuel booster rockets. After several months, the investigation blamed the explosion on defective O-rings produced by Morton Thiokol. A study of the contractor's stock prices showed an interesting happenstance. On the day of the *Challenger* explosion, Morton Thiokol stock was down 11.86% and the stock of the other three lost only 2 to 3%. Can we conclude that financial markets predicted the outcome of the investigation?

As another familiar example, recall in Chapter 4 we used the Applewood Auto Group data to show the relationship between two variables with a scatter diagram. We plotted the profit for each vehicle sold on the vertical axis and the age of the buyer on the horizontal axis. See page 116. In that graph, we observed that as the age of the buyer increased, the profit for each vehicle also increased.

Other examples of relationships between two variables are:

- Does the amount Healthtex spends per month on training its sales force affect its monthly sales?
- Is the number of square feet in a home related to the cost to heat the home in January?
- In a study of fuel efficiency, is there a relationship between miles per gallon and the weight of a car?
- Does the number of hours that students study for an exam influence the exam score?

In this chapter, we carry this idea further. That is, we develop numerical measures to express the relationship between two variables. Is the relationship strong or weak? Is it direct or inverse? In addition, we develop an equation to express the relationship between variables. This will allow us to estimate one variable on the basis of another.

To begin our study of relationships between two variables, we examine the meaning and purpose of **correlation analysis.** We continue by developing an equation that will allow us to estimate the value of one variable based on the value of another. This is called **regression analysis.** We will also evaluate the ability of the equation to accurately make estimations.

LO13-1

Explain the purpose of correlation analysis.

WHAT IS CORRELATION ANALYSIS?

When we study the relationship between two interval- or ratio-scale variables, we often start with a scatter diagram. This procedure provides a visual representation of the relationship between the variables. The next step is usually to calculate the correlation coefficient. It provides a quantitative measure of the strength of the relationship between

TABLE 13–1 Number of Sales Calls and Copiers Sold for 15 Salespeople

Sales Representative	Sales Calls	Copiers Sold
Brian Virost	96	41
Carlos Ramirez	40	41
Carol Saia	104	51
Greg Fish	128	60
Jeff Hall	164	61
Mark Reynolds	76	29
Meryl Rumsey	72	39
Mike Kiel	80	50
Ray Snarsky	36	28
Rich Niles	84	43
Ron Broderick	180	70
Sal Spina	132	56
Soni Jones	120	45
Susan Welch	44	31
Tom Keller	84	30

two variables. As an example, the sales manager of North American Copier Sales, which has a large sales force throughout the United States and Canada, wants to determine whether there is a relationship between the number of sales calls made in a month and the number of copiers sold that month. The manager selects a random sample of 15 representatives and determines, for each representative, the number of sales calls made and the number of copiers sold. This information is reported in Table 13–1.

By reviewing the data, we observe that there does seem to be some relationship between the number of sales calls and the number of units sold. That is, the salespeople who made the most sales calls sold the most units. However, the relationship is not "perfect" or exact. For example, Soni Jones made fewer sales calls than Jeff Hall, but she sold more units.

In addition to the graphical techniques in Chapter 4, we will develop numerical measures to precisely describe the relationship between the two variables, sales calls and copiers sold. This group of statistical techniques is called **correlation analysis.**

CORRELATION ANALYSIS A group of techniques to measure the relationship between two variables.

The basic idea of correlation analysis is to report the relationship between two variables. The usual first step is to plot the data in a **scatter diagram.** An example will show how a scatter diagram is used.

EXAMPLE

North American Copier Sales sells copiers to businesses of all sizes throughout the United States and Canada. Ms. Marcy Bancer was recently promoted to the position of national sales manager. At the upcoming sales meeting, the sales representatives from all over the country will be in attendance. She would like to impress upon them the importance of making that extra sales call each day. She decides to gather some information on the relationship between the number of sales calls and the number of copiers sold. She selects a random sample of 15 sales representatives and determines the number of sales calls they made last month and the number of copiers they sold. The sample information is reported in Table 13–1. What observations can you make about the relationship between the number of sales calls and the number of copiers sold? Develop a scatter diagram to display the information.

SOLUTION

Based on the information in Table 13–1, Ms. Bancer suspects there is a relationship between the number of sales calls made in a month and the number of copiers sold. Ron Broderick sold the most copiers last month and made 180 sales calls. On the other hand, Ray Snarsky, Carlos Ramirez, and Susan Welch made the fewest calls: 36, 40, and 44. They also had the lowest number of copiers sold among the sampled representatives.

The implication is that the number of copiers sold is related to the number of sales calls made. As the number of sales calls increases, it appears the number of copiers sold also increases. We refer to number of sales calls as the **independent variable** and number of copiers sold as the **dependent variable.**

The independent variable provides the basis for estimating or predicting the dependent variable. For example, we would like to predict the expected number of copiers sold if a salesperson makes 100 sales calls. In the randomly selected sample data, the independent variable—sales calls—is a random number.

The dependent variable is the variable that is being predicted or estimated. It can also be described as the result or outcome for a particular value of the independent variable. The dependent variable is random. That is, for a given value of the independent variable, there are many possible outcomes for the dependent variable.

It is common practice to scale the dependent variable (copiers sold) on the vertical or *Y*-axis and the independent variable (number of sales calls) on the horizontal or *X*-axis. To develop the scatter diagram of the North American Copier Sales information, we begin with the first sales representative, Brian Virost. Brian made 96 sales calls last month and sold 41 copiers, so $x = 96$ and $y = 41$. To plot this point, move along the horizontal axis to $x = 96$, then go vertically to $y = 41$ and place a dot at the intersection. This process is continued until all the paired data are plotted, as shown in Chart 13–1.

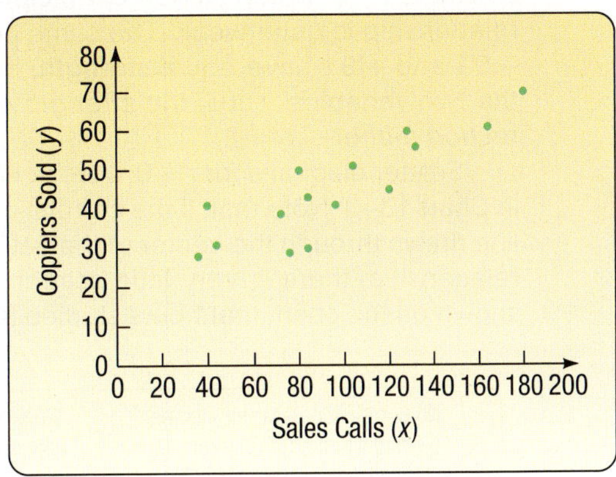

CHART 13–1 Scatter Diagram Showing Sales Calls and Copiers Sold

The scatter diagram shows graphically that the sales representatives who make more calls tend to sell more copiers. It is reasonable for Ms. Bancer, the national sales manager, to tell her salespeople that the more sales calls they make, the more copiers they can expect to sell. Note that, while there appears to be a positive relationship between the two variables, all the points do not fall on a straight line. In the following section, you will measure the strength and direction of this relationship between two variables by determining the correlation coefficient.

LO13-2
Calculate a correlation coefficient to test and interpret the relationship between two variables.

THE CORRELATION COEFFICIENT

Originated by Karl Pearson about 1900, the **correlation coefficient** describes the strength of the relationship between two sets of interval-scaled or ratio-scaled variables. Designated *r*, it is often referred to as *Pearson's r* and as the *Pearson product-moment correlation coefficient.* It can assume any value from −1.00 to +1.00 inclusive. A correlation coefficient of −1.00 or +1.00 indicates *perfect correlation.* For example, a correlation coefficient for the preceding example computed to be +1.00 would indicate that the number of sales calls and the number of copiers sold are perfectly related in a positive linear sense. A computed value of −1.00 would reveal that sales calls and the number of copiers sold are perfectly related in an inverse linear sense. How the scatter diagram would appear if the relationship between the two variables were linear and perfect is shown in Chart 13–2.

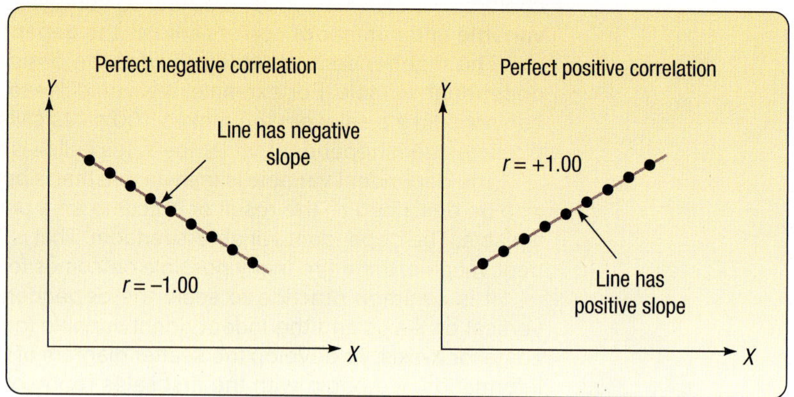

CHART 13–2 Scatter Diagrams Showing Perfect Negative Correlation and Perfect Positive Correlation

If there is absolutely no relationship between the two sets of variables, Pearson's *r* is zero. A correlation coefficient *r* close to 0 (say, .08) shows that the linear relationship is quite weak. The same conclusion is drawn if $r = -.08$. Coefficients of −.91 and +.91 have equal strength; both indicate very strong correlation between the two variables. Thus, *the strength of the correlation does not depend on the direction (either − or +).*

Scatter diagrams for $r = 0$, a weak *r* (say, −.23), and a strong *r* (say, +.87) are shown in Chart 13–3. Note that, if the correlation is weak, there is considerable scatter about a line drawn through the center of the data. For the scatter diagram representing a strong relationship, there is very little scatter about the line. This indicates, in the example shown on the chart, that hours studied is a good predictor of exam score.

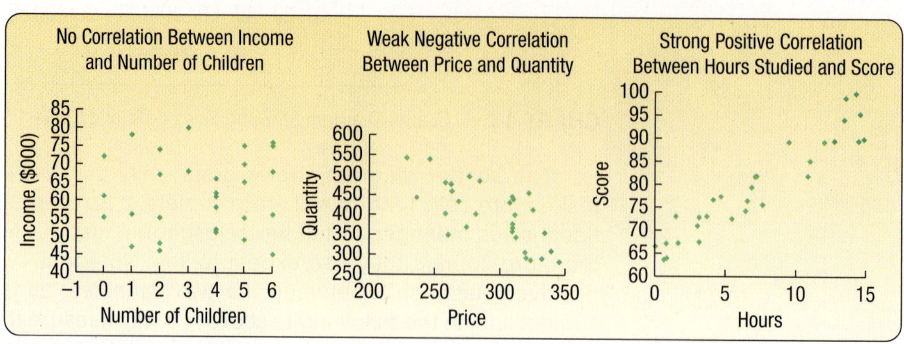

CHART 13–3 Scatter Diagrams Depicting Zero, Weak, and Strong Correlation

The following drawing summarizes the strength and direction of the correlation coefficient.

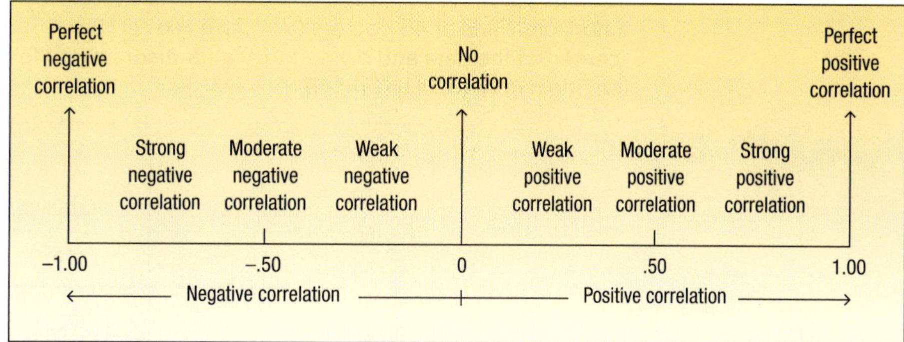

CORRELATION COEFFICIENT A measure of the strength of the linear relationship between two variables.

The characteristics of the correlation coefficient are summarized below.

CHARACTERISTICS OF THE CORRELATION COEFFICIENT

1. The sample correlation coefficient is identified by the lowercase letter *r*.
2. It shows the direction and strength of the linear relationship between two interval- or ratio-scale variables.
3. It ranges from −1 up to and including +1.
4. A value near 0 indicates there is little linear relationship between the variables.
5. A value near 1 indicates a direct or positive linear relationship between the variables.
6. A value near −1 indicates an inverse or negative linear relationship between the variables.

How is the value of the correlation coefficient determined? We will use the North American Copier Sales in Table 13–1 as an example. It is replicated in Table 13–2 for your convenience.

TABLE 13–2 Number of Sales Calls and Copiers Sold for 15 Salespeople

Sales Representative	Sales Calls	Copiers Sold
Brian Virost	96	41
Carlos Ramirez	40	41
Carol Saia	104	51
Greg Fish	128	60
Jeff Hall	164	61
Mark Reynolds	76	29
Meryl Rumsey	72	39
Mike Kiel	80	50
Ray Snarsky	36	28
Rich Niles	84	43
Ron Broderick	180	70
Sal Spina	132	56
Soni Jones	120	45
Susan Welch	44	31
Tom Keller	84	30
Total	1440	675

We begin with a scatter diagram, similar to Chart 13–2. Draw a vertical line through the data values at the mean of the x-values and a horizontal line at the mean of the y-values. In Chart 13–4, we've added a vertical line at 96 calls ($\bar{x} = \Sigma x/n = 1440/15 = 96$) and a horizontal line at 45 copiers ($\bar{y} = \Sigma y/n = 675/15 = 45$). These lines pass through the "center" of the data and divide the scatter diagram into four quadrants. Think of moving the origin from (0, 0) to (96, 45).

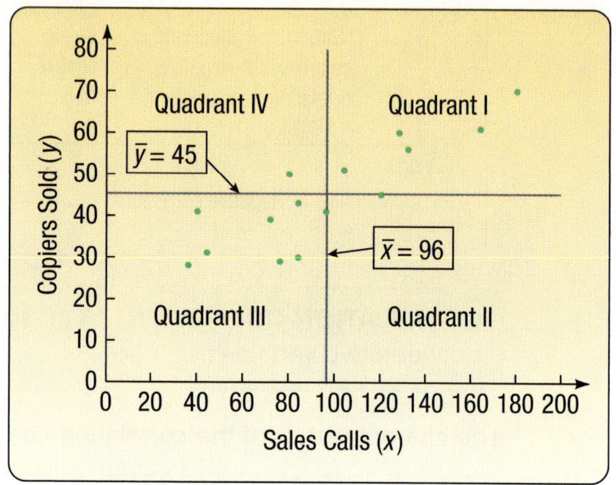

CHART 13–4 Computation of the Correlation Coefficient

Two variables are positively related when the number of copiers sold is above the mean and the number of sales calls is also above the mean. These points appear in the upper-right quadrant (labeled Quadrant I) of Chart 13–4. Similarly, when the number of copiers sold is less than the mean, so is the number of sales calls. These points fall in the lower-left quadrant of Chart 13–4 (labeled Quadrant III). For example, the third person on the list in Table 13–2, Carol Saia, made 104 sales calls and sold 51 copiers. These values are above their respective means, so this point is located in Quadrant I, which is in the upper-right quadrant. She made 8 more calls than the mean number of sales calls and sold 6 more than the mean number sold. Tom Keller, the last name on the list in Table 13–2, made 84 sales calls and sold 30 copiers. Both of these values are less than their respective means, hence this point is in the lower-left quadrant. Tom made 12 fewer sales calls and sold 15 fewer copiers than the respective means. The deviations from the mean number of sales calls and the mean number of copiers sold are summarized in Table 13–3 for the

TABLE 13–3 Deviations from the Mean and Their Products

Sales Representative	Sales Calls (x)	Copiers Sold (y)	$x - \bar{x}$	$x - \bar{y}$	$(x - \bar{x})(y - \bar{y})$
Brian Virost	96	41	0	−4	0
Carlos Ramirez	40	41	−56	−4	224
Carol Saia	104	51	8	6	48
Greg Fish	128	60	32	15	480
Jeff Hall	164	61	68	16	1,088
Mark Reynolds	76	29	−20	−16	320
Meryl Rumsey	72	39	−24	−6	144
Mike Kiel	80	50	−16	5	−80
Ray Snarsky	36	28	−60	−17	1,020
Rich Niles	84	43	−12	−2	24
Ron Broderick	180	70	84	25	2,100
Sal Spina	132	56	36	11	396
Soni Jones	120	45	24	0	0
Susan Welch	44	31	−52	−14	728
Tom Keller	84	30	−12	−15	180
Totals	1440	675	0	0	6,672

15 sales representatives. The sum of the products of the deviations from the respective means is 6672. That is, the term $\Sigma(x - \bar{x})(y - \bar{y}) = 6672$.

In both the upper-right and the lower-left quadrants, the product of $(x - \bar{x})(y - \bar{y})$ is positive because both of the factors have the same sign. In our example, this happens for all sales representatives except Mike Kiel. Mike made 80 sales calls (which is less than the mean) but sold 50 machines (which is more than the mean). We can therefore expect the correlation coefficient to have a positive value.

If the two variables are inversely related, one variable will be above the mean and the other below the mean. Most of the points in this case occur in the upper-left and lower-right quadrants, that is, Quadrants II and IV. Now $(x - \bar{x})$ and $(y - \bar{y})$ will have opposite signs, so their product is negative. The resulting correlation coefficient is negative.

What happens if there is no linear relationship between the two variables? The points in the scatter diagram will appear in all four quadrants. The negative products of $(x - \bar{x})(y - \bar{y})$ offset the positive products, so the sum is near zero. This leads to a correlation coefficient near zero. So, the term $\Sigma(x - \bar{x})(y - \bar{y})$ drives the strength as well as the sign of the relationship between the two variables.

The correlation coefficient is also unaffected by the units of the two variables. For example, if we had used hundreds of copiers sold instead of the number sold, the correlation coefficient would be the same. The correlation coefficient is independent of the scale used if we divide the term $\Sigma(x - \bar{x})(y - \bar{y})$ by the sample standard deviations. It is also made independent of the sample size and bounded by the values +1.00 and −1.00 if we divide by $(n - 1)$.

This reasoning leads to the following formula:

CORRELATION COEFFICIENT

$$r = \frac{\Sigma(x - \bar{x})(y - \bar{y})}{(n - 1)s_x s_y} \qquad [13\text{–}1]$$

To compute the correlation coefficient, we use the standard deviations of the sample of 15 sales calls and 15 copiers sold. We could use formula (3–9) to calculate the sample standard deviations or we could use a statistical software package. For the specific Excel and Minitab commands, see the **Software Commands** in Appendix C. The following is the Excel output. The standard deviation of the number of sales calls is 42.76 and of the number of copiers sold 12.89.

	A	B	C	D	E	F	G	H
1		Sales Representative	Sales Calls (x)	Copiers Sold (y)			Sales Calls (x)	Copiers Sold (y)
2		Brian Virost	96	41		Mean	96.00	45.00
3		Carlos Ramirez	40	41		Standard Error	11.04	3.33
4		Carol Saia	104	51		Median	84.00	43.00
5		Greg Fish	128	60		Mode	84.00	41.00
6		Jeff Hall	164	61		Standard Deviation	42.76	12.89
7		Mark Reynolds	76	29		Sample Variance	1828.57	166.14
8		Meryl Rumsey	72	39		Kurtosis	-0.32	-0.73
9		Mike Kiel	80	50		Skewness	0.46	0.36
10		Ray Snarsky	36	28		Range	144.00	42.00
11		Rich Niles	84	43		Minimum	36.00	28.00
12		Ron Broderick	180	70		Maximum	180.00	70.00
13		Sal Spina	132	56		Sum	1440.00	675.00
14		Soni Jones	120	45		Count	15.00	15.00
15		Susan Welch	44	31				
16		Tom Keller	84	30				
17		Total	1440	675				

We now insert these values into formula (13–1) to determine the correlation coefficient:

$$r = \frac{\Sigma(x - \bar{x})(y - \bar{y})}{(n - 1)s_x s_y} = \frac{6672}{(15 - 1)(42.76)(12.89)} = 0.865$$

How do we interpret a correlation of 0.865? First, it is positive, so we conclude there is a direct relationship between the number of sales calls and the number of copiers sold. This confirms our reasoning based on the scatter diagram, Chart 13–4. The value of 0.865 is fairly close to 1.00, so we conclude that the association is strong.

We must be careful with the interpretation. The correlation of 0.865 indicates a strong positive linear association between the variables. Ms. Bancer would be correct to encourage the sales personnel to make that extra sales call because the number of sales calls made is related to the number of copiers sold. However, does this mean that more sales calls *cause* more sales? No, we have not demonstrated cause and effect here, only that the two variables—sales calls and copiers sold—are statistically related.

If there is a strong relationship (say, .97) between two variables, we are tempted to assume that an increase or decrease in one variable *causes* a change in the other variable. For example, historically, the consumption of Georgia peanuts and the consumption of aspirin have a strong correlation. However, this does not indicate that an increase in the consumption of peanuts *caused* the consumption of aspirin to increase. Likewise, the incomes of professors and the number of inmates in mental institutions have increased proportionately. Further, as the population of donkeys has decreased, there has been an increase in the number of doctoral degrees granted. Relationships such as these are called **spurious correlations.** What we can conclude when we find two variables with a strong correlation is that there is a relationship or association between the two variables, not that a change in one causes a change in the other.

EXAMPLE

The Applewood Auto Group's marketing department believes younger buyers purchase vehicles on which lower profits are earned and the older buyers purchase vehicles on which higher profits are earned. They would like to use this information as part of an upcoming advertising campaign to try to attract older buyers, for whom the profits tend to be higher. Develop a scatter diagram depicting the relationship between vehicle profits and age of the buyer. Use statistical software to determine the correlation coefficient. Would this be a useful advertising feature?

SOLUTION

Using the Applewood Auto Group example, the first step is to graph the data using a scatter plot. It is shown in Chart 13–5.

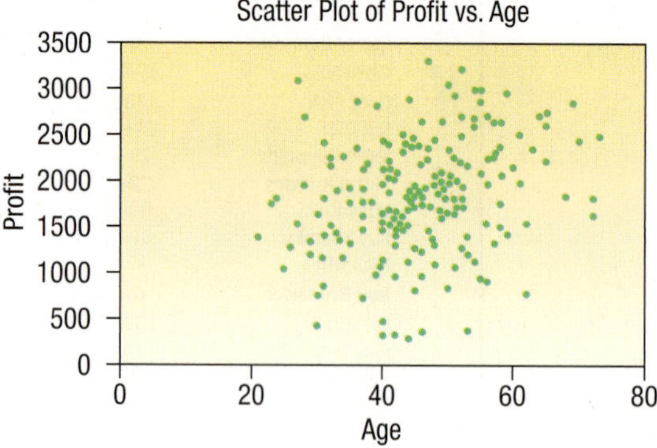

CHART 13–5 Scatter Diagram of Profit versus Age for the Applewood Auto Group Data

The scatter diagram suggests that a positive relationship does exist between age and profit; however, that relationship does not appear strong.

The next step is to calculate the correlation coefficient to evaluate the relative strength of the relationship. Statistical software provides an easy way to calculate the value of the correlation coefficient. The Excel output follows.

	A	B	C
1		*Age*	*Profit*
2	Age	1	
3	Profit	0.262	1

For these data, $r = 0.262$. To evaluate the relationship between a buyer's age and the profit on a car sale:

1. The relationship is positive or direct. Why? Because the sign of the correlation coefficient is positive. This confirms that as the age of the buyer increases, the profit on a car sale also increases.
2. The correlation coefficient is: $r = 0.262$. It is much closer to zero than one. Therefore, the relationship between the two variables is weak. We would observe that the relationship between the age of a buyer and the profit of their purchase is not very strong.

For Applewood Auto Group, the data does not support a business decision to create an advertising campaign to attract older buyers.

SELF-REVIEW 13–1

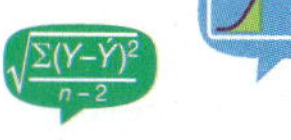

Haverty's Furniture is a family business that has been selling to retail customers in the Chicago area for many years. The company advertises extensively on radio, TV, and the Internet, emphasizing low prices and easy credit terms. The owner would like to review the relationship between sales and the amount spent on advertising. Below is information on sales and advertising expense for the last four months.

Month	Advertising Expense ($ million)	Sales Revenue ($ million)
July	2	7
August	1	3
September	3	8
October	4	10

(a) The owner wants to forecast sales on the basis of advertising expense. Which variable is the dependent variable? Which variable is the independent variable?
(b) Draw a scatter diagram.
(c) Determine the correlation coefficient.
(d) Interpret the strength of the correlation coefficient.

EXERCISES

1. **FILE** The following sample of observations were randomly selected.

x	4	5	3	6	10
y	4	6	5	7	7

Determine the correlation coefficient and interpret the relationship between x and y.

2. **FILE** The following sample of observations were randomly selected.

x	5	3	6	3	4	4	6	8
y	13	15	7	12	13	11	9	5

Determine the correlation coefficient and interpret the relationship between x and y.

3. **FILE** Bi-lo Appliance Super-Store has outlets in several large metropolitan areas in New England. The general sales manager aired a commercial for a digital camera on selected local TV stations prior to a sale starting on Saturday and ending Sunday. She obtained the information for Saturday–Sunday digital camera sales at the various outlets and paired it with the number of times the advertisement was shown on the local TV stations. The purpose is to find whether there is any relationship between the number of times the advertisement was aired and digital camera sales. The pairings are:

Location of TV Station	Number of Airings	Saturday–Sunday Sales ($ thousands)
Providence	4	15
Springfield	2	8
New Haven	5	21
Boston	6	24
Hartford	3	17

   a. What is the dependent variable?
   b. Draw a scatter diagram.
   c. Determine the correlation coefficient.
   d. Interpret these statistical measures.

4. **FILE** The production department of Celltronics International wants to explore the relationship between the number of employees who assemble a subassembly and the number produced. As an experiment, two employees were assigned to assemble the subassemblies. They produced 15 during a one-hour period. Then four employees assembled them. They produced 25 during a one-hour period. The complete set of paired observations follows.

Number of Assemblers	One-Hour Production (units)
2	15
4	25
1	10
5	40
3	30

The dependent variable is production; that is, it is assumed that different levels of production result from a different number of employees.
   a. Draw a scatter diagram.
   b. Based on the scatter diagram, does there appear to be any relationship between the number of assemblers and production? Explain.
   c. Compute the correlation coefficient.

5. **FILE** The city council of Pine Bluffs is considering increasing the number of police in an effort to reduce crime. Before making a final decision, the council asked the chief of police to survey other cities of similar size to determine the relationship between the number of police and the number of crimes reported. The chief gathered the following sample information.

City	Police	Number of Crimes	City	Police	Number of Crimes
Oxford	15	17	Holgate	17	7
Starksville	17	13	Carey	12	21
Danville	25	5	Whistler	11	19
Athens	27	7	Woodville	22	6

a. Which variable is the dependent variable and which is the independent variable? Hint: Which of the following makes better sense: Cities with more police have fewer crimes, or cities with fewer crimes have more police? Explain your choice.
b. Draw a scatter diagram.
c. Determine the correlation coefficient.
d. Interpret the correlation coefficient. Does it surprise you that the correlation coefficient is negative?

6. **FILE** The owner of Maumee Ford-Volvo wants to study the relationship between the age of a car and its selling price. Listed below is a random sample of 12 used cars sold at the dealership during the last year.

Car	Age (years)	Selling Price ($000)	Car	Age (years)	Selling Price ($000)
1	9	8.1	7	8	7.6
2	7	6.0	8	11	8.0
3	11	3.6	9	10	8.0
4	12	4.0	10	12	6.0
5	8	5.0	11	6	8.6
6	7	10.0	12	6	8.0

a. Draw a scatter diagram.
b. Determine the correlation coefficient.
c. Interpret the correlation coefficient. Does it surprise you that the correlation coefficient is negative?

Testing the Significance of the Correlation Coefficient

Recall that the sales manager of North American Copier Sales found the correlation between the number of sales calls and the number of copiers sold was 0.865. This indicated a strong positive association between the two variables. However, only 15 salespeople were sampled. Could it be that the correlation in the population is actually 0? This would mean the correlation of 0.865 was due to chance, or sampling error. The population in this example is all the salespeople employed by the firm.

Resolving this dilemma requires a test to answer the question: Could there be zero correlation in the population from which the sample was selected? To put it another way, did the computed r come from a population of paired observations with zero correlation? To continue our convention of allowing Greek letters to represent a population parameter, we will let ρ represent the correlation in the population. It is pronounced "rho."

We will continue with the illustration involving sales calls and copiers sold. We employ the same hypothesis testing steps described in Chapter 10. The null hypothesis and the alternate hypothesis are:

H_0: $\rho = 0$ (The correlation in the population is zero.)
H_1: $\rho \neq 0$ (The correlation in the population is different from zero.)

This is a two-tailed test. The null hypothesis can be rejected with either large or small sample values of the correlation coefficient.

The formula for *t* is:

t TEST FOR THE CORRELATION COEFFICIENT

$$t = \frac{r\sqrt{n-2}}{\sqrt{1-r^2}} \text{ with } n-2 \text{ degrees of freedom} \quad \textbf{[13–2]}$$

Using the .05 level of significance, the decision rule states that if the computed *t* falls in the area between plus 2.160 and minus 2.160, the null hypothesis is not rejected. To locate the critical value of 2.160, refer to Appendix B.5 for $df = n - 2 = 15 - 2 = 13$. See Chart 13–6.

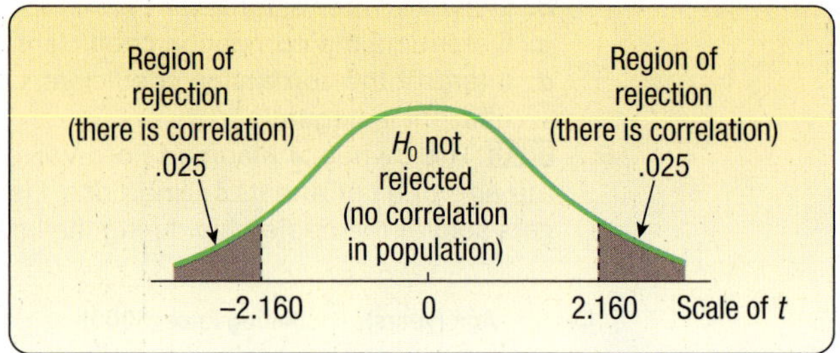

CHART 13–6 Decision Rule for Test of Hypothesis at .05 Significance Level and 13 *df*

Applying formula (13–2) to the example regarding the number of sales calls and units sold:

$$t = \frac{r\sqrt{n-2}}{\sqrt{1-r^2}} = \frac{.865\sqrt{15-2}}{\sqrt{1-.865^2}} = 6.216$$

The computed *t* is in the rejection region. Thus, H_0 is rejected at the .05 significance level. Hence we conclude the correlation in the population is not zero. This indicates to the sales manager that there is correlation with respect to the number of sales calls made and the number of copiers sold in the population of salespeople.

We can also interpret the test of hypothesis in terms of *p*-values. A *p*-value is the likelihood of finding a value of the test statistic more extreme than the one computed, when H_0 is true. To determine the *p*-value, go to the *t* distribution in Appendix B.5 and find the row for 13 degrees of freedom. The value of the test statistic is 6.216, so in the row for 13 degrees of freedom and a two-tailed test, find the value closest to 6.216. For a two-tailed test at the 0.001 significance level, the critical value is 4.221. Because 6.216 is greater than 4.221, we conclude that the *p*-value is less than 0.001.

Both Minitab and Excel will report the correlation between two variables. In addition to the correlation, Minitab reports the *p*-value for the test of hypothesis that the correlation in the population between the two variables is 0. The Minitab output follows.

Worksheet 1 ***

↓	C1-T Name	C2 Sales Calls	C3 Copiers Sold
1	Brian Virost	96	41
2	Carlos Ramirez	40	41
3	Carol Saia	104	51
4	Greg Fish	128	60
5	Jeff Hall	164	61
6	Mark Reynolds	76	29
7	Meryl Rumsey	72	39
8	Mike Kiel	80	50
9	Ray Snarsky	36	28
10	Rich Niles	84	43
11	Ron Broderick	180	70
12	Sal Spina	132	56
13	Soni Jones	120	45
14	Susan Welch	44	31
15	Tom Keller	84	30

Session

```
Correlations: Sales Calls, Copiers Sold

Pearson correlation of Sales Calls and Copiers Sold = 0.865
P-Value = 0.000
```

EXAMPLE

In the Applewood Auto Group example on page 444, we found that the correlation coefficient between the profit on the sale of a vehicle by the Applewood Auto Group and the age of the person that purchased the vehicle was 0.262. The sign of the correlation coefficient was positive, so we concluded there was a direct relationship between the two variables. However, because the value of the correlation coefficient was small—that is, near zero—we concluded that an advertising campaign directed toward the older buyers was not warranted. We can test our conclusion by conducting a hypothesis test that the correlation coefficient is greater than zero using the .05 significance level.

SOLUTION

To test the hypothesis, we need to clarify the sample and population issues. Let's assume that the data collected on the 180 vehicles sold by the Applewood Group is a sample from the population of *all* vehicles sold over many years by the Applewood Auto Group. The Greek letter ρ is the correlation coefficient in the population and r the correlation coefficient in the sample.

Our next step is to set up the null hypothesis and the alternate hypothesis. We test the null hypothesis that the correlation coefficient is equal to or less than zero. The alternate hypothesis is that there is positive correlation between the two variables.

H_0: $\rho \leq 0$ (The correlation in the population is negative or equal to zero.)
H_1: $\rho > 0$ (The correlation in the population is positive.)

This is a one-tailed test because we are interested in confirming a positive association between the variables. The test statistic follows the t distribution with $n - 2$ degrees of freedom, so the degrees of freedom are $180 - 2 = 178$. However, the value for 178 degrees of freedom is not in Appendix B.5. The closest value is 180, so we will use that value. Our decision rule is to reject the null hypothesis if the computed value of the test statistic is greater than 1.653.

We use formula (13–2) to find the value of the test statistic.

$$t = \frac{r\sqrt{n-2}}{\sqrt{1-r^2}} = \frac{0.262\sqrt{180-2}}{\sqrt{1-0.262^2}} = 3.622$$

Comparing the value of our test statistic of 3.622 to the critical value of 1.653, we reject the null hypothesis. We conclude that the sample correlation coefficient of 0.262 is too large to have come from a population with no correlation. To put our results another way, there is a positive correlation between profits and age in the population.

This result is confusing and seems contradictory. On one hand, we observed that the correlation coefficient did not indicate a very strong relationship and that the Applewood Auto Group marketing department should not use this information for its promotion and advertising decisions. On the other hand, the hypothesis test indicated that the correlation coefficient is not equal to zero and that a positive relationship between age and profit exists. How can this be? We must be very careful about the application of the hypothesis test results. The hypothesis test shows a statistically significant result. However, this result does not necessarily support a practical decision to start a new marketing and promotion campaign to older purchasers. In fact, the relatively low correlation coefficient is an indication that the outcome of a new marketing and promotion campaign to older potential purchasers is, at best, uncertain.

SELF-REVIEW 13–2

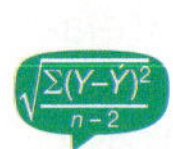

A sample of 25 mayoral campaigns in medium-sized cities with populations between 50,000 and 250,000 showed that the correlation between the percent of the vote received and the amount spent on the campaign by the candidate was .43. At the .05 significance level, is there a positive association between the variables?

EXERCISES

7. The following hypotheses are given.

$$H_0: \rho \leq 0$$
$$H_1: \rho > 0$$

A random sample of 12 paired observations indicated a correlation of .32. Can we conclude that the correlation in the population is greater than zero? Use the .05 significance level.

8. The following hypotheses are given.

$$H_0: \rho \geq 0$$
$$H_1: \rho < 0$$

A random sample of 15 paired observations has a correlation of −.46. Can we conclude that the correlation in the population is less than zero? Use the .05 significance level.

9. Pennsylvania Refining Company is studying the relationship between the pump price of gasoline and the number of gallons sold. For a sample of 20 stations last Tuesday, the correlation was .78. At the .01 significance level, is the correlation in the population greater than zero?
10. A study of 20 worldwide financial institutions showed the correlation between their assets and pretax profit to be .86. At the .05 significance level, can we conclude that there is positive correlation in the population?
11. The Airline Passenger Association studied the relationship between the number of passengers on a particular flight and the cost of the flight. It seems logical that more passengers on the flight will result in more weight and more luggage, which in turn will result in higher fuel costs. For a sample of 15 flights, the correlation between the number of passengers and total fuel cost was .667. Is it reasonable to conclude that there is positive association in the population between the two variables? Use the .01 significance level.
12. **FILE** The Student Government Association at Middle Carolina University wanted to demonstrate the relationship between the number of beers a student drinks and his or her blood alcohol content (BAC). A random sample of 18 students participated in a study in which each participating student was randomly assigned a number of 12-ounce cans of beer to drink. Thirty minutes after they consumed their assigned number of beers, a member of the local sheriff's office measured their blood alcohol content. The sample information is reported below.

Student	Beers	BAC	Student	Beers	BAC
Charles	6	0.10	Jaime	3	0.07
Ellis	7	0.09	Shannon	3	0.05
Harriet	7	0.09	Nellie	7	0.08
Marlene	4	0.10	Jeanne	1	0.04
Tara	5	0.10	Michele	4	0.07
Kerry	3	0.07	Seth	2	0.06
Vera	3	0.10	Gilberto	7	0.12
Pat	6	0.12	Lillian	2	0.05
Marjorie	6	0.09	Becky	1	0.02

Use a statistical software package to answer the following questions.

a. Develop a scatter diagram for the number of beers consumed and BAC. Comment on the relationship. Does it appear to be strong or weak? Does it appear to be positive or inverse?
b. Determine the correlation coefficient.
c. At the .01 significance level, is it reasonable to conclude that there is a positive relationship in the population between the number of beers consumed and the BAC? What is the *p*-value?

LO13-3
Apply regression analysis to estimate the linear relationship between two variables.

STATISTICS IN ACTION

In finance, investors are interested in the trade-off between returns and risk. One technique to quantify risk is a regression analysis of a company's stock price (dependent variable) and an average measure of the stock market (independent variable). Often the Standard and Poor's (S&P) 500 Index is used to estimate the market. The regression coefficient, called beta in finance, shows the change in a company's stock price for a one-unit change in the S&P Index. For example, if a stock has a beta of 1.5, then when the S&P index increases by 1%, the stock price will increase by 1.5%. The opposite is also true. If the S&P decreases by 1%, the stock price will decrease by 1.5%. If the beta is 1.0, then a 1% change in the index should show a 1% change in a stock price. If the beta is less than 1.0, then a 1% change in the index shows less than a 1% change in the stock price.

REGRESSION ANALYSIS

In the previous sections of this chapter, we evaluated the direction and the significance of the linear relationship between two variables by finding the correlation coefficient. Regression analysis is another method to examine a linear relationship between two variables. This analysis uses the basic concepts of correlation but provides much more information by expressing the linear relationship between two variables in the form of an equation. Using this equation, we will be able to estimate the value of the dependent variable *Y* based on a selected value of the independent variable *X*. The technique used to develop the equation and provide the estimates is called **regression analysis.**

© Image Source/Getty Images RF

In Table 13–1, we reported the number of sales calls and the number of units sold for a sample of 15 sales representatives employed by North American Copier Sales. Chart 13–1 portrayed this information in a scatter diagram. Recall that we tested the significance of the correlation coefficient ($r = 0.865$) and concluded that a significant relationship exists between the two variables. Now we want to develop a linear equation that expresses the relationship between the number of sales calls, the independent variable, and the number of units sold, the dependent variable. The equation for the line used to estimate *Y* on the basis of *X* is referred to as the **regression equation.**

REGRESSION EQUATION An equation that expresses the linear relationship between two variables.

Least Squares Principle

In regression analysis, our objective is to use the data to position a line that best represents the relationship between the two variables. Our first approach is to use a scatter diagram to visually position the line.

The scatter diagram in Chart 13–1 is reproduced in Chart 13–7, with a line drawn with a ruler through the dots to illustrate that a line would probably fit the data. However, the line drawn using a straight edge has one disadvantage: Its position is based in part on the judgment of the person drawing the line. The hand-drawn lines in Chart 13–8 represent the judgments of four people. All the lines except line *A* seem to be reasonable. That is, each line is centered among the graphed data. However, each would result in a different estimate of units sold for a particular number of sales calls.

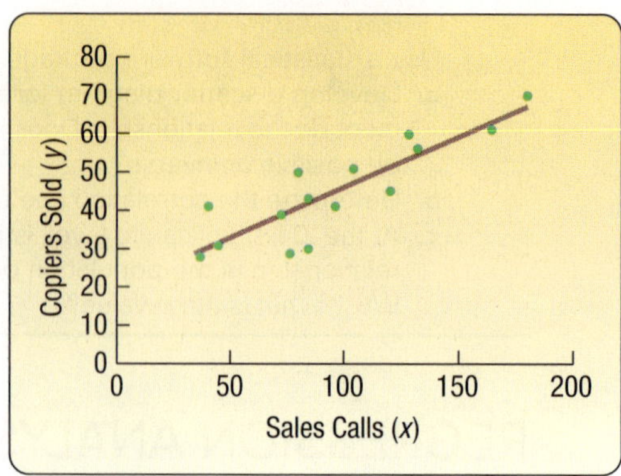

CHART 13–7 Sales Calls and Copiers Sold for 15 Sales Representatives

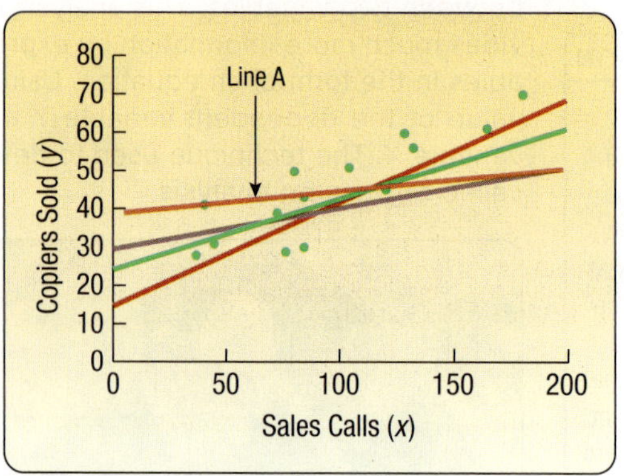

CHART 13–8 Four Lines Superimposed on the Scatter Diagram

We would prefer a method that results in a single, best regression line. This method is called the least squares principle. It gives what is commonly referred to as the "best-fitting" line.

LEAST SQUARES PRINCIPLE
A mathematical procedure that uses the data to position a line with the objective of minimizing the sum of the squares of the vertical distances between the actual *y* values and the predicted values of *y*.

To illustrate this concept, the same data are plotted in the three charts that follow. The dots are the actual values of *y*, and the asterisks are the predicted values of *y* for a given value of *x*. The regression line in Chart 13–9 was determined using the least squares method. It is the best-fitting line because the sum of the squares of the vertical deviations about it is at a minimum. The first plot ($x = 3$, $y = 8$) deviates by 2 from the line, found by 10 − 8. The deviation squared is 4. The squared deviation for the plot $x = 4$, $y = 18$ is 16. The squared deviation for the plot $x = 5$, $y = 16$ is 4. The sum of the squared deviations is 24, found by 4 + 16 + 4.

Assume that the lines in Charts 13–10 and 13–11 were drawn with a straight edge. The sum of the squared vertical deviations in Chart 13–10 is 44. For Chart 13–11, it is 132. Both sums are greater than the sum for the line in Chart 13–9, found by using the least squares method.

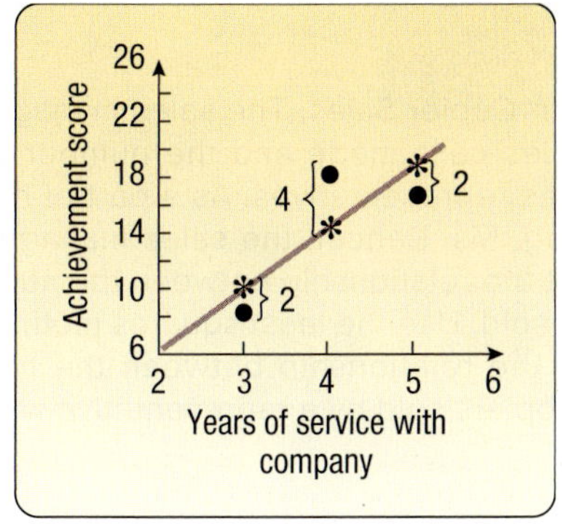

CHART 13–9 The Least Squares Line

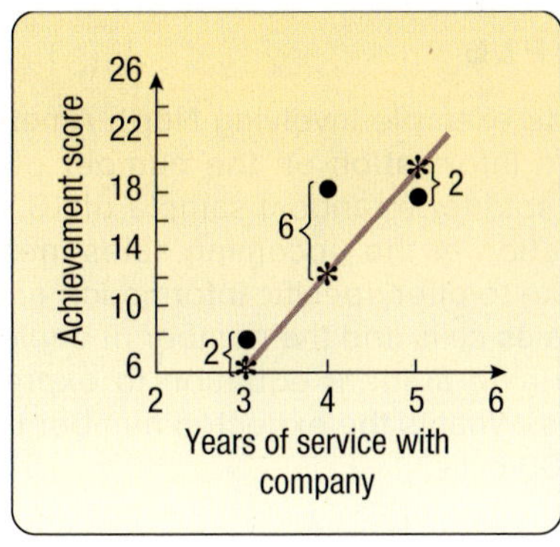

CHART 13–10 Line Drawn with a Straight Edge

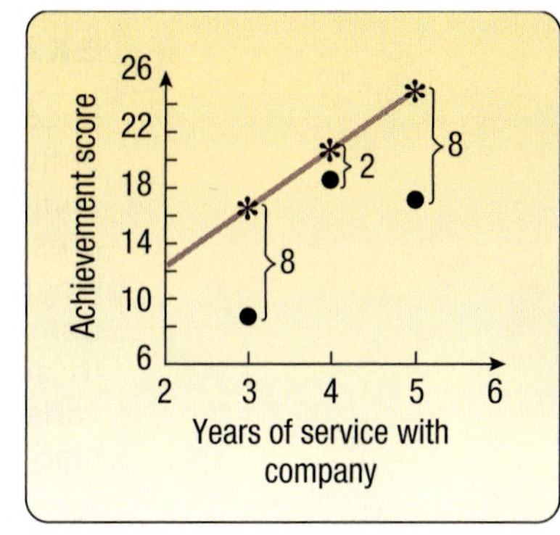

CHART 13–11 Different Line Drawn with a Straight Edge

The equation of a line has the form

GENERAL FORM OF LINEAR REGRESSION EQUATION	$\hat{y} = a + bx$	**[13–3]**

where:

$\hat{y}$, read *y* hat, is the estimated value of the *y* variable for a selected *x* value.
a is the *y*-intercept. It is the estimated value of *Y* when $x = 0$. Another way to put it is: *a* is the estimated value of *y* where the regression line crosses the *Y*-axis when *x* is zero.
b is the slope of the line, or the average change in $\hat{y}$ for each change of one unit (either increase or decrease) in the independent variable *x*.
x is any value of the independent variable that is selected.

The general form of the linear regression equation is exactly the same form as the equation of any line. *a* is the *Y* intercept and *b* is the slope. The purpose of regression analysis is to calculate the values of *a* and *b* to develop a linear equation that best fits the data.

The formulas for *a* and *b* are:

SLOPE OF THE REGRESSION LINE	$b = r\left(\frac{s_y}{s_x}\right)$	**[13–4]**

where:

r is the correlation coefficient.
s_y is the standard deviation of *y* (the dependent variable).
s_x is the standard deviation of *x* (the independent variable).

***Y*-INTERCEPT**	$a = \bar{y} - b\bar{x}$	**[13–5]**

where:

$\bar{y}$ is the mean of *y* (the dependent variable).
$\bar{x}$ is the mean of *x* (the independent variable).

EXAMPLE

Recall the example involving North American Copier Sales. The sales manager gathered information on the number of sales calls made and the number of copiers sold for a random sample of 15 sales representatives. As a part of her presentation at the upcoming sales meeting, Ms. Bancer, the sales manager, would like to offer specific information about the relationship between the number of sales calls and the number of copiers sold. Use the least squares method to determine a linear equation to express the relationship between the two variables. What is the expected number of copiers sold by a representative who made 100 calls?

SOLUTION

The first step in determining the regression equation is to find the slope of the least squares regression line. That is, we need the value of *b*. In the previous section on page 443, we determined the correlation coefficient *r* (0.865). In the Excel output on page 443, we determined the standard deviation of the independent variable *x* (42.76) and the standard deviation of the dependent variable *y* (12.89). The values are inserted in formula (13–4).

$$b = r\left(\frac{s_y}{s_x}\right) = .865\left(\frac{12.89}{42.76}\right) = 0.2608$$

Next, we need to find the value of *a*. To do this, we use the value for *b* that we just calculated as well as the means for the number of sales calls and the number of copiers sold. These means are also available in the Excel worksheet on page 443. From formula (13–5):

$$a = \bar{y} - b\bar{x} = 45 - .2608(96) = 19.9632$$

Thus, the regression equation is

$$\hat{y} = 19.9632 + 0.2608x.$$

So if a salesperson makes 100 calls, he or she can expect to sell 46.0432 copiers, found by

$$\hat{y} = 19.9632 + 0.2608x = 19.9632 + 0.2608(100) = 46.0432$$

The *b* value of .2608 indicates that for each additional sales call, the sales representative can expect to increase the number of copiers sold by about 0.2608. To put it another way, 20 additional sales calls in a month will result in about five more copiers being sold, found by 0.2608 (20) = 5.216.

The *a* value of 19.9632 is the point where the equation crosses the *Y*-axis. A literal translation is that if no sales calls are made, that is $x = 0$, 19.9632 copiers will be sold. Note that $x = 0$ is outside the range of values included in the sample and, therefore, should not be used to estimate the number of copiers sold. The sales calls ranged from 36 to 180, so estimates should be limited to that range.

Drawing the Regression Line

The least squares equation $\hat{y} = 19.9632 + 0.2608x$ can be drawn on the scatter diagram. The fifth sales representative in the sample is Jeff Hall. He made 164 calls. His estimated number of copiers sold is $\hat{y} = 19.9632 + 0.2608(164) = 62.7344$. The plot $x = 164$ and $\hat{y} = 62.7344$ is located by moving to 164 on the *X*-axis and then going vertically to 62.7344. The other points on the regression equation can be determined

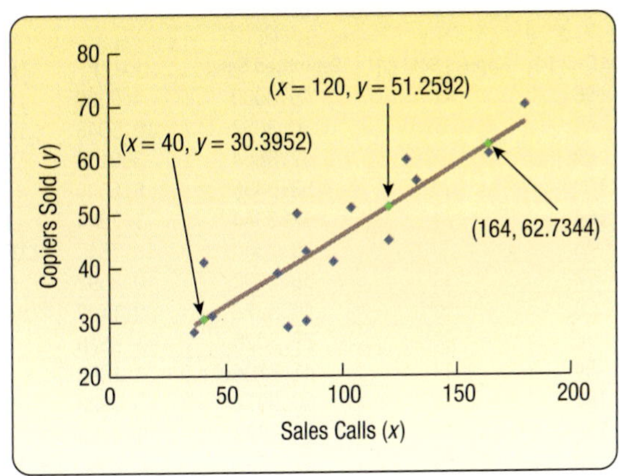

CHART 13–12 The Line of Regression Drawn on the Scatter Diagram

by substituting a particular value of x into the regression equation and calculating $\hat{y}$. All the points are connected to give the line. See Chart 13–12.

Sales Representative	Sales Calls (x)	Copiers Sold (y)	Estimated Sales ($\hat{y}$)
Brian Virost	96	41	45.0000
Carlos Ramirez	40	41	30.3952
Carol Saia	104	51	47.0864
Greg Fish	128	60	53.3456
Jeff Hall	164	61	62.7344
Mark Reynolds	76	29	39.7840
Meryl Rumsey	72	39	38.7408
Mike Kiel	80	50	40.8272
Ray Snarsky	36	28	29.3520
Rich Niles	84	43	41.8704
Ron Broderick	180	70	66.9072
Sal Spina	132	56	54.3888
Soni Jones	120	45	51.2592
Susan Welch	44	31	31.4384
Tom Keller	84	30	41.8704

The least squares regression line has some interesting and unique features. First, it will always pass through the point $(\bar{x}, \bar{y})$. To show this is true, we can use the mean number of sales calls to predict the number of copiers sold. In this example, the mean number of sales calls is 96, found by $\bar{x} = 1440/15$. The mean number of copiers sold is 45.0, found by $\bar{y} = 675/15$. If we let $x = 96$ and then use the regression equation to find the estimated value for $\hat{y}$ the result is:

$$\hat{y} = 19.9632 + 0.2608(96) = 45$$

The estimated number of copiers sold is exactly equal to the mean number of copiers sold. This simple example shows the regression line will pass through the point represented by the two means. In this case, the regression equation will pass through the point $x = 96$ and $y = 45$.

Second, as we discussed earlier in this section, there is no other line through the data where the sum of the squared deviations is smaller. To put it another way, the term $\Sigma(y - \hat{y})^2$ is smaller for the least squares regression equation than for any other equation. We use the Excel system to demonstrate this result in the following printout.

	A	B	C	D	E	F	G	H	I	J
1	**Sales Rep**	**Sales Calls (x)**	**Copiers Sold (y)**	**Estimated Sales**	**$(y-\hat{y})$**	**$(y-\hat{y})^2$**	**y^***	**$(y-y^*)^2$**	**y^{**}**	**$(y-y^{**})^2$**
2	Brian Virost	96	41	45.0000	−4.0000	16.0000	44.4000	11.5600	41.6000	0.3600
3	Carlos Ramirez	40	41	30.3952	10.6048	112.4618	29.0000	144.0000	29.0000	144.0000
4	Carol Saia	104	51	47.0864	3.9136	15.3163	46.6000	19.3600	43.4000	57.7600
5	Greg Fish	128	60	53.3456	6.6544	44.2810	53.2000	46.2400	48.8000	125.4400
6	Jeff Hall	164	61	62.7344	−1.7344	3.0081	63.1000	4.4100	56.9000	16.8100
7	Mark Reynolds	76	29	39.7840	−10.7840	116.2947	38.9000	98.0100	37.1000	65.6100
8	Meryl Rumsey	72	39	38.7408	0.2592	0.0672	37.8000	1.4400	36.2000	7.8400
9	Mike Kiel	80	50	40.8272	9.1728	84.1403	40.0000	100.0000	38.0000	144.0000
10	Ray Snarsky	36	28	29.3520	−1.3520	1.8279	27.9000	0.0100	28.1000	0.0100
11	Rich Niles	84	43	41.8704	1.1296	1.2760	41.1000	3.6100	38.9000	16.8100
12	Ron Broderick	180	70	66.9072	3.0928	9.5654	67.5000	6.2500	60.5000	90.2500
13	Sal Spina	132	56	54.3888	1.6112	2.5960	54.3000	2.8900	49.7000	39.6900
14	Soni Jones	120	45	51.2592	−6.2592	39.1776	51.0000	36.0000	47.0000	4.0000
15	Susan Welch	44	31	31.4384	−0.4384	0.1922	30.1000	0.8100	29.9000	1.2100
16	Tom Keller	84	30	41.8704	−11.8704	140.9064	41.1000	123.2100	38.9000	79.2100
17	**Total**				**0.0000**	**587.1108**		**597.8000**		**793.0000**

In columns A, B, and C in the Excel spreadsheet above, we duplicated the sample information on sales and copiers sold from Table 13–1. In column D, we provide the estimated sales values, the $\hat{y}$ values, as calculated above.

In column E, we calculate the **residuals,** or the error values. This is the difference between the actual values and the predicted values. That is, column E is $(y - \hat{y})$. For Soni Jones,

$$\hat{y} = 19{,}\ 9632 + 0.2608(120) = 51.2592$$

Her actual value is 45. So the residual, or error of estimate, is

$$(y - \hat{y}) = (45 - 51.2592) = -6.2592$$

This value reflects the amount the predicted value of sales is "off" from the actual sales value.

Next, in Column F, we square the residuals for each of the sales representatives and total the result. The total is 587.111.

$$\Sigma(y - \hat{y})^2 = 16.0000 + 112.4618 + \cdots + 140.9064 = 587.1108$$

This is the sum of the squared differences or the least squares value. There is no other line through these 15 data points where the sum of the squared differences is smaller.

We can demonstrate the least squares criterion by choosing two arbitrary equations that are close to the least squares equation and determining the sum of the squared differences for these equations. In column G, we use the equation $y^* = 18 + 0.275x$ to find the predicted value. Notice this equation is very similar to the least squares equation. In column H, we determine the residuals and square these residuals. For the first sales representative, Brian Virost,

$$y^* = 18 + 0.275(96) = 44.4$$

$$(y - y^*)^2 = (41 - 44.4)^2 = 11.56$$

This procedure is continued for the other 14 sales representatives and the squared residuals totaled. The result is 597.8. This is a larger value (597.8 is more than 587.1108) than the residuals for the least squares line.

In columns I and J on the output, we repeat the above process for yet another equation $y^{**} = 20 + 0.225x$. Again, this equation is similar to the least squares equation. The details for Brian Virost are:

$$y^{**} = 20 + 0.225x = 20 + 0.225(96) = 41.6$$

$$(y - y^{**})^2 = (41 - 41.6)^2 = 0.36$$

This procedure is continued for the other 14 sales representatives and the residuals totaled. The result is 793, which is also larger than the least squares values.

What have we shown with the example? The sum of the squared residuals $[\Sigma(y - \hat{y})^2]$ for the least squares equation is smaller than for other selected lines. The bottom line is you will not be able to find a line passing through these data points where the sum of the squared residuals is smaller.

SELF-REVIEW 13–3

Refer to Self-Review 13–1, where the owner of Haverty's Furniture Company was studying the relationship between sales and the amount spent on advertising. The advertising expense and sales revenue, both in millions of dollars, for the last 4 months are repeated below.

Month	Advertising Expense ($ million)	Sales Revenue ($ million)
July	2	7
August	1	3
September	3	8
October	4	10

(a) Determine the regression equation.
(b) Interpret the values of a and b.
(c) Estimate sales when $3 million is spent on advertising.

EXERCISES

13. FILE The following sample of observations was randomly selected.

x:	4	5	3	6	10
y:	4	6	5	7	7

a. Determine the regression equation.
b. Determine the value of when x is 7.

14. FILE The following sample of observations was randomly selected.

x:	5	3	6	3	4	4	6	8
y:	13	15	7	12	13	11	9	5

a. Determine the regression equation.
b. Determine the value of $\hat{y}$ when x is 7.

15. FILE Bradford Electric Illuminating Company is studying the relationship between kilowatt-hours (thousands) used and the number of rooms in a private single-family residence. A random sample of 10 homes yielded the following.

Number of Rooms	Kilowatt-Hours (thousands)	Number of Rooms	Kilowatt-Hours (thousands)
12	9	8	6
9	7	10	8
14	10	10	10
6	5	5	4
10	8	7	7

a. Determine the regression equation.
b. Determine the number of kilowatt-hours, in thousands, for a six-room house.

16. **FILE** Mr. James McWhinney, president of Daniel-James Financial Services, believes there is a relationship between the number of client contacts and the dollar amount of sales. To document this assertion, Mr. McWhinney gathered the following sample information. The *x* column indicates the number of client contacts last month and the *y* column shows the value of sales ($ thousands) last month for each client sampled.

Number of Contacts, x	Sales ($ thousands), y	Number of Contacts, x	Sales ($ thousands), y
14	24	23	30
12	14	48	90
20	28	50	85
16	30	55	120
46	80	50	110

a. Determine the regression equation.
b. Determine the estimated sales if 40 contacts are made.

17. **FILE** A recent article in *Bloomberg Businessweek* listed the "Best Small Companies." We are interested in the current results of the companies' sales and earnings. A random sample of 12 companies was selected and the sales and earnings, in millions of dollars, are reported below.

Company	Sales ($ millions)	Earnings ($ millions)	Company	Sales ($ millions)	Earnings ($ millions)
Papa John's International	$89.2	$4.9	Checkmate Electronics	$17.5	$ 2.6
Applied Innovation	18.6	4.4	Royal Grip	11.9	1.7
Integracare	18.2	1.3	M-Wave	19.6	3.5
Wall Data	71.7	8.0	Serving-N-Slide	51.2	8.2
Davidson & Associates	58.6	6.6	Daig	28.6	6.0
Chico's FAS	46.8	4.1	Cobra Golf	69.2	12.8

Let sales be the independent variable and earnings be the dependent variable.

a. Draw a scatter diagram.
b. Compute the correlation coefficient.
c. Determine the regression equation.
d. For a small company with $50.0 million in sales, estimate the earnings.

18. **FILE** We are studying mutual bond funds for the purpose of investing in several funds. For this particular study, we want to focus on the assets of a fund and its five-year performance. The question is: Can the five-year rate of return be estimated based on the assets of the fund? Nine mutual funds were selected at random, and their assets and rates of return are shown below.

Fund	Assets ($ millions)	Return (%)	Fund	Assets ($ millions)	Return (%)
AARP High Quality Bond	$622.2	10.8	MFS Bond A	$494.5	11.6
Babson Bond L	160.4	11.3	Nichols Income	158.3	9.5
Compass Capital Fixed Income	275.7	11.4	T. Rowe Price Short-term	681.0	8.2
Galaxy Bond Retail	433.2	9.1	Thompson Income B	241.3	6.8
Keystone Custodian B-1	437.9	9.2			

a. Draw a scatter diagram.
b. Compute the correlation coefficient.
c. Write a brief report of your findings for parts (a) and (b).
d. Determine the regression equation. Use assets as the independent variable.
e. For a fund with $400.0 million in sales, determine the five-year rate of return (in percent).

19. **FILE** Refer to Exercise 5. Assume the dependent variable is number of crimes.
   a. Determine the regression equation.
   b. Estimate the number of crimes for a city with 20 police officers.
   c. Interpret the regression equation.
20. **FILE** Refer to Exercise 6.
   a. Determine the regression equation.
   b. Estimate the selling price of a 10-year-old car.
   c. Interpret the regression equation.

LO13-4
Evaluate the significance of the slope of the regression equation.

TESTING THE SIGNIFICANCE OF THE SLOPE

In the prior section, we showed how to find the equation of the regression line that best fits the data. The method for finding the equation is based on the *least squares principle.* The purpose of the regression equation is to quantify a linear relationship between two variables.

The next step is to analyze the regression equation by conducting a test of hypothesis to see if the slope of the regression line is different from zero. Why is this important? If we can show that the slope of the line in the population is different from zero, then we can conclude that using the regression equation adds to our ability to predict or forecast the dependent variable based on the independent variable. If we cannot demonstrate that this slope is different from zero, then we conclude there is no merit to using the independent variable as a predictor. To put it another way, if we cannot show the slope of the line is different from zero, we might as well use the mean of the dependent variable as a predictor, rather than use the regression equation.

Following from the hypothesis-testing procedure in Chapter 10, the null and alternative hypotheses are:

$$H_0: \beta = 0$$
$$H_1: \beta \neq 0$$

We use β (the Greek letter beta) to represent the population slope for the regression equation. This is consistent with our policy to identify population parameters by Greek letters. We assumed the information regarding North American Copier Sales, Table 13–2, is a sample. Be careful here. Remember, this is a single sample of salespeople, but when we selected a particular salesperson we identified two pieces of information: how many customers they called on and how many copiers they sold.

We identified the slope value as b. So b is our computed slope based on a sample and is an estimate of the population's slope, identified as β. The null hypothesis is that the slope of the regression equation in the population is zero. If this is the case, the regression line is horizontal and there is no relationship between the independent variable, X, and the dependent variable, Y. In other words, the value of the dependent variable is the same for any value of the independent variable and does not offer us any help in estimating the value of the dependent variable.

What if the null hypothesis is rejected? If the null hypothesis is rejected and the alternate hypothesis accepted, this indicates that the slope of the regression line for the population is not equal to zero. To put it another way, a significant relationship exists between the two variables. Knowing the value of the independent variable allows us to estimate the value of the dependent variable.

Before we test the hypothesis, we use statistical software to determine the needed regression statistics. We continue to use the North American Copier Sales data from Table 13–2 and use Excel to perform the necessary calculations. The following spreadsheet shows three tables to the right of the sample data.

	A	B	C	D	E	F	G	H	I	J
1	**Sales Representive**	**Sales calls (x)**	**Copiers Sold (y)**		SUMMARY OUTPUT					
2	Brian Virost	96	41							
3	Carlos Ramirez	40	41		*Regression Statistics*					
4	Carol Saia	104	51		Multiple R	0.865				
5	Greg Fish	128	60		R Square	0.748				
6	Jeff Hall	164	61		Adjusted R Square	0.728				
7	Mark Reynolds	76	29		Standard Error	6.720				
8	Meryl Rumsey	72	39		Observations	15				
9	Mike Kiel	80	50							
10	Ray Snarsky	36	28		ANOVA					
11	Rich Niles	84	43			*df*	*SS*	*MS*	*F*	*Significance F*
12	Ron Broderick	180	70		Regression	1	1738.89	1738.89	38.5031	3.19277E-05
13	Sal Spina	132	56		Residual	13	587.11	45.1623		
14	Sani Jones	120	45		Total	14	2326			
15	Susan Welch	44	31							
16	Tom Keller	84	30			*Coefficients*	*Standard Error*	*t Stat*	*P-value*	
17					Intercept	19.9800	4.389675533	4.55159	0.00054	
18					Sales calls (x)	0.2606	0.042001817	6.20509	3.2E-05	

1. Starting on the top are the *Regression Statistics*. We will use this information later in the chapter, but notice that the "Multiple R" value is familiar. It is .865, which is the correlation coefficient we calculated using formula (13–1).
2. Next is an ANOVA table. This is a useful table for summarizing regression information. We will refer to it later in this chapter and use it extensively in the next chapter when we study multiple regression.
3. At the bottom, highlighted in blue, is the information needed to conduct our test of hypothesis regarding the slope of the line. It includes the value of the slope, which is 0.2606, and the intercept, which is 19.98. (Note that these values for the slope and the intercept are slightly different from those computed in the Example/Solution on page 454. These small differences are due to rounding.) In the column to the right of the regression coefficient is a column labeled "Standard Error." This is a value similar to the standard error of the mean. Recall that the standard error of the mean reports the variation in the sample means. In a similar fashion, these standard errors report the possible variation in slope and intercept values. The standard error of the slope coefficient is 0.0420.

To test the null hypothesis, we use the *t*-distribution with $(n - 2)$ and the following formula.

TEST FOR THE SLOPE $$t = \frac{b - 0}{s_b} \quad \text{with } n - 2 \text{ degrees of freedom} \qquad \textbf{[13–6]}$$

where:

b is the estimate of the regression line's slope calculated from the sample information.

s_b is the standard error of the slope estimate, also determined from sample information.

Our first step is to set the null and the alternative hypotheses. They are:

$$H_0: \beta \leq 0$$

$$H_1: \beta > 0$$

Notice that we have a one-tailed test. If we do not reject the null hypothesis, we conclude that the slope of the regression line in the population could be zero. This means the independent variable is of no value in improving our estimate of the dependent variable. In our case, this means that knowing the number of sales calls made by a representative does not help us predict the sales.

If we reject the null hypothesis and accept the alternative, we conclude the slope of the line is greater than zero. Hence, the independent variable is an aid in predicting the dependent variable. Thus, if we know the number of sales calls made by a salesperson, we can predict or forecast their sales. We also know, because we have demonstrated that the slope of the line is greater than zero—that is, positive—that more sales calls will result in the sale of more copiers.

The *t*-distribution is the test statistic; there are 13 degrees of freedom, found by $n - 2 = 15 - 2$. We use the .05 significance level. From Appendix B.5, the critical value is 1.771. Our decision rule is to reject the null hypothesis if the value computed from formula (13–6) is greater than 1.771. We apply formula (13–6) to find *t*.

$$t = \frac{b - 0}{s_b} = \frac{0.2606 - 0}{0.042} = 6.205$$

The computed value of 6.205 exceeds our critical value of 1.771, so we reject the null hypothesis and accept the alternative hypothesis. We conclude that the slope of the line is greater than zero. The independent variable, number of sales calls, is useful in estimating copier sales.

The table also provides us information on the *p*-value of this test. This cell is highlighted in purple. So we could select a significance level, say .05, and compare that value with the *p*-value. In this case, the calculated *p*-value in the table is reported in exponential notation and is equal to 0.0000319, so our decision is to reject the null hypothesis. An important caution is that the *p*-values reported in the statistical software are usually for a two-*tailed test.*

Before moving on, here is an interesting note. Observe that on page 448, when we conducted a test of hypothesis regarding the correlation coefficient for these same data using formula (13–2), we obtained the same value of the *t*-statistic, $t = 6.205$. Actually, when comparing the results of simple linear regression and correlation analysis, the two tests are equivalent and will always yield exactly the same values of *t* and the same *p*-values.

SELF-REVIEW 13–4

Refer to Self-Review 13–1, where the owner of Haverty's Furniture Company studied the relationship between the amount spent on advertising in a month and sales revenue for that month. The amount of sales is the dependent variable and advertising expense, the independent variable. The regression equation in that study was $\hat{y} = 1.5 + 2.2x$ for a sample of 5 months. Conduct a test of hypothesis to show there is a positive relationship between advertising and sales. From statistical software, the standard error of the regression coefficient is 0.42. Use the .05 significance level.

EXERCISES

21. **FILE** Refer to Exercise 5. The regression equation is $\hat{y} = 29.29 - 0.96x$, the sample size is 8, and the standard error of the slope is 0.22. Use the .05 significance level. Can we conclude that the slope of the regression line is less than zero?
22. **FILE** Refer to Exercise 6. The regression equation is $\hat{y} = 11.18 - 0.49x$, the sample size is 12, and the standard error of the slope is 0.23. Use the .05 significance level. Can we conclude that the slope of the regression line is less than zero?
23. **FILE** Refer to Exercise 17. The regression equation is $\hat{y} = 1.85 + .08x$, the sample size is 12, and the standard error of the slope is 0.03. Use the .05 significance level. Can we conclude that the slope of the regression line is *different from zero*?
24. **FILE** Refer to Exercise 18. The regression equation is $\hat{y} = 9.9198 - 0.00039x$, the sample size is 9, and the standard error of the slope is 0.0032. Use the .05 significance level. Can we conclude that the slope of the regression line is less than zero?

LO13-5
Evaluate a regression equation's ability to predict using the standard estimate of the error and the coefficient of determination.

EVALUATING A REGRESSION EQUATION'S ABILITY TO PREDICT

The Standard Error of Estimate

The results of the regression analysis for North American Copier Sales show a significant relationship between number of sales calls and the number of sales made. By substituting the names of the variables into the equation, it can be written as:

$$\text{Number of copiers sold} = 19.9632 + 0.2608 \text{ (Number of sales calls)}$$

The equation can be used to estimate the number of copiers sold for any given "number of sales calls" within the range of the data. For example, if the number of sales calls is 84, then we can predict the number of copiers sold. It is 41.8704, found by 19.9632 + 0.2608(84). However, the data show two sales representatives with 84 sales calls and 30 and 43 copiers sold. So, is the regression equation a good predictor of "Number of copiers sold"?

Perfect prediction, which is finding the exact outcome, is practically impossible in almost all disciplines including economics and business. For example:

- A large electronics firm, with production facilities throughout the United States, has a stock option plan for employees. Suppose there is a relationship between the number of years employed and the number of shares owned. This relationship is likely because, as number of years of service increases, the number of shares an employee earns also increases. If we observe all employees with 20 years of service, they would most likely own different numbers of shares.
- A real estate developer in the southwest United States studied the relationship between the income of buyers and the size, in square feet, of the home they purchased. The developer's analysis shows that as the income of a purchaser increases, the size of the home purchased will also increase. However, all buyers with an income of $70,000 will not purchase a home of exactly the same size.

What is needed, then, is a measure that describes how precise the prediction of Y is based on X or, conversely, how inaccurate the estimate might be. This measure is called the **standard error of estimate.** The standard error of estimate is symbolized by $s_{y \cdot x}$. The subscript, $y \cdot x$, is interpreted as the standard error of y for a given value of x. It is the same concept as the standard deviation discussed in Chapter 3. The standard deviation measures the dispersion around the mean. The standard error of estimate measures the dispersion about the regression line for a given value of x.

STANDARD ERROR OF ESTIMATE A measure of the dispersion, or scatter, of the observed values around the line of regression for a given value of x.

The standard error of estimate is found using formula (13–7).

STANDARD ERROR OF ESTIMATE

$$s_{y \cdot x} = \sqrt{\frac{\Sigma(y - \hat{y})^2}{n - 2}} \qquad \textbf{[13–7]}$$

The calculation of the standard error of estimate requires the sum of the squared differences between each observed value of y and the predicted value of y, which is identified as $\hat{y}$ in the numerator. This calculation is illustrated in the following spreadsheet. See the highlighted cell in the lower right corner.

	A	B	C	D	E	F
1	**Sales Rep**	**Sales Calls (x)**	**Copiers Sold (y)**	**Estimated Sales**	$(y-\hat{y})$	$(y-\hat{y})^2$
2	Brian Virost	96	41	45.0000	–4.0000	16.0000
3	Carlos Ramirez	40	41	30.3952	10.6048	112.4618
4	Carol Saia	104	51	47.0864	3.9136	15.3163
5	Greg Fish	128	60	53.3456	6.6544	44.2810
6	Jeff Hall	164	61	62.7344	–1.7344	3.0081
7	Mark Reynolds	76	29	39.7840	–10.7840	116.2947
8	Meryl Rumsey	72	39	38.7408	0.2592	0.0672
9	Mike Kiel	80	50	40.8272	9.1728	84.1403
10	Ray Snarsky	36	28	29.3520	–1.3520	1.8279
11	Rich Niles	84	43	41.8704	1.1296	1.2760
12	Ron Broderick	180	70	66.9072	3.0928	9.5654
13	Sal Spina	132	56	54.3888	1.6112	2.5960
14	Soni Jones	120	45	51.2592	–6.2592	39.1776
15	Susan Welch	44	31	31.4384	–0.4384	0.1922
16	Tom Keller	84	30	41.8704	–11.8704	140.9064
17	**Total**				**0.0000**	**587.1108**

The calculation of the standard error of estimate is:

$$s_{y \cdot x} = \sqrt{\frac{\Sigma(y-\hat{y})^2}{n-2}} = \sqrt{\frac{587.1108}{15-2}} = 6.720$$

The standard error of estimate can be calculated using statistical software such as Excel. It is included in Excel's regression analysis on page 460 and highlighted in yellow. Its value is 6.720.

If the standard error of estimate is small, this indicates that the data are relatively close to the regression line and the regression equation can be used to predict *y* with little error. If the standard error of estimate is large, this indicates that the data are widely scattered around the regression line and the regression equation will not provide a precise estimate of *y*.

The Coefficient of Determination

Using the standard error of estimate provides a relative measure of a regression equation's ability to predict. We will use it to provide more specific information about a prediction in the next section. In this section, another statistic is explained that will provide a more interpretable measure of a regression equation's ability to predict. It is called the coefficient of determination, or *R*-square.

COEFFICIENT OF DETERMINATION

The proportion of the total variation in the dependent variable *Y* that is explained, or accounted for, by the variation in the independent variable *X*.

The coefficient of determination is easy to compute. It is the correlation coefficient squared. Therefore, the term *R*-square is also used. With the North American Copier Sales data, the correlation coefficient for the relationship between the number of copiers sold and the number of sales calls is 0.865. If we compute $(0.865)^2$, the coefficient of determination is 0.748. See the blue (Multiple R) and green (*R*-square) highlighted cells in the spreadsheet on page 460. To better interpret the coefficient of determination, convert it to a percentage. Hence, we say that 74.8% of the variation in the number of copiers sold is explained, or accounted for, by the variation in the number of sales calls.

How well can the regression equation predict number of copiers sold with number of sales calls made? If it were possible to make perfect predictions, the coefficient of determination would be 100%. That would mean that the independent variable, number of sales calls, explains or accounts for all the variation in the number of copiers sold. A coefficient of determination of 100% is associated with a correlation coefficient of +1.0 or −1.0. Refer to Chart 13–2, which shows that a perfect prediction is associated with a perfect linear relationship where all the data points form a perfect line in a scatter diagram. Our analysis shows that only 74.8% of the variation in copiers sold is explained by the number of sales calls. Clearly, these data do not form a perfect line. Instead, the data are scattered around the best-fitting, least squares regression line, and there will be error in the predictions. In the next section, the standard error of estimate is used to provide more specific information regarding the error associated with using the regression equation to make predictions.

SELF-REVIEW 13–5

Refer to Self-Review 13–1, where the owner of Haverty's Furniture Company studied the relationship between the amount spent on advertising in a month and sales revenue for that month. The amount of sales is the dependent variable and advertising expense is the independent variable.

(a) Determine the standard error of estimate.
(b) Determine the coefficient of determination.
(c) Interpret the coefficient of determination.

EXERCISES

(You may wish to use a statistical software package such as Excel, Minitab, or Megastat to assist in your calculations.)

25. Refer to Exercise 5. Determine the standard error of estimate and the coefficient of determination. Interpret the coefficient of determination.
26. Refer to Exercise 6. Determine the standard error of estimate and the coefficient of determination. Interpret the coefficient of determination.
27. Refer to Exercise 15. Determine the standard error of estimate and the coefficient of determination. Interpret the coefficient of determination.
28. Refer to Exercise 16. Determine the standard error of estimate and the coefficient of determination. Interpret the coefficient of determination.

Relationships among the Correlation Coefficient, the Coefficient of Determination, and the Standard Error of Estimate

In formula 13-7 shown on page 462, we described the standard error of estimate. Recall that it measures how close the actual values are to the regression line. When the standard error is small, it indicates that the two variables are closely related. In the calculation of the standard error, the key term is

$$\Sigma(y - \hat{y})^2$$

If the value of this term is small, then the standard error will also be small.

The correlation coefficient measures the strength of the linear association between two variables. When the points on the scatter diagram appear close to the line, we note that the correlation coefficient tends to be large. Therefore, the correlation coefficient and the standard error of the estimate are inversely related. As the strength of a linear relationship between two variables increases, the correlation coefficient increases and the standard error of the estimate decreases.

We also noted that the square of the correlation coefficient is the coefficient of determination. The coefficient of determination measures the percentage of the variation in Y that is explained by the variation in X.

A convenient vehicle for showing the relationship among these three measures is an ANOVA table. See the highlighted portion of the spreadsheet below. This table is similar to the analysis of variance table developed in Chapter 12. In that chapter, the total variation was divided into two components: variation due to the *treatments* and variation due to *random error.* The concept is similar in regression analysis. The total variation is divided into two components: (1) variation explained by the *regression* (explained by the independent variable) and (2) the *error,* or *residual.* This is the unexplained variation. These three sources of variance (total, regression, and residual) are identified in the first column of the spreadsheet ANOVA table. The column headed "*df*" refers to the degrees of freedom associated with each category. The total number of degrees of freedom is $n - 1$. The number of degrees of freedom in the regression is 1 because there is only one independent variable. The number of degrees of freedom associated with the error term is $n - 2$. The term SS located in the middle of the ANOVA table refers to the sum of squares. You should note that the total degrees of freedom are equal to the sum of the regression and residual (error) degrees of freedom, and the total sum of squares is equal to the sum of the regression and residual (error) sum of squares. This is true for any ANOVA table.

	A	B	C	D	E	F	G	H	I	J
1	**Sales Representive**	**Sales Calls (x)**	**Copiers Sold (y)**		**SUMMARY OUTPUT**					
2	Brian Virost	96	41		***Regression Statistics***					
3	Carlos Ramirez	40	41		Multiple R	0.865				
4	Carol Saia	104	51		R Square	0.748				
5	Greg Fish	128	60		Adjusted R Square	0.728				
6	Jeff Hall	164	61		Standard Error	6.720				
7	Mark Reynolds	76	29		Observations	15				
8	Meryl Rumsey	72	39							
9	Mike Kiel	80	50		**ANOVA**					
10	Ray Snarsky	36	28			**df**	**SS**	**MS**	**F**	**Significance F**
11	Rich Niles	84	43		Regression	1	1738.890	1738.890	38.503	0.000
12	Ron Broderick	180	70		Residual	13	587.110	45.162		
13	Sal Spina	132	56		Total	14	2326			
14	Sani Jones	120	45							
15	Susan Welch	44	31			***Coefficients***	***Standard Error***	***t Stat***	***P-value***	
16	Tom Keller	84	30		Intercept	19.980	4.390	4.552	0.001	
17					Sales Calls (x)	0.261	0.042	6.205	0.000	

The ANOVA sum of squares are:

$$\text{Regression Sum of Squares} = \text{SSR} = \Sigma(\hat{y} - \bar{y})^2 = 1738.89$$

$$\text{Residual or Error Sum of Squares} = \text{SSE} = \Sigma(y - \hat{y})^2 = 587.11$$

$$\text{Total Sum of Squares} = \text{SS Total} = \Sigma(y - \bar{y})^2 = 2326.0$$

Recall that the coefficient of determination is defined as the percentage of the total variation (SS Total) explained by the regression equation (SSR). Using the ANOVA table, the reported value of R-square can be validated.

COEFFICIENT OF DETERMINATION

$$r^2 = \frac{\text{SSR}}{\text{SS Total}} = 1 - \frac{\text{SSE}}{\text{SS Total}} \qquad \textbf{[13–8]}$$

Using the values from the ANOVA table, the coefficient of determination is 1738.89/2326.0 = 0.748. Therefore, the more variation of the dependent variable (SS Total) explained by the independent variable (SSR), the higher the coefficient of determination.

We can also express the coefficient of determination in terms of the error or residual variation:

$$r^2 = 1 - \frac{\text{SSE}}{\text{SS Total}} = 1 - \frac{587.11}{2326.0} = 1 - 0.252 = 0.748$$

As illustrated in formula 13–8, the coefficient of determination and the residual or error sum of squares are inversely related. The higher the unexplained or error variation as a percentage of the total variation, the lower is the coefficient of determination. In this case, 25.2% of the total variation in the dependent variable is error or residual variation.

The final observation that relates the correlation coefficient, the coefficient of determination, and the standard error of estimate is to show the relationship between the standard error of estimate and SSE. By substituting [SSE Residual or Error Sum of Squares = SSE = $\Sigma(y - \hat{y})^2$] into the formula for the standard error of estimate, we find:

STANDARD ERROR OF ESTIMATE

$$s_{y \cdot x} = \sqrt{\frac{\text{SSE}}{n - 2}} \qquad \textbf{[13–9]}$$

Note that $s_{y \cdot x}$ can also be computed using the residual mean square from the ANOVA table.

STANDARD ERROR OF THE ESTIMATE

$$s_{y \cdot x} = \sqrt{\textit{Residual mean square}} \qquad \textbf{[13–10]}$$

In sum, regression analysis provides two statistics to evaluate the predictive ability of a regression equation: the standard error of the estimate and the coefficient of determination. When reporting the results of a regression analysis, the findings must be clearly explained, especially when using the results to make predictions of the dependent variable. The report must always include a statement regarding the coefficient of determination so that the relative precision of the prediction is known to the reader of the report. Objective reporting of statistical analysis is required so that the readers can make their own decisions.

EXERCISES

29. Given the following ANOVA table:

Source	*DF*	SS	MS	*F*
Regression	1	1000.0	1000.0	26.00
Error	13	500.0	38.46	
Total	14	1500.0		

a. Determine the coefficient of determination.

b. Assuming a direct relationship between the variables, what is the correlation coefficient?

c. Determine the standard error of estimate.

30. On the first statistics exam, the coefficient of determination between the hours studied and the grade earned was 80%. The standard error of estimate was 10. There were 20 students in the class. Develop an ANOVA table for the regression analysis of hours studied as a predictor of the grade earned on the first statistics exam.

LO13-6

Calculate and interpret confidence and prediction intervals.

INTERVAL ESTIMATES OF PREDICTION

The standard error of estimate and the coefficient of determination are two statistics that provide an overall evaluation of the ability of a regression equation to predict a dependent variable. Another way to report the ability of a regression equation to predict is specific to a stated value of the independent variable. For example, we can predict the number of copiers sold (y) for a selected value of number of sales calls made (x). In fact, we can calculate a confidence interval for the predicted value of the dependent variable for a selected value of the independent variable.

STATISTICS IN ACTION

Studies indicate that for both men and women, those who are considered good looking earn higher wages than those who are not. In addition, for men there is a correlation between height and salary. For each additional inch of height, a man can expect to earn an additional $250 per year. So a man 6′6″ tall receives a $3,000 "stature" bonus over his 5′6″ counterpart. Being overweight or underweight is also related to earnings, particularly among women. A study of young women showed the heaviest 10% earned about 6% less than their lighter counterparts.

Assumptions Underlying Linear Regression

Before we present the confidence intervals, the assumptions for properly applying linear regression should be reviewed. Chart 13–13 illustrates these assumptions.

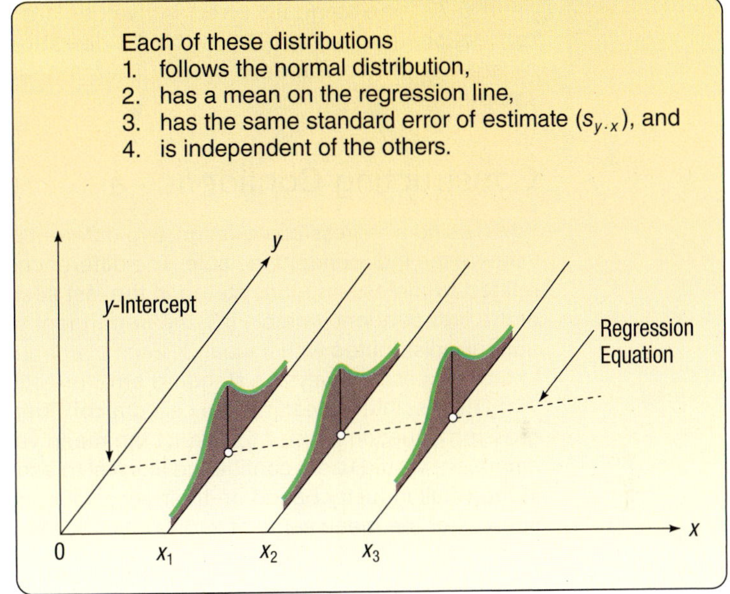

CHART 13–13 Regression Assumptions Shown Graphically

1. For each value of x, there are corresponding y values. These y values follow the normal distribution.
2. The means of these normal distributions lie on the regression line.
3. The standard deviations of these normal distributions are all the same. The best estimate we have of this common standard deviation is the standard error of estimate ($s_{y \cdot x}$).
4. The y values are statistically independent. This means that in selecting a sample, a particular x does not depend on any other value of x. This assumption is particularly important when data are collected over a period of time. In such situations, the errors for a particular time period are often correlated with those of other time periods.

Recall from Chapter 7 that if the values follow a normal distribution, then the mean plus or minus one standard deviation will encompass 68% of the observations, the mean plus or minus two standard deviations will encompass 95% of the observations, and the mean plus or minus three standard deviations will encompass virtually all of the observations. The same relationship exists between the predicted values $\hat{y}$ and the standard error of estimate ($s_{y \cdot x}$).

1. $\hat{y} \pm s_{y \cdot x}$ will include the middle 68% of the observations.
2. $\hat{y} \pm 2s_{y \cdot x}$ will include the middle 95% of the observations.
3. $\hat{y} \pm 3s_{y \cdot x}$ will include virtually all the observations.

We can now relate these assumptions to North American Copier Sales, where we studied the relationship between the number of sales calls and the number of copiers sold. If we drew a parallel line 6.72 units above the regression line and another 6.72 units below the regression line, about 68% of the points would fall between the two lines. Similarly, a line 13.44 [$2s_{y \cdot x} = 2(6.72)$] units above the regression line and another 13.44 units below the regression line should include about 95% of the data values.

As a rough check, refer to column E in the Excel spreadsheet appearing on page 456. Four of the 15 deviations exceed one standard error of estimate. That is, the deviations of Carlos Ramirez, Mark Reynolds, Mike Keil, and Tom Keller all exceed 6.72 (one standard error). All values are less than 13.44 units away from the regression line. In short, 11 of the 15 deviations are within one standard error and all are within two standard errors. That is a fairly good result for a relatively small sample.

Constructing Confidence and Prediction Intervals

When using a regression equation, two different predictions can be made for a selected value of the independent variable. The differences are subtle but very important and are related to the assumptions stated in the last section. Recall that for any selected value of the independent variable (*X*), the dependent variable (*Y*) is a random variable that is normally distributed with a mean $\hat{Y}$. Each distribution of *Y* has a standard deviation equal to the regression analysis's standard error of estimate.

The first interval estimate is called a **confidence interval.** This is used when the regression equation is used to predict the mean value of *Y* for a given value of *x*. For example, we would use a confidence interval to estimate the mean salary of all executives in the retail industry based on their years of experience. To determine the confidence interval for the mean value of *y* for a given *x*, the formula is:

CONFIDENCE INTERVAL FOR THE MEAN OF Y, GIVEN X

$$\hat{y} \pm ts_{y \cdot x}\sqrt{\frac{1}{n} + \frac{(x - \bar{x})^2}{\Sigma(x - \bar{x})^2}} \qquad \textbf{[13–11]}$$

The second interval estimate is called a prediction interval. This is used when the regression equation is used to predict an individual *y* for a given value of *x*. For example, we would estimate the salary of a particular retail executive who has 20 years of experience. To calculate a prediction interval, formula 13-11 is modified by adding a 1 under the radical. To determine the prediction interval for an estimate of an individual for a given *x*, the formula is:

PREDICTION INTERVAL FOR Y, GIVEN X

$$\hat{y} \pm ts_{y \cdot x}\sqrt{1 + \frac{1}{n} + \frac{(x - \bar{x})^2}{\Sigma(x - \bar{x})^2}} \qquad \textbf{[13–12]}$$

EXAMPLE

We return to the North American Copier Sales illustration. Determine a 95% confidence interval for all sales representatives who make 50 calls, and determine a prediction interval for Sheila Baker, a West Coast sales representative who made 50 calls.

SOLUTION

We use formula (13–11) to determine a confidence level. Table 13–4 includes the necessary totals and a repeat of the information of Table 13–2.

TABLE 13–4 Determining Confidence and Prediction Intervals

Sales Representative	Sales Calls (x)	Copiers Sold (y)	$(x - \bar{x})$	$(x - \bar{x})^2$
Brian Virost	96	41	0	0
Carlos Ramirez	40	41	−56	3,136
Carol Saia	104	51	8	64
Greg Fish	128	60	32	1,024
Jeff Hall	164	61	68	4,624
Mark Reynolds	76	29	−20	400
Meryl Rumsey	72	39	−24	576
Mike Kiel	80	50	−16	256
Ray Snarsky	36	28	−60	3,600
Rich Niles	84	43	−12	144
Ron Broderick	180	70	84	7,056
Sal Spina	132	56	36	1,296
Sani Jones	120	45	24	576
Susan Welch	44	31	−52	2,704
Tom Keller	84	30	−12	144
Total	1440	675	0	25,600

The first step is to determine the number of copiers we expect a sales representative to sell if he or she makes 50 calls. It is 33.0032, found by

$$\hat{y} = 19.9632 + 0.2608x = 19.9632 + 0.2608\,(50) = 33.0032$$

To find the t value, we need to first know the number of degrees of freedom. In this case, the degrees of freedom are $n - 2 = 15 - 2 = 13$. We set the confidence level at 95%. To find the value of t, move down the left-hand column of Appendix B.5 to 13 degrees of freedom, then move across to the column with the 95% level of confidence. The value of t is 2.160.

In the previous section, we calculated the standard error of estimate to be 6.720. We let $x = 50$, and from Table 13–4, the mean number of sales calls is 96.0 (1440/15) and $\Sigma(x - \bar{x})^2 = 25,600$ Inserting these values in formula (13–11), we can determine the confidence interval.

$$\text{Confidence Interval} = \hat{y} \pm ts_{y \cdot x}\sqrt{\frac{1}{n} + \frac{(x - \bar{x})^2}{\Sigma(x - \bar{x})^2}}$$

$$= 33.0032 \pm 2.160(6.720)\sqrt{\frac{1}{15} + \frac{(50 - 96)^2}{25,600}}$$

$$= 33.0032 \pm 5.6090$$

Thus, the 95% confidence interval for all sales representatives who make 50 calls is from 27.3942 up to 38.6122. To interpret, let's round the values. If a sales representative makes 50 calls, he or she can expect to sell 33 copiers. It is likely the sales will range from 27.4 to 38.6 copiers.

Suppose we want to estimate the number of copiers sold by Sheila Baker, who made 50 sales calls. Using formula (13–12), the 95% prediction interval is determined as follows:

$$\text{Prediction Interval} = \hat{y} \pm ts_{y\cdot x}\sqrt{1 + \frac{1}{n} + \frac{(x - \bar{x})^2}{\Sigma(x - \bar{x})^2}}$$

$$= 33.0032 \pm 2.160(6.720)\sqrt{1 + \frac{1}{15} + \frac{(50 - 96)^2}{25{,}600}}$$

$$= 33.0032 \pm 15.5612$$

Thus, the interval is from 17.442 up to 48.5644 copiers. We conclude that the number of office machines sold will be between about 17.4 and 48.6 for a particular sales representative, such as Sheila Baker, who makes 50 calls. This interval is quite large. It is much larger than the confidence interval for all sales representatives who made 50 calls. It is logical, however, that there should be more variation in the sales estimate for an individual than for a group.

The following Minitab graph shows the relationship between the least squares regression line (in the center), the confidence interval (shown in crimson), and the prediction interval (shown in green). The bands for the prediction interval are always further from the regression line than those for the confidence interval. Also, as the values of x move away from the mean number of calls (96) in either direction, the confidence interval and prediction interval bands widen. This is caused by the numerator of the right-hand term under the radical in formulas (13–11) and (13–12). That is, as the term increases, the widths of the confidence interval and the prediction interval also increase. To put it another way, there is less precision in our estimates as we move away, in either direction, from the mean of the independent variable.

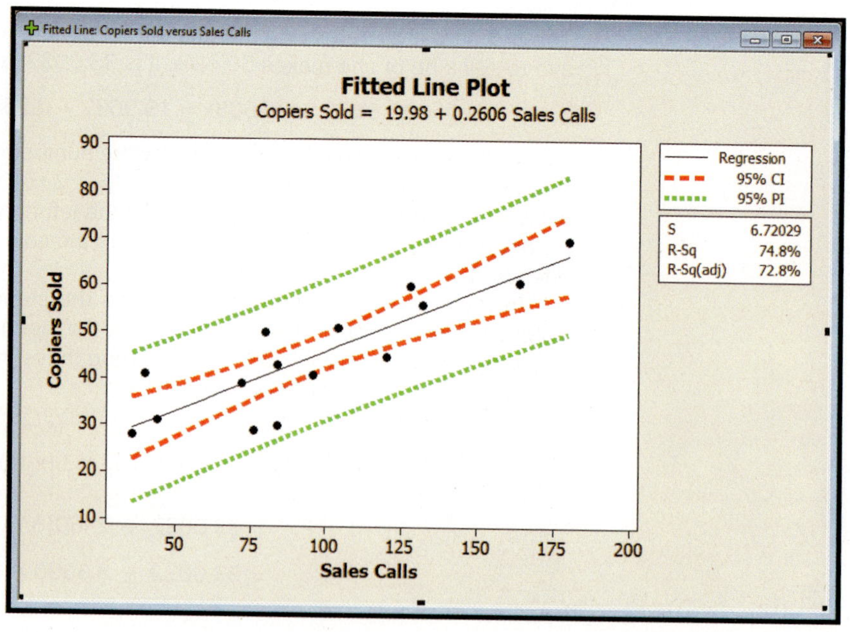

We wish to emphasize again the distinction between a confidence interval and a prediction interval. A confidence interval refers to the mean of all cases for a given value of x and is computed by formula (13–11). A prediction interval refers to a particular, single case for a given value of x and is computed using formula (13–12). The prediction interval will always be wider because of the extra 1 under the radical in the second equation.

SELF-REVIEW 13–6

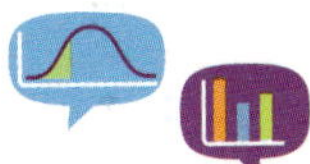

Refer to the sample data in Self-Review 13–1, where the owner of Haverty's Furniture was studying the relationship between sales and the amount spent on advertising. The advertising expense and sales revenue, both in millions of dollars, for the last 4 months are repeated below.

Month	Advertising Expense ($ million)	Sales Revenue ($ million)
July	2	7
August	1	3
September	3	8
October	4	10

The regression equation was computed to be $\hat{y} = 1.5 + 2.2x$ and the standard error 0.9487. Both variables are reported in millions of dollars. Determine the 90% confidence interval for the typical month in which $3 million was spent on advertising.

EXERCISES

31. Refer to Exercise 13.
   a. Determine the .95 confidence interval for the mean predicted when $x = 7$.
   b. Determine the .95 prediction interval for an individual predicted when $x = 7$.

32. Refer to Exercise 14.
   a. Determine the .95 confidence interval for the mean predicted when $x = 7$.
   b. Determine the .95 prediction interval for an individual predicted when $x = 7$.

33. Refer to Exercise 15.
   a. Determine the .95 confidence interval, in thousands of kilowatt-hours, for the mean of all six-room homes.
   b. Determine the .95 prediction interval, in thousands of kilowatt-hours, for a particular six-room home.

34. Refer to Exercise 16.
   a. Determine the .95 confidence interval, in thousands of dollars, for the mean of all sales personnel who make 40 contacts.
   b. Determine the .95 prediction interval, in thousands of dollars, for a particular salesperson who makes 40 contacts.

TRANSFORMING DATA

LO13-7
Use a log function to transform a nonlinear relationship.

Regression analysis describes the relationship between two variables. A requirement is that this relationship be linear. The same is true of the correlation coefficient. It measures the strength of a linear relationship between two variables. But what if the relationship is not linear? The remedy is to rescale one or both of the variables so the new relationship is linear. For example, instead of using the actual values of the dependent variable, y, we would create a new dependent variable by computing the log to the base 10 of *y*, Log(*y*). This calculation is called a transformation. Other common transformations include taking the square root, taking the reciprocal, or squaring one or both of the variables.

Thus, two variables could be closely related, but their relationship is not linear. Be cautious when you are interpreting the correlation coefficient or a regression equation. These statistics may indicate there is no linear relationship, but there could be a relationship of some other nonlinear or curvilinear form. The following example explains the details.

EXAMPLE

GroceryLand Supermarkets is a regional grocery chain with over 300 stores located in the midwestern United States. The corporate director of marketing for GroceryLand wishes to study the effect of price on the weekly sales of two-liter bottles of their private-brand diet cola. The objectives of the study are:

1. To determine whether there is a relationship between selling price and weekly sales. Is this relationship direct or indirect? Is it strong or weak?
2. To determine the effect of price increases or decreases on sales. Can we effectively forecast sales based on the price?

SOLUTION

To begin the project, the marketing director meets with the vice president of sales and other company staff members. They decide that it would be reasonable to price the two-liter bottle of their private-brand diet cola from $0.50 up to $2.00. To collect the data needed to analyze the relationship between price and sales, the marketing director selects a random sample of 20 stores and then randomly assigns a selling price for the two-liter bottle of diet cola between $0.50 and $2.00 to each selected store. The director contacts each of the 20 store managers included in the study to tell them the selling price and ask them to report the sales for the product at the end of the week. The results are reported below. For example, store number A-17 sold 181 two-liter bottles of diet cola at $0.50 each.

GroceryLand Sales and Price Data			GroceryLand Sales and Price Data		
Store Number	**Price**	**Sales**	**Store Number**	**Price**	**Sales**
A-17	0.50	181	A-30	0.76	91
A-121	1.35	33	A-127	1.79	13
A-227	0.79	91	A-266	1.57	22
A-135	1.71	13	A-117	1.27	34
A-6	1.38	34	A-132	0.96	74
A-282	1.22	47	A-120	0.52	164
A-172	1.03	73	A-272	0.64	129
A-296	1.84	11	A-120	1.05	55
A-143	1.73	15	A-194	0.72	107
A-66	1.62	20	A-105	0.75	119

To examine the relationship between Price and Sales, we use regression analysis setting *Price* as the independent variable and *Sales* as the dependent variable. The analysis will provide important information about the relationship between the variables. The analysis is summarized in the following Minitab output.

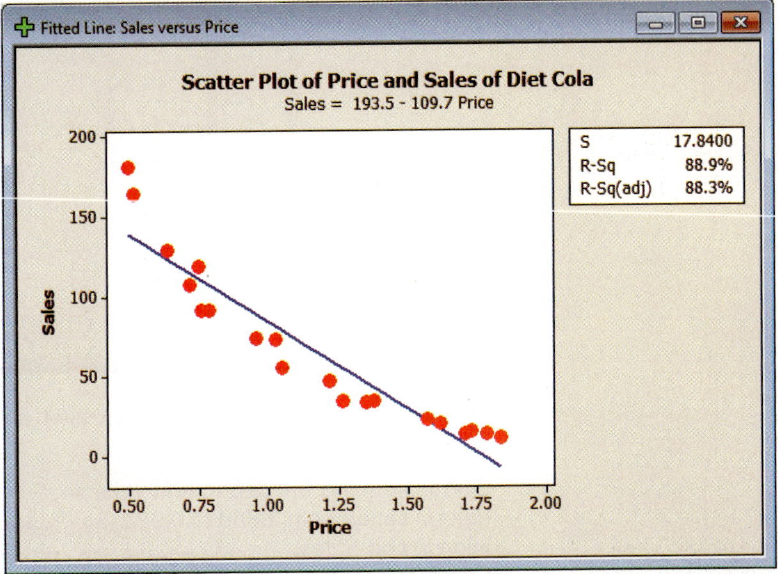

From the output, we can make these conclusions:

1. The relationship between the two variables is inverse or indirect. As the *Price* of the cola increases, the *Sales* of the product decreases. Given basic economic theory of price and demand, this is expected.
2. There is a strong relationship between the two variables. The coefficient of determination is 88.9%. So 88.9% of the variation in *Sales* is accounted for by the variation in *Price*. From the coefficient of determination, we can compute the correlation coefficient as the square root of the coefficient of determination. The correlation coefficient is the square root of 0.889, or 0.943. The sign of the correlation coefficient is negative because sales are inversely related to price. Therefore, the correlation coefficient is −0.943.
3. Before continuing our summary of conclusions, we should look carefully at the scatter diagram and the plot of the regression line. The assumption of a linear relationship is tenuous. If the relationship is linear, the data points should be distributed both above and below the line over the entire range of the independent variable. However, for the highest and lowest prices, the data points are above the regression line. For the selling prices in the middle, most of the data points are below the regression line. So the linear regression equation does not effectively describe the relationship between *Price* and *Sales*. A transformation of the data is needed to create a linear relationship.

By transforming one of the variables, we may be able to change the nonlinear relationship between the variables to a linear relationship. Of the possible choices, the director of marketing decides to transform the dependent variable, *Sales*, by taking the logarithm to the base 10 of each *Sales* value. Note the new variable, *Log-Sales*, in the following analysis. Now, the regression analysis uses *Log-Sales* as the dependent variable and *Price* as the independent variable. This analysis is reported below.

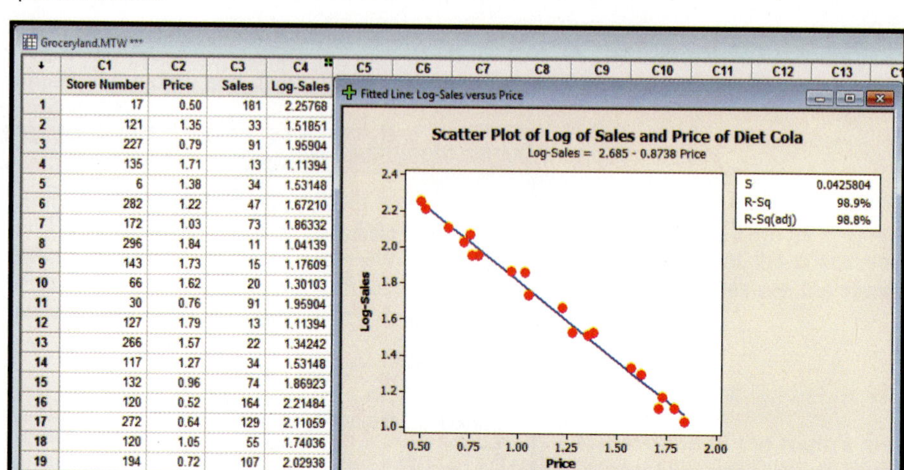

	C1 Store Number	C2 Price	C3 Sales	C4 Log-Sales
1	17	0.50	181	2.25768
2	121	1.35	33	1.51851
3	227	0.79	91	1.95904
4	135	1.71	13	1.11394
5	6	1.38	34	1.53148
6	282	1.22	47	1.67210
7	172	1.03	73	1.86332
8	296	1.84	11	1.04139
9	143	1.73	15	1.17609
10	66	1.62	20	1.30103
11	30	0.76	91	1.95904
12	127	1.79	13	1.11394
13	266	1.57	22	1.34242
14	117	1.27	34	1.53148
15	132	0.96	74	1.86923
16	120	0.52	164	2.21484
17	272	0.64	129	2.11059
18	120	1.05	55	1.74036
19	194	0.72	107	2.02938
20	105	0.75	119	2.07555

What can we conclude from the regression analysis using the transformation of the dependent variable *Sales?*

1. By transforming the dependent variable, *Sales,* we increase the coefficient of determination from 0.889 to 0.989. So *Price* now explains nearly all of the variation in *Log-Sales.*
2. Compare this result with the scatter diagram before we transformed the dependent variable. The transformed data seem to fit the linear relationship requirement much better. Observe that the data points are both above and below the regression line over the range of *Price.*
3. The regression equation is $\hat{y} = 2.685 - 0.8738x$. The sign of the slope value is negative, confirming the inverse association between the variables. We can use the new equation to estimate sales and study the effect of changes in price. For example, if we decided to sell the two-liter bottle of diet cola for \$1.25, the predicted *Log-Sales* is:

$$\hat{y} = 2.685 - 0.8738x = 2.685 - 0.8738\,(1.25) = 1.593$$

Remember that the regression equation now predicts the log, base10, of *Sales.* Therefore, we must undo the transformation by taking the antilog of 1.593, which is $10^{1.593}$, or 39.174. So, if we price the two-liter diet cola product at \$1.25, the predicted weekly sales are 39 bottles. If we increase the price to \$2.00, the regression equation would predict a value of .9374. Taking the antilog, $10^{.9374}$, the predicted sales decrease to 8.658, or, rounding, 9 two-liter bottles per week. Clearly, as price increases, sales decrease. This relationship will be very helpful to GroceryLand when making pricing decisions for this product.

EXERCISES

35. **FILE** Given the following sample of five observations, develop a scatter diagram, using *x* as the independent variable and *y* as the dependent variable, and compute the correlation coefficient. Does the relationship between the variables appear to be linear? Try squaring the *x* variable and then develop a scatter diagram and determine the correlation coefficient. Summarize your analysis.

x	−8	−16	12	2	18
y	58	247	153	3	341

36. **FILE** Every April, The Masters—one of the most prestigious golf tournaments on the PGA golf tour—is played in Augusta, Georgia. In 2016, 55 players received prize money. The 2016 winner, Danny Willett, earned a prize of $1,800,000. Jordan Spieth and Lee Westwood tied for second place, earning $880,000. Two amateur players finished "in the money" but they could not accept the prize money. They are not included in the data. The data are briefly summarized below. Each player has three corresponding variables: finishing position, score, and prize (in dollars). We want to study the relationship between score and prize.

Position	Player	Score	Prize
1	Danny Willett	283	$1,800,000
2(tied)	Jordan Spieth	286	$880,000
2(tied)	Lee Westwood	286	$880,000
4(tied)	Paul Casey	287	$413,333
4(tied)	J.B. Holmes	287	$413,333
4(tied)	Dustin Johnson	287	$413,333
..	..	..	..
..	..	..	..
..	..	..	..
52(tied)	Keegan Bradley	301	$24,900
52(tied)	Larry Mize	301	$24,900
54	Hunter Mahan	302	$24,000
55(tied)	Kevin Na	303	$23,400
55(tied)	Cameron Smith	303	$23,400
57	Thongchai Jaidee	307	$23,000

a. Using *Score* as the independent variable and *Prize* as the dependent variable, develop a scatter diagram. Does the relationship appear to be linear? Does it seem reasonable that as *Score* increases the *Prize* decreases?
b. What percentage of the variation in the dependent variable, *Prize,* is accounted for by the independent variable, *Score*?
c. Calculate a new variable, *Log-Prize*, computing the log to the base 10 of *Prize*. Draw a scatter diagram with *Log-Prize* as the dependent variable and *Score* as the independent variable.
d. Develop a regression equation and compute the coefficient of determination using *Log-Prize* as the dependent variable.
e. Compare the coefficient of determination in parts (b) and (d). What do you conclude?
f. Write out the regression equation developed in part (d). If a player shot an even par score of 288 for the four rounds, how much would you expect that player to earn?

CHAPTER SUMMARY

I. A scatter diagram is a graphic tool used to portray the relationship between two variables.
  A. The dependent variable is scaled on the *Y*-axis and is the variable being estimated.
  B. The independent variable is scaled on the *X*-axis and is the variable used as the predictor.

II. The correlation coefficient measures the strength of the linear association between two variables.
  A. Both variables must be at least the interval scale of measurement.
  B. The correlation coefficient can range from −1.00 to 1.00.

C. If the correlation between the two variables is 0, there is no association between them.
D. A value of 1.00 indicates perfect positive correlation, and a value of −1.00 indicates perfect negative correlation.
E. A positive sign means there is a direct relationship between the variables, and a negative sign means there is an inverse relationship.
F. It is designated by the letter *r* and found by the following equation:

$$r = \frac{\Sigma(x - \bar{x})(y - \bar{y})}{(n - 1)s_x s_y} \quad \textbf{[13–1]}$$

G. To test a hypothesis that a population correlation is different from 0, we use the following statistic:

$$t = \frac{r\sqrt{n - 2}}{\sqrt{1 - r^2}} \quad \text{with } n - 2 \text{ degrees of freedom} \quad \textbf{[13–2]}$$

III. In regression analysis, we estimate one variable based on another variable.
A. The variable being estimated is the dependent variable.
B. The variable used to make the estimate or predict the value is the independent variable.
1. The relationship between the variables is linear.
2. Both the independent and the dependent variables must be interval or ratio scale.
3. The least squares criterion is used to determine the regression equation.
IV. The least squares regression line is of the form $\hat{y} = a + bx$
A. $\hat{y}$ is the estimated value of *y* for a selected value of *x*.
B. *a* is the constant or intercept.
1. It is the value of $\hat{y}$ when $x = 0$.
2. *a* is computed using the following equation.

$$a = \bar{y} - b\bar{x} \quad \textbf{[13–5]}$$

C. *b* is the slope of the fitted line.
1. It shows the amount of change in $\hat{y}$ for a change of one unit in *x*.
2. A positive value for *b* indicates a direct relationship between the two variables. A negative value indicates an inverse relationship.
3. The sign of *b* and the sign of *r*, the correlation coefficient, are always the same.
4. *b* is computed using the following equation.

$$b = r\left(\frac{s_y}{s_x}\right) \quad \textbf{[13–4]}$$

D. *x* is the value of the independent variable.
V. For a regression equation, the slope is tested for significance.
A. We test the hypothesis that the slope of the line in the population is 0.
1. If we do not reject the null hypothesis, we conclude there is no relationship between the two variables.
2. The test is equivalent to the test for the correlation coefficient.
B. When testing the null hypothesis about the slope, the test statistic is with $n - 2$ degrees of freedom:

$$t = \frac{b - 0}{s_b} \quad \textbf{[13–6]}$$

VI. The standard error of estimate measures the variation around the regression line.
A. It is in the same units as the dependent variable.
B. It is based on squared deviations from the regression line.
C. Small values indicate that the points cluster closely about the regression line.
D. It is computed using the following formula.

$$s_{y \cdot x} = \sqrt{\frac{\Sigma(y - \hat{y})^2}{n - 2}} \quad \textbf{[13–7]}$$

VII. The coefficient of determination is the proportion of the variation of a dependent variable explained by the independent variable.

A. It ranges from 0 to 1.0.

B. It is the square of the correlation coefficient.

C. It is found from the following formula.

$$r^2 = \frac{\text{SSR}}{\text{SS Total}} = 1 - \frac{\text{SSE}}{\text{SS Total}} \qquad \textbf{[13–8]}$$

VIII. Inference about linear regression is based on the following assumptions.

A. For a given value of *x*, the values of *Y* are normally distributed about the line of regression.

B. The standard deviation of each of the normal distributions is the same for all values of *x* and is estimated by the standard error of estimate.

C. The deviations from the regression line are independent, with no pattern to the size or direction.

IX. There are two types of interval estimates.

A. In a confidence interval, the mean value of *y* is estimated for a given value of *x*.

1. It is computed from the following formula.

$$\hat{y} \pm t s_{y \cdot x}\sqrt{\frac{1}{n} + \frac{(x - \bar{x})^2}{\Sigma(x - \bar{x})^2}} \qquad \textbf{[13–11]}$$

2. The width of the interval is affected by the level of confidence, the size of the standard error of estimate, and the size of the sample, as well as the value of the independent variable.

B. In a prediction interval, the individual value of *y* is estimated for a given value of *x*.

1. It is computed from the following formula.

$$\hat{y} \pm t s_{y \cdot x}\sqrt{1 + \frac{1}{n} + \frac{(x - \bar{x})^2}{\Sigma(x - \bar{x})^2}} \qquad \textbf{[13–12]}$$

2. The difference between formulas (13–11) and (13–12) is the 1 under the radical.

a. The prediction interval will be wider than the confidence interval.

b. The prediction interval is also based on the level of confidence, the size of the standard error of estimate, the size of the sample, and the value of the independent variable.

PRONUNCIATION KEY

SYMBOL	MEANING	PRONUNCIATION
Σxy	Sum of the products of *x* and *y*	*Sum x y*
ρ	Correlation coefficient in the population	*Rho*
$\hat{y}$	Estimated value of *Y*	*y hat*
$s_{y \cdot x}$	Standard error of estimate	*s sub y dot x*
r^2	Coefficient of determination	*r square*

CHAPTER EXERCISES

37. A regional commuter airline selected a random sample of 25 flights and found that the correlation between the number of passengers and the total weight, in pounds, of luggage stored in the luggage compartment is 0.94. Using the .05 significance level, can we conclude that there is a positive association between the two variables?

38. A sociologist claims that the success of students in college (measured by their GPA) is related to their family's income. For a sample of 20 students, the correlation coefficient is 0.40. Using the 0.01 significance level, can we conclude that there is a positive correlation between the variables?

39. An Environmental Protection Agency study of 12 automobiles revealed a correlation of 0.47 between engine size and emissions. At the .01 significance level, can we conclude that there is a positive association between these variables? What is the *p*-value? Interpret.

40. FILE A suburban hotel derives its revenue from its hotel and restaurant operations. The owners are interested in the relationship between the number of rooms occupied on a nightly basis and the revenue per day in the restaurant. Below is a sample of 25 days (Monday through Thursday) from last year showing the restaurant income and number of rooms occupied.

Day	Revenue	Occupied	Day	Revenue	Occupied
1	$1,452	23	14	$1,425	27
2	1,361	47	15	1,445	34
3	1,426	21	16	1,439	15
4	1,470	39	17	1,348	19
5	1,456	37	18	1,450	38
6	1,430	29	19	1,431	44
7	1,354	23	20	1,446	47
8	1,442	44	21	1,485	43
9	1,394	45	22	1,405	38
10	1,459	16	23	1,461	51
11	1,399	30	24	1,490	61
12	1,458	42	25	1,426	39
13	1,537	54			

Use a statistical software package to answer the following questions.

a. Does the revenue seem to increase as the number of occupied rooms increases? Draw a scatter diagram to support your conclusion.

b. Determine the correlation coefficient between the two variables. Interpret the value.

c. Is it reasonable to conclude that there is a positive relationship between revenue and occupied rooms? Use the .10 significance level.

d. What percent of the variation in revenue in the restaurant is accounted for by the number of rooms occupied?

41. FILE The table below shows the number of cars (in millions) sold in the United States for various years and the percent of those cars manufactured by GM.

Year	Cars Sold (millions)	Percent GM	Year	Cars Sold (millions)	Percent GM
1950	6.0	50.2	1985	15.4	40.1
1955	7.8	50.4	1990	13.5	36.0
1960	7.3	44.0	1995	15.5	31.7
1965	10.3	49.9	2000	17.4	28.6
1970	10.1	39.5	2005	16.9	26.9
1975	10.8	43.1	2010	11.6	19.1
1980	11.5	44.0	2015	17.5	17.6

Use a statistical software package to answer the following questions.

a. Is the number of cars sold directly or indirectly related to GM's percentage of the market? Draw a scatter diagram to show your conclusion.

b. Determine the correlation coefficient between the two variables. Interpret the value.

c. Is it reasonable to conclude that there is a negative association between the two variables? Use the .01 significance level.

d. How much of the variation in GM's market share is accounted for by the variation in cars sold?

42. For a sample of 40 large U.S. cities, the correlation between the mean number of square feet per office worker and the mean monthly rental rate in the central business district is −0.363. At the .05 significance level, can we conclude that there is a negative association between the two variables.

43. FILE For each of the 32 National Football League teams, the numbers of points scored and allowed during the 2016 season are shown below.

TEAM	Conference	PTS Scored	PTS Allowed	TEAM	Conference	PTS Scored	PTS Allowed
Baltimore	AFC	343	321	Arizona	NFC	418	362
Buffalo	AFC	399	378	Atlanta	NFC	540	406
Cincinnati	AFC	325	315	Carolina	NFC	369	402
Cleveland	AFC	264	452	Chicago	NFC	279	399
Denver	AFC	333	297	Dallas	NFC	421	306
Houston	AFC	279	328	Detroit	NFC	346	358
Indianapolis	AFC	411	392	Green Bay	NFC	432	388
Jacksonville	AFC	318	400	Los Angeles	NFC	224	394
Kansas City	AFC	389	311	Minnesota	NFC	327	307
Miami	AFC	363	380	NY Giants	NFC	469	454
New England	AFC	441	250	New Orleans	NFC	310	284
NY Jets	AFC	275	409	Philadelphia	NFC	367	331
Oakland	AFC	416	385	San Francisco	NFC	309	480
Pittsburgh	AFC	399	327	Seattle	NFC	354	292
San Diego	AFC	410	423	Tampa Bay	NFC	354	369
Tennessee	AFC	381	378	Washington	NFC	396	383

Assuming these are sample data, answer the following questions. You may use statistical software to assist you.

a. What is the correlation coefficient between these variables? Are you surprised the association is negative? Interpret your results.
b. Find the coefficient of determination. What does it say about the relationship?
c. At the .05 significance level, can you conclude there is a negative association between "points scored" and "points allowed"?
d. At the .05 significance level, can you conclude there is a negative association between "points scored" and "points allowed" for each conference?

44. FILE The Cotton Mill is an upscale chain of women's clothing stores, located primarily in the southwest United States. Due to recent success, The Cotton Mill's top management is planning to expand by locating new stores in other regions of the country. The director of planning has been asked to study the relationship between yearly sales and the store size. As part of the study, the director selects a sample of 25 stores and determines the size of the store in square feet and the sales for last year. The sample data follow. The use of statistical software is suggested.

Store Size (thousands of square feet)	Sales (millions $)	Store Size (thousands of square feet)	Sales (millions $)
3.7	9.18	0.4	0.55
2.0	4.58	4.2	7.56
5.0	8.22	3.1	2.23
0.7	1.45	2.6	4.49
2.6	6.51	5.2	9.90
2.9	2.82	3.3	8.93
5.2	10.45	3.2	7.60
5.9	9.94	4.9	3.71
3.0	4.43	5.5	5.47
2.4	4.75	2.9	8.22
2.4	7.30	2.2	7.17
0.5	3.33	2.3	4.35
5.0	6.76		

a. Draw a scatter diagram. Use store size as the independent variable. Does there appear to be a relationship between the two variables. Is it positive or negative?
b. Determine the correlation coefficient and the coefficient of determination. Is the relationship strong or weak? Why?
c. At the .05 significance level, can we conclude there is a significant positive correlation?

45. FILE The manufacturer of Cardio Glide exercise equipment wants to study the relationship between the number of months since the glide was purchased and the time, in hours, the equipment was used last week.

Person	Months Owned	Hours Exercised	Person	Months Owned	Hours Exercised
Rupple	12	4	Massa	2	8
Hall	2	10	Sass	8	3
Bennett	6	8	Karl	4	8
Longnecker	9	5	Malrooney	10	2
Phillips	7	5	Veights	5	5

a. Plot the information on a scatter diagram. Let hours of exercise be the dependent variable. Comment on the graph.
b. Determine the correlation coefficient. Interpret.
c. At the .01 significance level, can we conclude that there is a negative association between the variables?

46. The following regression equation was computed from a sample of 20 observations:

$$\hat{y} = 15 - 5x$$

SSE was found to be 100 and SS total, 400.
a. Determine the standard error of estimate.
b. Determine the coefficient of determination.
c. Determine the correlation coefficient. (Caution: Watch the sign!)

47. FILE City planners believe that larger cities are populated by older residents. To investigate the relationship, data on population and median age in 10 large cities were collected.

City	Population City (in millions)	Median Age
Chicago, IL	2.833	31.5
Dallas, TX	1.233	30.5
Houston, TX	2.144	30.9
Los Angeles, CA	3.849	31.6
New York, NY	8.214	34.2
Philadelphia, PA	1.448	34.2
Phoenix, AZ	1.513	30.7
San Antonio, TX	1.297	31.7
San Diego, CA	1.257	32.5
San Jose, CA	0.930	32.6

a. Plot these data on a scatter diagram with median age as the dependent variable.
b. Find the correlation coefficient.
c. A regression analysis was performed and the resulting regression equation is Median Age = 31.4 + 0.272 Population. Interpret the meaning of the slope.
d. Estimate the median age for a city of 2.5 million people.
e. Here is a portion of the regression software output. What does it tell you?

```
Predictor        Coef    SE Coef       T        P
Constant      31.3672     0.6158   50.94    0.000
Population     0.2722     0.1901    1.43    0.190
```

f. Using the .10 significance level, test the significance of the slope. Interpret the result. Is there a significant relationship between the two variables?

48. **FILE** Emily Smith decides to buy a fuel-efficient used car. Here are several vehicles she is considering, with the estimated cost to purchase and the age of the vehicle.

Vehicle	Estimated Cost	Age
Honda Insight	$5,555	8
Toyota Prius	$17,888	3
Toyota Prius	$9,963	6
Toyota Echo	$6,793	5
Honda Civic Hybrid	$10,774	5
Honda Civic Hybrid	$16,310	2
Chevrolet Cruz	$2,475	8
Mazda3	$2,808	10
Toyota Corolla	$7,073	9
Acura Integra	$8,978	8
Scion xB	$11,213	2
Scion xA	$9,463	3
Mazda3	$15,055	2
Mini Cooper	$20,705	2

a. Plot these data on a scatter diagram with estimated cost as the dependent variable.
b. Find the correlation coefficient.
c. A regression analysis was performed and the resulting regression equation is Estimated Cost = 18358 − 1534 Age. Interpret the meaning of the slope.
d. Estimate the cost of a five-year-old car.
e. Here is a portion of the regression software output. What does it tell you?

```
Predictor        Coef     SE Coef        T        P
Constant        18358        1817    10.10    0.000
Age           -1533.6       306.3    -5.01    0.000
```

f. Using the .10 significance level, test the significance of the slope. Interpret the result. Is there a significant relationship between the two variables?

49. **FILE** The National Highway Association is studying the relationship between the number of bidders on a highway project and the winning (lowest) bid for the project. Of particular interest is whether the number of bidders increases or decreases the amount of the winning bid.

Project	Number of Bidders, x	Winning Bid ($ millions), y	Project	Number of Bidders, x	Winning Bid ($ millions), y
1	9	5.1	9	6	10.3
2	9	8.0	10	6	8.0
3	3	9.7	11	4	8.8
4	10	7.8	12	7	9.4
5	5	7.7	13	7	8.6
6	10	5.5	14	7	8.1
7	7	8.3	15	6	7.8
8	11	5.5			

a. Determine the regression equation. Interpret the equation. Do more bidders tend to increase or decrease the amount of the winning bid?
b. Estimate the amount of the winning bid if there were seven bidders.
c. A new entrance is to be constructed on the Ohio Turnpike. There are seven bidders on the project. Develop a 95% prediction interval for the winning bid.
d. Determine the coefficient of determination. Interpret its value.

50. **FILE** Mr. William Profit is studying companies going public for the first time. He is particularly interested in the relationship between the size of the offering and the price per share. A sample of 15 companies that recently went public revealed the following information.

Company	Size ($ millions), x	Price per Share, y	Company	Size ($ millions), x	Price per Share, y
1	9.0	10.8	9	160.7	11.3
2	94.4	11.3	10	96.5	10.6
3	27.3	11.2	11	83.0	10.5
4	179.2	11.1	12	23.5	10.3
5	71.9	11.1	13	58.7	10.7
6	97.9	11.2	14	93.8	11.0
7	93.5	11.0	15	34.4	10.8
8	70.0	10.7			

a. Determine the regression equation.
b. Conduct a test to determine whether the slope of the regression line is positive.
c. Determine the coefficient of determination. Do you think Mr. Profit should be satisfied with using the size of the offering as the independent variable?

51. **FILE** Bardi Trucking Co., located in Cleveland, Ohio, makes deliveries in the Great Lakes region, the Southeast, and the Northeast. Jim Bardi, the president, is studying the relationship between the distance a shipment must travel and the length of time, in days, it takes the shipment to arrive at its destination. To investigate, Mr. Bardi selected a random sample of 20 shipments made last month. Shipping distance is the independent variable and shipping time is the dependent variable. The results are as follows:

Shipment	Distance (miles)	Shipping Time (days)	Shipment	Distance (miles)	Shipping Time (days)
1	656	5	11	862	7
2	853	14	12	679	5
3	646	6	13	835	13
4	783	11	14	607	3
5	610	8	15	665	8
6	841	10	16	647	7
7	785	9	17	685	10
8	639	9	18	720	8
9	762	10	19	652	6
10	762	9	20	828	10

a. Draw a scatter diagram. Based on these data, does it appear that there is a relationship between how many miles a shipment has to go and the time it takes to arrive at its destination?
b. Determine the correlation coefficient. Can we conclude that there is a positive correlation between distance and time? Use the .05 significance level.
c. Determine and interpret the coefficient of determination.
d. Determine the standard error of estimate.
e. Would you recommend using the regression equation to predict shipping time? Why or why not.

52. **FILE** Super Markets Inc. is considering expanding into the Scottsdale, Arizona, area. You, as director of planning, must present an analysis of the proposed expansion to the operating committee of the board of directors. As a part of your proposal, you need to include information on the amount people in the region spend per month for grocery items. You would also like to include information on the relationship between the amount spent for grocery items and income. Your assistant gathered the following sample information.

Household	Amount Spent	Monthly Income
1	$ 555	$4,388
2	489	4,558
⋮	⋮	⋮
39	1,206	9,862
40	1,145	9,883

a. Let the amount spent be the dependent variable and monthly income the independent variable. Create a scatter diagram, using a software package.
b. Determine the regression equation. Interpret the slope value.
c. Determine the correlation coefficient. Can you conclude that it is greater than 0?

53. FILE Below is information on the price per share and the dividend for a sample of 30 companies.

Company	Price per Share	Dividend
1	$20.00	$ 3.14
2	22.01	3.36
⋮	⋮	⋮
29	77.91	17.65
30	80.00	17.36

a. Calculate the regression equation using selling price based on the annual dividend.
b. Test the significance of the slope.
c. Determine the coefficient of determination. Interpret its value.
d. Determine the correlation coefficient. Can you conclude that it is greater than 0 using the .05 significance level?

54. A highway employee performed a regression analysis of the relationship between the number of construction work-zone fatalities and the number of unemployed people in a state. The regression equation is Fatalities = 12.7 + 0.000114 (Unemp). Some additional output is:

```
Predictor          Coef        SE Coef       T        P
Constant         12.726          8.115    1.57    0.134
Unemp        0.00011386     0.00002896    3.93    0.001
Analysis of Variance
Source           DF       SS        MS         F        P
Regression        1    10354     10354     15.46    0.001
Residual Error   18    12054       670
Total            19    22408
```

a. How many states were in the sample?
b. Determine the standard error of estimate.
c. Determine the coefficient of determination.
d. Determine the correlation coefficient.
e. At the .05 significance level, does the evidence suggest there is a positive association between fatalities and the number unemployed?

55. A regression analysis relating the current market value in dollars to the size in square feet of homes in Greene County, Tennessee, follows. The regression equation is: Value = −37,186 + 65.0 Size.

```
Predictor          Coef      SE Coef        T        P
Constant         -37186         4629    -8.03    0.000
Size             64.993        3.047    21.33    0.000
Analysis of Variance
Source           DF            SS            MS          F        P
Regression        1   13548662082   13548662082     454.98    0.000
Residual Error   33     982687392      29778406
Total            34   14531349474
```

a. How many homes were in the sample?
b. Compute the standard error of estimate.
c. Compute the coefficient of determination.
d. Compute the correlation coefficient.
e. At the .05 significance level, does the evidence suggest a positive association between the market value of homes and the size of the home in square feet?

56. **FILE** The following table shows the mean annual percent return on capital (profitability) and the mean annual percentage sales growth for eight aerospace and defense companies.

Company	Profitability	Growth
Alliant Techsystems	23.1	8.0
Boeing	13.2	15.6
General Dynamics	24.2	31.2
Honeywell	11.1	2.5
L-3 Communications	10.1	35.4
Northrop Grumman	10.8	6.0
Rockwell Collins	27.3	8.7
United Technologies	20.1	3.2

a. Compute the correlation coefficient. Conduct a test of hypothesis to determine if it is reasonable to conclude that the population correlation is greater than zero. Use the .05 significance level.
b. Develop the regression equation for profitability based on growth. Can we conclude that the slope of the regression line is negative?
c. Use a software package to determine the residual for each observation. Which company has the largest residual?

57. **FILE** The following data show the retail price for 12 randomly selected laptop computers along with their corresponding processor speeds in gigahertz.

Computer	Speed	Price	Computer	Speed	Price
1	2.0	1008.50	7	2.0	1098.50
2	1.6	461.00	8	1.6	693.50
3	1.6	532.00	9	2.0	1057.00
4	1.8	971.00	10	1.6	1001.00
5	2.0	1068.50	11	1.0	468.50
6	1.2	506.00	12	1.4	434.50

a. Develop a linear equation that can be used to describe how the price depends on the processor speed.
b. Based on your regression equation, is there one machine that seems particularly over- or underpriced?
c. Compute the correlation coefficient between the two variables. At the .05 significance level, conduct a test of hypothesis to determine if the population correlation is greater than zero.

58. **FILE** A consumer buying cooperative tested the effective heating area of 20 different electric space heaters with different wattages. Here are the results.

Heater	Wattage	Area	Heater	Wattage	Area
1	1,500	205	11	1,250	116
2	750	70	12	500	72
3	1,500	199	13	500	82
4	1,250	151	14	1,500	206
5	1,250	181	15	2,000	245
6	1,250	217	16	1,500	219
7	1,000	94	17	750	63
8	2,000	298	18	1,500	200
9	1,000	135	19	1,250	151
10	1,500	211	20	500	44

a. Compute the correlation between the wattage and heating area. Is there a direct or an indirect relationship?
b. Conduct a test of hypothesis to determine if it is reasonable that the coefficient is greater than zero. Use the .05 significance level.
c. Develop the regression equation for effective heating based on wattage.
d. Which heater looks like the "best buy" based on the size of the residual?

59. FILE A dog trainer is exploring the relationship between the size of the dog (weight in pounds) and its daily food consumption (measured in standard cups). Below is the result of a sample of 18 observations.

Dog	Weight	Consumption	Dog	Weight	Consumption
1	41	3	10	91	5
2	148	8	11	109	6
3	79	5	12	207	10
4	41	4	13	49	3
5	85	5	14	113	6
6	111	6	15	84	5
7	37	3	16	95	5
8	111	6	17	57	4
9	41	3	18	168	9

a. Compute the correlation coefficient. Is it reasonable to conclude that the correlation in the population is greater than zero? Use the .05 significance level.
b. Develop the regression equation for cups based on the dog's weight. How much does each additional cup change the estimated weight of the dog?
c. Is one of the dogs a big undereater or overeater?

60. Waterbury Insurance Company wants to study the relationship between the amount of fire damage and the distance between the burning house and the nearest fire station. This information will be used in setting rates for insurance coverage. For a sample of 30 claims for the last year, the director of the actuarial department determined the distance from the fire station (x) and the amount of fire damage, in thousands of dollars (y). The MegaStat output is reported below.

ANOVA table

Source	SS	df	MS	F
Regression	1,864.5782	1	1,864.5782	38.83
Residual	1,344.4934	28	48.0176	
Total	3,209.0716	29		

Regression output

Variables	Coefficients	Std. Error	t(df = 28)
Intercept	12.3601	3.2915	3.755
Distance–X	4.7956	0.7696	6.231

Answer the following questions.
a. Write out the regression equation. Is there a direct or indirect relationship between the distance from the fire station and the amount of fire damage?
b. How much damage would you estimate for a fire 5 miles from the nearest fire station?
c. Determine and interpret the coefficient of determination.
d. Determine the correlation coefficient. Interpret its value. How did you determine the sign of the correlation coefficient?
e. Conduct a test of hypothesis to determine if there is a significant relationship between the distance from the fire station and the amount of damage. Use the .01 significance level and a two-tailed test.

61. FILE TravelAir.com samples domestic airline flights to explore the relationship between airfare and distance. The service would like to know if there is a correlation between airfare and flight distance. If there is a correlation, what percentage of the variation in airfare is accounted for by distance? How much does each additional mile add to the fare? The data follow.

Origin	Destination	Distance	Fare
Detroit, MI	Myrtle Beach, SC	636	$109
Baltimore, MD	Sacramento, CA	2,395	252
Las Vegas, NV	Philadelphia, PA	2,176	221
Sacramento, CA	Seattle, WA	605	151
Atlanta, GA	Orlando, FL	403	138
Boston, MA	Miami, FL	1,258	209
Chicago, IL	Covington, KY	264	254
Columbus, OH	Minneapolis, MN	627	259
Fort Lauderdale, FL	Los Angeles, CA	2,342	215
Chicago, IL	Indianapolis, IN	177	128
Philadelphia, PA	San Francisco, CA	2,521	348
Houston, TX	Raleigh/Durham, NC	1,050	224
Houston, TX	Midland/Odessa, TX	441	175
Cleveland, OH	Dallas/Ft.Worth, TX	1,021	256
Baltimore, MD	Columbus, OH	336	121
Boston, MA	Covington, KY	752	252
Kansas City, MO	San Diego, CA	1,333	206
Milwaukee, WI	Phoenix, AZ	1,460	167
Portland, OR	Washington, DC	2,350	308
Phoenix, AZ	San Jose, CA	621	152
Baltimore, MD	St. Louis, MO	737	175
Houston, TX	Orlando, FL	853	191
Houston, TX	Seattle, WA	1,894	231
Burbank, CA	New York, NY	2,465	251
Atlanta, GA	San Diego, CA	1,891	291
Minneapolis, MN	New York, NY	1,028	260
Atlanta, GA	West Palm Beach, FL	545	123
Kansas City, MO	Seattle, WA	1,489	211
Baltimore, MD	Portland, ME	452	139
New Orleans, LA	Washington, DC	969	243

a. Draw a scatter diagram with *Distance* as the independent variable and *Fare* as the dependent variable. Is the relationship direct or indirect?

b. Compute the correlation coefficient. At the .05 significance level, is it reasonable to conclude that the correlation coefficient is greater than zero?

c. What percentage of the variation in *Fare* is accounted for by *Distance* of a flight?

d. Determine the regression equation. How much does each additional mile add to the fare? Estimate the fare for a 1,500-mile flight.

e. A traveler is planning to fly from Atlanta to London Heathrow. The distance is 4,218 miles. She wants to use the regression equation to estimate the fare. Explain why it would not be a good idea to estimate the fare for this international flight with the regression equation.

DATA ANALYTICS

62. FILE The North Valley Real Estate data reports information on homes on the market.

a. Let selling price be the dependent variable and size of the home the independent variable. Determine the regression equation. Estimate the selling price for a home with an area of 2,200 square feet. Determine the 95% confidence interval for all 2,200 square foot homes and the 95% prediction interval for the selling price of a home with 2,200 square feet.

b. Let days-on-the-market be the dependent variable and price be the independent variable. Determine the regression equation. Estimate the days-on-the-market of a home that is priced at $300,000. Determine the 95% confidence interval of days-on-the-market for homes with a mean price of $300,000, and the 95% prediction interval of days-on-the-market for a home priced at $300,000.

c. Can you conclude that the independent variables "days on the market" and "selling price" are positively correlated? Are the size of the home and the selling price positively correlated? Use the .05 significance level. Report the *p*-value of the test. Summarize your results in a brief report.

63. FILE Refer to the Baseball 2016 data, which reports information on the 2016 Major League Baseball season. Let attendance be the dependent variable and total team salary be the independent variable. Determine the regression equation and answer the following questions.

a. Draw a scatter diagram. From the diagram, does there seem to be a direct relationship between the two variables?

b. What is the expected attendance for a team with a salary of $100.0 million?

c. If the owners pay an additional $30 million, how many more people could they expect to attend?

d. At the .05 significance level, can we conclude that the slope of the regression line is positive? Conduct the appropriate test of hypothesis.

e. What percentage of the variation in attendance is accounted for by salary?

f. Determine the correlation between attendance and team batting average and between attendance and team ERA. Which is stronger? Conduct an appropriate test of hypothesis for each set of variables.

64. FILE Refer to the Lincolnville School bus data. Develop a regression equation that expresses the relationship between age of the bus and maintenance cost. The age of the bus is the independent variable.

a. Draw a scatter diagram. What does this diagram suggest as to the relationship between the two variables? Is it direct or indirect? Does it appear to be strong or weak?

b. Develop a regression equation. How much does an additional year add to the maintenance cost. What is the estimated maintenance cost for a 10-year-old bus?

c. Conduct a test of hypothesis to determine whether the slope of the regression line is greater than zero. Use the .05 significance level. Interpret your findings from parts (a), (b), and (c) in a brief report.

14 Multiple Regression Analysis

THE MORTGAGE DEPARTMENT of the Bank of New England is studying data from recent loans. Of particular interest is how such factors as the value of the home being purchased, education level of the head of the household, age of the head of the household, current monthly mortgage payment, and gender of the head of the household relate to the family income. Are the proposed variables effective predictors of the dependent variable family income? (See the example/solution within the Review of Multiple Regression section.)

LEARNING OBJECTIVES

When you have completed this chapter, you will be able to:

LO14-1 Use multiple regression analysis to describe and interpret a relationship between several independent variables and a dependent variable.

LO14-2 Evaluate how well a multiple regression equation fits the data.

LO14-3 Test hypotheses about the relationships inferred by a multiple regression model.

LO14-4 Evaluate the assumptions of multiple regression.

LO14-5 Use and interpret a qualitative, dummy variable in multiple regression.

LO14-6 Include and interpret an interaction effect in multiple regression analysis.

LO14-7 Apply stepwise regression to develop a multiple regression model.

LO14-8 Apply multiple regression techniques to develop a linear model.

INTRODUCTION

In Chapter 13, we described the relationship between a pair of interval- or ratio-scaled variables. We began the chapter by studying the correlation coefficient, which measures the strength of the relationship. A coefficient near plus or minus 1.00 (−.88 or .78, for example) indicates a very strong linear relationship, whereas a value near 0 (−.12 or .18, for example) indicates that the relationship is weak. Next we developed a procedure to determine a linear equation to express the relationship between the two variables. We referred to this as a *regression line.* This line describes the relationship between the variables. It also describes the overall pattern of a dependent variable (y) to a single independent or explanatory variable (x).

In multiple linear correlation and regression, we use additional independent variables (denoted $x_1, x_2, \ldots$, and so on) that help us better explain or predict the dependent variable (y). Almost all of the ideas we saw in simple linear correlation and regression extend to this more general situation. However, the additional independent variables do lead to some new considerations. Multiple regression analysis can be used either as a descriptive or as an inferential technique.

LO14-1

Use multiple regression analysis to describe and interpret a relationship between several independent variables and a dependent variable.

MULTIPLE REGRESSION ANALYSIS

The general descriptive form of a multiple linear equation is shown in formula (14–1). We use k to represent the number of independent variables. So k can be any positive integer.

GENERAL MULTIPLE REGRESSION EQUATION

$$\hat{y} = a + b_1x_1 + b_2x_2 + b_3x_3 + \ldots + b_kx_k \quad \textbf{(14–1)}$$

where:

a is the intercept, the value of $\hat{y}$ when all the X's are zero.

b_j is the amount by which $\hat{y}$ changes when that particular x_j increases by one unit, with the values of all other independent variables held constant. The subscript j is simply a label that helps to identify each independent variable; it is not used in any calculations. Usually the subscript is an integer value between 1 and k, which is the number of independent variables. However, the subscript can also be a short or abbreviated label. For example, "age" could be used as a subscript to identify the independent variable, age.

In Chapter 13, the regression analysis described and tested the relationship between a dependent variable, $\hat{y}$ and a single independent variable, x. The relationship between ŷ and x was graphically portrayed by a line. When there are two independent variables, the regression equation is

$$\hat{y} = a + b_1x_1 + b_2x_2$$

Because there are two independent variables, this relationship is graphically portrayed as a plane and is shown in Chart 14–1. The chart shows the residuals as the difference between the actual y and the fitted $\hat{y}$ on the plane. If a multiple regression analysis includes more than two independent variables, we cannot use a graph to illustrate the analysis since graphs are limited to three dimensions.

To illustrate the interpretation of the intercept and the two regression coefficients, suppose the selling price of a home is directly related to the number of rooms and *inversely* related to its age. We let x_1 refer to the number of rooms, x_2 to the age of the home in years, and y to the selling price of the home in thousands of dollars ($000).

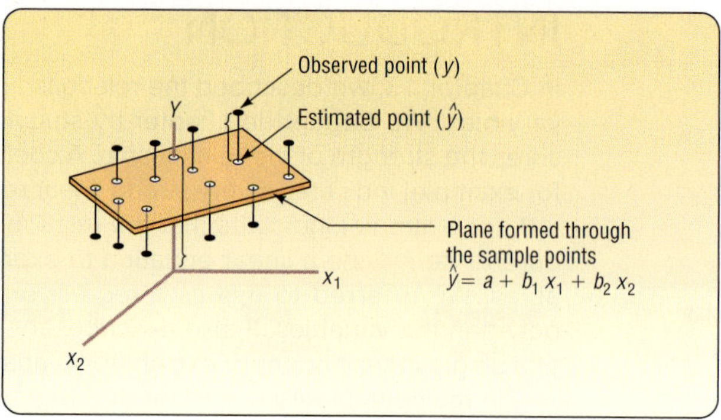

CHART 14–1 Regression Plane with 10 Sample Points

Suppose the regression equation, calculated using statistical software, is:

$$\hat{y} = 21.2 + 18.7x_1 - 0.25x_2$$

The intercept value of 21.2 indicates the regression equation (plane) intersects the *y*-axis at 21.2. This happens when both the number of rooms and the age of the home are zero. We could say that $21,200 is the average value of a property without a house.

The first regression coefficient, 18.7, indicates that for each increase of one room in the size of a home, the selling price will increase by $18.7 thousand ($18,700), regardless of the age of the home. The second regression coefficient, −0.25, indicates that for each increase of one year in age, the selling price will *decrease* by $.25 thousand ($250), regardless of the number of rooms. As an example, a seven-room home that is 30 years old is expected to sell for $144,600.

$$\hat{y} = 21.2 + 18.7x_1 - 0.25x_2 = 21.2 + 18.7(7) - 0.25(30) = 144.6$$

The values for the coefficients in the multiple linear equation are found by using the method of least squares. Recall from the previous chapter that the least squares method makes the sum of the squared differences between the fitted and actual values of *y* as small as possible, that is, the term $\Sigma(y - \hat{y})^2$ is minimized. The calculations are very tedious, so they are usually performed by a statistical software package.

In the following example, we show a multiple regression analysis using three independent variables employing Excel that produces a standard set of statistics and reports. Statistical software such as Minitab, MegaStat, and others provide advanced regression analysis techniques.

EXAMPLE

Salsberry Realty sells homes along the East Coast of the United States. One of the questions most frequently asked by prospective buyers is: If we purchase this home, how much can we expect to pay to heat it during the winter? The research department at Salsberry has been asked to develop some guidelines regarding heating costs for single-family homes. Three variables are thought to relate to the heating costs: (1) the mean daily outside temperature, (2) the number of inches of insulation in the attic, and (3) the age in years of the furnace. To investigate, Salsberry's research department selected a random sample of 20 recently sold homes. It determined the cost to heat each home last January, as well as the January outside temperature in the region, the number of inches of insulation in the attic, and the age of the furnace. The sample information is reported in Table 14–1.

TABLE 14–1 Factors in January Heating Cost for a Sample of 20 Homes

Home	Heating Cost ($)	Mean Outside Temperature (°F)	Attic Insulation (inches)	Age of Furnace (years)
1	$250	35	3	6
2	360	29	4	10
3	165	36	7	3
4	43	60	6	9
5	92	65	5	6
6	200	30	5	5
7	355	10	6	7
8	290	7	10	10
9	230	21	9	11
10	120	55	2	5
11	73	54	12	4
12	205	48	5	1
13	400	20	5	15
14	320	39	4	7
15	72	60	8	6
16	272	20	5	8
17	94	58	7	3
18	190	40	8	11
19	235	27	9	8
20	139	30	7	5

The data in Table 14–1 are available in Excel worksheet format at the textbook website, www.mhhe.com/Lind17e. The basic instructions for using Excel for these data are in the Software Commands in Appendix C.

Determine the multiple regression equation. Which variables are the independent variables? Which variable is the dependent variable? Discuss the regression coefficients. What does it indicate if some coefficients are positive and some coefficients are negative? What is the intercept value? What is the estimated heating cost for a home if the mean outside temperature is 30 degrees, there are 5 inches of insulation in the attic, and the furnace is 10 years old?

SOLUTION

We begin the analysis by defining the dependent and independent variables. The dependent variable is the January heating cost. It is represented by y. There are three independent variables:

- The mean outside temperature in January, represented by x_1.
- The number of inches of insulation in the attic, represented by x_2.
- The age in years of the furnace, represented by x_3.

Given these definitions, the general form of the multiple regression equation follows. The value $\hat{y}$ is used to estimate the value of y.

$$\hat{y} = a + b_1 x_1 + b_2 x_2 + b_3 x_3$$

Now that we have defined the regression equation, we are ready to use Excel to compute all the statistics needed for the analysis. The output from Excel is shown on the following page.

To use the regression equation to predict the January heating cost, we need to know the values of the regression coefficients: b_1, b_2, and b_3. These are highlighted in the software reports. The software uses the variable names or labels associated with each independent variable. The regression equation intercept, *a*, is labeled "intercept" in the Excel output.

	A	B	C	D
1	Cost	Temp	Insul	Age
2	250	35	3	6
3	360	29	4	10
4	165	36	7	3
5	43	60	6	9
6	92	65	5	6
7	200	30	5	5
8	355	10	6	7
9	290	7	10	10
10	230	21	9	11
11	120	55	2	5
12	73	54	12	4
13	205	48	5	1
14	400	20	5	15
15	320	39	4	7
16	72	60	8	6
17	272	20	5	8
18	94	58	7	3
19	190	40	8	11
20	235	27	9	8
21	139	30	7	5

E	F	G	H	I	J	K
	SUMMARY OUTPUT					
	Regression Statistics					
	Multiple R	0.897				
	R Square	0.804				
	Adjusted R Square	0.767				
	Standard Error	51.049				
	Observations	20				
	ANOVA					
		df	*SS*	*MS*	*F*	*Significance F*
	Regression	3	171220.473	57073.491	21.901	0.000
	Residual	16	41695.277	2605.955		
	Total	19	212915.750			
		Coefficients	*Standard Error*	*t Stat*	*P-value*	
	Intercept	427.194	59.601	7.168	0.000	
	Temp	-4.583	0.772	-5.934	0.000	
	Insul	-14.831	4.754	-3.119	0.007	
	Age	6.101	4.012	1.521	0.148	

In this case, the estimated regression equation is:

$$\hat{y} = 427.194 - 4.583x_1 - 14.831x_2 + 6.101x_3$$

We can now estimate or predict the January heating cost for a home if we know the mean outside temperature, the inches of insulation, and the age of the furnace. For an example home, the mean outside temperature for the month is 30 degrees (x_1), there are 5 inches of insulation in the attic (x_2), and the furnace is 10 years old (x_3). By substituting the values for the independent variables:

$$\hat{y} = 427.194 - 4.583(30) - 14.831(5) + 6.101(10) = 276.56$$

The estimated January heating cost is $276.56.

The regression coefficients, and their algebraic signs, also provide information about their individual relationships with the January heating cost. The regression coefficient for mean outside temperature is −4.583. The coefficient is negative and shows an inverse relationship between heating cost and temperature. This is not surprising. As the outside temperature increases, the cost to heat the home decreases. The numeric value of the regression coefficient provides more information. If the outside temperature increases by 1 degree and the other two independent variables remain constant, we can estimate a decrease of $4.583 in monthly heating cost. So if the mean temperature in Boston is 25 degrees and it is 35 degrees in Philadelphia, all other things being the same (insulation and age of furnace), we expect the heating cost would be $45.83 less in Philadelphia.

The attic insulation variable also shows an inverse relationship: the more insulation in the attic, the less the cost to heat the home. So the negative sign for this coefficient is logical. For each additional inch of insulation, we expect the cost to heat the home to decline $14.83 per month, holding the outside temperature and the age of the furnace constant.

The age of the furnace variable shows a direct relationship. With an older furnace, the cost to heat the home increases. Specifically, for each additional year older the furnace is, we expect the cost to increase $6.10 per month.

STATISTICS IN ACTION

Many studies indicate a woman will earn about 70% of what a man would for the same work. Researchers at the University of Michigan Institute for Social Research found that about one-third of the difference can be explained by such social factors as differences in education, seniority, and work interruptions. The remaining two-thirds is not explained by these social factors.

SELF-REVIEW 14–1

There are many restaurants in northeastern South Carolina. They serve beach vacationers in the summer, golfers in the fall and spring, and snowbirds in the winter. Bill and Joyce Tuneall manage several restaurants in the North Jersey area and are considering moving to Myrtle Beach, SC, to open a new restaurant. Before making a final decision, they wish to investigate existing restaurants and what variables seem to be related to profitability. They gather sample information where profit (reported in $000) is the dependent variable and the independent variables are:

x_1 the number of parking spaces near the restaurant.
x_2 the number of hours the restaurant is open per week.
x_3 the distance from the SkyWheel, a landmark in Myrtle Beach.
x_4 the number of servers employed.
x_5 the number of years the current owner operated the restaurant.

The following is part of the output obtained using statistical software.

Predictor	Coefficient	SE Coefficient	t
Constant	2.50	1.50	1.667
x_1	3.00	1.50	2.000
x_2	4.00	3.00	1.333
x_3	-3.00	0.20	-15.000
x_4	0.20	0.05	4.000
x_5	1.00	1.50	0.667

(a) What is the amount of profit for a restaurant with 40 parking spaces that is open 72 hours per week, is 10 miles from the SkyWheel, has 20 servers, and has been operated by the current owner for 5 years?
(b) Interpret the values of b_2 and b_3 in the multiple regression equation.

EXERCISES

1. The director of marketing at Reeves Wholesale Products is studying monthly sales. Three independent variables were selected as estimators of sales: regional population, per capita income, and regional unemployment rate. The regression equation was computed to be (in dollars):

$$\hat{y} = 64{,}100 + 0.394x_1 + 9.6x_2 - 11{,}600x_3$$

a. What is the full name of the equation?
b. Interpret the number 64,100.
c. What are the estimated monthly sales for a particular region with a population of 796,000, per capita income of $6,940, and an unemployment rate of 6.0%?

2. Thompson Photo Works purchased several new, highly sophisticated processing machines. The production department needed some guidance with respect to qualifications needed by an operator. Is age a factor? Is the length of service as an operator (in years) important? In order to explore further the factors needed to estimate performance on the new processing machines, four variables were listed:

x_1 = Length of time an employee was in the industry
x_2 = Mechanical aptitude test score
x_3 = Prior on-the-job rating
x_4 = Age

Performance on the new machine is designated y.

Thirty employees were selected at random. Data were collected for each, and their performances on the new machines were recorded. A few results are:

Name	Performance on New Machine, y	Length of Time in Industry, x_1	Mechanical Aptitude Score, x_2	Prior on-the-Job Performance, x_3	Age, x_4
Mike Miraglia	112	12	312	121	52
Sue Trythall	113	2	380	123	27

The equation is:

$$\hat{y} = 11.6 + 0.4x_1 + 0.286x_2 + 0.112x_3 + 0.002x_4$$

a. What is this equation called?
b. How many dependent variables are there? Independent variables?
c. What is the number 0.286 called?
d. As age increases by one year, how much does estimated performance on the new machine increase?
e. Carl Knox applied for a job at Photo Works. He has been in the business for 6 years and scored 280 on the mechanical aptitude test. Carl's prior on-the-job performance rating is 97, and he is 35 years old. Estimate Carl's performance on the new machine.

3. A consulting group was hired by the Human Resources Department at General Mills, Inc. to survey company employees regarding their degree of satisfaction with their quality of life. A special index, called the index of satisfaction, was used to measure satisfaction. Six factors were studied, namely, age at the time of first marriage (x_1), annual income (x_2), number of children living (x_3), value of all assets (x_4), status of health in the form of an index (x_5), and the average number of social activities per week—such as bowling and dancing (x_6). Suppose the multiple regression equation is:

$$\hat{y} = 16.24 + 0.017x_1 + 0.0028x_2 + 42x_3 + 0.0012x_4 + 0.19x_5 + 26.8x_6$$

a. What is the estimated index of satisfaction for a person who first married at 18, has an annual income of \$26,500, has three children living, has assets of \$156,000, has an index of health status of 141, and has 2.5 social activities a week on the average?
b. Which would add more to satisfaction, an additional income of \$10,000 a year or two more social activities a week?

4. Cellulon, a manufacturer of home insulation, wants to develop guidelines for builders and consumers on how the thickness of the insulation in the attic of a home and the outdoor temperature affect natural gas consumption. In the laboratory, it varied the insulation thickness and temperature. A few of the findings are:

Monthly Natural Gas Consumption (cubic feet), y	Thickness of Insulation (inches), x_1	Outdoor Temperature (°F), x_2
30.3	6	40
26.9	12	40
22.1	8	49

On the basis of the sample results, the regression equation is:

$$\hat{y} = 62.65 - 1.86x_1 - 0.52x_2$$

a. How much natural gas can homeowners expect to use per month if they install 6 inches of insulation and the outdoor temperature is 40 degrees F?
b. What effect would installing 7 inches of insulation instead of 6 have on the monthly natural gas consumption (assuming the outdoor temperature remains at 40 degrees F)?
c. Why are the regression coefficients b_1 and b_2 negative? Is this logical?

LO14-2
Evaluate how well a multiple regression equation fits the data.

EVALUATING A MULTIPLE REGRESSION EQUATION

Many statistics and statistical methods are used to evaluate the relationship between a dependent variable and more than one independent variable. Our first step was to write the relationship in terms of a multiple regression equation. The next step follows on the concepts presented in Chapter 13 by using the information in an ANOVA table to evaluate how well the equation fits the data.

The ANOVA Table

As in Chapter 13, the statistical analysis of a multiple regression equation is summarized in an ANOVA table. To review, the total variation of the dependent variable, y, is divided into two components: (1) *regression,* or the variation of y explained by all the independent variables, and (2) *the error or residual,* or unexplained variation of y. These two categories are identified in the first column of an ANOVA table below. The column headed "*df*" refers to the degrees of freedom associated with each category. The total number of degrees of freedom is $n - 1$. The number of degrees of freedom in the regression is equal to the number of independent variables in the multiple regression equation. We call the regression degrees of freedom k. The number of degrees of freedom associated with the error term is equal to the total degrees of freedom, $n - 1$, minus the regression degrees of freedom, k. So, the residual or error degrees of freedom is $(n - 1) - k$, and is the same as $n - (k + 1)$.

Source	*df*	SS	MS	*F*
Regression	k	SSR	MSR = SSR/k	MSR/MSE
Residual or error	$n - (k + 1)$	SSE	MSE = SSE/$[n - (k + 1)]$	
Total	$n - 1$	SS total		

In the ANOVA table, the column headed, "SS", lists the sum of squares for each source of variation: regression, residual or error, and total. The sum of squares is the amount of variation attributable to each source.

The total variation of the dependent variable, y, is summarized in "SS total". You should note that this is simply the numerator of the usual formula to calculate any variation—in other words, the sum of the squared deviations from the mean. It is computed as:

$$\text{Total Sum of Squares} = \text{SS total} = \Sigma(y - \bar{y})^2$$

As we have seen, the total sum of squares is the sum of the regression and residual sum of squares. The regression sum of squares is the sum of the squared differences between the estimated or predicted values, $\hat{y}$ and the overall mean of y. The regression sum of squares is found by:

$$\text{Regression Sum of Squares} = \text{SSR} = \Sigma(\hat{y} - \bar{y})^2$$

The residual sum of squares is the sum of the squared differences between the observed values of the dependent variable, y, and their corresponding estimated or predicted values, $\hat{y}$. Notice that this difference is the error of estimating or predicting the dependent variable with the multiple regression equation. It is calculated as:

$$\text{Residual or Error Sum of Squares} = \text{SSE} = \Sigma(y - \hat{y})^2$$

We will use the ANOVA table information from the previous example to evaluate the regression equation to estimate January heating costs.

	A	B	C	D
1	Cost	Temp	Insul	Age
2	250	35	3	6
3	360	29	4	10
4	165	36	7	3
5	43	60	6	9
6	92	65	5	6
7	200	30	5	5
8	355	10	6	7
9	290	7	10	10
10	230	21	9	11
11	120	55	2	5
12	73	54	12	4
13	205	48	5	1
14	400	20	5	15
15	320	39	4	7
16	72	60	8	6
17	272	20	5	8
18	94	58	7	3
19	190	40	8	11
20	235	27	9	8

SUMMARY OUTPUT

Regression Statistics	
Multiple R	0.897
R Square	0.804
Adjusted R Square	0.767
Standard Error	51.049
Observations	20

ANOVA

	df	*SS*	*MS*	*F*	*Significance F*
Regression	3	171220.473	57073.491	21.901	0.000
Residual	16	41695.277	2605.955		
Total	19	212915.750			

	Coefficients	*Standard Error*	*t Stat*	*P-value*
Intercept	427.194	59.601	7.168	0.000
Temp	-4.583	0.772	-5.934	0.000
Insul	-14.831	4.754	-3.119	0.007
Age	6.101	4.012	1.521	0.148

Multiple Standard Error of Estimate

We begin with the **multiple standard error of estimate.** Recall that the standard error of estimate is comparable to the standard deviation. To explain the details of the standard error of estimate, refer to the first sampled home in row 2 in the Excel spreadsheet on the previous page. The actual heating cost for the first observation, y, is $250; the outside temperature, x_1, is 35 degrees; the depth of insulation, x_2, is 3 inches; and the age of the furnace, x_3, is 6 years. Using the regression equation developed in the previous section, the estimated heating cost for this home is:

$$\begin{aligned}\hat{y} &= 427.194 - 4.583x_1 - 14.831x_2 + 6.101x_3 \\ &= 427.194 - 4.583(35) - 14.831(3) + 6.101(6) \\ &= 258.90\end{aligned}$$

So we would estimate that a home with a mean January outside temperature of 35 degrees, 3 inches of insulation, and a 6-year-old furnace would cost $258.90 to heat. The actual heating cost was $250, so the residual—which is the difference between the actual value and the estimated value—is $y - \hat{y} = 250 - 258.90 = -8.90$. This difference of $8.90 is the random or unexplained error for the first home sampled. Our next step is to square this difference—that is, find $(y - \hat{y})^2 = (250 - 258.90)^2 = (-8.90)^2 = 79.21$.

If we repeat this calculation for the other 19 observations and sum all 20 squared differences, the total will be the residual or error sum of squares from the ANOVA table. Using this information, we can calculate the multiple standard error of the estimate as:

MULTIPLE STANDARD ERROR OF ESTIMATE

$$s_{y \cdot 123 \ldots k} = \sqrt{\frac{\Sigma(y - \hat{y})^2}{n - (k + 1)}} = \sqrt{\frac{SSE}{n - (k + 1)}} \qquad \textbf{(14–2)}$$

where:

y is the actual observation.
$\hat{y}$ is the estimated value computed from the regression equation.
n is the number of observations in the sample.
k is the number of independent variables.
SSE is the Residual Sum of Squares from an ANOVA table.

There is more information in the ANOVA table that can be used to compute the multiple standard error of estimate. The column headed "MS" reports the mean squares for the regression and residual variation. These values are calculated as the sum of squares divided by the corresponding degrees of freedom. The multiple standard error of estimate is equal to the square root of the residual MS, which is also called the mean square error or the MSE.

$$s_{y \cdot 123 \dots k} = \sqrt{MSE} = \sqrt{2605.995} = \$51.05$$

How do we interpret the standard error of estimate of 51.05? It is the typical "error" when we use this equation to predict the cost. First, the units are the same as the dependent variable, so the standard error is in dollars, \$51.05. Second, we expect the residuals to be approximately normally distributed, so about 68% of the residuals will be within ±\$51.05 and about 95% within ±2(51.05), or ±\$102.10. As before with similar measures of dispersion, such as the standard error of estimate in Chapter 13, a smaller multiple standard error indicates a better or more effective predictive equation.

Coefficient of Multiple Determination

Next, let's look at the coefficient of multiple determination. Recall from the previous chapter the coefficient of determination is defined as the percent of variation in the dependent variable explained, or accounted for, by the independent variable. In the multiple regression case, we extend this definition as follows.

> **COEFFICIENT OF MULTIPLE DETERMINATION** The percent of variation in the dependent variable, *y*, explained by the set of independent variables, $x_1, x_2, x_3, \dots x_k$.

The characteristics of the coefficient of multiple determination are:

1. **It is symbolized by a capital *R* squared.** In other words, it is written as R^2 because it is calculated as the square of a correlation coefficient.
2. **It can range from 0 to 1.** A value near 0 indicates little association between the set of independent variables and the dependent variable. A value near 1 means a strong association.
3. **It cannot assume negative values.** Any number that is squared or raised to the second power cannot be negative.
4. **It is easy to interpret.** Because R^2 is a value between 0 and 1, it is easy to interpret, compare, and understand.

We can calculate the coefficient of determination from the information found in the ANOVA table. We look in the sum of squares column, which is labeled SS in the Excel output, and use the regression sum of squares, SSR, then divide by the total sum of squares, SS total.

COEFFICIENT OF MULTIPLE DETERMINATION

$$R^2 = \frac{SSR}{SS\ total} \qquad \textbf{(14–3)}$$

We can use the regression and the total sum of squares from the ANOVA table highlighted in the Excel output appearing earlier in this section and compute the coefficient of determination.

$$R^2 = \frac{SSR}{SS\ total} = \frac{171{,}220.473}{212{,}915.750} = .804$$

How do we interpret this value? We conclude that the independent variables (outside temperature, amount of insulation, and age of furnace) explain, or account for, 80.4% of the variation in heating cost. To put it another way, 19.6% of the variation is due to other sources, such as random error or variables not included in the analysis. Using the ANOVA table, 19.6% is the error sum of squares divided by the total sum of squares. Knowing that the SSR + SSE = SS total, the following relationship is true.

$$1 - R^2 = 1 - \frac{\text{SSR}}{\text{SS total}} = \frac{\text{SSE}}{\text{SS total}} = \frac{41{,}695.277}{212{,}915.750} = .196$$

Adjusted Coefficient of Determination

The coefficient of determination tends to increase as more independent variables are added to the multiple regression model. Each new independent variable causes the predictions to be more accurate. That, in turn, makes SSE smaller and SSR larger. Hence, R^2 increases only because the total number of independent variables increases and not because the added independent variable is a good predictor of the dependent variable. In fact, if the number of variables, k, and the sample size, n, are equal, the coefficient of determination is 1.0. In practice, this situation is rare and would also be ethically questionable. To balance the effect that the number of independent variables has on the coefficient of multiple determination, statistical software packages use an *adjusted* coefficient of multiple determination.

ADJUSTED COEFFICIENT OF DETERMINATION

$$R^2_{\text{adj}} = 1 - \frac{\dfrac{\text{SSE}}{n - (k + 1)}}{\dfrac{\text{SS total}}{n - 1}} \quad \textbf{(14–4)}$$

The error and total sum of squares are divided by their degrees of freedom. Notice especially the degrees of freedom for the error sum of squares include k, the number of independent variables. For the cost of heating example, the adjusted coefficient of determination is:

$$R^2_{\text{adj}} = 1 - \frac{\dfrac{41{,}695.277}{20 - (3 + 1)}}{\dfrac{212{,}915.750}{20 - 1}} = 1 - \frac{2{,}605.955}{11{,}206.092} = 1 - .233 = .767$$

If we compare the R^2 (0.80) to the adjusted R^2 (0.767), the difference in this case is small.

SELF-REVIEW 14–2

Refer to Self-Review 14–1 on the subject of restaurants in Myrtle Beach. The ANOVA portion of the regression output is presented below.

```
Analysis of Variance
Source            DF     SS     MS
Regression         5    100     20
Residual Error    20     40      2
Total             25    140
```

(a) How large was the sample?
(b) How many independent variables are there?
(c) How many dependent variables are there?
(d) Compute the standard error of estimate. About 95% of the residuals will be between what two values?
(e) Determine the coefficient of multiple determination. Interpret this value.
(f) Find the coefficient of multiple determination, adjusted for the degrees of freedom.

EXERCISES

5. Consider the ANOVA table that follows.

Analysis of Variance

Source	DF	SS	MS	F	P
Regression	2	77.907	38.954	4.14	0.021
Residual Error	62	583.693	9.414		
Total	64	661.600			

a. Determine the standard error of estimate. About 95% of the residuals will be between what two values?

b. Determine the coefficient of multiple determination. Interpret this value.

c. Determine the coefficient of multiple determination, adjusted for the degrees of freedom.

6. Consider the ANOVA table that follows.

Analysis of Variance

Source	DF	SS	MS	F
Regression	5	3710.00	742.00	12.89
Residual Error	46	2647.38	57.55	
Total	51	6357.38		

a. Determine the standard error of estimate. About 95% of the residuals will be between what two values?

b. Determine the coefficient of multiple determination. Interpret this value.

c. Determine the coefficient of multiple determination, adjusted for the degrees of freedom.

LO14-3

Test hypotheses about the relationships inferred by a multiple regression model.

INFERENCES IN MULTIPLE LINEAR REGRESSION

Thus far, multiple regression analysis has been viewed only as a way to describe the relationship between a dependent variable and several independent variables. However, the least squares method also has the ability to draw inferences or generalizations about the relationship for an entire population. Recall that when you create confidence intervals or perform hypothesis tests as a part of inferential statistics, you view the data as a random sample taken from some population.

In the multiple regression setting, we assume there is an unknown population regression equation that relates the dependent variable to the k independent variables. This is sometimes called a **model** of the relationship. In symbols we write:

$$Y = \alpha + \beta_1 X_1 + \beta_2 X_2 + \cdots + \beta_k X_k$$

This equation is analogous to formula (14–1) except the coefficients are now reported as Greek letters. We use the Greek letters to denote *population parameters*. Then under a certain set of assumptions, which will be discussed shortly, the computed values of a and b_i are sample statistics. These sample statistics are point estimates of the corresponding population parameters α and β_i. For example, the sample regression coefficient b_2 is a point estimate of the population parameter β_2. The sampling distribution of these point estimates follows the normal probability distribution. These sampling distributions are each centered at their respective parameter values. To put it another way, the means of the sampling distributions are equal to the parameter values to be estimated. Thus, by using the properties of the sampling distributions of these statistics, inferences about the population parameters are possible.

Global Test: Testing the Multiple Regression Model

We can test the ability of the independent variables $X_1, X_2, \ldots, X_k$ to explain the behavior of the dependent variable Y. To put this in question form: Can the dependent variable be estimated without relying on the independent variables? The test used is referred to as the **global test.** Basically, it investigates whether it is possible that all the independent variables have zero regression coefficients.

To relate this question to the heating cost example, we will test whether the three independent variables (amount of insulation in the attic, mean daily outside temperature, and age of furnace) effectively estimate home heating costs. In testing the hypothesis, we first state the null hypothesis and the alternate hypothesis in terms of the three population parameters, β_1, β_2, and β_3. Recall that b_1, b_2, and b_3 are sample regression coefficients and are not used in the hypothesis statements. In the null hypothesis, we test whether the regression coefficients in the population are all zero. The null hypothesis is:

$$H_0: \beta_1 = \beta_2 = \beta_3 = 0$$

The alternate hypothesis is:

$$H_1: \text{Not all the } \beta_i\text{'s are 0.}$$

If the hypothesis test fails to reject the null hypothesis, it implies the regression coefficients are all zero and, logically, are of no value in estimating the dependent variable (heating cost). Should that be the case, we would have to search for some other independent variables—or take a different approach—to predict home heating costs.

To test the null hypothesis that the multiple regression coefficients are all zero, we employ the *F* distribution introduced in Chapter 12. We will use the .05 level of significance. Recall these characteristics of the *F* distribution:

1. **There is a family of *F* distributions.** Each time the degrees of freedom in either the numerator or the denominator change, a new *F* distribution is created.
2. **The *F* distribution cannot be negative.** The smallest possible value is 0.
3. **It is a continuous distribution.** The distribution can assume an infinite number of values between 0 and positive infinity.
4. **It is positively skewed.** The long tail of the distribution is to the right-hand side. As the number of degrees of freedom increases in both the numerator and the denominator, the distribution approaches the normal probability distribution. That is, the distribution will move toward a symmetric distribution.
5. **It is asymptotic.** As the values of *X* increase, the *F* curve will approach the horizontal axis, but will never touch it.

The *F*-statistic to test the global hypothesis follows. As in Chapter 12, it is the ratio of two variances. In this case, the numerator is the regression sum of squares divided by its degrees of freedom, *k*. The denominator is the residual sum of squares divided by its degrees of freedom, $n - (k + 1)$. The formula follows.

GLOBAL TEST

$$F = \frac{\text{SSR}/k}{\text{SSE}/[n - (k + 1)]} \quad \textbf{(14–5)}$$

Using the values from the ANOVA table on page 492, the *F*-statistic is

$$F = \frac{\text{SSR}/k}{\text{SSE}/[n - (k + 1)]} = \frac{171{,}220.473/3}{41{,}695.277/[20 - (3 + 1)]} = 21.90$$

Remember that the *F*-statistic tests the basic null hypothesis that two variances or, in this case, two mean squares are equal. In our global multiple regression hypothesis test, we will reject the null hypothesis, H_0, that all regression coefficients are zero when the regression mean square is larger in comparison to the residual mean square. If this is true, the F-statistic will be relatively large and in the far right tail of the F distribution, and the p-value will be small, that is, less than our choice of significance level of 0.05. Thus, we will reject the null hypothesis.

As with other hypothesis-testing methods, the decision rule can be based on either of two methods: (1) comparing the test statistic to a critical value or (2) calculating a p-value based on the test statistic and comparing the p-value to the significance level. The critical value method using the F-statistic requires three pieces of information: (1) the numerator degrees of freedom, (2) the denominator degrees of freedom, and (3) the significance level. The degrees of freedom for the numerator and the denominator are reported in the Excel ANOVA table that follows. The ANOVA output is highlighted in light green. The top number in the column marked "*df*" is 3, indicating there are 3 degrees of freedom in the numerator. This value corresponds to the number of independent variables. The middle number in the "*df*" column (16) indicates that there are 16 degrees of freedom in the denominator. The number 16 is found by $n - (k - 1) = 20 - (3 - 1) = 16$.

	A	B	C	D	G	H	I	J	K	L	M
1	Cost	Temp	Insul	Age		SUMMARY OUTPUT					
2	250	35	3	6							
3	360	29	4	10		*Regression Statistics*					
4	165	36	7	3		Multiple R	0.897				
5	43	60	6	9		R Square	0.804				
6	92	65	5	6		Adjusted R Square	0.767				
7	200	30	5	5		Standard Error	51.049				
8	355	10	6	7		Observations	20				
9	290	7	10	10							
10	230	21	9	11		ANOVA					
11	120	55	2	5			*df*	*SS*	*MS*	*F*	*Significance F*
12	73	54	12	4		Regression	3	171220.473	57073.491	21.901	0.000
13	205	48	5	1		Residual	16	41695.277	2605.955		
14	400	20	5	15		Total	19	212915.750			
15	320	39	4	7							
16	72	60	8	6			*Coefficients*	*Standard Error*	*t Stat*	*P-value*	
17	272	20	5	8		Intercept	427.194	59.601	7.168	0.000	
18	94	58	7	3		Temp	-4.583	0.772	-5.934	0.000	
19	190	40	8	11		Insul	-14.831	4.754	-3.119	0.007	
20	235	27	9	8		Age	6.101	4.012	1.521	0.148	

The critical value of F is found in Appendix B.6. Using the table for the .05 significance level, move horizontally to 3 degrees of freedom in the numerator, then down to 16 degrees of freedom in the denominator, and read the critical value. It is 3.24. The region where H_0 is not rejected and the region where H_0 is rejected are shown in the following diagram.

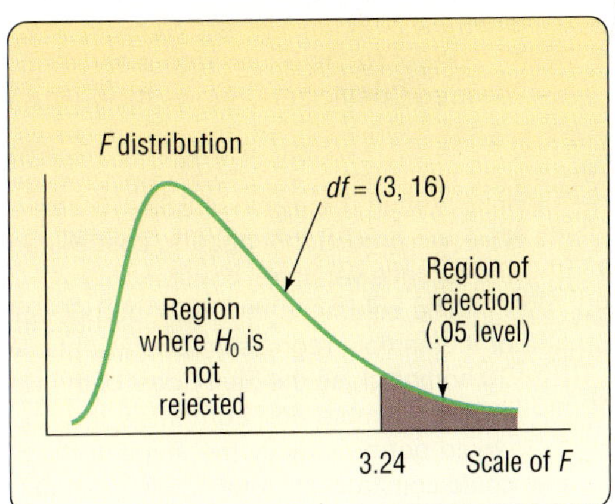

Continuing with the global test, the decision rule is: Do not reject the null hypothesis, H_0, that all the regression coefficients are 0 if the computed value of F is less than or equal to 3.24. If the computed F is greater than 3.24, reject H_0 and accept the alternate hypothesis, H_1.

The computed value of F is 21.90, which is in the rejection region. The null hypothesis that all the multiple regression coefficients are zero is therefore rejected. This means that at least one of the independent variables has the ability to explain the variation in the dependent variable (heating cost). We expected this decision. Logically, the outside temperature, the amount of insulation, or the age of the furnace has a great bearing on heating costs. The global test assures us that they do.

Testing the null hypothesis can also be based on a *p*-value, which is reported in the statistical software output for all hypothesis tests. In the case of the *F*-statistic, the *p*-value is defined as the probability of observing an *F*-value as large or larger than the *F* test statistic, assuming the null hypothesis is true. If the *p*-value is less than our selected significance level, then we decide to reject the null hypothesis. The ANOVA shows the *F*-statistic's *p*-value is equal to 0.000. It is clearly less than our significance level of 0.05. Therefore, we decide to reject the global null hypothesis and conclude that at least one of the regression coefficients is not equal to zero.

Evaluating Individual Regression Coefficients

So far we have shown that at least one, but not necessarily all, of the regression coefficients is not equal to zero and thus useful for predictions. The next step is to test the independent variables *individually* to determine which regression coefficients may be 0 and which are not.

Why is it important to know if any of the β_i's equal 0? If a β could equal 0, it implies that this particular independent variable is of no value in explaining any variation in the dependent value. If there are coefficients for which H_0 cannot be rejected, we may want to eliminate them from the regression equation.

Our strategy is to use three sets of hypotheses: one for temperature, one for insulation, and one for age of the furnace.

For temperature:	For insulation:	For furnace age:
$H_0: \beta_1 = 0$	$H_0: \beta_2 = 0$	$H_0: \beta_3 = 0$
$H_1: \beta_1 \neq 0$	$H_1: \beta_2 \neq 0$	$H_1: \beta_3 \neq 0$

We will test the hypotheses at the .05 level. Note that these are two-tailed tests.

The test statistic follows Student's *t* distribution with $n - (k + 1)$ degrees of freedom. The number of sample observations is *n*. There are 20 homes in the study, so $n = 20$. The number of independent variables is *k*, which is 3. Thus, there are $n - (k + 1) = 20 - (3 + 1) = 16$ degrees of freedom.

The critical value for *t* is in Appendix B.5. For a two-tailed test with 16 degrees of freedom using the .05 significance level, H_0 is rejected if *t* is less than −2.120 or greater than 2.120.

Refer to the Excel output earlier in this section. The column highlighted in orange, headed Coefficients, shows the values for the multiple regression equation:

$$\hat{y} = 427.194 - 4.583x_1 - 14.831x_2 + 6.101x_3$$

Interpreting the term $-4.583x_1$ in the equation: For each degree increase in temperature, we predict that heating cost will decrease \$4.58, holding the insulation and age of the furnace variables constant.

The column in the Excel output labeled "Standard Error" shows the standard error of the sample regression coefficients. Recall that Salsberry Realty selected a sample of 20 homes along the East Coast of the United States. If Salsberry Realty selected a second random sample and computed the regression coefficients for that sample, the values would not be exactly the same. If the sampling process was repeated many times, we could construct a sampling distribution for each of these regression coefficients. The column labeled "Standard Error" estimates the variability for each of these regression coefficients. The sampling distributions of the coefficients follow the *t* distribution with $n - (k + 1)$ degrees of freedom. Hence, we are able to test the independent variables individually to determine whether the regression coefficients differ from zero. The formula is:

TESTING INDIVIDUAL REGRESSION COEFFICIENTS

$$t = \frac{b_i - 0}{s_{b_i}} \quad \textbf{(14–6)}$$

The b_i refers to any one of the regression coefficients, and s_{b_i} refers to the standard deviation of that distribution of the regression coefficient. We include 0 in the equation because the null hypothesis is $\beta_i = 0$.

To illustrate this formula, refer to the test of the regression coefficient for the independent variable temperature. From the output earlier in this section, the regression coefficient for temperature is −4.583. The standard deviation of the sampling distribution of the regression coefficient for the independent variable temperature is 0.772. Inserting these values in formula (14–6):

$$t = \frac{b_1 - 0}{s_{b_1}} = \frac{-4.583 - 0}{0.772} = -5.937$$

The computed value of t is −5.937 for temperature (the small difference between the computed value and that shown on the Excel output is due to rounding) and −3.119 for insulation. Both of these t-values are in the rejection region to the left of −2.120. Thus, we conclude that the regression coefficients for the temperature and insulation variables are *not* zero. The computed t for the age of the furnace is 1.521, so we conclude that the coefficient could equal 0. The independent variable age of the furnace is not a significant predictor of heating cost. The results of these hypothesis tests indicate that the analysis should focus on temperature and insulation as predictors of heating cost.

We can also use p-values to test the individual regression coefficients. Again, these are commonly reported in statistical software output. The computed value of t for temperature on the Excel output is −5.934 and has a p-value of 0.000. Because the p-value is less than 0.05, the regression coefficient for the independent variable temperature is not equal to zero and should be included in the equation to predict heating costs. For insulation, the value of t is −3.119 and has a p-value of 0.007. As with temperature, the p-value is less than 0.05, so we conclude that the insulation regression coefficient is not equal to zero and should be included in the equation to predict heating cost. In contrast to temperature and insulation, the p-value to test the "age of the furnace" regression coefficient is 0.148. It is clearly greater than 0.05, so we conclude that the "age of furnace" regression coefficient could equal 0. Further, as an independent variable it is not a significant predictor of heating cost. Thus, age of furnace should not be included in the equation to predict heating costs.

At this point, we need to develop a strategy for deleting independent variables. In the Salsberry Realty case, there were three independent variables. For the age of the furnace variable, we failed to reject the null hypothesis that the regression coefficient was zero. It is clear that we should drop that variable and rerun the regression equation. Below is the Excel output where heating cost is the dependent variable and outside temperature and amount of insulation are the independent variables.

	A	B	C	D
1	Cost	Temp	Insul	Age
2	250	35	3	6
3	360	29	4	10
4	165	36	7	3
5	43	60	6	9
6	92	65	5	6
7	200	30	5	5
8	355	10	6	7
9	290	7	10	10
10	230	21	9	11
11	120	55	2	5
12	73	54	12	4
13	205	48	5	1
14	400	20	5	15
15	320	39	4	7
16	72	60	8	6
17	272	20	5	8
18	94	58	7	3
19	190	40	8	11
20	235	27	9	8

SUMMARY OUTPUT

Regression Statistics	
Multiple R	0.881
R Square	0.776
Adjusted R Square	0.749
Standard Error	52.982
Observations	20

ANOVA

	df	*SS*	*MS*	*F*	*Significance F*
Regression	2	165194.521	82597.261	29.424	0.000
Residual	17	47721.229	2807.131		
Total	19	212915.750			

	Coefficients	*Standard Error*	*t Stat*	*P-value*
Intercept	490.286	44.410	11.040	0.000
Temp	-5.150	0.702	-7.337	0.000
Insul	-14.718	4.934	-2.983	0.008

Summarizing the results from this new output:

1. The new regression equation is:

$$\hat{y} = 490.286 - 5.150x_1 - 14.718x_2$$

Notice that the regression coefficients for outside temperature (x_1) and amount of insulation (x_2) are similar to but not exactly the same as when we included the independent variable age of the furnace. Compare the above equation to that in the Excel output earlier in this section. Both of the regression coefficients are negative as in the earlier equation.

2. The details of the global test are as follows:

$$H_0 : \beta_1 = \beta_2 = 0$$
$$H_1 : \text{Not all of the } \beta_i\text{'s} = 0$$

The F distribution is the test statistic and there are $k = 2$ degrees of freedom in the numerator and $n - (k + 1) = 20 - (2 + 1) = 17$ degrees of freedom in the denominator. Using the .05 significance level and Appendix B.6, the decision rule is to reject H_0 if F is greater than 3.59. We compute the value of F as follows:

$$F = \frac{\text{SSR}/k}{\text{SSE}/[n - (k + 1)]} = \frac{165{,}194.521/2}{47{,}721.229/[20 - (2 + 1)]} = 29.424$$

Because the computed value of F (29.424) is greater than the critical value (3.59), the null hypothesis is rejected and the alternate accepted. We conclude that at least one of the regression coefficients is different from 0.

Using the p-value, the F test statistic (29.424) has a p-value (0.000), which is clearly less than 0.05. Therefore, we reject the null hypothesis and accept the alternate. We conclude that at least one of the regression coefficients is different from 0.

3. The next step is to conduct a test of the regression coefficients individually. We want to determine if one or both of the regression coefficients are different from 0. The null and alternate hypotheses for each of the independent variables are:

Outside Temperature	Insulation
$H_0: \beta_1 = 0$	$H_0: \beta_2 = 0$
$H_1: \beta_1 \neq 0$	$H_1: \beta_2 \neq 0$

The test statistic is the t distribution with $n - (k + 1) = 20 - (2 + 1) = 17$ degrees of freedom. Using the .05 significance level and Appendix B.5, the decision rule is to reject H_0 if the computed value of t is less than -2.110 or greater than 2.110.

Outside Temperature

$$t = \frac{b_1 - 0}{s_{b_1}} = \frac{-5.150 - 0}{0.702} = -7.337$$

Insulation

$$t = \frac{b_2 - 0}{s_{b_2}} = \frac{-14.718 - 0}{4.934} = -2.983$$

In both tests, we reject H_0 and accept H_1. We conclude that each of the regression coefficients is different from 0. Both outside temperature and amount of insulation are useful variables in explaining the variation in heating costs.

Using p-values, the p-value for the temperature t-statistic is 0.000 and the p-value for the insulation t-statistic is 0.008. Both p-values are less than 0.05, so in both tests we reject the null hypothesis and conclude that each of the regression coefficients is different from 0. Both outside temperature and amount of insulation are useful variables in explaining the variation in heating costs.

In the heating cost example, it was clear which independent variable to delete. However, in some instances which variable to delete may not be as clear-cut. To explain, suppose we develop a multiple regression equation based on five independent variables. We conduct the global test and find that some of the regression coefficients are different from zero. Next, we test the regression coefficients individually and find that three are significant and two are not. The preferred procedure is to drop the single independent variable with the *smallest absolute* t *value* or *largest* p-*value* and rerun the regression equation with the four remaining variables, then, on the new regression equation with four independent variables, conduct the individual tests. If there are still regression coefficients that are not significant, again drop the variable with the smallest absolute *t* value or the largest, nonsignificant *p*-value. To describe the process in another way, we should delete only one variable at a time. Each time we delete a variable, we need to rerun the regression equation and check the remaining variables.

This process of selecting variables to include in a regression model can be automated, using Excel, Minitab, MegaStat, or other statistical software. Most of the software systems include methods to sequentially remove and/or add independent variables and at the same time provide estimates of the percentage of variation explained (the *R*-square term). Two of the common methods are **stepwise regression** and **best subset regression.** It may take a long time, but in the extreme we could compute every regression between the dependent variable and any possible subset of the independent variables.

Unfortunately, on occasion, the software may work "too hard" to find an equation that fits all the quirks of your particular data set. The suggested equation may not represent the relationship in the population. Judgment is needed to choose among the equations presented. Consider whether the results are logical. They should have a simple interpretation and be consistent with your knowledge of the application under study.

SELF-REVIEW 14–3

The regression output about eating places in Myrtle Beach is repeated below (see earlier self-reviews).

Predictor	Coefficient	SE Coefficient	t	p-value	
Constant	2.50	1.50	1.667	0.111	
x_1	3.00	1.50	2.000	0.056	
x_2	4.00	3.00	1.333	0.194	
x_3	-3.00	0.20	-15.000	0.000	
x_4	0.20	0.05	4.000	0.000	
x_5	1.00	1.50	0.667	0.511	
Analysis of Variance					
Source	DF	SS	MS	F	p-value
Regression	5	100	20	10	0.000
Residual Error	20	40	2		
Total	25	140			

(a) Perform a global test of hypothesis to check if any of the regression coefficients are different from 0. What do you decide? Use the .05 significance level.

(b) Do an individual test of each independent variable. Which variables would you consider eliminating? Use the .05 significance level.

(c) Outline a plan for possibly removing independent variables.

EXERCISES

7. Given the following regression output,

Predictor	Coefficient	SE Coefficient	t	p-value	
Constant	84.998	1.863	45.62	0.000	
x_1	2.391	1.200	1.99	0.051	
x_2	-0.409	0.172	-2.38	0.021	
Analysis of Variance					
Source	DF	SS	MS	F	p-value
Regression	2	77.907	38.954	4.138	0.021
Residual Error	62	583.693	9.414		
Total	64	661.600			

answer the following questions:

a. Write the regression equation.

b. If x_1 is 4 and x_2 is 11, what is the expected or predicted value of the dependent variable?

c. How large is the sample? How many independent variables are there?

d. Conduct a global test of hypothesis to see if any of the set of regression coefficients could be different from 0. Use the .05 significance level. What is your conclusion?

e. Conduct a test of hypothesis for each independent variable. Use the .05 significance level. Which variable would you consider eliminating?

f. Outline a strategy for deleting independent variables in this case.

8. The following regression output was obtained from a study of architectural firms. The dependent variable is the total amount of fees in millions of dollars.

Predictor	Coefficient	SE Coefficient	t	p-value	
Constant	7.987	2.967	2.690	0.010	
x_1	0.122	0.031	3.920	0.000	
x_2	-1.220	0.053	-2.270	0.028	
x_3	-0.063	0.039	-1.610	0.114	
x_4	0.523	0.142	3.690	0.001	
x_5	-0.065	0.040	-1.620	0.112	
Analysis of Variance					
Source	DF	SS	MS	F	p-value
Regression	5	371000	742	12.89	0.000
Residual Error	46	2647.38	57.55		
Total	51	6357.38			

x_1 is the number of architects employed by the company.
x_2 is the number of engineers employed by the company.
x_3 is the number of years involved with health care projects.
x_4 is the number of states in which the firm operates.
x_5 is the percent of the firm's work that is health care–related.

a. Write out the regression equation.

b. How large is the sample? How many independent variables are there?

c. Conduct a global test of hypothesis to see if any of the set of regression coefficients could be different from 0. Use the .05 significance level. What is your conclusion?

d. Conduct a test of hypothesis for each independent variable. Use the .05 significance level. Which variable would you consider eliminating first?

e. Outline a strategy for deleting independent variables in this case.

LO14-4

Evaluate the assumptions of multiple regression.

EVALUATING THE ASSUMPTIONS OF MULTIPLE REGRESSION

In the previous section, we described the methods to statistically evaluate the multiple regression equation. The results of the test let us know if at least one of the coefficients was not equal to zero and we described a procedure of evaluating each regression coefficient. We also discussed the decision-making process for including and excluding independent variables in the multiple regression equation.

It is important to know that the validity of the statistical global and individual tests rely on several assumptions. So if the assumptions are not true, the results might be biased or misleading. However, strict adherence to the following assumptions is not always possible. Fortunately, the statistical techniques discussed in this chapter are robust enough to work effectively even when one or more of the assumptions are violated. Even if the values in the multiple regression equation are "off" slightly, our estimates using a multiple regression equation will be closer than any that could be made otherwise.

In Chapter 13, we listed the necessary assumptions for regression when we considered only a single independent variable. The assumptions for multiple regression are similar.

1. **There is a linear relationship.** That is, there is a straight-line relationship between the dependent variable and the set of independent variables.
2. **The variation in the residuals is the same for both large and small values of $\hat{y}$.** To put it another way, $(y - \hat{y})$ is unrelated to whether $\hat{y}$ is large or small.
3. **The residuals follow the normal probability distribution.** Recall the residual is the difference between the actual value of y and the estimated value $\hat{y}$. So the term $(y - \hat{y})$ is computed for every observation in the data set. These residuals should approximately follow a normal probability distribution with a mean of 0.
4. **The independent variables should not be correlated.** That is, we would like to select a set of independent variables that are not themselves correlated.
5. **The residuals are independent.** This means that successive observations of the dependent variable are not correlated. This assumption is often violated when time is involved with the sampled observations.

In this section, we present a brief discussion of each of these assumptions. In addition, we provide methods to validate these assumptions and indicate the consequences if these assumptions cannot be met. For those interested in additional discussion, search on the term "Applied Linear Models."

Linear Relationship

Let's begin with the linearity assumption. The idea is that the relationship between the set of independent variables and the dependent variable is linear. If we are considering two independent variables, we can visualize this assumption. The two independent variables and the dependent variable would form a three-dimensional space. The regression equation would then form a plane as shown on page 490. We can evaluate this assumption with scatter diagrams and residual plots.

Using Scatter Diagrams The evaluation of a multiple regression equation should always include a scatter diagram that plots the dependent variable against each independent variable. These graphs help us to visualize the relationships and provide some initial information about the direction (positive or negative), linearity, and strength of the relationship. For example, the scatter diagrams for the home heating example follow. The plots suggest a fairly strong negative, linear relationship between heating cost and temperature, and a negative relationship between heating cost and insulation.

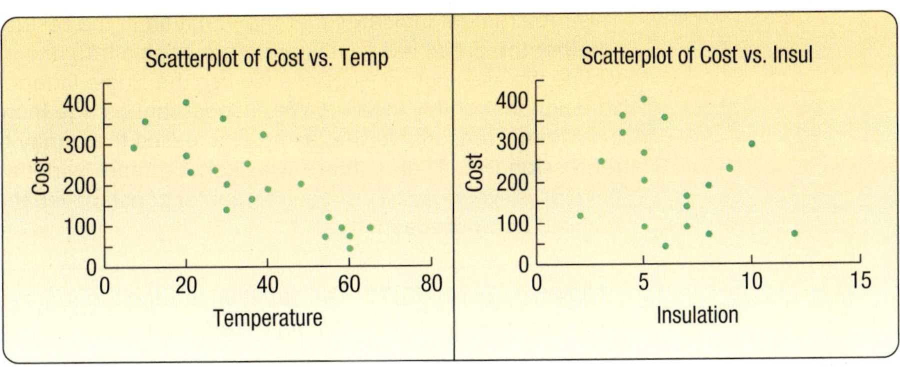

Using Residual Plots Recall that a residual $(y - \hat{y})$ can be computed using the multiple regression equation for each observation in a data set. In Chapter 13, we discussed the idea that the best regression line passed through the center of the data in a scatter plot. In this case, you would find a good number of the observations above the regression line (these residuals would have a positive sign) and a good number of the observations below the line (these residuals would have a negative sign). Further, the observations would be scattered above and below the line over the entire range of the independent variable.

The same concept is true for multiple regression, but we cannot graphically portray the multiple regression. However, plots of the residuals can help us evaluate the linearity of the multiple regression equation. To investigate, the residuals are plotted on the vertical axis against the predicted variable, $\hat{y}$. In the following graphs, the left graph shows the residual plots for the home heating cost example. Notice the following:

- The residuals are plotted on the vertical axis and are centered around zero. There are both positive and negative residuals.
- The residual plots show a random distribution of positive and negative values across the entire range of the variable plotted on the horizontal axis.
- The points are scattered and there is no obvious pattern, so there is no reason to doubt the linearity assumption.

The plot on the right shows nonrandom residuals. See that the residual plot does *not* show a random distribution of positive and negative values across the entire range of the variable plotted on the horizontal axis. In fact, the graph shows a non-linear pattern of the residuals. This indicates the relationship is probably not linear. In this case, we would evaluate different transformations of the variables in the equation as discussed in Chapter 13.

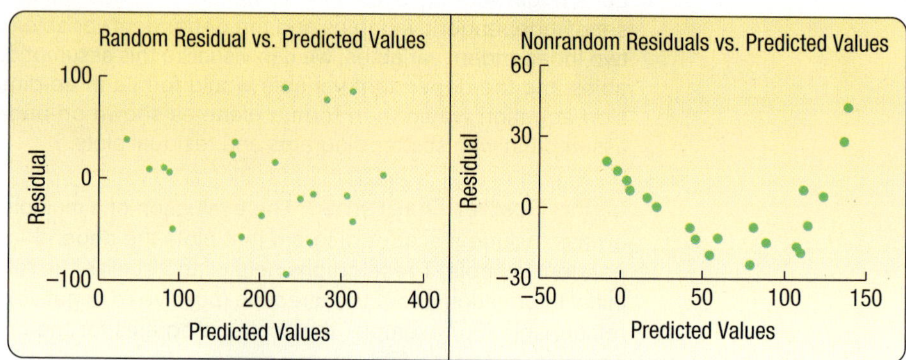

Variation in Residuals Same for Large and Small $\hat{y}$ Values

This requirement indicates that the variation in the residuals is constant, regardless of whether the predicted values are large or small. To cite a specific example which may violate the assumption, suppose we use the single independent variable age to explain variation in monthly income. We suspect that as age increases so does income, but it also seems reasonable that as age increases there may be more variation around the regression line. That is, there will likely be more variation in income for 50-year-olds than for 35-year-olds. The requirement for constant variation around the regression line is called **homoscedasticity.**

HOMOSCEDASTICITY The variation around the regression equation is the same for all of the values of the independent variables.

To check for homoscedasticity, the residuals are plotted against $\hat{y}$. This is the same graph that we used to evaluate the assumption of linearity. Based on the scatter diagram, it is reasonable to conclude that this assumption has not been violated.

Distribution of Residuals

To be sure that the inferences we make in the global and individual hypothesis tests are valid, we evaluate the distribution of residuals. Ideally, the residuals should follow a normal probability distribution.

To evaluate this assumption, we can organize the residuals into a frequency distribution. The Histogram of Residuals graph is shown on the left for the home heating cost example. Although it is difficult to show that the residuals follow a normal distribution with only 20 observations, it does appear the normality assumption is reasonable.

Another graph that helps to evaluate the assumption of normally distributed residuals is called a Normal Probability Plot and is shown to the right of the histogram. This graphical analysis is often included in statistical software. If the plotted points are fairly close to a straight line drawn from the lower left to the upper right of the graph, the normal probability plot supports the assumption of normally distributed residuals This plot supports the assumption of normally distributed residuals.

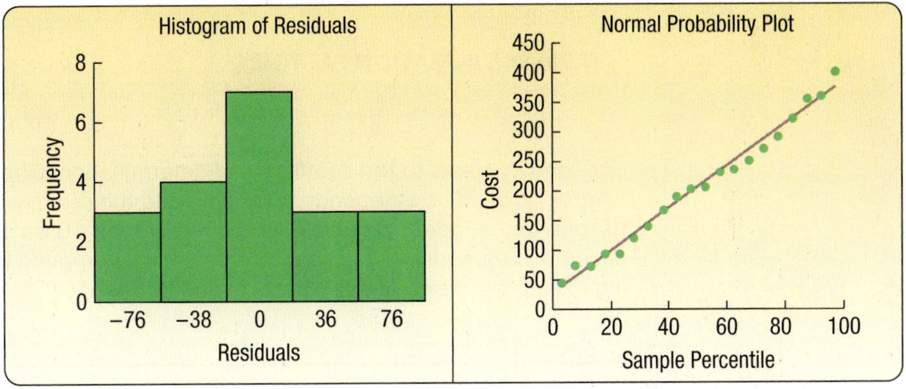

In this case, both graphs support the assumption that the residuals follow the normal probability distribution. Therefore, the inferences that we made based on the global and individual hypothesis tests are supported with the results of this evaluation.

Multicollinearity

Multicollinearity exists when independent variables are correlated. Correlated independent variables make it difficult to make inferences about the individual regression coefficients and their individual effects on the dependent variable. In practice, it is nearly impossible to select variables that are completely unrelated. To put it another way, it is nearly impossible to create a set of independent variables that are not correlated to some degree. However, a general understanding of the issue of multicollinearity is important.

First, multicollinearity does not affect a multiple regression equation's ability to predict the dependent variable. However, when we are interested in evaluating the relationship between each independent variable and the dependent variable, multicollinearity may show unexpected results.

For example, if we use two highly correlated independent variables, high school GPA and high school class rank, to predict the GPA of incoming college freshmen (dependent variable), we would expect that both independent variables would be positively related to the dependent variable. However, because the independent variables are highly correlated, one of the independent variables may have an unexpected and inexplicable negative sign. In essence, these two independent variables are redundant in that they explain the same variation in the dependent variable.

A second reason to avoid correlated independent variables is they may lead to erroneous results in the hypothesis tests for the individual independent variables. This is due to the instability of the standard error of estimate. Several clues that indicate problems with multicollinearity include the following:

1. An independent variable known to be an important predictor ends up having a regression coefficient that is not significant.
2. A regression coefficient that should have a positive sign turns out to be negative, or vice versa.
3. When an independent variable is added or removed, there is a drastic change in the values of the remaining regression coefficients.

In our evaluation of a multiple regression equation, an approach to reducing the effects of multicollinearity is to carefully select the independent variables that are included in the regression equation. A general rule is if the correlation between two independent variables is between −0.70 and 0.70, there likely is not a problem using both of the independent variables. A more precise test is to use the **variance inflation factor.** It is usually written *VIF*. The value of *VIF* is found as follows:

VARIANCE INFLATION FACTOR

$$VIF = \frac{1}{1 - R_j^2} \quad (14\text{–}7)$$

The term R_j^2 refers to the coefficient of determination, where the selected *independent variable* is used as a dependent variable and the remaining independent variables are used as independent variables. A *VIF* greater than 10 is considered unsatisfactory, indicating that the independent variable should be removed from the analysis. The following example will explain the details of finding the *VIF*.

EXAMPLE

Refer to the data in Table 14–1, which relate the heating cost to the independent variables: outside temperature, amount of insulation, and age of furnace. Develop a correlation matrix for all the independent variables. Does it appear there is a problem with multicollinearity? Find and interpret the variance inflation factor for each of the independent variables.

SOLUTION

We begin by finding the correlation matrix for the dependent variable and the three independent variables. A correlation matrix shows the correlation between all pairs of the variables. A portion of that output follows:

	Cost	*Temp*	*Insul*	*Age*
Cost	1.000			
Temp	−0.812	1.000		
Insul	−0.257	−0.103	1.000	
Age	0.537	−0.486	0.064	1.000

The highlighted area indicates the correlation among the independent variables. Because all of the correlations are between −.70 and .70, we do not suspect problems with multicollinearity. The largest correlation among the independent variables is −0.486 between age and temperature.

To confirm this conclusion, we compute the *VIF* for each of the three independent variables. We will consider the independent variable temperature first. We use the Regression Analysis in Excel to find the multiple coefficient of determination with temperature as the *dependent variable* and amount of insulation and age of the furnace as independent variables. The relevant regression output follows.

SUMMARY OUTPUT					
Regression Statistics					
Multiple R	0.491				
R Square	0.241				
Adjusted R Square	0.152				
Standard Error	16.031				
Observations	20				
ANOVA					
	df	*SS*	*MS*	*F*	*Significance F*
Regression	2	1390.291	695.145	2.705	0.096
Residual	17	4368.909	256.995		
Total	19	5759.200			

The coefficient of determination is .241, so inserting this value into the *VIF* formula:

$$VIF = \frac{1}{1 - R_1^2} = \frac{1}{1 - .241} = 1.32$$

The *VIF* value of 1.32 is less than the upper limit of 10. This indicates that the independent variable temperature is not strongly correlated with the other independent variables.

Again, to find the *VIF* for insulation we would develop a regression equation with insulation as the *dependent variable* and temperature and age of furnace as independent variables. For this equation, the R^2 is .011 and, using formula (14–7), the *VIF* for insulation would be 1.011. To find the *VIF* for age, we would develop a regression equation with age as the dependent variable and temperature and insulation as the independent variables. For this equation, the R^2 is .236 and, using formula (14–7), the *VIF* for age would be 1.310. All the *VIF* values are less than 10. Hence, we conclude there is not a problem with multicollinearity in this example.

Independent Observations

The fifth assumption about regression and correlation analysis is that successive residuals should be independent. This means that there is not a pattern to the residuals, the residuals are not highly correlated, and there are not long runs of positive or negative residuals. When successive residuals are correlated, we refer to this condition as **autocorrelation.**

Autocorrelation frequently occurs when the data are collected over a period of time. For example, we wish to predict yearly sales of Agis Software Inc. based on the time and the amount spent on advertising. The dependent variable is yearly sales and the independent variables are time and amount spent on advertising. It is likely that for a period of time the actual points will be above the regression plane (remember there are two independent variables) and then for a period of time the points will be below the regression plane. The graph below shows the residuals plotted on the vertical axis and the fitted values $\hat{y}$ on the horizontal axis. Note the run of residuals above the mean of the residuals, followed by a run below the mean. A scatter plot such as this would indicate possible autocorrelation.

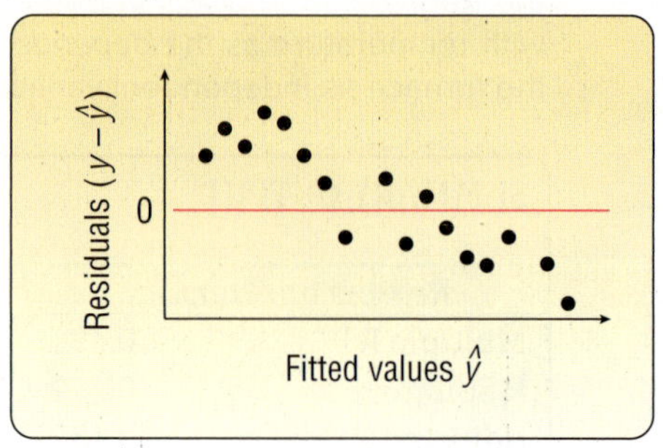

There is a test for autocorrelation, called the Durbin-Watson. It is discussed in Chapter 18.

LO14-5
Use and interpret a qualitative, dummy variable in multiple regression.

QUALITATIVE INDEPENDENT VARIABLES

In the previous example/solution regarding heating cost, the two independent variables outside temperature and insulation were quantitative; that is, numerical in nature. Frequently we wish to use nominal-scale variables—such as gender, whether the home has a swimming pool, or whether the sports team was the home or the visiting team—in our analysis. These are called **qualitative variables** because they describe a particular quality or attribute, such as gender measured as male or female. To use a qualitative variable in regression analysis, we use a scheme of **dummy variables** in which one of the two possible conditions is coded 0 and the other 1.

DUMMY VARIABLE A variable in which there are only two possible outcomes. For analysis, one of the outcomes is coded a 1 and the other a 0.

STATISTICS IN ACTION

Multiple regression has been used in a variety of legal proceedings. It is particularly useful in cases alleging discrimination by gender or race. As an example, suppose that a woman alleges that Company X's wage rates are unfair to women. To support the claim, the plaintiff produces data showing that, on the average, women earn less than men. In response, Company X argues that its wage rates are based on experience, training, and skill and that its female employees, on the average, are younger and less experienced than the male employees. In fact, the company might further argue that the current situation is actually due to its recent successful efforts to hire more women.

For example, we are interested in estimating an executive's salary on the basis of years of job experience and whether he or she graduated from college. "Graduation from college" can take on only one of two conditions: yes or no. Thus, it is considered a qualitative variable.

Suppose in the Salsberry Realty example that the independent variable "garage" is added. For those homes without an attached garage, 0 is used; for homes with an attached garage, a 1 is used. We will refer to the "garage" variable as x_4. The data from Table 14–2 are entered into the Excel system. Recall that the variable "age of the furnace" is not included in the analysis because we determined that it was not significantly related to heating cost.

The output from Excel is:

	A	B	C	D	E	F	G	H	I	J	K
1	Cost	Temp	Insul	Garage		SUMMARY OUTPUT					
2	250	35	3	0							
3	360	29	4	1		*Regression Statistics*					
4	165	36	7	0		Multiple R	0.933				
5	43	60	6	0		R Square	0.870				
6	92	65	5	0		Adjusted R Square	0.845				
7	200	30	5	0		Standard Error	41.618				
8	355	10	6	1		Observations	20				
9	290	7	10	1							
10	230	21	9	0		ANOVA					
11	120	55	2	0			*df*	*SS*	*MS*	*F*	*Significance F*
12	73	54	12	0		Regression	3	185202.269	61734.090	35.641	0.000
13	205	48	5	1		Residual	16	27713.481	1732.093		
14	400	20	5	1		Total	19	212915.750			
15	320	39	4	1							
16	72	60	8	0			*Coefficients*	*Standard Error*	*t Stat*	*P-value*	
17	272	20	5	1		Intercept	393.666	45.001	8.748	0.000	
18	94	58	7	0		Temp	-3.963	0.653	-6.072	0.000	
19	190	40	8	1		Insul	-11.334	4.002	-2.832	0.012	
20	235	27	9	0		Garage	77.432	22.783	3.399	0.004	

TABLE 14–2 Home Heating Costs, Temperature, Insulation, and Presence of a Garage for a Sample of 20 Homes

Cost, y	Temperature, x_1	Insulation, x_2	Garage, x_4
$250	35	3	0
360	29	4	1
165	36	7	0
43	60	6	0
92	65	5	0
200	30	5	0
355	10	6	1
290	7	10	1
230	21	9	0
120	55	2	0
73	54	12	0
205	48	5	1
400	20	5	1
320	39	4	1
72	60	8	0
272	20	5	1
94	58	7	0
190	40	8	1
235	27	9	0
139	30	7	0

What is the effect of the garage variable? Should it be included in the analysis? To show the effect of the variable, suppose we have two homes exactly alike next to each other in Buffalo, New York; one has an attached garage and the other does not. Both homes have 3 inches of insulation, and the mean January temperature in Buffalo is 20 degrees. For the house without an attached garage, a 0 is substituted for x_4 in the regression equation. The estimated heating cost is $280.404, found by:

$$\begin{aligned}\hat{y} &= 393.666 - 3.963x_1 - 11.334x_2 + 77.432x_4 \\ &= 393.666 - 3.963(20) - 11.334(3) + 77.432(0) = 280.404\end{aligned}$$

For the house with an attached garage, a 1 is substituted for x_4 in the regression equation. The estimated heating cost is $357.836, found by:

$$\begin{aligned}\hat{y} &= 393.666 - 3.963x_1 - 11.334x_2 + 77.432x_4 \\ &= 393.666 - 3.963(20) - 11.334(3) + 77.432(1) = 357.836\end{aligned}$$

The difference between the estimated heating costs is $77.432 ($357.836 − $280.404). Hence, we can expect the cost to heat a house with an attached garage to be $77.432 more than the cost for an equivalent house without a garage.

We have shown the difference between the two types of homes to be $77.432, but is the difference significant? We conduct the following test of hypothesis.

$$H_0: \beta_4 = 0$$
$$H_1: \beta_4 \neq 0$$

The information necessary to answer this question is in the output at the bottom of the previous page. The regression coefficient for the independent variable garage is $77.432, and the standard deviation of the sampling distribution is 22.783. We identify this as the fourth independent variable, so we use a subscript of 4. (Remember we dropped age of the furnace, the third independent variable.) Finally, we insert these values in formula (14–6).

$$t = \frac{b_4 - 0}{s_{b_4}} = \frac{77.432 - 0}{22.783} = 3.399$$

There are three independent variables in the analysis, so there are $n - (k + 1) = 20 - (3 + 1) = 16$ degrees of freedom. The critical value from Appendix B.5 is 2.120. The decision rule, using a two-tailed test and the .05 significance level, is to reject H_0 if the computed t is to the left of -2.120 or to the right of 2.120. Because the computed value of 3.399 is to the right of 2.120, the null hypothesis is rejected. We conclude that the regression coefficient is not zero. The independent variable garage should be included in the analysis.

Using the p-value approach, the computed t value of 3.399 has a p-value of 0.004. This value is less than the .05 significance level. Therefore, we reject the null hypothesis. We conclude that the regression coefficient is not zero and the independent variable garage should be included in the analysis.

Is it possible to use a qualitative variable with more than two possible outcomes? Yes, but the coding scheme becomes more complex and will require a series of dummy variables. To explain, suppose a company is studying its sales as they relate to advertising expense by quarter for the last 5 years. Let sales be the dependent variable and advertising expense be the first independent variable, x_1. To include the qualitative information regarding the quarter, we use three additional independent variables. For the variable x_2, the five observations referring to the first quarter of each of the 5 years are coded 1 and the other quarters 0. Similarly, for x_3 the five observations referring to the second quarter are coded 1 and the other quarters 0. For x_4, the five observations referring to the third quarter are coded 1 and the other quarters 0. An observation that does not refer to any of the first three quarters must refer to the fourth quarter, so a distinct independent variable referring to this quarter is not necessary.

SELF-REVIEW 14–4

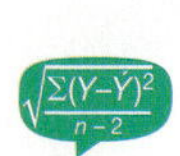

A study by the American Realtors Association investigated the relationship between the commissions earned by sales associates last year and the number of months since the associates earned their real estate licenses. Also of interest in the study is the gender of the sales associate. Below is a portion of the regression output. The dependent variable is commissions, which is reported in \$000, and the independent variables are months since the license was earned and gender (female = 1 and male = 0).

Regression Analysis

Regression Statistics	
Multiple R	0.801
R Square	0.642
Adjusted R Square	0.600
Standard Error	3.219
Observations	20

ANOVA

	df	*SS*	*MS*	*F*	*p-value*
Regression	2	315.9291	157.9645	15.2468	0.0002
Residual	17	176.1284	10.36049		
Total	19	492.0575			

	Coefficients	*Standard Error*	*t Stat*	*p-value*
Intercept	15.7625	3.0782	5.121	.0001
Months	0.4415	0.0839	5.262	.0001
Gender	3.8598	1.4724	2.621	.0179

(a) Write out the regression equation. How much commission would you expect a female agent to make who earned her license 30 months ago?
(b) Do the female agents on the average make more or less than the male agents? How much more?
(c) Conduct a test of hypothesis to determine if the independent variable gender should be included in the analysis. Use the .05 significance level. What is your conclusion?

LO14-6
Include and interpret an interaction effect in a multiple regression analysis.

REGRESSION MODELS WITH INTERACTION

In Chapter 12, we discussed interaction among independent variables. To explain, suppose we are studying weight loss and assume, as the current literature suggests, that diet and exercise are related. So the dependent variable is amount of change in weight and the independent variables are diet (yes or no) and exercise (none, moderate, significant). We are interested in whether there is interaction among the independent variables. That is, if those studied maintain their diet and exercise significantly, will that increase the mean amount of weight lost? Is total weight loss more than the sum of the loss due to the diet effect and the loss due to the exercise effect?

We can expand on this idea. Instead of having two nominal-scale variables, diet and exercise, we can examine the effect (interaction) of several ratio-scale variables. For example, suppose we want to study the effect of room temperature (68, 72, 76, or 80 degrees Fahrenheit) and noise level (60, 70, or 80 decibels) on the number of units produced. To put it another way, does the combination of noise level in the room and the temperature of the room have an effect on the productivity of the workers? Would workers produce more units in a quiet, cool room compared to a hot, noisy room?

In regression analysis, interaction is examined as a separate independent variable. An interaction prediction variable can be developed by multiplying the data values of one independent variable by the values of another independent variable, thereby creating a new independent variable. A two-variable model that includes an interaction term is:

$$Y = \alpha + \beta_1 X_1 + \beta_2 X_2 + \beta_3 X_1 X_2$$

The term X_1X_2 is the *interaction term.* We create this variable by multiplying the values of X_1 and X_2 to create a third independent variable. We then develop a regression equation using the three independent variables and test the significance of the third independent variable using the individual test for independent variables, described earlier in the chapter. An example will illustrate the details.

EXAMPLE

Refer to the heating cost example and the data in Table 14–1. Is there an interaction between the outside temperature and the amount of insulation? If both variables are increased, is the effect on heating cost greater than the sum of savings from warmer temperature and the savings from increased insulation separately?

SOLUTION

The information from Table 14–1 for the independent variables temperature and insulation is repeated below. We create the interaction variable by multiplying the value of temperature by the value insulation for each observation in the data set. For the first sampled home, the value temperature is 35 degrees and insulation is

3 inches so the value of the interaction variable is $35 \times 3 = 105$. The values of the other interaction products are found in a similar fashion.

	A	B	C	D	E	F	G	H	I	J	K
1	Cost	Temp	Insul	Temp X Insul		SUMMARY OUTPUT					
2	250	35	3	105							
3	360	29	4	116		*Regression Statistics*					
4	165	36	7	252		Multiple R	0.893				
5	43	60	6	360		R Square	0.798				
6	92	65	5	325		Adjusted R Square	0.760				
7	200	30	5	150		Standard Error	51.846				
8	355	10	6	60		Observations	20				
9	290	7	10	70							
10	230	21	9	189		ANOVA					
11	120	55	2	110			*df*	*SS*	*MS*	*F*	*Significance F*
12	73	54	12	648		Regression	3	169908.452	56636.151	21.070	0.000
13	205	48	5	240		Residual	16	43007.298	2687.956		
14	400	20	5	100		Total	19	212915.750			
15	320	39	4	156							
16	72	60	8	480			*Coefficients*	*Standard Error*	*t Stat*	*P-value*	
17	272	20	5	100		Intercept	598.070	92.265	6.482	0.000	
18	94	58	7	406		Temp	-7.811	2.124	-3.678	0.002	
19	190	40	8	320		Insul	-30.161	12.621	-2.390	0.030	
20	235	27	9	243		Temp X Insul	0.385	0.291	1.324	0.204	
21	139	30	7	210							

We find the multiple regression using temperature, insulation, and the interaction of temperature and insulation as independent variables. The regression equation is reported below.

$$\hat{y} = 598.070 - 7.811x_1 - 30.161x_2 + 0.385x_1x_2$$

The question we wish to answer is whether the interaction variable is significant. Note we use the subscript, 1×2, to indicate the coefficient of the interaction of variables 1 and 2. We will use the .05 significance level. In terms of a hypothesis:

$$H_0: \beta_{1\times2} = 0$$

$$H_1: \beta_{1\times2} \neq 0$$

There are $n - (k + 1) = 20 - (3 + 1) = 16$ degrees of freedom. Using the .05 significance level and a two-tailed test, the critical values of t are -2.120 and 2.120. We reject the null hypothesis if t is less than -2.120 or t is greater than 2.120. From the output, $b_{1\times2} = 0.385$ and $s_{b_{1\times2}} = 0.291$. To find the value of t, we use formula (14–6).

$$t = \frac{b_{1\times2} - 0}{s_{b_{1\times2}}} = \frac{0.385 - 0}{0.291} = 1.324$$

Because the computed value of 1.324 is less than the critical value of 2.120, we do not reject the null hypothesis. In addition, the p-value of .204 exceeds .05. We conclude that there is not a significant interaction effect of temperature and insulation on home heating costs.

There are other situations that can occur when studying interaction among independent variables.

1. It is possible to have a three-way interaction among the independent variables. In our heating example, we might have considered the three-way interaction between temperature, insulation, and age of the furnace.
2. It is possible to have an interaction where one of the independent variables is nominal scale. In our heating cost example, we could have studied the interaction between temperature and garage.

Studying all possible interactions can become very complex. However, careful consideration to possible interactions among independent variables can often provide useful insight into the regression models.

LO14-7

Apply stepwise regression to develop a multiple regression model.

STEPWISE REGRESSION

In our heating cost example (see sample information in Table 14–1), we considered three independent variables: the mean outside temperature, the amount of insulation in the home, and the age of the furnace. To obtain the equation, we first ran a global or "all at once" test to determine if any of the regression coefficients were significant. When we found at least one to be significant, we tested the regression coefficients individually to determine which were important. We kept the independent variables that had significant regression coefficients and left the others out. By retaining the independent variables with significant coefficients, we found the regression equation that used the fewest independent variables. This made the regression equation easier to interpret. Then we considered the qualitative variable, garage, and found that it was significantly related to heating cost. The variable, garage, was added to the equation.

Deciding the set of independent variables to include in a multiple regression equation can be accomplished using a a technique called **stepwise regression.** This technique efficiently builds an equation that only includes independent variables with significant regression coefficients.

STEPWISE REGRESSION A step-by-step method to determine a regression equation that begins with a single independent variable and adds or deletes independent variables one by one. Only independent variables with nonzero regression coefficients are included in the regression equation.

In the stepwise method, we develop a sequence of equations. The first equation contains only one independent variable. However, this independent variable is the one from the set of proposed independent variables that explains the most variation in the dependent variable. Stated differently, if we compute all the simple correlations between each independent variable and the dependent variable, the stepwise method first selects the independent variable with the strongest correlation with the dependent variable.

Next, the stepwise method looks at the remaining independent variables and then selects the one that will explain the largest percentage of the variation yet unexplained. We continue this process until all the independent variables with significant regression coefficients are included in the regression equation. The advantages to the stepwise method are:

1. Only independent variables with significant regression coefficients are entered into the equation.
2. The steps involved in building the regression equation are clear.
3. It is efficient in finding the regression equation with only significant regression coefficients.
4. The changes in the multiple standard error of estimate and the coefficient of determination are shown.

Stepwise regression procedures are included in many statistical software packages. For example, Minitab's stepwise regression analysis for the home heating cost problem follows. Note that the final equation, which is reported in the column labeled 3, includes the independent variables temperature, garage, and insulation. These are the same independent variables that were included in our equation using the global test and the test for individual independent variables. The independent variable age, indicating the furnace's age, is not included because it is not a significant predictor of cost.

Worksheet 1 ***

↓	C1 Cost	C2 Temp	C3 Insul	C4 Garage
1	250	35	3	0
2	360	29	4	1
3	165	36	7	0
4	43	60	6	0
5	92	65	5	0
6	200	30	5	0
7	355	10	6	1
8	290	7	10	1
9	230	21	9	0
10	120	55	2	0
11	73	54	12	0
12	205	48	5	1
13	400	20	5	1
14	320	39	4	1
15	72	60	8	0
16	272	20	5	1
17	94	58	7	0
18	190	40	8	1
19	235	27	9	0
20	139	30	7	0

Session

Stepwise Regression: Cost versus Temp, Insul, Garage

```
  Alpha-to-Enter: 0.15  Alpha-to-Remove: 0.15


Response is Cost on 3 predictors, with N = 20


Step              1       2       3
Constant      388.8   300.3   393.7

Temp          -4.93   -3.56   -3.96
T-Value       -5.89   -4.70   -6.07
P-Value       0.000   0.000   0.000

Garage                   93      77
T-Value                3.56    3.40
P-Value               0.002   0.004

Insul                         -11.3
T-Value                       -2.83
P-Value                       0.012

S              63.6    49.5    41.6
R-Sq          65.85   80.46   86.98
R-Sq(adj)     63.96   78.16   84.54
Mallows Cp     26.0    10.0     4.0
```

Reviewing the steps and interpreting output:

1. The stepwise procedure selects the independent variable temperature first. This variable explains more of the variation in heating cost than any of the other three proposed independent variables. Temperature explains 65.85% of the variation in heating cost. The regression equation is:

$$\hat{y} = 388.8 - 4.93x_1$$

   There is an inverse relationship between heating cost and temperature. For each degree the temperature increases, heating cost is reduced by $4.93.

2. The next independent variable to enter the regression equation is garage. When this variable is added to the regression equation, the coefficient of determination is increased from 65.85% to 80.46%. That is, by adding garage as an independent variable, we increase the coefficient of determination by 14.61 percentage points. The regression equation after step 2 is:

$$\hat{y} = 300.3 - 3.56x_1 + 93.0x_2$$

   Usually the regression coefficients will change from one step to the next. In this case, the coefficient for temperature retained its negative sign, but it changed from −4.93 to −3.56. This change is reflective of the added influence of the independent variable garage. Why did the stepwise method select the independent variable garage instead of either insulation or age? The increase in R^2, the coefficient of determination, is larger if garage is included rather than either of the other two variables.

3. At this point, there are two unused variables remaining, insulation and age. Notice on the third step the procedure selects insulation and then stops. This indicates the variable insulation explains more of the remaining variation in heating cost than the age variable does. After the third step, the regression equation is:

$$\hat{y} = 393.7 - 3.96x_1 + 77.0x_2 - 11.3x_3$$

   At this point, 86.98% of the variation in heating cost is explained by the three independent variables temperature, garage, and insulation. This is the same R^2 value and regression equation we found on page 512 except for rounding differences.

4. Here, the stepwise procedure stops. This means the independent variable age does not add significantly to the coefficient of determination.

The stepwise method developed the same regression equation, selected the same independent variables, and found the same coefficient of determination as the global and individual tests described earlier in the chapter. The advantage to the stepwise method is that it is more direct than using a combination of the global and individual procedures.

Other methods of variable selection are available. The stepwise method is also called the **forward selection method** because we begin with no independent variables and add one independent variable to the regression equation at each iteration. There is also the **backward elimination method,** which begins with the entire set of variables and eliminates one independent variable at each iteration.

The methods described so far look at one variable at a time and decide whether to include or eliminate that variable. Another approach is the **best-subset regression.** With this method, we look at the best model using one independent variable, the best model using two independent variables, the best model with three, and so on. The criterion is to find the model with the largest R^2 value, regardless of the number of independent variables. Also, each independent variable does not necessarily have a nonzero regression coefficient. Since each independent variable could either be included or not included, there are $2^k - 1$ possible models, where k refers to the number of independent variables. In our heating cost example, we considered four independent variables so there are 15 possible regression models, found by $2^4 - 1 = 16 - 1 = 15$. We would examine all regression models using one independent variable, all combinations using two variables, all combinations using three independent variables, and the possibility of using all four independent variables. The advantages to the best-subset method is it may examine combinations of independent variables not considered in the stepwise method. The process is available in Minitab and MegaStat.

EXERCISES

9. FILE The manager of High Point Sofa and Chair, a large furniture manufacturer located in North Carolina, is studying the job performance ratings of a sample of 15 electrical repairmen employed by the company. An aptitude test is required by the human resources department to become an electrical repairman. The manager was able to get the score for each repairman in the sample. In addition, he determined which of the repairmen were union members (code = 1) and which were not (code = 0). The sample information is reported below.

Worker	Job Performance Score	Aptitude Test Score	Union Membership
Abbott	58	5	0
Anderson	53	4	0
Bender	33	10	0
Bush	97	10	0
Center	36	2	0
Coombs	83	7	0
Eckstine	67	6	0
Gloss	84	9	0
Herd	98	9	1
Householder	45	2	1
Lori	97	8	1
Lindstrom	90	6	1
Mason	96	7	1
Pierse	66	3	1
Rohde	82	6	1

a. Use a statistical software package to develop a multiple regression equation using the job performance score as the dependent variable and aptitude test score and union membership as independent variables.

b. Comment on the regression equation. Be sure to include the coefficient of determination and the effect of union membership. Are these two variables effective in explaining the variation in job performance?

c. Conduct a test of hypothesis to determine if union membership should be included as an independent variable.

d. Repeat the analysis considering possible interaction terms.

10. FILE Cincinnati Paint Company sells quality brands of paints through hardware stores throughout the United States. The company maintains a large sales force who call on existing customers and look for new business. The national sales manager is investigating the relationship between the number of sales calls made and the miles driven by the sales representative. Also, do the sales representatives who drive the most miles and make the most calls necessarily earn the most in sales commissions? To investigate, the vice president of sales selected a sample of 25 sales representatives and determined:

- The amount earned in commissions last month (y)
- The number of miles driven last month (x_1)
- The number of sales calls made last month (x_2)

The information is reported below.

Commissions ($000)	Calls	Driven
22	139	2,371
13	132	2,226
33	144	2,731
⋮	⋮	⋮
25	127	2,671
43	154	2,988
34	147	2,829

Develop a regression equation including an interaction term. Is there a significant interaction between the number of sales calls and the miles driven?

11. FILE An art collector is studying the relationship between the selling price of a painting and two independent variables. The two independent variables are the number of bidders at the particular auction and the age of the painting, in years. A sample of 25 paintings revealed the following sample information.

Painting	Auction Price	Bidders	Age
1	3,470	10	67
2	3,500	8	56
3	3,700	7	73
⋮	⋮	⋮	⋮
23	4,660	5	94
24	4,710	3	88
25	4,880	1	84

a. Develop a multiple regression equation using the independent variables number of bidders and age of painting to estimate the dependent variable auction price. Discuss the equation. Does it surprise you that there is an inverse relationship between the number of bidders and the price of the painting?

b. Create an interaction variable and include it in the regression equation. Explain the meaning of the interaction. Is this variable significant?

c. Use the stepwise method and the independent variables for the number of bidders, the age of the painting, and the interaction between the number of bidders and the age of the painting. Which variables would you select?

12. **FILE** A real estate developer wishes to study the relationship between the size of home a client will purchase (in square feet) and other variables. Possible independent variables include the family income, family size, whether there is a senior adult parent living with the family (1 for yes, 0 for no), and the total years of education beyond high school for the husband and wife. The sample information is reported below.

Family	Square Feet	Income (000s)	Family Size	Senior Parent	Education
1	2,240	60.8	2	0	4
2	2,380	68.4	2	1	6
3	3,640	104.5	3	0	7
4	3,360	89.3	4	1	0
5	3,080	72.2	4	0	2
6	2,940	114	3	1	10
7	4,480	125.4	6	0	6
8	2,520	83.6	3	0	8
9	4,200	133	5	0	2
10	2,800	95	3	0	6

Develop an appropriate multiple regression equation. Which independent variables would you include in the final regression equation? Use the stepwise method.

LO14-8
Apply multiple regression techniques to develop a linear model.

REVIEW OF MULTIPLE REGRESSION

We described many topics involving multiple regression in this chapter. In this section of the chapter, we focus on a single example with a solution that reviews the procedure and guides your application of multiple regression analysis.

EXAMPLE

The Bank of New England is a large financial institution serving the New England states as well as New York and New Jersey. The mortgage department of the Bank of New England is studying data from recent loans. Of particular interest is how such factors as the value of the home being purchased ($000), education level of the head of the household (number of years, beginning with first grade), age of the head of the household, current monthly mortgage payment (in dollars), and gender of the head of the household (male = 1, female = 0) relate to the family income. The mortgage department would like to know whether these variables are effective predictors of family income.

SOLUTION

FILE Consider a random sample of 25 loan applications submitted to the Bank of New England last month. A portion of the sample information is shown in Table 14–3. The entire data set is available at the website (www.mhhe.com/Lind17e) and is identified as Bank of New England.

TABLE 14–3 Information on Sample of 25 Loans by the Bank of New England

Loan	Income ($000)	Value ($000)	Education	Age	Mortgage	Gender
1	100.7	190	14	53	230	1
2	99.0	121	15	49	370	1
3	102.0	161	14	44	397	1
⋮	⋮	⋮	⋮	⋮	⋮	⋮
23	102.3	163	14	46	142	1
24	100.2	150	15	50	343	0
25	96.3	139	14	45	373	0

We begin by calculating the correlation matrix shown below. It shows the relationship between each of the independent variables and the dependent variable. It helps to identify the independent variables that are more closely related to the dependent variable (family income). The correlation matrix also reveals the independent variables that are highly correlated and possibly redundant.

	Income	Value	Education	Age	Mortgage	Gender
Income	1					
Value	0.720	1				
Education	0.188	−0.144	1			
Age	0.243	0.220	0.621	1		
Mortgage	0.116	0.358	−0.210	−0.038	1	
Gender	0.486	0.184	0.062	0.156	−0.129	1

What can we learn from this correlation matrix?

1. The first column shows the correlations between each of the independent variables and the dependent variable family income. Observe that each of the independent variables is positively correlated with family income. The value of the home has the strongest correlation with family income. The level of education of the person applying for the loan and the current mortgage payment have a weak correlation with family income. These two variables are candidates to be dropped from the regression equation.
2. All possible correlations among the independent variables are identified with the green background. Our standard is to look for correlations that exceed an absolute value of .700. None of the independent variables are strongly correlated with each other. This indicates that multicollinearity is not likely.

Next, we compute the multiple regression equation using all the independent variables. The software output follows.

	A	B	C	D	E	F
1	SUMMARY OUTPUT					
2						
3	*Regression Statistics*					
4	Multiple R	0.866				
5	R Square	0.750				
6	Adjusted R Square	0.684				
7	Standard Error	1.478				
8	Observations	25				
9						
10	ANOVA					
11		*df*	*SS*	*MS*	*F*	*P-value*
12	Regression	5	124.322	24.864	11.385	0.000
13	Residual	19	41.494	2.184		
14	Total	24	165.815			
15						
16		*Coefficients*	*Standard Error*	*t Stat*	*P-value*	
17	Intercept	70.606	7.464	9.459	0.000	
18	Value ($000)	0.072	0.012	5.769	0.000	
19	Education	1.624	0.603	2.693	0.014	
20	Age	-0.122	0.078	-1.566	0.134	
21	Mortgage	-0.001	0.003	-0.319	0.753	
22	Gender	1.807	0.623	2.901	0.009	

The coefficients of determination, that is, both R^2 and adjusted R^2, are reported at the top of the summary output and highlighted in yellow. The R^2 value is 75.0%, so the five independent variables account for three-quarters of the variation in family income. The adjusted R^2 measures the strength of the relationship between the set of independent variables and family income and also accounts for the number of variables in the regression equation. The adjusted R^2 indicates that the five variables account for 68.4% of the variance of family income. Both of these suggest that the proposed independent variables are useful in predicting family income.

The output also includes the regression equation.

$$\hat{y} = 70.606 + 0.072(Value) + 1.624(Education) - 0.122(Age) - 0.001(Mortgage) + 1.807(Gender)$$

Be careful in this interpretation. Both income and the value of the home are in thousands of dollars. Here is a summary:

1. An increase of $1,000 in the value of the home suggests an increase of $72 in family income. An increase of 1 year of education increases income by $1,624, another year older reduces income by $122, and an increase of $1,000 in the mortgage reduces income by $1.
2. If a male is head of the household, the value of family income will increase by $1,807. Remember that "female" was coded 0 and "male" was coded 1, so a male head of household is positively related to home value.
3. The age of the head of household and monthly mortgage payment are inversely related to family income. This is true because the sign of the regression coefficient is negative.

Next we conduct the global hypothesis test. Here we check to see if any of the regression coefficients are different from 0. We use the .05 significance level.

$$H_0: \beta_1 = \beta_2 = \beta_3 = \beta_4 = \beta_5 = 0$$
$$H_1: \text{Not all the } \beta\text{'s are } 0$$

The p-value from the table (cell F12) is 0.000. Because the p-value is less than the significance level, we reject the null hypothesis and conclude that at least one of the regression coefficients is not equal to zero.

Next we evaluate the individual regression coefficients. The p-values to test each regression coefficient are reported in cells E18 through E22 in the software output on the previous page. The null hypothesis and the alternate hypothesis are:

$$H_0: \beta_i = 0$$
$$H_1: \beta_i \neq 0$$

The subscript i represents any particular independent variable. Again using .05 significance levels, the p-values for the regression coefficients for home value, years of education, and gender are all less than .05. We conclude that these regression coefficients are not equal to zero and are significant predictors of family income. The p-value for age and mortgage amount are greater than the significance level of .05, so we do not reject the null hypotheses for these variables. The regression coefficients are not different from zero and are not related to family income.

Based on the results of testing each of the regression coefficients, we conclude that the variables age and mortgage amount are not effective predictors of family income. Thus, they should be removed from the multiple regression equation. Remember that we must remove one independent variable at a time and redo the analysis to evaluate the overall effect of removing the variable. Our strategy is to remove the variable with the smallest t-statistic or the largest p-value. This variable is mortgage amount. The result of the regression analysis without the mortgage variable follows.

	A	B	C	D	E	F
1	SUMMARY OUTPUT					
2						
3	*Regression Statistics*					
4	Multiple R	0.865				
5	R Square	0.748				
6	Adjusted R Square	0.698				
7	Standard Error	1.444				
8	Observations	25				
9						
10	ANOVA					
11		*df*	*SS*	*MS*	*F*	*P-value*
12	Regression	4	124.099	31.025	14.874	0.000
13	Residual	20	41.716	2.086		
14	Total	24	165.815			
15						
16		*Coefficients*	*Standard Error*	*t Stat*	*P-value*	
17	Intercept	70.159	7.165	9.791	0.000	
18	Value ($000)	0.070	0.011	6.173	0.000	
19	Education	1.647	0.585	2.813	0.011	
20	Age	-0.122	0.076	-1.602	0.125	
21	Gender	1.846	0.596	3.096	0.006	

Observe that the R^2 and adjusted R^2 change very little without the mortgage variable. Also observe that the *p*-value associated with age is greater than the .05 significance level. So next we remove the age variable and redo the analysis. The regression output with the variables age and mortgage amount removed follows.

	A	B	C	D	E	F
1	SUMMARY OUTPUT					
2						
3	*Regression Statistics*					
4	Multiple R	0.846				
5	R Square	0.716				
6	Adjusted R Square	0.676				
7	Standard Error	1.497				
8	Observations	25				
9						
10	ANOVA					
11		*df*	*SS*	*MS*	*F*	*P-value*
12	Regression	3	118.743	39.581	17.658	0.000
13	Residual	21	47.072	2.242		
14	Total	24	165.815			
15						
16		*Coefficients*	*Standard Error*	*t Stat*	*P-value*	
17	Intercept	74.527	6.870	10.849	0.000	
18	Value ($000)	0.063	0.011	5.803	0.000	
19	Education	1.016	0.449	2.262	0.034	
20	Gender	1.770	0.616	2.872	0.009	

From this output, we conclude:

1. The R^2 and adjusted R^2 values have declined but only slightly. Using all five independent variables, the R^2 value was .750. With the two nonsignificant variables removed, the R^2 and adjusted R^2 values are .716 and .676, respectively. We prefer the equation with the fewer number of independent variables. It is easier to interpret.
2. In ANOVA, we observe that the *p*-value is less than .05. Hence, at least one of the regression coefficients is not equal to zero.

3. Reviewing the significance of the individual coefficients, the *p*-values associated with each of the remaining independent variables are less than .05. We conclude that all the regression coefficients are different from zero. Each independent variable is a useful predictor of family income.

Our final step is to examine the regression assumptions (Evaluating the Assumptions of Multiple Regression section on page 506) with our regression model. The first assumption is that there is a linear relationship between each independent variable and the dependent variable. It is not necessary to review the dummy variable Gender because there are only two possible outcomes. Below are the scatter plots of family income versus home value and family income versus years of education.

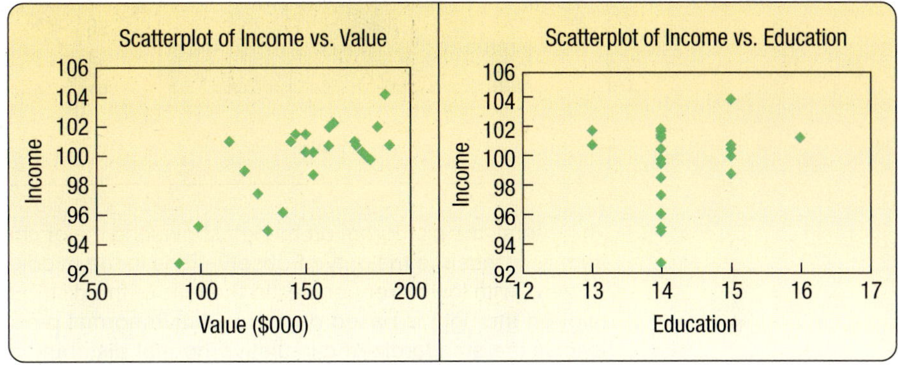

The scatter plot of income versus home value shows a general increasing trend. As the home value increases, so does family income. The points appear to be linear. That is, there is no observable nonlinear pattern in the data. The scatter plot on the right, of income versus years of education, shows that the data are measured to the nearest year. The measurement is to the nearest year and is a discrete variable. Given the measurement method, it is difficult to determine if the relationship is linear or not.

A plot of the residuals is also useful to evaluate the overall assumption of linearity. Recall that a residual is $(y - \hat{y})$, the difference between the actual value of the dependent variable (y) and the predicted value of the dependent variable ($\hat{y}$). Assuming a linear relationship, the distribution of the residuals should show about an equal proportion of negative residuals (points above the line) and positive residuals (points below the line) centered on zero. There should be no observable pattern to the plots. The graph follows.

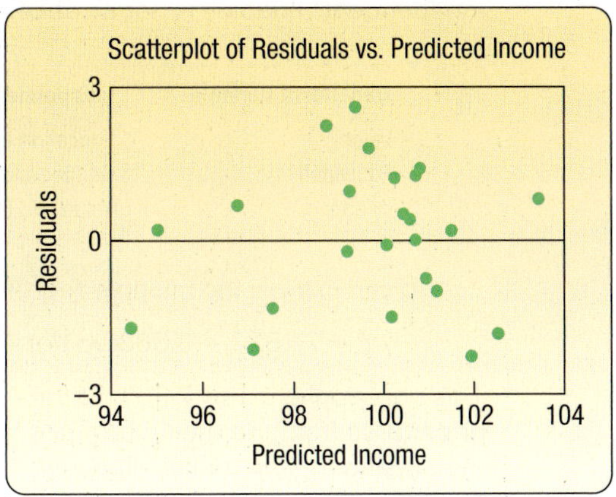

There is no discernable pattern to the plot, so we conclude that the linearity assumption is reasonable.

If the linearity assumption is valid, then the distribution of residuals should follow the normal probability distribution with a mean of zero. To evaluate this assumption, we will use a histogram and a normal probability plot.

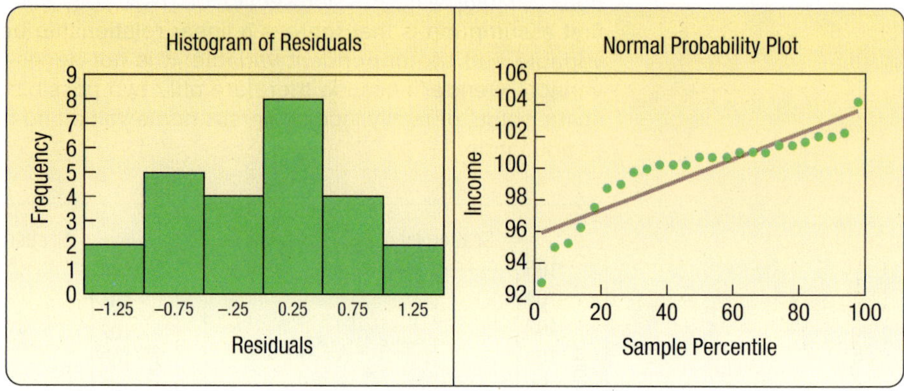

In general, the histogram on the left shows the major characteristics of a normal distribution, that is, a majority of observations in the middle and centered on the mean of zero, with lower frequencies in the tails of the distribution. The normal probability plot on the right is based on a cumulative normal probability distribution. The line shows the standardized cumulative normal distribution. The green dots show the cumulative distribution of the residuals. To confirm the normal distribution of the residuals, the green dots should be close to the line. This is true for most of the plot. However, we would note that there are departures and even perhaps a nonlinear pattern in the residuals in the lower part of the graph. As before, we are looking for serious departures from linearity and these are not indicated in these graphs.

The final assumption refers to multicollinearity. This means that the independent variables should not be highly correlated. We suggested a rule of thumb that multicollinearity would be a concern if the correlations among independent variables were close to 0.7 or −0.7. There are no violations of this guideline.

There is a statistic that is used to more precisely evaluate multicollinearity, the variance inflation factor (*VIF*). To calculate the *VIF*s, we need to do a regression analysis for each independent variable as a function of the other independent variables. From each of these regression analyses, we need the R^2 to compute the *VIF* using formula (14–7). The following table shows the R^2 for each regression analysis and the computed *VIF*. If the *VIF*s are less than 10, then multicollinearity is not a concern. In this case, the *VIF*s are all less than 10, so multicollinearity among the independent variables is not a concern.

Dependent Variable	Independent Variables	*R*-square	*VIF*
Value	Education and Gender	0.058	1.062
Education	Gender and Value	0.029	1.030
Gender	Value and Education	0.042	1.044

To summarize, the multiple regression equation is

$$\hat{y} = 74.527 + 0.063(Value) + 1.016(Education) + 1.770(Gender)$$

This equation explains 71.6% of the variation in family income. There are no major departures from the multiple regression assumptions of linearity, normally distributed residuals, and multicollinearity.

CHAPTER SUMMARY

I. The general form of a multiple regression equation is:

$$\hat{y} = a + b_1x_1 + b_2x_2 + \ldots + b_kx_k \tag{14–1}$$

where a is the Y-intercept when all x's are zero, b_j refers to the sample regression coefficients, and x_j refers to the value of the various independent variables.

A. There can be any number of independent variables.

B. The least squares criterion is used to develop the regression equation.

C. A statistical software package is needed to perform the calculations.

II. An ANOVA table summarizes the multiple regression analysis.

A. It reports the total amount of the variation in the dependent variable and divides this variation into that explained by the set of independent variables and that not explained.

B. It reports the degrees of freedom associated with the independent variables, the error variation, and the total variation.

III. There are two measures of the effectiveness of the regression equation.

A. The multiple standard error of estimate is similar to the standard deviation.

1. It is measured in the same units as the dependent variable.
2. It is based on squared deviations between the observed and predicted values of the dependent variable.
3. It ranges from 0 to plus infinity.
4. It is calculated from the following equation.

$$s_{y.123\ldots k} = \sqrt{\frac{\Sigma(y - \hat{y})^2}{n - (k + 1)}} \tag{14–2}$$

B. The coefficient of multiple determination reports the percent of the variation in the dependent variable explained by the variation in the set of independent variables.

1. It may range from 0 to 1.
2. It is also based on squared deviations from the regression equation.
3. It is found by the following equation.

$$R^2 = \frac{\text{SSR}}{\text{SS total}} \tag{14–3}$$

4. When the number of independent variables is large, we adjust the coefficient of determination for the degrees of freedom as follows.

$$R^2_{\text{adj}} = 1 - \frac{\dfrac{\text{SSE}}{n - (k + 1)}}{\dfrac{\text{SS total}}{n - 1}} \tag{14–4}$$

IV. A global test is used to investigate whether any of the independent variables have a regression coefficient that differs significantly from zero.

A. The null hypothesis is: All the regression coefficients are zero.

B. The alternate hypothesis is: At least one regression coefficient is not zero.

C. The test statistic is the F distribution with k (the number of independent variables) degrees of freedom in the numerator and $n - (k + 1)$ degrees of freedom in the denominator, where n is the sample size.

D. The formula to calculate the value of the test statistic for the global test is:

$$F = \frac{\text{SSR}/k}{\text{SSE}/[n - (k + 1)]} \tag{14–5}$$

V. The test for individual variables determines which independent variables have regression coefficients that differ significantly from zero.

A. The variables that have zero regression coefficients are usually dropped from the analysis.

B. The test statistic is the t distribution with $n - (k + 1)$ degrees of freedom.

C. The formula to calculate the value of the test statistic for the individual test is:

$$t = \frac{b_i - 0}{s_{b_i}} \qquad \textbf{(14–6)}$$

VI. There are five assumptions to use multiple regression analysis.
   A. The relationship between the dependent variable and the set of independent variables must be linear.
      1. To verify this assumption, develop a scatter diagram and plot the residuals on the vertical axis and the fitted values on the horizontal axis.
      2. If the plots appear random, we conclude the relationship is linear.
   B. The variation is the same for both large and small values of $\hat{y}$.
      1. Homoscedasticity means the variation is the same for all fitted values of the dependent variable.
      2. This condition is checked by developing a scatter diagram with the residuals on the vertical axis and the fitted values on the horizontal axis.
      3. If there is no pattern to the plots—that is, they appear random—the residuals meet the homoscedasticity requirement.
   C. The residuals follow the normal probability distribution.
      1. This condition is checked by developing a histogram of the residuals or a normal probability plot.
      2. The mean of the distribution of the residuals is 0.
   D. The independent variables are not correlated.
      1. A correlation matrix will show all possible correlations among independent variables. Signs of trouble are correlations larger than 0.70 or less than −0.70.
      2. Signs of correlated independent variables include when an important predictor variable is found insignificant, when an obvious reversal occurs in signs in one or more of the independent variables, or when a variable is removed from the solution, there is a large change in the regression coefficients.
      3. The variance inflation factor is used to identify correlated independent variables.

$$VIF = \frac{1}{1 - R_j^2} \qquad \textbf{(14–7)}$$

   E. Each residual is independent of other residuals.
      1. Autocorrelation occurs when successive residuals are correlated.
      2. When autocorrelation exists, the value of the standard error will be biased and will return poor results for tests of hypothesis regarding the regression coefficients.

VII. Several techniques help build a regression model.
   A. A dummy or qualitative independent variable can assume one of two possible outcomes.
      1. A value of 1 is assigned to one outcome and 0 to the other.
      2. Use formula (14–6) to determine if the dummy variable should remain in the equation.
   B. Interaction is the case in which one independent variable (such as x_2) affects the relationship with another independent variable (x_1) and the dependent variable (y).
   C. Stepwise regression is a step-by-step process to find the regression equation.
      1. Only independent variables with nonzero regression coefficients enter the equation.
      2. Independent variables are added one at a time to the regression equation.

PRONUNCIATION KEY

SYMBOL	MEANING	PRONUNCIATION
b_1	Regression coefficient for the first independent variable	*b sub 1*
b_k	Regression coefficient for any independent variable	*b sub k*
$s_{y.123...k}$	Multiple standard error of estimate	*s sub y dot 1, 2, 3 . . . k*

CHAPTER EXERCISES

13. A multiple regression analysis yields the following partial results.

Source	Sum of Squares	*df*
Regression	750	4
Error	500	35

- **a.** What is the total sample size?
- **b.** How many independent variables are being considered?
- **c.** Compute the coefficient of determination.
- **d.** Compute the standard error of estimate.
- **e.** Test the hypothesis that at least one of the regression coefficients is not equal to zero. Let $\alpha = .05$.

14. In a multiple regression analysis, two independent variables are considered, and the sample size is 25. The regression coefficients and the standard errors are as follows.

$$b_1 = 2.676 \qquad s_{b_1} = 0.56$$
$$b_2 = -0.880 \qquad s_{b_2} = 0.71$$

Conduct a test of hypothesis to determine whether either independent variable has a coefficient equal to zero. Would you consider deleting either variable from the regression equation? Use the .05 significance level.

15. The following output was obtained from a multiple regression analysis.

Analysis of Variance			
Source	DF	SS	MS
Regression	5	100	20
Residual Error	20	40	2
Total	25	140	
Predictor	Coefficient	SE Coefficient	t
Constant	3.00	1.50	2.00
X_1	4.00	3.00	1.33
X_2	3.00	0.20	15.00
X_3	0.20	0.05	4.00
X_4	-2.50	1.00	-2.50
X_5	3.00	4.00	0.75

- **a.** What is the sample size?
- **b.** Compute the value of R^2.
- **c.** Compute the multiple standard error of estimate.
- **d.** Conduct a global test of hypothesis to determine whether any of the regression coefficients are significant. Use the .05 significance level.
- **e.** Test the regression coefficients individually. Would you consider omitting any variable(s)? If so, which one(s)? Use the .05 significance level.

16. In a multiple regression analysis, $k = 5$ and $n = 20$, the MSE value is 5.10, and SS total is 519.68. At the .05 significance level, can we conclude that any of the regression coefficients are not equal to 0?

17. The district manager of Jasons, a large discount electronics chain, is investigating why certain stores in her region are performing better than others. She believes that three factors are related to total sales: the number of competitors in the region, the population in the surrounding area, and the amount spent on advertising. From her district, consisting of several hundred stores, she selects a random sample of 30 stores. For each store, she gathered the following information.

y = total sales last year (in \$ thousands)
x_1 = number of competitors in the region
x_2 = population of the region (in millions)
x_3 = advertising expense (in \$ thousands)

The results of a multiple regression analysis, using Minitab, follow.

Analysis of Variance			
Source	DF	SS	MS
Regression	3	3050	1016.67
Residual Error	26	2200	84.62
Total	29	5250	
Predictor	Coefficient	SE Coefficient	t
Constant	14.00	7.00	2.00
x_1	-1.00	0.70	-1.43
x_2	30.00	5.20	5.77
x_3	0.20	0.08	2.50

a. What are the estimated sales for the Bryne store, which has four competitors, a regional population of 0.4 (400,000), and an advertising expense of 30 ($30,000)?
b. Compute the R^2 value.
c. Compute the multiple standard error of estimate.
d. Conduct a global test of hypothesis to determine whether any of the regression coefficients are not equal to zero. Use the .05 level of significance.
e. Conduct tests of hypothesis to determine which of the independent variables have significant regression coefficients. Which variables would you consider eliminating? Use the .05 significance level.

18. Suppose that the sales manager of a large automotive parts distributor wants to estimate the total annual sales for each of the company's regions. Five factors appear to be related to regional sales: the number of retail outlets in the region, the number of automobiles in the region registered as of April 1, the total personal income recorded in the first quarter of the year, the average age of the automobiles (years), and the number of sales supervisors in the region. The data for each region were gathered for last year. For example, see the following table. In region 1 there were 1,739 retail outlets stocking the company's automotive parts, there were 9,270,000 registered automobiles in the region as of April 1, and so on. The region's sales for that year were $37,702,000.

Annual Sales ($ millions), y	Number of Retail Outlets, x_1	Number of Automobiles Registered (millions), x_2	Personal Income ($ billions), x_3	Average Age of Automobiles (years), x_4	Number of Supervisors, x_5
37.702	1,739	9.27	85.4	3.5	9.0
24.196	1,221	5.86	60.7	5.0	5.0
32.055	1,846	8.81	68.1	4.4	7.0
3.611	120	3.81	20.2	4.0	5.0
17.625	1,096	10.31	33.8	3.5	7.0
45.919	2,290	11.62	95.1	4.1	13.0
29.600	1,687	8.96	69.3	4.1	15.0
8.114	241	6.28	16.3	5.9	11.0
20.116	649	7.77	34.9	5.5	16.0
12.994	1,427	10.92	15.1	4.1	10.0

a. Consider the following correlation matrix. Which single variable has the strongest correlation with the dependent variable? The correlations between the independent variables outlets and income and between outlets and number of automobiles are fairly strong. Could this be a problem? What is this condition called?

```
                 sales     outlets        cars     income       age
outlets          0.899
automobiles      0.605       0.775
income           0.964       0.825       0.409
age             -0.323      -0.489      -0.447     -0.349
bosses           0.286       0.183       0.395      0.155     0.291
```

b. The output for all five variables is shown below. What percent of the variation is explained by the regression equation?

```
The regression equation is
Sales = -19.7 - 0.00063 outlets + 1.74 autos + 0.410 income
        + 2.04 age - 0.034 bosses

          Predictor          Coef      SE Coef         T         P
          Constant        -19.672        5.422     -3.63     0.022
          outlets       -0.000629     0.002638     -0.24     0.823
          automobiles      1.7399       0.5530      3.15     0.035
          income          0.40994      0.04385      9.35     0.001
          age              2.0357       0.8779      2.32     0.081
          bosses          -0.0344       0.1880     -0.18     0.864

Analysis of Variance
          SOURCE            DF        SS        MS         F         P
          Regression         5   1593.81    318.76    140.36     0.000
          Residual Error     4      9.08      2.27
          Total              9   1602.89
```

c. Conduct a global test of hypothesis to determine whether any of the regression coefficients are not zero. Use the .05 significance level.

d. Conduct a test of hypothesis on each of the independent variables. Would you consider eliminating "outlets" and "bosses"? Use the .05 significance level.

e. The regression has been rerun below with "outlets" and "bosses" eliminated. Compute the coefficient of determination. How much has R^2 changed from the previous analysis?

```
The regression equation is
Sales = -18.9 + 1.61 autos + 0.400 income + 1.96 age

          Predictor          Coef      SE Coef         T         P
          Constant        -18.924        3.636     -5.20     0.002
          automobiles      1.6129       0.1979      8.15     0.000
          income          0.40031      0.01569     25.52     0.000
          age              1.9637       0.5846      3.36     0.015

Analysis of Variance
          SOURCE            DF        SS        MS         F         P
          Regression         3   1593.66    531.22    345.25     0.000
          Residual Error     6      9.23      1.54
          Total              9   1602.89
```

f. Following is a histogram of the residuals. Does the normality assumption appear reasonable? Why?

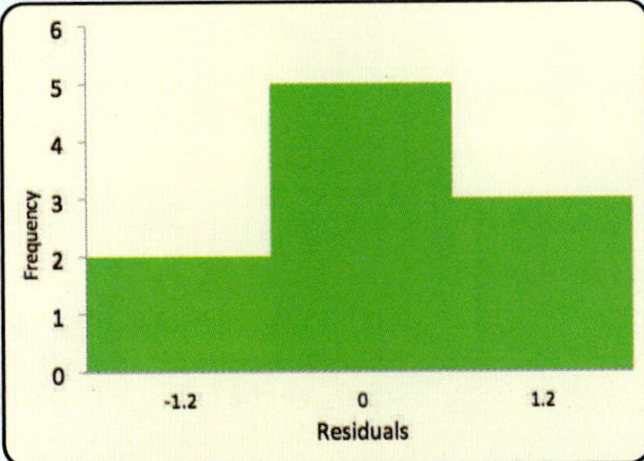

g. Following is a plot of the fitted values of y (i.e., $\hat{y}$) and the residuals. What do you observe? Do you see any violations of the assumptions?

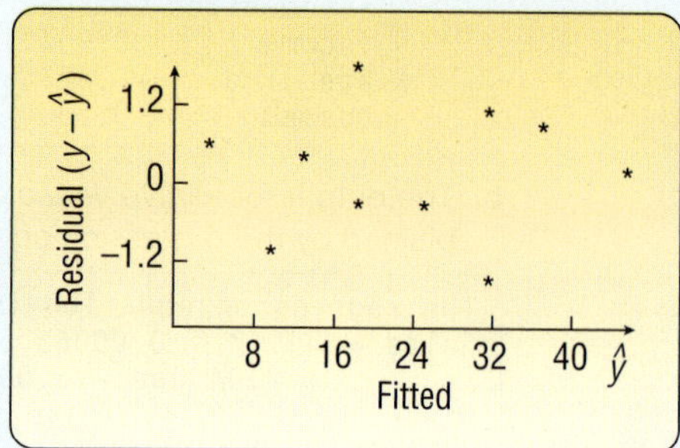

19. The administrator of a new paralegal program at Seagate Technical College wants to estimate the grade point average in the new program. He thought that high school GPA, the verbal score on the Scholastic Aptitude Test (SAT), and the mathematics score on the SAT would be good predictors of paralegal GPA. The data on nine students are:

Student	High School GPA	SAT Verbal	SAT Math	Paralegal GPA
1	3.25	480	410	3.21
2	1.80	290	270	1.68
3	2.89	420	410	3.58
4	3.81	500	600	3.92
5	3.13	500	490	3.00
6	2.81	430	460	2.82
7	2.20	320	490	1.65
8	2.14	530	480	2.30
9	2.63	469	440	2.33

a. Consider the following correlation matrix. Which variable has the strongest correlation with the dependent variable? Some of the correlations among the independent variables are strong. Does this appear to be a problem?

```
                Paralegal   High School
                      GPA           GPA  SAT Verbal
High School GPA     0.911
SAT Verbal          0.616         0.609
SAT Math            0.487         0.636       0.599
```

b. Consider the following output. Compute the coefficient of multiple determination.

```
The regression equation is
Paralegal GPA = -0.411 + 1.20 HSGPA + 0.00163 SAT_Verbal - 0.00194
SAT_Math

Predictor          Coef       SE Coef         T         P
Constant        -0.4111        0.7823     -0.53     0.622
HSGPA            1.2014        0.2955      4.07     0.010
SAT_Verbal     0.001629      0.002147      0.76     0.482
SAT_Math      -0.001939      0.002074     -0.94     0.393

Analysis of Variance
SOURCE            DF        SS        MS         F         P
Regression         3    4.3595    1.4532     10.33     0.014
Residual Error     5    0.7036    0.1407
Total              8    5.0631

SOURCE     DF    Seq SS
HSGPA       1    4.2061
SAT_Verbal 1     0.0303
SAT_Math    1    0.1231
```

c. Conduct a global test of hypothesis from the preceding output. Does it appear that any of the regression coefficients are not equal to zero?

d. Conduct a test of hypothesis on each independent variable. Would you consider eliminating the variables "SAT_Verbal" and "SAT_Math"? Let $\alpha = .05$.

e. The analysis has been rerun without "SAT_Verbal" and "SAT_Math." See the following output. Compute the coefficient of determination. How much has R^2 changed from the previous analysis?

```
The regression equation is
Paralegal GPA = −0.454 + 1.16 HSGPA

Predictor         Coef      SE Coef         T        P
Constant       −0.4542       0.5542     −0.82    0.439
HSGPA           1.1589       0.1977      5.86    0.001

Analysis of Variance
SOURCE            DF       SS        MS        F        P
Regression         1   4.2061    4.2061    34.35    0.001
Residual Error     7   0.8570    0.1224
Total              8   5.0631
```

f. Following is a histogram of the residuals. Does the normality assumption for the residuals seem reasonable?

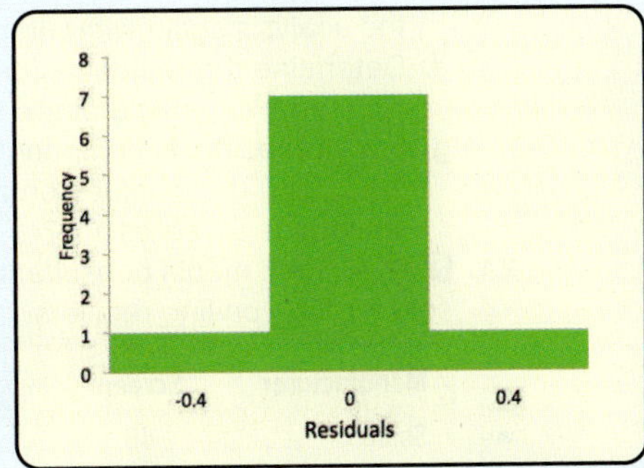

g. Following is a plot of the residuals and the $\hat{y}$ values. Do you see any violation of the assumptions?

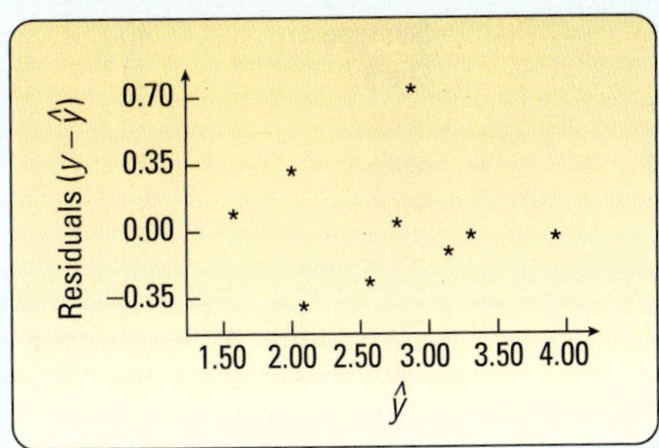

20. FILE Mike Wilde is president of the teachers' union for Otsego School District. In preparing for upcoming negotiations, he is investigating the salary structure of classroom teachers in the district. He believes there are three factors that affect a teacher's salary: years of experience, a teaching effectiveness rating given by the principal, and whether the teacher has a master's degree. A random sample of 20 teachers resulted in the following data.

Salary ($ thousands), y	Years of Experience, x_1	Principal's Rating, x_2	Master's Degree,* x_3
31.1	8	35	0
33.6	5	43	0
29.3	2	51	1
⋮	⋮	⋮	⋮
30.7	4	62	0
32.8	2	80	1
42.8	8	72	0

*1 = yes, 0 = no.

a. Develop a correlation matrix. Which independent variable has the strongest correlation with the dependent variable? Does it appear there will be any problems with multicollinearity?
b. Determine the regression equation. What salary would you estimate for a teacher with 5 years' experience, a rating by the principal of 60, and no master's degree?
c. Conduct a global test of hypothesis to determine whether any of the regression coefficients differ from zero. Use the .05 significance level.
d. Conduct a test of hypothesis for the individual regression coefficients. Would you consider deleting any of the independent variables? Use the .05 significance level.
e. If your conclusion in part (d) was to delete one or more independent variables, run the analysis again without those variables.
f. Determine the residuals for the equation of part (e). Use a stem-and-leaf chart or a histogram to verify that the distribution of the residuals is approximately normal.
g. Plot the residuals computed in part (f) in a scatter diagram with the residuals on the Y-axis and the $\hat{y}$ values on the X-axis. Does the plot reveal any violations of the assumptions of regression?

21. FILE A video media consultant collected the following data on popular LED televisions sold through on-line retailers.

Manufacturer	Screen	Price	Manufacturer	Screen	Price
Sharp	46	736.50	Sharp	37	657.25
Samsung	52	1150.00	Sharp	32	426.75
Samsung	46	895.00	Sharp	52	1389.00
Sony	40	625.00	Samsung	40	874.75
Sharp	42	773.25	Sharp	32	517.50
Samsung	46	961.25	Samsung	52	1475.00
Samsung	40	686.00	Sony	40	954.25
Sharp	37	574.75	Sony	52	1551.50
Sharp	46	1000.00	Sony	46	1303.00
Sony	40	722.25	Sony	46	1430.50
Sony	52	1307.50	Sony	52	1717.00
Samsung	32	373.75			

a. Does there appear to be a linear relationship between the screen size and the price?
b. Which variable is the "dependent" variable?
c. Using statistical software, determine the regression equation. Interpret the value of the slope in the regression equation.
d. Include the manufacturer in a multiple linear regression analysis using a "dummy" variable. Does it appear that some manufacturers can command a premium price? Hint: You will need to use a set of indicator variables.
e. Test each of the individual coefficients to see if they are significant.
f. Make a plot of the residuals and comment on whether they appear to follow a normal distribution.
g. Plot the residuals versus the fitted values. Do they seem to have the same amount of variation?

22. FILE A regional planner is studying the demographics of nine counties in the eastern region of an Atlantic seaboard state. She has gathered the following data:

County	Median Income	Median Age	Coastal
A	$48,157	57.7	1
B	48,568	60.7	1
C	46,816	47.9	1
D	34,876	38.4	0
E	35,478	42.8	0
F	34,465	35.4	0
G	35,026	39.5	0
H	38,599	65.6	0
J	33,315	27.0	0

a. Is there a linear relationship between the median income and median age?
b. Which variable is the "dependent" variable?
c. Use statistical software to determine the regression equation. Interpret the value of the slope in a simple regression equation.
d. Include the aspect that the county is "coastal" or not in a multiple linear regression analysis using a "dummy" variable. Does it appear to be a significant influence on incomes?
e. Test each of the individual coefficients to see if they are significant.
f. Make a plot of the residuals and comment on whether they appear to follow a normal distribution.
g. Plot the residuals versus the fitted values. Do they seem to have the same amount of variation?

23. FILE Great Plains Distributors, Inc. sells roofing and siding products to home improvement retailers, such as Lowe's and Home Depot, and commercial contractors. The owner is interested in studying the effects of several variables on the sales volume of fiber-cement siding products.

The company has 26 marketing districts across the United States. In each district, it collected information on the following variables: sales volume (in thousands of dollars), advertising dollars (in thousands), number of active accounts, number of competing brands, and a rating of market potential.

Sales (000s)	Advertising Dollars (000s)	Number of Accounts	Number of Competitors	Market Potential
79.3	5.5	31	10	8
200.1	2.5	55	8	6
163.2	8.0	67	12	9
200.1	3.0	50	7	16
146.0	3.0	38	8	15
177.7	2.9	71	12	17
⋮	⋮	⋮	⋮	⋮
93.5	4.2	26	8	3
259.0	4.5	75	8	19
331.2	5.6	71	4	9

Conduct a multiple regression analysis to find the best predictors of sales.

a. Draw a scatter diagram comparing sales volume with each of the independent variables. Comment on the results.
b. Develop a correlation matrix. Do you see any problems? Does it appear there are any redundant independent variables?
c. Develop a regression equation. Conduct the global test. Can we conclude that some of the independent variables are useful in explaining the variation in the dependent variable?

d. Conduct a test of each of the independent variables. Are there any that should be dropped?
e. Refine the regression equation so the remaining variables are all significant.
f. Develop a histogram of the residuals and a normal probability plot. Are there any problems?
g. Determine the variance inflation factor for each of the independent variables. Are there any problems?

24. FILE A market researcher is studying on-line subscription services. She is particularly interested in what variables relate to the number of subscriptions for a particular on-line service. She is able to obtain the following sample information on 25 on-line subscription services. The following notation is used:

Sub = Number of subscriptions (in thousands)
Web page hits = Average monthly count (in thousands)
Adv = The advertising budget of the service (in $ hundreds)
Price = Average monthly subscription price ($)

Service	Sub	Web Page Hits	Adv	Price
1	37.95	588.9	13.2	35.1
2	37.66	585.3	13.2	34.7
3	37.55	566.3	19.8	34.8
⋮	⋮	⋮	⋮	⋮
23	38.83	629.6	22.0	35.3
24	38.33	680.0	24.2	34.7
25	40.24	651.2	33.0	35.8

a. Determine the regression equation.
b. Conduct a global test of hypothesis to determine whether any of the regression coefficients are not equal to zero.
c. Conduct a test for the individual coefficients. Would you consider deleting any coefficients?
d. Determine the residuals and plot them against the fitted values. Do you see any problems?
e. Develop a histogram of the residuals. Do you see any problems with the normality assumption?

25. FILE Fred G. Hire is the manager of human resources at Crescent Custom Steel Products. As part of his yearly report to the CEO, he is required to present an analysis of the salaried employees. For each of the 30 salaried employees, he records monthly salary; service at Crescent, in months; age; gender (1 = male, 0 = female); and whether the employee has a management or engineering position. Those employed in management are coded 0, and those in engineering are coded 1.

Sampled Employee	Monthly Salary	Length of Service	Age	Gender	Job
1	$1,769	93	42	1	0
2	1,740	104	33	1	0
3	1,941	104	42	1	1
⋮	⋮	⋮	⋮	⋮	⋮
28	1,791	131	56	0	1
29	2,001	95	30	1	1
30	1,874	98	47	1	0

a. Determine the regression equation, using salary as the dependent variable and the other four variables as independent variables.
b. What is the value of R^2? Comment on this value.
c. Conduct a global test of hypothesis to determine whether any of the independent variables are different from 0.

d. Conduct an individual test to determine whether any of the independent variables can be dropped.
e. Rerun the regression equation, using only the independent variables that are significant. How much more does a man earn per month than a woman? Does it make a difference whether the employee has a management or engineering position?

26. **FILE** Many regions in North and South Carolina and Georgia have experienced rapid population growth over the last 10 years. It is expected that the growth will continue over the next 10 years. This has motivated many of the large grocery store chains to build new stores in the region. The Kelley's Super Grocery Stores Inc. chain is no exception. The director of planning for Kelley's Super Grocery Stores wants to study adding more stores in this region. He believes there are two main factors that indicate the amount families spend on groceries. The first is their income and the other is the number of people in the family. The director gathered the following sample information.

Family	Food	Income	Size
1	$5.04	$73.98	4
2	4.08	54.90	2
3	5.76	94.14	4
⋮	⋮	⋮	⋮
23	4.56	38.16	3
24	5.40	43.74	7
25	4.80	48.42	5

Food and income are reported in thousands of dollars per year, and the variable size refers to the number of people in the household.
a. Develop a correlation matrix. Do you see any problems with multicollinearity?
b. Determine the regression equation. Discuss the regression equation. How much does an additional family member add to the amount spent on food?
c. What is the value of R^2? Can we conclude that this value is greater than 0?
d. Would you consider deleting either of the independent variables?
e. Plot the residuals in a histogram. Is there any problem with the normality assumption?
f. Plot the fitted values against the residuals. Does this plot indicate any problems with homoscedasticity?

27. **FILE** An investment advisor is studying the relationship between a common stock's price to earnings (P/E) ratio and factors that she thinks would influence it. She has the following data on the earnings per share (EPS) and the dividend percentage (Yield) for a sample of 20 stocks.

Stock	P/E	EPS	Yield
1	20.79	$2.46	1.42
2	3.03	2.69	4.05
3	44.46	−0.28	4.16
⋮	⋮	⋮	⋮
18	30.21	1.71	3.07
19	32.88	0.35	2.21
20	15.19	5.02	3.50

a. Develop a multiple linear regression with P/E as the dependent variable.
b. Are either of the two independent variables an effective predictor of P/E?
c. Interpret the regression coefficients.
d. Do any of these stocks look particularly undervalued?
e. Plot the residuals and check the normality assumption. Plot the fitted values against the residuals.
f. Does there appear to be any problems with homoscedasticity?
g. Develop a correlation matrix. Do any of the correlations indicate multicollinearity?

28. FILE The Conch Café, located in Gulf Shores, Alabama, features casual lunches with a great view of the Gulf of Mexico. To accommodate the increase in business during the summer vacation season, Fuzzy Conch, the owner, hires a large number of servers as seasonal help. When he interviews a prospective server, he would like to provide data on the amount a server can earn in tips. He believes that the amount of the bill and the number of diners are both related to the amount of the tip. He gathered the following sample information.

Customer	Amount of Tip	Amount of Bill	Number of Diners
1	$7.00	$48.97	5
2	4.50	28.23	4
3	1.00	10.65	1
⋮	⋮	⋮	⋮
28	2.50	26.25	2
29	9.25	56.81	5
30	8.25	50.65	5

a. Develop a multiple regression equation with the amount of tips as the dependent variable and the amount of the bill and the number of diners as independent variables. Write out the regression equation. How much does another diner add to the amount of the tips?
b. Conduct a global test of hypothesis to determine if at least one of the independent variables is significant. What is your conclusion?
c. Conduct an individual test on each of the variables. Should one or the other be deleted?
d. Use the equation developed in part (c) to determine the coefficient of determination. Interpret the value.
e. Plot the residuals. Is it reasonable to assume they follow the normal distribution?
f. Plot the residuals against the fitted values. Is it reasonable to conclude they are random?

29. FILE The president of Blitz Sales Enterprises sells kitchen products through cable television infomercials. He gathered data from the last 15 weeks of sales to determine the relationship between sales and the number of infomercials.

Infomercials	Sales ($000s)	Infomercials	Sales ($000s)
20	3.2	22	2.5
15	2.6	15	2.4
25	3.4	25	3.0
10	1.8	16	2.7
18	2.2	12	2.0
18	2.4	20	2.6
15	2.4	25	2.8
12	1.5		

a. Determine the regression equation. Are the sales predictable from the number of commercials?
b. Determine the residuals and plot a histogram. Does the normality assumption seem reasonable?

30. FILE The director of special events for Sun City believed that the amount of money spent on fireworks displays for the 4th of July was predictive of attendance at the Fall Festival held in October. She gathered the following data to test her suspicion.

4th of July ($000)	Fall Festival (000)	4th of July ($000)	Fall Festival (000)
10.6	8.8	9.0	9.5
8.5	6.4	10.0	9.8
12.5	10.8	7.5	6.6
9.0	10.2	10.0	10.1
5.5	6.0	6.0	6.1
12.0	11.1	12.0	11.3
8.0	7.5	10.5	8.8
7.5	8.4		

Determine the regression equation. Is the amount spent on fireworks related to attendance at the Fall Festival? Evaluate the regression assumptions by examining the residuals.

31. **FILE** You are a new hire at Laurel Woods Real Estate, which specializes in selling foreclosed homes via public auction. Your boss has asked you to use the following data (mortgage balance, monthly payments, payments made before default, and final auction price) on a random sample of recent sales in order to estimate what the actual auction price will be.

Loan	Monthly Payments	Payments Made	Auction Price
$ 85,600	$ 985.87	1	$16,900
115,300	902.56	33	75,800
103,100	736.28	6	43,900
⋮	⋮	⋮	⋮
119,400	1,021.23	58	69,000
90,600	836.46	3	35,600
104,500	1,056.37	22	63,000

a. Carry out a global test of hypothesis to verify if any of the regression coefficients are different from zero.
b. Do an individual test of the independent variables. Would you remove any of the variables?
c. If it seems one or more of the independent variables is not needed, remove it and work out the revised regression equation.

32. **FILE** Think about the figures from the previous exercise. Add a new variable that describes the potential interaction between the loan amount and the number of payments made. Then do a test of hypothesis to check if the interaction is significant.

DATA ANALYTICS

(The data for these exercises are available at the text website: www.mhhe.com/Lind17e.)

33. The North Valley Real Estate data reports information on homes on the market. Use the selling price of the home as the dependent variable and determine the regression equation using the size of the house, number of bedrooms, days on the market, and number of bathrooms as independent variables.
a. Develop a correlation matrix. Which independent variables have strong or weak correlations with the dependent variable? Do you see any problems with multicollinearity?
b. Use a statistical software package to determine the multiple regression equation. How did you select the variables to include in the equation? How did you use the information from the correlation analysis? Show that your regression equation shows a significant relationship. Write out the regression equation and interpret its practical application. Report and interpret the *R*-square.
c. Using your results from part (b), evaluate the addition of the variables: pool or garage. Report your results and conclusions.

d. Develop a histogram or a stem-and-leaf display of the residuals from the final regression equation developed in part (c). Is it reasonable to conclude that the normality assumption has been met?
e. Plot the residuals against the fitted values from the final regression equation developed in part (c). Plot the residuals on the vertical axis and the fitted values on the horizontal axis.

34. Refer to the Baseball 2016 data, which report information on the 30 Major League Baseball teams for the 2016 season. Let the number of games won be the dependent variable and the following variables be independent variables: team batting average, team Earned Run Average (ERA), number of home runs, and whether the team plays in the American or the National League.
a. Develop a correlation matrix. Which independent variables have strong or weak correlations with the dependent variable? Do you see any problems with multicollinearity? Are you surprised that the correlation coefficient for ERA is negative?
b. Use a statistical software package to determine the multiple regression equation. How did you select the variables to include in the equation? How did you use the information from the correlation analysis? Show that your regression equation shows a significant relationship. Write out the regression equation and interpret its practical application. Report and interpret the *R*-square. Is the number of wins affected by whether the team plays in the National or the American League?
c. Conduct a global test on the set of independent variables. Interpret.
d. Conduct a test of hypothesis on each of the independent variables. Would you consider deleting any of the variables? If so, which ones?
e. Develop a histogram or a stem-and-leaf display of the residuals from the final regression equation developed in part (f). Is it reasonable to conclude that the normality assumption has been met?
f. Plot the residuals against the fitted values from the final regression equation developed in part (f). Plot the residuals on the vertical axis and the fitted values on the horizontal axis.

35. Refer to the Lincolnville School District bus data. First, add a variable to change the type of engine (diesel or gasoline) to a qualitative variable. If the engine type is diesel, then set the qualitative variable to 0. If the engine type is gasoline, then set the qualitative variable to 1. Develop a regression equation using statistical software with maintenance cost as the dependent variable and age, odometer miles, miles since last maintenance, and engine type as the independent variables.
a. Develop a correlation matrix. Which independent variables have strong or weak correlations with the dependent variable? Do you see any problems with multicollinearity?
b. Use a statistical software package to determine the multiple regression equation. How did you select the variables to include in the equation? How did you use the information from the correlation analysis? Show that your regression equation shows a significant relationship. Write out the regression equation and interpret its practical application. Report and interpret the *R*-square.
c. Develop a histogram or a stem-and-leaf display of the residuals from the final regression equation developed in part (f). Is it reasonable to conclude that the normality assumption has been met?
d. Plot the residuals against the fitted values from the final regression equation developed in part (f) against the fitted values of *Y*. Plot the residuals on the vertical axis and the fitted values on the horizontal axis.

A REVIEW OF CHAPTERS 13–14

This section is a review of the major concepts and terms introduced in Chapters 13 and 14. Chapter 13 noted that the strength of the relationship between the independent variable and the dependent variable is measured by the *correlation coefficient.* The correlation coefficient is designated by the letter *r.* It can assume any value between −1.00 and +1.00 inclusive. Coefficients of −1.00 and +1.00 indicate a perfect relationship, and 0 indicates no relationship. A value near 0, such as −.14 or .14, indicates a weak relationship. A value near −1 or +1, such as −.90 or +.90, indicates a strong relationship. The *coefficient of determination,* also called R^2, measures the proportion of the total variation in the dependent variable explained by the independent variable. It can be computed as the square of the correlation coefficient.

Likewise, the strength of the relationship between several independent variables and a dependent variable is measured by the *coefficient of multiple determination,* R^2. It measures the proportion of the variation in y explained by two or more independent variables.

The linear relationship in the simple case involving one independent variable and one dependent variable is described by the equation $\hat{y} = a + bx$. For k independent variables, $x_1, x_2, \ldots x_k$, the same multiple regression equation is

$$\hat{y} = a + b_1x_1 + b_2x_2 + \ldots + b_kx_k$$

Solving for $b_1, b_2, \ldots, b_k$ would involve tedious calculations. Fortunately, this type of problem can be quickly solved using one of the many statistical software packages and spreadsheet packages. Various measures, such as the coefficient of determination, the multiple standard error of estimate, the results of the global test, and the test of the individual variables, are reported in the output of most statistical software programs.

PROBLEMS

1. The accounting department at Box and Go Apparel wishes to estimate the net profit for each of the chain's many stores on the basis of the number of employees in the store, overhead costs, average markup, and theft loss. The data from two stores are:

Store	Net Profit ($ thousands) $\hat{y}$	Number of Employees x_1	Overhead Cost ($ thousands) x_2	Average Markup (percent) x_3	Theft Loss ($ thousands) x_4
1	$846	143	$79	69%	$52
2	513	110	64	50	45

a. The dependent variable is _________.
b. The general equation for this problem is _________.
c. The multiple regression equation was computed to be $\hat{y} = 67 + 8x_1 - 10x_2 + 0.004x_3 - 3x_4$. What are the predicted sales for a store with 112 employees, an overhead cost of $65,000, a markup rate of 50%, and a loss from theft of $50,000?
d. Suppose R^2 was computed to be .86. Explain.
e. Suppose that the multiple standard error of estimate was 3 (in $ thousands). Explain what this means in this problem.

2. Quick-print firms in a large downtown business area spend most of their advertising dollars on displays on bus benches. A research project involves predicting monthly sales based on the annual amount spent on placing ads on bus benches. A sample of quick-print firms revealed these advertising expenses and sales:

Firm	Annual Bus Bench Advertising ($ thousands)	Monthly Sales ($ thousands)
A	2	10
B	4	40
C	5	30
D	7	50
E	3	20

a. Draw a scatter diagram.
b. Determine the correlation coefficient.
c. What is the coefficient of determination?
d. Compute the regression equation.
e. Estimate the monthly sales of a quick-print firm that spends $4,500 on bus bench advertisements.
f. Summarize your findings.

3. The following ANOVA output is given.

Analysis of Variance			
Source	DF	SS	MS
Regression	4	1050.8	262.70
Residual Error	20	83.8	4.19
Total	24	1134.6	
Predictor	Coefficient	SE Coefficient	t
Constant	70.06	2.13	32.89
x_1	0.42	0.17	2.47
x_2	0.27	0.21	1.29
x_3	0.75	0.30	2.50
x_4	0.42	0.07	6.00

a. Compute the coefficient of determination.
b. Compute the multiple standard error of estimate.
c. Conduct a test of hypothesis to determine whether any of the regression coefficients are different from zero.
d. Conduct a test of hypothesis on the individual regression coefficients. Can any of the variables be deleted?

CASES

A. The Century National Bank

Refer to the Century National Bank data. Using checking account balance as the dependent variable and using as independent variables the number of ATM transactions, the number of other services used, whether the individual has a debit card, and whether interest is paid on the particular account, write a report indicating which of the variables seem related to the account balance and how well they explain the variation in account balances. Should all of the independent variables proposed be used in the analysis or can some be dropped?

B. Terry and Associates: The Time to Deliver Medical Kits

Terry and Associates is a specialized medical testing center in Denver, Colorado. One of the firm's major sources of revenue is a kit used to test for elevated amounts of lead in the blood. Workers in auto body shops, those in the lawn care industry, and commercial house painters are exposed to large amounts of lead and thus must be randomly tested. It is expensive to conduct the test, so the kits are delivered on demand to a variety of locations throughout the Denver area.

Kathleen Terry, the owner, is concerned about setting appropriate costs for each delivery. To investigate, Ms. Terry gathered information on a random sample of 50 recent deliveries. Factors thought to be related to the cost of delivering a kit were:

- Prep — The time in minutes between when the customized order is phoned into the company and when it is ready for delivery.
- Delivery — The actual travel time in minutes from Terry's plant to the customer.
- Mileage — The distance in miles from Terry's plant to the customer.

Sample Number	Cost	Prep	Delivery	Mileage	Sample Number	Cost	Prep	Delivery	Mileage
1	$32.60	10	51	20	6	$22.63	9	20	11
2	23.37	11	33	12	7	22.63	9	39	11
3	31.49	6	47	19	8	21.53	10	23	10
4	19.31	9	18	8	9	21.16	13	20	8
5	28.35	8	88	17	10	21.53	10	32	10

Sample Number	Cost	Prep	Delivery	Mileage	Sample Number	Cost	Prep	Delivery	Mileage
11	$28.17	5	35	16	31	$24.29	7	35	13
12	20.42	7	23	9	32	19.56	2	12	6
13	21.53	9	21	10	33	22.63	8	30	11
14	27.55	7	37	16	34	21.16	5	13	8
15	23.37	9	25	12	35	21.16	11	20	8
16	17.10	15	15	6	36	19.68	5	19	8
17	27.06	13	34	15	37	18.76	5	14	7
18	15.99	8	13	4	38	17.96	5	11	4
19	17.96	12	12	4	39	23.37	10	25	12
20	25.22	6	41	14	40	25.22	6	32	14
21	24.29	3	28	13	41	27.06	8	44	16
22	22.76	4	26	10	42	21.96	9	28	9
23	28.17	9	54	16	43	22.63	8	31	11
24	19.68	7	18	8	44	19.68	7	19	8
25	25.15	6	50	13	45	22.76	8	28	10
26	20.36	9	19	7	46	21.96	13	18	9
27	21.16	3	19	8	47	25.95	10	32	14
28	25.95	10	45	14	48	26.14	8	44	15
29	18.76	12	12	5	49	24.29	8	34	13
30	18.76	8	16	5	50	24.35	3	33	12

1. Develop a multiple linear regression equation that describes the relationship between the cost of delivery and the other variables. Do these three variables explain a reasonable amount of the variation in the dependent variable? Estimate the delivery cost for a kit that takes 10 minutes for preparation, takes 30 minutes to deliver, and must cover a distance of 14 miles.
2. Test to determine if one or more regression coefficient differs from zero. Also test to see whether any of the variables can be dropped from the analysis. If some of the variables can be dropped, rerun the regression equation until only significant variables are included.
3. Write a brief report interpreting the final regression equation.

PRACTICE TEST

Part 1—Objective

1. In a scatter diagram, the dependent variable is always scaled on which axis? **1.** ________
2. What level of measurement is required to compute the correlation coefficient? **2.** ________
3. If there is no correlation between two variables, what is the value of the correlation coefficient? **3.** ________
4. Which of the following values indicates the strongest correlation between two variables? (.65, −.77, 0, −.12) **4.** ________
5. Under what conditions will the coefficient of determination assume a value greater than 1? **5.** ________

Given the following regression equation, $\hat{Y} = 7 - .5X$, and that the coefficient of determination is .81, answer questions 6, 7, and 8.

6. At what point does the regression equation cross the Y-axis? **6.** ________
7. An increase of 1 unit in the independent variable will result in what amount of an increase or decrease in the dependent variable? **7.** ________
8. What is the correlation coefficient? (Be careful of the sign.) **8.** ________
9. If all the data points in a scatter diagram were on the regression line, what would be the value of the standard error of estimate? **9.** ________
10. In a multiple regression equation, what is the maximum number of independent variables allowed? (2, 10, 30, unlimited) **10.** ________

11. In multiple regression analysis, we assume what type of relationship between the dependent variable and the set of independent variables? (linear, multiple, curved, none of these) **11.** ______________

12. The difference between Y and $\hat{Y}$ is called a ______________. **12.** ______________

13. For a dummy variable, such as gender, how many different values are possible? **13.** ______________

14. What is the term given to a table that shows all possible correlation coefficients between the dependent variable and all the independent variables and among all the independent variables? **14.** ______________

15. If there is a linear relationship between the dependent variable and the set of independent variables, a graph of the residuals will show what type of distribution? **15.** ______________

Part 2—Problems

1. Given the following regression analysis output:

ANOVA Table

Source	SS	*df*	MS	*F*	*p*-value
Regression	129.7275	1	129.7275	14.50	.0007
Residual	250.4391	28	8.9443		
Total	380.1667	29			

Regression Output

Variables	Coefficients	Standard Error	t ($df = 28$)
Intercept	90.6190	1.5322	59.141
Slope	−0.9401	0.2468	−3.808

a. What is the sample size?
b. Write out the regression equation. Interpret the slope and intercept values.
c. If the value of the independent variable is 10, what is the value of the dependent variable?
d. Calculate the coefficient of determination. Interpret this value.
e. Calculate the correlation coefficient. Conduct a test of hypothesis to determine if there is a significant negative association between the variables.

2. Given the following regression analysis output.

ANOVA Table

Source	SS	*df*	MS	*F*	*p*-value
Regression	227.0928	4	56.7732	9.27	0.000
Residual	153.0739	25	6.1230		
Total	380.1667	29			

Regression Output

Variables	Coefficients	Standard Error	t ($df = 25$)	*p*-value
Intercept	68.3366	8.9752	7.614	0.000
x_1	0.8595	0.3087	2.784	0.010
x_2	−0.3380	0.8381	−0.403	0.690
x_3	−0.8179	0.2749	−2.975	0.006
x_4	−0.5824	0.2541	−2.292	0.030

a. What is the sample size?
b. How many independent variables are in the study?
c. Determine the coefficient of determination.
d. Conduct a global test of hypothesis. Can you conclude at least one of the independent variables does not equal zero? Use the .01 significance level.
e. Conduct an individual test of hypothesis on each of the independent variables. Would you consider dropping any of the independent variables? If so, which variable or variables would you drop? Use the .01 significance level.

Nonparametric Methods:

15

NOMINAL LEVEL HYPOTHESIS TESTS

© Matilde Gattoni/Getty Images

▲ **FOR MANY YEARS,** TV executives used the guideline that 30% of the audience were watching each of the traditional big three prime-time networks and 10% were watching cable stations on a weekday night. A random sample of 500 viewers in the Tampa–St. Petersburg, Florida, area last Monday night showed that 165 homes were tuned in to the ABC affiliate, 140 to the CBS affiliate, 125 to the NBC affiliate, and the remainder were viewing a cable station. At the .05 significance level, can we conclude that the guideline is still reasonable? (See Exercise 24 and LO15-3.)

LEARNING OBJECTIVES

When you have completed this chapter, you will be able to:

LO15-1 Test a hypothesis about a population proportion.

LO15-2 Test a hypothesis about two population proportions.

LO15-3 Test a hypothesis comparing an observed set of frequencies to an expected frequency distribution.

LO15-4 Explain the limitations of using the chi-square statistic in goodness-of-fit tests.

LO15-5 Test a hypothesis that an observed frequency distribution is normally distributed.

LO15-6 Perform a chi-square test for independence on a contingency table.

INTRODUCTION

In Chapters 9 through 12 we describe tests of hypothesis for data of interval or ratio scale. Examples of interval and ratio scale data include the scores on the first statistics examination in your class, the incomes of corporate executive officers in technology companies, or years of employment of production workers at the BMW plant in Greer, South Carolina.

We conducted hypothesis tests about a single population mean (Chapter 10), about two population means (Chapter 11), and about three or more population means (Chapter 12). For these tests we use interval or ratio data and assume the populations follow the normal probability distribution. However, there are hypothesis tests that do not require any assumption regarding the shape of the population. Hence, the assumption of a normal population is not necessary. These tests are referred to as nonparametric hypothesis tests.

In this chapter, we begin with tests of hypothesis for nominal scale data. Recall that nominal scale data are simply classified into mutually exclusive categories. In the first two sections of this chapter we describe tests of proportions. In these tests individuals or objects are classified into one of two mutually exclusive groups. Examples include gender (male or female), quality (acceptable or unacceptable), diabetes (yes or no), and airline flight arrivals (on time or late).

We also expand the nominal scale tests to include situations where data are classified into several mutually exclusive categories. The scale of measurement is still nominal, but there are several categories. Examples include the colors of M&M Plain Candies (red, green, blue, yellow, orange, and brown), brand of peanut butter purchased (Peter Pan, Jif, Skippy, and others), or days of the workweek (Monday, Tuesday, Wednesday, Thursday, and Friday). We introduce the chi-square distribution as a new test statistic. It is most often used when there are more than two nominal scale categories.

LO15-1
Test a hypothesis about a population proportion.

TEST A HYPOTHESIS OF A POPULATION PROPORTION

Beginning on page 300 in Chapter 9, we discussed confidence intervals for proportions. We can also conduct a test of hypothesis for a proportion. Recall that a proportion is the ratio of the number of successes to the number of observations. We let X refer to the number of successes and n the number of observations, so the proportion of successes in a fixed number of trials is X/n. Thus, the formula for computing a sample proportion, p, is $p = X/n$. Consider the following potential hypothesis-testing situations.

- Historically, General Motors reports that 70% of leased vehicles are returned with less than 36,000 miles. A recent sample of 200 vehicles returned at the end of their lease showed 158 had less than 36,000 miles. Has the proportion increased?
- The American Association of Retired Persons (AARP) reports that 60% of retired people under the age of 65 would return to work on a full-time basis if a suitable job were available. A sample of 500 retirees under 65 revealed 315 would return to work. Can we conclude that more than 60% would return to work?
- Able Moving and Storage Inc. advises its clients for long-distance residential moves that their household goods will be delivered in 3 to 5 days from the time they are picked up. Able's records show it is successful 90% of the time with this claim. A recent audit revealed it was successful 190 times out of 200. Can the company conclude its success rate has increased?

Some assumptions must be made and conditions met before testing a population proportion. To test a hypothesis about a population proportion, a random sample is chosen from the population. It is assumed that the binomial assumptions discussed in Chapter 6 are met: (1) the sample data collected are the result of counts; (2) the outcome of an experiment is classified into one of two mutually exclusive categories—a "success" or a "failure"; (3) the probability of a success is the same for each trial; and (4) the trials are independent, meaning the outcome of one trial does not affect the outcome of any other trial. This test is appropriate when both $n\pi$ and $n(1 - \pi)$ are at least 5. n is the sample size, and π is the population proportion. It takes advantage of the fact that a binomial distribution can be approximated by the normal distribution.

EXAMPLE

A Republican governor of a western state is thinking about running for reelection. Historically, to be reelected, a Republican candidate needs to earn at least 80% of the vote in the northern section of the state. The governor hires a polling organization to survey the voters in the northern section of the state and determine what percent would vote for him. The polling organization will survey 2,000 voters. Use a statistical hypothesis-testing procedure to assess the governor's chances of reelection.

SOLUTION

This situation regarding the governor's reelection meets the binomial conditions.

- There are only two possible outcomes. That is, a sampled voter will either vote or not vote for the governor.
- The probability of a success is the same for each trial. In this case, the likelihood a particular sampled voter will support reelection is .80.
- The trials are independent. This means, for example, the likelihood the 23rd voter sampled will support reelection is not affected by what the 24th or 52nd voter does.
- The sample data are the result of counts. We are going to count the number of voters who support reelection in the sample of 2,000.

We can use a normal approximation to the binomial distribution if both $n\pi$ and $n(1 - \pi)$ exceed 5. In this case, $n = 2{,}000$ and $\pi = 0.80$. (π is the proportion of the vote in the northern part of the state, or 80%, needed to be elected.) Thus, $n\pi = 2{,}000(.80) = 1{,}600$ and $n(1 - \pi) = 2{,}000(1 - .80) = 400$. Both 1,600 and 400 are clearly greater than 5.

Step 1: State the null hypothesis and the alternate hypothesis. The null hypothesis, H_0, is that the population proportion π is .80 or larger. The alternate hypothesis, H_1, is that the proportion is less than .80. From a practical standpoint, the incumbent governor is concerned only when the proportion is less than .80. If it is equal to or greater than .80, he will have no problem; that is, the sample data would indicate he will be reelected. These hypotheses are written symbolically as:

$$H_0\text{: } \pi \geq .80$$

$$H_1\text{: } \pi < .80$$

H_1 states a direction. Thus, as noted previously, the test is one-tailed with the inequality sign pointing to the tail of the distribution containing the region of rejection.

Step 2: Select the level of significance. The level of significance is .05. This is the likelihood that a true hypothesis will be rejected.

Step 3: Select the test statistic. z is the appropriate statistic, found by:

TEST OF HYPOTHESIS, ONE PROPORTION

$$z = \frac{p - \pi}{\sqrt{\frac{\pi(1 - \pi)}{n}}} \quad \textbf{(15–1)}$$

where:

π is the population proportion.
p is the sample proportion.
n is the sample size.

Step 4: Formulate the decision rule. The critical value or values of z form the dividing point or points between the regions where H_0 is rejected and where it is not rejected. Because the alternate hypothesis states a direction, this is a one-tailed test. The sign of the inequality points to the left, so only the left side of the curve is used. (See Chart 15–1.) The significance level is .05. This probability is in the left tail and determines the region of rejection. The area between zero and the critical value is .4500, found by .5000 – .0500. Referring to Appendix B.3, go to the column indicating a .05 significance level for a one-tailed test, find the row with infinite degrees of freedom, and read the z value of 1.645. The decision rule is, therefore: Reject the null hypothesis and accept the alternate hypothesis if the computed value of z falls to the left of –1.645; otherwise do not reject H_0.

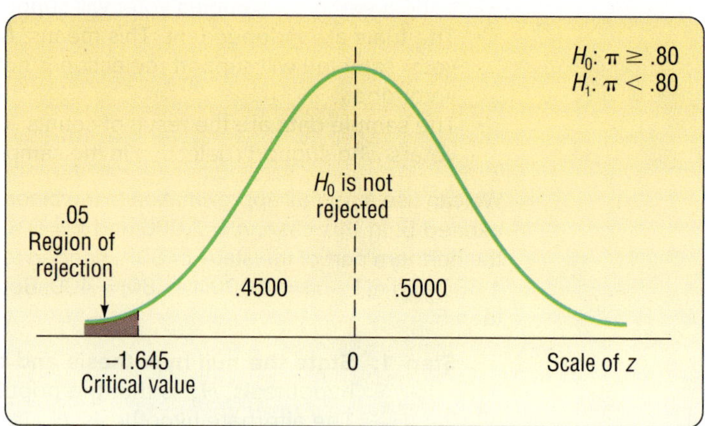

CHART 15–1 Rejection Region for the .05 Level of Significance, One-Tailed Test

Step 5: Make a decision. Select a sample and make a decision about H_0. A sample survey of 2,000 potential voters in the northern part of the state revealed that 1,550 planned to vote for the incumbent governor. Is the sample proportion of .775 (found by 1,550/2,000) close enough to .80 to conclude that the difference is due to sampling error? In this case:

p is .775, the proportion in the sample who plan to vote for the governor.
n is 2,000, the number of voters surveyed.
π is .80, the hypothesized population proportion.
z is a normally distributed test statistic. We can use it because the normal approximation assumptions are true.

Using formula (15–1) and computing z gives

$$z = \frac{p - \pi}{\sqrt{\frac{\pi(1 - \pi)}{n}}} = \frac{\frac{1,550}{2,000} - .80}{\sqrt{\frac{.80(1 - .80)}{2,000}}} = \frac{.775 - .80}{\sqrt{.00008}} = -2.80$$

The computed value of z (−2.80) is less than the critical value, so the null hypothesis is rejected at the .05 level. The difference of 2.5 percentage points between the sample percent (77.5%) and the hypothesized population percent in the northern part of the state necessary to carry the state (80%) is statistically significant. From Appendix B.3, the probability of a z value between zero and −2.80 is .4974. So the p-value is .0026, found by .5000 − .4974. Because the p-value is less than the significance level, the null hypothesis is rejected.

Step 6: Interpret the result. The governor can conclude that he does not have the necessary support in the northern section of the state to win reelection. To put it another way, the evidence at this point does not support the claim that the incumbent governor will return to the governor's mansion for another 4 years.

SELF-REVIEW 15–1

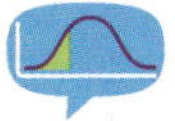

A recent insurance industry report indicated that 40% of those persons involved in minor traffic accidents this year have been involved in at least one other traffic accident in the last 5 years. An advisory group decided to investigate this claim, believing it was too large. A sample of 200 traffic accidents this year showed 74 persons were also involved in another accident within the last 5 years. Use the .01 significance level.

(a) Can we use z as the test statistic? Tell why or why not.
(b) State the null hypothesis and the alternate hypothesis.
(c) Show the decision rule graphically.
(d) Compute the value of z and state your decision regarding the null hypothesis.
(e) Determine and interpret the p-value.

EXERCISES

1. The following hypotheses are given.

$$H_0: \pi \leq .70$$
$$H_1: \pi > .70$$

A sample of 100 observations revealed that $p = .75$. At the .05 significance level, can the null hypothesis be rejected?

a. State the decision rule.
b. Compute the value of the test statistic.
c. What is your decision regarding the null hypothesis?

2. The following hypotheses are given.

$$H_0: \pi = .40$$
$$H_1: \pi \neq .40$$

A sample of 120 observations revealed that $p = .30$. At the .05 significance level, can the null hypothesis be rejected?

a. State the decision rule.
b. Compute the value of the test statistic.
c. What is your decision regarding the null hypothesis?

Note: It is recommended that you use the six-step hypothesis-testing procedure in solving the following problems.

3. The U.S. Department of Transportation estimates that 10% of Americans carpool. Does that imply that 10% of cars will have two or more occupants? A sample of 300 cars traveling southbound on the New Jersey Turnpike yesterday revealed that 63 had two or more occupants. At the .01 significance level, can we conclude that 10% of cars traveling on the New Jersey Turnpike have two or more occupants?
4. A recent article reported that a job awaits only one in three new college graduates. The major reasons given were an overabundance of college graduates and a weak economy. A survey of 200 recent graduates from your school revealed that 80 students had jobs. At the .01 significance level, can we conclude that a larger proportion of students at your school have jobs?
5. Chicken Delight claims that 90% of its orders are delivered within 10 minutes of the time the order is placed. A sample of 100 orders revealed that 82 were delivered within the promised time. At the .10 significance level, can we conclude that less than 90% of the orders are delivered in less than 10 minutes?
6. Research at the University of Toledo indicates that 50% of students change their major area of study after their first year in a program. A random sample of 100 students in the College of Business revealed that 48 had changed their major area of study after their first year of the program. Has there been a significant decrease in the proportion of students who change their major after the first year in this program? Test at the .05 level of significance.

LO15-2
Test a hypothesis about two population proportions.

TWO-SAMPLE TESTS ABOUT PROPORTIONS

In the previous section, we considered a test of a single population proportion. However, we are often interested also in whether two sample proportions come from populations that are equal. Here are several examples.

- The vice president of human resources wishes to know whether there is a difference in the proportion of hourly employees who miss more than 5 days of work per year at the Atlanta and the Houston plants.
- General Motors is considering a new design for the Chevy Malibu. The design is shown to a group of millennials and another group of baby-boomers. General Motors wishes to know whether there is a difference in the proportion of the two groups who like the new design.
- A consultant to the airline industry is investigating the fear of flying among adults. Specifically, the consultant wishes to know whether there is a difference in the proportion of men versus women who are fearful of flying.

In the above cases, each sampled item or individual can be classified as a "success" or a "failure." That is, in the Chevy Malibu example, each potential buyer is classified as "liking the new design" or "not liking the new design." We then compare the proportion in the millennial group with the proportion in the baby-boomer group who indicated they liked the new design. Can we conclude that the differences are due to chance? In this study, there is no measurement obtained, only classifying the individuals or objects.

To conduct the test, we assume each sample is large enough that the normal distribution will serve as a good approximation of the binomial distribution. The test statistic follows the standard normal distribution. We compute the value of z from the following formula:

TWO-SAMPLE TEST OF PROPORTIONS

$$z = \frac{p_1 - p_2}{\sqrt{\dfrac{p_c(1 - p_c)}{n_1} + \dfrac{p_c(1 - p_c)}{n_2}}} \quad \textbf{(15–2)}$$

where:

n_1 is the number of observations in the first sample.
n_2 is the number of observations in the second sample.
p_1 is the proportion in the first sample possessing the trait.
p_2 is the proportion in the second sample possessing the trait.
p_c is the pooled proportion possessing the trait in the combined samples. It is called the pooled estimate of the population proportion and is computed from the following formula.

POOLED PROPORTION

$$p_c = \frac{x_1 + x_2}{n_1 + n_2} \quad \textbf{(15–3)}$$

where:

x_1 is the number possessing the trait in the first sample.
x_2 is the number possessing the trait in the second sample.

The following example will illustrate the two-sample test of proportions.

EXAMPLE

Manelli Perfume Company recently developed a new fragrance that it plans to market under the name Heavenly. A number of market studies indicate that Heavenly has very good market potential. The sales department at Manelli is particularly interested in whether there is a difference in the proportions of working and stay-at-home women who would purchase Heavenly if it were marketed. There are two independent populations, a population consisting of working women and a population consisting of stay-at-home women. Each sampled woman will be asked to smell Heavenly and indicate whether she likes the fragrance well enough to purchase a bottle.

© Digital Vision/Punchstock

SOLUTION

We will use the usual six-step hypothesis-testing procedure.

Step 1: State H_0 and H_1. In this case, the null hypothesis is: "There is no difference in the proportion of working and stay-at-home women who prefer Heavenly." We designate π_1 as the proportion of working women who would purchase Heavenly and π_2 as the proportion of stay-at-home women who would purchase it. The alternate hypothesis is that the two proportions are not equal.

$$H_0: \pi_1 = \pi_2$$
$$H_1: \pi_1 \neq \pi_2$$

Step 2: Select the level of significance. We choose the .05 significance level in this example.

Step 3: Determine the test statistic. The two samples are sufficiently large so we use the standard normal distribution as the test statistic. The value of the test statistic is computed using formula (15–2).

Step 4: Formulate the decision rule. Recall that the alternate hypothesis from **Step 1** does not indicate a direction, so this is a two-tailed test. To find the critical value, go to Student's *t* distribution (Appendix B.5). In the table headings, find the row labeled **"Level of Significance for Two-Tailed Test"** and select the column for an alpha of .05. Go to the bottom row with infinite degrees of freedom. The *z* critical value is 1.960, so the critical values are −1.960 and 1.960. As before, if the computed test statistic is less than −1.960 or greater than 1.960, the null hypothesis is rejected. This information is summarized in Chart 15–2.

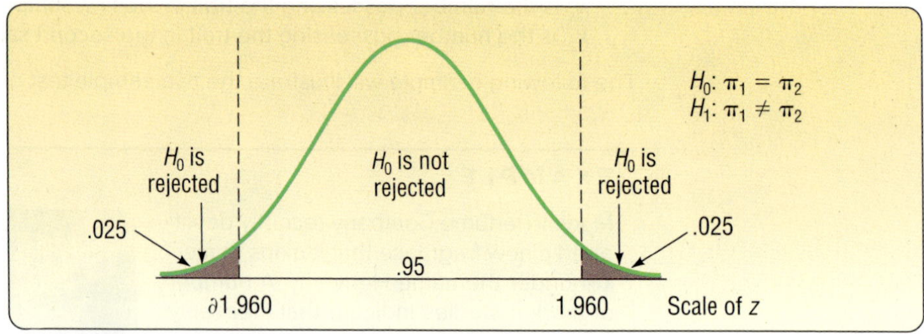

CHART 15–2 Decision Rules for Heavenly Fragrance Test, .05 Significance Level

Step 5: Select a sample and make a decision. A random sample of 100 working women revealed 19 liked the Heavenly fragrance well enough to purchase it. Similarly, a sample of 200 stay-at-home women revealed 62 liked the fragrance well enough to make a purchase. Let p_1 refer to working women and p_2 to stay-at-home women.

$$p_1 = \frac{x_1}{n_1} = \frac{19}{100} = .19 \qquad p_2 = \frac{x_2}{n_2} = \frac{62}{200} = .31$$

The research question is whether the difference of .12 in the two sample proportions is due to chance or whether there is a difference in the proportion of working and stay-at-home women who like the Heavenly fragrance.

Next, we combine or pool the sample proportions. We use formula (15–3).

$$p_c = \frac{x_1 + x_2}{n_1 + n_2} = \frac{19 + 62}{100 + 200} = \frac{81}{300} = 0.27$$

Note that the pooled proportion is closer to .31 than to .19 because more stay-at-home women than working women were sampled.

We use formula (15–2) to find the value of the test statistic.

$$z = \frac{p_1 - p_2}{\sqrt{\frac{p_c(1 - p_c)}{n_1} + \frac{p_c(1 - p_c)}{n_2}}} = \frac{.19 - .31}{\sqrt{\frac{.27(1 - .27)}{100} + \frac{.27(1 - .27)}{200}}} = -2.207$$

The computed value of −2.207 is in the area of rejection; that is, it is to the left of −1.960. Therefore, the null hypothesis is rejected at the .05 significance level. To put it another way, we reject the null hypothesis that the proportion of working women who would purchase Heavenly is equal to the proportion of stay-at-home women who would purchase Heavenly.

To find the *p*-value, we need to round the *z* test statistic from −2.207 to −2.21 so that we can use the table Areas under the Normal Curve in Appendix B.3. In the table, find the likelihood, or probability, of a *z* value less than −2.21 or greater than 2.21. The probability corresponding to 2.21 is .4864, so the likelihood of finding the value of the test statistic to be less than −2.21 or greater than 2.21 is:

$$p\text{-value} = 2(.5000 - .4864) = 2(.0136) = .0272$$

The *p*-value of .0272 is less than the significance level of .05, so our decision is to reject the null hypothesis.

Step 6: Interpret the result. The results of the hypothesis test indicate working and stay-at-home women would purchase Heavenly at different rates or proportions.

The MegaStat add-in for Excel has a procedure to determine the value of the test statistic and compute the *p*-value. Notice that the MegaStat output includes the two sample proportions, the value of *z*, and the *p*-value. The difference in the *p*-value is rounding. The results follow.

Hypothesis test for two independent proportions

p1	p2	p_c	
0.19	0.31	0.27	p (as decimal)
19/100	62/200	81/300	p (as fraction)
19.	62.	81.	X
100	200	300	n
	-0.12	difference	
	0.	hypothesized difference	
	0.0544	std. error	
	-2.21	z	
	.0273	p-value (two-tailed)	

SELF-REVIEW 15–2

Of 150 adults who tried a new peach-flavored Peppermint Pattie, 87 rated it excellent. Of 200 children sampled, 123 rated it excellent. Using the .10 level of significance, can we conclude that there is a significant difference in the proportion of adults and the proportion of children who rate the new flavor excellent?

(a) State the null hypothesis and the alternate hypothesis.
(b) What is the probability of a Type I error?
(c) Is this a one-tailed or a two-tailed test?
(d) What is the decision rule?
(e) What is the value of the test statistic?
(f) What is your decision regarding the null hypothesis?
(g) What is the *p*-value? Explain what it means in terms of this problem.

EXERCISES

7. The null and alternate hypotheses are:

$$H_0: \pi_1 \leq \pi_2$$
$$H_1: \pi_1 > \pi_2$$

A sample of 100 observations from the first population indicated that x_1 is 70. A sample of 150 observations from the second population revealed x_2 to be 90. Use the .05 significance level to test the hypothesis.

a. State the decision rule.
b. Compute the pooled proportion.
c. Compute the value of the test statistic.
d. What is your decision regarding the null hypothesis?

8. The null and alternate hypotheses are:

$$H_0: \pi_1 = \pi_2$$
$$H_1: \pi_1 \neq \pi_2$$

A sample of 200 observations from the first population indicated that x_1 is 170. A sample of 150 observations from the second population revealed x_2 to be 110. Use the .05 significance level to test the hypothesis.

a. State the decision rule.
b. Compute the pooled proportion.
c. Compute the value of the test statistic.
d. What is your decision regarding the null hypothesis?

Note: Use the six-step hypothesis-testing procedure in solving the following exercises.

9. The Damon family owns a large grape vineyard in western New York along Lake Erie. The grapevines must be sprayed at the beginning of the growing season to protect against various insects and diseases. Two new insecticides have just been marketed: Pernod 5 and Action. To test their effectiveness, three long rows were selected and sprayed with Pernod 5, and three others were sprayed with Action. When the grapes ripened, 400 of the vines treated with Pernod 5 were checked for infestation. Likewise, a sample of 400 vines sprayed with Action were checked. The results are:

Insecticide	Number of Vines Checked (sample size)	Number of Infested Vines
Pernod 5	400	24
Action	400	40

At the .05 significance level, can we conclude that there is a difference in the proportion of vines infested using Pernod 5 as opposed to Action?

10. GfK Research North America conducted identical surveys 5 years apart. One question asked of women was "Are most men basically kind, gentle, and thoughtful?" The earlier survey revealed that, of the 3,000 women surveyed, 2,010 said that they were. The later revealed 1,530 of the 3,000 women surveyed thought that men were kind, gentle, and thoughtful. At the .05 level, can we conclude that women think men are less kind, gentle, and thoughtful in the later survey compared with the earlier one?

11. A nationwide sample of influential Republicans and Democrats was asked as a part of a comprehensive survey whether they favored lowering environmental standards so that high-sulfur coal could be burned in coal-fired power plants. The results were:

	Republicans	Democrats
Number sampled	1,000	800
Number in favor	200	168

At the .02 level of significance, can we conclude that there is a larger proportion of Democrats in favor of lowering the standards? Determine the *p*-value.

12. The research department at the home office of New Hampshire Insurance conducts on-going research on the causes of automobile accidents, the characteristics of the drivers, and so on. A random sample of 400 policies written on single persons revealed 120 had at least one accident in the previous three-year period. Similarly, a sample of 600 policies written on married persons revealed that 150 had been in at least one accident. At the .05 significance level, is there a significant difference in the proportions of single and married persons having an accident during a three-year period? Determine the *p*-value.

LO15-3
Test a hypothesis comparing an observed set of frequencies to an expected frequency distribution.

GOODNESS-OF-FIT TESTS: COMPARING OBSERVED AND EXPECTED FREQUENCY DISTRIBUTIONS

Next, we discuss goodness-of-fit tests that compare an observed frequency distribution to an expected frequency distribution for variables measured on a nominal or ordinal scale. For example, a life insurance company classifies its policies into four categories using a nominal variable, policy type. Policy type has four categories: whole life, level term, decreasing term, and others. The table below shows the historical relative frequency distribution of the policy types. These would be the expected frequencies.

Policy Type	Percent
Whole life	40
Level term	25
Decreasing term	15
Other	20

The insurance company wishes to compare this historical distribution with an observed distribution of policy types for a sample of 2,000 current policies. The goodness-of-fit test would determine if the current distribution of policies "fits" the historical distribution or if it has changed. A goodness-of-fit test is one of the most commonly used statistical tests.

Hypothesis Test of Equal Expected Frequencies

Our first illustration of a goodness-of-fit test involves the case where we choose the expected frequencies to be equal. As the full name implies, the purpose of the goodness-of-fit test is to compare an observed frequency distribution to an expected frequency distribution.

EXAMPLE

Bubba's Fish and Pasta is a chain of restaurants located along the Gulf Coast of Florida. Bubba, the owner, is considering adding steak to his menu. Before doing so, he decides to hire Magnolia Research, LLC, to conduct a survey of adults as to their favorite meal when eating out. Magnolia selected a sample 120 adults and asked each to indicate his or her favorite meal when dining out. The results are reported below.

TABLE 15–1 Favorite Entrée as Selected by a Sample of 120 Adults

Favorite Entrée	Frequency
Chicken	32
Fish	24
Meat	35
Pasta	29
Total	120

Is it reasonable to conclude there is no preference among the four entrées?

SOLUTION

If there is no difference in the popularity of the four entrées, we would expect the observed frequencies to be equal—or nearly equal. To put it another way, we would expect as many adults to indicate they preferred chicken as fish. Thus, any discrepancy in the observed and expected frequencies is attributed to sampling error or chance.

What is the level of measurement in this problem? Notice that when a person is selected, we can only classify the selected adult as to the entrée preferred. We do not get a reading or a measurement of any kind. The "measurement" or "classification" is based on the selected entrée. In addition, there is no natural order to the favorite entrée. No one entrée is assumed better than another. Therefore, the nominal scale is appropriate.

© EQRoy/Shutterstock.com

If the entrées are equally popular, we would expect 30 adults to select each meal. Why is this so? If there are 120 adults in the sample and four categories, we expect that one-fourth of those surveyed would select each entrée. So 30, found by 120/4, is the expected frequency for each category, assuming there is no preference for any of the entrées. This information is summarized in Table 15–2. An examination of the data indicates meat is the entrée selected most frequently (35 out of 120) and fish is selected least frequently (24 out of 120). Is the difference in the number of

TABLE 15–2 Observed and Expected Frequencies for Survey of 120 Adults

Favorite Meal	Observed Frequency, f_o	Expected Frequency, f_e
Chicken	32	30
Fish	24	30
Meat	35	30
Pasta	29	30
Total	120	120

times each entrée is selected due to chance, or should we conclude that the entrées are not equally preferred?

To investigate the issue, we use the six-step hypothesis-testing procedure.

Step 1: State the null hypothesis and the alternate hypothesis. The null hypothesis, H_0, is that there is no difference between the set of observed frequencies and the set of expected frequencies. In other words, any difference between the two sets of frequencies is attributed to sampling error. The alternate hypothesis, H_1, is that there is a difference between the observed and expected sets of frequencies. If the null hypothesis is rejected and the alternate hypothesis is accepted, we conclude the preferences are not equally distributed among the four categories.

H_0: There is no difference in the proportion of adults selecting each entrée.

H_1: There is a difference in the proportion of adults selecting each entrée.

Step 2: Select the level of significance. We selected the .05 significance level. The probability is .05 that a true null hypothesis is rejected.

Step 3: Select the test statistic. The test statistic follows the chi-square distribution, designated by χ^2.

CHI-SQUARE TEST STATISTIC

$$\chi^2 = \Sigma\left[\frac{(f_o - f_e)^2}{f_e}\right] \quad \textbf{(15–4)}$$

with $k - 1$ degrees of freedom, where:

k is the number of categories.
f_o is an observed frequency in a particular category.
f_e is an expected frequency in a particular category.

We will examine the characteristics of the chi-square distribution in more detail shortly.

Step 4: Formulate the decision rule. Recall that the decision rule in hypothesis testing is the value that separates the region where we do not reject H_0 from the region where H_0 is rejected. This number is called the *critical value*. As we will soon see, the chi-square distribution is really a family of distributions. Each distribution has a slightly different shape, depending on the number of degrees of freedom. The number of degrees of freedom is $k - 1$, where k is the number of categories. In this particular problem, there are four categories, the four meal entrées. Because there are four categories, there are $k - 1 = 4 - 1 = 3$ degrees of freedom. The critical value for 3 degrees of freedom and the .05 level of significance is found in Appendix B.7. A portion of that table is shown in Table 15–3. The critical value is 7.815, found by locating 3 degrees of freedom in the left margin and then moving horizontally (to the right) and reading the critical value in the .05 column.

TABLE 15–3 A Portion of the Chi-Square Table

Degrees of Freedom	Right-Tail Area			
df	.10	.05	.02	.01
1	2.706	3.841	5.412	6.635
2	4.605	5.991	7.824	9.210
3	6.251	7.815	9.837	11.345
4	7.779	9.488	11.668	13.277
5	9.236	11.070	13.388	15.086

The decision rule is to reject the null hypothesis if the computed value of chi-square is greater than 7.815. If it is less than or equal to 7.815, we fail to reject the null hypothesis. Chart 15–3 shows the decision rule.

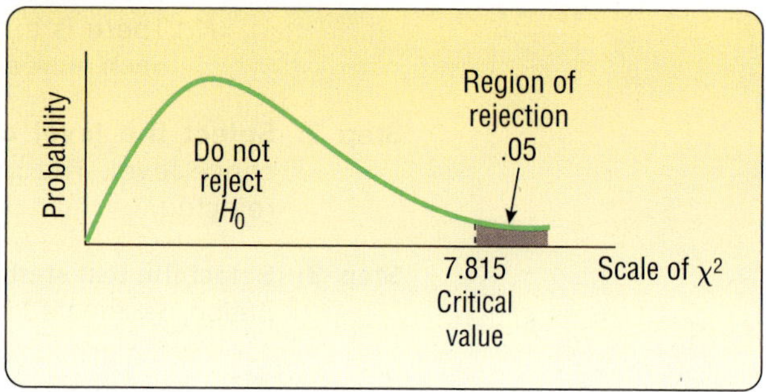

CHART 15–3 Chi-Square Probability Distribution for 3 Degrees of Freedom, Showing the Region of Rejection, .05 Level of Significance

The decision rule indicates that if there are large differences between the observed and expected frequencies, resulting in a computed χ^2 of more than 7.815, the null hypothesis should be rejected. However, if the differences between f_o and f_e are small, the computed χ^2 value will be 7.815 or less, and the null hypothesis should not be rejected. The reasoning is that such small differences between the observed and expected frequencies are probably due to chance. Remember, the 120 observations are a sample of the population.

Step 5: Compute the value of chi-square and make a decision. Of the 120 adults in the sample, 32 indicated their favorite entrée was chicken. The counts were reported in Table 15–1. The calculations for chi-square follow. (Note again that the expected frequencies are the same for each cell.)

Column D: Determine the differences between each f_o and f_e. That is, $f_o - f_e$. The sum of these differences is zero.

Column E: Square the difference between each observed and expected frequency, that is, $(f_o - f_e)^2$.

Column F: Divide the result for each observation by the expected frequency, that is, $(f_o - f_e)^2/f_e$. Finally, sum these values. The result is the value of χ^2, which is 2.20.

	A	B	C	D	E	F	G
1	Favorite Entrée	f_o	f_e	$(f_o - f_e)$	$(f_o - f_e)^2$	$(f_o - f_e)^2/f_e$	
2	Chicken	32	30	2	4	0.133	
3	Fish	24	30	-6	36	1.200	
4	Meat	35	30	5	25	0.833	χ^2 Value
5	Pasta	29	30	-1	1	0.033	
6	Total	120	120			2.200	

STATISTICS IN ACTION

For many years, researchers and statisticians believed that all variables were normally distributed. In fact, it was generally assumed to be a universal law. However, Karl Pearson observed that experimental data were not always normally distributed but there was no way to prove his observations were correct. To solve this problem, Pearson discovered the chi-square statistic that basically compares an observed frequency distribution with an assumed or expected normal distribution. His discovery proved that all variables were not normally distributed.

The computed χ^2 of 2.20 is not in the rejection region. It is less than the critical value of 7.815. The decision, therefore, is to not reject the null hypothesis.

Step 6: Interpret the results. We conclude that the differences between the observed and the expected frequencies could be due to chance. The data do not suggest that the preferences among the four entrées are different.

We can use MegaStat to compute the goodness-of-fit test as follows. The steps are shown in the **Software Commands** in Appendix C. The computed value of chi-square is 2.20, the same value obtained in our earlier calculations. Also note the *p*-value is .5319, much larger than .05.

Goodness-of-Fit Test

observed	expected	O – E	(O – E)²/E	% of chisq
32	30.000	2.000	0.133	6.06
24	30.000	–6.000	1.200	54.55
35	30.000	5.000	0.833	37.88
29	30.000	–1.000	0.033	1.52
120	120.000	0.000	2.200	100.00

2.20	chi-square
3	df
.5319	p-value

The Chi-square distribution has many applications in statistics. Its characteristics are:

1. **Chi-square values are never negative.** This is because the difference between f_o and f_e is squared, that is, $(f_o - f_e)^2$.
2. **There is a family of chi-square distributions.** There is a chi-square distribution for 1 degree of freedom, another for 2 degrees of freedom, another for 3 degrees of freedom, and so on. In this type of problem, the number of degrees of freedom is determined by $k - 1$, where k is the number of categories. Therefore, the shape of the chi-square distribution does *not* depend on the size of the sample, but on the number of categories used. For example, if 200 employees of an airline were classified into one of three categories—flight personnel, ground support, and administrative personnel—there would be $k - 1 = 3 - 1 = 2$ degrees of freedom.
3. **The chi-square distribution is positively skewed.** However, as the number of degrees of freedom increases, the distribution begins to approximate the normal probability distribution. Chart 15–4 shows the distributions for selected degrees of freedom. Notice that for 10 degrees of freedom the curve is approaching a normal distribution.

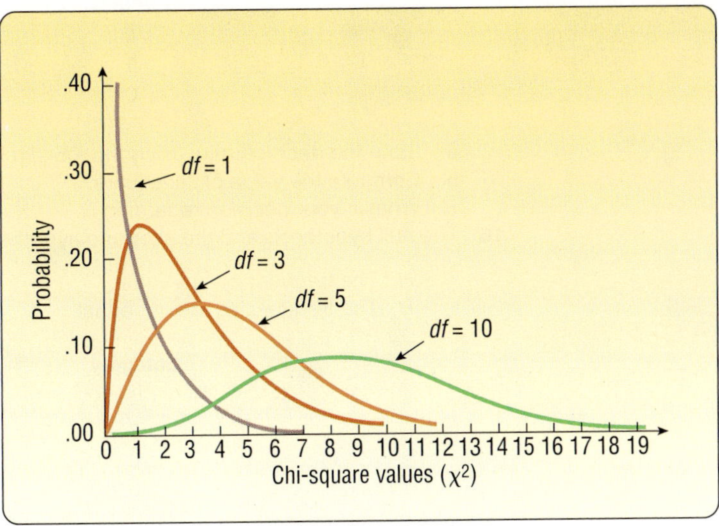

CHART 15–4 Chi-Square Distributions for Selected Degrees of Freedom

SELF-REVIEW 15–3

The human resources director at Georgetown Paper Inc. is concerned about absenteeism among hourly workers. She decides to sample the company records to determine whether absenteeism is distributed evenly throughout the six-day workweek. The hypotheses are:

H_0: Absenteeism is evenly distributed throughout the workweek.
H_1: Absenteeism is *not* evenly distributed throughout the workweek.

The sample results are:

	Number Absent		Number Absent
Monday	12	Thursday	10
Tuesday	9	Friday	9
Wednesday	11	Saturday	9

(a) What are the numbers 12, 9, 11, 10, 9, and 9 called?
(b) How many categories are there?
(c) What is the *expected* frequency for each day?
(d) How many degrees of freedom are there?
(e) What is the chi-square critical value at the 1% significance level?
(f) Compute the χ^2 test statistic.
(g) What is the decision regarding the null hypothesis?
(h) Specifically, what does this indicate to the human resources director?

EXERCISES

13. In a particular chi-square goodness-of-fit test, there are four categories and 200 observations. Use the .05 significance level.
   a. How many degrees of freedom are there?
   b. What is the critical value of chi-square?

14. In a particular chi-square goodness-of-fit test, there are six categories and 500 observations. Use the .01 significance level.
   a. How many degrees of freedom are there?
   b. What is the critical value of chi-square?

15. The null hypothesis and the alternate hypothesis are:

H_0: The frequencies are equal.
H_1: The frequencies are not equal.

Category	f_o
A	10
B	20
C	30

   a. State the decision rule, using the .05 significance level.
   b. Compute the value of chi-square.
   c. What is your decision regarding H_0?

16. The null hypothesis and the alternate hypothesis are:

H_0: The frequencies are equal.
H_1: The frequencies are not equal.

Category	f_o
A	10
B	20
C	30
D	20

a. State the decision rule, using the .05 significance level.
b. Compute the value of chi-square.
c. What is your decision regarding H_0?

17. A six-sided die is rolled 30 times and the numbers 1 through 6 appear as shown in the following frequency distribution. At the .10 significance level, can we conclude that the die is fair?

Outcome	Frequency	Outcome	Frequency
1	3	4	3
2	6	5	9
3	2	6	7

18. Classic Golf Inc. manages five courses in the Jacksonville, Florida, area. The director of golf wishes to study the number of rounds of golf played per weekday at the five courses. He gathered the following sample information. At the .05 significance level, is there a difference in the number of rounds played by day of the week?

Day	Rounds
Monday	124
Tuesday	74
Wednesday	104
Thursday	98
Friday	120

19. FILE A group of department store buyers viewed a new line of dresses and gave their opinions of them. The results were:

Opinion	Number of Buyers	Opinion	Number of Buyers
Outstanding	47	Good	39
Excellent	45	Fair	35
Very good	40	Undesirable	34

Because the largest number (47) indicated the new line is outstanding, the head designer thinks that this is a mandate to go into mass production of the dresses. The head sweeper (who somehow became involved in this) believes that there is not a clear mandate and claims that the opinions are evenly distributed among the six categories. He further states that the slight differences among the various counts are probably due to chance. Test the null hypothesis that there is no significant difference among the opinions of the buyers at the .01 level of significance.

20. FILE The safety director of a large steel mill took samples at random from company records of minor work-related accidents and classified them according to the time the accident took place.

Time	Number of Accidents	Time	Number of Accidents
8 up to 9 a.m.	6	1 up to 2 p.m.	7
9 up to 10 a.m.	6	2 up to 3 p.m.	8
10 up to 11 a.m.	20	3 up to 4 p.m.	19
11 up to 12 p.m.	8	4 up to 5 p.m.	6

Using the goodness-of-fit test and the .01 level of significance, determine whether the accidents are evenly distributed throughout the day. Write a brief explanation of your conclusion.

Hypothesis Test of Unequal Expected Frequencies

The expected frequencies (f_e) in the previous example/solution involving preferred entrées were all equal. According to the null hypothesis, it was expected that of the 120 adults in the study, an equal number would select each of the four entrées. So we expect 30 to select chicken, 30 to select fish, and so on. The chi-square test can also be used if the expected frequencies are not equal.

The following example illustrates the case of unequal frequencies and also gives a practical use of the chi-square goodness-of-fit test—namely, to find whether a local experience differs from the national experience.

EXAMPLE

The American Hospital Administrators Association (AHAA) reports the following information concerning the number of times senior citizens are admitted to a hospital during a one-year period. Forty percent are not admitted; 30% are admitted once; 20% are admitted twice, and the remaining 10% are admitted three or more times.

A survey of 150 residents of Bartow Estates, a community devoted to active seniors located in central Florida, revealed 55 residents were not admitted during the last year, 50 were admitted to a hospital once, 32 were admitted twice, and the rest of those in the survey were admitted three or more times. Can we conclude the survey at Bartow Estates is consistent with the information reported by the AHAA? Use the .05 significance level.

SOLUTION

We begin by organizing the above information into Table 15–4. Clearly, we cannot compare the percentages given in the AHAA study to the counts or frequencies reported for Bartow Estates residents. However, we can use the AHAA information to compute expected frequencies, f_e, for the Bartow Estates residents. According to AHAA, 40% of the seniors in their survey did not require hospitalization. Thus, if there is no difference between the national experience and the Bartow Estates' study, then the expectation is that 40% of the 150 Bartow seniors surveyed, or $f_e = 60$, would not have been hospitalized. Further, based on the AHAA information, 30% of the 150 Bartow seniors, or $f_e = 45$, would be expected to be admitted once, and so on. The observed and expected frequencies for Bartow residents are given in Table 15–4.

TABLE 15–4 Summary of Study by AHAA and a Survey of Bartow Estates

Number of Times Admitted	AHAA Relative Frequencies	Observed Frequency of Bartow Residents (f_o)	Expected Frequency of Bartow Residents (f_e)
0	40%	55	60 = (.40)(150)
1	30%	50	45 = (.30)(150)
2	20%	32	30 = (.20)(150)
3 or more	10%	13	15 = (.10)(150)
Total	100	150	

The null hypothesis and the alternate hypothesis are:

H_0: There is no difference between local and national experience for hospital admissions.

H_1: There is a difference between local and national experience for hospital admissions.

To find the decision rule, we use Appendix B.7 and the .05 significance level. There are four admitting categories, so the degrees of freedom are $df = 4 - 1 = 3$. The critical value is 7.815. Therefore, the decision rule is to reject the null hypothesis if $\chi^2 > 7.815$. The decision rule is portrayed in Chart 15–5.

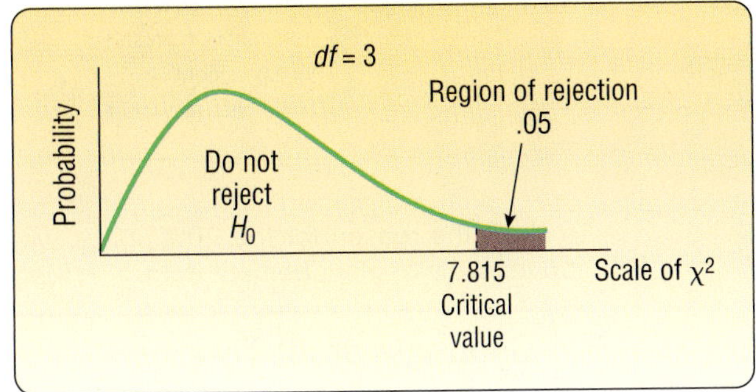

CHART 15–5 Decision Criteria for the Bartow Estates Research Study

STATISTICS IN ACTION

Many state governments operate lotteries to help fund education. In many lotteries, numbered balls are mixed and selected by a machine. In a Select Three game, numbered balls are selected randomly from three groups of balls numbered zero through nine. Randomness would predict that the frequency of each number is equal. How would you test if the machine ensured a random selection process? A chi-square, goodness-of-fit test could be used to investigate this question.

Now to compute the chi-square test statistic:

Number of Times Admitted	f_o	f_e	$(f_o - f_e)$	$(f_o - f_e)^2$	$(f_o - f_e)^2/f_e$
0	55	60	−5	25	0.4167
1	50	45	5	25	0.5556
2	32	30	2	4	0.1333
3 or more	13	15	−2	4	0.2667
Total	150				1.3723 (χ^2 value)

The computed value of χ^2 (1.3723) lies to the left of 7.815. Thus, we cannot reject the null hypothesis. We conclude that the survey results do not provide evidence of a difference between the local and national experience for hospital admissions.

LO15-4
Explain the limitations of using the chi-square statistic in goodness-of-fit tests.

LIMITATIONS OF CHI-SQUARE

If there is an unusually small expected frequency for a category, chi-square (if applied) might result in an erroneous conclusion. This can happen because f_e appears in the denominator, and dividing by a very small number makes the quotient quite large! Two generally accepted policies regarding small category frequencies are:

1. If there are only two cells, the *expected* frequency in each category should be at least 5. The computation of chi-square would be permissible in the following problem, involving a minimum f_e of 6.

Individual	f_o	f_e
Literate	641	642
Illiterate	7	6

2. For more than two categories, chi-square should *not* be used if more than 20% of the categories have expected frequencies less than 5. According to this policy, it would not be appropriate to use the goodness-of-fit test on the following data. Three of the seven categories, or 43%, have expected frequencies (f_e) of less than 5.

Level of Management	f_o	f_e
Foreman	30	32
Supervisor	110	113
Manager	86	87
Middle management	23	24
Assistant vice president	5	2
Vice president	5	4
Senior vice president	4	1
Total	263	263

To show the reason for the 20% policy, we conducted the goodness-of-fit test on the above levels-of-management data. The MegaStat output follows.

Goodness of Fit Test

observed	expected	O - E	$(O - E)^2 / E$	% of chisq
30	32.000	-2.000	0.125	0.89
110	113.000	-3.000	0.080	0.57
86	87.000	-1.000	0.011	0.08
23	24.000	-1.000	0.042	0.30
5	2.000	3.000	4.500	32.12
5	4.000	1.000	0.250	1.78
4	1.000	3.000	9.000	64.25
263	263.000	0.000	14.008	100.00

14.01 chi-square
6 df
.0295 p-value

For this test at the .05 significance level, H_0 is rejected if the computed value of chi-square is greater than 12.592. The computed value is 14.008, so we reject the null hypothesis that the observed and expected frequency distributions are the same. However, examine the MegaStat output critically. More than 98% of the computed chi-square value is accounted for by the three vice president categories [(4.500 + .250 + 9.000)/14.008 = 0.9815]. Logically, too much weight is being given to these categories.

The issue can be resolved by combining categories if it is logical to do so. In the above example, we combine the three vice president categories, which satisfies the 20% policy. Note that the degrees of freedom for the goodness of fit test change from 6 to 4.

Level of Management	f_o	f_e
Foreman	30	32
Supervisor	110	113
Manager	86	87
Middle management	23	24
Vice president	14	7
Total	263	263

The computed value of chi-square with the revised categories is 7.258. See the following MegaStat output. This value is less than the critical value of 9.488 (based on 4 degrees of freedom) for the .05 significance level. The null hypothesis is, therefore, not rejected at the .05 significance level. This indicates there is not a significant difference between the observed and expected distributions.

Goodness-of-Fit Test

Observed	Expected	O - E	(O - E)² / E	% of chisq
30	32.000	-2.000	0.125	1.72
110	113.000	-3.000	0.080	1.10
86	87.000	-1.000	0.011	0.16
23	24.000	-1.000	0.042	0.57
14	7.000	7.000	7.000	96.45
263	263.000	0.000	7.258	100.00

7.26 chi-square
4 df
.1229 p-value

SELF-REVIEW 15–4

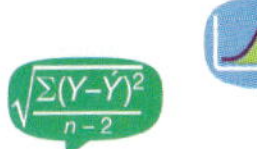

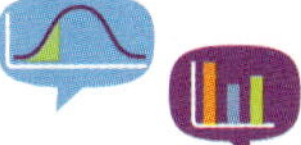

The American Accounting Association classifies accounts receivable as "current," "late," and "not collectible." Industry figures show that 60% of accounts receivable are current, 30% are late, and 10% are not collectible. Massa and Barr, a law firm in Greenville, Ohio, has 500 accounts receivable: 320 are current, 120 are late, and 60 are not collectible. Are these numbers in agreement with the industry distribution? Use the .05 significance level.

EXERCISES

21. For a particular population, a hypothesis states:

H_0: Forty percent of the observations are in category A, 40% are in B, and 20% are in C.
H_1: The distribution of the observations is not as described in H_0.

We took a sample of 60 observations from the population with the following results.

Category	f_o
A	30
B	20
C	10

a. For the hypothesis test, state the decision rule using the .01 significance level.
b. Compute the value of chi-square.
c. What is your decision regarding H_0?

22. The chief of security for the Mall of the Dakotas directed a study of theft. He selected a sample of 100 boxes that had been tampered with and ascertained that, for 60 of the boxes, the missing pants, shoes, and so on were attributed to shoplifting. For 30 boxes, employees had stolen the goods, and for the remaining 10 boxes he blamed poor inventory control. In his report to the mall management, can he say that shoplifting is *twice* as likely to be the cause of the loss as compared with either employee theft or poor inventory control and that employee theft and poor inventory control are equally likely? Use the .02 significance level.

23. From experience, the bank credit card department of Carolina Bank knows that 5% of its card holders have had some high school, 15% have completed high school, 25% have had some college, and 55% have completed college. Of the 500 card holders whose cards have been called in for failure to pay their charges this month, 50 had some high school, 100 had completed high school, 190 had some college, and 160 had completed college. Can we conclude that the distribution of card holders who do not pay their charges is different from all others? Use the .01 significance level.

24. For many years, TV executives used the guideline that 30% of the audience were watching each of the traditional big three prime-time networks and 10% were watching cable stations on a weekday night. A random sample of 500 viewers in the Tampa–St. Petersburg, Florida, area last Monday night showed that 165 homes were tuned in to the ABC affiliate, 140 to the CBS affiliate, and 125 to the NBC affiliate, with the remainder viewing a cable station. At the .05 significance level, can we conclude that the guideline is still reasonable?

LO15-5
Test a hypothesis that an observed frequency distribution is normally distributed.

TESTING THE HYPOTHESIS THAT A DISTRIBUTION IS NORMAL

We use a goodness-of-fit test to compare an observed frequency distribution to an expected frequency distribution. In the example/solution regarding Bubba's Fish and Pasta, the observed frequencies are the count of each entrée selected for a sample of 120 adults. We determine the expected frequencies by assuming there is no preference for any of the four entrées, so we expect that one-fourth of the sample, or 30 adults, selects each entrée. In this section, we want to test a hypothesis that a distribution is normal by using the goodness-of-fit test to compare an observed frequency distribution to an expected frequency distribution that is normal. Why is this test important? In Chapter 11, when we tested for differences in two population means, we assumed the two populations followed the normal distribution. We made the same assumption in Chapter 12 when we tested if several population means were equal. In Chapter 13 we assume the distribution of the residuals in a least squares regression analysis follow the normal probability distribution.

The following example/solution provides the details of a goodness-of-fit test to investigate the reasonableness of the normality assumption.

EXAMPLE

In Chapter 2 we use a frequency distribution to organize the profits from the Applewood Auto Group's sale of 180 vehicles. The frequency distribution is repeated in Table 15–5.

TABLE 15–5 Frequency Distribution of Profits for Vehicles Sold Last Month by Applewood Auto Group

Profit	Frequency
\$ 200 up to \$ 600	8
600 up to 1,000	11
1,000 up to 1,400	23
1,400 up to 1,800	38
1,800 up to 2,200	45
2,200 up to 2,600	32
2,600 up to 3,000	19
3,000 up to 3,400	4
Total	180

© Blend Images/Getty Images

Using statistical software, on page 64 in Chapter 3 we determined that the mean profit on a vehicle for the Applewood Auto Group was \$1,843.17 and that the standard deviation was \$643.63. Is it reasonable to conclude that the profit data is a sample obtained from a normal population? To put it another way, do the profit data follow a normal population? We use the .05 significance level.

SOLUTION

To test for a normal distribution, we need to find the expected frequencies for each class in the distribution, assuming that the expected distribution follows a normal probability distribution. We start with the normal distribution by calculating probabilities for each class. Then we use these probabilities to compute the expected frequencies for each class.

To begin, we need to find the area, or probability, for each of the eight classes in Table 15–5, assuming a normal population with a mean of \$1,843.17 and a standard deviation of \$643.63. To find this probability, we adapt formula (7–1) from Chapter 7 replacing μ with $\bar{x}$ and σ with s. So we use the following formula to determine the various values of z.

$$z = \frac{x - \bar{x}}{s}$$

In this case, z is the value of the standard normal statistic; $\bar{x}$, \$1,843.17, is the sample mean; and s, \$643.63, is the sample standard deviation. To illustrate, we select class \$200 up to \$600 from Table 15–5. We want to determine the expected frequency in this class, assuming the distribution of profits follows a normal distribution. First, we find the z value corresponding to \$200.

$$z = \frac{x - \bar{x}}{s} = \frac{\$200 - \$1{,}843.17}{\$643.63} = -2.55$$

This indicates that the lower limit of this class is 2.55 standard deviations below the mean. From Appendix B.3, the probability of finding a z value less than −2.55 is .5000 − .4946 = .0054.

For the upper limit of the \$200 up to \$600 class:

$$z = \frac{x - \bar{x}}{s} = \frac{\$600 - \$1{,}843.17}{\$643.63} = -1.93$$

The area to the left of $600 is the probability of a z value less than −1.93. To find this value, we again use Appendix B.3 and reason that .5000 − .4732 = .0268.

Finally, to find the area between $200 and $600:

$$P(\$200 < x < \$600) = P(-2.55 < z < -1.93) = .0268 - .0054 = .0214$$

That is, about 2.14% of the vehicles sold will result in a profit of between $200 and $600.

There is a chance that the profit earned is less than $200. To find this probability:

$$P(x < \$200) = P(z < -2.55) = .5000 - .4946 = .0054$$

We enter these two probabilities in the second and third rows of column 3 in Table 15–6.

TABLE 15–6 Profits at Applewood Auto Group, z Values, Areas under the Normal Distribution, and Expected Frequencies

Profit	z Values	Area	Found by	Expected Frequency
Under $200	Under −2.55	.0054	0.5000 − 0.4946	0.97
$ 200 up to $ 600	−2.55 up to −1.93	.0214	0.4946 − 0.4732	3.85
600 up to 1,000	−1.93 up to −1.31	.0683	0.4732 − 0.4049	12.29
1,000 up to 1,400	−1.31 up to −0.69	.1500	0.4049 − 0.2549	27.00
1,400 up to 1,800	−0.69 up to −0.07	.2270	0.2549 − 0.0279	40.86
1,800 up to 2,200	−0.07 up to 0.55	.2367	0.0279 + 0.2088	42.61
2,200 up to 2,600	0.55 up to 1.18	.1722	0.3810 − 0.2088	31.00
2,600 up to 3,000	1.18 up to 1.80	.0831	0.4641 − 0.3810	14.96
3,000 up to 3,400	1.80 up to 2.42	.0281	0.4922 − 0.4641	5.06
3,400 or more	2.42 or more	.0078	0.5000 − 0.4922	1.40
Total		1.0000		180.00

Logically, if we sold 180 vehicles, we would expect to earn a profit of between $200 and $600 on 3.85 vehicles, found by .0214(180). We would expect to sell 0.97 vehicle with a profit of less than $200, found by 180(.0054). We continue this process for the remaining classes. This information is summarized in Table 15–7. Don't be concerned that we are reporting fractional vehicles.

TABLE 15–7 Computations of the Chi-Square Statistic

Profit	f_o	f_e	$(f_o - f_e)$	$(f_o - f_e)^2$	$(f_o - f_e)^2/f_e$
Under $600	8	4.82	3.18	10.1124	2.098
$ 600 up to $1,000	11	12.29	−1.29	1.6641	.135
1,000 up to 1,400	23	27.00	−4.00	16.0000	.593
1,400 up to 1,800	38	40.86	−2.86	8.1796	.200
1,800 up to 2,200	45	42.61	2.39	5.7121	.134
2,200 up to 2,600	32	31.00	1.00	1.0000	.032
2,600 up to 3,000	19	14.96	4.04	16.3216	1.091
3,000 and over	4	6.46	−2.46	6.0516	.937
Total	180	180.00	0		5.220

Before continuing, we should emphasize one of the limitations of tests using chi-square as the test statistic. The second limitation on page 563 indicates that if more than 20% of the categories have *expected frequencies* of less than 5, some of the categories should be combined. In Table 15–6, there are three classes in which the expected frequencies are less than 5. Hence, we combine the "Under $200" class with the "$200 up to \$600" class and the "\$3,400 or more" class with the "\$3,000 up to \$3,400" class. So the expected frequency in the "Under \$600" class is now 4.82, found by 0.97 plus 3.85. We do the same for the "\$3,000 and over" class: 5.06 + 1.40 = 6.46. The results are shown in Table 15–7. The computed value of chi-square is 5.220.

Now let's put this information into the formal hypothesis-testing format. The null and alternate hypotheses are:

H_0: The population of profits follows the normal distribution.
H_1: The population of profits does not follow the normal distribution.

To determine the critical value of chi-square, we need to know the degrees of freedom. In this case, there are 8 categories, or classes, so the degrees of freedom are $k - 1 = 8 - 1 = 7$. In addition, the values \$1,843.17, the mean profit, and \$643.63, the standard deviation of the Applewood Auto Group profits, were computed from a sample. When we estimate population parameters from sample data, we lose a degree of freedom for each estimate. So we lose two more degrees of freedom for estimating the population mean and the population standard deviation. Thus, the number of degrees of freedom in this problem is 5, found by $k - 2 - 1 = 8 - 2 - 1 = 5$.

From Appendix B.7, using the .05 significance level, the critical value of chi-square is 11.070. Our decision rule is to reject the null hypothesis if the computed value of chi-square is more than 11.070.

Now, to compute the value of chi-square, we use formula (15–4):

$$\chi^2 = \Sigma\frac{(f_o - f_e)^2}{f_e} = \frac{(8 - 4.82)^2}{4.82} + \cdots + \frac{(4 - 6.46)^2}{6.46} = 5.220$$

The values for each class are shown in the right-hand column of Table 15–7, as well as the column total, which is 5.220. Because the computed value of 5.220 is less than the critical value, we do not reject the null hypothesis. We conclude the evidence does not suggest the distribution of profits is other than normal.

To expand on the calculation of the number of degrees of freedom, if we know the mean and the standard deviation of a population and wish to find whether some sample data conform to a normal, the degrees of freedom are $k - 1$. On the other hand, suppose we have sample data grouped into a frequency distribution, but we do not know the value of the population mean and the population standard deviation. In this case, the degrees of freedom are $k - 2 - 1$. In general, when we use sample statistics to estimate population parameters, we lose a degree of freedom for each parameter we estimate. This is parallel to the situation on page 500 of Chapter 14, the chapter on multiple regression, where we lost a degree of freedom in the denominator of the *F* statistic for each independent variable considered.

EXERCISES

25. FILE The IRS is interested in the number of individual tax forms prepared by small accounting firms. The IRS randomly sampled 50 public accounting firms with 10 or fewer employees in the Dallas–Fort Worth area. The following frequency table reports the results of the study. Assume the sample mean is 44.8 clients and the sample standard deviation is 9.37 clients. Is it reasonable to conclude that the sample data are from a population that follows a normal probability distribution? Use the .05 significance level.

Number of Clients	Frequency
20 up to 30	1
30 up to 40	15
40 up to 50	22
50 up to 60	8
60 up to 70	4

26. FILE Advertising expenses are a significant component of the cost of goods sold. Listed below is a frequency distribution showing the advertising expenditures for 60 manufacturing companies located in the Southwest. The mean expense is \$52.0 million and the standard deviation is \$11.32 million. Is it reasonable to conclude the sample data are from a population that follows a normal probability distribution? Use the .05 significance level.

Advertising Expense ($ Million)	Number of Companies
25 up to 35	5
35 up to 45	10
45 up to 55	21
55 up to 65	16
65 up to 75	8
Total	60

LO15-6
Perform a chi-square test for independence on a contingency table.

CONTINGENCY TABLE ANALYSIS

In Chapter 4, we discussed bivariate data, where we studied the relationship between two variables. We described a contingency table, which simultaneously summarizes two nominal-scale variables of interest. For example, a sample of students enrolled in the School of Business is classified by gender (male or female) and major (accounting, management, finance, marketing, or business analytics). This classification is based on the nominal scale because there is no natural order to the classifications.

We discussed contingency tables in Chapter 5. On page 151, we illustrated the relationship between the number of movies attended per month and the age of the attendee. We can use the chi-square distribution to test whether two nominal-scaled variables are related or not. To put it another way, is one variable *independent* of the other?

Here are some examples where we are interested in testing whether two nominal-scaled variables are related.

- Ford Motor Company operates an assembly plant in Dearborn, Michigan. The plant operates three shifts per day, 5 days a week. The quality control manager wishes to compare the quality level on the three shifts. Vehicles are classified by quality level (acceptable, unacceptable) and shift (day, afternoon, night). Is there a difference in the quality level on the three shifts? That is, is the quality of the product related to the shift when it was manufactured? Or is the quality of the product independent of the shift on which it was manufactured?
- A sample of 100 drivers who were stopped for speeding violations was classified by gender and whether or not they were wearing a seat belt. For this sample, is wearing a seatbelt related to gender?
- Does a male released from federal prison make a different adjustment to civilian life if he returns to his hometown or if he goes elsewhere to live? The two variables are adjustment to civilian life and place of residence. Note that both variables are measured on the nominal scale.

The following example/solution provides the details of the analysis and possible conclusions.

EXAMPLE

Rainbow Chemical, Inc. employs hourly and salaried employees. The vice president of human resources surveyed 380 employees about his/her satisfaction level with the current health care benefits program. The employees were then classified according to the pay type, i.e., salary or hourly. The results are shown in Table 15–8.

TABLE 15–8 Health Care Satisfaction Level for Rainbow Chemical Employees

Pay Type	Satisfied	Neutral	Dissatisfied	Total
Salary	30	17	8	55
Hourly	140	127	58	325
Total	170	144	66	380

At the .05 significance level, is it reasonable to conclude that pay type and level of satisfaction with the health care benefits are related?

SOLUTION

The first step is to state the null hypothesis and the alternate hypothesis.

H_0: There is no relationship between level of satisfaction and pay type.
H_1: There is a relationship between level of satisfaction and pay type.

The significance level, as requested by the HR vice president, is .05. The level of measurement for pay type is the nominal scale. The satisfaction level with health benefits is actually the ordinal scale, but we use it as a nominal-scale variable. Each sampled employee is classified by two criteria: the level of satisfaction with benefits and pay type. The information is tabulated into Table 15–8, which is called a contingency table.

We use the chi-square distribution as the test statistic. To determine the critical value of chi-square, we calculate the degrees of freedom (*df*) as:

$$df = (\text{Number of rows} - 1)(\text{Number of columns} - 1) = (r - 1)(c - 1)$$

In this example/solution there are 2 rows and 3 columns, so there are 2 degrees of freedom.

$$df = (r - 1)(c - 1) = (2 - 1)(3 - 1) = 2$$

To find the critical value for 2 degrees of freedom and the .05 level, refer to Appendix B.7. Move down the degrees of freedom column in the left margin to the row with 2 degrees of freedom. Move across this row to the column headed .05. At the intersection, the chi-square critical value is 5.991. The decision rule is to reject the null hypothesis if the computed value of χ^2 is greater than 5.991. See Chart 15–6.

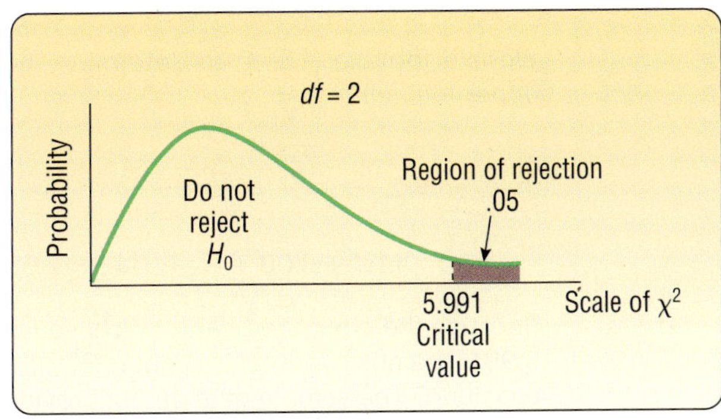

CHART 15–6 Chi-Square Distribution for 2 Degree of Freedom

Next we compute the chi-square value χ^2, using formula (15–4). The observed frequencies, f_o, are shown in Table 15–9. How are the corresponding expected frequencies, f_e, determined? To begin, notice from Table 15–8 that 55 of the 380 Rainbow Chemical employees sampled are salaried. So the fraction of salaried employees in the sample is 55/380 = .14474. *If there is no relationship* between pay type and level of satisfaction with the health care benefits program, we would expect about the same fraction of the employees who are satisfied with the health care to be salaried. There are 170 employees who are satisfied with the health care program, so the expected number of satisfied employees who are salaried is 24.61, found by (.14474)(170). Thus, the expected frequency for the upper-left cell is 24.61. Likewise, if there were no relationship between satisfaction level and pay type, we would expect .14474 of the 144 employees, or 20.84, who were neutral about the health care program to be salaried. We continue this process, filling in the remaining cells. It is not necessary to calculate each of these cell values. In fact we only need to calculate two cells. We can find the others by subtraction.

The expected frequency for any cell is determined by:

EXPECTED FREQUENCY $$f_e = \frac{(\text{Row total})(\text{Column total})}{(\text{Grand total})} \tag{15–5}$$

From this formula, the expected frequency for the upper-left cell in Table 15–8 is:

$$f_e = \frac{(\text{Row total})(\text{Column total})}{(\text{Grand total})} = \frac{(55)(170)}{380} = 24.61$$

The observed frequencies, f_o, and the expected frequencies, f_e, for all of the cells in the contingency table are listed in Table 15–9. Note there are slight differences due to rounding.

TABLE 15–9 Observed and Expected Frequencies

	Satisfaction Level with Health Care					
	Satisfied		Neutral		Dissatisfied	
Pay Type	f_o	f_e	f_o	f_e	f_o	f_e
Salary	30	24.61	17	20.84	8	9.55
Hourly	140	145.39	127	123.16	58	56.45
Total	170	170.00	144	144.00	66	66.00

We use formula (15–4) to determine the value of chi-square. Starting with the upper-left cell:

$$\chi^2 = \Sigma\frac{(f_o - f_e)^2}{f_e} = \frac{(30 - 24.61)^2}{24.61} + \frac{(17 - 20.84)^2}{20.84} + \cdots + \frac{(58 - 56.45)^2}{56.45}$$

$$= 1.181 + .708 + \cdots + .043 = 2.506$$

Because the computed value of chi-square (2.506) lies in the region to the left of 5.991, the null hypothesis is not rejected at the .05 significance level. What do we conclude? The sample data do not provide evidence that pay type and satisfaction level with health care benefits are related.

The following output is from the MegaStat Excel add-in.

Chi-square Contingency Table Test for Independence

Pay Type		Satisfaction Level with Health Care Satisfied	Neutral	Dissatisfied	Total
Salary	Observed	**30**	**17**	**8**	55
	Expected	24.61	20.84	9.55	55.00
Hourly	Observed	**140**	**127**	**58**	325
	Expected	145.39	123.16	56.45	325.00
Total	Observed	170	144	66	380
	Expected	170.00	144.00	66.00	380.00

2.506 chi-square
2 df
0.286 *p*-value

Observe that the value of chi-square is the same as that computed earlier, 2.506. In addition, the *p*-value, .286, is reported. So the probability of finding a value of the test statistic as large or larger, assuming the null hypothesis is true, is .286. The *p*-value also results in the same decision: do not reject the null hypothesis.

SELF-REVIEW 15–5

A social scientist sampled 140 people and classified them according to income level and whether or not they played a state lottery in the last month. The sample information is reported below. Is it reasonable to conclude that playing the lottery is related to income level? Use the .05 significance level.

	Income Low	Middle	High	Total
Played	46	28	21	95
Did not play	14	12	19	45
Total	60	40	40	140

(a) What is this table called?
(b) State the null hypothesis and the alternate hypothesis.
(c) What is the decision rule?
(d) Determine the value of chi-square.
(e) Make a decision on the null hypothesis. Interpret the result.

EXERCISES

27. FILE The director of advertising for the *Carolina Sun Times*, the largest newspaper in the Carolinas, is studying the relationship between the type of community in which a subscriber resides and the section of the newspaper he or she reads first. For a sample of readers, she collected the sample information in the following table.

	National News	Sports	Food
City	170	124	90
Suburb	120	112	100
Rural	130	90	88

At the .05 significance level, can we conclude there is a relationship between the type of community where the person resides and the section of the paper read first?

28. **FILE** Four brands of lightbulbs are being considered for use in the final assembly area of the Ford F-150 truck plant in Dearborn, Michigan. The director of purchasing asked for samples of 100 from each manufacturer. The numbers of acceptable and unacceptable bulbs from each manufacturer are shown below. At the .05 significance level, is there a difference in the quality of the bulbs?

	Manufacturer			
	A	**B**	**C**	**D**
Unacceptable	12	8	5	11
Acceptable	88	92	95	89
Total	100	100	100	100

29. **FILE** The quality control department at Food Town Inc., a grocery chain in upstate New York, conducts a monthly check on the comparison of scanned prices to posted prices. The chart below summarizes the results of a sample of 500 items last month. Company management would like to know whether there is any relationship between error rates on regularly priced items and specially priced items. Use the .01 significance level.

	Regular Price	Special Price
Undercharge	20	10
Overcharge	15	30
Correct price	200	225

30. **FILE** The use of cellular phones in automobiles has increased dramatically in the last few years. Of concern to traffic experts, as well as manufacturers of cellular phones, is the effect on accident rates. Is someone who is using a cellular phone more likely to be involved in a traffic accident? What is your conclusion from the following sample information? Use the .05 significance level.

	Had Accident in the Last Year	Did Not Have an Accident in the Last Year
Uses a cell phone	25	300
Does not use a cell phone	50	400

CHAPTER SUMMARY

I. This chapter considered tests of hypothesis for nominal level data.

II. When we sample from a single population and the variable of interest has only two possible outcomes, we call this a test of proportion.

A. The binomial conditions must be met.

B. Both $n\pi$ and $n(1-\pi)$ must be at least 5.

C. The test statistic is

$$z = \frac{p - \pi}{\sqrt{\frac{\pi(1 - \pi)}{n}}} \quad \textbf{(15–1)}$$

III. We can also test whether two samples came from populations with an equal proportion of successes.

A. The two sample proportions are pooled using the following formula:

$$p_c = \frac{x_1 + x_2}{n_1 + n_2} \tag{15–3}$$

B. We compute the value of the test statistic from the following formula:

$$z = \frac{p_1 - p_2}{\sqrt{\frac{p_c(1 - p_c)}{n_1} + \frac{p_c(1 - p_c)}{n_2}}} \tag{15–2}$$

IV. The characteristics of the chi-square distribution are:

A. The value of chi-square is never negative.

B. The chi-square distribution is positively skewed.

C. There is a family of chi-square distributions.

1. Each time the degrees of freedom change, a new distribution is formed.

2. As the degrees of freedom increase, the distribution approaches a normal distribution.

V. A goodness-of-fit test will show whether an observed set of frequencies could have come from a hypothesized population distribution.

A. The degrees of freedom are $k - 1$, where k is the number of categories.

B. The formula for computing the value of chi-square is

$$\chi^2 = \Sigma\frac{(f_o - f_e)^2}{f_e} \tag{15–4}$$

VI. A goodness-of-fit test can also be used to determine whether a sample of observations is from a normal population.

A. First, calculate the mean and standard deviation of the sample data.

B. Group the data into a frequency distribution.

C. Convert the class limits to z values and find the standard normal probability distribution for each class.

D. For each class, find the expected normally distributed frequency by multiplying the standard normal probability distribution by the class frequency.

E. Calculate the chi-square goodness-of-fit statistic based on the observed and expected class frequencies.

F. Find the expected frequency in each cell by determining the product of the probability of finding a value in each cell by the total number of observations.

G. If we use the information on the sample mean and the sample standard deviation from the sample data, the degrees of freedom are $k - 3$.

VII. A contingency table is used to test whether two traits or characteristics are related.

A. Each observation is classified according to two traits.

B. The expected frequency is determined as follows:

$$f_e = \frac{(\text{Row total})(\text{Column total})}{\text{Grand total}} \tag{15–5}$$

C. The degrees of freedom are found by:

$$df = (\text{Rows} - 1)(\text{Columns} - 1)$$

D. The usual hypothesis testing procedure is used.

PRONUNCIATION KEY

SYMBOL	MEANING	PRONUNCIATION
p_c	Pooled proportion	*p sub c*
χ^2	Chi-square statistic	*ki square*
f_o	Observed frequency	*f sub oh*
f_e	Expected frequency	*f sub e*

CHAPTER EXERCISES

31. A coin toss is used to decide which team gets the ball first in most sports. It involves little effort and is believed to give each side the same chance. In 50 Super Bowl games, the coin toss resulted in 24 heads and 26 tails. However, the National Football Conference has correctly called the coin flip 34 times. Meanwhile, the American Football Conference has correctly called the flip only 16 times. Use the six-step hypothesis-testing procedure at the .01 significance level to test whether these data suggest that the National Football Conference has an advantage in calling the coin flip.

a. Why can you use a *z*-statistic as the test statistic?
b. State the null and alternate hypotheses.
c. Make a diagram of the decision rule.
d. Evaluate the test statistic and make the decision.
e. What is the *p*-value and what does that imply?

32. According to a study by the American Pet Food Dealers Association, 63% of U.S. households own pets. A report is being prepared for an editorial in the *San Francisco Chronicle.* As a part of the editorial, a random sample of 300 households showed 210 own pets. Do these data disagree with the Pet Food Dealers Association's data? Use a .05 level of significance.

33. Tina Dennis is the comptroller for Meek Industries. She believes that the current cash-flow problem at Meek is due to the slow collection of accounts receivable. She believes that more than 60% of the accounts are more than 3 months in arrears. A random sample of 200 accounts showed that 140 were more than 3 months old. At the .01 significance level, can she conclude that more than 60% of the accounts are in arrears for more than three months?

34. The policy of the Suburban Transit Authority is to add a bus route if more than 55% of the potential commuters indicate they would use the particular route. A sample of 70 commuters revealed that 42 would use a proposed route from Bowman Park to the downtown area. Does the Bowman-to-downtown route meet the STA criterion? Use the .05 significance level.

35. Past experience at the Crowder Travel Agency indicated that 44% of those persons who wanted the agency to plan a vacation for them wanted to go to Europe. During the most recent season, a sampling of 1,000 persons was selected at random from the files. It was found that 480 persons wanted to go to Europe on vacation. Has there been a significant shift upward in the percentage of persons who want to go to Europe? Test at the .05 significance level.

36. Research in the gaming industry showed that 10% of all slot machines in the United States stop working each year. Short's Game Arcade has 60 slot machines and only 3 failed last year. At the .05 significance level, test whether these data contradict the research report.

a. Why can you use a *z*-statistic as the test statistic?
b. State the null and alternate hypotheses.
c. Evaluate the test statistic and make the decision.
d. What is the *p*-value and what does that imply?

37. An urban planner claims that, nationally, 20% of all families renting condominiums move during a given year. A random sample of 200 families renting condominiums in the Dallas Metroplex revealed that 56 moved during the past year. At the .01 significance level, does this evidence suggest that a larger proportion of condominium owners moved in the Dallas area? Determine the *p*-value.

38. After a losing season, there is a great uproar to fire the head football coach. In a random sample of 200 college alumni, 80 favor keeping the coach. Test at the .05 level of significance whether the proportion of alumni who support the coach is less than 50%.

39. During the 1990s, the fatality rate for lung cancer was 80 per 100,000 people. After the turn of the century and the establishment of newer treatments and adjustment in public health advertising, a random sample of 10,000 people exhibits only six deaths due to lung cancer. Test at the .05 significance level whether that data are proof of a reduced fatality rate for lung cancer.

40. Each month the National Association of Purchasing Managers surveys purchasing managers and publishes the NAPM index. One of the questions asked on the survey is: Do you think the economy is contracting? Last month, of the 300 responding managers, 160 answered yes to the question. This month, 170 of the 290 managers indicated they felt the economy was contracting. At the .05 significance level, can we conclude that a larger proportion of the purchasing managers believe the economy is contracting this month?

41. As part of a recent survey among dual-wage-earner couples, an industrial psychologist found that 990 men out of the 1,500 surveyed believed the division of household duties was fair. A sample of 1,600 women found 970 believed the division of household duties was fair. At the .01 significance level, is it reasonable to conclude that the proportion of men who believe the division of household duties is fair is larger? What is the *p*-value?

42. There are two major cell phone providers in the Colorado Springs, Colorado area, one called HTC and the other, Mountain Communications. We want to investigate the "churn rate" for each provider. Churn is the number of customers or subscribers who cut ties with a company during a given time period. At the beginning of the month, HTC had 10,000 customers; at the end of the month, HTC had 9810 customers for a loss of 190. For the same month, Mountain Communications started with 12,500 customers and ended the month with 12,285 customers, for a loss of 215. At the .01 significance level, is there a difference in the churn rate for the two providers?

43. The Consumer Confidence Survey is a monthly review that measures consumer confidence in the U.S. economy. It is based on a typical sample of 5,000 U.S. households. Last month 9.1% of consumers said conditions were "good." In the prior month, only 8.5% said they were "good." Use the six-step hypothesis-testing method at the .05 level of significance to see whether you can determine if there is an increase in the share asserting conditions are "good." Find the *p*-value and explain what it means.

44. A study was conducted to determine if there was a difference in the humor content in British and American trade magazine advertisements. In an independent random sample of 270 American trade magazine advertisements, 56 were humorous. An independent random sample of 203 British trade magazines contained 52 humorous ads. Do these data provide evidence at the .05 significance level that there is a difference in the proportion of humorous ads in British versus American trade magazines?

45. The AP-Petside.com poll contacted 300 married women and 200 married men. All owned pets. One hundred of the women and 36 of the men replied that their pets are better listeners than their spouses. At the .05 significance level, is there a difference between the responses of women and men?

46. The proportion of on-line shoppers who actually make a purchase appears to be relatively constant over time. In 2013, among a sample of 388 on-line shoppers, 160 purchased merchandise. In 2017, for a sample of 307 on-line shoppers, 144 purchased merchandise. At the .05 level of significance, did the proportion of on-line shoppers change from 2013 to 2017?

47. Vehicles heading west on Front Street may turn right, turn left, or go straight ahead at Elm Street. The city traffic engineer believes that half of the vehicles will continue straight through the intersection. Of the remaining half, equal proportions will turn right and left. Two hundred vehicles were observed, with the following results. Can we conclude that the traffic engineer is correct? Use the .10 significance level.

	Straight	Right Turn	Left Turn
Frequency	112	48	40

48. The publisher of a sports magazine plans to offer new subscribers one of three gifts: a sweatshirt with the logo of their favorite team, a coffee cup with the logo of their favorite team, or a pair of earrings also with the logo of their favorite team. In a sample of 500 new subscribers, the number selecting each gift is reported below. At the .05 significance level, is there a preference for the gifts or should we conclude that the gifts are equally well liked?

Gift	Frequency
Sweatshirt	183
Coffee cup	175
Earrings	142

49. In a particular metro area, there are three commercial television stations, each with its own news program from 6:00 to 6:30 p.m. According to a report in this morning's local newspaper, a random sample of 150 viewers last night revealed 53 watched the news on WNAE (channel 5), 64 watched on WRRN (channel 11), and 33 on WSPD (channel 13). At the .05 significance level, is there a difference in the proportion of viewers watching the three channels?

50. FILE There are four entrances to the Government Center Building in downtown Philadelphia. The building maintenance supervisor would like to know if the entrances are equally utilized. To investigate, 400 people were observed entering the building. The number using each entrance is reported below. At the .01 significance level, is there a difference in the use of the four entrances?

Entrance	Frequency
Main Street	140
Broad Street	120
Cherry Street	90
Walnut Street	50
Total	400

51. FILE The owner of a mail-order catalog would like to compare her sales with the geographic distribution of the population. According to the U.S. Bureau of the Census, 21% of the population lives in the Northeast, 24% in the Midwest, 35% in the South, and 20% in the West. Listed below is a breakdown of a sample of 400 orders randomly selected from those shipped last month. At the .01 significance level, does the distribution of the orders reflect the population?

Region	Frequency
Northeast	68
Midwest	104
South	155
West	73
Total	400

52. FILE Banner Mattress and Furniture Company wishes to study the number of credit applications received per day for the last 300 days. The sample information is reported below.

Number of Credit Applications	Frequency (Number of Days)
0	50
1	77
2	81
3	48
4	31
5 or more	13

To interpret, there were 50 days on which no credit applications were received, 77 days on which only one application was received, and so on. Would it be reasonable to conclude that the population distribution is Poisson with a mean of 2.0? Use the .05 significance level. (Hint: To find the expected frequencies use the Poisson distribution with a mean of 2.0. Find the probability of exactly one success given a Poisson distribution with a mean of 2.0. Multiply this probability by 300 to find the expected frequency for the number of days in which there was exactly one application. Determine the expected frequency for the other days in a similar manner.)

53. FILE Each of the digits in a raffle is thought to have the same chance of occurrence. The table shows the frequency of each digit for consecutive drawings in a California lottery.

Perform the chi-square test to see if you reject the hypothesis at the .05 significance level that the digits are from a uniform population.

Digit	Frequency	Digit	Frequency
0	44	5	24
1	32	6	31
2	23	7	27
3	27	8	28
4	23	9	21

54. FILE John Isaac Inc., a designer and installer of industrial signs, employs 60 people. The company recorded the type of the most recent visit to a doctor by each employee. A recent national survey found that 53% of all physician visits were to primary care physicians, 19% to medical specialists, 17% to surgical specialists, and 11% to emergency departments. Test at the .01 significance level if Isaac employees differ significantly from the survey distribution. Here are their results:

Visit Type	Number of Visits
Primary care	29
Medical specialist	11
Surgical specialist	16
Emergency	4

55. FILE The Eckel Manufacturing Company believes that their hourly wages follow a normal probability distribution. To confirm this, 270 employees were sampled and the results organized into the following frequency distribution. Use the methods on pages 82–83 of Chapter 3 to find the mean and standard deviation of these data grouped into a frequency distribution. At the .10 significance level, is it reasonable to conclude that the distribution of hourly wages follows a normal distribution?

Hourly Wage	Frequency
$5.50 up to $ 6.50	20
6.50 up to 7.50	24
7.50 up to 8.50	130
8.50 up to 9.50	68
9.50 up to 10.50	28
Total	270

56. FILE The National Cable and Telecommunications Association recently reported that the mean number of HDTVs per household in the United States is 2.30 with a standard deviation of 1.474 sets. A sample of 100 homes in Boise, Idaho, revealed the following sample information.

Number of HDTVs	Number of Households
0	7
1	27
2	28
3	18
4	10
5 or more	10
Total	100

At the .05 significance level, is it reasonable to conclude that the number of HDTVs per household follows a normal distribution? (Hint: Use limits such as 0.5 up to 1.5, 1.5 up to 2.5, and so on.)

57. FILE A survey investigated the public's attitude toward the federal deficit. Each sampled citizen was classified as to whether he or she felt the government should reduce the deficit or increase the deficit, or if the individual had no opinion. The sample results of the study by gender are reported below.

Gender	Reduce the Deficit	Increase the Deficit	No Opinion
Female	244	194	68
Male	305	114	25

At the .05 significance level, is it reasonable to conclude that gender is independent of a person's position on the deficit?

58. FILE A study regarding the relationship between age and the amount of pressure sales personnel feel in relation to their jobs revealed the following sample information. At the .01 significance level, is there a relationship between job pressure and age?

	Degree of Job Pressure		
Age (years)	Low	Medium	High
Less than 25	20	18	22
25 up to 40	50	46	44
40 up to 60	58	63	59
60 and older	34	43	43

59. FILE The claims department at Wise Insurance Company believes that younger drivers have more accidents and, therefore, should be charged higher insurance rates. Investigating a sample of 1,200 Wise policyholders revealed the following breakdown on whether a claim had been filed in the last 3 years and the age of the policyholder. Is it reasonable to conclude that there is a relationship between the age of the policyholder and whether or not the person filed a claim? Use the .05 significance level.

Age Group	No Claim	Claim
16 up to 25	170	74
25 up to 40	240	58
40 up to 55	400	44
55 or older	190	24
Total	1,000	200

60. FILE A sample of employees at a large chemical plant was asked to indicate a preference for one of three pension plans. The results are given in the following table. Does it seem that there is a relationship between the pension plan selected and the job classification of the employees? Use the .01 significance level.

	Pension Plan		
Job Class	Plan A	Plan B	Plan C
Supervisor	10	13	29
Clerical	19	80	19
Labor	81	57	22

61. FILE Did you ever purchase a bag of M&M's candies and wonder about the distribution of colors? Did you know in the beginning they were all brown? Now, peanut M&M's are 12% are brown, 15% yellow, 12% red, 23% blue, 23% orange, and 15% green. A 6-oz. bag purchased at the Book Store at Coastal Carolina University had 14 brown, 13 yellow, 14 red, 12 blue, 7 orange, and 12 green. Is it reasonable to conclude that the actual distribution agrees with the expected distribution? Use the .05 significance level. Conduct your own trial. Be sure to share with your instructor.

DATA ANALYTICS

(The data for these exercises are available at the text website: www.mhhe.com/Lind17e.)

62. The North Valley Real Estate data reports information on homes on the market.
 a. Determine the proportion of homes that have an attached garage. At the .05 significance level, can we conclude that more than 60% of the homes have an attached garage? What is the *p*-value?
 b. Determine the proportion of homes that have a pool. At the .05 significance level, can we conclude that more than 60% of the homes have a pool? What is the *p*-value?
 c. Develop a contingency table that shows whether a home has a pool and the township in which the house is located. Is there an association between the variables pool and township? Use the .05 significance level.
 d. Develop a contingency table that shows whether a home has an attached garage and the township in which the home is located. Is there an association between the variables attached garage and township? Use the .05 significance level.

63. Refer to the Baseball 2016 data, which report information on the 30 Major League Baseball teams for the 2016 season. Set up a variable that divides the teams into two groups, those that had a winning season and those that did not. There are 162 games in the season, so define a winning season as having won 81 or more games. Next, find the median team salary and divide the teams into two salary groups. Let the 15 teams with the largest salaries be in one group and the 15 teams with the smallest salaries be in the other. At the .05 significance level, is there a relationship between salaries and winning?

64. Refer to the Lincolnwood School District bus data.
 a. Suppose we consider a bus "old" if it has been in service more than 8 years. At the .01 significance level, can we conclude that less than 40% of the district's buses are old? Report the *p*-value.
 b. Find the median maintenance cost and the median age of the buses. Organize the data into a two-by-two contingency table, with buses above and below the median of each variable. Determine whether the age of the bus is related to the amount of the maintenance cost. Use the .05 significance level.
 c. Is there a relationship between the maintenance cost and the manufacturer of the bus? Use the breakdown in part (b) for the buses above and below the median maintenance cost and the bus manufacturers to create a contingency table. Use the .05 significance level.

Nonparametric Methods:

ANALYSIS OF ORDINAL DATA

▲ **ASSEMBLY WORKERS AT** Coastal Computers Inc. assemble one or two subassemblies and insert them in a frame. Executives at CC think that the employees would have more pride in their work if they assembled all components and tested the completed computer. A sample of 25 employees is selected to test the idea. Twenty liked assembling the entire unit and testing it. At the .05 level, can we conclude the employees preferred assembling the entire unit? (See Exercise 8 and LO16-1.)

LEARNING OBJECTIVES

When you have completed this chapter, you will be able to:

LO16-1 Use the sign test to compare two dependent populations.

LO16-2 Test a hypothesis about a median using the sign test.

LO16-3 Test a hypothesis of dependent populations using the Wilcoxon signed-rank test.

LO16-4 Test a hypothesis of independent populations using the Wilcoxon rank-sum test.

LO16-5 Test a hypothesis of several independent populations using the Kruskal-Wallis test.

LO16-6 Test and interpret a nonparametric hypothesis test of correlation.

INTRODUCTION

In Chapter 15, we introduced tests of hypothesis for *nominal-scale* variables. Recall from Chapter 1 that the nominal level of measurement implies the data can only be classified into categories, and there is no particular order to the categories. The purpose of these tests is to determine whether an observed set of frequencies, f_o, is significantly different from a corresponding set of expected frequencies, f_e. Likewise, if you are interested in the relationship between two characteristics—such as gender and his or her music preference—you would tally the data into a contingency table and use the chi-square distribution as the test statistic. For both these types of problems, no assumptions need to be made about the shape of the population. We do not have to assume, for example, that the population of interest follows the normal distribution, as we did with the tests of hypotheses in Chapters 10 through 12.

This chapter continues our discussion of hypothesis tests designed especially for nonparametric data. For these tests, we do not need to assume anything about the shape of the population distribution. Sometimes, we use the term *distribution-free tests*. These tests require that the variables in the data can be sorted and ranked. The variables must be measured with an ordinal, interval, or ratio scale. An example of an ordinal scale is executive title. Corporate executives can be ranked as assistant vice president, vice president, senior vice president, and president. A vice president is ranked higher than an assistant vice president, a senior vice president is ranked higher than a vice president, and so on.

In this chapter, we consider five distribution-free tests and the Spearman coefficient of rank correlation. The tests are the sign test, the median test, the Wilcoxon signed-rank test, the Wilcoxon rank-sum test, and the Kruskal-Wallis analysis of variance by ranks.

LO16-1
Use the sign test to compare two dependent populations.

THE SIGN TEST

The **sign test** is based on the sign of a difference between two related observations. We usually designate a plus sign for a positive difference and a minus sign for a negative difference. For example, a dietitian wishes to see if a person's cholesterol level decreases if the diet is supplemented by a certain mineral. She selects a sample of 20 production workers over the age of 40 and measures the workers' cholesterol level. After the 20 subjects take the mineral for six weeks, they are tested again. If the cholesterol level has dropped, a plus sign is recorded. If it has increased, a negative sign is recorded. If there is no change, a zero is recorded (and that person is dropped from the study). For the sign test, we are not concerned with the magnitude of the difference, only the direction of the difference.

The sign test has many applications. One is for "before/after" experiments. To illustrate, an auto repair shop wants to evaluate a new tune-up program for automobiles. We record the number of miles traveled per gallon of gasoline before the tune-up and again after the tune-up. If the tune-up is not effective—that is, it had no effect on performance—then about half of the automobiles tested would show an increase in miles per gallon and the other half a decrease. A "+" sign is assigned to an increase, a "−" sign to a decrease.

© digitalreflections/Shutterstock.com

A product-preference experiment illustrates another use of the sign test. Taster's Choice markets two kinds of coffee: decaffeinated and regular. Its market research department wants to determine whether coffee drinkers prefer decaffeinated or regular coffee. Coffee drinkers are given two small, unmarked cups of coffee, and each is asked his or her preference. Preference for decaffeinated could be coded "+" and preference for regular "−." In a sense, the data are ordinal level because the coffee drinkers give their preferred coffee the higher rank; they rank the other kind below it. Here again, if the population of consumers do not have a preference, we would expect half of the sample of coffee drinkers to prefer decaffeinated and the other half regular coffee.

We can best show the application of the sign test by an example. We will use a "before/after" experiment.

EXAMPLE

The director of information systems at Samuelson Chemicals recommended that an in-plant training program be instituted for certain managers. The objective is to improve the technology knowledge base in the Payroll, Accounting, and Production Planning Departments.

A sample of 15 managers is randomly selected from the three departments. The managers are rated on their technology knowledge based on an assessment of how they use technology to solve problems. Based on the results, they were rated as outstanding, excellent, good, fair, or poor. (See Table 16–1.) After the three-month training program, the same assessment rated each manager's technology knowledge again. The two ratings (before and after) are shown along with the sign of the difference. A "+" sign indicates improvement, and a "–" sign indicates that the manager's competence using technology had declined after the training program.

TABLE 16–1 Competence Before and After the Training Program

	Name	Before	After	Sign of Difference
	T. J. Bowers	Good	Outstanding	+
	Sue Jenkins	Fair	Excellent	+
	James Brown	Excellent	Good	–
	Tad Jackson	Poor	Good	+
Dropped from analysis	~~Andy Love~~	~~Excellent~~	~~Excellent~~	~~0~~
	Sarah Truett	Good	Outstanding	+
	Antonia Aillo	Poor	Fair	+
	Jean Unger	Excellent	Outstanding	+
	Coy Farmer	Good	Poor	–
	Troy Archer	Poor	Good	+
	V. A. Jones	Good	Outstanding	+
	Juan Guillen	Fair	Excellent	+
	Candy Fry	Good	Fair	–
	Arthur Seiple	Good	Outstanding	+
	Sandy Gumpp	Poor	Good	+

We are interested in whether the in-plant training program increased the managers' technology knowledge. That is, are the managers more knowledgeable after the training program than before?

SOLUTION

We will use the six-step hypothesis-testing procedure.

Step 1: State the null hypothesis and the alternate hypothesis.

H_0: $\pi \leq .50$ There has been no change in the technology knowledge base of the managers as a result of the training program.

H_1: $\pi > .50$ There has been an increase in the technology knowledge base of the managers as a result of the training program.

STATISTICS IN ACTION

A recent study of undergraduate students at the University of Michigan revealed the students with the worst attendance records also tended to earn the lowest grades. Does that surprise you? Students who were absent less than 10% of the time tended to earn a B or better. The same study also found that students who sat in the front of the class earned higher grades than those who sat in the back.

The symbol π refers to the proportion in the population with a particular characteristic. If we *do not reject* the null hypothesis, it will indicate the training program has produced no change in the knowledge base, or that knowledge actually decreased. If we *reject* the null hypothesis, it will indicate that the knowledge of the managers has increased as a result of the training program.

The test statistic follows the binomial probability distribution. It is appropriate because the sign test meets all the binomial assumptions, namely:

1. There are only two outcomes: a "success" and a "failure." A manager either increased his or her knowledge (a success) or did not.
2. For each trial, the probability of success is assumed to be .50. Thus, the probability of a success is the same for all trials (managers in this case).
3. The total number of trials is fixed (15 in this experiment).
4. Each trial is independent. This means, for example, that Arthur Seiple's performance in the three-month course is unrelated to Sandy Gumpp's performance.

Step 2: Select a level of significance. We chose the .10 level.

Step 3: Decide on the test statistic. It is the *number of plus signs* resulting from the experiment.

Step 4: Formulate a decision rule. Fifteen managers were enrolled in the training course, but Andy Love showed no increase or decrease in technology knowledge. (See Table 16–1.) He was, therefore, eliminated from the study because he could not be assigned to either group, so $n = 14$. From the binomial probability distribution table in Appendix B.1, for an n of 14 and a probability of .50, we copied the binomial probability distribution in Table 16–2. The number of successes is in column 1, the probabilities of success in column 2, and the cumulative probabilities in column 3. To arrive at the cumulative probabilities, we *add* the probabilities of success in column 2 from the bottom. For illustration, to get the cumulative probability of 11 or more successes, we add $.000 + .001 + .006 + .022 = .029$.

This is a one-tailed test because the alternate hypothesis gives a direction. The inequality (>) points to the right. Thus, the region of rejection is in the upper tail. If the inequality sign pointed toward the left tail (<), the region of rejection would be in the lower tail. If that were the case, we would add the probabilities in column 2 *down* to get the cumulative probabilities in column 3.

Recall that we selected the .10 level of significance. To arrive at the decision rule for this problem, we go to the cumulative probabilities in Table 16–2, column 3. We read up from the bottom until we reach the *cumulative probability nearest to but not exceeding the level of significance* (.10). That cumulative probability is .090. The number of successes (plus signs) corresponding to .090 in column 1 is 10. Therefore, the decision rule is: If the number of pluses in the sample is 10 or more, the null hypothesis is rejected and the alternate hypothesis accepted.

To put it another way, we add the probabilities from the bottom-up because the direction of the inequality (>) is toward the right, indicating that the region of rejection is in the upper tail. If the number of plus signs in the sample is 10 or more, we reject the null hypothesis; otherwise, we do not reject H_0. The region of rejection is portrayed in Chart 16–1.

TABLE 16–2 Binomial Probability Distribution for $n = 14$, $\pi = .50$

Number of Successes	Probability of Success		Cumulative Probability
0	0.000	↑	1.000
1	0.001		0.999
2	0.006		0.998
3	0.022		0.992
4	0.061		0.970
5	0.122		0.909
6	0.183		0.787
7	0.209	Add up	0.604
8	0.183	↑	0.395
9	0.122		0.212
10	0.061		0.090 ← .000 + .001 + .006 + .022 + .061
11	0.022		0.029
12	0.006		0.007
13	0.001		0.001
14	0.000		0.000

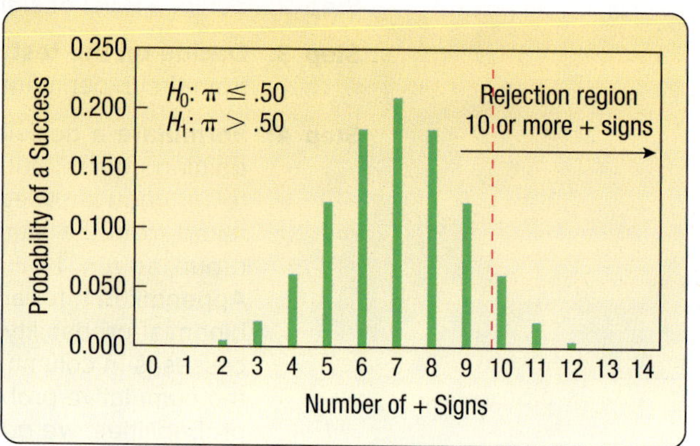

CHART 16–1 Binomial Distribution, $n = 14$, $\pi = .50$

What procedure is followed for a two-tailed test? We combine (add) the probabilities of success in the two tails until we come as close to the desired level of significance (α) as possible without exceeding it. In this example, α is .10. The probability of 3 or fewer successes is .029, found by .000 + .001 + .006 + .022. The probability of 11 or more successes is also .029. Adding the two probabilities gives .058. This is the closest we can come to .10 without exceeding it. Had we included the probabilities of 4 and 10 successes, the total would be .180, which exceeds .10. Hence, the decision rule for a two-tailed test would be to reject the null hypothesis if there are 3 or fewer plus signs, or 11 or more plus signs.

Step 5: Make a decision regarding the null hypothesis. Eleven out of the 14 managers in the training course increased their technology knowledge. The number 11 is in the rejection region, which starts at 10, so H_0 is rejected.

Step 6: Interpret the results. We conclude that the three-month training course was effective. It increased the managers' level of technology knowledge.

If the alternate hypothesis does not give a direction—for example, H_0: $\pi = .50$ and H_1: $\pi \neq .50$—the test of hypothesis is *two-tailed*. In such cases, there are two rejection regions, one in the lower tail and one in the upper tail. If $\alpha = .10$ and the test is two-tailed, the area in each tail is .05 ($\alpha/2 = .10/2 = .05$). Self-Review 16–1 illustrates this.

SELF-REVIEW 16–1

Recall the Taster's Choice example described on page 583, involving a consumer test to determine the preference for decaffeinated versus regular coffee. Use the .10 significance level. The null and alternate hypotheses are:

$$H_0: \pi = .50 \qquad n = 12$$
$$H_1: \pi \neq .50$$

(a) Is this a one-tailed or a two-tailed test of hypothesis?
(b) Show the decision rule in a chart.
(c) Letting consumer preference for decaffeinated coffee be a "+" and preference for regular coffee a "–," it was found that two customers preferred decaffeinated. What is your decision? Explain.

EXERCISES

1. The following hypothesis-testing situation is given: H_0: $\pi \leq .50$ and H_1: $\pi > .50$. The significance level is .10, and the sample size is 12.
   a. What is the decision rule?
   b. There were nine successes. What is your decision regarding the null hypothesis? Explain.
2. The following hypothesis-testing situation is given: H_0: $\pi = .50$ and H_1: $\pi \neq .50$. The significance level is .05, and the sample size is 9.
   a. What is the decision rule?
   b. There were five successes. What is your decision regarding the null hypothesis?
3. Calorie Watchers has low-calorie breakfasts, lunches, and dinners. If you join the club, you receive two packaged meals a day. Calorie Watchers claims that you can eat anything you want for the third meal and still lose at least 5 pounds the first month. Members of the club are weighed before commencing the program and again at the end of the first month. The experiences of a random sample of 11 enrollees are:

Name	Weight Change	Name	Weight Change
Foster	Lost	Hercher	Lost
Taoka	Lost	Camder	Lost
Lange	Gained	Hinckle	Lost
Rousos	Lost	Hinkley	Lost
Stephens	No change	Justin	Lost
Cantrell	Lost		

   We are interested in whether there has been a weight loss as a result of the Calorie Watchers program.
   a. State H_0 and H_1.
   b. Using the .05 level of significance, what is the decision rule?
   c. What is your conclusion about the Calorie Watchers program?

4. Many new stockbrokers resist giving presentations to bankers and certain other groups. Sensing this lack of self-confidence, management arranged to have a confidence-building seminar for a sample of new stockbrokers and enlisted Career Boosters for a three-week course. Before the first session, Career Boosters measured the level of confidence of each participant. It was measured again after the three-week seminar. The before and after levels of self-confidence for the 14 in the course are shown below. Self-confidence was classified as being either negative, low, high, or very high.

Stockbroker	Before Seminar	After Seminar	Stockbroker	Before Seminar	After Seminar
J. M. Martin	Negative	Low	F. M. Orphey	Low	Very high
T. D. Jagger	Negative	Negative	C. C. Ford	Low	High
A. D. Hammer	Low	High	A. R. Utz	Negative	Low
T. A. Jones Jr.	Very high	Low	M. R. Murphy	Low	High
B. G. Dingh	Low	High	P. A. Lopez	Negative	Low
D. A. Skeen	Low	High	B. K. Pierre	Low	High
C. B. Simmer	Negative	High	N. S. Walker	Low	Very high

The purpose of this study is to find whether Career Boosters was effective in raising the self-confidence of the new stockbrokers. That is, was the level of self-confidence higher after the seminar than before it? Use the .05 significance level.

a. State the null and alternate hypotheses.
b. Using the .05 level of significance, state the decision rule—either in words or in chart form.
c. Draw conclusions about the seminar offered by Career Boosters.

Using the Normal Approximation to the Binomial

If the number of observations in the sample is larger than 10, the normal distribution can be used to approximate the binomial. Using the normal distribution will simplify the sign test. In Chapter 6 on page 187, we computed the mean of the binomial distribution from $\mu = n\pi$ and the standard deviation from $\sigma = \sqrt{n\pi(1-\pi)}$. In this case, $\pi = .50$, so the equations reduce to $\mu = .50n$ and $\sigma = .50\sqrt{n}$, respectively.

The test statistic z is

SIGN TEST, $n > 10$

$$z = \frac{(x \pm .50) - \mu}{\sigma} \qquad [16–1]$$

If the number of pluses or minuses is *more than n/2*, we use the following form as the test statistic:

SIGN TEST, $n > 10$, + SIGNS MORE THAN $n/2$

$$z = \frac{(x - .50) - \mu}{\sigma} = \frac{(x - .50) - .50n}{.50\sqrt{n}} \qquad [16–2]$$

If the number of pluses or minuses is *less than n/2,* the test statistic z is

SIGN TEST, $n > 10$, + SIGNS LESS THAN $n/2$

$$z = \frac{(x + .50) - \mu}{\sigma} = \frac{(x + .50) - .50n}{.50\sqrt{n}} \qquad [16–3]$$

In the preceding formulas, x is the number of plus (or minus) signs. The value +.50 or −.50 is the *continuity correction factor,* discussed in Chapter 7 starting on page 230.

Briefly, it is applied when a continuous distribution such as the normal distribution (which we are using) is used to approximate a discrete distribution (the binomial).

The following example illustrates the details of the sign test when n is greater than 10.

EXAMPLE

The market research department of Cola, Inc. has the task of taste testing a new soft drink. There are two versions of the drink under consideration. One version is sweet and the other bitter. The market research department selects a random sample of 64 consumers. Each consumer will taste both the sweet cola (labeled A) and the bitter one (labeled B) and indicate a preference. Conduct a test of hypothesis to determine if there is a difference in the preference for the sweet and bitter tastes. Use the .05 significance level.

SOLUTION

Step 1: State the null and alternate hypotheses.

H_0: $\pi = .50$ There is no preference.

H_1: $\pi \neq .50$ There is a preference.

Step 2: Select a level of significance. It is .05, which is stated in the problem.

Step 3: Select the test statistic. It is z, given in formula (16–1).

$$z = \frac{(x \pm .50) - \mu}{\sigma}$$

where $\mu = .50n$ and $\sigma = .50\sqrt{n}$.

Step 4: Formulate the decision rule. Using Appendix B.5, *Student's t Distribution,* with infinite degrees of freedom, for a two-tailed test (because H_1 states that $\pi \neq .50$) and the .05 significance level, the critical values are + 1.960 and −1.960. Therefore, do not reject H_0 if the computed z value is between +1.960 and −1.960. Otherwise, reject H_0 and accept H_1.

Step 5: Compute *z*, compare the computed value with the critical value, and make a decision regarding H_0. Preference for cola A was given a "+" sign and preference for B a "−" sign. Out of the 64 in the sample, 42 preferred the sweet taste, which is cola A. Therefore, there are 42 pluses. Since 42 is *more than* $n/2 = 64/2 = 32$, we use formula (16–2) for z:

$$z = \frac{(x - .50) - .50n}{.50\sqrt{n}} = \frac{(42 - .50) - .50(64)}{.50\sqrt{64}} = 2.38$$

The computed z of 2.38 is beyond the critical value of 1.96. Therefore, the null hypothesis of no difference is rejected at the .05 significance level.

Step 6: Interpret the results. There is evidence of a difference in consumer preference. That is, we conclude consumers prefer one cola over another.

The p-value is the probability of finding a z value larger than 2.38 or smaller than −2.38. To compute the p-value, we first use Appendix B.3, *Areas under the Normal Curve,* and find the probability that a z value greater than 2.38 is .5000 − .4913 = .0087. For a two-tailed test, this probability is multiplied by two; the p-value is .0174. So the probability of obtaining a sample statistic this extreme when the null hypothesis is true is less than 2%.

SELF-REVIEW 16–2

The human resources department at Ford Motor Company began a pilot health education program at the beginning of the year. The study director randomly selected 100 employees to participate in the program. In the first week of January, the blood pressure of each employee was recorded. To evaluate the effectiveness of the program, the blood pressure of the same 100 employees was recorded in July. Eighty employees showed a reduction in blood pressure. Can we conclude that the program was effective in reducing blood pressure?

(a) State the null hypothesis and the alternate hypothesis.
(b) What is the decision rule for a significance level of .05?
(c) Compute the value of the test statistic.
(d) What is your decision regarding the null hypothesis?
(e) Interpret your decision.

EXERCISES

5. A sample of 45 overweight men participated in an exercise program. At the conclusion of the program, 32 had lost weight. At the .05 significance level, can we conclude the program is effective?

a. State the null hypothesis and the alternate hypothesis.
b. State the decision rule.
c. Compute the value of the test statistic.
d. What is your decision regarding the null hypothesis?

6. A sample of 60 college students was given a special training program designed to improve their time management skills. One month after completing the course, the students were contacted and asked whether the skills learned in the program were effective. A total of 42 responded yes. At the .05 significance level, can we conclude the program is effective?

a. State the null hypothesis and the alternate hypothesis.
b. State the decision rule.
c. Compute the value of the test statistic.
d. What is your decision regarding the null hypothesis?

7. Pierre's Restaurant announced that on Thursday night the menu would consist of unusual gourmet items, such as squid, rabbit, snails from Scotland, and dandelion greens. As part of a larger survey, a sample of 81 regular customers was asked whether they preferred the regular menu or the gourmet menu. Forty-three preferred the gourmet menu. At the .02 level, can we conclude the customers preferred the gourmet menu?

8. Assembly workers at Coastal Computers Inc. assemble just one or two subassemblies and insert them in a frame. The executives at CC think that the employees would have more pride in their work if they assembled all of the subassemblies and tested the complete computer. A sample of 25 employees was selected to experiment with the idea. After a training program, each was asked his or her preference. Twenty liked assembling the entire unit and testing it. At the .05 level, can we conclude the employees preferred assembling the entire unit? Explain the steps you used to arrive at your decision.

LO16-2
Test a hypothesis about a median using the sign test.

TESTING A HYPOTHESIS ABOUT A MEDIAN

Most of the tests of hypothesis we have conducted so far involved the population mean or a proportion. The sign test is one of the few tests that can be used to test the value of a median. Recall from Chapter 3 that the median is the value above which half of the observations lie and below which the other half lie. For hourly wages of \$7, \$9, \$11, and \$18, the median is \$10. Half of the wages are above \$10 an hour and the other half below \$10.

To conduct a test of hypothesis, a value above the median is assigned a plus sign, and a value below the median is assigned a minus sign. If a value is the same as the median, it is dropped from further analysis.

EXAMPLE

The U.S. Bureau of Labor Statistics reported in 2015 that the median amount spent eating out by American families is about \$3,000 annually. The food editor of the *Portland (Oregon) Tribune* wishes to know if the citizens of Portland differ from this national value in the last year in terms of eating out. She selected a random sample of 102 couples and found 60 spent more than \$3,000 last year eating out, 40 spent less than \$3,000, and surprisingly 2 spent exactly \$3,000. At the .10 significance level, is it reasonable to conclude that the median amount spent this year in Portland, Oregon, is not equal to \$3,000?

SOLUTION

If the population median is \$3,000, then we expect about half of the sampled couples spent more than \$3,000 last year and about half less than \$3,000. After discarding the two couples that spent exactly \$3,000, we would expect 50 to be above the median and 50 to be below the median. Is the difference between the 60 couples that spent more than \$3,000 and the number expected to spend more than \$3,000 attributable to chance? Is the median some value other than \$3,000? The statistical test for the median will help answer this question.

The null and the alternate hypotheses are:

$$H_0\text{: Median} = \$3{,}000$$
$$H_1\text{: Median} \neq \$3{,}000$$

This is a two-tailed test because the alternate hypothesis does not indicate a direction. That is, we are not interested in whether the median is less than or greater than \$3,000, only that it is different from \$3,000. The test statistic meets the binomial assumptions. That is:

1. An observation is either larger or smaller than the proposed median, so there are only two possible outcomes.
2. The probability of a success remains constant at .50. That is, $\pi = .50$.
3. The couples selected as part of the sample represent independent trials.
4. We count the number of successes in a fixed number of trials. In this case, we consider 100 couples and count the number who spend more than \$3,000 annually on eating out.

The usable sample size is 100 and π is .50, so $n\pi = 100(.50) = 50$ and $n(1 - \pi) = 100(1 - .50) = 50$, which are both larger than 5, so we use the normal distribution to approximate the binomial. That is, we actually use the standard normal distribution as the test statistic. The significance level is .10, so $\alpha/2 = .10/2 = .05$, which is the area in each tail of a normal distribution. From Appendix B.5, in the row with infinite degrees of freedom, the critical values are −1.645 and 1.645. The decision rule is to reject the null hypothesis if z is less than −1.645 or greater than 1.645.

We use formula (16–2) for z because 60 is greater than $n/2$ or $(100/2 = 50)$.

$$z = \frac{(x - .5) - .5n}{.50\sqrt{n}} = \frac{(60 - .5) - 50(100)}{.50\sqrt{100}} = 1.90$$

The null hypothesis is rejected because the computed value of 1.90 is greater than the critical value of 1.645. The sample evidence indicates that the median amount spent annually is *not* \$3,000. The food editor in Portland should conclude that there is a difference in the median amount spent annually last year in Portland as compared with that reported by the U.S. Bureau of Labor Statistics in 2015. The *p*-value is .0574, found by 2(.5000 − .4713). The *p*-value is smaller than the significance level of .10 for this test. So based on the *p*-value and a significance level of .10, we also reject the null hypothesis and conclude that Portland couples spend an amount that is different from the national median value.

SELF-REVIEW 16–3

After reading the results of the Portland, Oregon, study, the food editor of the *Tampa Times* decided to conduct a similar study. The Tampa food editor decides to alter the study slightly by investigating whether families in her region spend *more than* a median amount of \$3,000 A sample of 64 Tampa couples revealed 42 spent more than \$3,000 per year eating out. Using the .05 significance level, what should the editor conclude?

EXERCISES

9. The median salary for a chiropractor in the United States is \$81,500 per year, according to the U.S. Department of Labor. A group of recent graduates believe this amount is too low. In a random sample of 205 chiropractors who recently graduated, 170 began with a salary of more than \$81,500 and five earned a salary of exactly \$81,500.

a. State the null and alternate hypotheses.

b. State the decision rule. Use the .05 significance level.

c. Do the necessary computations and interpret the results.

10. Central Airlines claims that the median price of a round-trip ticket from Chicago to Jackson Hole, Wyoming, is \$503. This claim is being challenged by the Association of Travel Agents, who believe the median price is less than \$503. A random sample of 400 round-trip tickets from Chicago to Jackson Hole revealed 160 tickets were below \$503. None of the tickets was exactly \$503. Let $\alpha = .05$.

a. State the null and alternate hypotheses.

b. What is your decision regarding H_0? Interpret.

LO16-3
Test a hypothesis of dependent populations using the Wilcoxon signed-rank test.

WILCOXON SIGNED-RANK TEST FOR DEPENDENT POPULATIONS

The paired *t* test (page 370), described in Chapter 11, has two requirements. First, the samples must be dependent. Recall that dependent samples are characterized by a measurement, some type of intervention, and then another measurement. For example, a large company began a "wellness" program at the start of the year. Twenty workers were enrolled in the weight reduction portion of the program. To begin, all participants were weighed. Next they dieted, did the exercise, and so forth in an attempt to lose weight. At the end of the program, which lasted 6 months, all participants were weighed again. The difference in their weight between the start and the end of the program is the variable of interest. Note that there is a measurement, an intervention, and then another measurement.

The second requirement for the paired *t* test is that the distribution of the differences follow the normal probability distribution. In the company wellness example, this would require that the differences in the weights of the population of participants follow the normal probability distribution. In that case, this assumption is reasonable. However, there are instances when we want to study the differences between dependent observations where we cannot assume that the distribution of the differences approximates a normal distribution. Frequently, we encounter a problem with the normality assumption when the level of measurement in the samples is ordinal, rather than interval or ratio. For example, suppose there are 10 surgical patients on 3 East today. The nursing supervisor asks Nurse Benner and Nurse Jurris to rate each of the 10 patients on a scale

of 1 to 10, according to the difficulty of patient care. The distribution of the differences in the ratings probably would not approximate the normal distribution, and, therefore, the paired *t* test would not be appropriate.

In 1945, Frank Wilcoxon developed a nonparametric test, based on the differences in dependent samples, where the normality assumption is not required. This test is called the **Wilcoxon signed-rank test.** The following example details its application.

EXAMPLE

Fricker's is a family restaurant chain located primarily in the southeastern part of the United States. It offers a full dinner menu, but its specialty is chicken. Recently, Bernie Frick, the owner and founder, developed a new spicy flavor for the batter in which the chicken is cooked. Before replacing the current flavor, he wants to be sure that patrons will like the spicy flavor better.

To begin his taste test, Bernie selects a random sample of 15 customers. Each sampled customer is given a small piece of the current chicken and asked to rate its overall taste on a scale of 1 to 20. A value near 20 indicates the participant liked the flavor, whereas a rating near 0 indicates they did not like the flavor. Next, the same 15 participants are given a sample of the new chicken with the spicier flavor and again asked to rate its taste on a scale of 1 to 20. The results are reported below. Is it reasonable to conclude that the spicy flavor is preferred? Use the .05 significance level.

Participant	Spicy Flavor Rating	Current Flavor Rating
Arquette	14	12
Jones	8	16
Fish	6	2
Wagner	18	4
Badenhop	20	12
Hall	16	16
Fowler	14	5
Virost	6	16
Garcia	19	10
Sundar	18	10
Miller	16	13
Peterson	18	2
Boggart	4	13
Hein	7	14
Whitten	16	4

SOLUTION

Each participant is asked to rate both flavors of chicken. So the ratings are dependent or related and, for each participant, we compute the difference between the ratings for the spicy flavor and the current flavor. The resulting value shows the amount the participants favor one flavor over the other. If we choose to subtract the current flavor rating from the spicy flavor rating, a positive result is the "amount" the participant favors the spicy flavor. Negative differences indicate the participant favored the current flavor. Because of the subjective nature of the ratings, we are not confident that the distribution of the differences follows the normal distribution. We decide to use the nonparametric Wilcoxon signed-rank test.

As usual, we will use the six-step hypothesis-testing procedure. The null hypothesis is that there is no difference in the rating of the chicken flavors by the participants. The alternate hypothesis is that the ratings are higher for the spicy flavor. More formally:

H_0: There is no difference in the ratings of the two flavors.
H_1: The spicy ratings are higher.

This is a one-tailed test. Why? Because Bernie Frick, the owner of Fricker's, will want to change his chicken flavor only if the sample participants show that the population of customers like the new flavor better. The significance level is .05, as stated on the previous page.

The steps to conduct the Wilcoxon signed-rank test are as follows.

1. Compute the difference between the spicy flavor rating and the current flavor rating for each participant. For example, Arquette's spicy flavor rating was 14 and current flavor rating was 12, so the amount of the difference is 2. For Jones, the difference is −8, found by 8 − 16, and for Fish it is 4, found by 6 − 2. The differences for all participants are shown in column D of Table 16–3.

TABLE 16–3 Flavor Rating for Current and Spicy Flavors

A Participant	B Spicy Flavor Rating	C Current Flavor Rating	D Difference in Ratings	E Absolute Difference	F Rank	G Signed Rank R^+	H Signed Rank R^-
Arquette	14	12	2	2	1	1	
Jones	8	16	−8	8	6		6
Fish	6	2	4	4	3	3	
Wagner	18	4	14	14	13	13	
Badenhop	20	12	8	8	6	6	
Hall	16	16	0	*	*		
Fowler	14	5	9	9	9	9	
Virost	6	16	−10	10	11		11
Garcia	19	10	9	9	9	9	
Sundar	18	10	8	8	6	6	
Miller	16	13	3	3	2	2	
Peterson	18	2	16	16	14	14	
Boggart	4	13	−9	9	9		9
Hein	7	14	−7	7	4		4
Whitten	16	4	12	12	12	12	
					Sums	75	30

Smaller rank sum

2. Only the positive and negative differences are considered further. That is, if the difference in flavor ratings is 0, that participant is dropped from further analysis and the number in the sample reduced. From Table 16–3, Hall, the sixth participant, rated both the spicy and the current flavor a 16. Hence, Hall is dropped from the study and the usable sample size reduced from 15 to 14.
3. Determine the absolute differences for the values computed in column D. Recall that in an absolute difference we ignore the sign of the difference and focus on the magnitude of the differences in ratings. The absolute differences are shown in column E.

4. Next, rank the absolute differences from smallest to largest. Arquette, the first participant, rated the spicy chicken a 14 and the current a 12. The difference of 2 in the two taste ratings is the smallest absolute difference, so it is given a ranking of 1. The next largest difference is 3, given by Miller, so it is given a rank of 2. The other differences are ranked in a similar manner. There are three participants who rated the difference in the flavor as 8. That is, Jones, Badenhop, and Sundar each had a difference of 8 between their rating of the spicy flavor and the current flavor. To resolve this issue, we average the ranks involved and report the average rank for each. This situation involves the ranks 5, 6, and 7, so all three participants are assigned the rank of 6. The same situation occurs for those participants with a difference of 9. The ranks involved are 8, 9, and 10, so those participants are assigned a rank of 9.
5. Each assigned rank in column F is then given the same sign as the original difference, and the results are reported in column G or H. For example, the second participant has a difference of −8 and a rank of 6. So the value of 6 is recorded for Jones in the R^- section of column H.
6. Finally, the R^+ and R^- columns are totaled. The sum of the positive ranks is 75 and the sum of the negative ranks is 30. The smaller of the two rank sums is used as the test statistic and referred to as *T*.

The critical values for the Wilcoxon signed-rank test are located in Appendix B.8. A portion of that table is shown below. The α row is used for one-tailed tests and the 2α row for two-tailed tests. In this case, we want to show that customers like the spicy taste better, which is a one-tailed test, so we select the α row. We chose the .05 significance level, so move to the right to the column headed .05. Go down that column to the row where *n* is 14. (Recall that one person in the study rated the chicken flavors the same and was dropped from the study, making the usable sample size 14.) The value at the intersection is 25, so the critical value is 25. The decision rule is to reject the null hypothesis if the *smaller* of the rank sums is 25 or less. The value obtained from Appendix B.8 is the *largest value in the rejection region*. To put it another way, our decision rule is to reject H_0 if the smaller of the two rank sums is 25 or less. In this case, the smaller rank sum is 30, so the decision is not to reject the null hypothesis. We cannot conclude there is a difference in the flavor ratings between the current and the spicy. The study has failed to show that customers prefer the new flavor. Mr. Frick should stay with the current flavor of chicken.

	2α .15	**.10**	**.05**	**.04**	**.03**	**.02**	**.01**
n	**α .075**	**.05**	**.025**	**.02**	**.015**	**.01**	**.005**
4	0						
5	1	0					
6	2	2	0	0			
7	4	3	2	1	0	0	
8	7	5	3	3	2	1	0
9	9	8	5	5	4	3	1
10	12	10	8	7	6	5	3
11	16	13	10	9	8	7	5
12	19	17	13	12	11	9	7
13	24	21	17	16	14	12	9
14	28	25	21	19	18	15	12
15	33	30	25	23	21	19	15

SELF-REVIEW 16–4

The assembly area of Gotrac Products was recently redesigned. Installing a new lighting system and purchasing new workbenches were two features of the redesign. The production supervisor would like to know if the changes resulted in improved worker productivity. To investigate, she selected a sample of 11 workers and determined the production rate before and after the changes. The sample information is reported below.

Operator	Production Before	Production After	Operator	Production Before	Production After
S. M.	17	18	U. Z.	10	22
D. J.	21	23	Y. U.	20	19
M. D.	25	22	U. T.	17	20
B. B.	15	25	Y. H.	24	30
M. F.	10	28	Y. Y.	23	26
A. A.	16	16			

(a) How many usable pairs are there? That is, what is n?
(b) Use the Wilcoxon signed-rank test to determine whether the new procedures actually increased production. Use the .05 level and a one-tailed test.
(c) What assumption are you making about the distribution of the differences in production before and after redesign?

EXERCISES

11. **FILE** An industrial psychologist selected a random sample of seven young urban professional couples who own their homes. The size of their home (square feet) is compared with that of their parents. At the .05 significance level, can we conclude that the professional couples live in larger homes than their parents?

Couple Name	Professional	Parent	Couple Name	Professional	Parent
Gordon	1,725	1,175	Kuhlman	1,290	1,360
Sharkey	1,310	1,120	Welch	1,880	1,750
Uselding	1,670	1,420	Anderson	1,530	1,440
Bell	1,520	1,640			

12. **FILE** Toyota USA is studying the effect of regular versus high-octane gasoline on the fuel economy of its new high-performance, 3.5-liter, V6 engine. Ten executives are selected and asked to maintain records on the number of miles traveled per gallon of gas. The results are:

	Miles per Gallon			Miles per Gallon	
Executive	Regular	High-Octane	Executive	Regular	High-Octane
Bowers	25	28	Rau	38	40
Demars	33	31	Greolke	29	29
Grasser	31	35	Burns	42	37
DeToto	45	44	Snow	41	44
Kleg	42	47	Lawless	30	44

At the .05 significance level, is there a difference in the number of miles traveled per gallon between regular and high-octane gasoline?

13. **FILE** A new assembly-line procedure to increase production has been suggested. To test whether the new procedure is superior to the old procedure, a random sample of 15 assembly-line workers was selected. The number of units produced in an hour under the old procedure was determined, then the new procedure was

introduced. After an appropriate break-in period, their production was measured again using the new procedure. The results were:

Employee	Procedure Old	Procedure New	Employee	Procedure Old	Procedure New
A	60	64	I	87	84
B	40	52	J	80	80
C	59	58	K	56	57
D	30	37	L	21	21
E	70	71	M	99	108
F	78	83	N	50	56
G	43	46	O	56	62
H	40	52			

At the .05 significance level, can we conclude the production is greater using the new procedure?

a. State the null and alternate hypotheses.
b. State the decision rule.
c. Arrive at a decision regarding the null hypothesis.

14. FILE It has been suggested that daily production of a subassembly would be increased if better lighting were installed and background music and free coffee and doughnuts were provided during the day. Management agreed to try the scheme for a limited time. A listing of the number of subassemblies produced per week before and after the new work environment for each employee follows.

Employee	Past Production Record	Production after Installing Lighting, Music, etc.	Employee	Past Production Record	Production after Installing Lighting, Music, etc.
JD	23	33	WWJ	21	25
SB	26	26	OP	25	22
MD	24	30	CD	21	23
RCF	17	25	PA	16	17
MF	20	19	RRT	20	15
UHH	24	22	AT	17	9
IB	30	29	QQ	23	30

Using the Wilcoxon signed-rank test, determine whether the suggested changes are worthwhile.

a. State the null hypothesis.
b. You decide on the alternate hypothesis.
c. You decide on the level of significance.
d. State the decision rule.
e. Compute T and arrive at a decision.
f. What did you assume about the distribution of the differences?

LO16-4
Test a hypothesis of independent populations using the Wilcoxon rank-sum test.

WILCOXON RANK-SUM TEST FOR INDEPENDENT POPULATIONS

One test specifically designed to determine whether two *independent* samples came from equivalent populations is the **Wilcoxon rank-sum test.** This test is an alternative to the two-sample t test described starting on page 230 in Chapter 11. Recall that the t test requires that the two populations follow the normal distribution and have equal population variances. These conditions are not required for the Wilcoxon rank-sum test.

The Wilcoxon rank-sum test is based on the sum of ranks. The data are ranked as if the observations were from a single population. If the null hypothesis is true, then the ranks will be about evenly distributed between the two samples, and the sum of the ranks for the two samples will be about the same. That is, the low, medium, and high ranks should be about equally divided between the two samples. If the alternate hypothesis is true, one of the samples will have more of the lower ranks and, thus, a smaller rank sum. The other sample will have more of the higher ranks and, therefore, a larger rank sum. If each of the samples contains *at least eight observations,* the standard normal distribution is used as the test statistic. We use the following formula to find the value of the test statistic.

WILCOXON RANK-SUM TEST

$$z = \frac{W - \dfrac{n_1(n_1 + n_2 + 1)}{2}}{\sqrt{\dfrac{n_1 n_2(n_1 + n_2 + 1)}{12}}} \quad \textbf{(16–4)}$$

where:

n_1 is the number of observations from the first population.
n_2 is the number of observations from the second population.
W is the sum of the ranks from the first population.

EXAMPLE

Dan Thompson, the president of OTG Airlines, recently noted an increase in the number of bags that were checked-in at the gate (gate-checked bags) in Atlanta. He is particularly interested in determining whether there are more gate-checked bags from Atlanta compared with flights leaving Chicago. A sample of nine flights from Atlanta and eight from Chicago are reported in Table 16–4. At the .05 significance level, can we conclude that there are more gate-checked bags for flights originating in Atlanta?

TABLE 16–4 Number of Bags Checked at the Gate

Atlanta	Chicago
11	13
15	14
10	10
18	8
11	16
20	9
24	17
22	21
25	

SOLUTION

If the populations of gate-checked bags follow the normal probability distribution and have equal variances, the two-sample *t* test is appropriate. In this case, Mr. Thompson believes these two conditions cannot be met. Therefore, a nonparametric test, the Wilcoxon rank-sum test, is appropriate.

If the number of gate-checked bags is the same for Atlanta and Chicago, then we expect the sum of the ranks for the two distributions to be about the same. Or to put it another way, the average rank of the two groups will be about the same. If the number of gate-checked bags is not the same, we expect the average of the ranks to be quite different.

Mr. Thompson believes there are more gate-checked bags for Atlanta flights. Thus, a one-tailed test is appropriate. The null and alternate hypotheses are:

H_0: The number of gate-checked bags for Atlanta is the same or less than the number of gate-checked bags for Chicago.

H_1: The number gate-checked bags for Atlanta is more than the number of gate-checked bags for Chicago.

The test statistic follows the standard normal distribution. At the .05 significance level, we find from the last row in Appendix B.5 the critical value of z is 1.645. The null hypothesis is rejected if the computed value of z is greater than 1.645.

The alternate hypothesis is that there are more gate-checked bags in Atlanta, which means that the Atlanta distribution is located to the right of the Chicago distribution. The details of rank assignment are shown in Table 16–5. We rank the observations from *both* samples as if they were a single group. The Chicago flight with only 8 gate-checked bags had the fewest, so it is assigned a rank of 1. The Chicago flight with 9 gate-checked bags is ranked 2, and so on. The Atlanta flight with 25 gate-checked bags is the highest, so it is assigned the largest rank, 17. There are also two instances of tied ranks. There are Atlanta and Chicago flights that each have 10 gate-checked bags. There are also two Atlanta flights with 11 gate-checked bags. How do we handle these ties? The solution is to average the ranks involved and assign the average rank to both flights. In the case involving 10 gate-checked bags, the ranks involved are 3 and 4. The mean of these ranks is 3.5, so a rank of 3.5 is assigned to both the Atlanta and the Chicago flights with 10 gate-checked bags.

TABLE 16–5 Ranked Number of Gate-checked Bags

Atlanta		Chicago	
Gate-checked Bags	**Rank**	**Gate-checked Bags**	**Rank**
11	5.5	13	7
15	9	14	8
10	3.5	10	3.5
18	12	8	1
11	5.5	16	10
20	13	9	2
24	16	17	11
22	15	21	14
25	17		
	96.5		56.5

Atlanta Rank Sum

The sum of the ranks for the Atlanta flights is 96.5. This is the value of W in formula (16–4). From Table 16–5, there are nine flights originating in Atlanta and eight in Chicago, so $n_1 = 9$ and $n_2 = 8$. Computing z from formula (16–4) gives:

$$z = \frac{W - \frac{n_1(n_1 + n_2 + 1)}{2}}{\sqrt{\frac{n_1 n_2(n_1 + n_2 + 1)}{12}}} = \frac{96.5 - \frac{9(9 + 8 + 1)}{2}}{\sqrt{\frac{9(8)(9 + 8 + 1)}{12}}} = 1.49$$

Because the computed z value (1.49) is less than 1.645, the null hypothesis is not rejected. The evidence does not show a difference in the distributions of the number of gate-checked bags. That is, it appears that the number of gate-checked bags is the same in Atlanta as in Chicago. The p-value of .0681, found by determining the area to the right of 1.49 (.5000 − .4319), indicates the same result.

The Wilcoxon - Mann/Whitney test is available in MegaStat. It provides the following results. The p-value, .0679, is slightly different as the software corrects for ties.

Wilcoxon - Mann/Whitney Test

n	sum of ranks	
9	96.5	Atlanta
8	56.5	Chicago
17	153	total

81.000	expected value
10.392	standard deviation
1.491	z
.0679	p-value (one-tailed, upper)

In using the Wilcoxon rank-sum test, you may number the two populations in either order. However, once you have made a choice, W must be the sum of the ranks identified as population 1. If, in the gate-checked bags example, the population of Chicago was identified as number 1, the direction of the alternate hypothesis would be changed. The value of z would be the same but have the opposite sign.

H_0: The population distribution of gate-checked bags is the same or larger for Chicago than for Atlanta.

H_1: The population distribution of gate-checked bags is smaller for Chicago than for Atlanta.

The computed value of z is −1.49, found by:

$$z = \frac{W - \frac{n_1(n_1 + n_2 + 1)}{2}}{\sqrt{\frac{n_1 n_2(n_1 + n_2 + 1)}{12}}} = \frac{56.5 - \frac{8(8 + 9 + 1)}{2}}{\sqrt{\frac{8(9)(8 + 9 + 1)}{12}}} = -1.49$$

Our conclusion is the same as described earlier. There is no difference in the typical number of gate-checked bags for Chicago and Atlanta.

SELF-REVIEW 16–5

The research director for Top Flite wants to know whether there is a difference in the distribution of the distances traveled by two of the company's golf balls. Eight of its XL-5000 brand and eight of its D2 brand balls were hit by an automatic fairway metal. The distances (in yards) were as follows:

XL-5000:	252, 263, 279, 273, 271, 265, 257, 280
D2:	262, 242, 256, 260, 258, 243, 239, 265

Do not assume the distributions of the distances traveled follow the normal probability distribution. At the .05 significance level, is there a difference between the two distributions?

EXERCISES

15. FILE Eight observations were randomly selected from two populations (population A and population B) that were not normally distributed. Use the .05 significance level, a two-tailed test, and the Wilcoxon rank-sum test to determine whether there is a difference between the two populations.

Population A	38, 45, 56, 57, 61, 69, 70, 79
Population B	26, 31, 35, 42, 51, 52, 57, 62

16. FILE Nine observations were randomly selected from population A and eight observations were randomly selected from population B. The populations are not normally distributed. Use the .05 significance level, a two-tailed test, and the Wilcoxon rank-sum test to determine whether there is a difference between the two populations.

Population A	12, 14, 15, 19, 23, 29, 33, 40, 51
Population B	13, 16, 19, 21, 22, 33, 35, 43

17. FILE Tucson State University offers two MBA programs. In the first program, the students meet two nights per week at the university's main campus in downtown Tucson. In the second program, students only communicate online with the instructor. The director of the MBA experience at Tucson wishes to compare the number of hours studied last week by the two groups of students. A sample of 10 on-campus students and 12 online students revealed the following information.

Campus	28, 16, 42, 29, 31, 22, 50, 42, 23, 25
Online	26, 42, 65, 38, 29, 32, 59, 42, 27, 41, 46, 18

Do not assume the two distributions of study times (in hours) follow a normal distribution. At the .05 significance level, can we conclude the online students spend more time studying?

18. FILE In recent times, with mortgage rates at low levels, financial institutions have had to provide more customer convenience. One of the innovations offered by Coastal National Bank and Trust is online mortgage applications. Listed below are the times, in minutes, for eight customers to complete the application process for a 15-year fixed-rate mortgage and the times for nine customers to complete an application for a 30-year fixed-rate mortgage.

15 years, fixed rate	41, 36, 42, 39, 36, 48, 49, 38
30 years, fixed rate	21, 27, 36, 20, 19, 21, 39, 24, 22

At the .05 significance level, is it reasonable to conclude that it takes less time for those customers applying for the 30-year fixed-rate mortgage? Do not assume the distribution times follow a normal distribution for either group.

LO16-5

Test a hypothesis of several independent populations using the Kruskal-Wallis test.

KRUSKAL-WALLIS TEST: ANALYSIS OF VARIANCE BY RANKS

The analysis of variance (ANOVA) procedure discussed in Chapter 12 tests the hypothesis that several population means are equal. The data were interval or ratio level. Also, it was assumed the populations followed the normal probability distribution and their standard deviations were equal. What if the data are ordinal scale and/or the populations do not follow a normal distribution? Then we would use the **Kruskal-Wallis one-way analysis**

of variance by ranks. It requires ordinal, interval, or ratio scaled variables that can be ranked. The analysis makes no assumptions about the shape of the population distributions.

For the Kruskal-Wallis test to be applied, the populations must be *independent*. For example, if samples from three populations—executives, staff, and supervisors—are selected and interviewed, the responses of one group (say, the executives) must in no way influence the responses of the others.

To compute the Kruskal-Wallis test statistic, (1) all the samples are combined, (2) the combined values are ordered from low to high, and (3) the ordered values are *replaced by ranks, starting with 1 for the smallest value*. An example will clarify the details of the procedure.

EXAMPLE

The Hospital Systems of the Carolinas operate three hospitals in the Greater Charlotte area: St. Luke's Memorial on the west side of the city, Swedish Medical Center to the south, and Piedmont Hospital on the east side of town. The director of administration is concerned about the waiting time of patients with non-life-threatening injuries that arrive during weekday evenings at the three hospitals. Specifically, is there a difference in the waiting times at the three hospitals?

SOLUTION

To investigate, the director selected random samples of patients at the three locations and determined the time, in minutes, between entering the particular facility and when treatment was completed. The times in minutes are reported in Table 16–6.

TABLE 16–6 Waiting Times for Emergency Treatment at Hospital Systems of the Carolinas

St. Luke's Memorial	Swedish Medical Center	Piedmont Hospital
56	103	42
39	87	38
48	51	89
38	95	75
73	68	35
60	42	61
62	107	
	89	

From Table 16–6, we observe that the shortest waiting time is 35 minutes for the fifth sampled patient at Piedmont Hospital. The longest waiting time is 107 minutes by the seventh patient at the Swedish Medical Center.

Likely the first thought for comparing the waiting times is to determine whether there is a difference in the mean waiting time at the three hospitals, that is, use the one-way ANOVA described on page 392 of Chapter 12. However, there are three requirements for this test:

1. The samples are from independent populations.
2. The population variances must be equal.
3. The samples are from normal populations.

In this instance the samples are from independent populations, the three different hospitals. However, assumptions two and three may not be true. Specifically, the variances of the three samples are:

Sample variances		
St. Luke's Memorial	**Swedish Medical Center**	**Piedmont Hospital**
163.57	577.36	486.67

Notice that the variance for the Swedish Medical Center and Piedmont Hospital are more than twice that of St. Luke's. The equal variance assumption is tenuous. Also, with the small number of observations in each sample it would be difficult to support the assumption of normally distributed populations. Clearly, all the assumptions required for ANOVA techniques are not supported. So, we should use the Kruskal-Wallis test. It does not require these assumptions.

The first step in conducting the Kruskal-Wallis test is to state the null and the alternate hypotheses.

H_0: The population distributions of waiting times are the same for the three hospitals.

H_1: The population distributions are not all the same for the three hospitals.

The director of administration selected the .05 significance level.

The test statistic used for the Kruskal-Wallis test is designated H. Its formula is:

KRUSKAL-WALLIS TEST

$$H = \frac{12}{n(n+1)}\left[\frac{(\Sigma R_1)^2}{n_1} + \frac{(\Sigma R_2)^2}{n_2} + \cdots + \frac{(\Sigma R_k)^2}{n_k}\right] - 3(n+1) \qquad \textbf{(16–5)}$$

with $k - 1$ degrees of freedom (k is the number of populations), where:

$\Sigma R_1, \Sigma R_2, \ldots, \Sigma R_k$, are the sums of the ranks of samples 1, 2, . . . , k, respectively.

$n_1, n_2, \ldots, n_k$ are the sizes of samples 1, 2, . . . , k, respectively.

n is the combined number of observations for all samples.

The distribution of the sample H statistic follows the chi-square distribution with $k - 1$ degrees of freedom. We prefer that each sample include at least five observations. We use chi-square to formulate the decision rule. In this example, there are three populations—a population of waiting times for patients at St. Luke's Memorial, another for patients at the Swedish Medical Center, and a third for Piedmont Hospital patients. Thus, there are $k - 1$, or $3 - 1 = 2$ degrees of freedom. Refer to the chi-square table of critical values in Appendix B.7. The critical value for 2 degrees of freedom and the .05 level of significance is 5.991. So our decision rule is: Do not reject the null hypothesis if the computed value of the test statistic H is less than or equal to 5.991. If the computed value of H is greater than 5.991, reject the null hypothesis and accept the alternate hypothesis.

The next step is to determine the value of the test statistic. We assign the waiting times at the three hospitals with the corresponding ranks. Considering the waiting times as a single group, the Piedmont patient with a waiting time of 35 minutes waited the shortest time and hence is given the lowest rank of 1. There are two patients that waited 38 minutes, one at St. Luke's and one at Piedmont. To resolve this tie, each patient is given a rank of 2.5, found by (2 + 3)/2. This process is continued for all waiting times. The longest waiting time is 107 minutes, and that Swedish Medical Center patient is given a rank of 21. The scores, the ranks, and the sum of the ranks for each of the three hospitals are given in Table 16–7 on the following page.

Solving for H gives

$$H = \frac{12}{n(n+1)}\left[\frac{(\Sigma R_1)^2}{n_1} + \frac{(\Sigma R_2)^2}{n_2} + \frac{(\Sigma R_3)^2}{n_3}\right] - 3(n+1)$$

$$= \frac{12}{21(21+1)}\left[\frac{58.5^2}{7} + \frac{120^2}{8} + \frac{52.5^2}{6}\right] - 3(21+1) = 5.38$$

Because the computed value of H (5.38) is less than the critical value of 5.991, we do not reject the null hypothesis. There is not enough evidence to conclude that there is a difference among the distributions of waiting times at the three hospitals.

TABLE 16–7 Waiting Times for Emergency Treatment at Hospital Systems of the Carolinas

St. Luke's Memorial		Swedish Medical Center		Piedmont Hospital	
Time	**Rank**	**Time**	**Rank**	**Time**	**Rank**
56	9	103	20	42	5.5
39	4	87	16	38	2.5
48	7	51	8	89	17.5
38	2.5	95	19	75	15
73	14	68	13	35	1
60	10	42	5.5	61	11
62	12	107	21		
		89	17.5		
	$\Sigma R_1 = 58.5$		$\Sigma R_2 = 120$		$\Sigma R_3 = 52.5$

Waiting time rank sums

The Kruskal-Wallis procedure can be done using the MegaStat add-in for Excel. Output for the example regarding the hospital waiting time follows. The computed value of H is 5.39 and the p-value is .067. The values are slightly different because of rounding. Based on these results, the decision and conclusion are the same.

Kruskal-Wallis Test

Median	*n*	*Avg. Rank*	
56.00	7	8.36	St. Luke's
88.00	8	15.00	Swedish
51.50	6	8.75	Piedmont
61.00	21		Total
		5.39	H (corrected for ties)
		2	d.f.
		0.067	p-value

Recall from Chapter 12 that, for the analysis of variance technique to apply, we assume (1) the populations are normally distributed, (2) these populations have equal standard deviations, and (3) the samples are selected from independent populations. If these assumptions are met in the hospital waiting time example, we use the F distribution as the test statistic. If these assumptions cannot be met, we apply the distribution-free test by Kruskal-Wallis. To highlight the differences between the two approaches, we will solve the hospital waiting time example using the ANOVA technique.

To begin, we state the null and the alternate hypotheses for the three hospitals.

H_0: $\mu_1 = \mu_2 = \mu_3$

H_1: The treatment means are not all the same.

For the .05 significance level, with $k - 1 = 3 - 1 = 2$ degrees of freedom in the numerator and $n - k = 21 - 3 = 18$ degrees of freedom in the denominator, the critical value of F is 3.55. The decision rule is to reject the null hypothesis if the computed value of F is greater than 3.55. The output using Excel follows.

	A	B	C	D	E	F	G	H	I	J	K
1	St. Luke's	Swedish	Piedmont		Anova: Single Factor						
2	56	103	42								
3	39	87	38		SUMMARY						
4	48	51	89		*Groups*	*Count*	*Sum*	*Average*	*Variance*		
5	38	95	75		St. Luke's	7	376	53.714	163.571		
6	73	68	35		Swedish	8	642	80.250	577.357		
7	60	42	61		Piedmont	6	340	56.667	486.667		
8	62	107									
9		89									
10					ANOVA						
11					*Source of Variation*	*SS*	*df*	*MS*	*F*	*P-value*	*F crit*
12					Between Groups	3166.4	2	1583.202	3.822	0.041	3.555
13					Within Groups	7456.26	18	414.24			
14											
15					Total	10622.7	20				

Using the one-way ANOVA test, the computed value of F is 3.822 and the p-value is .041. Our decision is to reject the null hypothesis and conclude that the treatment means are not the same. That is, the mean waiting times at the three Hospital Systems of the Carolinas hospitals are different.

This comparison of the Kruskal-Wallis and ANOVA analyses shows important differences. The result of the Kruskal-Wallis test is to fail to reject the hypothesis that the samples are from identical populations. Remember that this test does not require any assumptions about the variances or distributions of the populations. The result of the ANOVA test is to reject the hypothesis and conclude that the population means are different. However, the assumption of equal population variances is most probably not true, and the assumption of normally distributed populations is difficult to validate. Therefore, we should suspect that the ANOVA results are not valid. Comparing the results of the Kruskal-Wallis and ANOVA serves to show the importance of validating the assumptions required for ANOVA. If the ANOVA assumptions are not supported, the results are not reliable. In this case, the Kruskal-Wallis analysis should be used.

SELF-REVIEW 16–6

The regional bank manager of Statewide Financial Bank is interested in the number of transactions occurring in personal checking accounts at four of the bank's branches. Each branch randomly samples a number of personal checking accounts and records the number of transactions made in each account over the last six months. The results are in the table below. Using the .01 level and the Kruskal-Wallis test, determine whether there is a difference in the number personal checking account transactions among the four branches.

Englewood Branch	West Side Branch	Great Northern Branch	Sylvania Branch
208	91	302	99
307	62	103	116
199	86	319	189
142	91	340	103
91	80	180	100
296			131

EXERCISES

19. Under what conditions should the Kruskal-Wallis test be used instead of ANOVA?

20. Under what conditions should the Kruskal-Wallis test be used instead of the Wilcoxon rank-sum test?

21. **FILE** The following sample data were obtained from three populations that did not follow a normal distribution.

Sample 1	Sample 2	Sample 3
50	48	39
54	49	41
59	49	44
59	52	47
65	56	51
	57	

a. State the null hypothesis.
b. Using the .05 level of risk, state the decision rule.
c. Compute the value of the test statistic.
d. What is your decision on the null hypothesis?

22. **FILE** The following sample data were obtained from three populations where the variances were not equal, and you wish to compare the populations.

Sample 1	Sample 2	Sample 3
21	15	38
29	17	40
35	22	44
45	27	51
56	31	53
71		

a. State the null hypothesis.
b. Using the .01 level of risk, state the decision rule.
c. Compute the value of the test statistic.
d. What is your decision on the null hypothesis?

23. **FILE** Davis Outboard Motors Inc. recently developed an epoxy painting process to protect exhaust components from corrosion. Bill Davis, the owner, wishes to determine whether the durability of the paint was equal for three different conditions: saltwater, freshwater without weeds, and freshwater with a heavy concentration of weeds. Accelerated-life tests were conducted in the laboratory, and the number of hours the paint lasted before peeling was recorded. Five boats were tested for each condition.

Saltwater	Freshwater	Freshwater with Weeds
167.3	160.6	182.7
189.6	177.6	165.4
177.2	185.3	172.9
169.4	168.6	169.2
180.3	176.6	174.7

Use the Kruskal-Wallis test and the .01 level to determine whether the number of hours the paint lasted is the same for the three water conditions.

24. **FILE** The National Turkey Association wants to experiment with the effects of three different feed mixtures on weight gain in poults. Because no experience exists regarding the three mixtures, no assumptions regarding the population distribution of weights exist. To study the effects of the three mixtures, five poults were given feed A, six were given feed B, and five were given feed C over a three-week time period. Test at the .05 level the hypothesis that there is no effect of feed mixture on weight.

Weight (in pounds)		
Feed Mixture A	**Feed Mixture B**	**Feed Mixture C**
11.2	12.6	11.3
12.1	10.8	11.9
10.9	11.3	12.4
11.3	11.0	10.6
12.0	12.0	12.0
	10.7	

LO16-6
Test and interpret a nonparametric hypothesis test of correlation.

RANK-ORDER CORRELATION

In Chapter 13 we described the correlation coefficient. Recall that it measures the association between two interval- or ratio-scaled variables. For example, the correlation coefficient reports the association between the salary of executives and their years of experience, or the association between the number of miles a shipment had to travel and the number of days it took to arrive at its destination. The correlation coefficient is a very versatile measure of association. However, there are several conditions when it is not appropriate or can be misleading. Those conditions include:

1. When the scale of measurement of one of the two variables is ordinal (ranked).
2. When the relationship between the variables is not linear.
3. When one or more of the data points are quite different from the others.

Charles Spearman, a British statistician, introduced a measure of correlation for ranked data. This measure allows us to describe the relationship between sets of ranked data. For example, two staff members in the Office of Research at the University of the Valley are asked to rank 10 faculty research proposals for funding purposes. We want to study the association between the ratings of the two staff members. That is, do the two staff members rate the same proposals as the most worthy and the least worthy of funding?

This coefficient of rank correlation is also applied to conditions 2 and 3 above. Instead of using the actual values in the data set, we rank the sample data and compute a correlation between the ranked values. Like Pearson's coefficient of correlation described in Chapter 13, it can range from −1.00 up to 1.00. Values of −1.00 or 1.00 indicate perfect association between the ranks. A value of 0 indicates no association between the ranks of the two variables. Values of −.84 and .84 both exhibit the same amount of association but −.84 indicates an inverse relationship and .84 a direct relationship. We denote Spearman's coefficient of rank correlation as r_s.

We can use formula (13–1) on page 443 to find the coefficient of rank correlation. However, we use the ranked values in place of the actual values. The values are always ranked from low to high. A simpler method is to use the following, which uses the actual ranks.

SPEARMAN'S COEFFICIENT OF RANK CORRELATION

$$r_s = 1 - \frac{6\Sigma d^2}{n(n^2 - 1)} \qquad \textbf{(16–6)}$$

where:

d is the difference between the ranks for each pair.
n is the number of paired observations.

The following example/solution provides the details of computing the coefficient of rank correlation.

EXAMPLE

Recent studies focus on the relationship between the age of online shoppers and the number of minutes spent browsing on the Internet. Table 16–8 shows a sample of 15 online shoppers who actually made a purchase last week. Included is their age and the time, in minutes, spent browsing on the Internet last week.

TABLE 16–8 Age and Browsing Minutes for a Sample of Internet Shoppers

Shopper	Age	Browsing Time (minutes)
Spina, Sal	28	342
Gordon, Ray	50	125
Schnur, Roberta	44	121
Alvear, Jose	32	257
Myers, Tom	55	56
Lyons, George	60	225
Harbin, Joe	38	185
Bobko, Jack	22	141
Koppel, Marty	21	342
Rowatti, Marty	45	169
Monahan, Joyce	52	218
Lanoue, Bernie	33	241
Roll, Judy	19	583
Goodall, Jody	17	394
Broderick, Ron	21	249

1. Draw a scatter diagram; plot age on the horizontal axis and browsing minutes on the vertical axis.
2. What type of association do the sample data suggest? Strong or weak, direct or inverse?
3. Do you see any issues with the relationship between the variables?
4. Find the coefficient of rank correlation.
5. Conduct a test of hypothesis to determine if there is a negative association between the ranks.

SOLUTION

Our first step is to create a scatter diagram, shown in Chart 16–2, to better understand the relationship between the two variables.

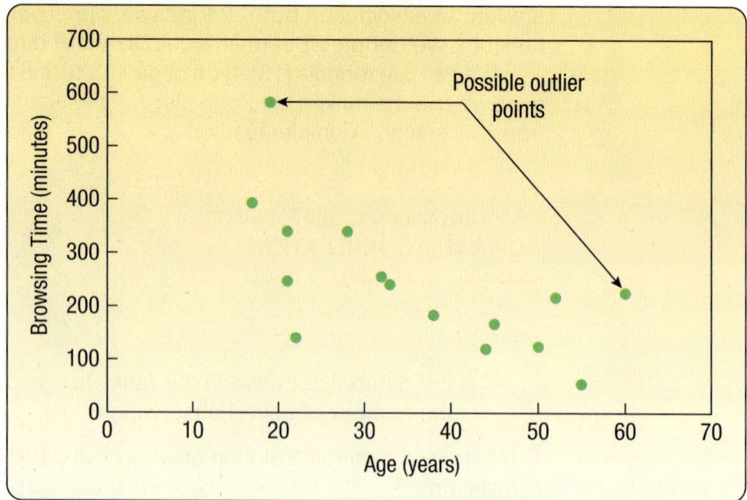

CHART 16–2 Scatter Diagram of Age and Internet Browsing Minutes

There appears to be a fairly strong inverse relationship between the Internet shopper's age and the amount of time spent browsing the Internet. That is, the younger shoppers seem to spend more time browsing. Not surprising. There are a couple of data points that seem quite different than the others. They are identified in Chart 16-2 on the previous page. Because of these points we decide to use the coefficient of rank correlation.

To calculate the coefficient of rank correlation, we first rank the age of the shoppers. The youngest shopper is Jody Goodall, who is 17, so she is ranked 1. The next youngest is Judy Roll, so she is ranked 2. There are two shoppers, Marty Koppel and Ron Broderick, who are 21 years old. This tie is resolved by giving each a rank of 3.5, which is the average of ranks 3 and 4. The oldest shopper in the sample is George Lyons; he is given a rank of 15. The same ranking strategy is used for browsing minutes. Tom Myers spent the fewest minutes browsing the Internet, so he has the rank of 1. Roberta Schnur is next with 141 minutes, so she has a browsing rank of 2. All the ranking data are shown in Table 16–9.

TABLE 16–9 Age, Browsing Time, Ranks, Differences, and Differences Squared

Shopper	Age	Age Rank	Browsing Time (minutes)	Browsing Rank	d	d^2
Spina, Sal	28	6.0	342	12.5	−6.50	42.25
Gordon, Ray	50	12.0	125	3.0	9.00	81.00
Schnur, Roberta	44	10.0	121	2.0	8.00	64.00
Alvear, Jose	32	7.0	257	11.0	−4.00	16.00
Myers, Tom	55	14.0	56	1.0	13.00	169.00
Lyons, George	60	15.0	225	8.0	7.00	49.00
Harbin, Joe	38	9.0	185	6.0	3.00	9.00
Bobko, Jack	22	5.0	141	4.0	1.00	1.00
Koppel, Marty	21	3.5	342	12.5	−9.00	81.00
Rowatti, Marty	45	11.0	169	5.0	6.00	36.00
Monahan, Joyce	52	13.0	218	7.0	6.00	36.00
Lanoue, Bernie	33	8.0	241	9.0	−1.00	1.00
Roll, Judy	19	2.0	583	15.0	−13.00	169.00
Goodall, Jody	17	1.0	394	14.0	−13.00	169.00
Broderick, Ron	21	3.5	249	10.0	−6.50	42.25
					Sum d^2	965.50

The coefficient of rank correlation is −.724, found by using formula (16–6).

$$r_s = 1 - \frac{6\Sigma d^2}{n(n^2 - 1)} = 1 - \frac{6(965.5)}{15(15^2 - 1)} = 1 - 1.724 = -0.724$$

The value of −0.724 indicates a fairly strong negative association between age of the Internet shopper and the minutes spent browsing. The younger shoppers tended to spend more time browsing the Internet.

Testing the Significance of r_s

Next we wish to investigate the question as to whether the degree of association between the ranked variables occurred by chance. Recall, in Chapter 13 starting on page 447, we investigated this same issue. In that instance, we used interval or ratio data; now we use ranks. In the preceding example/solution we found a rank correlation of −0.724. Is it possible that the correlation of −0.724 is due to chance and that the correlation among the ranks in the population is really 0? We can conduct a test of hypothesis to answer this question.

STATISTICS IN ACTION

Manatees are large mammals that like to float just below the water's surface. Because they float just below the surface, they are in danger from powerboat propellers. A study of the correlation between the number of powerboat registrations in coastal Florida counties and the number of accidental manatee deaths revealed a strong positive correlation. As a result, Florida created regions where powerboats are prohibited, so that manatees could thrive.

For a sample of 10 or more, the significance of r_s is determined by computing t using the following formula. The sampling distribution of r_s follows the t distribution with $n - 2$ degrees of freedom.

HYPOTHESIS TEST, RANK CORRELATION

$$t = r_s\sqrt{\frac{n-2}{1-r_s^2}} \qquad \textbf{(16–7)}$$

The null and the alternate hypotheses are:

H_0: The rank correlation in the population is zero.
H_1: There is a negative association among the ranks.

We use the .05 significance level. The decision rule is to reject the null hypothesis if the computed value is less than −1.771. Go to Appendix B.5 and use a one-tailed test with 15 − 2 = 13 degrees of freedom.

$$t = r_s\sqrt{\frac{n-2}{1-r_s^2}} = -0.724\sqrt{\frac{15-2}{1-(-0.724)^2}} = -3.784$$

The computed value of t is −3.784. The null hypothesis is rejected and the alternate hypothesis is accepted. The computed t of −3.784 is less than −1.771. There is evidence of a negative association between the age of the Internet shopper and the time spent browsing the Internet.

SELF-REVIEW 16–7

A sample of individuals applying for manufacturing jobs at Davis Enterprises revealed the following scores on an eye perception test (X) and a mechanical aptitude test (Y):

Subject	Eye Perception	Mechanical Aptitude	Subject	Eye Perception	Mechanical Aptitude
001	805	23	006	810	28
002	777	62	007	805	30
003	820	60	008	840	42
004	682	40	009	777	55
005	777	70	010	820	51

(a) Compute the coefficient of rank correlation between eye perception and mechanical aptitude.
(b) At the .05 significance level, can we conclude that the correlation in the population is different from 0?

EXERCISES

25. **FILE** Do husbands and wives like the same TV shows? A recent study by Nielsen Media Research asked a young married couple to rank 14 shows from best to worst. A rank of 1 indicates the best-liked show and a rank of 14 the least-liked show. The results for one married couple follow.

Program	Male Ranking	Female Ranking
60 Minutes	4	5
CSI — New York	6	4
Bones	7	8
SportsCenter	2	7
Late Show with Stephen Colbert	12	11
NBC Nightly News	8	6
Law and Order: Los Angeles	5	3
Miami Medical	3	9
Survivor	13	2
Parks and Recreation	14	10
American Idol	1	1
Grey's Anatomy	9	13
Doc Martin	10	12
Criminal Minds	11	14

a. Draw a scatter diagram. Place the male rankings on the horizontal axis and the female rankings on the vertical axis.

b. Compute the coefficient of rank correlation between the male and female rankings.

c. At the .05 significance level, is it reasonable to conclude there is a positive association between the two rankings?

26. **FILE** Far West University offers both day and evening classes in business administration. A survey of students inquires how they perceive the prestige associated with eight careers. A day student was asked to rank the careers from 1 to 8, with 1 having the most prestige and 8 the least prestige. An evening student was asked to do the same. The results follow.

Carrer	Ranking by Day Student	Ranking by Evening Student	Carrer	Ranking by Day Student	Ranking by Evening Student
Accountant	6	3	Statistician	1	7
Computer programmer	7	2	Marketing researcher	4	8
Branch bank manager	2	6	Stock analyst	3	5
Hospital administrator	5	4	Production manager	8	1

Find Spearman's coefficient of rank correlation.

27. **FILE** Ten new sales representatives for Clark Sprocket and Chain, Inc. were required to attend a training program before being assigned to a regional sales office. At the end of the program, the representatives took a series of tests and the scores were ranked. For example, Arden had the lowest test score and is ranked 1; Arbuckle had the highest test score and is ranked 10. At the end of the first sales year, the representatives' ranks based on test scores were paired with their first year sales.

Representative	Annual Sales ($ thousands)	Ranking in Training Program	Representative	Annual Sales ($ thousands)	Ranking in Training Program
Kitchen	319	8	Arden	300	1
Bond	150	2	Crane	280	6
Gross	175	5	Arthur	200	9
Arbuckle	460	10	Keene	190	4
Greene	348	7	Knopf	300	3

a. Compute and interpret the coefficient of rank correlation between first-year sales and class rank after the training program.
b. At the .05 significance level, can we conclude that there is a positive association between first-year sales dollars and ranking in the training program?

28. **FILE** Suppose Texas A & M University—Commerce has five scholarships available for the women's basketball team. The head coach provided the two assistant coaches with the names of 10 high school players with potential to play at the university. Each assistant coach attended three games and then ranked the 10 players with respect to potential. To explain, the first coach ranked Norma Tidwell as the best player among the 10 scouted and Jeannie Black the worst.

	Rank, by Assistant Coach			Rank, by Assistant Coach	
Player	Jean Cann	John Cannelli	Player	Jean Cann	John Cannelli
Cora Jean Seiple	7	5	Candy Jenkins	3	1
Bette Jones	2	4	Rita Rosinski	5	7
Jeannie Black	10	10	Anita Lockes	4	2
Norma Tidwell	1	3	Brenda Towne	8	9
Kathy Marchal	6	6	Denise Ober	9	8

a. Determine Spearman's rank correlation coefficient.
b. At the .05 significance level, can we conclude there is a positive association between the ranks?

CHAPTER SUMMARY

I. The sign test is based on the sign difference between two related observations.
- **A.** No assumptions need to be made about the shape of the two populations.
- **B.** It is based on paired or dependent samples.
- **C.** For small samples, find the number of + or − signs and refer to the binomial distribution for the critical value.
- **D.** For a sample of 10 or more, use the standard normal distribution and the following formula.

$$z = \frac{(x \pm .50) - .50n}{.50\sqrt{n}} \qquad \textbf{(16–2) (16–3)}$$

II. The median test is used to test a hypothesis about a population median.
- **A.** Find μ and σ for a binomial distribution.
- **B.** The z distribution is used as the test statistic.
- **C.** The value of z is computed from the following formula, where X is the number of observations above or below the median.

$$z = \frac{(x \pm .50) - \mu}{\sigma} \qquad \textbf{(16–1)}$$

III. The Wilcoxon signed-rank test is a nonparametric test for differences between two dependent populations.
- **A.** The assumption of normally distributed populations is not required.
- **B.** The steps to conduct the test are:
  1. Rank absolute differences between the related observations.
  2. Apply the sign of the differences to the ranks.
  3. Sum negative ranks and positive ranks.
  4. The smaller of the two sums is the computed T value.
  5. Refer to Appendix B.8 for the critical value, and make a decision regarding H_0.

IV. The Wilcoxon rank-sum test is used to test whether two independent samples came from equal populations.
- **A.** The assumption of normally distributed populations is not required.
- **B.** The data must be at least ordinal scale.

C. Each sample must contain at least eight observations.
D. To determine the value of the test statistic W, the sample observations are ranked from low to high as if they were from a single group.
E. The sum of ranks for each of the two samples is determined.
F. W is used to compute z, where W is the sum of the ranks for population 1.

$$z = \frac{W - \dfrac{n_1(n_1 + n_2 + 1)}{2}}{\sqrt{\dfrac{n_1 n_2(n_1 + n_2 + 1)}{12}}} \quad \textbf{(16–4)}$$

G. The standard normal distribution, found in Appendix B.3, is the test statistic.

V. The Kruskal-Wallis one-way ANOVA by ranks is used to test whether several population distributions are the same.
A. The assumption of normally distributed populations is not required.
B. The populations must be independent and at least ordinal scale.
C. The sample observations are ranked from smallest to largest as though they were a single group.
D. The test statistic follows the chi-square distribution, provided there are at least five observations in each sample.
E. The value of the test statistic is computed from the following:

$$H = \frac{12}{n(n+1)}\left[\frac{(\Sigma R_1)^2}{n_1} + \frac{(\Sigma R_2)^2}{n_2} + \cdots + \frac{(\Sigma R_k)^2}{n_k}\right] - 3(n+1) \quad \textbf{(16–5)}$$

VI. Spearman's coefficient of rank correlation is a measure of the association between two ordinal-scale variables.
A. It can range from −1 up to 1.
1. A value of 0 indicates there is no association between the variables.
2. A value of −1 indicates perfect negative correlation, and 1 indicates perfect positive correlation.
B. The value of r_s is computed from the following formula.

$$r_s = 1 - \frac{6\Sigma d^2}{n(n^2 - 1)} \quad \textbf{(16–6)}$$

C. Provided the sample size is at least 10, we can conduct a test of hypothesis using the following formula:

$$t = r_s\sqrt{\frac{n-2}{1-r_s^2}} \quad \textbf{(16–7)}$$

1. The test statistic follows the t distribution.
2. There are $n - 2$ degrees of freedom.

PRONUNCIATION KEY

SYMBOL	MEANING	PRONUNCIATION
$(\Sigma R_1)^2$	Square of the total of the first column ranks	*Sigma R sub 1 squared*
r_s	Spearman's coefficient of rank correlation	*r sub s*

CHAPTER EXERCISES

29. The vice president of programming at NBC is finalizing the prime-time schedule for the fall. She has decided to include a hospital drama but is unsure which of two possibilities to select. She has a pilot called *The Surgeon* and another called *Critical Care*. To help her make a final decision, a sample of 20 viewers from throughout the United States was asked to watch the two pilots and indicate which show they prefer. The results were that 12 liked *The Surgeon,* 7 liked *Critical Care,* and one had no preference. Is there a preference for one of the two shows? Use the .10 significance level.

30. IBM Inc. is going to award a contract for fine-line pens to be used nationally in its offices. Two suppliers, Bic and Pilot, have submitted bids. To determine the preference of office personnel, a preference test was conducted using a randomly selected sample of 20 employees. The .05 level of significance is to be used.

a. If the alternate hypothesis states that Bic is preferred over Pilot, is the sign test to be conducted as a one-tailed or a two-tailed test? Explain.

b. As each of the sampled employees told the researchers his or her preference, a "+" was recorded if it was Bic and a "–" if it was the Pilot fine-line pen. A count of the pluses revealed that 12 employees preferred Bic, 5 preferred Pilot, and 3 were undecided. What is *n*?

c. What is the decision rule in words?

d. What conclusion did you reach regarding pen preference? Explain.

31. Cornwall and Hudson, a large retail department store, wants to handle just one brand of MP3 player. The list has been narrowed to two brands: Sony and Panasonic. To help make a decision, a panel of 16 audio experts met. A music track using the Sony player was played. Then the same track was played using the Panasonic player. A "+" in the following table indicates an individual's preference for the Sony player, a "–" indicates preference for the Panasonic player, and a 0 signifies no preference.

Expert															
1	2	3	4	5	6	7	8	9	10	11	12	13	14	15	16
+	–	+	–	+	+	–	0	–	+	–	+	+	–	+	–

Conduct a test of hypothesis at the .10 significance level to determine whether there is a difference in preference between the two brands.

32. The Greater Jacksonville, Florida, Real Estate Association claims that the median rental for three-bedroom condominiums is more than $1,200 a month. A random sample of 149 units showed 5 rented for exactly $1,200 a month, and 75 rented for more than $1,200. At the .05 level, can we conclude that the median rental is more than $1,200?

a. State H_0 and H_1.

b. Give the decision rule.

c. Do the necessary calculations, and arrive at a decision.

33. The Citrus Council of America wants to determine whether consumers prefer orange juice with or without pulp. A random sample of 212 consumers was selected. Each member of the sample tasted a small, unlabeled cup of juice with pulp and a cup of juice without pulp. Twelve consumers said they had no preference, 40 preferred juice with pulp, and the remainder liked the juice without pulp better. Test at the .05 level that the preferences for orange juice with pulp and orange juice without pulp are equal.

34. **FILE** The objective of a community research project is to determine whether women are more community conscious before marriage or after 5 years of marriage. A test designed to measure community consciousness was administered to a sample of nine women before marriage, and the same test was given to them 5 years after marriage. The test scores are:

Name	Before Marriage	After Marriage	Name	Before Marriage	After Marriage
Beth	110	114	Carol	186	196
Jean	157	159	Lisa	116	116
Sue	121	120	Sandy	160	140
Cathy	96	103	Petra	149	142
Mary	130	139			

Test at the .05 level. H_0 is: There is no difference in community consciousness before and after marriage. H_1 is: There is a difference.

35. **FILE** Is there a difference in the annual divorce rates in predominantly rural counties among three geographic regions, namely, the Southwest, the Southeast, and the Northwest? Test at the .05 level. Annual divorce rates per 1,000 population for five randomly selected counties in the Southwest, six counties in the Southeast, and 5 counties in the Northwest are:

Southwest:	5.9, 6.2, 7.9, 8.6, 4.6
Southeast:	5.0, 6.4, 7.3, 6.2, 8.1, 5.1
Northwest:	6.7, 6.2, 4.9, 8.0, 5.5

36. FILE The production manager of MPS Audio Systems Inc. is concerned about the idle time of workers. In particular, he would like to know if there is a difference in the idle minutes for workers on the day shift and the evening shift. The information below is the number of idle minutes yesterday for the five day-shift workers and the six evening-shift workers. Use the .05 significance level.

Day Shift	Evening Shift
92	96
103	114
116	80
81	82
89	88
	91

37. FILE Drs. Trythall and Kerns are studying the mobility of executives in selected industries. Their research measures mobility using a score based on the number of times an executive has moved, changed companies, or changed jobs within a company over the last 10 years. The highest number of points is awarded for moving and changing companies; the fewest, for changing jobs within a company and not moving. They randomly sampled five executives in the chemical industry, six in the retail industry, five in the Internet industry, and five in the aerospace industry. The distribution of scores does not follow the normal probability distribution. Develop an appropriate test to determine if there is a difference in the mobility scores in the four industries. Use the .05 significance level.

Chemical	Retail	Internet	Aerospace
4	3	62	30
17	12	40	38
8	40	81	46
20	17	96	40
16	31	76	21
	19		

38. FILE A series of questions on sports and world events was asked of 14 randomly selected young adult naturalized citizens. The results were translated into sports and world events "knowledge" scores. The scores were:

Citizen	Sports	World Events	Citizen	Sports	World Events
J. C. McCarthy	47	49	L. M. Zaugg	87	75
A. N. Baker	12	10	J. B. Simon	59	86
B. B. Beebe	62	76	J. Goulden	40	61
L. D. Gaucet	81	92	A. A. Fernandez	87	18
C. A. Jones	90	86	A. M. Carbo	16	75
J. N. Lopez	35	42	A. O. Smithy	50	51
A. F. Nissen	61	61	J. J. Pascal	60	61

a. Determine the degree of association between how the citizens ranked with respect to knowledge of sports and how they ranked on world events.
b. At the .05 significance level, is the rank correlation between the sports and world events "knowledge" scores greater than zero?

39. FILE Early in the basketball season, 12 college teams appeared to be outstanding. A panel of sportswriters and a panel of college basketball coaches were asked to rank the 12 teams. Their composite rankings were as follows.

Team	Coaches	Sportswriters	Team	Coaches	Sportswriters
Duke	1	1	Syracuse	7	10
UNLV	2	5	Georgetown	8	11
Indiana	3	4	Villanova	9	7
North Carolina	4	6	LSU	10	12
Louisville	5	3	St. Johns	11	8
Ohio State	6	2	Michigan	12	9

Determine the correlation between the rankings of the coaches and the sportswriters. At the .05 significance level, can we conclude there is a positive correlation between the rankings?

40. FILE Professor Bert Forman believes the students who complete his examinations in the shortest time receive the highest grades and those who take the longest to complete them receive the lowest grades. To verify his suspicion, he assigns a rank to the order of finish and then grades the examinations. The results are shown below:

Student	Order of Completion	Score (50 possible)	Student	Order of Completion	Score (50 possible)
Gromney	1	48	Smythe	7	39
Bates	2	48	Arquette	8	30
MacDonald	3	43	Govito	9	37
Sosa	4	49	Gankowski	10	35
Harris	5	50	Bonfigilo	11	36
Cribb	6	47	Matsui	12	33

Convert the test scores to a rank and find the coefficient of rank correlation between the order of completion and the rank of the test score. At the .05 significance level, can Professor Forman conclude there is a positive association between the order of finish and the test scores?

DATA ANALYTICS

(The data for these exercises are available at the text website: www.mhhe.com/Lind17e.)

41. The North Valley Real Estate data report information on homes on the market.
   a. Use an appropriate nonparametric test to determine whether there is a difference in the typical selling price of the homes in the several townships. Assume the selling prices are not normally distributed. Use the .05 significance level.
   b. Combine the homes with six or more bedrooms into one group and determine whether there is a difference according to the number of bedrooms in the typical selling prices of the homes. Use the .05 significance level and assume the distribution of selling prices is not normally distributed.
   c. Compare the distribution of FICO scores for fixed and variable mortgages. FICO scores are people's credit rating. Higher ratings indicate better credit. Can we conclude there is a difference in the distributions of FICO scores based on the type of mortgage? Use the .05 significance level.

42. Refer to the Baseball 2016 data, which report information on the 2016 Major League Baseball season.
   a. Rank the teams by the number of wins and their total team salary. Compute the coefficient of rank correlation between the two variables. At the .01 significance level, can you conclude that it is greater than zero?
   b. Assume that the distributions of team salaries for the American League and National League do not follow the normal distribution. Conduct a test of hypothesis to see whether there is a difference in the two distributions.
   c. Rank the 30 teams by attendance and by team salary. Determine the coefficient of rank correlation between these two variables. At the .05 significance level, is it reasonable to conclude the ranks of these two variables are related?

43. Refer to the Lincolnville School District school bus data.
   a. Assume the distribution of the maintenance cost for the bus capacities does not follow a normal distribution. Conduct a test of hypothesis at the .05 significance level to determine whether the distributions differ.
   b. Assume the distribution of the maintenance cost for the fuel types, diesel or gasoline, does not follow a normal distribution. Conduct a test of hypothesis at the .05 significance level to determine whether the distributions differ.
   c. Assume the distribution of the maintenance cost for the three bus manufacturers does not follow a normal distribution. Conduct a test of hypothesis at the .05 significance level to determine whether the distributions differ.

A REVIEW OF CHAPTERS 15–16

In Chapters 15 and 16, we describe statistical methods to study data that are either the nominal or the ordinal scale of measurement. These methods are *nonparametric* or *distribution-free* statistics. They do not require assumptions regarding the shape of the population. Recall, for example, in Chapter 12 when investigating the means of several populations, we assume the populations follow the normal probability distribution.

In Chapter 15, we describe tests for the nominal level of data. We begin by studying one- and two-sample tests of proportions. A proportion is the fraction of individuals or objects that possess a certain characteristic. In a proportion the sampled individual or object either has the characteristic or does not. For example, in a one-sample test of proportions, we study 100 gasoline purchases at the local Kwick Fill station. The individual either purchased regular gasoline or did not. There are only two possible outcomes. In a two-sample test of proportions, we compare the proportion of purchasers who bought regular gasoline at the Corry, Texas Kwick Fill with the proportion of regular gasoline purchases at the Tyrone, Texas Kwick Fill. The test statistic is the standard normal distribution in both the one-sample and the two-sample tests.

We also use the chi-square distribution to compare an observed set of frequencies with the corresponding set of expected frequencies. The level of measurement is either the nominal or ordinal scale. In the previous example, there were only two possible outcomes: the purchaser bought regular gasoline or did not buy it. We use the chi-square distribution to investigate an instance where there are several possible nominal-scale outcomes. A gasoline purchaser can buy regular, midgrade, or premium. Recall that when data are measured at the nominal level, the observations can only be classified according to some label, name, or characteristic.

In Chapter 15, we also explore the relationship between two variables in a contingency table. That is, we observe two characteristics of each sampled individual or object. For example, is there a relationship between the quality of the product (acceptable or unacceptable) and the shift when it was manufactured (day, afternoon, or night)? The chi-square distribution is used as the test statistic.

In Chapter 16, we describe five nonparametric tests of hypothesis and the coefficient of rank correlation. Each of these tests requires at least the ordinal scale of measurement. That is, we are able to rank, or order, the variables of interest.

The *sign test* for dependent samples is based on the sign of the difference between related observations. The binomial distribution is the test statistic. In cases where the sample is greater than 10, the normal approximation to the binomial probability distribution serves as the test statistic.

The first step when using the *median test* is to count the number of observations above (or below) the proposed median. Next, we use the standard normal distribution to determine if this number is reasonable or too large to have occurred by chance.

The *Wilcoxon signed-rank test* requires dependent samples. It is an extension of the sign test in that it makes use of both the direction and the magnitude of the difference between related values. It has its own sampling distribution, which is reported in Appendix B.8.

The *Wilcoxon ranked-sum test* assumes independent populations, but does not require the populations to follow the normal probability distribution. It is an alternative to the *t* test for independent samples described in Chapter 11. When there are at least eight observations in each sample, the test statistic is the standard normal distribution.

The *Kruskal-Wallis test* is an extension of the Wilcoxon ranked-sum test in that it handles more than two populations. It is an alternative to the one-way ANOVA method described in Chapter 12. It does not require the populations to follow the normal probability distribution or that the populations have equal standard deviations.

The statistic *Spearman's coefficient of rank correlation* is a special case of the Pearson coefficient of correlation, described in Chapter 13. It is based on the correlation between the *ranks* of related observations. It may range from −1.00 to 1.00, with 0 indicating no association between the ranks.

PROBLEMS

1. The owner of Beach Front Snow Cones Inc. believes the median number of snow cones sold per day between Memorial Day and Labor Day is 60. Below is the number of snow-cones sold on 20 randomly selected days. Is it reasonable to conclude that the median is actually greater than 60? Use the .05 significance level.

65	70	65	64	66	54	68	61	62	67
65	50	64	55	74	57	67	72	66	65

2. The manufacturer of children's raincoats wants to know if there is a preference among children for blue, red, green, or yellow raincoats. The information below is the color preference for a sample of 50 children between the ages of 6 and 10. Use the .05 significance level to investigate.

Color	Frequency
Blue	17
Red	8
Green	12
Yellow	13

3. Is there a difference in the length of suspension bridges in the northeast, southeast, and far west parts of the United States? The following table shows the lengths (in feet) of seven bridges in the northeast, nine bridges in the southeast, and eight bridges in the far west. Conduct an appropriate test of hypothesis on the following data. Do not assume the bridge lengths follow a normal probability distribution. Use the .05 significance level.

Northeast	Southeast	Far West
3,645	3,502	3,547
3,727	3,645	3,636
3,772	3,718	3,659
3,837	3,746	3,673
3,873	3,758	3,728
3,882	3,845	3,736
3,894	3,940	3,788
	4,070	3,802
	4,081	

4. Research by the First Bank of Illinois revealed that 8% of its customers wait more than 5 minutes for a teller in a bank lobby. Management considers this reasonable and will not add more tellers unless the proportion waiting longer than 5 minutes becomes larger than 8%. The branch manager at the Litchfield Branch believes that the wait is longer than the standard at her branch and requested additional part-time tellers. To support her request, she found that, in a sample of 100 customers, 10 waited more than 5 minutes. At the .01 significance level, is it reasonable to conclude that more than 8% of the customers wait more than 5 minutes?

CASES

A. Century National Bank

Is there a relationship between the location of the branch bank and whether the customer has a debit card? Based on the information available, develop a table that shows the relationship between these two variables. At the .05 significance level, can we conclude there is a relationship between the branch location and whether the customer uses a debit card?

B. Thomas Testing Labs

John Thomas, the owner of Thomas Testing, has for some time done contract work for insurance companies regarding drunk driving. To improve his research capabilities, he recently purchased the Rupple Driving Simulator. This device will allow a subject to take a "road test" and provide a score indicating the number of driving errors committed during the test drive. Higher scores indicate more driving errors. Driving errors would include not coming to a complete stop at a stop sign, not using turning signals, not exercising caution on wet or snowy pavement, and so on. During the road test, problems appear at random and not all problems appear in each road test. These are major advantages to the Rupple Driving Simulator because subjects do not gain any advantage by taking the test several times.

With the new driving simulator, Mr. Thomas would like to study in detail the problem of drunk driving. He begins by selecting a random sample of 25 drivers. He asks each of the selected individuals to take the test drive on the Rupple Driving Simulator. The number of errors for each driver is recorded. Next, he has each of the individuals in the group drink three 16-ounce cans of beer in a 60-minute period and return to the Rupple Driving Simulator for another test drive. The number of driving errors after drinking the beer is also shown. The research question is: Does alcohol impair the driver's ability and, therefore, increase the number of driving errors?

Mr. Thomas believes the distribution of scores on the test drive does not follow a normal distribution and, therefore, a nonparametric test should be used. Because the observations are paired, he decides to use both the sign test and the Wilcoxon signed-rank test.

	Driving Errors			Driving Errors	
Subject	**Without Alcohol**	**With Alcohol**	**Subject**	**Without Alcohol**	**With Alcohol**
1	75	89	14	72	106
2	78	83	15	83	89
3	89	80	16	99	89
4	100	90	17	75	77
5	85	84	18	58	78
6	70	68	19	93	108
7	64	84	20	69	69
8	79	104	21	86	84
9	83	81	22	97	86
10	82	88	23	65	92
11	83	93	24	96	97
12	84	92	25	85	94
13	80	103			

a. Compare the results using these two procedures. Conduct an appropriate test of hypothesis to determine if alcohol is related to driving errors.

b. Write a report that summarizes your findings.

PRACTICE TEST

Part 1—Objective

1. The ____________ level of measurement is required for the chi-square goodness-of-fit test. 1. ____________
2. Which of the following is *not* a characteristic of the chi-square distribution? (positively skewed, based on degrees of freedom, cannot be negative, at least 30 observations) 2. ____________
3. In a contingency table, how many traits are considered for each observation? 3. ____________
4. In a contingency table, there are four rows and three columns. How many degrees of freedom are there? 4. ____________

5. In a goodness-of-fit test, the critical value of chi-square is based on ___________. (sample size, number of categories, number of variables, none of these) 5. ___________
6. In a sign test, are the samples dependent or independent? 6. ___________
7. In a sign test of eight paired observations, the test statistic is the ___________ distribution. (binomial, z, t, chi-square) 7. ___________
8. What is the major difference between the Kruskal-Wallis test and the Wilcoxon rank-sum test? (one is based on dependent samples and the other independent samples, one is for comparing two independent samples and the other two or more independent samples) 8. ___________
9. Under what conditions can the coefficient of rank correlation be less than −1.00? 9. ___________
10. The Kruskal-Wallis test is used in place of ANOVA when which two of the following criteria are not met? (normal population, equal standard deviations, more than 12 items in the sample, the populations are independent) 10. ___________

Part 2—Problems

Use the standard six-step hypothesis testing procedure.

1. A recent census report indicated that 65% of families have two parents present, 20% have only a mother present, 10% have only a father present, and 5% have no parent present. A random sample of 200 children from a large rural school district revealed the following frequencies of children with two parents, mother only, father only, no parent, and the total of 200.

Two Parents	Mother Only	Father Only	No Parent	Total
120	40	30	10	200

Is there sufficient evidence to conclude that the proportion of families by type of parent present in this particular school district differs from those reported in the recent census?

2. A book publisher wants to investigate the type of book selected for recreational reading by men and women. A random sample of 540 men and 500 women provided the following information regarding their preferences for mystery, romance, or self-help books. At the .05 significance level, should we conclude that gender is related or unrelated to type of book selected?

	Mystery	Romance	Self-Help	Total
Men	250	100	190	540
Women	130	170	200	500

3. An instructor has three sections of basic statistics: 8:00 a.m., 10:00 a.m., and 1:30 p.m. Listed below are the grades on the first exam for each section. Assume that the distributions do not follow the normal probability distribution. At the .05 significance level, is there a difference in the distributions of scores?

8 a.m.	10 a.m.	1:30 p.m.
68	59	67
84	59	69
75	63	75
78	62	76
70	78	79
77	76	83
88	80	86
71		86
		87

4. According to a study in *Health Magazine*, one in three children in the United States is obese or overweight. A health practitioner in Louisiana sampled 500 children and found 210 who were obese or overweight. Does this evidence suggest that the actual proportion of obese or overweight children is more than one out of three? Use the .01 significance level.

Index Numbers

17

▲ **INFORMATION ON PRICES** and quantities for margarine, shortening, milk, and potato chips for 2000 and 2016 is provided in Exercise 27. Compute a simple price index for each of the four items, using 2000 as the base period. (See Exercise 27 and LO17-1.)

LEARNING OBJECTIVES

When you have completed this chapter, you will be able to:

LO17-1 Compute and interpret a simple, unweighted index.

LO17-2 Compute and interpret an unweighted aggregate index.

LO17-3 Compute and interpret a weighted aggregate index.

LO17-4 List and describe special-purpose indexes.

LO17-5 Apply the Consumer Price Index.

INTRODUCTION

In this chapter, we will examine a useful descriptive tool called an **index.** An index expresses the relative change in a value from one period to another. No doubt you are familiar with indexes such as the **Consumer Price Index,** which is released monthly by the U.S. Department of Labor. There are many other indexes, such as the **Dow Jones Industrial Average** (DJIA), **NASDAQ, NIKKEI 225,** and **Standard & Poor's 500 Stock Average.** Indexes are published on a regular basis by the federal government, by business publications such as *Bloomberg Businessweek* and *Forbes,* in most daily newspapers, and on the Internet.

© Image Source/Getty Images

Of what importance is an index? Why is the Consumer Price Index so important and so widely reported? As the name implies, it measures the change in the price of a large group of items consumers purchase. The Federal Reserve Board, consumer groups, unions, management, senior citizens organizations, and others in business and economics are very concerned about changes in prices. These groups closely monitor the Consumer Price Index as well as the **Producer Price Index,** which measures price fluctuations at all stages of production. To combat sharp price increases, the Federal Reserve often raises the interest rate to "cool down" the economy. Likewise, the Dow Jones Industrial Average, which is updated continuously during the business day, describes the overall change in common stock prices of 30 large companies.

A few stock market indexes appear daily in the financial section of most newspapers. Many are also reported in real time. Shown below are the Dow Jones Industrial Average, NASDAQ, and other indexes from the Yahoo.com website (**http://financeyahoo.com**).

LO17-1
Compute and interpret a simple, unweighted index.

SIMPLE INDEX NUMBERS

What is an **index number**? An index or index number measures the change in a particular item (typically a product or service) between two time periods.

> **INDEX NUMBER** A number that expresses the relative change in price, quantity, or value compared to a base period.

If the index number is used to measure the relative change in just one variable, such as hourly wages in manufacturing, we refer to this as a simple index. It is the ratio of two variables converted to a percentage. The following four examples illustrate the use of index numbers. As noted in the definition, the main use of an index number in business is to show the percent change in one or more items from one time period to another.

EXAMPLE

According to the Bureau of Labor Statistics, in 2000 the average hourly earnings of production workers was \$14.02. In March 2016, it was \$21.37. What is the index of hourly earnings of production workers for March 2016 based on 2000 data?

SOLUTION

It is 152.43, found by:

$$P = \frac{\text{Average hourly earnings in 2016}}{\text{Average hourly earnings in 2000}}(100) = \frac{\$21.37}{\$14.02}(100) = 152.43$$

Thus, the hourly earnings in 2016 compared to 2000 were 152.43%. This means there was a 52.43% increase in hourly earnings during the period, found by 152.43 – 100.0 = 52.43.

You can check the latest information on wages, the Consumer Price Indexes, and other business-related values at the Bureau of Labor Statistics (BLS) website, http://www.bls.gov. The following chart shows some statistics from the BLS.

LATEST NUMBERS RSS

Consumer Price Index (CPI):
-0.2% in Feb 2016

Unemployment Rate:
5.0% in Mar 2016

Payroll Employment:
+215,000(p) in Mar 2016

Average Hourly Earnings:
+\$0.07(p) in Mar 2016

Producer Price Index - Final Demand:
-0.2%(p) in Feb 2016

Employment Cost Index (ECI):
+0.6% in 4th Qtr of 2015

Productivity:
-2.2%(r) in 4th Qtr of 2015

U.S. Import Price Index:
-0.3% in Feb 2016

U.S. Export Price Index:
-0.4% in Feb 2016

EXAMPLE

An index can also compare one item with another. The population of the Canadian province of British Columbia in 2014 was 4,657,947, and for Ontario it was 13,730,187. What is the population index of British Columbia compared to Ontario?

SOLUTION

The index of population for British Columbia is 33.9, found by:

$$P = \frac{\text{Population of British Columbia}}{\text{Population of Ontario}}(100) = \frac{4{,}657{,}947}{13{,}730{,}187}(100) = 33.9$$

This indicates that the population of British Columbia is 33.9% (about one-third) of the population of Ontario, or the population of British Columbia is 66.1% less than the population of Ontario (100 − 33.9 = 66.1).

EXAMPLE

The following chart shows the number of passengers (in millions) for the 10 busiest airports in the United States in 2014. Use the McCarran International Airport in Las Vegas as the base. What is the index for the other airports compared to Las Vegas?

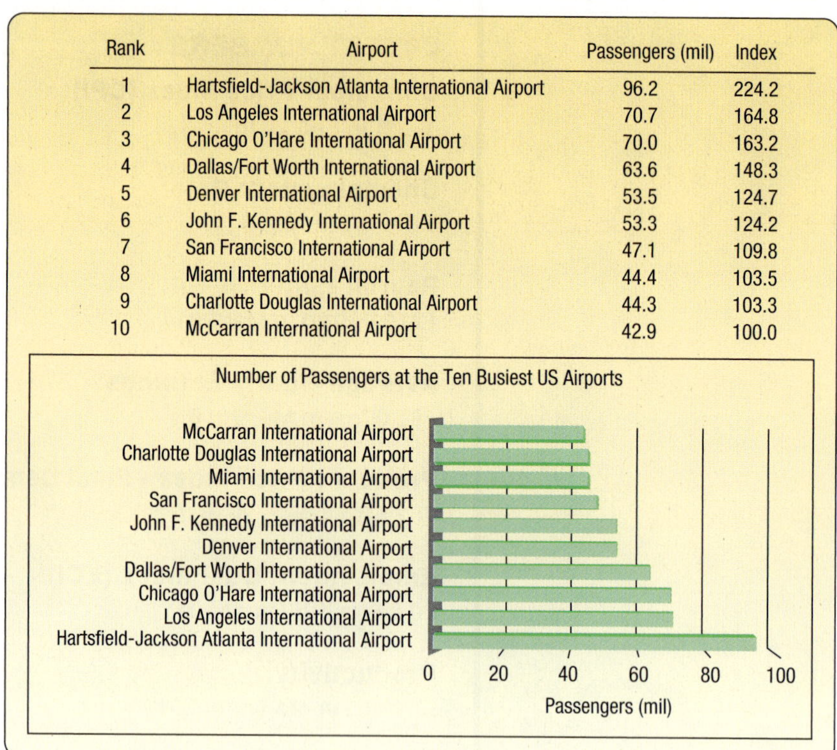

Rank	Airport	Passengers (mil)	Index
1	Hartsfield-Jackson Atlanta International Airport	96.2	224.2
2	Los Angeles International Airport	70.7	164.8
3	Chicago O'Hare International Airport	70.0	163.2
4	Dallas/Fort Worth International Airport	63.6	148.3
5	Denver International Airport	53.5	124.7
6	John F. Kennedy International Airport	53.3	124.2
7	San Francisco International Airport	47.1	109.8
8	Miami International Airport	44.4	103.5
9	Charlotte Douglas International Airport	44.3	103.3
10	McCarran International Airport	42.9	100.0

SOLUTION

To find the 10 indexes, we divide the passengers for Las Vegas into the passengers for the other nine airports. So the index for Atlanta is 224.2, found by (96.2/42.9)*(100). The index for San Francisco International is 109.8, found by

(47.1/42.9)*(100). So Atlanta has 124.2% more passengers than Las Vegas and San Francisco has 9.8 more than Las Vegas. The chart summarizes the indexes. The chart reveals that in 2014, Miami and Charlotte served about the same number of passengers as Las Vegas (all three of the indexes are close to 100). Atlanta, on the other hand, served more than twice as many passengers as McCarran International.

Note from the previous discussion that:

1. The index of average hourly earnings of production workers (152.43) is a percentage, but the percent symbol is usually omitted.
2. Indexes have either a **base** or a **base period.** In the example/solution regarding the average hourly earnings of production workers, we used 2000 as the base period. The Consumer Price Index uses 1982–84 as the base period. In contrast, in the example/solution about airport passengers, the McCarran International Airport in Las Vegas was used as the base for comparison.
3. Most business and economic indexes are reported to the nearest whole number, such as 214 or 96, or to the nearest tenth of a percent, such as 83.4 or 118.7.

Why Convert Data to Indexes?

Compiling index numbers is not a recent innovation. An Italian, G. R. Carli, is credited with originating index numbers in 1764. They were incorporated in a report he made regarding price fluctuations in Europe from 1500 to 1750. No systematic approach to collecting and reporting data in index form was evident in the United States until about 1900. The cost-of-living index (now called the Consumer Price Index) was introduced in 1913, and a long list of indexes has been compiled since then.

Why convert data to indexes? An index is a convenient way to express a change in a diverse group of items. The Consumer Price Index (CPI), for example, encompasses 200 categories of items summarized by 8 groups—food and beverages, housing, apparel, transportation, medical care, recreation, education and communication, and other goods and services. The prices of 80,000 goods and services in the 200 categories are collected. Prices are expressed in many different units such as dollars per pound or a dozen eggs. Only by summarizing these prices with an index number can the federal government and others concerned with inflation keep informed of the overall movement of consumer prices.

Converting data to indexes also makes it easier to assess the trend in a series composed of exceptionally large numbers. For example, the estimate of U.S. retail e-commerce sales in 2014 was $304,913,000 compared to $168,895,000 in 2010. This is an increase of $136,018,000 in the four-year period, but because of the very large numbers it is difficult to realize the increase. If we compute an index of 2014 sales based on 2010 sales, the index is 180.5. The index means that 2014 sales increased 80.5% compared to 2010 sales.

$$\text{Index} = \frac{\text{2014 e-commerce sales}}{\text{2010 e-commerce sales}}(100) = \frac{\$304{,}913{,}000}{\$168{,}895{,}000}(100) = 180.5$$

Construction of Index Numbers

We already discussed the construction of a simple price index. The price in a selected year (such as 2017) is divided by the price in the base year. The base-period price is designated as p_0, and a price other than the base period is often referred to as the *given period* or *selected period* and designated p_t. To calculate the simple price index P using 100 as the base value for any given period, use the formula:

SIMPLE INDEX

$$P = \frac{p_t}{p_0} \times 100 \qquad \textbf{(17–1)}$$

Suppose the price of a fall weekend package (including lodging and all meals) at Tryon Mountain Lodge in western North Carolina in 2000 was $450. The price rose to $795 in 2017. What is the price index for 2017 using 2000 as the base period and 100 as the base value? It is 176.7, found by:

$$P = \frac{p_t}{p_0}(100) = \frac{\$795}{\$450}(100) = 176.7$$

Interpreting this result, the price of the fall weekend package increased 76.7% from 2000 to 2017.

The base period need not be a single year. Note in Table 17–1 that if we use 2005 – 06 = 100, the base price for the stapler would be $21 [found by determining the mean price of 2005 and 2006, ($20 + $22)/2 = $21]. The prices $20, $22, and $23 are averaged if 2005—07 is selected as the base. The mean price would be $21.67. The indexes constructed using the three different base periods are presented in Table 17–1. (Note that when 2005 – 07 = 100, the index numbers for 2005, 2006, and 2007 average 100.0, as we would expect.) Logically, the index numbers for 2015 using the three different bases are not the same.

TABLE 17–1 Prices of a Benson Automatic Stapler, Model 3, Converted to Indexes Using Three Different Base Periods

Year	Price of Stapler	Price Index (2005 = 100)	Price Index (2005–06 = 100)	Price Index (2005–07 = 100)
2000	$18	90.0	$\frac{18}{21} \times 100 = 85.7$	$\frac{18}{21.67} \times 100 = 83.1$
2005	20	100.0	$\frac{20}{21} \times 100 = 95.2$	$\frac{20}{21.67} \times 100 = 92.3$
2006	22	110.0	$\frac{22}{21} \times 100 = 104.8$	$\frac{22}{21.67} \times 100 = 101.5$
2007	23	115.0	$\frac{23}{21} \times 100 = 109.5$	$\frac{23}{21.67} \times 100 = 106.1$
2015	38	190.0	$\frac{38}{21} \times 100 = 181.0$	$\frac{38}{21.67} \times 100 = 175.4$

SELF-REVIEW 17–1

1. Listed below are the top steel-producing countries for the year 2014 (http://www.worldsteel.org). Express the amount produced by China, Japan, India, and Russia as an index, using the United States as a base. What percent more steel does China produce than the United States?

Country	Amount (millions of tons)
China	822.7
Japan	110.7
United States	88.2
India	86.5
Russia	71.5

2. The average hourly earnings of production workers for selected years are given below.

Year	Average Hourly Earnings
1995	$11.65
2000	14.02
2005	16.13
2013	19.97
2016	21.37

(a) Using 1995 as the base period and 100 as the base value, determine the indexes for the other years. Interpret the index.

(b) Use the average of 1995 and 2000 as the base and determine indexes for the other years. Interpret the index.

EXERCISES

1. **FILE** PNC Bank Inc., which has its headquarters in Pittsburgh, reported the following commercial loan totals for years 2008 through 2015. Using 2008 as the base, develop a simple index of commercial loans for the following years

Year	Loans ($ Millions)
2008	69,220
2009	54,818
2010	55,177
2011	65,694
2012	83,040
2013	88,378
2014	97,420
2015	98,608

2. **FILE** The table below reports the earnings per share of common stock for Home Depot Inc. for 2003 through 2015. Develop an index, with 2003 as the base, for earnings per share for years 2004 through 2015.

Year	Earnings per Share	Year	Earnings per Share
2003	1.56	2010	1.57
2004	1.88	2011	2.01
2005	2.26	2012	2.47
2006	2.72	2013	3.76
2007	2.79	2014	4.71
2008	2.37	2015	5.46
2009	1.34		

3. **FILE** Listed below are the net sales for a San Francisco–area mail-order retailer for the years 2006 to 2015. Use the mean sales for the earliest three years to determine a base and then find the index for 2014 and 2015. By how much have net sales increased from the base period?

Year	Sales (millions)	Year	Sales (millions)
2006	$486.6	2011	$568.5
2007	506.8	2012	581.9
2008	522.2	2013	496.1
2009	574.6	2014	456.6
2010	580.7	2015	433.3

4. In January 2003, the price for a whole fresh chicken was $1.004 per pound. In February 2016, the price for the same chicken was $1.475 per pound. Use the January 2003 price as the base period and 100 as the base value to develop a simple index. By what percent has the cost of chicken increased?

LO17-2
Compute and interpret an unweighted aggregate index.

UNWEIGHTED INDEXES

In many situations, we wish to combine several items and develop an index to compare the cost of this aggregation of items in two different time periods. For example, we might be interested in an index for items that relate to the expense of operating and maintaining an automobile. The items in the index might include tires, oil changes, and gasoline prices. Or we might be interested in a college student index. This index might include the cost of books, tuition, housing, meals, and entertainment. There are several ways we can combine the items to determine the index.

Simple Average of the Price Indexes

Table 17–2 reports the prices for several food items for 2003 and 2015. We would like to develop an index for this group of food items for 2015, using the 2003 prices as the base. This is written in the abbreviated code 2003 = 100.

TABLE 17–2 Computation of the Index for Various Food Items, 2003 = 100

Item	2003 Price	2015 Price	Simple Index
Bread, white, cost per pound	$ 1.042	$ 1.440	138.2
Eggs, dozen	1.175	2.133	181.5
Milk, gallon, white	2.686	3.463	128.9
Apples, Red Delicious, 1 pound	0.911	1.265	138.9
Orange juice, 12 oz. concentrate	1.848	2.678	144.9
Coffee, 100% ground roast, 1 pound	2.999	4.827	161.0
Total	$10.661	$15.806	

We could begin by computing a **simple average** of the price indexes for each item using 2003 as the base. The simple index for bread is 138.2, found by using formula (17–1).

$$P = \frac{p_t}{p_0}(100) = \frac{1.440}{1.042}(100) = 138.2$$

We compute the simple index for the other items in Table 17–2 similarly. The largest price increase was 81.5% for eggs, and coffee was second at 61.0%.

We can also determine the percentage change in the group of foods by averaging the simple indexes. The formula is:

SIMPLE AVERAGE OF THE PRICE RELATIVES

$$P = \frac{\Sigma P_i}{n} \tag{17–2}$$

where P_i refers to the simple index for each of the items and n the number of items. In our example, the index is 148.9, found by:

$$P = \frac{\Sigma P_i}{n} = \frac{138.2 + \cdots + 161.0}{6} = \frac{893.4}{6} = 148.9$$

This indicates that the mean price of the group of food items increased 48.9% from 2003 to 2015.

A positive feature of the simple average of price indexes is that we would obtain the same value for the index regardless of the units of measure. In the above index, if apples were priced in tons, instead of pounds, the impact of apples on the combined index would not change. That is, the commodity "apples" represents one of six items in the index, so the impact of the item is not related to the units. A negative feature of this index is that it fails to consider the relative importance of the items included in the index. For example, milk and eggs receive the same weight, even though a typical family might spend far more over the year on milk than on eggs.

Simple Aggregate Index

A second possibility is to sum the prices (rather than the indexes) for the two periods and then determine the index based on the totals. The formula is:

SIMPLE AGGREGATE INDEX

$$P = \frac{\Sigma p_t}{\Sigma p_0} \times 100 \qquad \textbf{(17–3)}$$

This is called a **simple aggregate index.** The index for the food items on the previous page is found by dividing the sum of the prices in 2015 by the sum of the prices in 2003. The sum of the prices for the base period is $10.661 and for the given period it is $15.806. The simple aggregate index is 148.3. This means that the aggregate group of prices had increased 48.3% in the 13-year period.

$$P = \frac{\Sigma p_t}{\Sigma p_0} 100 = \frac{\$15.806}{\$10.661}(100) = 148.3$$

Because the value of a simple aggregate index can be influenced by the units of measurement, it is not used frequently. In our example, the value of the index would differ significantly if we were to report the price of apples in tons rather than pounds. Also, note the effect of coffee on the total index. For both the current year and the base year, coffee is a significant contributor to the total index, so the current price of coffee will drive the index much more than any other item. Therefore, we need a way to appropriately "weight" the items according to their relative importance.

LO17-3

Compute and interpret a weighted aggregate index.

WEIGHTED INDEXES

Two methods of computing a **weighted price index** are the **Laspeyres** method and the **Paasche** method. They differ only in the period used for weighting. The Laspeyres method uses *base-period weights;* that is, the original prices and quantities of the purchased items are used to find the percent change over a period of time in either price or quantity consumed, depending on the problem. The Paasche method uses *current-year weights*.

Laspeyres Price Index

Etienne Laspeyres developed a method in the latter part of the 18th century to determine a weighted price index using base-period quantities as weights. Applying his method, a weighted price index is computed by:

LASPEYRES PRICE INDEX

$$P = \frac{\Sigma p_t q_0}{\Sigma p_0 q_0} \times 100 \qquad \textbf{(17–4)}$$

where:

P is the price index.
p_t is the current price.
p_0 is the price in the base period.
q_0 is the quantity used in the base period.

EXAMPLE

The prices for the six food items from Table 17–2 are repeated on the following page in Table 17–3. Also included is the typical number of units consumed by a family in 2003 and 2015.

TABLE 17–3 Price and Quantity of Food Items in 2003 and 2015

	2003		2015	
Item	**Price**	**Quantity**	**Price**	**Quantity**
Bread, white, cost per pound	$1.042	50	$1.440	55
Eggs, dozen	1.175	26	2.133	20
Milk, gallon, white	2.686	102	3.463	130
Apples, Red Delicious, 1 pound	0.911	30	1.265	40
Orange juice, 12 oz. concentrate	1.848	40	2.678	41
Coffee, 100% ground roast, 1 pound	2.999	12	4.827	12

Determine a weighted price index using the Laspeyres method. Interpret the result.

SOLUTION

First we determine the total amount spent for the six items in the base period, 2003. To find this value, we multiply the base period, 2003, price for bread $1.042 by the base period, 2003, quantity of 50. The result is $52.10. This indicates that a total of $52.10 was spent in the base period on bread. We continue that for all items and total the results. The base period total is $493.86. The current period total is computed in a similar fashion. For the first item, bread, we multiply the quantity in 2003 by the price of bread in 2015, that is, $1.440(50). The result is $72.00. We make the same calculation for each item and total the results. The total is $683.68. Because of the repetitive nature of these calculations, a spreadsheet is very useful for creating the following table.

Laspeyres Index

	2003		03 Price*	2015		15 Price*
Item	**Price**	**Quantity**	**03 Quantity**	**Price**	**Quantity**	**03 Quantity**
Bread, white, cost per pound	$1.042	50	$ 52.10	$1.440	55	$ 72.00
Eggs, dozen	$1.175	26	$ 30.55	$2.133	20	$ 55.46
Milk, gallon, white	$2.686	102	$273.97	$3.463	130	$353.23
Apples, Red Delicious, 1 pound	$0.911	30	$ 27.33	$1.265	40	$ 37.95
Orange Juice, 12 oz concentrate	$1.848	40	$ 73.92	$2.678	41	$107.12
Coffee, 100% ground roast, 1 pound	$2.999	12	$ 35.99	$4.827	12	$ 57.92
			$493.86	Index	138.44	$683.68

The weighted price index for 2015 is 138.44, found by

$$P = \frac{\Sigma p_t q_0}{\Sigma p_0 q_0} 100 = \frac{\$683.68}{\$493.86}(100) = 138.44$$

Based on this analysis, we conclude that the price of this group of items has increased 38.44% in the 12 year period. The advantage of this method over the simple aggregate index is that the weight of each of the items is considered. In the simple aggregate index, coffee had about 40% of the weight in determining the index. In the Laspeyres index, the item with the most weight is milk because the product of the price and the units sold is the largest.

Paasche Price Index

The major disadvantage of the Laspeyres index is it assumes that the base-period quantities are still realistic in the given period. That is, the quantities used for the six items are about the same in 2003 as 2015. In this case, the quantity of eggs purchased declined by 23%, the quantity of milk increased by nearly 28%, and the quantity of apples increased by 33%.

The Paasche index is an alternative. The procedure is similar, but instead of using base-period quantities as weights, we use current-period quantities as weights. We use the sum of the products of the 2003 prices and the 2015 quantities. This has the advantage of using the more recent quantities. If there has been a change in the quantities consumed since the base period, such a change is reflected in the Paasche index.

PAASCHE PRICE INDEX

$$P = \frac{\Sigma p_t q_t}{\Sigma p_0 q_t} \times 100 \quad \textbf{(17–5)}$$

EXAMPLE

Use the information from Table 17–3 to determine the Paasche index. Discuss which of the indexes should be used.

SOLUTION

The following table shows the calculations to determine the Paasche index. Because of the repetitive calculations, Excel is very useful to compute the index.

Paasche Index

	2003		03 Price*	2015		15 Price*
Item	**Price**	**Quantity**	**13 Quantity**	**Price**	**Quantity**	**13 Quantity**
Bread, white, cost per pound	$1.04	50	$ 57.31	$1.44	55	$ 79.20
Eggs, dozen	$1.18	26	$ 23.50	$2.13	20	$ 42.66
Milk, gallon, white	$2.69	102	$349.18	$3.46	130	$450.19
Apples, Red Delicious, 1 pound	$0.91	30	$ 36.44	$1.27	40	$ 50.60
Orange Juice, 12 oz concentrate	$1.85	40	$ 75.77	$2.68	41	$109.80
Coffee, 100% ground roast, 1 pound	$3.00	12	$ 35.99	$4.83	12	$ 57.92
			$578.19	Index	136.7	$790.37

The Paasche index is 136.7, found by

$$P = \frac{\Sigma p_t q_t}{\Sigma p_0 q_t}100 = \frac{\$790.37}{\$578.19}(100) = 136.70$$

This result indicates that there has been an increase of 36.7% in the price of this "market basket" of goods between 2003 and 2015. That is, it costs 36.7% more to purchase these items in 2015 than it did in 2003.

How do we decide which index to use? When is Laspeyres most appropriate and when is Paasche the better choice?

Laspeyres

Advantages	Requires quantity data from only the base period. This allows a more meaningful comparison over time. The changes in the index can be attributed to changes in the price.
Disadvantages	Does not reflect changes in buying patterns over time. Also, it may overweight goods whose prices increase.

Paasche

Advantages	Because it uses quantities from the current period, it reflects current buying habits.
Disadvantages	It requires quantity data for the current year. Because different quantities are used each year, it is impossible to attribute changes in the index to changes in price alone. It tends to overweight the goods whose prices have declined. It requires the product of prices and quantities to be recomputed each year.

Fisher's Ideal Index

As noted earlier, Laspeyres' index tends to overweight goods whose prices have increased. Paasche's index, on the other hand, tends to overweight goods whose prices have decreased. In an attempt to offset these shortcomings, Irving Fisher, in his book *The Making of Index Numbers,* published in 1922, proposed an index called **Fisher's ideal index.** It is the geometric mean of the Laspeyres and Paasche indexes. We described the geometric mean in Chapter 3. It is determined by taking the kth root of the product of k positive numbers.

$$\text{Fisher's ideal index} = \sqrt{(\text{Laspeyres index})(\text{Paasche index})} \qquad \textbf{(17–6)}$$

Fisher's index seems to be theoretically ideal because it combines the best features of the Laspeyres and Paasche indexes. That is, it balances the effects of the two indexes. However, it is rarely used in practice because it has the same basic set of problems as the Paasche index. It requires that a new set of quantities be determined for each period.

EXAMPLE

Determine Fisher's ideal index for the data in Table 17–3.

SOLUTION

Fisher's ideal index is 137.57.

$$\begin{aligned}\text{Fisher's ideal index} &= \sqrt{(\text{Laspeyres index})(\text{Paasche index})}\\ &= \sqrt{(138.44)(136.70)} = 137.57\end{aligned}$$

SELF-REVIEW 17–2

Construct an index of clothing prices for 2016 based on 2000. The clothing items considered are shoes and dresses. The prices and quantities for both years are given below. Use 2000 as the base period and 100 as the base value.

	2000		2016	
Item	**Price**	**Quantity**	**Price**	**Quantity**
Dress (each)	$75	500	$85	520
Shoes (pair)	40	1,200	45	1,300

(a) Determine the simple average of the price indexes.
(b) Determine the aggregate price index for the two years.
(c) Determine Laspeyres price index.
(d) Determine the Paasche price index.
(e) Determine Fisher's ideal index.

EXERCISES

For exercises 5–8:

a. Determine the simple price indexes.
b. Determine the simple aggregate price index for the two years.
c. Determine Laspeyres price index.
d. Determine the Paasche price index.
e. Determine Fisher's ideal index.

5. **FILE** Below are the prices of toothpaste (9 oz.), shampoo (7 oz.), cough tablets (package of 100), and antiperspirant (2 oz.) for August 2000 and August 2017. Also included are the quantity purchased. Use August 2000 as the base.

	August 2000		August 2017	
Item	**Price**	**Quantity**	**Price**	**Quantity**
Toothpaste	$2.49	6	$3.35	6
Shampoo	3.29	4	4.49	5
Cough drops	1.59	2	4.19	3
Antiperspirant	1.79	3	2.49	4

6. **FILE** Fruit prices and the amounts consumed for 2000 and 2017 are below. Use 2000 as the base.

	2000		2017	
Fruit	**Price**	**Quantity**	**Price**	**Quantity**
Bananas (pound)	$0.23	100	$0.69	120
Grapefruit (each)	0.29	50	1.00	55
Apples (pound)	0.35	85	1.89	85
Strawberries (basket)	1.02	8	3.79	10
Oranges (bag)	0.89	6	2.99	8

7. **FILE** The prices and the numbers of various items produced by a small machine and stamping plant are reported below. Use 2000 as the base.

	2000		2017	
Item	Price	Quantity	Price	Quantity
Washer	$0.07	17,000	$0.10	20,000
Cotter pin	0.04	125,000	0.03	130,000
Stove bolt	0.15	40,000	0.15	42,000
Hex nut	0.08	62,000	0.10	65,000

8. FILE Following are the quantities and prices for the years 2000 and 2017 for Kinzua Valley Geriatrics. Use 2000 as the base period.

	2000		2017	
Item	Price	Quantity	Price	Quantity
Syringes (dozen)	$ 6.10	1,500	$ 6.83	2,000
Thermometers	8.10	10	9.35	12
Advil (bottle)	4.00	250	4.62	250
Patient record forms (box)	6.00	1,000	6.85	900
Copier paper (box)	12.00	30	13.65	40

Value Index

A **value index** measures changes in both the price and quantities involved. A value index, such as the index of department store sales, considers the base-year prices, the base-year quantities, the present-year prices, and the present-year quantities for its construction. Its formula is:

VALUE INDEX

$$V = \frac{\Sigma p_t q_t}{\Sigma p_0 q_0} \times 100 \qquad \textbf{(17–7)}$$

EXAMPLE

The prices and quantities sold at the Waleska Clothing Emporium for ties, suits, and shoes for May 2000 and May 2017 are:

	2000		2017	
Item	Price p_o	Quantity q_o	Price p_t	Quantity q_t
Ties (each)	$ 1.00	1,000	$ 2	900
Suits (each)	30.00	100	40	120
Shoes (pair)	10.00	500	8	500

What is the index of value for May 2017 using May 2000 as the base period?

SOLUTION

Total sales in May 2017 were $10,600 and the comparable figure for 2000 is $9,000. (See Table 17–4.) Thus, the value index for May 2017 using 2000 = 100 is 117.8. The value of apparel sales in 2017 was 117.8% of the 2000 sales.

To put it another way, the value of apparel sales increased 17.8% from May 2000 to May 2017.

$$V = \frac{\Sigma p_t q_t}{\Sigma p_0 q_0}(100) = \frac{\$10{,}600}{\$9{,}000}(100) = 117.8$$

TABLE 17–4 Construction of Value Index for 2017 (2000 = 100)

	2000			2017		
Item	**Price** p_0	**Quantity** q_0	**\$** p_0q_0	**Price** p_t	**Quantity** q_t	**\$** p_tq_t
Ties (each)	$ 1.00	1,000	$1,000	$ 2.00	900	$ 1,800.00
Suits (each)	30.00	100	3,000	40.00	120	4,800.00
Shoes (pair)	10.00	500	5,000	8.00	500	4,000.00
Total			$9,000	Index = 117.8		$10,600.00

SELF-REVIEW 17–3

The number of items produced by Houghton Products for 2001 and 2017 and the wholesale prices for the two periods are:

	Price		Number Produced	
Item Produced	**2001**	**2017**	**2001**	**2017**
Shear pins (box)	$ 3	$4	10,000	9,000
Cutting compound (pound)	1	5	600	200
Tie rods (each)	10	8	3,000	5,000

(a) Find the value index of production for 2017 using 2001 as the base period.
(b) Interpret the index.

EXERCISES

9. **FILE** The prices and production of grains for 2002 and 2015 (http://www.ers.usda.gov) are listed below.

Grain	2002 Price Per Bushel	2002 Production (millions of bushels)	2015 Price Per Bushel	2015 Production (millions of bushels)
Oats	$1.81	116	$2.09	90
Wheat	3.56	2	5.99	2
Corn	2.32	8,967	3.65	13,601
Barley	2.72	227	5.53	214

Using 2002 as the base period, find the value index of grains produced for 2015.

10. **FILE** Johnson Wholesale Company manufactures a variety of products. The prices and quantities produced for April 2000 and April 2017 are:

Product	2000 Price	2017 Price	2000 Quantity Produced	2017 Quantity Produced
Small motor (each)	$23.60	$28.80	1,760	4,259
Scrubbing compound (gallon)	2.96	3.08	86,450	62,949
Nails (pound)	0.40	0.48	9,460	22,370

Using April 2000 as the base period, find the value index of goods produced for April 2017.

LO17-4

List and describe special-purpose indexes.

SPECIAL-PURPOSE INDEXES

Many important indexes are prepared and published by private organizations. J. D. Power & Associates surveys automobile purchasers to determine how satisfied customers are with their vehicle after one year of ownership. This special index is called the *Consumer Satisfaction Index.* Financial institutions, utility companies, and university research centers often prepare indexes on employment, factory hours and wages, and retail sales for the regions they serve. Many trade associations prepare indexes of price and quantity that are vital to their particular area of interest. How are these special indexes prepared? An example will explain the details.

EXAMPLE

The Seattle Chamber of Commerce wants to develop a measure of general business activity for the northwest portion of the United States. The director of economic development has been assigned to develop the index. It will be called the *General Business Activity Index of the Northwest.*

SOLUTION

After considerable thought and research, the director concluded that four factors should be considered: the regional department store sales (which are reported in $ millions), the regional employment index (which has a 2005 base and is reported by the State of Washington), the freight car loadings (reported in millions), and exports for the Seattle Harbor (reported in thousands of tons). Table 17–5 shows this information for years 2005, 2010, and 2016.

TABLE 17–5 Data for Computation of the General Business Activity Index of the Northwest

Year	Department Store Sales	Index of Employment	Freight Car Loadings	Exports
2005	20	100	50	500
2010	41	110	30	900
2016	44	125	18	700

After review and consultation, the director assigned weights of 40% to department store sales, 30% to employment, 10% to freight car loadings, and 20% to exports. To develop the General Business Activity Index of the Northwest for

2016 using 2005 = 100, each 2016 value is expressed as a percentage, with the base-period value as the denominator. For illustration, department store sales for 2016 are converted to a percentage by ($44/$20)(100) = 220. This means that department store sales have increased 120% in the period. This percentage is then multiplied by the appropriate weight. For the department store sales, this is (220)(.40) = 88.0. The details of the calculations for the years 2010 and 2016 are shown below.

	2010	2016
Department store sales	[($41)/($20)][100][.40] = 82.0	[($44)/($20)][100][.40] = 88.0
Index of employment	[(110)/(100)][100][.30] = 33.0	[(125)/(100)][100][.30] = 37.5
Freight car loadings	[(30)/(50)][100][.10] = 6.0	[(18)/(50)][100][.10] = 3.6
Experts	[(900)/(500)][100][.20] = 36.0	[(700)/(500)][100][.20] = 28.0
Total	157.0	157.1

The General Business Activity Index of the Northwest for 2010 is 157.0 and for 2016 it is 157.1. Interpreting, business activity has increased 57.0% from 2005 to 2010 and 57.1% from the base period of 2005 to 2016.

As we stated at the start of the section, there are many special-purpose indexes. Here are a few examples.

Consumer Price Index

The U.S. Bureau of Labor Statistics reports this index monthly. It describes the changes in prices from one period to another for a "market basket" of goods and services. We discuss its history in detail and present some applications in the next section. You can access this information by going to http://www.bls.gov, then under **Data Tools** select **Inflation and Prices,** then select **All Urban Consumers (Current Series), Top Picks,** and then click on **U.S. All items 1982–84 = 100.** You may elect to include different periods. Following is a recent summary report.

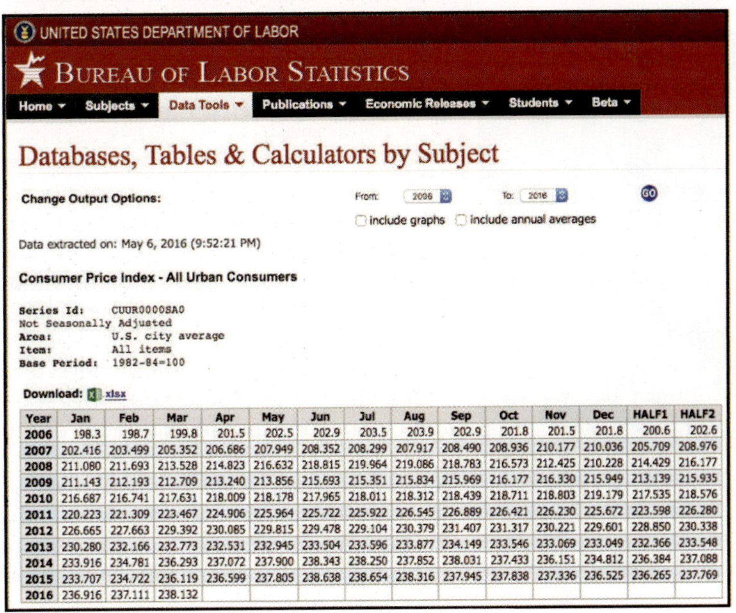

UNITED STATES DEPARTMENT OF LABOR

BUREAU OF LABOR STATISTICS

Home ▾ Subjects ▾ Data Tools ▾ Publications ▾ Economic Releases ▾ Students ▾ Beta ▾

Databases, Tables & Calculators by Subject

Change Output Options: From: 2006 To: 2016 GO

include graphs include annual averages

Data extracted on: May 6, 2016 (9:52:21 PM)

Consumer Price Index - All Urban Consumers

Series Id: CUUR0000SA0
Not Seasonally Adjusted
Area: U.S. city average
Item: All items
Base Period: 1982-84=100

Download: xlsx

Year	Jan	Feb	Mar	Apr	May	Jun	Jul	Aug	Sep	Oct	Nov	Dec	HALF1	HALF2
2006	198.3	198.7	199.8	201.5	202.5	202.9	203.5	203.9	202.9	201.8	201.5	201.8	200.6	202.6
2007	202.416	203.499	205.352	206.686	207.949	208.352	208.299	207.917	208.490	208.936	210.177	210.036	205.709	208.976
2008	211.080	211.693	213.528	214.823	216.632	218.815	219.964	219.086	218.783	216.573	212.425	210.228	214.429	216.177
2009	211.143	212.193	212.709	213.240	213.856	215.693	215.351	215.834	215.969	216.177	216.330	215.949	213.139	215.935
2010	216.687	216.741	217.631	218.009	218.178	217.965	218.011	218.312	218.439	218.711	218.803	219.179	217.535	218.576
2011	220.223	221.309	223.467	224.906	225.964	225.722	225.922	226.545	226.889	226.421	226.230	225.672	223.598	226.280
2012	226.665	227.663	229.392	230.085	229.815	229.478	229.104	230.379	231.407	231.317	230.221	229.601	228.850	230.338
2013	230.280	232.166	232.773	232.531	232.945	233.504	233.596	233.877	234.149	233.546	233.069	233.049	232.366	233.548
2014	233.916	234.781	236.293	237.072	237.900	238.343	238.250	237.852	238.031	237.433	236.151	234.812	236.384	237.088
2015	233.707	234.722	236.119	236.599	237.805	238.638	238.654	238.316	237.945	237.838	237.336	236.525	236.265	237.769
2016	236.916	237.111	238.132											

Producer Price Index

Formerly called the Wholesale Price Index, it dates back to 1890 and is also published by the U.S. Bureau of Labor Statistics. It reflects the prices of over 3,400 commodities. Price data are collected from the sellers of the commodities, and it usually refers to the first large-volume transaction for each commodity. It is a Laspeyres-type index. To access this information, go to http://www.bls.gov, then **Data Tools.** Select **Inflation and Prices,** then select **Commodity Data, Top Picks,** and finally select **Finished Goods.** You may select to include different periods. Below is a recent output.

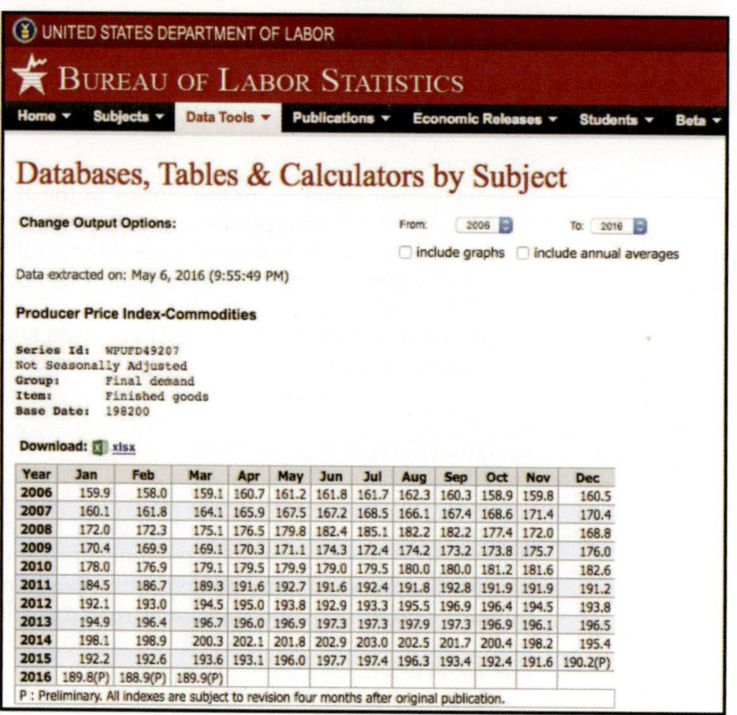

UNITED STATES DEPARTMENT OF LABOR

BUREAU OF LABOR STATISTICS

Home ▾ Subjects ▾ Data Tools ▾ Publications ▾ Economic Releases ▾ Students ▾ Beta ▾

Databases, Tables & Calculators by Subject

Change Output Options: From: 2006 To: 2016

include graphs include annual averages

Data extracted on: May 6, 2016 (9:55:49 PM)

Producer Price Index-Commodities

```
Series Id:   WPUFD49207
Not Seasonally Adjusted
Group:       Final demand
Item:        Finished goods
Base Date:   198200
```

Download: xlsx

Year	Jan	Feb	Mar	Apr	May	Jun	Jul	Aug	Sep	Oct	Nov	Dec
2006	159.9	158.0	159.1	160.7	161.2	161.8	161.7	162.3	160.3	158.9	159.8	160.5
2007	160.1	161.8	164.1	165.9	167.5	167.2	168.5	166.1	167.4	168.6	171.4	170.4
2008	172.0	172.3	175.1	176.5	179.8	182.4	185.1	182.2	182.2	177.4	172.0	168.8
2009	170.4	169.9	169.1	170.3	171.1	174.3	172.4	174.2	173.2	173.8	175.7	176.0
2010	178.0	176.9	179.1	179.5	179.9	179.0	179.5	180.0	180.0	181.2	181.6	182.6
2011	184.5	186.7	189.3	191.6	192.7	191.6	192.4	191.8	192.8	191.9	191.9	191.2
2012	192.1	193.0	194.5	195.0	193.8	192.9	193.3	195.5	196.9	196.4	194.5	193.8
2013	194.9	196.4	196.7	196.0	196.9	197.3	197.3	197.9	197.3	196.9	196.1	196.5
2014	198.1	198.9	200.3	202.1	201.8	202.9	203.0	202.5	201.7	200.4	198.2	195.4
2015	192.2	192.6	193.6	193.1	196.0	197.7	197.4	196.3	193.4	192.4	191.6	190.2(P)
2016	189.8(P)	188.9(P)	189.9(P)									

P : Preliminary. All indexes are subject to revision four months after original publication.

© Image Ideas Inc./Picture Quest

Dow Jones Industrial Average (DJIA)

This is an index of stock prices, but perhaps it would be better to say it is an "indicator" rather than an index. It is supposed to be the mean price of 30 specific industrial stocks. However, summing the 30 stock prices and dividing by 30 does not calculate its value because, over time, stocks split, companies merged, and stocks have been added or dropped. When changes in the 30 selected stocks occur, adjustments are made in the denominator used to compute the average. Today the DJIA is more of a psychological indicator than a representation of the general price movement on the New York Stock Exchange. The lack of representativeness of the stocks on the DJIA is one of the reasons for the development of the **New York Stock Exchange Index.** This index was developed as an average price of *all* stocks on the New York Stock Exchange. More information about the Dow Jones Industrial Average is available by going to the website: http://www.dowjones.com. You can find the current value of the DJIA by going to http://www.marketwatch.com. The default is to show the change in the Dow, NASDAQ, S&P 500, and others for the current day.

By clicking on **DJIA F** you can find additional detail on changes. At the bottom center of the chart you can change the horizontal scale to show the changes for a day, 5 days, and so on up to 5 years. In this case we changed the scale to show the changes for a year. Information on the NASDAQ and the S&P 500 is available by clicking on them as well.

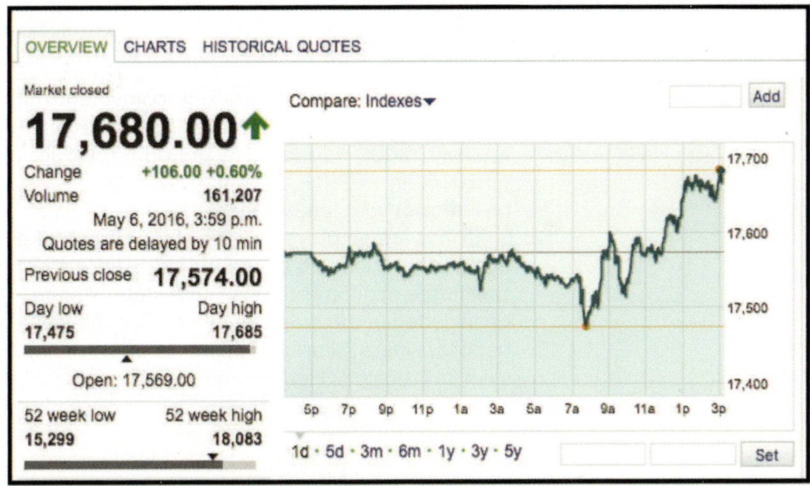

SELF-REVIEW 17–4

As an intern in the Fulton County Economic Development Office, you have been asked to develop a special-purpose index for your county. Three economic series seem to hold promise as the basis of an index. These data are the price of cotton (per pound), the number of new automobiles sold in the county, and the rate of money turnover (published by the local bank). After discussing the project with your supervisor and the director, you decide that money turnover should have a weight of .60, the number of new automobiles sold a weight of .30, and the cotton price a weight of .10. The base period is 2006.

Year	Cotton Price	Automobiles Sold	Money Turnover
2006	$0.20	1,000	80
2011	0.25	1,200	90
2016	0.50	900	75

(a) Construct the index for 2011 and 2016.
(b) Interpret the index for 2011 and 2016.

EXERCISES

11. FILE The index of leading economic indicators, compiled and published by the U.S. National Bureau of Economic Research, is composed of 12 time series, such as the average work hours of production in manufacturing, manufacturers' new orders, and money supply. This index and similar indexes are designed to move up or down before the economy begins to move the same way. Thus, an economist has statistical evidence to forecast future trends.

    You want to construct a leading indicator for Erie County in upstate New York. The index is to be based on 2000 data. Because of the time and work involved, you decide to use only four time series. As an experiment, you select these four series: unemployment in the county, a composite index of county stock prices, the County Price Index, and retail sales. Here are the figures for 2000 and 2016.

	2000	2016
Unemployment rate (percent)	5.3	6.8
Composite county stocks	265.88	362.26
County Price Index (1982 = 100)	109.6	125.0
Retail sales ($ millions)	529,917.0	622,864.0

    The weights you assign are unemployment rate 20%, stock prices 40%, County Price Index 25%, and retail sales 15%.
    a. Using 2000 as the base period, construct a leading economic indicator for 2016.
    b. Interpret your leading index.

12. FILE You are employed by the state bureau of economic development. There is a demand for a leading economic index to review past economic activity and to forecast future economic trends in the state. You decide that several key factors should be included in the index: number of new businesses started during the year, number of business failures, state income tax receipts, college enrollment, and the state sales tax receipts. Here are the data for 2000 and 2016.

	2000	2016
New businesses	1,088	1,162
Business failures	627	520
State income tax receipts ($ millions)	191.7	162.6
College student enrollment	242,119	290,841
State sales tax ($ millions)	41.6	39.9

    a. Decide on the weights to be applied to each item in the leading index.
    b. Compute the leading economic indicator for 2016.
    c. Interpret the indexes.

LO17-5
Apply the Consumer Price Index.

CONSUMER PRICE INDEX

Frequent mention has been made of the Consumer Price Index (CPI) in the preceding pages. It measures the change in price of a fixed market basket of goods and services from one period to another. In January 1978, the Bureau of Labor Statistics began publishing CPIs for two groups of the population. One index, called the Consumer Price Index—All Urban Consumers, covers about 87% of the total population. The other index is for urban wage earners and clerical workers and covers about 32% of the population.

STATISTICS IN ACTION

Does it seem that prices only increase? The Consumer Price Index, computed and reported by the U.S. Department of Labor, is a relative measure of price changes. It shows interesting price information for categories of products and services. For example, did you know that the CPI for personal computers and peripheral equipment was 45.269 in March 2016? Using a base of December 2007, this means that relative prices for computers and peripherals have decreased about 55% since December 2007.

The CPI serves several major functions. It allows consumers to determine the degree to which their purchasing power is being eroded by price increases. In that respect, it is a yardstick for revising wages, pensions, and other income payments to keep pace with changes in prices. Equally important, it is an economic indicator of the rate of inflation in the United States.

The index is based on the prices of 80,000 items collected monthly by about 250 agents. Prices are collected from thousands of U.S. retail stores, service establishments, rental units, and doctors' offices (http://stats.bls.gov/cpi/cpifaq.htm). Bread, beer, gasoline, haircuts, mortgage interest rates, physicians' fees, taxes, and operating-room charges are just a few of the items included in what is often termed a "market basket" of goods and services that a typical consumer purchases.

The CPI originated in 1913 and has been published regularly since 1921. The standard reference period (the base period) has been updated periodically. The current base period is 1982–84. The earlier base periods were 1967, 1957–59, 1947–49, 1935–39, and 1925–29. Why is it necessary to change the base? Our purchasing patterns that determine the "market basket" of goods and services change dramatically, and these changes must be reflected in the base period prices.

The CPI is actually not just one index. There are Consumer Price Indexes for New York, Chicago, Seattle, and Atlanta, as well as a number of other large cities. There are also price indexes for food, apparel, medical care, and other items. A few of them are shown below, 1982–84 = 100, for March 2016.

Item	CPI-U
All items	238.132
Food and beverage	247.677
Apparel	127.427
Transportation	191.257
Medical care	458.620
Housing	241.485

A review of this list shows that a weighted index of all items has increased 138.132% since 1982–84; medical care has increased the most, 358.620%; and apparel went up the least, 27.427%.

Special Uses of the Consumer Price Index

In addition to measuring changes in the prices of goods and services, both consumer price indexes have a number of other applications. The CPI is used to determine real disposable personal income, to deflate sales or other variables, to find the purchasing power of the dollar, and to establish cost-of-living increases. We first discuss the use of the CPI in determining **real income.**

Real Income As an example of the meaning and computation of *real income,* assume the Consumer Price Index is presently 200 with 1982–84 = 100. Also, assume that Ms. Watts earned $20,000 per year in the base period of 1982, 1983, and 1984. She has a current income of $40,000. Note that although her *money income* has doubled since the base period of 1982–84, the prices she paid for food, gasoline, clothing, and other items have also doubled. Thus, Ms. Watts' standard of living has remained the same from the base period to the present time. Price increases have exactly offset an increase in income, so her present buying power (real income) is still $20,000. (See Table 17–6 for computations.) In general:

REAL INCOME

$$\text{Real income} = \frac{\text{Money income}}{\text{CPI}} \times 100 \qquad \textbf{(17–8)}$$

TABLE 17–6 Computation of Real Income for 1982–84 and Present Year

Year	Annual Money Income	Consumer Price Index (1982–84 = 100)	Computation of Real Income	Real Income
1982–84	$20,000	100	$\frac{\$20{,}000}{100}(100)$	$20,000
Present year	40,000	200	$\frac{\$40{,}000}{200}(100)$	20,000

The concept of real income is sometimes called *deflated income,* and the CPI is called the *deflator.* Also, a popular term for deflated income is *income expressed in constant dollars.* Thus, in Table 17–6, to determine whether Ms. Watts' standard of living changed, her money income was converted to constant dollars. We found that her purchasing power, expressed in 1982–84 dollars (constant dollars), remained at $20,000.

SELF-REVIEW 17–5

The take-home pay of Jon Greene and the CPI for 2000 and 2016 are:

Year	Take-Home Pay	CPI (1982–84 = 100)
2000	$25,000	170.8
2016	41,200	238.132

(a) What was Jon's real income in 2000?
(b) What was his real income in 2016?
(c) Interpret your findings.

Deflating Sales A price index can also be used to "deflate" sales or similar money series. Deflated sales are determined by

USING AN INDEX AS A DEFLATOR

$$\text{Deflated sales} = \frac{\text{Actual sales}}{\text{An appropriate index}} \times 100 \quad \textbf{(17–9)}$$

EXAMPLE

The sales of Hill Enterprises, a small injection molding company in upstate New York, increased from 1982 to 2015. The following table shows the increase.

Year	$ Sales
1982	875,000
1990	1,482,000
1995	1,491,000
2000	1,502,000
2005	1.515,000
2010	1,596,000
2015	1,697,000

The owner, Harry Hill, realizes that the price of raw materials used in the process also has increased over the period, so Mr. Hill wants to deflate sales to account for the increase in raw material prices. What are the deflated sales for 1990, 1995, 2000, 2005, 2010, and 2015 expressed in constant 1982 dollars?

SOLUTION

The Producer Price Index (PPI) is an index released every month and published in the *Monthly Labor Review;* it is also available at the Bureau of Labor Statistics website. The prices included in the PPI reflect the prices the manufacturer pays for the metals, rubber, and other purchased raw materials. So the PPI seems an appropriate index to use to deflate the manufacturer's sales. The manufacturer's sales are listed in the second column of Table 17–7, and the PPI for each year is in the third column. The next column shows sales divided by the PPI. The right-hand column details the calculations.

TABLE 17–7 Calculation of Deflated Sales for Hill Enterprises

Year	Sales	PPI	Constant Dollars	Found by
1982	$ 875,000	100.0	$ 875,000.00	($875,000/100.0)*(100)
1990	1,482,000	119.2	1.243.288.59	($1,482,000/119.2)*(100)
1995	1,491,000	127.9	1,165,754.50	($1,491,000/127.9)*(100)
2000	1,502,000	138.0	1,088,405.80	($1,502,000/138.0)*(100)
2005	1,515,000	155.7	973,025.05	($1,515,000/155.7)*(100)
2010	1,596,000	179.8	887,652.95	($1,596,000/179.8)*(100)
2015	1,697,000	193.9	875,193.40	($1,697,000/193.9)*(100)

Sales increased from 1982 through 2015; in fact, they increased by 93.9% [($1,697,000/$875,000)*100] – 100.0. However, if we compare the sales in 1982 and 2015, they are nearly the same, $875,000 versus $875,193.

Purchasing Power of the Dollar The Consumer Price Index is also used to determine the *purchasing power of the dollar.*

USING AN INDEX TO FIND PURCHASING POWER

$$\text{Purchasing power of dollar} = \frac{\$1}{\text{CPI}} \times 100 \qquad \textbf{(17–10)}$$

EXAMPLE

Suppose the Consumer Price Index this month is 200.0 (1982–84 = 100). What is the purchasing power of the dollar?

SOLUTION

From formula (17–10), it is 50 cents, found by:

$$\text{Purchasing power of dollar} = \frac{\$1}{200.0}(100) = \$0.50$$

The CPI of 200.0 indicates that prices have doubled from the years 1982–84 to this month. Thus, the purchasing power of a dollar has been cut in half. That is, a 1982–84 dollar is worth only 50 cents this month. To put it another way, if you lost $1,000 in the period 1982–84 and just found it, the $1,000 could only buy half of what it could have bought in the years 1982, 1983, and 1984.

Cost-of-Living Adjustments The Consumer Price Index (CPI) is also the basis for cost-of-living adjustments, or COLAs, in many management–union contracts. The specific clause in the contract is often referred to as the "escalator clause." About 31 million

Social Security beneficiaries, 2.5 million retired military and federal civil service employees and survivors, and 600,000 postal workers have their incomes or pensions pegged to the CPI.

The CPI is also used to adjust alimony and child support payments; attorneys' fees; workers' compensation payments; rentals on apartments, homes, and office buildings; welfare payments; and so on. A retiree receives a pension of $500 a month and the CPI increases 5 points from 165 to 170. Suppose for each percentage point the CPI increases, the pension benefits increase 1 percent, so the monthly increase in benefits will be $15.15, found by [(170 − 165)/165] × 500. Now the retiree will receive $515.15 per month.

SELF-REVIEW 17–6

The Consumer Price Index for the latest month is 238.132 (1982–84 = 100). What is the purchasing power of the dollar? Interpret.

Shifting the Base

If two or more time series have the same base period, they can be compared directly. As an example, suppose we are interested in the trend in the prices of food and beverages, housing, apparel and upkeep, and medical care since the base period, 1982–84. Note in Table 17–8 that all of the consumer price indexes use the same base.

TABLE 17–8 Trend in Consumer Price to 2015 (1982–84 = 100)

Year	All Items	Food and Beverages	Housing	Apparel Upkeep	Medical Care
1982–84	100.0	100.0	100.0	100.0	100.0
1990	130.7	132.1	128.5	124.1	162.8
1995	152.4	148.9	148.5	132	220.5
2000	172.2	168.4	169.6	129.6	260.8
2005	195.3	191.2	195.7	119.5	323.2
2010	218.056	219.984	216.256	119.503	388.436
2015	237.017	246.804	238.060	125.903	446.752

Table 17–8 shows that the price of all consumer items combined increased 137.017% from the base period (1982–84) to the year 2015. (Beginning with January 2007, the CPI is reported to three decimal places instead of one.) Likewise, food and beverage prices increased 146.804%, housing prices increased 138.060%, apparel and upkeep increased 25.903%, and medical care increased 346.752%.

A problem arises, however, when comparing two or more series that do not have the same base period. The following example compares the two most widely reported stock market indexes, the DJIA and NASDAQ.

EXAMPLE

We want to compare the opening prices of the Dow Jones Industrial Average (DJIA) and the NASDAQ Composite on the first trading day of the year for 2004 through 2016.

Date	Opening Price DJIA	NASDAQ
1/2/04	$10,452.74	$2,011.08
1/3/05	10,783.75	2,184.75
1/5/06	10,718.30	2,216.53
1/3/07	12,459.54	2,429.72
1/2/08	13,261.82	2,653.91
1/2/09	8,772.25	1,578.87
1/4/10	10,430.69	2,294.41
1/3/11	11,577.43	2,676.65
1/3/12	12,221.19	2,657.39
1/2/13	13,104.30	3,091.33
1/2/14	16,572.17	4160.03
1/2/15	17,823.07	4760.24
1/4/16	17,405.48	4897.65

SOLUTION

A direct comparison of the DJIA and NASDAQ opening prices is not appropriate. Because we want to compare changes in the opening prices for the two markets, a logical approach is to compute indexes for each market using the 2004 opening price as the base. For the DJIA, the base is \$10,452.74, and for the NASDAQ it is \$2,011.08.

The calculation of the index for the DJIA in 2016 is:

$$\text{Index} = \frac{\$17{,}405.48}{\$10{,}452.74}(100) = 166.52$$

The following table reports the complete set of indexes.

	DJIA		NASDAQ	
Date	Value	Index	Value	Index
1/2/04	$10,452.74	100.0	$2,011.08	100.0
1/3/05	10,783.75	103.2	2,184.75	108.6
1/5/06	10,718.30	102.5	2,216.53	110.2
1/3/07	12,459.54	119.2	2,429.72	120.8
1/2/08	13,261.82	126.9	2,653.91	132.0
1/2/09	8,772.25	83.9	1,578.87	78.5
1/4/10	10,430.69	99.8	2,294.41	114.1
1/3/11	11,577.43	110.8	2,676.65	133.1
1/3/12	12,221.19	116.9	2,657.39	132.1
1/2/13	13,104.30	125.4	3,091.33	153.7
1/2/14	16,572.17	158.5	4160.03	206.9
1/2/15	17,823.07	170.5	4760.24	236.7
1/4/16	17,405.48	166.5	4897.65	243.5

We conclude that both indexes have increased over the period. The DJIA has increased 66.5% and the NASDAQ 143.5%.

The following chart shows the DJIA indexes in blue and NASDAQ indexes in brown. The graph shows the changes for both indexes starting from the base of January 2, 2004. From this graph we conclude that the NASDAQ reached its high at the start of the year 2016. The high for the Dow was in January 2016. In general, the two indexes seem to mirror each other rather closely. We should point out that if we select different periods as the base, the results may not be exactly the same. One should always be cautious of the base period selected for a chart or a graph.

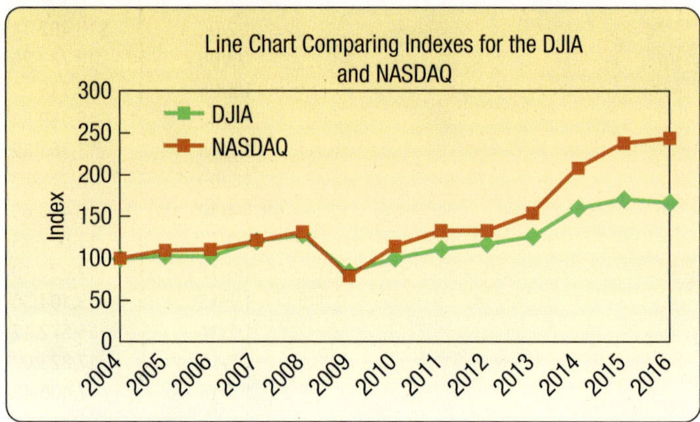

SELF-REVIEW 17–7

The changes in industrial production and in the prices manufacturers paid for raw materials are to be compared. Unfortunately, the index of industrial production, which measures changes in production, and the Producer Price Index for raw materials have different base periods. The production index has a 2012 base period and the Producer Price Index uses 1982 as the base period. The following table reports the value of each index at the start of the year. Compare the two series using 2010 as the base. Interpret the results.

Year	Industrial Production Index (2012 = 100)	Producer Price Index (1982 = 100)
2007	104.98	162.9
2008	101.25	175.8
2009	89.60	167.1
2010	94.52	175.4
2011	97.28	189.1
2012	100.00	193.9
2013	101.91	193.9
2014	104.89	195.5
2015	105.22	185.6

EXERCISES

13. In April 2013, the mean salary for a nurse manager with a bachelor's degree was $89,673. The Consumer Price Index for March 2016 was 238.132 (1982–84 = 100). The mean annual salary for a nurse in the base period of 1982–84 was $19,800. What was the real income of the nurse in March 2016? How much had the mean salary increased?

14. The Trade Union Association of Orlando, Florida, maintains indexes on the hourly wages for a number of the trades. Unfortunately, the indexes do not all have the same base periods. Listed below is information on plumbers and electricians. Shift the base periods to 2000 and compare the hourly wage increases for the period from 2000 to 2016.

Year	Plumbers (1995 = 100)	Electricians (1998 = 100)
2000	133.8	126.0
2016	159.4	158.7

15. In 2000, the mean salary of classroom teachers in Tinora School District was \$28,650. By 2010, the mean salary increased to \$33,972, and further increased in 2016 to \$37,382. The American Federation of Classroom Teachers maintains information on the trends throughout the United States in classroom teacher salaries. Its index, which has a base period of 2000, was 122.5 for 2010 and 136.9 for 2016. Compare the Tinora teachers to the national trends.
16. FILE Sam Steward is a freelance Web page designer. Listed below are his yearly wages for several years between 2013 and 2016. Also included is an industry index for Web page designers that reports the rate of wage inflation in the industry. This index has a base period of 2000.

Year	Wage (\$000)	Index (2000 = 100)
2013	134.8	160.6
2014	145.2	173.6
2015	156.6	187.9
2016	168.8	203.3

Compute Sam's real income for the selected years during the six-year period. Did his wages keep up with inflation, or did he lose ground?

CHAPTER SUMMARY

I. An index number measures the relative change from one period to another.
 A. The major characteristics of an index are:
  1. It is a percentage, but the percent sign is usually omitted.
  2. It has a base period.
 B. The reasons for computing an index are:
  1. It facilitates the comparison of unlike series.
  2. If the numbers are very large, often it is easier to comprehend the change of the index than the actual numbers.

II. There are two types of price indexes, unweighted and weighted.
 A. In an unweighted index, we do not consider the quantities.
  1. In a simple index, we compare the base period to the given period.

$$P = \frac{p_t}{p_0} \times 100 \qquad \textbf{(17–1)}$$

where p_t refers to the price in the current period and p_0 is the price in the base period.
  2. In the simple average of price indexes, we add the simple indexes for each item and divide by the number of items.

$$P = \frac{\Sigma P_i}{n} \qquad \textbf{(17–2)}$$

  3. In a simple aggregate price index, the price of the items in the group are totaled for both periods and compared.

$$P = \frac{\Sigma p_t}{\Sigma p_0} \times 100 \qquad \textbf{(17–3)}$$

 B. In a weighted index, the quantities are considered.
  1. In the Laspeyres method, the base period quantities are used in both the base period and the given period.

$$P = \frac{\Sigma p_t q_0}{\Sigma p_0 q_0} \times 100 \qquad \textbf{(17–4)}$$

2. In the Paasche method, current period quantities are used.

$$P = \frac{\Sigma p_t q_t}{\Sigma p_0 q_t} \times 100 \qquad \textbf{(17–5)}$$

3. Fisher's ideal index is the geometric mean of the Laspeyres and Paasche indexes.

$$\text{Fisher's ideal index} = \sqrt{(\text{Laspeyres index})(\text{Paasche index})} \qquad \textbf{(17–6)}$$

C. A value index uses both base period and current period prices and quantities.

$$V = \frac{\Sigma p_t q_t}{\Sigma p_0 q_0} \times 100 \qquad \textbf{(17–7)}$$

III. The most widely reported index is the Consumer Price Index (CPI).

A. It is often used to show the rate of inflation in the United States.
B. It is reported monthly by the U.S. Bureau of Labor Statistics.
C. The current base period is 1982–84.
D. CPI is used to compute "real" income and purchasing power and to adjust pensions and tax brackets.

CHAPTER EXERCISES

For exercises 17 through 22, use the following information taken from Johnson & Johnson annual reports. The principal office of Johnson & Johnson is in New Brunswick, New Jersey. Its common stock is listed on the New York Stock Exchange, using the symbol JNJ.

Year	Domestic Sales ($ million)	International Sales ($ million)	Employees (thousands)
2000	17,316	11,856	100.9
2001	19,825	12,492	101.8
2002	22,455	13,843	108.3
2003	25,274	16,588	110.6
2004	27,770	19,578	109.9
2005	28,377	22,137	115.6
2006	29,775	23,549	122.2
2007	32,444	28,651	119.2
2008	32,309	31,438	118.7
2009	30,889	31,008	115.5
2010	29,437	32,124	114.0
2011	28,907	36,107	117.9
2012	29,830	37,394	127.6
2013	31,910	39,402	128.1
2014	34,782	39,548	126.5
2015	35,687	34,387	127.1

17. FILE Using 2000 as the base period, compute a simple index of domestic sales for each year from 2004 until 2015. Interpret the trend in domestic sales.
18. FILE Using the period 2000–02 as the base period, compute a simple index of domestic sales for each year from 2004 to 2015.
19. FILE Using 2000 as the base period, compute a simple index of international sales for each year from 2004 until 2015. Interpret the trend in international sales.
20. FILE Using the period 2000–02 as the base period, compute a simple index of international sales for each year from 2004 to 2015.
21. FILE Using 2000 as the base period, compute a simple index of the number of employees for each year from 2004 until 2015. Interpret the trend in the number of employees.
22. FILE Using the period 2000–02 as the base period, compute a simple index of the number of employees for each year from 2004 to 2015.

For exercises 23 through 26, use the following information from General Electric Corporation's annual reports.

Year	Revenue ($ million)	Employees (000)	Year	Revenue ($ million)	Employees (000)
2004	134	325	2010	150	304
2005	152	307	2011	147	287
2006	157	316	2012	147	301
2007	168	319	2013	146	307
2008	177	327	2014	149	305
2009	183	323	2015	151	333

23. FILE Compute a simple index for the revenue of GE. Use 2004 as the base period. What can you conclude about the change in revenue over the period?

24. FILE Compute a simple index for the revenue of GE using the period 2004–06 as the base. What can you conclude about the change in revenue over the period?

25. FILE Compute a simple index for the number of employees for GE. Use 2004 as the base period. What can you conclude about the change in the number of employees over the period?

26. FILE Compute a simple index for the number of employees for GE using the period 2004–06 as the base. What can you conclude about the change in the number of employees over the period?

For exercises 27 through 32, use the following information on food items for the years 2000 and 2016.

	2000		2016	
Item	Price	Quantity	Price	Quantity
Margarine (pound)	$0.81	18	$2.00	27
Shortening (pound)	0.84	5	1.88	9
Milk (½ gallon)	1.44	70	2.89	65
Potato chips	2.91	27	3.99	33

27. FILE Compute a simple price index for each of the four items. Use 2000 as the base period.

28. FILE Compute a simple aggregate price index. Use 2000 as the base period.

29. FILE Compute Laspeyres' price index for 2016 using 2000 as the base period.

30. FILE Compute Paasche's index for 2016 using 2000 as the base period.

31. FILE Determine Fisher's ideal index using the values for the Laspeyres and Paasche indexes computed in the two previous problems.

32. FILE Determine a value index for 2016 using 2000 as the base period.

For exercises 33 through 38, use the following information. Betts Electronics purchases three replacement parts for robotic machines used in its manufacturing process. Information on the price of the replacement parts and the quantity purchased is given below.

	Price		Quantity	
Part	2000	2016	2000	2016
RC-33	$0.50	$0.60	320	340
SM-14	1.20	0.90	110	130
WC50	0.85	1.00	230	250

33. FILE Compute a simple price index for each of the three items. Use 2000 as the base period.

34. FILE Compute a simple aggregate price index for 2016. Use 2000 as the base period.

35. FILE Compute Laspeyres' price index for 2016 using 2000 as the base period.
36. FILE Compute Paasche's index for 2016 using 2000 as the base period.
37. FILE Determine Fisher's ideal index using the values for the Laspeyres and Paasche indexes computed in the two previous problems.
38. FILE Determine a value index for 2016 using 2000 as the base period.

For exercises 39 through 44, use the following price information for selected foods for 2000 and 2016 given in the following table.

	Price		Quantity	
Item	**2000**	**2016**	**2000**	**2016**
Cabbage (pound)	$0.06	$0.05	2,000	1,500
Carrots (bunch)	0.10	0.12	200	200
Peas (quart)	0.20	0.18	400	500
Endive (bunch)	0.15	0.15	100	200

39. FILE Compute a simple price index for each of the four items. Use 2000 as the base period.
40. FILE Compute a simple aggregate price index. Use 2000 as the base period.
41. FILE Compute Laspeyres' price index for 2016 using 2000 as the base period.
42. FILE Compute Paasche's index for 2016 using 2000 as the base period.
43. FILE Determine Fisher's ideal index using the values for the Laspeyres and Paasche indexes computed in the two previous problems.
44. FILE Determine a value index for 2016 using 2000 as the base period.

For exercises 45 through 50, use the following price information for selected items for 1990 and 2016. Production figures for those two periods are also given.

	Price		Quantity	
Item	**1990**	**2016**	**1990**	**2016**
Aluminum (cents per pound)	$ 0.287	$ 0.73	1,000	1,200
Natural gas (1,000 cu. ft.)	0.17	2.12	5,000	4,000
Petroleum (barrel)	3.18	44.08	60,000	60,000
Platinum (troy ounce)	133.00	1,904.30	500	600

45. FILE Compute a simple price index for each of the four items. Use 1990 as the base period.
46. FILE Compute a simple aggregate price index. Use 1990 as the base period.
47. FILE Compute Laspeyres' price index for 2016 using 1990 as the base period.
48. FILE Compute Paasche's index for 2016 using 1990 as the base period.
49. FILE Determine Fisher's ideal index using the values for the Laspeyres and Paasche indexes computed in the two previous problems.
50. FILE Determine a value index for 2016 using 1990 as the base period.
51. FILE A special-purpose index is to be designed to monitor the overall economy of the Southwest. Four key series were selected. After considerable deliberation, it was decided to weight retail sales 20%, total bank deposits 10%, industrial production in the area 40%, and nonagricultural employment 30%. The data for 1996 and 2016 are:

Year	Retail Sales ($ millions)	Bank Deposits ($ billions)	Industrial Production (1990 = 100)	Employment
1996	1,159.0	87	110.6	1,214,000
2016	1,971.0	91	114.7	1,501,000

Construct a special-purpose index for 2016 using 1996 as the base period and interpret.

52. FILE We are making a historical study of the American economy from 1950 to 1980. Data on prices, the labor force, productivity, and the GNP were collected. Note in the

following table that the CPI has a base period of 1967, employment is in millions of persons, and so on. A direct comparison, therefore, is not feasible.

a. Make whatever calculations are necessary to compare the trend in the four series from 1950 to 1980.

b. Interpret.

Year	Consumer Price Index (1967 = 100)	Total Labor Force (millions)	Index of Productivity in Manufacturing (1967 = 100)	Gross National Product ($ billions)
1950	72.1	64	64.9	286.2
1967	100.0	81	100.0	789.6
1971	121.3	87	110.3	1,063.4
1975	161.2	95	114.9	1,516.3
1980	246.8	107	146.6	2,626.0

53. FILE The management of Ingalls Super Discount stores, with several stores in the Oklahoma City area, wants to construct an index of economic activity for the metropolitan area. Management contends that, if the index reveals that the economy is slowing down, inventory should be kept at a low level.

Three series seem to hold promise as predictors of economic activity–area retail sales, bank deposits, and employment. All of these data can be secured monthly from the U.S. government. Retail sales is to be weighted 40%, bank deposits 35%, and employment 25%. Seasonally adjusted data for the first 3 months of the year are:

Month	Retail Sales ($ millions)	Bank Deposits ($ billions)	Employment (thousands)
January	8.0	20	300
February	6.8	23	303
March	6.4	21	297

Construct an index of economic activity for each of the 3 months, using January as the base period.

54. FILE The following table gives information on the Consumer Price Index (Base = 1982–84) and the monthly take-home pay of Bill Martin, an employee at Ford Motor Corporation.

Year	Consumer Price Index (1982–84 = 100)	Mr. Martin's Monthly Take-Home Pay
1982–84	100.0	$ 600
2016	238.132	7,000

a. What is the purchasing power of the dollar in 2016, based on the period 1982–84?

b. Determine Mr. Martin's "real" monthly income for 2016.

55. Suppose that the Producer Price Index and the sales of Hoskin's Wholesale Distributors for 2006 and 2016 are:

Year	Producer Price Index	Sales
2006	160.5	$2,400,000
2016	109.7	3,500,000

What are Hoskin's real sales (also called deflated sales) for the 2 years?

DATA ANALYTICS

(The data for this exercise is available at the text website: www.mhhe.com/lind17e.)

56. Refer to the Baseball 2016 data, which include information on the 2016 Major League Baseball season. The data also include the mean player salary since 1989.

a. Use the year 2000 salary as the base period and 100 as the base value to develop a simple index for the years since 2000. By what percent has the typical salary increased?

b. The Consumer Price Index values for 2001, 2003, 2011, 2012, and 2016 are 177.1, 184.0, 224.94, 229.594, and 238.132, respectively. What are the average player's real (or deflated) salaries for those years? Describe the trend in the deflated salaries in a few sentences. Compare these results with your reply in part (a).

Time Series and Forecasting

18

© Bob Levey/Getty Images

▲ **TEAM SPORTS INC.** sells sporting goods to high schools and colleges via a nationally distributed catalog. Management at Team Sports estimates it will sell 2,000 Wilson Model A2000 catcher's mitts next year. The deseasonalized sales are projected to be the same for each of the four quarters next year. The seasonal factor for the second quarter is 145. Determine the seasonally adjusted sales for the second quarter of next year. (See Exercise 12 and LO18-6.)

LEARNING OBJECTIVES

When you have completed this chapter, you will be able to:

LO18-1 Define and describe the components of a time series.

LO18-2 Smooth a time series by computing a moving average.

LO18-3 Smooth a time series by computing a weighted moving average.

LO18-4 Use regression analysis to fit a linear trend line to a time series.

LO18-5 Use regression analysis to fit a nonlinear time series.

LO18-6 Compute and apply seasonal indexes to make seasonally adjusted forecasts.

LO18-7 Deseasonalize a time series using seasonal indexes.

LO18-8 Conduct a hypothesis test of autocorrelation.

INTRODUCTION

The emphasis in this chapter is on time series analysis and forecasting. A **time series** is a collection of data recorded over a period of time—weekly, monthly, quarterly, or yearly. Two examples of time series are Microsoft Corporation sales by quarter since 1985 and the daily reports of the Dow Jones Industrial Average over the last three months.

© Flying Colors Ltd/Photodisc/Getty Images

An analysis of history—a time series—is used by management to make current decisions and plans based on long-term forecasting. We usually assume past patterns will continue into the future. Long-term forecasts extend more than 1 year into the future; 2-, 5-, and 10-year projections are common. Long-range predictions are essential to allow sufficient time for the procurement, manufacturing, sales, finance, and other departments of a company to develop plans for possible new plants, financing, development of new products, and new methods of assembling.

Forecasting the level of sales, both short-term and long-term, is practically dictated by the very nature of business organizations in the United States and around the world. Competition for the consumer's dollar, stress on earning a profit for the stockholders, a desire to procure a larger share of the market, and the ambitions of executives are some of the prime motivating forces in business. Thus, a forecast of the future is necessary to plan for the raw materials, production facilities, and staff needed to meet the projected demand.

This chapter shows how to use time-series data to forecast future events. First, we look at the components of a time series. Then, we examine some of the techniques used to analyze time-series data. Finally, we use these techniques to forecast future events.

LO18-1
Define and describe the components of a time series.

COMPONENTS OF A TIME SERIES

There are four components to a time series: secular trend, cyclical variation, seasonal variation, and irregular variation.

Secular Trend

The trend of sales, unemployment, stock prices, and other business and economic series follow various patterns. Some move steadily upward, others decline, and still others stay the same over time. The change over time may be linear and follow a straight line, or it may increase at an exponential rate. The long-run change (or lack of change) is called the trend of the time series or, more precisely, the **secular trend.**

SECULAR TREND The smoothed long-term direction of a time series.

The following are several examples of a secular trend.

- Home Depot, Inc. was founded in 1978 and is the world's largest home improvement retailer. The following chart shows the number of associates working for Home Depot, Inc. You can see the number of associates increased from just over 98,000 in 1996 to 364,400 in 2006. Since then, the number of associates decreased from 2007 through 2009. From 2009 through 2015, the number of associates has increased steadily. A time series graph is always used to summarize the data.

Year	Associates	Year	Associates
1996	98.1	2006	364.4
1997	124.4	2007	331.0
1998	156.7	2008	322.0
1999	201.4	2009	317.0
2000	227.3	2010	321.0
2001	256.3	2011	331.0
2002	280.9	2012	340.0
2003	298.8	2013	365.0
2004	323.1	2014	371.0
2005	344.8	2015	385.0

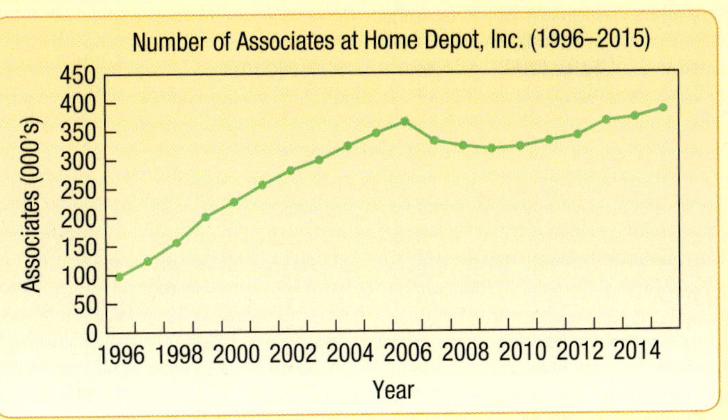

- The average price for a gallon of regular gasoline was below $2.00 until 2005. From 2005 until 2013, except for a period between 2009 and 2010, price increased steadily by almost $0.20 per year. Since 2013, price declined. This information is shown in the time series chart below.

Year	Cost/Gallon	Year	Cost/Gallon
1996	1.20	2006	2.57
1997	1.20	2007	2.80
1998	1.03	2008	3.25
1999	1.14	2009	2.35
2000	1.48	2010	2.78
2001	1.42	2011	3.52
2002	1.35	2012	3.62
2003	1.56	2013	3.49
2004	1.85	2014	3.34
2005	2.27	2015	2.40

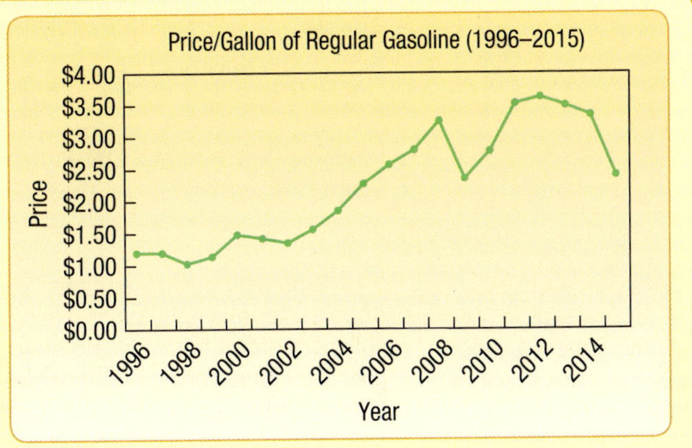

Cyclical Variation

The second component of a time series is **cyclical variation.** A typical business cycle consists of a period of prosperity followed by periods of recession, depression, and then recovery. There are sizable fluctuations unfolding over more than one year in time above and below the secular trend. In a recession, for example, employment, production, the Dow Jones Industrial Average, and many other business and economic series are below the long-term trend lines. Conversely, in periods of prosperity they are above their long-term trend lines.

CYCLICAL VARIATION The rise and fall of a time series over periods longer than 1 year.

Chart 18–1 shows the annual unit sales of batteries sold by National Battery Retailers, Inc. from 1996 through 2016. The cyclical nature of business is highlighted. There are periods of recovery, followed by prosperity, then contraction, and finally the cycle bottoms out with depression.

Year	Battery Sales (000)	Year	Battery Sales (000)
1996	24.0	2007	41.0
1997	30.0	2008	42.0
1998	31.0	2009	38.0
1999	26.5	2010	39.0
2000	27.0	2011	46.0
2001	27.5	2012	52.0
2002	34.0	2013	53.5
2003	35.0	2014	47.0
2004	31.0	2015	51.0
2005	32.0	2016	48.0
2006	35.5		

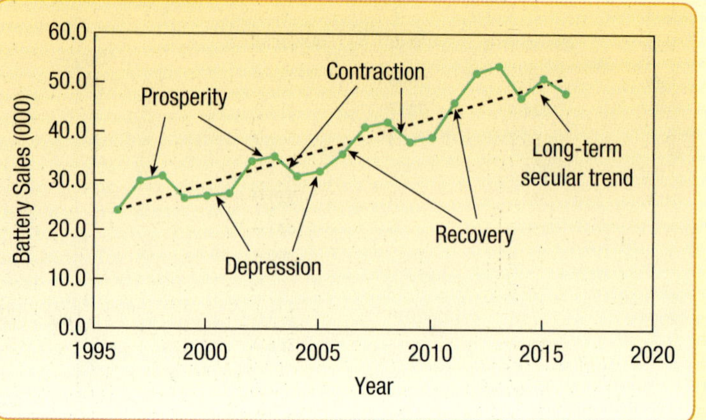

CHART 18–1 Battery Sales for National Battery Retailers, Inc. 1996 to 2016

Seasonal Variation

The third component of a time series is the **seasonal variation.** Many sales, production, and other series fluctuate with the seasons. The unit of time reported is usually quarterly or monthly but could be weekly.

SEASONAL VARIATION Patterns of change in a time series within a year. These patterns tend to repeat themselves each year.

STATISTICS IN ACTION

Statisticians, economists, and business executives are constantly looking for variables that will forecast the country's economy. The production of crude oil, price of gold on world markets, and the Dow Jones average, as well as many published government indexes, are variables that have been used with some success. Variables such as the length of hemlines and the winner of the Super Bowl have also been tried. The variable that seems overall to be the most successful is the price of scrap metal. Why? Scrap metal is the beginning of the manufacturing chain. When its demand increases, this is an indication that manufacturing is also increasing.

Almost all businesses tend to have recurring seasonal patterns. Men's and women's apparel, for example, have extremely high sales just prior to Christmas and relatively low sales just after Christmas and during the summer. Beach rental properties are another example. They have very low rental rates in the winter but during the summer when the temperature is warm, rentals increase significantly. Toy sales are another example with an extreme seasonal pattern. More than half of the annual toy sales usually occur in the months of November and December. The lawn care business is seasonal in the northeast and north-central states. Many businesses try to even out the seasonal effects by engaging in an offsetting seasonal business. In the Northeast, the operator of a lawn care business will attach a snowplow to the front of a truck in an effort to earn income in the off-season. At ski resorts throughout the country, you will often find golf courses nearby. The owners of the lodges attract skiers in the winter and golfers in the summer. This is an effective method of spreading their fixed costs over the entire year rather than a few months.

Chart 18–2 shows the quarterly sales, in millions of dollars, of Hercher Sporting Goods, Inc. The Chicago-area sporting goods company specializes in selling baseball and softball equipment to high schools, colleges, and youth leagues. It also has several retail outlets in some of the larger shopping malls. There is a distinct seasonal pattern to its business. Most of its sales are in the first and second quarters of the year, when schools and organizations are purchasing equipment for the upcoming season. During the early summer, it keeps busy by selling replacement equipment. It does some business during the holidays (fourth quarter). The late summer (third quarter) is its slow season.

Irregular Variation

Many analysts prefer to subdivide the **irregular variation** into *episodic* and *residual* variations. Episodic fluctuations are unpredictable, but they can be identified. The initial

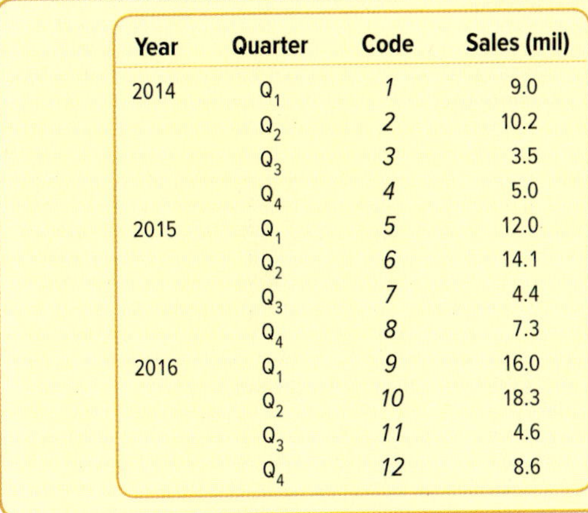

Year	Quarter	Code	Sales (mil)
2014	Q_1	1	9.0
	Q_2	2	10.2
	Q_3	3	3.5
	Q_4	4	5.0
2015	Q_1	5	12.0
	Q_2	6	14.1
	Q_3	7	4.4
	Q_4	8	7.3
2016	Q_1	9	16.0
	Q_2	10	18.3
	Q_3	11	4.6
	Q_4	12	8.6

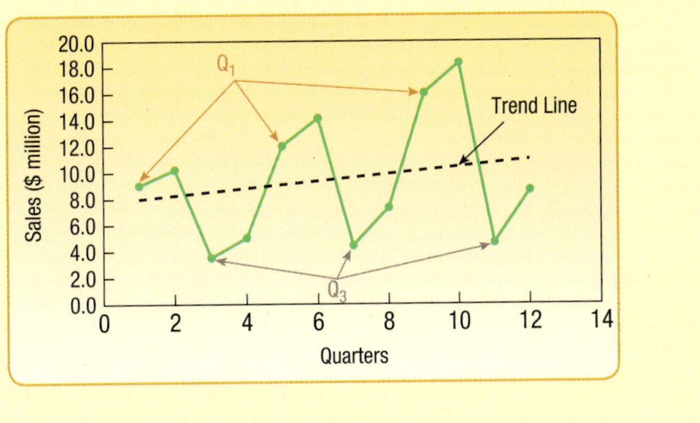

CHART 18–2 Sales of Baseball and Softball Equipment, Hercher Sporting Goods 2014–2016 by Quarter

STATISTICS IN ACTION

Forecasts are not always correct. The reality is that a forecast may just be a best guess as to what will happen. What are the reasons forecasts are not correct? One expert lists eight common errors: (1) failure to carefully examine the assumptions, (2) limited expertise, (3) lack of imagination, (4) neglect of constraints, (5) excessive optimism, (6) reliance on mechanical extrapolation, (7) premature closure, and (8) overspecification.

impact on the economy of a major labor strike or a war can be identified, but a strike or war cannot be predicted. After the episodic fluctuations have been removed, the remaining variation is called the residual variation. The residual fluctuations, often called chance fluctuations or noise, are unpredictable, and they cannot be identified. Of course, neither episodic nor residual variation can be projected into the future.

A MOVING AVERAGE

LO18-2
Smooth a time series by computing a moving average.

A **moving average** is useful in smoothing a time series to see its trend. It is also the basic method used in measuring seasonal fluctuation, described later in the chapter. In contrast to the least squares method, which expresses the trend in terms of a mathematical equation ($\hat{y} = a + bt$), the moving-average method merely smooths the fluctuations in the data. This is accomplished by "moving" the arithmetic mean values through the time series.

To apply the moving average to a time series, the data should follow a fairly linear trend and have a definite rhythmic pattern of fluctuations (repeating, say, every three years). The data in the following example have three components—trend, cycle, and irregular, abbreviated *T, C,* and *I*. There is no seasonal variation because the data are recorded annually. What the moving average accomplishes is to average out *C* and *I*. What is left is the trend.

If the duration of the cycles is constant, and if the amplitudes of the cycles are equal, the cyclical and irregular fluctuations are removed entirely using the moving average. The result is a line. For example, in the following time series, the cycle repeats itself every 7 years, and the amplitude of each cycle is 4; that is, there are exactly four units from the trough (lowest time period) to the peak. The seven-year moving average, therefore, averages out the cyclical and irregular fluctuations perfectly, and the residual is a linear trend.

The first step in computing the seven-year moving average is to determine the seven-year moving totals. The total sales for the first 7 years (1991–97 inclusive) are $22 million, found by $1 + 2 + 3 + 4 + 5 + 4 + 3$. (See Table 18–1.) The total of $22 million is divided by 7 to determine the arithmetic mean sales per year. The seven-year total (22) and the seven-year mean (3.143) are positioned opposite the middle year for that group of seven, namely, 1994, as shown in Table 18–1. Then the total sales for the next seven years (1992–98 inclusive) are determined. (A convenient way of doing this is to subtract the sales for 1991 [$1 million] from the first seven-year total [$22 million] and add the sales for 1998 [$2 million], to give the new total of $23 million.) The mean of this total, $3.286 million, is positioned opposite the middle year, 1995. The sales data and seven-year moving average are shown graphically in Chart 18–3.

TABLE 18–1 Computation of Seven-Year Moving Average

Year	Sales ($ Mil)	Seven-Year Moving Total	Seven-Year Moving Average
1991	1		
1992	2		
1993	3		
1994	4	22	3.143
1995	5	23	3.286
1996	4	24	3.429
1997	3	25	3.571
1998	2	26	3.714
1999	3	27	3.857
2000	4	28	4.000
2001	5	29	4.143
2002	6	30	4.286
2003	5	31	4.429
2004	4	32	4.571
2005	3	33	4.714
2006	4	34	4.857
2007	5	35	5.000
2008	6	36	5.143
2009	7	37	5.286
2010	6	38	5.429
2011	5	39	5.571
2012	4	40	5.714
2013	5	41	5.857
2014	6		
2015	7		
2016	8		

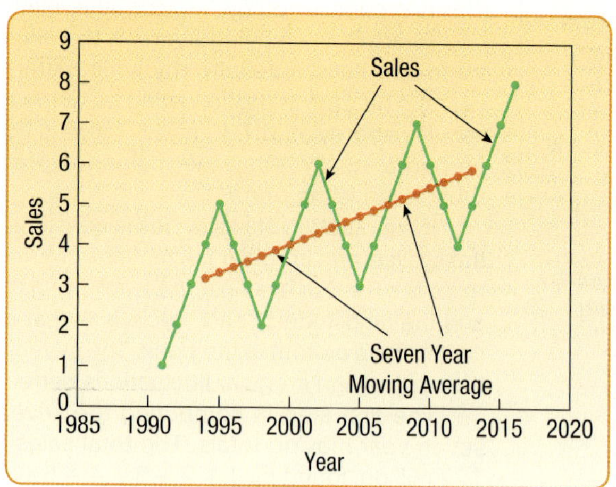

CHART 18–3 Sales and Seven-Year Moving Average

The number of data values to include in a moving average depends on the data collected. If the data are quarterly, then four values is typical because there are four quarters in a year. If the data are daily, then seven values is appropriate because there are 7 days in a week. You might also use trial and error to determine a number that best levels out the chance fluctuations. For example, Table 18–2 and Chart 18–4 show three-year and five-year moving averages for a series of production data.

TABLE 18–2 Production, Three-Year Moving Average, and Five-Year Moving Average

Year	Production	Three-Year Moving Total	Three-Year Moving Average	Five-Year Moving Total	Five-Year Moving Average
1998	5				
1999	6	19	6.33		
2000	8	24	8.00	34	6.80
2001	10	23	7.67	32	6.40
2002	5	18	6.00	33	6.60
2003	3	15	5.00	35	7.00
2004	7	20	6.67	37	7.40
2005	10	29	9.67	43	8.60
2006	12	33	11.00	49	9.80
2007	11	32	10.67	55	11.00
2008	9	33	11.00	60	12.00
2009	13	37	12.33	66	13.20
2010	15	46	15.33	70	14.00
2011	18	48	16.00	72	14.40
2012	15	44	14.67	73	14.60
2013	11	40	13.33	75	15.00
2014	14	42	14.00	79	15.80
2015	17	53	17.67		
2016	22				

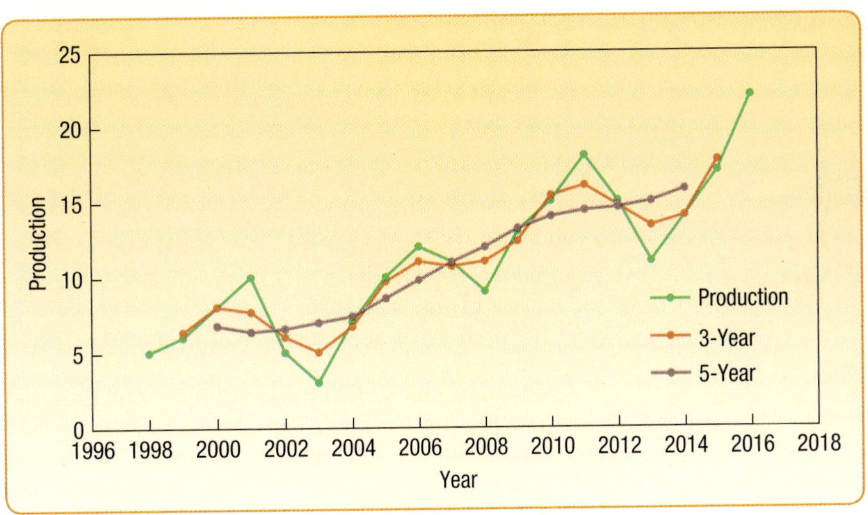

CHART 18–4 Time Series Plot of Production, Three-Year Moving Average, and Five-Year Moving Average

Sales, production, and other economic and business series usually do not have (1) periods of oscillation that are of equal length or (2) oscillations that have identical amplitudes. Thus, in practice, the application of a moving average does not result precisely in a line. For example, the production series in Table 18–2 repeats about every 5 years, but the amplitude of the data varies from one oscillation to another. The trend appears to be upward and somewhat linear. Both moving averages—the three-year and the five-year—seem to adequately describe the trend in production since 1998.

Four-year, six-year, and other even-numbered-year moving averages present one minor problem regarding the centering of the moving totals and moving averages. Note in Table 18–3 below there is no center time period, so the moving totals are positioned *between* two time periods. The total for the first 4 years ($42) is positioned between 2009 and 2010. The total for the next 4 years is $43. The averages of the first four years and the second 4 years ($10.50 and $10.75, respectively) are averaged, and the resulting figure is centered on 2010. This procedure is repeated until all possible four-year averages are computed.

TABLE 18–3 Calculations of a Four-Year Moving Average

Year	Sales	Four-Year Moving Total	Four-Year Moving Average	Centered Moving Average
2008	8			
2009	11			
		42 (8 + 11 + 9 + 14)	10.50 (42/4)	
2010	9			10.625
		43 (11 + 9 + 14 + 9)	10.75 (43/4)	
2011	14			10.625
		42	10.50	
2012	9			10.625
		43	10.75	
2013	10			10.000
		37	9.25	
2014	10			9.625
		40	10.00	
2015	8			
2016	12			

LO18-3
Smooth a time series by computing a weighted moving average.

WEIGHTED MOVING AVERAGE

A moving average uses the same weight for each observation. For example, a three-year moving total is divided by the value 3 to yield the three-year moving average. To put it another way, each data value has a weight of one-third in this case. Similarly, you can see that for a five-year moving, average, each data value has a weight of one-fifth.

A natural extension of the weighted mean discussed in Chapter 3 is to compute a weighted moving average. This involves selecting a different weight for each data value and then computing a weighted average of the most recent *n* values as the smoothed value. In the majority of applications, we use the smoothed value as a forecast of the future. So, the most recent observation receives the most weight, and the weight decreases for older data values. Of course, the sum of the weights must be equal to 1.

Suppose, for example, we compute a two-year weighted moving average for the data in Table 18–3 giving twice as much weight to the most recent value. In other words, give a weight of two-thirds to the last year and one-third to the value immediately before that. Then "forecast" sales for 2010 would be found by (1/3)($8) + (2/3)($11) = $10. The next moving average would be computed as (1/3)($11) + (2/3)($9) = $9.667. Proceeding in the same fashion, the final, or 2016, weighted moving average would be (1/3)($10) + (2/3)($8) = $10.667. To summarize the technique of using moving averages, its purpose is to help identify the long-term trend in a time series (because it will smooth out short-term fluctuations). It is used to reveal any cyclical and seasonal fluctuations.

EXAMPLE

Cedar Fair operates eleven amusement parks, three outdoor water parks, one indoor water park, and five hotels. Its combined attendance (in thousands) for the last 20 years is given in the following table. A partner asks you to study the trend in attendance. Compute a three-year moving average and a three-year weighted moving average with weights of 0.2, 0.3, and 0.5 for successive years.

Year	Attendance (000)
1996	7,445
1997	7,405
1998	11,450
1999	11,224
2000	11,703
2001	11,890
2002	12,380
2003	12,181
2004	12,557
2005	12,700
2006	19,300
2007	22,100
2008	22,720
2009	21,136
2010	22,785
2011	23,377
2012	23,300
2013	23,500
2014	23,300
2015	24,400

SOLUTION

The three-year moving average is:

Year	Attendance (000)	3-Year Moving Average	Found by
1996	7,445		
1997	7,405	8766.67	(7,445 + 7,405 + 11,450)/3
1998	11,450	10026.33	(7,405 + 11,450 + 11,224)/3
1999	11,224	11459.00	↑
2000	11,703	11605.67	
2001	11,890	11991.00	
2002	12,380	12150.33	
2003	12,181	12372.67	
2004	12,557	12479.33	
2005	12,700	14852.33	
2006	19,300	18033.33	
2007	22,100	21373.33	
2008	22,720	21985.33	
2009	21,136	22213.67	
2010	22,785	22432.67	
2011	23,377	23154.00	
2012	23,300	23392.33	
2013	23,500	23366.67	↓
2014	23,300	23733.33	(23,500 + 23,300 + 24,400)/3
2015	24,400		

The three-year weighted moving average is:

Year	Attendance (000)	3-Year Weighted Moving Average	Found by
1996	7,445		
1997	7,405	9,435.50	.2(7,445) + .3(7,405) + .5(11,450)
1998	11,450	10,528.00	.2(7,405) + .3(11,450) + .5(11,224)
1999	11,224	11,508.70	▲
2000	11,703	11,700.70	
2001	11,890	12,097.60	
2002	12,380	12,182.50	
2003	12,181	12,408.80	
2004	12,557	12,553.30	
2005	12,700	15,971.40	
2006	19,300	19,380.00	
2007	22,100	21,850.00	
2008	22,720	21,804.00	
2009	21,136	22,277.30	
2010	22,785	22,751.20	
2011	23,377	23,220.10	
2012	23,300	23,415.40	
2013	23,500	23,360.00	▼
2014	23,300	23,890.00	.2(23,500) + .3(23,300) + .5(24,400)
2015	24,400		

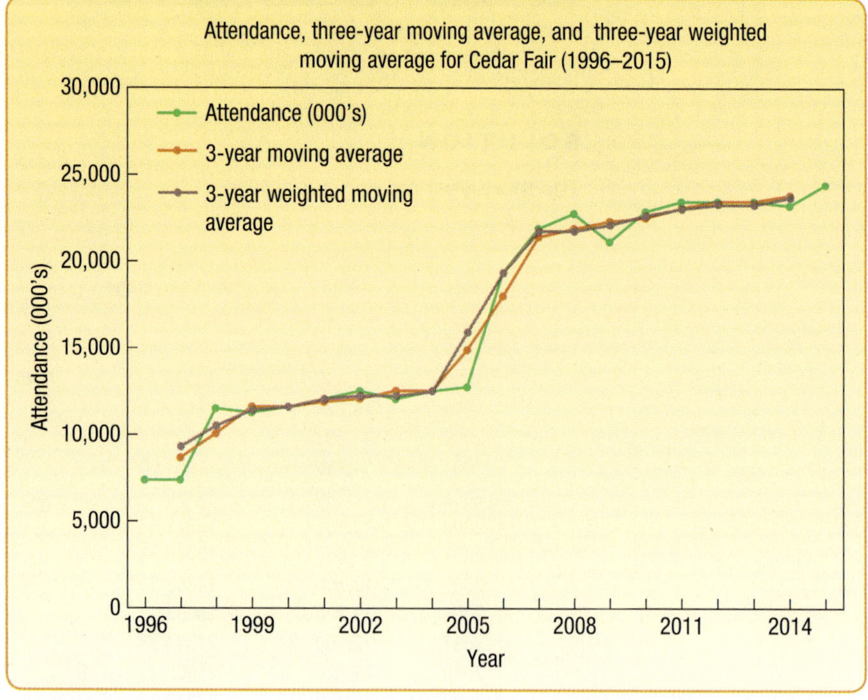

Study the graph carefully. You will see that the attendance trend is evenly upward with approximately 400,000 additional visitors each year. However, there is a "hop" of approximately 3 million per year between 1997 and 1998. At this time, Cedar Fair acquired Knott's Berry Farm (located in Southern California) in late 1997, leading to a boost in attendance. A similar boost occurred in 2006 with the purchase of King's Island near Cincinnati, Ohio. You can also observe the financial crisis in 2009 followed by a steady recovery in attendance.

The weighted moving average follows the data more closely than the moving average. This reflects the additional influence given to the most recent period. In other words, the weighted method, where the most recent period is given the largest weight, won't be quite as smooth.

SELF-REVIEW 18–1

Determine a three-year moving average for the sales of Waccamaw Machine Tool Inc. Plot both the original data and the moving average.

Year	Number Produced (thousands)	Year	Number Produced (thousands)
2011	2	2014	5
2012	6	2015	3
2013	4	2016	10

EXERCISES

1. **FILE** Calculate a four-quarter weighted moving average for the number of shares outstanding for the Boxley Box Company for the nine quarters of data. The data are reported in thousands. Apply weights of .1, .2, .3, and .4, respectively, for the past three quarters and current quarter. In a few words, describe the trend in the number of subscribers.

1st Quarter 2015	28,766
2nd Quarter 2015	30,057
3rd Quarter 2015	31,336
4th Quarter 2015	33,240
1st Quarter 2016	34,610
2nd Quarter 2016	35,102
3rd Quarter 2016	35,308
4th Quarter 2016	35,203
1st Quarter 2017	34,386

2. **FILE** Listed below is the number of movie tickets sold at the Library Cinema-Complex, in thousands, for the period from 2004 to 2016. Compute a five-year weighted moving average using weights of .1, .1, .2, .3, and .3, respectively. Describe the trend in yield.

2004	8.61	2011	6.61
2005	8.14	2012	5.58
2006	7.67	2013	5.87
2007	6.59	2014	5.94
2008	7.37	2015	5.49
2009	6.88	2016	5.43
2010	6.71		

LO18-4
Use regression analysis to fit a linear trend line to a time series.

LINEAR TREND

The long-term trend of many business series, such as sales, exports, and production, often approximates a straight line. If so, the equation to describe this trend is:

LINEAR TREND EQUATION $$\hat{y} = a + bt \quad \text{(18–1)}$$

where:

$\hat{y}$, read *y*, hat, is the projected value of the *y* variable for a selected value of *t*.
a is the *y*-intercept. It is the estimated value of *y* where the line crosses the *y*-axis, or when $t = 0$.
b is the slope of the line, or the average change in $\hat{y}$ for each increase of one unit in *t*.
t is any value of time that is selected.

To illustrate the meaning of $\hat{y}$, a, b, and t in a time-series problem, a line is drawn in Chart 18–5 to represent the typical trend of sales. Assume that this company started in business in 2008. This beginning year (2008) has been arbitrarily coded as time period 1. Note that sales increased an average of $2 million every year; that is, based on the straight line drawn through the sales data, sales increased from $3 million in 2008 to $5 million in 2009, to $7 million in 2010, to $9 million in 2011, and so on. The slope, or *b*, is therefore 2. The slope is the average change in sales for each unit increase in the time period. Note too that the line intercepts the *y*-axis (when $t = 0$, which is the year 2007) at $1 million. This point is *a*. Another way of determining *b* is to locate the starting place of the straight line in year 1. It is 3 for 2008 in this example. Then locate the value on the straight line for the last year. It is 19 for 2016.

Time Period	Year	Sales	Trend Line
1	2008	6	3
2	2009	2	5
3	2010	9	7
4	2011	8	9
5	2012	16	11
6	2013	10	13
7	2014	12	15
8	2015	21	17
9	2016	18	19

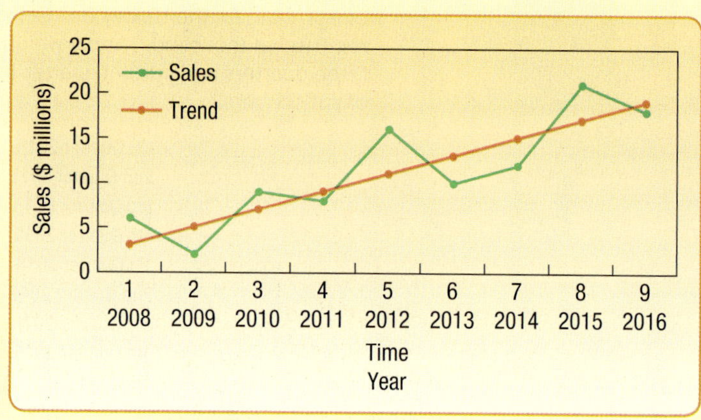

CHART 18–5 A Straight Line Fitted to Sales Data

The equation for the line in Chart 18–5 is:

$$\hat{y} = 1 + 2t$$

where:

$\hat{y}$ is sales in millions of dollars.
1 is the intercept with the *Y*-axis. It is also the sales in millions of dollars for year 0, or 2007.
t is the coded time period for each year.

In Chapter 13, we drew a line through points on a scatter diagram to approximate the regression line. We stressed, however, that this method for determining the regression equation has a serious drawback—namely, the position of the line depends on the judgment of the individual who drew the line. Three people would probably draw three different lines through the scatter plots. Likewise, the line we drew through the sales data in Chart 18–5 might not be the best-fitting line. Because of the subjective judgment involved, this method should be used only when a quick approximation of the straight-line equation is needed, or to check the reasonableness of the least squares line, which is discussed next.

Least Squares Method

In the discussion of simple linear regression in Chapter 13, we showed how the least squares method is used to find the best linear relationship between two variables. In forecasting methods, time is the independent variable and the value of the time series is the dependent variable. Furthermore, we often code the independent variable, time, to make the equations easier to interpret. In other words, we let *t* be 1 for the first year, 2 for the second, and so on. If a time series includes the sales of General Electric for 5 years starting in 2012 and continuing through 2016, we would code the year 2012 as 1, 2013 as 2, and 2016 as 5.

When the least squares method is used to find the trend line for a time series, the errors or residuals are usually correlated and not independent. Therefore, the results of the hypothesis tests for regression analysis presented in Chapter 13 may not be valid in time series analysis. However, simple linear regression can still be used to find a line of best fit for a time series.

STATISTICS IN ACTION

Investors frequently use regression analysis to study the relationship between a particular stock and the general condition of the market. The dependent variable is the monthly percentage change in the value of the stock, and the independent variable is the monthly percentage change in a market index, such as the Standard & Poor's 500 Composite Index. The value of *b* in the regression equation is the particular stock's *beta coefficient,* or just the *beta*. If *b* is greater than 1, the implication is that the stock is sensitive to market changes. If *b* is between 0 and 1, the implication is that the stock is not sensitive to market changes.

EXAMPLE

The sales of Jensen Foods, a small grocery chain located in southwest Texas, for 2012 through 2016 are:

Year	Time (t)	Sales ($ million)
2012	1	7.0
2013	2	10.0
2014	3	9.0
2015	4	11.0
2016	5	13.0

Determine the regression equation. How much are sales increasing each year? What is the sales forecast for 2018?

SOLUTION

To determine the trend equation, we could use formula (13–4) to find the slope, or *b* value, and formula (13–5) to locate the intercept, or *a* value. We would substitute *t*, the coded values for the year, for *X* in these equations. Another approach is to use a software package. Chart 18–6 shows the plot of sales and the fitted or trended sales for each year.

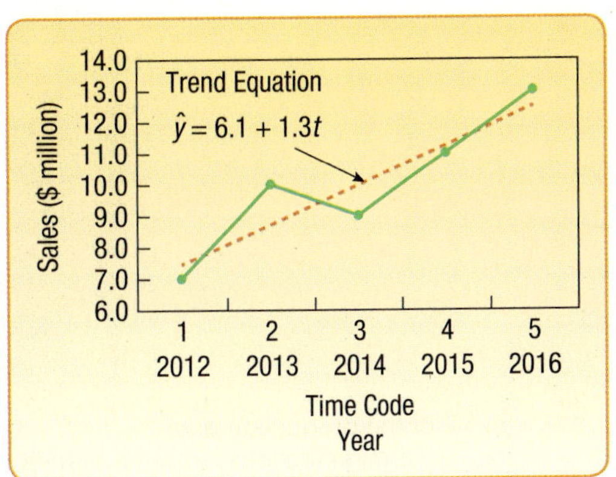

CHART 18–6 Sales and Trend Line for Jensen Foods (2012 to 2016)

From the regression analysis, the trend equation is $\hat{y} = 6.1 + 1.3t$. How do we interpret this equation? The sales are in millions of dollars. So the value 1.3 tells us that sales increased at a rate of 1.3 million dollars per year. The value 6.1 is the estimated value of sales in the year 0. That is the estimate for 2011, which is called the base year. For example, to determine the point on the line for 2015, insert the t value of 4 in the equation. Then $\hat{y} = 6.1 + 1.3(4) = 11.3$.

If sales, production, or other data approximate a linear trend, the equation developed by the least squares technique can be used to estimate future values. For Jensen Foods, the sales data appears to follow a linear trend, so we can use the trend equation to forecast future sales.

See Table 18–4. The year 2012 is coded 1, the year 2014 is coded 3, and year 2016 is coded 5. Logically, we code 2018 as 7 and 2019 as 8. So we substitute 7 into the trend equation and solve for $\hat{y}$.

TABLE 18–4 Calculations for Determining the Points on Trend Line

Year	Sales ($ million)	Code (t)	y	Found by
2012	7.0	1	7.4	6.1 + 1.3(1)
2013	10.0	2	8.7	6.1 + 1.3(2)
2014	9.0	3	10.0	6.1 + 1.3(3)
2015	11.0	4	11.3	6.1 + 1.3(4)
2016	13.0	5	12.6	6.1 + 1.3(5)

$$\hat{y} = 6.1 + 1.3t = 6.1 + 1.3(7) = 15.2$$

Thus, on the basis of past sales, the estimate for 2018 is $15.2 million.

In this time series example, there were 5 years of sales data. Based on those five sales figures, we estimated sales for 2018. Many researchers suggest that we do not project sales, production, and other business and economic series more than $n/2$ time periods into the future where n is the number of data points. If, for example, there are 10 years of data, we would make estimates only up to 5 years into the future ($n/2 = 10/2 = 5$). Others suggest the forecast may be for no longer than 2 years, especially in rapidly changing economic times.

SELF-REVIEW 18–2

Annual production of king-size rockers by Wood Products Inc. for 2009 through 2016 follows.

Year	Time	Production (thousands)
2009	1	4
2010	2	8
2011	3	5
2012	4	8
2013	5	11
2014	6	9
2015	7	11
2016	8	14

(a) Plot the production data.
(b) Determine the least squares equation using a software package.
(c) Using the least squares equation, determine the points on the line for 2009 and 2016.
(d) Based on the linear trend equation, what is the estimated production for 2019?

EXERCISES

3. **FILE** Listed below is the number of rooms rented at Plantation Resorts of Georgia for the years from 2006 to 2016. Remember to code the years starting at 1 for year 2006.

Year	Rental	Year	Rental	Year	Rental
2006	6,714	2010	9,762	2014	6,162
2007	7,991	2011	10,180	2015	6,897
2008	9,075	2012	8,334	2016	8,285
2009	9,775	2013	8,272		

Determine the least squares equation. According to this information, what is the estimated number of rentals for 2017?

4. **FILE** Listed below are the net sales in $ million for Home Depot Inc. and its subsidiaries from 1993 to 2015. Remember to code the years starting at 1 for year 1993.

Year	Net Sales	Year	Net Sales	Year	Net Sales
1993	$ 9,239	2001	53,553	2009	66,176
1994	12,477	2002	58,247	2010	67,997
1995	15,470	2003	64,816	2011	70,395
1996	19,535	2004	73,094	2012	74,754
1997	24,156	2005	81,511	2013	78,812
1998	30,219	2006	90,837	2014	83,176
1999	38,434	2007	77,349	2015	88,519
2000	45,738	2008	71,288		

Determine the least squares equation. On the basis of this information, what are the estimated sales for 2016 and 2017?

5. **FILE** The following table lists the annual amounts of glass cullet produced by Kimble Glass Works Inc. for 2013 through 2017.

Year	Code	Scrap (tons)	Year	Code	Scrap (tons)
2013	1	2	2016	4	5
2014	2	4	2017	5	6
2015	3	3			

Determine the least squares trend equation. Estimate the amount of scrap for the year 2019.

6. **FILE** The sales by Walker's Milk and Dairy Products in millions of dollars for the period from 2011 to 2017 are reported in the following table.

Year	Code	Sales ($ millions)	Year	Code	Sales ($ millions)
2011	1	17.5	2015	5	24.5
2012	2	19.0	2016	6	26.7
2013	3	21.0	2017	7	27.3
2014	4	22.7			

Determine the least squares regression trend equation. Estimate the sales for 2019.

LO18-5
Use regression analysis to fit a nonlinear time series.

NONLINEAR TRENDS

The emphasis in the previous discussion was on a time series whose growth or decline approximated a straight line. A linear trend equation is used to represent the time series when it is believed that the data are increasing (or decreasing) by *equal amounts,* on the average, from one period to another.

Data that increase (or decrease) by *increasing amounts* over a period of time appear *curvilinear* when plotted on an arithmetic scale. To put it another way, data that increase (or decrease) by *equal percents* or *proportions* over a period of time appear curvilinear. (See Chart 18–7.)

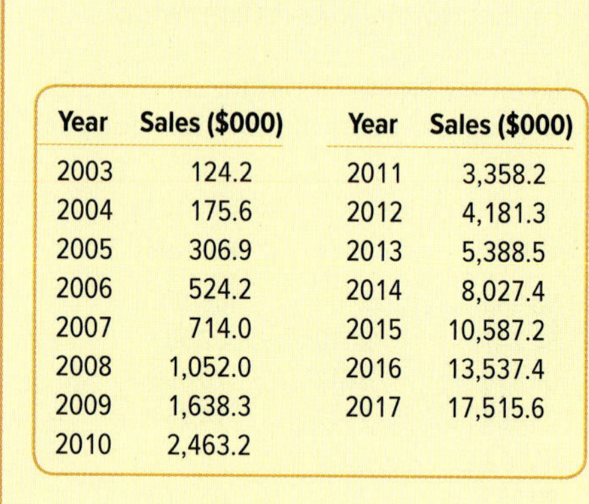

Year	Sales ($000)	Year	Sales ($000)
2003	124.2	2011	3,358.2
2004	175.6	2012	4,181.3
2005	306.9	2013	5,388.5
2006	524.2	2014	8,027.4
2007	714.0	2015	10,587.2
2008	1,052.0	2016	13,537.4
2009	1,638.3	2017	17,515.6
2010	2,463.2		

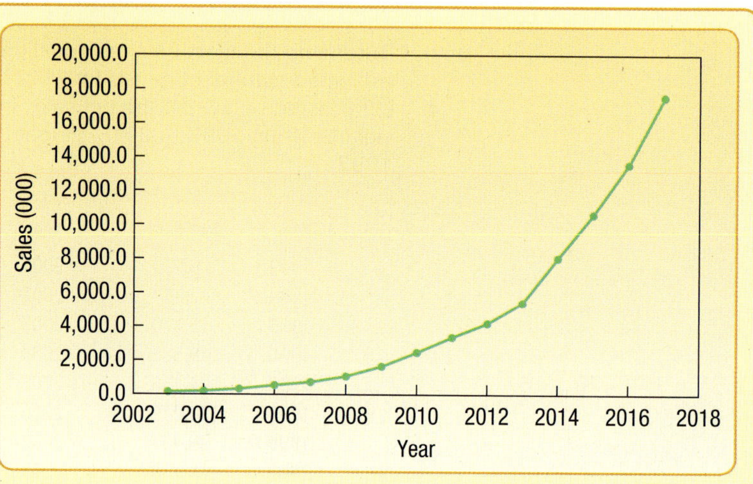

CHART 18–7 Sales for Gulf Shores Importers (2003–2017)

The trend equation for a time series that does approximate a curvilinear trend, such as the one portrayed in Chart 18–7, is computed by using the logarithms of the data and the least squares method. The general equation for the logarithmic trend equation is:

LOG TREND EQUATION $\log \hat{y} = \log a + \log b(t)$ **(18–2)**

The logarithmic trend equation can be determined for the Gulf Shores Importers data in Chart 18–7 using Excel. The first step is to enter the data, then find the log base 10 of each year's imports. Finally, use the regression procedure to find the least squares equation. That is, use the log of each year's data, then use the logs as the dependent variable and the coded year as the independent variable.

Code	Year	Sales ($000)	Log-sales
1	2003	124.2	2.094122
2	2004	175.6	2.244525
3	2005	306.9	2.486997
4	2006	524.2	2.719497
5	2007	714.0	2.853698
6	2008	1052.0	3.022016
7	2009	1638.3	3.214393
8	2010	2463.2	3.391500
9	2011	3358.2	3.526107
10	2012	4181.3	3.621311
11	2013	5388.5	3.731468
12	2014	8027.4	3.904575
13	2015	10587.2	4.024781
14	2016	13537.4	4.131535
15	2017	17515.6	4.243425

SUMMARY OUTPUT

Regression Statistics	
Multiple R	0.994
R Square	0.988
Adjusted R Square	0.987
Standard Error	0.079
Observations	15

ANOVA

	df	*SS*	*MS*	*F*
Regression	1	6.585	6.585	1065.2279
Residual	13	0.080	0.006	
Total	14	6.666		

	Coefficients
Intercept	2.053805
Code	0.153357

Regression Equation
$y = 2.053805 + 0.153357t$

The regression equation is $\hat{y} = 2.053805 + 0.153357t$. This equation is the log form. We now have a trend equation in terms of percent of change. That is, the value 0.153357 is the percent of change in $\hat{y}$ for each unit increase in t. This value is similar to the geometric mean described in Chapter 3.

The log of b is 0.153357 and its antilog or inverse is 1.423498. If we subtract 1 from this value, as we did in Chapter 3, the value 0.423498 indicates the geometric mean annual rate of increase from 2003 to 2017. We conclude that imports increased at a rate of 42.35% annually during the period.

We also can use the logarithmic trend equation to make estimates of future values. Suppose we want to estimate the imports in the year 2019. The first step is to determine the code for the year 2019. It is 19. To explain, the year 2017 has a code of 15 and the year 2019 is 4 years later, so 15 + 4 = 19. The log of imports for the year 2019 is

$$\hat{y} = 2.053805 + 0.153357t = 2.053805 + 0.153357(19) = 4.967588$$

To find the estimated imports for the year 2019, we need the antilog of 4.967588. It is 92,809. This is our estimate of the number of imports for 2019. Recall that the data were in thousands of dollars, so the estimate is $92,809,000.

SELF-REVIEW 18–3

Sales at Tomlin Manufacturing from 2013 to 2017 are:

Year	Sales ($ millions)
2013	2.13
2014	18.10
2015	39.80
2016	81.40
2017	112.00

(a) Determine the logarithmic trend equation for the sales data.
(b) Sales increased by what percentage annually from 2013–2017?
(c) What is the projected sales amount for 2018?

EXERCISES

7. **FILE** Sally's Software Inc. is a rapidly growing supplier of computer software to the Sarasota area. Sales for the last 5 years, 2013 to 2017, are given below.

Year	Sales ($ millions)
2013	1.1
2014	1.5
2015	2.0
2016	2.4
2017	3.1

   a. Determine the logarithmic trend equation.
   b. By what percent did sales increase, on the average, during the period?
   c. Estimate sales for the year 2020.

8. **FILE** It appears that the imports of carbon black have been increasing by about 10% annually.

Year	Imports of Carbon Black (thousands of tons)	Year	Imports of Carbon Black (thousands of tons)
2010	92.0	2014	135.0
2011	101.0	2015	149.0
2012	112.0	2016	163.0
2013	124.0	2017	180.0

a. Determine the logarithmic trend equation.
b. By what percent did imports increase, on the average, during the period?
c. Estimate imports for the year 2020.

LO18-6
Compute and apply seasonal indexes to make seasonally adjusted forecasts.

SEASONAL VARIATION

We mentioned that *seasonal variation* is another of the components of a time series. Time series data, such as automobile sales, shipments of soft-drink bottles, and residential construction, have periods of above-average and below-average activity each year. In the area of production, one of the reasons for analyzing seasonal fluctuations is to have a sufficient supply of raw materials on hand to meet the varying seasonal demand. The glass container division of a large glass company, for example, manufactures nonreturnable beer bottles, iodine bottles, aspirin bottles, bottles for rubber cement, and so on. The production scheduling department must know how many bottles to produce and when to produce each kind. A run of too many bottles of one kind may cause a serious storage problem. Production cannot be based entirely on orders on hand because many orders are telephoned in for immediate shipment. Since the demand for many of the bottles varies according to the season, a forecast a year or two in advance, by month, is essential to good scheduling.

© Goran Bogicevic/Shutterstock.com

An analysis of seasonal fluctuations over a period of years can also help in evaluating current sales. The typical sales of department stores in the United States, excluding mail-order sales, are expressed as indexes in Table 18–5. Each index represents the average sales for a period of several years. The actual sales for some months were above average (which is represented by an index over 100.0), and the sales for other months were below average. The index of 126.8 for December indicates that, typically, sales for December are 26.8% above an average month; the index of 86.0 for July indicates that department store sales for July are typically 14% below an average month.

TABLE 18–5 Typical Seasonal Indexes for U.S. Department Store Sales, Excluding Mail-Order Sales

January	87.0	July	86.0
February	83.2	August	99.7
March	100.5	September	101.4
April	106.5	October	105.8
May	101.6	November	111.9
June	89.6	December	126.8

Suppose an enterprising store manager, in an effort to stimulate sales during December, introduced a number of unique promotions, including bands of carolers strolling through the store singing holiday songs, large mechanical exhibits, and clerks dressed in Santa Claus costumes. When the index of sales was computed for that December, it was 150.0. Compared with the typical December sales of 126.8, it was concluded that the promotional program was a huge success.

Determining a Seasonal Index

A typical set of monthly indexes consists of 12 indexes that are representative of the data for a 12-month period. Logically, there are four typical seasonal indexes for data reported quarterly. Each index is a percent, with the average for the year equal to 100.0; that is, each monthly index indicates the level of sales, production, or another variable in relation to the annual average of 100.0. A typical index of 96.0 for January indicates that sales (or whatever the variable is) are usually 4% below the average for the year. An index of 107.2 for October means that the variable is typically 7.2% above the annual average.

Several methods have been developed to measure the typical seasonal fluctuation in a time series. The method most commonly used to compute the typical seasonal pattern is called the *ratio-to-moving-average method.* It eliminates the trend, cyclical, and irregular components from the original data (Y). In the following discussion, T refers to trend, C to cyclical, S to seasonal, and I to irregular variation. The numbers that result are called the *typical seasonal index.*

We will discuss in detail the steps followed in arriving at typical seasonal indexes using the ratio-to-moving-average method. The data of interest might be monthly or quarterly. To illustrate, we have chosen the quarterly sales of Toys International. First, we will show the steps needed to arrive at a set of typical quarterly indexes. Then we use the MegaStat add-in for Excel to calculate the seasonal indexes.

EXAMPLE

Table 18–6 shows the quarterly sales for Toys International for the years 2012 through 2017. The sales are reported in millions of dollars. Determine a quarterly seasonal index using the ratio-to-moving-average method.

TABLE 18–6 Toys International Quarterly Sales ($ million), 2012 to 2017

Year	Winter	Spring	Summer	Fall
2012	6.7	4.6	10.0	12.7
2013	6.5	4.6	9.8	13.6
2014	6.9	5.0	10.4	14.1
2015	7.0	5.5	10.8	15.0
2016	7.1	5.7	11.1	14.5
2017	8.0	6.2	11.4	14.9

SOLUTION

Chart 18–8 depicts the quarterly sales for Toys International over the six-year period. Notice the seasonal nature of the sales. For each year, the fall, 4th-quarter sales are the largest and the spring, 2nd-quarter sales are the smallest. Also, there is a moderate increase in the sales from one year to the next. To observe this feature, look only at the six fall quarter sales values. Over the six-year period, the sales in the fall quarter increased. You would expect a similar seasonal pattern for 2018.

Year	Quarter	Time	Sales ($ Million)	Year	Quarter	Time	Sales ($ Million)
2012	Winter	1	6.7	2015	Winter	13	7.0
	Spring	2	4.6		Spring	14	5.5
	Summer	3	10.0		Summer	15	10.8
	Fall	4	12.7		Fall	16	15.0
2013	Winter	5	6.5	2016	Winter	17	7.1
	Spring	6	4.6		Spring	18	5.7
	Summer	7	9.8		Summer	19	11.1
	Fall	8	13.6		Fall	20	14.5
2014	Winter	9	6.9	2017	Winter	21	8.0
	Spring	10	5.0		Spring	22	6.2
	Summer	11	10.4		Summer	23	11.4
	Fall	12	14.1		Fall	24	14.9

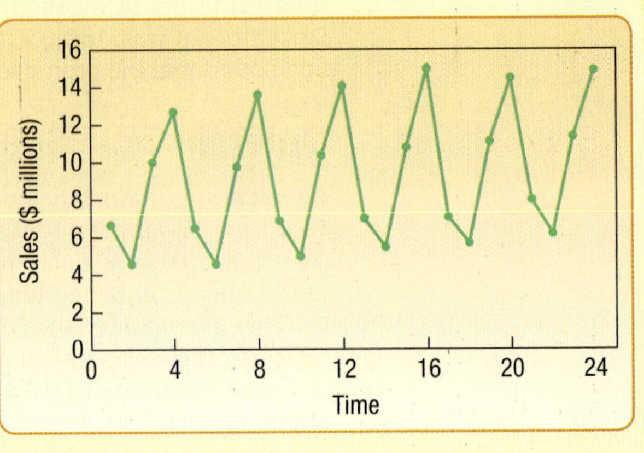

CHART 18–8 Toys International Quarterly Sales in ($ Million), 2012 to 2017

There are six steps to determining the quarterly seasonal indexes.

Step 1: For the following discussion, refer to Table 18–7. The first step is to determine the four-quarter moving total for 2012. Starting with the winter quarter of 2012, we add $6.7, $4.6, $10.0, and $12.7. The total is $34.0 (million). The four-quarter total is "moved along" by adding the spring, summer, and fall sales of 2012 to the winter sales of 2013. The total is $33.8 (million), found by 4.6 + 10.0 + 12.7 + 6.5. This procedure is continued for the quarterly sales for each of the six years. Column 2 of Table 18–7 shows all of the moving totals. Note that the moving total 34.0 is positioned between the spring and summer sales of 2012. The next moving total, 33.8, is positioned between sales for summer and fall 2012, and so on. Check the totals frequently to avoid arithmetic errors.

Step 2: Each quarterly moving total in column 2 is divided by 4 to give the four-quarter moving average. (See column 3.) All the moving averages are still positioned between the quarters. For example, the first moving average (8.500) is positioned between spring and summer 2012.

Step 3: The moving averages are then centered. The first centered moving average is found by (8.500 + 8.450)/2 = 8.475 and centered opposite summer 2012. The second moving average is found by (8.450 + 8.450)/2 = 8.450. The others are found similarly. Note in column 4 that a centered moving average is positioned on a particular quarter.

Step 4: The **specific seasonal index** for each quarter is then computed by dividing the sales in column 1 by the centered moving average in column 4. The specific seasonal index reports the ratio of the original time series value to the moving average. To explain further, if the time series is represented by *TSCI* and the moving average by *TC*, then, algebraically, if we compute *TSCI*/*TC*, the result is the specified seasonal component *SI*. The specific seasonal index for the summer quarter of 2012 is 1.180, found by 10.0/8.475.

TABLE 18–7 Computations Needed for the Specific Seasonal Indexes

Year	Quarter	(1) Sales ($ millions)	(2) Four-Quarter Total	(3) Four-Quarter Moving Average	(4) Centered Moving Average	(5) Specific Seasonal
2012	Winter	6.7				
	Spring	4.6				
			34.0	8.500		
	Summer	10.0			8.475	1.180
			33.8	8.450		
	Fall	12.7			8.450	1.503
			33.8	8.450		
2013	Winter	6.5			8.425	0.772
			33.6	8.400		
	Spring	4.6			8.513	0.540
			34.5	8.625		
	Summer	9.8			8.675	1.130
			34.9	8.725		
	Fall	13.6			8.775	1.550
			35.3	8.825		
2014	Winter	6.9			8.900	0.775
			35.9	8.975		
	Spring	5.0			9.038	0.553
			36.4	9.100		
	Summer	10.4			9.113	1.141
			36.5	9.125		
	Fall	14.1			9.188	1.535
			37.0	9.250		
2015	Winter	7.0			9.300	0.753
			37.4	9.350		
	Spring	5.5			9.463	0.581
			38.3	9.575		
	Summer	10.8			9.588	1.126
			38.4	9.600		
	Fall	15.0			9.625	1.558
			38.6	9.650		
2016	Winter	7.1			9.688	0.733
			38.9	9.725		
	Spring	5.7			9.663	0.590
			38.4	9.600		
	Summer	11.1			9.713	1.143
			39.3	9.825		
	Fall	14.5			9.888	1.466
			39.8	9.950		
2017	Winter	8.0			9.888	0.801
			40.1	10.025		
	Spring	6.2			10.075	0.615
			40.5	10.125		
	Summer	11.4				
	Fall	14.9				

Step 5: The specific seasonal indexes are organized in Table 18–8. This table will help us locate the specific seasonals for the corresponding quarters. The values 1.180, 1.130, 1.141, 1.126, and 1.143 all represent estimates of the typical seasonal index for the summer quarter. A reasonable method to find a typical seasonal index is to average these values in order to eliminate the irregular component. So we find the typical index for the summer quarter by (1.180 + 1.130 + 1.141 + 1.126 + 1.143)/5 = 1.144.

TABLE 18–8 Calculations Needed for Typical Quarterly Indexes

Year	Winter	Spring	Summer	Fall	
2012			1.180	1.503	
2013	0.772	0.540	1.130	1.550	
2014	0.775	0.553	1.141	1.535	
2015	0.753	0.581	1.126	1.558	
2016	0.733	0.590	1.143	1.466	
2017	0.801	0.615			
Total	3.834	2.879	5.720	7.612	
Mean	0.767	0.576	1.144	1.522	4.009
Adjusted	0.765	0.575	1.141	1.519	4.000
Index	76.5	57.5	114.1	151.9	

Step 6: The four quarterly means (0.767, 0.576, 1.144, and 1.522) should theoretically total 4.00 because the average is set at 1.0. The total of the four quarterly means may not exactly equal 4.00 due to rounding. In this problem, the total of the means is 4.009. A *correction factor* is therefore applied to each of the four means to force them to total 4.00.

CORRECTION FACTOR FOR ADJUSTING QUARTERLY MEANS

$$\text{Correction factor} = \frac{4.00}{\text{Total of four means}} \tag{18–3}$$

In this example,

$$\text{Correction factor} = \frac{4.00}{4.009} = 0.997755$$

The adjusted winter quarterly index is, therefore, .767(.997755) = .765. Each of the means is adjusted downward so that the total of the four quarterly means is 4.00. Usually indexes are reported as percentages, so each value in the last row of Table 18–8 has been multiplied by 100. So the index for the winter quarter is 76.5 and for the fall it is 151.9. How are these values interpreted? Sales for the fall quarter are 51.9% above the typical quarter, and for winter they are 23.5% below the typical quarter (100.0 − 76.5). These findings should not surprise you. The period prior to Christmas (the fall quarter) is when toy sales are brisk. After Christmas (the winter quarter), sales of the toys decline drastically.

Statistical software can perform these calculations. For example, the output from the MegaStat add-in for Excel is shown below. Use of software will greatly reduce the computational time and the chance of an error in arithmetic, but you should understand the steps in the process, as outlined earlier. There can be slight differences in the answers, due to the number of digits carried in the calculations.

Centered Moving Average and Deseasonalization

t	Year	Quarter	Sales	Centered Moving Average	Ratio to CMA	Seasonal Indexes	Deseasonalized Sales
1	2012	1	6.70			0.765	8.759
2	2012	2	4.60			0.575	8.004
3	2012	3	10.00	8.475	1.180	1.141	8.761
4	2012	4	12.70	8.450	1.503	1.519	8.361
5	2013	1	6.50	8.425	0.772	0.765	8.498
6	2013	2	4.60	8.513	0.540	0.575	8.004
7	2013	3	9.80	8.675	1.130	1.141	8.586
8	2013	4	13.60	8.775	1.550	1.519	8.953
9	2014	1	6.90	8.900	0.775	0.765	9.021
10	2014	2	5.00	9.038	0.553	0.575	8.700
11	2014	3	10.40	9.113	1.141	1.141	9.112
12	2014	4	14.10	9.188	1.535	1.519	9.283
13	2015	1	7.00	9.300	0.753	0.765	9.151
14	2015	2	5.50	9.463	0.581	0.575	9.570
15	2015	3	10.80	9.588	1.126	1.141	9.462
16	2015	4	15.00	9.625	1.558	1.519	9.875
17	2016	1	7.10	9.688	0.733	0.765	9.282
18	2016	2	5.70	9.663	0.590	0.575	9.918
19	2016	3	11.10	9.713	1.143	1.141	9.725
20	2016	4	14.50	9.888	1.466	1.519	9.546
21	2017	1	8.00	9.988	0.801	0.765	10.459
22	2017	2	6.20	10.075	0.615	0.575	10.788
23	2017	3	11.40			1.141	9.988
24	2017	4	14.90			1.519	9.809

Calculation of Seasonal Indexes

	1	2	3	4	
2012			1.180	1.503	
2013	0.772	0.540	1.130	1.550	
2014	0.775	0.553	1.141	1.535	
2015	0.753	0.581	1.126	1.558	
2016	0.733	0.590	1.143	1.466	
2017	0.801	0.615			
Mean:	0.767	0.576	1.144	1.522	4.009
Adjusted:	0.765	0.575	1.141	1.519	4.000

Now we briefly summarize the reasoning underlying the preceding calculations. The original data in column 1 of Table 18–7 contain trend (*T*), cyclical (*C*), seasonal (*S*), and irregular (*I*) components. The ultimate objective is to remove seasonal (*S*) from the original sales valuation.

Columns 2 and 3 in Table 18–7 are concerned with deriving the centered moving average given in column 4. Basically, we "average out" the seasonal and irregular fluctuations from the original data in column 1. Thus, in column 4 we have only trend and cyclical (*TC*).

Next, we divide the sales data in column 1 (*TCSI*) by the centered fourth-quarter moving average in column 4 (*TC*) to arrive at the specific seasonals in column 5 (*SI*). In terms of letters, $TCSI/TC = SI$. We multiply *SI* by 100.0 to express the typical seasonal in index form.

Finally, we take the mean of all the winter typical indexes, all the spring indexes, and so on. This averaging eliminates most of the irregular fluctuations from the specific seasonals, and the resulting four indexes indicate the typical seasonal sales pattern.

SELF-REVIEW 18–4

Teton Village, Wyoming, near Grand Teton Park and Yellowstone Park, contains shops, restaurants, and motels. The village has two peak seasons—winter, for skiing on the 10,000-foot slopes, and summer, for tourists visiting the parks. The number of visitors (in thousands) by quarter for 5 years, 2013 through 2017, follows.

	Quarter			
Year	**Winter**	**Spring**	**Summer**	**Fall**
2013	117.0	80.7	129.6	76.1
2014	118.6	82.5	121.4	77.0
2015	114.0	84.3	119.9	75.0
2016	120.7	79.6	130.7	69.6
2017	125.2	80.2	127.6	72.0

(a) Develop the typical seasonal pattern for Teton Village using the ratio-to-moving-average method.
(b) Explain the typical index for the winter season.

EXERCISES

9. FILE Victor Anderson, the owner of Anderson Belts Inc., is studying absenteeism among his employees. His workforce is small, consisting of only five employees. For the last 3 years, 2014 through 2016, he recorded the following number of employee absences, in days, for each quarter.

	Quarter			
Year	**I**	**II**	**III**	**IV**
2014	4	10	7	3
2015	5	12	9	4
2016	6	16	12	4

Determine a typical seasonal index for each of the four quarters.

10. FILE Appliance Center sells a variety of electronic equipment and home appliances. For the last 4 years, 2013 through 2016, the following quarterly sales (in $ millions) were reported.

	Quarter			
Year	**I**	**II**	**III**	**IV**
2013	5.3	4.1	6.8	6.7
2014	4.8	3.8	5.6	6.8
2015	4.3	3.8	5.7	6.0
2016	5.6	4.6	6.4	5.9

Determine a typical seasonal index for each of the four quarters.

LO18-7
Deseasonalize a time series using seasonal indexes.

DESEASONALIZING DATA

A set of typical indexes is very useful in adjusting a sales series, for example, for seasonal fluctuations. The resulting sales series is called **deseasonalized sales** or **seasonally adjusted sales.** The reason for deseasonalizing the sales series is to remove the seasonal fluctuations so that the trend and cycle can be studied. To illustrate the procedure, the quarterly sales totals of Toys International from Table 18–6 are repeated in column 1 of Table 18–9.

TABLE 18–9 Actual and Deseasonalized Sales for Toys International

Year	Quarter	(1) Sales	(2) Seasonal Index	(3) Deseasonalized Sales
2012	Winter	6.7	0.765	8.759
	Spring	4.6	0.575	8.004
	Summer	10.0	1.141	8.761
	Fall	12.7	1.519	8.361
2013	Winter	6.5	0.765	8.498
	Spring	4.6	0.575	8.004
	Summer	9.8	1.141	8.586
	Fall	13.6	1.519	8.953
2014	Winter	6.9	0.765	9.021
	Spring	5.0	0.575	8.700
	Summer	10.4	1.141	9.112
	Fall	14.1	1.519	9.283
2015	Winter	7.0	0.765	9.151
	Spring	5.5	0.575	9.570
	Summer	10.8	1.141	9.462
	Fall	15.0	1.519	9.875
2016	Winter	7.1	0.765	9.282
	Spring	5.7	0.575	9.918
	Summer	11.1	1.141	9.725
	Fall	14.5	1.519	9.546
2017	Winter	8.0	0.765	10.459
	Spring	6.2	0.575	10.788
	Summer	11.4	1.141	9.988
	Fall	14.9	1.519	9.809

To remove the effect of seasonal variation, the sales amount for each quarter (which contains trend, cyclical, irregular, and seasonal effects) is divided by the seasonal index for that quarter, that is, *TSCI/S*. For example, the actual sales for the first, winter quarter of 2012 were $6.7 million. The seasonal index for the winter quarter is 76.5%, using the results on page 674. The index of 76.5 indicates that sales for the winter quarter are typically 23.5% below the average for a typical quarter. By dividing the actual sales of $6.7 million by 76.5 and multiplying the result by 100, we find the *deseasonalized sales* value—that is, removed the seasonal effect on sales—for the winter quarter of 2012. It is $8,758,170, found by ($6,700,000/76.5)100. We continue this process for the other quarters in column 3 of Table 18–9, with the results reported in millions of dollars. Because the seasonal component has been removed (divided out) from the quarterly sales, the deseasonalized sales value contains only the trend (*T*), cyclical (*C*), and irregular (*I*) components. Scanning the deseasonalized sales in column 3 of Table 18–9, we see that the sales of toys showed a moderate increase over the six-year period. Chart 18–9 shows both the actual sales and the deseasonalized sales. It is clear that removing the seasonal factor allows us to focus on the overall long-term trend of sales.

We will also be able to determine the regression equation of the trend data and use it to forecast future sales.

Year	Time	Sales ($ Million)	Deseasonalized Sales ($ Million)	Year	Time	Sales ($ Million)	Deseasonalized Sales ($ Million)
2012	1	6.7	8.759	2015	13	7.0	9.151
	2	4.6	8.004		14	5.5	9.570
	3	10.0	8.761		15	10.8	9.462
	4	12.7	8.361		16	15.0	9.875
2013	5	6.5	8.498	2016	17	7.1	9.282
	6	4.6	8.004		18	5.7	9.918
	7	9.8	8.586		19	11.1	9.725
	8	13.6	8.953		20	14.5	9.546
2014	9	6.9	9.021	2017	21	8.0	10.459
	10	5.0	8.700		22	6.2	10.788
	11	10.4	9.112		23	11.4	9.988
	12	14.1	9.283		24	14.9	9.809

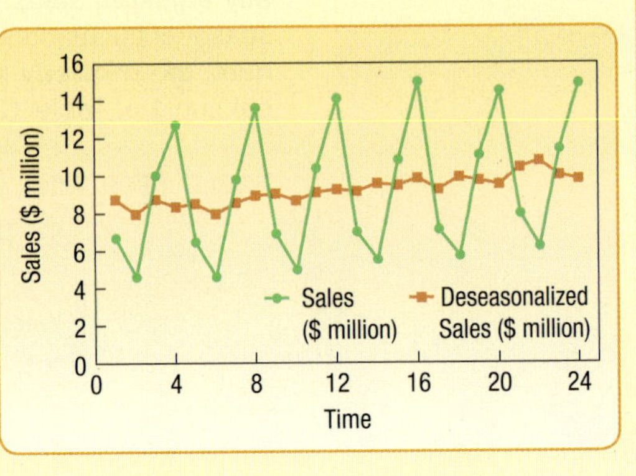

CHART 18–9 Actual and Deseasonalized Sales for Toys International (2012 to 2017)

Using Deseasonalized Data to Forecast

The procedure for identifying trend and the seasonal adjustments can be combined to yield seasonally adjusted forecasts. To identify the trend, we determine the least squares trend equation on the deseasonalized historical data. Then we project this trend into future periods, and finally we adjust these trend values to account for the seasonal factors. The following example will help to clarify.

EXAMPLE

Toys International would like to forecast its sales for each quarter of 2018. Use the information in Table 18–9 to determine the forecast.

SOLUTION

The deseasonalized data depicted in Chart 18–9 seem to follow a straight line. Hence, it is reasonable to develop a linear trend equation based on these data. The deseasonalized trend equation is:

$$\hat{y} = a + bt$$

where:

$\hat{y}$ is the estimated trend value for Toys International sales for the period t.
a is the intercept of the trend line at time 0.
b is the slope of the line.
t is the coded time period.

The winter quarter of 2012 is the first quarter, so it is coded 1, the spring quarter of 2012 is coded 2, and so on. The last quarter of 2017 is coded 24.

We use Excel to find the regression equation. The output follows. The output includes a scatter diagram of the coded time periods and the deseasonalized sales as well as the regression line.

The equation for the trend line is:

$$\hat{y} = 8.11043 + 0.08988t$$

The slope of the trend line is 0.08988. This shows that over the 24 quarters the deseasonalized sales increased at a rate of 0.08988 ($ million) per quarter, or $89,880 per quarter. The value of 8.11043 is the intercept of the trend line on the Y-axis (i.e., for $t = 0$).

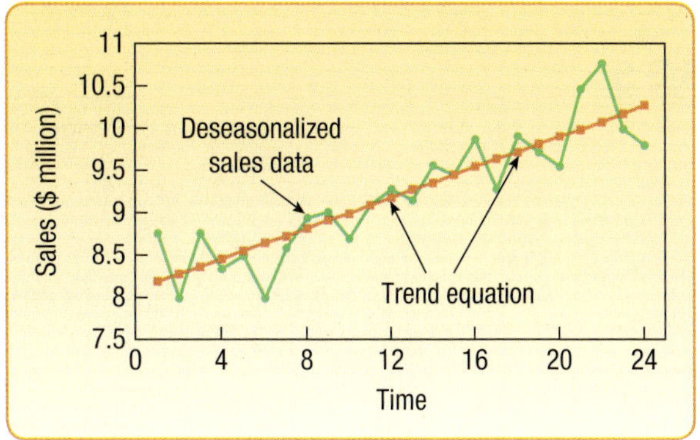

The coefficient of determination is .785. This value is computed using Excel and is shown in the text box on the graph. We can use this value as an indication of the fit of the data. Because this is *not* sample information, technically we should not use R^2 for judging a regression equation. However, it will serve to quickly evaluate the fit of the deseasonalized sales data. In this instance, because R^2 is rather large, we conclude the deseasonalized sales of Toys International are effectively explained by a linear trend equation.

If we assume that the past 24 periods are a good indicator of future sales, we can use the trend equation to estimate future sales. For example, for the winter quarter of 2018 the value of t is 25. Therefore, the estimated sales of that period are 10.35743, found by

$$\hat{y} = 8.11043 + 0.08988t = 8.11043 + 0.08988(25) = 10.35743$$

The estimated deseasonalized sales for the winter quarter of 2018 are $10,357,430. This is the sales forecast, before we consider the effects of seasonality.

We use the same procedure and an Excel spreadsheet to determine a forecast for each of the four quarters of 2018. A partial Excel output follows.

Quarterly Forecast for Toys International 2018

Quarter	Time	Estimated Sales	Seasonal Index	Quarterly Forecast
Winter	25	10.35743	0.765	7.92343
Spring	26	10.44731	0.575	6.00720
Summer	27	10.53719	1.141	12.02293
Fall	28	10.62707	1.519	16.14252

Now that we have the forecasts for the four quarters of 2018, we can seasonally adjust them. The index for a winter quarter is 0.765. So we can seasonally adjust the forecast for the winter quarter of 2018 by 10.35743(.765) = 7.92343. The estimates for each of the four quarters of 2018 are in the right-hand column of the Excel output. Notice how the seasonal adjustments drastically increase the sales estimates for the last two quarters of the year.

SELF-REVIEW 18–5

Westberg Electric Company sells electric motors to customers in the Jamestown, New York, area. The monthly trend equation, based on 5 years of monthly data, is

$$\hat{y} = 4.4 + 0.5t$$

The seasonal factor for the month of January is 120, and it is 95 for February. Determine the seasonally adjusted forecast for January and February of the sixth year.

EXERCISES

11. The planning department of Padget and Kure Shoes, the manufacturer of an exclusive brand of women's shoes, developed the following trend equation, in millions of pairs, based on 5 years of quarterly data.

$$\hat{y} = 3.30 + 1.75t$$

The following table gives the seasonal factors for each quarter.

	Quarter			
	I	II	III	IV
Index	110.0	120.0	80.0	90.0

Determine the seasonally adjusted forecast for each of the four quarters of the sixth year.

12. Team Sports Inc. sells sporting goods to high schools and colleges via a nationally distributed catalog. Management at Team Sports estimates it will sell 2,000 Wilson Model A2000 catcher's mitts next year. The deseasonalized sales are projected to be the same for each of the four quarters next year. The seasonal factor for the second quarter is 145. Determine the seasonally adjusted sales for the second quarter of next year.
13. Refer to Exercise 9 regarding the absences at Anderson Belts, Inc. Use the seasonal indexes you computed to determine the deseasonalized absences. Determine the linear trend equation based on the quarterly data for the 3 years. Forecast the seasonally adjusted absences for 2017.
14. Refer to Exercise 10, regarding sales at Appliance Center. Use the seasonal indexes you computed to determine the deseasonalized sales. Determine the linear trend equation based on the quarterly data for the 4 years. Forecast the seasonally adjusted sales for 2017.

LO18-8
Conduct a hypothesis test of autocorrelation.

THE DURBIN-WATSON STATISTIC

Time series data or observations collected successively over a period of time present a particular difficulty when you use the technique of regression. One of the assumptions traditionally used in regression is that the successive residuals are independent. This means that there is not a pattern to the residuals, the residuals are not highly correlated, and there are not long runs of positive or negative residuals. In Chart 18–10, the residuals are scaled on the vertical axis and the $\hat{y}$ values along the horizontal axis. Notice there are "runs" of residuals above and below the 0 line. If we computed the correlation between successive residuals, it is likely the correlation would be strong.

This condition is called **autocorrelation** or serial correlation.

AUTOCORRELATION Successive residuals are correlated.

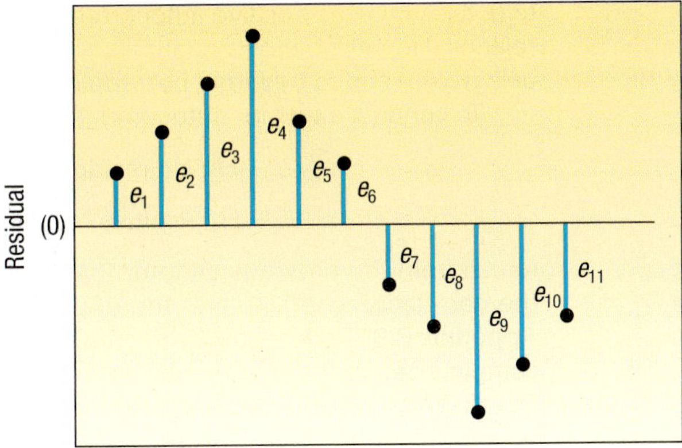

CHART 18–10 Correlated Residuals

Successive residuals are correlated in time series data because an event in one time period often influences the event in the next period. To explain, the owner of a furniture store decides to have a sale this month and spends a large amount of money advertising the event. We would expect a correlation between sales and advertising expense, but all the results of the increase in advertising are not experienced this month. It is likely that some of the effect of the advertising carries over into next month. Therefore, we expect correlation among the residuals.

The regression relationship in a time series is written

$$Y_t = \alpha + \beta_1 X_t + \varepsilon_t$$

where the subscript *t* is used in place of *i* to suggest the data were collected over time.

If the residuals are correlated, problems occur when we try to conduct tests of hypotheses about the regression coefficients. Also, a confidence interval or a prediction interval, where the multiple standard error of estimate is used, may not yield the correct results.

The autocorrelation, reported as *r*, is the strength of the association among the residuals. The *r* has the same characteristics as the coefficient of correlation. That is, values close to −1.00 or 1.00 indicate a strong association, and values near 0 indicate no association. Instead of directly conducting a hypothesis test on *r*, we use the **Durbin-Watson statistic.**

The Durbin-Watson statistic, identified by the letter *d*, is computed by first determining the residuals for each observation. That is, $e_t = (y_t - \hat{y}_t)$. Next, we compute *d* using the following relationship.

DURBIN-WATSON STATISTIC

$$d = \frac{\sum_{t=2}^{n}(e_t - e_{t-1})^2}{\sum_{t=1}^{n}(e_t)^2} \quad \textbf{(18–4)}$$

To determine the numerator of formula (18–4), we lag each of the residuals one period and then square the difference between consecutive residuals. This may also be called finding the differences. This accounts for summing the observations from 2, rather than from 1, up to *n*. In the denominator, we square the residuals and sum over all *n* observations.

The value of the Durbin-Watson statistic can range from 0 to 4. The value of *d* is 2.00 when there is no autocorrelation among the residuals. When the value of *d* is close to 0, this indicates positive autocorrelation. Values beyond 2 indicate negative autocorrelation. Negative autocorrelation seldom exists in practice. To occur, successive residuals would tend to be large, but would have opposite signs.

To conduct a test for autocorrelation, the null and alternate hypotheses are:

$$H_0\text{: No residual correlation } (\rho = 0)$$

$$H_1\text{: Positive residual correlation } (\rho > 0)$$

Recall from the previous chapter that r refers to the sample correlation and that ρ is the correlation coefficient in the population. The critical values for d are reported in Appendix B.9. To determine the critical value, we need α (the significance level), n (the sample size), and k (the number of independent variables). The decision rule for the Durbin-Watson test is altered from what we are used to. As usual, there is a range of values where the null hypothesis is rejected and a range where it is not rejected. However, there is also a range of values where d is inconclusive. That is, in the inconclusive range the null hypothesis is neither rejected nor not rejected. To state this more formally:

- Values less than d_l cause the rejection of the null hypothesis.
- Values greater then d_u will result in the null hypothesis not being rejected.
- Values of d between d_l and d_u yield inconclusive results.

The subscript l refers to the lower limit of d and the subscript u the upper limit.

How do we interpret the various decisions for the test for residual correlation? If the null hypothesis is not rejected, we conclude that autocorrelation is not present. The residuals are not correlated, there is no autocorrelation present, and the regression assumption has been met. There will not be any problem with the estimated value of the standard error of estimate. If the null hypothesis is rejected, then we conclude that autocorrelation is present.

The usual remedy for autocorrelation is to include another predictor variable that captures time order. For example, we might use the square root of y instead of y. This transformation will result in a change in the distribution of the residuals. If the result falls in the inconclusive range, more sophisticated tests are needed, or conservatively, we treat the conclusion as rejecting the null hypothesis.

An example will show the details of the Durbin-Watson test and how the results are interpreted.

EXAMPLE

© Arthur Tilley/Getty Images

Banner Rocker Company manufactures and markets rocking chairs. The company developed a special rocker for senior citizens, which it advertises extensively on TV. Banner's market for the special chair is the Carolinas, Florida, and Arizona where there are many senior citizens and retired people. The president of Banner Rocker is studying the association between his advertising expense (X) and the number of rockers sold over the last 20 months (Y). He collected the following data. He would like to create a model to forecast sales, based on the amount spent on advertising, but is concerned that, because he gathered these data over consecutive months, there might be problems with autocorrelation.

Month	Sales (000)	Advertising ($ millions)	Month	Sales (000)	Advertising ($ millions)
1	153	$5.5	11	169	6.3
2	156	5.5	12	176	5.9
3	153	5.3	13	176	6.1
4	147	5.5	14	179	6.2
5	159	5.4	15	184	6.2
6	160	5.3	16	181	6.5
7	147	5.5	17	192	6.7
8	147	5.7	18	205	6.9
9	152	5.9	19	215	6.5
10	160	6.2	20	209	6.4

Determine the regression equation. Is advertising a good predictor of sales? If the owner were to increase the amount spent on advertising by $1,000,000, how many additional chairs can he expect to sell? Investigate the possibility of autocorrelation.

SOLUTION

The first step is to determine the regression equation.

SUMMARY OUTPUT

Regression Statistics	
Multiple R	0.828
R Square	0.685
Adjusted R Square	0.668
Standard Error	12.347
Observations	20

ANOVA

	df	*SS*	*MS*	*F*
Regression	1	5967.731456	5967.73146	39.1430957
Residual	18	2744.268544	152.459364	
Total	19	8712		

	Coefficients	*Standard Error*	*t Stat*	*P-value*
Intercept	-43.80	34.44	-1.27	0.22
Advertising	35.95	5.75	6.256	0.00

The coefficient of determination is 68.5%. So we know there is a strong positive association between the variables. We conclude that, as we increase the amount spent on advertising, we can expect to sell more chairs. Of course this is what we had hoped.

How many more chairs can we expect to sell if we increase advertising by $1,000,000? We must be careful with the units of the data. Sales are in thousands of chairs and advertising expense is in millions of dollars. The regression equation is:

$$\hat{y} = -43.80 + 35.95x$$

This equation indicates that an increase of 1 in X will result in an increase of 35.95 in y. So an increase of $1,000,000 in advertising will increase sales by 35,950 chairs. To put it another way, it will cost $27.82 in additional advertising expense per chair sold, found by $1,000,000/35,950.

What about the potential issue of autocorrelation? Many software packages will calculate the value of the Durbin-Watson test and output the results. To understand the nature of the test and to see the details of formula (18–4), we use an Excel spreadsheet.

A	B	C	D	E	F	G	H
Month	Sales (000) y	Advertising ($ Millions) x	Predicted Sales $\hat{y}$	Residuals $e_t = y - \hat{y}$	Lagged Residuals e_{t-1}	$(e_t - e_{t-1})^2$	e_t^2
1	153	5.5	153.925	-0.925			0.8556
2	156	5.5	153.925	2.075	-0.925	9.000	4.3056
3	153	5.3	146.735	6.265	2.075	17.556	39.2502
4	147	5.5	153.925	-6.925	6.265	173.976	47.9556
5	159	5.4	150.330	8.670	-6.925	243.204	75.1689
6	160	5.3	146.735	13.265	8.670	21.114	175.9602
7	147	5.5	153.925	-6.925	13.265	407.636	47.9556
8	147	5.7	161.115	-14.115	-6.925	51.696	199.2332
9	152	5.9	168.305	-16.305	-14.115	4.796	265.8530
10	160	6.2	179.090	-19.090	-16.305	7.756	364.4281
11	169	6.3	182.685	-13.685	-19.090	29.214	187.2792
12	176	5.9	168.305	7.695	-13.685	457.104	59.2130
13	176	6.1	175.495	0.505	7.695	51.696	0.2550
14	179	6.2	179.090	-0.090	0.505	0.354	0.0081
15	184	6.2	179.090	4.910	-0.090	25.000	24.1081
16	181	6.5	189.875	-8.875	4.910	190.026	78.7656
17	192	6.7	197.065	-5.065	-8.875	14.516	25.6542
18	205	6.9	204.255	0.745	-5.065	33.756	0.5550
19	215	6.5	189.875	25.125	0.745	594.384	631.2656
20	209	6.4	186.280	22.720	25.125	5.784	516.1984
						2338.570	2744.26858

$\sum_{t=1}^{n}(e_t)^2$

$\sum_{t=2}^{n}(e_t - e_{t-1})^2$

To investigate the possible autocorrelation, we need to determine the residuals for each observation. We find the fitted values—that is, the $\hat{y}$—for each of the 20 months. This information is shown in the fourth column, column D. Next we find the residual, which is the difference between the actual value and the fitted values. So for the first month:

$$\hat{y} = -43.80 + 35.950x = -43.80 + 35.950(5.5) = 153.925$$

$$e_1 = y_1 - \hat{y}_1 = 153 - 153.925 = -0.925$$

The residual, reported in column E, is slightly different due to rounding in the software. Notice in particular the string of five negative residuals for months 7 through 11. In column F, we lag the residuals one period. In column G, we find the difference between the current residual and the residual in the previous and square this difference. Using the values from the software:

$$(e_t - e_{t-1})^2 = (e_2 - e_{2-1})^2 = [2.075 - (-.925)]^2 = (3.0000)^2 = 9.0000$$

The other values in column G are found the same way. The values in column H are the squares of those in column E.

$$(e_1)^2 = (-0.925)^2 = 0.8556$$

To find the value of d, we need the sums of columns G and H. These sums are noted in blue in the spreadsheet.

$$d = \frac{\sum_{t=2}^{n}(e_t - e_{t-1})^2}{\sum_{t=1}^{n}(e_t)^2} = \frac{2338.570}{2744.269} = 0.8522$$

Now to answer the question as to whether there is significant autocorrelation. The null and the alternate hypotheses are stated as follows.

H_0: No residual correlation

H_1: Positive residual correlation

The critical value of d is found in Appendix B.9, a portion of which is shown below. There is one independent variable, so $k = 1$, the level of significance is 0.05, and the sample size is 20. We move to the .05 table, the columns where $k = 1$, and the row of 20. The reported values are $d_l = 1.20$ and $d_u = 1.41$. The null hypothesis is rejected if $d < 1.20$ and not rejected if $d > 1.41$. No conclusion is reached if d is between 1.20 and 1.41.

n	k 1		2	
	d_l	d_u	d_l	d_u
15	1.08	1.36	0.95	1.54
16	1.10	1.37	0.98	1.54
17	1.13	1.38	1.02	1.54
18	1.16	1.39	1.05	1.53
19	1.18	1.40	1.08	1.53
20	1.20	1.41	1.10	1.54
21	1.22	1.42	1.13	1.54
22	1.24	1.43	1.15	1.54
23	1.26	1.44	1.17	1.54
24	1.27	1.45	1.19	1.55
25	1.29	1.45	1.21	1.55

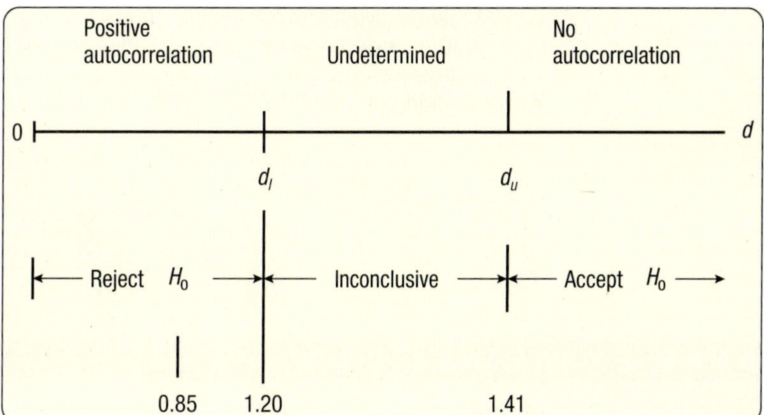

Because the computed value of d is 0.8522, which is less than the d_l, we reject the null hypothesis and accept the alternate hypothesis. We conclude that the residuals are autocorrelated. We have violated one of the regression assumptions. What do we do? The presence of autocorrelation usually means that the regression model has not been correctly specified. It is likely we need to add one or more independent variables that have some time-ordered effects on the dependent variable. The simplest independent variable to add is one that represents the time periods.

EXERCISES

15. FILE Recall Exercise 9 from Chapter 14 and the regression equation to predict job performance. See page 519.
    a. Plot the residuals in the order in which the data are presented.
    b. Test for autocorrelation at the .05 significance level.
16. FILE Consider the data in Exercise 10 from Chapter 14 and the regression equation to predict commissions earned. See page 520.
    a. Plot the residuals in the order in which the data are presented.
    b. Test for autocorrelation at the .01 significance level.

CHAPTER SUMMARY

I. A time series is a collection of data over a period of time.
  A. The trend is the long-run direction of the time series.
  B. The cyclical component is the fluctuation above and below the long-term trend line over a longer period of time.
  C. The seasonal variation is the pattern in a time series within a year. These patterns tend to repeat themselves from year to year for most businesses.
  D. The irregular variation is divided into two components.
    1. The episodic variations are unpredictable, but they can usually be identified. A flood is an example.
    2. The residual variations are random in nature.

II. A moving average is used to smooth the trend in a time series.

III. The linear trend equation is $\hat{y} = a + bt$, where a is the y-intercept, b is the slope of the line, and t is the coded time.
  A. We use least squares to determine the trend equation.
  B. If the trend is not linear, but rather the increases tend to be a constant percent, the y values are converted to logarithms, and a least squares equation is determined using the logarithms.

IV. The seasonal factor is estimated using the ratio-to-moving-average method.
  A. The six-step procedure yields a seasonal index for each period.
    1. Seasonal factors are usually computed on a monthly or a quarterly basis.
    2. The seasonal factor is used to adjust forecasts, taking into account the effects of the season.

V. The Durbin-Watson statistic [18–4] is used to test for autocorrelation.

$$d = \frac{\sum_{t=2}^{n}(e_t - e_{t-1})^2}{\sum_{t=1}^{n}(e_t)^2} \qquad \textbf{(18–4)}$$

CHAPTER EXERCISES

17. FILE The asset turnovers, excluding cash and short-term investments, for RNC Company from 2007 to 2017 are:

2007	2008	2009	2010	2011	2012	2013	2014	2015	2016	2017
1.11	1.28	1.17	1.10	1.06	1.14	1.24	1.33	1.38	1.50	1.65

  a. Plot the data.
  b. Determine the least squares trend equation.

c. Calculate the points on the trend line for 2010 and 2015, and plot the line on the graph.
d. Estimate the asset turnover for 2022.
e. How much did the asset turnover increase per year, on the average, from 2007 to 2017?

18. **FILE** The sales, in billions of dollars, of Keller Overhead Door Inc. for 2012 to 2017 are:

Year	Sales	Year	Sales
2012	7.45	2015	7.94
2013	7.83	2016	7.76
2014	8.07	2017	7.90

a. Plot the data.
b. Determine the least squares trend equation.
c. Use the trend equation to calculate the points for 2014 and 2017. Plot them on the graph and draw the regression line.
d. Estimate the net sales for 2020.
e. By how much have sales increased (or decreased) per year on the average during the period?

19. **FILE** The number of employees, in thousands, of Keller Overhead Door Inc. for the years 2012 to 2017 are:

Year	Employees (000's)	Year	Employees (000's)
2012	45.6	2015	39.3
2013	42.2	2016	34.0
2014	41.1	2017	30.0

a. Plot the data.
b. Determine the least squares trend equation.
c. Use the trend equation to calculate the points for 2014 and 2017. Plot them on the graph and draw the regression line.
d. Estimate the number of employees in 2020.
e. By how much has the number of employees increased (or decreased) per year, on the average, during the period?

20. **FILE** Listed below is the selling price for a share of PepsiCo Inc. at the close of each year from 1998 to 2015.

Year	Price	Year	Price	Year	Price	Year	Price
1998	40.6111	2003	46.62	2008	54.77	2013	82.94
1999	35.0230	2004	52.20	2009	60.80	2014	94.56
2000	49.5625	2005	59.85	2010	65.33	2015	99.92
2001	48.68	2006	62.00	2011	66.35		
2002	42.22	2007	77.51	2012	68.43		

a. Plot the data.
b. Determine the least squares trend equation.
c. Calculate the points for the years 2008 and 2013.
d. Estimate the selling price in 2018. Does this seem like a reasonable estimate based on the historical data?
e. By how much has the stock price increased or decreased (per year) on average during the period?

21. **FILE** If plotted, the following sales series would appear curvilinear. This indicates that sales are increasing at a somewhat constant annual rate (percent). To fit the sales, therefore, a logarithmic equation should be used.

Year	Sales ($ millions)	Year	Sales ($ millions)
2007	8.0	2013	39.4
2008	10.4	2014	50.5
2009	13.5	2015	65.0
2010	17.6	2016	84.1
2011	22.8	2017	109.0
2012	29.3		

a. Determine the logarithmic equation.
b. Determine the coordinates of the points on the logarithmic straight line for 2007 and 2014.
c. By what percent did sales increase per year, on the average, during the period from 2007 to 2017?
d. Based on the equation, what are the estimated sales for 2018?

22. **FILE** Reported below are the amounts spent on advertising ($ millions) by a large firm from 2007 to 2017.

Year	Amount	Year	Amount
2007	88.1	2013	132.6
2008	94.7	2014	141.9
2009	102.1	2015	150.9
2010	109.8	2016	157.9
2011	118.1	2017	162.6
2012	125.6		

a. Determine the logarithmic trend equation.
b. Estimate the advertising expenses for 2020.
c. By what percent per year did advertising expense increase during the period?

23. **FILE** Listed below is the selling price for a share of Oracle Inc. stock at the close of the year for 1998 through 2015.

Year	Price	Year	Price	Year	Price	Year	Price
1998	7.1875	2003	13.23	2008	17.73	2013	37.78
1999	28.0156	2004	13.72	2009	24.53	2014	45.02
2000	29.0625	2005	12.21	2010	31.30	2015	36.01
2001	13.81	2006	19.11	2011	26.33		
2002	10.80	2007	20.23	2012	34.08		

a. Plot the data.
b. Determine the least squares trend equation. Use both the actual stock price and the logarithm of the price. Which seems to yield a more accurate forecast?
c. Using the equation with the logarithm of price, calculate the points for the years 2001 and 2006.
d. Using the equation with the logarithm of price, estimate the selling price in 2018. Does this seem like a reasonable estimate based on the historical data?
e. Using the equation with the logarithm of price, how much has the stock price increased or decreased (per year) on average during the period?

24. **FILE** The production of Reliable Manufacturing Company for 2012 and part of 2013 follows.

Month	2012 Production (thousands)	2013 Production (thousands)	Month	2012 Production (thousands)	2013 Production (thousands)
January	6	7	July	3	4
February	7	9	August	5	
March	12	14	September	14	
April	8	9	October	6	
May	4	5	November	7	
June	3	4	December	6	

a. Using the ratio-to-moving-average method, determine the specific seasonals for July, August, and September 2012.
b. Assume that the specific seasonal indexes in the following table are correct. Insert in the table the specific seasonals you computed in part (a) for July, August, and September 2012, and determine the 12 typical seasonal indexes.

Year	Jan.	Feb.	Mar.	Apr.	May	June	July	Aug.	Sept.	Oct.	Nov.	Dec.
2012							?	?	?	92.1	106.5	92.9
2013	88.9	102.9	178.9	118.2	60.1	43.1	44.0	74.0	200.9	90.0	101.9	90.9
2014	87.6	103.7	170.2	125.9	59.4	48.6	44.2	77.2	196.5	89.6	113.2	80.6
2015	79.8	105.6	165.8	124.7	62.1	41.7	48.2	72.1	203.6	80.2	103.0	94.2
2016	89.0	112.1	182.9	115.1	57.6	56.9						

c. Interpret the typical seasonal index.

25. **FILE** The sales of Andre's Boutique for 2012 and part of 2013 are:

Month	2012 Sales (thousands)	2013 Sales (thousands)	Month	2012 Sales (thousands)	2013 Sales (thousands)
January	78	65	July	81	65
February	72	60	August	85	61
March	80	72	September	90	75
April	110	97	October	98	
May	92	86	November	115	
June	86	72	December	130	

a. Using the ratio-to-moving-average method, determine the specific seasonals for July, August, September, and October 2012.
b. Assume that the seasonal indexes in the following table are correct. Insert in the table the seasonal indexes you computed in part (a) for July, August, September, and October 2012, and determine the 12 typical seasonal indexes.

Year	Jan.	Feb.	Mar.	Apr.	May	June	July	Aug.	Sept.	Oct.	Nov.	Dec.
2012							?	?	?	?	123.6	150.9
2013	83.9	77.6	86.1	118.7	99.7	92.0	87.0	91.4	97.3	105.4	124.9	140.1
2014	86.7	72.9	86.2	121.3	96.6	92.0	85.5	93.6	98.2	103.2	126.1	141.7
2015	85.6	65.8	89.2	125.6	99.6	94.4	88.9	90.2	100.2	102.7	121.6	139.6
2016	77.3	81.2	85.8	115.7	100.3	89.7						

c. Interpret the typical seasonal index.

26. FILE The quarterly production of pine lumber, in millions of board feet, by Northwest Lumber for 2012 through 2016 is:

	Quarter			
Year	**Winter**	**Spring**	**Summer**	**Fall**
2012	7.8	10.2	14.7	9.3
2013	6.9	11.6	17.5	9.3
2014	8.9	9.7	15.3	10.1
2015	10.7	12.4	16.8	10.7
2016	9.2	13.6	17.1	10.3

a. Determine the typical seasonal pattern for the production data using the ratio-to-moving-average method.
b. Interpret the pattern.
c. Deseasonalize the data and determine the linear trend equation.
d. Project the seasonally adjusted production for the four quarters of 2017.

27. FILE Work Gloves Corp. is reviewing its quarterly sales of Toughie, the most durable glove it produces. The numbers of pairs produced (in thousands) by quarter for 2011 through 2016 are:

	Quarter			
Year	**I Jan.–Mar.**	**II Apr.–June**	**III July–Sept.**	**IV Oct.–Dec.**
2011	142	312	488	208
2012	146	318	512	212
2013	160	330	602	187
2014	158	338	572	176
2015	162	380	563	200
2016	162	362	587	205

a. Using the ratio-to-moving-average method, determine the four typical quarterly indexes.
b. Interpret the typical seasonal pattern.

28. FILE Sales of roof material, by quarter, for 2010 through 2016, by Carolina Home Construction Inc. are shown below (in $000).

	Quarter			
Year	**I**	**II**	**III**	**IV**
2010	210	180	60	246
2011	214	216	82	230
2012	246	228	91	280
2013	258	250	113	298
2014	279	267	116	304
2015	302	290	114	310
2016	321	291	120	320

a. Determine the typical seasonal patterns for sales using the ratio-to-moving-average method.
b. Deseasonalize the data and determine the trend equation.
c. Project sales for the four quarters of next year using the trend equation and seasonally adjust these values to find the predicted sales for each quarter.

29. **FILE** Blueberry Farms Golf and Fish Club of Hilton Head, South Carolina, wants to find monthly seasonal indexes for package play, nonpackage play, and total play. The package play refers to golfers who visit the area as part of a golf package. Typically, the greens fees, cart fees, lodging, maid service, and meals are included as part of a golfing package. The course earns a certain percentage of this total. The nonpackage play includes play by local residents and visitors to the area who wish to play golf. The following data, beginning with July 2014 and ending with June 2017, report the package and nonpackage play by month, as well as the total amount, in thousands of dollars.

Year	Month	Package	Local	Total	Year	Month	Package	Local	Total
2014	July	$ 18.36	$43.44	$ 61.80	2016	January	30.60	9.48	40.08
	August	28.62	56.76	85.38		February	63.54	30.96	94.50
	September	101.34	34.44	135.78		March	167.67	47.64	215.31
	October	182.70	38.40	221.10		April	299.97	59.40	359.37
	November	54.72	44.88	99.60		May	173.61	40.56	214.17
	December	36.36	12.24	48.60		June	64.98	63.96	128.94
2015	January	25.20	9.36	34.56		July	25.56	67.20	92.76
	February	67.50	25.80	93.30		August	31.14	52.20	83.34
	March	179.37	34.44	213.81		September	81.09	37.44	118.53
	April	267.66	34.32	301.98		October	213.66	62.52	276.18
	May	179.73	40.80	220.53		November	96.30	35.04	131.34
	June	63.18	40.80	103.98		December	16.20	33.24	49.44
	July	16.20	77.88	94.08	2017	January	26.46	15.96	42.42
	August	23.04	76.20	99.24		February	72.27	35.28	107.55
	September	102.33	42.96	145.29		March	131.67	46.44	178.11
	October	224.37	51.36	275.73		April	293.40	67.56	360.96
	November	65.16	25.56	90.72		May	158.94	59.40	218.34
	December	22.14	15.96	38.10		June	79.38	60.60	139.98

Using statistical software:

a. Develop a seasonal index for each month for the package sales. What do you note about the various months?

b. Develop a seasonal index for each month for the nonpackage sales. What do you note about the various months?

c. Develop a seasonal index for each month for the total sales. What do you note about the various months?

d. Compare the indexes for package sales, nonpackage sales, and total sales. Are the busiest months the same?

30. **FILE** The following is the number of retirees receiving benefits from the State Teachers Retirement System of Ohio from 1996 until 2015.

Year	Retirees	Year	Retirees	Year	Retirees	Year	Retirees
1996	70,448	2001	83,918	2006	99,248	2011	117,138
1997	72,601	2002	86,666	2007	102,771	2012	112,136
1998	75,482	2003	89,257	2008	106,099	2013	127,797
1999	78,341	2004	92,574	2009	109,031	2014	130,521
2000	81,111	2005	95,843	2010	112,483	2015	136,018

a. Plot the data.

b. Determine the least squares trend equation. Use a linear equation.

c. Calculate the points for the years 2005 and 2015.

d. Estimate the number of retirees that will be receiving benefits in 2018. Does this seem like a reasonable estimate based on the historical data?

e. By how much has the number of retirees increased or decreased (per year) on average during the period?

31. FILE Ray Anderson, owner of Anderson Ski Lodge in upstate New York, is interested in forecasting the number of visitors for the upcoming year. The following data are available, by quarter, from the first quarter of 2010 to the fourth quarter of 2016. Develop a seasonal index for each quarter. How many visitors would you expect for each quarter of 2017, if Ray projects that there will be a 10% increase from the total number of visitors in 2016? Determine the trend equation, project the number of visitors for 2017, and seasonally adjust the forecast. Which forecast would you choose?

Year	Quarter	Visitors	Year	Quarter	Visitors
2010	I	86	2014	I	188
	II	62		II	172
	III	28		III	128
	IV	94		IV	198
2011	I	106	2015	I	208
	II	82		II	202
	III	48		III	154
	IV	114		IV	220
2012	I	140	2016	I	246
	II	120		II	240
	III	82		III	190
	IV	154		IV	252
2013	I	162			
	II	140			
	III	100			
	IV	174			

32. FILE The enrollment in the College of Business at Midwestern University by quarter from 2013 to spring 2017 is:

	Quarter			
Year	Winter	Spring	Summer	Fall
2013	2,033	1,871	714	2,318
2014	2,174	2,069	840	2,413
2015	2,370	2,254	927	2,704
2016	2,625	2,478	1,136	3,001
2017	2,803	2,668	—	—

Using the ratio-to-moving-average method:

a. Determine the four quarterly indexes.

b. Interpret the quarterly pattern of enrollment. Does the seasonal variation surprise you?

c. Compute the trend equation, and forecast enrollment for the next four quarters.

33. FILE At the beginning of this chapter, we presented a graph showing the price per gallon of gasoline from 1996 until 2015. The actual data for each year are given below.

Year	Cost/Gallon	Year	Cost/Gallon
1996	1.20	2006	2.57
1997	1.20	2007	2.80
1998	1.03	2008	3.25
1999	1.14	2009	2.35
2000	1.48	2010	2.78
2001	1.42	2011	3.52
2002	1.35	2012	3.62
2003	1.56	2013	3.49
2004	1.85	2014	3.34
2005	2.27	2015	2.40

Determine the trend line using both linear and nonlinear equations. Which would you suggest? Why? Based on your recommendation as the better equation, what cost per gallon would you estimate for 2016 and 2017?

DATA ANALYTICS

(The data for this exercise is available at the text website: www.mhhe.com/lind17e.)

Use the following information obtained from annual reports of Home Depot to solve Exercises 34, 35, and 36. You will need the help of a software package such as Excel and perhaps a companion package such as MegaStat. For the years 1993 through 2015, the data include a coded time variable (1 through 23), the number of associates in thousands, net sales in millions of dollars, the mean dollar amount per transaction, and the Consumer Price Index (CPI) for each year.

Year	Time	Associates (000)	Net Sales ($ million)	Mean Amount per Transaction	CPI
1993	1	50.6	9,239	39.13	144.500
1994	2	67.3	12,477	41.29	148.200
1995	3	80.8	15,470	41.78	152.400
1996	4	98.1	19,535	42.09	156.900
1997	5	124.4	24,156	43.63	160.500
1998	6	156.7	30,219	45.05	163.000
1999	7	201.4	38,454	47.87	166.000
2000	8	227.3	45,738	48.65	172.200
2001	9	256.3	53,553	48.64	177.100
2002	10	280.9	58,247	49.43	179.900
2003	11	298.8	64,816	51.15	184.000
2004	12	323.1	73,094	54.89	188.900
2005	13	344.8	81,511	57.98	195.300
2006	14	364.4	79,022	58.90	201.600
2007	15	331.0	77,349	57.48	207.342
2008	16	322.0	71,288	55.61	215.303
2009	17	317.0	66,176	51.76	214.537
2010	18	321.0	67,997	51.93	218.056
2011	19	331.0	70,395	53.28	224.939
2012	20	340.0	74,754	54.89	229.594
2013	21	365.0	78,812	56.76	232.957
2014	22	371.0	83,176	57.87	236.736
2015	23	385.0	88,519	58.77	237.017

34. Develop a trend equation for the net sales ($ million) for Home Depot. Consider both a linear trend and a nonlinear trend. Which one would you select and why? Given the trend equation you selected, forecast the net sales for 2016 and 2017.

35. Consider the variable mean amount per transaction in the Home Depot data presented above. This variable indicates, for example, that the average customer spent $39.13 on goods during a store visit in 1993. By 2012 this amount increased to $54.89. During that same period the Consumer Price Index (CPI) as reported by the Bureau of Labor Statistics increased from 144.5 to 229.594. Convert the CPI to a 1993 base, as described on page 644 in chapter 17, and convert the mean amount per transaction to 1993 dollars. Develop a linear trend equation for the constant 1993 dollars of the mean amount per transaction. Is it reasonable that the trend is linear? Can we conclude that the value of the amount the customer spent is less?

36. Use the variables mean amount per transaction and number of associates to forecast net sales. Are these two independent variables reasonable predictors of net sales?

(Hints: What is the R^2 value? Is it large? Look at the p-values for each of the independent variables. Is this value less than .05 for each?) Because all of these variables are associated with time, it may be that there is autocorrelation. Conduct the appropriate test of hypothesis to determine if there is autocorrelation present. What is your conclusion? Again, use the .05 significance level.

37. Refer to the Baseball 2016 data, which include information on the 2016 Major League Baseball season. The data include the mean player salary since 2000. Plot the information and develop a linear trend equation. Write a brief report on your findings.

A REVIEW OF CHAPTERS 17–18

Chapter 17 presents index numbers. An *index number* describes the relative change in value from one period, called the base period, to another called the given period. It is actually a percent, but the percent sign is usually omitted. Indexes are used to compare the change in unlike series over time. For example, a company might wish to compare the change in sales with the change in the number of sales representatives employed over the same period of time. A direct comparison is not meaningful because the units for one set of data are dollars and the other people. Index numbers also facilitate the comparison of very large values, where the amount of change in the actual values is very large and therefore difficult to interpret.

There are two types of price indexes. In an *unweighted price index,* the quantities are not considered. To form an unweighted index, we divide the base period value into the current period (also called the given period) and report the percent change. So if sales were \$12,000,000 in 2011 and \$18,600,000 in 2017, the simple unweighted price index for 2017 is:

$$p = \frac{p_t}{p_0}(100) = \frac{\$18{,}600{,}000}{\$12{,}000{,}000}(100) = 155.0$$

We conclude there is a 55% increase in sales during the six-year period.

In a *weighted price index, quantities* are considered. The most widely used weighted index is the *Laspeyres price index.* It uses the base period quantities as weights to compare changes in prices. It is computed by multiplying the base period quantities by the base period price for each product considered and summing the result. This result is the denominator of the fraction. The numerator of the fraction is the product of the base period quantities and the current price. For example, an appliance store sold 50 computers at \$1,000 and 200 DVDs at \$150 each in year 2011. In 2017, the same store sold 60 computers at \$1,200 and 230 DVDs at \$175. The Laspeyres price index is:

$$p = \frac{\Sigma p_t q_0}{\Sigma p_0 q_0}(100) = \frac{\$1{,}200 \times 50 + \$175 \times 200}{\$1{,}000 \times 50 + \$150 \times 200}(100) = \frac{\$95{,}000}{\$80{,}000}(100) = 118.75$$

Notice the same base period quantities are used as weights in both the numerator and the denominator. The index indicates there has been an 18.75% increase in the value of sales during the six-year period.

The most widely used and reported index is the *Consumer Price Index (CPI).* The CPI is a Laspeyres type index. It is reported monthly by the U.S. Department of Labor and is often used to report the rate of inflation in the prices of goods and services in the United States. The current base period is 1982–84.

In Chapter 18, we studied time series and forecasting. A *time series* is a collection of data over a period of time. The earnings per share of General Electric common stock over the last 10 years is an example of a time series. There are four components to a time series: the secular trend, cyclic effects, seasonal effects, and irregular effects.

Trend is the long-term direction of the time series. It can be either increasing or decreasing.

The *cyclical component* is the fluctuation above and below the trend line over a period of several years. Economic cycles are examples of the cyclical component. Most businesses shift between relative expansion and reduction periods over a cycle of several years.

Seasonal variation is the recurring pattern of the time series within a year. The consumption of many products and services is seasonal. Beach homes along the Gulf Coast are seldom rented during the winter and ski lodges in Wyoming are not used in the summer months. Hence, we say the rentals of beach front properties and ski lodges are seasonal.

The *irregular component* includes any unpredictable events. In other words, the irregular component includes events that cannot be forecast. There are two types of irregular components. Episodic variations are unpredictable, but can usually be identified. The Houston flooding in the spring of 2016 is an example. The residual variation is random in nature and not predicted or identified.

The linear trend for a time series is given by the equation $\hat{y} = a + bt$, where $\hat{y}$ is the estimated trend value, a is the intercept with the y-axis, b is the slope of the trend line (the rate of change), and t refers to the coded values for the time periods. We use the least squares method described in Chapter 13 to determine the trend line. Autocorrelation is often a problem when using the trend equation. Autocorrelation means that successive values of the time series are correlated.

PROBLEMS

1. Listed below are the net sales (in millions of euros) for the Adidas Group from 2008 to 2015.

Year	Net Sales
2008	10,799
2009	10,381
2010	11,990
2011	13,332
2012	14,883
2013	14,203
2014	14,534
2015	16,915

a. Determine the index for 2015, using 2008 as the base period.
b. Use the period 2008 to 2010 as the base period and find the index for 2015.
c. With 2008 as the base year, use the least squares method to find the trend equation. What is the estimated consolidated revenue for 2017? What is the rate of increase per year?

2. The table below shows the labor force and the unemployment rate for three counties in northwest Pennsylvania for 2004 and 2015.

	2004		2015	
County	Labor Force	Percent Unemployed	Labor Force	Percent Unemployed
Erie	134,538	6.1	134,873	5.3
Warren	20,158	5.0	19,980	4.8
McKean	19,302	5.7	18,987	5.9

a. In 2004, the national unemployment rate was 5.5%. For 2004, compute a simple average unemployment index for the region using the national unemployment rate as the base. Interpret the simple average index.
b. In 2015, the national unemployment rate was 5.0%. For 2015, compute a simple average unemployment index for the region using the national unemployment rate as the base. Interpret the simple average index.
c. Use the data for this region of northwest Pennsylvania to create a weighted unemployment index using the Laspeyres method. Use 2004 as the base period. Interpret the index.

3. Based on five years of monthly data (the period from January 2011 to December 2015), the trend equation for a small company is $\hat{y} = 3.5 + 0.7t$. The seasonal index for January is 120 and for June it is 90. What are the seasonally adjusted sales forecasts for January 2016 and June 2016?

PRACTICE TEST

Part 1—Objective

1. To compute an index, the base period is always in the ____________. (numerator, denominator, can be in either, always 100) 1. ____________
2. A number that measures the relative change from one period to another is called a/an ____________. 2. ____________
3. In a weighted index, both the price and the ____________ are considered. 3. ____________
4. In a Laspeyres index, the ____________ quantities are used in both the numerator and denominator. (base period, given period, oldest, newest—pick one) 4. ____________
5. The current base period for the Consumer Price Index is ____________. 5. ____________
6. The long-term direction of a time series is called the ____________. 6. ____________
7. One method used to smooth the trend in a time series is a ____________. 7. ____________
8. When successive residuals are correlated, this condition is called ____________. 8. ____________
9. Irregular variation in a time series that is random in nature is called ____________. 9. ____________
10. In a three-year moving average, the weights given to each period are ____________. (the same, oldest year has the most weight, oldest year has the least weight) 10. ____________

Part 2—Problems

1. Listed below are the sales at Roberta's Ice Cream Stand for the last 5 years, 2012 through 2016.

Year	Sales
2012	$130,000
2013	145,000
2014	120,000
2015	170,000
2016	190,000

   a. Find the simple index for each year using 2012 as the base year.
   b. Find the simple index for each year using 2012–2013 as the base year.

2. Listed below are the price and quantity of several golf items purchased by members of the men's golf league at Indigo Creek Golf and Tennis Club for 2012 and 2016.

	2012		2016	
	Price	Quantity	Price	Quantity
Driver	$250.00	5	$275.00	6
Putter	60.00	12	75.00	10
Irons	700.00	3	750.00	4

   a. Determine the simple aggregate price index, with 2012 as the base period.
   b. Determine a Laspeyres price index.
   c. Determine the Paasche price index.
   d. Determine a value index.

3. The monthly linear trend equation for the Hoopes ABC Beverage Store is:

$$\hat{y} = 5.50 + 1.25t$$

The equation is based on 4 years of monthly data and is reported in thousands of dollars. The index for January is 105.0 and for February it is 98.3. Determine the seasonally adjusted forecast for January and February of the fifth year.

Statistical Process Control and Quality Management

▲ **A BICYCLE MANUFACTURER** randomly selects 10 frames each day and tests for defects. The numbers of defective frames found over the last 14 days are 3, 2, 1, 3, 2, 2, 8, 2, 0, 3, 5, 2, 0, and 4. Construct a control chart for this process and comment on whether the process is "in control." (See Exercise 11 and LO19-6.)

LEARNING OBJECTIVES

When you have completed this chapter, you will be able to:

LO19-1 Explain the purpose of quality control in production and service operations.

LO19-2 Define the two sources of process variation and explain how they are used to monitor quality.

LO19-3 Explain the use of charts to investigate the sources of process variation.

LO19-4 Compute control limits for mean and range control charts for a variable measure of quality.

LO19-5 Evaluate control charts to determine if a process is out of control.

LO19-6 Compute control limits of control charts for an attribute measure of quality.

LO19-7 Explain the process of acceptance sampling.

INTRODUCTION

Throughout this text, we present many applications of hypothesis testing. In Chapter 10, we describe methods for testing a hypothesis regarding a single population value. In Chapter 11, we describe methods for testing a hypothesis about two populations. In this chapter, we present another, somewhat different application of hypothesis testing, called **statistical process control** or **SPC.**

Statistical process control is a collection of strategies, techniques, and actions taken by an organization to ensure it is producing a quality product or providing a quality service. SPC begins at the product planning stage, when we specify the attributes of the product or service. It continues through the production stage. Each attribute throughout the process contributes to the overall quality of the product. To effectively use quality control, measurable attributes and specifications are developed against which the actual attributes of the product or service are compared.

LO19-1
Explain the purpose of quality control in production and service operations.

A BRIEF HISTORY OF QUALITY CONTROL

Prior to the 1900s, U.S. industry was largely characterized by small shops making relatively simple products, such as candles or furniture. In these small shops, the individual worker was generally a craftsman who was completely responsible for the quality of the work. The worker could ensure the quality through the personal selection of the materials, skillful manufacturing, and selective fitting and adjustment.

In the early 1900s, factories sprang up where people with limited training were formed into large assembly lines. Products became much more complex. The individual worker no longer had complete control over the quality of the product. A semiprofessional staff, usually called the Inspection Department, became responsible for the quality of the product. The quality responsibility was usually fulfilled by a 100% inspection of all the important characteristics. If there were any discrepancies noted, these problems were handled by the manufacturing department supervisor. In essence, quality was attained by "inspecting the quality into the product."

During the 1920s, Dr. Walter A. Shewhart, of Bell Telephone Laboratories, developed the concepts of statistical quality control. He introduced the concept of "controlling" the quality of a product as it was being manufactured, rather than inspecting the quality into the product after it was manufactured. For the purpose of controlling quality, Shewhart developed charting techniques for controlling in-process manufacturing operations. In addition, he introduced the concept of statistical sample inspection to estimate the quality of a product as it was being manufactured. This replaced the old method of inspecting each part after it was completed in the production operation.

Statistical quality control came into its own during World War II. The need for mass-produced war-related items, such as bomb sights, accurate radar, and other electronic equipment, at the lowest possible cost hastened the use of statistical sampling and quality control charts. Since World War II, these statistical techniques have been refined and sharpened. The use of computers has also widened the use of these techniques.

World War II virtually destroyed the Japanese production capability. Rather than retool their old production methods, the Japanese enlisted the aid of the late Dr. W. Edwards Deming, of the U.S. Department of Agriculture, to help them develop an overall plan. In a series of seminars with Japanese planners, he stressed a philosophy that is known today as Deming's 14 points. These 14 points are listed on the following page. He emphasized that quality originates from improving the process, not from inspection, and that quality is determined by the customers. The manufacturer must be able, via market research, to anticipate the needs of customers. Senior management has the responsibility for long-term improvement. Another of his points, and one that the Japanese strongly endorsed, is that every member of the company must contribute to long-term improvement. To achieve this improvement, ongoing education and training are necessary.

Deming had some ideas that did not mesh with contemporary management philosophies in the United States. Two areas where Deming's ideas differed from U.S. management philosophy were with production quotas and merit ratings. He believed these two practices, which are both common in the United States, are not productive and should be eliminated. He also pointed out that U.S. managers are mostly interested in good news. Good news, however, does not provide an opportunity for improvement. On the other hand, bad news opens the door for new products and allows for company improvement.

Listed below, in a condensed form, are Dr. Deming's 14 points. He was adamant that the 14 points needed to be adopted as a package in order to be successful. The underlying theme is cooperation, teamwork, and the belief that workers want to do their jobs in a quality fashion.

DEMING'S 14 POINTS

1. Create constancy of purpose for the continual improvement of products and service to society.
2. Adopt a philosophy that we can no longer live with commonly accepted levels of delays, mistakes, defective materials, and defective workmanship.
3. Eliminate the need for mass inspection as the way to achieve quality. Instead, achieve quality by building the product correctly in the first place.
4. End the practice of awarding business solely on the basis of price. Instead, require meaningful measures of quality along with the price.
5. Improve constantly and forever every process for planning, production, and service.
6. Institute modern methods of training on the job for all employees, including managers. This will lead to better utilization of each employee.
7. Adopt and institute leadership aimed at helping people do a better job.
8. Encourage effective two-way communication and other means to drive out fear throughout the organization so that everyone may work more effectively and more productively for the company.
9. Break down barriers between departments and staff areas.
10. Eliminate the use of slogans, posters, and exhortations demanding zero defects and new levels of productivity without providing methods.
11. Eliminate work standards that prescribe quotas for the workforce and numerical goals for people in management. Substitute aids and helpful leadership in order to achieve continual improvement in quality and productivity.
12. Remove the barriers that rob hourly workers and the people in management of their right to pride of workmanship.
13. Institute a vigorous program of education and encourage self-improvement for everyone. What an organization needs is good people and people who are improving with education. Advancement to a competitive position will have its roots in knowledge.
14. Define clearly management's permanent commitment to ever-improving quality and productivity to implement all of these principles.

Deming's 14 points did not ignore statistical quality control, which is often abbreviated as SQC. The objective of statistical quality control is to monitor production through many stages of manufacturing. We use the tools of statistical quality control, such as *X*-bar and *R* charts, to monitor the quality of many processes and services. Control charts allow us to identify when a process or service is "out of control," that is, when an excessive number of defective units are being produced.

Courtesy of National Institute of Standards and Technology

Interest in quality has accelerated dramatically in the United States since the late 1980s. Turn on the television and watch the commercials sponsored by Ford, Nissan, and GM to verify the emphasis on quality control on the assembly line. It is now one of the "in" topics in all facets of business. V. Daniel Hunt, a noted American quality control consultant, reports that in the United States 20 to 25% of the cost of production is currently spent finding and correcting mistakes. And, he added, the additional cost incurred in repairing or replacing faulty products in the field drives the total cost of poor quality to nearly 30%. In Japan, he indicated, this cost is about 3%!

In recent years, companies have been motivated to improve quality by the challenge of being recognized for their quality achievements. The Malcolm Baldrige National Quality Award, established in 1988, is awarded annually to U.S. companies that demonstrate excellence in quality achievement and management. The award categories include manufacturing, service, small business, health care, and education. Past winners include Xerox, IBM, the University of Wisconsin–Stout, Ritz-Carlton Hotel Corporation, Federal Express, and Cadillac. The 2016 winners were:

- Don Chalmers Ford, an independent business franchised by the Ford Motor Company and located in Rio Rancho, New Mexico won in the small business category. The company motto, "Real Value, Real People, Real Simple", is implemented through a commitment to "customers, quality and community."
- The Momentum Group, with headquarters in Irvine, California started in 1994 as a small contract textile distributor. Now they specialize in customized commercial interiors. In the last twenty years, Momentum Groups' sales grew more than 400 percent.
- Kindred Nursing and Rehabilitation Center, located in Mountain View, California won the award in the health care category. One hundred percent of the residents and family members surveyed expressed either "very" or "extreme" overall satisfaction levels since 2013, well above the national average assessment of similar facilities.
- Memorial Hermann Sugar Land Hospital is the largest not-for-profit health system in Southeast Texas. The hospital's focus on patient safety resulted in zero medical errors related to pressure ulcers, ventilator-associated pneumonia, transfusion reactions, and deaths from normally low mortality conditions.

You can obtain more information on these and other winners by visiting the website http://www.nist.gov/baldrige.

STATISTICS IN ACTION

Does excellence in quality management lead to higher financial performance? Recent research compared the financial performance of companies that received the Baldrige National Quality Award to similar companies that did not receive the award. The research showed that the companies receiving the award had an average of 39% higher operating income and 26% higher sales, and were 1.22% lower in their cost per sales dollar.

Six Sigma

Many service, manufacturing, and nonprofit organizations are committed to improving the quality of their services and products. "Six Sigma" is a name given to an organizationwide program designed to improve quality and performance throughout an organization. The focus of the program is to reduce the variation in any process used to produce and deliver services and products to customers. Six Sigma programs apply to production processes as well as accounting and other organizational support processes. The ultimate outcomes of a Six Sigma program are to reduce the costs of defects and errors, increase customer satisfaction and sales of products and services, and increase profits.

Six Sigma gets its name from the normal distribution. The term *sigma* means standard deviation, and "plus or minus" three standard deviations gives a total range of six standard deviations. So Six Sigma means that a process should not generate more than 3.4 defects per million for any product or service. Many companies strive for even fewer defects.

To attain this goal, a Six Sigma program trains every organization member in processes to identify sources of process variation that significantly affect quality. The process includes identifying and defining problems, collecting and analyzing data to investigate and become knowledgeable about the problem, making process improvements to reduce process variation, and implementing procedures for improving the process.

Six Sigma uses many statistical techniques to collect and analyze the data needed to reduce process variation. The following are included in this text: histograms, analysis of variation, chi-square test of independence, regression, and correlation.

General Electric, Motorola, and AlliedSignal (now a part of Honeywell) are large companies that have used Six Sigma methods and achieved significant quality improvement and cost savings. Even cities like Fort Wayne, Indiana, have used Six Sigma techniques to improve their operations. The city is reported to have saved $10 million since 2000 and improved customer service at the same time. For example, the city reduced missed trash pickups by 50% and cut the response time to repair potholes from 21 to 3 hours. You can learn more about Six Sigma ideas, methods, and training at http://www.6sigma.us.

LO19-2
Define the two sources of process variation and explain how they are used to monitor quality.

SOURCES OF VARIATION

No two products are *exactly* the same. There is always some variation. The weight of each McDonald's Quarter Pounder is not exactly 0.25 pound. Some will weigh more than 0.25 pound, others less. The standard time for the TARTA (Toledo Area Regional Transit Authority) bus run from downtown Toledo, Ohio, to Perrysburg is 25 minutes. However, each run does not take *exactly* 25 minutes. Some runs take longer. Other times the TARTA driver must wait in Perrysburg before returning to Toledo. In some cases, there is a reason for the bus being late, an accident on the expressway or a snowstorm, for example. In other cases, the driver may not "hit" the green lights or the traffic is unusually heavy and slow for no apparent reason. There are two general sources of variation in a process—chance and assignable.

Internal machine friction, slight variations in material or process conditions (such as the temperature of the mold being used to make glass bottles), atmospheric conditions (such as temperature, humidity, and the dust content of the air), and vibrations transmitted to a machine from a passing forklift are a few examples of sources of **chance variation.**

CHANCE VARIATION Variation that is random in nature. This type of variation cannot be completely eliminated unless there is a major change in the techniques, technologies, methods, equipment, or materials used in the process.

If the hole drilled in a piece of steel is too large due to a dull drill, the drill may be sharpened or a new drill inserted. An operator who continually sets up the machine incorrectly can be replaced or retrained. If the roll of steel to be used in the process does not have the correct tensile strength, it can be rejected. These are examples of **assignable variation.**

ASSIGNABLE VARIATION Variation that is not random. It can be eliminated or reduced by investigating the problem and finding the cause.

There are several reasons why we should be concerned with variation. Two are stated below.

1. It will change the shape, dispersion, and central location of the distribution of the product characteristic being measured.
2. Assignable variation is usually correctable, whereas chance variation usually cannot be corrected or stabilized economically.

LO19-3
Explain the use of charts to investigate the sources of process variation.

DIAGNOSTIC CHARTS

There are a variety of diagnostic techniques available to investigate quality problems. Two of the more prominent of these techniques are **Pareto charts** and **fishbone diagrams.**

Pareto Charts

Pareto analysis is a technique for tallying the number and type of defects that happen within a product or service. The chart is named after a 19-century Italian scientist, Vilfredo Pareto. He noted that most of the "activity" in a process is caused by relatively few of the "factors." His concept, often called the 80–20 rule, is that 80% of the activity is caused by 20% of the factors. By concentrating on 20% of the factors, managers can attack 80% of the problem. For example, Emily's Family Restaurant, located at the junction of Interstates 75 and 70, is investigating "customer complaints." The five complaints heard most frequently are discourteous service, cold food, long wait for seating, few menu choices, and unruly young children. Suppose discourteous service was mentioned most frequently and cold food second. The data show these two factors are more than 85% of the total complaints. Addressing these two complaints first will yield the largest reduction in complaints and the largest increase in customer satisfaction.

To develop a Pareto chart, we begin by tallying the type of defects. Next, we rank the defects in terms of frequency of occurrence from largest to smallest. Finally, we produce a vertical bar chart, with the height of the bars corresponding to the frequency of each defect. The following example illustrates these ideas.

EXAMPLE

The city manager of Grove City, Utah, is concerned with water usage, particularly in single-family homes. She would like to develop a plan to reduce the water usage in Grove City. To investigate, she selects a sample of 100 homes and determines the typical daily water usage for various purposes. These sample results are as follows.

Reasons for Water Usage	Gallons per Day
Laundering	24.9
Watering lawn	143.7
Personal bathing	106.7
Cooking	5.1
Swimming pool	28.3
Dishwashing	12.3
Car washing	10.4
Drinking	7.9

What is the area of greatest usage? Where should she concentrate her efforts to reduce the water usage?

SOLUTION

A Pareto chart is useful for identifying the major areas of water usage and focusing on those areas where the greatest reduction can be achieved. The first step is to convert each of the activities to a percent and then to order them from largest to smallest. The total water usage per day is 339.3 gallons, found by totaling the gallons used in the eight activities. The activity with the largest use is watering lawns. It accounts for 143.7 gallons of water per day, or 42.4% of the amount of water used. The next largest category is personal bathing, which accounts for 31.4% of the water used. These two activities account for 73.8% of the water usage.

Reasons for Water Usage	Gallons per Day	Percent
Laundering	24.9	7.3
Watering lawn	143.7	42.4
Personal bathing	106.7	31.4
Cooking	5.1	1.5
Swimming pool usage	28.3	8.3
Dishwashing	12.3	3.6
Car washing	10.4	3.1
Drinking	7.9	2.3
Total	339.3	100.0

To draw the Pareto chart, we begin by scaling the number of gallons used on the left vertical axis and the corresponding percent on the right vertical axis. Next we draw a vertical bar with the height of the bar corresponding to the activity with the largest number of occurrences. In the Grove City example, we draw a vertical bar for the activity watering lawns to a height of 143.7 gallons. (We call this the count.) We continue this procedure for the other activities, as shown in the Minitab output in Chart 19–1.

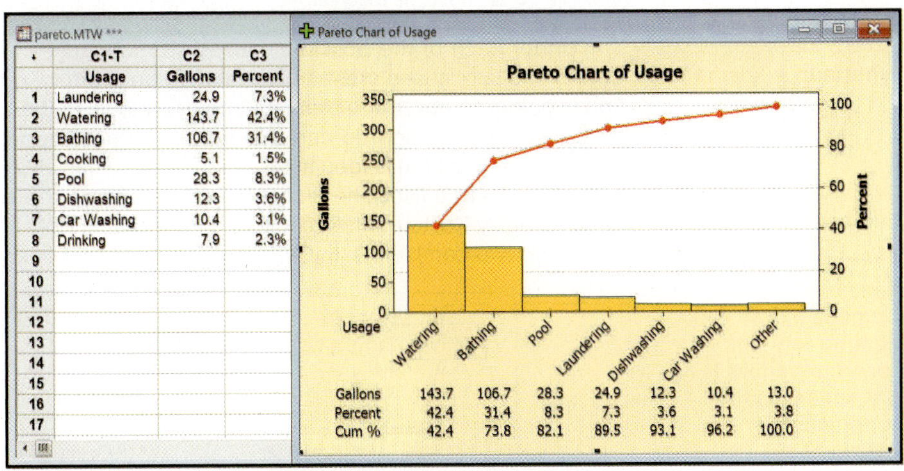

	C1-T Usage	C2 Gallons	C3 Percent
1	Laundering	24.9	7.3%
2	Watering	143.7	42.4%
3	Bathing	106.7	31.4%
4	Cooking	5.1	1.5%
5	Pool	28.3	8.3%
6	Dishwashing	12.3	3.6%
7	Car Washing	10.4	3.1%
8	Drinking	7.9	2.3%

CHART 19–1 Pareto Chart for Water Usage in Grove City, Utah

Below the chart, we list the activities, their frequency of occurrence, and the percent of the time each activity occurs. In the last row, we list the cumulative percentage. This cumulative row will allow us to quickly determine which set of activities account for most of the activity. These cumulative percents are plotted above the vertical bars. In the Grove City example, the activities of watering lawn, personal bathing, and pools account for 82.1% of the water usage. The city manager can attain the greatest gain by looking to reduce the water usage in these three areas.

Fishbone Diagrams

Another diagnostic chart is a **cause-and-effect diagram** or a **fishbone diagram.** It is called a cause-and-effect diagram to emphasize the relationship between an effect and a set of possible causes that produce the particular effect. This diagram is useful to help organize ideas and to identify relationships. It is a tool that encourages open brainstorming for ideas. By identifying these relationships, we can determine factors that are the cause of variability in our process. The name *fishbone* comes from the manner in which the various causes and effects are organized on the diagram. The effect is usually a particular problem, or perhaps a goal, and it is shown on the right-hand side of the diagram. The major causes are listed on the left-hand side of the diagram.

The usual approach to a fishbone diagram is to consider four problem areas, namely, methods, materials, equipment, and personnel. The problem, or the effect, is the head of the fish. See Chart 19–2.

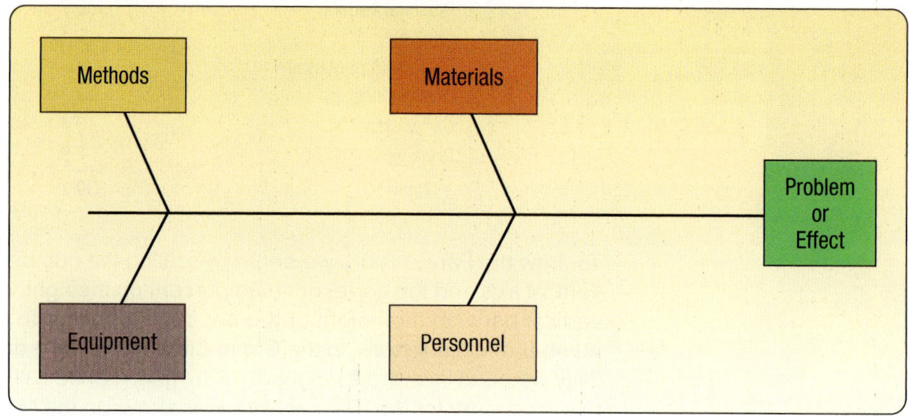

CHART 19–2 Fishbone Diagram

Under each of the possible causes are subcauses that are identified and investigated. The subcauses are factors that may be producing the particular effect. Information is gathered about the problem and used to fill in the fishbone diagram. Each of the subcauses is investigated and those that are not important eliminated, until the real cause of the problem is identified.

To illustrate a fishbone diagram, we investigate the causes of cold food served at Emily's Family Restaurant. Recall that a Pareto analysis showed that cold food was one of the top two complaints. In Chart 19–3, notice that each of the subcauses is listed as

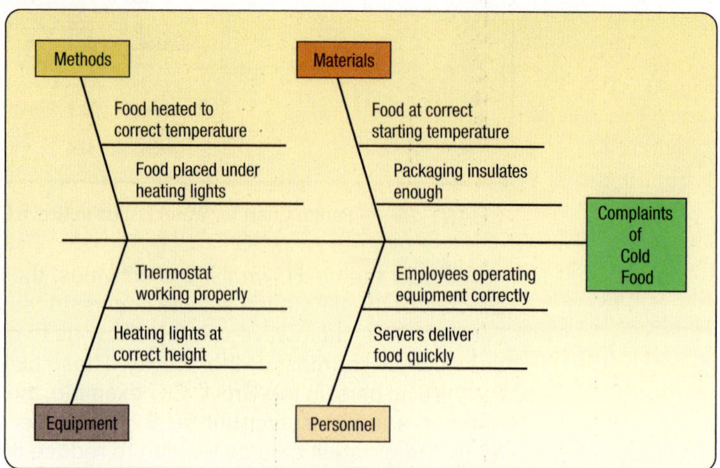

CHART 19–3 Fishbone Diagram for a Restaurant Investigation of Cold Food Complaints

an assumption. Each of these subcauses must be investigated to find the real problem regarding the cold food. In a fishbone diagram, there is no weighting of the subcauses.

SELF-REVIEW 19–1

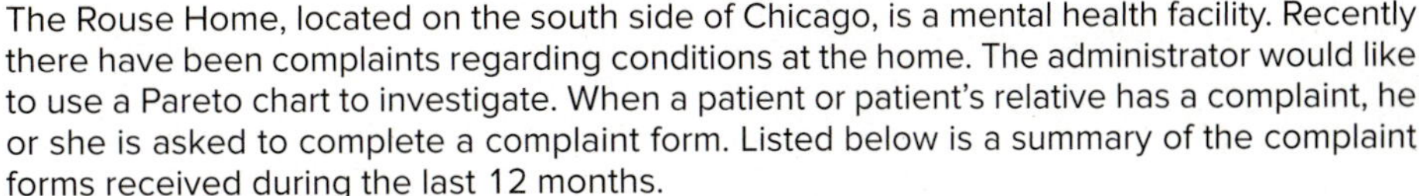

The Rouse Home, located on the south side of Chicago, is a mental health facility. Recently there have been complaints regarding conditions at the home. The administrator would like to use a Pareto chart to investigate. When a patient or patient's relative has a complaint, he or she is asked to complete a complaint form. Listed below is a summary of the complaint forms received during the last 12 months.

Complaint	Number	Complaint	Number
Nothing to do	45	Dirty conditions	63
Poor care by staff	71	Poor quality of food	84
Medication error	2	Lack of respect by staff	35

Develop a Pareto chart. What complaints would you suggest the administrator work on first to achieve the most significant improvement?

EXERCISES

1. Tom Sharkey is the owner of Sharkey Chevy, Buick, GMC. At the start of the year, Tom instituted a customer opinion program to find ways to improve service. The day after the service is performed, Tom's administrative assistant calls the customer to find out whether the service was performed satisfactorily and how the service might be improved. A summary of the complaints for the first six months follows. Develop a Pareto chart. How should Tom prioritize the complaints to improve the quality of service?

Complaint	Frequency	Complaint	Frequency
Problem not corrected	38	Price too high	23
Error on invoice	8	Wait too long for service	10
Unfriendly atmosphere	12		

2. Out of 110 diesel engines tested, a rework and repair facility found 9 had leaky water pumps, 15 had faulty cylinders, 4 had ignition problems, 52 had oil leaks, and 30 had cracked blocks. Draw a Pareto chart to identify the key problem in the engines.

LO19-4
Compute control limits for mean and range control charts for a variable measure of quality.

PURPOSE AND TYPES OF QUALITY CONTROL CHARTS

Control charts identify when assignable causes of variation or changes have entered the process. For example, Wheeling Company makes vinyl-coated aluminum replacement windows for older homes. The vinyl coating must have a thickness between certain limits. If the coating becomes too thick, it will cause the windows to jam. On the other hand, if the coating becomes too thin, the window will not seal properly. The mechanism that determines how much coating is put on each window becomes worn and begins making the coating too thick. Thus, a change has occurred in the process. Control charts are useful for detecting the change in process conditions. It is important to know when changes have entered the process, so that the cause may be identified and corrected before a large number of unacceptable windows are produced.

© Bloomberg/Getty Images

Control charts are similar to the scoreboard in a baseball game. By looking at the scoreboard, the fans, coaches, and players can tell which team is winning the game. However, the scoreboard can do nothing to win or lose the game. Control charts provide a similar function. These charts indicate to the workers, group leaders, quality control engineers, production supervisor, and management whether the production of the part or service is "in control" or "out of control." If the production is "out of control," the control chart will not fix the situation; it is just a piece of paper with numbers and dots on it. Instead, the person responsible must adjust the machine manufacturing the part or do what is necessary to return production to "in control."

There are two types of control charts. A **variable control chart** portrays measurements, such as the amount of cola in a two-liter bottle or the outside diameter of a piece of pipe. A variable control chart requires the interval or the ratio scale of measurement. An **attribute control chart** classifies a product or service as either acceptable or unacceptable. It is based on the nominal scale of measurement. The Marines stationed at Camp Lejeune are asked to rate the meals served as acceptable or unacceptable; bank loans are either repaid or defaulted.

Control Charts for Variables

To develop control charts for variables, we rely on the sampling theory discussed in connection with the central limit theorem in Chapter 8. Suppose a sample of five pieces is selected each hour from the production process and the mean of each sample computed. The sample means are $\bar{x}_1$, $\bar{x}_2$, $\bar{x}_3$, and so on. The mean of these sample means is denoted as $\bar{\bar{x}}$. We use k to indicate the number of sample means. The overall or grand mean is found by:

GRAND MEAN

$$\bar{\bar{x}} = \frac{\Sigma \text{ of the sample means}}{\text{Number of sample means}} = \frac{\Sigma \bar{x}}{k} \quad \textbf{(19–1)}$$

The standard error of the distribution of the sample means is designated by $s_{\bar{x}}$. It is found by:

STANDARD ERROR OF THE MEAN

$$s_{\bar{x}} = \frac{s}{\sqrt{n}} \quad \textbf{(19–2)}$$

These relationships allow us to establish limits for the sample means to show how much variation can be expected for a given sample size. These expected limits are called the **upper control limit** (*UCL*) and the **lower control limit** (*LCL*). An example will illustrate the use of control limits and how the limits are determined.

EXAMPLE

Statistical Software Inc. offers a toll-free number where customers can call with problems involving the use of their products from 7 a.m. until 11 p.m. daily. It is impossible to have every call answered immediately by a technical representative. The company knows that the length of waiting time is related to a customer's perception of service quality. To understand its service-call process, Statistical Software decides to develop a control chart describing the total time from when a call is received until the representative answers the call and resolves the issue raised by the caller. Yesterday, for the 16 hours of operation, five calls were sampled each hour and the total time to resolve a customer's problem, in minutes, was recorded. This information is reported below.

	Sample Number				
Time	1	2	3	4	5
a.m. 7	8	9	15	4	11
8	7	10	7	6	8
9	11	12	10	9	10
10	12	8	6	9	12
11	11	10	6	14	11
p.m. 12	7	7	10	4	11
1	10	7	4	10	10
2	8	11	11	7	7
3	8	11	8	14	12
4	12	9	12	17	11
5	7	7	9	17	13
6	9	9	4	4	11
7	10	12	12	12	12
8	8	11	9	6	8
9	10	13	9	4	9
10	9	11	8	5	11

Based on this information, develop a control chart for the mean duration of the call. Does there appear to be a trend in the calling times? Is there any period in which it appears that customers wait longer than others?

SOLUTION

A mean chart has two limits, an upper control limit (*UCL*) and a lower control limit (*LCL*). These upper and lower control limits are computed by:

CONTROL LIMITS FOR THE MEAN

$$UCL = \bar{\bar{x}} + 3\frac{s}{\sqrt{n}} \quad \text{and} \quad LCL = \bar{\bar{x}} - 3\frac{s}{\sqrt{n}} \qquad \textbf{(19–3)}$$

where *s* is an estimate of the standard deviation of the population, σ. Notice that in the calculation of the upper and lower control limits the number 3 appears. It represents the 99.74% confidence limits. The limits are often called the 3-sigma limits. However, other levels of confidence (such as 90 or 95%) can be used.

This application was developed before computers were widely available, and computing standard deviations was difficult. Rather than calculate the standard deviation from each sample as a measure of variation, it is easier to use the range. For fixed-sized samples, there is a constant relationship between the range and the standard deviation, so we can use the following formulas to determine the 99.74% control limits for the mean. It can be demonstrated that the term $3(s/\sqrt{n})$ from formula (19–3) is equivalent to $A_2\bar{R}$ in the following formula.

CONTROL LIMITS FOR THE MEAN

$$UCL = \bar{\bar{x}} + A_2\bar{R} \qquad LCL = \bar{\bar{x}} - A_2\bar{R} \qquad \textbf{(19–4)}$$

where:

A_2 is a constant used in computing the upper and the lower control limits. It is based on the average range, $\bar{R}$. The factors for various sample sizes are available in Appendix B.10. (*Note: n* in this table refers to the number of items in the sample.) A portion of Appendix B.10 is shown below. To locate the A_2 factor for this problem, find the sample size for *n* in the left margin. It is 5. Then move horizontally to the A_2 column and read the factor. It is 0.577.

n	A_2	d_2	D_3	D_4
2	1.880	1.128	0	3.267
3	1.023	1.693	0	2.575
4	0.729	2.059	0	2.282
5	0.577	2.326	0	2.115
6	0.483	2.534	0	2.004

$\bar{\bar{x}}$ is the mean of the sample means, computed by $\Sigma\bar{x}/k$ where k is the number of samples selected. In this problem, a sample of five observations is taken each hour for 16 hours, so $k = 16$.

$\bar{R}$ is the mean of the ranges of the sample. It is $\Sigma R/k$. Remember the range is the difference between the largest and the smallest value in each sample. It describes the variability occurring in that particular sample. (See Table 19–1.)

TABLE 19–1 Sixteen Samples of Call Duration Data for Statistical Software, Inc.

Time	1	2	3	4	5	Mean	Range
a.m. 7	8	9	15	4	11	9.4	11
8	7	10	7	6	8	7.6	4
9	11	12	10	9	10	10.4	3
10	12	8	6	9	12	9.4	6
11	11	10	6	14	11	10.4	8
p.m. 12	7	7	10	4	11	7.8	7
1	10	7	4	10	10	8.2	6
2	8	11	11	7	7	8.8	4
3	8	11	8	14	12	10.6	6
4	12	9	12	17	11	12.2	8
5	7	7	9	17	13	10.6	10
6	9	9	4	4	11	7.4	7
7	10	12	12	12	12	11.6	2
8	8	11	9	6	8	8.4	5
9	10	13	9	4	9	9.0	9
10	9	11	8	5	11	8.8	6
Total						150.6	102

The centerline for the chart is $\bar{\bar{x}}$. It is 9.413 minutes, found by 150.6/16. The mean of the ranges ($\bar{R}$) is 6.375 minutes, found by 102/16. Thus, the upper control limit of the mean chart is:

$$UCL = \bar{\bar{x}} + A_2\bar{R} = 9.413 + 0.577(6.375) = 13.091$$

The lower control limit of the mean chart is:

$$LCL = \bar{\bar{x}} - A_2\bar{R} = 9.413 - 0.577(6.375) = 5.735$$

$\bar{\bar{x}}$, *UCL, LCL,* and the sample means are portrayed in Chart 19–4. The mean, $\bar{\bar{x}}$, is 9.413 minutes, the upper control limit is located at 13.091 minutes, and the lower control limit is located at 5.735. There is some variation in the duration of the calls, but all sample means are within the control limits. Thus, based on 16 samples of five calls, we conclude that 99.74% of the time the mean length of a sample of five calls will be between 5.735 minutes and 13.091 minutes.

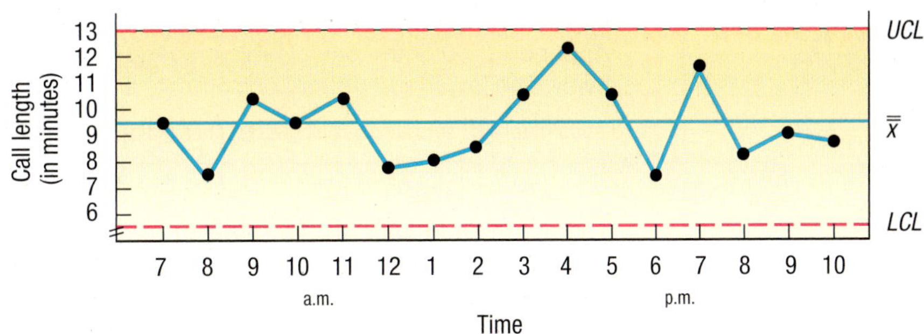

CHART 19–4 Control Chart for Mean Call Duration for Statistical Software Inc.

Because the statistical theory is based on the normality of large samples, control charts should be based on a stable process, that is, a fairly large sample, taken over a long period of time. Before using control charts in practice, at least 25 samples need to be collected to establish control chart limits.

Range Charts

In addition to the central location in a sample, we must also monitor the amount of variation from sample to sample. A **range chart** shows the variation in the sample ranges. If the points representing the ranges fall between the upper and the lower limits, it is concluded that the operation is in control. According to chance, about 997 times out of 1,000 the range of the samples will fall within the limits. If the range should fall above the limits, we conclude that an assignable cause affected the operation and an adjustment to the process is needed. Why are we not as concerned about the lower control limit of the range? For small samples, the lower limit is often zero. Actually, for any sample of six or less, the lower control limit is 0. If the range is zero, then logically all the parts are the same and there is not a problem with the variability of the operation.

The upper and lower control limits of the range chart are determined from the following equations.

STATISTICS IN ACTION

Control charts were used to help convict a person who bribed jai alai players to lose. Mean and range charts showed unusual betting patterns and that some contestants did not win as much as expected when they made certain bets. A quality control expert was able to identify times when assignable variation stopped, and prosecutors were able to tie those times to the arrest of the suspect.

CONTROL CHART FOR RANGES $UCL = D_4\bar{R}$ $LCL = D_3\bar{R}$ **(19–5)**

The values for D_3 and D_4, which reflect the usual three σ (sigma) limits for various sample sizes, are found in Appendix B.10 or in the table on page 708.

EXAMPLE

The length of time customers of Statistical Software Inc. waited from the time their call was answered until a technical representative answered their question or solved their problem is recorded in Table 19–1. Develop a control chart for the range. Does it appear that there is any time when there is too much variation in the operation?

SOLUTION

The first step is to find the mean of the sample ranges. The range for the five calls sampled in the 7 a.m. hour is 11 minutes. The longest call selected from that hour was 15 minutes and the shortest 4 minutes; the difference in the lengths is 11 minutes. In the 8 a.m. hour, the range is 4 minutes. The total of the 16 ranges is 102 minutes, so the average range is 6.375 minutes, found by $\bar{R} = 102/16$. Referring to Appendix B.10 or the partial table on page 708, D_3 and D_4 are 0 and 2.115, respectively. The lower and upper control limits are 0 and 13.483.

$$UCL = D_4\bar{R} = 2.115(6.375) = 13.483$$

$$LCL = D_3\bar{R} = 0(6.375) = 0$$

The range chart with the 16 sample ranges plotted is shown in Chart 19–5. This chart shows all the ranges are well within the control limits. Hence, we conclude the variation in the time to service the customers' calls is within normal limits, that is, "in control." Of course, we should be determining the control limits based on one set of data and then applying them to evaluate future data, not the data we already know.

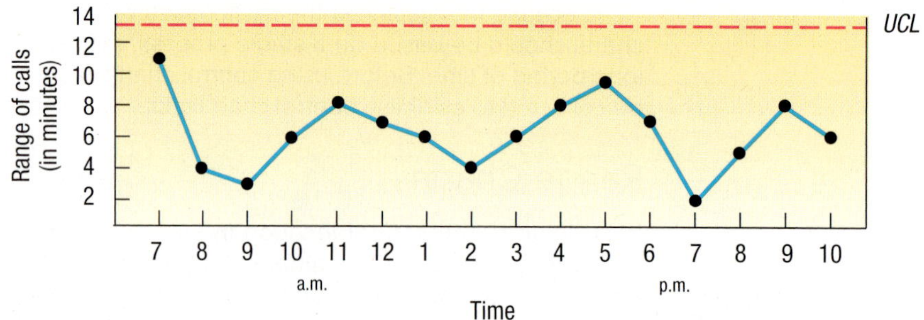

CHART 19–5 Control Chart for Ranges of Length of Customer Calls to Statistical Software Inc.

Statistical software packages will compute all the statistics and draw control charts. The following is the Minitab analysis for the Statistical Software example showing the mean and range charts. The minor differences in the control limits are due to rounding.

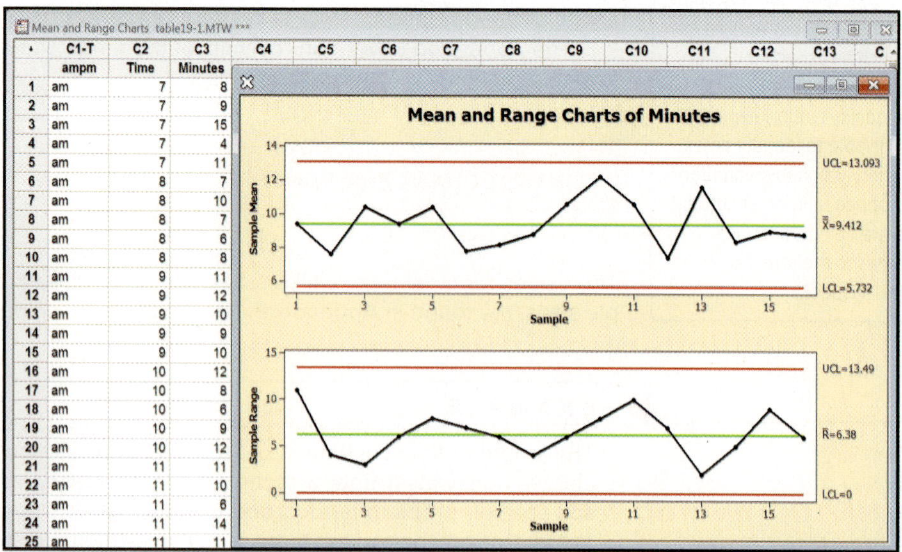

↓	C1-T ampm	C2 Time	C3 Minutes
1	am	7	8
2	am	7	9
3	am	7	15
4	am	7	4
5	am	7	11
6	am	8	7
7	am	8	10
8	am	8	7
9	am	8	6
10	am	8	8
11	am	9	11
12	am	9	12
13	am	9	10
14	am	9	9
15	am	9	10
16	am	10	12
17	am	10	8
18	am	10	6
19	am	10	9
20	am	10	12
21	am	11	11
22	am	11	10
23	am	11	6
24	am	11	14
25	am	11	11

LO19-5
Evaluate control charts to determine if a process is out of control.

IN-CONTROL AND OUT-OF-CONTROL SITUATIONS

Three illustrations of in-control and out-of-control processes follow.

1. The mean chart and the range chart together indicate that the process is in control. Note the sample means and sample ranges are clustered close to the centerlines. Some are above and some below the centerlines, indicating the process is quite stable. That is, there is no visible tendency for the means and ranges to move toward the out-of-control areas.

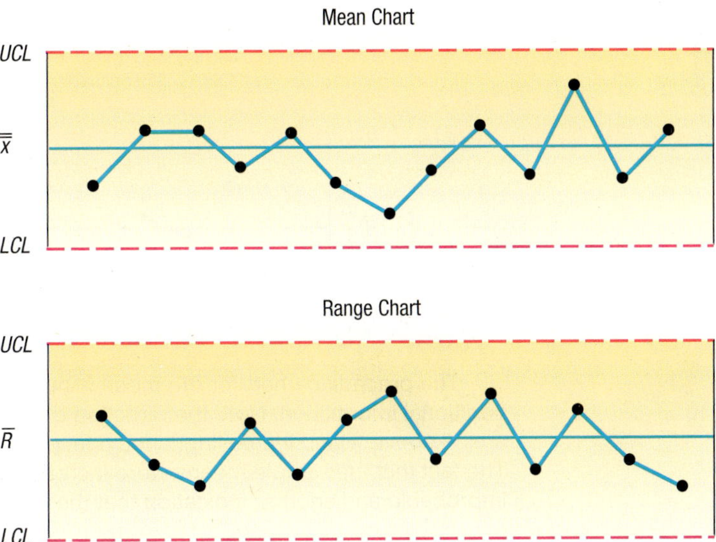

2. The sample means are in control, but the ranges of the last two samples are out of control. This indicates there is considerable variation in the samples. Some sample ranges are large; others are small. An adjustment in the process is probably necessary.

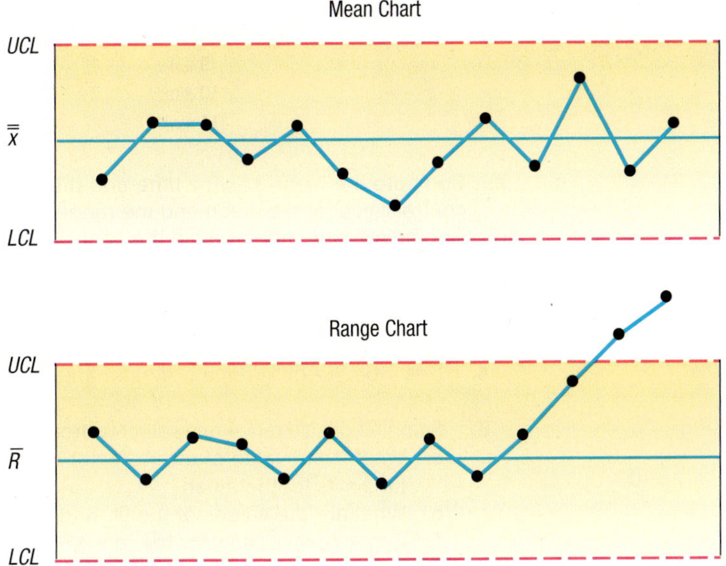

3. The mean is in control for the first samples, but there is an upward trend toward the *UCL*. The last two sample means are out of control. An adjustment in the process is indicated.

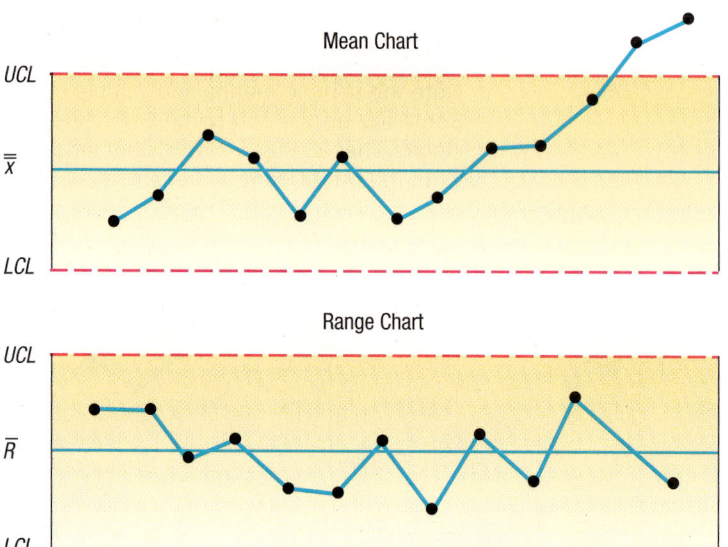

The preceding chart for the mean is an example of a control chart that offers some additional information. Note the direction of the last five observations of the mean. They are all above $\overline{\overline{x}}$ and increasing, and, in fact, the last two observations are out of control. The fact that the sample means were increasing for six consecutive observations is very improbable and another indication that the process is out of control.

SELF-REVIEW 19–2

The manager of River City McDonald's randomly selects four customers during three hours of the day: 9 a.m., 10 a.m., and 11 a.m. For these selected customers, she determines the time, in minutes, between order entry and order delivery. The results are shown below.

	Sample Times			
Time	**1**	**2**	**3**	**4**
9 a.m.	1	4	5	2
10 a.m.	2	3	2	1
11 a.m.	1	7	3	5

(a) Compute the mean service time and the mean range of service time, determine the control limits for the mean and the range, and create control charts.
(b) Are the measurements within the control limits? Interpret the chart.

EXERCISES

3. Describe the difference between assignable variation and chance variation.

4. Describe the difference between an attribute control chart and a variable control chart.

5. Samples of size $n = 4$ are selected from a production line.
   a. What is the value of the A_2 factor used to determine the upper and lower control limits for the mean?
   b. What are the values of the D_3 and D_4 factors used to determine the lower and upper control limits for the range?

6. Samples of size 5 are selected from a manufacturing process. The mean of the sample ranges is .50. What is the estimate of the standard deviation of the population?
7. FILE A new industrial oven has just been installed at Piatt Bakery. To develop experience regarding the oven temperature, an inspector reads the temperature at four different places inside the oven each half hour starting at 8:00 a.m. The last reading was at 10:30 a.m., for a total of six samples. The first reading, taken at 8:00 a.m., was 340 degrees Fahrenheit. (Only the last two digits are given in the following table to make the computations easier.)

	Reading			
Time	**1**	**2**	**3**	**4**
8:00 a.m.	40	50	55	39
8:30 a.m.	44	42	38	38
9:00 a.m.	41	45	47	43
9:30 a.m.	39	39	41	41
10:00 a.m.	37	42	46	41
10:30 a.m.	39	40	39	40

   a. On the basis of this initial experience, determine the control limits for the mean temperature. Determine the grand mean. Plot the results on a control chart.
   b. Interpret the chart. Does there seem to be a time when the temperature is out of control?
8. FILE Refer to Exercise 7.
   a. On the basis of this initial experience, determine the control limits for the range. Plot the plot results on a control chart.
   b. Does there seem to be a time when there is too much variation in the temperature?

LO19-6

Compute control limits of control charts for an attribute measure of quality.

ATTRIBUTE CONTROL CHARTS

Often the data we collect are the result of counting rather than measuring. That is, we observe the presence or absence of some attribute. For example, the screw top on a bottle of shampoo either fits onto the bottle and does not leak (an "acceptable" condition) or does not seal and a leak results (an "unacceptable" condition), or a bank makes a loan to a customer and the loan is either repaid or not repaid. In other cases, we are interested in the number of defects in a sample. British Airways might count the number of its flights arriving late per day at Gatwick Airport in London. In this section, we discuss two types of attribute charts: the *p*-chart (proportion defective) and the *c*-bar chart (number of defectives per unit).

p-Charts

If the item recorded is the proportion of unacceptable parts made in a larger batch of parts, the appropriate control chart is the ***p*-chart.** This chart is based on the binomial distribution, discussed in Chapter 6, and proportions, discussed in Chapter 15. The centerline is at p, the mean proportion defective. The p replaces the $\bar{\bar{x}}$ of the variable control chart. The mean proportion defective is found by:

MEAN PROPORTION DEFECTIVE

$$p = \frac{\text{Total number defective}}{\text{Total number of items sampled}} \qquad \textbf{(19–6)}$$

The variation in the sample proportion is described by the standard error of a proportion. It is found by:

STANDARD ERROR OF THE SAMPLE PROPORTION

$$s_p = \sqrt{\frac{p(1-p)}{n}} \tag{19–7}$$

Hence, the upper control limit (*UCL*) and the lower control limit (*LCL*) are computed as the mean proportion defective plus or minus three times the standard error of the proportions. The formula for the control limits is:

CONTROL LIMITS FOR PROPORTIONS

$$LCL, UCL = p \pm 3\sqrt{\frac{p(1-p)}{n}} \tag{19–8}$$

An example will show the details of the calculations and the conclusions.

EXAMPLE

Jersey Glass Company Inc. produces small hand mirrors. Jersey Glass runs day and evening shifts each weekday. The quality assurance department (QA) monitors the quality of the mirrors twice during the day shift and twice during the evening shift. QA selects and carefully inspects a random sample of 50 mirrors once every four hours. Each mirror is classified as either acceptable or unacceptable. Finally, QA counts the number of mirrors in the sample that do not conform to quality specifications. Listed next are the results of these checks over the last 10 business days.

Date	Number Sampled	Defects	Date	Number Sampled	Defects
10-Oct	50	1	17-Oct	50	7
	50	0		50	9
	50	9		50	0
	50	9		50	8
11-Oct	50	4	18-Oct	50	6
	50	4		50	9
	50	5		50	6
	50	3		50	1
12-Oct	50	9	19-Oct	50	4
	50	3		50	5
	50	10		50	2
	50	2		50	5
13-Oct	50	2	20-Oct	50	0
	50	4		50	0
	50	9		50	4
	50	4		50	7
14-Oct	50	6	21-Oct	50	5
	50	9		50	1
	50	2		50	9
	50	4		50	9

Construct a *p*-chart for this process. What are the upper and lower control limits? Interpret the results. Does it appear the process is out of control during the period?

SOLUTION

The first step is to determine the overall proportion defective. We use formula (19–6).

$$p = \frac{\text{Total number defective}}{\text{Total number of items sampled}} = \frac{196}{2{,}000} = .098$$

So we estimate that .098 of the mirrors produced during the period do not meet specifications.

Date	Number Sampled	Defects	Proportion Defective	Date	Number Sampled	Defects	Proportion Defective
10-Oct	50	1	0.02	13-Oct	50	2	0.04
	50	0	0.00		50	4	0.08
	50	9	0.18		50	9	0.18
	50	9	0.18		50	4	0.08
11-Oct	50	4	0.08	14-Oct	50	6	0.12
	50	4	0.08		50	9	0.18
	50	5	0.10		50	2	0.04
	50	3	0.06		50	4	0.08
12-Oct	50	9	0.18	17-Oct	50	7	0.14
	50	3	0.06		50	9	0.18
	50	10	0.20		50	0	0.00
	50	2	0.04		50	8	0.16
18-Oct	50	6	0.12	20-Oct	50	0	0.00
	50	9	0.18		50	0	0.00
	50	6	0.12		50	4	0.08
	50	1	0.02		50	7	0.14
19-Oct	50	4	0.08	21-Oct	50	5	0.10
	50	5	0.10		50	1	0.02
	50	2	0.04		50	9	0.18
	50	5	0.10		50	9	0.18
				Total	2,000	196	

The upper and lower control limits are computed by using formula (19–8).

$$LCL, UCL = p \pm 3\sqrt{\frac{p(1-p)}{n}} = .098 \pm 3\sqrt{\frac{.098(1-.098)}{50}} = .098 \pm .1261$$

From the above calculations, the upper control limit is .2241, found by .098 + .1261. The lower control limit is 0. Why? The lower limit by the formula is .098 − .1261 = −0.0281. However, a negative proportion defective is not possible, so the smallest value is 0. We set the control limits at 0 and 0.2241. Any sample outside these limits indicates the quality level of the process has changed.

This information is summarized in Chart 19–6, which is output from the Minitab system.

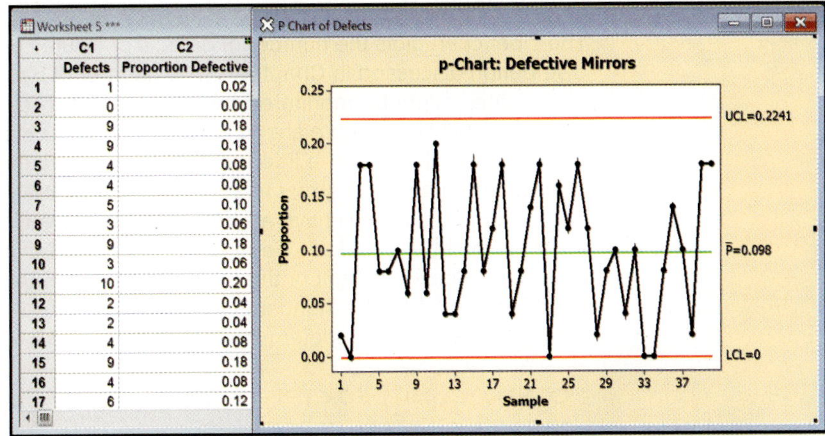

CHART 19–6 p-Chart for Mirrors at Jersey Glass

After establishing the limits, the process is monitored for the next week—five days, two shifts per day—with two quality checks per shift. The results are shown below.

Date	Number Sampled	Defects	Proportion Defective	Date	Number Sampled	Defects	Proportion Defective
24-Oct	50	1	0.02	27-Oct	50	2	0.04
	50	13	0.26		50	1	0.02
	50	10	0.20		50	7	0.14
	50	7	0.14		50	12	0.24
25-Oct	50	4	0.08	28-Oct	50	5	0.10
	50	5	0.10		50	5	0.10
	50	6	0.12		50	10	0.20
	50	10	0.20		50	9	0.18
26-Oct	50	6	0.12				
	50	1	0.02				
	50	8	0.16				
	50	4	0.08				

The process was out of control on two occasions, on October 24 when the proportion of defects was 0.26 and again on October 27 when the proportion of defects was 0.24. QA should report this information to the production department for the appropriate action. The Minitab output follows.

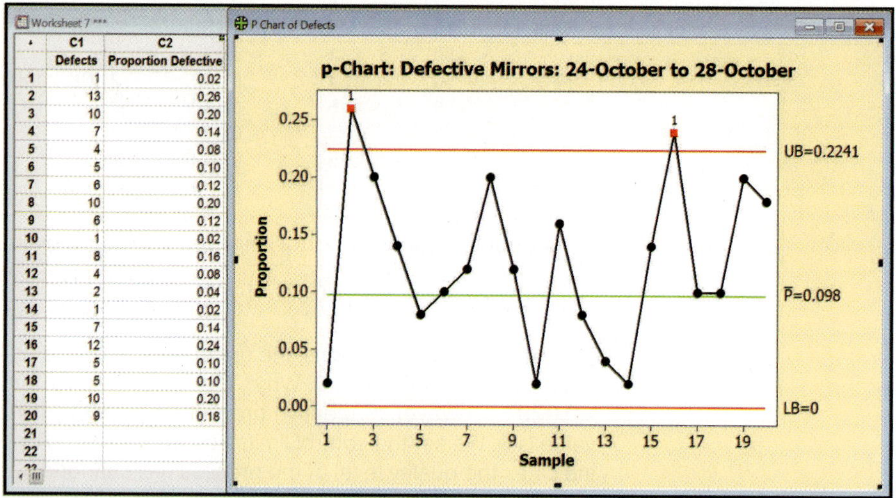

c-Bar Charts

The *c*-bar chart plots the number of defects or failures per unit. It is based on the Poisson distribution discussed in Chapter 6. The number of bags mishandled on a flight by Blue Sky Airlines might be monitored by a *c*-bar chart. The "unit" under consideration is the flight. On most flights, there are no bags mishandled. On others, there may be only one, on others two, and so on. The Internal Revenue Service might count and develop a control chart for the number of errors in arithmetic per tax return. Most returns will not have any errors, some returns will have a single error, others will have two, and so on. We let $\bar{c}$ be the mean number of defects per unit. Thus, $\bar{c}$ is the mean number of bags mishandled by Blue Sky Airlines per flight or the mean number of arithmetic errors per tax return. Recall from Chapter 6 that the standard deviation of a Poisson distribution is the square root of the mean. Thus, we can determine the 3-sigma, or 99.74%, limits on a *c*-bar chart by:

CONTROL LIMITS FOR THE NUMBER OF DEFECTS PER UNIT

$$LCL, UCL = \bar{c} \pm 3\sqrt{\bar{c}} \quad \textbf{(19–9)}$$

EXAMPLE

The publisher of the *Oak Harbor Daily Telegraph* is concerned about the number of misspelled words in the daily newspaper. In an effort to control the problem and promote the need for correct spelling, a control chart will be used. The numbers of misspelled words found in the final edition of the paper for the last 10 days are 5, 6, 3, 0, 4, 5, 1, 2, 7, and 4. Determine the appropriate control limits and interpret the chart. Were there any days during the period that the number of misspelled words was out of control?

SOLUTION

During the 10-day period, there were a total of 37 misspelled words. The mean number of misspelled words per edition is 3.7. The number of misspelled words per edition follows the Poisson probability distribution. The standard deviation is the square root of the mean.

$$\bar{c} = \frac{\Sigma x}{n} = \frac{5 + 6 + \cdots + 4}{10} = \frac{37}{10} = 3.7 \qquad s = \sqrt{\bar{c}} = \sqrt{3.7} = 1.924$$

To find the upper control limit, we use formula (19–9). The lower control limit is zero.

$$UCL = \bar{c} + 3\sqrt{\bar{c}} = 3.7 + 3\sqrt{3.7} = 3.7 + 5.77 = 9.47$$

The computed lower control limit would be 3.7 − 3(1.924) = −2.07. However, the number of misspelled words cannot be less than 0, so we use 0 as the lower limit. The lower control limit is 0 and the upper limit is 9.47. When we compare each of the data points to the value of 9.47, we see they are all less than the upper control limit; the number of misspelled words is "in control." Of course, newspapers are going to strive to eliminate all misspelled words, but control charting techniques offer a means of tracking daily results and determining whether there has been a change. For example, if a new proofreader was hired, her work could be compared with others. These results are summarized in Chart 19–7, which is output from the Minitab system.

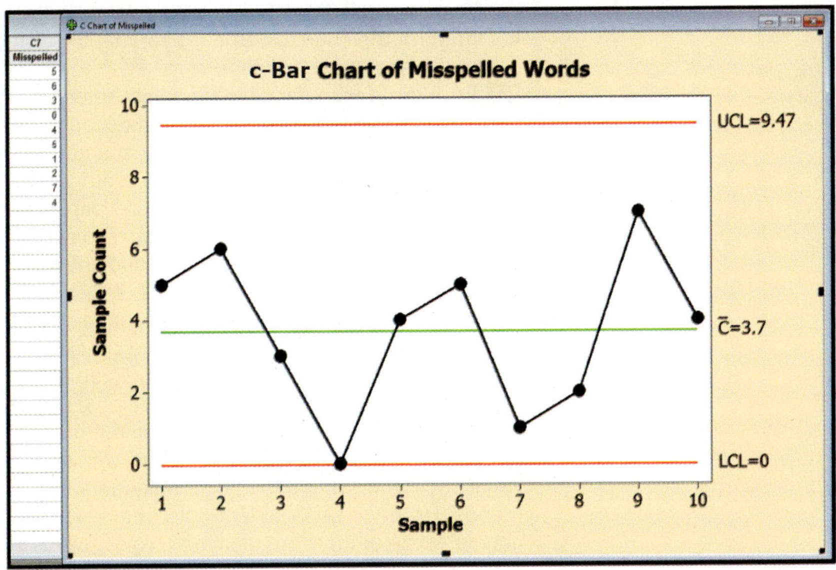

CHART 19–7 *c*-Bar Chart for Number of Misspelled Words per Edition of the *Oak Harbor Daily Telegraph*

SELF-REVIEW 19–3

Auto-Lite Company manufactures car batteries. At the end of each shift, the quality assurance department selects a sample of batteries and tests them. The numbers of defective batteries found over the last 12 shifts are 2, 1, 0, 2, 1, 1, 7, 1, 1, 2, 6, and 1. Construct a control chart for the process and comment on whether the process is in control.

EXERCISES

9. Below is a p-chart for a manufacturing process.

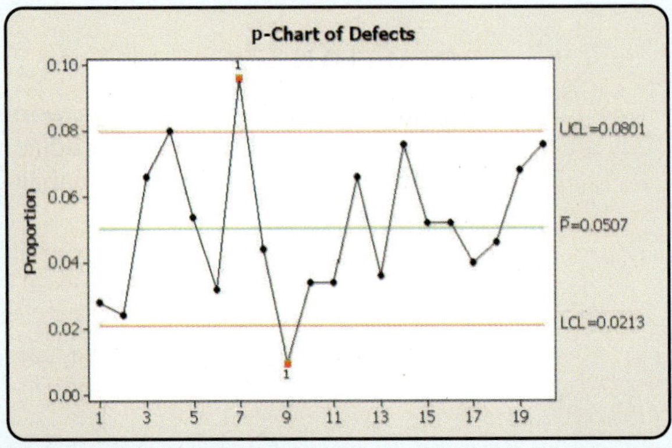

   a. What is the mean proportion defective? What are the upper and lower control limits?
   b. Are there any sample observations that indicate the process is out of control? Which sample numbers are they?
   c. Does there seem to be any trend in the process? That is, does the process seem to be getting better, getting worse, or staying the same?

10. **FILE** Inter-State Moving and Storage Company is setting up a control chart to monitor the proportion of residential moves that result in written complaints due to late delivery, lost items, or damaged items. A sample of 50 moves is selected for each of the last 12 months. The number of written complaints in each sample is 8, 7, 4, 8, 2, 7, 11, 6, 7, 6, 8, and 12.
   a. Design a p-chart and label the mean proportion defective, *UCL*, and *LCL*.
   b. Plot the proportion of written complaints in the last 12 months.
   c. Interpret the chart. Does it appear that the number of complaints is out of control for any of the months?

11. **FILE** A bicycle manufacturer randomly selects 10 frames each day and tests for defects. The numbers of defective frames found over the last 14 days are 3, 2, 1, 3, 2, 2, 8, 2, 0, 3, 5, 2, 0, and 4. Construct a control chart for this process and comment on whether the process is "in control."

12. **FILE** During the process of producing toilet paper, Scott Paper randomly selects a toilet paper roll 5 times throughout the day and subjects each roll to a stress test to see how often the paper tears. Over a 3-day period, the testing of 15 rolls found the following number of defectives in each roll: 2, 3, 1, 2, 2, 1, 3, 2, 2, 1, 2, 2, 1, 0, and 0. Construct a control chart for the process and comment on whether the process is "in control."

13. **FILE** Sam's Supermarkets monitors the checkout scanners by randomly examining the receipts for scanning errors. On October 27th, they recorded the following number of scanner errors on each receipt: 0, 1, 1, 0, 0, 1, 1, 0, 1, 1, 0. Construct a control chart for this process and comment on whether the process is "in control."

14. **FILE** Dave Christi runs a car wash chain with outlets scattered throughout Chicago. He is concerned that some local managers are giving away free washes to their friends. He decides to collect data on the number of "voided" sales receipts. Of course, some of them are legitimate voids. Would the following data indicate a reasonable number of voids at his facilities: 3, 8, 3, 4, 6, 5, 0, 1, 2, 4? Construct a control chart for this process and comment on whether the process is "in control."

LO19-7

Explain the process of acceptance sampling.

ACCEPTANCE SAMPLING

© Ingram Publishing

The previous section was concerned with maintaining the *quality of the product as it is being produced.* In many business situations, we are also concerned with the *quality of the incoming finished product.* What do the following cases have in common?

- Sims Software Inc. purchases DVDs from DVD International. The normal purchase order is for 100,000 DVDs, packaged in lots of 1,000. Todd Sims, president, does not expect each DVD to be perfect. In fact, he has agreed to accept lots of 1,000 with up to 10% defective. He would like to develop a plan to inspect incoming lots, to ensure that the quality standard is met. The purpose of the inspection procedure is to separate the acceptable from the unacceptable lots.
- Zenith Electric purchases magnetron tubes from Bono Electronics for use in its new microwave oven. The tubes are shipped to Zenith in lots of 10,000. Zenith allows the incoming lots to contain up to 5% defective tubes. It would like to develop a sampling plan to determine which lots meet the criterion and which do not.
- General Motors purchases windshields from many suppliers. GM insists that the windshields be in lots of 1,000, and is willing to accept 50 or fewer defects in each lot, that is, 5% defective. They would like to develop a sampling procedure to verify that incoming shipments meet the criterion.

The common thread in these cases is a need to verify that an incoming product meets the stipulated requirements. The situation can be likened to a screen door, which allows the warm summer air to enter the room while keeping the bugs out. Acceptance sampling lets the lots of acceptable quality into the manufacturing area and screens out lots that are not acceptable.

Of course, the situation in modern business is more complex. The buyer wants protection against accepting lots that are below the quality standard. The best protection against inferior quality is 100% inspection. Unfortunately, the cost of 100% inspection is often prohibitive. Another problem with checking each item is that the test may be destructive. If all lightbulbs were tested until burning out before they were shipped, there would be none left to sell. Also, 100% inspection may not lead to the identification of all defects because boredom might cause a loss of perception on the part of the inspectors. Thus, complete inspection is rarely employed in practical situations.

To evaluate the quality of incoming parts, we use a statistical sampling plan. According to this plan, a sample of n units is randomly selected from the lots of N units (the population). This is called **acceptance sampling.** The inspection will determine the number of defects in the sample. This number is compared with a predetermined number called the **critical number** or the **acceptance number.** The acceptance number is usually designated c. If the number of defects in the sample of size n is less than or equal to c, the lot is accepted. If the number of defects exceeds c, the lot is rejected and returned to the supplier, or perhaps submitted to 100% inspection.

Acceptance sampling is a decision-making process. There are two possible decisions: accept or reject the lot. In addition, there are two situations under which the decision is made: the lot is good or the lot is bad. These are the states of nature. If the lot is good and the sample inspection reveals the lot to be good, or if the lot is bad and the sample inspection indicates it is bad, then a correct decision is made. However, there are two other possibilities. The lot may actually contain more defects than it should, but it is accepted. This is called **consumer's risk.** Similarly, the lot may be within the agreed-upon limits, but it is rejected during the sample inspection. This is called the **producer's risk.** The following summary table for acceptance decisions shows these possibilities.

Notice how this discussion is very similar to the ideas of Type I and Type II errors discussed in Chapter 10.

	States of Nature	
Decision	**Good Lot**	**Bad Lot**
Accept lot	Correct	Consumer's risk
Reject lot	Producer's risk	Correct

To evaluate a sampling plan and determine that it is fair to both the producer and the consumer, the usual procedure is to develop an **operating characteristic curve,** or an **OC curve.** An OC curve reports the percent defective along the horizontal axis and the probability of accepting that percent defective along the vertical axis. A smooth curve is usually drawn connecting all the possible levels of quality. The binomial distribution is used to develop the probabilities for an OC curve.

EXAMPLE

Sims Software, as mentioned earlier, purchases DVDs from DVD International. The DVDs are packaged in lots of 1,000 each. Todd Sims, president of Sims Software, has agreed to accept lots with 10% or fewer defective DVDs. Todd has directed his inspection department to select a random sample of 20 DVDs and examine them carefully. He will accept the lot if it has two or fewer defectives in the sample. Develop an OC curve for this inspection plan. What is the probability of accepting a lot that is 10% defective?

SOLUTION

This type of sampling is called **attribute sampling** because the sampled item, a DVD in this case, is classified as acceptable or unacceptable. No "reading" or "measurement" is obtained on the DVD. Let π represent the actual proportion defective in the population.

The lot is good if $\pi \leq .10$.
The lot is bad if $\pi > .10$.

Let x be the number of defects in the sample. The decision rule is:

Accept the lot if $x \leq 2$.
Reject the lot if $x \geq 3$.

Here the acceptable lot is one with 10% or fewer defective DVDs. If the lot is acceptable when it has exactly 10% defectives, it would be even more acceptable if it contained fewer than 10% defectives. Hence, it is the usual practice to work with the upper limit of the percent of defectives.

The binomial distribution is used to compute the various values on the OC curve. Recall that for us to use the binomial, there are four requirements:

1. There are only two possible outcomes: the DVD is either acceptable or unacceptable.
2. There are a fixed number of trials. The number of trials is the sample size of 20.
3. There is a constant probability of success. A success is finding a defective DVD. The probability of success is assumed to be .10.
4. The trials are independent. The probability of obtaining a defective DVD on the third one selected is not related to the likelihood of finding a defect on the fourth DVD selected.

Appendix B.1 gives various binomial probabilities. However, the tables in Appendix B.1 go up to only 15, that is, $n = 15$. For this problem, $n = 20$, so we will use Excel to compute the various binomial probabilities. The following Excel output shows the binomial probabilities for $n = 20$ when π is equal to .05, .10, .15, .20, .25, and .30.

We need to convert the terms used in Chapter 6 to acceptance sampling vocabulary. We let π refer to the probability of finding a defect, c the number of defects allowed, and n the number of items sampled. In this case, we will allow up to two defects, so $c = 2$. This means that we will allow 0, 1, or 2 of the 20 items sampled to be defective and still accept the incoming shipment of DVDs.

To begin, we determine the probability of accepting a lot that is 5% defective. This means that $\pi = .05$, $c = 2$, and $n = 20$. From the Excel output, the likelihood of selecting a sample of 20 items from a shipment that contained 5% defective and finding exactly 0 defects is .358. The likelihood of finding exactly 1 defect is .377, and finding 2 is .189. Hence, the likelihood of 2 or fewer defects is .924, found by .358 + .377 + .189. This result is usually written in shorthand notation as follows (recall that bar "|" means "given that").

$$P(x \leq 2 \mid \pi = .05 \text{ and } n = 20) = .358 + .377 + .189 = .924$$

lot fraction defective.xlsx

Incoming Lot Fraction Defective

Number of Defects	Probability 0.05	0.10	0.15	0.20	0.25	0.30
0	0.358	0.122	0.039	0.012	0.003	0.001
1	0.377	0.270	0.137	0.058	0.021	0.007
2	0.189	0.285	0.229	0.137	0.067	0.028
3	0.060	0.190	0.243	0.205	0.134	0.072
4	0.013	0.090	0.182	0.218	0.190	0.130
5	0.002	0.032	0.103	0.175	0.202	0.179
6	0.000	0.009	0.045	0.109	0.169	0.192
7	0.000	0.002	0.016	0.055	0.112	0.164
8	0.000	0.000	0.005	0.022	0.061	0.114
9	0.000	0.000	0.001	0.007	0.027	0.065
10	0.000	0.000	0.000	0.002	0.010	0.031
11	0.000	0.000	0.000	0.000	0.003	0.012
12	0.000	0.000	0.000	0.000	0.001	0.004
13	0.000	0.000	0.000	0.000	0.000	0.001
14	0.000	0.000	0.000	0.000	0.000	0.000
•	•	•	•	•	•	•
20	0.000	0.000	0.000	0.000	0.000	0.000

Continuing, the likelihood of accepting a lot that is actually 10% defective is .677. That is:

$$P(x \leq 2 \mid \pi = .10 \text{ and } n = 20) = .122 + .270 + .285 = .677$$

The complete OC curve in Chart 19–8 shows the smoothed curve for all values of π between 0 and about 30%. There is no need to show values larger than 30% because their probability is very close to 0. The likelihood of accepting lots of selected quality levels is shown in table form on the right-hand side of Chart 19–8. With the OC curve, the management of Sims Software will be able to quickly evaluate the probabilities of various quality levels.

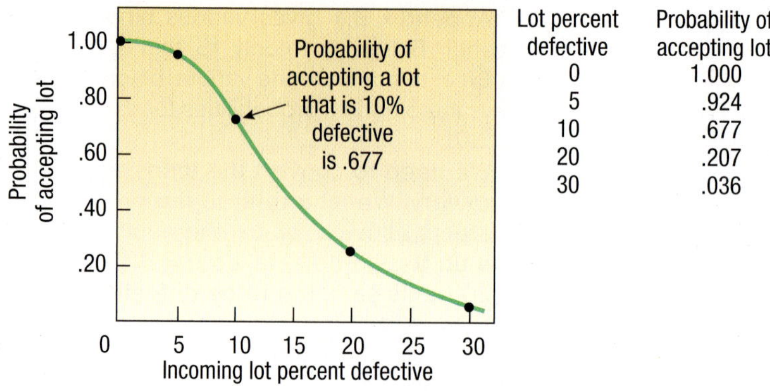

Lot percent defective	Probability of accepting lot
0	1.000
5	.924
10	.677
20	.207
30	.036

CHART 19–8 OC Curve for Sampling Plan ($n = 20$, $c = 2$)

SELF-REVIEW 19–4

Compute the probability of accepting a lot of DVDs that is actually 30% defective, using the sampling plan for Sims Software.

EXERCISES

15. Determine the probability of accepting lots that are 10%, 20%, 30%, and 40% defective using a sample of size 12 and an acceptance number of 2.

16. Determine the probability of accepting lots that are 10%, 20%, 30%, and 40% defective using a sample of size 14 and an acceptance number of 3.

17. Warren Electric manufactures fuses for many customers. To ensure the quality of the outgoing product, it tests 10 fuses each hour. If no more than one fuse is defective, it packages the fuses and prepares them for shipment. Develop an OC curve for this sampling plan. Compute the probabilities of accepting lots that are 10%, 20%, 30%, and 40% defective. Draw the OC curve for this sampling plan using the four quality levels.

18. Grills Video Products purchases LCDs from Mira Electronics. According to his sampling plan, Art Grills, owner of Grills Video, will accept a shipment of LCDs if 3 or fewer are defective in a sample of 25. Develop an OC curve for these percents defective: 10%, 20%, 30%, and 40%. You will need a statistical software package.

CHAPTER SUMMARY

I. The objective of statistical quality control is to monitor the quality of the product or service as it is being developed.

II. A Pareto chart is a technique for tallying the number and type of defects that happen within a product or service.
- **A.** This chart was named after an Italian scientist, Vilfredo Pareto.
- **B.** The concept of the chart is that 80% of the activity is caused by 20% of the factors.

III. A fishbone diagram emphasizes the relationship between a possible problem cause that will produce the particular effect.
- **A.** It is also called a cause-and-effect diagram.
- **B.** The usual approach is to consider four problem areas: methods, materials, equipment, and personnel.

IV. The purpose of a control chart is to monitor graphically the quality of a product or service.
- **A.** There are two types of control charts.
  - **1.** A variable control chart is the result of a measurement.
  - **2.** An attribute chart shows whether the product or service is acceptable or not acceptable.

B. There are two sources of variation in the quality of a product or service.
  1. Chance variation is random in nature and cannot be controlled or eliminated.
  2. Assignable variation is not due to random causes and can be eliminated.

C. Four control charts were considered in this chapter.
  1. A mean chart shows the mean of a variable, and a range chart shows the range of the variable.
    a. The upper and lower control limits are set at plus and minus 3 standard errors from the mean.
    b. The formulas for the upper and lower control limits for the mean are:

$$UCL = \bar{\bar{x}} + A_2\bar{R} \qquad LCL = \bar{\bar{x}} - A_2\bar{R} \tag{19–4}$$

    c. The formulas for the upper and lower control limits for the range are:

$$UCL = D_4\bar{R} \qquad LCL = D_3\bar{R} \tag{19–5}$$

  2. A p-chart is an attribute chart that shows the proportion of the product or service that does not conform to the standard.
    a. The mean proportion defective is found by

$$p = \frac{\text{Total number defective}}{\text{Total number of items sampled}} \tag{19–6}$$

    b. The control limits for the proportion defective are determined from the equation

$$LCL, UCL = p \pm 3\sqrt{\frac{p(1-p)}{n}} \tag{19–8}$$

  3. A *c*-bar chart refers to the number of defects per unit.
    a. It is based on the Poisson distribution.
    b. The mean number of defects per unit is $\bar{c}$.
    c. The control limits are determined from the following equation.

$$LCL, UCL = \bar{c} \pm 3\sqrt{\bar{c}} \tag{19–9}$$

V. Acceptance sampling is a method to determine whether an incoming lot of a product meets specified standards.

A. It is based on random sampling techniques.

B. A random sample of *n* units is selected from a population of *N* units.

C. *c* is the maximum number of defective units that may be found in the sample of *n* and the lot is still considered acceptable.

D. An OC (operating characteristic) curve is developed using the binomial probability distribution to determine the probability of accepting lots of various quality levels.

PRONUNCIATION KEY

SYMBOL	MEANING	PRONUNCIATION
$\bar{\bar{x}}$	Mean of the sample means	*x double bar*
$s_{\bar{x}}$	Standard error of the mean	*s sub x bar*
A_2	Constant used to determine the upper and lower control limit for the mean	*A sub 2*
$\bar{R}$	Mean of the sample ranges	*R bar*
D_4	Constant used to determine the upper control limit for the range	*D sub 4*
$\bar{c}$	Mean number of defects per unit	*c bar*

CHAPTER EXERCISES

19. The production supervisor at Westburg Electric Inc. noted an increase in the number of electric motors rejected at the time of final inspection. Of the last 200 motors rejected, 80 of the defects were due to poor wiring, 60 contained a short in the coil, 50 involved a defective plug, and 10 involved other defects. Develop a Pareto chart to show the major problem areas.

20. FILE The manufacturer of running shoes conducted a study on its newly developed jogging shoe. Listed below are the type and frequency of the nonconformities and failures found. Develop a Pareto chart to show the major problem areas.

Type of Nonconformity	Frequency	Type of Nonconformity	Frequency
Sole separation	34	Lace breakage	14
Heel separation	98	Eyelet failure	10
Sole penetration	62	Other	16

21. At Rumsey's Old Fashion Roast Beef, cola drinks are filled by an automatic machine whose operation is based on the weight of the drink. When the process is in control, the machine fills each cup so that the grand mean is 10.0 ounces and the mean range is 0.25 for samples of 5.

a. Determine the upper and lower control limits for the process for both the mean and the range.

b. The manager of the I-280 store tested five soft drinks served last hour and found that the mean was 10.16 ounces and the range was 0.35 ounce. Is the process in control? Should other action be taken?

22. FILE A new machine has just been installed to produce printed circuit boards. One of the critical measurements is the thickness of the resistance layer. The quality control inspector randomly selects five boards each half-hour, measures the thickness, and records the results. The measurements (in millimeters) for the period 8:00 a.m. to 10:30 a.m. follow.

	Thickness (millimeters)				
Time	1	2	3	4	5
8:00	87.1	87.3	87.9	87.0	87.0
8:30	86.9	88.5	87.6	87.5	87.4
9:00	87.5	88.4	86.9	87.6	88.2
9:30	86.0	88.0	87.2	87.6	87.1
10:00	87.1	87.1	87.1	87.1	87.1
10:30	88.0	86.2	87.4	87.3	87.8

a. Determine the control limits for the mean and the range.

b. Plot the control limits for the mean outside diameter and the range.

c. Are there any points on the mean or the range chart that are out of control? Comment on the chart.

23. FILE Long Last Tire Company, as part of its inspection process, tests its tires for tread wear under simulated road conditions. Twenty samples of three tires each were selected from different shifts over the last month of operation. The tread wear is reported below in hundredths of an inch.

Sample	Tread Wear			Sample	Tread Wear		
1	44	41	19	11	11	33	34
2	39	31	21	12	51	34	39
3	38	16	25	13	30	16	30
4	20	33	26	14	22	21	35
5	34	33	36	15	11	28	38
6	28	23	39	16	49	25	36
7	40	15	34	17	20	31	33
8	36	36	34	18	26	18	36
9	32	29	30	19	26	47	26
10	29	38	34	20	34	29	32

a. Determine the control limits for the mean and the range.
b. Plot the control limits for the mean tread wear and the range.
c. Are there any points on the mean or the range chart that are "out of control"? Comment on the chart.

24. FILE Charter National Bank has a staff of loan officers located in its branch offices throughout the Southwest. Robert Kerns, vice president of consumer lending, would like some information on the typical amount of loans and the range in the amount of the loans. A staff analyst of the vice president selected a sample of 10 loan officers and from each officer selected a sample of five loans he or she made last month. The data are reported below. Develop a control chart for the mean and the range. Do any of the officers appear to be "out of control"? Comment on your findings.

	Loan Amount ($000)						Loan Amount ($000)				
Officer	**1**	**2**	**3**	**4**	**5**	**Officer**	**1**	**2**	**3**	**4**	**5**
Weinraub	59	74	53	48	65	Bowyer	66	80	54	68	52
Visser	42	51	70	47	67	Kuhlman	74	43	45	65	49
Moore	52	42	53	87	85	Ludwig	75	53	68	50	31
Brunner	36	70	62	44	79	Longnecker	42	65	70	41	52
Wolf	34	59	39	78	61	Simonetti	43	38	10	19	47

25. During the 2016 Masters Golf tournament Jordan Spieth failed to repeat as champion. His scores relative to par in each round, on each hole are reported in the table below. Develop and review appropriate control charts for his performance. Report your findings.

Hole	Round 1	Round 2	Round 3	Round 4
1	0	−1	0	0
2	0	0	−1	−1
3	−1	−1	0	0
4	0	0	0	0
5	0	2	0	1
6	−1	0	0	−1
7	0	0	1	−1
8	−1	−1	−1	−1
9	0	1	0	−1
10	−1	1	0	1
11	0	0	2	1
12	0	0	−1	4
13	−1	0	0	−1
14	0	0	−1	0
15	0	−1	−1	−1
16	0	1	0	0
17	0	1	1	1
18	−1	0	2	0

26. FILE Early Morning Delivery Service guarantees delivery of small packages by 10:30 a.m. Of course, some of the packages are not delivered by 10:30 a.m. For a sample of 200 packages delivered each of the last 15 working days, the following numbers of packages were delivered after the deadline: 9, 14, 2, 13, 9, 5, 9, 3, 4, 3, 4, 3, 3, 8, and 4.
a. Determine the mean proportion of packages delivered after 10:30 a.m.
b. Determine the control limits for the proportion of packages delivered after 10:30 a.m. Were any of the sampled days out of control?
c. If 10 packages out of 200 in the sample were delivered after 10:30 a.m. today, is this sample within the control limits?

27. FILE An automatic machine produces 5.0-millimeter bolts at a high rate of speed. A quality control program has been initiated to control the number of defectives. The quality control inspector selects 50 bolts at random and determines how many are defective. The numbers of defectives in the first 10 samples are 3, 5, 0, 4, 1, 2, 6, 5, 7, and 7.

a. Design a p-chart. Insert the mean proportion defective, *UCL*, and *LCL*.
b. Plot the proportion defective for the first 10 samples on the chart.
c. Interpret the chart.

28. FILE Steele Breakfast Foods Inc. produces a popular brand of raisin bran cereal. The package indicates it contains 25.0 ounces of cereal. To ensure the product quality, the Steele inspection department makes hourly checks on the production process. As a part of the hourly check, four boxes are selected and their contents weighed. The results for 25 samples are reported below.

Sample	Weights				Sample	Weights			
1	26.1	24.4	25.6	25.2	14	23.1	23.3	24.4	24.7
2	25.2	25.9	25.1	24.8	15	24.6	25.1	24.0	25.3
3	25.6	24.5	25.7	25.1	16	24.4	24.4	22.8	23.4
4	25.5	26.8	25.1	25.0	17	25.1	24.1	23.9	26.2
5	25.2	25.2	26.3	25.7	18	24.5	24.5	26.0	26.2
6	26.6	24.1	25.5	24.0	19	25.3	27.5	24.3	25.5
7	27.6	26.0	24.9	25.3	20	24.6	25.3	25.5	24.3
8	24.5	23.1	23.9	24.7	21	24.9	24.4	25.4	24.8
9	24.1	25.0	23.5	24.9	22	25.7	24.6	26.8	26.9
10	25.8	25.7	24.3	27.3	23	24.8	24.3	25.0	27.2
11	22.5	23.0	23.7	24.0	24	25.4	25.9	26.6	24.8
12	24.5	24.8	23.2	24.2	25	26.2	23.5	23.7	25.0
13	24.4	24.5	25.9	25.5					

Develop an appropriate control chart. What are the limits? Is the process out of control at any time?

29. FILE An investor believes there is a 50–50 chance that a stock will increase on a particular day. To investigate this idea, for 30 consecutive trading days the investor selects a random sample of 50 stocks and counts the number that increase. The number of stocks in the sample that increased is reported below.

14	12	13	17	10	18	10	13	13	14
13	10	12	11	9	13	14	11	12	11
15	13	10	16	10	11	12	15	13	10

Develop p-chart and write a brief report summarizing your findings. Based on these sample results, is it reasonable that the odds are 50–50 that a stock will increase? What percent of the stocks would need to increase in a day for the process to be "out of control"?

30. FILE Lahey Motors specializes in selling cars to buyers with a poor credit history. Listed below is the number of cars that were repossessed from Lahey customers because they did not meet the payment obligations over each of the last 36 months.

6	5	8	20	11	10	9	3	9	9
15	12	4	11	9	9	6	18	6	8
9	7	13	7	11	8	11	13	6	14
13	5	5	8	10	11				

Develop a c-bar chart for the number repossessed. Were there any months when the number was out of control? Write a brief report summarizing your findings.

31. A process engineer is considering two sampling plans. In the first, a sample of 10 will be selected and the lot accepted if 3 or fewer are found defective. In the second, the sample size is 20 and the acceptance number is 5. Develop an OC curve for each. Compare the probability of acceptance for lots that are 5, 10, 20, and 30% defective. Which of the plans would you recommend if you were the supplier?

32. FILE Christina Sanders is a member of the women's basketball team at Windy City College. Last season, she made 55% of her free throw attempts. In an effort to improve this statistic, she attended a summer camp devoted to shooting techniques. The next 20 days she shot 100 free throws each day. She carefully recorded the number of free throws that she made each day. The results are reported below.

55	61	52	59	67	57	61	59	69	58
57	66	63	63	63	65	63	68	64	67

To interpret, the first day she made 55 out of 100, or 55%. The second day she made 61 shots, the third day, 52 shots, the tenth day 58, the eleventh day 57 shots. The last day she made 67 out of 100, or 67%.

a. Develop a control chart for the proportion of shots made. Over the 20 days of practice, what percent of attempts did she make? What are the upper and lower control limits for the proportion of shots made?

b. Is there any trend in her proportion made? Does she seem to be improving, staying the same, or getting worse?

c. Find the percent of attempts made for the last 5 days of practice. Use the hypothesis testing procedure, formula (15-1), to determine if there is an improvement from 55%.

33. FILE Eric's Cookie House sells chocolate chip cookies in shopping malls. Of concern is the number of chocolate chips in each cookie. Eric, the owner and president, would like to establish a control chart for the number of chocolate chips per cookie. He selects a sample of 15 cookies from today's production and counts the number of chocolate chips in each. The results are as follows: 6, 8, 20, 12, 20, 19, 11, 23, 12, 14, 15, 16, 12, 13, and 12.

a. Determine the centerline and the control limits.

b. Develop a control chart and plot the number of chocolate chips per cookie.

c. Interpret the chart. Does it appear that the number of chocolate chips is out of control in any of the cookies sampled?

34. FILE The numbers of "near misses" recorded for the last 20 months at Lima International Airport are 3, 2, 3, 2, 2, 3, 5, 1, 2, 2, 4, 4, 2, 6, 3, 5, 2, 5, 1, and 3. Develop an appropriate control chart. Determine the mean number of misses per month and the limits on the number of misses per month. Are there any months where the number of near misses is out of control?

35. FILE The following numbers of robberies were reported during the last 10 days to the robbery division of the Metro City Police: 10, 8, 8, 7, 8, 5, 8, 5, 4, and 7. Develop an appropriate control chart. Determine the mean number of robberies reported per day and determine the control limits. Are there any days when the number of robberies reported is out of control?

36. Swiss Watches, Ltd. purchases watch stems for their watches in lots of 10,000. Their sampling plan calls for checking 20 stems, and if 3 or fewer stems are defective, the lot is accepted.

a. Based on the sampling plan, what is the probability that a lot of 40% defective will be accepted?

b. Design an OC curve for incoming lots that have zero, 10%, 20%, 30%, and 40% defective stems.

37. Automatic Screen Door Manufacturing Company purchases door latches from a number of vendors. The purchasing department is responsible for inspecting the incoming latches. Automatic purchases 10,000 door latches per month and inspects 20 latches selected at random. Develop an OC curve for the sampling plan if three latches can be defective and the incoming lot is still accepted.

38. At the beginning of each football season, Team Sports, the local sporting goods store, purchases 5,000 footballs. A sample of 25 balls is selected, and they are inflated, tested, and then deflated. If more than two balls are found defective, the lot of 5,000 is returned to the manufacturer. Develop an OC curve for this sampling plan.

a. What are the probabilities of accepting lots that are 10%, 20%, and 30% defective?

b. Estimate the probability of accepting a lot that is 15% defective.

c. John Brennen, owner of Team Sports, would like the probability of accepting a lot that is 5% defective to be more than 90%. Does this appear to be the case with this sampling plan?

20 An Introduction to Decision Theory

© Mark Horn/Getty Images

▲ **BLACKBEARD'S PHANTOM FIREWORKS** is considering introducing two new bottle rockets. The company can add both to the current line, neither, or just one of the two. The success of these products depends on consumers' reactions. These reactions can be summarized as good, fair, or poor. The company's revenues are estimated in the payoff table in Exercise 11. Compute the expected monetary value for each decision. (See Exercise 11a and LO20-2.)

LEARNING OBJECTIVES

When you have completed this chapter, you will be able to:

LO20-1 Identify and apply the three components of a decision.

LO20-2 Analyze a decision using expected monetary value.

LO20-3 Analyze a decision using opportunity loss.

LO20-4 Apply maximin, maximax, and minimax regret strategies to make a decision.

LO20-5 Compute and explain the expected value of perfect information.

LO20-6 Apply sensitivity analysis to evaluate a decision subject to uncertainty.

LO20-7 Use a decision tree to illustrate and analyze decision making under uncertainty.

INTRODUCTION

Decision theory is a branch of statistics that evaluates two or more decision alternatives in the face of an uncertain future. Probabilities are used to forecast the likelihood of future events. As the name implies, the focus is on the process of making decisions and explicitly includes the payoffs that may result from selecting a particular decision alternative. In contrast, classical statistics focuses on estimating a parameter, such as the population mean, constructing a confidence interval, or conducting a hypothesis test. Classical statistics does not address the consequences.

Statistical decision theory is concerned with determining which decision, from a set of possible alternatives, is optimal for a particular set of conditions. Consider the following examples of decision-theory problems.

- Ford Motor Company must decide whether to purchase assembled door locks for the 2017 Ford F-150 truck or to manufacture and assemble the door locks at its Louisville, Kentucky, plant. If sales of the F-150 truck continue to increase, it will be more profitable to manufacture and assemble the parts. If sales level off or decline, it will be more profitable to purchase the door locks assembled. Should it make or buy the door locks?
- Banana Republic developed a new line of summer rain jackets that are very popular in the cold-weather regions of the country. It would like to purchase commercial television time during the upcoming NCAA basketball final. If both teams that play in the game are from warm parts of the country, it estimates that only a small proportion of the viewers will be interested in the jackets. However, a matchup between two teams who come from cold climates would reach a large proportion of viewers who wear jackets. Should it purchase commercial television time?
- General Electric is considering three options regarding the prices of refrigerators for next year. GE could (1) raise the prices 5%, (2) raise the prices 2.5%, or (3) leave the prices as they are. The final decision will be based on sales estimates and on GE's knowledge of what other refrigerator manufacturers might do.

© Jeff Kowalsky/Bloomberg/Getty Images

In each of these cases, the decision is characterized by several alternative courses of action and several factors not under the control of the decision maker. For example, Banana Republic has no control over which teams reach the NCAA basketball final. These cases characterize the nature of decision making. Possible decision alternatives can be listed, possible future events determined, and even probabilities established, but the decisions are *made in the face of uncertainty.*

LO20-1
Identify and apply the three components of a decision.

ELEMENTS OF A DECISION

There are three components to any decision: (1) the choices available, or alternatives; (2) the states of nature, which are not under the control of the decision maker; and (3) the payoffs. These concepts will be explained in the following paragraphs.

The **alternatives,** or **acts,** are the choices available to the decision maker. Ford can decide to manufacture and assemble the door locks in Louisville, or it can decide to purchase them. Banana Republic has two advertising alternatives: to purchase commercial television time or not. GE is considering three pricing alternatives regarding the marketing of refrigerators. To simplify our presentation, we assume the decision maker can select from a rather small number of outcomes. With the help of computers, however, the decision alternatives can be expanded to a large number of possibilities.

The **states of nature** are the uncontrollable future events. The state of nature that actually happens is outside the control of the decision maker. Ford does not know whether demand will remain high for the F-150. Banana Republic cannot determine whether warm-weather or cold-weather teams will play in the NCAA basketball final. GE does not know how competitors will price refrigerators.

A **payoff** is needed to compare each combination of decision alternative and state of nature. Ford may estimate that if it assembles door locks at its Louisville plant and the demand for F-150 trucks is low, the payoff will be $40,000. Conversely, if it purchases the door locks assembled and the demand is high, the payoff is estimated to be $22,000. Banana Republic needs to estimate the payoffs for purchasing commercial television time given estimates of the potential audience for the rain jacket. GE needs to estimate the payoffs for each pricing alternative given estimates of competitors' pricing.

The main elements of the decision under conditions of uncertainty are identified schematically:

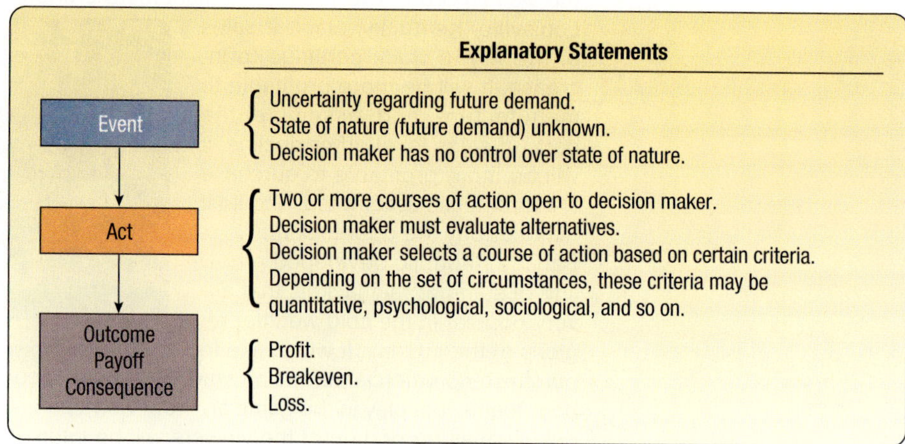

In many cases, we can make better decisions if we establish probabilities for the states of nature. These probabilities may be based on historical data or subjective estimates. Ford may estimate the probability of continued high demand as .70. Banana Republic may estimate a probability of .75 that the commercial will reach the targeted audience. GE may estimate the probability to be .25 that Amana and other manufacturers will raise the prices of their refrigerators.

LO20-2

Analyze a decision using expected monetary value.

DECISION MAKING UNDER CONDITIONS OF UNCERTAINTY

We begin this section with an example of decision making under uncertainty. The purpose of the example is to explain a logical process to evaluate a set of alternatives and select an alternative as the decision. The first step is to set up a payoff table.

Payoff Table

Bob Hill, a small investor, has $1,100 to invest. He has studied several common stocks and narrowed his choices to three, namely, Kayser Chemicals, Rim Homes, and Texas Electronics. He estimated that, if his $1,100 were invested in Kayser Chemicals and a strong bull market developed by the end of the year (that is, stock prices increased drastically), the value of his Kayser stock would more than double, to $2,400. However, if there was a bear market (i.e., stock prices declined), the value of his Kayser stock could conceivably drop to $1,000 by the end of the year. His predictions regarding the value of his $1,100 investment for the three stocks for a bull market and for a bear market are shown in Table 20–1. This table is a **payoff table.**

TABLE 20–1 Payoff Table for Three Common Stocks under Two Market Conditions

Purchase	Bull Market, S_1	Bear Market, S_2
Kayser Chemicals (A_1)	$2,400	$1,000
Rim Homes (A_2)	2,200	1,100
Texas Electronics (A_3)	1,900	1,150

The various choices are called the **decision alternatives** or the **acts.** There are three in this situation. Let A_1 be the purchase of Kayser Chemicals, A_2 the purchase of Rim Homes, and A_3 the purchase of Texas Electronics. Whether the market turns out to be bear or bull is not under the control of Bob Hill. These uncontrolled future events are the **states of nature.** Let the bull market be represented by S_1 and the bear market by S_2.

Expected Payoff

If the payoff table was the only information available, the investor might take a conservative action and buy Texas Electronics to be assured of at least $1,150 at the end of the year (a slight profit). A speculative venture, however, might be to buy Kayser Chemicals, with the possibility of more than doubling the $1,100 investment.

Any decision regarding the purchase of one of the three common stocks made solely on the information in the payoff table would ignore the valuable historical records kept by Moody's, Value Line, and other investment services relative to stock price movements over a long period. Suppose a study of these investment services revealed that during the past 10 years stock market prices increased six times and declined only four times. According to this information, the probability of a market rise is .60 and the probability of a market decline is .40.

Assuming these historical frequencies are reliable, the payoff table and the probability estimates (.60 and .40) are combined to arrive at the **expected payoff** of buying each of the three stocks. Expected payoff is also called **expected monetary value,** shortened to EMV. It can also be described as the **mean payoff.** The calculations needed to determine the expected payoff for the act of purchasing Kayser Chemicals are shown in Table 20–2.

TABLE 20–2 Expected Payoff for the Act of Buying Kayser Chemicals, EMV (A_1)

State of Nature	Payoff	Probability of State of Nature	Expected Value
Market rise, S_1	$2,400	.60	$1,440
Market decline, S_2	1,000	.40	400
			$1,840

To explain one expected monetary value calculation, note that if the investor had purchased Kayser Chemicals and the market prices declined, the value of the stock would be only $1,000 at the end of the year (from Table 20–1). Past experience, however, revealed that this event (a market decline) occurred only 40% of the time. In the long run, therefore, a market decline would contribute $400 to the total expected payoff from the stock, found by ($1,000)(.40). Adding the $400 to the $1,440 expected under rising market conditions gives $1,840, the "expected" payoff in the long run.

These calculations are summarized as follows.

EXPECTED MONETARY VALUE $$\text{EMV}(A_i) = \Sigma[P(S_j) \cdot V(A_i, S_j)] \quad \textbf{(20–1)}$$

where:

$EMV(A_i)$ refers to the expected monetary value of decision alternative *i*. There may be many decisions possible. We will let 1 refer to the first decision, 2 to the second, and so on. The lowercase letter *i* represents the entire set of decisions.

$P(S_j)$ refers to the probability of the states of nature. There can be an unlimited number, so we will let *j* represent this possible outcome.

$V(A_i, S_j)$ refers to the value of the payoffs. Note that each payoff is the result of a combination of a decision alternative and a state of nature.

$EMV(A_1)$, the expected monetary value for the decision alternative of purchasing Kayser Chemicals stock, is computed by:

$$EMV(A_1) = [P(S_1) \cdot V(A_1, S_1)] + [P(S_2) \cdot V(A_1, S_2)]$$
$$= .60(\$2{,}400) + .40(\$1{,}000) = \$1{,}840$$

Purchasing Kayser Chemicals stock is only one possible choice. The expected payoffs for the acts of buying Kayser Chemicals, Rim Homes, and Texas Electronics are given in Table 20–3.

TABLE 20–3 Expected Payoffs for Three Stocks

Purchase	Expected Payoff
Kayser Chemicals	$1,840
Rim Homes	1,760
Texas Electronics	1,600

An analysis of the expected payoffs in Table 20–3 indicates that purchasing Kayser Chemicals would yield the greatest expected profit. This outcome is based on (1) the investor's estimated future value of the stocks and (2) historical experience with respect to the rise and decline of stock prices. It should be emphasized that although purchasing Kayser stock represents the best action under the expected-value criterion, the investor still might decide to buy Texas Electronics stock in order to minimize the risk of losing some of the $1,100 investment.

SELF-REVIEW 20–1

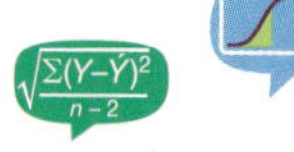

Verify the conclusion, shown in Table 20–3, that the expected payoff for the act of purchasing Rim Homes stock is $1,760.

EXERCISES

1. The following payoff table was developed. Let $P(S_1) = .30$, $P(S_2) = .50$, and $P(S_3) = .20$. Compute the expected monetary value for each of the alternatives. What decision would you recommend?

Alternative	State of Nature S_1	S_2	S_3
A_1	$50	$70	$100
A_2	90	40	80
A_3	70	60	90

2. Wilhelms Cola Company plans to market a new lime-flavored cola this summer. The decision is whether to package the cola in returnable or in nonreturnable bottles. Currently, the state legislature is considering eliminating nonreturnable bottles. Tybo Wilhelms, president of Wilhelms Cola Company, has discussed the problem with his state representative and established the probability to be .70 that nonreturnable bottles will be eliminated. The following table shows the estimated monthly profits (in thousands of dollars) if the lime cola is bottled in returnable versus nonreturnable bottles. Of course, if the law is passed and the decision is to bottle the cola in nonreturnable bottles, all profits would be from out-of-state sales. Compute the expected profit for both bottling decisions. Which decision do you recommend?

Alternative	Law Is Passed ($000), S_1	Law Is Not Passed ($000), S_2
Returnable bottle	80	40
Nonreturnable bottle	25	60

LO20-3
Analyze a decision using opportunity loss.

OPPORTUNITY LOSS

Another method to analyze a decision regarding which common stock to purchase is to determine the profit that might be lost because the state of nature (the market behavior) was not known at the time the investor bought the stock. This potential loss is called **opportunity loss** or **regret.** To illustrate, suppose the investor had purchased the common stock of Rim Homes, and a bull market developed. Further, suppose the value of his Rim Homes stock increased from $1,100 to $2,200, as anticipated. But had the investor bought Kayser Chemicals stock and market values increased, the value of his Kayser stock would be $2,400 (from Table 20–1). Thus, the investor missed making an extra profit of $200 by buying Rim Homes instead of Kayser Chemicals. To put it another way, the $200 represents the opportunity loss for not knowing the future state of nature. If market prices did increase, the investor would have *regretted* buying Rim Homes. However, had the investor bought Kayser Chemicals and market prices increased, he would have had no regret, that is, no opportunity loss.

The opportunity losses corresponding to this example are given in Table 20–4. Each amount is the outcome (opportunity loss) of a particular combination of acts and a state of nature, that is, stock purchase and market reaction.

TABLE 20–4 Opportunity Losses for Various Combinations of Stock Purchase and Market Movement

	Opportunity Loss	
Purchase	**Market Rise**	**Market Decline**
Kayser Chemicals	$ 0	$150
Rim Homes	200	50
Texas Electronics	500	0

Notice that the stock of Kayser Chemicals would be a good investment choice in a rising (bull) market, Texas Electronics would be the best buy in a declining (bear) market, and Rim Homes is somewhat of a compromise.

SELF-REVIEW 20–2

Refer to Table 20–4. Verify that the opportunity loss for:
(a) Rim Homes, given a market decline, is $50.
(b) Texas Electronics, given a market rise, is $500.

EXERCISES

3. Refer to Exercise 1. Develop an opportunity loss table. Determine the opportunity loss for each decision.
4. Refer to Exercise 2, involving Wilhelms Cola Company. Develop an opportunity loss table, and determine the opportunity loss for each decision.

Expected Opportunity Loss

The opportunity losses in Table 20–4 again ignore the historical experience of market movements. Recall that the probability of a market rise is .60 and that of a market decline .40. These probabilities and the opportunity losses can be combined to determine the **expected opportunity loss.** These calculations are shown in Table 20–5 for the decision to purchase Rim Homes. The expected opportunity loss is $140.

TABLE 20–5 Expected Opportunity Loss for the Act of Buying Rim Homes Stock

State of Nature	Opportunity Loss	Probability of State of Nature	Expected Opportunity Loss
Market rise, S_1	$200	.60	$120
Market decline, S_2	50	.40	20
			$140

Interpreting, the expected opportunity loss of $140 means that, in the long run, the investor would lose the opportunity to make an additional profit of $140 if he decided to buy Rim Homes stock. This expected loss would be incurred because the investor was unable to accurately predict the trend of the stock market. In a bull market, he could earn an additional $200 by purchasing the common stock of Kayser Chemicals, but in a bear market an investor could earn an additional $50 by buying Texas Electronics stock. When weighted by the probability of the event, the expected opportunity loss is $140.

These calculations are summarized as follows:

EXPECTED OPPORTUNITY LOSS $$\text{EOL}(A_i) = \Sigma[P(S_j) \cdot R(A_i, S_j)] \qquad \textbf{(20–2)}$$

where:

$\text{EOL}(A_i)$ refers to the expected opportunity loss for a particular decision alternative.

$P(S_j)$ refers to the probability associated with the states of nature j.

$R(A_i, S_j)$ refers to the regret or loss for a particular combination of a state of nature and a decision alternative.

$\text{EOL}(A_2)$, the regret, or expected opportunity loss, for selecting Rim Homes, is computed as follows:

$$\begin{aligned}\text{EOL}(A_2) &= [P(S_1) \cdot R(A_2, S_1)] + [P(S_2) \cdot R(A_2, S_2)] \\ &= .60(\$200) + .40(\$50) = \$140\end{aligned}$$

The expected opportunity losses for the three decision alternatives are given in Table 20–6. The lowest expected opportunity loss is $60, meaning that the investor would experience the least regret on average if he purchased Kayser Chemicals.

TABLE 20–6 Expected Opportunity Losses for the Three Stocks

Purchase	Expected Opportunity Loss
Kayser Chemicals	$ 60
Rim Homes	140
Texas Electronics	300

Incidentally, note that the decision to purchase Kayser Chemicals stock because it offers the lowest expected opportunity loss reinforces the decision made previously, that Kayser stock would ultimately result in the highest expected payoff ($1,840). These two approaches (lowest expected opportunity loss and highest expected payoff) will always lead to the same decision concerning which course of action to follow.

SELF-REVIEW 20–3

Referring to Table 20–6, verify that the expected opportunity loss for the act of purchasing Texas Electronics is $300.

EXERCISES

5. Refer to Exercises 1 and 3. Compute the expected opportunity losses.
6. Refer to Exercises 2 and 4. Compute the expected opportunity losses.

LO20-4
Apply maximin, maximax, and minimax regret strategies to make a decision.

MAXIMIN, MAXIMAX, AND MINIMAX REGRET STRATEGIES

Suppose several financial advisors believe the decision to purchase Kayser Chemicals stock is too risky. They note that the payoff might not be $1,840, but only $1,000 (from Table 20–1). Arguing that the stock market is too unpredictable, they urge the investor to take a more conservative position and buy Texas Electronics. This is called a **maximin strategy:** it maximizes the minimum gain. On the basis of the payoff table (Table 20–1), they reason that the investor would be assured a profit of at least $1,150. Those who subscribe to this somewhat pessimistic strategy are sometimes called **maximiners.**

At the other extreme are the optimistic **maximaxers,** who would select the stock that maximizes the maximum gain. If their **maximax strategy** was followed, the investor would purchase Kayser Chemicals stock. These optimists stress that there is a possibility of selling the stock in the future for $2,400 instead of only $1,150, as advocated by the maximiners.

Another strategy is the **minimax regret strategy.** Advisors advocating this approach would scan the opportunity losses in Table 20–4 and select the stock that minimizes the maximum regret. In this example, it would be Kayser Chemicals stock, with a maximum opportunity loss of $150. Recall that you wish to *avoid* opportunity losses! The maximum regrets were $200 for Rim Homes and $500 for Texas Electronics.

LO20-5
Compute and explain the expected value of perfect information.

VALUE OF PERFECT INFORMATION

Before deciding on a stock, the investor might want to consider ways of predicting the movement of the stock market. If he knew precisely what the market would do, he could maximize profit by always purchasing the correct stock. The question is: What is this advance information worth? The dollar value of this information is called the **expected value of perfect information,** written EVPI. In this example, if perfect information is available, Bob Hill would know what will happen in the future and whether the stock market will rise or decline. If Bob had this information, he would always make the best decision. The question is: What is the most that Bob should be willing to pay for perfect information?

An acquaintance who is an analyst with a large brokerage firm said that he would be willing to supply Bob with information that he might find valuable in predicting market rises and declines. Of course, there would be a fee, as yet undetermined, for this information, regardless of whether the investor used it. What is the maximum amount that Bob should pay for this special service? \$10? \$100? \$500?

The value of the information from the analyst is, in essence, the expected value of perfect information because the investor would then be assured of buying the most profitable stock.

VALUE OF PERFECT INFORMATION The difference between the maximum expected payoff under conditions of certainty and the maximum expected payoff under uncertainty.

In this example, it is the difference between the maximum value of the stock at the end of the year under conditions of certainty and the value associated with the optimum decision using the expected-value criterion.

To explain, the maximum expected value under conditions of certainty means that the investor would buy Kayser Chemicals if a market rise were predicted and Texas Electronics if a market decline were imminent. The expected payoff under conditions of certainty is \$1,900. (See Table 20–7.)

TABLE 20–7 Calculations for the Expected Payoff under Conditions of Certainty

State of Nature	Decision	Payoff	Probability of State of Nature	Expected Payoff
Market rise, S_1	Buy Kayser	\$2,400	.60	\$1,440
Market decline, S_2	Buy Texas Electronics	1,150	.40	460
				\$1,900

Recall that if the actual behavior of the stock market was unknown (conditions of uncertainty), the stock to buy would be Kayser Chemicals; its expected value at the end of the period was computed to be \$1,840 (from Table 20–3). The value of perfect information is, therefore, \$60, found by:

\$1,900	Expected value of stock purchased under conditions of certainty
−1,840	Expected value of purchase (Kayser) under conditions of uncertainty
\$ 60	Expected value of perfect information

In general, the expected value of perfect information is computed as follows:

EXPECTED VALUE OF PERFECT INFORMATION

$$\text{EVPI} = \text{Expected value under conditions of certainty} - \text{Expected value under conditions of uncertainty} \quad \textbf{(20–3)}$$

It would be worth up to $60 for the information the stock analyst might supply. In essence, the analyst would be "guaranteeing" a selling price on average of $1,900, and if the analyst asked $40 for the information, the investor would be assured of a $1,860 payoff, found by $1,900 – $40. Thus, it would be worthwhile for the investor to agree to this fee ($40) because the expected outcome ($1,860) would be greater than the expected value under conditions of uncertainty ($1,840). However, if his acquaintance wanted a fee of $100 for the service, the investor would realize only $1,800 on average, found by $1,900 – $100. Logically, the service would not be worth $100 because the investor could expect $1,840 on average without agreeing to this financial arrangement. Notice that the expected value of perfect information ($60) is the same as the minimum of the expected regrets (Table 20–6). That is not an accident.

Payoff Table			
Purchase	Bull Market	Bear Market	Expected Value
Kayser	$2,400	$1,000	$1,840
Rim	2,200	1,100	1,760
Texas	1,900	1,150	1,600

Opportunity Loss Table			
Purchase	Bull Market	Bear Market	Expected Value
Kayser	$ 0	$ 150	$ 60
Rim	200	50	140
Texas	500	1,150	760

The expected payoff and the expected opportunity loss are the same as reported in Table 20–3 and Table 20–6, respectively. The calculations in the preceding investment example were kept at a minimum to emphasize the new terms and the decision-making procedures. When the number of decision alternatives and the number of states of nature become large, a computer package or spreadsheet is recommended.

LO20-6

Apply sensitivity analysis to evaluate a decision subject to uncertainty.

SENSITIVITY ANALYSIS

In the foregoing stock selection situation, the set of probabilities applied to the payoff values was derived from historical experience with similar market conditions. Objections may be voiced, however, that future market behavior may be different from past experiences. Despite these differences, *the rankings of the decision alternatives are frequently not highly sensitive to changes within a plausible range.* As an example, suppose the investor's brother believes that instead of a 60% chance of a market rise and a 40% chance of a decline, the reverse is true—that is, there is a .40 probability that the stock market will rise and a .60 probability of a decline. Further, the investor's cousin thinks the probability of a market rise is .50 and that of a decline is .50. A comparison of the original expected payoffs (left column), the expected payoffs for the set of probabilities suggested by the investor's brother (center column), and those cited by the cousin (right column) is shown in Table 20–8. The decision is the same in all three cases—purchase Kayser Chemicals.

TABLE 20–8 Expected Payoffs for Three Sets of Probabilities

	Expected Payoffs		
Purchase	**Historical Experience (probability of .60 rise, .40 decline)**	**Brother's Estimate (probability of .40 rise, .60 decline)**	**Cousin's Estimate (probability of .50 rise, .50 decline)**
Kayser Chemicals	$1,840	$1,560	$1,700
Rim Homes	1,760	1,540	1,650
Texas Electronics	1,600	1,450	1,525

SELF-REVIEW 20–4

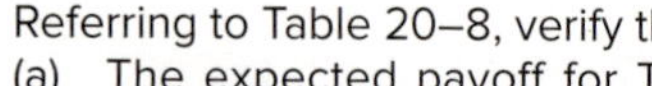

Referring to Table 20–8, verify that:

(a) The expected payoff for Texas Electronics for the brother's set of probabilities is $1,450.

(b) The expected payoff for Kayser Chemicals for the cousin's set of probabilities is $1,700.

A comparison of the three sets of expected payoffs in Table 20–8 reveals the best alternative would still be to purchase Kayser Chemicals. As might be expected, there are some differences in the expected future values for each of the three stocks.

If there are drastic changes in the assigned probabilities, the expected values and the optimal decision may change. As an example, suppose the likelihood of a market rise was .20 and for a market decline .80. The expected payoffs would be as shown in Table 20–9. In the long run, the best alternative would be to buy Rim Homes stock. Thus, sensitivity analysis lets you see how accurate the probability estimates need to be in order to feel comfortable with your choice.

TABLE 20–9 Expected Values for Purchasing the Three Stocks

Purchase	**Expected Payoff**
Kayser Chemicals	$1,280
Rim Homes	1,320
Texas Electronics	1,300

SELF-REVIEW 20–5

Is there any choice of probabilities for which the best alternative would be to purchase Texas Electronics stock? (Hint: This can be arrived at algebraically or by using a trial-and-error method. Try a somewhat extreme probability for a market rise.)

EXERCISES

7. Refer to Exercises 1, 3, and 5. Compute the expected value of perfect information.

8. Refer to Exercises 2, 4, and 6. Compute the expected value of perfect information.

9. Refer to Exercise 1. Revise the probabilities as follows: $P(S_1) = .50$, $P(S_2) = .20$, and $P(S_3) = .30$ and use Expected Monetary Value to evaluate the decision. Does this change the decision?

10. Refer to Exercise 2. Reverse the probabilities; that is, let $P(S_1) = .30$ and $P(S_2) = .70$ and use Expected Monetary Value to evaluate the decision. Does this alter your decision?

LO20-7

Use a decision tree to illustrate and analyze decision making under uncertainty.

DECISION TREES

An analytic tool introduced in Chapter 5 that is also useful for studying a decision situation is a **decision tree.** It is a picture of all the possible courses of action and the consequent possible outcomes. A box is used to indicate the point at which a decision must be made, and the branches going out from the box indicate the alternatives under consideration. Referring to Chart 20–1, on the left is the box with three branches radiating from it, representing the acts of purchasing Kayser Chemicals, Rim Homes, or Texas Electronics.

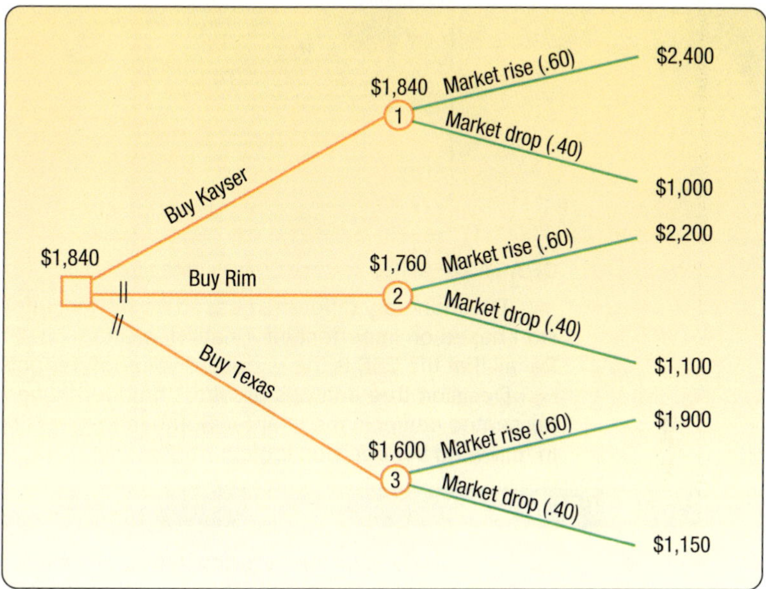

CHART 20–1 Decision Tree for the Investor's Decision

The three nodes, or circles, numbered 1, 2, and 3, represent the expected payoff of each of the three stocks. The branches going out to the right of the nodes show the chance events (market rise or decline) and their corresponding probabilities in parentheses. The numbers at the extreme ends of the branches are the estimated future values of ending the decision process at those points. This is sometimes called the *conditional payoff* to denote that the payoff depends on a particular choice of action and a particular chance outcome. Thus, if the investor purchased Rim Homes stock and the market rose, the conditional value of the stock would be $2,200.

After the decision tree has been constructed, the best decision strategy is found by what is termed *backward induction.* For example, suppose the investor is considering the act of purchasing Texas Electronics. Starting at the lower right in Chart 20–1 with the anticipated payoff given a market rise ($1,900) versus a market decline ($1,150) and going backward (moving left), the appropriate probabilities are applied to give the expected payoff of $1,600 [found by .60($1,900) + .40($1,150)]. The investor would mark the expected value of $1,600 above circled node 3 as shown in Chart 20–1. Similarly, the investor would determine the expected values for Rim Homes and Kayser Chemicals.

Assuming the investor wants to maximize the expected value of his stock purchase, $1,840 would be preferred over $1,760 or $1,600. Continuing to the left toward the box, the investor would draw a double bar across branches representing the two alternatives he rejected (numbers 2 and 3, representing Rim Homes and Texas Electronics). The unmarked branch that leads to the box is clearly the best action to follow, namely, buy Kayser Chemicals stock.

The expected value under *conditions of certainty* can also be portrayed via a decision tree analysis (see Chart 20–2). Recall that under conditions of certainty the investor would know *before the stock is purchased* whether the stock market would rise or decline. Hence, he would purchase Kayser Chemicals in a rising market and Texas

Electronics in a falling market, and the expected payoff would be $1,900. Again, backward induction would be used to arrive at the expected payoff of $1,900.

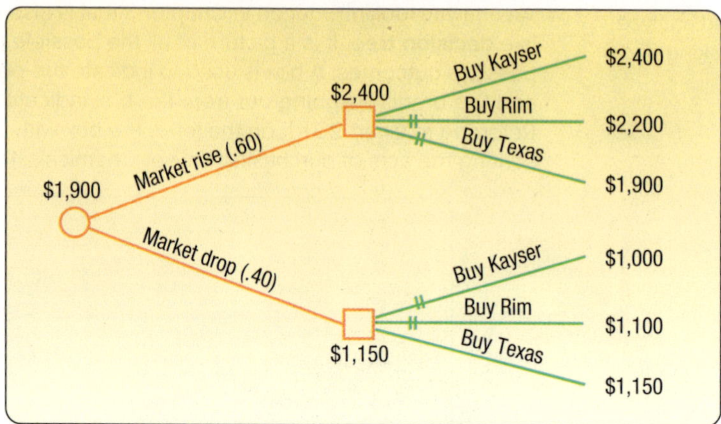

CHART 20–2 Decision Tree Given Perfect Information

The monetary difference based on perfect information in Chart 20–2 and the decision based on imperfect information in Chart 20–1 is $60, found by $1,900 – $1,840. Recall that the $60 is the expected value of perfect information.

Decision tree analysis provides an alternative method to perform the calculations presented earlier in the chapter. Some managers find these graphic sketches help them in following the decision logic.

CHAPTER SUMMARY

I. Statistical decision theory is concerned with making decisions from a set of alternatives.
- **A.** The various courses of action are called the acts or alternatives.
- **B.** The uncontrollable future events are called the states of nature. Probabilities are assigned to the states of nature.
- **C.** The consequence of a particular decision alternative and state of nature is the payoff.
- **D.** All possible combinations of decision alternatives and states of nature result in a payoff table.

II. There are several criteria for selecting the best decision alternative.
- **A.** The expected monetary value (EMV) computes the expected value for each decision. If the payoffs are costs, the decision with the smallest EMV is selected. If the payoffs are profits, the decision with the largest EMV is selected.
- **B.** A decision can be selected using an opportunity loss table.
  1. To construct an opportunity loss table, first calculate the difference between the best payoff and the payoffs of the other decision alternatives for each state of nature.
  2. The difference between the optimal decision and any other decision is the opportunity loss or regret due to making a decision other than the optimum.
  3. The expected opportunity loss (EOL) is similar to the expected monetary value. The opportunity loss is combined with the probabilities of the various states of nature for each decision alternative to determine the expected opportunity loss.
- **C.** A maximin strategy compares the lowest payoffs of the decision alternatives and selects the decision alternative with the maximum of these payoffs.
- **D.** A maximax strategy selects the decision alternative with the highest payoff.
- **E.** A minimax regret strategy, first, converts payoffs to regrets or opportunity losses. Then, decision alternatives are compared based on the maximum regrets and the alternative with the smallest of the maximum regrets is selected.

III. The expected value of perfect information (EVPI) is the difference between the best expected payoff under certainty and the best expected payoff under uncertainty.

IV. Sensitivity analysis examines the effects of various probabilities for the states of nature on the expected values.

V. Decision trees are useful for structuring the various alternatives. They present a picture of the various courses of action and the possible states of nature.

CHAPTER EXERCISES

11. Blackbeard's Phantom Fireworks is considering introducing two new bottle rockets. The company can add both to the current line, neither, or just one of the two. The success of these products depends on consumers' reactions. These reactions can be summarized as good, $P(S_1) = .30$; fair, $P(S_2) = .50$; or poor, $P(S_3) = .20$. The company's revenues, in thousands of dollars, are estimated in the following payoff table.

	State of Nature		
Decision	S_1	S_2	S_3
Neither	0	0	0
Product 1 only	125	65	30
Product 2 only	105	60	30
Both	220	110	40

a. Compute the expected monetary value for each decision.
b. What decision would you recommend ?
c. Develop an opportunity loss table.
d. Compute the expected opportunity loss for each decision.
e. Compute the expected value of perfect information.

12. A financial executive for Fidelity Investments lives in Boston but frequently must travel to New York. She can go to New York by car, train, or plane. The cost for a plane ticket from Boston to New York is \$200, and it is estimated that the trip takes 30 minutes in good weather and 45 minutes in bad weather. The cost for a train ticket is \$100, and the trip takes an hour in good weather and two hours in bad weather. The cost to drive her own car from Boston to New York is \$40, and this trip takes three hours in good weather and four in bad weather. The executive places a value of \$60 per hour on her time. The weather forecast is for a 60% chance of bad weather tomorrow. What decision would you recommend? (*Hint:* Set up a payoff table, and remember that you want to minimize costs.) What is the expected value of perfect information?

13. Thomas Manufacturing Company has \$100,000 available to invest. John Thomas, the president and CEO of the company, would like to either expand his production, invest the money in stocks, or purchase a certificate of deposit from the bank. Of course, the unknown is whether the economy will continue at a high level or there will be a recession. He estimates the likelihood of a recession at .20. Whether there is a recession or not, the certificate of deposit will result in a gain of 6%. If there is a recession, he predicts a 10% loss if he expands his production and a 5% loss if he invests in stocks. If there is not a recession, an expansion of production will result in a 15% gain, and stock investment will produce a 12% gain.
a. What decision should he make if he uses the maximin strategy?
b. What decision should John Thomas make if the maximax strategy is used?
c. What decision would be made if he uses the expected monetary value criterion?
d. What is the expected value of perfect information?

14. The quality assurance department at Malcomb Products must either inspect each part in a lot or not inspect any of the parts. That is, there are two decision alternatives: inspect all the parts or inspect none of the parts. The proportion of parts defective in the lot, S_j, is known from historical data to assume the following probability distribution.

State of Nature, S_j	Probability, $P(S_j)$
.02	.70
.04	.20
.06	.10

For the decision not to inspect any parts, the cost of quality is $C = NS_jK$. For inspecting all the items in the lot, it is $C = Nk$, where:

$N = 20$ (lot size)
$K = \$18.00$ (the cost of finding a defect)
$k = \$0.50$ (the cost of sampling one item)

a. Develop a payoff table.
b. What decision should be made if the expected value criterion is used?
c. What is the expected value of perfect information?

15. Dude Ranches Incorporated was founded on the idea that many families in the eastern and southern areas of the United States do not have a sufficient amount of vacation time to drive to the dude ranches in the Southwest and Rocky Mountain areas for their vacations. Various surveys indicated, however, that there was a considerable interest in this type of family vacation, which includes horseback riding, cattle drives, swimming, fishing, and the like. Dude Ranches Incorporated bought a large farm near several eastern cities and constructed a lake, a swimming pool, and other facilities. However, to build a number of family cottages on the ranch would have required a considerable investment. Further, the owners reasoned that most of this investment would be lost should the ranch–farm complex be a financial failure. Instead, they decided to enter into an agreement with Mobile Homes Manufacturing Company to supply a very attractive authentic ranch-type mobile home. Mobile Homes agreed to deliver a mobile home on Saturday for $300 a week. Mobile Homes must know early Saturday morning how many mobile homes Dude Ranches Incorporated wants for the forthcoming week. It has other customers to supply and can only deliver the homes on Saturday. This presents a problem. Dude Ranches will have some reservations by Saturday, but indications are that many families do not make them. Instead, they prefer to examine the facilities before making a decision. An analysis of the various costs involved indicated that $350 a week should be charged for a ranch home, including all privileges. The basic problem is how many mobile ranch homes to order from Mobile Homes each week. Should Dude Ranches Incorporated order 10 (considered the minimum), 11, 12, 13, or 14 (considered the maximum)?

Any decision made solely on the information in the payoff table would ignore, however, the valuable experience that Dude Ranches Incorporated has acquired in the past 4 years (about 200 weeks) actually operating a dude ranch in the Southwest. Its records showed that it always had nine advance reservations. Also, it never had a demand for 15 or more cottages. The occupancy of 10, 11, 12, 13, or 14 ranch cottages, in part, represented families who drove in and inspected the facilities before renting. A frequency distribution showing the number of weeks in which 10, 11, . . . , 14 ranch cottages were rented during the 200-week period is found in the following table.

Number of Cottages Rented	Number of Weeks
10	26
11	50
12	60
13	44
14	20
	200

a. Construct a payoff table.
b. Determine the expected payoffs, and arrive at a decision.
c. Set up an opportunity loss table.
d. Compute the expected opportunity losses, and arrive at a decision.
e. Determine the expected value of perfect information.

16. The proprietor of the newly built White Mountain Ski and Swim Lodge has been considering purchasing or leasing several snowmobiles for the use of guests. The owner found that other financial obligations made it impossible to purchase the machines. Snowmobiles Incorporated (SI) will lease a machine for $20 a week, including any needed maintenance. According to SI, the usual rental charge to the guests of the lodge is $25 a week. Gasoline and oil are extra. Snowmobiles Incorporated only leases a machine for the full season. The proprietor of Ski and Swim, knowing that leasing an excessive number of snowmobiles might cause a net loss for the lodge, investigated the records of other resort owners. The combined experience at several other lodges was found to be:

Number of Snowmobiles Demanded by Guests	Number of Weeks
7	10
8	25
9	45
10	20

a. Design a payoff table.
b. Compute the expected profits for leasing 7, 8, 9, and 10 snowmobiles based on the cost of leasing of $20, the rental charge of $25, and the experience of other lodges.
c. Which alternative is the most profitable?
d. Design an opportunity loss table.
e. Find the expected opportunity losses for leasing 7, 8, 9, and 10 snowmobiles.
f. Which act would give the least expected opportunity loss?
g. Determine the expected value of perfect information.
h. Suggest a course of action to the proprietor of the Ski and Swim Lodge. Include in your explanation the various figures, such as expected profit.

17. Casual Furniture World has had numerous inquiries regarding the availability of furniture and equipment that could be rented for large outdoor summer parties. This includes such items as folding chairs and tables, a deluxe grill, propane gas, and lights. No rental equipment of this nature is available locally, and the management of the furniture store is considering forming a subsidiary to handle rentals.

An investigation revealed that most people interested in renting wanted a complete group of party essentials (about 12 chairs, four tables, a deluxe grill, a bottle of propane gas, tongs, etc.). Management decided not to buy a large number of complete sets because of the financial risk involved. That is, if the demand for the rental groups was not as large as anticipated, a large financial loss might be incurred. Further, outright purchase would mean that the equipment would have to be stored during the off-season.

It was then discovered that a firm in Boston leased a complete party set for $560 for the summer season. This amounts to about $5 a day. In the promotional literature from the Boston firm, a rental fee of $15 was suggested. For each set rented, a profit of $10 would thus be earned. It was then decided to lease from the Boston firm, at least for the first season.

The Boston firm suggested that, based on the combined experience of similar rental firms in other cities, either 41, 42, 43, 44, 45, or 46 complete sets be leased for the season. Based on this suggestion, management must now decide on the most profitable number of complete sets to lease for the season.

The leasing firm in Boston also made available some additional information gathered from several rental firms similar to the newly formed subsidiary. Note in the following table (which is based on the experience of the other rental firms) that for 360 days of the total of 6,000 days' experience—or about 6% of the days—these rental firms rented out 41 complete party sets. On 10% of the days during a typical summer, they rented 42 complete sets, and so on.

Number of Sets Rented	Number of Days	Number of Sets Rented	Number of Days
40	0	44	2,400
41	360	45	1,500
42	600	46	300
43	840	47	0

a. Construct a payoff table. (As a check figure, for the act of having 41 complete sets available and the event of renting 41, the payoff is $410.)
b. The expected daily profit for leasing 43 complete sets from the Boston firm is $426.70; for 45 sets, $431.70; and for 46 sets, $427.45. Organize these expected daily profits into a table, and complete the table by finding the expected daily profit for leasing 41, 42, and 44 sets from the Boston firm.
c. On the basis of the expected daily profit, what is the most profitable action to take?
d. The expected opportunity loss for leasing 43 party sets from the Boston firm is $11.60; for 45 sets, $6.60; for 46 sets, $10.85. Organize these into an expected

opportunity loss table, and complete the table by computing the expected opportunity loss for 41, 42, and 44.

e. According to the expected opportunity loss table, what is the most profitable course of action to take? Does this agree with your decision for part (c)?

f. Determine the expected value of perfect information. Explain what it indicates in this problem.

18. Tim Waltzer owns and operates Waltzer's Wrecks, a discount car rental agency near Cleveland Hopkins International Airport. He rents a wreck for $20 a day. He has an arrangement with Landrum Leasing to purchase used cars at $6,000 each. His cars receive only needed maintenance and, as a result, are worth only $2,000 at the end of the year of operation. Tim has decided to sell all his wrecks every year and purchase a complete set of wrecks from Landrum Leasing.

His clerk-accountant provided him with a probability distribution with respect to the number of cars rented per day.

	Numbers of Cars Rented per Day			
	20	**21**	**22**	**23**
Probability	.10	.20	.50	.20

Tim is an avid golfer and tennis player. He is either on the golf course on weekends or playing tennis indoors. Thus, his car rental agency is only open weekdays. Also, he closes for 2 weeks during the summer and goes on a golfing tour.

The clerk-accountant estimated that it cost $1.50 per car rental for minimal maintenance and cleaning.

a. How many cars should he purchase to maximize profit?

b. What is the expected value of perfect information?

19. You sign up for a cell phone plan and are presented with this chart showing how your plan "automatically adjusts" to the minutes you use each month. For example: If you select Option 1 and you use 700 minutes the first month, you'll only pay $79.99. If your usage then goes down to 200 minutes the second month, you'll only pay $29.99. You guess your monthly usage will be 100, 300, 500, or 700 anytime minutes. Assume the probabilities for each event are the same.

Option 1—Starting at $29.99 per Month	
Anytime Minutes	**Cost**
0–200	$29.99
201–700	$5 for each 50 minutes
Above 700	Additional anytime minutes only 10¢ each
Option 2—Starting at $34.99 per Month	
Anytime Minutes	**Cost**
0–400	$34.99
401–900	$5 for each 50 minutes
Above 900	Additional anytime minutes only 10¢ each
Option 3—Starting at $59.99 per Month	
Anytime Minutes	**Cost**
0–1,000	$59.99
1,001–1,500	$5 for each 50 minutes
Above 1,500	Additional anytime minutes only 10¢ each

a. Create a payoff (cost) table for this decision.

b. Using the expected monetary value principle, which decision would you suggest?

c. Using the optimistic (maximax cost) approach, which decision would you suggest?

d. Using the pessimistic (maximin cost) strategy, which decision would you suggest?

e. Work out an opportunity loss table for this decision.

f. Using the minimax regret strategy, which choice would you suggest?

g. What is the expected value of perfect information?

20. You're about to drive to New York. If your car's engine is out of tune, your gas cost will increase by $100. Having the engine tested will cost $20. If it's out of tune, repairs will cost $60. Before testing, the probability is 30% that the engine is out of tune. What should you do?

Appendixes Introduction

APPENDIX A: DATA SETS

APPENDIX B: TABLES

APPENDIX C: SOFTWARE COMMANDS

APPENDIX D: ANSWERS TO ODD-NUMBERED CHAPTER EXERCISES & REVIEW EXERCISES & SOLUTIONS TO PRACTICE TESTS

APPENDIX E: ANSWERS TO SELF-REVIEW

APPENDIX A

A.1 Data Set 1—North Valley Real Estate Data

Variables

Record = Property identification number
Agent = Name of the real estate agent assigned to the property
Price = Market price in dollars
Size = Livable square feet of the property
Bedrooms = Number of bedrooms
Baths = Number of bathrooms
Pool = Does the home have a pool? (1 = yes, 0 = no)
Garage = Does the home have an attached garage (1 = yes, 0 = no)
Days = Number of days of the property on the market
Township = Area where the property is located
Mortgage type = Fixed or adjustable. The fixed mortgage is a 30 year, fixed interest rate loan. The adjustable rate loan begins with an introductory interest rate of 3% for the first five years, then the interest rate is based on the current interest rates plus 1% (i.e. the interest rate AND the payment is likely to change each year after the 5th year)
Years = the number of years that the mortgage loan has been paid
FICO = the credit score of the mortgage loan holder. The highest score is 850; an average score is 680, a low score is below 680. The score reflects a person's ability to pay their debts.
Default = Is the mortgage loan in default? (1 = yes, 0 = no)

Record	Agent	Price	Size	Bedrooms	Baths	Pool (Yes is 1)	Garage (Yes is 1)	Days	Township	Mortgage type	Years	FICO	Default (Yes is 1)
1	Marty	206424	1820	2	1.5	1	1	33	2	Fixed	2	824	0
2	Rose	346150	3010	3	2	0	0	36	4	Fixed	9	820	0
3	Carter	372360	3210	4	3	0	1	21	2	Fixed	18	819	0
4	Peterson	310622	3330	3	2.5	1	0	26	3	Fixed	17	817	0
5	Carter	496100	4510	6	4.5	0	1	13	4	Fixed	17	816	0
6	Peterson	294086	3440	4	3	1	1	31	4	Fixed	19	813	0
7	Carter	228810	2630	4	2.5	0	1	39	4	Adjustable	10	813	0
8	Isaacs	384420	4470	5	3.5	0	1	26	2	Fixed	6	812	0
9	Peterson	416120	4040	5	3.5	0	1	26	4	Fixed	3	810	0
10	Isaacs	487494	4380	6	4	1	1	32	3	Fixed	6	808	0
11	Rose	448800	5280	6	4	0	1	35	4	Fixed	8	806	1
12	Peterson	388960	4420	4	3	0	1	50	2	Adjustable	9	805	1
13	Marty	335610	2970	3	2.5	0	1	25	3	Adjustable	9	801	1
14	Rose	276000	2300	2	1.5	0	0	34	1	Fixed	20	798	0
15	Rose	346421	2970	4	3	1	1	17	3	Adjustable	10	795	0
16	Isaacs	453913	3660	6	4	1	1	12	3	Fixed	18	792	0
17	Carter	376146	3290	5	3.5	1	1	28	2	Adjustable	9	792	1
18	Peterson	694430	5900	5	3.5	1	1	36	3	Adjustable	10	788	0
19	Rose	251269	2050	3	2	1	1	38	3	Fixed	16	786	0
20	Rose	547596	4920	6	4.5	1	1	37	5	Fixed	2	785	0
21	Marty	214910	1950	2	1.5	1	0	20	4	Fixed	6	784	0
22	Rose	188799	1950	2	1.5	1	0	52	1	Fixed	10	782	0
23	Carter	459950	4680	4	3	1	1	31	4	Fixed	8	781	0
24	Isaacs	264160	2540	3	2.5	0	1	40	1	Fixed	18	780	0
25	Carter	393557	3180	4	3	1	1	54	1	Fixed	20	776	0
26	Isaacs	478675	4660	5	3.5	1	1	26	5	Adjustable	9	773	0
27	Carter	384020	4220	5	3.5	0	1	23	4	Adjustable	9	772	1
28	Marty	313200	3600	4	3	0	1	31	3	Fixed	19	772	0
29	Isaacs	274482	2990	3	2	1	0	37	3	Fixed	5	769	0
30	Marty	167962	1920	2	1.5	1	1	31	5	Fixed	6	769	0

(continued)

A.1 Data Set 1—North Valley Real Estate Data (*continued*)

Record	Agent	Price	Size	Bedrooms	Baths	Pool (Yes is 1)	Garage (Yes is 1)	Days	Township	Mortgage type	Years	FICO	Default (Yes is 1)
31	Isaacs	175823	1970	2	1.5	1	0	28	5	Adjustable	9	766	1
32	Isaacs	226498	2520	4	3	1	1	28	3	Fixed	8	763	1
33	Carter	316827	3150	4	3	1	1	22	4	Fixed	2	759	1
34	Carter	189984	1550	2	1.5	1	0	22	2	Fixed	17	758	0
35	Marty	366350	3090	3	2	1	1	23	3	Fixed	5	754	1
36	Isaacs	416160	4080	4	3	0	1	25	4	Fixed	12	753	0
37	Isaacs	308000	3500	4	3	0	1	37	2	Fixed	18	752	0
38	Rose	294357	2620	4	3	1	1	15	4	Fixed	10	751	0
39	Carter	337144	2790	4	3	1	1	19	3	Fixed	15	749	0
40	Peterson	299730	2910	3	2	0	0	31	2	Fixed	13	748	0
41	Rose	445740	4370	4	3	0	1	19	3	Fixed	5	746	0
42	Rose	410592	4200	4	3	1	1	27	1	Adjustable	9	741	1
43	Peterson	667732	5570	5	3.5	1	1	29	5	Fixed	4	740	0
44	Rose	523584	5050	6	4	1	1	19	5	Adjustable	10	739	0
45	Marty	336000	3360	3	2	0	0	32	3	Fixed	6	737	0
46	Marty	202598	2270	3	2	1	0	28	1	Fixed	10	737	0
47	Marty	326695	2830	3	2.5	1	0	30	4	Fixed	8	736	0
48	Rose	321320	2770	3	2	0	1	23	4	Fixed	6	736	0
49	Isaacs	246820	2870	4	3	0	1	27	5	Fixed	13	735	0
50	Isaacs	546084	5910	6	4	1	1	35	5	Adjustable	10	731	0
51	Isaacs	793084	6800	8	5.5	1	1	27	4	Fixed	6	729	0
52	Isaacs	174528	1600	2	1.5	1	0	39	2	Fixed	15	728	0
53	Peterson	392554	3970	4	3	1	1	30	4	Fixed	17	726	0
54	Peterson	263160	3060	3	2	0	1	26	3	Fixed	10	726	0
55	Rose	237120	1900	2	1.5	1	0	14	3	Fixed	18	723	0
56	Carter	225750	2150	2	1.5	1	1	27	2	Fixed	15	715	0
57	Isaacs	848420	7190	6	4	0	1	49	1	Fixed	5	710	0
58	Carter	371956	3110	5	3.5	1	1	29	5	Fixed	8	710	0
59	Carter	404538	3290	5	3.5	1	1	24	2	Fixed	14	707	0
60	Rose	250090	2810	4	3	0	1	18	5	Fixed	11	704	0
61	Peterson	369978	3830	4	2.5	1	1	27	4	Fixed	10	703	0
62	Peterson	209292	1630	2	1.5	1	0	18	3	Fixed	10	701	0
63	Isaacs	190032	1850	2	1.5	1	1	30	4	Adjustable	2	675	0
64	Isaacs	216720	2520	3	2.5	0	0	2	4	Adjustable	5	674	1
65	Marty	323417	3220	4	3	1	1	22	4	Adjustable	2	673	0
66	Isaacs	316210	3070	3	2	0	0	30	1	Adjustable	1	673	0
67	Peterson	226054	2090	2	1.5	1	1	28	1	Adjustable	6	670	0
68	Marty	183920	2090	3	2	0	0	30	2	Adjustable	8	669	1
69	Rose	248400	2300	3	2.5	1	1	50	2	Adjustable	4	667	0
70	Isaacs	466560	5760	5	3.5	0	1	42	4	Adjustable	3	665	0
71	Rose	667212	6110	6	4	1	1	21	3	Adjustable	8	662	1
72	Peterson	362710	4370	4	2.5	0	1	24	1	Adjustable	2	656	0
73	Rose	265440	3160	5	3.5	1	1	22	5	Adjustable	3	653	0
74	Rose	706596	6600	7	5	1	1	40	3	Adjustable	7	652	1
75	Marty	293700	3300	3	2	0	0	14	4	Adjustable	7	647	1
76	Marty	199448	2330	2	1.5	1	1	25	3	Adjustable	5	644	1
77	Carter	369533	4230	4	3	1	1	32	2	Adjustable	2	642	0
78	Marty	230121	2030	2	1.5	1	0	21	2	Adjustable	3	639	0
79	Marty	169000	1690	2	1.5	0	0	20	1	Adjustable	7	639	1
80	Peterson	190291	2040	2	1.5	1	1	31	4	Adjustable	6	631	1
81	Rose	393584	4660	4	3	1	1	34	3	Adjustable	7	630	1
82	Marty	363792	2860	3	2.5	1	1	48	5	Adjustable	3	626	0
83	Carter	360960	3840	6	4.5	0	1	32	2	Adjustable	5	626	1
84	Carter	310877	3180	3	2	1	1	40	1	Adjustable	6	624	1
85	Peterson	919480	7670	8	5.5	1	1	30	4	Adjustable	1	623	0
86	Carter	392904	3400	3	2	1	0	40	2	Adjustable	8	618	1
87	Carter	200928	1840	2	1.5	1	1	36	4	Adjustable	3	618	1

(*continued*)

A.1 Data Set 1—North Valley Real Estate Data (*concluded*)

Record	Agent	Price	Size	Bedrooms	Baths	Pool (Yes is 1)	Garage (Yes is 1)	Days	Township	Mortgage type	Years	FICO	Default (Yes is 1)
88	Carter	537900	4890	6	4	0	1	23	1	Adjustable	7	614	0
89	Rose	258120	2390	3	2.5	0	1	23	1	Adjustable	6	614	1
90	Carter	558342	6160	6	4	1	1	24	3	Adjustable	7	613	0
91	Marty	302720	3440	4	2.5	0	1	38	3	Adjustable	3	609	1
92	Isaacs	240115	2220	2	1.5	1	0	39	5	Adjustable	1	609	0
93	Carter	793656	6530	7	5	1	1	53	4	Adjustable	3	605	1
94	Peterson	218862	1930	2	1.5	1	0	58	4	Adjustable	1	604	0
95	Peterson	383081	3510	3	2	1	1	27	2	Adjustable	6	601	1
96	Marty	351520	3380	3	2	0	1	35	2	Adjustable	8	599	1
97	Peterson	841491	7030	6	4	1	1	50	4	Adjustable	8	596	1
98	Marty	336300	2850	3	2.5	0	0	28	1	Adjustable	6	595	1
99	Isaacs	312863	3750	6	4	1	1	12	4	Adjustable	2	595	0
100	Carter	275033	3060	3	2	1	1	27	3	Adjustable	3	593	0
101	Peterson	229990	2110	2	1.5	0	0	37	3	Adjustable	6	591	1
102	Isaacs	195257	2130	2	1.5	1	0	11	5	Adjustable	8	591	1
103	Marty	194238	1650	2	1.5	1	1	30	2	Adjustable	7	590	1
104	Peterson	348528	2740	4	3	1	1	27	5	Adjustable	3	584	1
105	Peterson	241920	2240	2	1.5	0	1	34	5	Adjustable	8	583	1

A.2 Data Set 2—Baseball Statistics, 2015 Season

Variables

Team = Team's name
League = American or National League
Year Opened = First year the team's stadium was used
Team Salary = Total team salary expressed in millions of dollars
Attendance = Total number of people attending regular season games
Wins = Number of regular season games won
ERA = Team earned run average
BA = Team batting average
HR = Team home runs
Year = Year of operation
Average salary = Average annual player salary in dollars

Team	League	Year Opened	Team Salary	Attendance	Wins	ERA	BA	HR
Arizona	National	1998	65.80	2,080,145	79	4.04	0.264	154
Atlanta	National	1996	89.60	2,001,392	67	4.41	0.251	100
Baltimore	American	1992	118.90	2,281,202	81	4.05	0.250	217
Boston	American	1912	168.70	2,880,694	78	4.31	0.265	161
Chicago Cubs	National	1914	117.20	2,959,812	97	3.36	0.244	171
Chicago Sox	American	1991	110.70	1,755,810	76	3.98	0.250	136
Cincinnati	National	2003	117.70	2,419,506	64	4.33	0.248	167
Cleveland	American	1994	87.70	1,388,905	81	3.67	0.256	141
Colorado	National	1995	98.30	2,506,789	68	5.04	0.265	186
Detroit	American	2000	172.80	2,726,048	74	4.64	0.270	151
Houston	American	2000	69.10	2,153,585	86	3.57	0.250	230
Kansas City	American	1973	112.90	2,708,549	95	3.73	0.269	139
LA Angels	American	1966	146.40	3,012,765	85	3.94	0.246	176
LA Dodgers	National	1962	230.40	3,764,815	92	3.44	0.250	187
Miami	National	2012	84.60	1,752,235	71	4.02	0.260	120
Milwaukee	National	2001	98.70	2,542,558	68	4.28	0.251	145
Minnesota	American	2010	108.30	2,220,054	83	4.07	0.247	156
NY Mets	National	2009	100.10	2,569,753	90	3.43	0.244	177
NY Yankees	American	2009	213.50	3,193,795	87	4.05	0.251	212
Oakland	American	1966	80.80	1,768,175	68	4.14	0.251	146
Philadelphia	National	2004	133.00	1,831,080	63	4.69	0.249	130
Pittsburgh	National	2001	85.90	2,498,596	98	3.21	0.260	140
San Diego	National	2004	126.60	2,459,742	74	4.09	0.243	148
San Francisco	National	2000	166.50	3,375,882	84	3.72	0.267	136
Seattle	American	1999	123.20	2,193,581	76	4.16	0.249	198
St. Louis	National	2006	120.30	3,520,889	100	2.94	0.253	137
Tampa Bay	American	1990	74.80	1,287,054	80	3.74	0.252	167
Texas	American	1994	144.80	2,491,875	88	4.24	0.257	172
Toronto	American	1989	116.40	2,794,891	93	3.8	0.269	232
Washington	National	2008	174.50	2,619,843	83	3.62	0.251	177

(continued)

A.2 Data Set 2—Baseball Statistics, 2015 Season (*concluded*)

Year	Average salary
2000	1,988,034
2001	2,264,403
2002	2,383,235
2003	2,555,476
2004	2,486,609
2005	2,632,655
2006	2,866,544
2007	2,944,556
2008	3,154,845
2009	3,240,206
2010	3,297,828
2011	3,305,393
2012	3,440,000
2013	3,650,000
2014	3,950,000
2015	4,250,000

A.3 Data Set 3—Lincolnville School District Bus Data

Variables

ID = Bus identification number
Manufacturer = Source of the bus (Bluebird, Keiser, or Thompson)
Engine type = If the engine is diesel then engine type = 0; if the engine is gasoline, then engine type = 1)
Capacity = number of seats on the bus
Maintenance cost = dollars spent to maintain a bus last year
Age = number of years since the bus left the manufacturer
Odometer Miles = total number of miles traveled by a bus
Miles = number of miles traveled since last maintenance

ID	Manufacturer	Engine Type (0=diesel)	Capacity	Maintenance cost	Age	Odometer Miles	Miles
10	Keiser	1	14	4646	5	54375	11973
396	Thompson	0	14	1072	2	21858	11969
122	Bluebird	1	55	9394	10	116580	11967
751	Keiser	0	14	1078	2	22444	11948
279	Bluebird	0	55	1008	2	22672	11925
500	Bluebird	1	55	5329	5	50765	11922
520	Bluebird	0	55	4794	10	119130	11896
759	Keiser	0	55	3952	8	87872	11883
714	Bluebird	0	42	3742	7	73703	11837
875	Bluebird	0	55	4376	9	97947	11814
600	Bluebird	0	55	4832	10	119860	11800
953	Bluebird	0	55	5160	10	117700	11798
101	Bluebird	0	55	1955	4	41096	11789
358	Bluebird	0	55	2775	6	70086	11782
29	Bluebird	1	55	5352	6	69438	11781
365	Keiser	0	55	3065	6	63384	11778
162	Keiser	1	55	3143	3	31266	11758
686	Bluebird	0	55	1569	3	34674	11757
370	Keiser	1	55	7766	8	86528	11707
887	Bluebird	0	55	3743	8	93672	11704
464	Bluebird	1	55	2540	3	34530	11698
948	Keiser	0	42	4342	9	97956	11691
678	Keiser	0	55	3361	7	75229	11668
481	Keiser	1	6	3097	3	34362	11662
43	Bluebird	1	55	8263	9	102969	11615
704	Bluebird	0	55	4218	8	83424	11610
814	Bluebird	0	55	2028	4	40824	11576
39	Bluebird	1	55	5821	6	69444	11533
699	Bluebird	1	55	9069	9	98307	11518
75	Bluebird	0	55	3011	6	71970	11462
693	Keiser	1	55	9193	9	101889	11461
989	Keiser	0	55	4795	9	106605	11418
982	Bluebird	0	55	505	1	10276	11359
321	Bluebird	0	42	2732	6	70122	11358
724	Keiser	0	42	3754	8	91968	11344
732	Keiser	0	42	4640	9	101196	11342
880	Keiser	1	55	8410	9	97065	11336
193	Thompson	0	14	5922	11	128711	11248
884	Bluebird	0	55	4364	9	92457	11231
57	Bluebird	0	55	3190	7	79240	11222
731	Bluebird	0	42	3213	6	68526	11168
61	Keiser	0	55	4139	9	103536	11148

(continued)

A.3 Data Set 3—Lincolnville School District Bus Data (*concluded*)

ID	Manufacturer	Engine Type (0=diesel)	Capacity	Maintenance cost	Age	Odometer Miles	Miles
135	Bluebird	0	55	3560	7	76426	11127
833	Thompson	0	14	3920	8	90968	11112
671	Thompson	1	14	6733	8	89792	11100
692	Bluebird	0	55	3770	8	93248	11048
200	Bluebird	0	55	5168	10	103700	11018
754	Keiser	0	14	7380	14	146860	11003
540	Bluebird	1	55	3656	4	45284	10945
660	Bluebird	1	55	6213	6	64434	10911
353	Keiser	1	55	4279	4	45744	10902
482	Bluebird	1	55	10575	10	116534	10802
398	Thompson	0	6	4752	9	95922	10802
984	Bluebird	0	55	3809	8	87664	10760
977	Bluebird	0	55	3769	7	79422	10759
705	Keiser	0	42	2152	4	47596	10755
767	Keiser	0	55	2985	6	71538	10726
326	Bluebird	0	55	4563	9	107343	10724
120	Keiser	0	42	4723	10	110320	10674
554	Bluebird	0	42	1826	4	44604	10662
695	Bluebird	0	55	1061	2	23152	10633
9	Keiser	1	55	3527	4	46848	10591
861	Bluebird	1	55	9669	10	106040	10551
603	Keiser	0	14	2116	4	44384	10518
156	Thompson	0	14	6212	12	140460	10473
427	Keiser	1	55	6927	7	73423	10355
883	Bluebird	1	55	1881	2	20742	10344
168	Thompson	1	14	7004	7	83006	10315
954	Bluebird	0	42	5284	10	101000	10235
768	Bluebird	0	42	3173	7	71778	10227
490	Bluebird	1	55	10133	10	106240	10210
725	Bluebird	0	55	2356	5	57065	10209
45	Keiser	0	55	3124	6	60102	10167
38	Keiser	1	14	5976	6	61662	10140
314	Thompson	0	6	5408	11	128117	10128
507	Bluebird	0	55	3690	7	72849	10095
40	Bluebird	1	55	9573	10	118470	10081
918	Bluebird	0	55	2470	5	53620	10075
387	Bluebird	1	55	6863	8	89960	10055
418	Bluebird	0	55	4513	9	104715	10000

A.4 Data Set 4—Applewood Auto Group

Age = the age of the buyer at the time of the purchase
Profit = the amount earned by the dealership on the sale of each vehicle
Location = the dealership where the vehicle was purchased
Vehicle type = SUV, sedan, compact, hybrid, or truck
Previous = the number of vehicles previously purchased at any of the four Applewood dealerships by the customer

Age	Profit	Location	Vehicle-Type	Previous
21	$1,387	Tionesta	Sedan	0
23	1,754	Sheffield	SUV	1
24	1,817	Sheffield	Hybrid	1
25	1,040	Sheffield	Compact	0
26	1,273	Kane	Sedan	1
27	1,529	Sheffield	Sedan	1
27	3,082	Kane	Truck	0
28	1,951	Kane	SUV	1
28	2,692	Tionesta	Compact	0
29	1,206	Sheffield	Sedan	0
29	1,342	Kane	Sedan	2
30	443	Kane	Sedan	3
30	754	Olean	Sedan	2
30	1,621	Sheffield	Truck	1
31	870	Tionesta	Sedan	1
31	1,174	Kane	Truck	0
31	1,412	Sheffield	Sedan	1
31	1,809	Tionesta	Sedan	1
31	2,415	Kane	Sedan	0
32	1,546	Sheffield	Truck	3
32	2,148	Tionesta	SUV	2
32	2,207	Sheffield	Compact	0
32	2,252	Tionesta	SUV	0
33	1,428	Kane	SUV	2
33	1,889	Olean	SUV	1
34	1,166	Olean	Sedan	1
34	1,320	Tionesta	Sedan	1
34	2,265	Olean	Sedan	0
35	1,323	Olean	Sedan	2
35	1,761	Kane	Sedan	1
35	1,919	Tionesta	SUV	1
36	2,357	Kane	SUV	2
36	2,866	Kane	Sedan	1
37	732	Olean	SUV	1
37	1,464	Olean	Sedan	3
37	1,626	Tionesta	Compact	4
37	1,761	Olean	SUV	1
37	1,915	Tionesta	SUV	2
37	2,119	Kane	Hybrid	1
38	1,766	Sheffield	SUV	0
38	2,201	Sheffield	Truck	2
39	996	Kane	Compact	2
39	2,813	Tionesta	SUV	0
40	323	Kane	Sedan	0
40	352	Sheffield	Compact	0
40	482	Olean	Sedan	1
40	1,144	Tionesta	Truck	0
40	1,485	Sheffield	Compact	0
40	1,509	Kane	SUV	2
40	1,638	Sheffield	Sedan	0
40	1,961	Sheffield	Sedan	1
40	2,127	Olean	Truck	0
40	2,430	Tionesta	Sedan	1
41	1,704	Sheffield	Sedan	1
41	1,876	Kane	Sedan	2
41	2,010	Tionesta	Sedan	1
41	2,165	Tionesta	SUV	0
41	2,231	Tionesta	SUV	2
41	2,389	Kane	Truck	1
42	335	Olean	SUV	1
42	963	Kane	Sedan	0
42	1,298	Tionesta	Sedan	1
42	1,410	Kane	SUV	2
42	1,553	Tionesta	Compact	0
42	1,648	Olean	SUV	0
42	2,071	Kane	SUV	0
42	2,116	Kane	Compact	2
43	1,500	Tionesta	Sedan	0
43	1,549	Kane	SUV	2
43	2,348	Tionesta	Sedan	0
43	2,498	Tionesta	SUV	1
44	294	Kane	SUV	1
44	1,115	Kane	Truck	0
44	1,124	Tionesta	Compact	2
44	1,532	Tionesta	SUV	3
44	1,688	Kane	Sedan	4
44	1,822	Kane	SUV	0
44	1,897	Sheffield	Compact	0
44	2,445	Kane	SUV	0
44	2,886	Olean	SUV	1
45	820	Kane	Compact	1
45	1,266	Olean	Sedan	0
45	1,741	Olean	Compact	2
45	1,772	Olean	Compact	1
45	1,932	Tionesta	Sedan	1
45	2,350	Sheffield	Compact	0
45	2,422	Kane	Sedan	1
45	2,446	Olean	Compact	1
46	369	Olean	Sedan	1
46	978	Kane	Sedan	1
46	1,238	Sheffield	Compact	1
46	1,818	Kane	SUV	0
46	1,824	Olean	Truck	0
46	1,907	Olean	Sedan	0
46	1,938	Kane	Sedan	0
46	1,940	Kane	Truck	3

(continued)

A.4 Data Set 4—Applewood Auto Group (*concluded*)

Age	Profit	Location	Vehicle-Type	Previous
46	2,197	Sheffield	Sedan	1
46	2,646	Tionesta	Sedan	2
47	1,461	Kane	Sedan	0
47	1,731	Tionesta	Compact	0
47	2,230	Tionesta	Sedan	1
47	2,341	Sheffield	SUV	1
47	3,292	Olean	Sedan	2
48	1,108	Sheffield	Sedan	1
48	1,295	Sheffield	SUV	1
48	1,344	Sheffield	SUV	0
48	1,906	Kane	Sedan	1
48	1,952	Tionesta	Compact	1
48	2,070	Kane	SUV	1
48	2,454	Kane	Sedan	1
49	1,606	Olean	Compact	0
49	1,680	Kane	SUV	3
49	1,827	Tionesta	Truck	3
49	1,915	Tionesta	SUV	1
49	2,084	Tionesta	Sedan	0
49	2,639	Sheffield	SUV	0
50	842	Kane	SUV	0
50	1,963	Sheffield	Sedan	1
50	2,059	Sheffield	Sedan	1
50	2,338	Tionesta	SUV	0
50	3,043	Kane	Sedan	0
51	1,059	Kane	SUV	1
51	1,674	Sheffield	Sedan	1
51	1,807	Tionesta	Sedan	1
51	2,056	Sheffield	Hybrid	0
51	2,236	Tionesta	SUV	2
51	2,928	Kane	SUV	0
52	1,269	Tionesta	Sedan	1
52	1,717	Sheffield	SUV	3
52	1,797	Kane	Sedan	1
52	1,955	Olean	Hybrid	2
52	2,199	Tionesta	SUV	0
52	2,482	Olean	Compact	0
52	2,701	Sheffield	SUV	0
52	3,210	Olean	Truck	4
53	377	Olean	SUV	1
53	1,220	Olean	Sedan	0
53	1,401	Tionesta	SUV	2
53	2,175	Olean	Sedan	1
54	1,118	Sheffield	Compact	1
54	2,584	Olean	Compact	2
54	2,666	Tionesta	Truck	0
54	2,991	Tionesta	SUV	0
55	934	Sheffield	Truck	1
55	2,063	Kane	SUV	1
55	2,083	Sheffield	Sedan	1
55	2,856	Olean	Hybrid	1
55	2,989	Tionesta	Compact	1
56	910	Sheffield	SUV	0
56	1,536	Kane	SUV	0
56	1,957	Sheffield	SUV	1
56	2,240	Olean	Sedan	0
56	2,695	Kane	Sedan	2
57	1,325	Olean	Sedan	1
57	2,250	Sheffield	Sedan	2
57	2,279	Sheffield	Hybrid	1
57	2,626	Sheffield	Sedan	2
58	1,501	Sheffield	Hybrid	1
58	1,752	Kane	Sedan	3
58	2,058	Kane	SUV	1
58	2,370	Tionesta	Compact	0
58	2,637	Sheffield	SUV	1
59	1,426	Sheffield	Sedan	0
59	2,944	Olean	SUV	2
60	2,147	Olean	Compact	2
61	1,973	Kane	SUV	3
61	2,502	Olean	Sedan	0
62	783	Sheffield	Hybrid	1
62	1,538	Olean	Truck	1
63	2,339	Olean	Compact	1
64	2,700	Kane	Truck	0
65	2,222	Kane	Truck	1
65	2,597	Sheffield	Truck	0
65	2,742	Tionesta	SUV	2
68	1,837	Sheffield	Sedan	1
69	2,842	Kane	SUV	0
70	2,434	Olean	Sedan	4
72	1,640	Olean	Sedan	1
72	1,821	Tionesta	SUV	1
73	2,487	Olean	Compact	4

A.5 Banking Data Set—Century National Bank Case

Balance = Account balance in $
ATM = Number of ATM transactions in the month
Services = Number of other bank services used
Debit = Account has a debit card (1 = yes, 0 = no)
Interest = Receives interest on the account (1 = yes, 0 = no)
City = City where banking is done
60 Accounts

Balance	ATM	Services	Debit	Interest	City
1,756	13	4	0	1	2
748	9	2	1	0	1
1,501	10	1	0	0	1
1,831	10	4	0	1	3
1,622	14	6	0	1	4
1,886	17	3	0	1	1
740	6	3	0	0	3
1,593	10	8	1	0	1
1,169	6	4	0	0	4
2,125	18	6	0	0	2
1,554	12	6	1	0	3
1,474	12	7	1	0	1
1,913	6	5	0	0	1
1,218	10	3	1	0	1
1,006	12	4	0	0	1
2,215	20	3	1	0	4
137	7	2	0	0	3
167	5	4	0	0	4
343	7	2	0	0	1
2,557	20	7	1	0	4
2,276	15	4	1	0	3
1,494	11	2	0	1	1
2,144	17	3	0	0	3
1,995	10	7	0	0	2
1,053	8	4	1	0	3
1,526	8	4	0	1	2
1,120	8	6	1	0	3
1,838	7	5	1	1	3
1,746	11	2	0	0	2
1,616	10	4	1	1	2

Balance	ATM	Services	Debit	Interest	City
1,958	6	2	1	0	2
634	2	7	1	0	4
580	4	1	0	0	1
1,320	4	5	1	0	1
1,675	6	7	1	0	2
789	8	4	0	0	4
1,735	12	7	0	1	3
1,784	11	5	0	0	1
1,326	16	8	0	0	3
2,051	14	4	1	0	4
1,044	7	5	1	0	1
1,885	10	6	1	1	2
1,790	11	4	0	1	3
765	4	3	0	0	4
1,645	6	9	0	1	4
32	2	0	0	0	3
1,266	11	7	0	0	4
890	7	1	0	1	1
2,204	14	5	0	0	2
2,409	16	8	0	0	2
1,338	14	4	1	0	2
2,076	12	5	1	0	2
1,708	13	3	1	0	1
2,138	18	5	0	1	4
2,375	12	4	0	0	2
1,455	9	5	1	1	3
1,487	8	4	1	0	4
1,125	6	4	1	0	2
1,989	12	3	0	1	2
2,156	14	5	1	0	2

APPENDIX B: TABLES

B.1 Binomial Probability Distribution

n = 1

Probability

x	0.05	0.10	0.20	0.30	0.40	0.50	0.60	0.70	0.80	0.90	0.95
0	0.950	0.900	0.800	0.700	0.600	0.500	0.400	0.300	0.200	0.100	0.050
1	0.050	0.100	0.200	0.300	0.400	0.500	0.600	0.700	0.800	0.900	0.950

n = 2

Probability

x	0.05	0.10	0.20	0.30	0.40	0.50	0.60	0.70	0.80	0.90	0.95
0	0.903	0.810	0.640	0.490	0.360	0.250	0.160	0.090	0.040	0.010	0.003
1	0.095	0.180	0.320	0.420	0.480	0.500	0.480	0.420	0.320	0.180	0.095
2	0.003	0.010	0.040	0.090	0.160	0.250	0.360	0.490	0.640	0.810	0.903

n =3

Probability

x	0.05	0.10	0.20	0.30	0.40	0.50	0.60	0.70	0.80	0.90	0.95
0	0.857	0.729	0.512	0.343	0.216	0.125	0.064	0.027	0.008	0.001	0.000
1	0.135	0.243	0.384	0.441	0.432	0.375	0.288	0.189	0.096	0.027	0.007
2	0.007	0.027	0.096	0.189	0.288	0.375	0.432	0.441	0.384	0.243	0.135
3	0.000	0.001	0.008	0.027	0.064	0.125	0.216	0.343	0.512	0.729	0.857

n = 4

Probability

x	0.05	0.10	0.20	0.30	0.40	0.50	0.60	0.70	0.80	0.90	0.95
0	0.815	0.656	0.410	0.240	0.130	0.063	0.026	0.008	0.002	0.000	0.000
1	0.171	0.292	0.410	0.412	0.346	0.250	0.154	0.076	0.026	0.004	0.000
2	0.014	0.049	0.154	0.265	0.346	0.375	0.346	0.265	0.154	0.049	0.014
3	0.000	0.004	0.026	0.076	0.154	0.250	0.346	0.412	0.410	0.292	0.171
4	0.000	0.000	0.002	0.008	0.026	0.063	0.130	0.240	0.410	0.656	0.815

n = 5

Probability

x	0.05	0.10	0.20	0.30	0.40	0.50	0.60	0.70	0.80	0.90	0.95
0	0.774	0.590	0.328	0.168	0.078	0.031	0.010	0.002	0.000	0.000	0.000
1	0.204	0.328	0.410	0.360	0.259	0.156	0.077	0.028	0.006	0.000	0.000
2	0.021	0.073	0.205	0.309	0.346	0.313	0.230	0.132	0.051	0.008	0.001
3	0.001	0.008	0.051	0.132	0.230	0.313	0.346	0.309	0.205	0.073	0.021
4	0.000	0.000	0.006	0.028	0.077	0.156	0.259	0.360	0.410	0.328	0.204
5	0.000	0.000	0.000	0.002	0.010	0.031	0.078	0.168	0.328	0.590	0.774

(continued)

B.1 Binomial Probability Distribution (*continued*)

n = 6

Probability

x	**0.05**	**0.10**	**0.20**	**0.30**	**0.40**	**0.50**	**0.60**	**0.70**	**0.80**	**0.90**	**0.95**
0	0.735	0.531	0.262	0.118	0.047	0.016	0.004	0.001	0.000	0.000	0.000
1	0.232	0.354	0.393	0.303	0.187	0.094	0.037	0.010	0.002	0.000	0.000
2	0.031	0.098	0.246	0.324	0.311	0.234	0.138	0.060	0.015	0.001	0.000
3	0.002	0.015	0.082	0.185	0.276	0.313	0.276	0.185	0.082	0.015	0.002
4	0.000	0.001	0.015	0.060	0.138	0.234	0.311	0.324	0.246	0.098	0.031
5	0.000	0.000	0.002	0.010	0.037	0.094	0.187	0.303	0.393	0.354	0.232
6	0.000	0.000	0.000	0.001	0.004	0.016	0.047	0.118	0.262	0.531	0.735

n = 7

Probability

x	**0.05**	**0.10**	**0.20**	**0.30**	**0.40**	**0.50**	**0.60**	**0.70**	**0.80**	**0.90**	**0.95**
0	0.698	0.478	0.210	0.082	0.028	0.008	0.002	0.000	0.000	0.000	0.000
1	0.257	0.372	0.367	0.247	0.131	0.055	0.017	0.004	0.000	0.000	0.000
2	0.041	0.124	0.275	0.318	0.261	0.164	0.077	0.025	0.004	0.000	0.000
3	0.004	0.023	0.115	0.227	0.290	0.273	0.194	0.097	0.029	0.003	0.000
4	0.000	0.003	0.029	0.097	0.194	0.273	0.290	0.227	0.115	0.023	0.004
5	0.000	0.000	0.004	0.025	0.077	0.164	0.261	0.318	0.275	0.124	0.041
6	0.000	0.000	0.000	0.004	0.017	0.055	0.131	0.247	0.367	0.372	0.257
7	0.000	0.000	0.000	0.000	0.002	0.008	0.028	0.082	0.210	0.478	0.698

n = 8

Probability

x	**0.05**	**0.10**	**0.20**	**0.30**	**0.40**	**0.50**	**0.60**	**0.70**	**0.80**	**0.90**	**0.95**
0	0.663	0.430	0.168	0.058	0.017	0.004	0.001	0.000	0.000	0.000	0.000
1	0.279	0.383	0.336	0.198	0.090	0.031	0.008	0.001	0.000	0.000	0.000
2	0.051	0.149	0.294	0.296	0.209	0.109	0.041	0.010	0.001	0.000	0.000
3	0.005	0.033	0.147	0.254	0.279	0.219	0.124	0.047	0.009	0.000	0.000
4	0.000	0.005	0.046	0.136	0.232	0.273	0.232	0.136	0.046	0.005	0.000
5	0.000	0.000	0.009	0.047	0.124	0.219	0.279	0.254	0.147	0.033	0.005
6	0.000	0.000	0.001	0.010	0.041	0.109	0.209	0.296	0.294	0.149	0.051
7	0.000	0.000	0.000	0.001	0.008	0.031	0.090	0.198	0.336	0.383	0.279
8	0.000	0.000	0.000	0.000	0.001	0.004	0.017	0.058	0.168	0.430	0.663

(continued)

B.1 Binomial Probability Distribution (*continued*)

$n = 9$

Probability

x	0.05	0.10	0.20	0.30	0.40	0.50	0.60	0.70	0.80	0.90	0.95
0	0.630	0.387	0.134	0.040	0.010	0.002	0.000	0.000	0.000	0.000	0.000
1	0.299	0.387	0.302	0.156	0.060	0.018	0.004	0.000	0.000	0.000	0.000
2	0.063	0.172	0.302	0.267	0.161	0.070	0.021	0.004	0.000	0.000	0.000
3	0.008	0.045	0.176	0.267	0.251	0.164	0.074	0.021	0.003	0.000	0.000
4	0.001	0.007	0.066	0.172	0.251	0.246	0.167	0.074	0.017	0.001	0.000
5	0.000	0.001	0.017	0.074	0.167	0.246	0.251	0.172	0.066	0.007	0.001
6	0.000	0.000	0.003	0.021	0.074	0.164	0.251	0.267	0.176	0.045	0.008
7	0.000	0.000	0.000	0.004	0.021	0.070	0.161	0.267	0.302	0.172	0.063
8	0.000	0.000	0.000	0.000	0.004	0.018	0.060	0.156	0.302	0.387	0.299
9	0.000	0.000	0.000	0.000	0.000	0.002	0.010	0.040	0.134	0.387	0.630

$n = 10$

Probability

x	0.05	0.10	0.20	0.30	0.40	0.50	0.60	0.70	0.80	0.90	0.95
0	0.599	0.349	0.107	0.028	0.006	0.001	0.000	0.000	0.000	0.000	0.000
1	0.315	0.387	0.268	0.121	0.040	0.010	0.002	0.000	0.000	0.000	0.000
2	0.075	0.194	0.302	0.233	0.121	0.044	0.011	0.001	0.000	0.000	0.000
3	0.010	0.057	0.201	0.267	0.215	0.117	0.042	0.009	0.001	0.000	0.000
4	0.001	0.011	0.088	0.200	0.251	0.205	0.111	0.037	0.006	0.000	0.000
5	0.000	0.001	0.026	0.103	0.201	0.246	0.201	0.103	0.026	0.001	0.000
6	0.000	0.000	0.006	0.037	0.111	0.205	0.251	0.200	0.088	0.011	0.001
7	0.000	0.000	0.001	0.009	0.042	0.117	0.215	0.267	0.201	0.057	0.010
8	0.000	0.000	0.000	0.001	0.011	0.044	0.121	0.233	0.302	0.194	0.075
9	0.000	0.000	0.000	0.000	0.002	0.010	0.040	0.121	0.268	0.387	0.315
10	0.000	0.000	0.000	0.000	0.000	0.001	0.006	0.028	0.107	0.349	0.599

$n = 11$

Probability

x	0.05	0.10	0.20	0.30	0.40	0.50	0.60	0.70	0.80	0.90	0.95
0	0.569	0.314	0.086	0.020	0.004	0.000	0.000	0.000	0.000	0.000	0.000
1	0.329	0.384	0.236	0.093	0.027	0.005	0.001	0.000	0.000	0.000	0.000
2	0.087	0.213	0.295	0.200	0.089	0.027	0.005	0.001	0.000	0.000	0.000
3	0.014	0.071	0.221	0.257	0.177	0.081	0.023	0.004	0.000	0.000	0.000
4	0.001	0.016	0.111	0.220	0.236	0.161	0.070	0.017	0.002	0.000	0.000
5	0.000	0.002	0.039	0.132	0.221	0.226	0.147	0.057	0.010	0.000	0.000
6	0.000	0.000	0.010	0.057	0.147	0.226	0.221	0.132	0.039	0.002	0.000
7	0.000	0.000	0.002	0.017	0.070	0.161	0.236	0.220	0.111	0.016	0.001
8	0.000	0.000	0.000	0.004	0.023	0.081	0.177	0.257	0.221	0.071	0.014
9	0.000	0.000	0.000	0.001	0.005	0.027	0.089	0.200	0.295	0.213	0.087
10	0.000	0.000	0.000	0.000	0.001	0.005	0.027	0.093	0.236	0.384	0.329
11	0.000	0.000	0.000	0.000	0.000	0.000	0.004	0.020	0.086	0.314	0.569

(continued)

B.1 Binomial Probability Distribution (*continued*)

$n = 12$

Probability

x	0.05	0.10	0.20	0.30	0.40	0.50	0.60	0.70	0.80	0.90	0.95
0	0.540	0.282	0.069	0.014	0.002	0.000	0.000	0.000	0.000	0.000	0.000
1	0.341	0.377	0.206	0.071	0.017	0.003	0.000	0.000	0.000	0.000	0.000
2	0.099	0.230	0.283	0.168	0.064	0.016	0.002	0.000	0.000	0.000	0.000
3	0.017	0.085	0.236	0.240	0.142	0.054	0.012	0.001	0.000	0.000	0.000
4	0.002	0.021	0.133	0.231	0.213	0.121	0.042	0.008	0.001	0.000	0.000
5	0.000	0.004	0.053	0.158	0.227	0.193	0.101	0.029	0.003	0.000	0.000
6	0.000	0.000	0.016	0.079	0.177	0.226	0.177	0.079	0.016	0.000	0.000
7	0.000	0.000	0.003	0.029	0.101	0.193	0.227	0.158	0.053	0.004	0.000
8	0.000	0.000	0.001	0.008	0.042	0.121	0.213	0.231	0.133	0.021	0.002
9	0.000	0.000	0.000	0.001	0.012	0.054	0.142	0.240	0.236	0.085	0.017
10	0.000	0.000	0.000	0.000	0.002	0.016	0.064	0.168	0.283	0.230	0.099
11	0.000	0.000	0.000	0.000	0.000	0.003	0.017	0.071	0.206	0.377	0.341
12	0.000	0.000	0.000	0.000	0.000	0.000	0.002	0.014	0.069	0.282	0.540

$n = 13$

Probability

x	0.05	0.10	0.20	0.30	0.40	0.50	0.60	0.70	0.80	0.90	0.95
0	0.513	0.254	0.055	0.010	0.001	0.000	0.000	0.000	0.000	0.000	0.000
1	0.351	0.367	0.179	0.054	0.011	0.002	0.000	0.000	0.000	0.000	0.000
2	0.111	0.245	0.268	0.139	0.045	0.010	0.001	0.000	0.000	0.000	0.000
3	0.021	0.100	0.246	0.218	0.111	0.035	0.006	0.001	0.000	0.000	0.000
4	0.003	0.028	0.154	0.234	0.184	0.087	0.024	0.003	0.000	0.000	0.000
5	0.000	0.006	0.069	0.180	0.221	0.157	0.066	0.014	0.001	0.000	0.000
6	0.000	0.001	0.023	0.103	0.197	0.209	0.131	0.044	0.006	0.000	0.000
7	0.000	0.000	0.006	0.044	0.131	0.209	0.197	0.103	0.023	0.001	0.000
8	0.000	0.000	0.001	0.014	0.066	0.157	0.221	0.180	0.069	0.006	0.000
9	0.000	0.000	0.000	0.003	0.024	0.087	0.184	0.234	0.154	0.028	0.003
10	0.000	0.000	0.000	0.001	0.006	0.035	0.111	0.218	0.246	0.100	0.021
11	0.000	0.000	0.000	0.000	0.001	0.010	0.045	0.139	0.268	0.245	0.111
12	0.000	0.000	0.000	0.000	0.000	0.002	0.011	0.054	0.179	0.367	0.351
13	0.000	0.000	0.000	0.000	0.000	0.000	0.001	0.010	0.055	0.254	0.513

(*continued*)

B.1 Binomial Probability Distribution (*concluded*)

$n = 14$

Probability

x	0.05	0.10	0.20	0.30	0.40	0.50	0.60	0.70	0.80	0.90	0.95
0	0.488	0.229	0.044	0.007	0.001	0.000	0.000	0.000	0.000	0.000	0.000
1	0.359	0.356	0.154	0.041	0.007	0.001	0.000	0.000	0.000	0.000	0.000
2	0.123	0.257	0.250	0.113	0.032	0.006	0.001	0.000	0.000	0.000	0.000
3	0.026	0.114	0.250	0.194	0.085	0.022	0.003	0.000	0.000	0.000	0.000
4	0.004	0.035	0.172	0.229	0.155	0.061	0.014	0.001	0.000	0.000	0.000
5	0.000	0.008	0.086	0.196	0.207	0.122	0.041	0.007	0.000	0.000	0.000
6	0.000	0.001	0.032	0.126	0.207	0.183	0.092	0.023	0.002	0.000	0.000
7	0.000	0.000	0.009	0.062	0.157	0.209	0.157	0.062	0.009	0.000	0.000
8	0.000	0.000	0.002	0.023	0.092	0.183	0.207	0.126	0.032	0.001	0.000
9	0.000	0.000	0.000	0.007	0.041	0.122	0.207	0.196	0.086	0.008	0.000
10	0.000	0.000	0.000	0.001	0.014	0.061	0.155	0.229	0.172	0.035	0.004
11	0.000	0.000	0.000	0.000	0.003	0.022	0.085	0.194	0.250	0.114	0.026
12	0.000	0.000	0.000	0.000	0.001	0.006	0.032	0.113	0.250	0.257	0.123
13	0.000	0.000	0.000	0.000	0.000	0.001	0.007	0.041	0.154	0.356	0.359
14	0.000	0.000	0.000	0.000	0.000	0.000	0.001	0.007	0.044	0.229	0.488

$n = 15$

Probability

x	0.05	0.10	0.20	0.30	0.40	0.50	0.60	0.70	0.80	0.90	0.95
0	0.463	0.206	0.035	0.005	0.000	0.000	0.000	0.000	0.000	0.000	0.000
1	0.366	0.343	0.132	0.031	0.005	0.000	0.000	0.000	0.000	0.000	0.000
2	0.135	0.267	0.231	0.092	0.022	0.003	0.000	0.000	0.000	0.000	0.000
3	0.031	0.129	0.250	0.170	0.063	0.014	0.002	0.000	0.000	0.000	0.000
4	0.005	0.043	0.188	0.219	0.127	0.042	0.007	0.001	0.000	0.000	0.000
5	0.001	0.010	0.103	0.206	0.186	0.092	0.024	0.003	0.000	0.000	0.000
6	0.000	0.002	0.043	0.147	0.207	0.153	0.061	0.012	0.001	0.000	0.000
7	0.000	0.000	0.014	0.081	0.177	0.196	0.118	0.035	0.003	0.000	0.000
8	0.000	0.000	0.003	0.035	0.118	0.196	0.177	0.081	0.014	0.000	0.000
9	0.000	0.000	0.001	0.012	0.061	0.153	0.207	0.147	0.043	0.002	0.000
10	0.000	0.000	0.000	0.003	0.024	0.092	0.186	0.206	0.103	0.010	0.001
11	0.000	0.000	0.000	0.001	0.007	0.042	0.127	0.219	0.188	0.043	0.005
12	0.000	0.000	0.000	0.000	0.002	0.014	0.063	0.170	0.250	0.129	0.031
13	0.000	0.000	0.000	0.000	0.000	0.003	0.022	0.092	0.231	0.267	0.135
14	0.000	0.000	0.000	0.000	0.000	0.000	0.005	0.031	0.132	0.343	0.366
15	0.000	0.000	0.000	0.000	0.000	0.000	0.000	0.005	0.035	0.206	0.463

B.2 Poisson Distribution

	μ								
x	**0.1**	**0.2**	**0.3**	**0.4**	**0.5**	**0.6**	**0.7**	**0.8**	**0.9**
0	0.9048	0.8187	0.7408	0.6703	0.6065	0.5488	0.4966	0.4493	0.4066
1	0.0905	0.1637	0.2222	0.2681	0.3033	0.3293	0.3476	0.3595	0.3659
2	0.0045	0.0164	0.0333	0.0536	0.0758	0.0988	0.1217	0.1438	0.1647
3	0.0002	0.0011	0.0033	0.0072	0.0126	0.0198	0.0284	0.0383	0.0494
4	0.0000	0.0001	0.0003	0.0007	0.0016	0.0030	0.0050	0.0077	0.0111
5	0.0000	0.0000	0.0000	0.0001	0.0002	0.0004	0.0007	0.0012	0.0020
6	0.0000	0.0000	0.0000	0.0000	0.0000	0.0000	0.0001	0.0002	0.0003
7	0.0000	0.0000	0.0000	0.0000	0.0000	0.0000	0.0000	0.0000	0.0000

	μ								
x	**1.0**	**2.0**	**3.0**	**4.0**	**5.0**	**6.0**	**7.0**	**8.0**	**9.0**
0	0.3679	0.1353	0.0498	0.0183	0.0067	0.0025	0.0009	0.0003	0.0001
1	0.3679	0.2707	0.1494	0.0733	0.0337	0.0149	0.0064	0.0027	0.0011
2	0.1839	0.2707	0.2240	0.1465	0.0842	0.0446	0.0223	0.0107	0.0050
3	0.0613	0.1804	0.2240	0.1954	0.1404	0.0892	0.0521	0.0286	0.0150
4	0.0153	0.0902	0.1680	0.1954	0.1755	0.1339	0.0912	0.0573	0.0337
5	0.0031	0.0361	0.1008	0.1563	0.1755	0.1606	0.1277	0.0916	0.0607
6	0.0005	0.0120	0.0504	0.1042	0.1462	0.1606	0.1490	0.1221	0.0911
7	0.0001	0.0034	0.0216	0.0595	0.1044	0.1377	0.1490	0.1396	0.1171
8	0.0000	0.0009	0.0081	0.0298	0.0653	0.1033	0.1304	0.1396	0.1318
9	0.0000	0.0002	0.0027	0.0132	0.0363	0.0688	0.1014	0.1241	0.1318
10	0.0000	0.0000	0.0008	0.0053	0.0181	0.0413	0.0710	0.0993	0.1186
11	0.0000	0.0000	0.0002	0.0019	0.0082	0.0225	0.0452	0.0722	0.0970
12	0.0000	0.0000	0.0001	0.0006	0.0034	0.0113	0.0263	0.0481	0.0728
13	0.0000	0.0000	0.0000	0.0002	0.0013	0.0052	0.0142	0.0296	0.0504
14	0.0000	0.0000	0.0000	0.0001	0.0005	0.0022	0.0071	0.0169	0.0324
15	0.0000	0.0000	0.0000	0.0000	0.0002	0.0009	0.0033	0.0090	0.0194
16	0.0000	0.0000	0.0000	0.0000	0.0000	0.0003	0.0014	0.0045	0.0109
17	0.0000	0.0000	0.0000	0.0000	0.0000	0.0001	0.0006	0.0021	0.0058
18	0.0000	0.0000	0.0000	0.0000	0.0000	0.0000	0.0002	0.0009	0.0029
19	0.0000	0.0000	0.0000	0.0000	0.0000	0.0000	0.0001	0.0004	0.0014
20	0.0000	0.0000	0.0000	0.0000	0.0000	0.0000	0.0000	0.0002	0.0006
21	0.0000	0.0000	0.0000	0.0000	0.0000	0.0000	0.0000	0.0001	0.0003
22	0.0000	0.0000	0.0000	0.0000	0.0000	0.0000	0.0000	0.0000	0.0001

B.3 Areas under the Normal Curve

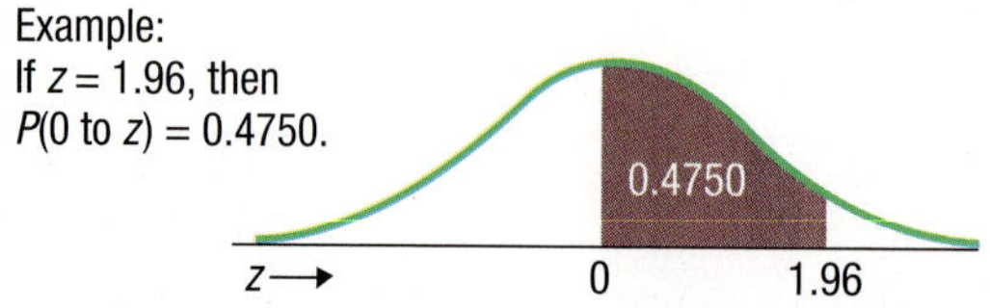

z	0.00	0.01	0.02	0.03	0.04	0.05	0.06	0.07	0.08	0.09
0.0	0.0000	0.0040	0.0080	0.0120	0.0160	0.0199	0.0239	0.0279	0.0319	0.0359
0.1	0.0398	0.0438	0.0478	0.0517	0.0557	0.0596	0.0636	0.0675	0.0714	0.0753
0.2	0.0793	0.0832	0.0871	0.0910	0.0948	0.0987	0.1026	0.1064	0.1103	0.1141
0.3	0.1179	0.1217	0.1255	0.1293	0.1331	0.1368	0.1406	0.1443	0.1480	0.1517
0.4	0.1554	0.1591	0.1628	0.1664	0.1700	0.1736	0.1772	0.1808	0.1844	0.1879
0.5	0.1915	0.1950	0.1985	0.2019	0.2054	0.2088	0.2123	0.2157	0.2190	0.2224
0.6	0.2257	0.2291	0.2324	0.2357	0.2389	0.2422	0.2454	0.2486	0.2517	0.2549
0.7	0.2580	0.2611	0.2642	0.2673	0.2704	0.2734	0.2764	0.2794	0.2823	0.2852
0.8	0.2881	0.2910	0.2939	0.2967	0.2995	0.3023	0.3051	0.3078	0.3106	0.3133
0.9	0.3159	0.3186	0.3212	0.3238	0.3264	0.3289	0.3315	0.3340	0.3365	0.3389
1.0	0.3413	0.3438	0.3461	0.3485	0.3508	0.3531	0.3554	0.3577	0.3599	0.3621
1.1	0.3643	0.3665	0.3686	0.3708	0.3729	0.3749	0.3770	0.3790	0.3810	0.3830
1.2	0.3849	0.3869	0.3888	0.3907	0.3925	0.3944	0.3962	0.3980	0.3997	0.4015
1.3	0.4032	0.4049	0.4066	0.4082	0.4099	0.4115	0.4131	0.4147	0.4162	0.4177
1.4	0.4192	0.4207	0.4222	0.4236	0.4251	0.4265	0.4279	0.4292	0.4306	0.4319
1.5	0.4332	0.4345	0.4357	0.4370	0.4382	0.4394	0.4406	0.4418	0.4429	0.4441
1.6	0.4452	0.4463	0.4474	0.4484	0.4495	0.4505	0.4515	0.4525	0.4535	0.4545
1.7	0.4554	0.4564	0.4573	0.4582	0.4591	0.4599	0.4608	0.4616	0.4625	0.4633
1.8	0.4641	0.4649	0.4656	0.4664	0.4671	0.4678	0.4686	0.4693	0.4699	0.4706
1.9	0.4713	0.4719	0.4726	0.4732	0.4738	0.4744	0.4750	0.4756	0.4761	0.4767
2.0	0.4772	0.4778	0.4783	0.4788	0.4793	0.4798	0.4803	0.4808	0.4812	0.4817
2.1	0.4821	0.4826	0.4830	0.4834	0.4838	0.4842	0.4846	0.4850	0.4854	0.4857
2.2	0.4861	0.4864	0.4868	0.4871	0.4875	0.4878	0.4881	0.4884	0.4887	0.4890
2.3	0.4893	0.4896	0.4898	0.4901	0.4904	0.4906	0.4909	0.4911	0.4913	0.4916
2.4	0.4918	0.4920	0.4922	0.4925	0.4927	0.4929	0.4931	0.4932	0.4934	0.4936
2.5	0.4938	0.4940	0.4941	0.4943	0.4945	0.4946	0.4948	0.4949	0.4951	0.4952
2.6	0.4953	0.4955	0.4956	0.4957	0.4959	0.4960	0.4961	0.4962	0.4963	0.4964
2.7	0.4965	0.4966	0.4967	0.4968	0.4969	0.4970	0.4971	0.4972	0.4973	0.4974
2.8	0.4974	0.4975	0.4976	0.4977	0.4977	0.4978	0.4979	0.4979	0.4980	0.4981
2.9	0.4981	0.4982	0.4982	0.4983	0.4984	0.4984	0.4985	0.4985	0.4986	0.4986
3.0	0.4987	0.4987	0.4987	0.4988	0.4988	0.4989	0.4989	0.4989	0.4990	0.4990

B.4 Table of Random Numbers

02711	08182	75997	79866	58095	83319	80295	79741	74599	84379
94873	90935	31684	63952	09865	14491	99518	93394	34691	14985
54921	78680	06635	98689	17306	25170	65928	87709	30533	89736
77640	97636	37397	93379	56454	59818	45827	74164	71666	46977
61545	00835	93251	87203	36759	49197	85967	01704	19634	21898
17147	19519	22497	16857	42426	84822	92598	49186	88247	39967
13748	04742	92460	85801	53444	65626	58710	55406	17173	69776
87455	14813	50373	28037	91182	32786	65261	11173	34376	36408
08999	57409	91185	10200	61411	23392	47797	56377	71635	08601
78804	81333	53809	32471	46034	36306	22498	19239	85428	55721
82173	26921	28472	98958	07960	66124	89731	95069	18625	92405
97594	25168	89178	68190	05043	17407	48201	83917	11413	72920
73881	67176	93504	42636	38233	16154	96451	57925	29667	30859
46071	22912	90326	42453	88108	72064	58601	32357	90610	32921
44492	19686	12495	93135	95185	77799	52441	88272	22024	80631
31864	72170	37722	55794	14636	05148	54505	50113	21119	25228
51574	90692	43339	65689	76539	27909	05467	21727	51141	72949
35350	76132	92925	92124	92634	35681	43690	89136	35599	84138
46943	36502	01172	46045	46991	33804	80006	35542	61056	75666
22665	87226	33304	57975	03985	21566	65796	72915	81466	89205
39437	97957	11838	10433	21564	51570	73558	27495	34533	57808
77082	47784	40098	97962	89845	28392	78187	06112	08169	11261
24544	25649	43370	28007	06779	72402	62632	53956	24709	06978
27503	15558	37738	24849	70722	71859	83736	06016	94397	12529
24590	24545	06435	52758	45685	90151	46516	49644	92686	84870
48155	86226	40359	28723	15364	69125	12609	57171	86857	31702
20226	53752	90648	24362	83314	00014	19207	69413	97016	86290
70178	73444	38790	53626	93780	18629	68766	24371	74639	30782
10169	41465	51935	05711	09799	79077	88159	33437	68519	03040
81084	03701	28598	70013	63794	53169	97054	60303	23259	96196
69202	20777	21727	81511	51887	16175	53746	46516	70339	62727
80561	95787	89426	93325	86412	57479	54194	52153	19197	81877
08199	26703	95128	48599	09333	12584	24374	31232	61782	44032
98883	28220	39358	53720	80161	83371	15181	11131	12219	55920
84568	69286	76054	21615	80883	36797	82845	39139	90900	18172
04269	35173	95745	53893	86022	77722	52498	84193	22448	22571
10538	13124	36099	13140	37706	44562	57179	44693	67877	01549
77843	24955	25900	63843	95029	93859	93634	20205	66294	41218
12034	94636	49455	76362	83532	31062	69903	91186	65768	55949
10524	72829	47641	93315	80875	28090	97728	52560	34937	79548
68935	76632	46984	61772	92786	22651	07086	89754	44143	97687
89450	65665	29190	43709	11172	34481	95977	47535	25658	73898
90696	20451	24211	97310	60446	73530	62865	96574	13829	72226
49006	32047	93086	00112	20470	17136	28255	86328	07293	38809
74591	87025	52368	59416	34417	70557	86746	55809	53628	12000
06315	17012	77103	00968	07235	10728	42189	33292	51487	64443
62386	09184	62092	46617	99419	64230	95034	85481	07857	42510
86848	82122	04028	36959	87827	12813	08627	80699	13345	51695
65643	69480	46598	04501	40403	91408	32343	48130	49303	90689
11084	46534	78957	77353	39578	77868	22970	84349	09184	70603

B.5 Student's *t* Distribution

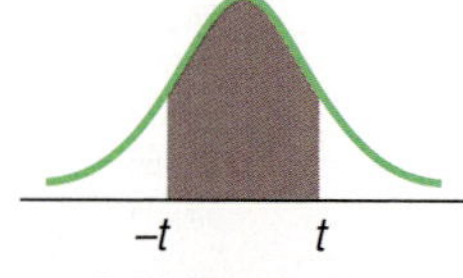

Confidence interval

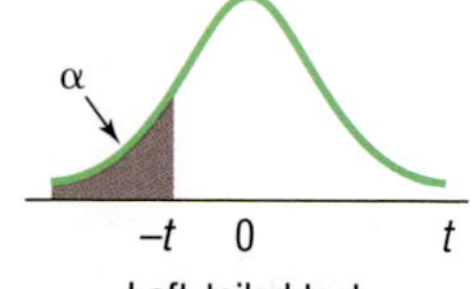

Left-tailed test

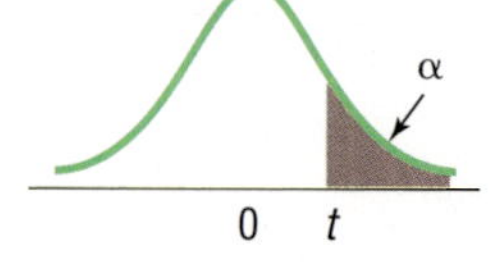

Right-tailed test

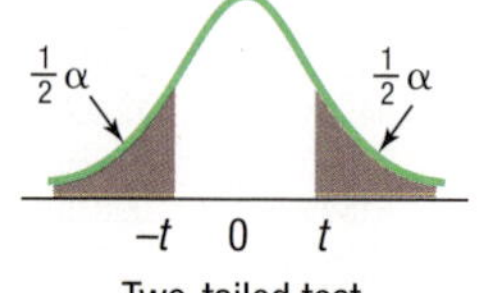

Two-tailed test

	Confidence Intervals, *c*					
	80%	**90%**	**95%**	**98%**	**99%**	**99.9%**
	Level of Significance for One-Tailed Test, α					
df	**0.10**	**0.05**	**0.025**	**0.01**	**0.005**	**0.0005**
	Level of Significance for Two-Tailed Test, α					
	0.20	**0.10**	**0.05**	**0.02**	**0.01**	**0.001**
1	3.078	6.314	12.706	31.821	63.657	636.619
2	1.886	2.920	4.303	6.965	9.925	31.599
3	1.638	2.353	3.182	4.541	5.841	12.924
4	1.533	2.132	2.776	3.747	4.604	8.610
5	1.476	2.015	2.571	3.365	4.032	6.869
6	1.440	1.943	2.447	3.143	3.707	5.959
7	1.415	1.895	2.365	2.998	3.499	5.408
8	1.397	1.860	2.306	2.896	3.355	5.041
9	1.383	1.833	2.262	2.821	3.250	4.781
10	1.372	1.812	2.228	2.764	3.169	4.587
11	1.363	1.796	2.201	2.718	3.106	4.437
12	1.356	1.782	2.179	2.681	3.055	4.318
13	1.350	1.771	2.160	2.650	3.012	4.221
14	1.345	1.761	2.145	2.624	2.977	4.140
15	1.341	1.753	2.131	2.602	2.947	4.073
16	1.337	1.746	2.120	2.583	2.921	4.015
17	1.333	1.740	2.110	2.567	2.898	3.965
18	1.330	1.734	2.101	2.552	2.878	3.922
19	1.328	1.729	2.093	2.539	2.861	3.883
20	1.325	1.725	2.086	2.528	2.845	3.850
21	1.323	1.721	2.080	2.518	2.831	3.819
22	1.321	1.717	2.074	2.508	2.819	3.792
23	1.319	1.714	2.069	2.500	2.807	3.768
24	1.318	1.711	2.064	2.492	2.797	3.745
25	1.316	1.708	2.060	2.485	2.787	3.725
26	1.315	1.706	2.056	2.479	2.779	3.707
27	1.314	1.703	2.052	2.473	2.771	3.690
28	1.313	1.701	2.048	2.467	2.763	3.674
29	1.311	1.699	2.045	2.462	2.756	3.659
30	1.310	1.697	2.042	2.457	2.750	3.646
31	1.309	1.696	2.040	2.453	2.744	3.633
32	1.309	1.694	2.037	2.449	2.738	3.622
33	1.308	1.692	2.035	2.445	2.733	3.611
34	1.307	1.691	2.032	2.441	2.728	3.601
35	1.306	1.690	2.030	2.438	2.724	3.591
36	1.306	1.688	2.028	2.434	2.719	3.582
37	1.305	1.687	2.026	2.431	2.715	3.574
38	1.304	1.686	2.024	2.429	2.712	3.566
39	1.304	1.685	2.023	2.426	2.708	3.558
40	1.303	1.684	2.021	2.423	2.704	3.551
41	1.303	1.683	2.020	2.421	2.701	3.544
42	1.302	1.682	2.018	2.418	2.698	3.538
43	1.302	1.681	2.017	2.416	2.695	3.532
44	1.301	1.680	2.015	2.414	2.692	3.526
45	1.301	1.679	2.014	2.412	2.690	3.520
46	1.300	1.679	2.013	2.410	2.687	3.515
47	1.300	1.678	2.012	2.408	2.685	3.510
48	1.299	1.677	2.011	2.407	2.682	3.505
49	1.299	1.677	2.010	2.405	2.680	3.500
50	1.299	1.676	2.009	2.403	2.678	3.496
51	1.298	1.675	2.008	2.402	2.676	3.492
52	1.298	1.675	2.007	2.400	2.674	3.488
53	1.298	1.674	2.006	2.399	2.672	3.484
54	1.297	1.674	2.005	2.397	2.670	3.480
55	1.297	1.673	2.004	2.396	2.668	3.476
56	1.297	1.673	2.003	2.395	2.667	3.473
57	1.297	1.672	2.002	2.394	2.665	3.470
58	1.296	1.672	2.002	2.392	2.663	3.466
59	1.296	1.671	2.001	2.391	2.662	3.463
60	1.296	1.671	2.000	2.390	2.660	3.460
61	1.296	1.670	2.000	2.389	2.659	3.457
62	1.295	1.670	1.999	2.388	2.657	3.454
63	1.295	1.669	1.998	2.387	2.656	3.452
64	1.295	1.669	1.998	2.386	2.655	3.449
65	1.295	1.669	1.997	2.385	2.654	3.447
66	1.295	1.668	1.997	2.384	2.652	3.444
67	1.294	1.668	1.996	2.383	2.651	3.442
68	1.294	1.668	1.995	2.382	2.650	3.439
69	1.294	1.667	1.995	2.382	2.649	3.437
70	1.294	1.667	1.994	2.381	2.648	3.435

(continued)

B.5 Student's *t* Distribution (*concluded*)

	Confidence Intervals, *c*					
	80%	90%	95%	98%	99%	99.9%
	Level of Significance for One-Tailed Test, α					
df	0.10	0.05	0.025	0.01	0.005	0.0005
	Level of Significance for Two-Tailed Test, α					
	0.20	0.10	0.05	0.02	0.01	0.001
71	1.294	1.667	1.994	2.380	2.647	3.433
72	1.293	1.666	1.993	2.379	2.646	3.431
73	1.293	1.666	1.993	2.379	2.645	3.429
74	1.293	1.666	1.993	2.378	2.644	3.427
75	1.293	1.665	1.992	2.377	2.643	3.425
76	1.293	1.665	1.992	2.376	2.642	3.423
77	1.293	1.665	1.991	2.376	2.641	3.421
78	1.292	1.665	1.991	2.375	2.640	3.420
79	1.292	1.664	1.990	2.374	2.640	3.418
80	1.292	1.664	1.990	2.374	2.639	3.416
81	1.292	1.664	1.990	2.373	2.638	3.415
82	1.292	1.664	1.989	2.373	2.637	3.413
83	1.292	1.663	1.989	2.372	2.636	3.412
84	1.292	1.663	1.989	2.372	2.636	3.410
85	1.292	1.663	1.988	2.371	2.635	3.409
86	1.291	1.663	1.988	2.370	2.634	3.407
87	1.291	1.663	1.988	2.370	2.634	3.406
88	1.291	1.662	1.987	2.369	2.633	3.405

	Confidence Intervals, *c*					
	80%	90%	95%	98%	99%	99.9%
	Level of Significance for One-Tailed Test, α					
df	0.10	0.05	0.025	0.01	0.005	0.0005
	Level of Significance for Two-Tailed Test, α					
	0.20	0.10	0.05	0.02	0.01	0.001
89	1.291	1.662	1.987	2.369	2.632	3.403
90	1.291	1.662	1.987	2.368	2.632	3.402
91	1.291	1.662	1.986	2.368	2.631	3.401
92	1.291	1.662	1.986	2.368	2.630	3.399
93	1.291	1.661	1.986	2.367	2.630	3.398
94	1.291	1.661	1.986	2.367	2.629	3.397
95	1.291	1.661	1.985	2.366	2.629	3.396
96	1.290	1.661	1.985	2.366	2.628	3.395
97	1.290	1.661	1.985	2.365	2.627	3.394
98	1.290	1.661	1.984	2.365	2.627	3.393
99	1.290	1.660	1.984	2.365	2.626	3.392
100	1.290	1.660	1.984	2.364	2.626	3.390
120	1.289	1.658	1.980	2.358	2.617	3.373
140	1.288	1.656	1.977	2.353	2.611	3.361
160	1.287	1.654	1.975	2.350	2.607	3.352
180	1.286	1.653	1.973	2.347	2.603	3.345
200	1.286	1.653	1.972	2.345	2.601	3.340
∞	1.282	1.645	1.960	2.326	2.576	3.291

B.6A Critical Values of the F Distribution ($\alpha = .05$)

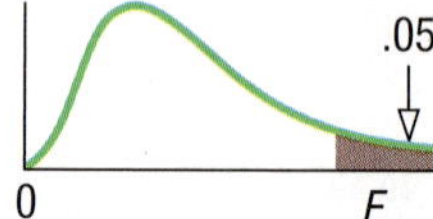

Degrees of Freedom for the Denominator	Degrees of Freedom for the Numerator															
	1	**2**	**3**	**4**	**5**	**6**	**7**	**8**	**9**	**10**	**12**	**15**	**20**	**24**	**30**	**40**
1	161	200	216	225	230	234	237	239	241	242	244	246	248	249	250	251
2	18.5	19.0	19.2	19.2	19.3	19.3	19.4	19.4	19.4	19.4	19.4	19.4	19.4	19.5	19.5	19.5
3	10.1	9.55	9.28	9.12	9.01	8.94	8.89	8.85	8.81	8.79	8.74	8.70	8.66	8.64	8.62	8.59
4	7.71	6.94	6.59	6.39	6.26	6.16	6.09	6.04	6.00	5.96	5.91	5.86	5.80	5.77	5.75	5.72
5	6.61	5.79	5.41	5.19	5.05	4.95	4.88	4.82	4.77	4.74	4.68	4.62	4.56	4.53	4.50	4.46
6	5.99	5.14	4.76	4.53	4.39	4.28	4.21	4.15	4.10	4.06	4.00	3.94	3.87	3.84	3.81	3.77
7	5.59	4.74	4.35	4.12	3.97	3.87	3.79	3.73	3.68	3.64	3.57	3.51	3.44	3.41	3.38	3.34
8	5.32	4.46	4.07	3.84	3.69	3.58	3.50	3.44	3.39	3.35	3.28	3.22	3.15	3.12	3.08	3.04
9	5.12	4.26	3.86	3.63	3.48	3.37	3.29	3.23	3.18	3.14	3.07	3.01	2.94	2.90	2.86	2.83
10	4.96	4.10	3.71	3.48	3.33	3.22	3.14	3.07	3.02	2.98	2.91	2.85	2.77	2.74	2.70	2.66
11	4.84	3.98	3.59	3.36	3.20	3.09	3.01	2.95	2.90	2.85	2.79	2.72	2.65	2.61	2.57	2.53
12	4.75	3.89	3.49	3.26	3.11	3.00	2.91	2.85	2.80	2.75	2.69	2.62	2.54	2.51	2.47	2.43
13	4.67	3.81	3.41	3.18	3.03	2.92	2.83	2.77	2.71	2.67	2.60	2.53	2.46	2.42	2.38	2.34
14	4.60	3.74	3.34	3.11	2.96	2.85	2.76	2.70	2.65	2.60	2.53	2.46	2.39	2.35	2.31	2.27
15	4.54	3.68	3.29	3.06	2.90	2.79	2.71	2.64	2.59	2.54	2.48	2.40	2.33	2.29	2.25	2.20
16	4.49	3.63	3.24	3.01	2.85	2.74	2.66	2.59	2.54	2.49	2.42	2.35	2.28	2.24	2.19	2.15
17	4.45	3.59	3.20	2.96	2.81	2.70	2.61	2.55	2.49	2.45	2.38	2.31	2.23	2.19	2.15	2.10
18	4.41	3.55	3.16	2.93	2.77	2.66	2.58	2.51	2.46	2.41	2.34	2.27	2.19	2.15	2.11	2.06
19	4.38	3.52	3.13	2.90	2.74	2.63	2.54	2.48	2.42	2.38	2.31	2.23	2.16	2.11	2.07	2.03
20	4.35	3.49	3.10	2.87	2.71	2.60	2.51	2.45	2.39	2.35	2.28	2.20	2.12	2.08	2.04	1.99
21	4.32	3.47	3.07	2.84	2.68	2.57	2.49	2.42	2.37	2.32	2.25	2.18	2.10	2.05	2.01	1.96
22	4.30	3.44	3.05	2.82	2.66	2.55	2.46	2.40	2.34	2.30	2.23	2.15	2.07	2.03	1.98	1.94
23	4.28	3.42	3.03	2.80	2.64	2.53	2.44	2.37	2.32	2.27	2.20	2.13	2.05	2.01	1.96	1.91
24	4.26	3.40	3.01	2.78	2.62	2.51	2.42	2.36	2.30	2.25	2.18	2.11	2.03	1.98	1.94	1.89
25	4.24	3.39	2.99	2.76	2.60	2.49	2.40	2.34	2.28	2.24	2.16	2.09	2.01	1.96	1.92	1.87
30	4.17	3.32	2.92	2.69	2.53	2.42	2.33	2.27	2.21	2.16	2.09	2.01	1.93	1.89	1.84	1.79
40	4.08	3.23	2.84	2.61	2.45	2.34	2.25	2.18	2.12	2.08	2.00	1.92	1.84	1.79	1.74	1.69
60	4.00	3.15	2.76	2.53	2.37	2.25	2.17	2.10	2.04	1.99	1.92	1.84	1.75	1.70	1.65	1.59
120	3.92	3.07	2.68	2.45	2.29	2.18	2.09	2.02	1.96	1.91	1.83	1.75	1.66	1.61	1.55	1.50
∞	3.84	3.00	2.60	2.37	2.21	2.10	2.01	1.94	1.88	1.83	1.75	1.67	1.57	1.52	1.46	1.39

B.6B Critical Values of the *F* Distribution ($\alpha = .01$)

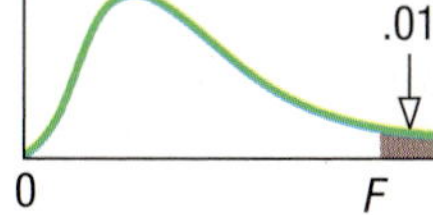

Degrees of Freedom for the Denominator	Degrees of Freedom for the Numerator: 1	2	3	4	5	6	7	8	9	10	12	15	20	24	30	40
1	4052	5000	5403	5625	5764	5859	5928	5981	6022	6056	6106	6157	6209	6235	6261	6287
2	98.5	99.0	99.2	99.2	99.3	99.3	99.4	99.4	99.4	99.4	99.4	99.4	99.4	99.5	99.5	99.5
3	34.1	30.8	29.5	28.7	28.2	27.9	27.7	27.5	27.3	27.2	27.1	26.9	26.7	26.6	26.5	26.4
4	21.2	18.0	16.7	16.0	15.5	15.2	15.0	14.8	14.7	14.5	14.4	14.2	14.0	13.9	13.8	13.7
5	16.3	13.3	12.1	11.4	11.0	10.7	10.5	10.3	10.2	10.1	9.89	9.72	9.55	9.47	9.38	9.29
6	13.7	10.9	9.78	9.15	8.75	8.47	8.26	8.10	7.98	7.87	7.72	7.56	7.40	7.31	7.23	7.14
7	12.2	9.55	8.45	7.85	7.46	7.19	6.99	6.84	6.72	6.62	6.47	6.31	6.16	6.07	5.99	5.91
8	11.3	8.65	7.59	7.01	6.63	6.37	6.18	6.03	5.91	5.81	5.67	5.52	5.36	5.28	5.20	5.12
9	10.6	8.02	6.99	6.42	6.06	5.80	5.61	5.47	5.35	5.26	5.11	4.96	4.81	4.73	4.65	4.57
10	10.0	7.56	6.55	5.99	5.64	5.39	5.20	5.06	4.94	4.85	4.71	4.56	4.41	4.33	4.25	4.17
11	9.65	7.21	6.22	5.67	5.32	5.07	4.89	4.74	4.63	4.54	4.40	4.25	4.10	4.02	3.94	3.86
12	9.33	6.93	5.95	5.41	5.06	4.82	4.64	4.50	4.39	4.30	4.16	4.01	3.86	3.78	3.70	3.62
13	9.07	6.70	5.74	5.21	4.86	4.62	4.44	4.30	4.19	4.10	3.96	3.82	3.66	3.59	3.51	3.43
14	8.86	6.51	5.56	5.04	4.69	4.46	4.28	4.14	4.03	3.94	3.80	3.66	3.51	3.43	3.35	3.27
15	8.68	6.36	5.42	4.89	4.56	4.32	4.14	4.00	3.89	3.80	3.67	3.52	3.37	3.29	3.21	3.13
16	8.53	6.23	5.29	4.77	4.44	4.20	4.03	3.89	3.78	3.69	3.55	3.41	3.26	3.18	3.10	3.02
17	8.40	6.11	5.18	4.67	4.34	4.10	3.93	3.79	3.68	3.59	3.46	3.31	3.16	3.08	3.00	2.92
18	8.29	6.01	5.09	4.58	4.25	4.01	3.84	3.71	3.60	3.51	3.37	3.23	3.08	3.00	2.92	2.84
19	8.18	5.93	5.01	4.50	4.17	3.94	3.77	3.63	3.52	3.43	3.30	3.15	3.00	2.92	2.84	2.76
20	8.10	5.85	4.94	4.43	4.10	3.87	3.70	3.56	3.46	3.37	3.23	3.09	2.94	2.86	2.78	2.69
21	8.02	5.78	4.87	4.37	4.04	3.81	3.64	3.51	3.40	3.31	3.17	3.03	2.88	2.80	2.72	2.64
22	7.95	5.72	4.82	4.31	3.99	3.76	3.59	3.45	3.35	3.26	3.12	2.98	2.83	2.75	2.67	2.58
23	7.88	5.66	4.76	4.26	3.94	3.71	3.54	3.41	3.30	3.21	3.07	2.93	2.78	2.70	2.62	2.54
24	7.82	5.61	4.72	4.22	3.90	3.67	3.50	3.36	3.26	3.17	3.03	2.89	2.74	2.66	2.58	2.49
25	7.77	5.57	4.68	4.18	3.85	3.63	3.46	3.32	3.22	3.13	2.99	2.85	2.70	2.62	2.54	2.45
30	7.56	5.39	4.51	4.02	3.70	3.47	3.30	3.17	3.07	2.98	2.84	2.70	2.55	2.47	2.39	2.30
40	7.31	5.18	4.31	3.83	3.51	3.29	3.12	2.99	2.89	2.80	2.66	2.52	2.37	2.29	2.20	2.11
60	7.08	4.98	4.13	3.65	3.34	3.12	2.95	2.82	2.72	2.63	2.50	2.35	2.20	2.12	2.03	1.94
120	6.85	4.79	3.95	3.48	3.17	2.96	2.79	2.66	2.56	2.47	2.34	2.19	2.03	1.95	1.86	1.76
∞	6.63	4.61	3.78	3.32	3.02	2.80	2.64	2.51	2.41	2.32	2.18	2.04	1.88	1.79	1.70	1.59

B.7 Critical Values of Chi-Square

This table contains the values of χ^2 that correspond to a specific right-tail area and specific number of degrees of freedom.

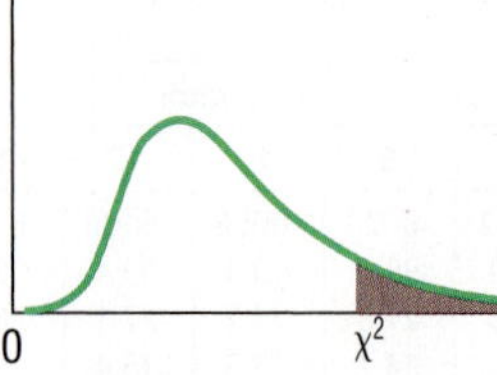

Example: With 17 *df* and a .02 area in the upper tail, $\chi^2 = 30.995$

Degrees of Freedom, *df*	Right-Tail Area			
	0.10	**0.05**	**0.02**	**0.01**
1	2.706	3.841	5.412	6.635
2	4.605	5.991	7.824	9.210
3	6.251	7.815	9.837	11.345
4	7.779	9.488	11.668	13.277
5	9.236	11.070	13.388	15.086
6	10.645	12.592	15.033	16.812
7	12.017	14.067	16.622	18.475
8	13.362	15.507	18.168	20.090
9	14.684	16.919	19.679	21.666
10	15.987	18.307	21.161	23.209
11	17.275	19.675	22.618	24.725
12	18.549	21.026	24.054	26.217
13	19.812	22.362	25.472	27.688
14	21.064	23.685	26.873	29.141
15	22.307	24.996	28.259	30.578
16	23.542	26.296	29.633	32.000
17	24.769	27.587	30.995	33.409
18	25.989	28.869	32.346	34.805
19	27.204	30.144	33.687	36.191
20	28.412	31.410	35.020	37.566
21	29.615	32.671	36.343	38.932
22	30.813	33.924	37.659	40.289
23	32.007	35.172	38.968	41.638
24	33.196	36.415	40.270	42.980
25	34.382	37.652	41.566	44.314
26	35.563	38.885	42.856	45.642
27	36.741	40.113	44.140	46.963
28	37.916	41.337	45.419	48.278
29	39.087	42.557	46.693	49.588
30	40.256	43.773	47.962	50.892

B.8 Wilcoxon *T* Values

	2α						
	.15	.10	.05	.04	.03	.02	.01
	α						
n	.075	.050	.025	.020	.015	.010	.005
4	0						
5	1	0					
6	2	2	0	0			
7	4	3	2	1	0	0	
8	7	5	3	3	2	1	0
9	9	8	5	5	4	3	1
10	12	10	8	7	6	5	3
11	16	13	10	9	8	7	5
12	19	17	13	12	11	9	7
13	24	21	17	16	14	12	9
14	28	25	21	19	18	15	12
15	33	30	25	23	21	19	15
16	39	35	29	28	26	23	19
17	45	41	34	33	30	27	23
18	51	47	40	38	35	32	27
19	58	53	46	43	41	37	32
20	65	60	52	50	47	43	37
21	73	67	58	56	53	49	42
22	81	75	65	63	59	55	48
23	89	83	73	70	66	62	54
24	98	91	81	78	74	69	61
25	108	100	89	86	82	76	68
26	118	110	98	94	90	84	75
27	128	119	107	103	99	92	83
28	138	130	116	112	108	101	91
29	150	140	126	122	117	110	100
30	161	151	137	132	127	120	109
31	173	163	147	143	137	130	118
32	186	175	159	154	148	140	128
33	199	187	170	165	159	151	138
34	212	200	182	177	171	162	148
35	226	213	195	189	182	173	159
40	302	286	264	257	249	238	220
50	487	466	434	425	413	397	373
60	718	690	648	636	620	600	567
70	995	960	907	891	872	846	805
80	1,318	1,276	1,211	1,192	1,168	1,136	1,086
90	1,688	1,638	1,560	1,537	1,509	1,471	1,410
100	2,105	2,045	1,955	1,928	1,894	1,850	1,779

B.9A Critical Values for the Durbin–Watson d Statistic ($\alpha = .05$)

n	$k = 1$		$k = 2$		$k = 3$		$k = 4$		$k = 5$	
	$d_{L,.05}$	$d_{U,.05}$	$d_{L,.05}$	$d_{U,.05}$	$d_{L,.05}$	$d_{U,.05}$	$d_{L,.05}$	$d_{U,.05}$	$d_{L,.05}$	$d_{U,.05}$
15	1.08	1.36	0.95	1.54	0.82	1.75	0.69	1.97	0.56	2.21
16	1.10	1.37	0.98	1.54	0.86	1.73	0.74	1.93	0.62	2.15
17	1.13	1.38	1.02	1.54	0.90	1.71	0.78	1.90	0.67	2.10
18	1.16	1.39	1.05	1.53	0.93	1.69	0.82	1.87	0.71	2.06
19	1.18	1.40	1.08	1.53	0.97	1.68	0.86	1.85	0.75	2.02
20	1.20	1.41	1.10	1.54	1.00	1.68	0.90	1.83	0.79	1.99
21	1.22	1.42	1.13	1.54	1.03	1.67	0.93	1.81	0.83	1.96
22	1.24	1.43	1.15	1.54	1.05	1.66	0.96	1.80	0.86	1.94
23	1.26	1.44	1.17	1.54	1.08	1.66	0.99	1.79	0.90	1.92
24	1.27	1.45	1.19	1.55	1.10	1.66	1.01	1.78	0.93	1.90
25	1.29	1.45	1.21	1.55	1.12	1.66	1.04	1.77	0.95	1.89
26	1.30	1.46	1.22	1.55	1.14	1.65	1.06	1.76	0.98	1.88
27	1.32	1.47	1.24	1.56	1.16	1.65	1.08	1.76	1.01	1.86
28	1.33	1.48	1.26	1.56	1.18	1.65	1.10	1.75	1.03	1.85
29	1.34	1.48	1.27	1.56	1.20	1.65	1.12	1.74	1.05	1.84
30	1.35	1.49	1.28	1.57	1.21	1.65	1.14	1.74	1.07	1.83
31	1.36	1.50	1.30	1.57	1.23	1.65	1.16	1.74	1.09	1.83
32	1.37	1.50	1.31	1.57	1.24	1.65	1.18	1.73	1.11	1.82
33	1.38	1.51	1.32	1.58	1.26	1.65	1.19	1.73	1.13	1.81
34	1.39	1.51	1.33	1.58	1.27	1.65	1.21	1.73	1.15	1.81
35	1.40	1.52	1.34	1.58	1.28	1.65	1.22	1.73	1.16	1.80
36	1.41	1.52	1.35	1.59	1.29	1.65	1.24	1.73	1.18	1.80
37	1.42	1.53	1.36	1.59	1.31	1.66	1.25	1.72	1.19	1.80
38	1.43	1.54	1.37	1.59	1.32	1.66	1.26	1.72	1.21	1.79
39	1.43	1.54	1.38	1.60	1.33	1.66	1.27	1.72	1.22	1.79
40	1.44	1.54	1.39	1.60	1.34	1.66	1.29	1.72	1.23	1.79
45	1.48	1.57	1.43	1.62	1.38	1.67	1.34	1.72	1.29	1.78
50	1.50	1.59	1.46	1.63	1.42	1.67	1.38	1.72	1.34	1.77
55	1.53	1.60	1.49	1.64	1.45	1.68	1.41	1.72	1.38	1.77
60	1.55	1.62	1.51	1.65	1.48	1.69	1.44	1.73	1.41	1.77
65	1.57	1.63	1.54	1.66	1.50	1.70	1.47	1.73	1.44	1.77
70	1.58	1.64	1.55	1.67	1.52	1.70	1.49	1.74	1.46	1.77
75	1.60	1.65	1.57	1.68	1.54	1.71	1.51	1.74	1.49	1.77
80	1.61	1.66	1.59	1.69	1.56	1.72	1.53	1.74	1.51	1.77
85	1.62	1.67	1.60	1.70	1.57	1.72	1.55	1.75	1.52	1.77
90	1.63	1.68	1.61	1.70	1.59	1.73	1.57	1.75	1.54	1.78
95	1.64	1.69	1.62	1.71	1.60	1.73	1.58	1.75	1.56	1.78
100	1.65	1.69	1.63	1.72	1.61	1.74	1.59	1.76	1.57	1.78

SOURCE: J. Durbin and G. S. Watson, "Testing for Serial Correlation in Least Squares Regression, II," *Biometrika* 30 (1951), pp. 159–178. Reproduced by permission of the Biometrika Trustees.

B.9B Critical Values for the Durbin–Watson *d* Statistic ($\alpha = .025$)

	$k = 1$		$k = 2$		$k = 3$		$k = 4$		$k = 5$	
n	$d_{L,.025}$	$d_{U,.025}$	$d_{L,.025}$	$d_{U,.025}$	$d_{L,.025}$	$d_{U,.025}$	$d_{L,.025}$	$d_{U,.025}$	$d_{L,.025}$	$d_{U,.025}$
15	0.95	1.23	0.83	1.40	0.71	1.61	0.59	1.84	0.48	2.09
16	0.98	1.24	0.86	1.40	0.75	1.59	0.64	1.80	0.53	2.03
17	1.01	1.25	0.90	1.40	0.79	1.58	0.68	1.77	0.57	1.98
18	1.03	1.26	0.93	1.40	0.82	1.56	0.72	1.74	0.62	1.93
19	1.06	1.28	0.96	1.41	0.86	1.55	0.76	1.72	0.66	1.90
20	1.08	1.28	0.99	1.41	0.89	1.55	0.79	1.70	0.70	1.87
21	1.10	1.30	1.01	1.41	0.92	1.54	0.83	1.69	0.73	1.84
22	1.12	1.31	1.04	1.42	0.95	1.54	0.86	1.68	0.77	1.82
23	1.14	1.32	1.06	1.42	0.97	1.54	0.89	1.67	0.80	1.80
24	1.16	1.33	1.08	1.43	1.00	1.54	0.91	1.66	0.83	1.79
25	1.18	1.34	1.10	1.43	1.02	1.54	0.94	1.65	0.86	1.77
26	1.19	1.35	1.12	1.44	1.04	1.54	0.96	1.65	0.88	1.76
27	1.21	1.36	1.13	1.44	1.06	1.54	0.99	1.64	0.91	1.75
28	1.22	1.37	1.15	1.45	1.08	1.54	1.01	1.64	0.93	1.74
29	1.24	1.38	1.17	1.45	1.10	1.54	1.03	1.63	0.96	1.73
30	1.25	1.38	1.18	1.46	1.12	1.54	1.05	1.63	0.98	1.73
31	1.26	1.39	1.20	1.47	1.13	1.55	1.07	1.63	1.00	1.72
32	1.27	1.40	1.21	1.47	1.15	1.55	1.08	1.63	1.02	1.71
33	1.28	1.41	1.22	1.48	1.16	1.55	1.10	1.63	1.04	1.71
34	1.29	1.41	1.24	1.48	1.17	1.55	1.12	1.63	1.06	1.70
35	1.30	1.42	1.25	1.48	1.19	1.55	1.13	1.63	1.07	1.70
36	1.31	1.43	1.26	1.49	1.20	1.56	1.15	1.63	1.09	1.70
37	1.32	1.43	1.27	1.49	1.21	1.56	1.16	1.62	1.10	1.70
38	1.33	1.44	1.28	1.50	1.23	1.56	1.17	1.62	1.12	1.70
39	1.34	1.44	1.29	1.50	1.24	1.56	1.19	1.63	1.13	1.69
40	1.35	1.45	1.30	1.51	1.25	1.57	1.20	1.63	1.15	1.69
45	1.39	1.48	1.34	1.53	1.30	1.58	1.25	1.63	1.21	1.69
50	1.42	1.50	1.38	1.54	1.34	1.59	1.30	1.64	1.26	1.69
55	1.45	1.52	1.41	1.56	1.37	1.60	1.33	1.64	1.30	1.69
60	1.47	1.54	1.44	1.57	1.40	1.61	1.37	1.65	1.33	1.69
65	1.49	1.55	1.46	1.59	1.43	1.62	1.40	1.66	1.36	1.69
70	1.51	1.57	1.48	1.60	1.45	1.63	1.42	1.66	1.39	1.70
75	1.53	1.58	1.50	1.61	1.47	1.64	1.45	1.67	1.42	1.70
80	1.54	1.59	1.52	1.62	1.49	1.65	1.47	1.67	1.44	1.70
85	1.56	1.60	1.53	1.63	1.51	1.65	1.49	1.68	1.46	1.71
90	1.57	1.61	1.55	1.64	1.53	1.66	1.50	1.69	1.48	1.71
95	1.58	1.62	1.56	1.65	1.54	1.67	1.52	1.69	1.50	1.71
100	1.59	1.63	1.57	1.65	1.55	1.67	1.53	1.70	1.51	1.72

SOURCE: J. Durbin and G. S. Watson, "Testing for Serial Correlation in Least Squares Regression, II," *Biometrika* 30 (1951), pp. 159–178. Reproduced by permission of the Biometrika Trustees.

B.9C Critical Values for the Durbin–Watson *d* Statistic ($\alpha = .01$)

	$k = 1$		$k = 2$		$k = 3$		$k = 4$		$k = 5$	
n	$d_{L,.01}$	$d_{U,.01}$	$d_{L,.01}$	$d_{U,.01}$	$d_{L,.01}$	$d_{U,.01}$	$d_{L,.01}$	$d_{U,.01}$	$d_{L,.01}$	$d_{U,.01}$
15	0.81	1.07	0.70	1.25	0.59	1.46	0.49	1.70	0.39	1.96
16	0.84	1.09	0.74	1.25	0.63	1.44	0.53	1.66	0.44	1.90
17	0.87	1.10	0.77	1.25	0.67	1.43	0.57	1.63	0.48	1.85
18	0.90	1.12	0.80	1.26	0.71	1.42	0.61	1.60	0.52	1.80
19	0.93	1.13	0.83	1.26	0.74	1.41	0.65	1.58	0.56	1.77
20	0.95	1.15	0.86	1.27	0.77	1.41	0.68	1.57	0.60	1.74
21	0.97	1.16	0.89	1.27	0.80	1.41	0.72	1.55	0.63	1.71
22	1.00	1.17	0.91	1.28	0.83	1.40	0.75	1.54	0.66	1.69
23	1.02	1.19	0.94	1.29	0.86	1.40	0.77	1.53	0.70	1.67
24	1.04	1.20	0.96	1.30	0.88	1.41	0.80	1.53	0.72	1.66
25	1.05	1.21	0.98	1.30	0.90	1.41	0.83	1.52	0.75	1.65
26	1.07	1.22	1.00	1.31	0.93	1.41	0.85	1.52	0.78	1.64
27	1.09	1.23	1.02	1.32	0.95	1.41	0.88	1.51	0.81	1.63
28	1.10	1.24	1.04	1.32	0.97	1.41	0.90	1.51	0.83	1.62
29	1.12	1.25	1.05	1.33	0.99	1.42	0.92	1.51	0.85	1.61
30	1.13	1.26	1.07	1.34	1.01	1.42	0.94	1.51	0.88	1.61
31	1.15	1.27	1.08	1.34	1.02	1.42	0.96	1.51	0.90	1.60
32	1.16	1.28	1.10	1.35	1.04	1.43	0.98	1.51	0.92	1.60
33	1.17	1.29	1.11	1.36	1.05	1.43	1.00	1.51	0.94	1.59
34	1.18	1.30	1.13	1.36	1.07	1.43	1.01	1.51	0.95	1.59
35	1.19	1.31	1.14	1.37	1.08	1.44	1.03	1.51	0.97	1.59
36	1.21	1.32	1.15	1.38	1.10	1.44	1.04	1.51	0.99	1.59
37	1.22	1.32	1.16	1.38	1.11	1.45	1.06	1.51	1.00	1.59
38	1.23	1.33	1.18	1.39	1.12	1.45	1.07	1.52	1.02	1.58
39	1.24	1.34	1.19	1.39	1.14	1.45	1.09	1.52	1.03	1.58
40	1.25	1.34	1.20	1.40	1.15	1.46	1.10	1.52	1.05	1.58
45	1.29	1.38	1.24	1.42	1.20	1.48	1.16	1.53	1.11	1.58
50	1.32	1.40	1.28	1.45	1.24	1.49	1.20	1.54	1.16	1.59
55	1.36	1.43	1.32	1.47	1.28	1.51	1.25	1.55	1.21	1.59
60	1.38	1.45	1.35	1.48	1.32	1.52	1.28	1.56	1.25	1.60
65	1.41	1.47	1.38	1.50	1.35	1.53	1.31	1.57	1.28	1.61
70	1.43	1.49	1.40	1.52	1.37	1.55	1.34	1.58	1.31	1.61
75	1.45	1.50	1.42	1.53	1.39	1.56	1.37	1.59	1.34	1.62
80	1.47	1.52	1.44	1.54	1.42	1.57	1.39	1.60	1.36	1.62
85	1,48	1.53	1.46	1.55	1.43	1.58	1.41	1.60	1.39	1.63
90	1.50	1.54	1.47	1.56	1.45	1.59	1.43	1.61	1.41	1.64
95	1.51	1.55	1.49	1.57	1.47	1.60	1.45	1.62	1.42	1.64
100	1.52	1.56	1.50	1.58	1.48	1.60	1.46	1.63	1.44	1.65

SOURCE: J. Durbin and G. S. Watson, "Testing for Serial Correlation in Least Squares Regression, II," *Biometrika* 30 (1951), pp. 159–178. Reproduced by permission of the Biometrika Trustees.

B.10 Factors for Control Charts

Number of Items in Sample,	Chart for Averages	Chart for Ranges		
	Factors for Control Limits	Factors for Central Line	Factors for Control Limits	
n	A_2	d_2	D_3	D_4
2	1.880	1.128	0	3.267
3	1.023	1.693	0	2.575
4	.729	2.059	0	2.282
5	.577	2.326	0	2.115
6	.483	2.534	0	2.004
7	.419	2.704	.076	1.924
8	.373	2.847	.136	1.864
9	.337	2.970	.184	1.816
10	.308	3.078	.223	1.777
11	.285	3.173	.256	1.744
12	.266	3.258	.284	1.716
13	.249	3.336	.308	1.692
14	.235	3.407	.329	1.671
15	.223	3.472	.348	1.652

SOURCE: Adapted from American Society for Testing and Materials, *Manual on Quality Control of Materials,* 1951, Table B2, p. 115. For a more detailed table and explanation, see J. Duncan Acheson, *Quality Control and Industrial Statistics,* 3d ed. (Homewood, Ill.: Richard D. Irwin, 1974), Table M, p. 927.

APPENDIX C: SOFTWARE COMMANDS

CHAPTER 2

2–1. The Excel commands to use the PivotTable Wizard to create the frequency table, bar chart, and pie chart on page 22 are:

a. Open the Applewood Auto Group data file.

b. Click on a cell somewhere in the data set, such as cell *C5*.

c. Click on the *Insert* menu on the toolbar. Then click *PivotTable* on the far left of the *Ribbon*.

d. The following screen will appear. Click on "*Select a table or range*" to select the data range as shown in the *Table/ Range* row. Next, click on "*Existing Worksheet*" and select a cell location, such a *N1,* and click *OK*.

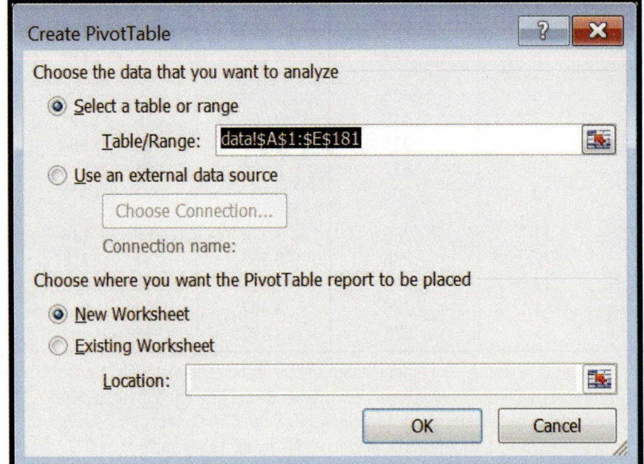

e. On the right-hand side of the spreadsheet, a *PivotTable Field List* will appear with a list of the data set variables. To summarize the "Vehicle-Type" variable, click on the "Vehicle-Type" variable and it will appear in the lower left box called *Row Label*. You will note that the frequency table is started in cell *N1* with the rows labeled with the values of the variable "Vehicle-Type." Next, return to the top box, and select and drag the "Vehicle-Type" variable to the "Σ Values" box. A column of frequencies will be added to the table. Note that you can format the table to center the values and also relabel the column headings as needed.

f. To create the bar chart, select any cell in the PivotTable. Next, select the *Insert* menu from the tool bar and within the *Charts* group, select a bar chart from the *Column* drop-down menu. A bar chart appears. Click on the chart heading and label the chart as needed.

g. To create the pie chart, the frequencies should be converted to relative frequencies. Click in the body of the PivotTable and the *PivotTable Field List* will appear to the right. In the "Σ Values" box, click on the pull-down menu for "Count of Vehicle Type" and select the *Value Field Settings* option. You will see a number of different selections that can be used to summarize the variables in a PivotTable. Click on the tab "*Show Values As*" and, in the pull-down menu, select "*% of Grand Total*." The frequencies will be converted to relative frequencies.

To create the pie chart, select any cell in the PivotTable. Next, select the *Insert* menu from the tool bar, and within the *Charts* group, select a pie chart from the *Column* drop-down menu. A pie chart appears. Click on the chart heading and label the chart as needed. To add the percentages, click on the pie chart and a menu will appear. Click on "Add Data Labels."

2–2. The Excel commands to use the PivotTable Wizard to create the frequency and relative frequency distributions on page 30 and the histogram on page 33 follow.

a. Open the Applewood Auto Group data file.

b. Click on a cell somewhere in the data set, such as cell *C5*.

c. Click on the *Insert* menu on the toolbar. Then click on *PivotTable* on the far left of the *Ribbon*.

d. The following screen will appear. Click on "*Select a table or range*" to select the data range as shown in the *Table/ Range* row. Next, click on "*New Worksheet*" and the PivotTable will be created in a new worksheet.

e. On the right-hand side of the spreadsheet, a *PivotTable Field List* will appear with a list of the data set variables. To summarize the "Profit" variable, click on the "Profit" variable and drag it to the "Row Labels" box. Then return to the top box, click on "Profits" again and drag it to the "Σ Values" box. Staying in this box, click on the pull-down menu for "Sum of Profit." You will see a number of different selections that can be used to summarize the variables in a PivotTable. In the "*Summarize Values As*" tab, select "Count" to create frequencies for the variable "Profit." A PivotTable will appear in the new worksheet.

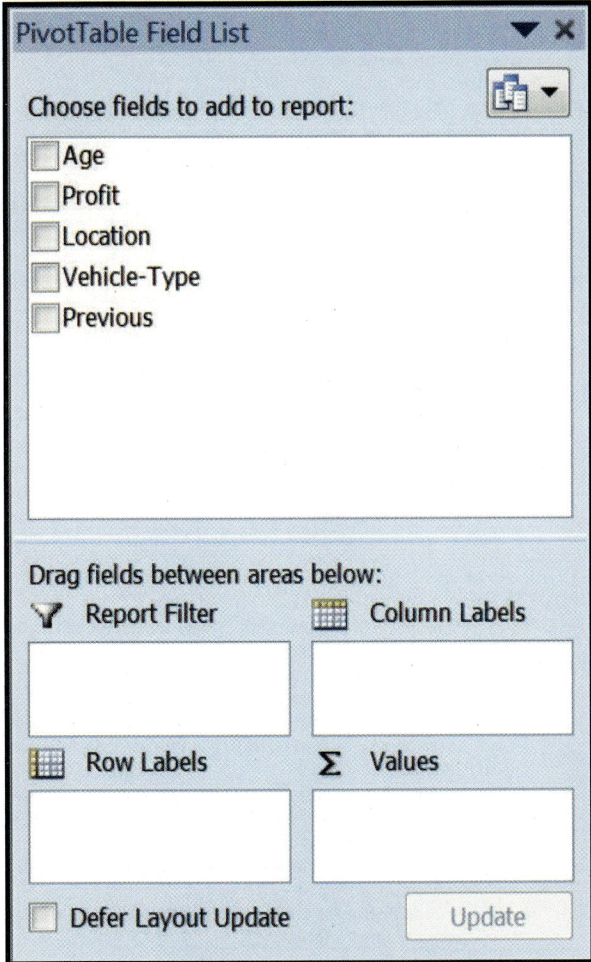

f. In the PivotTable, the left column shows each value of the variable "Profit." To create classes for "Profit," select any cell in the column and right-click. A menu appears. Select "Group" from the menu to create the classes. First, uncheck both boxes. Then, in the dialogue box, enter the lower limit of the first class as the "Starting at" value. Enter the upper limit of the last class as the "Ending at" value. Then enter the class interval as the "By" value. Click OK. A frequency distribution appears.

g. To create a relative frequency distribution, point and click on one of the cells in the PivotTable and the "PivotTable Field List" appears to the right. Click and drag the variable "Profits" to the "Σ Values" box. A second "Counts of Profit" appears. In the "Σ Values," click on the second "Counts of Profit" and select the "Value Fields Setting." You will see a number of different selections that can be used to summarize the variables in a PivotTable. Click on the tab "*Show Values As*" and, in the pull-down menu, select "*% of Grand Total.*" The relative frequencies will be added to the table. You can format the table by relabeling the column headings such as "Frequency" and "Relative Frequency."

h. To create a histogram, select a cell in the PivotTable, choose the *Insert* menu from the tool bar, and within the *Charts* group, select a *column* chart from the *Column* drop-down menu. A histogram appears with both "Count of Profit" and "Count of Profit2." On the "Count of Profit2" bubble at the top of the chart, right-click and select "Remove Field." Then the chart and PivotTable only report the frequencies. To eliminate the space between the bars, select the entire chart area, and "PivotChart Tools" will appear at the top. Select "Design." In the "Chart Layouts" choices, select the option that shows no spaces between the bars. The option is illustrated in the figure to the right. To add data labels, select the histogram, right-click, and select "Add Data Labels." Relabel the chart and axes as needed.

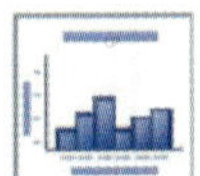

CHAPTER 3

3–1. The Excel Commands for the descriptive statistics on page 64 are:

a. From the website, **www.mhhe.com/Lind17e**, retrieve the Applewood data.

b. From the menu bar, select **Data** and then **Data Analysis.** Select **Descriptive Statistics** and then click **OK.**

c. For the **Input Range,** type *C1:C181,* indicate that the data are grouped by column and that the labels are in the first row. Click on **Output Range,** indicate that the output should go in *G1* (or any place you wish), click on **Summary statistics,** then click **OK.**

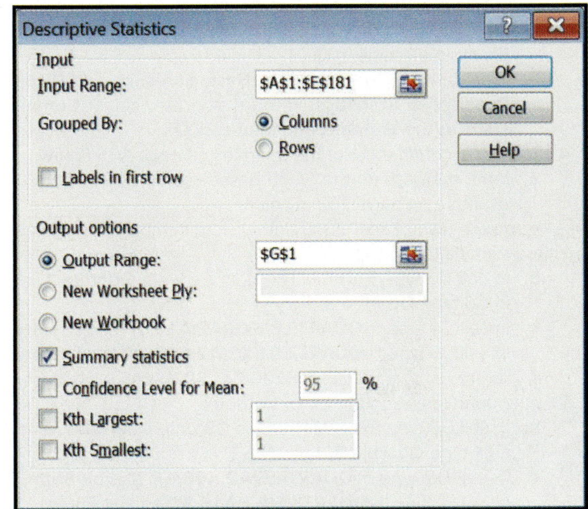

d. After you get your results, double-check the count in the output to be sure it contains the correct number of items.

CHAPTER 4

4–1. The Minitab commands for the dot plot on page 96 are:

a. Enter the number of vehicles serviced at Tionesta Ford Lincoln Mercury in column *C1* and Sheffield Motors in *C2.* Name the variables accordingly.

b. Select **Graph** and **Dotplot.** In the first dialog box, select **Multiple Y's, Simple** in the lower left corner, and click **OK.** In the next dialog box, select **Tionesta** and **Sheffield** as the variables to **Graph,** click on **Labels,** and write an appropriate title. Then click **OK.**

c. To calculate the descriptive statistics shown in the output, select **Stat, Basic statistics,** and then **Display Descriptive statistics.** In the dialog box, select **Tionesta** and **Sheffield** as the variables, click on **Statistics,** select the desired statistics to be output, and finally click **OK** twice.

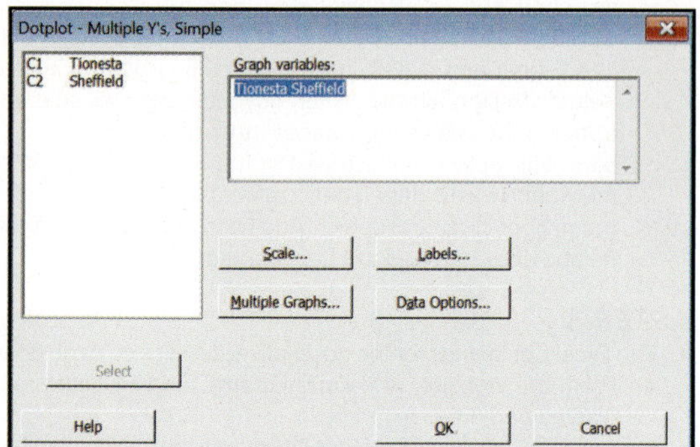

4–2. The Minitab commands for the stem-and-leaf display on page 99 are:
  a. Import the data for **Table 4–1** from **www.mhhe.com/lind17e**.
  b. Select **Graph,** and click on **Stem-and-Leaf.**
  c. Select the variable **Spots,** enter *10* for the **Increment,** and then click **OK.**

4–3. The Minitab commands for the descriptive summary on page 105 are:
  a. Input the data on the Smith Barney commissions from the Example on page 103.
  b. From the toolbar, select **Stat, Basic Statistics,** and **Display Descriptive Statistics.** In the dialog box, select **Commissions** as the **Variable,** and then click **OK.**

4–4. The Excel commands for the quartiles on page 105 follow.
  a. Input the data on the Smith Barney commissions from the example on page 103 in column A.
  If you are using Excel 2010 and wish to compute quartiles using formula (4–1), the steps are:
  b. In cell *C3* type **Formula (4–1),** in *C4* write **Quartile 1,** and in *C6* type **Quartile 3.**
  c. In cell *D4* type **"=QUARTILE.EXC(A2:A16,1)"** and hit **Enter.** In cell *D6* type **"=QUARTILE.EXC(A2:A16,3)"** and hit **Enter.**
  If you are using either Excel 2007 or 2010 and wish to compute quartiles using the Excel Method:
  b. In cell *C8* type **Excel Method,** in *C9* write **Quartile 1,** and in *C11* type **Quartile 3.**
  c. In cell *D8* type **"=QUARTILE(A2:A16,1)"** and hit **Enter.** In cell *D11* type **"=QUARTILE(A2:A16,3)"** and hit **Enter.**

4–5. The Minitab commands for the box plot on page 108 are:
  a. Import the Applewood Auto Group data from **www.mhhe.com/lind17e**.

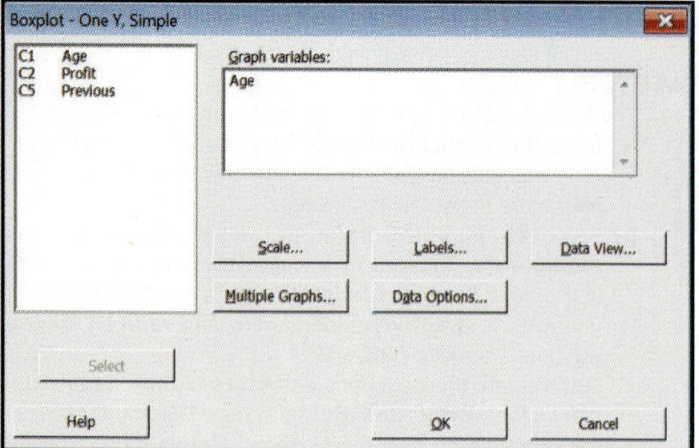

  b. Select **Graph** and then **Boxplot.** In the dialog box, select **Simple** in the upper left corner and click **OK.** Select **Age** as the **Graph Variable,** click on **Labels** and include an appropriate heading, and then click **OK.**

4–6. The Minitab commands for the descriptive summary on page 113 are:
  a. Enter the data in the first column. In the cell below *C1,* enter the variable *Earnings.*
  b. Select **Stat, Basic Statistics,** and then click on **Graphical Summary.** Select **Earnings** as the variable, and then click **OK.**

4–7. The Excel commands for the scatter diagram on page 116 are:
  a. Retrieve the Applewood Auto data.
  b. Using the mouse, highlight the column of age and profit. Include the first row.
  c. Select the **Insert** tab. Select **Scatter** from the **Chart** options. Select the top left option. The scatter plot will appear.
  d. With **Chart Tools** displayed at the top, select the **Layout** tab. Select **Chart Title** and type in a title for the plot. Next, under the same **Layout** tab, select **AxisTitles.** Using **Primary Vertical Axis Title,** name the vertical axis *Profit.* Using the **Primary Horizontal Axis Title,** name the horizontal axis *Age.* Next, select **Legend** and select **None.**

CHAPTER 5

5–1. The Excel Commands to determine the number of permutations shown on page 165 are:
  a. Click on the **Formulas** tab in the top menu, then, on the far left, select **Insert Function** ***fx.***
  b. In the **Insert Function** box, select **Statistical** as the category, then scroll down to **PERMUT** in the **Select a function list.** Click **OK.**
  c. In the **PERM** box after **Number,** enter *8* and in the **Number_chosen** box enter *3.* The correct answer of *336* appears twice in the box.

5–2. The Excel Commands to determine the number of combinations shown on page 165 are:
  a. Click on the **Formulas** tab in the top menu, then, on the far left, select **Insert Function** ***fx.***
  b. In the **Insert Function** box, select **Math & Trig** as the category, then scroll down to **COMBIN** in the **Select a function list.** Click **OK.**
  c. In the **COMBIN** box after **Number,** enter *7,* and in the **Number_chosen** box enter *3.* The correct answer of *35* appears twice in the box.

CHAPTER 6

6–1. The Excel commands necessary to determine the binomial probability distribution on page 189 are:
  a. On a blank Excel worksheet, write the word *Success* in cell A1 and the word *Probability* in B1. In cells A2 through A17, write the integers *0* to *15.* Click on *B2* as the active cell.
  b. Click on the **Formulas** tab in the top menu, then, on the far left, select **Insert Function** ***fx.***
  c. In the first dialog box, select **Statistical** in the function category and **BINOM.DIST** in the function name category, then click **OK.**
  d. In the second dialog box, enter the four items necessary to compute a binomial probability.
    1. Enter *0* for the **Number_s.**
    2. Enter *40* for the **Trials.**
    3. Enter *.09* for the probability of a success.
    4. Enter the word *false* or the *0* for **Cumulative** and click on **OK.**
    5. Excel will compute the probability of 0 successes in 40 trials, with a .09 probability of success. The result, .02299618, is stored in cell B2.

e. To complete the probability distribution for successes of 1 through 15, double-click on cell **B2.** The binomial function should appear. Replace the **0** to the right of the open parentheses with the cell reference **A2.**

f. Move the mouse to the lower right corner of cell B2 until a solid black + symbol appears, then click and hold and highlight the B column to cell B17. The probability of a success for the various values of the random variable will appear.

6–2. The Excel commands necessary to determine the hypergeometric distribution on page 196 are:

a. On a blank Excel worksheet, write the word *Union Members* in cell A1 and the word *Probability* in B1. In cells A2 through A7, enter the numbers *0* through *5*. Click on cell **B2.**

b. Click the **Formulas** tab in the top menu, then, on the far left, select **Insert Function** ***fx*****.**

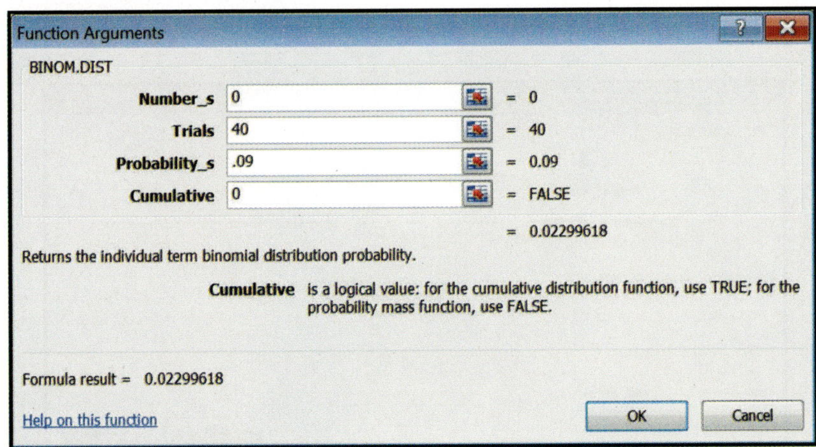

c. In the first dialog box, select **Statistical** and **HYPGEOM.DIST** and then click **OK.**

d. In the second dialog box, enter the four items necessary to compute a hypergeometric probability.

1. Enter *0* for the **Sample_s.**
2. Enter *5* for the **Number_sample.**
3. Enter *40* for the **Population_s.**
4. Enter *50* for the **Number_pop.**
5. Enter *0* for the **Cumulative** and click **OK.**
6. Excel will compute the probability of 0 successes in 5 trials (.000118937) and store that result in cell **B2.**

e. To complete the probability distribution for successes of 1 through 5, double-click on cell **B2.** The hypergeometric function should appear. Replace the **0** to the right of the open parentheses with the cell reference **A2.**

f. Move the mouse to the lower right corner of cell **B2** till a solid black + symbol appears, then click and hold and highlight the **B** column to cell **B7.** The probability of a success for the various outcomes will appear.

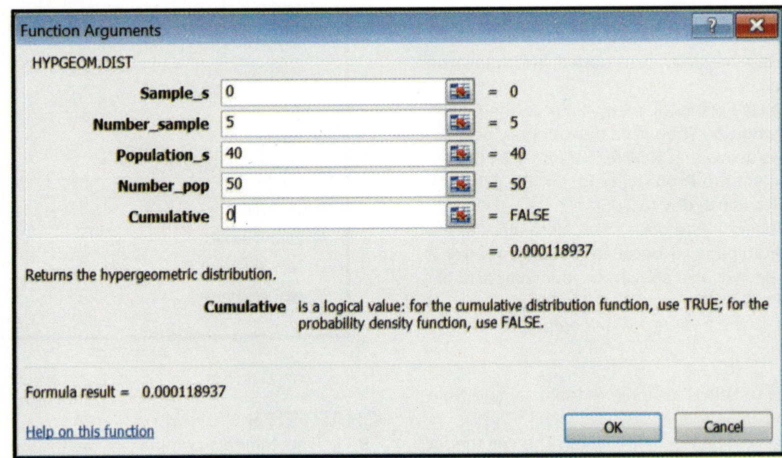

6–3. The Excel commands necessary to determine the Poisson probability distribution on page 199 are:

a. On a blank Excel worksheet, write the word ***Success*** in cell **A1** and the word Probability in **B1.** In cells **A2** through **A9,** write the integers *0* to *7*. Click on **B2** as the active cell.

b. Click on the **Formulas** tab in the top menu, then, on the far left, select **Insert Function** ***fx*****.**

c. In the first dialog box, select **Statistical** in the function category and **POISSON.DIST** in the function name category, then click **OK.**

d. In the second dialog box, enter the three items necessary to compute a Poisson probability.
   1. Enter *0* for **X.**
   2. Enter *0.3* for the **Mean.**
   3. Enter the word *false* or the number *0* for **Cumulative** and click **OK.**
   4. Excel will compute the probability of 0 successes for a Poisson probability distribution with a mean of 0.3. The result, .74081822, is stored in cell **B2.**

e. To complete the probability distribution for successes of 1 through 7, double-click on cell **B2.** The Poisson function should appear. Replace the **0** to the right of the open parentheses with the cell reference **A2.**

f. Move the mouse to the lower right corner of cell **B2** until a solid black + symbol appears, then click and hold and highlight the **B** column to cell **B9.** The probability of a success for the various values of the random variable will appear.

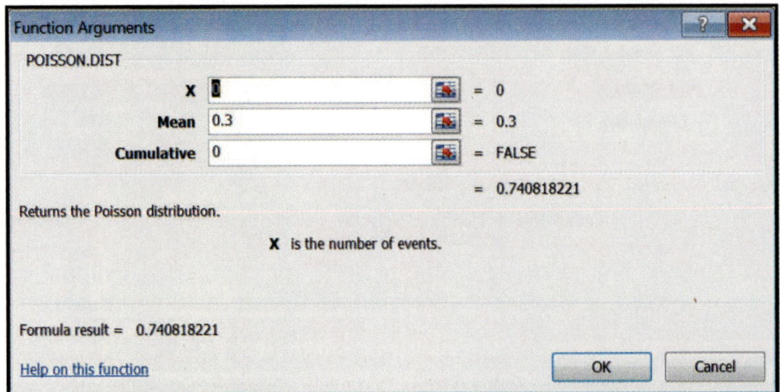

CHAPTER 7

7–1. The Excel commands necessary to produce the output on page 222 are:

a. Click on the **Formulas** tab in the top menu, then, on the far left, select **Insert Function *fx*.** Then from the category box, select **Statistical** and below that **NORM.DIST** and click **OK.**

b. In the dialog box, put *1100* in the box for **X,** *1000* for the **Mean,** *100* for the **Standard_dev,** and *True* in the **Cumulative** box, and click **OK.**

c. The result will appear in the dialog box. If you click **OK,** the answer appears in your spreadsheet.

7–2. The Excel commands necessary to produce the output on page 228 are:

a. Click the **Formulas** tab in the top menu, then, on the far left, select **Insert Function *fx*.** Then from the category box, select **Statistical** and below that **NORM.INV** and click **OK.**

b. In the dialog box, set the **Probability** to *.04,* the **Mean** to *67900,* and the **Standard_dev** to *2050.*

c. The results will appear in the dialog box. Note that the answer is different from page ••• because of rounding error. If you click **OK,** the answer also appears in your spreadsheet.

d. Try entering a **Probability** of *.04,* a **Mean** of *0,* and a **Standard_dev** of *1.* The *z* value will be computed.

CHAPTER 8

8–1. The Excel commands to select a simple random sample from the rental data on page 254 are:

a. Select the **Data** tab on the top of the menu. Then on the far right select **Data Analysis,** then **Sampling** and **OK.**

b. For **Input Range,** insert *B1:B31.* Since the column is named, click the **Labels** box. Select **Random,** and enter the sample size for the **Number of Samples,** in this case *5.* Click on **Output Range** and indicate the place in the spreadsheet where you want the sample information. Note that your sample results will differ from those in the text. Also recall that Excel samples with replacement, so it is possible for a population value to appear more than once in the sample.

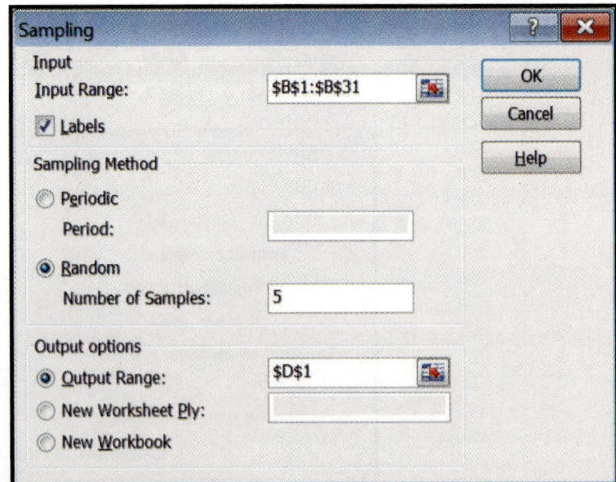

CHAPTER 9

9–1. The Minitab commands for the confidence interval for the amount spent at the Inlet Square Mall on page 297 are:

a. Enter the 20 amounts spent in column **C1** and name the variable *Amount.*

b. On the Toolbar, select **Stat, Basic Statistics,** and click on **1-Sample t.**

c. Select **Samples in columns:** and select **Amount** and click **OK.**

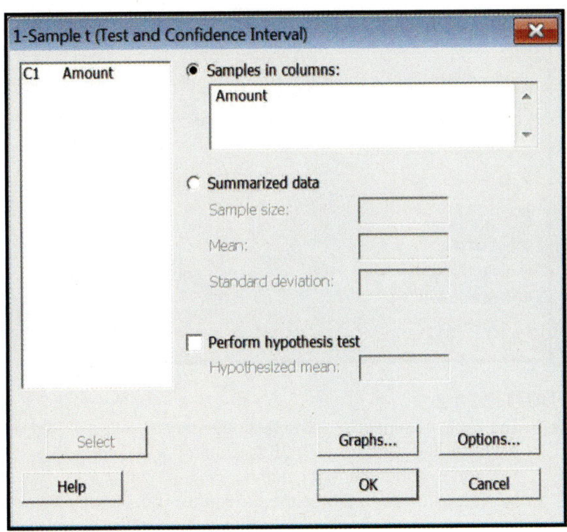

9–2. The Excel commands for the confidence interval for the amounts spent at the Inlet Square Mall on page 298 are:

a. Select the **Data** tab on the top menu. Then, on the far right, select **Data Analysis,** and then **Descriptive Statistics,** and click **OK.**

b. For the **Input Range,** type *A1:A21,* click on **Labels in first row,** type *C1* as the **Output Range,** click on **Summary statistics** and **Confidence Level for Mean,** and then click on **OK.**

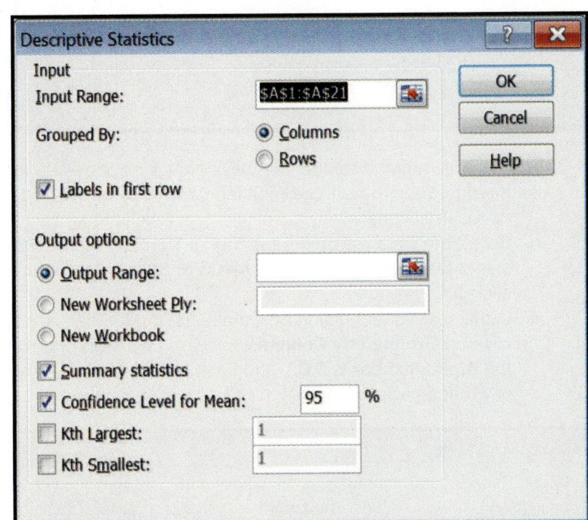

CHAPTER 10

10–1. The Minitab commands for the histogram and the descriptive statistics on page 335 are:

a. Enter the 26 sample observations in column **C1** and name the variable *Cost.*

b. From the menu bar, select **Stat, Basic Statistics,** and **Graphical Summary.** In the dialog box, select **Cost** as the variable and click **OK.**

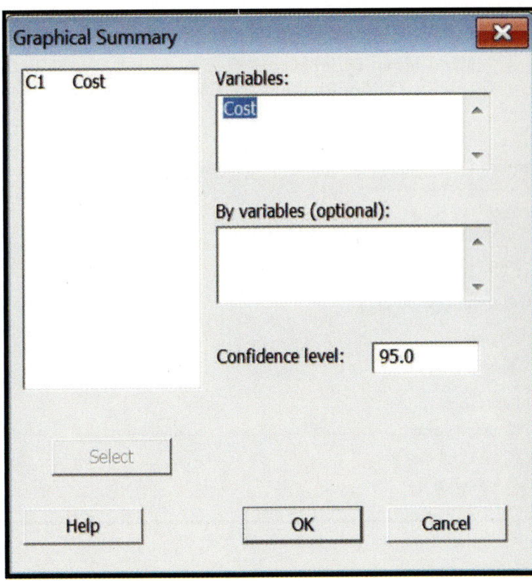

10–2. The Minitab commands for the one-sample *t* test on page 340 are:

a. Enter the sample data into column **C1** and name the variable *Minutes.*

b. From the menu bar, select **Stat, Basic Statistics,** and **1-Sample *t*,** and then hit **Enter.**

c. Select **Minutes** as the variable, select **Perform hypothesized mean,** insert the value *40.* Click **Options.** Under **Alternate,** select **greater than.** Finally, click **OK** twice.

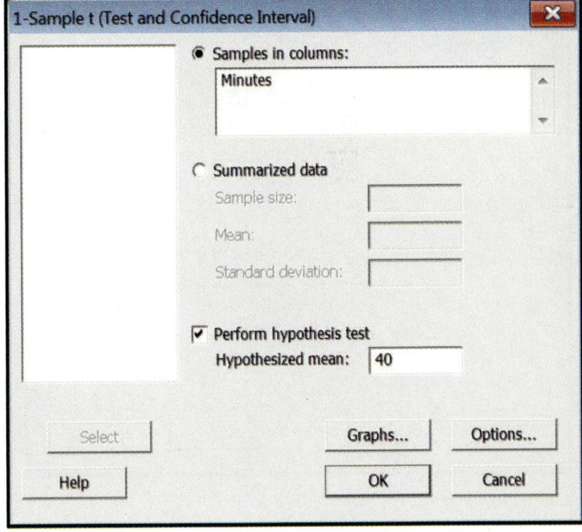

CHAPTER 11

11–1. The Excel commands for the two-sample *t*-test on page 364 are:

a. Enter the data into columns A and B (or any other columns) in the spreadsheet. Use the first row of each column to enter the variable name.

b. Select the **Data** tab on the top menu. Then, on the far right, select **Data Analysis.** Select **t-Test: Two Sample Assuming Equal Variances,** and then click **OK.**

c. In the dialog box, indicate that the range of **Variable 1** is from *A1* to *A6* and **Variable 2** from *B1* to *B7*, the **Hypothesized Mean Difference** is *0*, click **Labels, Alpha** is *0.05*, and the **Output Range** is *D1*. Click **OK.**

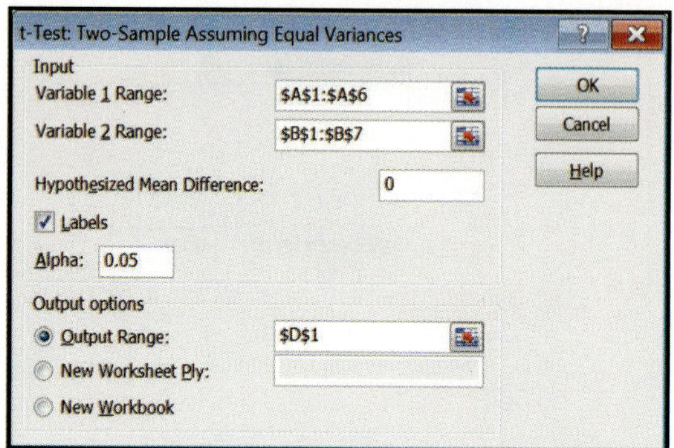

11–2. The Minitab commands for the two-sample *t*-test on page 368 are:

a. Put the amount absorbed by the Store brand in *C1* and the amount absorbed by the Name brand paper towel in *C2*.
b. From the toolbar, select **Stat, Basic Statistics,** and then **2-Sample,** and click **OK.**
c. In the next dialog box, select **Samples in different columns,** select *C1* Store for the **First** column and *C2* Name of the **Second,** click the box next to **Assume equal variances,** and click **OK.**

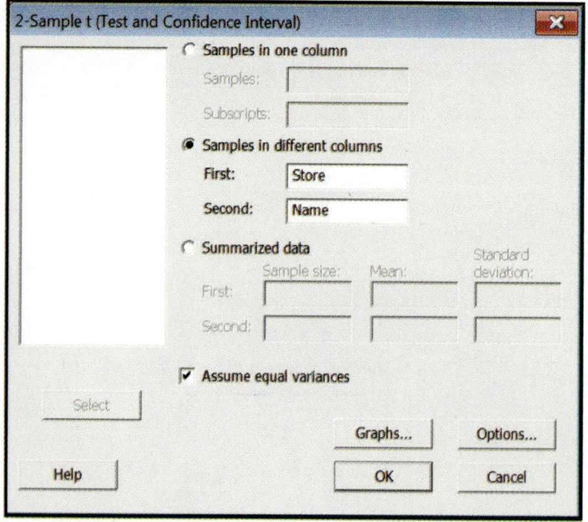

11–3. The Excel commands for the paired *t*-test on page 373 are:

a. Enter the data into columns B and C (or any other two columns) in the spreadsheet, with the variable names in the first row.
b. Select the **Data** tab on the top menu. Then, on the far right, select **Data Analysis.** Select **t-Test: Paired Two Sample for Means,** and then click **OK.**
c. In the dialog box, indicate that the range of **Variable 1** is from *B1* to *B11* and **Variable 2** from *C1* to *C11*, the **Hypothesized Mean Difference** is *0*, click **Labels, Alpha** is *.05*, and the **Output Range** is *E1*. Click **OK.**

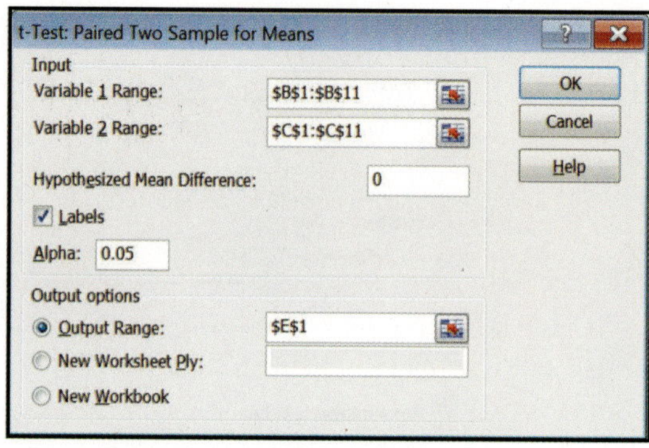

CHAPTER 12

12–1. The Excel commands for the test of variances on page 391 are:

a. Enter the data for U.S. 25 in column A and for I-75 in column B. Label the two columns.
b. Select the **Data** tab on the top menu. Then, on the far right, select **Data Analysis.** Select **F-Test: Two-Sample for Variances,** then click **OK.**
c. The range of the first variable is *A1:A8*, and *B1:B9* for the second. Click on **Labels,** enter *0.05* for **Alpha,** select *D1* for the **Output Range,** and click **OK.**

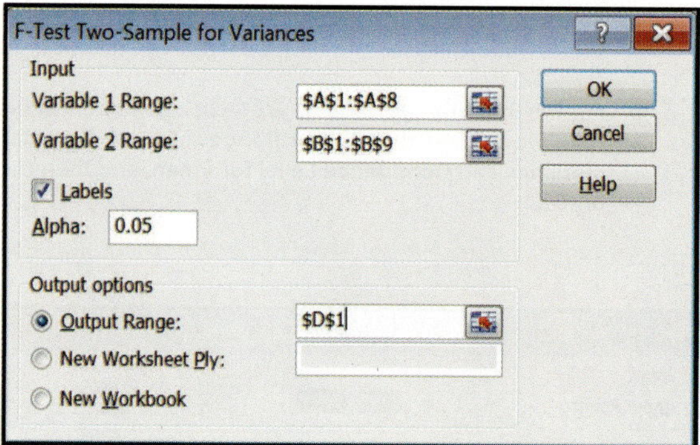

12–2. The Excel commands for the one-way ANOVA on page 400 are:

a. Key in data into four columns labeled *Northern, WTA, Pocono,* and *Branson.*
b. Select the **Data** tab on the top menu. Then, on the far right, select **Data Analysis.** Select **ANOVA: Single Factor,** then click **OK.**
c. In the subsequent dialog box, make the input range *A1:D8*, click on **Grouped by Columns,** click on **Labels in first row,** the **Alpha** text box is *0.05*, and finally select **Output Range** as *F1* and click **OK.**

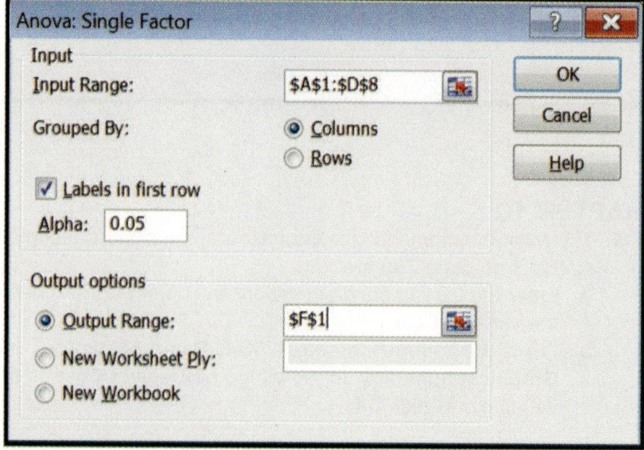

12–3. The Minitab commands for the pairwise comparisons on page 403 are:

a. Input the data into four columns and identify the columns as *Northern, WTA, Pocono,* and *Branson.*

b. Select **Stat, ANOVA,** and **One-way,** select "Response data are in a separate column for each factor level", select and enter the variable names into the **Responses** box by clicking on the variable names in the following order: *Branson, Pocono, WTA, and Northern.* Then select **Comparisons** and then select **Fisher's, individual error rate.** Then **OK.**

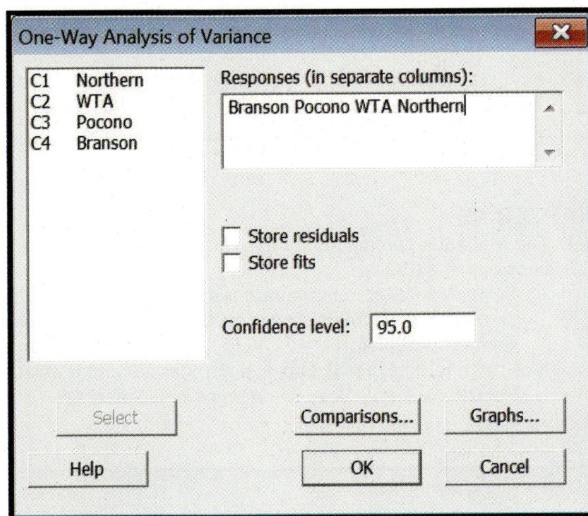

12–4. The Excel commands for the two-way ANOVA on page 408 are:

a. In the first row of the first column, write the word *Driver,* then list the five drivers in the first column. In the first row of the next four columns, enter the names of the routes. Enter the data under each route name.

b. Select the **Data** tab on the top menu. Then, on the far right, select **Data Analysis.** Select **ANOVA: Two-Factor Without Replication,** then click **OK.**

c. In the dialog box, the **Input Range** is *A3:E8,* click on **Labels,** enter *0.05* for **Alpha,** select **G3** for the **Output Range,** and then click **OK.**

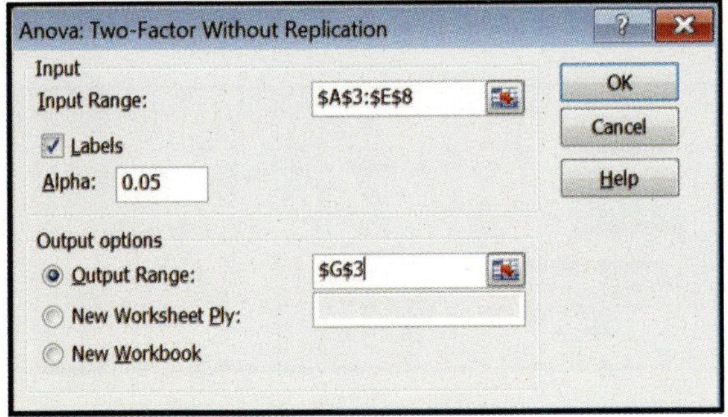

12–5. The Excel commands for the two-way ANOVA with interaction on page 410 are:

a. Enter the data into Excel as shown on page 410.

b. Select the **Data** tab on the top menu. Then, on the far right, select **Data Analysis.** Select **ANOVA: Two-Factor With Replication,** then click **OK.**

c. In the dialog box, for the **Input Range** highlight the entire range for the data including row and column labels, enter **Rows per sample** as *3,* enter *0.05* for **Alpha, Output Range** and cell H1.

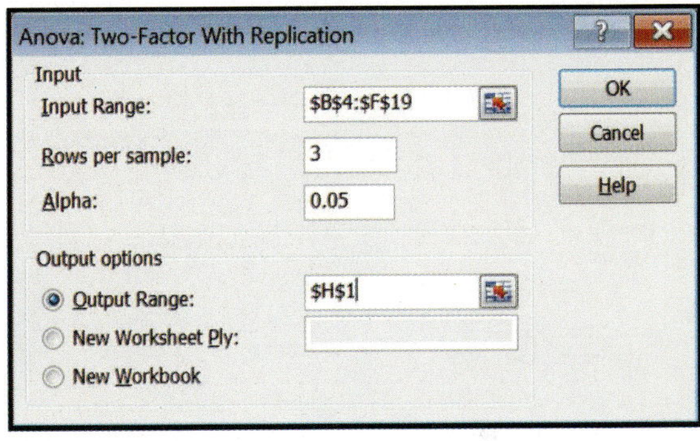

CHAPTER 13

13–1. The Excel commands for calculating the correlation coefficient on page 445 are:

a. Access the Applewood Auto Group dataset (www.mhhe.com/lind17e).

b. Select the **Data** tab on the top of the ribbon. Then, on the far right, select **Data Analysis.** Select **Correlation,** and click **OK.**

c. For the **Input Range,** highlight the **Age** and **Profit** columns, including the labels in row 1. The data are grouped by **Columns.** Check the **Labels in first row** box. Select a cell in the worksheet as the beginning of the range to output the correlation. Click **OK.**

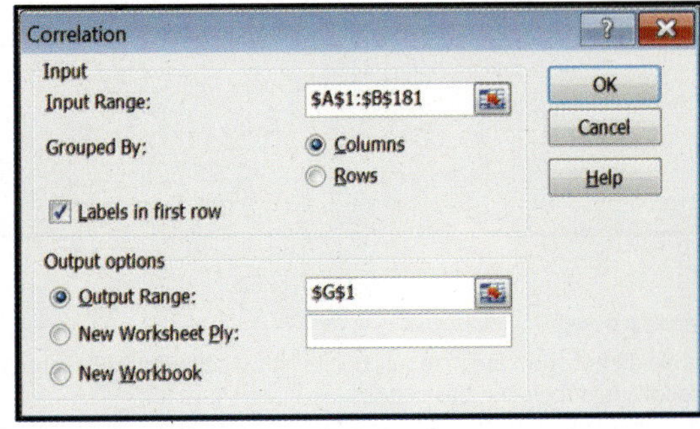

13–2. The computer commands for the Excel output on page 460 are:

a. Enter the variable names in row 1 of columns A, B, and C. Enter the data in rows 2 through 16 in the same columns.

b. Select the **Data** tab on the top of the menu. Then, on the far right, select **Data Analysis.** Select **Regression,** then click **OK.**

c. For our spreadsheet, we have *Calls* in column B and *Sales* in column C. The **Input Y Range** is *C1:C16* and the **Input X Range** is *B1:B16.* Click on **Labels,** select *E1* as the **Output Range,** and click **OK.**

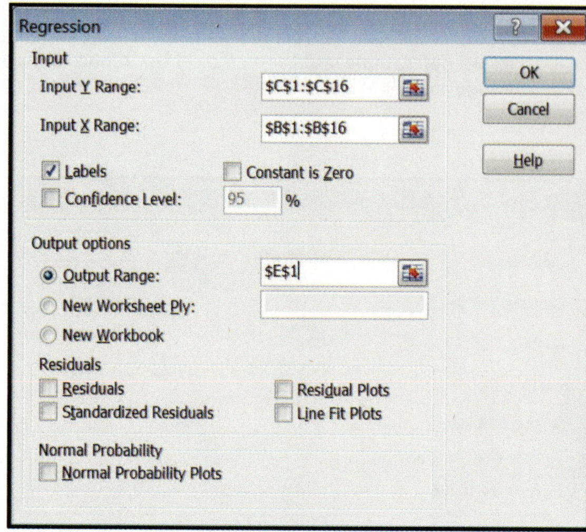

13–3. The Minitab commands to the confidence intervals and prediction intervals on page 470 are:

a. Select **Stat, Regression,** and **Fitted line plot.**
b. In the next dialog box, the **Response (Y)** is *Copiers Sold* and **Predictor (X)** is *Sales Calls*. Select **Linear** for the type of regression model and then click on **Options.**
c. In the **Options** dialog box, click on **Display confidence interval and prediction interval,** use the **95.0 for confidence level,** type an appropriate heading in the **Title** box, then click **OK** and then **OK** again.

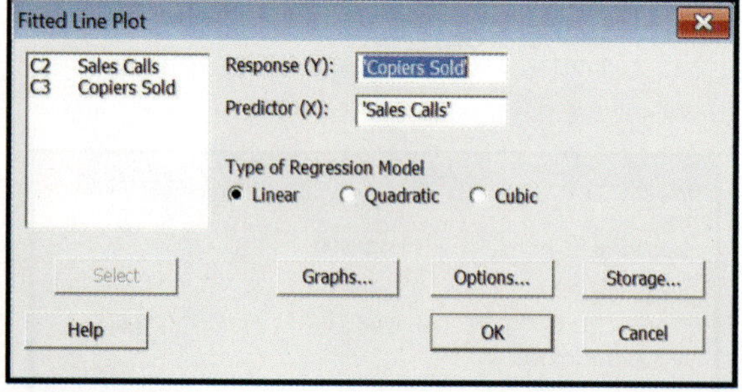

CHAPTER 14

Note: We do not show steps for all the statistical software in Chapter 14. The following shows the basic steps.

14–1. The Excel commands to produce the multiple regression output on page 492 are:

a. Import the data from the text website: www.mhhe.com/lind17e. The file name is **Tbl14.**
b. Select the **Data** tab on the top menu. Then on the far right, select **Data analysis.** Select **Regression** and click **OK.**
c. Make the **Input Y Range** *A1:A21,* the **Input X Range** *B1:D21,* check the **Labels** box, the **Output Range** is *F1,* then click **OK.**

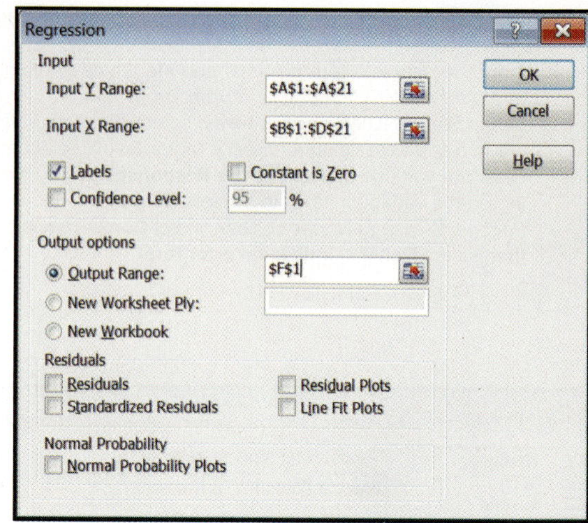

CHAPTER 15

15–1. The MegaStat commands for the two-sample test of proportions on page 553 are:

a. Select **MegaStat** from the **Add-Ins** tab. From the menu, select **Hypothesis Tests,** and then **Compare Two Independent Proportions.**
b. Enter the data. For **Group 1,** enter **x** as *19* and **n** as *100.* For **Group 2,** enter **x** as *62* and **n** as *200.* Select **OK.**

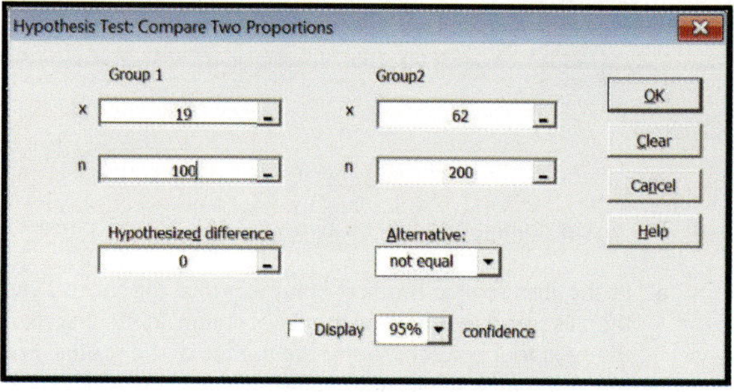

15–2. The MegaStat commands to create the chi-square goodness-of-fit test on page 559 are:

a. Enter the information from Table 15–2 into a worksheet as shown.
b. Select **MegaStat, Chi-Square/Crosstabs,** and **Goodness of Fit Test** and hit **Enter.**
c. In the dialog box, select *B2:B5* as the **Observed values,** *C2:C5* as the **Expected values,** and enter *0* as the **Number of parameters estimated from the data.** Click **OK.**

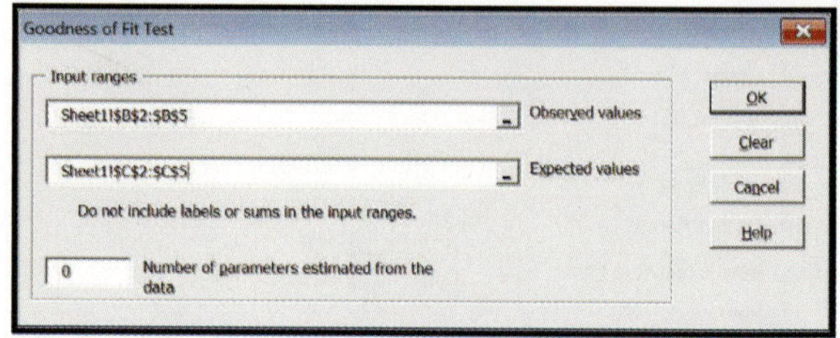

15–3. The MegaStat commands to create the chi-square goodness-of-fit tests on pages 564 and 565 are the same except for the number of items in the observed and expected frequency columns. Only one dialog box is shown.

a. Enter the Levels of Management information shown on page 564.

b. Select **MegaStat, Chi-Square/Crosstabs,** and **Goodness of Fit Test** and hit **Enter.**

c. In the dialog box, select *B1:B7* as the **Observed values,** *C1:C7* as the **Expected values,** and enter *0* as the **Number of parameters estimated from the data.** Click **OK.**

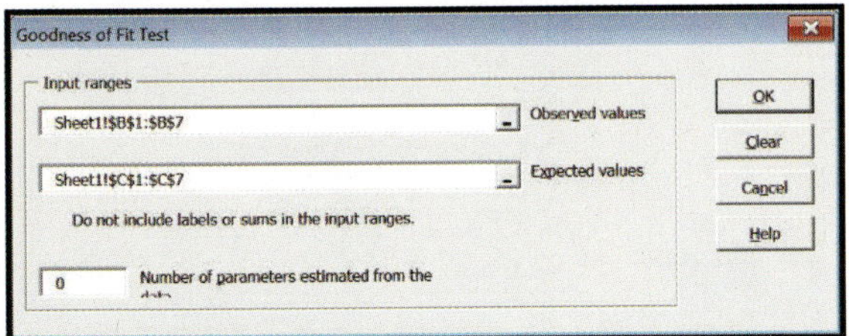

15–4. The MegaStat commands for the contingency table analysis on page 573 are:

a. Enter Table 15–8 on page 571 into cells **A1** through **D3.** Include the row and column labels. DO NOT include the Total column or row.

b. Select **MegaStat** from the **Add-Ins** tab. From the menu select **Chi-square/Crosstab,** then select **Contingency Table.**

c. For the **Input Range,** select cells **A1** through **D3.** Check the **chi-square** and **Expected values** boxes. Select **OK.**

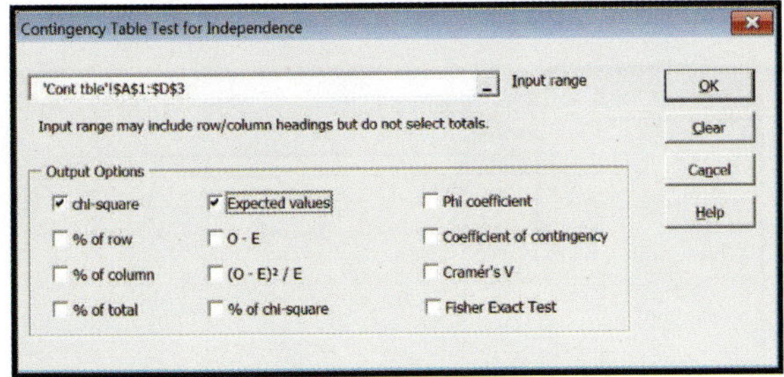

CHAPTER 16

16–1. The MegaStat for Excel commands necessary for the Wilcoxon rank-sum test on page 600 are:

a. Enter the number of no-shows for Atlanta in column A and for Chicago in column B.

b. Select **MegaStat, Nonparametric Tests,** and **Wilcoxon-Mann/Whitney Test,** then hit **Enter.**

c. For **Group 1,** use the data on Atlanta flights (*A1:A9*) and for **Group 2** use the data on Chicago flights (*B1:B8*). Click on **Correct for ties** and **one-tailed,** and *greater than* as the **Alternative,** then click on **OK.**

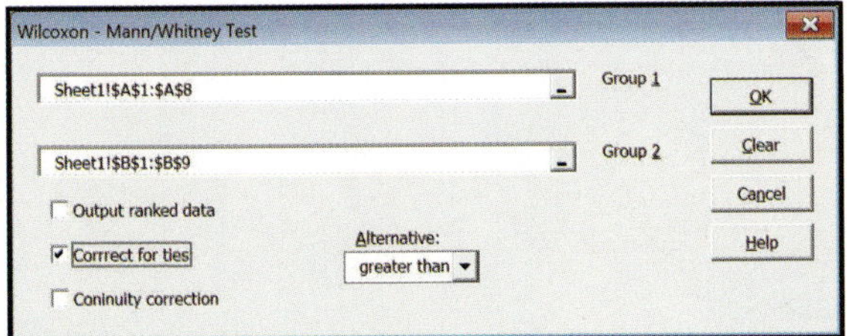

16–2. The MegaStat commands for the Kruskal-Wallis Test on page 604 are:

a. Enter the data in Table 16–6 into an Excel worksheet including labels into columns A, B, and C starting in row 1.

b. Select **MegaStat** from the **Add-Ins** tab. From the menu select **Nonparametric Tests,** then select **Kruskal-Wallis Test.**

c. For the **Input Range,** select cells *A1* through *C9.* Check the **Correct for Ties** box. Select **OK.**

16–3. The Excel commands for the one-way ANOVA on page 605 are:

a. Enter the data in Table 16–6 into an Excel worksheet including labels into columns A, B, and C starting in row 1.

b. Select the **Data** tab on the top of the menu. Then, on the far right, select **Data Analysis.** Select **ANOVA: Single Factor,** then click **OK.**

c. In the dialog box, the **Input Range** is *A1:C9,* click on **Labels in first row,** and enter *E1* as the **Output Range,** then click **OK.**

CHAPTER 18

18–1. The MegaStat commands for creating the seasonal indexes on page 675 are:

a. Enter the coded time period and the value of the time series in two columns. You may also want to include information on the years and quarters.

b. Select **MegaStat, Time Series/Forecasting,** and **Deseasonalization,** and hit **Enter.**

c. Input only the range of the sales data, indicate the data are in the first quarter, and click **OK.**

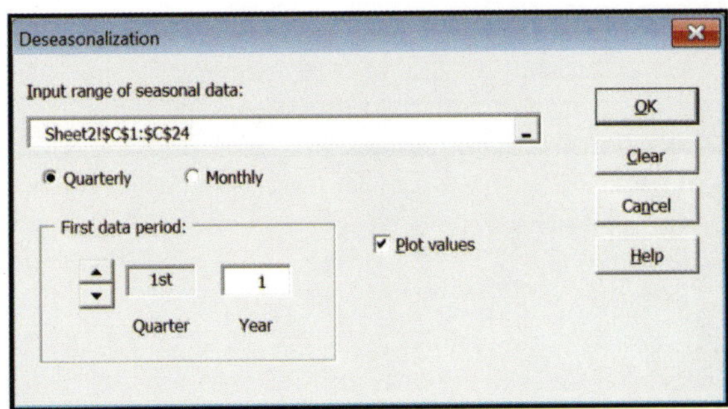

CHAPTER 19

19–1. The Minitab commands for the Pareto chart on page 703 are:

a. Enter the reasons for water usage in column **C1** and the gallons used in **C2.** Give the columns appropriate names.

b. Click on **Stat, Quality Tools, Pareto Chart,** and then hit **Enter.**

c. Indicate **Defects of attribute data** as the variable *Usage* and **Frequencies** as the variable *Gallons*. Click on **Options** and type a chart title, and click **OK.**

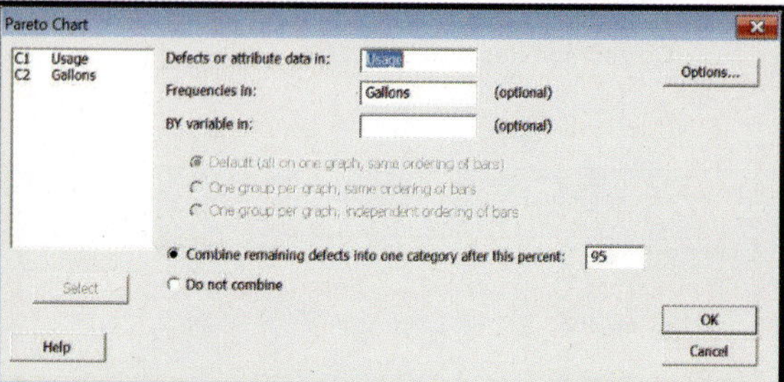

19–2. The Minitab commands for the mean and range charts on page 610 are:

a. Enter the information in Table 19–1 or from the text website, www.mhhe.com/lind17e. The file name is Table 19–1.

b. Click on **Stat, Control Charts, Variables Charts for Subgroups, Xbar-R,** and hit **Enter.**

c. Select **All observations for a chart are in one column.** Then in the box below, select the variable **Minutes.** For **Subgroup sizes,** enter the variable *Time*.

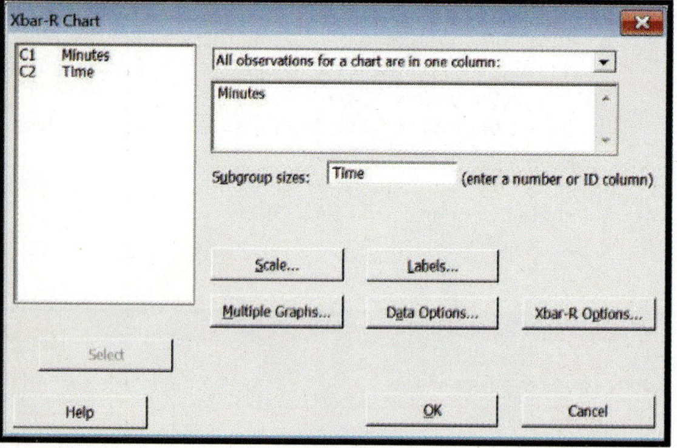

19–3. The Minitab commands for the p-chart on page 715 are:

a. Enter the data on the number of defects from page 715.

b. Click on **Stat, Control Charts, Attribute Charts, P,** and hit **Enter.**

c. Under **Variables,** select *Defects,* then enter *50* for **Subgroup sizes.** Click on **Labels,** type in the title, and click **OK** twice.

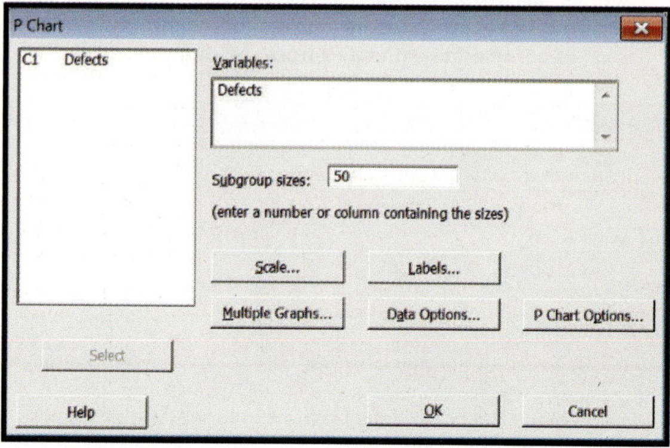

19–4. The Minitab commands for the c-bar chart on page 717 are:

a. Enter the data on the number of misspelled words from page 717.

b. Click on **Stat, Control Charts, Attribute Charts, C,** and hit **Enter.**

c. Select the **Variable** indicating the number of misspelled words, then click on **Labels** and type the title in the space provided, and click **OK** twice.

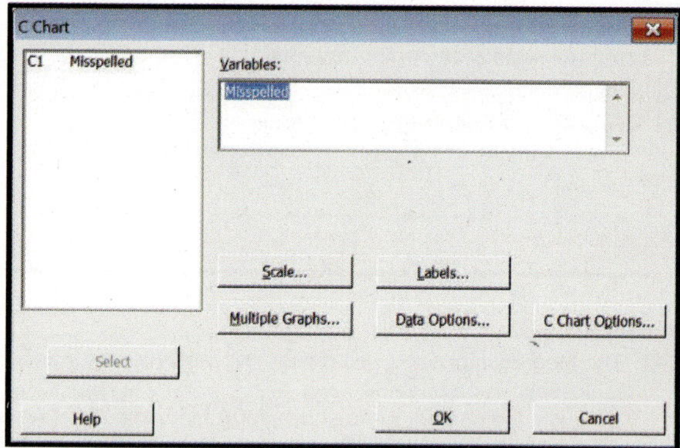

APPENDIX D: ANSWERS TO ODD-NUMBERED CHAPTER EXERCISES & REVIEW EXERCISES & SOLUTIONS TO PRACTICE TESTS

Answers to Odd-Numbered Chapter Exercises

CHAPTER 1

1. **a.** Interval
   b. Ratio
   c. Nominal
   d. Nominal
   e. Ordinal
   f. Ratio
3. Answers will vary.
5. Qualitative data are not numerical, whereas quantitative data are numerical. Examples will vary by student.
7. A discrete variable may assume only certain values. A continuous variable may assume an infinite number of values within a given range. The number of traffic citations issued each day during February in Garden City Beach, South Carolina, is a discrete variable. The weight of commercial trucks passing the weigh station at milepost 195 on Interstate 95 in North Carolina is a continuous variable.
9. **a.** Ordinal
   b. Ratio
   c. The newer system provides information on the distance between exits.
11. If you were using this store as typical of all Best Buy stores, then the daily number sold last month would be a sample. However, if you considered the store as the only store of interest, then the daily number sold last month would be a population.
13.

	Discrete Variable	Continuous Variable
Qualitative	b. Gender d. Soft drink preference g. Student rank in class h. Rating of a finance professor	
Quantitative	c. Sales volume of MP3 players f. SAT scores i. Number of home computers	a. Salary e. Temperature

	Discrete	Continuous
Nominal	b. Gender	
Ordinal	d. Soft drink preference g. Student rank in class h. Rating of a finance professor	
Interval	f. SAT scores	e. Temperature
Ratio	c. Sales volume of MP3 players i. Number of home computers	a. Salary

15. According to the sample information, 120/300 or 40% would accept a job transfer.
17. **a.**

Manufacturer	Difference
General Motors Corp.	128,133
Chrysler	126,955
Ford Motor Company	112,975
Toyota Motor Sales USA Inc.	96,078
Nissan North America Inc.	72,146
Subaru of America Inc.	61,834
American Honda Motor Co Inc.	38,440
Kia Motors America Inc.	36,313
Hyundai Motor America	30,656
Mercedes-Benz	20,187
Audi of America Inc.	18,970
Mitsubishi Motors N A, Inc.	16,119
Land Rover	13,535
BMW of North America Inc.	12,202
Mazda Motor of America Inc.	7,407
Volvo	5,980
Mini	4,573
Porsche Cars NA Inc.	4,337
Tesla	1,850
Lamborghini	372
Ferrari	164
Rolls Royce	19
Bentley	−351
Jaguar	−633
Maserati	−783
Smart	−2,512
Fiat	−3,650
Volkswagen of America Inc.	−6,585

b. Percentage differences with top five and bottom five.

Manufacturer	% change from 2014
Lamborghini	75%
Land Rover	32%
Mitsubishi Motors N A, Inc.	25%
Subaru of America Inc.	15%
Audi of America Inc.	13%
Volvo	13%
Tesla	12%
Porsche Cars NA Inc.	11%
Mini	10%
Ferrari	9%
Chrysler	8%
Kia Motors America Inc.	7%
Mercedes-Benz	7%
Nissan North America Inc.	6%
Ford Motor Company	5%
General Motors Corp.	5%
Hyundai Motor America	5%
Toyota Motor Sales USA Inc.	5%
BMW of North America Inc.	5%
American Honda Motor Co Inc.	3%
Mazda Motor of America Inc.	3%
Rolls Royce	3%
Volkswagen of America Inc.	−2%
Jaguar	−5%
Maserati	−8%
Fiat	−9%
Bentley	−15%
Smart	−29%

c.

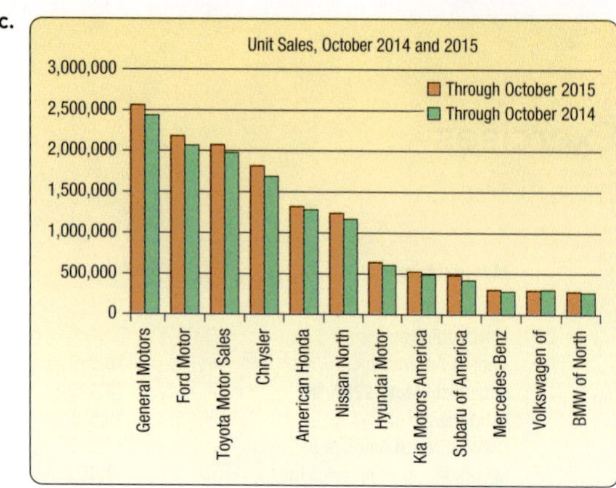

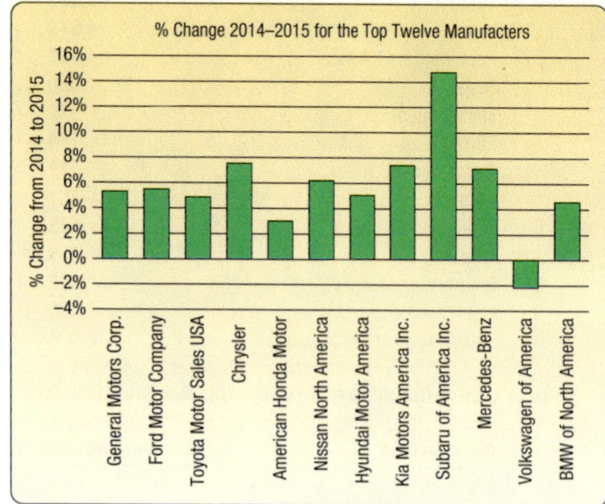

19. The graph shows a gradual increase from 2003 to 2006 with a large increase in 2008. However, during the recession of 2009, earnings decreased, then increased to 2008 levels over the years 2010 through 2012. Over 2013 and 2014, earnings were steady at a bit over $30 billion.

21. **a.** League is a qualitative variable; the others are quantitative.
b. League is a nominal-level variable; the others are ratio-level variables.

CHAPTER 2

1. 25% market share.

3.

Season	Frequency	Relative Frequency
Winter	100	.10
Spring	300	.30
Summer	400	.40
Fall	200	.20
	1,000	1.00

5. **a.** A frequency table.

Color	Frequency	Relative Frequency
Bright White	130	0.10
Metallic Black	104	0.08
Magnetic Lime	325	0.25
Tangerine Orange	455	0.35
Fusion Red	286	0.22
Total	1,300	1.00

b.

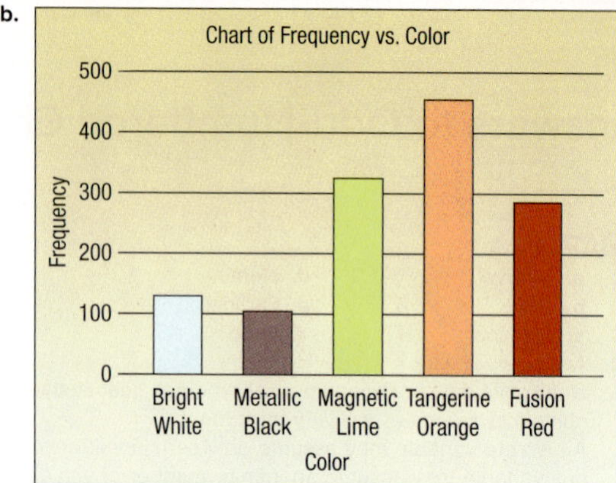

c.

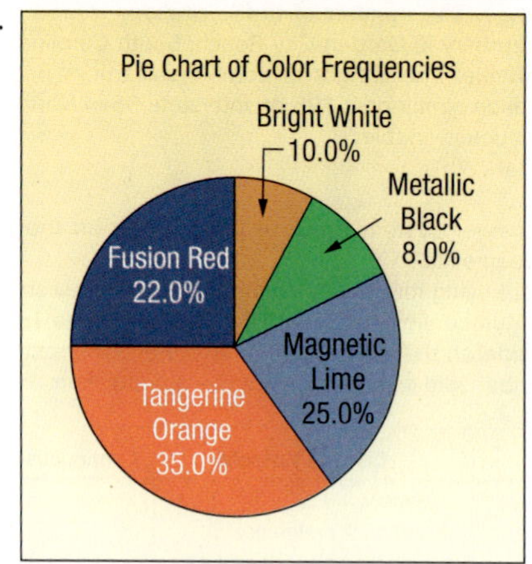

d. 350,000 orange, 250,000 lime, 220,000 red, 100,000 white, and 80,000 black, found by multiplying relative frequency by 1,000,000 production.

7. $2^5 = 32$, $2^6 = 64$, therefore, 6 classes

9. $2^7 = 128$, $2^8 = 256$, suggests 8 classes

$i \geq \frac{\$567 - \$235}{8} = 41$ Class intervals of 45 or 50 would be acceptable.

11. **a.** $2^4 = 16$ Suggests 5 classes.

b. $i \geq \frac{31 - 25}{5} = 1.2$ Use interval of 1.5.

c. 24

d.

Units	f	Relative Frequency
24.0 up to 25.5	2	0.125
25.5 up to 27.0	4	0.250
27.0 up to 28.5	8	0.500
28.5 up to 30.0	0	0.000
30.0 up to 31.5	2	0.125
Total	16	1.000

e. The largest concentration is in the 27.0 up to 28.5 class (8).

13. **a.**

Number of Visits	f
0 up to 3	9
3 up to 6	21
6 up to 9	13
9 up to 12	4
12 up to 15	3
15 up to 18	1
Total	51

b. The largest group of shoppers (21) shop at the BiLo Supermarket 3, 4, or 5 times during a month period. Some customers visit the store only 1 time during the month, but others shop as many as 15 times.

c.

Number of Visits	Percent of Total
0 up to 3	17.65
3 up to 6	41.18
6 up to 9	25.49
9 up to 12	7.84
12 up to 15	5.88
15 up to 18	1.96
Total	100.00

15. a. Histogram
b. 100
c. 5
d. 28
e. 0.28
f. 12.5
g. 13

17. a. 50
b. 1.5 thousand miles, or 1,500 miles.
c.

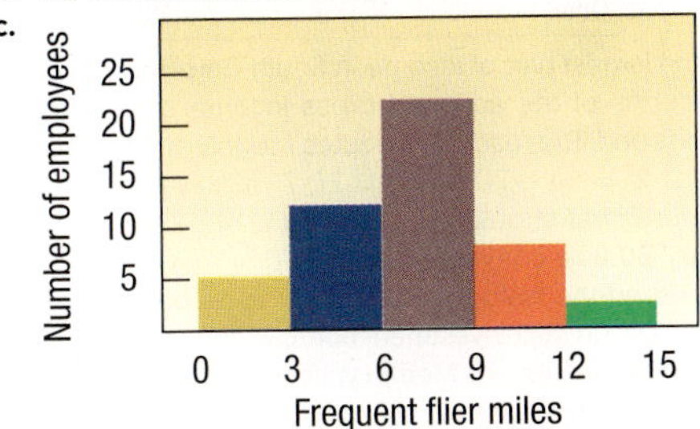

d. $X = 1.5$, $Y = 5$
e.

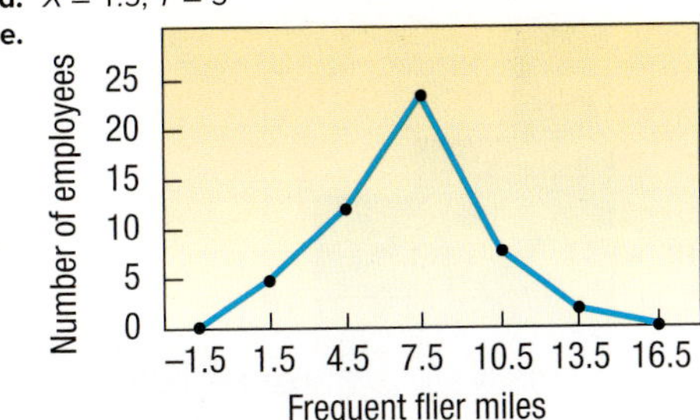

f. For the 50 employees, about half traveled between 6,000 and 9,000 miles. Five employees traveled less than 3,000 miles, and 2 traveled more than 12,000 miles.

19. a. 40
b. 5
c. 11 or 12
d. About $18/hr
e. About $9/hr
f. About 75%

21. a. 5
b.

Miles	*CF*
Less than 3	5
Less than 6	17
Less than 9	40
Less than 12	48
Less than 15	50

c.

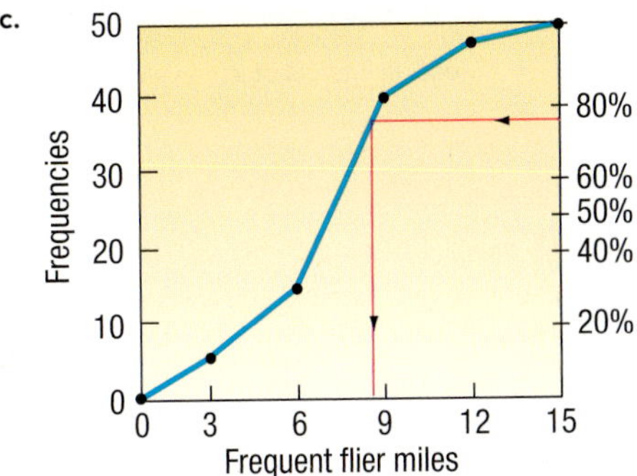

d. About 8.7 thousand miles

23. a. A qualitative variable uses either the nominal or ordinal scale of measurement. It is usually the result of counts. Quantitative variables are either discrete or continuous. There is a natural order to the results for a quantitative variable. Quantitative variables can use either the interval or ratio scale of measurement.
b. Both types of variables can be used for samples and populations.

25. a. Frequency table
b.

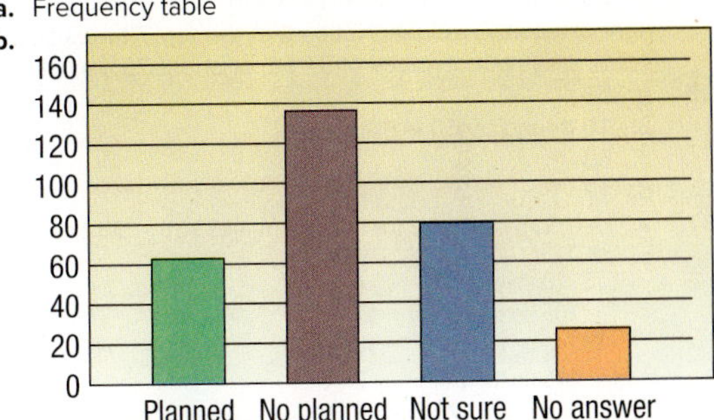

c.

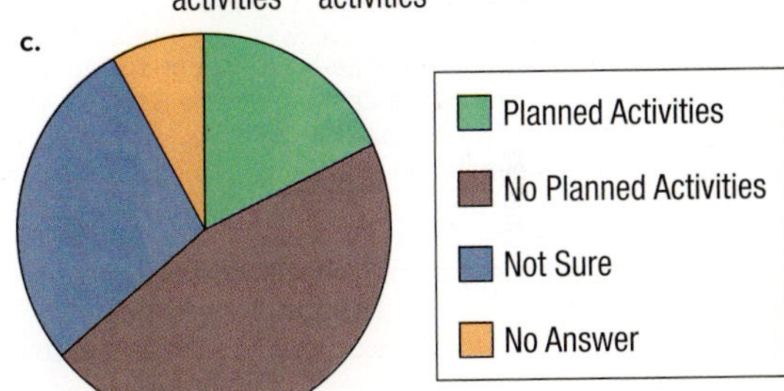

d. A pie chart would be better because it clearly shows that nearly half of the customers prefer no planned activities.

27. $2^6 = 64$ and $2^7 = 128$, suggest 7 classes

29. a. 5, because $2^4 = 16 < 25$ and $2^5 = 32 > 25$
b. $i \geq \frac{48 - 16}{5} = 6.4$ Use interval of 7.
c. 15
d.

Class	Frequency	
15 up to 22	III	3
22 up to 29	~~IIII~~ III	8
29 up to 36	~~IIII~~ II	7
36 up to 43	~~IIII~~	5
43 up to 50	II	2
		25

e. It is fairly symmetric, with most of the values between 22 and 36.

31. **a.** $2^5 = 32$, $2^6 = 64$, 6 classes recommended.

b. $i = \dfrac{10 - 1}{6} = 1.5$ use an interval of 2.

c. 0

d.

Class	Frequency
0 up to 2	1
2 up to 4	5
4 up to 6	12
6 up to 8	17
8 up to 10	8
10 up to 12	2

e. The distribution is fairly symmetric or bell-shaped with a large peak in the middle of the two classes of 4 up to 8.

33.

Class	Frequency
0 up to 200	19
200 up to 400	1
400 up to 600	4
600 up to 800	1
800 up to 1,000	2

This distribution is positively skewed with a large "tail" to the right or positive values. Notice that the top 7 tunes account for 4,342 plays out of a total of 5,968, or about 73% of all plays.

35. **a.** 56

b. 10 (found by 60 – 50)

c. 55

d. 17

37. **a.** Use \$35 because the minimum is (\$265 – \$82)/6 = \$30.5.

b.

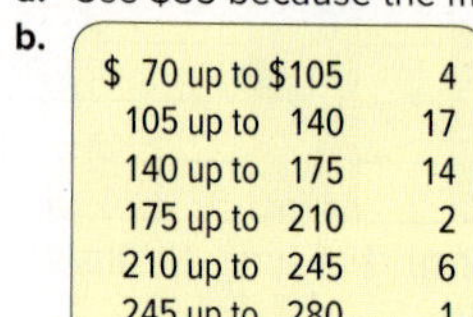

\$ 70 up to \$105	4
105 up to 140	17
140 up to 175	14
175 up to 210	2
210 up to 245	6
245 up to 280	1

c. The purchases range from a low of about \$70 to a high of about \$280. The concentration is in the \$105 up to \$140 and \$140 up to \$175 classes.

39. Bar charts are preferred when the goal is to compare the actual amount in each category.

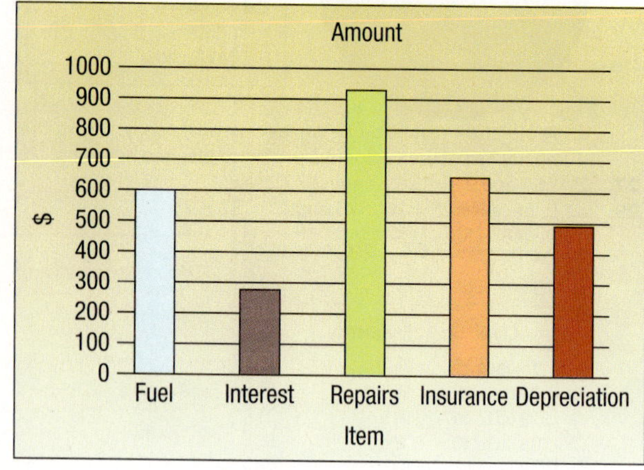

41.

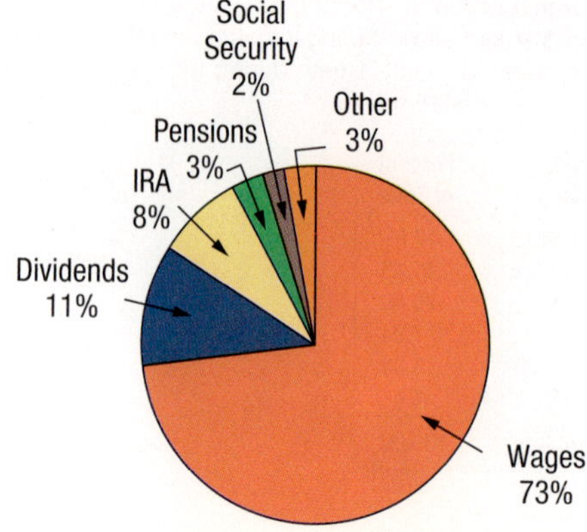

SC Income	Percent	Cumulative
Wages	73	73
Dividends	11	84
IRA	8	92
Pensions	3	95
Social Security	2	97
Other	3	100

By far the largest part of income in South Carolina is wages. Almost three-fourths of the adjusted gross income comes from wages. Dividends and IRAs each contributes roughly another 10%.

43. **a.** Since $2^6 = 64 < 70 < 128 = 2^7$, 7 classes are recommended. The interval should be at least (1,002.2 – 3.3)/7 = 142.7. Use 150 as a convenient value.

b. Based on the histogram, the majority of people has less than \$500,000 in their investment portfolio and may not have enough money for retirement. Merrill Lynch financial advisors need to promote the importance of investing for retirement in this age group.

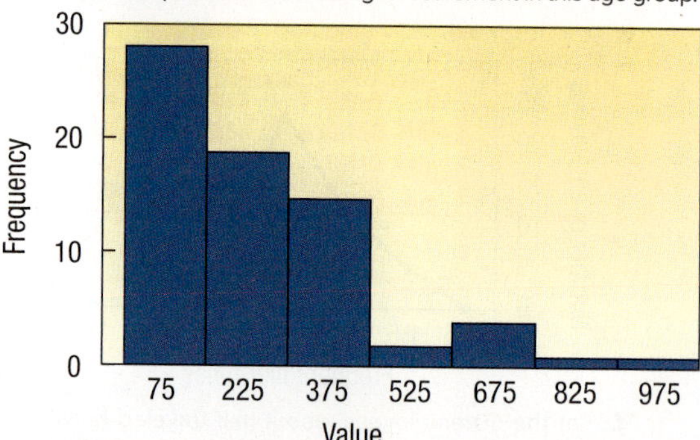

45. **a.** Pie chart

b. 700, found by 0.7(1,000)

c. Yes, 0.70 + 0.20 = 0.90

47. **a.**

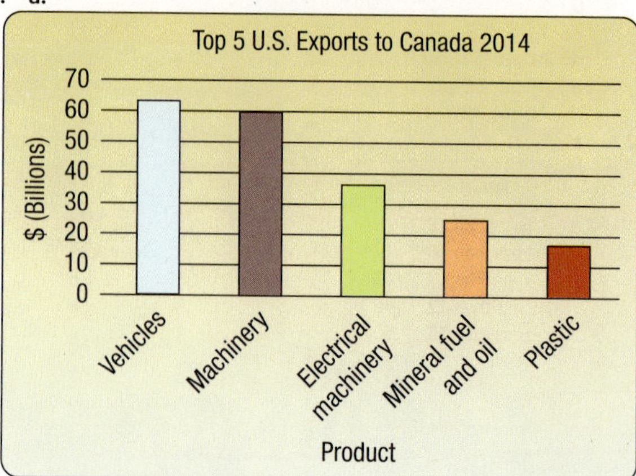

b. 25.5%, found by (59.7 + 36.6)/376

c. 47.8% found by (59.7 + 36.6)/(63.3 + 59.7 + 36.6 + 24.8 + 17))

49.

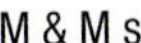

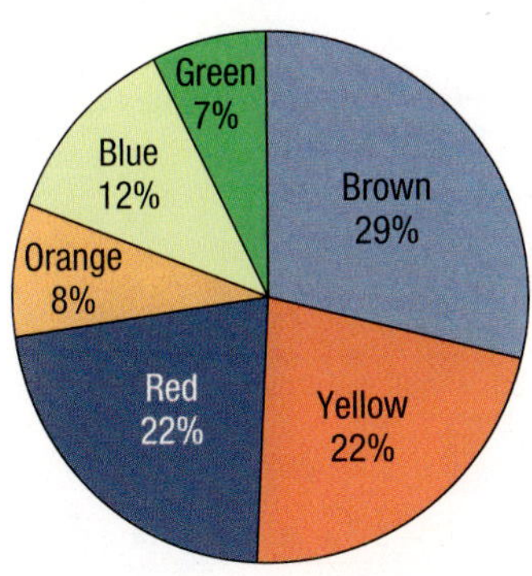

Brown, yellow, and red make up almost 75 percent of the candies. The other 25 percent is composed of blue, orange, and green.

51. There are many choices and possibilities here. For example you could choose to start the first class at 160,000 rather than 120,000. The choice is yours!

i > = (919,480 − 167,962)/7 = 107,360. Use intervals of 120,000

Selling Price (000)	Frequency	Cumulative Frequency
120 up to 240	26	26
240 up to 360	36	62
360 up to 480	27	89
480 up to 600	7	96
600 up to 720	4	100
720 up to 840	2	102
840 up to 960	1	105

a. Most homes (60%) sell between $240,000 and $480,000.

b. The typical price in the first class is $180,000 and in the last class it is $900,000

c.

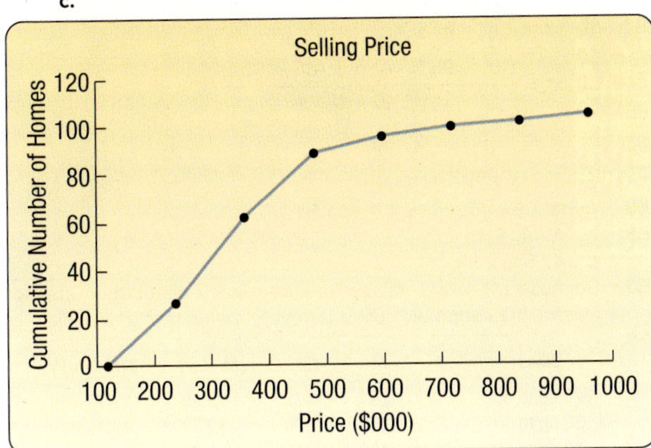

Fifty percent (about 52) of the homes sold for about $320,000 or less.
The top ten percent (about 90) of homes sold for at least $520,000
About 41 (about 41) percent of the homes sold for less than $300,000.

d.

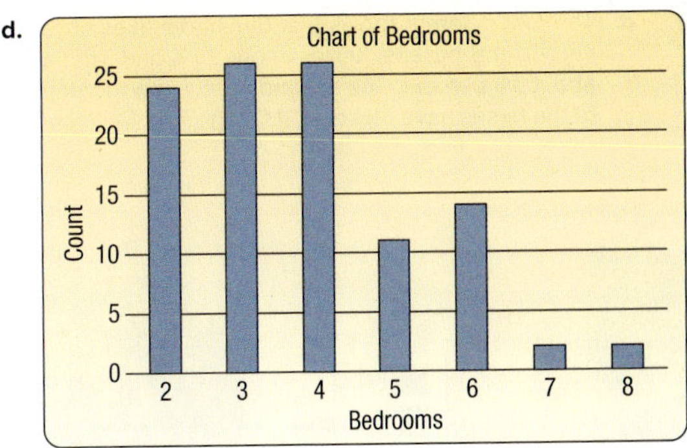

2,3 and 4 bedroom houses are most common with about 25 houses each. 7 and 8 bedroom houses are rather rare. **(LO2-3)**

53. Since $2^6 = 64 < 80 < 128 = 2^7$, use 7 classes. The interval should be at least (11973 − 10000)/7 = 281 miles. Use 300. The resulting frequency distribution is:

Class	*f*
9900 up to 10200	8
10200 up to 10500	8
10500 up to 10800	11
10800 up to 11100	8
11110 up to 11400	13
11400 up to 11700	12
11700 up to 12000	20

a. The typical amount driven, or the middle of the distribution is about 11100 miles. Based on the frequency distribution, the range is from 9900 up to 12000 miles.

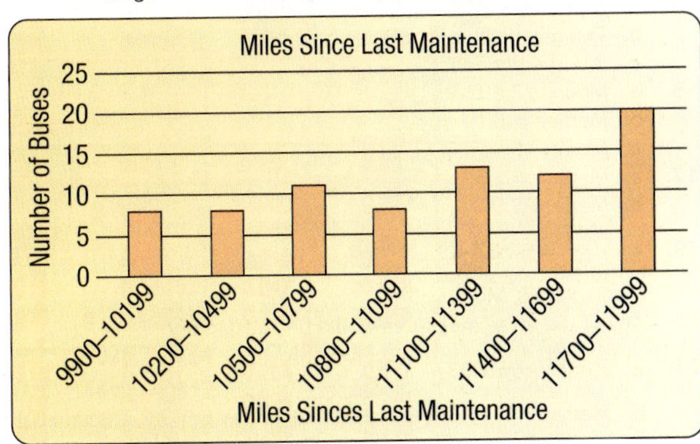

b. The distribution is somewhat "skewed" with a longer "tail" to the left and no outliers. **(LO2-3)**

c.

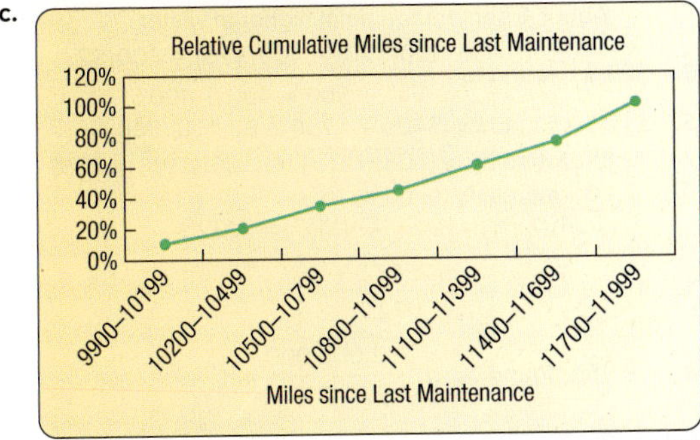

Forty percent of the buses were driven fewer than about 10800 miles. About 30% of the 80 busses (about 24) were driven less than 10500 miles. **(LO2-3)**

d. The first diagram shows that Bluebird makes about 59 percent of the busses, Keiser about 31% and Thompson only about 10 percent. The second chart shows that nearly 69% of the buses have 55 seats. **(LO2-2)**

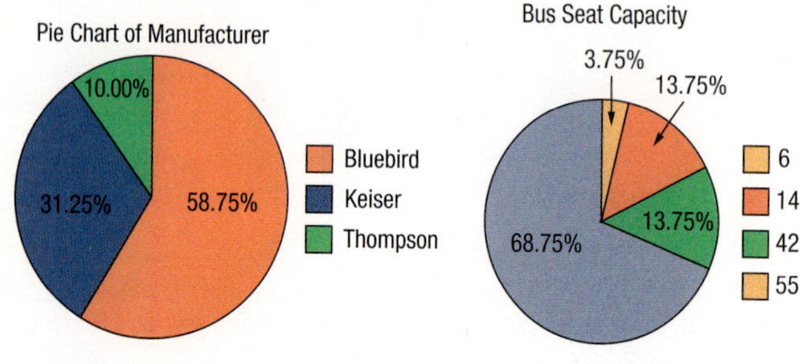

CHAPTER 3

1. $\mu = 5.4$, found by 27/5

3. **a.** $\bar{x} = 7.0$, found by 28/4
b. $(5 - 7) + (9 - 7) + (4 - 7) + (10 - 7) = 0$

5. $\bar{x} = 14.58$, found by 43.74/3

7. **a.** 15.4, found by 154/10
b. Population parameter, since it includes all the salespeople at Midtown Ford

9. **a.** $54.55, found by $1,091/20
b. A sample statistic—assuming that the power company serves more than 20 customers

11. $\bar{x} = \frac{\Sigma x}{n}$ so

$\Sigma x = \bar{x} \cdot n = (\$5,430)(30) = \$162,900$

13. **a.** No mode
b. The given value would be the mode.
c. 3 and 4 bimodal

15. **a.** Mean = 3.583
b. Median = 5
c. Mode = 5

17. **a.** Median = 2.9
b. Mode = 2.9

19. $\bar{x} = \frac{647}{11} = 58.82$

Median = 58, Mode = 58

Any of the three measures would be satisfactory.

21. **a.** $\bar{x} = \frac{90.4}{12} = 7.53$
b. Median = 7.45. There are several modes: 6.5, 7.3, 7.8, and 8.7.
c. $\bar{x} = \frac{33.8}{4} = 8.45$,

Median = 8.7

About 1 percentage point higher in winter

23. $22.91, found by $\frac{300(\$20) + 400(\$25) + 400(\$23)}{300 + 400 + 400}$

25. $17.75, found by ($400 + $750 + $2,400)/200

27. 12.8%, found by $\sqrt[5]{(1.08)(1.12)(1.14)(1.26)(1.05)} = 1.128$

29. 12.28% increase, found by $\sqrt[5]{(1.094)(1.138)(1.117)(1.119)(1.147)} = 1.1228$

31. 2.14%, found by $\sqrt[15]{\frac{236.525}{172.2}} - 1$

33. 58.95%, found by $\sqrt[15]{\frac{752,000,000}{720,000}} - 1$

35. **a.** 7, found by 10 − 3
b. 6, found by 30/5
c. 6.8, found by 34/5
d. The difference between the highest number sold (10) and the smallest number sold (3) is 7. The typical squared deviation from 6 is 6.8.

37. **a.** 30, found by 54 − 24
b. 38, found by 380/10
c. 74.4, found by 744/10
d. The difference between 54 and 24 is 30. The average of the squared deviations from 38 is 74.4.

39.

State	Mean	Median	Range
California	33.10	34.0	32
Iowa	24.50	25.0	19

The mean and median ratings were higher, but there was also more variation in California.

41. **a.** 5
b. 4.4, found by

$$\frac{(8 - 5)^2 + (3 - 5)^2 + (7 - 5)^2 + (3 - 5)^2 + (4 - 5)^2}{5}$$

43. **a.** $2.77
b. 1.26, found by

$$\frac{(2.68 - 2.77)^2 + (1.03 - 2.77)^2 + (2.26 - 2.77)^2 + (4.30 - 2.77)^2 + (3.58 - 2.77)^2}{5}$$

45. **a.** Range: 7.3, found by 11.6 − 4.3. Arithmetic mean: 6.94, found by 34.7/5. Variance: 6.5944, found by 32.972/5. Standard deviation: 2.568, found by $\sqrt{6.5944}$.
b. Dennis has a higher mean return (11.76 > 6.94). However, Dennis has greater spread in its returns on equity (16.89 > 6.59).

47. **a.** $\bar{x} = 4$

$$s^2 = \frac{(7 - 4)^2 + \cdots + (3 - 4)^2}{5 - 1} = \frac{22}{5 - 1} = 5.5$$

b. $s = 2.3452$

49. **a.** $\bar{x} = 38$

$$s^2 = \frac{(28 - 38)^2 + \cdots + (42 - 38)^2}{10 - 1}$$

$$= \frac{744}{10 - 1} = 82.667$$

b. $s = 9.0921$

51. **a.** $\bar{x} = \frac{951}{10} = 95.1$

$$s^2 = \frac{(101 - 95.1)^2 + \cdots + (88 - 95.1)^2}{10 - 1}$$

$$= \frac{1,112.9}{9} = 123.66$$

b. $s = \sqrt{123.66} = 11.12$

53. About 69%, found by $1 - 1/(1.8)^2$

55. **a.** About 95%
b. 47.5%, 2.5%

57. Because the exact values in a frequency distribution are not known, the midpoint is used for every member of that class.

59.

Class	f	M	fM	$(M - \bar{x})$	$f(M - \bar{x})^2$
20 up to 30	7	25	175	−22.29	3,477.909
30 up to 40	12	35	420	−12.29	1,812.529
40 up to 50	21	45	945	−2.29	110.126
50 up to 60	18	55	990	7.71	1,069.994
60 up to 70	12	65	780	17.71	3,763.729
	70		3,310		10,234.287

$$\bar{x} = \frac{3,310}{70} = 47.29$$

$$s = \sqrt{\frac{10,234.287}{70 - 1}} = 12.18$$

61.

Number of Clients	f	M	fM	$(M - \bar{x})$	$f(M - \bar{x})^2$
20 up to 30	1	25	25	−19.8	392.04
30 up to 40	15	35	525	−9.8	1,440.60
40 up to 50	22	45	990	0.2	0.88
50 up to 60	8	55	440	10.2	832.32
60 up to 70	4	65	260	20.2	1,632.16
	50		2,240		4,298.00

$\bar{x} = \frac{2,240}{50} = 44.8$

$s = \sqrt{\frac{4,298}{50 - 1}} = 9.37$

63. a. Mean = 5, found by (6 + 4 + 3 + 7 + 5)/5.
Median is 5, found by rearranging the values and selecting the middle value.
b. Population, because all partners were included
c. $\Sigma(x - \mu) = (6 - 5) + (4 - 5) + (3 - 5) + (7 - 5) + (5 - 5) = 0$

65. $\bar{x} = \frac{545}{16} = 34.06$
Median = 37.50

67. The mean is 35.675, found by 1,427/40. The median is 36, found by sorting the data and averaging the 20th and 21st observations.

69. $\bar{x}_w = \frac{\$5.00(270) + \$6.50(300) + \$8.00(100)}{270 + 300 + 100} = \$6.12$

71. $\bar{x}_w = \frac{15,300(4.5) + 10,400(3.0) + 150,600(10.2)}{176,300} = 9.28$

73. $GM = \sqrt[50]{\frac{4,600,000}{42,000}} - 1 = 0.0985$, So about 9.85%

75. a. 55, found by 72 − 17
b. 17.6245, found by the square root of 2795.6/9

77. a. This is a population because it includes all the public universities in Ohio.
b. The mean is 25,165.4.
c. The median is 20,595.
d. The range is 60,560.
e. The standard deviation is 16,344.9.

79. a. There were 13 flights, so all items are considered.
b. $\mu = \frac{2,259}{13} = 173.77$
c. Range = 301 − 7 = 294
$s = \sqrt{\frac{133,846}{13}} = 101.47$

81. a. The mean is \$717.20, found by \$17,930/25. The median is \$717.00 and there are two modes, \$710 and \$722.
b. The range is \$90, found by \$771 − \$681, and the standard deviation is \$24.87, found by the square root of 14,850/24.
c. From \$667.46 up to \$766.94, found by \$717.20 ± 2(\$24.87)

83. a. $\bar{x} = \frac{273}{30} = 9.1$, Median = 9
b. Range = 18 − 4 = 14
$s = \sqrt{\frac{368.7}{30 - 1}} = 3.57$
c. $2^5 = 32$, so suggest 5 classes
$i = \frac{18 - 4}{5} = 2.8$ use $i = 3$

Class	M	f	fM	$M - \bar{x}$	$(M - \bar{x})^2$	$f(M - \bar{x})^2$
3.5 up to 6.5	5	10	50	−4	16	160
6.5 up to 9.5	8	6	48	−1	1	6
9.5 up to 12.5	11	9	99	2	4	36
12.5 up to 15.5	14	4	56	5	25	100
15.5 up to 18.5	17	1	17	8	64	64
			270			366

d. $\bar{x} = \frac{270}{30} = 9.0$
$s = \sqrt{\frac{366}{30 - 1}} = 3.552$
The mean and standard deviation from grouped data are estimates of the mean and standard deviations of the actual values.

85. $\bar{x} = 13 = \frac{910}{70}$
$s = 5.228 = \sqrt{1807.5/69}$

87. a. 1. The mean team salary is \$121.12 million and the median is \$112.91 million. Since the distribution is skewed, the median value of \$112.91 million is more typical.
2. The range is \$154.29 million found by \$223.35 million − \$69.06. The population standard deviation is \$39.66. At least 95% of the team salaries are between \$74.97 million and \$233.61 million; found by \$154.29 million plus or minus 2(\$39.66 million).
b. 4.78% per year, found by $\sqrt[17]{\frac{4.40}{1.99}} - 1 = 0.0478 = 4.78\%$

CHAPTER 4

1. In a histogram, observations are grouped so their individual identity is lost. With a dot plot, the identity of each observation is maintained.

3. a. Dot plot
b. 15
c. 1, 7
d. 2 and 3

5. a. 620 to 629
b. 5
c. 621, 623, 623, 627, 629

7. a. 25
b. One
c. 38,106
d. 60, 61, 63, 63, 65, 65, 69
e. No values
f. 9
g. 9
h. 76
i. 16

9.

Stem	Leaves
0	5
1	28
2	
3	0024789
4	12366
5	2

There were a total of 16 calls studied. The number of calls ranged from 5 to 52. Seven of the 16 subscribers made between 30 and 39 calls.

11. Median = 53, found by $(11 + 1)(\frac{1}{2})$ ∴ 6th value in from lowest
$Q_1 = 49$, found by $(11 + 1)(\frac{1}{4})$ ∴ 3rd value in from lowest
$Q_3 = 55$, found by $(11 + 1)(\frac{3}{4})$ ∴ 9th value in from lowest

13. a. $Q_1 = 33.25$, $Q_3 = 50.25$
b. $D_2 = 27.8$, $D_8 = 52.6$
c. $P_{67} = 47$

15. a. 350
b. $Q_1 = 175$, $Q_3 = 930$
c. 930 − 175 = 755
d. Less than 0, or more than about 2,060
e. There are no outliers.
f. The distribution is positively skewed.

17.
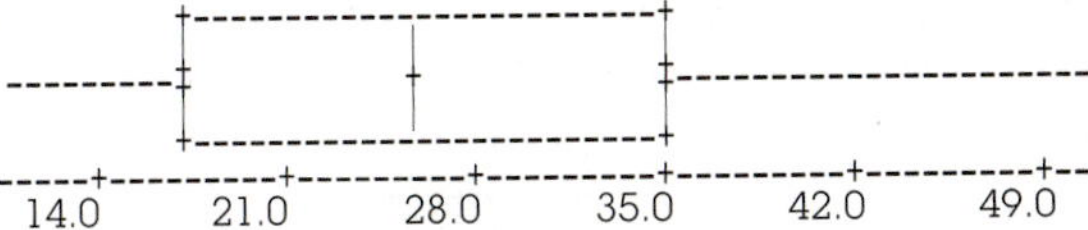

The distribution is somewhat positively skewed. Note that the dashed line above 35 is longer than below 18.

19. a. The mean is 30.8, found by 154/5. The median is 31.0, and the standard deviation is 3.96, found by
$s = \sqrt{\frac{62.8}{4}} = 3.96$

b. −0.15, found by $\dfrac{3(30.8 - 31.0)}{3.96}$

c.

Salary	$\left(\dfrac{x - \bar{x}}{s}\right)$	$\left(\dfrac{x - \bar{x}}{s}\right)^3$
36	1.313131	2.264250504
26	−1.212121	−1.780894343
33	0.555556	0.171467764
28	−0.707071	−0.353499282
31	0.050505	0.000128826
		0.301453469

0.125, found by $[5/(4 \times 3)] \times 0.301$

21. **a.** The mean is 21.93, found by 328.9/15. The median is 15.8, and the standard deviation is 21.18, found by

$$s = \sqrt{\frac{6{,}283}{14}} = 21.18$$

b. 0.868, found by $[3(21.93 - 15.8)]/21.18$

c. 2.444, found by $[15/(14 \times 13)] \times 29.658$

23.

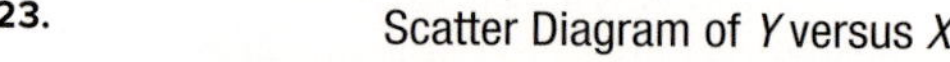

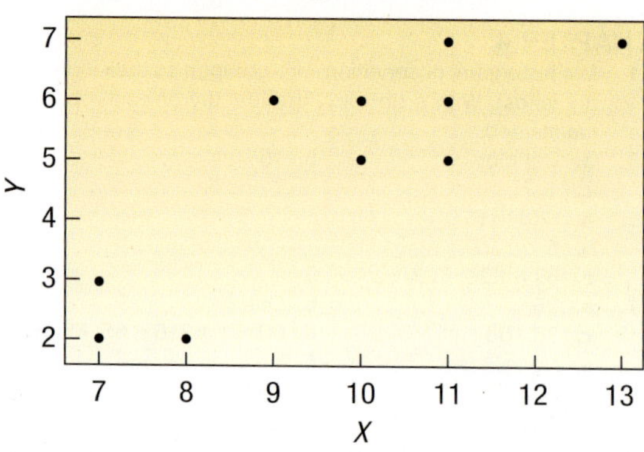

There is a positive relationship between the variables.

25. **a.** Both variables are nominal scale. **b.** Contingency table

c. Men are about twice as likely to order a dessert. From the table, 32% of the men ordered dessert, but only 15% of the women.

27. **a.** Dot plot **b.** 15 **c.** 5

29. Stem-and-leaf $N = 23$

3	3	222
5	3	77
11	4	000002
(6)	4	666666
6	5	222222

31. **a.** $L_{50} = (20 + 1)\frac{50}{100} = 10.50$

$\text{Median} = \dfrac{83.7 + 85.6}{2} = 84.65$

$L_{25} = (21)(.25) = 5.25$

$Q_1 = 66.6 + .25(72.9 - 66.6) = 68.175$

$L_{75} = 21(.75) = 15.75$

$Q_3 = 87.1 + .75(90.2 - 87.1) = 89.425$

b. $L_{26} = 21(.26) = 5.46$

$P_{26} = 66.6 + .46(72.9 - 66.6) = 69.498$

$L_{83} = 21(.83) = 17.43$

$P_{83} = 93.3 + .43(98.6 - 93.3)$
$= 95.579$

c.

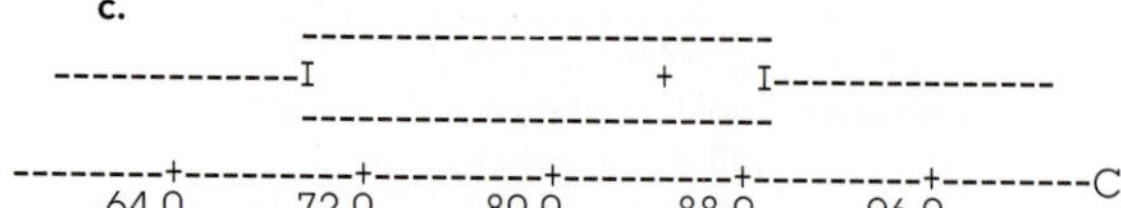

33. **a.** $Q_1 = 26.25$, $Q_3 = 35.75$, Median = 31.50

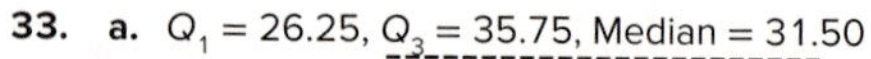

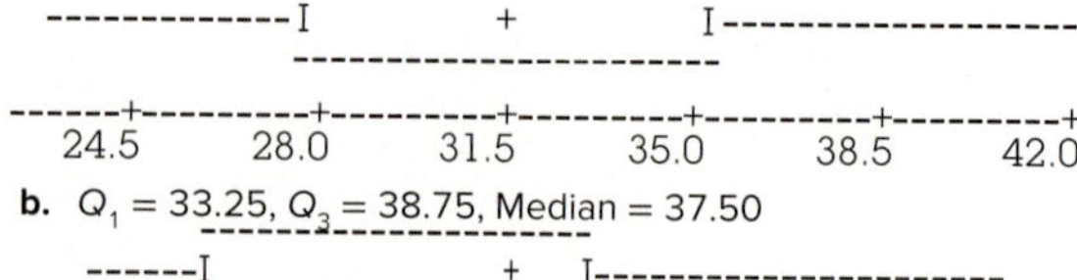

b. $Q_1 = 33.25$, $Q_3 = 38.75$, Median = 37.50

```
                 -----------------------
------I                   +   I-----------------------
                 -----------------------

------+----------+----------+----------+----------+----------+
    32.5       35.0       37.5       40.0       42.5       45.0
```

c. The median time for public transportation is about 6 minutes less. There is more variation in public transportation. The difference between Q_1 and Q_3 is 9.5 minutes for public transportation and 5.5 minutes for private transportation.

35. The distribution is positively skewed. The first quartile is about \$20 and the third quartile is about \$90. There is one outlier located at \$255. The median is about \$50.

37. **a.**

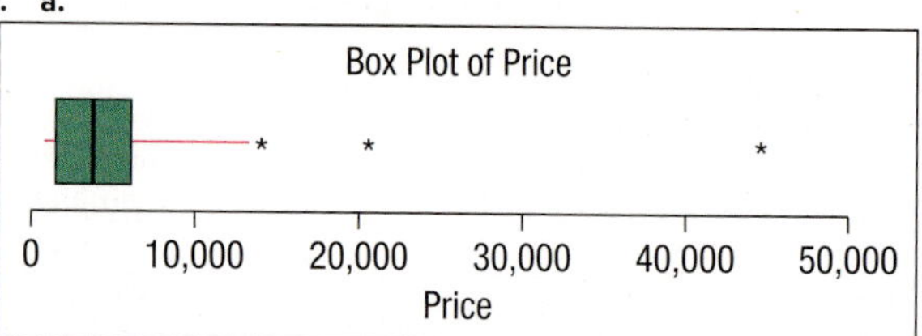

Median is 3,733. First quartile is 1,478. Third quartile is 6,141. So prices over 13,135.5, found by $6{,}141 + 1.5 \times (6{,}141 - 1{,}478)$, are outliers. There are three (13,925; 20,413; and 44,312).

b.

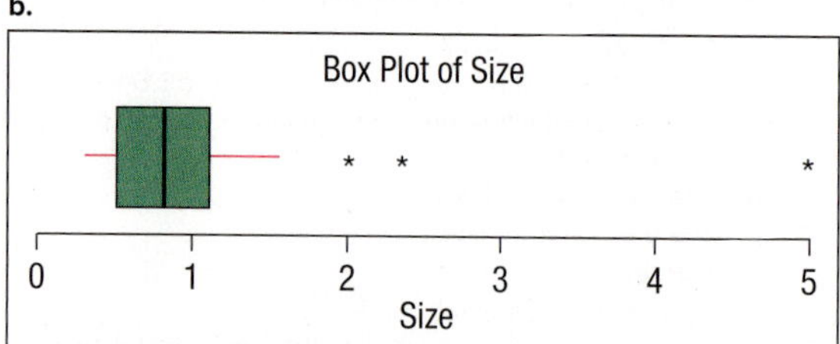

Median is 0.84. First quartile is 0.515. Third quartile is 1.12. So sizes over 2.0275, found by $1.12 + 1.5\,(1.12 - 0.515)$, are outliers. There are three (2.03; 2.35; and 5.03).

c.

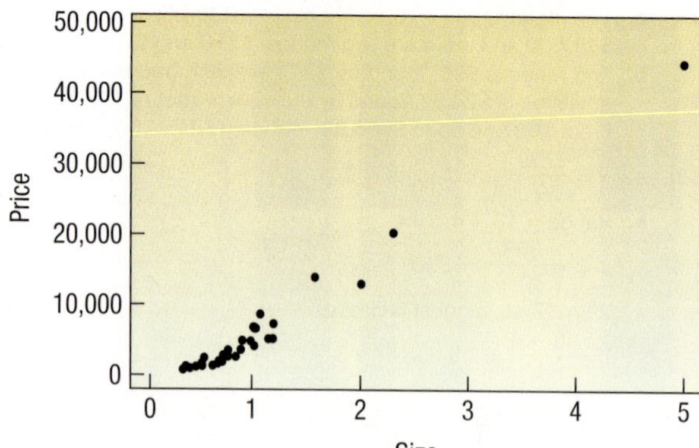

There is a direct association between them. The first observation is larger on both scales.

d.

Shape/ Cut	Average	Good	Ideal	Premium	Ultra Ideal	All
Emerald	0	0	1	0	0	1
Marquise	0	2	0	1	0	3
Oval	0	0	0	1	0	1
Princess	1	0	2	2	0	5
Round	1	3	3	13	3	23
Total	2	5	6	17	3	33

The majority of the diamonds are round (23). Premium cut is most common (17). The Round Premium combination occurs most often (13).

39. $sk = 0.065$ or $sk = \frac{3(7.7143 - 8.0)}{3.9036} = -0.22$

41.

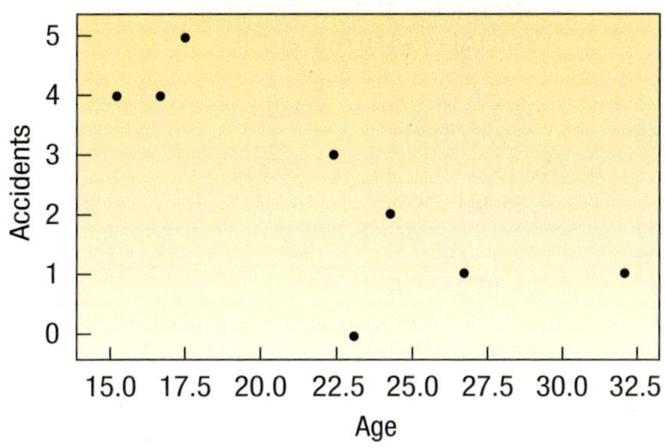

As age increases, the number of accidents decreases.

43. **a.** 139,340,000
b. 5.4% unemployed, found by (7,523/139,340)100
c. Men = 5.64%
Women = 5.12%

45. **a.** Box plot of age assuming the current year is 2016.

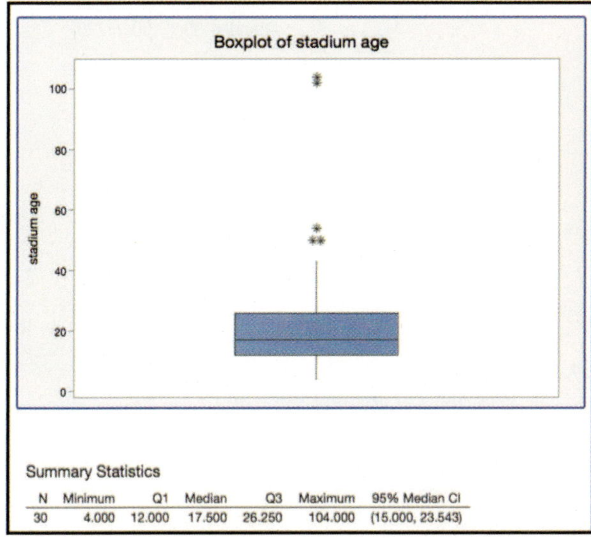

Distribution of stadium is highly skewed to the right. Any stadium older than 47.625 years (Q3 + 1.5(Q3–Q1) = 26.25 + 1.5(26.25–12) is an outlier. Boston, Chicago Cubs, La Dodgers, Oakland, and LA Angels.

b.

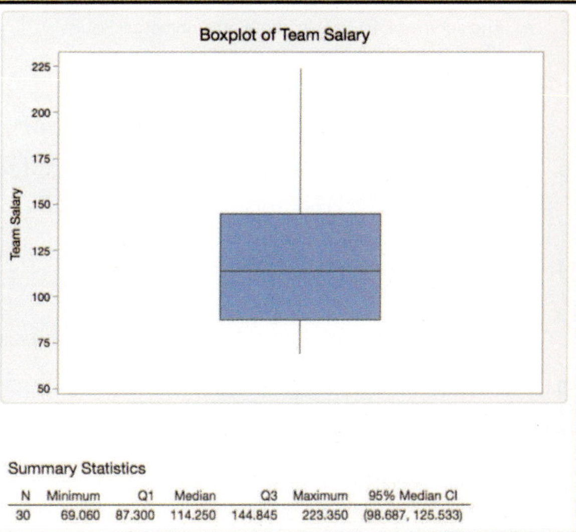

The first quartile is $87.3 million and the third is $144.35 million. Outliers are greater than (Q3 + 1.5(Q3–Q1)) or 144.35 = 1.5*(144.35–87.3) = $229.925 million. The distribution is positively skewed. However in 2016, there were no outliers. **(LO4–4)**

c.

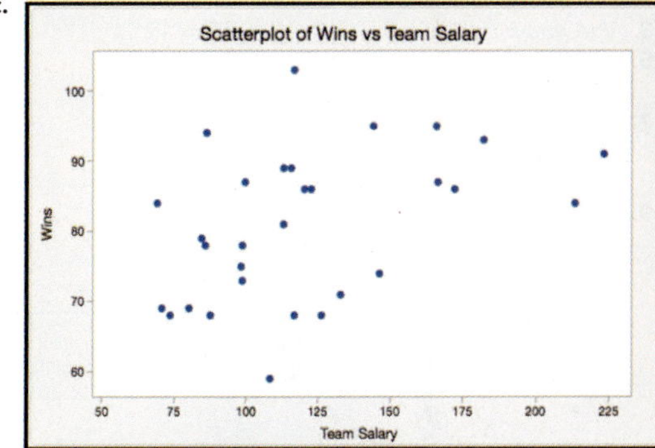

Higher salaries do not necessarily lead to more wins. **(LO4-6)**

d.

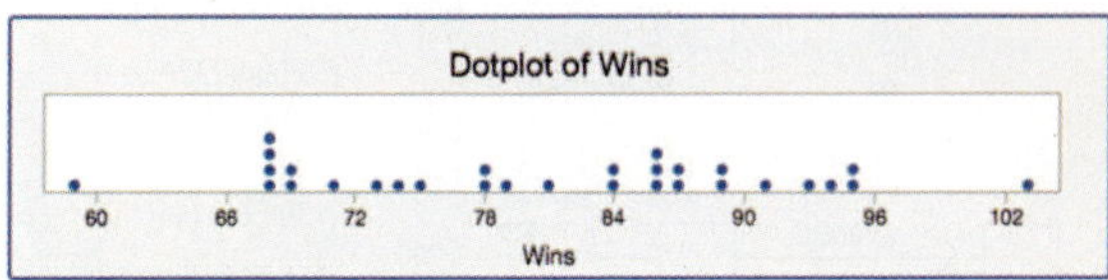

The distribution is fairly uniform between 59 and 103. **(LO4-1)**

CHAPTER 5

1.

Outcome	Person 1	Person 2
1	A	A
2	A	F
3	F	A
4	F	F

3. **a.** .176, found by $\frac{6}{34}$ **b.** Empirical

5. **a.** Empirical
b. Classical

c. Classical
d. Empirical, based on seismological data

7. a. The survey of 40 people about environmental issues
b. 26 or more respond yes, for example.
c. 10/40 = .25
d. Empirical
e. The events are not equally likely, but they are mutually exclusive.

9. a. Answers will vary. Here are some possibilities: 123, 124, 125, 999
b. $(1/10)^3$
c. Classical

11. $P(A \text{ or } B) = P(A) + P(B) = .30 + .20 = .50$
$P(\text{neither}) = 1 - .50 = .50.$

13. a. 102/200 = .51
b. .49, found by 61/200 + 37/200 = .305 + .185. Special rule of addition.

15. $P(\text{above } C) = .25 + .50 = .75$

17. $P(A \text{ or } B) = P(A) + P(B) - P(A \text{ and } B) = .20 + .30 - .15 = .35$

19. When two events are mutually exclusive, it means that if one occurs, the other event cannot occur. Therefore, the probability of their joint occurrence is zero.

21. Let A denote the event the fish is green and B be the event the fish is male.
a. $P(A) = 80/140 = 0.5714$
b. $P(B) = 60/140 = 0.4286$
c. $P(A \text{ and } B) = 36/140 = 0.2571$
d. $P(A \text{ or } B) = P(A) + P(B) - P(A \text{ and } B) = 80/140 + 60/140 - 36/140 = 104/140 = 0.7429$

23. $P(A \text{ and } B) = P(A) \times P(B|A) = .40 \times .30 = .12$

25. .90, found by (.80 + .60) − .5.
.10, found by (1 − .90).

27. a. $P(A_1) = 3/10 = .30$
b. $P(B_1|A_2) = 1/3 = .33$
c. $P(B_2 \text{ and } A_3) = 1/10 = .10$

29. a. A contingency table
b. .27, found by 300/500 × 135/300
c. The tree diagram would appear as:

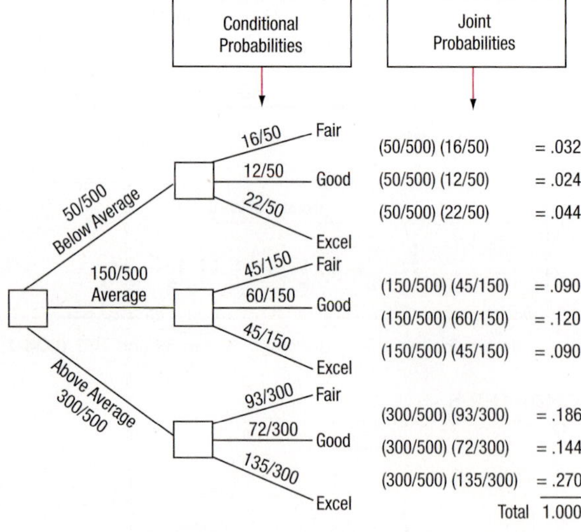

31. a. Out of all 545 students, 171 prefer skiing. So the probability is 171/545, or 0.3138.
b. Out of all 545 students, 155 are in junior college. Thus, the probability is 155/545, or 0.2844.
c. Out of 210 four-year students, 70 prefer ice skating. So the probability is 70/210, or 0.3333.
d. Out of 211 students who prefer snowboarding, 68 are in junior college. So the probability is 68/211, or 0.3223.
e. Out of 180 graduate students, 74 prefer skiing and 47 prefer ice skating. So the probability is (74 + 47)/180 = 121/180, or 0.6722.

33. $$P(A_1 | B_1) = \frac{P(A_1) \times P(B_1 | A_1)}{P(A_1) \times P(B_1 | A_1) + P(A_2) \times P(B_1 | A_2)}$$
$$= \frac{.60 \times .05}{(.60 \times .05) + (.40 \times .10)} = .4286$$

35. $$P(\text{night} | \text{win}) = \frac{P(\text{night})P(\text{win} | \text{night})}{P(\text{night})P(\text{win} | \text{night}) + P(\text{day})P(\text{win} | \text{day})}$$
$$= \frac{(.70)(.50)}{[(.70)(.50)] + [(.30)(.90)]} = .5645$$

37. $P(\text{cash} \mid > \$50)$
$$= \frac{P(\text{cash})\, P(> \$50 | \text{cash})}{[P(\text{cash})\, P(> \$50 | \text{cash}) + P(\text{credit})\, P(> \$50 | \text{credit}) + P(\text{debit})\, P(> \$50 | \text{debit})]}$$
$$= \frac{(.30)(.20)}{(.30)(.20) + (.30)(.90) + (.40)(.60)} = .1053$$

39. a. 78,960,960
b. 840, found by (7)(6)(5)(4). That is 7!/3!
c. 10, found by 5!/3!2!

41. 210, found by (10)(9)(8)(7)/(4)(3)(2)

43. 120, found by 5!

45. (4)(8)(3) = 96 combinations

47. a. Asking teenagers to compare their reactions to a newly developed soft drink.
b. Answers will vary. One possibility is more than half of the respondents like it.

49. Subjective

51. a. 4/9, found by (2/3) · (2/3)
b. 3/4, because (3/4) · (2/3) = 0.5

53. a. .8145, found by $(.95)^4$
b. Special rule of multiplication
c. $P(A \text{ and } B \text{ and } C \text{ and } D) = P(A) \times P(B) \times P(C) \times P(D)$

55. a. .08, found by .80 × .10
b. No; 90% of females attended college, 78% of males
c.

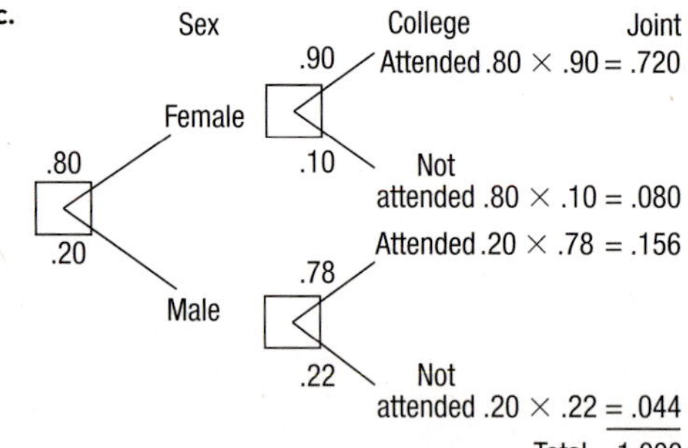

d. Yes, because all the possible outcomes are shown on the tree diagram.

57. a. 0.57, found by 57/100
b. 0.97, found by (57/100) + (40/100)
c. Yes, because an employee cannot be both
d. 0.03, found by 1 − 0.97

59. a. 1/2, found by (2/3)(3/4)
b. 1/12, found by (1/3)(1/4)
c. 11/12, found by 1 − 1/12

61. a. 0.9039, found by $(0.98)^5$
b. 0.0961, found by 1 − 0.9039

63. a. 0.0333, found by (4/10)(3/9)(2/8)
b. 0.1667, found by (6/10)(5/9)(4/8)
c. 0.8333, found by 1 − 0.1667
d. Dependent

65. **a.** 0.3818, found by (9/12)(8/11)(7/10)
b. 0.6182, found by 1 − 0.3818

67. **a.** $P(S) \cdot P(R|S) = .60(.85) = 0.51$
b. $P(S) \cdot P(PR|S) = .60(1 - .85) = 0.09$

69. **a.** $P(\text{not perfect}) = P(\text{bad sector}) + P(\text{defective})$
$$= \frac{112}{1{,}000} + \frac{31}{1{,}000} = .143$$
b. $P(\text{defective} \mid \text{not perfect}) = \frac{.031}{.143} = .217$

71. $$P(\text{poor} \mid \text{profit}) = \frac{.10(.20)}{.10(.20) + .60(.80) + .30(.60)} = .0294$$

73. **a.** 0.1 + 0.02 = 0.12
b. 1 − 0.12 = 0.88
c. $(0.88)^3 = 0.6815$
d. 1 − .6815 = 0.3185

75. Yes, 256 is found by 2^8.

77. .9744, found by $1 - (.40)^4$

79. **a.** 0.193, found by .15 + .05 − .0075 = .193
b. .0075, found by (.15)(.05)

81. **a.** $P(F \text{ and } >60) = .25$, found by solving with the general rule of multiplication: $P(F) \cdot P(>60|F) = (.5)(.5)$
b. 0
c. .3333, found by 1/3

83. $26^4 = 456{,}976$

85. 1/3, 628,800

87. **a.** $P(D) = .20(.03) + .30(.04) + .25(.07) + .25(.065) = .05175$
b. $$P(\text{Tyson} \mid \text{defective}) = \frac{.20(.03)}{[.20(.03) + .30(.04) + .25(.07) + .25(.065)]} = .1159$$

Supplier	Joint	Revised
Tyson	.00600	.1159
Fuji	.01200	.2319
Kirkpatricks	.01750	.3382
Parts	.01625	.3140
	.05175	1.0000

89. 0.512, found by $(0.8)^3$

91. .525, found by $1 - (.78)^3$

93. **a.**

Winning Season	Low Attendance	Moderate Attendance	High Attendance	Total
No	7	6	1	14
Yes	1	9	6	16
Total	8	15	7	30

1. 0.5333 found by 16/30
2. 0.5667 found by 16/30 + 5/30 − 4/30 = 17/30
3. 0.8571 found by 6/7
4. 0.0333 found by 1/30

b.

	Losing Season	Winning Season	Total
New	8	8	16
Old	6	8	14
Total	14	16	30

1. 0.4667 found by 14/30
2. 0.2667 found by 8/30
3. 0.8000 found by 16/30 + 16/30 − 8/30 = 24/30

CHAPTER 6

1. Mean = 1.3, variance = .81, found by:
$$\mu = 0(.20) + 1(.40) + 2(.30) + 3(.10) = 1.3$$
$$\sigma^2 = (0 - 1.3)^2(.2) + (1 - 1.3)^2(.4) + (2 - 1.3)^2(.3) + (3 - 1.3)^2(.1) = .81$$

3. Mean = 14.5, variance = 27.25, found by:
$$\mu = 5(.1) + 10(.3) + 15(.2) + 20(.4) = 14.5$$
$$\sigma^2 = (5 - 14.5)^2(.1) + (10 - 14.5)^2(.3) + (15 - 14.5)^2(.2) + (20 - 14.5)^2(.4) = 27.25$$

5. **a.**

Calls, x	Frequency	$P(x)$	$xP(x)$	$(x - \mu)^2 P(x)$
0	8	.16	0	.4624
1	10	.20	.20	.0980
2	22	.44	.88	.0396
3	9	.18	.54	.3042
4	1	.02	.08	.1058
	50		1.70	1.0100

b. Discrete distribution, because only certain outcomes are possible.
c. $\mu = \Sigma x \cdot P(x) = 1.70$
d. $\sigma = \sqrt{1.01} = 1.005$

7.

Amount	$P(x)$	$xP(x)$	$(x - \mu)^2 P(x)$
10	.50	5	60.50
25	.40	10	6.40
50	.08	4	67.28
100	.02	2	124.82
		21	259.00

a. $\mu = \Sigma xP(x) = 21$
b. $\sigma^2 = \Sigma(x - \mu)^2 P(x) = 259$
$\sigma = \sqrt{259} = 16.093$

9. **a.** $P(2) = \frac{4!}{2!(4-2)!}(.25)^2(.75)^{4-2} = .2109$
b. $P(3) = \frac{4!}{3!(4-3)!}(.25)^3(.75)^{4-3} = .0469$

11. **a.**

x	$P(x)$
0	.064
1	.288
2	.432
3	.216

b. $\mu = 1.8$
$\sigma^2 = 0.72$
$\sigma = \sqrt{0.72} = .8485$

13. **a.** .2668, found by $P(2) = \frac{9!}{(9-2)!2!}(.3)^2(.7)^7$
b. .1715, found by $P(4) = \frac{9!}{(9-4)!4!}(.3)^4(.7)^5$
c. .0404, found by $P(0) = \frac{9!}{(9-0)!0!}(.3)^0(.7)^9$

15. **a.** .2824, found by $P(0) = \frac{12!}{(12-0)!0!}(.1)^0(.9)^{12}$
b. .3766, found by $P(1) = \frac{12!}{(12-1)!1!}(.1)^1(.9)^{11}$
c. .2301, found by $P(2) = \frac{12!}{(12-2)!2!}(.1)^2(.9)^{10}$
d. $\mu = 1.2$, found by 12(.1)
$\sigma = 1.0392$, found by $\sqrt{1.08}$

17. a. 0.1858, found by $\frac{15!}{2!13!}(0.23)^2(0.77)^{13}$
b. 0.1416, found by $\frac{15!}{5!10!}(0.23)^5(0.77)^{10}$
c. 3.45, found by (0.23)(15)

19. a. 0.296, found by using Appendix B.1 with n of 8, π of 0.30, and x of 2
b. $P(x \leq 2) = 0.058 + 0.198 + 0.296 = 0.552$
c. 0.448, found by $P(x \geq 3) = 1 - P(x \leq 2) = 1 - 0.552$

21. a. 0.387, found from Appendix B.1 with n of 9, π of 0.90, and x of 9
b. $P(x < 5) = 0.001$
c. 0.992, found by 1 – 0.008
d. 0.947, found by 1 – 0.053

23. a. $\mu = 10.5$, found by 15(0.7) and $\sigma = \sqrt{15(0.7)(0.3)} = 1.7748$
b. 0.2061, found by $\frac{15!}{10!5!}(0.7)^{10}(0.3)^5$
c. 0.4247, found by 0.2061 + 0.2186
d. 0.5154, found by
0.2186 + 0.1700 + 0.0916 + 0.0305 + 0.0047

25. $P(2) = \frac{[{}_6C_2][{}_4C_1]}{{}_{10}C_3} = \frac{15(4)}{120} = .50$

27. N is 10, the number of loans in the population; S is 3, the number of underwater loans in the population; x is 0, the number of selected underwater loans in the sample; and n is 2, the size of the sample. Use formula (6–6) to find

$$P(0) = \frac{({}_7C_2)({}_3C_0)}{{}_{10}C_2} = \frac{21(1)}{45} = 0.4667.$$

29. $P(2) = \frac{[{}_9C_3][{}_6C_2]}{[{}_{15}C_5]} = \frac{84(15)}{3003} = .4196$

31. a. .6703
b. .3297

33. a. .0613
b. .0803

35. $\mu = 6$
$P(x \geq 5) = 1 - (.0025 + .0149 + .0446 + .0892 + .1339)$
$= .7149$

37. A random variable is an outcome that results from a chance experiment. A probability distribution also includes the likelihood of each possible outcome.

39. $\mu = \$1{,}000(.25) + \$2{,}000(.60) + \$5{,}000(.15) = \$2{,}200$
$\sigma^2 = (1{,}000 - 2{,}200)^2 .25 + (2{,}000 - 2{,}200)^2 .60 + (5{,}000 - 2{,}200)^2 .15$
$= 1{,}560{,}000$

41. $\mu = 12(.25) + \cdots + 15(.1) = 13.2$
$\sigma^2 = (12 - 13.2)^2 .25 + \cdots + (15 - 13.2)^2 .10 = 0.86$
$\sigma = \sqrt{0.86} = .927$

43. a. 5 10(.35) = 3.5
b. $P(x = 4) = {}_{10}C_4 (.35)^4 (.65)^6 = 210(.0150)(.0754) = .2375$
c. $P(x \geq 4) = {}_{10}C_x (.35)^x (.65)^{10-x}$
$= 2375 + .1536 + \cdots + .0000 = .4862$

45. a. 6, found by 0.4 × 15
b. 0.0245, found by $\frac{15!}{10!5!}(0.4)^{10}(0.6)^5$
c. 0.0338, found by
0.0245 + 0.0074 + 0.0016 + 0.0003 + 0.0000
d. 0.0093, found by 0.0338 – 0.0245

47. a. $\mu = 20(0.075) = 1.5$
$\sigma = \sqrt{20(0.075)(0.925)} = 1.1779$
b. 0.2103, found by $\frac{20!}{0!20!}(0.075)^0(0.925)^{20}$
c. 0.7897, found by 1 – 0.2103

49. a. 0.1311, found by $\frac{16!}{4!12!}(0.15)^4(0.85)^{12}$
b. 2.4, found by (0.15)(16)
c. 0.2100, found by 1 – 0.0743 – 0.2097 – 0.2775 – 0.2285

51. 0.2784, found by 0.1472 + 0.0811 + 0.0348 + 0.0116 + 0.0030 + 0.0006 + 0.0001 + 0.0000

53. a.

0	0.0002	7	0.2075
1	0.0019	8	0.1405
2	0.0116	9	0.0676
3	0.0418	10	0.0220
4	0.1020	11	0.0043
5	0.1768	12	0.0004
6	0.2234		

b. $\mu = 12(0.52) = 6.24$ $\sigma = \sqrt{12(0.52)(0.48)} = 1.7307$
c. 0.1768
d. 0.3343, found by
0.0002 + 0.0019 + 0.0116 + 0.0418 + 0.1020 + 0.1768

55. a. $P(1) = \frac{[{}_7C_2][{}_3C_1]}{[{}_{10}C_3]} = \frac{(21)(3)}{120} = .5250$
b. $P(0) = \frac{[{}_7C_3][{}_3C_0]}{[{}_{10}C_3]} = \frac{(35)(1)}{120} = .2917$
$P(x \geq 1) = 1 - P(0) = 1 - .2917 = .7083$

57. $P(x = 0) = \frac{[{}_8C_4][{}_4C_0]}{[{}_{12}C_4]} = \frac{70}{495} = .141$

59. a. .0498 b. .7746, found by $(1 - .0498)^5$

61. a. .0183 b. .1954
c. .6289 d. .5665

63. a. 0.1733, found by $\frac{(3.1)^4 e^{-3.1}}{4!}$
b. 0.0450, found by $\frac{(3.1)^0 e^{-3.1}}{0!}$
c. 0.9550, found by 1 – 0.0450

65. $\mu = n\pi = 23\left(\frac{2}{113}\right) = .407$

$$P(2) = \frac{(.407)^2 e^{-.407}}{2!} = 0.0551$$

$$P(0) = \frac{(.407)^0 e^{-.407}}{0!} = 0.6656$$

67. Let $\mu = n\pi = 155(1/3{,}709) = 0.042$

$$P(4) = \frac{0.042^4 e^{-0.042}}{4!} = 0.00000012$$

Very unlikely!

69. a. $\mu = n\pi = 15(.67) = 10.05$
$\sigma = \sqrt{n\pi(1 - \pi)} = \sqrt{15(.67)(.33)} = 1.8211$
b. $P(8) = {}_{15}C_8(.67)^8(.33)^7 = 6435(.0406)(.000426) = .1114$
c. $P(x \geq 8) = .1114 + .1759 + \cdots + .0025 = .9163$

71. The mean number of home runs per game is 2.3, found. The average season home runs per team is 187. Then (187 × 2)/162 = 2.3.
a. $P(0) = \frac{2.3^0 e^{-2.3}}{0!} = 0.1003$
b. $P(2) = \frac{2.3^2 e^{-2.3}}{2!} = 0.2652$
c. $P(x \geq 4) = 0.1981$, found by
1 – (0.1169 + 0.0538 + 0.0206 + 0.0068)

CHAPTER 7

1. a. $b = 10, a = 6$ b. $\mu = \frac{6 + 10}{2} = 8$
c. $\sigma = \sqrt{\frac{(10 - 6)^2}{12}} = 1.1547$
d. $\text{Area} = \frac{1}{(10 - 6)} \cdot \frac{(10 - 6)}{1} = 1$
e. $P(x > 7) = \frac{1}{(10 - 6)} \cdot \frac{10 - 7}{1} = \frac{3}{4} = .75$
f. $P(7 \leq x \leq 9) = \frac{1}{(10 - 6)} \cdot \frac{(9 - 7)}{1} = \frac{2}{4} = .50$

3. a. 0.30, found by (30 − 27)/(30 − 20)
   b. 0.40, found by (24 − 20)/(30 − 20)

5. a. $a = 0.5, b = 3.00$
   b. $\mu = \frac{0.5 + 3.00}{2} = 1.75$

   $\sigma = \sqrt{\frac{(3.00 - .50)^2}{12}} = .72$

   c. $P(x < 1) = \frac{1}{(3.0 - 0.5)} \cdot \frac{1 - .5}{1} = \frac{.5}{2.5} = 0.2$

   d. 0, found by $\frac{1}{(3.0 - 0.5)} \frac{(1.0 - 1.0)}{1}$

   e. $P(x > 1.5) = \frac{1}{(3.0 - 0.5)} \cdot \frac{3.0 - 1.5}{1} = \frac{1.5}{2.5} = 0.6$

7. The actual shape of a normal distribution depends on its mean and standard deviation. Thus, there is a normal distribution, and an accompanying normal curve, for a mean of 7 and a standard deviation of 2. There is another normal curve for a mean of $25,000 and a standard deviation of $1,742, and so on.

9. a. 490 and 510, found by 500 ± 1(10)
   b. 480 and 520, found by 500 ± 2(10)
   c. 470 and 530, found by 500 ± 3(10)

11. $z_{Rob} = \frac{\$50,000 - \$60,000}{\$5,000} = -2$

    $z_{Rachel} = \frac{\$50,000 - \$35,000}{\$8,000} = 1.875$

    Adjusting for their industries, Rob is well below average and Rachel well above.

13. a. 1.25, found by $z = \frac{25 - 20}{4.0} = 1.25$
    b. 0.3944, found in Appendix B.3
    c. 0.3085, found by $z = \frac{18 - 20}{2.5} = -0.5$

    Find 0.1915 in Appendix B.3 for $z = -0.5$, then 0.5000 − 0.1915 = 0.3085

15. a. 0.3413, found by $z = \frac{\$24 - \$20.50}{\$3.50} = 1.00$, then find 0.3413 in Appendix B.3 for $z = 1$
    b. 0.1587, found by 0.5000 − 0.3413 = 0.1587
    c. 0.3336, found by $z = \frac{\$19.00 - \$20.50}{\$3.50} = -0.43$

    Find 0.1664 in Appendix B.3, for $z = -0.43$, then 0.5000 − 0.1664 = 0.3336

17. a. 0.8276: First find $z = -1.5$, found by (44 − 50)/4 and $z = 1.25 = (55 - 50)/4$. The area between −1.5 and 0 is 0.4332 and the area between 0 and 1.25 is 0.3944, both from Appendix B.3. Then adding the two areas we find that 0.4332 + 0.3944 = 0.8276.
    b. 0.1056, found by 0.5000 − .3944, where $z = 1.25$
    c. 0.2029: Recall that the area for $z = 1.25$ is 0.3944, and the area for $z = 0.5$, found by (52 − 50)/4, is 0.1915. Then subtract 0.3944 − 0.1915 and find 0.2029.

19. a. 0.2514: Begin by using formula (7–5) to find the z value for $3,100, which is (3,100 − 2,800)/450, or 0.67. Then see Appendix B.3 to find the area between 0 and 0.67, which is 0.2486. Finally, since the area of interest is beyond 0.67, subtract that probability from 0.5000. The result is 0.5000 − 0.2486, or 0.2514.
    b. 0.1908: Use formula (7–5) to find the z value for $3,500, which is (3,500 − 2,800)/450, or 1.56. Then see Appendix B.3 for the area under the standard normal curve. That probability is 0.4406. Since the two points (1.56 and 0.66) are on the same side of the mean, subtract the smaller probability from the larger. The result is 0.4406 − 0.2486 = 0.1920.
    c. 0.8294: Use formula (7–5) to find the z value for $2,250, which is −1.22, found by (2,250 − 2,800)/450. The corresponding area is 0.3888. Since 1.56 and −1.22 are on different sides of the mean, add the corresponding probabilities. Thus, we find 0.3888 + 0.4406 = 0.8294.

21. a. 0.0764, found by $z = (20 - 15)/3.5 = 1.43$, then 0.5000 − 0.4236 = 0.0764
    b. 0.9236, found by 0.5000 + 0.4236, where $z = 1.43$
    c. 0.1185, found by $z = (12 - 15)/3.5 = -0.86$.
    The area under the curve is 0.3051, then $z = (10 - 15)/3.5 = -1.43$. The area is 0.4236. Finally, 0.4236 − 0.3051 = 0.1185.

23. $x = 56.60$, found by adding 0.5000 (the area left of the mean) and then finding a z value that forces 45% of the data to fall inside the curve. Solving for x: $1.65 = (x - 50)/4$, so $x = 56.60$.

25. $1,630, found by $2,100 − 1.88($250)

27. a. 214.8 hours: Find a z value where 0.4900 of area is between 0 and z. That value is $z = 2.33$. Then solve for x: $2.33 = (x - 195)/8.5$, so $x = 214.8$ hours.
    b. 270.2 hours: Find a z value where 0.4900 of area is between 0 and $(-z)$. That value is $z = -2.33$. Then solve for x: $-2.33 = (x - 290)/8.5$, so $x = 270.2$ hours.

29. 41.7%, found by 12 + 1.65(18)

31. a. $\mu = n\pi = 50(0.25) = 12.5$

    $\sigma^2 = n\pi(1 - \pi) = 12.5(1 - 0.25) = 9.375$

    $\sigma = \sqrt{9.375} = 3.0619$

    b. 0.2578, found by (14.5 − 12.5)/3.0619 = 0.65.
    The area is 0.2422. Then 0.5000 − 0.2422 = 0.2578.
    c. 0.2578, found by (10.5 − 12.5)/3.0619 = −0.65.
    The area is 0.2422. Then 0.5000 − 0.2422 = 0.2578.

33. a. $\mu = n\pi = 80(0.07) = 5.6 \qquad \sigma = \sqrt{5.208} = 2.2821$
    0.3483, found from $z = (6.5 - 5.6)/2.2821 = 0.39$ with the corresponding area of 0.1517, then 0.5000 − 0.1517 = 0.3483
    b. 0.5160, found from $z = (5.5 - 5.6)/2.2821 = -0.04$ with the corresponding area of 0.0160, then 0.5000 + 0.0160 = 0.5160
    c. .1677, found by .5160 − 0.3483.

35. a. Yes. (1) There are two mutually exclusive outcomes: overweight and not overweight. (2) It is the result of counting the number of successes (overweight members). (3) Each trial is independent. (4) The probability of 0.30 remains the same for each trial.
    b. 0.0084, found by

    $\mu = 500(0.30) = 150$

    $\sigma^2 = 500(.30)(.70) = 105$

    $\sigma = \sqrt{105} = 10.24695$

    $z = \frac{x - \mu}{\sigma} = \frac{174.5 - 150}{10.24695} = 2.39$

    The area under the curve for 2.39 is 0.4916.
    Then 0.5000 − 0.4916 = 0.0084.

    c. 0.8461, found by $z = \frac{139.5 - 150}{10.24695} = -1.02$

    The area between 139.5 and 150 is 0.3461.
    Adding 0.3461 + 0.5000 = 0.8461.

37. a. 0.3935, found by $1 - e^{[(-1/60)(30)]}$
    b. 0.1353, found by $e^{[(-1/60)(120)]}$
    c. 0.1859, found by $e^{[(-1/60)(45)]} - e^{[(-1/60)(75)]}$
    d. 41.59 seconds, found by −60 ln(0.5)

39. a. 0.5654, found by $1 - e^{[(-1/18)(15)]}$, and 0.2212, found by $1 - e^{[(-1/60)(15)]}$
    b. 0.0013, found by $e^{[(-1/18)(120)]}$, and 0.1353, found by $e^{[(-1/60)(120)]}$
    c. 0.1821, found by $e^{[(-1/18)(30)]} - e^{[(-1/18)(90)]}$, and 0.3834, found by $e^{[(-1/60)(30)]} - e^{[(-1/60)(90)]}$
    d. 4 minutes, found by −18 ln(0.8), and 13.4 minutes, found by −60 ln(0.8)

41. a. $\mu = \frac{11.96 + 12.05}{2} = 12.005$

    b. $\sigma = \sqrt{\frac{(12.05 - 11.96)^2}{12}} = .0260$

    c. $P(x < 12) = \frac{1}{(12.05 - 11.96)} \frac{12.00 - 11.96}{1} = \frac{.04}{.09} = .44$

d. $P(x > 11.98) = \frac{1}{(12.05 - 11.96)}\left(\frac{12.05 - 11.98}{1}\right)$
$= \frac{.07}{.09} = .78$

e. All cans have more than 11.00 ounces, so the probability is 100%.

43. a. $\mu = \frac{4 + 10}{2} = 7$

b. $\sigma = \sqrt{\frac{(10 - 4)^2}{12}} = 1.732$

c. $P(x < 6) = \frac{1}{(10 - 4)} \cdot \left(\frac{6 - 4}{1}\right) = \frac{2}{6} = .33$

d. $P(x > 5) = \frac{1}{(10 - 4)} \cdot \left(\frac{10 - 5}{1}\right) = \frac{5}{6} = .83$

45. a. −0.4 for net sales, found by (170 − 180)/25. 2.92 for employees, found by (1,850 − 1,500)/120.

b. Net sales are 0.4 standard deviation below the mean. Employees is 2.92 standard deviation above the mean.

c. 65.54% of the aluminum fabricators have greater net sales compared with Clarion, found by 0.1554 + 0.5000. Only 0.18% have more employees than Clarion, found by 0.5000 − 0.4982.

47. a. 0.5000, because $z = \frac{430 - 890}{90} = -5.11$

b. 0.2514, found by 0.5000 − 0.2486

c. 0.6374, found by 0.2486 + 0.3888

d. 0.3450, found by 0.3888 − 0.0438

49. a. 0.3015, found by 0.5000 − 0.1985

b. 0.2579, found by 0.4564 − 0.1985

c. 0.0011, found by 0.5000 − 0.4989

d. 1,818, found by 1,280 + 1.28(420)

51. a. 90.82%: First find $z = 1.33$, found by (40 − 34)/4.5. The area between 0 and 1.33 is 0.4082 hours/week for women. Then add 0.5000 and 0.4082 and find 0.9082, or 90.82%.

b. 78.23%: First find $z = -0.78$, found by (25 − 29)/5.1. The area between 0 and (−0.78) is 0.2823. Then add 0.5000 and 0.2823 and find 0.7823, or 78.23%.

c. Find a z value where 0.4900 of the area is between 0 and z. That value is 2.33. Then solve for x: $2.33 = (x - 34)/4.5$, so $x =$ 44.5 hours/week for women.
40.9 hours/week for men: $2.33 = (x - 29)/5.1$,
so $x = 40.9$ hours/week.

53. About 4,099 units, found by solving for x. $1.65 = (x - 4{,}000)/60$

55. a. 15.39%, found by (8 − 10.3)/2.25 = −1.02,
then 0.5000 − 0.3461 = 0.1539.

b. 17.31%, found by:
$z = (12 - 10.3)/2.25 = 0.76$. Area is 0.2764.
$z = (14 - 10.3)/2.25 = 1.64$. Area is 0.4495.
The area between 12 and 14 is 0.1731, found by 0.4495 − 0.2764.

c. On 99.73% of the days, returns are between 3.55 and 17.05, found by 10.3 ± 3(2.25). Thus, the chance of less than 3.55 returns is rather remote.

57. a. 0.9678, found by:
$\mu = 60(0.64) = 38.4$
$\sigma^2 = 60(0.64)(0.36) = 13.824$
$\sigma = \sqrt{13.824} = 3.72$
Then (31.5 − 38.4)/3.72 = −1.85, for which the area is 0.4678.
Then 0.5000 + 0.4678 = 0.9678.

b. 0.0853, found by (43.5 − 38.4)/3.72 = 1.37, for which the area is 0.4147. Then 0.5000 − 0.4147 = .0853.

c. 0.8084, found by 0.4441 + 0.3643

d. 0.0348, found by 0.4495 − 0.4147

59. 0.0968, found by:
$\mu = 50(0.40) = 20$
$\sigma^2 = 50(0.40)(0.60) = 12$
$\sigma = \sqrt{12} = 3.46$
$z = (24.5 - 20)/3.46 = 1.30.$
The area is 0.4032. Then, for 25 or more, 0.5000 − 0.4032 = 0.0968.

61. a. $1.65 = (45 - \mu)/5$ $\mu = 36.75$

b. $1.65 = (45 - \mu)/10$ $\mu = 28.5$

c. $z = (30 - 28.5)/10 = 0.15$, then 0.5000 + 0.0596 = 0.5596

63. a. 21.19%, found by $z = (9.00 - 9.20)/0.25 = -0.80$, so 0.5000 − 0.2881 = 0.2119

b. Increase the mean. $z = (9.00 - 9.25)/0.25 = -1.00$, $P =$ 0.5000 − 0.3413 = 0.1587.
Reduce the standard deviation. $\sigma = (9.00 - 9.20)/0.15 =$ −1.33; $P = 0.5000 - 0.4082 = 0.0918$.
Reducing the standard deviation is better because a smaller percent of the hams will be below the limit.

65. a. $z = (60 - 52)/5 = 1.60$, so 0.5000 − 0.4452 = 0.0548

b. Let $z = 0.67$, so $0.67 = (x - 52)/5$ and $x = 55.35$, set mileage at 55,350

c. $z = (45 - 52)/5 = -1.40$, so 0.5000 − 0.4192 = 0.0808

67. $\frac{470 - \mu}{\sigma} = 0.25$ $\frac{500 - \mu}{\sigma} = 1.28$ $\sigma = 29{,}126$ and
$\mu = 462{,}718$

69. $\mu = 150(0.15) = 22.5$ $\sigma = \sqrt{150(0.15)(0.85)} = 4.37$
$z = (29.5 - 22.5)/4.37 = 1.60$
$P(z > 1.60) = .05000 - 0.4452 = 0.0548$

71. a. 0.4262, found by $1 - e^{[(-1/27)(15)]}$

b. 0.1084, found by $e^{[(-1/27)(60)]}$

c. 0.1403, found by $e^{[(-1/27)(30)]} - e^{[(-1/27)(45)]}$

d. 2.84 secs, found by −27 ln(0.9)

73. a. 0.2835, found by $1 - e^{[(-1/300{,}000)(100{,}000)]}$

b. 0.1889, found by $e^{[(-1/300{,}000)(500{,}000)]}$

c. 0.2020, found by $e^{[(-1/300{,}000)(200{,}000)]} - e^{[(-1/300{,}000)(350{,}000)]}$

d. Both the mean and standard deviation are 300,000 hours.

75. a. 0.0427, found by 0.5000 − 0.4573 with $z = (3.500 - 2.439)/0.618 = 1.72$; leads to 1.3 teams, found by 30(0.0427). One team actually had attendance of more than 3.5 million. So the estimate is accurate.

b. 0.7019, found by 0.5000 + 0.2019 with $z = (100 - 121)/40.0 = 0.53$; leads to 21.1 teams with salaries of more than $100 million, found by 30(0.7019). 18 teams actually had salaries of more than $100 million. We may want to try another comparison to assess if the normal probability distribution is a good description of salary.

CHAPTER 8

1. a. 303 Louisiana, 5155 S. Main, 3501 Monroe, 2652 W. Central

b. Answers will vary.

c. 630 Dixie Hwy, 835 S. McCord Rd, 4624 Woodville Rd

d. Answers will vary.

3. a. Bob Schmidt Chevrolet
Great Lakes Ford Nissan
Grogan Towne Chrysler
Southside Lincoln Mercury
Rouen Chrysler Jeep Eagle

b. Answers will vary.

c. York Automotive
Thayer Chevrolet Toyota
Franklin Park Lincoln Mercury
Mathews Ford Oregon Inc.
Valiton Chrysler

5. a.

Sample	Values	Sum	Mean
1	12, 12	24	12
2	12, 14	26	13
3	12, 16	28	14
4	12, 14	26	13
5	12, 16	28	14
6	14, 16	30	15

b. $\mu_{\bar{x}} = (12 + 13 + 14 + 13 + 14 + 15)/6 = 13.5$

$\mu = (12 + 12 + 14 + 16)/4 = 13.5$

c. More dispersion with population data compared to the sample means. The sample means vary from 12 to 15, whereas the population varies from 12 to 16.

7. a.

Sample	Values	Sum	Mean
1	12, 12, 14	38	12.66
2	12, 12, 15	39	13.00
3	12, 12, 20	44	14.66
4	14, 15, 20	49	16.33
5	12, 14, 15	41	13.66
6	12, 14, 15	41	13.66
7	12, 15, 20	47	15.66
8	12, 15, 20	47	15.66
9	12, 14, 20	46	15.33
10	12, 14, 20	46	15.33

b. $\mu_{\bar{x}} = \dfrac{(12.66 + \cdots + 15.33 + 15.33)}{10} = 14.6$

$\mu = (12 + 12 + 14 + 15 + 20)/5 = 14.6$

c. The dispersion of the population is greater than that of the sample means. The sample means vary from 12.66 to 16.33, whereas the population varies from 12 to 20.

9. a. 20, found by ${}_6C_3$

b.

Sample	Cases	Sum	Mean
Ruud, Wu, Sass	3, 6, 3	12	4.00
Ruud, Sass, Flores	3, 3, 3	9	3.00
⋮	⋮	⋮	⋮
Sass, Flores, Schueller	3, 3, 1	7	2.33

c. $\mu_{\bar{x}} = 2.67$, found by $\dfrac{53.33}{20}$

$\mu = 2.67$, found by $(3 + 6 + 3 + 3 + 0 + 1)/6$.
They are equal.

d.

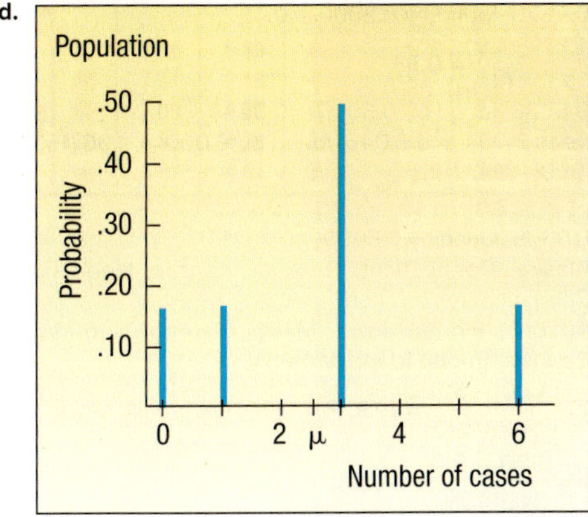

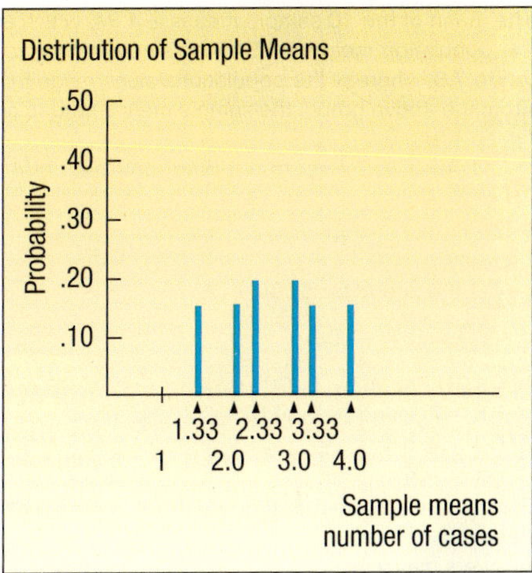

Sample Mean	Number of Means	Probability
1.33	3	.1500
2.00	3	.1500
2.33	4	.2000
3.00	4	.2000
3.33	3	.1500
4.00	3	.1500
	20	1.0000

The population has more dispersion than the sample means. The sample means vary from 1.33 to 4.0. The population varies from 0 to 6.

11. a.

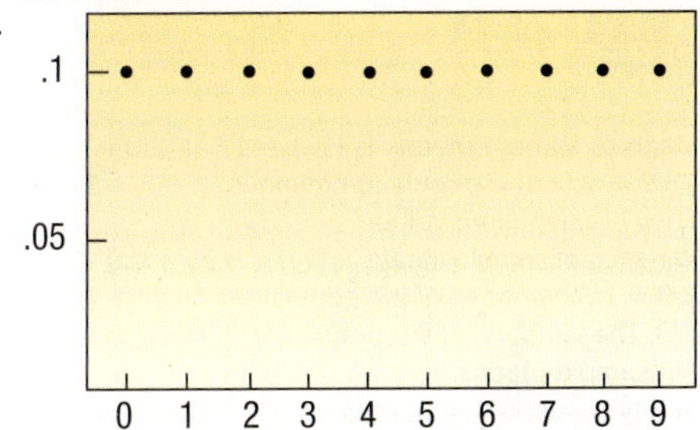

$\mu = \dfrac{0 + 1 + \cdots + 9}{10} = 4.5$

b.

Sample	Sum	$\bar{x}$	Sample	Sum	$\bar{x}$
1	11	2.2	6	20	4.0
2	31	6.2	7	23	4.6
3	21	4.2	8	29	5.8
4	24	4.8	9	35	7.0
5	21	4.2	10	27	5.4

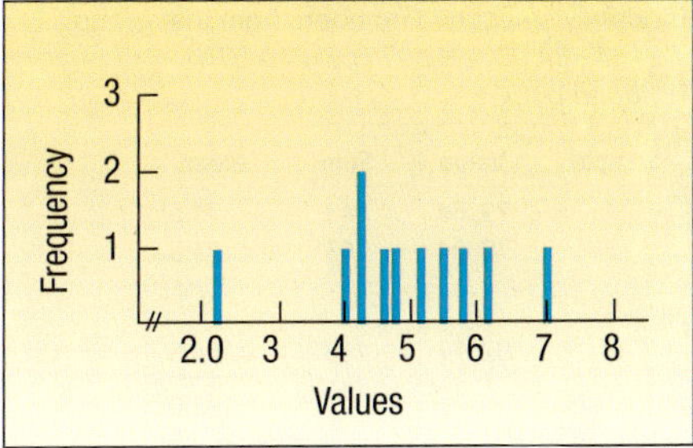

The mean of the 10 sample means is 4.84, which is close to the population mean of 4.5. The sample means range from 2.2 to 7.0, whereas the population values range from 0 to 9. From the above graph, the sample means tend to cluster between 4 and 5.

13. a.–c. Answers will vary depending on the coins in your possession.

15. a. $z = \frac{63 - 60}{12/\sqrt{9}} = 0.75$

$p = .2266$, found by $.5000 - .2734$

b. $z = \frac{56 - 60}{12/\sqrt{9}} = -1.00$

$p = .1587$, found by $.5000 - .3413$

c. $p = .6147$, found by $0.3413 + 0.2734$

17. $z = \frac{1{,}950 - 2{,}200}{250/\sqrt{50}} = -7.07 \quad p = 1,$ or virtually certain

19. a. Formal Man, Summit Stationers, Bootleggers, Leather Ltd., Petries

b. Answers may vary.

c. Elder-Beerman, Frederick's of Hollywood, Summit Stationers, Lion Store, Leather Ltd., Things Remembered, County Seat, Coach House Gifts, Regis Hairstylists

21. a.

Samples	Mean	Deviation from Mean	Square of Deviation
1, 1	1.0	−1.0	1.0
1, 2	1.5	−0.5	0.25
1, 3	2.0	0.0	0.0
2, 1	1.5	−0.5	0.25
2, 2	2.0	0.0	0.0
2, 3	2.5	0.5	0.25
3, 1	2.0	0.0	0.0
3, 2	2.5	0.5	0.25
3, 3	3.0	1.0	1.0

b. Mean of sample means is $(1.0 + 1.5 + 2.0 + \cdots + 3.0)/9 = 18/9 = 2.0$. The population mean is $(1 + 2 + 3)/3 = 6/3 = 2$. They are the same value.

c. Variance of sample means is $(1.0 + 0.25 + 0.0 + \cdots + 3.0)/9 = 3/9 = 1/3$. Variance of the population values is $(1 + 0 + 1)/3 = 2/3$. The variance of the population is twice as large as that of the sample means.

d. Sample means follow a triangular shape peaking at 2. The population is uniform between 1 and 3.

23. Larger samples provide narrower estimates of a population mean. So the company with 200 sampled customers can provide more precise estimates. In addition, they selected consumers who are familiar with laptop computers and may be better able to evaluate the new computer.

25. a. We selected 60, 104, 75, 72, and 48. Answers will vary.

b. We selected the third observation. So the sample consists of 75, 72, 68, 82, 48. Answers will vary.

c. Number the first 20 motels from 00 to 19. Randomly select three numbers. Then number the last five numbers 20 to 24. Randomly select two numbers from that group.

27. a. (79+64+84+82+92+77)/6 =79.67%

b. 15 found by $_6C_2$

c.

Sample	Value	Sum	Mean
1	79, 64	143	71.5
2	79, 84	163	81.5
⋮	⋮	⋮	⋮
15	92, 77	169	84.5
			1,195.0

d. $\mu_{\bar{x}} = 79.67$, found by 1,195/15.

$\mu = 79.67$, found by 478/6.

They are equal.

e. Answers will vary. Not likely as the student is not graded on all available information. Based on these test sores however, this student has a 8/15 chance of receiving a higher grade with this method than the average and a 7/15 chance of receiving a lower grade.

29. a. 10, found by $_5C_2$

b.

Number of Shutdowns	Mean	Number of Shutdowns	Mean
4, 3	3.5	3, 3	3.0
4, 5	4.5	3, 2	2.5
4, 3	3.5	5, 3	4.0
4, 2	3.0	5, 2	3.5
3, 5	4.0	3, 2	2.5

Sample Mean	Frequency	Probability
2.5	2	.20
3.0	2	.20
3.5	3	.30
4.0	2	.20
4.5	1	.10
	10	1.00

c. $\mu_{\bar{x}} = (3.5 + 4.5 + \cdots + 2.5)/10 = 3.4$

$\mu = (4 + 3 + 5 + 3 + 2)/5 = 3.4$

The two means are equal.

d. The population values are relatively uniform in shape. The distribution of sample means tends toward normality.

31. a. The distribution will be normal.

b. $\sigma_{\bar{x}} = \frac{5.5}{\sqrt{25}} = 1.1$

c. $z = \frac{36 - 35}{5.5/\sqrt{25}} = 0.91$

$p = 0.1814$, found by $0.5000 + 0.3186$

d. $z = \frac{34.5 - 35}{5.5/\sqrt{25}} = -0.45$

$p = 0.6736$, found by $0.5000 + 0.1736$

e. 0.4922, found by $0.3186 + 0.1736$

33. $z = \frac{\$335 - \$350}{\$45/\sqrt{40}} = -2.11$

$p = 0.9826$, found by $0.5000 + 0.4826$

35. $z = \frac{29.3 - 29}{2.5/\sqrt{60}} = 0.93$

$p = 0.8238$, found by $0.5000 + 0.3238$

37. Between 5,954 and 6,046, found by $6{,}000 \pm 1.96\,(150/\sqrt{40})$

39. $z = \frac{900 - 947}{205/\sqrt{60}} = -1.78$

$p = 0.0375$, found by $0.5000 - 0.4625$

41. a. Alaska, Connecticut, Georgia, Kansas, Nebraska, South Carolina, Virginia, Utah

b. Arizona, Florida, Iowa, Massachusetts, Nebraska, North Carolina, Rhode Island, Vermont

43. a. $z = \frac{600 - 510}{14.28/\sqrt{10}} = 19.9$, $P = 0.00$, or virtually never

b. $z = \frac{500 - 510}{14.28/\sqrt{10}} = -2.21,$

$p = 0.4864 + 0.5000 = 0.9864$

c. $z = \frac{500 - 510}{14.28/\sqrt{10}} = -2.21,$

$p = 0.5000 - 0.4864 = 0.0136$

45. **a.** $\sigma_{\bar{x}} = \dfrac{2.1}{\sqrt{81}} = 0.23$

b. $z = \dfrac{7.0 - 6.5}{2.1/\sqrt{81}} = 2.14,\ z = \dfrac{6.0 - 6.5}{2.1/\sqrt{81}} = -2.14,$
$p = .4838 + .4838 = .9676$

c. $z = \dfrac{6.75 - 6.5}{2.1/\sqrt{81}} = 1.07,\ z = \dfrac{6.25 - 6.5}{2.1/\sqrt{81}} = -1.07,$
$p = .3577 + .3577 = .7154$

d. .0162, found by .5000 – .4838

47. Mean 2016 attendance is 2.439 million. Likelihood of a sample mean this large or larger is 0.5359, found by 0.5000 + 0.0359, where $z = \dfrac{2.439 - 2.45}{\dfrac{0.71}{\sqrt{30}}} = -0.09.$

CHAPTER 9

1. 51.314 and 58.686, found by $55 \pm 2.58(10/\sqrt{49})$

3. **a.** 1.581, found by $\sigma_{\bar{x}} = 25/\sqrt{250}$

b. The population is normally distributed and the population variance is known. In addition, the Central Limit Theorem says that the sampling distribution of sample means will be normally distributed.

c. 16.901 and 23.099, found by 20 ± 3.099

5. **a.** \$20. It is our best estimate of the population mean.

b. \$18.60 and \$21.40, found by $\$20 \pm 1.96(\$5/\sqrt{49})$. About 95% of the intervals similarly constructed will include the population mean.

7. **a.** 8.60 gallons

b. 7.83 and 9.37, found by $8.60 \pm 2.58(2.30/\sqrt{60})$

c. If 100 such intervals were determined, the population mean would be included in about 99 intervals.

9. **a.** 2.201

b. 1.729

c. 3.499

11. **a.** The population mean is unknown, but the best estimate is 20, the sample mean.

b. Use the *t* distribution since the standard deviation is unknown. However, assume the population is normally distributed.

c. 2.093

d. Between 19.06 and 20.94, found by $20 \pm 2.093(2/\sqrt{20})$

e. Neither value is reasonable because they are not inside the interval.

13. Between 95.39 and 101.81, found by $98.6 \pm 1.833(5.54/\sqrt{10})$

15. **a.** 0.8, found by 80/100

b. Between 0.72 and 0.88, found by
$0.8 \pm 1.96\left(\sqrt{\dfrac{0.8(1 - 0.8)}{100}}\right)$

c. We are reasonably sure the population proportion is between 72 and 88%.

17. **a.** 0.625, found by 250/400

b. Between 0.563 and 0.687, found by
$0.625 \pm 2.58\left(\sqrt{\dfrac{0.625(1 - 0.625)}{400}}\right)$

c. We are reasonably sure the population proportion is between 56 and 69%. Because the estimated population proportion is more than 50%, the results indicate that Fox TV should schedule the new comedy show.

19. 97, found by $n = \left(\dfrac{1.96 \times 10}{2}\right)^2 = 96.04$

21. 196, found by $n = 0.15(0.85)\left(\dfrac{1.96}{0.05}\right)^2 = 195.9216$

23. 554, found by $n = \left(\dfrac{1.96 \times 3}{0.25}\right)^2 = 553.19$

25. **a.** 577, found by $n = 0.60(0.40)\left(\dfrac{1.96}{0.04}\right)^2 = 576.24$

b. 601, found by $n = 0.50(0.50)\left(\dfrac{1.96}{0.04}\right)^2 = 600.25$

27. 33.41 and 36.59, found by
$35 \pm 2.030\left(\dfrac{5}{\sqrt{36}}\right)\sqrt{\dfrac{300 - 36}{300 - 1}}$

29. 1.683 and 2.037, found by
$1.86 \pm 2.680\left(\dfrac{0.5}{\sqrt{50}}\right)\sqrt{\dfrac{400 - 50}{400 - 1}}$

31. 6.13 years to 6.87 years, found by $6.5 \pm 1.989(1.7/\sqrt{85})$

33. **a.** Between \$864.82 and 903.18, found by
$884 \pm 2.426\left(\dfrac{50}{\sqrt{40}}\right).$

b. \$950 is not reasonable because it is outside of the confidence interval.

35. **a.** The population mean is unknown.

b. Between 7.50 and 9.14, found by $8.32 \pm 1.685(3.07/\sqrt{40})$

c. 10 is not reasonable because it is outside the confidence interval.

37. **a.** 65.49 up to 71.71 hours, found by
$68.6 \pm 2.680(8.2/\sqrt{50})$

b. The value suggested by the NCAA is included in the confidence interval. Therefore, it is reasonable.

c. Changing the confidence interval to 95 would reduce the width of the interval. The value of 2.680 would change to 2.010.

39. 61.47, rounded to 62. Found by solving for *n* in the equation: $1.96(16/\sqrt{n}) = 4$

41. Between \$55,461.23 up to \$57,769.43 found by $55{,}051 \pm 1.711\left(\dfrac{7{,}568}{\sqrt{25}}\right)$. 55,000 is reasonable because it is inside of the confidence interval.

43. **a.** 82.58, found by 991/12

b. Between 80.54 and \$84.62, found by
$82.58 \pm 1.796\left(\dfrac{3.94}{\sqrt{12}}\right).$

c. 80 hours per week is not reasonable because it is outside the confidence interval.

45. **a.** 89.4667, found by 1,342/15

b. Between 84.99 and 93.94, found by
$89.4667 \pm 2.145(8.08/\sqrt{15})$

c. Yes, because even the lower limit of the confidence interval is above 80.

47. The confidence interval is between 0.011 and 0.059, found by $0.035 \pm 2.576\left(\sqrt{\dfrac{0.035(1 - 0.035)}{400}}\right)$. It would not be reasonable to conclude that fewer than 5% of the employees are now failing the test because 0.05 is inside the confidence interval.

49. Between 0.648 and 0.752, found by
$0.70 \pm 2.576\left(\sqrt{\dfrac{0.70(1 - 0.70)}{500}}\right)\left(\sqrt{\dfrac{20{,}000 - 500}{20{,}000 - 1}}\right).$
Yes, because even the lower limit of the confidence interval is above 0.500.

51. \$52.51 and \$55.49, found by
$\$54.00 \pm 2.032\dfrac{\$4.50}{\sqrt{35}}\sqrt{\dfrac{(500 - 35)}{500 - 1}}$

53. 369, found by $n = 0.60(1 - 0.60)(1.96/0.05)^2$

55. 97, found by $[(1.96 \times 500)/100]^2$

57. **a.** Between 7,849 and 8,151, found by
$8{,}000 \pm 2.756(300/\sqrt{30})$

b. 554, found by $n = \left(\dfrac{(1.96)(300)}{25}\right)^2$

59. a. Between 75.44 and 80.56, found by $78 \pm 2.010(9/\sqrt{50})$

b. 220, found by $n = \left(\frac{(1.645)(9)}{1.0}\right)^2$

61. a. 4, found by $24/\sqrt{36}$

b. Between \$641.88 and \$658.12, found by $650 \pm 2.030\left(\frac{24}{\sqrt{36}}\right)$

c. 23, found by $n = \{(1.96 \times 24)/10\}^2 = 22.13$

63. a. 708.13, rounded up to 709, found by $0.21(1 - 0.21)(1.96/0.03)^2$

b. 1,068, found by $0.50(0.50)(1.96/0.03)^2$

65. a. Between 0.156 and 0.184, found by $0.17 \pm 1.96\sqrt{\frac{(0.17)(1 - 0.17)}{2700}}$

b. Yes, because 18% are inside the confidence interval.

c. 21,682; found by $0.17(1 - 0.17)[1.96/0.005]^2$

67. Between 12.69 and 14.11, found by $13.4 \pm 1.96(6.8/\sqrt{352})$

69. a. Answers will vary.

b. Answers will vary.

c. Answers will vary.

d. Answers may vary.

e. Select a different sample of 20 homes and compute a confidence interval using the new sample. There is a 5% probability that a sample mean will be more than 1.96 standard errors from the mean. If this happens, the confidence interval will not include the population mean.

71. a. Between \$4,033.1476 and \$5,070.6274, found by $4{,}551.8875 \pm 518.7399$.

b. Between 71,040.0894 and 84,877.1106, found by $77{,}958.6000 \pm 6{,}918.5106$.

c. In general, the confidence intervals indicate that the average maintenance cost and the average odometer reading suggest an aging bus fleet.

CHAPTER 10

1. a. Two-tailed

b. Reject H_0 when z does not fall in the region between −1.96 and 1.96.

c. −1.2, found by $z = (49 - 50)/(5/\sqrt{36}) = -1.2$

d. Fail to reject H_0.

e. $p = .2302$, found by 2(.5000 − .3849). A 23.02% chance of finding a z value this large when H_0 is true.

3. a. One-tailed

b. Reject H_0 when $z > 1.65$.

c. 1.2, found by $z = (21 - 20)/(5/\sqrt{36})$

d. Fail to reject H_0 at the .05 significance level

e. $p = .1151$, found by .5000 − .3849. An 11.51% chance of finding a z value this large or larger.

5. a. H_0: $\mu = 60{,}000$ $\quad H_1$: $\mu \neq 60{,}000$

b. Reject H_0 if $z < -1.96$ or $z > 1.96$.

c. −0.69, found by:

$$z = \frac{59{,}500 - 60{,}000}{(5{,}000/\sqrt{48})}$$

d. Do not reject H_0.

e. $p = .4902$, found by 2(.5000 − .2549). Crosset's experience is not different from that claimed by the manufacturer. If H_0 is true, the probability of finding a value more extreme than this is .4902.

7. a. H_0: $\mu \geq 6.8$ $\quad H_1$: $\mu < 6.8$

b. Reject H_0 if $z < -1.65$

c. $z = \frac{6.2 - 6.8}{1.8/\sqrt{36}} = -2.0$

d. H_0 is rejected.

e. $p = 0.0228$. The mean number of DVDs watched is less than 6.8 per month. If H_0 is true, you will get a statistic this small less than one time out of 40 tests.

9. a. Reject H_0 when $t < 1.833$

b. $t = \frac{12 - 10}{(3/\sqrt{10})} = 2.108$

c. Reject H_0. The mean is greater than 10.

11. H_0: $\mu \leq 40$ $\quad H_1$: $\mu > 40$
Reject H_0 if $t > 1.703$.

$$t = \frac{42 - 40}{(2.1/\sqrt{28})} = 5.040$$

Reject H_0 and conclude that the mean number of calls is greater than 40 per week.

13. H_0: $\mu \leq 50{,}000$ $\quad H_1$: $\mu > 50{,}000$
Reject H_0 if $t > 1.833$.

$$t = \frac{(60000 - 50000)}{(10000/\sqrt{10})} = 3.16$$

Reject H_0 and conclude that the mean income in Wilmington is greater than \$50,000.

15. a. Reject H_0 if $t < -3.747$.

b. $\bar{x} = 17$ and $s = \sqrt{\frac{50}{5 - 1}} = 3.536$

$$t = \frac{17 - 20}{(3.536/\sqrt{5})} = -1.90$$

c. Do not reject H_0. We cannot conclude the population mean is less than 20.

d. Between .05 and .10, about .065

17. H_0: $\mu \leq 1.4$ $\quad H_1$: $\mu > 1.4$
Reject H_0 if $t > 2.821$.

$$t = \frac{1.6 - 1.4}{0.216/\sqrt{10}} = 2.93$$

Reject H_0 and conclude that water consumption has increased. The p-value is between 0.01 and 0.005. There is a slight probability (between one chance in 100 and one chance in 200) this rise could have arisen by chance.

19. H_0: $\mu \leq 67$ $\quad H_1$: $\mu > 67$
Reject H_0 if $t > 1.796$

$$t = \frac{(82.5 - 67)}{(59.5/\sqrt{12})} = 0.902$$

Fail to reject H_0 and conclude that the mean number of text messages is not greater than 67. The p-value is greater than 0.05. There is a good probability (about 18%) this could happen by chance. **(LO10-7)**

21. 1.05, found by $z = (9{,}992 - 9{,}880)/(400/\sqrt{100})$. Then 0.5000 − 0.3531 = 0.1469, which is the probability of a Type II error.

23. H_0: $\mu \geq 60$ $\quad H_1$: $\mu < 60$
Reject H_0 if $z < -1.282$; the critical value is 59.29.

$$z = \frac{58 - 60}{(2.7/\sqrt{24})} = -3.629$$

Reject H_0. The mean assembly time is less than 60 minutes. Using the sample mean, 58, as μ_1, the z-score for 59.29 is 2.34. So the probability for values between 58 and 59.29 is .4904. The Type II error is the area to the right of 59.29 or .5000 − .4904 = .0096.

25. H_0: $\mu = \$45{,}000$ $\quad H_1$: $\mu \neq \$45{,}000$
Reject H_0 if $z < -1.65$ or $z > 1.65$.

$$z = \frac{\$45{,}500 - \$45{,}000}{\$3000/\sqrt{120}} = 1.83$$

Reject H_0. We can conclude that the mean salary is not \$45,000. p-value 0.0672, found by 2(0.5000 − 0.4664).

27. H_0: $\mu \geq 10$ $\quad H_1$: $\mu < 10$
Reject H_0 if $z < -1.65$.

$$z = \frac{9.0 - 10.0}{2.8/\sqrt{50}} = -2.53$$

Reject H_0. The mean weight loss is less than 10 pounds. p-value = 0.5000 − 0.4943 = 0.0057

29. H_0: $\mu \geq 7.0$ H_1: $\mu < 7.0$
Assuming a 5% significance level, reject H_0 if $t < -1.677$.

$$t = \frac{6.8 - 7.0}{0.9/\sqrt{50}} = -1.57$$

Do not reject H_0. West Virginia students are not sleeping less than 6 hours. *p*-value is between .05 and .10.

31. H_0: $\mu \geq 3.13$ H_1: $\mu < 3.13$
Reject H_0 if $t < -1.711$

$$t = \frac{2.86 - 3.13}{1.20/\sqrt{25}} = -1.13$$

We fail to reject H_0 and conclude that the mean number of residents is not necessarily less than 3.13.

33. H_0: $\mu \leq \$6,658$ H_1: $\mu > \$6,658$
Reject H_0 if $t > 1.796$

$$\bar{x} = \frac{85,963}{12} = 7,163.58 \qquad s = \sqrt{\frac{9,768,674.92}{12 - 1}} = 942.37$$

$$t = \frac{7163.58 - 6,658}{942.37/\sqrt{12}} = 1.858$$

Reject H_0. The mean interest paid is greater than $6,658.

35. H_0: $\mu = 3.1$ H_1: $\mu \neq 3.1$ Assume a normal population.
Reject H_0 if $t < -2.201$ or $t > 2.201$.

$$\bar{x} = \frac{41.1}{12} = 3.425$$

$$s = \sqrt{\frac{4.0625}{12 - 1}} = .6077$$

$$t = \frac{3.425 - 3.1}{.6077/\sqrt{12}} = 1.853$$

Do not reject H_0. Cannot show a difference between senior citizens and the national average. *p*-value is about 0.09.

37. H_0: $\mu \geq 6.5$ H_1: $\mu < 6.5$ Assume a normal population.
Reject H_0 if $t < -2.718$.
$\bar{x} = 5.1667$ $s = 3.1575$

$$t = \frac{5.1667 - 6.5}{3.1575/\sqrt{12}} = -1.463$$

Do not reject H_0. The *p*-value is greater than 0.05.

39. H_0: $\mu = 0$ H_1: $\mu \neq 0$
Reject H_0 if $t < -2.110$ or $t > 2.110$.
$\bar{x} = -0.2322$ $s = 0.3120$

$$t = \frac{-0.2322 - 0}{0.3120/\sqrt{18}} = -3.158$$

Reject H_0. The mean gain or loss does not equal 0. The *p*-value is less than 0.01, but greater than 0.001.

41. H_0: $\mu \leq 100$ H_1: $\mu > 100$ Assume a normal population.
Reject H_0 if $t > 1.761$.

$$\bar{x} = \frac{1,641}{15} = 109.4$$

$$s = \sqrt{\frac{1,389.6}{15 - 1}} = 9.9628$$

$$t = \frac{109.4 - 100}{9.9628/\sqrt{15}} = 3.654$$

Reject H_0. The mean number with the scanner is greater than 100. *p*-value is 0.001.

43. H_0: $\mu = 1.5$ H_1: $\mu \neq 1.5$
Reject H_0 if $t > 3.250$ or $t < -3.250$.

$$t = \frac{1.3 - 1.5}{0.9/\sqrt{10}} = -0.703$$

Fail to reject H_0.

45. H_0: $\mu \geq 30$ H_1: $\mu < 30$
Reject H_0 if $t < -1.895$.

$$\bar{x} = \frac{238.3}{8} = 29.7875 \qquad s = \sqrt{\frac{5.889}{8 - 1}} = 0.9172$$

$$t = \frac{29.7875 - 30}{0.9172/\sqrt{8}} = -0.655$$

Do not reject H_0. The cost is not less than $30,000.

47. **a.** $9.00 \pm 1.645(1/\sqrt{36}) = 9.00 \pm 0.274$.
So the limits are 8.726 and 9.274.

b. $z = \dfrac{8.726 - 8.6}{1/\sqrt{36}} = 0.756$.

$P(z < 0.756) = 0.5000 + 0.2764 = .7764$

c. $z = \dfrac{9.274 - 9.6}{1/\sqrt{36}} = -1.956$.

$P(z > -1.96) = 0.4750 + 0.5000 = .9750$

49. $50 + 2.33 \dfrac{10}{\sqrt{n}} = 55 - .525 \dfrac{10}{\sqrt{n}}$ $\qquad n = (5.71)^2 = 32.6$
Let $n = 33$

51. H_0: $\mu \geq 8$ H_1: $\mu < 8$
Reject H_0 if $t < -1.714$.

$$t = \frac{7.5 - 8}{3.2/\sqrt{24}} = -0.77$$

Do not reject the null hypothesis. The time is not less.

53. **a.** H_0: $\mu = 100$ H_1: $\mu \neq 100$
Reject H_0 if t is not between -2.045 and 2.045.

$$t = \frac{121.12 - 100}{39.66/\sqrt{30}} = 2.92$$

Reject the null. The mean salary is probably not $100.0 million.

b. H_0: $\mu \leq 2,000,000$ H_1: $\mu > 2,000,000$
Reject H_0 if t is > 1.699.

$$t = \frac{2,438,636 - 2,000,000}{617,670/\sqrt{30}} = 3.89$$

Reject the null. The mean attendance was more than 2,000,000.

CHAPTER 11

1. **a.** Two-tailed test
b. Reject H_0 if $z < -2.05$ or $z > 2.05$
c. $z = \dfrac{102 - 99}{\sqrt{\dfrac{5^2}{40} + \dfrac{6^2}{50}}} = 2.59$
d. Reject H_0
e. *p*-value = .0096, found by 2(.5000 −.4952)

3. **Step 1** H_0: $\mu_1 \geq \mu_2$ H_1: $\mu_1 < \mu_2$
Step 2 The .05 significance level was chosen.
Step 3 Reject H_0 if $z < -1.65$.
Step 4 −0.94, found by:

$$z = \frac{7.6 - 8.1}{\sqrt{\dfrac{(2.3)^2}{40} + \dfrac{(2.9)^2}{55}}} = -0.94$$

Step 5 Fail to reject H_0.
Step 6 Babies using the Gibbs brand did not gain less weight. *p*-value = .1736, found by .5000 −.3264.

5. **Step 1** H_0: $\mu_{married} = \mu_{unmarried}$ H_1: $\mu_{married} \neq \mu_{unmarried}$
Step 2 The 0.05 significance level was chosen
Step 3 Use a *z*-statistic as both population standard deviations are known.
Step 4 If $z < -1.960$ or $z > 1.960$, reject H_0.
Step 5 $z = \dfrac{3.0 - 3.4}{\sqrt{\dfrac{(1.2)^2}{45} + \dfrac{(1.1)^2}{39}}} = -1.59$

Fail to reject the null.
Step 6 It is reasonable to conclude that the time that married and unmarried women spend each week is not significantly different. The *p*-value is greater than 0.05. The difference of 0.4 hours per week could be explained by sampling error.

7. **a.** Reject H_0 if $t > 2.120$ or $t < -2.120$. $df = 10 + 8 - 2 = 16$
b. $s_p^2 = \dfrac{(10 - 1)(4)^2 + (8 - 1)(5)^2}{10 + 8 - 2} = 19.9375$
c. $t = \dfrac{23 - 26}{\sqrt{19.9375\left(\dfrac{1}{10} + \dfrac{1}{8}\right)}} = -1.416$

d. Do not reject H_0.
e. p-value is greater than .10 and less than .20.

9. **Step 1** H_0: $\mu_{\text{Pitchers}} = \mu_{\text{Position Players}}$
H_1: $\mu_{\text{Pitchers}} \neq \mu_{\text{Position Players}}$
Step 2 The 0.01 significance level was chosen.
Step 3 Use a t-statistic assuming a pooled variance with the standard deviation unknown.
Step 4 $df = 12 + 13 - 2 = 23$. Reject H_0 if t is not between -2.807 and 2.807.

$$s_p^2 = \frac{(12-1)(8.597)^2 + (13-1)(8.578)^2}{12+13-2} = 73.738$$

$$t = \frac{6.091 - 10.684}{\sqrt{73.738\left(\frac{1}{12} + \frac{1}{13}\right)}} = -1.336$$

Step 5 Do not reject H_0.
Step 6 There is no difference in the mean salaries of pitchers and position players.

11. **Step 1** H_0: $\mu_s \leq \mu_a$ $\quad H_1$: $\mu_s > \mu_a$
Step 2 The .10 significance level was chosen.
Step 3 $df = 6 + 7 - 2 = 11$
Reject H_0 if $t > 1.363$.

Step 4 $$s_p^2 = \frac{(6-1)(12.2)^2 + (7-1)(15.8)^2}{6+7-2} = 203.82$$

$$t = \frac{142.5 - 130.3}{\sqrt{203.82\left(\frac{1}{6} + \frac{1}{7}\right)}} = 1.536$$

Step 5 Reject H_0.
Step 6 The mean daily expenses are greater for the sales staff. The p-value is between .05 and .10.

13. **a.** $$df = \frac{\left(\frac{25}{15} + \frac{225}{12}\right)^2}{\frac{\left(\frac{25}{15}\right)^2}{15-1} + \frac{\left(\frac{225}{12}\right)^2}{12-1}} = \frac{416.84}{0.1984 + 31.9602}$$
$= 12.96 \rightarrow 12df$

b. H_0: $\mu_1 = \mu_2$ $\quad H_1$: $\mu_1 \neq \mu_2$
Reject H_0 if $t > 2.179$ or $t < -2.179$.

c. $$t = \frac{50 - 46}{\sqrt{\frac{25}{15} + \frac{225}{12}}} = 0.8852$$

d. Fail to reject the null hypothesis.

15. **a.** $$df = \frac{\left(\frac{697{,}225}{16} + \frac{2{,}387{,}025}{18}\right)^2}{\frac{\left(\frac{697{,}225}{16}\right)^2}{16-1} + \frac{\left(\frac{2{,}387{,}025}{18}\right)^2}{18-1}} = 26.7 \rightarrow 26df$$

b. H_0: $\mu_{\text{Private}} \leq \mu_{\text{Public}}$ $\quad H_1$: $\mu_{\text{Private}} > \mu_{\text{Public}}$
Reject H_0 if $t > 1.706$.

c. $$t = \frac{12{,}840 - 11{,}045}{\sqrt{\frac{2{,}387{,}025}{18} + \frac{697{,}225}{16}}} = 4.276$$

d. Reject the null hypothesis. The mean adoption cost from a private agency is greater than the mean adoption cost from a public agency.

17. **a.** Reject H_0 if $t > 2.353$.

b. $\bar{d} = \frac{12}{4} = 3.00 \qquad s_d = \sqrt{\frac{2}{3}} = 0.816$

c. $$t = \frac{3.00}{0.816/\sqrt{4}} = 7.35$$

d. Reject H_0. There are more defective parts produced on the day shift.
e. p-value is less than .005 but greater than .0005.

19. H_0: $\mu_d \leq 0 \qquad H_1$: $\mu_d > 0$
$\bar{d} = 25.917$
$s_d = 40.791$
Reject H_0 if $t > 1.796$

$$t = \frac{25.917}{40.791/\sqrt{12}} = 2.20$$

Reject H_0. The incentive plan resulted in an increase in daily income. The p-value is about .025.

21. H_0: $\mu_M = \mu_W \qquad H_1$: $\mu_M \neq \mu_W$
Reject H_0 if $t < -2.645$ or $t > 2.645$ ($df = 35 + 40 - 2$).

$$s_p^2 = \frac{(35-1)(4.48)^2 + (40-1)(3.86)^2}{35+40-2} = 17.3079$$

$$t = \frac{24.51 - 22.69}{\sqrt{17.3079\left(\frac{1}{35} + \frac{1}{40}\right)}} = 1.890$$

Do not reject H_0. There is no difference in the number of times men and women buy take-out dinner in a month. The p-value is between .05 and .10.

23. H_0: $\mu_1 = \mu_2 \qquad H_1$: $\mu_1 \neq \mu_2$
Reject H_0 if $z < -1.96$ or $z > 1.96$.

$$z = \frac{4.77 - 5.02}{\sqrt{\frac{(1.05)^2}{40} + \frac{(1.23)^2}{50}}} = -1.04$$

H_0 is not rejected. There is no difference in the mean number of calls. p-value $= 2(.5000 - .3508) = .2984$.

25. H_0: $\mu_B \leq \mu_A \qquad H_1$: $\mu_B > \mu_A$
Reject H_0 if $t > 1.668$

$$t = \frac{\$61{,}000 - \$57{,}000}{\sqrt{\frac{(\$7{,}100)^2}{30} + \frac{(\$9{,}200)^2}{40}}} = \frac{\$4{,}000.00}{\$1{,}948.42} = 2.05$$

Reject H_0. The mean income is larger for Plan B. The p-value $= .5000 - .4798 = .0202$.

27. **a.** $$df = \frac{\left(\frac{0.3136}{12} + \frac{0.0900}{12}\right)^2}{\frac{\left(\frac{0.3136}{12}\right)^2}{12-1} + \frac{\left(\frac{0.0900}{12}\right)^2}{12-1}}$$

$$= \frac{0.0011}{0.000062 + 0.0000051} = 16.37 \rightarrow 16df$$

b. H_0: $\mu_a = \mu_w \qquad H_1$: $\mu_a \neq \mu_w$
Reject H_0 if $t > 2.120$ or $t < -2.120$.

c. $$t = \frac{1.65 - 2.20}{\sqrt{\frac{0.3136}{12} + \frac{0.0900}{12}}} = -3.00$$

d. Reject the null hypothesis. There is a difference.

29. Assume equal population standard deviations.
H_0: $\mu_n = \mu_s \qquad H_1$: $\mu_n \neq \mu_s$
Reject H_0 if $t < -2.086$ or $t > 2.086$.

$$s_p^2 = \frac{(10-1)(10.5)^2 + (12-1)(14.25)^2}{10+12-2} = 161.2969$$

$$t = \frac{83.55 - 78.8}{\sqrt{161.2969\left(\frac{1}{10} + \frac{1}{12}\right)}} = 0.874$$

p-value $> .10$. Do not reject H_0. There is no difference in the mean number of hamburgers sold at the two locations.

31. Assume equal population standard deviations.
H_0: $\mu_1 = \mu_2$ H_1: $\mu_1 \neq \mu_2$
Reject H_0 if $t > 2.819$ or $t < -2.819$.

$$s_p^2 = \frac{(10-1)(2.33)^2 + (14-1)(2.55)^2}{10+14-2} = 6.06$$

$$t = \frac{15.87 - 18.29}{\sqrt{6.06\left(\frac{1}{10} + \frac{1}{14}\right)}} = -2.374$$

Do not reject H_0. There is no difference in the mean amount purchased.

33. Assume equal population standard deviations.
H_0: $\mu_1 \leq \mu_2$ H_1: $\mu_1 > \mu_2$ Reject H_0 if $t > 2.567$.

$$s_p^2 = \frac{(8-1)(2.2638)^2 + (11-1)(2.4606)^2}{8+11-2} = 5.672$$

$$t = \frac{10.375 - 5.636}{\sqrt{5.672\left(\frac{1}{8} + \frac{1}{11}\right)}} = 4.28$$

Reject H_0. The mean number of transactions by the young adults is more than for the senior citizens.

35. H_0: $\mu_1 \leq \mu_2$ H_1: $\mu_1 > \mu_2$ Reject H_0 if $t > 2.650$.
$\bar{X}_1 = 125.125$ $s_1 = 15.094$
$\bar{X}_2 = 117.714$ $s_2 = 19.914$

$$s_p^2 = \frac{(8-1)(15.094)^2 + (7-1)(19.914)^2}{8+7-2} = 305.708$$

$$t = \frac{125.125 - 117.714}{\sqrt{305.708\left(\frac{1}{8} + \frac{1}{7}\right)}} = 0.819$$

H_0 is not rejected. There is no difference in the mean number sold at the regular price and the mean number sold at the reduced price.

37. H_0: $\mu_d \leq 0$ H_1: $\mu_d > 0$ Reject H_0 if $t > 1.895$.
$\bar{d} = 1.75$ $s_d = 2.9155$

$$t = \frac{1.75}{2.9155/\sqrt{8}} = 1.698$$

Do not reject H_0. There is no difference in the mean number of absences. The p-value is greater than .05 but less than .10.

39. H_0: $\mu_1 = \mu_2$ H_1: $\mu_1 \neq \mu_2$
Reject H_0 if $t < -2.024$ or $t > 2.204$.

$$s_p^2 = \frac{(15-1)(40)^2 + (25-1)(30)^2}{15+25-2} = 1{,}157.89$$

$$t = \frac{150 - 180}{\sqrt{1{,}157.89\left(\frac{1}{15} + \frac{1}{25}\right)}} = -2.699$$

Reject the null hypothesis. The population means are different.

41. H_0: $\mu_d \leq 0$ H_1: $\mu_d > 0$
Reject H_0 if $t > 1.895$.
$\bar{d} = 3.11$ $s_d = 2.91$

$$t = \frac{3.11}{2.91/\sqrt{8}} = 3.02$$

Reject H_0. The mean is lower.

43. H_0: $\mu_O = \mu_R$, H_1: $\mu_O \neq \mu_R$
$df = 25 + 28 - 2 = 51$
Reject H_0 if $t < -2.008$ or $t > 2.008$.
$\bar{X}_O = 86.24$, $s_O = 23.43$
$X_R = 92.04$, $s_R = 24.12$

$$s_p^2 = \frac{(25-1)(23.43)^2 + (28-1)(24.12)^2}{25+28-2} = 566.335$$

$$t = \frac{86.24 - 92.04}{\sqrt{566.335\left(\frac{1}{25} + \frac{1}{28}\right)}} = -0.886$$

Do not reject H_0. There is no difference in the mean number of cars in the two lots.

45. H_0: $\mu_d \leq 0$ H_1: $\mu_d > 0$ Reject H_0 if $t > 1.711$.
$\bar{d} = 2.8$ $s_d = 6.59$

$$t = \frac{2.8}{6.59/\sqrt{25}} = 2.124$$

Reject H_0. There are on average more cars in the US 17 lot.

47. a. Using statistical software, the result is that we fail to reject the null hypothesis that the mean prices of homes with and without pools are equal. Assuming equal population variances, the p-value is 0.4908.
b. Using statistical software, the result is that we reject the null hypothesis that the mean prices of homes with and without garages are equal. There is a large difference in mean prices between homes with and without garages. Assuming equal population variances, the p-value is less than 0.0001.
c. Using statistical software, the result is that we fail to reject the null hypothesis that the mean prices of homes are equal with mortgages in default and not in default. Assuming equal population variances, the p-value is 0.6980.

49. Using statistical software, the result is that we reject the null hypothesis that the mean maintenance cost of buses powered by diesel and gasoline engines is the same. Assuming equal population variances, the p-value is less than 0.0001.

CHAPTER 12

1. a. 9.01, from Appendix B.6

3. Reject H_0 if $F > 10.5$, where degrees of freedom in the numerator are 7 and 5 in the denominator. Computed $F = 2.04$, found by:

$$F = \frac{s_1^2}{s_2^2} = \frac{(10)^2}{(7)^2} = 2.04$$

Do not reject H_0. There is no difference in the variations of the two populations.

5. H_0: $\sigma_1^2 = \sigma_2^2$ H_1: $\sigma_1^2 \neq \sigma_2^2$
Reject H_0 where $F > 3.10$. (3.10 is about halfway between 3.14 and 3.07.) Computed $F = 1.44$, found by:

$$F = \frac{(12)^2}{(10)^2} = 1.44$$

Do not reject H_0. There is no difference in the variations of the two populations.

7. a. H_0: $\mu_1 = \mu_2 = \mu_3$; H_1: Treatment means are not all the same.
b. Reject H_0 if $F > 4.26$.

c & d.

Source	SS	*df*	MS	*F*
Treatment	62.17	2	31.08	21.94
Error	12.75	9	1.42	
Total	74.92	11		

e. Reject H_0. The treatment means are not all the same.

9. H_0: $\mu_1 = \mu_2 = \mu_3$; H_1: Treatment means are not all the same. Reject H_0 if $F > 4.26$.

Source	SS	*df*	MS	*F*
Treatment	276.50	2	138.25	14.18
Error	87.75	9	9.75	

Reject H_0. The treatment means are not all the same.

11. a. H_0: $\mu_1 = \mu_2 = \mu_3$; H_1: Not all means are the same.
b. Reject H_0 if $F > 4.26$.
c. SST = 107.20, SSE = 9.47, SS total = 116.67
d.

Source	SS	*df*	MS	*F*
Treatment	107.20	2	53.600	50.96
Error	9.47	9	1.052	
Total	116.67	11		

e. Since 50.96 > 4.26, H_0 is rejected. At least one of the means differs.

f. $(\bar{x}_1 - \bar{x}_2) \pm t\sqrt{\text{MSE}(1/n_1 + 1/n_2)}$
$= (9.667 - 2.20) \pm 2.262\sqrt{1.052(1/3 + 1/5)}$
$= 7.467 \pm 1.69$
$= [5.777, 9.157]$
Yes, we can conclude that treatments 1 and 2 have different means.

13. H_0: $\mu_1 = \mu_2 = \mu_3 = \mu_4$; H_1: Not all means are equal.
H_0 is rejected if $F > 3.71$.

Source	SS	df	MS	F
Treatment	32.33	3	10.77	2.36
Error	45.67	10	4.567	
Total	78.00	13		

Because 2.36 is less than 3.71, H_0 is not rejected. There is no difference in the mean number of weeks.

15. a. H_0: $\mu_1 = \mu_2$; H_1: Not all treatment means are equal.
b. Reject H_0 if $F > 18.5$.
c. H_0: $\mu_1 = \mu_2 = \mu_3$; H_1: Not all block means are equal.
H_0 is rejected if $F > 19.0$.
d. SS total $= (46.0 - 36.5)^2 + \cdots + (35 - 36.5)^2 = 289.5$
$\text{SST} = 3(42.33 - 36.5)^2 + 3(30.67 - 36.5)^2$
$= 204.167$
$\text{SSB} = 2(38.5 - 36.5)^2 + 2(31.5 - 36.5)^2 + 2(39.5 - 36.5)^2 = 8 + 50 + 18 = 76$
$\text{SSE} = 289.50 - 204.1667 - 76 = 9.3333$
e.

Source	SS	df	MS	F
Treatment	204.167	1	204.167	43.75
Blocks	76.000	2	38.000	8.14
Error	9.333	2	4.667	
Total	289.5000	5		

f. 43.75 > 18.5, so reject H_0. There is a difference in the treatments. 8.14 < 19.0, so do not reject H_0 for blocks. There is no difference among blocks.

17.

Source	SS	df	MS	F
Treatment	62.53	2	31.2650	5.75
Blocks	33.73	4	8.4325	1.55
Error	43.47	8	5.4338	
Total	139.73			

There is a difference in shifts, but not by employee.

19.

Source	SS	df	MS	F	P
Size	156.333	2	78.1667	1.98	0.180
Weight	98.000	1	98.000	2.48	0.141
Interaction	36.333	2	18.1667	0.46	0.642
Error	473.333	12	39.444		
Total	764.000	17			

a. Since the p-value (0.18) is greater than 0.05, there is no difference in the Size means.
b. The p-value for Weight (0.141) is also greater than 0.05. Thus, there is no difference in those means.
c. There is no significant interaction because the p-value (0.642) is greater than 0.05.

21. a.

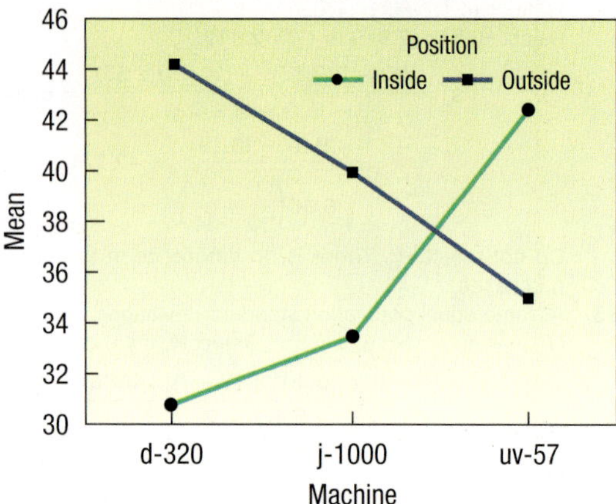

Yes, there appears to be an interaction effect. Sales are different based on machine position, either in the inside or outside position.

b.

Two-way ANOVA: Sales versus Position, Machine

Source	df	SS	MS	F	P
Position	1	104.167	104.167	9.12	0.007
Machine	2	16.333	8.167	0.72	0.502
Interaction	2	457.333	228.667	20.03	0.000
Error	18	205.500	11.417		
Total	23	783.333			

The position and the interaction of position and machine effects are significant. The effect of machine on sales is not significant.

c.

One-way ANOVA: D-320 Sales versus Position

Source	df	SS	MS	F	P
Position	1	364.50	364.50	40.88	0.001
Error	6	53.50	8.92		
Total	7	418.00			

One-way ANOVA: J-1000 Sales versus Position

Source	df	SS	MS	F	P
Position	1	84.5	84.5	5.83	0.052
Error	6	87.0	14.5		
Total	7	171.5			

One-way ANOVA: UV-57 Sales versus Position

Source	df	SS	MS	F	P
Position	1	112.5	112.5	10.38	0.018
Error	6	65.0	10.8		
Total	7	177.5			

Recommendations using the statistical results and mean sales plotted in part (a): Position the D-320 machine outside. Statistically, the position of the J-1000 does not matter. Position the UV-57 machine inside.

23. H_0: $\sigma_1^2 \le \sigma_2^2$; H_1: $\sigma_1^2 > \sigma_2^2$. $df_1 = 21 - 1 = 20$; $df_2 = 18 - 1 = 17$. H_0 is rejected if $F > 3.16$.

$$F = \frac{(45{,}600)^2}{(21{,}330)^2} = 4.57$$

Reject H_0. There is more variation in the selling price of oceanfront homes.

25. Sharkey: $n = 7$ $s_s = 14.79$
White: $n = 8$ $s_w = 22.95$
H_0: $\sigma_w^2 \leq \sigma_s^2$; H_1: $\sigma_w^2 > \sigma_s^2$. $df_s = 7 - 1 = 6$; $df_w = 8 - 1 = 7$. Reject H_0 if $F > 8.26$.

$$F = \frac{(22.95)^2}{(14.79)^2} = 2.41$$

Cannot reject H_0. There is no difference in the variation of the monthly sales.

27. **a.** H_0: $\mu_1 = \mu_2 = \mu_3 = \mu_4$
H_1: Treatment means are not all equal.
b. $\alpha = .05$ Reject H_0 if $F > 3.10$.
c.

Source	SS	df	MS	F
Treatment	50	4 − 1 = 3	50/3	1.67
Error	200	24 − 4 = 20	10	
Total	250	24 − 1 = 23		

d. Do not reject H_0.

29. H_0: $\mu_1 = \mu_2 = \mu_3$; H_1: Not all treatment means are equal.
H_0 is rejected if $F > 3.89$.

Source	SS	df	MS	F
Treatment	63.33	2	31.667	13.38
Error	28.40	12	2.367	
Total	91.73	14		

H_0 is rejected. There is a difference in the treatment means.

31. H_0: $\mu_1 = \mu_2 = \mu_3 = \mu_4$; H_1: Not all means are equal.
H_0 is rejected if $F > 3.10$.

Source	SS	df	MS	F
Factor	87.79	3	29.26	9.12
Error	64.17	20	3.21	
Total	151.96	23		

Because the computed F of $9.12 > 3.10$, the null hypothesis of no difference is rejected at the .05 level.

33. **a.** H_0: $\mu_1 = \mu_2$; H_1: $\mu_1 \neq \mu_2$. Critical value of $F = 4.75$.

Source	SS	df	MS	F
Treatment	219.43	1	219.43	23.10
Error	114.00	12	9.5	
Total	333.43	13		

b. $$t = \frac{37 - 45}{\sqrt{9.5\left(\frac{1}{6} + \frac{1}{8}\right)}} = -4.806$$

Since $t^2 = F$. That is $(-4.806)2 \approx 23.10$ (actually 23.098, difference due to rounding). The p-value for this statistic is 0.0004 as well. Reject H_0 in favor of the alternative.
c. H_0 is rejected. There is a difference in the mean scores.

35. The null hypothesis is rejected because the F statistic (8.26) is greater than the critical value (5.61) at the .01 significance level. The p-value (.0019) is also less than the significance level. The mean mile per gallon are not the same.

37. H_0: $\mu_1 = \mu_2 = \mu_3 = \mu_4$. H_1: At least one mean is different. Reject H_0 if $F > 2.7395$. Since $13.74 > 2.74$, reject H_0. You can also see this from the p-value of $0.0001 < 0.05$. Priority mail express is faster than all three of the other classes, and priority mail is faster than either first-class or standard. However, first-class and standard mail may be the same.

39. For color, the critical value of F is 4.76; for size, it is 5.14.

Source	SS	df	MS	F
Treatment	25.0	3	8.3333	5.88
Blocks	21.5	2	10.75	7.59
Error	8.5	6	1.4167	
Total	55.0	11		

H_0s for both treatment and blocks (color and size) are rejected. At least one mean differs for color and at least one mean differs for size.

41. **a.** Critical value of F is 3.49. Computed F is 0.668. Do not reject H_0.
b. Critical value of F is 3.26. Computed F value is 100.204. Reject H_0 for block means.
There is a difference in homes but not assessors.

43. For gasoline:
H_0: $\mu_1 = \mu_2 = \mu_3$; H_1: Mean mileage is not the same.
Reject H_0 if $F > 3.89$.
For automobile:
H_0: $\mu_1 = \mu_2 = \ldots = \mu_7$; H_1: Mean mileage is not the same.
Reject H_0 if $F > 3.00$.

ANOVA Table

Source	SS	df	MS	F
Gasoline	44.095	2	22.048	26.71
Autos	77.238	6	12.873	15.60
Error	9.905	12	0.825	
Total	131.238	20		

There is a difference in both autos and gasoline.

45. H_0: $\mu_1 = \mu_2 = \mu_3 = \mu_4 = \mu_5 = \mu_6$; H_1: The treatment means are not equal. Reject H_0 if $F > 2.37$.

Source	SS	df	MS	F
Treatment	0.03478	5	0.00696	3.86
Error	0.10439	58	0.0018	
Total	0.13917	63		

H_0 is rejected. There is a difference in the mean weight of the colors.

47. **a.**

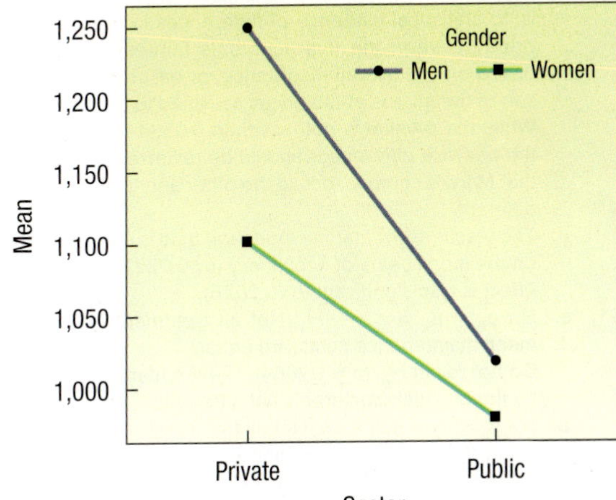

b. Two-way ANOVA: Wage versus Gender, Sector

```
Source       DF      SS      MS      F      P
Gender        1   44086   44086  11.44  0.004
Sector        1  156468  156468  40.61  0.000
Interaction   1   14851   14851   3.85  0.067
Error        16   61640    3853
Total        19  277046
```

There is no interaction effect of gender and sector on wages. However, there are significant differences in mean wages based on gender and significant differences in mean wages based on sector.

c. One-way ANOVA: Wage versus Sector

```
Source   DF      SS        MS       F       P
Sector    1   156468    156468   23.36   0.000
Error    18   120578      6699
Total    19   277046

s = 81.85   R-Sq = 56.48%   R-Sq(adj) = 54.06%
```

```
One-way ANOVA: Wage versus Gender
Source   DF      SS       MS      F       P
Gender    1    44086    44086   3.41   0.081
Error    18   232960    12942
Total    19   277046

s = 113.8  R-Sq = 15.91%  R-Sq(adj) = 11.24%
```

d. The statistical results show that only sector, private or public, has a significant effect on the wages of accountants.

49. a. H_0: $\sigma_p^2 = \sigma_{np}^2$ H_1: $\sigma_p^2 \neq \sigma_{np}^2$.
Reject H_0. The p-value is less than 0.05. There is a difference in the variance of average selling prices between houses with pools and houses without pools.

b. H_0: $\sigma_g^2 = \sigma_{ng}^2$ H_1: $\sigma_g^2 \neq \sigma_{ng}^2$
Reject H_0. There is a difference in the variance of average selling prices between house with garages and houses without garages. The p-value is < 0.0001.

c. H_0: $\mu_1 = \mu_2 = \mu_3 = \mu_4 = \mu_5$; H_1: Not all treatment means are equal
Fail to reject H_0. The p-value is much larger than 0.05. There is no statistical evidence of differences in the mean selling price between the five townships.

d. H_0: $\mu_c = \mu_l = \mu_m = \mu_p = \mu_r$ H_1: Not all treatment means are equal
Fail to reject H_0. The p-value is much larger than 0.05. There is no statistical evidence of differences in the mean selling price between the five agents. Is fairness of assignment based on the overall mean price, or based on the comparison of the means of the prices assigned to the agents?
While the p-value is not less than 0.05, it may indicate that the pairwise differences should be reviewed. These indicate that Marty's comparisons to the other agents are significantly different.

e. The results show that the mortgage type is a significant effect on the mean years of occupancy (p=0.0227). The interaction effect is also significant (p=0.0026).

51. a. H_0: $\mu_B = \mu_K = \mu_T$ H_1: Not all treatment (manufacturer) mean maintenance costs, are equal.
Do not reject H_0. ($p = 0.7664$). The mean maintenance costs by the bus manufacturer is not different.

b. H_0: $\mu_B = \mu_K = \mu_T$ H_1: Not all treatments have equal mean miles since the last maintenance.
Do not reject H_0. The mean miles since the last maintenance by the bus manufacturer is not different. P-value = 0.4828.

CHAPTER 13

1. $\Sigma(x - \bar{x})(y - \bar{y}) = 10.6$, $s_x = 2.7$, $s_y = 1.3$

$$r = \frac{10.6}{(5-1)(2.709)(1.38)} = 0.75$$

3. a. Sales.

b.

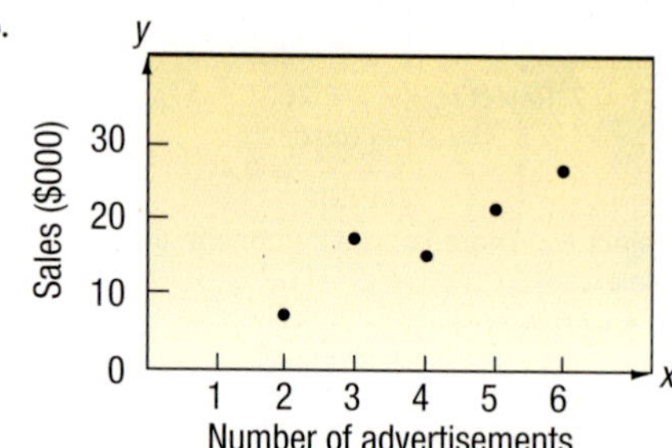

c. $\Sigma(x - \bar{x})(y - \bar{y}) = 36$, $n = 5$, $s_x = 1.5811$, $s_y = 6.1237$

$$r = \frac{36}{(5-1)(1.5811)(6.1237)} = 0.9295$$

d. There is a strong positive association between the variables.

5. a. Either variable could be independent. In the scatter plot, police is the independent variable.

b.

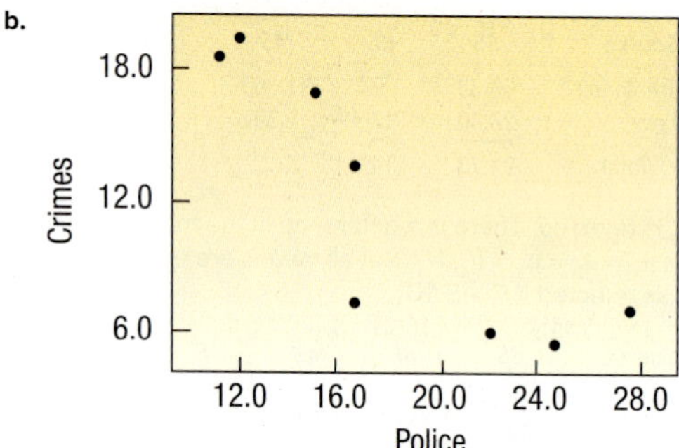

c. $n = 8$, $\Sigma(x - \bar{x})(y - \bar{y}) = -231.75$, $s_x = 5.8737$, $s_y = 6.4462$

$$r = \frac{-231.75}{(8-1)(5.8737)(6.4462)} = -0.8744$$

d. Strong inverse relationship. As the number of police increases, the crime decreases or, as crime increases the number of police decrease.

7. Reject H_0 if $t > 1.812$.

$$t = \frac{.32\sqrt{12-2}}{\sqrt{1-(.32)^2}} = 1.068$$

Do not reject H_0.

9. H_0: $\rho \leq 0$; H_1: $\rho > 0$. Reject H_0 if $t > 2.552$. $df = 18$.

$$t = \frac{.78\sqrt{20-2}}{\sqrt{1-(.78)^2}} = 5.288$$

Reject H_0. There is a positive correlation between gallons sold and the pump price.

11. H_0: $\rho \leq 0$ H_1: $\rho > 0$
Reject H_0 if $t > 2.650$ with $df = 13$.

$$t = \frac{0.667\sqrt{15-2}}{\sqrt{1-0.667^2}} = 3.228$$

Reject H_0. There is a positive correlation between the number of passengers and plane weight.

13. a. $\hat{y} = 3.7671 + 0.3630x$

$$b = 0.7522\left(\frac{1.3038}{2.7019}\right) = 0.3630$$

$$a = 5.8 - 0.3630(5.6) = 3.7671$$

b. 6.3081, found by $\hat{y} = 3.7671 + 0.3630(7)$

15. **a.** $\Sigma(x-\bar{x})(y-\bar{y}) = 44.6$, $s_x = 2.726$, $s_y = 2.011$

$$r = \frac{44.6}{(10-1)(2.726)(2.011)} = .904$$

$$b = .904\left(\frac{2.011}{2.726}\right) = 0.667$$

$$a = 7.4 - .677(9.1) = 1.333$$

b. $\hat{Y} = 1.333 + .667(6) = 5.335$

17. **a.**

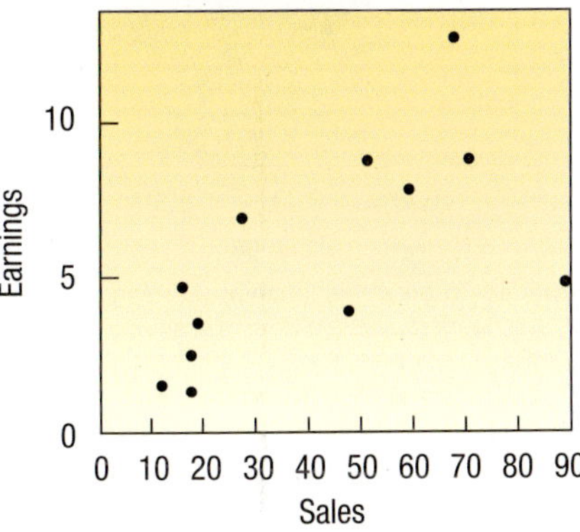

b. $\Sigma(x-\bar{x})(y-\bar{y}) = 629.64$, $s_x = 26.17$, $s_y = 3.248$

$$r = \frac{629.64}{(12-1)(26.17)(3.248)} = .6734$$

c. $b = .6734\left(\frac{3.248}{26.170}\right) = 0.0836$

$$a = \frac{64.1}{12} - 0.0836\left(\frac{501.10}{12}\right) = 1.8507$$

d. $\hat{y} = 1.8507 + 0.0836(50.0) = 6.0307$ ($ millions)

19. **a.** $b = -.8744\left(\frac{6.4462}{5.8737}\right) = -0.9596$

$$a = \frac{95}{8} - (-0.9596)\left(\frac{146}{8}\right) = 29.3877$$

b. 10.1957, found by 29.3877 – 0.9596(20)

c. For each policeman added, crime goes down by almost one.

21. $H_0: \beta \geq 0 \quad H_1: \beta < 0 \quad df = n - 2 = 8 - 2 = 6$
Reject H_0 if $t < -1.943$.

$$t = -0.96/0.22 = -4.364$$

Reject H_0 and conclude the slope is less than zero.

23. $H_0: \beta = 0 \quad H_1: \beta \neq 0 \quad df = n - 2 = 12 - 2 = 10$
Reject H_0 if t not between −2.228 and 2.228.

$$t = 0.08/0.03 = 2.667$$

Reject H_0 and conclude the slope is different from zero.

25. The standard error of estimate is 3.378, found by $\sqrt{\frac{68.4814}{8-2}}$.

The coefficient of determination is 0.76, found by $(-0.874)^2$. Seventy-six percent of the variation in crimes can be explained by the variation in police.

27. The standard error of estimate is 0.913, found by $\sqrt{\frac{6.667}{10-2}}$.

The coefficient of determination is 0.82, found by 29.733/36.4. Eighty-two percent of the variation in kilowatt hours can be explained by the variation in the number of rooms.

29. **a.** $r^2 = \frac{1{,}000}{1{,}500} = .6667$

b. $r = \sqrt{.6667} = .8165$

c. $s_{y \cdot x} = \sqrt{\frac{500}{13}} = 6.2017$

31. **a.** $6.308 \pm (3.182)(.993)\sqrt{.2 + \frac{(7-5.6)^2}{29.2}}$
$= 6.308 \pm 1.633$
$= [4.675, 7.941]$

b. $6.308 \pm (3.182)(.993)\sqrt{1 + 1/5 + .0671}$
$= [2.751, 9.865]$

33. **a.** 4.2939, 6.3721

b. 2.9854, 7.6806

35. The correlation between the two variables is 0.298. By squaring x, the correlation increases to .998.

37. $H_0: \rho \leq 0$; $H_1: \rho > 0$. Reject H_0 if $t > 1.714$.

$$t = \frac{.94\sqrt{25-2}}{\sqrt{1-(.94)^2}} = 13.213$$

Reject H_0. There is a positive correlation between passengers and weight of luggage.

39. $H_0: \rho \leq 0$; $H_1: \rho > 0$. Reject H_0 if $t > 2.764$.

$$t = \frac{.47\sqrt{12-2}}{\sqrt{1-(.47)^2}} = 1.684$$

Do not reject H_0. There is not a positive correlation between engine size and performance. p-value is greater than .05 but less than .10.

41. **a.** The sales volume is inversely related to their market share.

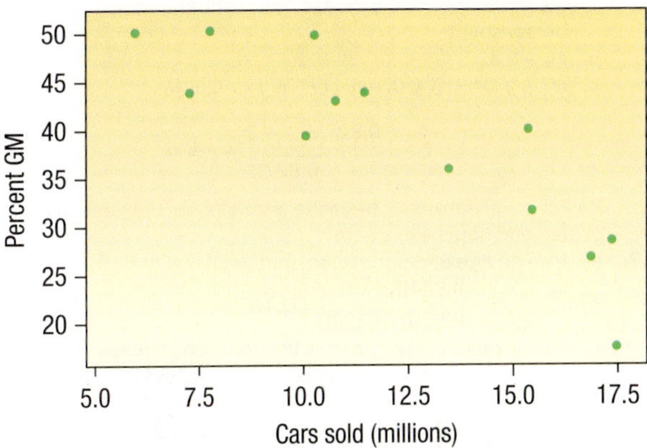

b. The correlation coefficient is −0.876; there is an inverse linear relationship between the two variables.

c. $H_0: \rho \geq 0 \quad H_1: \rho < 0 \quad$ Reject H_0 if $t < -2.681 \quad df = 12$

$$t = \frac{-0.876\sqrt{14-2}}{\sqrt{1-(-0.876)^2}} = -6.29$$

Reject H_0. There is a negative correlation between cars sold and market share.

d. 76.7%, found by $(-0.876)^2$, of the variation in market share is accounted for by variation in cars sold.

43. **a.** $r = -0.024$

b. The coefficient of determination is 0.00058, found by squaring (−0.024).

c. $H_0: \rho \geq 0 \quad H_1: \rho < 0 \quad$ Reject H_0 if $t < -1.697$

$$t = \frac{-0.024\sqrt{32-2}}{\sqrt{1-(-0.024)^2}} = -0.13$$

Reject H_0. There is a negative correlation between points scored and points allowed.

d. For the National conference (NFC): H_0: $\rho \geq 0$ H_1: $\rho < 0$
Reject H_0 if $t < -1.761$.

$$t = \frac{-0.139\sqrt{16-2}}{\sqrt{1-(-0.139)^2}} = -0.53$$

Do not reject H_0. We *cannot* say there is a negative correlation between points scored and points allowed in the NFC.
For the American conference (AFC): H_0: $\rho \geq 0$ H_1: $\rho < 0$
Reject H_0 if $t < -1.761$.

$$t = \frac{-0.292\sqrt{16-2}}{\sqrt{1-(-0.292)^2}} = -1.142$$

Do not reject H_0. We *cannot* say there is a negative correlation between points scored and points allowed in the AFC.

45. a.

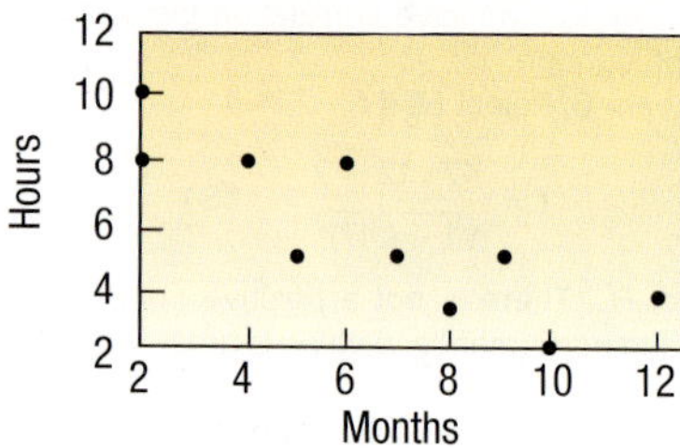

There is an inverse relationship between the variables. As the months owned increase, the number of hours exercised decreases.

b. $r = -0.827$

c. H_0: $\rho \geq 0$; H_1: $\rho < 0$. Reject H_0 if $t < -2.896$.

$$t = \frac{-0.827\sqrt{10-2}}{\sqrt{1-(-0.827)^2}} = -4.16$$

Reject H_0. There is a negative association between months owned and hours exercised.

47. a. Median age and population are directly related.

b. $r = \dfrac{11.93418}{(10-1)(2.207)(1.330)} = 0.452$

c. The slope of 0.272 indicates that for each increase of 1 million in the population, the median age increases on average by 0.272 year.

d. The median age is 32.08 years, found by 31.4 + 0.272(2.5).

e. The *p*-value (0.190) for the population variable is greater than, say, .05. A test for significance of that coefficient would fail to be rejected. In other words, it is possible the population coefficient is zero.

f. H_0: $\rho = 0$ H_1: $\rho \neq 0$ Reject H_0 if t is not between −1.86 and 1.86.

$df = 8$ $t = \dfrac{0.452\sqrt{10-2}}{\sqrt{1-(0.452)^2}} = 1.433$ Do not reject H_0.

There may be no relationship between age and population.

49. a. $b = -0.4667$, $a = 11.2358$

b. $\hat{y} = 11.2358 - 0.4667(7.0) = 7.9689$

c. $7.9689 \pm (2.160)(1.114)\sqrt{1 + \dfrac{1}{15} + \dfrac{(7-7.1333)^2}{73.7333}}$

$= 7.9689 \pm 2.4854$
$= [5.4835, 10.4543]$

d. $R^2 = 0.499$. Nearly 50% of the variation in the amount of the bid is explained by the number of bidders.

51. a.

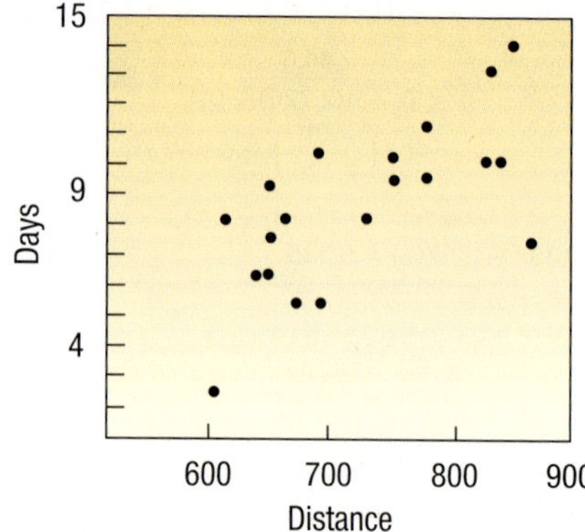

There appears to be a relationship between the two variables. As the distance increases, so does the shipping time.

b. $r = 0.692$
H_0: $\rho \leq 0$; H_1: $\rho > 0$. Reject H_0 if $t > 1.734$.

$$t = \frac{0.692\sqrt{20-2}}{\sqrt{1-(0.692)^2}} = 4.067$$

H_0 is rejected. There is a positive association between shipping distance and shipping time.

c. $R^2 = 0.479$. Nearly half of the variation in shipping time is explained by shipping distance.

d. $s_{y \cdot x} = 2.004$

53. a. $b = 2.41$
$a = 26.8$
The regression equation is: Price = 26.8 + 2.41 × Dividend. For each additional dollar of dividend, the price increases by $2.41.

b. To test the significance of the slope, we use $n - 2$, or $30 - 2 = 28$ degrees of freedom. For a 0.05 level of significance, the critical values are −2.048 and 2.048. The *t*-test statistic is $t = \dfrac{b-0}{s_b} = \dfrac{2.408}{0.328} = 7.34$. We reject the null hypothesis that the slope is equal to zero.

c. $R^2 = \dfrac{5{,}057.6}{7{,}682.7} = 0.658$ Thus, 65.8% of the variation in price is explained by the dividend.

d. $r = \sqrt{.658} = 0.811$ H_0: $\rho \leq 0$ H_1: $\rho > 0$
At the 5% level, reject H_0 when $t > 1.701$.

$$t = \frac{0.811\sqrt{30-2}}{\sqrt{1-(0.811)^2}} = 7.34$$

Thus, H_0 is rejected. The population correlation is positive.

55. a. 35

b. $s_{y \cdot x} = \sqrt{29{,}778{,}406} = 5{,}456.96$

c. $r^2 = \dfrac{13{,}548{,}662{,}082}{14{,}531{,}349{,}474} = 0.932$

d. $r = \sqrt{0.932} = 0.966$

e. H_0: $\rho \leq 0$, H_1: $\rho > 0$; reject H_0 if $t > 1.692$.

$$t = \frac{.966\sqrt{35-2}}{\sqrt{1-(.966)^2}} = 21.46$$

Reject H_0. There is a direct relationship between size of the house and its market value.

57. a. The regression equation is Price = −386.5 + 704.0 Speed.

b. The computers 2, 3, and 10 have errors in excess of $200.00.

c. The correlation of Speed and Price is 0.835.
$H_0: \rho \leq 0 \quad H_1: \rho > 0 \quad$ Reject H_0 if $t > 1.8125$.

$$t = \frac{0.835\sqrt{12-2}}{\sqrt{1-(0.835)^2}} = 4.799$$

Reject H_0. It is reasonable to say the population correlation is positive.

59. a. $r = .987$, $H_0: \rho \leq 0$, $H_1: \rho > 0$. Reject H_0 if $t > 1.746$.

$$t = \frac{.987\sqrt{18-2}}{\sqrt{1-(.987)^2}} = 24.564$$

b. $\hat{y} = -29.7 + 22.93x$; an additional cup increases the dog's weight by almost 23 pounds.

c. Dog number 4 is an overeater.

61. a.

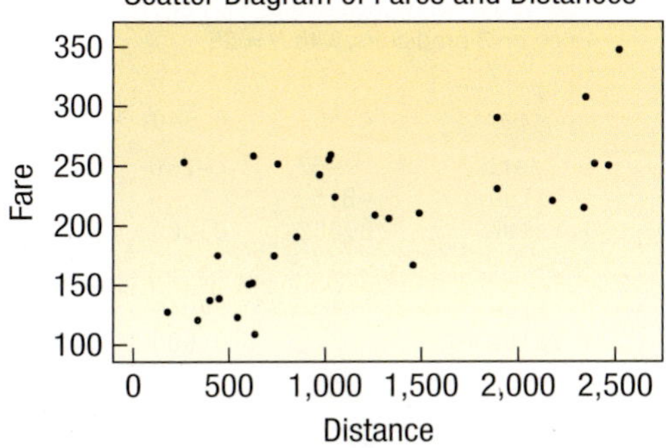

The relationship is direct. Fares increase for longer flights.

b. The correlation of Distance and Fare is 0.656.
$H_0: \rho \leq 0 \quad H_1: \rho > 0 \quad$ Reject H_0 if $t > 1.701$. $\quad df = 28$

$$t = \frac{0.656\sqrt{30-2}}{\sqrt{1-(0.656)^2}} = 4.599$$

Reject H_0. There is a significant positive correlation between fares and distances.

c. 43%, found by $(0.656)^2$, of the variation in fares is explained by the variation in distance.

d. The regression equation is Fare = 147.08 + 0.05265 Distance. Each additional mile adds $0.05265 to the fare.
A 1,500-mile flight would cost $226.06, found by $147.08 + 0.05265(1,500).

e. A flight of 4,218 miles is outside the range of the sampled data, so the regression equation may not be useful.

63. a. There does seem to be a direct relationship between the variables.

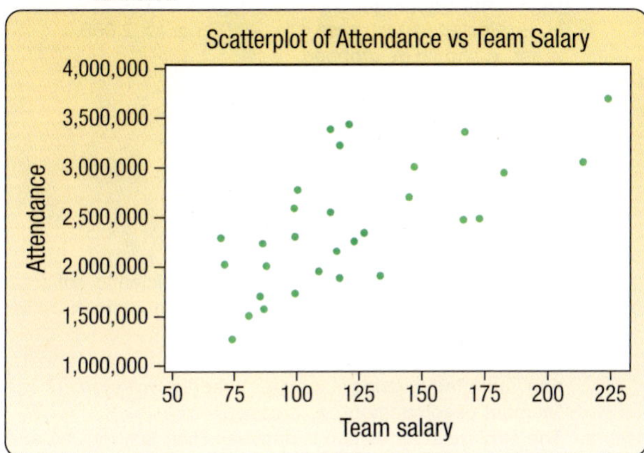

b. Expected Attendance with a salary of $100 million is 2,224,268, found by 1,208,968 + 10,153(100)

c. Increasing the salary by 30 million will increase attendance by 304,590 on average, found by 10,153 (30). This is also the difference between the expected attendance with a salary of 130 and the expected attendance of 100 million.

d. The regression output from *Excel* is below.

SUMMARY OUTPUT

Regression Statistics	
Multiple R	0.652
R Square	0.425
Adjusted R Square	0.404
Standard Error	484846.605
Observations	30.000

ANOVA

	df	SS	MS	F	Significance F
Regression	1	4863338397693.920	4863338397693.920	20.688	0.000
Residual	28	6582134442815.280	235076230100.546		
Total	29	11445472840509.200			

	Coefficients	Standard Error	t Stat	P-value
Intercept	1208968.430	284472.197	4.250	0.000
Team Salary	10152.694	2232.124	4.548	0.000

$H_0: \beta \leq 0 \quad H_1: \beta > 0 \quad df = n - 2 = 30 - 2 = 28$ Reject H_0 if $t > 1.701 \quad t = 10152.694/2232.124 = 4.548$. Reject H_0 and conclude the slope is positive.

e. 0.4249 or 42.49% of the variation in attendance is explained by variation in salary.

f. The correlation between attendance and batting average is 0.1472.
$H_0: \rho \leq 0 \quad H_1: \rho > 0 \quad$ At the 5% level, reject H_0 if $t > 1.701$.

$$t = \frac{0.1472\sqrt{30-2}}{\sqrt{1-(0.1472)^2}} = 0.787$$

Fail to reject H_0.
p-value = 0.4377
The batting average and attendance are not positively correlated.
The correlation between attendance and ERA is −0.4745. The correlation between attendance and ERA is stronger than the correlation between attendance and batting average.
$H_0: \rho \geq 0 \quad H_1: \rho < 0 \quad$ At the 5% level, reject H_0 if $t < -1.701$.

$$t = \frac{-0.4745\sqrt{30-2}}{\sqrt{1-(-0.4745)^2}} = -2.8524$$

Fail to reject H_0.
p-value = 0.0081
The ERA and attendance are not negatively correlated.

CHAPTER 14

1. a. Multiple regression equation

b. The y-intercept

c. $\hat{y} = 64{,}100 + 0.394(796{,}000) + 9.6(6{,}940) - 11{,}600(6.0) = \$374{,}748$

3. a. 497.736, found by
$\hat{y} = 16.24 + 0.017(18) + 0.0028(26{,}500) + 42(3) + 0.0012(156{,}000) + 0.19(141) + 26.8(2.5)$

b. Two more social activities. Income added only 28 to the index; social activities added 53.6.

5. **a.** $s_{Y\cdot12} = \sqrt{\frac{SSE}{n-(k+1)}} = \sqrt{\frac{583.693}{65-(2+1)}}$

$= \sqrt{9.414} = 3.068$

95% of the residuals will be between ±6.136, found by 2(3.068).

b. $R^2 = \frac{\text{SSR}}{\text{SS total}} = \frac{77.907}{661.6} = .118$

The independent variables explain 11.8% of the variation.

c. $R^2_{adj} = 1 - \frac{\frac{\text{SSE}}{n-(k+1)}}{\frac{\text{SS total}}{n-1}} = 1 - \frac{\frac{583.693}{65-(2+1)}}{\frac{661.6}{65-1}}$

$= 1 - \frac{9.414}{10.3375} = 1 - .911 = .089$

7. **a.** $\hat{y} = 84.998 + 2.391x_1 - 0.4086x_2$

b. 90.0674, found by $\hat{y} = 84.998 + 2.391(4) - 0.4086(11)$

c. $n = 65$ and $k = 2$

d. H_0: $\beta_1 = \beta_2 = 0$ H_1: Not all βs are 0

Reject H_0 if $F > 3.15$.

$F = 4.14$, reject H_0. Not all net regression coefficients equal zero.

e. For x_1 For x_2

H_0: $\beta_1 = 0$ H_0: $\beta_2 = 0$

H_1: $\beta_1 \neq 0$ H_1: $\beta_2 \neq 0$

$t = 1.99$ $t = -2.38$

Reject H_0 if $t > 2.0$ or $t < -2.0$.

Delete variable 1 and keep 2.

f. The regression analysis should be repeated with only x_2 as the independent variable.

9. **a.** The regression equation is: Performance = 29.3 + 5.22 Aptitude + 22.1 Union

Predictor	Coef	SE Coef	T	P
Constant	29.28	12.77	2.29	0.041
Aptitude	5.222	1.702	3.07	0.010
Union	22.135	8.852	2.50	0.028

S = 16.9166 R-Sq = 53.3% R-Sq (adj) = 45.5%

Analysis of Variance

Source	DF	SS	MS	F	P
Regression	2	3919.3	1959.6	6.85	0.010
Residual Error	12	3434.0	286.2		
Total	14	7353.3			

b. These variables are effective in predicting performance. They explain 53.3% of the variation in performance. In particular, union membership increases the typical performance by 22.1.

c. H_0: $\beta_2 = 0$ H_1: $\beta_2 \neq 0$

Reject H_0 if $t < -2.179$ or $t > 2.179$. Since 2.50 is greater than 2.179, we reject the null hypothesis and conclude that union membership is significant and should be included.

d. When you consider the interaction variable, the regression equation is Performance = 38.7 + 3.80 Aptitude − 0.1 Union + 3.61 x_1x_2

Predictor	Coef	SE Coef	T	P
Constant	38.69	15.62	2.48	0.031
Aptitude	3.802	2.179	1.74	0.109
Union	−0.10	23.14	−0.00	0.997
X_1X_2	3.610	3.473	1.04	0.321

The t value corresponding to the interaction term is 1.04. This is not significant. So we conclude there is no interaction between aptitude and union membership when predicting job performance.

11. **a.** The regression equation is

Price = 3,080 − 54.2 Bidders + 16.3 Age

Predictor	Coef	SE Coef	T	P
Constant	3080.1	343.9	8.96	0.000
Bidders	−54.19	12.28	−4.41	0.000
Age	16.289	3.784	4.30	0.000

The price decreases 54.2 as each additional bidder participates. Meanwhile the price increases 16.3 as the painting gets older. While one would expect older paintings to be worth more, it is unexpected that the price goes down as more bidders participate!

b. The regression equation is

Price = 3,972 − 185 Bidders + 6.35 Age + 1.46 x_1x_2

Predictor	Coef	SE Coef	T	P
Constant	3971.7	850.2	4.67	0.000
Bidders	−185.0	114.9	−1.61	0.122
Age	6.353	9.455	0.67	0.509
X_1X_2	1.462	1.277	1.15	0.265

The t value corresponding to the interaction term is 1.15. This is not significant. So we conclude there is no interaction.

c. In the stepwise procedure, the number of bidders enters the equation first. Then the interaction term enters. The variable age would not be included as it is not significant. Response is Price on 3 predictors, with $N = 25$.

Step	1	2
Constant	4,507	4,540
Bidders	−57	−256
T-Value	−3.53	−5.59
P-Value	0.002	0.000
X_1X_2		2.25
T-Value		4.49
P-Value		0.000
S	295	218
R-Sq	35.11	66.14
R-Sq(adj)	32.29	63.06

13. **a.** $n = 40$

b. 4

c. $R^2 = \frac{750}{1{,}250} = .60$

d. $s_{y\cdot1234} = \sqrt{500/35} = 3.7796$

e. H_0: $\beta_1 = \beta_2 = \beta_3 = \beta_4 = 0$

H_1: Not all the βs equal zero.

H_0 is rejected if $F > 2.65$.

$F = \frac{750/4}{500/35} = 13.125$

H_0 is rejected. At least one β_i does not equal zero.

15. **a.** $n = 26$

b. $R^2 = 100/140 = .7143$

c. 1.4142, found by $\sqrt{2}$

d. H_0: $\beta_1 = \beta_2 = \beta_3 = \beta_4 = \beta_5 = 0$

H_1: Not all the βs are 0.

H_0 is rejected if $F > 2.71$.

Computed $F = 10.0$. Reject H_0. At least one regression coefficient is not zero.

e. H_0 is rejected in each case if $t < -2.086$ or $t > 2.086$. x_1 and x_5 should be dropped.

17. **a.** $28,000

b. $R^2 = \frac{\text{SSR}}{\text{SS total}} = \frac{3{,}050}{5{,}250} = .5809$

c. 9.199, found by $\sqrt{84.62}$

d. H_0 is rejected if $F > 2.97$ (approximately)

$$\text{Computed } F = \frac{1{,}016.67}{84.62} = 12.01$$

H_0 is rejected. At least one regression coefficient is not zero.

e. If computed t is to the left of −2.056 or to the right of 2.056, the null hypothesis in each of these cases is rejected. Computed t for x_2 and x_3 exceed the critical value. Thus, "population" and "advertising expenses" should be retained and "number of competitors," x_1, dropped.

19. **a.** The strongest correlation is between High School GPA and Paralegal GPA. No problem with multicollinearity.

b. $R^2 = \dfrac{4.3595}{5.0631} = .8610$

c. H_0 is rejected if $F > 5.41$.

$$F = \frac{1.4532}{0.1407} = 10.328$$

At least one coefficient is not zero.

d. Any H_0 is rejected if $t < -2.571$ or $t > 2.571$. It appears that only High School GPA is significant. Verbal and math could be eliminated.

e. $R^2 = \dfrac{4.2061}{5.0631} = .8307$

R^2 has only been reduced .0303.

f. The residuals appear slightly skewed (positive) but acceptable.

g. There does not seem to be a problem with the plot.

21. **a.** The correlation of Screen and Price is 0.893. So there does appear to be a linear relationship between the two.

b. Price is the "dependent" variable.

c. The regression equation is Price = −1242.1 + 50.671 (screen size). For each inch increase in screen size, the price increases $50.671 on average.

d. Using a "dummy" variable for Sony, the regression equation is Price = 11145.6 + 46.955 (Screen) + 187.10 (Sony). If we set "Sony" = 0, then the manufacturer is Samsung and the price is predicted only by screen size. If we set "Sony" = 1, then the manufacturer is Sony. Therefore, Sony TV's are, on average, $187.10 higher in price than Samsung TVs.

e. Here is some of the output.

Coefficients

Term	Coef	SE Coef	95% CI	*T*-Value	*P*-Value
Constant	−1145.6	220.7	(−1606.1, −685.2)	−5.19	<0.0001
Screen	46.955	5.149	(36.215, 57.695)	9.12	<0.0001
Sony					
1	187.10	71.84	(37.24, 336.96)	2.60	0.0170

Based on the *p*-values, screen size and manufacturer are both significant in predicting price.

f. A histogram of the residuals indicates they follow a normal distribution.

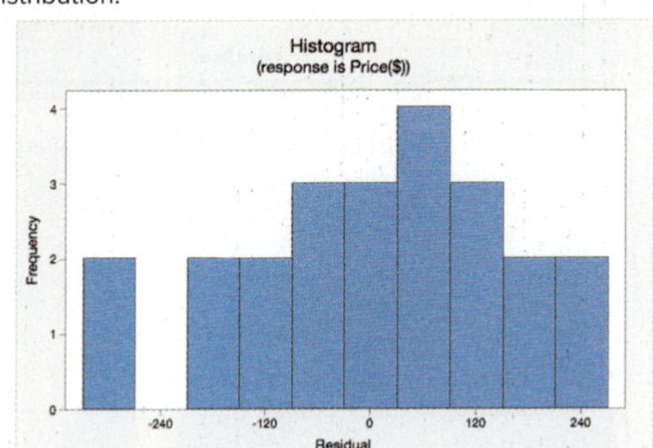

g. There is no apparent relationship in the residuals, but the residual variation may be increasing with larger fitted values.

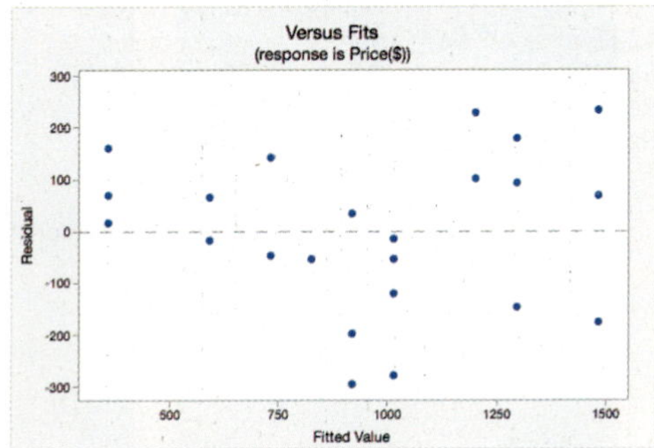

23. **a.**

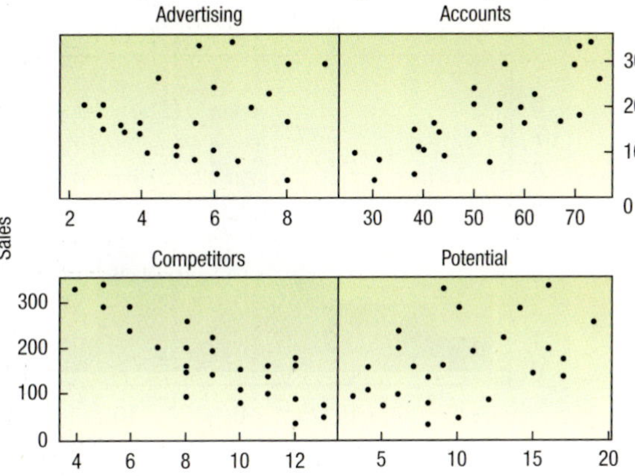

Sales seem to fall with the number of competitors and rise with the number of accounts and potential.

b. Pearson correlations

	Sales	Advertising	Accounts	Competitors
Advertising	0.159			
Accounts	0.783	0.173		
Competitors	−0.833	−0.038	−0.324	
Potential	0.407	−0.071	0.468	−0.202

The number of accounts and the market potential are moderately correlated.

c. The regression equation is:

Sales = 178 + 1.81 Advertising + 3.32 Accounts − 21.2 Competitors + 0.325 Potential

Predictor	Coef	SE Coef	T	P
Constant	178.32	12.96	13.76	0.000
Advertising	1.807	1.081	1.67	0.109
Accounts	3.3178	0.1629	20.37	0.000
Competitors	−21.1850	0.7879	−26.89	0.000
Potential	0.3245	0.4678	0.69	0.495

S = 9.60441 R-Sq = 98.9% R-Sq(adj) = 98.7%

Analysis of Variance

Source	DF	SS	MS	F	P
Regression	4	176777	44194	479.10	0.000
Residual Error	21	1937	92		
Total	25	178714			

The computed *F* value is quite large. So we can reject the null hypothesis that all of the regression coefficients are zero. We conclude that some of the independent variables are effective in explaining sales.

d. Market potential and advertising have large *p*-values (0.495 and 0.109, respectively). You would probably drop them.

e. If you omit potential, the regression equation is:

Sales = 180 + 1.68 Advertising + 3.37 Accounts − 21.2 Competitors

Predictor	Coef	SE Coef	T	P
Constant	179.84	12.62	14.25	0.000
Advertising	1.677	1.052	1.59	0.125
Accounts	3.3694	0.1432	23.52	0.000
Competitors	−21.2165	0.7773	−27.30	0.000

Now advertising is not significant. That would also lead you to cut out the advertising variable and report that the polished regression equation is: Sales = 187 + 3.41 Accounts − 21.2 Competitors

Predictor	Coef	SE Coef	T	P
Constant	186.69	12.26	15.23	0.000
Accounts	3.4081	0.1458	23.37	0.000
Competitors	−21.1930	0.8028	−26.40	0.000

f.

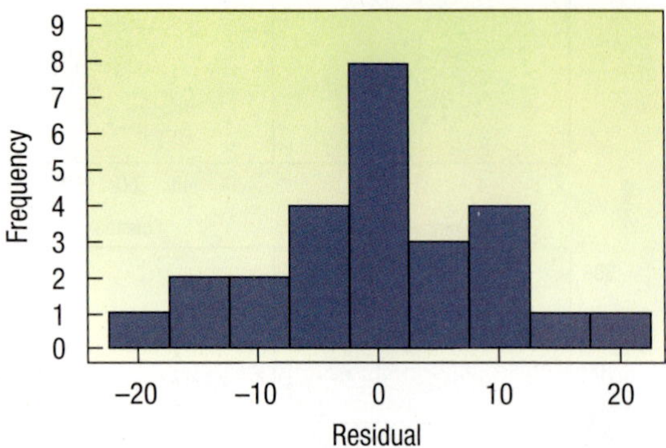

The histogram looks to be normal. There are no problems shown in this plot.

g. The variance inflation factor for both variables is 1.1. They are less than 10. There are no troubles as this value indicates the independent variables are not strongly correlated with each other.

25. The computer output is:

```
Predictor      Coef   StDev   t-ratio      p
Constant      651.9   345.3      1.89  0.071
Service      13.422   5.125      2.62  0.015
Age          -6.710   6.349     -1.06  0.301
Gender       205.65   90.27      2.28  0.032
Job          -33.45   89.55     -0.37  0.712

Analysis of Variance
SOURCE       DF       SS       MS     F      p
Regression    4  1066830   266708  4.77  0.005
Error        25  1398651    55946
Total        29  2465481
```

a. $\hat{y} = 651.9 + 13.422x_1 - 6.710x_2 + 205.65x_3 - 33.45x_4$

b. $R^2 = .433$, which is somewhat low for this type of study.

c. H_0: $\beta_1 = \beta_2 = \beta_3 = \beta_4 = 0$; H_1: Not all βs equal zero
Reject H_0 if $F > 2.76$.

$$F = \frac{1{,}066{,}830/4}{1{,}398{,}651/25} = 4.77$$

H_0 is rejected. Not all the β_is equal 0.

d. Using the .05 significance level, reject the hypothesis that the regression coefficient is 0 if $t < -2.060$ or $t > 2.060$. Service and gender should remain in the analyses; age and job should be dropped.

e. Following is the computer output using the independent variables service and gender.

```
Predictor      Coef   StDev   t-ratio      p
Constant      784.2   316.8      2.48  0.020
Service       9.021   3.106      2.90  0.007
Gender       224.41   87.35      2.57  0.016

Analysis of Variance
SOURCE       DF       SS       MS     F      p
Regression    2   998779   499389  9.19  0.001
Error        27  1466703    54322
Total        29  2465481
```

A man earns $224 more per month than a woman. The difference between management and engineering positions is not significant.

27. a. $\hat{y} = 29.913 - 5.324x_1 + 1.449x_2$

b. EPS is ($t = -3.26$, p-value $= .005$). Yield is not ($t = 0.81$, p-value $= .431$).

c. An increase of 1 in EPS results in a decline of 5.324 in P/E.

d. Stock number 2 is undervalued.

e. Below is a residual plot. It does *not* appear to follow the normal distribution.

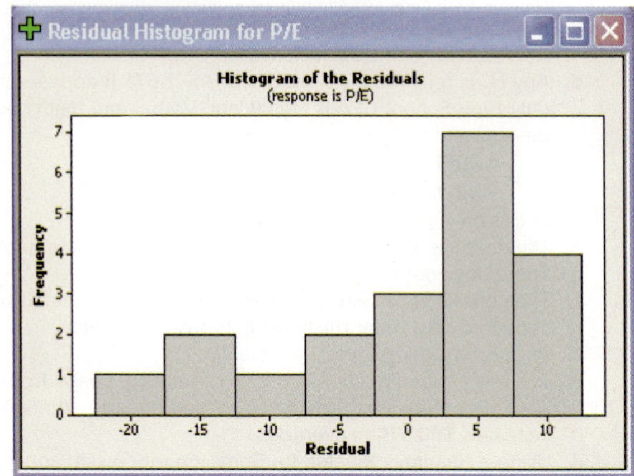

f. There does not seem to be a problem with the plot of the residuals versus the fitted values.

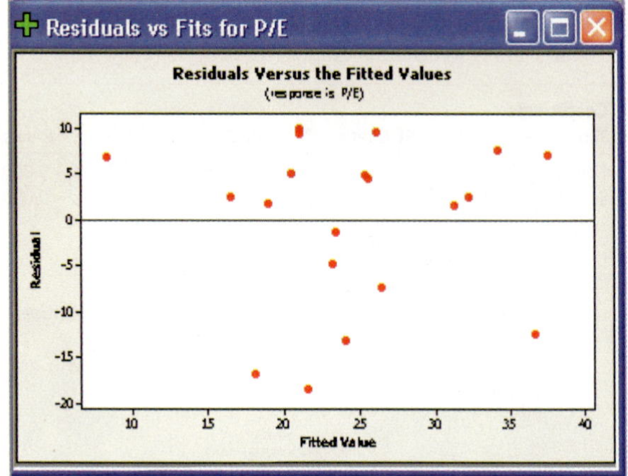

g. The correlation between yield and EPS is not a problem. No problem with multicollinearity.

	P/E	EPS
EPS	−0.602	
Yield	.054	.162

29. a. The regression equation is
Sales (000) = 1.02 + 0.0829 Infomercials

```
Predictor          Coef   SE Coef      T      P
Constant         1.0188    0.3105   3.28  0.006
Infomercials    0.08291   0.01680   4.94  0.000

Analysis of Variance
Source           DF      SS      MS      F      P
Regression        1  2.3214  2.3214  24.36  0.000
Residual Error   13  1.2386  0.0953
Total            14  3.5600
```

The global test demonstrates there is a relationship between sales and the number of infomercials.

b.

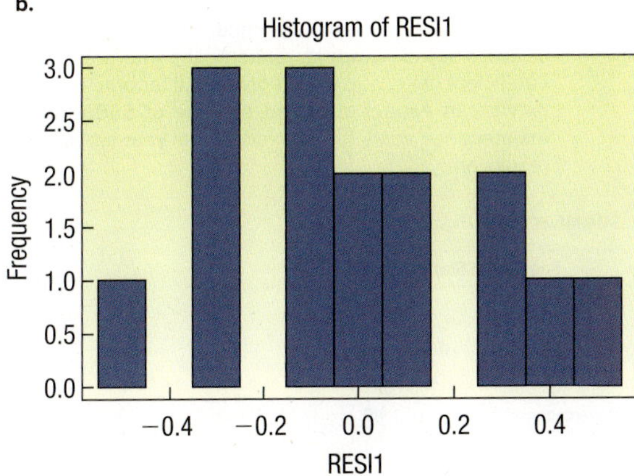

The residuals appear to follow the normal distribution.

31. a. The regression equation is
Auction Price = −118,929 + 1.63 Loan + 2.1 Monthly Payment + 50 Payments Made

```
Analysis of Variance
Source      DF          SS          MS      F      P
Regression   3  5966725061  1988908354  39.83  0.000
Residual
  Error     16   798944439    49934027
Total       19  6765669500
```

The computed *F* is 39.83. It is much larger than the critical value 3.24. The *p*-value is also quite small. Thus, the null hypothesis that all the regression coefficients are zero can be rejected. At least one of the multiple regression coefficients is different from zero.

b.

```
Predictor        Coef    SE Coef      T      P
Constant      -118929      19734  -6.03  0.000
Loan           1.6268     0.1809   8.99  0.000
Monthly
  Payment        2.06      14.95   0.14  0.892
Payments
  Made           50.3      134.9   0.37  0.714
```

The null hypothesis is that the coefficient is zero in the individual test. It would be rejected if *t* is less than −2.120 or more than 2.120. In this case, the *t* value for the loan variable is larger than the critical value. Thus, it should not be removed. However, the monthly payment and payments made variables would likely be removed.

c. The revised regression equation is: Auction Price = −119,893 + 1.67 Loan

33. a. The correlation matrix is as follows:

	Price	Bedrooms	Size (square feet)	baths	Days on Market
Price	1.000				
Bedrooms	0.844	1.000			
Size (square feet)	0.952	0.877	1.000		
Baths	0.825	0.985	0.851	1.000	
Days on Market	0.185	0.002	0.159	−0.002	1

The correlations for strong, positive relationships between "Price" and the independent variables "Bedrooms", "Size", and "Baths". There appears to be no relationship between "Price" and "Days on the Market". The correlations among the independent variables are very strong. So, there would be a high degree of multicollinearity in a multiple regression equation if all the variables were included. We will need to be careful in selecting the best independent variable to predict price.

b.

SUMMARY OUTPUT

Regression Statistics	
Multiple *R*	0.952
R Square	0.905
Adjusted *R* Square	0.905
Standard Error	49655.822
Observations	105.000

ANOVA

	df	SS	MS	*F*	Significance *F*
Regression	1	2.432E+12	2.432E+12	9.862E+02	1.46136E-54
Residual	103	2.540E+11	2.466E+09		
Total	104	2.686E+12			

	Coefficients	Standard Error	*t* Stat	*P*-value
Intercept	−15775.955	12821.967	−1.230	0.221
Size (square feet)	108.364	3.451	31.405	0.000

The regression analysis shows a significant relationship between price and house size. The *p*-value of the *F*-statistic is 0.00, so the null hypothesis of "no relationship" is rejected. Also, the *p*-value associated with the regression coefficient of "size" is 0.000. Therefore, this coefficient is clearly different from zero.

The regression equation is: Price = −15775.995 + 108.364 Size.

In terms of pricing, the regression equation suggests that houses are priced at about $108 per square foot.

c. The regression analyses of price and size with the qualitative variables pool and garage follow. The results show that the variable "pool" is statistically significant in the equation. The regression coefficient indicates that if a house has a pool, it adds about $28,575 to the price. The analysis of including "garage" to the analysis indicates that it does not affect the pricing of the house.

Adding pool to the regression equation increases the *R*-square by about 1%.

SUMMARY OUTPUT

Regression Statistics	
Multiple *R*	0.955
R Square	0.913
Adjusted *R* Square	0.911
Standard Error	47914.856
Observations	105

ANOVA

	df	SS	MS	*F*	Significance *F*
Regression	2.00	2451577033207.43	1225788516603.72	533.92	0.00
Residual	102.00	234175013207.24	2295833462.82		
Total	104.00	2685752046414.68			

	Coefficients	Standard Error	*t* Stat	*P*-value
Intercept	−34640.573	13941.203	−2.485	0.015
Size (square feet)	108.547	3.330	32.595	0.000
Pool (yes is 1)	28575.145	9732.223	2.936	0.004

d. The following histogram was developed using the residuals from part c. The normality assumption is reasonable.

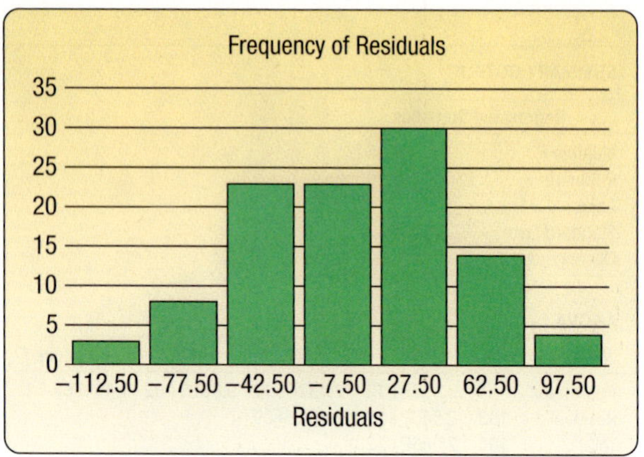

e. The following scatter diagram is based on the residuals in part c with the predicted dependent variable on the horizontal axis and residuals on the vertical axis. There does appear that the variance of the residuals increases with higher values of the predicted price. You can experiment with transformations such as the Log of Price or the square root of price and observe the changes in the graphs of residuals. Note that the transformations will make the interpretation of the regression equation more difficult. **(LO14-6)**

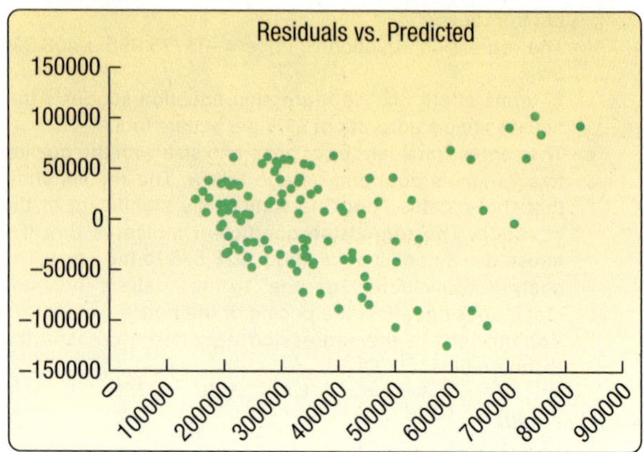

35. a.

	Maintenance cost($)	Age (years)	Odometer Miles	Miles since last Maintenance
Maintenance cost($)	1			
Age(years)	0.710194278	1		
Odometer Miles	0.700439797	0.990675674	1	
Miles since last Maint.	−0.160275988	−0.140196856	−0.118982823	1

The correlation analysis shows that age and odometer miles are positively correlated with cost and that "miles since last maintenance" shows that costs increase with fewer miles between maintenance. The analysis also shows a strong correlation between age and odometer miles. This indicates the strong possibility of multicollinearity if age and odometer miles are included in a regression equation.

b. There are a number of analyses to do. First, using Age or Odometer Miles as an independent variable. When you review these analyses, both result in significant relationships. However, Age has a slightly higher R^2. So I would select age as the first independent variable. The interpretation of the coefficient using age is bit more useful for practical use. That is, we can expect about an average of $600 increase in maintenance costs for each additional year a bus ages. The results are:

SUMMARY OUTPUT

Regression Statistics	
Multiple *R*	0.708
R Square	0.501
Adjusted *R* Square	0.494
Standard Error	1658.097
Observations	80

ANOVA

	df	SS	MS	*F*	Significance *F*
Regression	1	215003471.845	215003471.845	78.203	0.000
Residual	78	214444212.142	2749284.771		
Total	79	429447683.988			

	Coefficients	Standard Error	*t* Stat	*P*-value
Intercept	337.297	511.372	0.660	0.511
Age (years)	603.161	68.206	8.843	0.000

We can also explore including the variable "miles since last maintenance" with Age. Your analysis will show that "miles since last maintenance" is not significantly related to costs.

Last, it is possible that maintenance costs are different for diesel versus gasoline engines. So, adding this variable to the analysis shows:

SUMMARY OUTPUT

Regression Statistics	
Multiple *R*	0.960
R Square	0.922
Adjusted *R* Square	0.920
Standard Error	658.369
Observations	80

ANOVA

	df	SS	MS	*F*	Significance *F*
Regression	2	396072093.763	198036046.881	456.884	0.000
Residual	77	33375590.225	433449.224		
Total	79	429447683.988			

	Coefficients	Standard Error	*t* Stat	*P*-value
Intercept	−1028.539	213.761	−4.812	0.000
Age (years)	644.528	27.157	23.733	0.000
Engine Type (0=diesel)	3190.481	156.100	20.439	0.000

The results show that the engine type is statistically significant and increases the R^2 to 92.2%. Now the practical interpretation of the analysis is that, on average, buses with gasoline engines cost about $3,190 more to maintain. Also, the maintenance costs increase with bus age at an average of $644 per year of bus age.

c. The normality conjecture appears realistic.

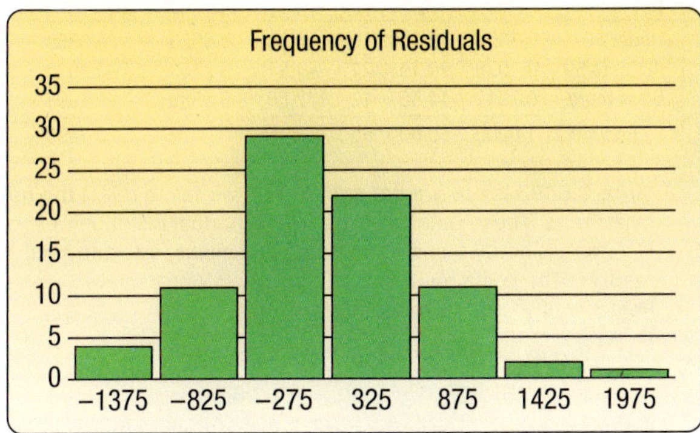

d. The plot of residuals versus predicted values shows the following. There are clearly patterns in the graph that indicate that the residuals do not follow the assumptions required for the tests of hypotheses.

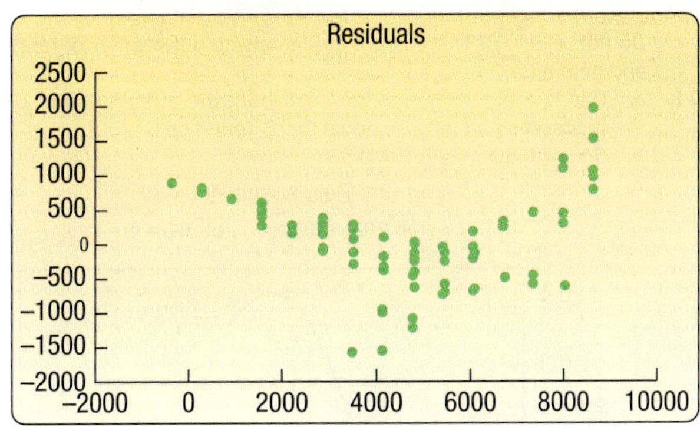

Lets remember the scatter plot of costs versus age. The graph clearly shows the effect of engine type on costs. So there are essentially two regression equations depending on the type of engine.

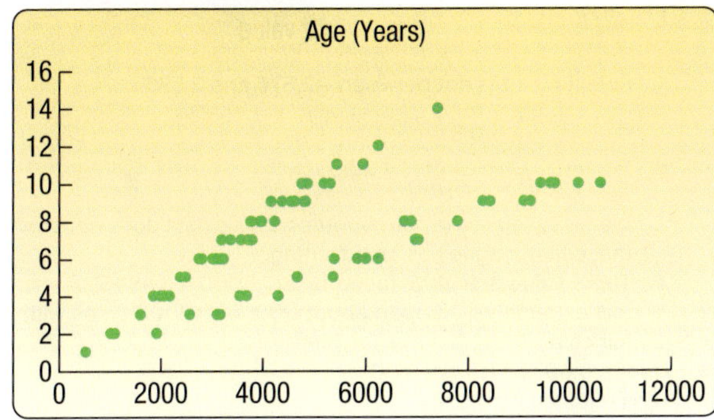

So based on our knowledge of the data, lets create a residual plot of costs for each engine type.

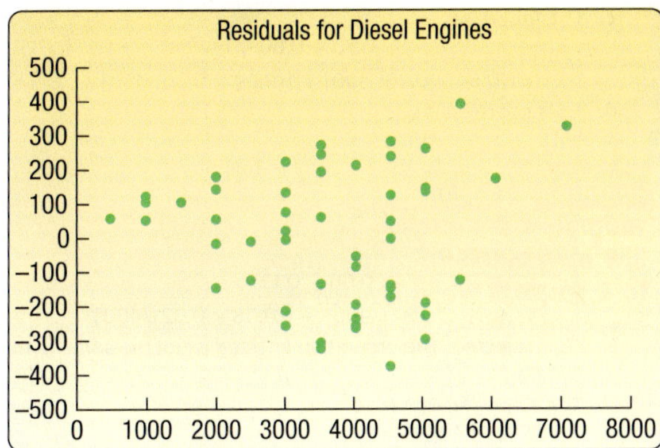

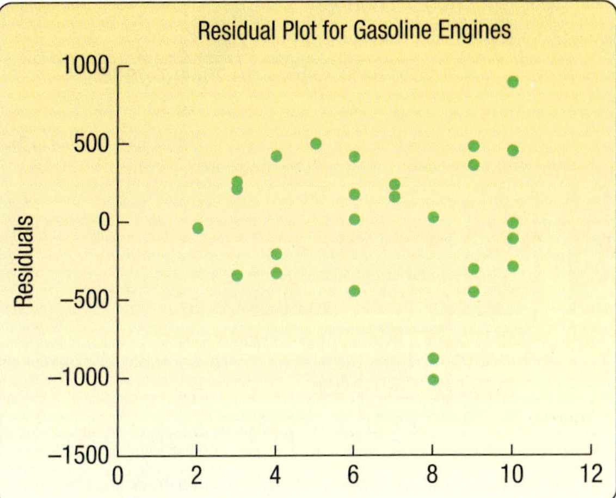

The graphs show a much better distribution of residuals. **(LO14-5)**

CHAPTER 15

1. **a.** H_0 is rejected if $z > 1.65$.
  b. 1.09, found by $z = (0.75 - 0.70)/\sqrt{(0.70 \times 0.30)/100}$
  c. H_0 is not rejected.

3. Step 1: H_0: $\pi = 0.10$ H_1: $\pi \neq 0.10$
  Step 2: The 0.01 significance level was chosen
  Step 3: Use the z-statistic as the binomial distribution can be approximated by the normal distribution as $n\pi = 30 > 5$ and $n(1-\pi) = 270 > 5$.
  Step 4: Reject H_0 if $z > 2.326$
  Step 5:

$$z = \frac{\{(^{63}/_{300}) - 0.10\}}{\sqrt{\{^{0.10(0.90)}/_{300}\}}} = 6.35,$$

  Reject H_0.
  Step 6: We conclude that the proportion of carpooling cars on the Turnpike is not 10%.

5. **a.** H_0: $\pi \geq 0.90$ H_1: $\pi < 0.90$
  b. H_0 is rejected if $z < -1.28$.
  c. −2.67, found by $z = (0.82 - 0.90)/\sqrt{(0.90 \times 0.10)/100}$
  d. H_0 is rejected. Fewer than 90% of the customers receive their orders in less than 10 minutes.

7. **a.** H_0 is rejected if $z > 1.65$.
  b. 0.64, found by $p_c = \dfrac{70 + 90}{100 + 150}$

c. 1.61, found by

$$z = \frac{0.70 - 0.60}{\sqrt{[(0.64 \times 0.36)/100] + [(0.64 \times 0.36)/150]}}$$

d. H_0 is not rejected.

9. a. H_0: $\pi_1 = \pi_2$ $\quad H_1$: $\pi_1 \neq \pi_2$

b. H_0 is rejected if $z < -1.96$ or $z > 1.96$.

c. $p_c = \frac{24 + 40}{400 + 400} = 0.08$

d. −2.09, found by

$$z = \frac{0.06 - 0.10}{\sqrt{[(0.08 \times 0.92)/400] + [(0.08 \times 0.92)/400]}}$$

e. H_0 is rejected. The proportion infested is not the same in the two fields.

11. H_0: $\pi_d \leq \pi_r$ $\quad H_1$: $\pi_d > \pi_r$
H_0 is rejected if $z > 2.05$.

$$p_c = \frac{168 + 200}{800 + 1{,}000} = 0.2044$$

$$z = \frac{0.21 - 0.20}{\sqrt{\frac{(0.2044)(0.7956)}{800} + \frac{(0.2044)(0.7956)}{1{,}000}}} = 0.52$$

H_0 is not rejected. We cannot conclude that a larger proportion of Democrats favor lowering the standards. p-value = .3015.

13. a. 3

b. 7.815

15. a. Reject H_0 if $\chi^2 > 5.991$

b. $\chi^2 = \frac{(10 - 20)^2}{20} + \frac{(20 - 20)^2}{20} + \frac{(30 - 20)^2}{20} = 10.0$

c. Reject H_0. The proportions are not equal.

17. H_0: The outcomes are the same; H_1: The outcomes are not the same. Reject H_0 if $\chi^2 > 9.236$.

$$\chi^2 = \frac{(3 - 5)^2}{5} + \cdots + \frac{(7 - 5)^2}{5} = 7.60$$

Do not reject H_0. Cannot reject H_0 that outcomes are the same.

19. H_0: There is no difference in the proportions.
H_1: There is a difference in the proportions.
Reject H_0 if $\chi^2 > 15.086$.

$$\chi^2 = \frac{(47 - 40)^2}{40} + \cdots + \frac{(34 - 40)^2}{40} = 3.400$$

Do not reject H_0. There is no difference in the proportions.

21. a. Reject H_0 if $\chi^2 > 9.210$.

b. $\chi^2 = \frac{(30 - 24)^2}{24} + \frac{(20 - 24)^2}{24} + \frac{(10 - 12)^2}{12} = 2.50$

c. Do not reject H_0.

23. H_0: Proportions are as stated; H_1: Proportions are not as stated. Reject H_0 if $\chi^2 > 11.345$.

$$\chi^2 = \frac{(50 - 25)^2}{25} + \cdots + \frac{(160 - 275)^2}{275} = 115.22$$

Reject H_0. The proportions are not as stated.

25.

Number of Clients	z-values	Area	Found by	f_e
Under 30	Under −1.58	0.0571	0.5000 − 0.4429	2.855
30 up to 40	−1.58 up to −0.51	0.2479	0.4429 − 0.1950	12.395
40 up to 50	−0.51 up to 0.55	0.4038	0.1950 + 0.2088	20.19
50 up to 60	0.55 up to 1.62	0.2386	0.4474 − 0.2088	11.93
60 or more	1.62 or more	0.0526	0.5000 − 0.4474	2.63

The first and last class both have expected frequencies smaller than 5. They are combined with adjacent classes.
H_0: The population of clients follows a normal distribution.
H_1: The population of clients does not follow a normal distribution.
Reject the null if $\chi^2 > 5.991$.

Number of Clients	Area	f_e	f_o	$f_e - f_o$	$(f_o - f_e)^2$	$[(f_o - f_e)^2]/f_e$
Under 40	0.3050	15.25	16	−0.75	0.5625	0.0369
40 up to 50	0.4038	20.19	22	−1.81	3.2761	0.1623
50 or more	0.2912	14.56	12	2.56	6.5536	0.4501
Total	1.0000	50.00	50	0		0.6493

Since 0.6493 is not greater than 5.991, we fail to reject the null hypothesis. These data could be from a normal distribution.

27. H_0: There is no relationship between community size and section read. H_1: There is a relationship.
Reject H_0 if $\chi^2 > 9.488$.

$$\chi^2 = \frac{(170 - 157.50)^2}{157.50} + \cdots + \frac{(88 - 83.62)^2}{83.62} = 7.340$$

Do not reject H_0. There is no relationship between community size and section read.

29. H_0: No relationship between error rates and item type.
H_1: There is a relationship between error rates and item type.
Reject H_0 if $\pi^2 > 9.21$.

$$\chi^2 = \frac{(20 - 14.1)^2}{14.1} + \cdots + \frac{(225 - 225.25)^2}{225.25} = 8.033$$

Do not reject H_0. There is not a relationship between error rates and item type.

31. a. This is a binomial situation with both the mean number of successes and failures equal to 25, found by 0.5(50).

b. H_0: $\pi = 0.50$ $\quad H_1$: $\pi \neq 0.50$

c.

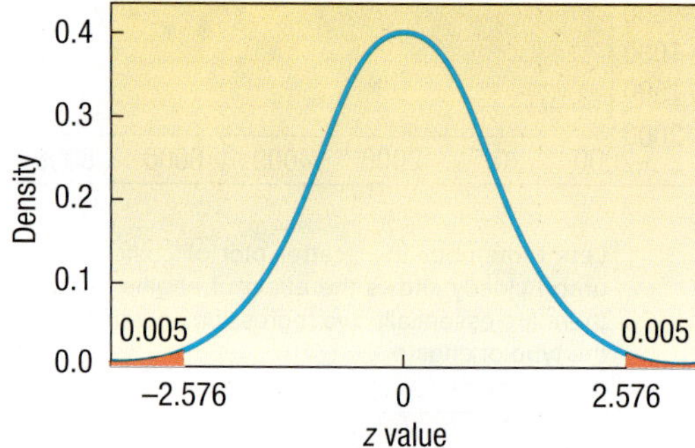

Reject H_0 if z is not between −2.576 and 2.576.

d. $z = \frac{\frac{34}{50} - 0.5}{\sqrt{0.5(1 - 0.5)/50}} = 2.55$

We fail to reject the null hypothesis. This data does not prove that either league has an advantage.

e. The p-value is 0.0108, found by 2(0.5000 − 0.4946). A value this extreme will happen about once out of 100 times with a fair coin.

33. H_0: $\pi \leq 0.60$ $\quad H_1$: $\pi > 0.60$
H_0 is rejected if $z > 2.33$.

$$z = \frac{.70 - .60}{\sqrt{\frac{.60(.40)}{200}}} = 2.89$$

H_0 is rejected. Ms. Dennis is correct. More than 60% of the accounts are more than three months old.

35. $H_0: \pi \leq 0.44 \quad H_1: \pi > 0.44$
H_0 is rejected if $z > 1.65$.

$$z = \frac{0.480 - 0.44}{\sqrt{(0.44 \times 0.56)/1.000}} = 2.55$$

H_0 is rejected. We conclude that there has been an increase in the proportion of people wanting to go to Europe.

37. $H_0: \pi \leq 0.20 \quad H_1: \pi > 0.20$
H_0 is rejected if $z > 2.33$

$$z = \frac{(56/200) - 0.20}{\sqrt{(0.20 \times 0.80)/200}} = 2.83$$

H_0 is rejected. More than 20% of the owners move during a particular year. p-value = 0.5000 − 0.4977 = 0.0023.

39. $H_0: \pi \geq 0.0008 \quad H_1: \pi < 0.0008$
H_0 is rejected if $z < -1.645$.

$$z = \frac{0.0006 - 0.0008}{\sqrt{\dfrac{0.0008\,(0.9992)}{10{,}000}}} = -0.707 \qquad H_0 \text{ is not rejected.}$$

These data do not prove there is a reduced fatality rate.

41. $H_0: \pi_1 \leq \pi_2 \quad H_1: \pi_1 > \pi_2$
If $z > 2.33$, reject H_0.

$$p_c = \frac{990 + 970}{1{,}500 + 1{,}600} = 0.63$$

$$z = \frac{.6600 - .60625}{\sqrt{\dfrac{.63(.37)}{1{,}500} + \dfrac{.63(.37)}{1{,}600}}} = 3.10$$

Reject the null hypothesis. We can conclude the proportion of men who believe the division is fair is greater.

43. $H_0: \pi_1 \leq \pi_2 \quad H_1: \pi_1 > \pi_2 \quad H_0$ is rejected if $z > 1.65$.

$$p_c = \frac{.091 + .085}{2} = .088$$

$$z = \frac{0.091 - 0.085}{\sqrt{\dfrac{(0.088)(0.912)}{5{,}000} + \dfrac{(0.088)(0.912)}{5{,}000}}} = 1.059$$

H_0 is not rejected. There has not been an increase in the proportion calling conditions "good." The p-value is .1446, found by .5000 − .3554. The increase in the percentages will happen by chance in one out of every seven cases.

45. $H_0: \pi_1 = \pi_2 \quad H_1: \pi_1 \neq \pi_2$
H_0 is rejected if z is not between −1.96 and 1.96.

$$p_c = \frac{100 + 36}{300 + 200} = .272$$

$$z = \frac{\dfrac{100}{300} - \dfrac{36}{200}}{\sqrt{\dfrac{(0.272)(0.728)}{300} + \dfrac{(0.272)(0.728)}{200}}} = 3.775$$

H_0 is rejected. There is a difference in the replies of the sexes.

47. $H_0: \pi_s = 0.50, \pi_r = \pi_e = 0.25$
H_1: Distribution is not as given above.
$df = 2$. Reject H_0 if $\chi^2 > 4.605$.

Turn	f_o	f_e	$f_o - f_e$	$(f_o - f_e)^2/f_e$
Straight	112	100	12	1.44
Right	48	50	−2	0.08
Left	40	50	−10	2.00
Total	200	200		3.52

H_0 is not rejected. The proportions are as given in the null hypothesis.

49. H_0: There is no preference with respect to TV stations.
H_1: There is a preference with respect to TV stations.
$df = 3 - 1 = 2$. H_0 is rejected if $\chi^2 > 5.991$.

TV Station	f_o	f_e	$f_o - f_e$	$(f_o - f_e)^2$	$(f_o - f_e)^2/f_e$
WNAE	53	50	3	9	0.18
WRRN	64	50	14	196	3.92
WSPD	33	50	−17	289	5.78
	150	150	0		9.88

H_0 is rejected. There is a preference for TV stations.

51. $H_0: \pi_n = 0.21, \pi_m = 0.24, \pi_s = 0.35, \pi_w = 0.20$
H_1: The distribution is not as given.
Reject H_0 if $\chi^2 > 11.345$.

Region	f_o	f_e	$f_o - f_e$	$(f_o - f_e)^2/f_e$
Northeast	68	84	−16	3.0476
Midwest	104	96	8	0.6667
South	155	140	15	1.6071
West	73	80	−7	0.6125
Total	400	400	0	5.9339

H_0 is not rejected. The distribution of order destinations reflects the population.

53. H_0: The proportions are the same.
H_1: The proportions are not the same.
Reject H_0 if $\chi^2 > 16.919$.

f_o	f_e	$f_o - f_e$	$(f_o - f_e)^2$	$(f_o - f_e)^2/f_e$
44	28	16	256	9.143
32	28	4	16	0.571
23	28	−5	25	0.893
27	28	−1	1	0.036
23	28	−5	25	0.893
24	28	−4	16	0.571
31	28	3	9	0.321
27	28	−1	1	0.036
28	28	0	0	0.000
21	28	−7	49	1.750
				14.214

Do not reject H_0. The digits are evenly distributed.

55.

Hourly Wage	f	M	fM	$M - x$	$(M - x)^2$	$f(M - x)^2$
$5.50 up to 6.50	20	6	120	−2.222	4.938	98.8
6.50 up to 7.50	24	7	168	−1.222	1.494	35.9
7.50 up to 8.50	130	8	1040	−0.222	0.049	6.4
8.50 up to 9.50	68	9	612	0.778	0.605	41.1
9.50 up to 10.50	28	10	280	1.778	3.161	88.5
Total	270		2220			270.7

The sample mean is 8.222, found by 2,220/270.
The sample standard deviation is 1.003, found as the square root of 270.7/269.
H_0: The population of wages follows a normal distribution.
H_1: The population of hourly wages does not follow a normal distribution.

Reject the null if $\chi^2 > 4.605$.

Wage	z-values	Area	Found by	f_e	f_o	$f_e - f_o$	$(f_o - f_e)^2$	$[(f_o - f_e)^2]/f_e$
Under $6.50	Under −1.72	0.0427	0.5000 − 0.4573	11.529	20	−8.471	71.7578	6.2241
6.50 up to 7.50	−1.72 up to −0.72	0.1931	0.4573 − 0.2642	52.137	24	28.137	791.6908	15.1848
7.50 up to 8.50	−0.72 up to 0.28	0.3745	0.2642 + 0.1103	101.115	130	−28.885	834.3432	8.2514
8.50 up to 9.50	0.28 up to 1.27	0.2877	0.3980 − 0.1103	77.679	68	9.679	93.6830	1.2060
9.50 or more	1.27 or more	0.1020	0.5000 − 0.3980	27.54	28	−0.46	0.2116	0.0077
Total		1.0000		270	270	0		30.874

Since 30.874 is greater than 4.605, we reject the null hypothesis not from a normal distribution.

57. H_0: Gender and attitude toward the deficit are not related.
H_1: Gender and attitude toward the deficit are related.
Reject H_0 if $\chi^2 > 5.991$.

$$\chi^2 = \frac{(244 - 292.41)^2}{292.41} + \frac{(194 - 164.05)^2}{164.05} + \frac{(68 - 49.53)^2}{49.53} + \frac{(305 - 256.59)^2}{256.59} + \frac{(114 - 143.95)^2}{143.95} + \frac{(25 - 43.47)^2}{43.47} = 43.578$$

Since $43.578 > 5.991$, you reject H_0. A person's position on the deficit is influenced by his or her gender.

59. H_0: Whether a claim is filed and age are not related.
H_1: Whether a claim is filed and age are related.
Reject H_0 if $\chi^2 > 7.815$.

$$\chi^2 = \frac{(170 - 203.33)^2}{203.33} + \cdots + \frac{(24 - 35.67)^2}{35.67} = 53.639$$

Reject H_0. Age is related to whether a claim is filed.

61. H_0: $\pi_{BL} = \pi_O = .23$, $\pi_Y = \pi_G = .15$, $\pi_{BR} = \pi_R = .12$.
H_1: The proportions are not as given. Reject H_0 if $\chi^2 > 15.086$.

Color	f_o	f_e	$(f_o - f_e)^2/f_e$
Blue	12	16.56	1.256
Brown	14	8.64	3.325
Yellow	13	10.80	0.448
Red	14	8.64	3.325
Orange	7	16.56	5.519
Green	12	10.80	0.133
Total	72		14.006

Do not reject H_0. The color distribution agrees with the manufacturer's information.

63. H_0: Salary and winning are not related
H_1: Salary and winning are related
Reject H_0 if $\chi^2 > 3.841$ with 1 degree of freedom.

	Salary		
Winning	Lower half	Top half	Total
No	10	4	14
Yes	5	11	16
Total	15	15	

$$\chi^2 = \frac{(10 - 7)^2}{7} + \frac{(4 - 7)^2}{7} + \frac{(5 - 8)^2}{8} + \frac{(11 - 8)^2}{8} = 4.82$$

Reject H_0. Conclude that salary and winning are related.

CHAPTER 16

1. **a.** If the number of pluses (successes) in the sample is 9 or more, reject H_0.

b. Reject H_0 because the cumulative probability associated with nine or more successes (.073) does not exceed the significance level (.10).

3. **a.** H_0: $\pi \leq .50$; H_1: $\pi > .50$; $n = 10$

b. H_0 is rejected if there are nine or more plus signs. A "+" represents a loss.

c. Reject H_0. It is an effective program because there were nine people who lost weight.

5. **a.** H_0: $\pi \leq .50$ (There is no change in weight.) H_1: $\pi > .50$ (There is a loss of weight.)

b. Reject H_0 if $z > 1.65$.

c. $z = \dfrac{(32 - .50) - .50(45)}{.50\sqrt{45}} = 2.68$

d. Reject H_0. The weight loss program is effective.

7. H_0: $\pi \geq .50$, H_1: $\pi \geq .50$. H_0 is rejected if $z > 2.05$.

$$z = \frac{42.5 - 40.5}{4.5} = .44$$

Because $.44 < 2.05$, do not reject H_0. No preference.

9. **a.** H_0: Median ≤ $81,500; H_1: Median > $81,500

b. H_0 is rejected if $z > 1.65$.

c. $z = \dfrac{170 - .50 - 100}{7.07} = 9.83$

H_0 is rejected. The median income is greater than $81,500.

11.

Couple	Difference	Rank
1	550	7
2	190	5
3	250	6
4	−120	3
5	−70	1
6	130	4
7	90	2

Sums: −4, +24. So $T = 4$ (the smaller of the two sums). From Appendix B.8, .05 level, one-tailed test, $n = 7$, the critical value is 3. Since the T of $4 > 3$, do not reject H_0 (one-tailed test). There is no difference in square footage. Professional couples do not live in larger homes.

13. **a.** H_0: The production is the same for the two systems.
H_1: Production using the new procedure is greater.

b. H_0 is rejected if $T \leq 21$, $n = 13$.

c. The calculations for the first three employees are:

Employee	Old	new	d	Rank	R^1	R^2
A	60	64	4	6	6	
B	40	52	12	12.5	12.5	
C	59	58	−1	2		2

The sum of the negative ranks is 6.5. Since 6.5 is less than 21, H_0 is rejected. Production using the new procedure is greater.

15. H_0: The distributions are the same. H_1: The distributions are not the same. Reject H_0 if z, 21.96 or $z > 1.96$.

A		B	
Score	Rank	Score	Rank
38	4	26	1
45	6	31	2
56	9	35	3
57	10.5	42	5
61	12	51	7
69	14	52	8
70	15	57	10.5
79	16	62	13
	86.5		49.5

$$z = \frac{86.5 - \frac{8(8+8+1)}{2}}{\sqrt{\frac{8(8)(8+8+1)}{12}}} = 1.943$$

H_0 is not rejected. There is no difference in the two populations.

17. H_0: The distributions are the same. H_1: The distribution of Campus is to the right. Reject H_0 if $z > 1.65$.

Campus		Online	
Age	**Rank**	**Age**	**Rank**
26	6	28	8
42	16.5	16	1
65	22	42	16.5
38	13	29	9.5
29	9.5	31	11
32	12	22	3
59	21	50	20
42	16.5	42	16.5
27	7	23	4
41	14	25	5
46	19		94.5
18	2		
	158.5		

$$z = \frac{158.5 - \frac{12(12+10+1)}{2}}{\sqrt{\frac{12(10)(12+10+1)}{12}}} = 1.35$$

H_0 is not rejected. There is no difference in the distributions.

19. ANOVA requires that we have two or more populations, the data are interval- or ratio-level, the populations are normally distributed, and the population standard deviations are equal. Kruskal-Wallis requires only ordinal-level data, and no assumptions are made regarding the shape of the populations.

21. **a.** H_0: The three population distributions are equal. H_1: Not all of the distributions are the same.

b. Reject H_0 if $H > 5.991$.

c.

Sample 1 Rank	Sample 2 Rank	Sample 3 Rank
8	5	1
11	6.5	2
14.5	6.5	3
14.5	10	4
16	12	9
64	13	19
	53	

$$H = \frac{12}{16(16+1)}\left[\frac{(64)^2}{5} + \frac{(53)^2}{6} + \frac{(19)^2}{5}\right] - 3(16+1)$$

$$= 59.98 - 51 = 8.98$$

d. Reject H_0 because $8.98 > 5.991$. The three distributions are not equal.

23. H_0: The distributions of the lengths of life are the same. H_1: The distributions of the lengths of life are not the same. H_0 is rejected if $H > 9.210$.

Salt		Fresh		Others	
Hours	**Rank**	**Hours**	**Rank**	**Hours**	**Rank**
167.3	3	160.6	1	182.7	13
189.6	15	177.6	11	165.4	2
177.2	10	185.3	14	172.9	7
169.4	6	168.6	4	169.2	5
180.3	12	176.6	9	174.7	8
	46		39		35

$$H = \frac{12}{15(16)}\left[\frac{(46)^2}{5} + \frac{(39)^2}{5} + \frac{(35)^2}{5}\right] - 3(16) = 0.62$$

H_0 is not rejected. There is no difference in the three distributions.

25. **a.**

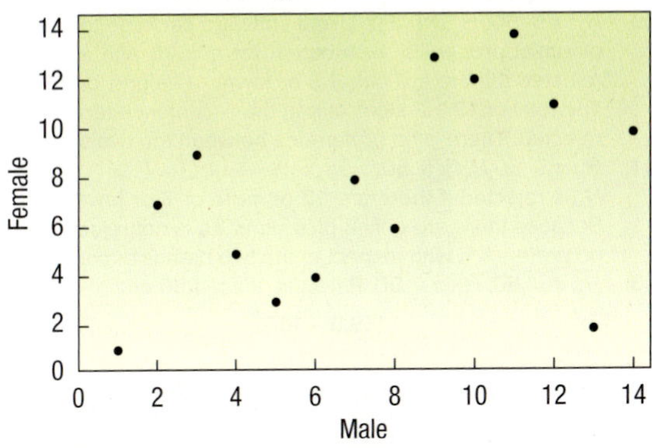

b.

Male	Female	d	d^2	
4	5	−1	1	
6	4	2	4	
7	8	−1	1	
2	7	−5	25	
12	11	1	1	
8	6	2	4	
5	3	2	4	found by 69220/69220
3	9	−6	36	found by 54818/69220
13	2	11	121	found by 55177/69220
14	10	4	16	found by 65694/69220
1	1	0	0	found by 83040/69220
9	13	−4	16	found by 88378/69220
10	12	−2	4	found by 97420/69220
11	14	−3	9	found by 98608/69220
		Total	242	

$$r_s = 1 - \frac{6(242)}{14(14^2 - 1)} = 0.47$$

c. H_0: No correlation among the ranks. H_1: A positive correlation among the ranks. Reject H_0 if $t > 1.782$.

$$t = 0.47\sqrt{\frac{14-2}{1-(0.47)^2}} = 1.84$$

H_0 is rejected. We conclude the correlation in population among the ranks is positive. Husbands and wives generally like the same shows.

27.

Representative	Sales	Rank	Training Rank	d	d^2
1	319	8	8	0	0
2	150	1	2	1	1
3	175	2	5	3	9
4	460	10	10	0	0
5	348	9	7	−2	4
6	300	6.5	1	5.5	30.25
7	280	5	6	1	1
8	200	4	9	5	25
9	190	3	4	1	1
10	300	6.5	3	−3.5	12.25
					83.50

a. $r_s = 1 - \frac{6(83.5)}{10(10^2 - 1)} = 0.494$

A moderate positive correlation

b. H_0: No correlation among the ranks. H_1: A positive correlation among the ranks. Reject H_0 if $t > 1.860$.

$$t = 0.494\sqrt{\frac{10 - 2}{1 - (0.494)^2}} = 1.607$$

H_0 is not rejected. The correlation in population among the ranks could be 0.

29. H_0: π 5 .50. H_1: π fi .50. Use a software package to develop the binomial probability distribution for n = 19 and π 5 .50. H_0 is rejected if there are either 5 or fewer "+" signs, or 14 or more. The total of 12 "+" signs falls in the acceptance region. H_0 is not rejected. There is no preference between the two shows.

31. H_0: π 5 .50 H_1: π fi .50
H_0 is rejected if there are 12 or more or 3 or fewer plus signs. Because there are only 8 plus signs, H_0 is not rejected. There is no preference with respect to the two brands of components.

33. H_0: $\pi = .50$; H_1: π fi .50. Reject H_0 if $z > 1.96$ or $z < -1.96$.

$$z = \frac{159.5 - 100}{7.071} = 8.415$$

Reject H_0. There is a difference in the preference for the two types of orange juice.

35. H_0: Rates are the same; H_1: The rates are not the same.
H_0 is rejected if $H > 5.991$. $H = .082$. Do not reject H_0.

37. H_0: The populations are the same. H_1: The populations differ. Reject H_0 if $H > 7.815$. $H = 14.30$. Reject H_0.

39. $r_s = 1 - \dfrac{6(78)}{12(12^2 - 1)} = 0.727$

H_0: There is no correlation between the rankings of the coaches and of the sportswriters.
H_1: There is a positive correlation between the rankings of the coaches and of the sportswriters. Reject H_0 if $t > 1.812$.

$$t = 0.727\sqrt{\frac{12 - 2}{1 - (.727)^2}} = 3.348$$

H_0 is rejected. There is a positive correlation between the sportswriters and the coaches.

41. a. H_0: There is no difference in the distributions of the selling prices in the five townships.
H_1: There is a difference in the distributions of the selling prices of the five townships.
H_0 is rejected if H is greater than 9.488. The computed value of H is 2.70, so the null hypothesis is not rejected. The sample data does not suggest a difference in the distributions of selling prices.

b. H_0: There is no difference in the distributions of the selling prices depending on the number of bedrooms.
H_1: There is a difference in the distributions of the selling prices depending on the number of bedrooms.
H_0 is rejected if H is greater than 9.488. The computed value of H is 75.71 so the null hypothesis is rejected. The sample data indicates there is a difference in the distributions of selling prices based on the number of bedrooms.

c. H_0: There is no difference in the distributions of FICO scores depending on the type of mortgage the occupant has on the home.
H_1: There is a difference in the distributions of FICO scores depending on the type of mortgage the occupant has on the home.
H_0 is rejected if H is greater than 3.841. The computed value of H is 41.04, so the null hypothesis is rejected. The sample data suggests a difference in the distributions of the FICO scores. The data shows that home occupants with lower FICO scores tended to use adjustable rate mortgages.

43. a. H_0: The distributions of the maintenance costs are the same for all capacities.
H_1: The distributions of the costs are not the same
H_0 is rejected if $H > 7.815$, from χ^2 with 3 degrees of freedom.

$$H = \frac{12}{80(81)}\left[\frac{(132)^2}{3} + \frac{(501)^2}{11} + \frac{(349)^2}{11} + \frac{(2258)^2}{55}\right] - 3(81) = 2.186$$

Fail to reject H_0. There is no difference in the maintenance cost for the four bus capacities.

b. H_0: The distributions of maintenance costs by fuel type are the same.
H_1: The distributions are different.
Reject H_0 if $z < -1.96$ or $z > 1.96$.

$$z = \frac{1693 - \dfrac{53(53 + 27 + 1)}{2}}{\sqrt{\dfrac{(53)(27)(53 + 27 + 1)}{12}}} = -4.614$$

We reject reject H_0 and conclude that maintenance costs are different for diesel and gasoline fueled buses.

c. H_0: The distributions of the maintenance costs are the same for the three bus manufacturers.
H_1: The distributions of the costs are not the same
H_0 is rejected if $H > 5.991$, from χ^2 with 2 degrees of freedom.

$$H = \frac{12}{80(81)}\left[\frac{(414)^2}{8} + \frac{(1005)^2}{25} + \frac{(1821)^2}{47}\right] - 3(81) = 2.147$$

H_0 is not rejected. There may be no difference in the maintenance cost for the three different manufacturers. The distributions could be the same.

CHAPTER 17

1.

Year	Loans ($ Millions)	Index (Base = 2008)
2008	69220	100.0
2009	54818	79.2
2010	55177	79.7
2011	65694	94.9
2012	83040	120.0
2013	88378	127.7
2014	97420	140.7
2015	98608	142.5

3. The mean sales for the earliest three years is $(486.6 + 506.8 + 522.2)/3 or $505.2.
2014: 90.4, found by (456.6/505.2) (100)
2015: 85.8, found by (433.3/505.2) (100)
Net sales decreased by 9.6 and 14.2 percent from the 2003–2005 period to 2014 and 2015 respectively.

5. a. $P_t = \dfrac{3.35}{2.49}(100) = 134.54$ $\quad P_s = \dfrac{4.49}{3.29}(100) = 136.47$

$P_c = \dfrac{4.19}{1.59}(100) = 263.52$ $\quad P_a = \dfrac{2.49}{1.79}(100) = 139.11$

b. $P = \dfrac{14.52}{9.16}(100) = 158.52$

c. $P = \dfrac{\$3.35(6) + 4.49(4) + 4.19(2) + 2.49(3)}{\$2.49(6) + 3.29(4) + 1.59(2) + 1.79(3)}(100) = 147.1$

d. $P = \dfrac{\$3.35(6) + 4.49(5) + 4.19(3) + 2.49(4)}{\$2.49(6) + 3.29(5) + 1.59(3) + 1.79(4)}(100) = 150.2$

e. $I = \sqrt{(147.1)(150.2)} = 148.64$

7. a. $P_W = \dfrac{0.10}{0.07}(100) = 142.9$ $\quad P_C = \dfrac{0.03}{0.04}(100) = 75.0$

$P_S = \dfrac{0.15}{0.15}(100) = 100$ $\quad P_H = \dfrac{0.10}{0.08}(100) = 125.0$

b. $P = \dfrac{0.38}{0.34}(100) = 111.8$

c.
$$P = \frac{0.10(17{,}000) + 0.03(125{,}000) + 0.15(40{,}000) + 0.10(62{,}000)}{0.07(17{,}000) + 0.04(125{,}000) + 0.15(40{,}000) + 0.08(62{,}000)} \times (100) = 102.92$$

d.
$$P = \frac{0.10(20{,}000) + 0.03(130{,}000) + 0.15(42{,}000) + 0.10(65{,}000)}{0.07(20{,}000) + 0.04(130{,}000) + 0.15(42{,}000) + 0.08(65{,}000)} \times (100) = 103.32$$

e. $I = \sqrt{102.92(103.32)} = 103.12$

9.
$$V = \frac{\$2.09(90) + 5.99(2) + 3.65(13{,}601) + 5.53(214)}{\$1.81(116) + 3.56(2) + 2.32(8{,}967) + 2.72(227)}(100) = 235.82$$

11. a. $I = \frac{6.8}{5.3}(0.20) + \frac{362.26}{265.88}(0.40) + \frac{125.0}{109.6}(0.25) + \frac{622{,}864}{529{,}917}(0.15) = 1.263.$

Index is 126.3.

b. Business activity increased 26.3% from 200 to 2016.

13. The real income is $X = (\$89{,}673)/2.38132 = \$37{,}657$. "Real" salary increased \$37,657 – \$19,800 = \$17,857.

15.

Year	Tinora	Tinora Index	National Index
2000	\$28,650	100.0	100
2010	\$33,972	118.6	122.5
2016	\$37,382	130.5	136.9

The Tinora teachers received smaller increases than the national average

17.

Domestic sales: The index (2000=100) for selected years

Year	Index
2004	160.4
2005	163.9
2006	172.0
2007	187.4
2008	186.6
2009	178.4
2010	170.0
2011	166.9
2012	172.3
2013	184.3
2014	200.9
2015	206.1

Domestic sales increased by about 26% by 2008, then declined by 20% by 2011 and increased overall from 2004 to 2015 about 66%. **(LO17-1)**

19.

International sales: The index (2000=100) for selected years

Year	Index
2004	165.1
2005	186.7
2006	198.6
2007	241.7
2008	265.2
2009	261.5
2010	271.0
2011	304.5
2012	315.4
2013	332.3
2014	333.6
2015	290.0

International sales more than tripled from 2000 to 2014. International sales declined more 43% from 2014 to 2015. This is the largest decrease since 2004.

21.

Number of employees: The index (2000=100) for selected years

Year	Index
2004	108.9
2005	114.6
2006	121.1
2007	118.1
2008	117.6
2009	114.5
2010	113.0
2011	116.8
2012	126.5
2013	127.0
2014	125.4
2015	126.0

The number of employees increased about 15% between 2000 and 2005, then decreases from 2006 through 2011. The number of employees has remained about the same since, only changing about 1%.

23.

GE Revenue (2004=100)

Year	Index
2005	113.4
2006	117.2
2007	125.4
2008	132.1
2009	136.6
2010	111.9
2011	109.7
2012	109.7
2013	109
2014	111.2
2015	112.7

Revenue increased about 37% until 2009. It has been relatively stable since 2009.

25.

GE Employees (2004=100)

Year	Index
2005	94.5
2006	97.2
2007	98.2
2008	100.6
2009	99.4
2010	93.5
2011	90.8
2012	95.3
2013	97.2
2014	96.5
2015	105.4

Number of employees increased about 6% until 2008, and then in 2011 declined 10%. From 2011 to 2015 employees have increased about 15%.

27. $P_{ma} = \frac{2.00}{0.81}(100) = 246.91 \qquad P_{sh} = \frac{1.88}{0.84}(100) = 223.81$

$P_{mi} = \frac{2.89}{1.44}(100) = 200.69 \qquad P_{po} = \frac{3.99}{2.91}(100) = 137.11$

29. $P = \frac{\$2.00(18) + 1.88(5) + 2.89(70) + 3.99(27)}{\$0.81(18) + 0.84(5) + 1.44(70) + 2.91(27)}(100) = 179.37$

31. $I = \sqrt{179.37(178.23)} = 178.80$

33. $P_R = \frac{0.60}{0.50}(100) = 120 \qquad P_S = \frac{0.90}{1.20}(100) = 75.0$

$P_W = \frac{1.00}{0.85}(100) = 117.65$

35. $P = \frac{0.60(320) + 0.90(110) + 1.00(230)}{0.50(320) + 1.20(110) + 0.85(230)}(100) = 106.87$

37. $P = \sqrt{(106.87)(106.04)} = 106.45$

39. $P_C = \frac{0.05}{0.06}(100) = 83.33 \qquad P_C = \frac{0.12}{0.10}(100) = 120$

$P_P = \frac{0.18}{0.20}(100) = 90 \qquad P_E = \frac{.015}{0.15}(100) = 100$

41. $P = \frac{0.05(2{,}000) + 0.12(200) + 0.18(400) + 0.15(100)}{0.06(2{,}000) + 0.10(200) + 0.20(400) + 0.15(100)}(100)$
$= 89.79$

43. $I = \sqrt{(89.79)(91.25)} = 90.52$

45. $P_A = \frac{0.73}{0.287}(100) = 254.36 \qquad P_N = \frac{2.12}{0.17}(100) = 1247.06$

$P_P = \frac{44.08}{3.18}(100) = 1386.16 \qquad P_P = \frac{1904.30}{133}(100) = 1431.80$

(LO17-1)

47. $P = \frac{0.73(1{,}000) + 2.12(5{,}000) + 44.08(60{,}000) + 1904.30(500)}{0.287(1{,}000) + 0.17(5{,}000) + 3.18(60{,}000) + 133(500)} \times (100) = 1396.19$

49. $I = \sqrt{(1396.19)(1397.79)} = 1396.99$

51. $I = 100\left[\frac{1971.0}{1159.0}(0.20) + \frac{91}{87}(0.10) + \frac{114.7}{110.6}(0.40) + \frac{1501000}{1214000}(0.30)\right] = 123.05$

The economy is up 23.05 percent from 1996 to 2016.

53. February: $I = 100\left[\frac{6.8}{8.0}(0.40) + \frac{23}{20}(0.35) + \frac{303}{300}(0.25)\right] = 99.50$

March: $I = 100\left[\frac{6.4}{8.0}(0.40) + \frac{21}{20}(0.35) + \frac{297}{300}(0.25)\right] = 93.50$

55. For 2006: \$1,495,327, found by \$2,400,000/1.605
For 2016: \$3,190,520, found by \$3,500,000/1.097

CHAPTER 18

1. The weighted moving averages are: 31,584.8, 33,088.9, 34,205.4, 34,899.8, 35,155.0, 34,887.1
3. The regression equation is: $\hat{Y} = 8842.1273 - 88.1273t$ where $t = 1$ in 2006. For 2017, $t = 12$ and $\hat{Y} = 8842.1273 - 88.1273(12) = 7784.5997$
5. $\hat{y} = 1.30 + 0.90t$
$\hat{y} = 1.30 + 0.90(7) = 7.6$
7. **a.** $b = \frac{5.274318 - (1.390087)(15)/5}{55 - (15)^2/5}$
$= \frac{1.104057}{10} = 0.1104057$
$a = \frac{1.390087}{5} - 0.1104057\left(\frac{15}{5}\right) = -0.0531997$
b. 28.95%, found by 1.28945 − 1.0
c. $\hat{y} = -0.0531997 + 0.1104057t$ for 2010, $t = 8$
$\hat{y} = -0.0531997 + 0.1104057(8) = 0.8300459$
Antilog of 0.8300459 = 6.76
9.

Quarter	Average SI Component	Seasonal Index
1	0.6859	0.6911
2	1.6557	1.6682
3	1.1616	1.1704
4	0.4732	0.4768

11.

t	Estimated Pairs (millions)	Seasonal Index	Quarterly Forecast (millions)
21	40.05	110.0	44.055
22	41.80	120.0	50.160
23	43.55	80.0	34.840
24	45.30	90.0	40.770

13. $\hat{y} = 5.1658 + .37805t$. The following are the sales estimates.

Estimate	Index	Seasonally Adjusted
10.080	0.6911	6.966
10.458	1.6682	17.446
10.837	1.1704	12.684
11.215	0.4768	5.343

15. **a.** The ordered residuals are 2.61, 2.83, −48.50, 15.50, −3.72, 17.17, 6.39, 7.72, −0.41, −16.86, 3.81, 7.25, 8.03, −1.08, and −0.75.

Time Series Plot of RESI1

b. There are 2 independent variables (k) and the sample size (n) is 15. For a significance level of .05, the upper value is 1.54. Since the computed value of the Durbin-Watson statistic is 2.48, which is above the upper limit, the null hypothesis is not rejected. There is no autocorrelation among these residuals.

17. **a.**

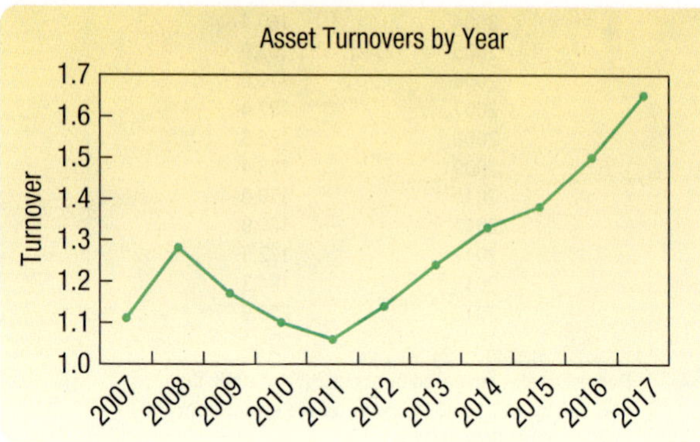

b. $\hat{y} = 1.00455 + 0.04409t$, using $t = 1$ for 2007

c.

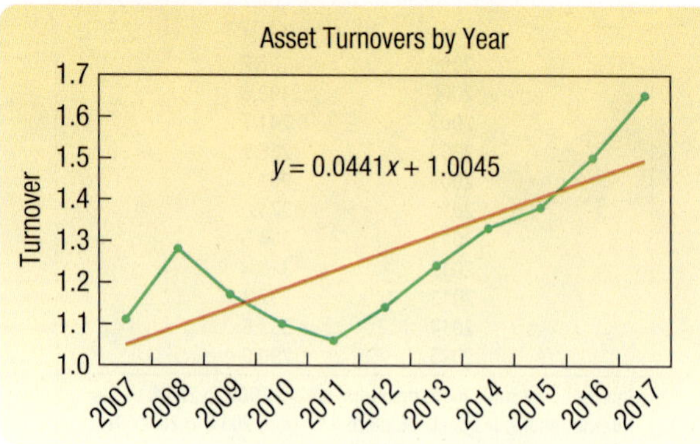

for 2010, $\hat{Y} = 1.18091$, and for 2015 $\hat{Y} = 1.40136$

d. for 2022, $\hat{Y} = 1.70999$

e. Each asset turned over 0.044 times.

19. a.

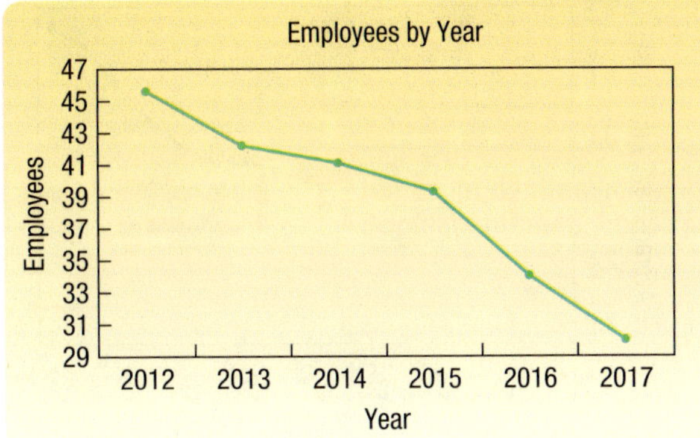

b. $\hat{Y} = 49.140 - 2.9829t$

c.

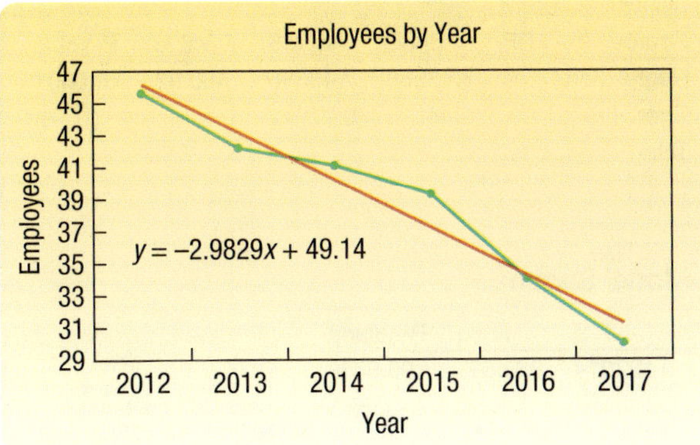

for 2014, $\hat{Y} = 40.1913$ and for 2017, $\hat{Y} = 34.2426$

d. for 2020 $\hat{Y} = 22.2939$

e. The number of employees decreases at a rate of 2983 per year.

21. a. Log $\hat{y} = 0.790231 + .113669t$

b. Log $\hat{y} = 0.9039$, found by $0.790231 + 0.113669(1)$, antilog is 8.015

Log $\hat{y} = 1.699583$, found by $0.790231 + .113699(8)$, antilog is 50.071

c. 29.92, which is the antilog of .113669 minus 1

d. Log $\hat{y} = 2.154258$, antilog is 142.65.

23. a.

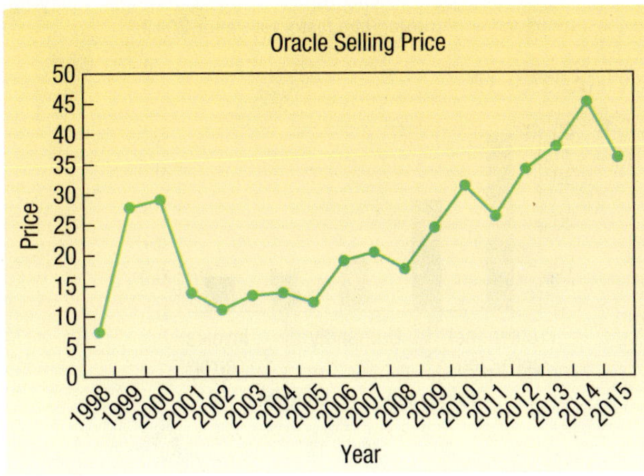

b. The equations are $\hat{Y} = 9.4269 + 1.4647t$ and log $\hat{Y} = 1.03837 + 0.02957t$.

The equation using the logarithm has an R^2 of 0.51 compared to 0.53, so in terms of R^2 the equations are very close.

c. *Using the logarithmic equation.*

log $\hat{Y} = 1.03837 + 0.02957(4) = 1.15665$, antilog is 14.3433.

log $\hat{Y} = 1.03837 + 0.02957(9) = 1.3045$, antilog is 20.1604.

Using the linear equation.

$\hat{Y} = 9.4269 + 1.4647(4) = 15.2859.$

$\hat{Y} = 9.4269 + 1.4647(9) = 22.6096$

d. log $\hat{Y} = 1.03837 + 0.02957(21) = 1.65934$, antilog is 45.6394. The linear estimate is $\hat{Y} = 9.4269 + 1.4647(21) = 40.1865$, which is reasonable if the increase per year remains constant.

e. Using the logarithmic approach, the annual rate of increase in stock price is 7.04%, found by the antilog of 0.02957 minus 1. The linear approach indicates the stock price increase by \$1.4647 each year on average.

25. a. July 87.5; August 92.9; September 99.3; October 109.1

b.

Month	Total	Mean	Corrected
July	348.9	87.225	86.777
Aug.	368.1	92.025	91.552
Sept.	395.0	98.750	98.242
Oct.	420.4	105.100	104.560
Nov.	496.2	124.050	123.412
Dec.	572.3	143.075	142.340
Jan.	333.5	83.375	82.946
Feb.	297.5	74.375	73.993
March	347.3	86.825	86.379
April	481.3	120.325	119.707
May	396.2	99.050	98.541
June	368.1	92.025	91.552
		1,206.200	

Correction = 1,200/1,206.2 = 0.99486

c. April, November, and December are periods of high sales, while February's sales are lowest.

Note: The solutions to Exercises 27 to 31 may vary due to rounding and the particular software package used.

27. a.

Seasonal Index by Quarter

Quarter	Average SI Component	Seasonal Index
1	0.5014	0.5027
2	1.0909	1.0936
3	1.7709	1.7753
4	0.6354	0.6370

b. Production is the largest in the third quarter. It is 77.5% above the average quarter. The second quarter is also above average. The first and fourth quarters are well below average, with the first quarter at about 50% of a typical quarter.

29. a. The seasonal indices for package play are shown below. Recall that period 1 is actually July because the data begin with July.

Period	Index	Period	Index
1	0.19792	7	0.26874
2	0.25663	8	0.63189
3	0.87840	9	1.67943
4	2.10481	10	2.73547
5	0.77747	11	1.67903
6	0.18388	12	0.60633

Notice the 4th period (October) and the 10th period (April) are more than twice the average.

b. The seasonal indices for nonpackage play are:

Period	Index	Period	Index
1	1.73270	7	0.23673
2	1.53389	8	0.69732
3	0.94145	9	1.00695
4	1.29183	10	1.13226
5	0.66928	11	0.98282
6	0.52991	12	1.24486

These indices are more constant. Notice the very low values in the 6th (December) and 7th (January) periods.

c. The seasonal indices for total play are:

Period	Index	Period	Index
1	0.63371	7	0.25908
2	0.61870	8	0.65069
3	0.89655	9	1.49028
4	1.86415	10	2.28041
5	0.74353	11	1.48235
6	0.29180	12	0.78876

These indices show both the peaks in October (4th period) and April (10th period) and the valleys in December (6th period) and January (7th period).

d. Package play is relatively highest in April. Nonpackage play is relatively high in July. Since 70% of total play comes from package play, total play is very similar to package play.

31.

Seasonal Index by Quarter		
Quarter	Average SI Component	Seasonal Index
1	1.1962	1.2053
2	1.0135	1.0212
3	0.6253	0.6301
4	1.1371	1.1457

The regression equation is $\hat{y} = 43.611 + 7.21153t$

Period	Visitors	Index	Forecast
29	252.86	1.2053	304.77
30	260.07	1.0212	265.58
31	267.29	0.6301	168.42
32	274.50	1.1457	314.50

In 2016 there were a total of 928 visitors. A 10% increase in 2017 means there will be 1,021 visitors. The quarterly estimates are 1,021/4 = 255.25 visitors per quarter.

33. The linear trend line is $\hat{Y} = 0.7965 + 0.1366{*}t$ and the logarithmic trend line is $\log \hat{Y} = 0.0083 + 0.0289{*}t$.
The equation using the logarithm appears better because R^2 is larger at 0.831 compared to 0.796.
The years 2016 and 2017 would be coded $t = 21$ and 22, respectively.
For 2016: $\log \hat{Y} = 0.0083 + 0.0289(21) = 0.6152$ and its antilog is 4.12.
For 2017: $\log \hat{Y} = 0.0083 + 0.0289(22) = 0.6441$ and its antilog is 4.71.

35. The linear trend line for the mean amount per transaction (expressed in constant dollars) is $\hat{y} = 41.58 - 0.238528t$.
Customer spending is definitely declining about $0.24 per year.
Here is an output for the regression of transactions over time (notice the *p*-value for time):
The regression equation is CPI = 41.6 – 0.239 Time

```
Predictor       Coef   SE Coef       T       P
Constant      41.583     1.078   38.56   0.000
Time        -0.23853   0.09003   -2.65   0.016
```

37.

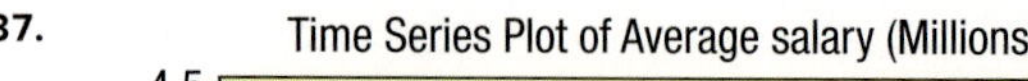

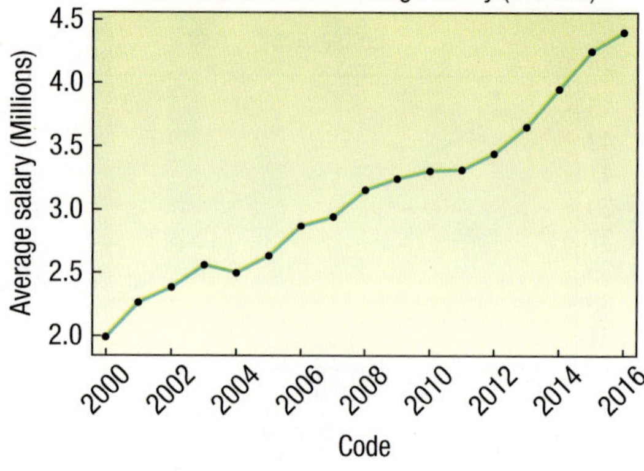

Analysis of Variance

Source	DF	Adj SS	Adj MS	F-Value	P-Value
Regression	1	7.43580	7.43580	460.92	<0.0001
Error	15	0.24199	0.01613		
Total	16	7.67779			

Model Summary

S	R-sq	R-sq(adj)
0.127014	96.85%	96.64%

Coefficients

Term	Coef	SE Coef	T-Value	P-Value
Constant	1.89147	0.06443	29.36	<0.0001
code	0.135000	0.006288	21.47	<0.0001

With 2000 coded as $t = 1$, the regression equation is: $\hat{y} = 1.89147 + 0.135t$. Average player salary increased at a rate of $135,000 per year over the period. R2 = 96.85%. The trend is fairly consistent over time. However, the rate of average salary increase appears to change about 2012. Average salary appears to be increasing at a faster rate after 2012.

CHAPTER 19

1.

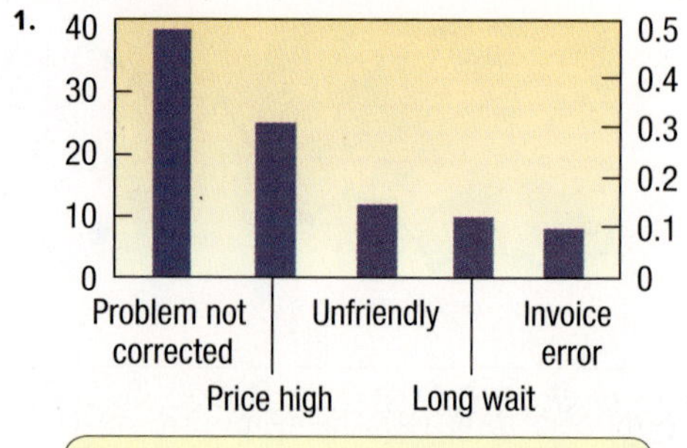

Count	38	23	12	10	8
Percent	42	25	13	11	9
Cum %	42	67	80	91	100

About 67% of the complaints concern the problem not being corrected and the price being too high.

3. Chance variation is random in nature; because the cause is a variety of factors, it cannot be entirely eliminated. Assignable variation is not random; it is usually due to a specific cause and can be eliminated.

5. a. The A_2 factor is 0.729.
   b. The value for D_3 is 0, and for D_4 it is 2.282.

7. a.

UCL 46.78

$\bar{\bar{X}}$ 41.92

LCL 37.06

8 8:30 9 9:30 10 10:30

Time	$\bar{x}$, Arithmetic Means	*R*, Range
8:00 a.m.	46	16
8:30 a.m.	40.5	6
9:00 a.m.	44	6
9:30 a.m.	40	2
10:00 a.m.	41.5	9
10:30 a.m.	39.5	1
	251.5	40

$$\bar{\bar{x}} = \frac{251.5}{6} = 41.92 \qquad \bar{R} = \frac{40}{6} = 6.67$$

$$UCL = 41.92 + 0.729(6.67) = 46.78$$

$$LCL = 41.92 - 0.729(6.67) = 37.06$$

   b. Interpreting, the mean reading was 341.92 degrees Fahrenheit. If the oven continues operating as evidenced by the first six hourly readings, about 99.7% of the mean readings will lie between 337.06 degrees and 346.78 degrees.

9. a. The fraction defective is 0.0507. The upper control limit is 0.0801 and the lower control limit is 0.0213.
   b. Yes, the 7th and 9th samples indicate the process is out of control.
   c. The process appears to stay the same.

11. $\bar{c} = \frac{37}{14} = 2.64$

$2.64 \pm 3\sqrt{2.64}$

The control limits are 0 and 7.5. The process is out of control on the seventh day.

13. $\bar{c} = \frac{6}{11} = 0.545$

$0.545 \pm 2\sqrt{0.545} = 0.545 \pm 2.215$

The control limits are from 0 to 2.760, so there are no receipts out of control.

15.

Percent Defective	Probability of Accepting Lot
10	.889
20	.558
30	.253
40	.083

17. $P(x \leq 1 \mid n = 10, \pi = .10) = .736$
$P(x \leq 1 \mid n = 10, \pi = .20) = .375$
$P(x \leq 1 \mid n = 10, \pi = .30) = .149$
$P(x \leq 1 \mid n = 10, \pi = .40) = .046$

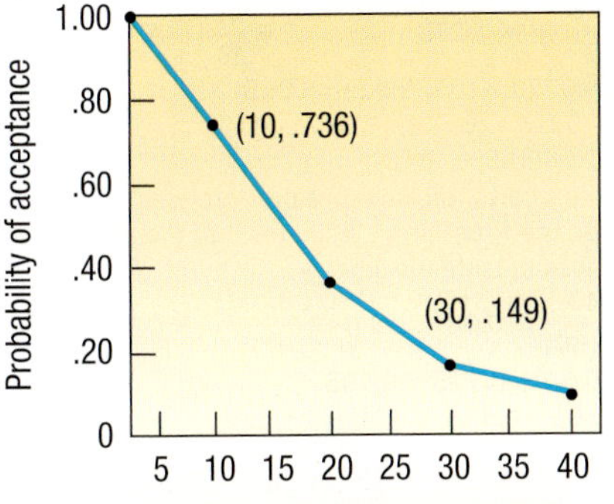

19.

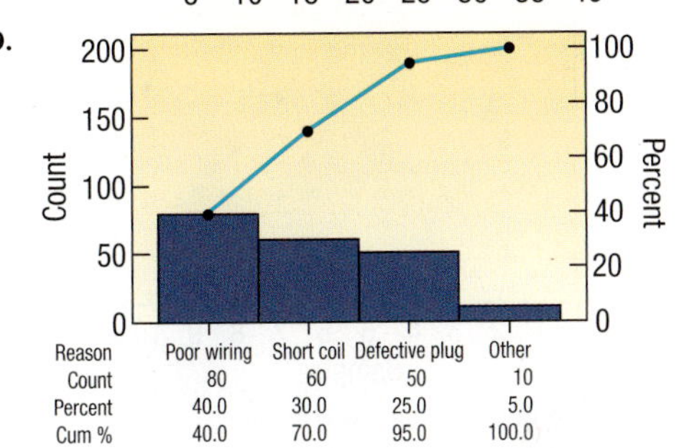

21. a. Mean: $UCL = 10.0 + 0.577(0.25) = 10.0 + 0.14425 = 10.14425$
$LCL = 10.0 - 0.577(0.25) = 10.0 - 0.14425 = 9.85575$
Range: $UCL = 2.115(0.25) = 0.52875$
$LCL = 0(0.25) = 0$
   b. The mean is 10.16, which is above the upper control limit and is out of control. There is too much cola in the soft drinks. The process is in control for variation; an adjustment is needed.

23. a. $\bar{\bar{x}} = \frac{611.3333}{20} = 30.57$

$\bar{R} = \frac{312}{20} = 15.6$

Mean: $UCL = 30.5665 + (1.023)(15.6) = 46.53$
$LCL = 30.5665 - (1.023)(15.6) = 14.61$
Range: $UCL = 2.575(15.6) = 40.17$

   b.

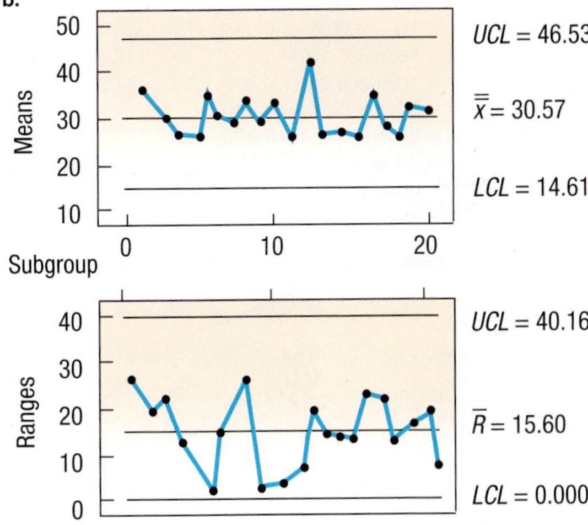

   c. The points all seem to be within the control limits. No adjustments are necessary.

25. $\bar{\bar{X}} = \frac{-0.5}{18} = -0.0278$ $\quad\quad \bar{R} = \frac{27}{18} = 1.5$

$UCL = -.0278 + (0.729)(1.5) = 1.065$

$LCL = -.0278 - (0.729)(1.5) = -1.121$

$UCL = 2.282(1.5) = 3.423$

The X-bar chart indicates that the "process" was in control. However, the R-bar chart indicates that the performance on hole 12 was outside the limits.

27. a. $p = \frac{40}{10(50)} = 0.08 \quad 3\sqrt{\frac{0.08(0.92)}{50}} = 0.115$

$UCL = 0.08 + 0.115 = 0.195$

$LCL = 0.08 - 0.115 = 0$

b.

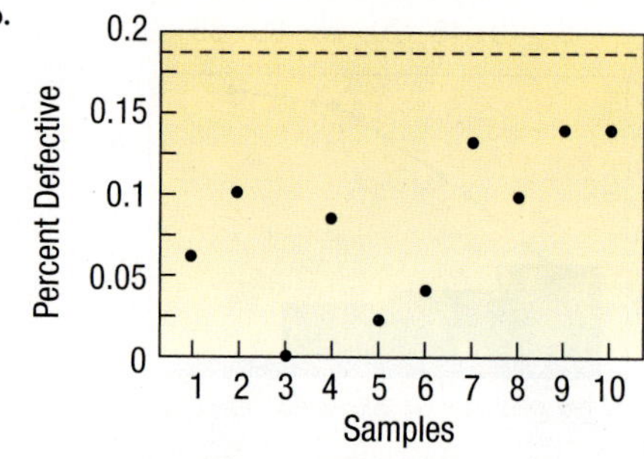

c. There are no points that exceed the limits.

29.

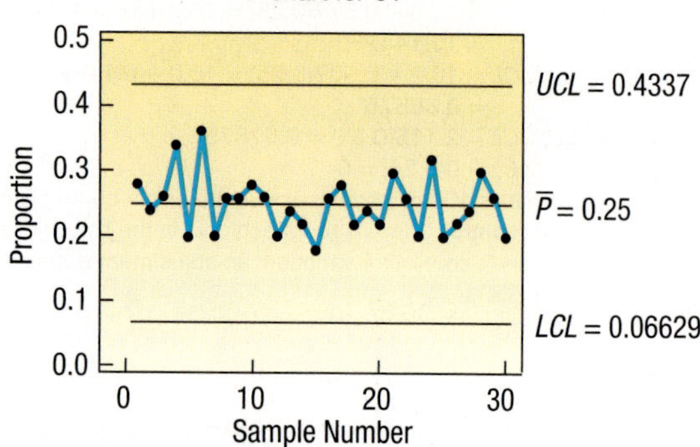

These sample results indicate that the odds are much less than 50-50 for an increase. The percent of stocks that increase is "in control" around 0.25, or 25%. The control limits are 0.06629 and 0.4337.

31. $P(x \le 3 \mid n = 10, \pi = 0.05) = 0.999$

$P(x \le 3 \mid n = 10, \pi = 0.10) = 0.987$

$P(x \le 3 \mid n = 10, \pi = 0.20) = 0.878$

$P(x \le 3 \mid n = 10, \pi = 0.30) = 0.649$

$P(x \le 5 \mid n = 20, \pi = 0.05) = 0.999$

$P(x \le 5 \mid n = 20, \pi = 0.10) = 0.989$

$P(x \le 5 \mid n = 20, \pi = 0.20) = 0.805$

$P(x \le 5 \mid n = 20, \pi = 0.30) = 0.417$

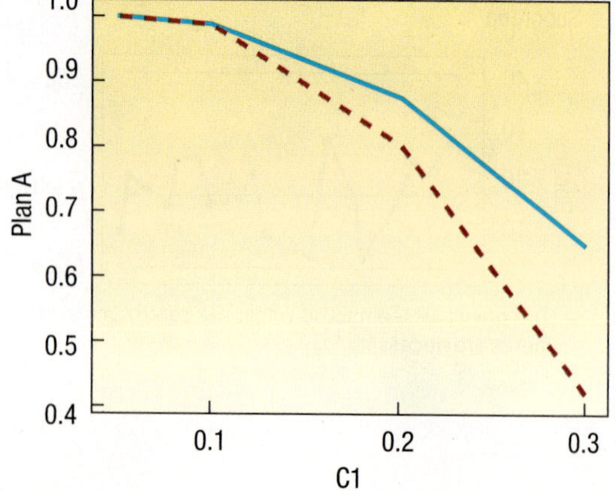

The solid line is the operating characteristic curve for the first plan, and the dashed line, the second. The supplier would prefer the first because the probability of acceptance is higher (above). However, if he is really sure of his quality, the second plan seems higher at the very low range of defect percentages and might be preferred.

33. a. $\bar{c} = \frac{213}{15} = 14.2;\ 3\sqrt{14.2} = 11.30$

$UCL = 14.2 + 11.3 = 25.5$

$LCL = 14.2 - 11.3 = 2.9$

b.

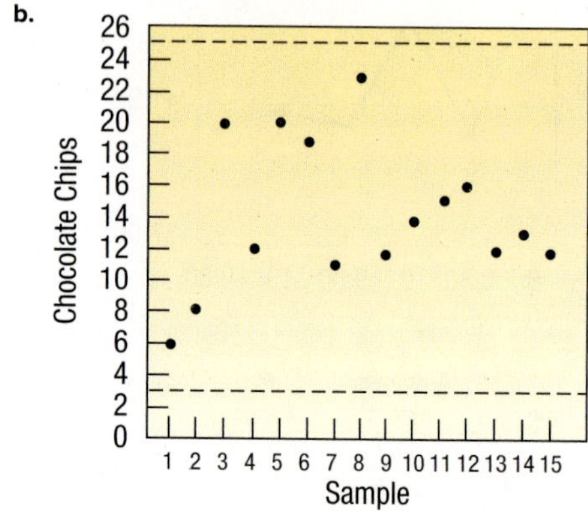

c. All the points are in control.

35. $\bar{c} = \frac{70}{10} = 7.0$

$UCL = 7.0 + 3\sqrt{7} = 14.9$

$LCL = 7.0 - 3\sqrt{7} = 0$

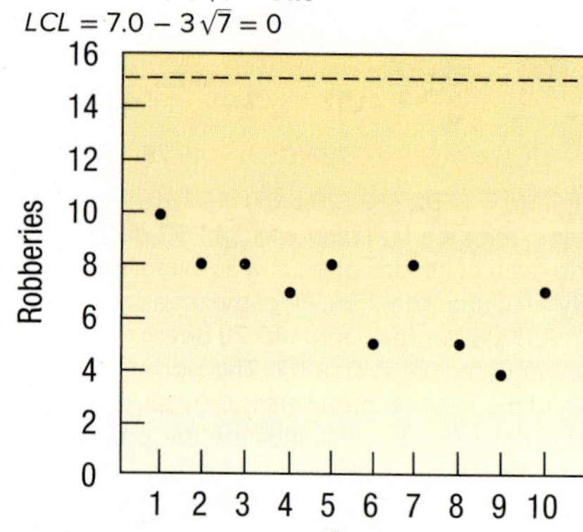

37. $P(x \le 3 \mid n = 20, \pi = .10) = .867$

$P(x \le 3 \mid n = 20, \pi = .20) = .412$

$P(x \le 3 \mid n = 20, \pi = .30) = .108$

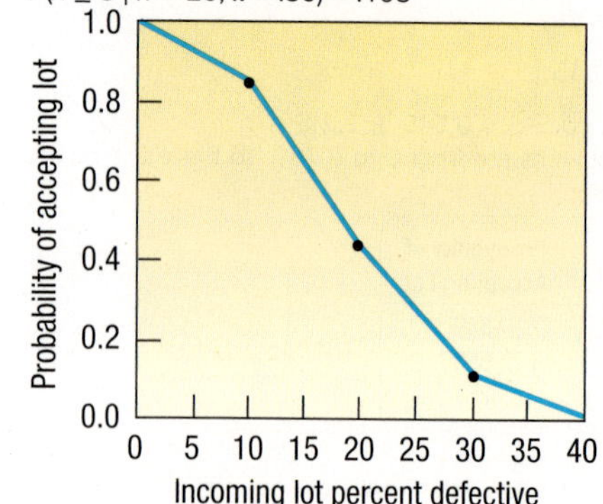

APPENDIX D: ANSWERS

Answers to Odd-Numbered Review Exercises

REVIEW OF CHAPTERS 1–4
PROBLEMS

1. a. Mean is 147.9. Median is 148.5. Standard deviation is 69.24.
   b. The first quartile is 106. The third quartile is 186.25.
   c.

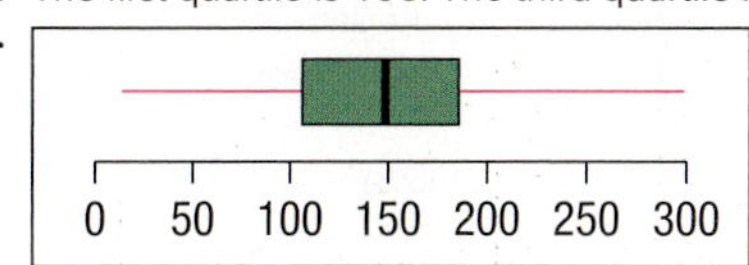

There are no outliers. The distribution is symmetric. The whiskers and the boxes are about equal on the two sides.

   d. $2^6 = 64$, use 6 classes; $i = \frac{299 - 14}{6} = 47.5$, use $i = 50$.

Amount	Frequency
\$ 0 up to \$ 50	3
50 up to 100	8
100 up to 150	15
150 up to 200	13
200 up to 250	7
250 up to 300	7
Total	50

   e. Answers will vary but include all of the above information.

3. a. Mean is \$55,224. Median is \$54,916. Standard deviation is \$9,208.
   b. The first quartile is \$48,060. The third quartile is 60,730.
   c.

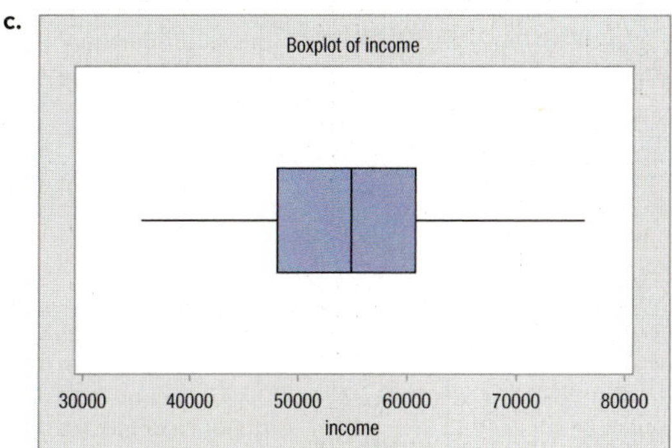

The distribution is symmetric with no outliers.

   d.

Amounts	Frequency
35000–42999	5
43000–50999	12
51000–58999	18
59000–66999	9
67000–74999	6
75000–82999	1
Total	**51**

   e. Answers will vary but include all of the above information.

5. a. Box plot.
   b. Median is 48, the first quartile is 24, and the third quartile is 84.
   c. Positively skewed with the long tail to the right.
   d. You cannot determine the number of observations.

REVIEW OF CHAPTERS 5–7
PROBLEMS

1. a. .035
   b. .018
   c. .648
3. a. .0401
   b. .6147
   c. 7,440
5. a. $\mu = 1.10$
   $\sigma = 1.18$
   b. About 550
   c. $\mu = 1.833$

REVIEW OF CHAPTERS 8 AND 9
PROBLEMS

1. $z = \frac{8.8 - 8.6}{2.0/\sqrt{35}} = 0.59$, $.5000 - .2224 = .2776$
3. $160 \pm 2.426 \frac{20}{\sqrt{40}}$, 152.33 up to 167.67
5. $985.5 \pm 2.571 \frac{115.5}{\sqrt{6}}$, 864.27 up to 1,106.73
7. $240 \pm 2.131 \frac{35}{\sqrt{16}}$, 221.35 up to 258.65

   Because 250 is in the interval, the evidence does *not* indicate an increase in production.
9. $n = \left[\frac{1.96(25)}{4}\right]^2 = 150$
11. $n = .08(.92)\left(\frac{2.33}{0.22}\right)^2 = 999$
13. $n = .4(.6)\left(\frac{2.33}{0.03}\right)^2 = 1{,}448$

REVIEW OF CHAPTERS 10–12
PROBLEMS

1. $H_0: \mu \geq 36$; $H_1: \mu < 36$. Reject H_0 if $t < -1.683$.

$$t = \frac{35.5 - 36.0}{0.9/\sqrt{42}} = -3.60$$

   Reject H_0. The mean height is less than 36 inches.

3. $H_0: \mu_1 = \mu_2$ $H_1: \mu_1 \neq \mu_2$
   Reject H_0 if $t < -2.845$ or $t > 2.845$.

$$s_p^2 = \frac{(12 - 1)(5)^2 + (10 - 1)(8)^2}{12 + 10 + 2} = 42.55$$

$$t = \frac{250 - 252}{\sqrt{42.55\left(\frac{1}{12} + \frac{1}{10}\right)}} = -0.716$$

   H_0 is not rejected. There is no difference in the mean strength of the two glues.

5. $H_0: \mu_1 = \mu_2 = \mu_3 = \mu_4$ H_1: The means are not all the same
   H_0 rejected if $F > 3.29$.

Source	SS	df	MS	F
Treatments	20.736	3	6.91	1.04
Error	100.00	15	6.67	
Total	120.736	18		

   H_0 is not rejected. There is no difference in the mean sales.

7. **a.** From the graph, marketing salaries may be acting differently.
   b. H_0: $\mu_1 = \mu_2 = \mu_3 = \mu_4$
   H_1: At least one mean is different (for four majors)
   H_0: $\mu_1 = \mu_2 = \mu_3$
   H_1: At least one mean is different (for three years)
   H_0: There is no interaction
   H_1: There is interaction
   c. The *p*-value (.482) is high. Do not reject the hypothesis of no interaction.
   d. The *p*-value for majors is small (.034 < .05), so there is a difference among mean salaries by major. There is no difference from one year to the next in mean salaries (.894 > .05).

REVIEW OF CHAPTERS 13 AND 14 PROBLEMS

1. **a.** Profit
   b. $\hat{y} = a + b_1x_1 + b_2x_2 + b_3x_3 + b_4x_4$
   c. $163,200
   d. About 86% of the variation in net profit is explained by the four variables.
   e. About 68% of the net profits would be within $3,000 of the estimates; about 95% would be within 2($3,000), or $6,000, of the estimates; and virtually all would be within 3($3,000), or $9,000, of the estimates.
3. **a.** 0.9261
   b. 2.0469, found by $\sqrt{83.8/20}$
   c. H_0: $\beta_1 = \beta_2 = \beta_3 = \beta_4 = 0$
   H_1: Not all coefficients are zero.
   Reject if $F > 2.87$; computed $F = 62.697$, found by 162.70/4.19.
   d. Could delete x_2 because *t*-ratio (1.29) is less than the critical *t* value of 2.086. Otherwise, reject H_0 for x_1, x_3, and x_4 because all of those *t*-ratios are greater than 2.086.

REVIEW OF CHAPTERS 15 AND 16 PROBLEMS

1. H_0: Median $\leq$ 60
   H_1: Median > 60
   $\mu = 20(.5) = 10$
   $\sigma = \sqrt{20(.5)(.5)} = 2.2361$
   H_0 is rejected if $z > 1.65$. There are 16 observations greater than 60.
   $$z = \frac{15.5 - 10.0}{2.2361} = 2.46$$
   Reject H_0. The median sales per day are greater than 60.
3. H_0: The population lengths are the same.
   H_1: The population lengths are not the same.
   H_0 is rejected if H is > 5.991.
   $$H = \frac{12}{24(24+1)}\left[\frac{(104.5)^2}{7} + \frac{(125.5)^2}{9} + \frac{(70)^2}{8}\right] - 3(24+1)$$
   $$= 78.451 - 75 = 3.451$$
   Do not reject H_0. The population lengths are the same.

REVIEW OF CHAPTERS 17 AND 18 PROBLEMS

1. **a.** 156.6, found by (16,915/10,799)100
   b. 153.0, found by (16,615/11,056.7)100. Note: 11,056.7 is the average for the period 2008 to 2010.
   c. 9,535 + 854.4*t* and 18,079, found by 9,535 + 854.4 (10)
3. 55.44, found by 1.20[3.5 + (0.7)(61)], and 44.73, found by 0.90[3.5 + (0.7)(66)]

APPENDIX D: ANSWERS

Solutions to Practice Tests

PRACTICE TEST (AFTER CHAPTER 4)
PART 1

1. statistics
2. descriptive statistics
3. population
4. quantitative and qualitative
5. discrete
6. nominal
7. nominal
8. zero
9. seven
10. 50
11. variance
12. never
13. median

PART 2

1. $\sqrt[3]{(1.18)(1.04)(1.02)} = 1.0777$, *or* 7.77%
2. **a.** 30 thousands of dollars
   b. 105
   c. 52
   d. 0.19, found by 20/105
   e. 165
   f. 120 and 330
3. **a.** 70
   b. 71.5
   c. 67.8
   d. 28
   e. 9.34
4. $44.20, found by [(200)$36 + (300)$40 + (500)$50]/1,000
5. **a.** pie chart
   b. 11.1
   c. three times
   d. 65%

PRACTICE TEST (AFTER CHAPTER 7)
PART 1

1. never
2. experiment
3. event
4. joint
5. **a.** permutation
   b. combination
6. one
7. three or more outcomes
8. infinite
9. one
10. 0.2764
11. 0.0475
12. independent
13. mutually exclusive
14. only two outcomes
15. bell-shaped

PART 2

1. **a.** 0.0526, found by (5/20)(4/19)
   b. 0.4474, found by 1 – (15/20)(14/19)
2. **a.** 0.2097, found by $16(.15)(.85)^{15}$
   b. 0.9257, found by $1 - (.85)^{16}$
3. 720, found by $6 \cdot 5 \cdot 4 \cdot 3 \cdot 2$
4. **a.** 2.2, found by .2(1) + .5(2) + .2(3) + .1(4)
   b. 0.76, found by .2(1.44) + .5(0.04) + .2(0.64) + .1(3.24)
5. **a.** 0.1808. The z value for $2,000 is 0.47, found by (2,000 – 1,600)/850.
   b. 0.4747, found by 0.2939 + 0.1808
   c. 0.0301, found by 0.5000 – 0.4699
6. **a.** contingency table
   b. 0.625, found by 50/80
   c. 0.75, found by 60/80
   d. 0.40, found by 20/50
   e. 0.125, found by 10/80
7. **a.** 0.0498, found by $\frac{3^0 e^{-3}}{0!}$
   b. 0.2240, found by $\frac{3^3 e^{-3}}{3!}$
   c. 0.1847, found by 1 – [0.0498 + 0.1494 + 0.2240 + 0.2240 + 0.1680]
   d. .0025

PRACTICE TEST (AFTER CHAPTER 9)
PART 1

1. random sample
2. sampling error
3. standard error
4. become smaller
5. point estimate
6. confidence interval
7. population size
8. proportion
9. positively skewed
10. 0.5

PART 2

1. 0.0351, found by 0.5000 – 0.4649. The corresponding
   $z = \frac{11 - 12.2}{2.3/\sqrt{12}} = -1.81$
2. **a.** The population mean is unknown.
   b. 9.3 years, which is the sample mean
   c. 0.3922, found by $2/\sqrt{26}$
   d. The confidence interval is from 8.63 up to 9.97, found by
   $9.3 \pm 1.708\left(\frac{2}{\sqrt{26}}\right)$
3. 2,675, found by $.27(1 - .27)\left(\frac{2.33}{.02}\right)^2$
4. The confidence interval is from 0.5459 up to 0.7341, found by
   $.64 \pm 1.96\sqrt{\frac{.64(1 - .64)}{100}}$

PRACTICE TEST (AFTER CHAPTER 12)
PART 1

1. null hypothesis
2. significance level
3. *p*-value
4. standard deviation
5. normality
6. test statistic
7. split evenly between the two tails
8. range from negative infinity to positive infinity

9. independent
10. three and 20

PART 2

1. $H_0: \mu \leq 90 \quad H_1: \mu > 90 \quad$ If $t > 2.567$, reject H_0.

$$t = \frac{96 - 90}{12/\sqrt{18}} = 2.12$$

Do not reject the null. The mean time in the park could be 90 minutes.

2. $H_0: \mu_1 = \mu_2 \quad H_1: \mu_1 \neq \mu_2$.
$df = 14 + 12 - 2 = 24$
If $t < -2.064$ or $t > 2.064$, then reject H_0.

$$s_p^2 = \frac{(14-1)(30)^2 + (12-1)(40)^2}{14 + 12 - 2} = 1{,}220.83$$

$$t = \frac{837 - 797}{\sqrt{1{,}220.83\left(\frac{1}{14} + \frac{1}{12}\right)}} = \frac{40.0}{13.7455} = 2.910$$

Reject the null hypothesis. There is a difference in the mean miles traveled.

3. a. three, because there are 2 *df* between groups.
   b. 21, found by the total degrees of freedom plus 1.
   c. If the significance level is .05, the critical value is 3.55.
   d. $H_0: \mu_1 = \mu_2 = \mu_3 \quad H_1$: Treatment means are not all the same.
   e. At a 5% significance level, the null hypothesis is rejected.
   f. At a 5% significance level, we can conclude the treatment means differ.

PRACTICE TEST (AFTER CHAPTER 14) PART 1

1. vertical
2. interval
3. zero
4. −0.77
5. never
6. 7
7. decrease of .5
8. −0.9
9. zero
10. unlimited
11. linear
12. residual
13. two
14. correlation matrix
15. normal distribution

PART 2

1. a. 30
   b. The regression equation is $\hat{y} = 90.619X - 0.9401$. If X is zero, the line crosses the vertical axis at −0.9401. As the independent variable increases by one unit, the dependent variable increases by 90.619 units.
   c. 905.2499
   d. 0.3412, found by 129.7275/380.1667. Thirty-four percent of the variation in the dependent variable is explained by the independent variable.
   e. 0.5842, found by $\sqrt{0.3412} \quad H_0: \rho \geq 0 \quad H_1: \rho < 0$
   Using a significance level of .01, reject H_0 if $t > 2.467$.

$$t = \frac{0.5842\sqrt{30 - 2}}{\sqrt{1 - (0.5842)^2}} = 3.81$$

   Reject H_0. There is a negative correlation between the variables.

2. a. 30
   b. 4
   c. 0.5974, found by 227.0928/380.1667
   d. $H_0: \beta_1 = \beta_2 = \beta_3 = \beta_4 = 0 \quad H_1$: Not all βs are 0. Reject H_0 if $F > 4.18$ (using a 1% level of significance). Since the computed value of F is 9.27, reject H_0. Not all of the regression coefficients are zero.
   e. Reject H_0 if $t > 2.787$ or $t < -2.787$ (using a 1% level of significance). Drop variable 2 initially and then rerun. Perhaps you will delete variable(s) 1 and/or 4 also.

PRACTICE TEST (AFTER CHAPTER 16) PART 1

1. nominal
2. at least 30 observations
3. two
4. 6
5. number of categories
6. dependent
7. binomial
8. comparing two or more independent samples
9. never
10. normal populations, equal standard deviations

PART 2

1. H_0: The proportions are as stated.
H_1: The proportions are not as stated.
Using a significance level of .05, reject H_0 if $\chi^2 > 7.815$.

$$x^2 = \frac{(120-130)^2}{130} + \frac{(40-40)^2}{40} + \frac{(30-20)^2}{20} + \frac{(10-10)^2}{10} = 5.769$$

Do not reject H_0. Proportions could be as declared.

2. H_0: No relationship between gender and book type.
H_1: There is a relationship between gender and book type.
Using a significance level of .01, reject H_0 if $\chi^2 > 9.21$.

$$x^2 = \frac{(250 - 197.3)^2}{197.3} + \cdots + \frac{(200 - 187.5)^2}{187.5} = 54.84$$

Reject H_0. There is a relationship between gender and book type.

3. H_0: The distributions are the same.
H_1: The distributions are not the same.
H_0 is rejected if $H > 5.99$.

8:00 a.m. Ranks		10:00 a.m. Ranks		1:30 p.m. Ranks	
68	6	59	1.5	67	5
84	20	59	1.5	69	7
75	10.5	63	4	75	10.5
78	15.5	62	3	76	12.5
70	8	78	15.5	79	17
77	14	76	12.5	83	19
88	24	80	18	86	21.5
71	9			86	21.5
				87	23
Sums	107		56		137
Count	8		7		9

$$H = \frac{12}{24(25)}\left[\frac{107^2}{8} + \frac{56^2}{7} + \frac{137^2}{9}\right] - 3(25) = 4.29$$

H_0 is not rejected. There is no difference in the three distributions.

4. $H_0: \pi \leq 1/3 \quad H_1: \pi > 1/3$
At the .01 significance level, the decision rule is to reject H_0 if $z > 2.326$.

$$z = \frac{\left[\frac{210}{500} - \frac{1}{3}\right]}{\sqrt{\frac{(\frac{1}{3})(1 - \frac{1}{3})}{500}}} = \frac{0.08667}{0.02108} = 4.11$$

Reject the null hypothesis.
The actual proportion of Louisiana children who were obese or overweight is more than one out of three.

PRACTICE TEST (AFTER CHAPTER 18) PART 1

1. denominator
2. index
3. quantity
4. base period
5. 1982–1984
6. trend
7. moving average
8. autocorrelation
9. residual
10. same

PART 2

1. a. 111.54, found by (145,000/130,000) × 100 for 2013 92.31, found by (120,000/130,000) × 100 for 2014 130.77, found by (170,000/130,000) × 100 for 2015 146.15, found by (190,000/130,000) × 100 for 2016
   b. 87.27, found by (120,000/137,500) × 100 for 2014 126.64, found by (170,000/137,500) × 100 for 2015 138.18, found by (190,000/137,500) × 100 for 2016
2. a. 108.91, found by (1,100/1,010) × 100
   b. 111.18, found by (4,525/4,070) × 100
   c. 110.20, found by (5,400/4,900) × 100
   d. 110.69, found by the square root of (111.18) × (110.20)
3. For January of the fifth year, the seasonally adjusted forecast is 70.0875, found by 1.05 × [5.50 + 1.25(49)].
   For February of the fifth year, the seasonally adjusted forecast is 66.844, found by 0.983 × [5.50 + 1.25(50)].

APPENDIX E: ANSWERS TO SELF-REVIEW

CHAPTER 1

1.1 **a.** Inferential statistics, because a sample was used to draw a conclusion about how all consumers in the population would react if the chicken dinner were marketed.

b. On the basis of the sample of 1,960 consumers, we estimate that, if it is marketed, 60% of all consumers will purchase the chicken dinner: (1,176/1,960) × 100 = 60%.

1.2 **a.** Age is a ratio-scale variable. A 40-year-old is twice as old as someone 20 years old.

b. The two variables are: 1) if a person owns a luxury car, and 2) the state of residence. Both are measured on a nominal scale.

CHAPTER 2

2.1 **a.** Qualitative data, because the customers' response to the taste test is the name of a beverage.

b. Frequency table. It shows the number of people who prefer each beverage.

c.

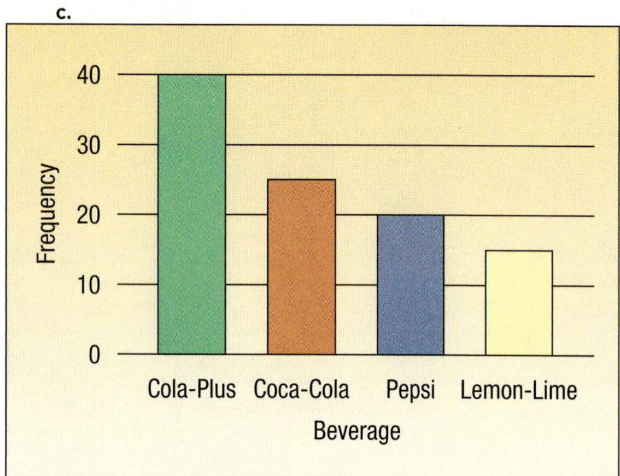

d.

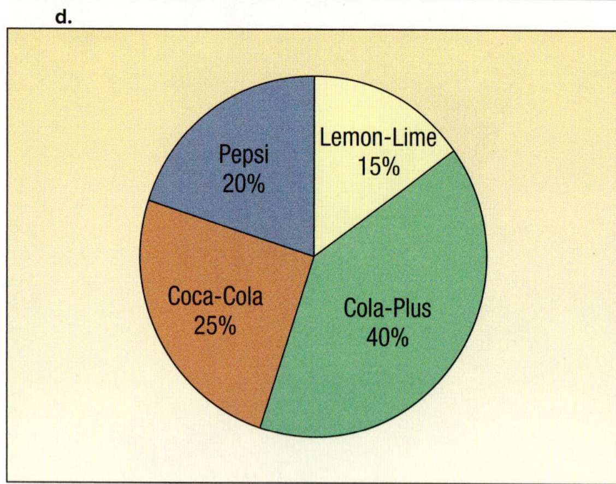

2.2 **a.** The raw data or ungrouped data.

b.

Commission	Number of Salespeople
\$1,400 up to \$1,500	2
1,500 up to 1,600	5
1,600 up to 1,700	3
1,700 up to 1,800	1
Total	11

c. Class frequencies.

d. The largest concentration of commissions is \$1,500 up to \$1,600. The smallest commission is about \$1,400 and the largest is about \$1,800. The typical amount earned is \$1,550.

2.3 **a.** $2^6 = 64 < 73 < 128 = 2^7$, so seven classes are recommended.

b. The interval width should be at least (488 − 320)/7 = 24. Class intervals of either 25 or 30 are reasonable.

c. Assuming a class interval of 25 and beginning with a lower limit of 300, eight classes are required. If we use an interval of 30 and begin with a lower limit of 300, only 7 classes are required. Seven classes is the better alternative.

Distance Classes	Frequency	Percent
300 up to 330	2	2.7%
330 up to 360	2	2.7
360 up to 390	17	23.3
390 up to 420	27	37.0
420 up to 450	22	30.1
450 up to 480	1	1.4
480 up to 510	2	2.7
Grand Total	73	100.00

d. 17

e. 23.3%, found by 17/73

f. 71.2%, found by (27 + 22 + 1 + 2)/73

2.4 **a.**

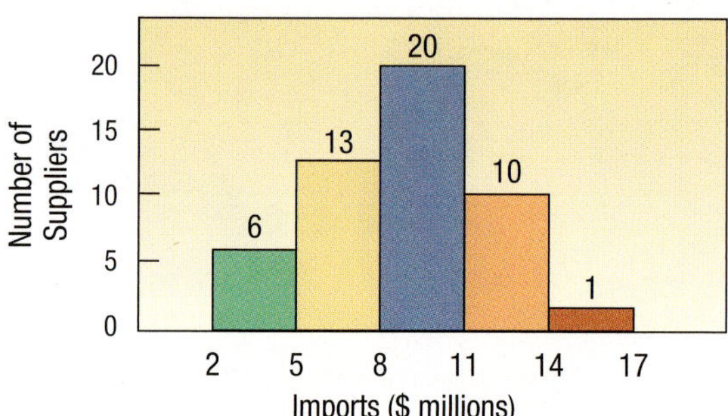

b.

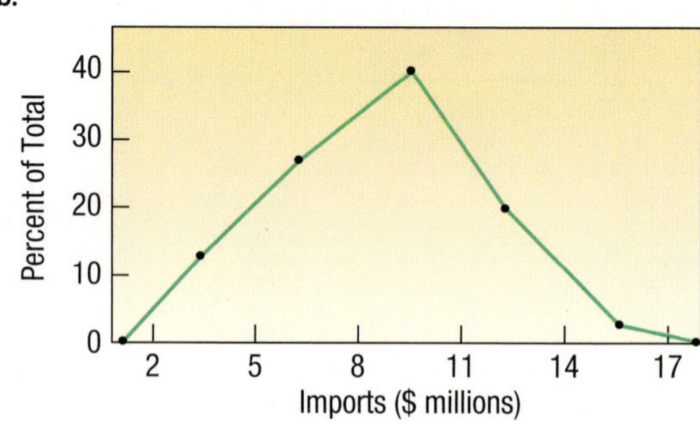

The plots are: (3.5, 12), (6.5, 26), (9.5, 40), (12.5, 20), and (15.5, 2).

c. The smallest annual volume of imports by a supplier is about \$2 million, the largest about \$17 million. The highest frequency is between \$8 million and \$11 million.

2.5 **a.** A frequency distribution.

b.

Hourly Wages	Cumulative Number
Less than \$8	0
Less than \$10	3
Less than \$12	10
Less than \$14	14
Less than \$16	15

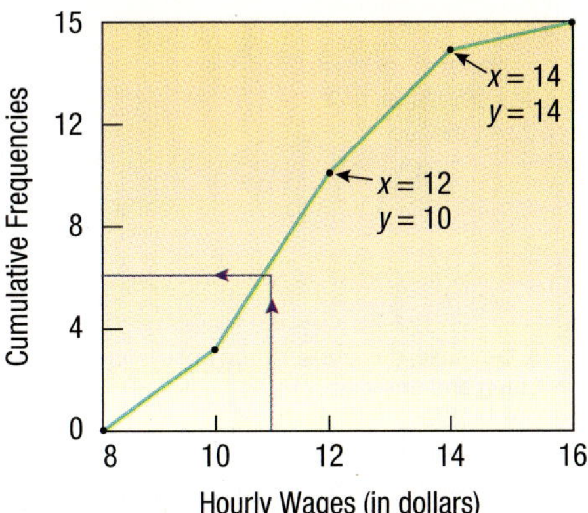

c. About seven employees earn \$11.00 or less.

CHAPTER 3

3–1 **1. a.** $\bar{x} = \frac{\Sigma x}{n}$

b. $\bar{x} = \frac{\$267{,}100}{4} = \$66{,}775$

c. Statistic, because it is a sample value.

d. \$66,775. The sample mean is our best estimate of the population mean.

2. a. $\mu = \frac{\Sigma x}{N}$

b. $\mu = \frac{498}{6} = 83$

c. Parameter, because it was computed using all the population values.

3–2 **1. a.** \$878

b. 3, 3

2. a. 17, found by (15 + 19)/2 = 17

b. 5, 5

c. There are 3 values that occur twice: 11, 15, and 19. There are three modes.

3–3 **a.**

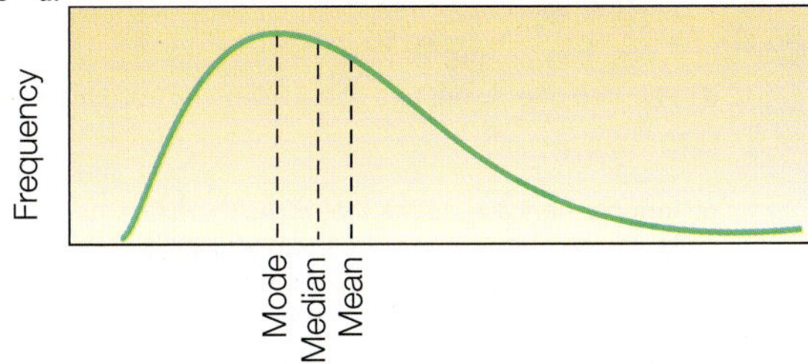

b. Positively skewed, because the mean is the largest average and the mode is the smallest.

3–4 **a.** \$237, found by:

$$\frac{(95 \times \$400) + (126 \times \$200) + (79 \times \$100)}{95 + 126 + 79} = \$237.00$$

b. The profit per suit is \$12, found by \$237 − \$200 cost − \$25 commission. The total profit for the 300 suits is \$3,600, found by 300 × \$12.

3–5 **1. a.** About 9.9%, found by $\sqrt[4]{1.458602236}$, then 1.099 − 1.00 = .099

b. About 10.095%

c. Greater than, because 10.095 > 9.9

2. 8.63%, found by $\sqrt[20]{\frac{120{,}520}{23{,}000}} - 1 = 1.0863 - 1$

3–6 **a.** 22 thousands of pounds, found by 112 − 90

b. $\bar{x} = \frac{824}{8} = 103$ thousands of pounds

c. Variance $= \frac{373}{8} = 46.625$

3–7 **a.** $\mu = \frac{\$16{,}900}{5} = \$3{,}380$

b. $\sigma^2 = \frac{(3{,}536 - 3{,}380)^2 + \cdots + (3{,}622 - 3{,}380)^2}{5}$

$$= \frac{(156)^2 + (-207)^2 + (68)^2 + (-259)^2 + (242)^2}{5}$$

$$= \frac{197{,}454}{5} = 39{,}490.8$$

c. $\sigma = \sqrt{39{,}490.8} = 198.72$

d. There is more variation in the Pittsburgh office because the standard deviation is larger. The mean is also larger in the Pittsburgh office.

3–8 2.33, found by:

$$\bar{x} = \frac{\Sigma x}{n} = \frac{28}{7} = 4$$

$$s^2 = \frac{\Sigma(x - \bar{x})^2}{n - 1} = \frac{14}{7 - 1} = 2.33$$

$$s = \sqrt{2.33} = 1.53$$

3–9 **a.** $k = \frac{14.15 - 14.00}{.10} = 1.5$

$$k = \frac{13.85 - 14.0}{.10} = -1.5$$

$$1 - \frac{1}{(1.5)^2} = 1 - .44 = .56$$

b. 13.8 and 14.2

3–10 **a.** Frequency distribution.

b. $\bar{x} = \frac{\Sigma fM}{M} = \frac{\$244}{20} = \$12.20$

c. $s = \sqrt{\frac{303.20}{20 - 1}} = \$3.99$

CHAPTER 4

4–1 **1. a.** 79, 105

b. 15

c. From 88 to 97; 75% of the stores are in this range.

2. a. 8

b. 10.1, 10.2, 10.4, 10.8

c. 9.5

d. 11.6, 7.7

4–2 **a.** 7.9

b. $Q_1 = 7.76$, $Q_3 = 8.015$

4–3 The smallest value is 10 and the largest 85; the first quartile is 25 and the third 60. About 50% of the values are between 25 and 60. The median value is 40. The distribution is positively skewed. There are no outliers.

4–4 **a.** $\bar{x} = \frac{407}{5} = 81.4$,

$$s = \sqrt{\frac{923.2}{5 - 1}} = 15.19, \text{ Median} = 84$$

b. $sk = \frac{3(81.4 - 84.0)}{15.19} = -0.51$

c. $sk = \frac{5}{(4)(3)}[-1.3154] = -0.5481$

d. The distribution is somewhat negatively skewed.

4–5 **a.** Scatter diagram

b. 16

c. $7,500

d. Strong and direct

CHAPTER 5

5–1 **a.** Count the number who think the new game is playable.

b. Seventy-three players found the game playable. Many other answers are possible.

c. No. Probability cannot be greater than 1. The probability that the game, if put on the market, will be successful is 65/80, or .8125.

d. Cannot be less than 0. Perhaps a mistake in arithmetic.

e. More than half of the players testing the game liked it. (Of course, other answers are possible.)

5–2 **1.** $\frac{\text{4 queens in deck}}{\text{52 cards total}} = \frac{4}{52} = .0769$

Classical.

2. $\frac{182}{539} = .338$ Empirical.

3. The probability of the outcome is estimated by applying the subjective approach to estimating a probability. If you think that it is likely that you will save $1 million, then your probability should be between .5 and 1.0.

5–3 **a.** **i.** $\frac{(50 + 68)}{2{,}000} = .059$

ii. $1 - \frac{302}{2{,}000} = .849$

b.

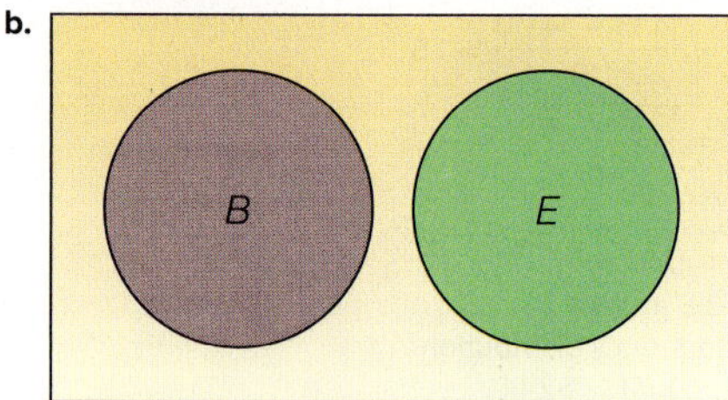

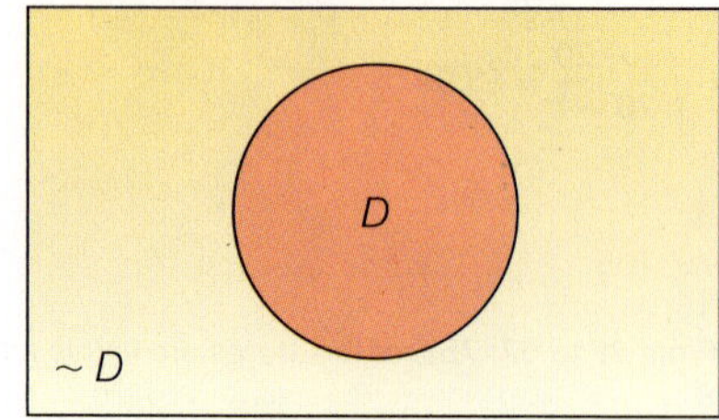

c. They are not complementary, but are mutually exclusive.

5–4 **a.** Need for corrective shoes is event A. Need for major dental work is event B.

$$P(A \text{ or } B) = P(A) + P(B) - P(A \text{ and } B) = .08 + .15 - .03 = .20$$

b. One possibility is:

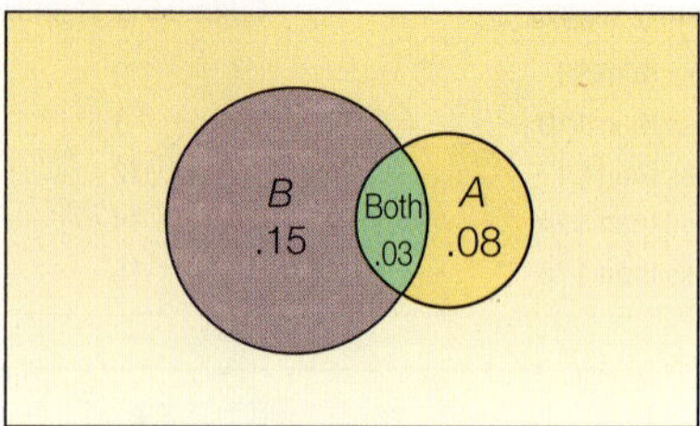

5–5 $(.95)(.95)(.95)(.95) = .8145$

5–6 **a.** .002, found by:

$$\left(\frac{4}{12}\right)\left(\frac{3}{11}\right)\left(\frac{2}{10}\right)\left(\frac{1}{9}\right) = \frac{24}{11{,}880} = .002$$

b. .14, found by:

$$\left(\frac{8}{12}\right)\left(\frac{7}{11}\right)\left(\frac{6}{10}\right)\left(\frac{5}{9}\right) = \frac{1{,}680}{11{,}880} = .1414$$

c. No, because there are other possibilities, such as three women and one man.

5–7 **a.** $P(B_2) = \frac{225}{500} = .45$

b. The two events are mutually exclusive, so apply the special rule of addition.

$$P(B_1 \text{ or } B_2) = P(B_1) + P(B_2) = \frac{100}{500} + \frac{225}{500} = .65$$

c. The two events are not mutually exclusive, so apply the general rule of addition.

$$P(B_1 \text{ or } A_1) = P(B_1) + P(A_1) - P(B_1 \text{ and } A_1) = \frac{100}{500} + \frac{75}{500} - \frac{15}{500} = .32$$

d. As shown in the example/solution, movies attended per month and age are not independent, so apply the general rule of multiplication.

$$P(B_1 \text{ and } A_1) = P(B_1)P(A_1 \mid B_1) = \left(\frac{100}{500}\right)\left(\frac{15}{100}\right) = .03$$

5–8 **a.** $P(\text{visited often}) = \frac{80}{195} = .41$

b. $P(\text{visited a store in an enclosed mall}) = \frac{90}{195} = .46$

c. The two events are not mutually exclusive, so apply the general rule of addition.

P(visited often or visited a Sears in an enclosed mall)
$= P(\text{often}) + P(\text{enclosed mall}) - P(\text{often and enclosed mall})$
$= \frac{80}{195} + \frac{90}{195} - \frac{60}{195} = .56$

d. P(visited often|went to a Sears in an enclosed mall)
$= \frac{60}{90} = .67$

e. Independence requires that $P(A|B) = P(A)$. One possibility is: P(visit often|visited an enclosed mall) $= P$(visit often). Does $60/90 = 80/195$? No, the two variables are not independent. Therefore, any joint probability in the table must be computed by using the general rule of multiplication.

f. As shown in part (e), visits often and enclosed mall are not independent, so apply the general rule of multiplication.

$$P(\text{often and enclosed mall}) = P(\text{often})P(\text{enclosed} \mid \text{often}) = \left(\frac{80}{195}\right)\left(\frac{60}{80}\right) = .31$$

g.

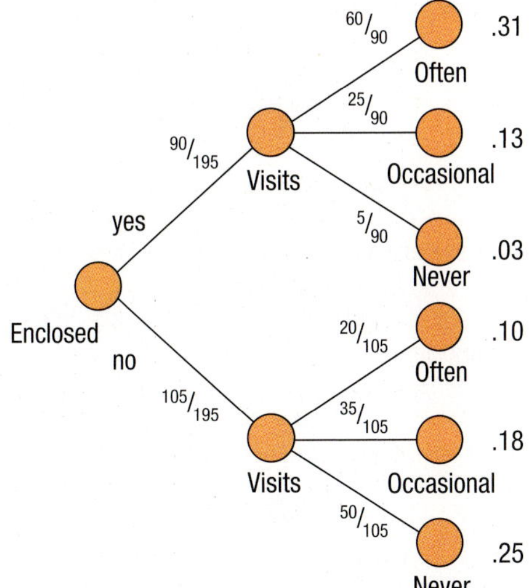

5–9 **a.** $P(A_3 \mid B_2) = \dfrac{P(A_3)P(B_2 \mid A_3)}{P(A_1)P(B_2 \mid A_1) + P(A_2)P(B_2 \mid A_2) + P(A_3)P(B_2 \mid A_3)}$

b. $= \dfrac{(.50)(.96)}{(.30)(.97) + (.20)(.95) + (.50)(.96)}$

$= \dfrac{.480}{.961} = .499$

5–10 **1.** (5)(4) = 20

2. (3)(2)(4)(3) = 72

5–11 **1.** **a.** 60, found by (5)(4)(3).

b. 60, found by:

$\dfrac{5!}{(5-3)!} = \dfrac{5 \cdot 4 \cdot 3 \cdot \cancel{2 \cdot 1}}{\cancel{2 \cdot 1}}$

2. 5,040, found by:

$\dfrac{10!}{(10-4)!} = \dfrac{10 \cdot 9 \cdot 8 \cdot 7 \cdot \cancel{6 \cdot 5 \cdot 4 \cdot 3 \cdot 2 \cdot 1}}{\cancel{6 \cdot 5 \cdot 4 \cdot 3 \cdot 2 \cdot 1}}$

3. **a.** 35 is correct, found by:

${}_7C_3 = \dfrac{n!}{r!(n-r)!} = \dfrac{7!}{3!(7-3)!} = 35$

b. Yes. There are 21 combinations, found by:

${}_7C_5 = \dfrac{n!}{r!(n-r)!} = \dfrac{7!}{5!(7-5)!} = 21$

4. **a.** ${}_{50}P_3 = \dfrac{50!}{(50-3)!} = 117{,}600$

b. ${}_{50}C_3 = \dfrac{50!}{3!\,(50-3)!} = 19{,}600$

CHAPTER 6

6–1 **a.**

Number of Spots	Probability
1	$\frac{1}{6}$
2	$\frac{1}{6}$
3	$\frac{1}{6}$
4	$\frac{1}{6}$
5	$\frac{1}{6}$
6	$\frac{1}{6}$
Total	$\frac{6}{6} = 1.00$

b.

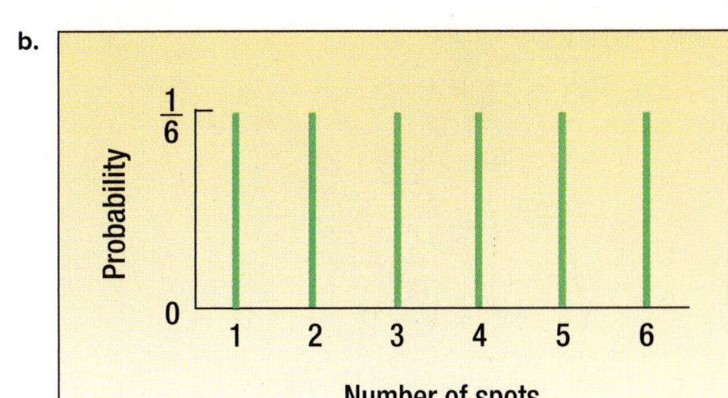

c. $\dfrac{6}{6}$ or 1.

6–2 **a.** It is discrete because the values $1.99, $2.49, and $2.89 are clearly separated from each other. Also the sum of the probabilities is 1.00, and the outcomes are mutually exclusive.

b.

x	$P(x)$	$xP(x)$
1.99	.30	0.597
2.49	.50	1.245
2.89	.20	0.578
		Sum is 2.42

Mean is 2.42

c.

x	$P(x)$	$(x-\mu)$	$(x-\mu)^2P(x)$
1.99	.30	−0.43	0.05547
2.49	.50	0.07	0.00245
2.89	.20	0.47	0.04418
			0.10210

The variance is 0.10208, and the standard deviation is 31.95 cents.

6–3 **a.** It is reasonable because each employee either uses direct deposit or does not; employees are independent; the probability of using direct deposit is 0.95 for all; and we count the number using the service out of 7.

b. $P(7) = {}_7C_7\,(.95)^7\,(.05)^0 = .6983$

c. $P(4) = {}_7C_4\,(.95)^4\,(.05)^3 = .0036$

d. Answers are in agreement.

6–4 **a.** $n = 8, \pi = .40$

b. $P(x = 3) = .2787$

c. $P(x > 0) = 1 - P(x = 0) = 1 - .0168 = .9832$

6–5 $P(3) = \dfrac{{}_8C_3\,{}_4C_2}{{}_{12}C_5} = \dfrac{\left(\dfrac{8!}{3!5!}\right)\left(\dfrac{4!}{2!2!}\right)}{\dfrac{12!}{5!7!}}$

$= \dfrac{(56)(6)}{792} = .424$

6–6 $\mu = 4{,}000(.0002) = 0.8$

$P(1) = \dfrac{0.8^1 e^{-0.8}}{1!} = .3595$

CHAPTER 7

7–1 **a.**

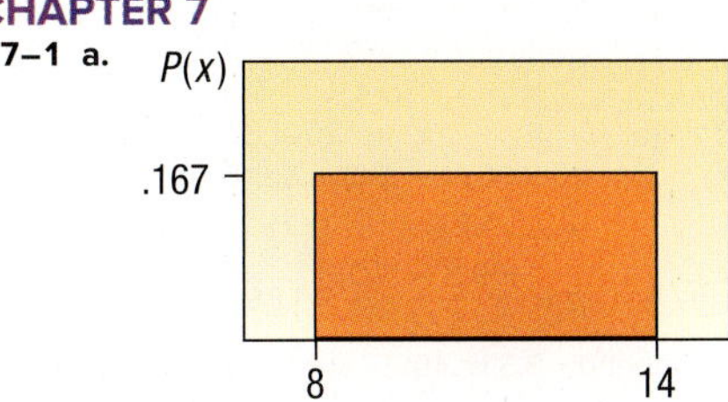

b. $P(x) = \text{(height)(base)}$

$$= \left(\frac{1}{14-8}\right)(14-8)$$

$$= \left(\frac{1}{6}\right)(6) = 1.00$$

c. $\mu = \frac{a+b}{2} = \frac{14+8}{2} = \frac{22}{2} = 11$

$$\sigma = \sqrt{\frac{(b-a)^2}{12}} = \sqrt{\frac{(14-8)^2}{12}} = \sqrt{\frac{36}{12}} = \sqrt{3}$$

$$= 1.73$$

d. $P(10 < x < 14) = \text{(height)(base)}$

$$= \left(\frac{1}{14-8}\right)(14-10)$$

$$= \frac{1}{6}(4)$$

$$= .667$$

e. $P(x < 9) = \text{(height)(base)}$

$$= \left(\frac{1}{14-8}\right)(9-8)$$

$$= 0.167$$

7–2 a. $z = (64 - 48)/12.8 = 1.25$. This person's difference of 16 ounces more than average is 1.25 standard deviations above the average.

b. $z = (32 - 48)/12.8 = -1.25$. This person's difference of 16 ounces less than average is 1.25 standard deviations below the average.

7–3 a. \$46,400 and \$48,000, found by \$47,200 ± 1(\$800).

b. \$45,600 and \$48,800, found by \$47,200 ± 2(\$800).

c. \$44,800 and \$49,600, found by \$47,200 ± 3(\$800).

d. \$47,200. The mean, median, and mode are equal for a normal distribution.

e. Yes, a normal distribution is symmetrical.

7–4 a. Computing z:

$$z = \frac{154 - 150}{5} = 0.80$$

Referring to Appendix B.3, the area is .2881. So $P(150 < \text{temp} < 154) = .2881$.

b. Computing z:

$$z = \frac{164 - 150}{5} = 2.80$$

Referring to Appendix B.3, the area is .4974. So $P(164 > \text{temp}) = .5000 - .4974 = .0026$

7–5 a. Computing the z-values:

$$z = \frac{146 - 150}{5} = -0.80 \quad \text{and} \quad z = \frac{156 - 150}{5} = 1.20$$

$$P(146 < \text{temp} < 156) = P(-0.80 < z < 1.20)$$
$$= .2881 + .3849 = .6730$$

b. Computing the z-values:

$$z = \frac{162 - 150}{5} = 2.40 \quad \text{and} \quad z = \frac{156 - 150}{5} = 1.20$$

$$P(156 < \text{temp} < 162) = P(1.20 < z < 2.40)$$
$$= .4918 - .3849 = .1069$$

7–6 85.24 (instructor would no doubt make it 85). The closest area to .4000 is .3997; z is 1.28. Then:

$$1.28 = \frac{x - 75}{8}$$

$$10.24 = x - 75$$

$$x = 85.24$$

7–7 a. .0465, found by $\mu = n\pi = 200(.80) = 160$, and $\sigma^2 = n\pi(1 - \pi) = 200(.80)(1 - .80) = 32$. Then,

$$\sigma = \sqrt{32} = 5.66$$

$$z = \frac{169.5 - 160}{5.66} = 1.68$$

Area from Appendix B.3 is .4535. Subtracting from .5000 gives .0465.

b. .9686, found by .4686 + .5000. First calculate z:

$$z = \frac{149.5 - 160}{5.66} = -1.86$$

Area from Appendix B.3 is .4686.

7–8 a. .7769, found by:

$$P(\text{Arrival} < 15) = 1 - e^{-\frac{1}{10}(15)}$$
$$= 1 - .2231 = .7769$$

b. .0821, found by:

$$P(\text{Arrival} > 25) = e^{-\frac{1}{10}(25)} = .0821$$

c. .1410, found by

$$P(15 < x < 25) = P(\text{Arrival} < 25) - P(\text{Arrival} < 15)$$
$$= .9179 - .7769 = .1410$$

d. 16.09 minutes, found by:

$$.80 = 1 - e^{-\frac{1}{10}(x)}$$

$$-\ln 0.20 = \frac{1}{10}x$$

$$x = -(-1.609)(10) = 1.609(10) = 16.09$$

CHAPTER 8

8–1 a. Students selected are Price, Detley, and Molter.

b. Answers will vary.

c. Skip it and move to the next random number.

8–2 The students selected are Berry, Francis, Kopp, Poteau, and Swetye.

8–3 a. 10, found by:

$$_5C_2 = \frac{5!}{2!(5-2)!}$$

b.

	Service	Sample Mean
Snow, Tolson	20, 22	21
Snow, Kraft	20, 26	23
Snow, Irwin	20, 24	22
Snow, Jones	20, 28	24
Tolson, Kraft	22, 26	24
Tolson, Irwin	22, 24	23
Tolson, Jones	22, 28	25
Kraft, Irwin	26, 24	25
Kraft, Jones	26, 28	27
Irwin, Jones	24, 28	26

c.

Mean	Number	Probability
21	1	.10
22	1	.10
23	2	.20
24	2	.20
25	2	.20
26	1	.10
27	1	.10
	10	1.00

d. Identical: population mean, μ, is 24, and mean of sample means, is also 24.

e. Sample means range from 21 to 27. Population values go from 20 to 28.

f. No, the population is uniformly distributed.

g. Yes.

8–4 The answers will vary. Here is one solution.

	Sample Number									
	1	2	3	4	5	6	7	8	9	10
	8	2	2	19	3	4	0	4	1	2
	19	1	14	9	2	5	8	2	14	4
	8	3	4	2	4	4	1	14	4	1
	0	3	2	3	1	2	16	1	2	3
	2	1	7	2	19	18	18	16	3	7
Total	37	10	29	35	29	33	43	37	24	17
$\bar{x}$	7.4	2	5.8	7.0	5.8	6.6	8.6	7.4	4.8	3.4

Mean of the 10 sample means is 5.88.

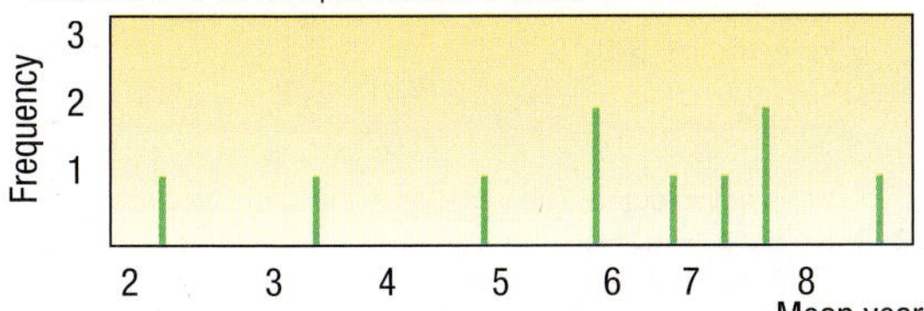

8–5 $z = \dfrac{31.08 - 31.20}{0.4/\sqrt{16}} = -1.20$

The probability that z is greater than -1.20 is $.5000 + .3849 = .8849$. There is more than an 88% chance the filling operation will produce bottles with at least 31.08 ounces.

CHAPTER 9

9–1 **a.** Unknown. This is the value we wish to estimate.

b. The sample mean of \$20,000 is the point estimate of the population mean daily franchise sales.

c. $\$20,000 \pm 1.960 \dfrac{\$3,000}{\sqrt{40}} = \$20,000 \pm \$930$

d. The estimate of the population mean daily sales for the Bun-and-Run franchises is between \$19,070 and \$20,930. About 95% all possible samples of 40 Bun-and-Run franchises would include the population mean.

9–2 **a.** $\bar{x} = \dfrac{18}{10} = 1.8 \qquad s = \sqrt{\dfrac{11.6}{10 - 1}} = 1.1353$

b. The population mean is not known. The best estimate is the sample mean, 1.8 days.

c. $1.80 \pm 2.262 \dfrac{1.1353}{\sqrt{10}} = 1.80 \pm 0.81$

The endpoints are 0.99 and 2.61.

d. t is used because the population standard deviation is unknown.

e. The value of 0 is not in the interval. It is unreasonable to conclude that the mean number of days of work missed is 0 per employee.

9–3 **a.** $p = \dfrac{420}{1,400} = .30$

b. $.30 \pm 2.576(.0122) = .30 \pm .03$

c. The interval is between .27 and .33. About 99% of the similarly constructed intervals would include the population mean.

9–4 $n = \left(\dfrac{2.576(.279)}{.05}\right)^2 = 206.6$. The sample should be rounded to 207.

9–5 $.375 \pm 1.96 \sqrt{\dfrac{.375(1 - .375)}{40}} \sqrt{\dfrac{250 - 40}{250 - 1}} =$

$.375 \pm 1.96(.0765)(.9184) = .375 \pm .138$

CHAPTER 10

10–1 **a.** H_0: $\mu = 16.0$; H_1: $\mu \neq 16.0$

b. .05

c. $z = \dfrac{\bar{x} - \mu}{\sigma/\sqrt{n}}$

d. Reject H_0 if $z < -1.96$ or $z > 1.96$.

e. $z = \dfrac{16.017 - 16.0}{0.15/\sqrt{50}} = \dfrac{0.0170}{0.0212} = 0.80$

f. Do not reject H_0.

g. We cannot conclude the mean amount dispensed is different from 16.0 ounces.

10–2 **a.** H_0: $\mu \leq 16.0$; H_1: $\mu > 16.0$

b. Reject H_0 if $z > 1.645$.

c. $z = \dfrac{16.040 - 16.0}{0.15/\sqrt{50}} = \dfrac{.0400}{.0212} = 1.89$

d. Reject H_0.

e. The mean amount dispensed is more than 16.0 ounces.

f. p-value $= .5000 - .4706 = .0294$. The p-value is less than α (.05), so H_0 is rejected. It is the same conclusion as in part (d).

10–3 **a.** H_0: $\mu \leq 305$; H_1: $\mu > 305$

b. $df = n - 1 = 20 - 1 = 19$

The decision rule is to reject H_0 if $t > 1.729$.

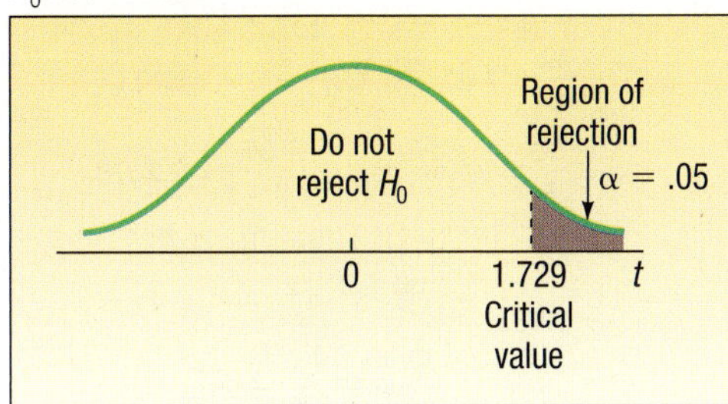

c. $t = \dfrac{\bar{X} - \mu}{s/\sqrt{n}} = \dfrac{311 - 305}{12/\sqrt{20}} = 2.236$

Reject H_0 because $2.236 > 1.729$. The modification increased the mean battery life to more than 305 days.

10–4 **a.** H_0: $\mu \geq 9.0$; H_1: $\mu < 9.0$

b. 7, found by $n - 1 = 8 - 1 = 7$

c. Reject H_0 if $t < -2.998$.

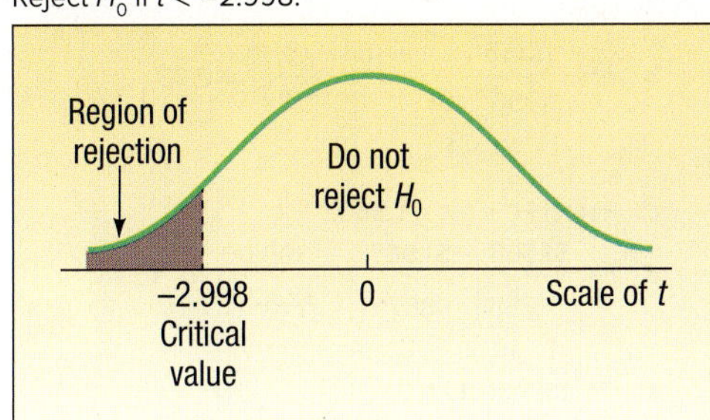

d. $t = -2.494$, found by:

$$s = \sqrt{\frac{0.36}{8 - 1}} = 0.2268$$

$$\bar{x} = \frac{70.4}{8} = 8.8$$

Then

$$t = \frac{8.8 - 9.0}{0.2268/\sqrt{8}} = -2.494$$

Since -2.494 lies to the right of -2.998, H_0 is not rejected. We have not shown that the mean is less than 9.0.

e. The p-value is between .025 and .010.

10–5 .0054, found by determining the area under the curve between 10,078 and 10,180.

$$z = \frac{\bar{x}_c - \mu_1}{\sigma/\sqrt{n}}$$
$$= \frac{10{,}078 - 10{,}180}{400/\sqrt{100}} = -2.55$$

The area under the curve for a z of −2.55 is .4946 (Appendix B.3), and .5000 − .4946 = .0054.

CHAPTER 11

11–1 **a.** H_0: $\mu_W \le \mu_M$ H_1: $\mu_W > \mu_M$
The subscript W refers to the women and M to the men.
b. Reject H_0 if $z > 1.645$.
c. $z = \dfrac{\$1{,}500 - \$1{,}400}{\sqrt{\dfrac{(\$250)^2}{50} + \dfrac{(\$200)^2}{40}}} = 2.11$
d. Reject the null hypothesis.
e. p-value = .5000 − .4826 = .0174
f. The mean amount sold per day is larger for women.

11–2 **a.** H_0: $\mu_d = \mu_a$ H_1: $\mu_d \ne \mu_a$
b. $df = 6 + 8 - 2 = 12$
Reject H_0 if $t < -2.179$ or $t > 2.179$.
c. $\bar{x}_1 = \dfrac{42}{6} = 7.00 \quad s_1 = \sqrt{\dfrac{10}{6-1}} = 1.4142$

$\bar{x}_2 = \dfrac{80}{8} = 10.00 \quad s_2 = \sqrt{\dfrac{36}{8-1}} = 2.2678$

$s_p^2 = \dfrac{(6-1)(1.4142)^2 + (8-1)(2.2678)^2}{6+8-2}$
$= 3.8333$
$t = \dfrac{7.00 - 10.00}{\sqrt{3.8333\left(\dfrac{1}{6} + \dfrac{1}{8}\right)}} = -2.837$

d. Reject H_0 because −2.837 is less than the critical value.
e. The p-value is less than .02.
f. The mean number of defects is not the same on the two shifts.
g. Independent populations, populations follow the normal distribution, populations have equal standard deviations.

11–3 **a.** H_0: $\mu_c \ge \mu_a$ H_1: $\mu_c < \mu_a$
b. $df = \dfrac{[(356^2/10) + (857^2/8)]^2}{\dfrac{(356^2/10)^2}{10-1} + \dfrac{(857^2/8)^2}{8-1}} = 8.93$
so $df = 8$
c. Reject H_0 if $t < -1.860$.
d. $t = \dfrac{\$1{,}568 - \$1{,}967}{\sqrt{\dfrac{356^2}{10} + \dfrac{857^2}{8}}} = \dfrac{-399.00}{323.23} = -1.234$
e. Do not reject H_0.
f. There is no difference in the mean account balance of those who applied for their card or were contacted by a telemarketer.

11–4 **a.** H_0: $\mu_d \ge 0$, H_1: $\mu_d > 0$
b. Reject H_0 if $t > 2.998$.
c.

Name	Before	After	d	$(d - \bar{d})$	$(d - d)^2$
Hunter	155	154	1	−7.875	62.0156
Cashman	228	207	21	12.125	147.0156
Mervine	141	147	−6	−14.875	221.2656
Massa	162	157	5	−3.875	15.0156
Creola	211	196	15	6.125	37.5156
Peterson	164	150	14	5.125	26.2656
Redding	184	170	14	5.125	26.2656
Poust	172	165	7	−1.875	3.5156
			71		538.8750

$\bar{d} = \dfrac{71}{8} = 8.875$

$s_d = \sqrt{\dfrac{538.875}{8-1}} = 8.774$

$t = \dfrac{8.875}{8.774/\sqrt{8}} = 2.861$

d. Do not reject H_0. We cannot conclude that the students lost weight. The p-value is less than .025 but larger than .01.
e. The distribution of the differences must be approximately normal.

CHAPTER 12

12–1 Let Mark's assemblies be population 1, then H_0: $\sigma_1^2 \le \sigma_2^2$; H_1: $\sigma_1^2 > \sigma_2^2$; $df_1 = 10 - 1 = 9$; and df_2 also equals 9. H_0 is rejected if $F > 3.18$.

$$F = \frac{(2.0)^2}{(1.5)^2} = 1.78$$

H_0 is not rejected. The variation is the same for both employees.

12–2 **a.** H_0: $\mu_1 = \mu_2 = \mu_3$
H_1: At least one treatment mean is different.
b. Reject H_0 if $F > 4.26$.
c. $\bar{x} = \dfrac{240}{12} = 20$
SS total $= (18 - 20)^2 + \cdots + (32 - 20)^2$
$= 578$
SSE $= (18 - 17)^2 + (14 - 17)^2 + \cdots + (32 - 29)^2$
$= 74$
SST $= 578 - 74 = 504$
d.

Source	Sum of Squares	Degrees of Freedom	Mean Square	F
Treatment	504	2	252	30.65
Error	74	9	8.22	
Total	578	11		

e. H_0 is rejected. There is a difference in the mean number of bottles sold at the various locations.

12–3 **a.** H_0: $\mu_1 = \mu_2 = \mu_3$
H_1: Not all means are equal.
b. H_0 is rejected if $F > 3.98$.
c.

ANOVA: Single Factor

Groups	Count	Sum	Average	Variance
Northeast	5	205	41	1
Southeast	4	155	38.75	0.916667
West	5	184	36.8	0.7

ANOVA

Source of Variation	SS	df	MS	F	P-value
Between Groups	44.16429	2	22.08214	25.43493	7.49E-05
Within Groups	9.55	11	0.868182		
Total	53.71429	13			

d. H_0 is rejected. The treatment means differ.
e. $(41 - 36.8) \pm 2.201\sqrt{0.8682(\frac{1}{5} + \frac{1}{5})} = 4.2 \pm 1.3 = 2.9$ *and* 5.50
These treatment means differ because both endpoints of the confidence interval are of the same sign. Zero is not in the interval.

12–4 For types:
H_0: $\mu_1 = \mu_2 = \mu_3$
H_1: The treatment means are not equal.
Reject H_0 if $F > 4.46$.
For months:
H_0: $\mu_1 = \mu_2 = \mu_3 = \mu_4 = \mu_5$
H_1: The block means are not equal.
Reject H_0 if $F > 3.84$.

The analysis of variance table is as follows:

Source	df	SS	MS	F
Types	2	3.60	1.80	0.39
Months	4	31.73	7.93	1.71
Error	8	37.07	4.63	
Total	14	72.40		

The null hypotheses cannot be rejected for either types or months. There is no difference in the mean sales among types or months.

12–5 **a.** There are four levels of Factor A. The *p*-value is less than .05, so Factor A means differ.

b. There are three levels of Factor B. The *p*-value is less than .05, so the Factor B means differ.

c. There are three observations in each cell. There is an interaction between Factor A and Factor B means because the *p*-value is less than .05.

CHAPTER 13

13–1 **a.** Advertising expense is the independent variable, and sales revenue is the dependent variable.

b.

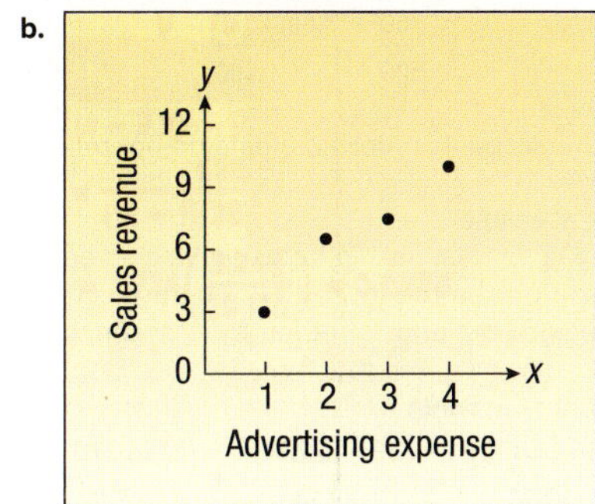

c.

x	y	$(x - \bar{x})$	$(x - \bar{x})^2$	$(y - \bar{y})$	$(y - \bar{y})^2$	$(x - \bar{x})(y - \bar{y})$
2	7	−0.5	.25	0	0	0
1	3	−1.5	2.25	−4	16	6
3	8	0.5	.25	1	1	0.5
4	10	1.5	2.25	3	9	4.5
10	28		5.00		26	11.0

$\bar{x} = \frac{10}{4} = 2.5 \qquad \bar{y} = \frac{28}{4} = 7$

$s_x = \sqrt{\frac{5}{3}} = 1.2910$

$s_y = \sqrt{\frac{26}{3}} = 2.9439$

$r = \frac{\Sigma(X - \bar{X})(y - \bar{y})}{(n-1)s_x s_y} = \frac{11}{(4-1)(1.2910)(2.9439)}$

$= 0.9648$

d. There is a strong correlation between the advertising expense and sales.

13–2 H_0: $\rho \le 0$, H_1: $\rho > 0$. H_0 is rejected if $t > 1.714$.

$$t = \frac{.43\sqrt{25-2}}{\sqrt{1-(.43)^2}} = 2.284$$

H_0 is rejected. There is a positive correlation between the percent of the vote received and the amount spent on the campaign.

13–3 **a.** See the calculations in Self-Review 13–1, part (c).

$$b = \frac{rs_y}{s_x} = \frac{(0.9648)(2.9439)}{1.2910} = 2.2$$

$$a = \frac{28}{4} - 2.2\left(\frac{10}{4}\right) = 7 - 5.5 = 1.5$$

b. The slope is 2.2. This indicates that an increase of \$1 million in advertising will result in an increase of \$2.2 million in sales. The intercept is 1.5. If there was no expenditure for advertising, sales would be \$1.5 million.

c. $\hat{Y} = 1.5 + 2.2(3) = 8.1$

13–4 H_0: $\beta_1 \le 0$; H_1: $\beta > 0$. Reject H_0 if $t > 3.182$.

$$t = \frac{2.2 - 0}{0.4243} = 5.1850$$

Reject H_0. The slope of the line is greater than 0.

13–5 **a.**

y	$\hat{y}$	$(y - \hat{y})$	$(y - \hat{y})^2$
7	5.9	1.1	1.21
3	3.7	−0.7	.49
8	8.1	−0.1	.01
10	10.3	−0.3	.09
			1.80

$$s_{y \cdot x} = \sqrt{\frac{\Sigma(y - \hat{y})^2}{n-2}} = \sqrt{\frac{1.80}{4-2}} = .9487$$

b. $r^2 = (.9648)^2 = .9308$

c. Ninety-three percent of the variation in sales is accounted for by advertising expense.

13–6 6.58 and 9.62, since for an x of 3 is 8.1, found by $\hat{y} = 1.5 + 2.2(3) = 8.1$, then $\bar{x} = 2.5$ and $\Sigma(x - \bar{x})^2 = 5$. t from Appendix B.5 for $4 - 2 = 2$ degrees of freedom at the .10 level is 2.920.

$$\hat{y} \pm t(s_{y \cdot x})\sqrt{\frac{1}{n} + \frac{(x - \bar{x})^2}{\Sigma(x - \bar{x})^2}}$$

$$= 8.1 \pm 2.920(0.9487)\sqrt{\frac{1}{4} + \frac{(3 - 2.5)^2}{5}}$$

$$= 8.1 \pm 2.920(0.9487)(0.5477)$$

$= 6.58$ and 9.62 (in \$ millions)

CHAPTER 14

14–1 **a.** \$389,500 or 389.5 (in \$000); found by $2.5 + 3(40) + 4(72) - 3(10) + .2(20) + 1(5) = 3{,}895$

b. The b_2 of 4 shows profit will go up \$4,000 for each extra hour the restaurant is open (if none of the other variables change). The b_3 of −3 implies profit will fall \$3,000 for each added mile away from the central area (if none of the other variables change).

14–2 **a.** The total degrees of freedom $(n - 1)$ is 25. So the sample size is 26.

b. There are 5 independent variables.

c. There is only 1 dependent variable (profit).

d. $S_{Y.12345} = 1.414$, found by $\sqrt{2}$. Ninety-five percent of the residuals will be between −2.828 and 2.828, found by ±2(1.414).

e. $R^2 = .714$, found by 100/140. 71.4% of the deviation in profit is accounted for by these five variables.

f. $R^2_{adj} = .643$, found by

$$1 - \left[\frac{40}{(26 - (5+1))}\right] \Big/ \left[\frac{140}{(26-1)}\right]$$

14–3 **a.** H_0: $\beta_1 = \beta_2 = \beta_3 = \beta_4 = \beta_5 = 0$

H_1: Not all of the βs are 0.

The decision rule is to reject H_0 if $F > 2.71$. The computed value of F is 10, found by 20/2. So, you reject H_0, which indicates at least one of the regression coefficients is different from zero.

Based on *p*-values, the decision rule is to reject the null hypothesis if the *p*-value is less than .05. The computed value of F is 10, found by 20/2, and has a *p*-value of .000. Thus, we reject the null hypothesis, which indicates that at least one of the regression coefficients is different from zero.

b. For variable 1: H_0: $\beta_1 = 0$ and H_1: $\beta_1 \neq 0$
The decision rule is to reject H_0 if $t < -2.086$ or $t > 2.086$. Since 2.000 does not go beyond either of those limits, we fail to reject the null hypothesis. This regression coefficient could be zero. We can consider dropping this variable. By parallel logic, the null hypothesis is rejected for variables 3 and 4.

For variable 1, the decision rule is to reject H_0: $\beta_1 = 0$ if the *p*-value is less than .05. Because the *p*-value is .056, we cannot reject the null hypothesis. This regression coefficient could be zero. Therefore, we can consider dropping this variable. By parallel logic, we reject the null hypothesis for variables 3 and 4.

c. We should consider dropping variables 1, 2, and 5. Variable 5 has the smallest absolute value of *t* or largest *p*-value. So delete it first and compute the regression equation again.

14–4 a. $\hat{y} = 15.7625 + 0.4415x_1 + 3.8598x_2$
$\hat{y} = 15.7625 + 0.4415(30) + 3.8598(1)$
$= 32.87$

b. Female agents make $3,860 more than male agents.

c. H_0: $\beta_3 = 0$
H_1: $\beta_3 \neq 0$
$df = 17$; reject H_0 if $t < -2.110$ or $t > 2.110$

$$t = \frac{3.8598 - 0}{1.4724} = 2.621$$

The *t* statistic exceeds the critical value of 2.110. Also, the *p*-value = .0179 and is less than .05. Reject H_0. Gender should be included in the regression equation.

CHAPTER 15

15–1 a. Yes, because both $n\pi$ and $n(1 - \pi)$ exceed 5: $n\pi = 200(.40) = 80$, and $n(1 - \pi) = 200(.60) = 120$.

b. H_0: $\pi \geq .40$
H_1: $\pi < .40$

c. Reject H_0 if $z < -2.326$.

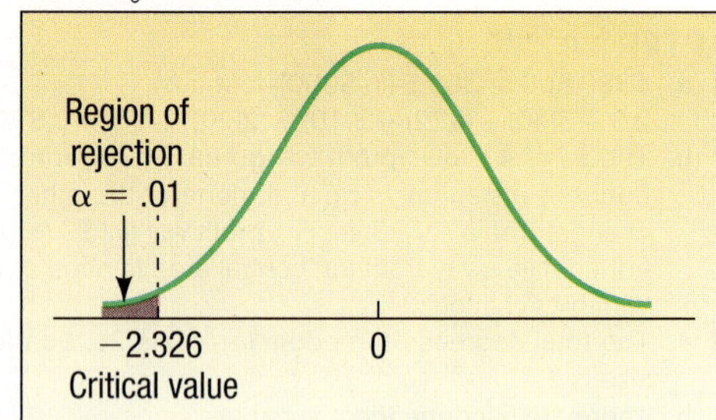

d. $z = -0.87$, found by:

$$z = \frac{.37 - .40}{\sqrt{\frac{.40(1 - .40)}{200}}} = \frac{-.03}{\sqrt{.0012}} = -0.87$$

Do not reject H_0.

e. The *p*-value is .1922, found by .5000 – .3078.

15–2 a. H_0: $\pi_a = \pi_{ch}$
H_1: $\pi_a \neq \pi_{ch}$

b. .10

c. Two-tailed

d. Reject H_0 if $z < -1.645$ or $z > 1.645$.

e. $$p_c = \frac{87 + 123}{150 + 200} = \frac{210}{350} = .60$$

$$p_a = \frac{87}{150} = .58 \qquad p_{ch} = \frac{123}{200} = .615$$

$$z = \frac{.58 - .615}{\sqrt{\frac{.60(.40)}{150} + \frac{.60(.40)}{200}}} = -0.66$$

f. Do not reject H_0.

g. *p*-value = 2(.5000 – .2454) = .5092

There is no difference in the proportion of adults and children that liked the proposed flavor.

15–3 a. Observed frequencies

b. Six (six days of the week)

c. 10. Total observed frequencies ÷ 6 = 60/6 = 10.

d. 5; $k - 1 = 6 - 1 = 5$

e. 15.086 (from the chi-square table in Appendix B.7).

f. $$\chi^2 = \Sigma\left[\frac{(f_o - f_e)^2}{f_e}\right] = \frac{(12 - 10)^2}{10} + \cdots + \frac{(9 - 10)^2}{10} = 0.8$$

g. Do not reject H_0.

h. Evidence fails to show a difference in the proportion of absences by day of the week.

15–4 H_0: $P_C = .60$, $P_L = .30$, and $P_U = .10$.
H_1: Distribution is not as above.
Reject H_0 if $\chi^2 > 5.991$.

Category	f_o	f_e	$\frac{(f_o - f_e)^2}{f_e}$
Current	320	300	1.33
Late	120	150	6.00
Uncollectible	60	50	2.00
	500	500	9.33

Reject H_0. The accounts receivable data do not reflect the national average.

15–5 a. Contingency table

b. H_0: There is no relationship between income and whether the person played the lottery. H_1: There is a relationship between income and whether the person played the lottery.

c. Reject H_0 if $\chi^2 > 5.991$.

d. $$\chi^2 = \frac{(46 - 40.71)^2}{40.71} + \frac{(28 - 27.14)^2}{27.14} + \frac{(21 - 27.14)^2}{27.14} + \frac{(14 - 19.29)^2}{19.29} + \frac{(12 - 12.86)^2}{12.86} + \frac{(19 - 12.86)^2}{12.86}$$
$$= 6.544$$

e. Reject H_0. There is a relationship between income level and playing the lottery.

CHAPTER 16

16–1 a. Two-tailed because H_1 does not state a direction.

b.

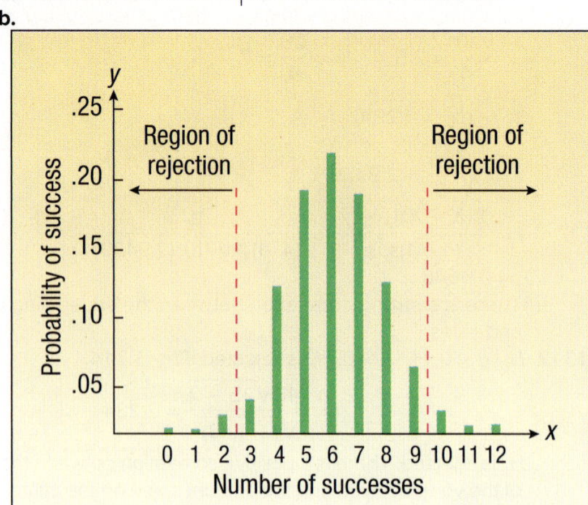

Adding down, .000 + .003 + .016 = .019. This is the largest cumulative probability up to but not exceeding .050, which is half the level of significance. The decision rule is to reject H_0 if the number of plus signs is 2 or less or 10 or more.

c. Reject H_0; accept H_1. There is a preference.

16–2 **a.** H_0: $\pi \leq 0.50$, H_1: $\pi > 0.50$.

b. Reject H_0 if $z > 1.645$.

c. Since 80 is more than $n/2 = 100/2 = 50$, we use:

$$z = \frac{(80 - .50) - .50(100)}{.50\sqrt{100}} = \frac{29.5}{5} = 5.9$$

d. H_0 is rejected.

e. The screening was effective.

16–3 H_0: The median $\leq$ \$3,000, H_1: The median is more than \$3,000. The decision rule is to reject H_0 if $z > 1.645$.

$$z = \frac{(42 - .50) - 32}{.50\sqrt{64}} = \frac{9.5}{4} = 2.38$$

Reject H_0 because 2.38 is larger than 1.645. The median amount spent is more than \$3,000.

16–4 **a.** $n = 10$ (because there was no change for A. A.)

b.

Before	After	Difference	Absolute Difference	Rank	R^-	R^+
17	18	−1	1	1.5	1.5	
21	23	−2	2	3.0	3.0	
25	22	3	3	5.0		5.0
15	25	−10	10	8.0	8.0	
10	28	−18	18	10.0	10.0	
16	16	—	—	—	—	—
10	22	−12	12	9.0	9.0	
20	19	1	1	1.5		1.5
17	20	−3	3	5.0	5.0	
24	30	−6	6	7.0	7.0	
23	26	−3	3	5.0	5.0	
					48.5	6.5

H_0: Production is the same.
H_1: Production has increased.

The sum of the positive signed ranks is 6.5; the negative sum is 48.5. From Appendix B.8, one-tailed test, $n = 10$, the critical value is 10. Since 6.5 is less than 10, reject the null hypothesis and accept the alternate. New procedures did increase production.

c. No assumption regarding the shape of the distribution is necessary.

16–5 H_0: There is no difference in the distances traveled by the XL-5000 and by the D2.

H_1: There is a difference in the distances traveled by the XL-5000 and by the D2.

Do not reject H_0 if the computed z is between 1.96 and −1.96 (from Appendix B.3); otherwise, reject H_0 and accept H_1. $n_1 = 8$, the number of observations in the first sample.

XL-5000		D2	
Distance	Rank	Distance	Rank
252	4	262	9
263	10	242	2
279	15	256	5
273	14	260	8
271	13	258	7
265	11.5	243	3
257	6	239	1
280	16	265	11.5
Total	89.5		46.5

$W = 89.5$

$$z = \frac{89.5 - \dfrac{8(8+8+1)}{2}}{\sqrt{\dfrac{(8)(8)(8+8+1)}{12}}}$$

$$= \frac{21.5}{9.52} = 2.26$$

Reject H_0; accept H_1. There is evidence of a difference in the distances traveled by the two golf balls.

16–6

Ranks			
Englewood	West Side	Great Northern	Sylvania
17	5	19	7
20	1	9.5	11
16	3	21	15
13	5	22	9.5
5	2	14	8
18			12

$\Sigma R_1 = 89$ $\quad \Sigma R_2 = 16$ $\quad \Sigma R_3 = 85.5$ $\quad \Sigma R_4 = 62.5$

$n_1 = 6$ $\quad n_2 = 5$ $\quad n_3 = 5$ $\quad n_4 = 6$

H_0: The population distributions are identical.
H_1: The population distributions are not identical.

$$H = \frac{12}{22(22+1)}\left[\frac{(89)^2}{6} + \frac{(16)^2}{5} + \frac{(85.5)^2}{5} + \frac{(62.5)^2}{6}\right] - 3(22+1)$$
$$= 13.635$$

The critical value of chi-square for $k - 1 = 4 - 1 = 3$ degrees of freedom is 11.345. Since the computed value of 13.635 is greater than 11.345, the null hypothesis is rejected. We conclude that the number of transactions is not the same.

16–7 **a.**

		Rank			
x	y	x	y	d	d^2
805	23	5.5	1	4.5	20.25
777	62	3.0	9	−6.0	36.00
820	60	8.5	8	0.5	0.25
682	40	1.0	4	−3.0	9.00
777	70	3.0	10	−7.0	49.00
810	28	7.0	2	5.0	25.00
805	30	5.5	3	2.5	6.25
840	42	10.0	5	5.0	25.00
777	55	3.0	7	−4.0	16.00
820	51	8.5	6	2.5	6.25
				0	193.00

$$r_s = 1 - \frac{6(193)}{10(99)} = -.170$$

b. H_0: $\rho = 0$; H_1: $\rho \neq 0$. Reject H_0 if $t < -2.306$ or $t > 2.306$.

$$t = -.170\sqrt{\frac{10 - 2}{1 - (-0.170)^2}} = -0.488$$

H_0 is not rejected. We have not shown a relationship between the two tests.

CHAPTER 17

17–1 **1.**

Country	Amount	Index (Based=US)
China	822.7	932.8
Japan	110.7	125.5
United States	88.2	100.0
India	86.5	98.1
Russia	71.5	81.1

China produced 832.8% more steel than the US

2. a.

Year	Average Hourly Earnings	Index (1995 = Base)
1995	11.65	100.0
2000	14.02	120.3
2005	16.13	138.5
2013	19.97	171.4
2016	21.37	183.4

2016 Average wage Increased 83.4% from 1995

b.

Year	Average Hourly Earnings	Index (1995 – 2000 = Base)
1995	11.65	90.8
2000	14.02	109.2
2005	16.13	125.7
2013	19.97	155.6
2016	21.37	166.5

2016 Average wage Increased 86.5% from the average of 1995, 2000

17–2 1. **a.** $P_1 = (\$85/\$75)(100) = 113.3$

$P_2 = (\$45/\$40)(100) = 112.5$

$P = (113.3 + 112.5)/2 = 112.9$

b. $P = (\$130/\$115)(100) = 113.0$

c. $$P = \frac{\$85(500) + \$45(1{,}200)}{\$75(500) + \$40(1{,}200)}(100) = \frac{\$96{,}500}{85{,}500}(100) = 112.9$$

d. $$P = \frac{\$85(520) + \$45(1{,}300)}{\$75(520) + \$40(1{,}300)}(100) = \frac{\$102{,}700}{\$91{,}000}(100) = 112.9$$

e. $P = \sqrt{(112.9)(112.9)} = 112.9$

17–3 **a.** $$P = \frac{\$4(9{,}000) + \$5(200) + \$8(5{,}000)}{\$3(10{,}000) + \$1(600) + \$10(3{,}000)}(100) = \frac{\$77{,}000}{60{,}600}(100) = 127.1$$

b. The value of sales went up 27.1% from 2001 to 2017

17–4 **a.**

For 2011	
Item	**Weight**
Cotton	($0.25/$0.20)(100)(.10) = 12.50
Autos	(1,200/1,000)(100)(.30) = 36.00
Money turnover	(90/80)(100)(.60) = 67.50
Total	116.00

For 2016	
Item	**Weight**
Cotton	($0.50/$0.20)(100)(.10) = 25.00
Autos	(900/1,000)(100)(.30) = 27.00
Money turnover	(75/80)(100)(.60) = 56.25
Total	108.25

b. Business activity increased 16% from 2004 to 2009. It increased 8.25% from 2004 to 2014.

17–5 In terms of the base period, Jon's salary was $14,637 in 2000 and $17,944 in 2016. This indicates that take-home pay increased at a faster rate than the rate of prices paid for food, transportation, etc.

17–6 $0.42, round by ($1.00/238.132)(100). The purchasing power has declined by $0.58.

17–7

Year	IPI	PPI
2007	111.07	92.9
2008	107.12	100.2
2009	94.80	95.3
2010	100.00	100.0
2011	102.93	107.8
2012	105.80	110.1
2013	107.83	110.5
2014	110.98	111.5
2015	111.32	105.8

The Industrial Production Index (IPI) increased 11.32% from 2010 to 2015. The Producer Price Index (PPI) increased 5.8%.

CHAPTER 18

18–1

Year	Number Produced	Moving Average
2011	2	
2012	6	4
2013	4	5
2014	5	4
2015	3	6
2016	10	

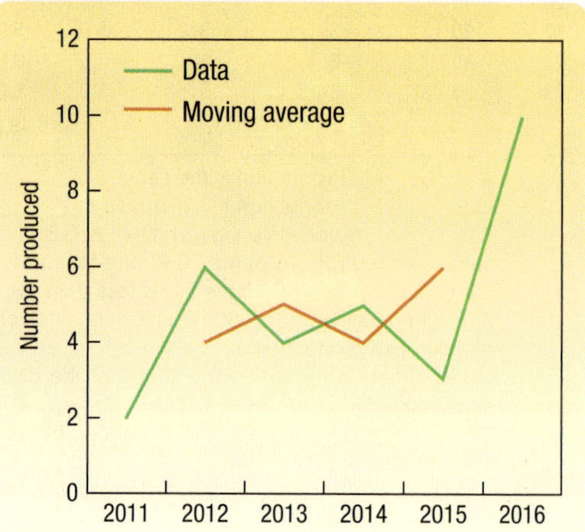

18–2 **a.**

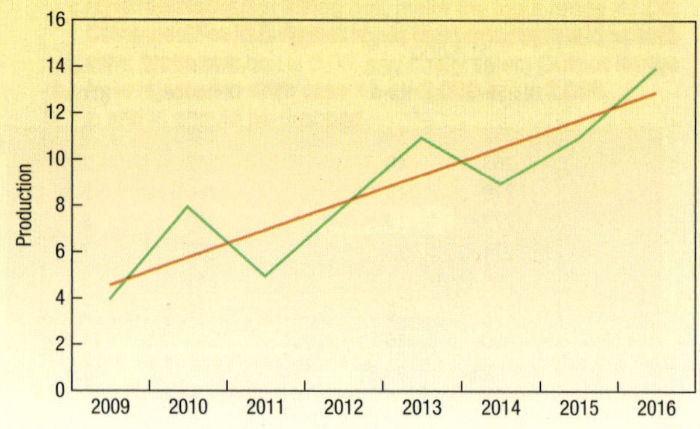

b. $\hat{y} = a + bt = 3.3928 + 1.1905t$ (in thousands)

c.

Year	Predicted values	Year code	Found by
2009	4.58	1	3.39+1.19(1)
2010	5.77	2	3.39+1.19(2)
2011	6.96	3	3.39+1.19(3)
2012	8.15	4	3.39+1.19(4)
2013	9.35	5	3.39+1.19(5)
2014	10.54	6	3.39+1.19(6)
2015	11.73	7	3.39+1.19(7)
2016	12.92	8	3.39+1.19(8)

d.

Year	Predicted values	Year code	Found by
2019	16.49	11	3.39+1.19(11)

18–3 a.

Year	t	Sales	Log Sales
2013	1	2.13	0.3284
2014	2	18.10	1.2577
2015	3	39.80	1.5999
2016	4	81.40	1.9106
2017	5	112.00	2.0492
b=0.40945			
a=0.20081			

b. About 156.7%. The antilog of 0.40945 is 2.567. Subtracting 1 yields 1.567.

c. About 454.5, found by $\hat{y} = 0.20081 + .40945(6) = 2.65751$. The antilog of 2.65751 is 454.5.

18–4 a. The following values are from a software package. Due to rounding, your figures might be slightly different.

	Winter	Spring	Summer	Fall
Mean	119.35	81.66	125.31	74.24
Typical seasonal	119.18	81.55	125.13	74.13

The correction factor is 0.9986.

b. Total sales at Teton Village for the winter season are typically 19.18% above the annual average.

18–5 The forecast value for January of the sixth year is 34.9, found by

$$\hat{y} = 4.4 + 0.5(61) = 34.9$$

Seasonally adjusting the forecast, 34.9(120)/100 = 41.88. For February, $\hat{y} = 4.4 + 0.5(62) = 35.4$. Then, (35.4)95/100 = 33.63.

CHAPTER 19

19–1

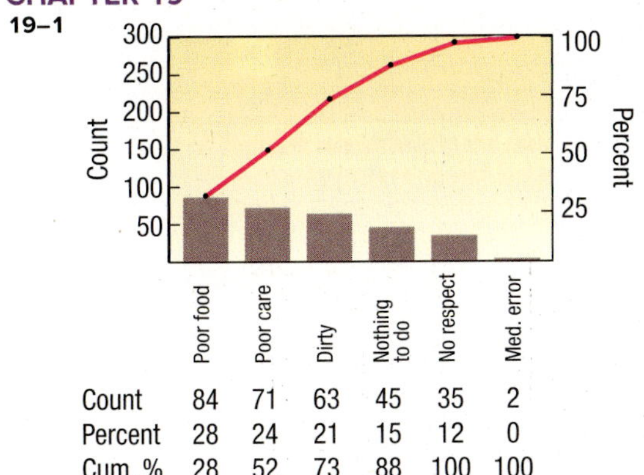

Count	84	71	63	45	35	2
Percent	28	24	21	15	12	0
Cum. %	28	52	73	88	100	100

Seventy-three percent of the complaints involve poor food, poor care, or dirty conditions. These are the factors the administrator should address.

19–2 a.

Sample Times						
1	2	3	4	Total	Average	Range
1	4	5	2	12	3	4
2	3	2	1	8	2	2
1	7	3	5	16	4	6
					9	12

$$\bar{\bar{x}} = \frac{9}{3} = 3 \qquad \bar{R} = \frac{12}{3} = 4$$

$$UCL \text{ and } LCL = \bar{\bar{x}} \pm A_2\bar{R}$$
$$= 3 \pm 0.729(4)$$
$$UCL = 5.916 \qquad LCL = 0.084$$

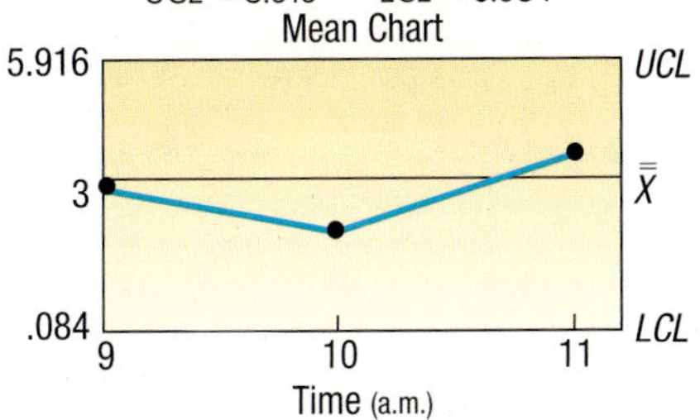

$$LCL = D_3\bar{R} = 0(4) = 0$$
$$UCL = D_4\bar{R} = 2.282(4) = 9.128$$

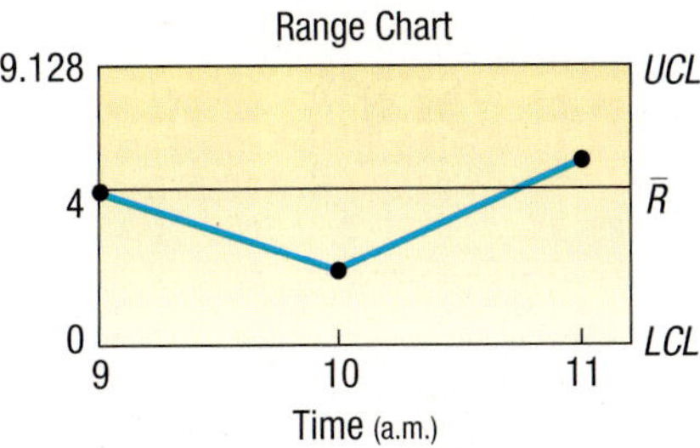

b. Yes. Both the mean chart and the range chart indicate that the process is in control.

19–3 $\bar{c} = \frac{25}{12} = 2.083$

$$UCL = 2.083 + 3\sqrt{2.083} = 6.413$$
$$LCL = 2.083 - 3\sqrt{2.083} = -2.247$$

Because LCL is a negative value, we set $LCL = 0$. The shift with seven defects is out of control.

19–4 $P(x \leq 2|\pi = .30 \text{ and } n = 20) = .036$

CHAPTER 20

20–1

Event	Payoff	Probability of Event	Expected Value
Market rise	$2,200	.60	$1,320
Market decline	1,100	.40	440
			$1,760

20–2 a. Suppose the investor purchased Rim Homes stock, and the value of the stock in a bear market dropped to $1,100 as anticipated (Table 20–1). Instead, had the investor purchased Texas Electronics and the market declined, the value of the Texas Electronics stock would be $1,150. The difference of $50, found by $1,150 – $1,100, represents the investor's regret for buying Rim Homes stock.

b. Suppose the investor purchased Texas Electronics stock, and then a bull market developed. The stock rose to $1,900, as anticipated (Table 20–1). However, had the investor bought Kayser Chemicals stock and the market value increased to $2,400 as anticipated, the difference of $500 represents the extra profit the investor could have made by purchasing Kayser Chemicals stock.

20–3

Event	Payoff	Probability of Event	Expected Opportunity Value
Market rise	$500	.60	$300
Market decline	0	.40	0
			$300

20–4 a.

Event	Payoff	Probability of Event	Expected Value
Market rise	$1,900	.40	$ 760
Market decline	1,150	.60	690
			$1,450

b.

Event	Payoff	Probability of Event	Expected Value
Market rise	$2,400	.50	$1,200
Market decline	1,000	.50	500
			$1,700

20–5 For probabilities of a market rise (or decline) down to .333, Kayser Chemicals stock would provide the largest expected profit. For probabilities .333 to .143, Rim Homes would be the best buy. For .143 and below, Texas Electronics would give the largest expected profit. Algebraic solutions:

Kayser: $2{,}400p + (1 - p)1{,}000$
Rim: $2{,}200p + (1 - p)1{,}100$

$$1{,}400p + 1{,}000 = 1{,}100p + 1{,}100$$
$$p = .333$$

Rim: $2{,}200p + (1 - p)1{,}100$
Texas: $1{,}900p + (1 - p)1{,}150$

$$1{,}100p + 1{,}100 = 750p + 1{,}150$$
$$p = .143$$

Glossary

Alternate hypothesis A statement that is accepted if the sample data provide sufficient evidence that the null hypothesis is false.

Analysis of variance (ANOVA) A technique used to test simultaneously whether the means of several populations are equal. It uses the *F* distribution as the distribution of the test statistic.

Assignable variation Variation that is not random. It can be eliminated or reduced by investigating the problem and finding the cause.

Attribute control chart An attribute control chart plots a count of a nominal variable over time.

Autocorrelation Successive residuals in a time series are correlated.

Bar chart A graph that shows qualitative classes on the horizontal axis and the class frequencies on the vertical axis. The class frequencies are proportional to the heights of the bars.

Bayes' theorem Developed by Reverend Bayes in the 1700s, it is designed to find the probability of one event, *A*, occurring, given that another event, *B*, has already occurred.

Binomial probability distribution A probability distribution based on a discrete random variable. Its major characteristics are: 1. Each outcome can be classified into one of two mutually exclusive categories. 2. The distribution is the result of counting the number of successes. 3. Each trial is independent, meaning that the answer to trial 1 (correct or wrong) in no way affects the answer to trial 2. 4. The probability of a success stays the same from trial to trial.

Blocking variable A second treatment variable that when included in the ANOVA analysis will have the effect of reducing the SSE term.

Box plot A graphic display that shows the general shape of a variable's distribution. It is based on five descriptive statistics: the maximum and minimum values, the first and third quartiles, and the median.

Cause-and-effect diagram A diagram used to illustrate the relationship between a problem and a set of the problem's possible causes.

Central limit theorem If all samples of a particular size are selected from any population, the sampling distribution of the sample mean is approximately a normal distribution. This approximation improves with larger samples.

Chance variation Variation that is random in nature. This type of variation cannot be completely eliminated unless there is a major change in the techniques, technologies, methods, equipment, or materials used in the process.

Chebyshev's theorem For any set of observations (sample or population), the proportion of the values that lie within k standard deviations of the mean is at least $1 - 1/k^2$, where k is any value greater than 1.

Classical probability Probability based on the assumption we know the number of possible outcomes and that each of the outcomes is equally likely.

Cluster sampling A population is divided into clusters using naturally occurring geographic or other boundaries. Then, clusters are randomly selected and a sample is collected by randomly selecting from each cluster.

Collectively exhaustive At least one of the events must occur when an experiment is conducted.

Combination formula A formula to count the number of possible arrangements when the order of the outcomes is not important. For example, the outcome {a, b, c} is considered the same as {c, b, a}.

Conditional probability The probability of a particular event occurring, given that another event has occurred.

Confidence interval A range of values constructed from sample data so that the population parameter is likely to occur within that range at a specified probability. The specified probability is called the *level of confidence*.

Consumer Price Index An index reported monthly by the U.S. Department of Labor. It describes the change in a market basket of goods and services from the base period of 1982–84 to the present.

Consumer's risk The error of accepting a lot, when the lot should be rejected.

Contingency table A table used to classify sample observations according to two identifiable characteristics.

Continuity correction factor Used to improve the accuracy of estimating or approximating a discrete distribution with a continuous distribution.

Continuous random variable A random variable that may assume an infinite number of values within a given range.

Correlation analysis A group of techniques to measure the relationship between two variables.

Correlation coefficient A measure of the strength of association between two variables.

Critical value The dividing point between the region where the null hypothesis is rejected and the region where it is not rejected.

Cyclical variation The rise and fall of a time series over periods longer than 1 year.

Deciles Values of an ordered (minimum to maximum) data set that divide the data into 10 equal parts.

Dependent variable The variable that is being predicted or estimated.

Descriptive statistics The techniques used to describe the important characteristics of a set of data. This includes organizing the data values into a frequency distribution, computing measures of location, and computing measures of dispersion and skewness.

Discrete random variable A random variable that can assume only certain clearly separated values.

Dot plot A dot plot summarizes the distribution of one variable by stacking dots at points on a number line that shows the values of the variable. A dot plot shows all values.

Dummy variable A variable in which there are only two possible outcomes. For analysis, one of the outcomes is coded a 1 and the other a 0.

Empirical probability The probability of an event happening is the fraction of the time similar events happened in the past.

Empirical rule For a symmetrical, bell-shaped frequency distribution, approximately 68% of the observations lie within ± 1 standard deviation of the mean; about 95% of the observations lie within ± 2 standard deviations of the mean; and practically all (99.7%) lie within ± 3 standard deviations of the mean.

Event A collection of one or more outcomes of an experiment.

Experiment A process that leads to the occurrence of one and only one of several possible results.

Finite-population correction factor (FPC) When sampling without replacement from a finite population, a correction term is used to reduce the standard error of the mean according to the relative size of the sample to the size of the population. The correction factor is used when the sample is more than 5% of a finite population.

Fishbone diagram A diagram used to illustrate the relationship between a problem and a set of the problem's possible causes.

Frequency distribution A grouping of quantitative data into mutually exclusive and collectively exhaustive classes showing the number of observations in each class.

Frequency table A grouping of qualitative data into mutually exclusive classes showing the number of observations in each class.

Global test A test used to determine if any of the set of independent variables has regression coefficients different from zero.

Histogram A graph in which the classes are marked on the horizontal axis and the class frequencies on the vertical axis. The class frequencies are represented by the heights of the bars, and the bars are drawn adjacent to each other.

Homoscedasticity The variation around the regression equation is the same for all of the values of the independent variables.

Hypergeometric distribution A probability distribution based on a discrete random variable. Its major characteristics are a fixed number of trials, only two possible outcomes, and the probability of success is not the same on each trial.

Independent events The occurrence of one event has no effect on the probability of another event.

Independent variable A variable that provides the basis for estimation.

Index number A number that expresses the relative change in price, quantity, or value compared to a base period.

Inferential statistics The methods used to estimate a property of a population on the basis of a sample.

Interaction The effect of one factor on a response variable differs depending on the value of another factor.

Interquartile range The absolute numerical difference between the first and third quartiles. Fifty percent of a distribution's values occur in this range.

Interval level of measurement For data recorded at the interval level of measurement, the interval or the distance between values is meaningful. The interval level of measurement is based on a scale with a known unit of measurement.

Irregular variation Variation in a time series that is random in nature and does not regularly repeat itself.

Joint probability A probability that measures the likelihood two or more events will happen concurrently.

Kruskal-Wallis one-way analysis of variance by ranks A test used when the assumptions for parametric analysis of variance (ANOVA) cannot be met. Its purpose is to test whether several populations are the same. The data must be at least ordinal scale.

Law of large numbers Over a large number of trials, the empirical probability of an event will approach its true probability.

Measure of dispersion A value that shows the spread of a data set. The range, variance, and standard deviation are measures of dispersion.

Measure of location A single value that is typical of the data. It pinpoints the center of a distribution. The arithmetic mean, weighted mean, median, mode, and geometric mean are measures of location.

Median The value of the middle observation after all the observations have been arranged from low to high. For example, if observations 6, 9, 4 are rearranged to read 4, 6, 9, the median is 6, the middle value.

Mode The value that appears most frequently in a set of data. For grouped data, it is the midpoint of the class containing the largest number of values.

Multiplication formula If there are m ways of doing one thing and n ways of doing another thing, there are $m \times n$ ways of doing both.

Mutually exclusive The occurence of one event means that none of the other events can occur at the same time.

Nominal level of measurement Data recorded at the nominal level of measurement is represented as labels or names. They have no order. They can only be classified and counted.

Null hypothesis A statement about the value of a population parameter developed for the purpose of testing numerical evidence.

Ordinal level of measurement Data recorded at the ordinal level of measurement is based on a relative ranking or rating of items based on a defined attribute or qualitative variable. Variables based on this level of measurement are only ranked or counted.

Outcome A particular result of an experiment.

Outlier A data point that is unusually far from the others. An accepted rule is to classify an observation as an outlier if it is 1.5 times the interquartile range above the third quartile or below the first quartile.

***p*-value** The probability of observing a sample value as extreme as, or more extreme than, the value observed, given that the null hypothesis is true.

Parameter A characteristic of a population.

Percentiles Values of an ordered (minimum to maximum) data set that divide the data into 100 intervals.

Permutation Any arrangement of r objects selected from a single group of n possible objects.

Permutation formula A formula to count the number of possible arrangements when the order of the outcomes is important. For example, the outcome {a, b, c} is considered different from {c, b, a}.

Pie chart A chart that shows the proportion or percentage that each class represents of the total number of frequencies.

Point estimate A single value computed from a sample and used to estimate a population parameter. Example: If the sample mean is 1,020, it is the best estimate of the population mean.

Point estimates The statistic, computed from sample information, that estimates a population parameter.

Poisson probability distribution A discrete probability distribution often used to approximate binomial probabilities when n is large and π is small.

Population The entire set of individuals or objects of interest or the measurements obtained from all individuals or objects of interest.

Posterior probability A revised probability based on additional information.

Prior probability The initial probability based on the present level of information.

Probability A value between 0 and 1, inclusive, that reports the likelihood that a specific event will occur.

Probability distribution A listing of all possible outcomes of an experiment and the probability associated with each outcome.

Producer Price Index Producer Price Index measures change over time in the selling prices received by domestic producers for their output.

Producer's risk The error of rejecting a lot, when the lot is acceptable.

Qualitative variables A nominal-scale variable coded to assume only one nonnumeric outcome or category. For example, a person is considered either employed or unemployed.

Quartiles Values of an ordered (minimum to maximum) data set that divide the data into four intervals.

Random variable A variable measured or observed as the result of an experiment. By chance, the variable can have different values.

Random variation The sum of the squared differences between each observation and its treatment mean.

Range A measure of dispersion found by subtracting the minimum value from the maximum value.

Ratio level of measurement Data recorded at the ratio level of measurement are based on a scale with a known unit of measurement and a meaningful interpretation of zero on the scale.

Regression equation An equation that expresses the linear relationship between two variables.

Residual The difference between the actual value of the dependent variable and the estimated value of the dependent variable, that is, $y - \hat{y}$.

Sample A portion, or part, of the population of interest.

Sampling distribution of the sample mean A probability distribution of all possible sample means of a given sample size.

Sampling error The difference between a sample statistic and its corresponding population parameter.

Scatter diagram Graphical technique used to show the relationship between two variables measured with interval or ratio scales.

Seasonal variation Patterns of change in a time series within a year. These patterns of change repeat themselves each year.

Secular trend The smoothed long-term direction of a time series.

Sign test A test used for dependent samples. The sign test is used to find whether there is a brand preference for two products or to determine whether performance after an experiment is greater than before the experiment. Also, the sign test is used to test a hypothesis about the median.

Simple random sample A sample selected so that each item or person in the population has the same chance of being included.

Special rule of addition A rule used to find the probabilities of events made up of A or B when the events are mutually exclusive.

Special rule of multiplication A rule used to find the probability of the joint occurrence of independent events.

Standard error of estimate A measure of the dispersion, or scatter, of the observed values around the line of regression for a given value of x.

Statistic A characteristic of a sample.

Statistics The science of collecting, organizing, analyzing, and interpreting data for the purpose of making more effective decisions.

Stem-and-leaf display A method to display a variable's distribution using every value. Values are classified by the data's leading digit. For example, if a data set contains values between 13 and 84, eight classes based on the 10s digit would be used for the stems. The 1s digits would be the leaves.

Stepwise regression A step-by-step method to determine a regression equation that begins with a single independent variable and adds or deletes independent variables one by one. Only independent variables with nonzero regression coefficients are included in the regression equation.

Stratified random sample a population is divided into subgroups, called strata, and a sample is randomly selected from each stratum.

Subjective concept of probability The probability or likelihood of a event that is assigned by an individual based on their experience and knowledge.

Systematic random sampling A random starting point is selected, and then every kth member of the population is selected.

Test statistic A value, determined from sample information, used to decide whether to reject or fail to reject the null hypothesis.

Total variation The sum of the squared differences between each observation and the overall mean.

Treatment variation The sum of the squared differences between each treatment mean and the grand or overall mean. Each squared difference is multiplied by the number of observations in the treatment.

Value of perfect information The difference between the maximum payoff under conditions of certainty and the maximum payoff under uncertainty.

Variable control chart A variable control chart plots the mean of an interval or ratio measurement over time.

Variance A measure of dispersion based on the average squared differences from the arithmetic mean.

Variance inflation factor A test used to detect correlation among independent variables.

Weighted index The prices in the base period and the given period are multiplied by quantities (weights).

Wilcoxon rank-sum test A nonparametric test requiring independent samples. The data must be at least ordinal level. That is, the data must be capable of being ranked. The test is used when the assumptions for the parametric Student's *t* test cannot be met. The objective of the test is to find whether two independent samples can be considered as coming from the same population. It is used if the assumptions required for the paired *t* test cannot be met.

***z*-value** It is the distance between a selected value and the mean measured in units of the standard deviation.

Index

KEY FORMULAS Lind, Marchal, and Wathen • *Statistical Techniques in Business & Economics,* 17th edition

CHAPTER 3

- Population mean

$$\mu = \frac{\Sigma x}{N} \quad [3\text{–}1]$$

- Sample mean, raw data

$$\bar{x} = \frac{\Sigma x}{n} \quad [3\text{–}2]$$

- Weighted mean

$$\bar{x}_w = \frac{w_1x_1 + w_2x_2 + \cdots + w_nx_n}{w_1 + w_2 + \cdots + w_n} \quad [3\text{–}3]$$

- Geometric mean

$$GM = \sqrt[n]{(x_1)(x_2)(x_3)\ldots(x_n)} \quad [3\text{–}4]$$

- Geometric mean rate of increase

$$GM = \sqrt[n]{\frac{\text{Value at end of period}}{\text{Value at start of period}}} - 1.0 \quad [3\text{–}5]$$

- Range

$$\text{Range} = \text{Maximum value} - \text{Minimum value} \quad [3\text{–}6]$$

- Population variance

$$\sigma^2 = \frac{\Sigma(x - \mu)^2}{N} \quad [3\text{–}7]$$

- Population standard deviation

$$\sigma = \sqrt{\frac{\Sigma(x - \mu)^2}{N}} \quad [3\text{–}8]$$

- Sample variance

$$s^2 = \frac{\Sigma(x - \bar{x})^2}{n - 1} \quad [3\text{–}9]$$

- Sample standard deviation

$$s = \sqrt{\frac{\Sigma(x - \bar{x})^2}{n - 1}} \quad [3\text{–}10]$$

- Sample mean, grouped data

$$\bar{x} = \frac{\Sigma fM}{n} \quad [3\text{–}11]$$

- Sample standard deviation, grouped data

$$s = \sqrt{\frac{\Sigma f(M - \bar{x})^2}{n - 1}} \quad [3\text{–}12]$$

CHAPTER 4

- Location of a percentile

$$L_p = (n + 1)\frac{P}{100} \quad [4\text{–}1]$$

- Pearson's coefficient of skewness

$$sk = \frac{3(\bar{x} - \text{Median})}{s} \quad [4\text{–}2]$$

- Software coefficient of skewness

$$sk = \frac{n}{(n - 1)(n - 2)}\left[\Sigma\left(\frac{x - \bar{x}}{s}\right)^3\right] \quad [4\text{–}3]$$

CHAPTER 5

- Special rule of addition

$$P(A \text{ or } B) = P(A) + P(B) \quad [5\text{–}2]$$

- Complement rule

$$P(A) = 1 - P(\sim A) \quad [5\text{–}3]$$

- General rule of addition

$$P(A \text{ or } B) = P(A) + P(B) - P(A \text{ and } B) \quad [5\text{–}4]$$

- Special rule of multiplication

$$P(A \text{ and } B) = P(A)P(B) \quad [5\text{–}5]$$

- General rule of multiplication

$$P(A \text{ and } B) = P(A)P(B|A) \quad [5\text{–}6]$$

- Bayes' Theorem

$$P(A_1|B) = \frac{P(A_1)P(B|A_1)}{P(A_1)P(B|A_1) + P(A_2)P(B|A_2)} \quad [5\text{–}7]$$

- Multiplication formula

$$\text{Total arrangements} = (m)(n) \quad [5\text{–}8]$$

- Number of permutations

$$_nP_r = \frac{n!}{(n - r)!} \quad [5\text{–}9]$$

- Number of combinations

$$_nC_r = \frac{n!}{r!(n - r)!} \quad [5\text{–}10]$$

CHAPTER 6

- Mean of a probability distribution

$$\mu = \Sigma[xP(x)] \quad [6\text{–}1]$$

- Variance of a probability distribution

$$\sigma^2 = \Sigma[(x - \mu)^2P(x)] \quad [6\text{–}2]$$

- Binomial probability distribution

$$P(x) = {_nC_x}\,\pi^x(1 - \pi)^{n - x} \quad [6\text{–}3]$$

- Mean of a binomial distribution

$$\mu = n\pi \quad [6\text{–}4]$$

- Variance of a binomial distribution

$$\sigma^2 = n\pi(1 - \pi) \quad [6\text{–}5]$$

- Hypergeometric probability distribution

$$P(x) = \frac{({_SC_x})({_{N-S}C_{n-x}})}{_NC_n} \quad [6\text{–}6]$$

- Poisson probability distribution

$$P(x) = \frac{\mu^x e^{-\mu}}{x!} \quad [6\text{–}7]$$

- Mean of a Poisson distribution

$$\mu = n\pi \quad [6\text{–}8]$$

CHAPTER 7

- Mean of a uniform distribution

$$\mu = \frac{a + b}{2} \qquad [7\text{–}1]$$

- Standard deviation of a uniform distribution

$$\sigma = \sqrt{\frac{(b - a)^2}{12}} \qquad [7\text{–}2]$$

- Uniform probability distribution

$$P(x) = \frac{1}{b - a} \qquad [7\text{–}3]$$

if $a \leq x \leq b$ and 0 elsewhere

- Normal probability distribution

$$P(x) = \frac{1}{\sigma\sqrt{2\pi}} e^{-\left[\frac{(x-\mu)^2}{2\sigma^2}\right]} \qquad [7\text{–}4]$$

- Standard normal value

$$z = \frac{x - \mu}{\sigma} \qquad [7\text{–}5]$$

- Exponential distribution

$$P(x) = \lambda e^{-\lambda x} \qquad [7\text{–}6]$$

- Finding a probability using the exponential distribution

$$P(\text{Arrival time} < x) = 1 - e^{-\lambda x} \qquad [7\text{–}7]$$

CHAPTER 8

- Standard error of mean

$$\sigma_{\bar{X}} = \frac{\sigma}{\sqrt{n}} \qquad [8\text{–}1]$$

- z-value, μ and σ known

$$z = \frac{\bar{x} - \mu}{\sigma/\sqrt{n}} \qquad [8\text{–}2]$$

CHAPTER 9

- Confidence interval for μ, with σ known

$$\bar{x} \pm z\frac{\sigma}{\sqrt{n}} \qquad [9\text{–}1]$$

- Confidence interval for μ, σ unknown

$$\bar{x} \pm t\frac{s}{\sqrt{n}} \qquad [9\text{–}2]$$

- Sample proportion

$$p = \frac{x}{n} \qquad [9\text{–}3]$$

- Confidence interval for proportion

$$p \pm z\sqrt{\frac{p(1 - p)}{n}} \qquad [9\text{–}4]$$

- Sample size for estimating mean

$$n = \left(\frac{z\sigma}{E}\right)^2 \qquad [9\text{–}5]$$

- Sample size for a proportion

$$n = \pi(1 - \pi)\left(\frac{z}{E}\right)^2 \qquad [9\text{–}6]$$

CHAPTER 10

- Testing a mean, σ known

$$z = \frac{\bar{x} - \mu}{\sigma/\sqrt{n}} \qquad [10\text{–}1]$$

- Testing a mean, σ unknown

$$t = \frac{\bar{x} - \mu}{s/\sqrt{n}} \qquad [10\text{–}2]$$

- Type II error

$$z = \frac{\bar{x}_c - \mu_1}{\sigma/\sqrt{n}} \qquad [10\text{–}3]$$

CHAPTER 11

- Variance of the distribution of difference in means

$$\sigma^2_{\bar{x}_1 - \bar{x}_2} = \frac{\sigma_1^2}{n_1} + \frac{\sigma_2^2}{n_2} \qquad [11\text{–}1]$$

- Two-sample test of means, known σ

$$z = \frac{\bar{x}_1 - \bar{x}_2}{\sqrt{\frac{\sigma_1^2}{n_1} + \frac{\sigma_2^2}{n_2}}} \qquad [11\text{–}2]$$

- Pooled variance

$$s_p^2 = \frac{(n_1 - 1)\, s_1^2 + (n_2 - 1)\, s_2^2}{n_1 + n_2 - 2} \qquad [11\text{–}3]$$

- Two-sample test of means, unknown but equal σ^2s

$$t = \frac{\bar{x}_1 - \bar{x}_2}{\sqrt{s_p^2\left(\frac{1}{n_1} + \frac{1}{n_2}\right)}} \qquad [11\text{–}4]$$

- Two-sample tests of means, unknown and unequal σ^2s

$$t = \frac{\bar{x}_1 - \bar{x}_2}{\sqrt{\frac{s_1^2}{n_1} + \frac{s_2^2}{n_2}}} \qquad [11\text{–}5]$$

- Degrees of freedom for unequal variance test

$$df = \frac{[(s_1^2/n_1) + (s_2^2/n_2)]^2}{\frac{(s_1^2/n_1)^2}{n_1 - 1} + \frac{(s_2^2/n_2)^2}{n_2 - 1}} \qquad [11\text{–}6]$$

- Paired t test

$$t = \frac{\bar{d}}{s_d/\sqrt{n}} \qquad [11\text{–}7]$$

CHAPTER 12

- Test for comparing two variances

$$F = \frac{s_1^2}{s_2^2} \qquad [12\text{–}1]$$

- Sum of squares, total

$$\text{SS total} = \Sigma(x - \bar{x}_G)^2 \qquad [12\text{–}2]$$

- Sum of squares, error

$$SSE = \Sigma(x - \bar{x}_c)^2 \quad [12\text{–}3]$$

- Sum of squares, treatments

$$SST = SS\ total - SSE \quad [12\text{–}4]$$

- Confidence interval for differences in treatment means

$$(\bar{x}_1 - \bar{x}_2) \pm t\sqrt{MSE\left(\frac{1}{n_1} + \frac{1}{n_2}\right)} \quad [12\text{–}5]$$

- Sum of squares, blocks

$$SSB = k\Sigma(\bar{x}_b - \bar{x}_G)^2 \quad [12\text{–}6]$$

- Sum of squares error, two-way ANOVA

$$SSE = SS\ total - SST - SSB \quad [12\text{–}7]$$

CHAPTER 13

- Correlation coefficient

$$r = \frac{\Sigma(x - \bar{x})(y - \bar{y})}{(n - 1)\, s_x s_y} \quad [13\text{–}1]$$

- Test for significant correlation

$$t = \frac{r\sqrt{n-2}}{\sqrt{1-r^2}} \quad [13\text{–}2]$$

- Linear regression equation

$$\hat{y} = a + bx \quad [13\text{–}3]$$

- Slope of the regression line

$$b = r\frac{s_y}{s_x} \quad [13\text{–}4]$$

- Intercept of the regression line

$$a = \bar{y} - b\bar{x} \quad [13\text{–}5]$$

- Test for a zero slope

$$t = \frac{b - 0}{s_b} \quad [13\text{–}6]$$

- Standard error of estimate

$$s_{y \cdot x} = \sqrt{\frac{\Sigma(y - \hat{y})^2}{n - 2}} \quad [13\text{–}7]$$

- Coefficient of determination

$$r^2 = \frac{SSR}{SS\ Total} = 1 - \frac{SSE}{SS\ Total} \quad [13\text{–}8]$$

- Standard error of estimate

$$s_{y \cdot x} = \sqrt{\frac{SSE}{n - 2}} \quad [13\text{–}9]$$

- Confidence interval

$$\hat{y} \pm t s_{y \cdot x}\sqrt{\frac{1}{n} + \frac{(x - \bar{x})^2}{\Sigma(x - \bar{x})^2}} \quad [13\text{–}10]$$

- Prediction interval

$$\hat{y} \pm t s_{y \cdot x}\sqrt{1 + \frac{1}{n} + \frac{(x - \bar{x})^2}{\Sigma(x - \bar{x})^2}} \quad [13\text{–}11]$$

CHAPTER 14

- Multiple regression equation

$$\hat{y} = a + b_1x_1 + b_2x_2 + \cdots + b_kx_k \quad [14\text{–}1]$$

- Multiple standard error of estimate

$$s_{y \cdot 123\ldots k} = \sqrt{\frac{\Sigma(y - \hat{y})^2}{n - (k + 1)}} = \sqrt{\frac{SSE}{n - (k + 1)}} \quad [14\text{–}2]$$

- Coefficient of multiple determination

$$R^2 = \frac{SSR}{SS\ total} \quad [14\text{–}3]$$

- Adjusted coefficient of determination

$$R^2_{adj} = 1 - \frac{\dfrac{SSE}{n - (k + 1)}}{\dfrac{SS\ total}{n - 1}} \quad [14\text{–}4]$$

- Global test of hypothesis

$$F = \frac{SSR/k}{SSE/[n - (k + 1)]} \quad [14\text{–}5]$$

- Testing for a particular regression coefficient

$$t = \frac{b_i - 0}{s_{b_i}} \quad [14\text{–}6]$$

- Variance inflation factor

$$VIF = \frac{1}{1 - R_j^2} \quad [14\text{–}7]$$

CHAPTER 15

- Test of hypothesis, one proportion

$$z = \frac{p - \pi}{\sqrt{\dfrac{\pi(1 - \pi)}{n}}} \quad [15\text{–}1]$$

- Two-sample test of proportions

$$z = \frac{p_1 - p_2}{\sqrt{\dfrac{p_c(1 - p_c)}{n_1} + \dfrac{p_c(1 - p_c)}{n_2}}} \quad [15\text{–}2]$$

- Pooled proportion

$$p_c = \frac{x_1 + x_2}{n_1 + n_2} \quad [15\text{–}3]$$

- Chi-square test statistic

$$\chi^2 = \Sigma\left[\frac{(f_o - f_e)^2}{f_e}\right] \quad [15\text{–}4]$$

- Expected frequency

$$f_e = \frac{(\text{Row total})(\text{Column total})}{\text{Grand total}} \quad [15\text{–}5]$$

CHAPTER 16

- Sign test, $n > 10$

$$z = \frac{(x \pm .50) - \mu}{\sigma} \quad [16\text{–}1]$$

- Wilcoxon rank-sum test

$$z = \frac{W - \frac{n_1(n_1 + n_2 + 1)}{2}}{\sqrt{\frac{n_1 n_2(n_1 + n_2 + 1)}{12}}} \quad \textbf{[16–4]}$$

- Kruskal-Wallis test

$$H = \frac{12}{n(n+1)}\left[\frac{(\Sigma R_1)^2}{n_1} + \frac{(\Sigma R_2)^2}{n_2} + \cdots + \frac{(\Sigma R_k)^2}{n_k}\right] - 3(n+1) \quad \textbf{[16–5]}$$

- Spearman coefficient of rank correlation

$$r_s = 1 - \frac{6\Sigma d^2}{n(n^2 - 1)} \quad \textbf{[16–6]}$$

- Hypothesis test, rank correlation

$$t = r_s\sqrt{\frac{n-2}{1-r_s^2}} \quad \textbf{[16–7]}$$

CHAPTER 17

- Simple index

$$P = \frac{p_t}{p_0}(100) \quad \textbf{[17–1]}$$

- Simple average of price relatives

$$P = \frac{\Sigma P_i}{n} \quad \textbf{[17–2]}$$

- Simple aggregate index

$$P = \frac{\Sigma p_t}{\Sigma p_0}(100) \quad \textbf{[17–3]}$$

- Laspeyres' price index

$$P = \frac{\Sigma p_t q_0}{\Sigma p_0 q_0}(100) \quad \textbf{[17–4]}$$

- Paasche's price index

$$P = \frac{\Sigma p_t q_t}{\Sigma p_0 q_t}(100) \quad \textbf{[17–5]}$$

- Fisher's ideal index

$$\sqrt{(\text{Laspeyres' price index})(\text{Paasche's price index})} \quad \textbf{[17–6]}$$

- Value index

$$V = \frac{\Sigma p_t q_t}{\Sigma p_0 q_0}(100) \quad \textbf{[17–7]}$$

- Real income

$$\text{Real income} = \frac{\text{Money income}}{\text{CPI}}(100) \quad \textbf{[17–8]}$$

- Using an index as a deflator

$$\text{Deflated sales} = \frac{\text{Actual sales}}{\text{Index}}(100) \quad \textbf{[17–9]}$$

- Purchasing power

$$\text{Purchasing power} = \frac{\$1}{\text{CPI}}(100) \quad \textbf{[17–10]}$$

CHAPTER 18

- Linear trend

$$\hat{y} = a + bt \quad \textbf{[18–1]}$$

- Log trend equation

$$\log \hat{y} = \log a + \log b(t) \quad \textbf{[18–2]}$$

- Correction factor for adjusting quarterly means

$$\text{Correction factor} = \frac{4.00}{\text{Total of four means}} \quad \textbf{[18–3]}$$

- Durbin-Watson statistic

$$d = \frac{\sum_{t=2}^{n}(e_t - e_{t-1})^2}{\sum_{t=1}^{n} e_t^2} \quad \textbf{[18–4]}$$

CHAPTER 19

- Grand mean

$$\bar{\bar{x}} = \frac{\Sigma \bar{x}}{k} \quad \textbf{[19–1]}$$

- Control limits, mean

$$\text{UCL} = \bar{\bar{x}} + A_2\bar{R} \qquad \text{LCL} = \bar{\bar{x}} - A_2\bar{R} \quad \textbf{[19–4]}$$

- Control limits, range

$$\text{UCL} = D_4\bar{R} \qquad \text{LCL} = D_3\bar{R} \quad \textbf{[19–5]}$$

- Mean proportion defective

$$p = \frac{\text{Total number defective}}{\text{Total number of items sampled}} \quad \textbf{[19–6]}$$

- Control limits, proportion

$$\text{UCL and LCL} = p \pm 3\sqrt{\frac{p(1-p)}{n}} \quad \textbf{[19–8]}$$

- Control limits, *c*-bar chart

$$\text{UCL and LCL} = \bar{c} \pm 3\sqrt{\bar{c}} \quad \textbf{[19–9]}$$

CHAPTER 20

- Expected monetary value

$$\text{EMV}(A_i) = \Sigma[P(S_j) \cdot V(A_i, S_j)] \quad \textbf{[20–1]}$$

- Expected opportunity loss

$$\text{EOL}(A_i) = \Sigma[P(S_j) \cdot R(A_i, S_j)] \quad \textbf{[20–2]}$$

- Expected value of perfect information

EVPI = Expected value under conditions of certainty
– Expected value of optimal decision under conditions of uncertainty **[20–3]**

Student's *t* Distribution

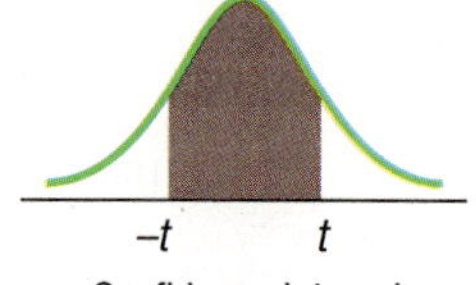

Confidence interval

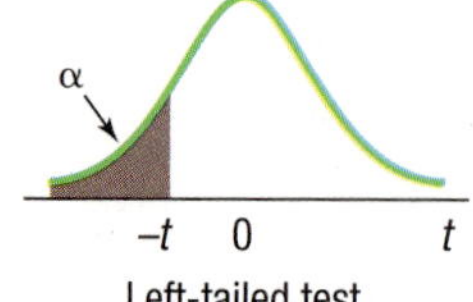

Left-tailed test

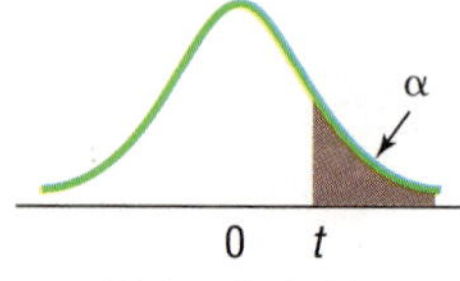

Right-tailed test

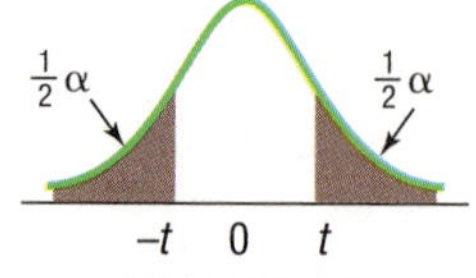

Two-tailed test

df (degrees of freedom)	Confidence Intervals, *c*					
	80%	**90%**	**95%**	**98%**	**99%**	**99.9%**
	Level of Significance for One-Tailed Test, α					
	0.10	**0.05**	**0.025**	**0.01**	**0.005**	**0.0005**
	Level of Significance for Two-Tailed Test, α					
	0.20	**0.10**	**0.05**	**0.02**	**0.01**	**0.001**
1	3.078	6.314	12.706	31.821	63.657	636.619
2	1.886	2.920	4.303	6.965	9.925	31.599
3	1.638	2.353	3.182	4.541	5.841	12.924
4	1.533	2.132	2.776	3.747	4.604	8.610
5	1.476	2.015	2.571	3.365	4.032	6.869
6	1.440	1.943	2.447	3.143	3.707	5.959
7	1.415	1.895	2.365	2.998	3.499	5.408
8	1.397	1.860	2.306	2.896	3.355	5.041
9	1.383	1.833	2.262	2.821	3.250	4.781
10	1.372	1.812	2.228	2.764	3.169	4.587
11	1.363	1.796	2.201	2.718	3.106	4.437
12	1.356	1.782	2.179	2.681	3.055	4.318
13	1.350	1.771	2.160	2.650	3.012	4.221
14	1.345	1.761	2.145	2.624	2.977	4.140
15	1.341	1.753	2.131	2.602	2.947	4.073
16	1.337	1.746	2.120	2.583	2.921	4.015
17	1.333	1.740	2.110	2.567	2.898	3.965
18	1.330	1.734	2.101	2.552	2.878	3.922
19	1.328	1.729	2.093	2.539	2.861	3.883
20	1.325	1.725	2.086	2.528	2.845	3.850
21	1.323	1.721	2.080	2.518	2.831	3.819
22	1.321	1.717	2.074	2.508	2.819	3.792
23	1.319	1.714	2.069	2.500	2.807	3.768
24	1.318	1.711	2.064	2.492	2.797	3.745
25	1.316	1.708	2.060	2.485	2.787	3.725
26	1.315	1.706	2.056	2.479	2.779	3.707
27	1.314	1.703	2.052	2.473	2.771	3.690
28	1.313	1.701	2.048	2.467	2.763	3.674
29	1.311	1.699	2.045	2.462	2.756	3.659
30	1.310	1.697	2.042	2.457	2.750	3.646
31	1.309	1.696	2.040	2.453	2.744	3.633
32	1.309	1.694	2.037	2.449	2.738	3.622
33	1.308	1.692	2.035	2.445	2.733	3.611
34	1.307	1.691	2.032	2.441	2.728	3.601
35	1.306	1.690	2.030	2.438	2.724	3.591

(continued-top right)

(continued)

df (degrees of freedom)	Confidence Intervals, *c*					
	80%	**90%**	**95%**	**98%**	**99%**	**99.9%**
	Level of Significance for One-Tailed Test, α					
	0.10	**0.05**	**0.025**	**0.01**	**0.005**	**0.0005**
	Level of Significance for Two-Tailed Test, α					
	0.20	**0.10**	**0.05**	**0.02**	**0.01**	**0.001**
36	1.306	1.688	2.028	2.434	2.719	3.582
37	1.305	1.687	2.026	2.431	2.715	3.574
38	1.304	1.686	2.024	2.429	2.712	3.566
39	1.304	1.685	2.023	2.426	2.708	3.558
40	1.303	1.684	2.021	2.423	2.704	3.551
41	1.303	1.683	2.020	2.421	2.701	3.544
42	1.302	1.682	2.018	2.418	2.698	3.538
43	1.302	1.681	2.017	2.416	2.695	3.532
44	1.301	1.680	2.015	2.414	2.692	3.526
45	1.301	1.679	2.014	2.412	2.690	3.520
46	1.300	1.679	2.013	2.410	2.687	3.515
47	1.300	1.678	2.012	2.408	2.685	3.510
48	1.299	1.677	2.011	2.407	2.682	3.505
49	1.299	1.677	2.010	2.405	2.680	3.500
50	1.299	1.676	2.009	2.403	2.678	3.496
51	1.298	1.675	2.008	2.402	2.676	3.492
52	1.298	1.675	2.007	2.400	2.674	3.488
53	1.298	1.674	2.006	2.399	2.672	3.484
54	1.297	1.674	2.005	2.397	2.670	3.480
55	1.297	1.673	2.004	2.396	2.668	3.476
56	1.297	1.673	2.003	2.395	2.667	3.473
57	1.297	1.672	2.002	2.394	2.665	3.470
58	1.296	1.672	2.002	2.392	2.663	3.466
59	1.296	1.671	2.001	2.391	2.662	3.463
60	1.296	1.671	2.000	2.390	2.660	3.460
61	1.296	1.670	2.000	2.389	2.659	3.457
62	1.295	1.670	1.999	2.388	2.657	3.454
63	1.295	1.669	1.998	2.387	2.656	3.452
64	1.295	1.669	1.998	2.386	2.655	3.449
65	1.295	1.669	1.997	2.385	2.654	3.447
66	1.295	1.668	1.997	2.384	2.652	3.444
67	1.294	1.668	1.996	2.383	2.651	3.442
68	1.294	1.668	1.995	2.382	2.650	3.439
69	1.294	1.667	1.995	2.382	2.649	3.437
70	1.294	1.667	1.994	2.381	2.648	3.435

(continued)

Student's *t* Distribution (*concluded*)

(*continued*)

df (degrees of freedom)	Confidence Intervals, *c*					
	80%	90%	95%	98%	99%	99.9%
	Level of Significance for One-Tailed Test, α					
	0.10	0.05	0.025	0.01	0.005	0.0005
	Level of Significance for Two-Tailed Test, α					
	0.20	0.10	0.05	0.02	0.01	0.001
71	1.294	1.667	1.994	2.380	2.647	3.433
72	1.293	1.666	1.993	2.379	2.646	3.431
73	1.293	1.666	1.993	2.379	2.645	3.429
74	1.293	1.666	1.993	2.378	2.644	3.427
75	1.293	1.665	1.992	2.377	2.643	3.425
76	1.293	1.665	1.992	2.376	2.642	3.423
77	1.293	1.665	1.991	2.376	2.641	3.421
78	1.292	1.665	1.991	2.375	2.640	3.420
79	1.292	1.664	1.990	2.374	2.640	3.418
80	1.292	1.664	1.990	2.374	2.639	3.416
81	1.292	1.664	1.990	2.373	2.638	3.415
82	1.292	1.664	1.989	2.373	2.637	3.413
83	1.292	1.663	1.989	2.372	2.636	3.412
84	1.292	1.663	1.989	2.372	2.636	3.410
85	1.292	1.663	1.988	2.371	2.635	3.409
86	1.291	1.663	1.988	2.370	2.634	3.407
87	1.291	1.663	1.988	2.370	2.634	3.406
88	1.291	1.662	1.987	2.369	2.633	3.405
89	1.291	1.662	1.987	2.369	2.632	3.403
90	1.291	1.662	1.987	2.368	2.632	3.402
91	1.291	1.662	1.986	2.368	2.631	3.401
92	1.291	1.662	1.986	2.368	2.630	3.399
93	1.291	1.661	1.986	2.367	2.630	3.398
94	1.291	1.661	1.986	2.367	2.629	3.397
95	1.291	1.661	1.985	2.366	2.629	3.396
96	1.290	1.661	1.985	2.366	2.628	3.395
97	1.290	1.661	1.985	2.365	2.627	3.394
98	1.290	1.661	1.984	2.365	2.627	3.393
99	1.290	1.660	1.984	2.365	2.626	3.392
100	1.290	1.660	1.984	2.364	2.626	3.390
120	1.289	1.658	1.980	2.358	2.617	3.373
140	1.288	1.656	1.977	2.353	2.611	3.361
160	1.287	1.654	1.975	2.350	2.607	3.352
180	1.286	1.653	1.973	2.347	2.603	3.345
200	1.286	1.653	1.972	2.345	2.601	3.340
∞	1.282	1.645	1.960	2.326	2.576	3.291

Areas under the Normal Curve

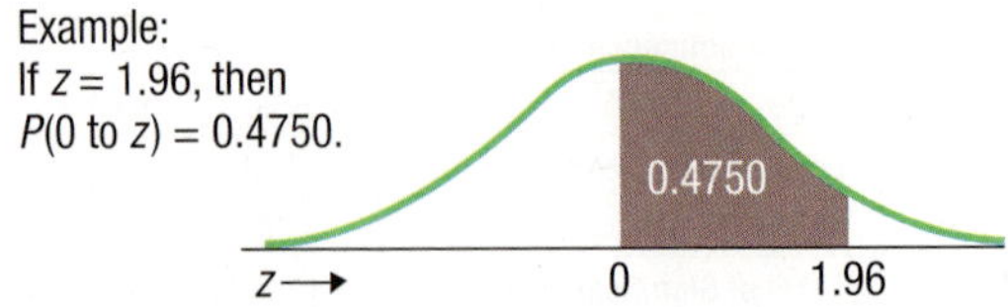

z	0.00	0.01	0.02	0.03	0.04	0.05	0.06	0.07	0.08	0.09
0.0	0.0000	0.0040	0.0080	0.0120	0.0160	0.0199	0.0239	0.0279	0.0319	0.0359
0.1	0.0398	0.0438	0.0478	0.0517	0.0557	0.0596	0.0636	0.0675	0.0714	0.0753
0.2	0.0793	0.0832	0.0871	0.0910	0.0948	0.0987	0.1026	0.1064	0.1103	0.1141
0.3	0.1179	0.1217	0.1255	0.1293	0.1331	0.1368	0.1406	0.1443	0.1480	0.1517
0.4	0.1554	0.1591	0.1628	0.1664	0.1700	0.1736	0.1772	0.1808	0.1844	0.1879
0.5	0.1915	0.1950	0.1985	0.2019	0.2054	0.2088	0.2123	0.2157	0.2190	0.2224
0.6	0.2257	0.2291	0.2324	0.2357	0.2389	0.2422	0.2454	0.2486	0.2517	0.2549
0.7	0.2580	0.2611	0.2642	0.2673	0.2704	0.2734	0.2764	0.2794	0.2823	0.2852
0.8	0.2881	0.2910	0.2939	0.2967	0.2995	0.3023	0.3051	0.3078	0.3106	0.3133
0.9	0.3159	0.3186	0.3212	0.3238	0.3264	0.3289	0.3315	0.3340	0.3365	0.3389
1.0	0.3413	0.3438	0.3461	0.3485	0.3508	0.3531	0.3554	0.3577	0.3599	0.3621
1.1	0.3643	0.3665	0.3686	0.3708	0.3729	0.3749	0.3770	0.3790	0.3810	0.3830
1.2	0.3849	0.3869	0.3888	0.3907	0.3925	0.3944	0.3962	0.3980	0.3997	0.4015
1.3	0.4032	0.4049	0.4066	0.4082	0.4099	0.4115	0.4131	0.4147	0.4162	0.4177
1.4	0.4192	0.4207	0.4222	0.4236	0.4251	0.4265	0.4279	0.4292	0.4306	0.4319
1.5	0.4332	0.4345	0.4357	0.4370	0.4382	0.4394	0.4406	0.4418	0.4429	0.4441
1.6	0.4452	0.4463	0.4474	0.4484	0.4495	0.4505	0.4515	0.4525	0.4535	0.4545
1.7	0.4554	0.4564	0.4573	0.4582	0.4591	0.4599	0.4608	0.4616	0.4625	0.4633
1.8	0.4641	0.4649	0.4656	0.4664	0.4671	0.4678	0.4686	0.4693	0.4699	0.4706
1.9	0.4713	0.4719	0.4726	0.4732	0.4738	0.4744	0.4750	0.4756	0.4761	0.4767
2.0	0.4772	0.4778	0.4783	0.4788	0.4793	0.4798	0.4803	0.4808	0.4812	0.4817
2.1	0.4821	0.4826	0.4830	0.4834	0.4838	0.4842	0.4846	0.4850	0.4854	0.4857
2.2	0.4861	0.4864	0.4868	0.4871	0.4875	0.4878	0.4881	0.4884	0.4887	0.4890
2.3	0.4893	0.4896	0.4898	0.4901	0.4904	0.4906	0.4909	0.4911	0.4913	0.4916
2.4	0.4918	0.4920	0.4922	0.4925	0.4927	0.4929	0.4931	0.4932	0.4934	0.4936
2.5	0.4938	0.4940	0.4941	0.4943	0.4945	0.4946	0.4948	0.4949	0.4951	0.4952
2.6	0.4953	0.4955	0.4956	0.4957	0.4959	0.4960	0.4961	0.4962	0.4963	0.4964
2.7	0.4965	0.4966	0.4967	0.4968	0.4969	0.4970	0.4971	0.4972	0.4973	0.4974
2.8	0.4974	0.4975	0.4976	0.4977	0.4977	0.4978	0.4979	0.4979	0.4980	0.4981
2.9	0.4981	0.4982	0.4982	0.4983	0.4984	0.4984	0.4985	0.4985	0.4986	0.4986
3.0	0.4987	0.4987	0.4987	0.4988	0.4988	0.4989	0.4989	0.4989	0.4990	0.4990